TEXAS

RULES OF COURT

VOLUME II – FEDERAL

2019

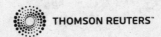
THOMSON REUTERS™

Mat#42146549

PREFACE

Designed for use in the office or courtroom, this pamphlet contains the Texas federal rules.

WHAT'S NEW

Texas Court Rules, Volume II – Federal, 2019, includes rules and associated material governing practice before the Texas federal courts. It is current with amendments received through February 1, 2019.

CONTACT US

For additional information or research assistance, call the reference attorneys at 1-800-REF-ATTY (1-800-733-2889). Contact our U.S. legal editorial department directly with your questions and suggestions by e-mail at editors.us-legal@tr.com.

Thank you for subscribing to this product. Should you have any questions regarding this product please contact Customer Service at 1-800-328-4880 or by fax at 1-800-340-9378. If you would like to inquire about related publications, or to place an order, please contact us at 1-888-728-7677 or visit us at legalsolutions.thomsonreuters.com.

THE PUBLISHER

March 2019

THOMSON REUTERS PROVIEW™

This title is one of many now available on your tablet as an eBook.

Take your research mobile. Powered by the Thomson Reuters ProView™ app, our eBooks deliver the same trusted content as your print resources, but in a compact, on-the-go format.

ProView eBooks are designed for the way you work. You can add your own notes and highlights to the text, and all of your annotations will transfer electronically to every new edition of your eBook.

You can also instantly verify primary authority with built-in links to WestlawNext® and KeyCite®, so you can be confident that you're accessing the most current and accurate information.

To find out more about ProView eBooks and available discounts, call 1-800-344-5009.

TABLE OF CONTENTS

FEDERAL
RULES OF CIVIL PROCEDURE

Including Amendments Effective December 1, 2018

TITLE I. SCOPE OF RULES; FORM OF ACTION

RULE 1. SCOPE AND PURPOSE

These rules govern the procedure in all civil actions and proceedings in the United States district courts, except as stated in Rule 81. They should be construed, administered, and employed by the court and the parties to secure the just, speedy, and inexpensive determination of every action and proceeding.

(Amended December 29, 1948, effective October 20, 1949; February 28, 1966, effective July 1, 1966; April 22, 1993, effective December 1, 1993; April 30, 2007, effective December 1, 2007; April 29, 2015, effective December 1, 2015.)

RULE 2. ONE FORM OF ACTION

There is one form of action—the civil action.

(Amended April 30, 2007, effective December 1, 2007.)

TITLE II. COMMENCING AN ACTION; SERVICE OF PROCESS, PLEADINGS, MOTIONS, AND ORDERS

RULE 3. COMMENCING AN ACTION

A civil action is commenced by filing a complaint with the court.

(Amended April 30, 2007, effective December 1, 2007.)

RULE 4. SUMMONS

(a) Contents; Amendments.

(1) *Contents.* A summons must:

(A) name the court and the parties;

(B) be directed to the defendant;

(C) state the name and address of the plaintiff's attorney or—if unrepresented—of the plaintiff;

(D) state the time within which the defendant must appear and defend;

(E) notify the defendant that a failure to appear and defend will result in a default judgment against the defendant for the relief demanded in the complaint;

(F) be signed by the clerk; and

(G) bear the court's seal.

(2) *Amendments.* The court may permit a summons to be amended.

(b) Issuance. On or after filing the complaint, the plaintiff may present a summons to the clerk for signature and seal. If the summons is properly completed, the clerk must sign, seal, and issue it to the plaintiff for service on the defendant. A summons—or a copy of a summons that is addressed to multiple defendants—must be issued for each defendant to be served.

(c) Service.

(1) *In General.* A summons must be served with a copy of the complaint. The plaintiff is responsible for having the summons and complaint served within the time allowed by Rule 4(m) and must furnish the necessary copies to the person who makes service.

(2) ***By Whom.*** Any person who is at least 18 years old and not a party may serve a summons and complaint.

(3) ***By a Marshal or Someone Specially Appointed.*** At the plaintiff's request, the court may order that service be made by a United States marshal or deputy marshal or by a person specially appointed by the court. The court must so order if the plaintiff is authorized to proceed in forma pauperis under 28 U.S.C. § 1915 or as a seaman under 28 U.S.C. § 1916.

(d) Waiving Service.

(1) ***Requesting a Waiver.*** An individual, corporation, or association that is subject to service under Rule 4(e), (f), or (h) has a duty to avoid unnecessary expenses of serving the summons. The plaintiff may notify such a defendant that an action has been commenced and request that the defendant waive service of a summons. The notice and request must:

(A) be in writing and be addressed:

(i) to the individual defendant; or

(ii) for a defendant subject to service under Rule 4(h), to an officer, a managing or general agent, or any other agent authorized by appointment or by law to receive service of process;

(B) name the court where the complaint was filed;

(C) be accompanied by a copy of the complaint, 2 copies of the waiver form appended to this Rule 4, and a prepaid means for returning the form;

(D) inform the defendant, using the form appended to this Rule 4, of the consequences of waiving and not waiving service;

(E) state the date when the request is sent;

(F) give the defendant a reasonable time of at least 30 days after the request was sent—or at least 60 days if sent to the defendant outside any judicial district of the United States—to return the waiver; and

(G) be sent by first-class mail or other reliable means.

(2) ***Failure to Waive.*** If a defendant located within the United States fails, without good cause, to sign and return a waiver requested by a plaintiff located within the United States, the court must impose on the defendant:

(A) the expenses later incurred in making service; and

(B) the reasonable expenses, including attorney's fees, of any motion required to collect those service expenses.

(3) ***Time to Answer After a Waiver.*** A defendant who, before being served with process, timely returns a waiver need not serve an answer to the complaint until 60 days after the request was sent—or until 90 days after it was sent to the defendant outside any judicial district of the United States.

(4) ***Results of Filing a Waiver.*** When the plaintiff files a waiver, proof of service is not required and these rules apply as if a summons and complaint had been served at the time of filing the waiver.

(5) ***Jurisdiction and Venue Not Waived.*** Waiving service of a summons does not waive any objection to personal jurisdiction or to venue.

(e) Serving an Individual Within a Judicial District of the United States. Unless federal law provides otherwise, an individual—other than a minor, an incompetent person, or a person whose waiver has been filed—may be served in a judicial district of the United States by:

(1) following state law for serving a summons in an action brought in courts of general jurisdiction in the state where the district court is located or where service is made; or

(2) doing any of the following:

(A) delivering a copy of the summons and of the complaint to the individual personally;

(B) leaving a copy of each at the individual's dwelling or usual place of abode with someone of suitable age and discretion who resides there; or

(C) delivering a copy of each to an agent authorized by appointment or by law to receive service of process.

(f) Serving an Individual in a Foreign Country. Unless federal law provides otherwise, an individual—other than a minor, an incompetent person, or a person whose waiver has been filed—may be served at a place not within any judicial district of the United States:

(1) by any internationally agreed means of service that is reasonably calculated to give notice, such as those authorized by the Hague Convention on the Service Abroad of Judicial and Extrajudicial Documents;

(2) if there is no internationally agreed means, or if an international agreement allows but does not specify other means, by a method that is reasonably calculated to give notice:

(A) as prescribed by the foreign country's law for service in that country in an action in its courts of general jurisdiction;

(B) as the foreign authority directs in response to a letter rogatory or letter of request; or

(C) unless prohibited by the foreign country's law, by:

(i) delivering a copy of the summons and of the complaint to the individual personally; or

(ii) using any form of mail that the clerk addresses and sends to the individual and that requires a signed receipt; or

(3) by other means not prohibited by international agreement, as the court orders.

(g) Serving a Minor or an Incompetent Person. A minor or an incompetent person in a judicial district of the United States must be served by following state law for serving a summons or like process on such a defendant in an action brought in the courts of general jurisdiction of the state where service is made. A minor or an incompetent person who is not within any judicial district of the United States must be served in the manner prescribed by Rule 4(f)(2)(A), (f)(2)(B), or (f)(3).

(h) Serving a Corporation, Partnership, or Association. Unless federal law provides otherwise or the defendant's waiver has been filed, a domestic or foreign corporation, or a partnership or other unincorporated association that is subject to suit under a common name, must be served:

    (1) in a judicial district of the United States:

        (A) in the manner prescribed by Rule 4(e)(1) for serving an individual; or

        (B) by delivering a copy of the summons and of the complaint to an officer, a managing or general agent, or any other agent authorized by appointment or by law to receive service of process and—if the agent is one authorized by statute and the statute so requires—by also mailing a copy of each to the defendant; or

    (2) at a place not within any judicial district of the United States, in any manner prescribed by Rule 4(f) for serving an individual, except personal delivery under (f)(2)(C)(i).

(i) Serving the United States and Its Agencies, Corporations, Officers, or Employees.

    (1) *United States.* To serve the United States, a party must:

        (A)(i) deliver a copy of the summons and of the complaint to the United States attorney for the district where the action is brought—or to an assistant United States attorney or clerical employee whom the United States attorney designates in a writing filed with the court clerk—or

        (ii) send a copy of each by registered or certified mail to the civil-process clerk at the United States attorney's office;

        (B) send a copy of each by registered or certified mail to the Attorney General of the United States at Washington, D.C.; and

        (C) if the action challenges an order of a nonparty agency or officer of the United States, send a copy of each by registered or certified mail to the agency or officer.

    (2) *Agency; Corporation; Officer or Employee Sued in an Official Capacity.* To serve a United States agency or corporation, or a United States officer or employee sued only in an official capacity, a party must serve the United States and also send a copy of the summons and of the complaint by registered or certified mail to the agency, corporation, officer, or employee.

    (3) *Officer or Employee Sued Individually.* To serve a United States officer or employee sued in an individual capacity for an act or omission occurring in connection with duties performed on the United States' behalf (whether or not the officer or employee is also sued in an official capacity), a party must serve the United States and also serve the officer or employee under Rule 4(e), (f), or (g).

    (4) *Extending Time.* The court must allow a party a reasonable time to cure its failure to:

        (A) serve a person required to be served under Rule 4(i)(2), if the party has served either the United States attorney or the Attorney General of the United States; or

        (B) serve the United States under Rule 4(i)(3), if the party has served the United States officer or employee.

(j) Serving a Foreign, State, or Local Government.

    (1) *Foreign State.* A foreign state or its political subdivision, agency, or instrumentality must be served in accordance with 28 U.S.C. § 1608.

    (2) *State or Local Government.* A state, a municipal corporation, or any other state-created governmental organization that is subject to suit must be served by:

        (A) delivering a copy of the summons and of the complaint to its chief executive officer; or

        (B) serving a copy of each in the manner prescribed by that state's law for serving a summons or like process on such a defendant.

(k) Territorial Limits of Effective Service.

    (1) *In General.* Serving a summons or filing a waiver of service establishes personal jurisdiction over a defendant:

        (A) who is subject to the jurisdiction of a court of general jurisdiction in the state where the district court is located;

        (B) who is a party joined under Rule 14 or 19 and is served within a judicial district of the United States and not more than 100 miles from where the summons was issued; or

        (C) when authorized by a federal statute.

    (2) *Federal Claim Outside State–Court Jurisdiction.* For a claim that arises under federal law, serving a summons or filing a waiver of service establishes personal jurisdiction over a defendant if:

        (A) the defendant is not subject to jurisdiction in any state's courts of general jurisdiction; and

        (B) exercising jurisdiction is consistent with the United States Constitution and laws.

(l) Proving Service.

    (1) *Affidavit Required.* Unless service is waived, proof of service must be made to the court. Except for service by a United States marshal or deputy marshal, proof must be by the server's affidavit.

    (2) *Service Outside the United States.* Service not within any judicial district of the United States must be proved as follows:

        (A) if made under Rule 4(f)(1), as provided in the applicable treaty or convention; or

        (B) if made under Rule 4(f)(2) or (f)(3), by a receipt signed by the addressee, or by other evidence satisfying the court that the summons and complaint were delivered to the addressee.

    (3) *Validity of Service; Amending Proof.* Failure to prove service does not affect the validity of service. The court may permit proof of service to be amended.

(m) Time Limit for Service. If a defendant is not served within (90 days) after the complaint is filed, the court—on motion or on its own after notice to the plaintiff—must dismiss the action without prejudice against that defendant or order that service be made within a specified time. But if the plaintiff shows good cause for the failure, the court must extend the time for service for an appropriate period. This subdivision (m) does not apply to service in a foreign country under Rule 4(f), 4(h)(2), or 4(j)(1), or to service of a notice under Rule 71.1(d)(3)(A).

(n) Asserting Jurisdiction over Property or Assets.

(1) *Federal Law.* The court may assert jurisdiction over property if authorized by a federal statute. Notice to claimants of the property must be given as provided in the statute or by serving a summons under this rule.

(2) *State Law.* On a showing that personal jurisdiction over a defendant cannot be obtained in the district where the action is brought by reasonable efforts to serve a summons under this rule, the court may assert jurisdiction over the defendant's assets found in the district. Jurisdiction is acquired by seizing the assets under the circumstances and in the manner provided by state law in that district.

Rule 4   Notice of a Lawsuit and Request to Waive Service of Summons.

(Caption)

To (*name the defendant or — if the defendant is a corporation, partnership, or association — name an officer or agent authorized to receive service*):

Why are you getting this?

A lawsuit has been filed against you, or the entity you represent, in this court under the number shown above. A copy of the complaint is attached.

This is not a summons, or an official notice from the court. It is a request that, to avoid expenses, you waive formal service of a summons by signing and returning the enclosed waiver. To avoid these expenses, you must return the signed waiver within (*give at least 30 days or at least 60 days if the defendant is outside any judicial district of the United States*) from the date shown below, which is the date this notice was sent. Two copies of the waiver form are enclosed, along with a stamped, self-addressed envelope or other prepaid means for returning one copy. You may keep the other copy.

What happens next?

If you return the signed waiver, I will file it with the court. The action will then proceed as if you had been served on the date the waiver is filed, but no summons will be served on you and you will have 60 days from the date this notice is sent (see the date below) to answer the complaint (or 90 days if this notice is sent to you outside any judicial district of the United States).

If you do not return the signed waiver within the time indicated, I will arrange to have the summons and complaint served on you. And I will ask the court to require you, or the entity you represent, to pay the expenses of making service.

Please read the enclosed statement about the duty to avoid unnecessary expenses.

I certify that this request is being sent to you on the date below.

Date: _____

_____
(Signature of the attorney
or unrepresented party)

_____
(Printed name)

_____
(Address)

_____
(E–mail address)

_____
(Telephone number)

Rule 4   Waiver of the Service of Summons.

(Caption)

To (*name the plaintiff's attorney or the unrepresented plaintiff*):

I have received your request to waive service of a summons in this action along with a copy of the complaint, two copies of this waiver form, and a prepaid means of returning one signed copy of the form to you.

I, or the entity I represent, agree to save the expense of serving a summons and complaint in this case.

I understand that I, or the entity I represent, will keep all defenses or objections to the lawsuit, the court's jurisdiction, and the venue of the action, but that I waive any objections to the absence of a summons or of service.

I also understand that I, or the entity I represent, must file and serve an answer or a motion under Rule 12 within 60 days from_____, the date when this request was sent (or 90 days if it was sent outside the United States). If I fail to do so, a default judgment will be entered against me or the entity I represent.

Date: _____

_____
(Signature of the attorney
or unrepresented party)

_____
(Printed name)

_____
(Address)

_____
(E–mail address)

_____
(Telephone number)

(Attach the following)

**Duty to Avoid Unnecessary Expenses
of Serving a Summons**

Rule 4 of the Federal Rules of Civil Procedure requires certain defendants to cooperate in saving unnecessary expenses of serving a summons and complaint. A defendant who is located in the United States and who fails to return a signed waiver of service requested by a plaintiff located in the United States will be required to pay the expenses of service, unless the defendant shows good cause for the failure.

"Good cause" does not include a belief that the lawsuit is groundless, or that it has been brought in an improper venue, or that the court has no jurisdiction over this matter or over the defendant or the defendant's property.

If the waiver is signed and returned, you can still make these and all other defenses and objections, but you cannot object to the absence of a summons or of service.

If you waive service, then you must, within the time specified on the waiver form, serve an answer or a motion under Rule 12 on the plaintiff and file a copy with the court. By signing and returning the waiver form, you are allowed more time to respond than if a summons had been served.

(Amended January 21, 1963, effective July 1, 1963; February 28, 1966, effective July 1, 1966; April 29, 1980, effective August 1, 1980; amended by Pub.L. 97-462, § 2, January 12, 1983, 96 Stat. 2527, effective 45 days after January 12, 1983; amended March 2, 1987, effective August 1, 1987; April 22, 1993, effective December 1, 1993; April 17, 2000, effective December 1, 2000; April 30, 2007, effective December 1, 2007; April 29, 2015, effective December 1, 2015; April 28, 2016, effective December 1, 2016; April 27, 2017, effective December 1, 2017.)

RULE 4.1. SERVING OTHER PROCESS

(a) **In General.** Process—other than a summons under Rule 4 or a subpoena under Rule 45—must be served by a United States marshal or deputy marshal or by a person specially appointed for that purpose. It may be served anywhere within the territorial limits of the state where the district court is located and, if authorized by a federal statute, beyond those limits. Proof of service must be made under Rule 4(*l*).

(b) **Enforcing Orders: Committing for Civil Contempt.** An order committing a person for civil contempt of a decree or injunction issued to enforce federal law may be served and enforced in any district. Any other order in a civil-contempt proceeding may be served only in the state where the issuing court is located or elsewhere in the United States within 100 miles from where the order was issued.

(Adopted April 22, 1993, effective December 1, 1993; amended April 30, 2007, effective December 1, 2007.)

RULE 5. SERVING AND FILING PLEADINGS AND OTHER PAPERS

(a) **Service: When Required.**

(1) *In General.* Unless these rules provide otherwise, each of the following papers must be served on every party:

(A) an order stating that service is required;

(B) a pleading filed after the original complaint, unless the court orders otherwise under Rule 5(c) because there are numerous defendants;

(C) a discovery paper required to be served on a party, unless the court orders otherwise;

(D) a written motion, except one that may be heard ex parte; and

(E) a written notice, appearance, demand, or offer of judgment, or any similar paper.

(2) *If a Party Fails to Appear.* No service is required on a party who is in default for failing to appear. But a pleading that asserts a new claim for relief against such a party must be served on that party under Rule 4.

(3) *Seizing Property.* If an action is begun by seizing property and no person is or need be named as a defendant, any service required before the filing of an appearance, answer, or claim must be made on the person who had custody or possession of the property when it was seized.

(b) **Service: How Made.**

(1) *Serving an Attorney.* If a party is represented by an attorney, service under this rule must be made on the attorney unless the court orders service on the party.

(2) *Service in General.* A paper is served under this rule by:

(A) handing it to the person;

(B) leaving it:

(i) at the person's office with a clerk or other person in charge or, if no one is in charge, in a conspicuous place in the office; or

(ii) if the person has no office or the office is closed, at the person's dwelling or usual place of abode with someone of suitable age and discretion who resides there;

(C) mailing it to the person's last known address—in which event service is complete upon mailing;

(D) leaving it with the court clerk if the person has no known address;

(E) sending it to a registered user by filing it with the court's electronic-filing system or sending it by other electronic means that the person consented to in writing—in either of which events service is complete upon filing or sending, but is not effective if the filer or sender learns that it did not reach the person to be served; or

(F) delivering it by any other means that the person consented to in writing—in which event service is complete when the person making service delivers it to the agency designated to make delivery.

(3) *Using Court Facilities.* [Abrogated (Apr. 26, 2018, eff. Dec. 1, 2018.)]

(c) **Serving Numerous Defendants.**

(1) *In General.* If an action involves an unusually large number of defendants, the court may, on motion or on its own, order that:

(A) defendants' pleadings and replies to them need not be served on other defendants;

(B) any crossclaim, counterclaim, avoidance, or affirmative defense in those pleadings and replies to them will be treated as denied or avoided by all other parties; and

(C) filing any such pleading and serving it on the plaintiff constitutes notice of the pleading to all parties.

(2) *Notifying Parties.* A copy of every such order must be served on the parties as the court directs.

(d) Filing.

(1) *Required Filings; Certificate of Service.*

(A) *Papers after the Complaint.* Any paper after the complaint that is required to be served must be filed no later than a reasonable time after service. But disclosures under Rule 26(a)(1) or (2) and the following discovery requests and responses must not be filed until they are used in the proceeding or the court orders filing: depositions, interrogatories, requests for documents or tangible things or to permit entry onto land, and requests for admission.

(B) *Certificate of Service.* No certificate of service is required when a paper is served by filing it with the court's electronic-filing system. When a paper that is required to be served is served by other means:

(i) if the paper is filed, a certificate of service must be filed with it or within a reasonable time after service; and

(ii) if the paper is not filed, a certificate of service need not be filed unless filing is required by court order or by local rule.

(2) *Nonelectronic Filing.* A paper not filed electronically is filed by delivering it:

(A) to the clerk; or

(B) to a judge who agrees to accept it for filing, and who must then note the filing date on the paper and promptly send it to the clerk.

(3) *Electronic Filing and Signing.*

(A) *By a Represented Person—Generally Required; Exceptions.* A person represented by an attorney must file electronically, unless nonelectronic filing is allowed by the court for good cause or is allowed or required by local rule.

(B) *By an Unrepresented Person—When Allowed or Required.* A person not represented by an attorney:

(i) may file electronically only if allowed by court order or by local rule; and

(ii) may be required to file electronically only by court order, or by a local rule that includes reasonable exceptions.

(C) *Signing.* A filing made through a person's electronic-filing account and authorized by that person, together with that person's name on a signature block, constitutes the person's signature.

(D) *Same as a Written Paper.* A paper filed electronically is a written paper for purposes of these rules.

(4) *Acceptance by the Clerk.* The clerk must not refuse to file a paper solely because it is not in the form prescribed by these rules or by a local rule or practice.

(Amended January 21, 1963, effective July 1, 1963; March 30, 1970, effective July 1, 1970; April 29, 1980, effective August 1, 1980; March 2, 1987, effective August 1, 1987; April 30, 1991, effective December 1, 1991; April 22, 1993, effective December 1, 1993; April 23, 1996, effective December 1, 1996; April 17, 2000, effective December 1, 2000; April 23, 2001, effective December 1, 2001; April 12, 2006, effective December 1, 2006; April 30, 2007, effective December 1, 2007; April 26, 2018, effective December 1, 2018.)

RULE 5.1. CONSTITUTIONAL CHALLENGE TO A STATUTE—NOTICE, CERTIFICATION, AND INTERVENTION

(a) Notice by a Party. A party that files a pleading, written motion, or other paper drawing into question the constitutionality of a federal or state statute must promptly:

(1) file a notice of constitutional question stating the question and identifying the paper that raises it, if:

(A) a federal statute is questioned and the parties do not include the United States, one of its agencies, or one of its officers or employees in an official capacity; or

(B) a state statute is questioned and the parties do not include the state, one of its agencies, or one of its officers or employees in an official capacity; and

(2) serve the notice and paper on the Attorney General of the United States if a federal statute is questioned—or on the state attorney general if a state statute is questioned—either by certified or registered mail or by sending it to an electronic address designated by the attorney general for this purpose.

(b) Certification by the Court. The court must, under 28 U.S.C. § 2403, certify to the appropriate attorney general that a statute has been questioned.

(c) Intervention; Final Decision on the Merits. Unless the court sets a later time, the attorney general may intervene within 60 days after the notice is filed or after the court certifies the challenge, whichever is earlier. Before the time to intervene expires, the court may reject the constitutional challenge, but may not enter a final judgment holding the statute unconstitutional.

(d) No Forfeiture. A party's failure to file and serve the notice, or the court's failure to certify, does not forfeit a constitutional claim or defense that is otherwise timely asserted.

(Adopted April 12, 2006, effective December 1, 2006; amended April 30, 2007, effective December 1, 2007.)

RULE 5.2. PRIVACY PROTECTION FOR FILINGS MADE WITH THE COURT

(a) Redacted Filings. Unless the court orders otherwise, in an electronic or paper filing with the court that contains an individual's social-security number, taxpayer-identification number, or birth date, the name of an individual known to be a minor, or a financial-account number, a party or nonparty making the filing may include only:

(1) the last four digits of the social-security number and taxpayer-identification number;

(2) the year of the individual's birth;

(3) the minor's initials; and

(4) the last four digits of the financial-account number.

(b) Exemptions from the Redaction Requirement. The redaction requirement does not apply to the following:

(1) a financial-account number that identifies the property allegedly subject to forfeiture in a forfeiture proceeding;

(2) the record of an administrative or agency proceeding;

(3) the official record of a state-court proceeding;

(4) the record of a court or tribunal, if that record was not subject to the redaction requirement when originally filed;

(5) a filing covered by Rule 5.2(c) or (d); and

(6) a pro se filing in an action brought under 28 U.S.C. §§ 2241, 2254, or 2255.

(c) Limitations on Remote Access to Electronic Files; Social–Security Appeals and Immigration Cases. Unless the court orders otherwise, in an action for benefits under the Social Security Act, and in an action or proceeding relating to an order of removal, to relief from removal, or to immigration benefits or detention, access to an electronic file is authorized as follows:

(1) the parties and their attorneys may have remote electronic access to any part of the case file, including the administrative record;

(2) any other person may have electronic access to the full record at the courthouse, but may have remote electronic access only to:

(A) the docket maintained by the court; and

(B) an opinion, order, judgment, or other disposition of the court, but not any other part of the case file or the administrative record.

(d) Filings Made Under Seal. The court may order that a filing be made under seal without redaction. The court may later unseal the filing or order the person who made the filing to file a redacted version for the public record.

(e) Protective Orders. For good cause, the court may by order in a case:

(1) require redaction of additional information; or

(2) limit or prohibit a nonparty's remote electronic access to a document filed with the court.

(f) Option for Additional Unredacted Filing Under Seal. A person making a redacted filing may also file an unredacted copy under seal. The court must retain the unredacted copy as part of the record.

(g) Option for Filing a Reference List. A filing that contains redacted information may be filed together with a reference list that identifies each item of redacted information

and specifies an appropriate identifier that uniquely corresponds to each item listed. The list must be filed under seal and may be amended as of right. Any reference in the case to a listed identifier will be construed to refer to the corresponding item of information.

(h) Waiver of Protection of Identifiers. A person waives the protection of Rule 5.2(a) as to the person's own information by filing it without redaction and not under seal.

(Adopted April 30, 2007, effective December 1, 2007.)

RULE 6. COMPUTING AND EXTENDING TIME; TIME FOR MOTION PAPERS

(a) Computing Time. The following rules apply in computing any time period specified in these rules, in any local rule or court order, or in any statute that does not specify a method of computing time.

(1) *Period Stated in Days or a Longer Unit.* When the period is stated in days or a longer unit of time:

(A) exclude the day of the event that triggers the period;

(B) count every day, including intermediate Saturdays, Sundays, and legal holidays; and

(C) include the last day of the period, but if the last day is a Saturday, Sunday, or legal holiday, the period continues to run until the end of the next day that is not a Saturday, Sunday, or legal holiday.

(2) *Period Stated in Hours.* When the period is stated in hours:

(A) begin counting immediately on the occurrence of the event that triggers the period;

(B) count every hour, including hours during intermediate Saturdays, Sundays, and legal holidays; and

(C) if the period would end on a Saturday, Sunday, or legal holiday, the period continues to run until the same time on the next day that is not a Saturday, Sunday, or legal holiday.

(3) *Inaccessibility of the Clerk's Office.* Unless the court orders otherwise, if the clerk's office is inaccessible:

(A) on the last day for filing under Rule 6(a)(1), then the time for filing is extended to the first accessible day that is not a Saturday, Sunday, or legal holiday; or

(B) during the last hour for filing under Rule 6(a)(2), then the time for filing is extended to the same time on the first accessible day that is not a Saturday, Sunday, or legal holiday.

(4) *"Last Day" Defined.* Unless a different time is set by a statute, local rule, or court order, the last day ends:

(A) for electronic filing, at midnight in the court's time zone; and

(B) for filing by other means, when the clerk's office is scheduled to close.

(5) *"Next Day" Defined.* The "next day" is determined by continuing to count forward when the period is measured after an event and backward when measured before an event.

(6) "Legal Holiday" Defined. "Legal holiday" means:

(A) the day set aside by statute for observing New Year's Day, Martin Luther King Jr.'s Birthday, Washington's Birthday, Memorial Day, Independence Day, Labor Day, Columbus Day, Veterans' Day, Thanksgiving Day, or Christmas Day;

(B) any day declared a holiday by the President or Congress; and

(C) for periods that are measured after an event, any other day declared a holiday by the state where the district court is located.

(b) Extending Time.

(1) In General. When an act may or must be done within a specified time, the court may, for good cause, extend the time:

(A) with or without motion or notice if the court acts, or if a request is made, before the original time or its extension expires; or

(B) on motion made after the time has expired if the party failed to act because of excusable neglect.

(2) Exceptions. A court must not extend the time to act under Rules 50(b) and (d), 52(b), 59(b), (d), and (e), and 60(b).

(c) Motions, Notices of Hearing, and Affidavits.

(1) In General. A written motion and notice of the hearing must be served at least 14 days before the time specified for the hearing, with the following exceptions:

(A) when the motion may be heard ex parte;

(B) when these rules set a different time; or

(C) when a court order—which a party may, for good cause, apply for ex parte—sets a different time.

(2) Supporting Affidavit. Any affidavit supporting a motion must be served with the motion. Except as Rule 59(c) provides otherwise, any opposing affidavit must be served at least 7 days before the hearing, unless the court permits service at another time.

(d) Additional Time After Certain Kinds of Service. When a party may or must act within a specified time after being served and service is made under Rule 5(b)(2)(C) (mail), (D) (leaving with the clerk), or (F) (other means consented to), 3 days are added after the period would otherwise expire under Rule 6(a).

(Amended December 27, 1946, effective March 19, 1948; January 21, 1963, effective July 1, 1963; February 28, 1966, effective July 1, 1966; December 4, 1967, effective July 1, 1968; March 1, 1971, effective July 1, 1971; April 28, 1983, effective August 1, 1983; April 29, 1985, effective August 1, 1985; March 2, 1987, effective August 1, 1987; April 26, 1999, effective December 1, 1999; April 23, 2001, effective December 1, 2001; April 25, 2005, effective December 1, 2005; April 30, 2007, effective December 1, 2007; March 26, 2009, effective December 1, 2009; April 28, 2016, effective December 1, 2016.)

TITLE III. PLEADINGS AND MOTIONS

RULE 7. PLEADINGS ALLOWED; FORM OF MOTIONS AND OTHER PAPERS

(a) Pleadings. Only these pleadings are allowed:

(1) a complaint;

(2) an answer to a complaint;

(3) an answer to a counterclaim designated as a counterclaim;

(4) an answer to a crossclaim;

(5) a third-party complaint;

(6) an answer to a third-party complaint; and

(7) if the court orders one, a reply to an answer.

(b) Motions and Other Papers.

(1) In General. A request for a court order must be made by motion. The motion must:

(A) be in writing unless made during a hearing or trial;

(B) state with particularity the grounds for seeking the order; and

(C) state the relief sought.

(2) Form. The rules governing captions and other matters of form in pleadings apply to motions and other papers.

(Amended December 27, 1946, effective March 19, 1948; January 21, 1963, effective July 1, 1963; April 28, 1983, effective August 1, 1983; April 30, 2007, effective December 1, 2007.)

RULE 7.1. DISCLOSURE STATEMENT

(a) Who Must File; Contents. A nongovernmental corporate party must file two copies of a disclosure statement that:

(1) identifies any parent corporation and any publicly held corporation owning 10% or more of its stock; or

(2) states that there is no such corporation.

(b) Time to File; Supplemental Filing. A party must:

(1) file the disclosure statement with its first appearance, pleading, petition, motion, response, or other request addressed to the court; and

(2) promptly file a supplemental statement if any required information changes.

(Adopted April 29, 2002, effective December 1, 2002; April 30, 2007, effective December 1, 2007.)

RULE 8. GENERAL RULES OF PLEADING

(a) Claim for Relief. A pleading that states a claim for relief must contain:

(1) a short and plain statement of the grounds for the court's jurisdiction, unless the court already has jurisdiction and the claim needs no new jurisdictional support;

(2) a short and plain statement of the claim showing that the pleader is entitled to relief; and

(3) a demand for the relief sought, which may include relief in the alternative or different types of relief.

(b) Defenses; Admissions and Denials.

(1) *In General.* In responding to a pleading, a party must:

    (A) state in short and plain terms its defenses to each claim asserted against it; and

    (B) admit or deny the allegations asserted against it by an opposing party.

(2) *Denials—Responding to the Substance.* A denial must fairly respond to the substance of the allegation.

(3) *General and Specific Denials.* A party that intends in good faith to deny all the allegations of a pleading—including the jurisdictional grounds—may do so by a general denial. A party that does not intend to deny all the allegations must either specifically deny designated allegations or generally deny all except those specifically admitted.

(4) *Denying Part of an Allegation.* A party that intends in good faith to deny only part of an allegation must admit the part that is true and deny the rest.

(5) *Lacking Knowledge or Information.* A party that lacks knowledge or information sufficient to form a belief about the truth of an allegation must so state, and the statement has the effect of a denial.

(6) *Effect of Failing to Deny.* An allegation—other than one relating to the amount of damages—is admitted if a responsive pleading is required and the allegation is not denied. If a responsive pleading is not required, an allegation is considered denied or avoided.

(c) Affirmative Defenses.

(1) *In General.* In responding to a pleading, a party must affirmatively state any avoidance or affirmative defense, including:

- accord and satisfaction;
- arbitration and award;
- assumption of risk;
- contributory negligence;
- duress;
- estoppel;
- failure of consideration;
- fraud;
- illegality;
- injury by fellow servant;
- laches;
- license;
- payment;
- release;
- res judicata;
- statute of frauds;
- statute of limitations; and

- waiver.

(2) *Mistaken Designation.* If a party mistakenly designates a defense as a counterclaim, or a counterclaim as a defense, the court must, if justice requires, treat the pleading as though it were correctly designated, and may impose terms for doing so.

(d) Pleading to Be Concise and Direct; Alternative Statements; Inconsistency.

(1) *In General.* Each allegation must be simple, concise, and direct. No technical form is required.

(2) *Alternative Statements of a Claim or Defense.* A party may set out 2 or more statements of a claim or defense alternatively or hypothetically, either in a single count or defense or in separate ones. If a party makes alternative statements, the pleading is sufficient if any one of them is sufficient.

(3) *Inconsistent Claims or Defenses.* A party may state as many separate claims or defenses as it has, regardless of consistency.

(e) Construing Pleadings. Pleadings must be construed so as to do justice.

(Amended February 28, 1966, effective July 1, 1966; March 2, 1987, effective August 1, 1987; April 30, 2007, effective December 1, 2007; April 28, 2010, effective December 1, 2010.)

RULE 9.   PLEADING SPECIAL MATTERS

(a) Capacity or Authority to Sue; Legal Existence.

(1) *In General.* Except when required to show that the court has jurisdiction, a pleading need not allege:

    (A) a party's capacity to sue or be sued;

    (B) a party's authority to sue or be sued in a representative capacity; or

    (C) the legal existence of an organized association of persons that is made a party.

(2) *Raising Those Issues.* To raise any of those issues, a party must do so by a specific denial, which must state any supporting facts that are peculiarly within the party's knowledge.

(b) Fraud or Mistake; Conditions of Mind. In alleging fraud or mistake, a party must state with particularity the circumstances constituting fraud or mistake. Malice, intent, knowledge, and other conditions of a person's mind may be alleged generally.

(c) Conditions Precedent. In pleading conditions precedent, it suffices to allege generally that all conditions precedent have occurred or been performed. But when denying that a condition precedent has occurred or been performed, a party must do so with particularity.

(d) Official Document or Act. In pleading an official document or official act, it suffices to allege that the document was legally issued or the act legally done.

(e) Judgment. In pleading a judgment or decision of a domestic or foreign court, a judicial or quasi-judicial tribunal, or a board or officer, it suffices to plead the judgment or decision without showing jurisdiction to render it.

(f) Time and Place. An allegation of time or place is material when testing the sufficiency of a pleading.

(g) Special Damages. If an item of special damage is claimed, it must be specifically stated.

(h) Admiralty or Maritime Claim.

(1) *How Designated.* If a claim for relief is within the admiralty or maritime jurisdiction and also within the court's subject-matter jurisdiction on some other ground, the pleading may designate the claim as an admiralty or maritime claim for purposes of Rules 14(c), 38(e), and 82 and the Supplemental Rules for Admiralty or Maritime Claims and Asset Forfeiture Actions. A claim cognizable only in the admiralty or maritime jurisdiction is an admiralty or maritime claim for those purposes, whether or not so designated.

(2) *Designation for Appeal.* A case that includes an admiralty or maritime claim within this subdivision (h) is an admiralty case within 28 U.S.C. § 1292(a)(3).

(Amended February 28, 1966, effective July 1, 1966; December 4, 1967, effective July 1, 1968; March 30, 1970, effective July 1, 1970; March 2, 1987, effective August 1, 1987; April 11, 1997, effective December 1, 1997; April 12, 2006, effective December 1, 2006; April 30, 2007, effective December 1, 2007.)

RULE 10. FORM OF PLEADINGS

(a) Caption; Names of Parties. Every pleading must have a caption with the court's name, a title, a file number, and a Rule 7(a) designation. The title of the complaint must name all the parties; the title of other pleadings, after naming the first party on each side, may refer generally to other parties.

(b) Paragraphs; Separate Statements. A party must state its claims or defenses in numbered paragraphs, each limited as far as practicable to a single set of circumstances. A later pleading may refer by number to a paragraph in an earlier pleading. If doing so would promote clarity, each claim founded on a separate transaction or occurrence—and each defense other than a denial—must be stated in a separate count or defense.

(c) Adoption by Reference; Exhibits. A statement in a pleading may be adopted by reference elsewhere in the same pleading or in any other pleading or motion. A copy of a written instrument that is an exhibit to a pleading is a part of the pleading for all purposes.

(Amended April 30, 2007, effective December 1, 2007.)

RULE 11. SIGNING PLEADINGS, MOTIONS, AND OTHER PAPERS; REPRESENTATIONS TO THE COURT; SANCTIONS

(a) Signature. Every pleading, written motion, and other paper must be signed by at least one attorney of record in the attorney's name—or by a party personally if the party is unrepresented. The paper must state the signer's address, e-mail address, and telephone number. Unless a rule or statute specifically states otherwise, a pleading need not be verified or accompanied by an affidavit. The court must strike an un-signed paper unless the omission is promptly corrected after being called to the attorney's or party's attention.

(b) Representations to the Court. By presenting to the court a pleading, written motion, or other paper—whether by signing, filing, submitting, or later advocating it—an attorney or unrepresented party certifies that to the best of the person's knowledge, information, and belief, formed after an inquiry reasonable under the circumstances:

(1) it is not being presented for any improper purpose, such as to harass, cause unnecessary delay, or needlessly increase the cost of litigation;

(2) the claims, defenses, and other legal contentions are warranted by existing law or by a nonfrivolous argument for extending, modifying, or reversing existing law or for establishing new law;

(3) the factual contentions have evidentiary support or, if specifically so identified, will likely have evidentiary support after a reasonable opportunity for further investigation or discovery; and

(4) the denials of factual contentions are warranted on the evidence or, if specifically so identified, are reasonably based on belief or a lack of information.

(c) Sanctions.

(1) *In General.* If, after notice and a reasonable opportunity to respond, the court determines that Rule 11(b) has been violated, the court may impose an appropriate sanction on any attorney, law firm, or party that violated the rule or is responsible for the violation. Absent exceptional circumstances, a law firm must be held jointly responsible for a violation committed by its partner, associate, or employee.

(2) *Motion for Sanctions.* A motion for sanctions must be made separately from any other motion and must describe the specific conduct that allegedly violates Rule 11(b). The motion must be served under Rule 5, but it must not be filed or be presented to the court if the challenged paper, claim, defense, contention, or denial is withdrawn or appropriately corrected within 21 days after service or within another time the court sets. If warranted, the court may award to the prevailing party the reasonable expenses, including attorney's fees, incurred for the motion.

(3) *On the Court's Initiative.* On its own, the court may order an attorney, law firm, or party to show cause why conduct specifically described in the order has not violated Rule 11(b).

(4) *Nature of a Sanction.* A sanction imposed under this rule must be limited to what suffices to deter repetition of the conduct or comparable conduct by others similarly situated. The sanction may include nonmonetary directives; an order to pay a penalty into court; or, if imposed on motion and warranted for effective deterrence, an order directing payment to the movant of part or all of the reasonable attorney's fees and other expenses directly resulting from the violation.

(5) *Limitations on Monetary Sanctions.* The court must not impose a monetary sanction:

(A) against a represented party for violating Rule 11(b)(2); or

(B) on its own, unless it issued the show-cause order under Rule 11(c)(3) before voluntary dismissal or settlement of the claims made by or against the party that is, or whose attorneys are, to be sanctioned.

(6) *Requirements for an Order.* An order imposing a sanction must describe the sanctioned conduct and explain the basis for the sanction.

(d) **Inapplicability to Discovery.** This rule does not apply to disclosures and discovery requests, responses, objections, and motions under Rules 26 through 37.

(Amended April 28, 1983, effective August 1, 1983; March 2, 1987, effective August 1, 1987; April 22, 1993, effective December 1, 1993; April 30, 2007, effective December 1, 2007.)

RULE 12. DEFENSES AND OBJECTIONS: WHEN AND HOW PRESENTED; MOTION FOR JUDGMENT ON THE PLEADINGS; CONSOLIDATING MOTIONS; WAIVING DEFENSES; PRETRIAL HEARING

(a) **Time to Serve a Responsive Pleading.**

(1) *In General.* Unless another time is specified by this rule or a federal statute, the time for serving a responsive pleading is as follows:

(A) A defendant must serve an answer:

(i) within 21 days after being served with the summons and complaint; or

(ii) if it has timely waived service under Rule 4(d), within 60 days after the request for a waiver was sent, or within 90 days after it was sent to the defendant outside any judicial district of the United States.

(B) A party must serve an answer to a counterclaim or crossclaim within 21 days after being served with the pleading that states the counterclaim or crossclaim.

(C) A party must serve a reply to an answer within 21 days after being served with an order to reply, unless the order specifies a different time.

(2) *United States and Its Agencies, Officers, or Employees Sued in an Official Capacity.* The United States, a United States agency, or a United States officer or employee sued only in an official capacity must serve an answer to a complaint, counterclaim, or crossclaim within 60 days after service on the United States attorney.

(3) *United States Officers or Employees Sued in an Individual Capacity.* A United States officer or employee sued in an individual capacity for an act or omission occurring in connection with duties performed on the United States' behalf must serve an answer to a complaint, counterclaim, or crossclaim within 60 days after service on the officer or employee or service on the United States attorney, whichever is later.

(4) *Effect of a Motion.* Unless the court sets a different time, serving a motion under this rule alters these periods as follows:

(A) if the court denies the motion or postpones its disposition until trial, the responsive pleading must be served within 14 days after notice of the court's action; or

(B) if the court grants a motion for a more definite statement, the responsive pleading must be served within 14 days after the more definite statement is served.

(b) **How to Present Defenses.** Every defense to a claim for relief in any pleading must be asserted in the responsive pleading if one is required. But a party may assert the following defenses by motion:

(1) lack of subject-matter jurisdiction;

(2) lack of personal jurisdiction;

(3) improper venue;

(4) insufficient process;

(5) insufficient service of process;

(6) failure to state a claim upon which relief can be granted; and

(7) failure to join a party under Rule 19.

A motion asserting any of these defenses must be made before pleading if a responsive pleading is allowed. If a pleading sets out a claim for relief that does not require a responsive pleading, an opposing party may assert at trial any defense to that claim. No defense or objection is waived by joining it with one or more other defenses or objections in a responsive pleading or in a motion.

(c) **Motion for Judgment on the Pleadings.** After the pleadings are closed—but early enough not to delay trial—a party may move for judgment on the pleadings.

(d) **Result of Presenting Matters Outside the Pleadings.** If, on a motion under Rule 12(b)(6) or 12(c), matters outside the pleadings are presented to and not excluded by the court, the motion must be treated as one for summary judgment under Rule 56. All parties must be given a reasonable opportunity to present all the material that is pertinent to the motion.

(e) **Motion for a More Definite Statement.** A party may move for a more definite statement of a pleading to which a responsive pleading is allowed but which is so vague or ambiguous that the party cannot reasonably prepare a response. The motion must be made before filing a responsive pleading and must point out the defects complained of and the details desired. If the court orders a more definite statement and the order is not obeyed within 14 days after notice of the order or within the time the court sets, the court may strike the pleading or issue any other appropriate order.

(f) **Motion to Strike.** The court may strike from a pleading an insufficient defense or any redundant, immaterial, impertinent, or scandalous matter. The court may act:

(1) on its own; or

(2) on motion made by a party either before responding to the pleading or, if a response is not allowed, within 21 days after being served with the pleading.

(g) **Joining Motions.**

(1) *Right to Join.* A motion under this rule may be joined with any other motion allowed by this rule.

(2) *Limitation on Further Motions.* Except as provided in Rule 12(h)(2) or (3), a party that makes a motion under this rule must not make another motion under this rule raising a defense or objection that was available to the party but omitted from its earlier motion.

(h) Waiving and Preserving Certain Defenses.

(1) *When Some Are Waived.* A party waives any defense listed in Rule 12(b)(2)-(5) by:

(A) omitting it from a motion in the circumstances described in Rule 12(g)(2); or

(B) failing to either:

(i) make it by motion under this rule; or

(ii) include it in a responsive pleading or in an amendment allowed by Rule 15(a)(1) as a matter of course.

(2) *When to Raise Others.* Failure to state a claim upon which relief can be granted, to join a person required by Rule 19(b), or to state a legal defense to a claim may be raised:

(A) in any pleading allowed or ordered under Rule 7(a);

(B) by a motion under Rule 12(c); or

(C) at trial.

(3) *Lack of Subject–Matter Jurisdiction.* If the court determines at any time that it lacks subject-matter jurisdiction, the court must dismiss the action.

(i) Hearing Before Trial. If a party so moves, any defense listed in Rule 12(b)(1)-(7)—whether made in a pleading or by motion—and a motion under Rule 12(c) must be heard and decided before trial unless the court orders a deferral until trial.

(Amended December 27, 1946, effective March 19, 1948; January 21, 1963, effective July 1, 1963; February 28, 1966, effective July 1, 1966; March 2, 1987, effective August 1, 1987; April 22, 1993, effective December 1, 1993; April 17, 2000, effective December 1, 2000; April 30, 2007, effective December 1, 2007; March 26, 2009, effective December 1, 2009.)

RULE 13. COUNTERCLAIM AND CROSSCLAIM

(a) Compulsory Counterclaim.

(1) *In General.* A pleading must state as a counterclaim any claim that—at the time of its service—the pleader has against an opposing party if the claim:

(A) arises out of the transaction or occurrence that is the subject matter of the opposing party's claim; and

(B) does not require adding another party over whom the court cannot acquire jurisdiction.

(2) *Exceptions.* The pleader need not state the claim if:

(A) when the action was commenced, the claim was the subject of another pending action; or

(B) the opposing party sued on its claim by attachment or other process that did not establish personal jurisdiction over the pleader on that claim, and the pleader does not assert any counterclaim under this rule.

(b) Permissive Counterclaim. A pleading may state as a counterclaim against an opposing party any claim that is not compulsory.

(c) Relief Sought in a Counterclaim. A counterclaim need not diminish or defeat the recovery sought by the opposing party. It may request relief that exceeds in amount or differs in kind from the relief sought by the opposing party.

(d) Counterclaim Against the United States. These rules do not expand the right to assert a counterclaim—or to claim a credit—against the United States or a United States officer or agency.

(e) Counterclaim Maturing or Acquired After Pleading. The court may permit a party to file a supplemental pleading asserting a counterclaim that matured or was acquired by the party after serving an earlier pleading.

(f) [Abrogated]

(g) Crossclaim Against a Coparty. A pleading may state as a crossclaim any claim by one party against a coparty if the claim arises out of the transaction or occurrence that is the subject matter of the original action or of a counterclaim, or if the claim relates to any property that is the subject matter of the original action. The crossclaim may include a claim that the coparty is or may be liable to the cross-claimant for all or part of a claim asserted in the action against the cross-claimant.

(h) Joining Additional Parties. Rules 19 and 20 govern the addition of a person as a party to a counterclaim or crossclaim.

(i) Separate Trials; Separate Judgments. If the court orders separate trials under Rule 42(b), it may enter judgment on a counterclaim or crossclaim under Rule 54(b) when it has jurisdiction to do so, even if the opposing party's claims have been dismissed or otherwise resolved.

(Amended December 27, 1946, effective March 19, 1948; January 21, 1963, effective July 1, 1963; February 28, 1966, effective July 1, 1966; March 2, 1987, effective August 1, 1987; April 30, 2007, effective December 1, 2007; March 26, 2009, effective December 1, 2009.)

RULE 14. THIRD–PARTY PRACTICE

(a) When a Defending Party May Bring in a Third Party.

(1) *Timing of the Summons and Complaint.* A defending party may, as third-party plaintiff, serve a summons and complaint on a nonparty who is or may be liable to it for all or part of the claim against it. But the third-party plaintiff must, by motion, obtain the court's leave if it files the third-party complaint more than 14 days after serving its original answer.

(2) *Third–Party Defendant's Claims and Defenses.* The person served with the summons and third-party complaint—the "third-party defendant":

(A) must assert any defense against the third-party plaintiff's claim under Rule 12;

(B) must assert any counterclaim against the third-party plaintiff under Rule 13(a), and may assert any counterclaim against the third-party plaintiff under Rule

13(b) or any crossclaim against another third-party defendant under Rule 13(g);

(C) may assert against the plaintiff any defense that the third-party plaintiff has to the plaintiff's claim; and

(D) may also assert against the plaintiff any claim arising out of the transaction or occurrence that is the subject matter of the plaintiff's claim against the third-party plaintiff.

(3) *Plaintiff's Claims Against a Third–Party Defendant.* The plaintiff may assert against the third-party defendant any claim arising out of the transaction or occurrence that is the subject matter of the plaintiff's claim against the third-party plaintiff. The third-party defendant must then assert any defense under Rule 12 and any counterclaim under Rule 13(a), and may assert any counterclaim under Rule 13(b) or any crossclaim under Rule 13(g).

(4) *Motion to Strike, Sever, or Try Separately.* Any party may move to strike the third-party claim, to sever it, or to try it separately.

(5) *Third–Party Defendant's Claim Against a Nonparty.* A third-party defendant may proceed under this rule against a nonparty who is or may be liable to the third-party defendant for all or part of any claim against it.

(6) *Third–Party Complaint In Rem.* If it is within the admiralty or maritime jurisdiction, a third-party complaint may be in rem. In that event, a reference in this rule to the "summons" includes the warrant of arrest, and a reference to the defendant or third-party plaintiff includes, when appropriate, a person who asserts a right under Supplemental Rule C(6)(a)(i) in the property arrested.

(b) When a Plaintiff May Bring in a Third Party. When a claim is asserted against a plaintiff, the plaintiff may bring in a third party if this rule would allow a defendant to do so.

(c) Admiralty or Maritime Claim.

(1) *Scope of Impleader.* If a plaintiff asserts an admiralty or maritime claim under Rule 9(h), the defendant or a person who asserts a right under Supplemental Rule C(6)(a)(i) may, as a third-party plaintiff, bring in a third-party defendant who may be wholly or partly liable—either to the plaintiff or to the third-party plaintiff—for remedy over, contribution, or otherwise on account of the same transaction, occurrence, or series of transactions or occurrences.

(2) *Defending Against a Demand for Judgment for the Plaintiff.* The third-party plaintiff may demand judgment in the plaintiff's favor against the third-party defendant. In that event, the third-party defendant must defend under Rule 12 against the plaintiff's claim as well as the third-party plaintiff's claim; and the action proceeds as if the plaintiff had sued both the third-party defendant and the third-party plaintiff.

(Amended December 27, 1946, effective March 19, 1948; January 21, 1963, effective July 1, 1963; February 28, 1966, effective July 1, 1966; March 2, 1987, effective August 1, 1987; April 17, 2000, effective December 1, 2000; April 12, 2006, effective December 1, 2006; April 30, 2007, effective December 1, 2007; March 26, 2009, effective December 1, 2009.)

RULE 15. AMENDED AND SUPPLEMENTAL PLEADINGS

(a) Amendments Before Trial.

(1) *Amending as a Matter of Course.* A party may amend its pleading once as a matter of course within:

(A) 21 days after serving it, or

(B) if the pleading is one to which a responsive pleading is required, 21 days after service of a responsive pleading or 21 days after service of a motion under Rule 12(b), (e), or (f), whichever is earlier.

(2) *Other Amendments.* In all other cases, a party may amend its pleading only with the opposing party's written consent or the court's leave. The court should freely give leave when justice so requires.

(3) *Time to Respond.* Unless the court orders otherwise, any required response to an amended pleading must be made within the time remaining to respond to the original pleading or within 14 days after service of the amended pleading, whichever is later.

(b) Amendments During and After Trial.

(1) *Based on an Objection at Trial.* If, at trial, a party objects that evidence is not within the issues raised in the pleadings, the court may permit the pleadings to be amended. The court should freely permit an amendment when doing so will aid in presenting the merits and the objecting party fails to satisfy the court that the evidence would prejudice that party's action or defense on the merits. The court may grant a continuance to enable the objecting party to meet the evidence.

(2) *For Issues Tried by Consent.* When an issue not raised by the pleadings is tried by the parties' express or implied consent, it must be treated in all respects as if raised in the pleadings. A party may move—at any time, even after judgment—to amend the pleadings to conform them to the evidence and to raise an unpleaded issue. But failure to amend does not affect the result of the trial of that issue.

(c) Relation Back of Amendments.

(1) *When an Amendment Relates Back.* An amendment to a pleading relates back to the date of the original pleading when:

(A) the law that provides the applicable statute of limitations allows relation back;

(B) the amendment asserts a claim or defense that arose out of the conduct, transaction, or occurrence set out—or attempted to be set out—in the original pleading; or

(C) the amendment changes the party or the naming of the party against whom a claim is asserted, if Rule 15(c)(1)(B) is satisfied and if, within the period provided by Rule 4(m) for serving the summons and complaint, the party to be brought in by amendment:

(i) received such notice of the action that it will not be prejudiced in defending on the merits; and

(ii) knew or should have known that the action would have been brought against it, but for a mistake concerning the proper party's identity.

(2) *Notice to the United States.* When the United States or a United States officer or agency is added as a defendant by amendment, the notice requirements of Rule 15(c)(1)(C)(i) and (ii) are satisfied if, during the stated period, process was delivered or mailed to the United States attorney or the United States attorney's designee, to the Attorney General of the United States, or to the officer or agency.

(d) Supplemental Pleadings. On motion and reasonable notice, the court may, on just terms, permit a party to serve a supplemental pleading setting out any transaction, occurrence, or event that happened after the date of the pleading to be supplemented. The court may permit supplementation even though the original pleading is defective in stating a claim or defense. The court may order that the opposing party plead to the supplemental pleading within a specified time.

(Amended January 21, 1963, effective July 1, 1963; February 28, 1966, effective July 1, 1966; March 2, 1987, effective August 1, 1987; April 30, 1991, effective December 1, 1991; amended by Pub.L. 102–198, § 11, December 9, 1991, 105 Stat. 1626; amended April 22, 1993, effective December 1, 1993; April 30, 2007, effective December 1, 2007; March 26, 2009, effective December 1, 2009.)

RULE 16. PRETRIAL CONFERENCES; SCHEDULING; MANAGEMENT

(a) Purposes of a Pretrial Conference. In any action, the court may order the attorneys and any unrepresented parties to appear for one or more pretrial conferences for such purposes as:

(1) expediting disposition of the action;

(2) establishing early and continuing control so that the case will not be protracted because of lack of management;

(3) discouraging wasteful pretrial activities;

(4) improving the quality of the trial through more thorough preparation; and

(5) facilitating settlement.

(b) Scheduling.

(1) *Scheduling Order.* Except in categories of actions exempted by local rule, the district judge—or a magistrate judge when authorized by local rule—must issue a scheduling order:

(A) after receiving the parties' report under Rule 26(f); or

(B) after consulting with the parties' attorneys and any unrepresented parties at a scheduling conference.

(2) *Time to Issue.* The judge must issue the scheduling order as soon as practicable, but unless the judge finds good cause for delay, the judge must issue it within the earlier of 90 days after any defendant has been served with the complaint or 60 days after any defendant has appeared.

(3) *Contents of the Order.*

(A) *Required Contents.* The scheduling order must limit the time to join other parties, amend the pleadings, complete discovery, and file motions.

(B) *Permitted Contents.* The scheduling order may:

(i) modify the timing of disclosures under Rules 26(a) and 26(e)(1);

(ii) modify the extent of discovery;

(iii) provide for disclosure, discovery, or preservation of electronically stored information;

(iv) include any agreements the parties reach for asserting claims of privilege or of protection as trial-preparation material after information is produced, including agreements reached under Federal Rule of Evidence 502;

(v) direct that before moving for an order relating to discovery, the movant must request a conference with the court;

(vi) set dates for pretrial conferences and for trial; and

(vii) include other appropriate matters.

(4) *Modifying a Schedule.* A schedule may be modified only for good cause and with the judge's consent.

(c) Attendance and Matters for Consideration at a Pretrial Conference.

(1) *Attendance.* A represented party must authorize at least one of its attorneys to make stipulations and admissions about all matters that can reasonably be anticipated for discussion at a pretrial conference. If appropriate, the court may require that a party or its representative be present or reasonably available by other means to consider possible settlement.

(2) *Matters for Consideration.* At any pretrial conference, the court may consider and take appropriate action on the following matters:

(A) formulating and simplifying the issues, and eliminating frivolous claims or defenses;

(B) amending the pleadings if necessary or desirable;

(C) obtaining admissions and stipulations about facts and documents to avoid unnecessary proof, and ruling in advance on the admissibility of evidence;

(D) avoiding unnecessary proof and cumulative evidence, and limiting the use of testimony under Federal Rule of Evidence 702;

(E) determining the appropriateness and timing of summary adjudication under Rule 56;

(F) controlling and scheduling discovery, including orders affecting disclosures and discovery under Rule 26 and Rules 29 through 37;

(G) identifying witnesses and documents, scheduling the filing and exchange of any pretrial briefs, and setting dates for further conferences and for trial;

(H) referring matters to a magistrate judge or a master;

(I) settling the case and using special procedures to assist in resolving the dispute when authorized by statute or local rule;

(J) determining the form and content of the pretrial order;

(K) disposing of pending motions;

(L) adopting special procedures for managing potentially difficult or protracted actions that may involve complex issues, multiple parties, difficult legal questions, or unusual proof problems;

(M) ordering a separate trial under Rule 42(b) of a claim, counterclaim, crossclaim, third-party claim, or particular issue;

(N) ordering the presentation of evidence early in the trial on a manageable issue that might, on the evidence, be the basis for a judgment as a matter of law under Rule 50(a) or a judgment on partial findings under Rule 52(c);

(O) establishing a reasonable limit on the time allowed to present evidence; and

(P) facilitating in other ways the just, speedy, and inexpensive disposition of the action.

(d) Pretrial Orders. After any conference under this rule, the court should issue an order reciting the action taken. This order controls the course of the action unless the court modifies it.

(e) Final Pretrial Conference and Orders. The court may hold a final pretrial conference to formulate a trial plan, including a plan to facilitate the admission of evidence. The conference must be held as close to the start of trial as is reasonable, and must be attended by at least one attorney who will conduct the trial for each party and by any unrepresented party. The court may modify the order issued after a final pretrial conference only to prevent manifest injustice.

(f) Sanctions.

(1) *In General.* On motion or on its own, the court may issue any just orders, including those authorized by Rule 37(b)(2)(A)(ii)-(vii), if a party or its attorney:

(A) fails to appear at a scheduling or other pretrial conference;

(B) is substantially unprepared to participate—or does not participate in good faith—in the conference; or

(C) fails to obey a scheduling or other pretrial order.

(2) *Imposing Fees and Costs.* Instead of or in addition to any other sanction, the court must order the party, its attorney, or both to pay the reasonable expenses—including attorney's fees—incurred because of any noncompliance with this rule, unless the noncompliance was substantially justified or other circumstances make an award of expenses unjust.

(Amended April 28, 1983, effective August 1, 1983; March 2, 1987, effective August 1, 1987; April 22, 1993, effective December 1, 1993; April 12, 2006, effective December 1, 2006; April 30, 2007, effective December 1, 2007; April 29, 2015, effective December 1, 2015.)

TITLE IV. PARTIES

RULE 17. PLAINTIFF AND DEFENDANT; CAPACITY; PUBLIC OFFICERS

(a) Real Party in Interest.

(1) *Designation in General.* An action must be prosecuted in the name of the real party in interest. The following may sue in their own names without joining the person for whose benefit the action is brought:

(A) an executor;

(B) an administrator;

(C) a guardian;

(D) a bailee;

(E) a trustee of an express trust;

(F) a party with whom or in whose name a contract has been made for another's benefit; and

(G) a party authorized by statute.

(2) *Action in the Name of the United States for Another's Use or Benefit.* When a federal statute so provides, an action for another's use or benefit must be brought in the name of the United States.

(3) *Joinder of the Real Party in Interest.* The court may not dismiss an action for failure to prosecute in the name of the real party in interest until, after an objection, a reasonable time has been allowed for the real party in interest to ratify, join, or be substituted into the action. After ratification, joinder, or substitution, the action proceeds as if it had been originally commenced by the real party in interest.

(b) Capacity to Sue or Be Sued. Capacity to sue or be sued is determined as follows:

(1) for an individual who is not acting in a representative capacity, by the law of the individual's domicile;

(2) for a corporation, by the law under which it was organized; and

(3) for all other parties, by the law of the state where the court is located, except that:

(A) a partnership or other unincorporated association with no such capacity under that state's law may sue or be sued in its common name to enforce a substantive right existing under the United States Constitution or laws; and

(B) 28 U.S.C. §§ 754 and 959(a) govern the capacity of a receiver appointed by a United States court to sue or be sued in a United States court.

(c) Minor or Incompetent Person.

(1) *With a Representative.* The following representatives may sue or defend on behalf of a minor or an incompetent person:

(A) a general guardian;

(B) a committee;

(C) a conservator; or

(D) a like fiduciary.

(2) *Without a Representative.* A minor or an incompetent person who does not have a duly appointed representative may sue by a next friend or by a guardian ad litem. The court must appoint a guardian ad litem—or issue another appropriate order—to protect a minor or incompetent person who is unrepresented in an action.

(d) Public Officer's Title and Name. A public officer who sues or is sued in an official capacity may be designated by official title rather than by name, but the court may order that the officer's name be added.

(Amended December 27, 1946, effective March 19, 1948; December 29, 1948, effective October 20, 1949; February 28, 1966, effective July 1, 1966; March 2, 1987, effective August 1, 1987; April 25, 1988, effective August 1, 1988; amended by Pub.L. 100–690, Title VII, § 7049, November 18, 1988, 102 Stat. 4401 (although amendment by Pub.L. 100–690 could not be executed due to prior amendment by Court order which made the same change effective August 1, 1988); April 30, 2007, effective December 1, 2007.)

RULE 18.   JOINDER OF CLAIMS

(a) In General. A party asserting a claim, counterclaim, crossclaim, or third-party claim may join, as independent or alternative claims, as many claims as it has against an opposing party.

(b) Joinder of Contingent Claims. A party may join two claims even though one of them is contingent on the disposition of the other; but the court may grant relief only in accordance with the parties' relative substantive rights. In particular, a plaintiff may state a claim for money and a claim to set aside a conveyance that is fraudulent as to that plaintiff, without first obtaining a judgment for the money.

(Amended February 28, 1966, effective July 1, 1966; March 2, 1987, effective August 1, 1987; April 30, 2007, effective December 1, 2007.)

RULE 19.   REQUIRED JOINDER OF PARTIES

(a) Persons Required to Be Joined if Feasible.

(1) *Required Party.* A person who is subject to service of process and whose joinder will not deprive the court of subject-matter jurisdiction must be joined as a party if:

(A) in that person's absence, the court cannot accord complete relief among existing parties; or

(B) that person claims an interest relating to the subject of the action and is so situated that disposing of the action in the person's absence may:

(i) as a practical matter impair or impede the person's ability to protect the interest; or

(ii) leave an existing party subject to a substantial risk of incurring double, multiple, or otherwise inconsistent obligations because of the interest.

(2) *Joinder by Court Order.* If a person has not been joined as required, the court must order that the person be made a party. A person who refuses to join as a plaintiff may be made either a defendant or, in a proper case, an involuntary plaintiff.

(3) *Venue.* If a joined party objects to venue and the joinder would make venue improper, the court must dismiss that party.

(b) When Joinder Is Not Feasible. If a person who is required to be joined if feasible cannot be joined, the court must determine whether, in equity and good conscience, the action should proceed among the existing parties or should be dismissed. The factors for the court to consider include:

(1) the extent to which a judgment rendered in the person's absence might prejudice that person or the existing parties;

(2) the extent to which any prejudice could be lessened or avoided by:

(A) protective provisions in the judgment;

(B) shaping the relief; or

(C) other measures;

(3) whether a judgment rendered in the person's absence would be adequate; and

(4) whether the plaintiff would have an adequate remedy if the action were dismissed for nonjoinder.

(c) Pleading the Reasons for Nonjoinder. When asserting a claim for relief, a party must state:

(1) the name, if known, of any person who is required to be joined if feasible but is not joined; and

(2) the reasons for not joining that person.

(d) Exception for Class Actions. This rule is subject to Rule 23.

(Amended February 28, 1966, effective July 1, 1966; March 2, 1987, effective August 1, 1987; April 30, 2007, effective December 1, 2007.)

RULE 20.   PERMISSIVE JOINDER OF PARTIES

(a) Persons Who May Join or Be Joined.

(1) *Plaintiffs.* Persons may join in one action as plaintiffs if:

(A) they assert any right to relief jointly, severally, or in the alternative with respect to or arising out of the same transaction, occurrence, or series of transactions or occurrences; and

(B) any question of law or fact common to all plaintiffs will arise in the action.

(2) *Defendants.* Persons—as well as a vessel, cargo, or other property subject to admiralty process in rem—may be joined in one action as defendants if:

(A) any right to relief is asserted against them jointly, severally, or in the alternative with respect to or arising out of the same transaction, occurrence, or series of transactions or occurrences; and

(B) any question of law or fact common to all defendants will arise in the action.

(3) *Extent of Relief.* Neither a plaintiff nor a defendant need be interested in obtaining or defending against all the relief demanded. The court may grant judgment to one or more plaintiffs according to their rights, and against one or more defendants according to their liabilities.

(b) **Protective Measures.** The court may issue orders—including an order for separate trials—to protect a party against embarrassment, delay, expense, or other prejudice that arises from including a person against whom the party asserts no claim and who asserts no claim against the party.

(Amended February 28, 1966, effective July 1, 1966; March 2, 1987, effective August 1, 1987; April 30, 2007, effective December 1, 2007.)

RULE 21. MISJOINDER AND NONJOINDER OF PARTIES

Misjoinder of parties is not a ground for dismissing an action. On motion or on its own, the court may at any time, on just terms, add or drop a party. The court may also sever any claim against a party.

(Amended April 30, 2007, effective December 1, 2007.)

RULE 22. INTERPLEADER

(a) **Grounds.**

(1) *By a Plaintiff.* Persons with claims that may expose a plaintiff to double or multiple liability may be joined as defendants and required to interplead. Joinder for interpleader is proper even though:

(A) the claims of the several claimants, or the titles on which their claims depend, lack a common origin or are adverse and independent rather than identical; or

(B) the plaintiff denies liability in whole or in part to any or all of the claimants.

(2) *By a Defendant.* A defendant exposed to similar liability may seek interpleader through a crossclaim or counterclaim.

(b) **Relation to Other Rules and Statutes.** This rule supplements—and does not limit—the joinder of parties allowed by Rule 20. The remedy this rule provides is in addition to—and does not supersede or limit—the remedy provided by 28 U.S.C. §§ 1335, 1397, and 2361. An action under those statutes must be conducted under these rules.

(Amended December 29, 1948, effective October 20, 1949; March 2, 1987, effective August 1, 1987; April 30, 2007, effective December 1, 2007.)

RULE 23. CLASS ACTIONS

(a) **Prerequisites.** One or more members of a class may sue or be sued as representative parties on behalf of all members only if:

(1) the class is so numerous that joinder of all members is impracticable;

(2) there are questions of law or fact common to the class;

(3) the claims or defenses of the representative parties are typical of the claims or defenses of the class; and

(4) the representative parties will fairly and adequately protect the interests of the class.

(b) **Types of Class Actions.** A class action may be maintained if Rule 23(a) is satisfied and if:

(1) prosecuting separate actions by or against individual class members would create a risk of:

(A) inconsistent or varying adjudications with respect to individual class members that would establish incompatible standards of conduct for the party opposing the class; or

(B) adjudications with respect to individual class members that, as a practical matter, would be dispositive of the interests of the other members not parties to the individual adjudications or would substantially impair or impede their ability to protect their interests;

(2) the party opposing the class has acted or refused to act on grounds that apply generally to the class, so that final injunctive relief or corresponding declaratory relief is appropriate respecting the class as a whole; or

(3) the court finds that the questions of law or fact common to class members predominate over any questions affecting only individual members, and that a class action is superior to other available methods for fairly and efficiently adjudicating the controversy. The matters pertinent to these findings include:

(A) the class members' interests in individually controlling the prosecution or defense of separate actions;

(B) the extent and nature of any litigation concerning the controversy already begun by or against class members;

(C) the desirability or undesirability of concentrating the litigation of the claims in the particular forum; and

(D) the likely difficulties in managing a class action.

(c) **Certification Order; Notice to Class Members; Judgment; Issues Classes; Subclasses.**

(1) *Certification Order.*

(A) *Time to Issue.* At an early practicable time after a person sues or is sued as a class representative, the court must determine by order whether to certify the action as a class action.

(B) *Defining the Class; Appointing Class Counsel.* An order that certifies a class action must define the class and the class claims, issues, or defenses, and must appoint class counsel under Rule 23(g).

(C) *Altering or Amending the Order.* An order that grants or denies class certification may be altered or amended before final judgment.

(2) *Notice.*

(A) *For (b)(1) or (b)(2) Classes.* For any class certified under Rule 23(b)(1) or (b)(2), the court may direct appropriate notice to the class.

(B) *For (b)(3) Classes.* For any class certified under Rule 23(b)(3)—or upon ordering notice under Rule 23(e)(1) to a class proposed to be certified for purposes of settlement under Rule 23(b)(3)—the court must direct to class members the best notice that is practicable under the circumstances, including individual notice to all members who can be identified through reasonable effort. The notice may be by one or more of the following: United States mail, electronic means, or other appropriate means. The notice must clearly and concisely state in plain, easily understood language:

(i) the nature of the action;

(ii) the definition of the class certified;

(iii) the class claims, issues, or defenses;

(iv) that a class member may enter an appearance through an attorney if the member so desires;

(v) that the court will exclude from the class any member who requests exclusion;

(vi) the time and manner for requesting exclusion; and

(vii) the binding effect of a class judgment on members under Rule 23(c)(3).

(3) *Judgment.* Whether or not favorable to the class, the judgment in a class action must:

(A) for any class certified under Rule 23(b)(1) or (b)(2), include and describe those whom the court finds to be class members; and

(B) for any class certified under Rule 23(b)(3), include and specify or describe those to whom the Rule 23(c)(2) notice was directed, who have not requested exclusion, and whom the court finds to be class members.

(4) *Particular Issues.* When appropriate, an action may be brought or maintained as a class action with respect to particular issues.

(5) *Subclasses.* When appropriate, a class may be divided into subclasses that are each treated as a class under this rule.

(d) Conducting the Action.

(1) *In General.* In conducting an action under this rule, the court may issue orders that:

(A) determine the course of proceedings or prescribe measures to prevent undue repetition or complication in presenting evidence or argument;

(B) require—to protect class members and fairly conduct the action—giving appropriate notice to some or all class members of:

(i) any step in the action;

(ii) the proposed extent of the judgment; or

(iii) the members' opportunity to signify whether they consider the representation fair and adequate, to intervene and present claims or defenses, or to otherwise come into the action;

(C) impose conditions on the representative parties or on intervenors;

(D) require that the pleadings be amended to eliminate allegations about representation of absent persons and that the action proceed accordingly; or

(E) deal with similar procedural matters.

(2) *Combining and Amending Orders.* An order under Rule 23(d)(1) may be altered or amended from time to time and may be combined with an order under Rule 16.

(e) Settlement, Voluntary Dismissal, or Compromise. The claims, issues, or defenses of a certified class—or a class proposed to be certified for purposes of settlement—may be settled, voluntarily dismissed, or compromised only with the court's approval. The following procedures apply to a proposed settlement, voluntary dismissal, or compromise:

(1) *Notice to the Class.*

(A) *Information That Parties Must Provide to the Court.* The parties must provide the court with information sufficient to enable it to determine whether to give notice of the proposal to the class.

(B) *Grounds for a Decision to Give Notice.* The court must direct notice in a reasonable manner to all class members who would be bound by the proposal if giving notice is justified by the parties' showing that the court will likely be able to:

(i) approve the proposal under Rule 23(e)(2); and

(ii) certify the class for purposes of judgment on the proposal.

(2) *Approval of the Proposal.* If the proposal would bind class members, the court may approve it only after a hearing and only on finding that it is fair, reasonable, and adequate after considering whether:

(A) the class representatives and class counsel have adequately represented the class;

(B) the proposal was negotiated at arm's length;

(C) the relief provided for the class is adequate, taking into account:

(i) the costs, risks, and delay of trial and appeal;

(ii) the effectiveness of any proposed method of distributing relief to the class, including the method of processing class-member claims;

(iii) the terms of any proposed award of attorney's fees, including timing of payment; and

(iv) any agreement required to be identified under Rule 23(e)(3); and

(D) the proposal treats class members equitably relative to each other.

(3) *Identifying Agreements.* The parties seeking approval must file a statement identifying any agreement made in connection with the proposal.

(4) *New Opportunity to be Excluded.* If the class action was previously certified under Rule 23(b)(3), the court may refuse to approve a settlement unless it affords a new opportunity to request exclusion to individual class members who had an earlier opportunity to request exclusion but did not do so.

(5) *Class–Member Objections.*

(A) *In General.* Any class member may object to the proposal if it requires court approval under this subdivision (e). The objection must state whether it applies only to the objector, to a specific subset of the class, or to the entire class, and also state with specificity the grounds for the objection.

(B) *Court Approval Required for Payment in Connection with an Objection.* Unless approved by the court after a hearing, no payment or other consideration may be provided in connection with:

(i) forgoing or withdrawing an objection, or

(ii) forgoing, dismissing, or abandoning an appeal from a judgment approving the proposal.

(C) *Procedure for Approval After an Appeal.* If approval under Rule 23(e)(5)(B) has not been obtained before an appeal is docketed in the court of appeals, the procedure of Rule 62.1 applies while the appeal remains pending.

(f) Appeals. A court of appeals may permit an appeal from an order granting or denying class-action certification under this rule, but not from an order under Rule 23(e)(1). A party must file a petition for permission to appeal with the circuit clerk within 14 days after the order is entered, or within 45 days after the order is entered if any party is the United States, a United States agency, or a United States officer or employee sued for an act or omission occurring in connection with duties performed on the United States' behalf. An appeal does not stay proceedings in the district court unless the district judge or the court of appeals so orders.

(g) Class Counsel.

(1) *Appointing Class Counsel.* Unless a statute provides otherwise, a court that certifies a class must appoint class counsel. In appointing class counsel, the court:

(A) must consider:

(i) the work counsel has done in identifying or investigating potential claims in the action;

(ii) counsel's experience in handling class actions, other complex litigation, and the types of claims asserted in the action;

(iii) counsel's knowledge of the applicable law; and

(iv) the resources that counsel will commit to representing the class;

(B) may consider any other matter pertinent to counsel's ability to fairly and adequately represent the interests of the class;

(C) may order potential class counsel to provide information on any subject pertinent to the appointment and to propose terms for attorney's fees and nontaxable costs;

(D) may include in the appointing order provisions about the award of attorney's fees or nontaxable costs under Rule 23(h); and

(E) may make further orders in connection with the appointment.

(2) *Standard for Appointing Class Counsel.* When one applicant seeks appointment as class counsel, the court may appoint that applicant only if the applicant is adequate under Rule 23(g)(1) and (4). If more than one adequate applicant seeks appointment, the court must appoint the applicant best able to represent the interests of the class.

(3) *Interim Counsel.* The court may designate interim counsel to act on behalf of a putative class before determining whether to certify the action as a class action.

(4) *Duty of Class Counsel.* Class counsel must fairly and adequately represent the interests of the class.

(h) Attorney's Fees and Nontaxable Costs. In a certified class action, the court may award reasonable attorney's fees and nontaxable costs that are authorized by law or by the parties' agreement. The following procedures apply:

(1) A claim for an award must be made by motion under Rule 54(d)(2), subject to the provisions of this subdivision (h), at a time the court sets. Notice of the motion must be served on all parties and, for motions by class counsel, directed to class members in a reasonable manner.

(2) A class member, or a party from whom payment is sought, may object to the motion.

(3) The court may hold a hearing and must find the facts and state its legal conclusions under Rule 52(a).

(4) The court may refer issues related to the amount of the award to a special master or a magistrate judge, as provided in Rule 54(d)(2)(D).

(Amended February 28, 1966, effective July 1, 1966; March 2, 1987, effective August 1, 1987; April 24, 1998, effective December 1, 1998; March 27, 2003, effective December 1, 2003; April 30, 2007, effective December 1, 2007; March 26, 2009, effective December 1, 2009; April 26, 2018, effective December 1, 2018.)

RULE 23.1. DERIVATIVE ACTIONS

(a) Prerequisites. This rule applies when one or more shareholders or members of a corporation or an unincorporated association bring a derivative action to enforce a right that the corporation or association may properly assert but has failed to enforce. The derivative action may not be maintained if it appears that the plaintiff does not fairly and adequately represent the interests of shareholders or members who are similarly situated in enforcing the right of the corporation or association.

(b) Pleading Requirements. The complaint must be verified and must:

(1) allege that the plaintiff was a shareholder or member at the time of the transaction complained of, or that the plaintiff's share or membership later devolved on it by operation of law;

(2) allege that the action is not a collusive one to confer jurisdiction that the court would otherwise lack; and

(3) state with particularity:

(A) any effort by the plaintiff to obtain the desired action from the directors or comparable authority and, if necessary, from the shareholders or members; and

(B) the reasons for not obtaining the action or not making the effort.

(c) Settlement, Dismissal, and Compromise. A derivative action may be settled, voluntarily dismissed, or compromised only with the court's approval. Notice of a proposed settlement, voluntary dismissal, or compromise must be given to shareholders or members in the manner that the court orders.

(Adopted February 28, 1966, effective July 1, 1966; amended March 2, 1987, effective August 1, 1987; April 30, 2007, effective December 1, 2007.)

RULE 23.2. ACTIONS RELATING TO UNINCORPORATED ASSOCIATIONS

This rule applies to an action brought by or against the members of an unincorporated association as a class by naming certain members as representative parties. The action may be maintained only if it appears that those parties will fairly and adequately protect the interests of the association and its members. In conducting the action, the court may issue any appropriate orders corresponding with those in Rule 23(d), and the procedure for settlement, voluntary dismissal, or compromise must correspond with the procedure in Rule 23(e).

(Adopted February 28, 1966, effective July 1, 1966; amended April 30, 2007, effective December 1, 2007.)

RULE 24. INTERVENTION

(a) Intervention of Right. On timely motion, the court must permit anyone to intervene who:

(1) is given an unconditional right to intervene by a federal statute; or

(2) claims an interest relating to the property or transaction that is the subject of the action, and is so situated that disposing of the action may as a practical matter impair or impede the movant's ability to protect its interest, unless existing parties adequately represent that interest.

(b) Permissive Intervention.

(1) *In General.* On timely motion, the court may permit anyone to intervene who:

(A) is given a conditional right to intervene by a federal statute; or

(B) has a claim or defense that shares with the main action a common question of law or fact.

(2) *By a Government Officer or Agency.* On timely motion, the court may permit a federal or state governmental officer or agency to intervene if a party's claim or defense is based on:

(A) a statute or executive order administered by the officer or agency; or

(B) any regulation, order, requirement, or agreement issued or made under the statute or executive order.

(3) *Delay or Prejudice.* In exercising its discretion, the court must consider whether the intervention will unduly delay or prejudice the adjudication of the original parties' rights.

(c) Notice and Pleading Required. A motion to intervene must be served on the parties as provided in Rule 5. The motion must state the grounds for intervention and be accompanied by a pleading that sets out the claim or defense for which intervention is sought.

(Amended December 27, 1946, effective March 19, 1948; December 29, 1948, effective October 20, 1949; January 21, 1963, effective July 1, 1963; February 28, 1966, effective July 1, 1966; March 2, 1987, effective August 1, 1987; April 30, 1991, effective December 1, 1991; April 12, 2006, effective December 1, 2006; April 30, 2007, effective December 1, 2007.)

RULE 25. SUBSTITUTION OF PARTIES

(a) Death.

(1) *Substitution if the Claim Is Not Extinguished.* If a party dies and the claim is not extinguished, the court may order substitution of the proper party. A motion for substitution may be made by any party or by the decedent's successor or representative. If the motion is not made within 90 days after service of a statement noting the death, the action by or against the decedent must be dismissed.

(2) *Continuation Among the Remaining Parties.* After a party's death, if the right sought to be enforced survives only to or against the remaining parties, the action does not abate, but proceeds in favor of or against the remaining parties. The death should be noted on the record.

(3) *Service.* A motion to substitute, together with a notice of hearing, must be served on the parties as provided in Rule 5 and on nonparties as provided in Rule 4. A statement noting death must be served in the same manner. Service may be made in any judicial district.

(b) Incompetency. If a party becomes incompetent, the court may, on motion, permit the action to be continued by or against the party's representative. The motion must be served as provided in Rule 25(a)(3).

(c) Transfer of Interest. If an interest is transferred, the action may be continued by or against the original party unless the court, on motion, orders the transferee to be substituted in the action or joined with the original party. The motion must be served as provided in Rule 25(a)(3).

(d) Public Officers; Death or Separation from Office. An action does not abate when a public officer who is a party in an official capacity dies, resigns, or otherwise ceases to hold office while the action is pending. The officer's successor is automatically substituted as a party. Later proceedings should be in the substituted party's name, but any misnomer not affecting the parties' substantial rights must be disregarded. The court may order substitution at any time, but the absence of such an order does not affect the substitution.

(Amended December 29, 1948, effective October 20, 1949; April 17, 1961, effective July 19, 1961; January 21, 1963, effective July 1, 1963; March 2, 1987, effective August 1, 1987; April 30, 2007, effective December 1, 2007.)

TITLE V. DISCLOSURES AND DISCOVERY

RULE 26. DUTY TO DISCLOSE; GENERAL PROVISIONS GOVERNING DISCOVERY

(a) Required Disclosures.

(1) *Initial Disclosure.*

(A) *In General.* Except as exempted by Rule 26(a)(1)(B) or as otherwise stipulated or ordered by the court, a party must, without awaiting a discovery request, provide to the other parties:

(i) the name and, if known, the address and telephone number of each individual likely to have discoverable information—along with the subjects of that information—that the disclosing party may use to support its claims or defenses, unless the use would be solely for impeachment;

(ii) a copy—or a description by category and location—of all documents, electronically stored information, and tangible things that the disclosing party has in its possession, custody, or control and may use to support its claims or defenses, unless the use would be solely for impeachment;

(iii) a computation of each category of damages claimed by the disclosing party—who must also make available for inspection and copying as under Rule 34 the documents or other evidentiary material, unless privileged or protected from disclosure, on which each computation is based, including materials bearing on the nature and extent of injuries suffered; and

(iv) for inspection and copying as under Rule 34, any insurance agreement under which an insurance business may be liable to satisfy all or part of a possible judgment in the action or to indemnify or reimburse for payments made to satisfy the judgment.

(B) *Proceedings Exempt from Initial Disclosure.* The following proceedings are exempt from initial disclosure:

(i) an action for review on an administrative record;

(ii) a forfeiture action in rem arising from a federal statute;

(iii) a petition for habeas corpus or any other proceeding to challenge a criminal conviction or sentence;

(iv) an action brought without an attorney by a person in the custody of the United States, a state, or a state subdivision;

(v) an action to enforce or quash an administrative summons or subpoena;

(vi) an action by the United States to recover benefit payments;

(vii) an action by the United States to collect on a student loan guaranteed by the United States;

(viii) a proceeding ancillary to a proceeding in another court; and

(ix) an action to enforce an arbitration award.

(C) *Time for Initial Disclosures—In General.* A party must make the initial disclosures at or within 14 days after the parties' Rule 26(f) conference unless a different time is set by stipulation or court order, or unless a party objects during the conference that initial disclosures are not appropriate in this action and states the objection in the proposed discovery plan. In ruling on the objection, the court must determine what disclosures, if any, are to be made and must set the time for disclosure.

(D) *Time for Initial Disclosures—For Parties Served or Joined Later.* A party that is first served or otherwise joined after the Rule 26(f) conference must make the initial disclosures within 30 days after being served or joined, unless a different time is set by stipulation or court order.

(E) *Basis for Initial Disclosure; Unacceptable Excuses.* A party must make its initial disclosures based on the information then reasonably available to it. A party is not excused from making its disclosures because it has not fully investigated the case or because it challenges the sufficiency of another party's disclosures or because another party has not made its disclosures.

(2) *Disclosure of Expert Testimony.*

(A) *In General.* In addition to the disclosures required by Rule 26(a)(1), a party must disclose to the other parties the identity of any witness it may use at trial to present evidence under Federal Rule of Evidence 702, 703, or 705.

(B) *Witnesses Who Must Provide a Written Report.* Unless otherwise stipulated or ordered by the court, this disclosure must be accompanied by a written report—prepared and signed by the witness—if the witness is one retained or specially employed to provide expert testimony in the case or one whose duties as the party's employee regularly involve giving expert testimony. The report must contain:

(i) a complete statement of all opinions the witness will express and the basis and reasons for them;

(ii) the facts or data considered by the witness in forming them;

(iii) any exhibits that will be used to summarize or support them;

(iv) the witness's qualifications, including a list of all publications authored in the previous 10 years;

(v) a list of all other cases in which, during the previous 4 years, the witness testified as an expert at trial or by deposition; and

(vi) a statement of the compensation to be paid for the study and testimony in the case.

(C) *Witnesses Who Do Not Provide a Written Report.* Unless otherwise stipulated or ordered by the court, if the witness is not required to provide a written report, this disclosure must state:

(i) the subject matter on which the witness is expected to present evidence under Federal Rule of Evidence 702, 703, or 705; and

(ii) a summary of the facts and opinions to which the witness is expected to testify.

(D) *Time to Disclose Expert Testimony.* A party must make these disclosures at the times and in the sequence that the court orders. Absent a stipulation or a court order, the disclosures must be made:

(i) at least 90 days before the date set for trial or for the case to be ready for trial; or

(ii) if the evidence is intended solely to contradict or rebut evidence on the same subject matter identified by another party under Rule 26(a)(2)(B) or (C), within 30 days after the other party's disclosure.

(E) *Supplementing the Disclosure.* The parties must supplement these disclosures when required under Rule 26(e).

(3) *Pretrial Disclosures.*

(A) *In General.* In addition to the disclosures required by Rule 26(a)(1) and (2), a party must provide to the other parties and promptly file the following information about the evidence that it may present at trial other than solely for impeachment:

(i) the name and, if not previously provided, the address and telephone number of each witness—separately identifying those the party expects to present and those it may call if the need arises;

(ii) the designation of those witnesses whose testimony the party expects to present by deposition and, if not taken stenographically, a transcript of the pertinent parts of the deposition; and

(iii) an identification of each document or other exhibit, including summaries of other evidence—separately identifying those items the party expects to offer and those it may offer if the need arises.

(B) *Time for Pretrial Disclosures; Objections.* Unless the court orders otherwise, these disclosures must be made at least 30 days before trial. Within 14 days after they are made, unless the court sets a different time, a party may serve and promptly file a list of the following objections: any objections to the use under Rule 32(a) of a deposition designated by another party under Rule 26(a)(3)(A)(ii); and any objection, together with the grounds for it, that may be made to the admissibility of materials identified under Rule 26(a)(3)(A)(iii). An objection not so made—except for one under Federal Rule of Evidence 402 or 403—is waived unless excused by the court for good cause.

(4) *Form of Disclosures.* Unless the court orders otherwise, all disclosures under Rule 26(a) must be in writing, signed, and served.

(b) **Discovery Scope and Limits.**

(1) *Scope in General.* Unless otherwise limited by court order, the scope of discovery is as follows: Parties may obtain discovery regarding any nonprivileged matter that is relevant to any party's claim or defense and proportional to the needs of the case, considering the importance of the issues at stake in the action, the amount in controversy, the parties' relative access to relevant information, the parties' resources, the importance of the discovery in resolving the issues, and whether the burden or expense of the proposed discovery outweighs its likely benefit. Information within this scope of discovery need not be admissible in evidence to be discoverable.

(2) *Limitations on Frequency and Extent.*

(A) *When Permitted.* By order, the court may alter the limits in these rules on the number of depositions and interrogatories or on the length of depositions under Rule 30. By order or local rule, the court may also limit the number of requests under Rule 36.

(B) *Specific Limitations on Electronically Stored Information.* A party need not provide discovery of electronically stored information from sources that the party identifies as not reasonably accessible because of undue burden or cost. On motion to compel discovery or for a protective order, the party from whom discovery is sought must show that the information is not reasonably accessible because of undue burden or cost. If that showing is made, the court may nonetheless order discovery from such sources if the requesting party shows good cause, considering the limitations of Rule 26(b)(2)(C). The court may specify conditions for the discovery.

(C) *When Required.* On motion or on its own, the court must limit the frequency or extent of discovery otherwise allowed by these rules or by local rule if it determines that:

(i) the discovery sought is unreasonably cumulative or duplicative, or can be obtained from some other source that is more convenient, less burdensome, or less expensive;

(ii) the party seeking discovery has had ample opportunity to obtain the information by discovery in the action; or

(iii) the proposed discovery is outside the scope permitted by Rule 26(b)(1).

(3) *Trial Preparation: Materials.*

(A) *Documents and Tangible Things.* Ordinarily, a party may not discover documents and tangible things that are prepared in anticipation of litigation or for trial by or for another party or its representative (including the other party's attorney, consultant, surety, indemnitor, insurer, or agent). But, subject to Rule 26(b)(4), those materials may be discovered if:

(i) they are otherwise discoverable under Rule 26(b)(1); and

(ii) the party shows that it has substantial need for the materials to prepare its case and cannot, without undue hardship, obtain their substantial equivalent by other means.

(B) *Protection Against Disclosure.* If the court orders discovery of those materials, it must protect against disclosure of the mental impressions, conclusions, opinions, or legal theories of a party's attorney or other representative concerning the litigation.

(C) *Previous Statement.* Any party or other person may, on request and without the required showing, obtain the person's own previous statement about the action or its subject matter. If the request is refused, the person may move for a court order, and Rule 37(a)(5) applies to the award of expenses. A previous statement is either:

(i) a written statement that the person has signed or otherwise adopted or approved; or

(ii) a contemporaneous stenographic, mechanical, electrical, or other recording—or a transcription of it—that recites substantially verbatim the person's oral statement.

(4) *Trial Preparation: Experts.*

(A) *Deposition of an Expert Who May Testify.* A party may depose any person who has been identified as an expert whose opinions may be presented at trial. If Rule 26(a)(2)(B) requires a report from the expert, the deposition may be conducted only after the report is provided.

(B) *Trial–Preparation Protection for Draft Reports or Disclosures.* Rules 26(b)(3)(A) and (B) protect drafts of any report or disclosure required under Rule 26(a)(2), regardless of the form in which the draft is recorded.

(C) *Trial–Preparation Protection for Communications Between a Party's Attorney and Expert Witnesses.* Rules 26(b)(3)(A) and (B) protect communications between the party's attorney and any witness required to provide a report under Rule 26(a)(2)(B), regardless of the form of the communications, except to the extent that the communications:

(i) relate to compensation for the expert's study or testimony;

(ii) identify facts or data that the party's attorney provided and that the expert considered in forming the opinions to be expressed; or

(iii) identify assumptions that the party's attorney provided and that the expert relied on in forming the opinions to be expressed.

(D) *Expert Employed Only for Trial Preparation.* Ordinarily, a party may not, by interrogatories or deposition, discover facts known or opinions held by an expert who has been retained or specially employed by another party in anticipation of litigation or to prepare for trial and who is not expected to be called as a witness at trial. But a party may do so only:

(i) as provided in Rule 35(b); or

(ii) on showing exceptional circumstances under which it is impracticable for the party to obtain facts or opinions on the same subject by other means.

(E) *Payment.* Unless manifest injustice would result, the court must require that the party seeking discovery:

(i) pay the expert a reasonable fee for time spent in responding to discovery under Rule 26(b)(4)(A) or (D); and

(ii) for discovery under (D), also pay the other party a fair portion of the fees and expenses it reasonably incurred in obtaining the expert's facts and opinions.

(5) *Claiming Privilege or Protecting Trial-Preparation Materials.*

(A) *Information Withheld.* When a party withholds information otherwise discoverable by claiming that the information is privileged or subject to protection as trial-preparation material, the party must:

(i) expressly make the claim; and

(ii) describe the nature of the documents, communications, or tangible things not produced or disclosed—and do so in a manner that, without revealing information itself privileged or protected, will enable other parties to assess the claim.

(B) *Information Produced.* If information produced in discovery is subject to a claim of privilege or of protection as trial-preparation material, the party making the claim may notify any party that received the information of the claim and the basis for it. After being notified, a party must promptly return, sequester, or destroy the specified information and any copies it has; must not use or disclose the information until the claim is resolved; must take reasonable steps to retrieve the information if the party disclosed it before being notified; and may promptly present the information to the court under seal for a determination of the claim. The producing party must preserve the information until the claim is resolved.

(c) **Protective Orders.**

(1) *In General.* A party or any person from whom discovery is sought may move for a protective order in the court where the action is pending — or as an alternative on matters relating to a deposition, in the court for the district where the deposition will be taken. The motion must include a certification that the movant has in good faith conferred or attempted to confer with other affected parties in an effort to resolve the dispute without court action. The court may, for good cause, issue an order to protect a party or person from annoyance, embarrassment, oppression, or undue burden or expense, including one or more of the following:

(A) forbidding the disclosure or discovery;

(B) specifying terms, including time and place or the allocation of expenses, for the disclosure or discovery;

(C) prescribing a discovery method other than the one selected by the party seeking discovery;

(D) forbidding inquiry into certain matters, or limiting the scope of disclosure or discovery to certain matters;

(E) designating the persons who may be present while the discovery is conducted;

(F) requiring that a deposition be sealed and opened only on court order;

F, G, H = classic exs

(G) requiring that a trade secret or other confidential research, development, or commercial information not be revealed or be revealed only in a specified way; and

(H) requiring that the parties simultaneously file specified documents or information in sealed envelopes, to be opened as the court directs.

(2) *Ordering Discovery.* If a motion for a protective order is wholly or partly denied, the court may, on just terms, order that any party or person provide or permit discovery.

(3) *Awarding Expenses.* Rule 37(a)(5) applies to the award of expenses.

(d) Timing and Sequence of Discovery.

(1) *Timing.* A party may not seek discovery from any source before the parties have conferred as required by Rule 26(f), except in a proceeding exempted from initial disclosure under Rule 26(a)(1)(B), or when authorized by these rules, by stipulation, or by court order.

(2) *Early Rule 34 Requests.*

(A) Time to Deliver. More than 21 days after the summons and complaint are served on a party, a request under Rule 34 may be delivered:

(i) to that party by any other party, and

(ii) by that party to any plaintiff or to any other party that has been served.

(B) *When Considered Served.* The request is considered to have been served at the first Rule 26(f) conference.

(3) *Sequence.* Unless the parties stipulate or the court orders otherwise for the parties' and witnesses' convenience and in the interests of justice:

(A) methods of discovery may be used in any sequence; and

(B) discovery by one party does not require any other party to delay its discovery.

(e) Supplementing Disclosures and Responses.

(1) *In General.* A party who has made a disclosure under Rule 26(a)—or who has responded to an interrogatory, request for production, or request for admission—must supplement or correct its disclosure or response:

(A) in a timely manner if the party learns that in some material respect the disclosure or response is incomplete or incorrect, and if the additional or corrective information has not otherwise been made known to the other parties during the discovery process or in writing; or

(B) as ordered by the court.

(2) *Expert Witness.* For an expert whose report must be disclosed under Rule 26(a)(2)(B), the party's duty to supplement extends both to information included in the report and to information given during the expert's deposition. Any additions or changes to this information must be disclosed by the time the party's pretrial disclosures under Rule 26(a)(3) are due.

(f) Conference of the Parties; Planning for Discovery.

(1) *Conference Timing.* Except in a proceeding exempted from initial disclosure under Rule 26(a)(1)(B) or when the court orders otherwise, the parties must confer as soon as practicable—and in any event at least 21 days before a scheduling conference is to be held or a scheduling order is due under Rule 16(b).

(2) *Conference Content; Parties' Responsibilities.* In conferring, the parties must consider the nature and basis of their claims and defenses and the possibilities for promptly settling or resolving the case; make or arrange for the disclosures required by Rule 26(a)(1); discuss any issues about preserving discoverable information; and develop a proposed discovery plan. The attorneys of record and all unrepresented parties that have appeared in the case are jointly responsible for arranging the conference, for attempting in good faith to agree on the proposed discovery plan, and for submitting to the court within 14 days after the conference a written report outlining the plan. The court may order the parties or attorneys to attend the conference in person.

(3) *Discovery Plan.* A discovery plan must state the parties' views and proposals on:

(A) what changes should be made in the timing, form, or requirement for disclosures under Rule 26(a), including a statement of when initial disclosures were made or will be made;

(B) the subjects on which discovery may be needed, when discovery should be completed, and whether discovery should be conducted in phases or be limited to or focused on particular issues;

(C) any issues about disclosure, discovery, or preservation of electronically stored information, including the form or forms in which it should be produced;

(D) any issues about claims of privilege or of protection as trial-preparation materials, including — if the parties agree on a procedure to assert these claims after production — whether to ask the court to include their agreement in an order under Federal Rule of Evidence 502;

(E) what changes should be made in the limitations on discovery imposed under these rules or by local rule, and what other limitations should be imposed; and

(F) any other orders that the court should issue under Rule 26(c) or under Rule 16(b) and (c).

(4) *Expedited Schedule.* If necessary to comply with its expedited schedule for Rule 16(b) conferences, a court may by local rule:

(A) require the parties' conference to occur less than 21 days before the scheduling conference is held or a scheduling order is due under Rule 16(b); and

(B) require the written report outlining the discovery plan to be filed less than 14 days after the parties' conference, or excuse the parties from submitting a written report and permit them to report orally on their discovery plan at the Rule 16(b) conference.

(g) Signing Disclosures and Discovery Requests, Responses, and Objections.

(1) *Signature Required; Effect of Signature.* Every disclosure under Rule 26(a)(1) or (a)(3) and every discovery request, response, or objection must be signed by at least one attorney of record in the attorney's own name—or by the party personally, if unrepresented—and must state the signer's address, e-mail address, and telephone number. By signing, an attorney or party certifies that to the best of the person's knowledge, information, and belief formed after a reasonable inquiry:

(A) with respect to a disclosure, it is complete and correct as of the time it is made; and

(B) with respect to a discovery request, response, or objection, it is:

(i) consistent with these rules and warranted by existing law or by a nonfrivolous argument for extending, modifying, or reversing existing law, or for establishing new law;

(ii) not interposed for any improper purpose, such as to harass, cause unnecessary delay, or needlessly increase the cost of litigation; and

(iii) neither unreasonable nor unduly burdensome or expensive, considering the needs of the case, prior discovery in the case, the amount in controversy, and the importance of the issues at stake in the action.

(2) *Failure to Sign.* Other parties have no duty to act on an unsigned disclosure, request, response, or objection until it is signed, and the court must strike it unless a signature is promptly supplied after the omission is called to the attorney's or party's attention.

(3) *Sanction for Improper Certification.* If a certification violates this rule without substantial justification, the court, on motion or on its own, must impose an appropriate sanction on the signer, the party on whose behalf the signer was acting, or both. The sanction may include an order to pay the reasonable expenses, including attorney's fees, caused by the violation.

(Amended December 27, 1946, effective March 19, 1948; January 21, 1963, effective July 1, 1963; February 28, 1966, effective July 1, 1966; March 30, 1970, effective July 1, 1970; April 29, 1980, effective August 1, 1980; April 28, 1983, effective August 1, 1983; March 2, 1987, effective August 1, 1987; April 22, 1993, effective December 1, 1993; April 17, 2000, effective December 1, 2000; April 12, 2006, effective December 1, 2006; April 30, 2007, effective December 1, 2007; April 28, 2010, effective December 1, 2010; April 29, 2015, effective December 1, 2015.)

RULE 27.   DEPOSITIONS TO PERPETUATE TESTIMONY

(a) Before an Action Is Filed.

(1) *Petition.* A person who wants to perpetuate testimony about any matter cognizable in a United States court may file a verified petition in the district court for the district where any expected adverse party resides. The petition must ask for an order authorizing the petitioner to depose the named persons in order to perpetuate their testimony. The petition must be titled in the petitioner's name and must show:

(A) that the petitioner expects to be a party to an action cognizable in a United States court but cannot presently bring it or cause it to be brought;

(B) the subject matter of the expected action and the petitioner's interest;

(C) the facts that the petitioner wants to establish by the proposed testimony and the reasons to perpetuate it;

(D) the names or a description of the persons whom the petitioner expects to be adverse parties and their addresses, so far as known; and

(E) the name, address, and expected substance of the testimony of each deponent.

(2) *Notice and Service.* At least 21 days before the hearing date, the petitioner must serve each expected adverse party with a copy of the petition and a notice stating the time and place of the hearing. The notice may be served either inside or outside the district or state in the manner provided in Rule 4. If that service cannot be made with reasonable diligence on an expected adverse party, the court may order service by publication or otherwise. The court must appoint an attorney to represent persons not served in the manner provided in Rule 4 and to cross-examine the deponent if an unserved person is not otherwise represented. If any expected adverse party is a minor or is incompetent, Rule 17(c) applies.

(3) *Order and Examination.* If satisfied that perpetuating the testimony may prevent a failure or delay of justice, the court must issue an order that designates or describes the persons whose depositions may be taken, specifies the subject matter of the examinations, and states whether the depositions will be taken orally or by written interrogatories. The depositions may then be taken under these rules, and the court may issue orders like those authorized by Rules 34 and 35. A reference in these rules to the court where an action is pending means, for purposes of this rule, the court where the petition for the deposition was filed.

(4) *Using the Deposition.* A deposition to perpetuate testimony may be used under Rule 32(a) in any later-filed district-court action involving the same subject matter if the deposition either was taken under these rules or, although not so taken, would be admissible in evidence in the courts of the state where it was taken.

(b) Pending Appeal.

(1) *In General.* The court where a judgment has been rendered may, if an appeal has been taken or may still be taken, permit a party to depose witnesses to perpetuate their testimony for use in the event of further proceedings in that court.

(2) *Motion.* The party who wants to perpetuate testimony may move for leave to take the depositions, on the same notice and service as if the action were pending in the district court. The motion must show:

(A) the name, address, and expected substance of the testimony of each deponent; and

(B) the reasons for perpetuating the testimony.

(3) *Court Order.* If the court finds that perpetuating the testimony may prevent a failure or delay of justice, the court may permit the depositions to be taken and may issue orders like those authorized by Rules 34 and 35. The depositions may be taken and used as any other deposition taken in a pending district-court action.

(c) Perpetuation by an Action. This rule does not limit a court's power to entertain an action to perpetuate testimony.

(Amended December 27, 1946, effective March 19, 1948; December 29, 1948, effective October 20, 1949; March 1, 1971, effective July 1, 1971; March 2, 1987, effective August 1, 1987; April 25, 2005, effective December 1, 2005; April 30, 2007, effective December 1, 2007; March 26, 2009, effective December 1, 2009.)

RULE 28. PERSONS BEFORE WHOM DEPOSITIONS MAY BE TAKEN

(a) Within the United States.

(1) *In General.* Within the United States or a territory or insular possession subject to United States jurisdiction, a deposition must be taken before:

(A) an officer authorized to administer oaths either by federal law or by the law in the place of examination; or

(B) a person appointed by the court where the action is pending to administer oaths and take testimony.

(2) *Definition of "Officer."* The term "officer" in Rules 30, 31, and 32 includes a person appointed by the court under this rule or designated by the parties under Rule 29(a).

(b) In a Foreign Country.

(1) *In General.* A deposition may be taken in a foreign country:

(A) under an applicable treaty or convention;

(B) under a letter of request, whether or not captioned a "letter rogatory";

(C) on notice, before a person authorized to administer oaths either by federal law or by the law in the place of examination; or

(D) before a person commissioned by the court to administer any necessary oath and take testimony.

(2) *Issuing a Letter of Request or a Commission.* A letter of request, a commission, or both may be issued:

(A) on appropriate terms after an application and notice of it; and

(B) without a showing that taking the deposition in another manner is impracticable or inconvenient.

(3) *Form of a Request, Notice, or Commission.* When a letter of request or any other device is used according to a treaty or convention, it must be captioned in the form prescribed by that treaty or convention. A letter of request may be addressed "To the Appropriate Authority in [name of country]." A deposition notice or a commission must designate by name or descriptive title the person before whom the deposition is to be taken.

(4) *Letter of Request—Admitting Evidence.* Evidence obtained in response to a letter of request need not be excluded merely because it is not a verbatim transcript, because the testimony was not taken under oath, or because of any similar departure from the requirements for depositions taken within the United States.

(c) Disqualification. A deposition must not be taken before a person who is any party's relative, employee, or attorney; who is related to or employed by any party's attorney; or who is financially interested in the action.

(Amended December 27, 1946, effective March 19, 1948; January 21, 1963, effective July 1, 1963; April 29, 1980, effective August 1, 1980; March 2, 1987, effective August 1, 1987; April 22, 1993, effective December 1, 1993; April 30, 2007, effective December 1, 2007.)

RULE 29. STIPULATIONS ABOUT DISCOVERY PROCEDURE

Unless the court orders otherwise, the parties may stipulate that:

(a) a deposition may be taken before any person, at any time or place, on any notice, and in the manner specified—in which event it may be used in the same way as any other deposition; and

(b) other procedures governing or limiting discovery be modified—but a stipulation extending the time for any form of discovery must have court approval if it would interfere with the time set for completing discovery, for hearing a motion, or for trial.

(Amended March 30, 1970, effective July 1, 1970; April 22, 1993, effective December 1, 1993; April 30, 2007, effective December 1, 2007.)

RULE 30. DEPOSITIONS BY ORAL EXAMINATION

(a) When a Deposition May Be Taken.

(1) *Without Leave.* A party may, by oral questions, depose any person, including a party, without leave of court except as provided in Rule 30(a)(2). The deponent's attendance may be compelled by subpoena under Rule 45.

(2) *With Leave.* A party must obtain leave of court, and the court must grant leave to the extent consistent with Rule 26(b)(1) and (2):

(A) if the parties have not stipulated to the deposition and:

(i) the deposition would result in more than 10 depositions being taken under this rule or Rule 31 by the plaintiffs, or by the defendants, or by the third-party defendants;

(ii) the deponent has already been deposed in the case; or

(iii) the party seeks to take the deposition before the time specified in Rule 26(d), unless the party certifies in the notice, with supporting facts, that the deponent is expected to leave the United States and be unavailable for examination in this country after that time; or

(B) if the deponent is confined in prison.

(b) Notice of the Deposition; Other Formal Requirements.

(1) *Notice in General.* A party who wants to depose a person by oral questions must give reasonable written notice to every other party. The notice must state the time and place of the deposition and, if known, the deponent's name and address. If the name is unknown, the notice must provide a general description sufficient to identify the person or the particular class or group to which the person belongs.

(2) *Producing Documents.* If a subpoena duces tecum is to be served on the deponent, the materials designated for production, as set out in the subpoena, must be listed in the notice or in an attachment. The notice to a party deponent may be accompanied by a request under Rule 34 to produce documents and tangible things at the deposition.

(3) *Method of Recording.*

(A) *Method Stated in the Notice.* The party who notices the deposition must state in the notice the method for recording the testimony. Unless the court orders otherwise, testimony may be recorded by audio, audiovisual, or stenographic means. The noticing party bears the recording costs. Any party may arrange to transcribe a deposition.

(B) *Additional Method.* With prior notice to the deponent and other parties, any party may designate another method for recording the testimony in addition to that specified in the original notice. That party bears the expense of the additional record or transcript unless the court orders otherwise.

(4) *By Remote Means.* The parties may stipulate—or the court may on motion order—that a deposition be taken by telephone or other remote means. For the purpose of this rule and Rules 28(a), 37(a)(2), and 37(b)(1), the deposition takes place where the deponent answers the questions.

(5) *Officer's Duties.*

(A) *Before the Deposition.* Unless the parties stipulate otherwise, a deposition must be conducted before an officer appointed or designated under Rule 28. The officer must begin the deposition with an on-the-record statement that includes:

(i) the officer's name and business address;

(ii) the date, time, and place of the deposition;

(iii) the deponent's name;

(iv) the officer's administration of the oath or affirmation to the deponent; and

(v) the identity of all persons present.

(B) *Conducting the Deposition; Avoiding Distortion.* If the deposition is recorded non-stenographically, the officer must repeat the items in Rule 30(b)(5)(A)(i)-(iii) at the beginning of each unit of the recording medium. The deponent's and attorneys' appearance or demeanor must not be distorted through recording techniques.

(C) *After the Deposition.* At the end of a deposition, the officer must state on the record that the deposition is complete and must set out any stipulations made by the attorneys about custody of the transcript or recording and of the exhibits, or about any other pertinent matters.

(6) *Notice or Subpoena Directed to an Organization.* In its notice or subpoena, a party may name as the deponent a public or private corporation, a partnership, an association, a governmental agency, or other entity and must describe with reasonable particularity the matters for examination. The named organization must then designate one or more officers, directors, or managing agents, or designate other persons who consent to testify on its behalf; and it may set out the matters on which each person designated will testify. A subpoena must advise a nonparty organization of its duty to make this designation. The persons designated must testify about information known or reasonably available to the organization. This paragraph (6) does not preclude a deposition by any other procedure allowed by these rules.

(c) Examination and Cross–Examination; Record of the Examination; Objections; Written Questions.

(1) *Examination and Cross–Examination.* The examination and cross-examination of a deponent proceed as they would at trial under the Federal Rules of Evidence, except Rules 103 and 615. After putting the deponent under oath or affirmation, the officer must record the testimony by the method designated under Rule 30(b)(3)(A). The testimony must be recorded by the officer personally or by a person acting in the presence and under the direction of the officer.

(2) *Objections.* An objection at the time of the examination—whether to evidence, to a party's conduct, to the officer's qualifications, to the manner of taking the deposition, or to any other aspect of the deposition—must be noted on the record, but the examination still proceeds; the testimony is taken subject to any objection. An objection must be stated concisely in a nonargumentative and nonsuggestive manner. A person may instruct a deponent not to answer only when necessary to preserve a privilege, to enforce a limitation ordered by the court, or to present a motion under Rule 30(d)(3).

(3) *Participating Through Written Questions.* Instead of participating in the oral examination, a party may serve written questions in a sealed envelope on the party noticing the deposition, who must deliver them to the officer. The officer must ask the deponent those questions and record the answers verbatim.

(d) Duration; Sanction; Motion to Terminate or Limit.

(1) *Duration.* Unless otherwise stipulated or ordered by the court, a deposition is limited to one day of 7 hours. The court must allow additional time consistent with Rule 26(b)(1) and (2) if needed to fairly examine the deponent or if the deponent, another person, or any other circumstance impedes or delays the examination.

(2) *Sanction.* The court may impose an appropriate sanction—including the reasonable expenses and attorney's fees incurred by any party—on a person who impedes, delays, or frustrates the fair examination of the deponent.

(3) *Motion to Terminate or Limit.*

(A) *Grounds.* At any time during a deposition, the deponent or a party may move to terminate or limit it on the ground that it is being conducted in bad faith or in a manner that unreasonably annoys, embarrasses, or oppresses the deponent or party. The motion may be filed in the court where the action is pending or the deposition is being taken. If the objecting deponent or party so demands, the deposition must be suspended for the time necessary to obtain an order.

(B) *Order.* The court may order that the deposition be terminated or may limit its scope and manner as provided in Rule 26(c). If terminated, the deposition may be resumed only by order of the court where the action is pending.

(C) *Award of Expenses.* Rule 37(a)(5) applies to the award of expenses.

(e) Review by the Witness; Changes.

(1) *Review; Statement of Changes.* On request by the deponent or a party before the deposition is completed, the deponent must be allowed 30 days after being notified by the officer that the transcript or recording is available in which:

(A) to review the transcript or recording; and

(B) if there are changes in form or substance, to sign a statement listing the changes and the reasons for making them.

(2) *Changes Indicated in the Officer's Certificate.* The officer must note in the certificate prescribed by Rule 30(f)(1) whether a review was requested and, if so, must attach any changes the deponent makes during the 30–day period.

(f) Certification and Delivery; Exhibits; Copies of the Transcript or Recording; Filing.

(1) *Certification and Delivery.* The officer must certify in writing that the witness was duly sworn and that the deposition accurately records the witness's testimony. The certificate must accompany the record of the deposition. Unless the court orders otherwise, the officer must seal the deposition in an envelope or package bearing the title of the action and marked "Deposition of [witness's name]" and must promptly send it to the attorney who arranged for the transcript or recording. The attorney must store it under conditions that will protect it against loss, destruction, tampering, or deterioration.

(2) *Documents and Tangible Things.*

(A) *Originals and Copies.* Documents and tangible things produced for inspection during a deposition must, on a party's request, be marked for identification and attached to the deposition. Any party may inspect and copy them. But if the person who produced them wants to keep the originals, the person may:

(i) offer copies to be marked, attached to the deposition, and then used as originals—after giving all parties a fair opportunity to verify the copies by comparing them with the originals; or

(ii) give all parties a fair opportunity to inspect and copy the originals after they are marked—in which event the originals may be used as if attached to the deposition.

(B) *Order Regarding the Originals.* Any party may move for an order that the originals be attached to the deposition pending final disposition of the case.

(3) *Copies of the Transcript or Recording.* Unless otherwise stipulated or ordered by the court, the officer must retain the stenographic notes of a deposition taken stenographically or a copy of the recording of a deposition taken by another method. When paid reasonable charges, the officer must furnish a copy of the transcript or recording to any party or the deponent.

(4) *Notice of Filing.* A party who files the deposition must promptly notify all other parties of the filing.

(g) Failure to Attend a Deposition or Serve a Subpoena; Expenses. A party who, expecting a deposition to be taken, attends in person or by an attorney may recover reasonable expenses for attending, including attorney's fees, if the noticing party failed to:

(1) attend and proceed with the deposition; or

(2) serve a subpoena on a nonparty deponent, who consequently did not attend.

(Amended January 21, 1963, effective July 1, 1963; March 30, 1970, effective July 1, 1970; March 1, 1971, effective July 1, 1971; November 20, 1972, effective July 1, 1975; April 29, 1980, effective August 1, 1980; March 2, 1987, effective August 1, 1987; April 22, 1993, effective December 1, 1993; April 17, 2000, effective December 1, 2000; April 30, 2007, effective December 1, 2007; April 29, 2015, effective December 1, 2015.)

RULE 31. DEPOSITIONS BY WRITTEN QUESTIONS

(a) When a Deposition May Be Taken.

(1) *Without Leave.* A party may, by written questions, depose any person, including a party, without leave of court except as provided in Rule 31(a)(2). The deponent's attendance may be compelled by subpoena under Rule 45.

(2) *With Leave.* A party must obtain leave of court, and the court must grant leave to the extent consistent with Rule 26(b)(1) and (2):

(A) if the parties have not stipulated to the deposition and:

(i) the deposition would result in more than 10 depositions being taken under this rule or Rule 30 by the plaintiffs, or by the defendants, or by the third-party defendants;

(ii) the deponent has already been deposed in the case; or

(iii) the party seeks to take a deposition before the time specified in Rule 26(d); or

(B) if the deponent is confined in prison.

(3) *Service; Required Notice.* A party who wants to depose a person by written questions must serve them on every other party, with a notice stating, if known, the deponent's name and address. If the name is unknown, the notice must provide a general description sufficient to identify the person or the particular class or group to which the person belongs. The notice must also state the name or descriptive title and the address of the officer before whom the deposition will be taken.

(4) Questions Directed to an Organization. A public or private corporation, a partnership, an association, or a governmental agency may be deposed by written questions in accordance with Rule 30(b)(6).

(5) Questions from Other Parties. Any questions to the deponent from other parties must be served on all parties as follows: cross-questions, within 14 days after being served with the notice and direct questions; redirect questions, within 7 days after being served with cross-questions; and recross-questions, within 7 days after being served with redirect questions. The court may, for good cause, extend or shorten these times.

(b) Delivery to the Officer; Officer's Duties. The party who noticed the deposition must deliver to the officer a copy of all the questions served and of the notice. The officer must promptly proceed in the manner provided in Rule 30(c), (e), and (f) to:

(1) take the deponent's testimony in response to the questions;

(2) prepare and certify the deposition; and

(3) send it to the party, attaching a copy of the questions and of the notice.

(c) Notice of Completion or Filing.

(1) Completion. The party who noticed the deposition must notify all other parties when it is completed.

(2) Filing. A party who files the deposition must promptly notify all other parties of the filing.

(Amended March 30, 1970, effective July 1, 1970; March 2, 1987, effective August 1, 1987; April 22, 1993, effective December 1, 1993; April 30, 2007, effective December 1, 2007; April 29, 2015, effective December 1, 2015.)

RULE 32. USING DEPOSITIONS IN COURT PROCEEDINGS

(a) Using Depositions.

(1) In General. At a hearing or trial, all or part of a deposition may be used against a party on these conditions:

(A) the party was present or represented at the taking of the deposition or had reasonable notice of it;

(B) it is used to the extent it would be admissible under the Federal Rules of Evidence if the deponent were present and testifying; and

(C) the use is allowed by Rule 32(a)(2) through (8).

(2) Impeachment and Other Uses. Any party may use a deposition to contradict or impeach the testimony given by the deponent as a witness, or for any other purpose allowed by the Federal Rules of Evidence.

(3) Deposition of Party, Agent, or Designee. An adverse party may use for any purpose the deposition of a party or anyone who, when deposed, was the party's officer, director, managing agent, or designee under Rule 30(b)(6) or 31(a)(4).

(4) Unavailable Witness. A party may use for any purpose the deposition of a witness, whether or not a party, if the court finds:

(A) that the witness is dead;

(B) that the witness is more than 100 miles from the place of hearing or trial or is outside the United States, unless it appears that the witness's absence was procured by the party offering the deposition;

(C) that the witness cannot attend or testify because of age, illness, infirmity, or imprisonment;

(D) that the party offering the deposition could not procure the witness's attendance by subpoena; or

(E) on motion and notice, that exceptional circumstances make it desirable—in the interest of justice and with due regard to the importance of live testimony in open court—to permit the deposition to be used.

(5) Limitations on Use.

(A) Deposition Taken on Short Notice. A deposition must not be used against a party who, having received less than 14 days' notice of the deposition, promptly moved for a protective order under Rule 26(c)(1)(B) requesting that it not be taken or be taken at a different time or place—and this motion was still pending when the deposition was taken.

(B) Unavailable Deponent; Party Could Not Obtain an Attorney. A deposition taken without leave of court under the unavailability provision of Rule 30(a)(2)(A)(iii) must not be used against a party who shows that, when served with the notice, it could not, despite diligent efforts, obtain an attorney to represent it at the deposition.

(6) Using Part of a Deposition. If a party offers in evidence only part of a deposition, an adverse party may require the offeror to introduce other parts that in fairness should be considered with the part introduced, and any party may itself introduce any other parts.

(7) Substituting a Party. Substituting a party under Rule 25 does not affect the right to use a deposition previously taken.

(8) Deposition Taken in an Earlier Action. A deposition lawfully taken and, if required, filed in any federal- or state-court action may be used in a later action involving the same subject matter between the same parties, or their representatives or successors in interest, to the same extent as if taken in the later action. A deposition previously taken may also be used as allowed by the Federal Rules of Evidence.

(b) Objections to Admissibility. Subject to Rules 28(b) and 32(d)(3), an objection may be made at a hearing or trial to the admission of any deposition testimony that would be inadmissible if the witness were present and testifying.

(c) Form of Presentation. Unless the court orders otherwise, a party must provide a transcript of any deposition testimony the party offers, but may provide the court with the testimony in nontranscript form as well. On any party's request, deposition testimony offered in a jury trial for any purpose other than impeachment must be presented in non-transcript form, if available, unless the court for good cause orders otherwise.

(d) Waiver of Objections.

(1) *To the Notice.* An objection to an error or irregularity in a deposition notice is waived unless promptly served in writing on the party giving the notice.

(2) *To the Officer's Qualification.* An objection based on disqualification of the officer before whom a deposition is to be taken is waived if not made:

(A) before the deposition begins; or

(B) promptly after the basis for disqualification becomes known or, with reasonable diligence, could have been known.

(3) *To the Taking of the Deposition.*

(A) *Objection to Competence, Relevance, or Materiality.* An objection to a deponent's competence—or to the competence, relevance, or materiality of testimony—is not waived by a failure to make the objection before or during the deposition, unless the ground for it might have been corrected at that time.

(B) *Objection to an Error or Irregularity.* An objection to an error or irregularity at an oral examination is waived if:

(i) it relates to the manner of taking the deposition, the form of a question or answer, the oath or affirmation, a party's conduct, or other matters that might have been corrected at that time; and

(ii) it is not timely made during the deposition.

(C) *Objection to a Written Question.* An objection to the form of a written question under Rule 31 is waived if not served in writing on the party submitting the question within the time for serving responsive questions or, if the question is a recross-question, within 7 days after being served with it.

(4) *To Completing and Returning the Deposition.* An objection to how the officer transcribed the testimony—or prepared, signed, certified, sealed, endorsed, sent, or otherwise dealt with the deposition—is waived unless a motion to suppress is made promptly after the error or irregularity becomes known or, with reasonable diligence, could have been known.

(Amended March 30, 1970, effective July 1, 1970; November 20, 1972, effective July 1, 1975; April 29, 1980, effective August 1, 1980; March 2, 1987, effective August 1, 1987; April 22, 1993, effective December 1, 1993; April 30, 2007, effective December 1, 2007; March 26, 2009, effective December 1, 2009.)

RULE 33. INTERROGATORIES TO PARTIES

(a) In General.

(1) *Number.* Unless otherwise stipulated or ordered by the court, a party may serve on any other party no more than 25 written interrogatories, including all discrete subparts. Leave to serve additional interrogatories may be granted to the extent consistent with Rule 26(b)(1) and (2).

(2) *Scope.* An interrogatory may relate to any matter that may be inquired into under Rule 26(b). An interrogatory is not objectionable merely because it asks for an opinion or contention that relates to fact or the application of law to fact, but the court may order that the interrogatory need not be answered until designated discovery is complete, or until a pretrial conference or some other time.

(b) Answers and Objections.

(1) *Responding Party.* The interrogatories must be answered:

(A) by the party to whom they are directed; or

(B) if that party is a public or private corporation, a partnership, an association, or a governmental agency, by any officer or agent, who must furnish the information available to the party.

(2) *Time to Respond.* The responding party must serve its answers and any objections within 30 days after being served with the interrogatories. A shorter or longer time may be stipulated to under Rule 29 or be ordered by the court.

(3) *Answering Each Interrogatory.* Each interrogatory must, to the extent it is not objected to, be answered separately and fully in writing under oath.

(4) *Objections.* The grounds for objecting to an interrogatory must be stated with specificity. Any ground not stated in a timely objection is waived unless the court, for good cause, excuses the failure.

(5) *Signature.* The person who makes the answers must sign them, and the attorney who objects must sign any objections.

(c) Use. An answer to an interrogatory may be used to the extent allowed by the Federal Rules of Evidence.

(d) Option to Produce Business Records. If the answer to an interrogatory may be determined by examining, auditing, compiling, abstracting, or summarizing a party's business records (including electronically stored information), and if the burden of deriving or ascertaining the answer will be substantially the same for either party, the responding party may answer by:

(1) specifying the records that must be reviewed, in sufficient detail to enable the interrogating party to locate and identify them as readily as the responding party could; and

(2) giving the interrogating party a reasonable opportunity to examine and audit the records and to make copies, compilations, abstracts, or summaries.

(Amended December 27, 1946, effective March 19, 1948; March 30, 1970, effective July 1, 1970; April 29, 1980, effective August 1, 1980; April 22, 1993, effective December 1, 1993; April 12, 2006, effective December 1, 2006; April 30, 2007, effective December 1, 2007; April 29, 2015, effective December 1, 2015.)

RULE 34. PRODUCING DOCUMENTS, ELECTRONICALLY STORED INFORMATION, AND TANGIBLE THINGS, OR ENTERING ONTO LAND, FOR INSPECTION AND OTHER PURPOSES

(a) In General. A party may serve on any other party a request within the scope of Rule 26(b):

(1) to produce and permit the requesting party or its representative to inspect, copy, test, or sample the following items in the responding party's possession, custody, or control:

(A) any designated documents or electronically stored information—including writings, drawings, graphs, charts, photographs, sound recordings, images, and other data or data compilations—stored in any medium from which information can be obtained either directly or, if necessary, after translation by the responding party into a reasonably usable form; or

(B) any designated tangible things; or

(2) to permit entry onto designated land or other property possessed or controlled by the responding party, so that the requesting party may inspect, measure, survey, photograph, test, or sample the property or any designated object or operation on it.

(b) Procedure.

(1) *Contents of the Request.* The request:

(A) must describe with reasonable particularity each item or category of items to be inspected;

(B) must specify a reasonable time, place, and manner for the inspection and for performing the related acts; and

(C) may specify the form or forms in which electronically stored information is to be produced.

(2) *Responses and Objections.*

(A) *Time to Respond.* The party to whom the request is directed must respond in writing within 30 days after being served or — if the request was delivered under Rule 26(d)(2) — within 30 days after the parties' first Rule 26(f) conference. A shorter or longer time may be stipulated to under Rule 29 or be ordered by the court.

(B) *Responding to Each Item.* For each item or category, the response must either state that inspection and related activities will be permitted as requested or state with specificity the grounds for objecting to the request, including the reasons. The responding party may state that it will produce copies of documents or of electronically stored information instead of permitting inspection. The production must then be completed no later than the time for inspection specified in the request or another reasonable time specified in the response.

(C) *Objections.* An objection must state whether any responsive materials are being withheld on the basis of that objection. An objection to part of a request must specify the part and permit inspection of the rest.

(D) *Responding to a Request for Production of Electronically Stored Information.* The response may state an objection to a requested form for producing electronically stored information. If the responding party objects to a requested form—or if no form was specified in the request—the party must state the form or forms it intends to use.

(E) *Producing the Documents or Electronically Stored Information.* Unless otherwise stipulated or ordered by the court, these procedures apply to producing documents or electronically stored information:

(i) A party must produce documents as they are kept in the usual course of business or must organize and label them to correspond to the categories in the request;

(ii) If a request does not specify a form for producing electronically stored information, a party must produce it in a form or forms in which it is ordinarily maintained or in a reasonably usable form or forms; and

(iii) A party need not produce the same electronically stored information in more than one form.

(c) Nonparties. As provided in Rule 45, a nonparty may be compelled to produce documents and tangible things or to permit an inspection.

(Amended December 27, 1946, effective March 19, 1948; March 30, 1970, effective July 1, 1970; April 29, 1980, effective August 1, 1980; March 2, 1987, effective August 1, 1987; April 30, 1991, effective December 1, 1991; April 22, 1993, effective December 1, 1993; April 12, 2006, effective December 1, 2006; April 30, 2007, effective December 1, 2007; April 29, 2015, effective December 1, 2015.)

RULE 35. PHYSICAL AND MENTAL EXAMINATIONS

(a) Order for an Examination.

(1) *In General.* The court where the action is pending may order a party whose mental or physical condition—including blood group—is in controversy to submit to a physical or mental examination by a suitably licensed or certified examiner. The court has the same authority to order a party to produce for examination a person who is in its custody or under its legal control.

(2) *Motion and Notice; Contents of the Order.* The order:

(A) may be made only on motion for good cause and on notice to all parties and the person to be examined; and

(B) must specify the time, place, manner, conditions, and scope of the examination, as well as the person or persons who will perform it.

(b) Examiner's Report.

(1) *Request by the Party or Person Examined.* The party who moved for the examination must, on request, deliver to the requester a copy of the examiner's report, together with like reports of all earlier examinations of the same condition. The request may be made by the party against whom the examination order was issued or by the person examined.

(2) *Contents.* The examiner's report must be in writing and must set out in detail the examiner's findings, including diagnoses, conclusions, and the results of any tests.

(3) *Request by the Moving Party.* After delivering the reports, the party who moved for the examination may request—and is entitled to receive—from the party against whom the examination order was issued like reports of all earlier or later examinations of the same condition. But those reports need not be delivered by the party with custody or control of the person examined if the party shows that it could not obtain them.

(4) *Waiver of Privilege.* By requesting and obtaining the examiner's report, or by deposing the examiner, the party examined waives any privilege it may have—in that action or any other action involving the same controversy—concerning testimony about all examinations of the same condition.

(5) *Failure to Deliver a Report.* The court on motion may order—on just terms—that a party deliver the report of an examination. If the report is not provided, the court may exclude the examiner's testimony at trial.

(6) *Scope.* This subdivision (b) applies also to an examination made by the parties' agreement, unless the agreement states otherwise. This subdivision does not preclude obtaining an examiner's report or deposing an examiner under other rules.

(Amended March 30, 1970, effective July 1, 1970; March 2, 1987, effective August 1, 1987; amended by Pub.L. 100–690, Title VII, § 7047(b), November 18, 1988, 102 Stat. 4401; amended April 30, 1991, effective December 1, 1991; April 30, 2007, effective December 1, 2007.)

RULE 36.   REQUESTS FOR ADMISSION

(a) Scope and Procedure.

(1) *Scope.* A party may serve on any other party a written request to admit, for purposes of the pending action only, the truth of any matters within the scope of Rule 26(b)(1) relating to:

    (A) facts, the application of law to fact, or opinions about either; and

    (B) the genuineness of any described documents.

(2) *Form; Copy of a Document.* Each matter must be separately stated. A request to admit the genuineness of a document must be accompanied by a copy of the document unless it is, or has been, otherwise furnished or made available for inspection and copying.

(3) *Time to Respond; Effect of Not Responding.* A matter is admitted unless, within 30 days after being served, the party to whom the request is directed serves on the requesting party a written answer or objection addressed to the matter and signed by the party or its attorney. A shorter or longer time for responding may be stipulated to under Rule 29 or be ordered by the court.

(4) *Answer.* If a matter is not admitted, the answer must specifically deny it or state in detail why the answering party cannot truthfully admit or deny it. A denial must fairly respond to the substance of the matter; and when good faith requires that a party qualify an answer or deny only a part of a matter, the answer must specify the part admitted and qualify or deny the rest. The answering party may assert lack of knowledge or information as a reason for failing to admit or deny only if the party states that it has made reasonable inquiry and that the information it knows or can readily obtain is insufficient to enable it to admit or deny.

(5) *Objections.* The grounds for objecting to a request must be stated. A party must not object solely on the ground that the request presents a genuine issue for trial.

(6) *Motion Regarding the Sufficiency of an Answer or Objection.* The requesting party may move to determine the sufficiency of an answer or objection. Unless the court finds an objection justified, it must order that an answer be served. On finding that an answer does not comply with this rule, the court may order either that the matter is admitted or that an amended answer be served. The court may defer its final decision until a pretrial conference or a specified time before trial. Rule 37(a)(5) applies to an award of expenses.

(b) Effect of an Admission; Withdrawing or Amending It. A matter admitted under this rule is conclusively established unless the court, on motion, permits the admission to be withdrawn or amended. Subject to Rule 16(e), the court may permit withdrawal or amendment if it would promote the presentation of the merits of the action and if the court is not persuaded that it would prejudice the requesting party in maintaining or defending the action on the merits. An admission under this rule is not an admission for any other purpose and cannot be used against the party in any other proceeding.

(Amended December 27, 1946, effective March 19, 1948; March 30, 1970, effective July 1, 1970; March 2, 1987, effective August 1, 1987; April 22, 1993, effective December 1, 1993; April 30, 2007, effective December 1, 2007.)

RULE 37.   FAILURE TO MAKE DISCLOSURES OR TO COOPERATE IN DISCOVERY; SANCTIONS

(a) Motion for an Order Compelling Disclosure or Discovery.

(1) *In General.* On notice to other parties and all affected persons, a party may move for an order compelling disclosure or discovery. The motion must include a certification that the movant has in good faith conferred or attempted to confer with the person or party failing to make disclosure or discovery in an effort to obtain it without court action.

(2) *Appropriate Court.* A motion for an order to a party must be made in the court where the action is pending. A motion for an order to a nonparty must be made in the court where the discovery is or will be taken.

(3) *Specific Motions.*

    (A) *To Compel Disclosure.* If a party fails to make a disclosure required by Rule 26(a), any other party may move to compel disclosure and for appropriate sanctions.

    (B) *To Compel a Discovery Response.* A party seeking discovery may move for an order compelling an answer, designation, production, or inspection. This motion may be made if:

        (i) a deponent fails to answer a question asked under Rule 30 or 31;

        (ii) a corporation or other entity fails to make a designation under Rule 30(b)(6) or 31(a)(4);

(iii) a party fails to answer an interrogatory submitted under Rule 33; or

(iv) a party fails to produce documents or fails to respond that inspection will be permitted — or fails to permit inspection — as requested under Rule 34.

(C) *Related to a Deposition.* When taking an oral deposition, the party asking a question may complete or adjourn the examination before moving for an order.

(4) *Evasive or Incomplete Disclosure, Answer, or Response.* For purposes of this subdivision (a), an evasive or incomplete disclosure, answer, or response must be treated as a failure to disclose, answer, or respond.

(5) *Payment of Expenses; Protective Orders.*

(A) *If the Motion Is Granted (or Disclosure or Discovery Is Provided After Filing).* If the motion is granted— or if the disclosure or requested discovery is provided after the motion was filed—the court must, after giving an opportunity to be heard, require the party or deponent whose conduct necessitated the motion, the party or attorney advising that conduct, or both to pay the movant's reasonable expenses incurred in making the motion, including attorney's fees. But the court must not order this payment if:

(i) the movant filed the motion before attempting in good faith to obtain the disclosure or discovery without court action;

(ii) the opposing party's nondisclosure, response, or objection was substantially justified; or

(iii) other circumstances make an award of expenses unjust.

(B) *If the Motion Is Denied.* If the motion is denied, the court may issue any protective order authorized under Rule 26(c) and must, after giving an opportunity to be heard, require the movant, the attorney filing the motion, or both to pay the party or deponent who opposed the motion its reasonable expenses incurred in opposing the motion, including attorney's fees. But the court must not order this payment if the motion was substantially justified or other circumstances make an award of expenses unjust.

(C) *If the Motion Is Granted in Part and Denied in Part.* If the motion is granted in part and denied in part, the court may issue any protective order authorized under Rule 26(c) and may, after giving an opportunity to be heard, apportion the reasonable expenses for the motion.

(b) Failure to Comply with a Court Order.

(1) *Sanctions Sought in the District Where the Deposition Is Taken.* If the court where the discovery is taken orders a deponent to be sworn or to answer a question and the deponent fails to obey, the failure may be treated as contempt of court. If a deposition-related motion is transferred to the court where the action is pending, and that court orders a deponent to be sworn or to answer a question and the deponent fails to obey, the failure may be treated as contempt of either the court where the discovery is taken or the court where the action is pending.

(2) *Sanctions Sought in the District Where the Action Is Pending.*

(A) *For Not Obeying a Discovery Order.* If a party or a party's officer, director, or managing agent—or a witness designated under Rule 30(b)(6) or 31(a)(4)—fails to obey an order to provide or permit discovery, including an order under Rule 26(f), 35, or 37(a), the court where the action is pending may issue further just orders. They may include the following:

(i) directing that the matters embraced in the order or other designated facts be taken as established for purposes of the action, as the prevailing party claims;

(ii) prohibiting the disobedient party from supporting or opposing designated claims or defenses, or from introducing designated matters in evidence;

(iii) striking pleadings in whole or in part;

(iv) staying further proceedings until the order is obeyed;

(v) dismissing the action or proceeding in whole or in part;

(vi) rendering a default judgment against the disobedient party; or

(vii) treating as contempt of court the failure to obey any order except an order to submit to a physical or mental examination.

(B) *For Not Producing a Person for Examination.* If a party fails to comply with an order under Rule 35(a) requiring it to produce another person for examination, the court may issue any of the orders listed in Rule 37(b)(2)(A)(i)-(vi), unless the disobedient party shows that it cannot produce the other person.

(C) *Payment of Expenses.* Instead of or in addition to the orders above, the court must order the disobedient party, the attorney advising that party, or both to pay the reasonable expenses, including attorney's fees, caused by the failure, unless the failure was substantially justified or other circumstances make an award of expenses unjust.

(c) Failure to Disclose, to Supplement an Earlier Response, or to Admit.

(1) *Failure to Disclose or Supplement.* If a party fails to provide information or identify a witness as required by Rule 26(a) or (e), the party is not allowed to use that information or witness to supply evidence on a motion, at a hearing, or at a trial, unless the failure was substantially justified or is harmless. In addition to or instead of this sanction, the court, on motion and after giving an opportunity to be heard:

(A) may order payment of the reasonable expenses, including attorney's fees, caused by the failure;

(B) may inform the jury of the party's failure; and

(C) may impose other appropriate sanctions, including any of the orders listed in Rule 37(b)(2)(A)(i)-(vi).

(2) *Failure to Admit.* If a party fails to admit what is requested under Rule 36 and if the requesting party later proves a document to be genuine or the matter true, the requesting party may move that the party who failed to admit pay the reasonable expenses, including attorney's fees, incurred in making that proof. The court must so order unless:

    (A) the request was held objectionable under Rule 36(a);

    (B) the admission sought was of no substantial importance;

    (C) the party failing to admit had a reasonable ground to believe that it might prevail on the matter; or

    (D) there was other good reason for the failure to admit.

(d) Party's Failure to Attend Its Own Deposition, Serve Answers to Interrogatories, or Respond to a Request for Inspection.

    (1) *In General.*

    (A) *Motion; Grounds for Sanctions.* The court where the action is pending may, on motion, order sanctions if:

    (i) a party or a party's officer, director, or managing agent—or a person designated under Rule 30(b)(6) or 31(a)(4)—fails, after being served with proper notice, to appear for that person's deposition; or

    (ii) a party, after being properly served with interrogatories under Rule 33 or a request for inspection under Rule 34, fails to serve its answers, objections, or written response.

    (B) *Certification.* A motion for sanctions for failing to answer or respond must include a certification that the movant has in good faith conferred or attempted to confer with the party failing to act in an effort to obtain the answer or response without court action.

    (2) *Unacceptable Excuse for Failing to Act.* A failure described in Rule 37(d)(1)(A) is not excused on the ground that the discovery sought was objectionable, unless the party failing to act has a pending motion for a protective order under Rule 26(c).

    (3) *Types of Sanctions.* Sanctions may include any of the orders listed in Rule 37(b)(2)(A)(i)-(vi). Instead of or in addition to these sanctions, the court must require the party failing to act, the attorney advising that party, or both to pay the reasonable expenses, including attorney's fees, caused by the failure, unless the failure was substantially justified or other circumstances make an award of expenses unjust.

(e) Failure to Preserve Electronically Stored Information. If electronically stored information that should have been preserved in the anticipation or conduct of litigation is lost because a party failed to take reasonable steps to preserve it, and it cannot be restored or replaced through additional discovery, the court:

    (1) upon finding prejudice to another party from loss of the information, may order measures no greater than necessary to cure the prejudice; or

    (2) only upon finding that the party acted with the intent to deprive another party of the information's use in the litigation may:

    (A) presume that the lost information was unfavorable to the party;

    (B) instruct the jury that it may or must presume the information was unfavorable to the party; or

    (C) dismiss the action or enter a default judgment.

(f) Failure to Participate in Framing a Discovery Plan. If a party or its attorney fails to participate in good faith in developing and submitting a proposed discovery plan as required by Rule 26(f), the court may, after giving an opportunity to be heard, require that party or attorney to pay to any other party the reasonable expenses, including attorney's fees, caused by the failure.

(Amended December 29, 1948, effective October 20, 1949; March 30, 1970, effective July 1, 1970; April 29, 1980, effective August 1, 1980; amended by Pub.L. 96–481, Title II, § 205(a), October 21, 1980, 94 Stat. 2330, effective October 1, 1981; amended March 2, 1987, effective August 1, 1987; April 22, 1993, effective December 1, 1993; April 17, 2000, effective December 1, 2000; April 12, 2006, effective December 1, 2006; April 30, 2007, effective December 1, 2007; April 16, 2013, effective December 1, 2013; April 29, 2015, effective December 1, 2015.)

TITLE VI.   TRIALS

RULE 38.   RIGHT TO A JURY TRIAL; DEMAND

    (a) Right Preserved. The right of trial by jury as declared by the Seventh Amendment to the Constitution—or as provided by a federal statute—is preserved to the parties inviolate.

    (b) Demand. On any issue triable of right by a jury, a party may demand a jury trial by:

    (1) serving the other parties with a written demand—which may be included in a pleading—no later than 14 days after the last pleading directed to the issue is served; and

    (2) filing the demand in accordance with Rule 5(d).

    (c) Specifying Issues. In its demand, a party may specify the issues that it wishes to have tried by a jury; otherwise, it is considered to have demanded a jury trial on all the issues so triable. If the party has demanded a jury trial on only some issues, any other party may—within 14 days after being served with the demand or within a shorter time ordered by the court—serve a demand for a jury trial on any other or all factual issues triable by jury.

    (d) Waiver; Withdrawal. A party waives a jury trial unless its demand is properly served and filed. A proper demand may be withdrawn only if the parties consent.

    (e) Admiralty and Maritime Claims. These rules do not create a right to a jury trial on issues in a claim that is an admiralty or maritime claim under Rule 9(h).

(Amended February 28, 1966, effective July 1, 1966; March 2, 1987, effective August 1, 1987; April 22, 1993, effective December 1, 1993; April 30, 2007, effective December 1, 2007; March 26, 2009, effective December 1, 2009.)

RULE 39.   TRIAL BY JURY OR BY THE COURT

(a) When a Demand Is Made. When a jury trial has been demanded under Rule 38, the action must be designated on the docket as a jury action. The trial on all issues so demanded must be by jury unless:

(1) the parties or their attorneys file a stipulation to a nonjury trial or so stipulate on the record; or

(2) the court, on motion or on its own, finds that on some or all of those issues there is no federal right to a jury trial.

(b) When No Demand Is Made. Issues on which a jury trial is not properly demanded are to be tried by the court. But the court may, on motion, order a jury trial on any issue for which a jury might have been demanded.

(c) Advisory Jury; Jury Trial by Consent. In an action not triable of right by a jury, the court, on motion or on its own:

(1) may try any issue with an advisory jury; or

(2) may, with the parties' consent, try any issue by a jury whose verdict has the same effect as if a jury trial had been a matter of right, unless the action is against the United States and a federal statute provides for a nonjury trial.

(Amended April 30, 2007, effective December 1, 2007.)

RULE 40.   SCHEDULING CASES FOR TRIAL

Each court must provide by rule for scheduling trials. The court must give priority to actions entitled to priority by a federal statute.

(Amended April 30, 2007, effective December 1, 2007.)

RULE 41.   DISMISSAL OF ACTIONS

(a) Voluntary Dismissal.

(1) *By the Plaintiff.*

(A) *Without a Court Order.* Subject to Rules 23(e), 23.1(c), 23.2, and 66 and any applicable federal statute, the plaintiff may dismiss an action without a court order by filing:

(i) a notice of dismissal before the opposing party serves either an answer or a motion for summary judgment; or

(ii) a stipulation of dismissal signed by all parties who have appeared.

(B) *Effect.* Unless the notice or stipulation states otherwise, the dismissal is without prejudice. But if the plaintiff previously dismissed any federal- or state-court action based on or including the same claim, a notice of dismissal operates as an adjudication on the merits.

(2) *By Court Order; Effect.* Except as provided in Rule 41(a)(1), an action may be dismissed at the plaintiff's request only by court order, on terms that the court considers proper. If a defendant has pleaded a counterclaim before being served with the plaintiff's motion to dismiss, the action may be dismissed over the defendant's objection only if the counterclaim can remain pending for independent adjudica-

tion. Unless the order states otherwise, a dismissal under this paragraph (2) is without prejudice.

(b) Involuntary Dismissal; Effect. If the plaintiff fails to prosecute or to comply with these rules or a court order, a defendant may move to dismiss the action or any claim against it. Unless the dismissal order states otherwise, a dismissal under this subdivision (b) and any dismissal not under this rule—except one for lack of jurisdiction, improper venue, or failure to join a party under Rule 19—operates as an adjudication on the merits.

(c) Dismissing a Counterclaim, Crossclaim, or Third–Party Claim. This rule applies to a dismissal of any counterclaim, crossclaim, or third-party claim. A claimant's voluntary dismissal under Rule 41(a)(1)(A)(i) must be made:

(1) before a responsive pleading is served; or

(2) if there is no responsive pleading, before evidence is introduced at a hearing or trial.

(d) Costs of a Previously Dismissed Action. If a plaintiff who previously dismissed an action in any court files an action based on or including the same claim against the same defendant, the court:

(1) may order the plaintiff to pay all or part of the costs of that previous action; and

(2) may stay the proceedings until the plaintiff has complied.

(Amended December 27, 1946, effective March 19, 1948; January 21, 1963, effective July 1, 1963; February 28, 1966, effective July 1, 1966; December 4, 1967, effective July 1, 1968; March 2, 1987, effective August 1, 1987; April 30, 1991, effective December 1, 1991; April 30, 2007, effective December 1, 2007.)

RULE 42.   CONSOLIDATION; SEPARATE TRIALS

(a) Consolidation. If actions before the court involve a common question of law or fact, the court may:

(1) join for hearing or trial any or all matters at issue in the actions;

(2) consolidate the actions; or

(3) issue any other orders to avoid unnecessary cost or delay.

(b) Separate Trials. For convenience, to avoid prejudice, or to expedite and economize, the court may order a separate trial of one or more separate issues, claims, crossclaims, counterclaims, or third-party claims. When ordering a separate trial, the court must preserve any federal right to a jury trial.

(Amended February 28, 1966, effective July 1, 1966; April 30, 2007, effective December 1, 2007.)

RULE 43.   TAKING TESTIMONY

(a) In Open Court. At trial, the witnesses' testimony must be taken in open court unless a federal statute, the Federal Rules of Evidence, these rules, or other rules adopted by the Supreme Court provide otherwise. For good cause in compelling circumstances and with appropriate safeguards, the court may permit testimony in open court by contemporaneous transmission from a different location.

(b) Affirmation Instead of an Oath. When these rules require an oath, a solemn affirmation suffices.

(c) Evidence on a Motion. When a motion relies on facts outside the record, the court may hear the matter on affidavits or may hear it wholly or partly on oral testimony or on depositions.

(d) Interpreter. The court may appoint an interpreter of its choosing; fix reasonable compensation to be paid from funds provided by law or by one or more parties; and tax the compensation as costs.

(Amended February 28, 1966, effective July 1, 1966; November 20, 1972, and December 18, 1972, effective July 1, 1975; March 2, 1987, effective August 1, 1987; April 23, 1996, effective December 1, 1996; April 30, 2007, effective December 1, 2007.)

RULE 44. PROVING AN OFFICIAL RECORD

(a) Means of Proving.

(1) *Domestic Record.* Each of the following evidences an official record—or an entry in it—that is otherwise admissible and is kept within the United States, any state, district, or commonwealth, or any territory subject to the administrative or judicial jurisdiction of the United States:

(A) an official publication of the record; or

(B) a copy attested by the officer with legal custody of the record—or by the officer's deputy—and accompanied by a certificate that the officer has custody. The certificate must be made under seal:

(i) by a judge of a court of record in the district or political subdivision where the record is kept; or

(ii) by any public officer with a seal of office and with official duties in the district or political subdivision where the record is kept.

(2) *Foreign Record.*

(A) *In General.* Each of the following evidences a foreign official record—or an entry in it—that is otherwise admissible:

(i) an official publication of the record; or

(ii) the record—or a copy—that is attested by an authorized person and is accompanied either by a final certification of genuineness or by a certification under a treaty or convention to which the United States and the country where the record is located are parties.

(B) *Final Certification of Genuineness.* A final certification must certify the genuineness of the signature and official position of the attester or of any foreign official whose certificate of genuineness relates to the attestation or is in a chain of certificates of genuineness relating to the attestation. A final certification may be made by a secretary of a United States embassy or legation; by a consul general, vice consul, or consular agent of the United States; or by a diplomatic or consular official of the foreign country assigned or accredited to the United States.

(C) *Other Means of Proof.* If all parties have had a reasonable opportunity to investigate a foreign record's authenticity and accuracy, the court may, for good cause, either:

(i) admit an attested copy without final certification; or

(ii) permit the record to be evidenced by an attested summary with or without a final certification.

(b) Lack of a Record. A written statement that a diligent search of designated records revealed no record or entry of a specified tenor is admissible as evidence that the records contain no such record or entry. For domestic records, the statement must be authenticated under Rule 44(a)(1). For foreign records, the statement must comply with (a)(2)(C)(ii).

(c) Other Proof. A party may prove an official record—or an entry or lack of an entry in it—by any other method authorized by law.

(Amended February 28, 1966, effective July 1, 1966; March 2, 1987, effective August 1, 1987; April 30, 1991, effective December 1, 1991; April 30, 2007, effective December 1, 2007.)

RULE 44.1. DETERMINING FOREIGN LAW

A party who intends to raise an issue about a foreign country's law must give notice by a pleading or other writing. In determining foreign law, the court may consider any relevant material or source, including testimony, whether or not submitted by a party or admissible under the Federal Rules of Evidence. The court's determination must be treated as a ruling on a question of law.

(Adopted February 28, 1966, effective July 1, 1966; amended November 20, 1972, effective July 1, 1975; March 2, 1987, effective August 1, 1987; April 30, 2007, effective December 1, 2007.)

RULE 45. SUBPOENA

(a) In General.

(1) *Form and Contents.*

(A) *Requirements—In General.* Every subpoena must:

(i) state the court from which it issued;

(ii) state the title of the action and its civil-action number;

(iii) command each person to whom it is directed to do the following at a specified time and place: attend and testify; produce designated documents, electronically stored information, or tangible things in that person's possession, custody, or control; or permit the inspection of premises; and

(iv) set out the text of Rule 45(d) and (e).

(B) *Command to Attend a Deposition—Notice of the Recording Method.* A subpoena commanding attendance at a deposition must state the method for recording the testimony.

(C) *Combining or Separating a Command to Produce or to Permit Inspection; Specifying the Form for Electronically Stored Information.* A command to produce documents, electronically stored information, or tangible things or to permit the inspection of premises may be included in a subpoena commanding attendance at a deposition, hearing, or trial, or may be set out in a separate subpoena. A subpoena may specify the form or forms in which electronically stored information is to be produced.

(D) *Command to Produce; Included Obligations.* A command in a subpoena to produce documents, electronically stored information, or tangible things requires the responding person to permit inspection, copying, testing, or sampling of the materials.

(2) *Issuing Court.* A subpoena must issue from the court where the action is pending.

(3) *Issued by Whom.* The clerk must issue a subpoena, signed but otherwise in blank, to a party who requests it. That party must complete it before service. An attorney also may issue and sign a subpoena if the attorney is authorized to practice in the issuing court.

(4) *Notice to Other Parties Before Service.* If the subpoena commands the production of documents, electronically stored information, or tangible things or the inspection of premises before trial, then before it is served on the person to whom it is directed, a notice and a copy of the subpoena must be served on each party.

(b) Service.

(1) *By Whom and How; Tendering Fees.* Any person who is at least 18 years old and not a party may serve a subpoena. Serving a subpoena requires delivering a copy to the named person and, if the subpoena requires that person's attendance, tendering the fees for 1 day's attendance and the mileage allowed by law. Fees and mileage need not be tendered when the subpoena issues on behalf of the United States or any of its officers or agencies.

(2) *Service in the United States.* A subpoena may be served at any place within the United States.

(3) *Service in a Foreign Country.* 28 U.S.C. § 1783 governs issuing and serving a subpoena directed to a United States national or resident who is in a foreign country.

(4) *Proof of Service.* Proving service, when necessary, requires filing with the issuing court a statement showing the date and manner of service and the names of the persons served. The statement must be certified by the server.

(c) Place of Compliance.

(1) *For a Trial, Hearing, or Deposition.* A subpoena may command a person to attend a trial, hearing, or deposition only as follows:

(A) within 100 miles of where the person resides, is employed, or regularly transacts business in person; or

(B) within the state where the person resides, is employed, or regularly transacts business in person, if the person

(i) is a party or a party's officer; or

(ii) is commanded to attend a trial and would not incur substantial expense.

(2) *For Other Discovery.* A subpoena may command:

(A) production of documents, electronically stored information, or tangible things at a place within 100 miles of where the person resides, is employed, or regularly transacts business in person; and

(B) inspection of premises at the premises to be inspected.

(d) Protecting a Person Subject to a Subpoena; Enforcement.

(1) *Avoiding Undue Burden or Expense; Sanctions.* A party or attorney responsible for issuing and serving a subpoena must take reasonable steps to avoid imposing undue burden or expense on a person subject to the subpoena. The court for the district where compliance is required must enforce this duty and impose an appropriate sanction—which may include lost earnings and reasonable attorney's fees—on a party or attorney who fails to comply.

(2) *Command to Produce Materials or Permit Inspection.*

(A) *Appearance Not Required.* A person commanded to produce documents, electronically stored information, or tangible things, or to permit the inspection of premises, need not appear in person at the place of production or inspection unless also commanded to appear for a deposition, hearing, or trial.

(B) *Objections.* A person commanded to produce documents or tangible things or to permit inspection may serve on the party or attorney designated in the subpoena a written objection to inspecting, copying, testing, or sampling any or all of the materials or to inspecting the premises—or to producing electronically stored information in the form or forms requested. The objection must be served before the earlier of the time specified for compliance or 14 days after the subpoena is served. If an objection is made, the following rules apply:

(i) At any time, on notice to the commanded person, the serving party may move the court for the district where compliance is required for an order compelling production or inspection.

(ii) These acts may be required only as directed in the order, and the order must protect a person who is neither a party nor a party's officer from significant expense resulting from compliance.

(3) *Quashing or Modifying a Subpoena.*

(A) *When Required.* On timely motion, the court for the district where compliance is required must quash or modify a subpoena that:

(i) fails to allow a reasonable time to comply;

(ii) requires a person to comply beyond the geographical limits specified in Rule 45(c);

(iii) requires disclosure of privileged or other protected matter, if no exception or waiver applies; or

(iv) subjects a person to undue burden.

(B) *When Permitted.* To protect a person subject to or affected by a subpoena, the court for the district where compliance is required may, on motion, quash or modify the subpoena if it requires:

(i) disclosing a trade secret or other confidential research, development, or commercial information; or

(ii) disclosing an unretained expert's opinion or information that does not describe specific occurrences in dispute and results from the expert's study that was not requested by a party.

(C) *Specifying Conditions as an Alternative.* In the circumstances described in Rule 45(d)(3)(B), the court may, instead of quashing or modifying a subpoena, order appearance or production under specified conditions if the serving party:

(i) shows a substantial need for the testimony or material that cannot be otherwise met without undue hardship; and

(ii) ensures that the subpoenaed person will be reasonably compensated.

(e) Duties in Responding to a Subpoena.

(1) *Producing Documents or Electronically Stored Information.* These procedures apply to producing documents or electronically stored information:

(A) *Documents.* A person responding to a subpoena to produce documents must produce them as they are kept in the ordinary course of business or must organize and label them to correspond to the categories in the demand.

(B) *Form for Producing Electronically Stored Information Not Specified.* If a subpoena does not specify a form for producing electronically stored information, the person responding must produce it in a form or forms in which it is ordinarily maintained or in a reasonably usable form or forms.

(C) *Electronically Stored Information Produced in Only One Form.* The person responding need not produce the same electronically stored information in more than one form.

(D) *Inaccessible Electronically Stored Information.* The person responding need not provide discovery of electronically stored information from sources that the person identifies as not reasonably accessible because of undue burden or cost. On motion to compel discovery or for a protective order, the person responding must show that the information is not reasonably accessible because of undue burden or cost. If that showing is made, the court may nonetheless order discovery from such sources if the requesting party shows good cause, considering the limitations of Rule 26(b)(2)(C). The court may specify conditions for the discovery.

(2) *Claiming Privilege or Protection.*

(A) *Information Withheld.* A person withholding subpoenaed information under a claim that it is privileged or subject to protection as trial-preparation material must:

(i) expressly make the claim; and

(ii) describe the nature of the withheld documents, communications, or tangible things in a manner that, without revealing information itself privileged or protected, will enable the parties to assess the claim.

(B) *Information Produced.* If information produced in response to a subpoena is subject to a claim of privilege or of protection as trial-preparation material, the person making the claim may notify any party that received the information of the claim and the basis for it. After being notified, a party must promptly return, sequester, or destroy the specified information and any copies it has; must not use or disclose the information until the claim is resolved; must take reasonable steps to retrieve the information if the party disclosed it before being notified; and may promptly present the information under seal to the court for the district where compliance is required for a determination of the claim. The person who produced the information must preserve the information until the claim is resolved.

(f) Transferring a Subpoena–Related Motion. When the court where compliance is required did not issue the subpoena, it may transfer a motion under this rule to the issuing court if the person subject to the subpoena consents or if the court finds exceptional circumstances. Then, if the attorney for a person subject to a subpoena is authorized to practice in the court where the motion was made, the attorney may file papers and appear on the motion as an officer of the issuing court. To enforce its order, the issuing court may transfer the order to the court where the motion was made.

(g) Contempt. The court for the district where compliance is required—and also, after a motion is transferred, the issuing court—may hold in contempt a person who, having been served, fails without adequate excuse to obey the subpoena or an order related to it.

(Amended December 27, 1946, effective March 19, 1948; December 29, 1948, effective October 20, 1949; March 30, 1970, effective July 1, 1970; April 29, 1980, effective August 1, 1980; April 29, 1985, effective August 1, 1985; March 2, 1987, effective August 1, 1987; April 30, 1991, effective December 1, 1991; April 25, 2005, effective December 1, 2005; April 12, 2006, effective December 1, 2006; April 30, 2007, effective December 1, 2007; April 16, 2013, effective December 1, 2013.)

RULE 46. OBJECTING TO A RULING OR ORDER

A formal exception to a ruling or order is unnecessary. When the ruling or order is requested or made, a party need only state the action that it wants the court to take or objects to, along with the grounds for the request or objection. Failing to object does not prejudice a party who had no opportunity to do so when the ruling or order was made.

(Amended March 2, 1987, effective August 1, 1987; April 30, 2007, effective December 1, 2007.)

RULE 47. SELECTING JURORS

(a) Examining Jurors. The court may permit the parties or their attorneys to examine prospective jurors or may itself do so. If the court examines the jurors, it must permit the parties or their attorneys to make any further inquiry it considers proper, or must itself ask any of their additional questions it considers proper.

(b) Peremptory Challenges. The court must allow the number of peremptory challenges provided by 28 U.S.C. § 1870.

(c) Excusing a Juror. During trial or deliberation, the court may excuse a juror for good cause.

(Amended February 28, 1966, effective July 1, 1966; April 30, 1991, effective December 1, 1991; April 30, 2007, effective December 1, 2007.)

RULE 48.   NUMBER OF JURORS; VERDICT; POLLING

(a) Number of Jurors. A jury must begin with at least 6 and no more than 12 members, and each juror must participate in the verdict unless excused under Rule 47(c).

(b) Verdict. Unless the parties stipulate otherwise, the verdict must be unanimous and must be returned by a jury of at least 6 members.

(c) Polling. After a verdict is returned but before the jury is discharged, the court must on a party's request, or may on its own, poll the jurors individually. If the poll reveals a lack of unanimity or lack of assent by the number of jurors that the parties stipulated to, the court may direct the jury to deliberate further or may order a new trial.

(Amended April 30, 1991, effective December 1, 1991; April 30, 2007, effective December 1, 2007; March 26, 2009, effective December 1, 2009.)

RULE 49.   SPECIAL VERDICT; GENERAL VERDICT AND QUESTIONS

(a) Special Verdict.

(1) *In General.* The court may require a jury to return only a special verdict in the form of a special written finding on each issue of fact. The court may do so by:

(A) submitting written questions susceptible of a categorical or other brief answer;

(B) submitting written forms of the special findings that might properly be made under the pleadings and evidence; or

(C) using any other method that the court considers appropriate.

(2) *Instructions.* The court must give the instructions and explanations necessary to enable the jury to make its findings on each submitted issue.

(3) *Issues Not Submitted.* A party waives the right to a jury trial on any issue of fact raised by the pleadings or evidence but not submitted to the jury unless, before the jury retires, the party demands its submission to the jury. If the party does not demand submission, the court may make a finding on the issue. If the court makes no finding, it is considered to have made a finding consistent with its judgment on the special verdict.

(b) General Verdict with Answers to Written Questions.

(1) *In General.* The court may submit to the jury forms for a general verdict, together with written questions on one or more issues of fact that the jury must decide. The court must give the instructions and explanations necessary to enable the jury to render a general verdict and answer the questions in writing, and must direct the jury to do both.

(2) *Verdict and Answers Consistent.* When the general verdict and the answers are consistent, the court must approve, for entry under Rule 58, an appropriate judgment on the verdict and answers.

(3) *Answers Inconsistent with the Verdict.* When the answers are consistent with each other but one or more is inconsistent with the general verdict, the court may:

(A) approve, for entry under Rule 58, an appropriate judgment according to the answers, notwithstanding the general verdict;

(B) direct the jury to further consider its answers and verdict; or

(C) order a new trial.

(4) *Answers Inconsistent with Each Other and the Verdict.* When the answers are inconsistent with each other and one or more is also inconsistent with the general verdict, judgment must not be entered; instead, the court must direct the jury to further consider its answers and verdict, or must order a new trial.

(Amended January 21, 1963, effective July 1, 1963; March 2, 1987, effective August 1, 1987; April 30, 2007, effective December 1, 2007.)

RULE 50.   JUDGMENT AS A MATTER OF LAW IN A JURY TRIAL; RELATED MOTION FOR A NEW TRIAL; CONDITIONAL RULING

(a) Judgment as a Matter of Law.

(1) *In General.* If a party has been fully heard on an issue during a jury trial and the court finds that a reasonable jury would not have a legally sufficient evidentiary basis to find for the party on that issue, the court may:

(A) resolve the issue against the party; and

(B) grant a motion for judgment as a matter of law against the party on a claim or defense that, under the controlling law, can be maintained or defeated only with a favorable finding on that issue.

(2) *Motion.* A motion for judgment as a matter of law may be made at any time before the case is submitted to the jury. The motion must specify the judgment sought and the law and facts that entitle the movant to the judgment.

(b) Renewing the Motion After Trial; Alternative Motion for a New Trial. If the court does not grant a motion for judgment as a matter of law made under Rule 50(a), the court is considered to have submitted the action to the jury subject to the court's later deciding the legal questions raised by the motion. No later than 28 days after the entry of judgment—or if the motion addresses a jury issue not decided by a verdict, no later than 28 days after the jury was discharged—the movant may file a renewed motion for judgment as a matter of law and may include an alternative or joint request for a new trial under Rule 59. In ruling on the renewed motion, the court may:

    (1) allow judgment on the verdict, if the jury returned a verdict;

    (2) order a new trial; or

    (3) direct the entry of judgment as a matter of law.

(c) Granting the Renewed Motion; Conditional Ruling on a Motion for a New Trial.

    (1) *In General.* If the court grants a renewed motion for judgment as a matter of law, it must also conditionally rule on any motion for a new trial by determining whether a new trial should be granted if the judgment is later vacated or reversed. The court must state the grounds for conditionally granting or denying the motion for a new trial.

    (2) *Effect of a Conditional Ruling.* Conditionally granting the motion for a new trial does not affect the judgment's finality; if the judgment is reversed, the new trial must proceed unless the appellate court orders otherwise. If the motion for a new trial is conditionally denied, the appellee may assert error in that denial; if the judgment is reversed, the case must proceed as the appellate court orders.

(d) Time for a Losing Party's New–Trial Motion. Any motion for a new trial under Rule 59 by a party against whom judgment as a matter of law is rendered must be filed no later than 28 days after the entry of the judgment.

(e) Denying the Motion for Judgment as a Matter of Law; Reversal on Appeal. If the court denies the motion for judgment as a matter of law, the prevailing party may, as appellee, assert grounds entitling it to a new trial should the appellate court conclude that the trial court erred in denying the motion. If the appellate court reverses the judgment, it may order a new trial, direct the trial court to determine whether a new trial should be granted, or direct the entry of judgment.

(Amended January 21, 1963, effective July 1, 1963; March 2, 1987, effective August 1, 1987; April 30, 1991, effective December 1, 1991; April 22, 1993, effective December 1, 1993; April 27, 1995, effective December 1, 1995; April 12, 2006, effective December 1, 2006; April 30, 2007, effective December 1, 2007; March 26, 2009, effective December 1, 2009.)

RULE 51. INSTRUCTIONS TO THE JURY; OBJECTIONS; PRESERVING A CLAIM OF ERROR

(a) Requests.

    (1) *Before or at the Close of the Evidence.* At the close of the evidence or at any earlier reasonable time that the court orders, a party may file and furnish to every other party written requests for the jury instructions it wants the court to give.

    (2) *After the Close of the Evidence.* After the close of the evidence, a party may:

        (A) file requests for instructions on issues that could not reasonably have been anticipated by an earlier time that the court set for requests; and

        (B) with the court's permission, file untimely requests for instructions on any issue.

(b) Instructions. The court:

    (1) must inform the parties of its proposed instructions and proposed action on the requests before instructing the jury and before final jury arguments;

    (2) must give the parties an opportunity to object on the record and out of the jury's hearing before the instructions and arguments are delivered; and

    (3) may instruct the jury at any time before the jury is discharged.

(c) Objections.

    (1) *How to Make.* A party who objects to an instruction or the failure to give an instruction must do so on the record, stating distinctly the matter objected to and the grounds for the objection.

    (2) *When to Make.* An objection is timely if:

        (A) a party objects at the opportunity provided under Rule 51(b)(2); or

        (B) a party was not informed of an instruction or action on a request before that opportunity to object, and the party objects promptly after learning that the instruction or request will be, or has been, given or refused.

(d) Assigning Error; Plain Error.

    (1) *Assigning Error.* A party may assign as error:

        (A) an error in an instruction actually given, if that party properly objected; or

        (B) a failure to give an instruction, if that party properly requested it and—unless the court rejected the request in a definitive ruling on the record—also properly objected.

    (2) *Plain Error.* A court may consider a plain error in the instructions that has not been preserved as required by Rule 51(d)(1) if the error affects substantial rights.

(Amended March 2, 1987, effective August 1, 1987; March 27, 2003, effective December 1, 2003; April 30, 2007, effective December 1, 2007.)

RULE 52. FINDINGS AND CONCLUSIONS BY THE COURT; JUDGMENT ON PARTIAL FINDINGS

(a) Findings and Conclusions.

    (1) *In General.* In an action tried on the facts without a jury or with an advisory jury, the court must find the facts specially and state its conclusions of law separately. The findings and conclusions may be stated on the record after the close of the evidence or may appear in an opinion or a memorandum of decision filed by the court. Judgment must be entered under Rule 58.

    (2) *For an Interlocutory Injunction.* In granting or refusing an interlocutory injunction, the court must similarly state the findings and conclusions that support its action.

(3) *For a Motion.* The court is not required to state findings or conclusions when ruling on a motion under Rule 12 or 56 or, unless these rules provide otherwise, on any other motion.

(4) *Effect of a Master's Findings.* A master's findings, to the extent adopted by the court, must be considered the court's findings.

(5) *Questioning the Evidentiary Support.* A party may later question the sufficiency of the evidence supporting the findings, whether or not the party requested findings, objected to them, moved to amend them, or moved for partial findings.

(6) *Setting Aside the Findings.* Findings of fact, whether based on oral or other evidence, must not be set aside unless clearly erroneous, and the reviewing court must give due regard to the trial court's opportunity to judge the witnesses' credibility.

(b) Amended or Additional Findings. On a party's motion filed no later than 28 days after the entry of judgment, the court may amend its findings—or make additional findings—and may amend the judgment accordingly. The motion may accompany a motion for a new trial under Rule 59.

(c) Judgment on Partial Findings. If a party has been fully heard on an issue during a nonjury trial and the court finds against the party on that issue, the court may enter judgment against the party on a claim or defense that, under the controlling law, can be maintained or defeated only with a favorable finding on that issue. The court may, however, decline to render any judgment until the close of the evidence. A judgment on partial findings must be supported by findings of fact and conclusions of law as required by Rule 52(a).

(Amended December 27, 1946, effective March 19, 1948; January 21, 1963, effective July 1, 1963; April 28, 1983, effective August 1, 1983; April 29, 1985, effective August 1, 1985; April 30, 1991, effective December 1, 1991; April 22, 1993, effective December 1, 1993; April 27, 1995, effective December 1, 1995; April 30, 2007, effective December 1, 2007; March 26, 2009, effective December 1, 2009.)

RULE 53.   MASTERS

(a) Appointment.

(1) *Scope.* Unless a statute provides otherwise, a court may appoint a master only to:

   (A) perform duties consented to by the parties;

   (B) hold trial proceedings and make or recommend findings of fact on issues to be decided without a jury if appointment is warranted by:

      (i) some exceptional condition; or

      (ii) the need to perform an accounting or resolve a difficult computation of damages; or

   (C) address pretrial and posttrial matters that cannot be effectively and timely addressed by an available district judge or magistrate judge of the district.

(2) *Disqualification.* A master must not have a relationship to the parties, attorneys, action, or court that would require disqualification of a judge under 28 U.S.C. § 455, unless the parties, with the court's approval, consent to the appointment after the master discloses any potential grounds for disqualification.

(3) *Possible Expense or Delay.* In appointing a master, the court must consider the fairness of imposing the likely expenses on the parties and must protect against unreasonable expense or delay.

(b) Order Appointing a Master.

(1) *Notice.* Before appointing a master, the court must give the parties notice and an opportunity to be heard. Any party may suggest candidates for appointment.

(2) *Contents.* The appointing order must direct the master to proceed with all reasonable diligence and must state:

   (A) the master's duties, including any investigation or enforcement duties, and any limits on the master's authority under Rule 53(c);

   (B) the circumstances, if any, in which the master may communicate ex parte with the court or a party;

   (C) the nature of the materials to be preserved and filed as the record of the master's activities;

   (D) the time limits, method of filing the record, other procedures, and standards for reviewing the master's orders, findings, and recommendations; and

   (E) the basis, terms, and procedure for fixing the master's compensation under Rule 53(g).

(3) *Issuing.* The court may issue the order only after:

   (A) the master files an affidavit disclosing whether there is any ground for disqualification under 28 U.S.C. § 455; and

   (B) if a ground is disclosed, the parties, with the court's approval, waive the disqualification.

(4) *Amending.* The order may be amended at any time after notice to the parties and an opportunity to be heard.

(c) Master's Authority.

(1) *In General.* Unless the appointing order directs otherwise, a master may:

   (A) regulate all proceedings;

   (B) take all appropriate measures to perform the assigned duties fairly and efficiently; and

   (C) if conducting an evidentiary hearing, exercise the appointing court's power to compel, take, and record evidence.

(2) *Sanctions.* The master may by order impose on a party any noncontempt sanction provided by Rule 37 or 45, and may recommend a contempt sanction against a party and sanctions against a nonparty.

(d) Master's Orders. A master who issues an order must file it and promptly serve a copy on each party. The clerk must enter the order on the docket.

(e) Master's Reports. A master must report to the court as required by the appointing order. The master must file the report and promptly serve a copy on each party, unless the court orders otherwise.

(f) Action on the Master's Order, Report, or Recommendations.

(1) *Opportunity for a Hearing; Action in General.* In acting on a master's order, report, or recommendations, the court must give the parties notice and an opportunity to be heard; may receive evidence; and may adopt or affirm, modify, wholly or partly reject or reverse, or resubmit to the master with instructions.

(2) *Time to Object or Move to Adopt or Modify.* A party may file objections to—or a motion to adopt or modify—the master's order, report, or recommendations no later than 21 days after a copy is served, unless the court sets a different time.

(3) *Reviewing Factual Findings.* The court must decide de novo all objections to findings of fact made or recommended by a master, unless the parties, with the court's approval, stipulate that:

(A) the findings will be reviewed for clear error; or

(B) the findings of a master appointed under Rule 53(a)(1)(A) or (C) will be final.

(4) *Reviewing Legal Conclusions.* The court must decide de novo all objections to conclusions of law made or recommended by a master.

(5) *Reviewing Procedural Matters.* Unless the appointing order establishes a different standard of review, the court may set aside a master's ruling on a procedural matter only for an abuse of discretion.

(g) Compensation.

(1) *Fixing Compensation.* Before or after judgment, the court must fix the master's compensation on the basis and terms stated in the appointing order, but the court may set a new basis and terms after giving notice and an opportunity to be heard.

(2) *Payment.* The compensation must be paid either:

(A) by a party or parties; or

(B) from a fund or subject matter of the action within the court's control.

(3) *Allocating Payment.* The court must allocate payment among the parties after considering the nature and amount of the controversy, the parties' means, and the extent to which any party is more responsible than other parties for the reference to a master. An interim allocation may be amended to reflect a decision on the merits.

(h) Appointing a Magistrate Judge. A magistrate judge is subject to this rule only when the order referring a matter to the magistrate judge states that the reference is made under this rule.

(Amended February 28, 1966, effective July 1, 1966; April 28, 1983, effective August 1, 1983; March 2, 1987, effective August 1, 1987; April 30, 1991, effective December 1, 1991; April 22, 1993, effective December 1, 1993; March 27, 2003, effective December 1, 2003; April 30, 2007, effective December 1, 2007; March 26, 2009, effective December 1, 2009.)

TITLE VII. JUDGMENT

RULE 54. JUDGMENT; COSTS

(a) Definition; Form. "Judgment" as used in these rules includes a decree and any order from which an appeal lies. A judgment should not include recitals of pleadings, a master's report, or a record of prior proceedings.

(b) Judgment on Multiple Claims or Involving Multiple Parties. When an action presents more than one claim for relief—whether as a claim, counterclaim, crossclaim, or third-party claim—or when multiple parties are involved, the court may direct entry of a final judgment as to one or more, but fewer than all, claims or parties only if the court expressly determines that there is no just reason for delay. Otherwise, any order or other decision, however designated, that adjudicates fewer than all the claims or the rights and liabilities of fewer than all the parties does not end the action as to any of the claims or parties and may be revised at any time before the entry of a judgment adjudicating all the claims and all the parties' rights and liabilities.

(c) Demand for Judgment; Relief to Be Granted. A default judgment must not differ in kind from, or exceed in amount, what is demanded in the pleadings. Every other final judgment should grant the relief to which each party is entitled, even if the party has not demanded that relief in its pleadings.

(d) Costs; Attorney's Fees.

(1) *Costs Other Than Attorney's Fees.* Unless a federal statute, these rules, or a court order provides otherwise, costs—other than attorney's fees—should be allowed to the prevailing party. But costs against the United States, its officers, and its agencies may be imposed only to the extent allowed by law. The clerk may tax costs on 14 days' notice. On motion served within the next 7 days, the court may review the clerk's action.

(2) *Attorney's Fees.*

(A) *Claim to Be by Motion.* A claim for attorney's fees and related nontaxable expenses must be made by motion unless the substantive law requires those fees to be proved at trial as an element of damages.

(B) *Timing and Contents of the Motion.* Unless a statute or a court order provides otherwise, the motion must:

(i) be filed no later than 14 days after the entry of judgment;

(ii) specify the judgment and the statute, rule, or other grounds entitling the movant to the award;

(iii) state the amount sought or provide a fair estimate of it; and

(iv) disclose, if the court so orders, the terms of any agreement about fees for the services for which the claim is made.

(C) *Proceedings.* Subject to Rule 23(h), the court must, on a party's request, give an opportunity for adversary submissions on the motion in accordance with Rule 43(c) or 78. The court may decide issues of liability for fees before receiving submissions on the value of services. The court must find the facts and state its conclusions of law as provided in Rule 52(a).

(D) *Special Procedures by Local Rule; Reference to a Master or a Magistrate Judge.* By local rule, the court may establish special procedures to resolve fee-related issues without extensive evidentiary hearings. Also, the court may refer issues concerning the value of services to a special master under Rule 53 without regard to the limitations of Rule 53(a)(1), and may refer a motion for attorney's fees to a magistrate judge under Rule 72(b) as if it were a dispositive pretrial matter.

(E) *Exceptions.* Subparagraphs (A)-(D) do not apply to claims for fees and expenses as sanctions for violating these rules or as sanctions under 28 U.S.C. § 1927.

(Amended December 27, 1946, effective March 19, 1948; April 17, 1961, effective July 19, 1961; March 2, 1987, effective August 1, 1987; April 22, 1993, effective December 1, 1993; April 29, 2002, effective December 1, 2002; March 27, 2003, effective December 1, 2003; April 30, 2007, effective December 1, 2007; March 26, 2009, effective December 1, 2009.)

RULE 55. DEFAULT; DEFAULT JUDGMENT

(a) Entering a Default. When a party against whom a judgment for affirmative relief is sought has failed to plead or otherwise defend, and that failure is shown by affidavit or otherwise, the clerk must enter the party's default.

(b) Entering a Default Judgment.

(1) *By the Clerk.* If the plaintiff's claim is for a sum certain or a sum that can be made certain by computation, the clerk—on the plaintiff's request, with an affidavit showing the amount due—must enter judgment for that amount and costs against a defendant who has been defaulted for not appearing and who is neither a minor nor an incompetent person.

(2) *By the Court.* In all other cases, the party must apply to the court for a default judgment. A default judgment may be entered against a minor or incompetent person only if represented by a general guardian, conservator, or other like fiduciary who has appeared. If the party against whom a default judgment is sought has appeared personally or by a representative, that party or its representative must be served with written notice of the application at least 7 days before the hearing. The court may conduct hearings or make referrals—preserving any federal statutory right to a jury trial—when, to enter or effectuate judgment, it needs to:

(A) conduct an accounting;

(B) determine the amount of damages;

(C) establish the truth of any allegation by evidence; or

(D) investigate any other matter.

(c) Setting Aside a Default or a Default Judgment. The court may set aside an entry of default for good cause, and it may set aside a final default judgment under Rule 60(b).

(d) Judgment Against the United States. A default judgment may be entered against the United States, its officers, or its agencies only if the claimant establishes a claim or right to relief by evidence that satisfies the court.

(Amended March 2, 1987, effective August 1, 1987; April 30, 2007, effective December 1, 2007; March 26, 2009, effective December 1, 2009; April 29, 2015, effective December 1, 2015.)

RULE 56. SUMMARY JUDGMENT

(a) Motion for Summary Judgment or Partial Summary Judgment. A party may move for summary judgment, identifying each claim or defense—or the part of each claim or defense—on which summary judgment is sought. The court shall grant summary judgment if the movant shows that there is no genuine dispute as to any material fact and the movant is entitled to judgment as a matter of law. The court should state on the record the reasons for granting or denying the motion.

(b) Time to File a Motion. Unless a different time is set by local rule or the court orders otherwise, a party may file a motion for summary judgment at any time until 30 days after the close of all discovery.

(c) Procedures.

(1) *Supporting Factual Positions.* A party asserting that a fact cannot be or is genuinely disputed must support the assertion by:

(A) citing to particular parts of materials in the record, including depositions, documents, electronically stored information, affidavits or declarations, stipulations (including those made for purposes of the motion only), admissions, interrogatory answers, or other materials; or

(B) showing that the materials cited do not establish the absence or presence of a genuine dispute, or that an adverse party cannot produce admissible evidence to support the fact.

(2) *Objection That a Fact Is Not Supported by Admissible Evidence.* A party may object that the material cited to support or dispute a fact cannot be presented in a form that would be admissible in evidence.

(3) *Materials Not Cited.* The court need consider only the cited materials, but it may consider other materials in the record.

(4) *Affidavits or Declarations.* An affidavit or declaration used to support or oppose a motion must be made on personal knowledge, set out facts that would be admissible in evidence, and show that the affiant or declarant is competent to testify on the matters stated.

(d) When Facts Are Unavailable to the Nonmovant. If a nonmovant shows by affidavit or declaration that, for specified reasons, it cannot present facts essential to justify its opposition, the court may:

(1) defer considering the motion or deny it;

(2) allow time to obtain affidavits or declarations or to take discovery; or

(3) issue any other appropriate order.

(e) Failing to Properly Support or Address a Fact. If a party fails to properly support an assertion of fact or fails to properly address another party's assertion of fact as required by Rule 56(c), the court may:

(1) give an opportunity to properly support or address the fact;

(2) consider the fact undisputed for purposes of the motion;

(3) grant summary judgment if the motion and supporting materials—including the facts considered undisputed— show that the movant is entitled to it; or

(4) issue any other appropriate order.

(f) Judgment Independent of the Motion. After giving notice and a reasonable time to respond, the court may:

(1) grant summary judgment for a nonmovant;

(2) grant the motion on grounds not raised by a party; or

(3) consider summary judgment on its own after identifying for the parties material facts that may not be genuinely in dispute.

(g) Failing to Grant All the Requested Relief. If the court does not grant all the relief requested by the motion, it may enter an order stating any material fact—including an item of damages or other relief—that is not genuinely in dispute and treating the fact as established in the case.

(h) Affidavit or Declaration Submitted in Bad Faith. If satisfied that an affidavit or declaration under this rule is submitted in bad faith or solely for delay, the court—after notice and a reasonable time to respond—may order the submitting party to pay the other party the reasonable expenses, including attorney's fees, it incurred as a result. An offending party or attorney may also be held in contempt or subjected to other appropriate sanctions.

(Amended December 27, 1946, effective March 19, 1948; January 21, 1963, effective July 1, 1963; March 2, 1987, effective August 1, 1987; April 30, 2007, effective December 1, 2007; March 26, 2009, effective December 1, 2009; April 28, 2010, effective December 1, 2010.)

RULE 57.   DECLARATORY JUDGMENT

These rules govern the procedure for obtaining a declaratory judgment under 28 U.S.C. § 2201. Rules 38 and 39 govern a demand for a jury trial. The existence of another adequate remedy does not preclude a declaratory judgment that is otherwise appropriate. The court may order a speedy hearing of a declaratory-judgment action.

(Amended December 29, 1948, effective October 20, 1949; April 30, 2007, effective December 1, 2007.)

RULE 58.   ENTERING JUDGMENT

(a) Separate Document. Every judgment and amended judgment must be set out in a separate document, but a separate document is not required for an order disposing of a motion:

(1) for judgment under Rule 50(b);

(2) to amend or make additional findings under Rule 52(b);

(3) for attorney's fees under Rule 54;

(4) for a new trial, or to alter or amend the judgment, under Rule 59; or

(5) for relief under Rule 60.

(b) Entering Judgment.

(1) *Without the Court's Direction.* Subject to Rule 54(b) and unless the court orders otherwise, the clerk must, without awaiting the court's direction, promptly prepare, sign, and enter the judgment when:

(A) the jury returns a general verdict;

(B) the court awards only costs or a sum certain; or

(C) the court denies all relief.

(2) *Court's Approval Required.* Subject to Rule 54(b), the court must promptly approve the form of the judgment, which the clerk must promptly enter, when:

(A) the jury returns a special verdict or a general verdict with answers to written questions; or

(B) the court grants other relief not described in this subdivision (b).

(c) Time of Entry. For purposes of these rules, judgment is entered at the following times:

(1) if a separate document is not required, when the judgment is entered in the civil docket under Rule 79(a); or

(2) if a separate document is required, when the judgment is entered in the civil docket under Rule 79(a) and the earlier of these events occurs:

(A) it is set out in a separate document; or

(B) 150 days have run from the entry in the civil docket.

(d) Request for Entry. A party may request that judgment be set out in a separate document as required by Rule 58(a).

(e) Cost or Fee Awards. Ordinarily, the entry of judgment may not be delayed, nor the time for appeal extended, in order to tax costs or award fees. But if a timely motion for attorney's fees is made under Rule 54(d)(2), the court may act before a notice of appeal has been filed and become effective to order that the motion have the same effect under Federal Rule of Appellate Procedure 4(a)(4) as a timely motion under Rule 59.

(Amended December 27, 1946, effective March 19, 1948; January 21, 1963, effective July 1, 1963; April 22, 1993, effective December 1, 1993; April 29, 2002, effective December 1, 2002; April 30, 2007, effective December 1, 2007.)

RULE 59.   NEW TRIAL; ALTERING OR AMENDING A JUDGMENT

(a) In General.

(1) *Grounds for New Trial.* The court may, on motion, grant a new trial on all or some of the issues—and to any party—as follows:

(A) after a jury trial, for any reason for which a new trial has heretofore been granted in an action at law in federal court; or

(B) after a nonjury trial, for any reason for which a rehearing has heretofore been granted in a suit in equity in federal court.

(2) *Further Action After a Nonjury Trial.* After a nonjury trial, the court may, on motion for a new trial, open the judgment if one has been entered, take additional testimony, amend findings of fact and conclusions of law or make new ones, and direct the entry of a new judgment.

(b) Time to File a Motion for a New Trial. A motion for a new trial must be filed no later than 28 days after the entry of judgment.

(c) Time to Serve Affidavits. When a motion for a new trial is based on affidavits, they must be filed with the motion. The opposing party has 14 days after being served to file opposing affidavits. The court may permit reply affidavits.

(d) New Trial on the Court's Initiative or for Reasons Not in the Motion. No later than 28 days after the entry of judgment, the court, on its own, may order a new trial for any reason that would justify granting one on a party's motion. After giving the parties notice and an opportunity to be heard, the court may grant a timely motion for a new trial for a reason not stated in the motion. In either event, the court must specify the reasons in its order.

(e) Motion to Alter or Amend a Judgment. A motion to alter or amend a judgment must be filed no later than 28 days after the entry of the judgment.

(Amended December 27, 1946, effective March 19, 1948; February 28, 1966, effective July 1, 1966; April 27, 1995, effective December 1, 1995; April 30, 2007, effective December 1, 2007; March 26, 2009, effective December 1, 2009.)

RULE 60. RELIEF FROM A JUDGMENT OR ORDER

(a) Corrections Based on Clerical Mistakes; Oversights and Omissions. The court may correct a clerical mistake or a mistake arising from oversight or omission whenever one is found in a judgment, order, or other part of the record. The court may do so on motion or on its own, with or without notice. But after an appeal has been docketed in the appellate court and while it is pending, such a mistake may be corrected only with the appellate court's leave.

(b) Grounds for Relief from a Final Judgment, Order, or Proceeding. On motion and just terms, the court may relieve a party or its legal representative from a final judgment, order, or proceeding for the following reasons:

(1) mistake, inadvertence, surprise, or excusable neglect;

(2) newly discovered evidence that, with reasonable diligence, could not have been discovered in time to move for a new trial under Rule 59(b);

(3) fraud (whether previously called intrinsic or extrinsic), misrepresentation, or misconduct by an opposing party;

(4) the judgment is void;

(5) the judgment has been satisfied, released, or discharged; it is based on an earlier judgment that has been reversed or vacated; or applying it prospectively is no longer equitable; or

(6) any other reason that justifies relief.

(c) Timing and Effect of the Motion.

(1) *Timing.* A motion under Rule 60(b) must be made within a reasonable time—and for reasons (1), (2), and (3) no more than a year after the entry of the judgment or order or the date of the proceeding.

(2) *Effect on Finality.* The motion does not affect the judgment's finality or suspend its operation.

(d) Other Powers to Grant Relief. This rule does not limit a court's power to:

(1) entertain an independent action to relieve a party from a judgment, order, or proceeding;

(2) grant relief under 28 U.S.C. § 1655 to a defendant who was not personally notified of the action; or

(3) set aside a judgment for fraud on the court.

(e) Bills and Writs Abolished. The following are abolished: bills of review, bills in the nature of bills of review, and writs of coram nobis, coram vobis, and audita querela.

(Amended December 27, 1946, effective March 19, 1948; December 29, 1948, effective October 20, 1949; March 2, 1987, effective August 1, 1987; April 30, 2007, effective December 1, 2007.)

RULE 61. HARMLESS ERROR

Unless justice requires otherwise, no error in admitting or excluding evidence—or any other error by the court or a party—is ground for granting a new trial, for setting aside a verdict, or for vacating, modifying, or otherwise disturbing a judgment or order. At every stage of the proceeding, the court must disregard all errors and defects that do not affect any party's substantial rights.

(Amended April 30, 2007, effective December 1, 2007.)

RULE 62. STAY OF PROCEEDINGS TO ENFORCE A JUDGMENT

(a) Automatic Stay. Except as provided in Rule 62(c) and (d), execution on a judgment and proceedings to enforce it are stayed for 30 days after its entry, unless the court orders otherwise.

(b) Stay by Bond or Other Security. At any time after judgment is entered, a party may obtain a stay by providing a bond or other security. The stay takes effect when the court approves the bond or other security and remains in effect for the time specified in the bond or other security.

(c) Stay of an Injunction, Receivership, or Patent Accounting Order. Unless the court orders otherwise, the following are not stayed after being entered, even if an appeal is taken:

(1) an interlocutory or final judgment in an action for an injunction or receivership; or

(2) a judgment or order that directs an accounting in an action for patent infringement.

(d) Injunction Pending an Appeal. While an appeal is pending from an interlocutory order or final judgment that grants, continues, modifies, refuses, dissolves, or refuses to dissolve or modify an injunction, the court may suspend, modify, restore, or grant an injunction on terms for bond or other terms that secure the opposing party's rights. If the judgment appealed from is rendered by a statutory three-judge district court, the order must be made either:

(1) by that court sitting in open session; or

(2) by the assent of all its judges, as evidenced by their signatures.

(e) Stay Without Bond on an Appeal by the United States, Its Officers, or Its Agencies. The court must not require a bond, obligation, or other security from the appellant when granting a stay on an appeal by the United States, its officers, or its agencies or on an appeal directed by a department of the federal government.

(f) Stay in Favor of a Judgment Debtor Under State Law. If a judgment is a lien on the judgment debtor's property under the law of the state where the court is located, the judgment debtor is entitled to the same stay of execution the state court would give.

(g) Appellate Court's Power Not Limited. This rule does not limit the power of the appellate court or one of its judges or justices:

(1) to stay proceedings—or suspend, modify, restore, or grant an injunction—while an appeal is pending; or

(2) to issue an order to preserve the status quo or the effectiveness of the judgment to be entered.

(h) Stay with Multiple Claims or Parties. A court may stay the enforcement of a final judgment entered under Rule 54(b) until it enters a later judgment or judgments, and may prescribe terms necessary to secure the benefit of the stayed judgment for the party in whose favor it was entered.

(Amended December 27, 1946, effective March 19, 1948; December 29, 1948, effective October 20, 1949; April 17, 1961, effective July 19, 1961; March 2, 1987, effective August 1, 1987; April 30, 2007, effective December 1, 2007; March 26, 2009, effective December 1, 2009; April 26, 2018, effective December 1, 2018.)

RULE 62.1. INDICATIVE RULING ON A MOTION FOR RELIEF THAT IS BARRED BY A PENDING APPEAL

(a) Relief Pending Appeal. If a timely motion is made for relief that the court lacks authority to grant because of an appeal that has been docketed and is pending, the court may:

(1) defer considering the motion;

(2) deny the motion; or

(3) state either that it would grant the motion if the court of appeals remands for that purpose or that the motion raises a substantial issue.

(b) Notice to the Court of Appeals. The movant must promptly notify the circuit clerk under Federal Rule of Appellate Procedure 12.1 if the district court states that it would grant the motion or that the motion raises a substantial issue.

(c) Remand. The district court may decide the motion if the court of appeals remands for that purpose.

(Added March 26, 2009, effective December 1, 2009.)

RULE 63. JUDGE'S INABILITY TO PROCEED

If a judge conducting a hearing or trial is unable to proceed, any other judge may proceed upon certifying familiarity with the record and determining that the case may be completed without prejudice to the parties. In a hearing or a nonjury trial, the successor judge must, at a party's request, recall any witness whose testimony is material and disputed and who is available to testify again without undue burden. The successor judge may also recall any other witness.

(Amended March 2, 1987, effective August 1, 1987; April 30, 1991, effective December 1, 1991; April 30, 2007, effective December 1, 2007.)

TITLE VIII. PROVISIONAL AND FINAL REMEDIES

RULE 64. SEIZING A PERSON OR PROPERTY

(a) Remedies Under State Law—In General. At the commencement of and throughout an action, every remedy is available that, under the law of the state where the court is located, provides for seizing a person or property to secure satisfaction of the potential judgment. But a federal statute governs to the extent it applies.

(b) Specific Kinds of Remedies. The remedies available under this rule include the following—however designated and regardless of whether state procedure requires an independent action:

- arrest;
- attachment;
- garnishment;

- replevin;
- sequestration; and
- other corresponding or equivalent remedies.

(Amended April 30, 2007, effective December 1, 2007.)

RULE 65. INJUNCTIONS AND RESTRAINING ORDERS

(a) Preliminary Injunction.

(1) *Notice.* The court may issue a preliminary injunction only on notice to the adverse party.

(2) *Consolidating the Hearing with the Trial on the Merits.* Before or after beginning the hearing on a motion for a preliminary injunction, the court may advance the trial on the merits and consolidate it with the hearing. Even

when consolidation is not ordered, evidence that is received on the motion and that would be admissible at trial becomes part of the trial record and need not be repeated at trial. But the court must preserve any party's right to a jury trial.

(b) Temporary Restraining Order.

(1) *Issuing Without Notice.* The court may issue a temporary restraining order without written or oral notice to the adverse party or its attorney only if:

(A) specific facts in an affidavit or a verified complaint clearly show that immediate and irreparable injury, loss, or damage will result to the movant before the adverse party can be heard in opposition; and

(B) the movant's attorney certifies in writing any efforts made to give notice and the reasons why it should not be required.

(2) *Contents; Expiration.* Every temporary restraining order issued without notice must state the date and hour it was issued; describe the injury and state why it is irreparable; state why the order was issued without notice; and be promptly filed in the clerk's office and entered in the record. The order expires at the time after entry—not to exceed 14 days—that the court sets, unless before that time the court, for good cause, extends it for a like period or the adverse party consents to a longer extension. The reasons for an extension must be entered in the record.

(3) *Expediting the Preliminary–Injunction Hearing.* If the order is issued without notice, the motion for a preliminary injunction must be set for hearing at the earliest possible time, taking precedence over all other matters except hearings on older matters of the same character. At the hearing, the party who obtained the order must proceed with the motion; if the party does not, the court must dissolve the order.

(4) *Motion to Dissolve.* On 2 days' notice to the party who obtained the order without notice—or on shorter notice set by the court—the adverse party may appear and move to dissolve or modify the order. The court must then hear and decide the motion as promptly as justice requires.

(c) Security. The court may issue a preliminary injunction or a temporary restraining order only if the movant gives security in an amount that the court considers proper to pay the costs and damages sustained by any party found to have been wrongfully enjoined or restrained. The United States, its officers, and its agencies are not required to give security.

(d) Contents and Scope of Every Injunction and Restraining Order.

(1) *Contents.* Every order granting an injunction and every restraining order must:

(A) state the reasons why it issued;

(B) state its terms specifically; and

(C) describe in reasonable detail—and not by referring to the complaint or other document—the act or acts restrained or required.

(2) *Persons Bound.* The order binds only the following who receive actual notice of it by personal service or otherwise:

(A) the parties;

(B) the parties' officers, agents, servants, employees, and attorneys; and

(C) other persons who are in active concert or participation with anyone described in Rule 65(d)(2)(A) or (B).

(e) Other Laws Not Modified. These rules do not modify the following:

(1) any federal statute relating to temporary restraining orders or preliminary injunctions in actions affecting employer and employee;

(2) 28 U.S.C. § 2361, which relates to preliminary injunctions in actions of interpleader or in the nature of interpleader; or

(3) 28 U.S.C. § 2284, which relates to actions that must be heard and decided by a three-judge district court.

(f) Copyright Impoundment. This rule applies to copyright-impoundment proceedings.

(Amended December 27, 1946, effective March 19, 1948; December 29, 1948, effective October 20, 1949; February 28, 1966, effective July 1, 1966; March 2, 1987, effective August 1, 1987; April 23, 2001, effective December 1, 2001; April 30, 2007, effective December 1, 2007; March 26, 2009, effective December 1, 2009.)

RULE 65.1. PROCEEDINGS AGAINST A SECURITY PROVIDER

Whenever these rules (including the Supplemental Rules for Admiralty or Maritime Claims and Asset Forfeiture Actions) require or allow a party to give security, and security is given with one or more security providers, each provider submits to the court's jurisdiction and irrevocably appoints the court clerk as its agent for receiving service of any papers that affect its liability on the security. The security provider's liability may be enforced on motion without an independent action. The motion and any notice that the court orders may be served on the court clerk, who must promptly send a copy of each to every security provider whose address is known.

(Adopted February 28, 1966, effective July 1, 1966; amended March 2, 1987, effective August 1, 1987; April 12, 2006, effective December 1, 2006; April 30, 2007, effective December 1, 2007; April 26, 2018, effective December 1, 2018.)

RULE 66. RECEIVERS

These rules govern an action in which the appointment of a receiver is sought or a receiver sues or is sued. But the practice in administering an estate by a receiver or a similar court-appointed officer must accord with the historical practice in federal courts or with a local rule. An action in which a receiver has been appointed may be dismissed only by court order.

(Amended December 27, 1946, effective March 19, 1948; December 29, 1948, effective October 20, 1949; April 30, 2007, effective December 1, 2007.)

RULE 67. DEPOSIT INTO COURT

(a) Depositing Property. If any part of the relief sought is a money judgment or the disposition of a sum of money or some other deliverable thing, a party—on notice to every other party and by leave of court—may deposit with the court all or part of the money or thing, whether or not that party claims any of it. The depositing party must deliver to the clerk a copy of the order permitting deposit.

(b) Investing and Withdrawing Funds. Money paid into court under this rule must be deposited and withdrawn in accordance with 28 U.S.C. §§ 2041 and 2042 and any like statute. The money must be deposited in an interest-bearing account or invested in a court-approved, interest-bearing instrument.

(Amended December 29, 1948, effective October 20, 1949; April 28, 1983, effective August 1, 1983; April 30, 2007, effective December 1, 2007.)

RULE 68.   OFFER OF JUDGMENT

(a) Making an Offer; Judgment on an Accepted Offer. At least 14 days before the date set for trial, a party defending against a claim may serve on an opposing party an offer to allow judgment on specified terms, with the costs then accrued.   If, within 14 days after being served, the opposing party serves written notice accepting the offer, either party may then file the offer and notice of acceptance, plus proof of service.   The clerk must then enter judgment.

(b) Unaccepted Offer. An unaccepted offer is considered withdrawn, but it does not preclude a later offer. Evidence of an unaccepted offer is not admissible except in a proceeding to determine costs.

(c) Offer After Liability is Determined.   When one party's liability to another has been determined but the extent of liability remains to be determined by further proceedings, the party held liable may make an offer of judgment.   It must be served within a reasonable time—but at least 14 days—before the date set for a hearing to determine the extent of liability.

(d) Paying Costs After an Unaccepted Offer. If the judgment that the offeree finally obtains is not more favorable than the unaccepted offer, the offeree must pay the costs incurred after the offer was made.

(Amended December 27, 1946, effective March 19, 1948; February 28, 1966, effective July 1, 1966; March 2, 1987, effective August 1, 1987; April 30, 2007, effective December 1, 2007; March 26, 2009, effective December 1, 2009.)

RULE 69.   EXECUTION

(a) In General.

(1) *Money Judgment; Applicable Procedure.* A money judgment is enforced by a writ of execution, unless the court directs otherwise. The procedure on execution—and in proceedings supplementary to and in aid of judgment or execution—must accord with the procedure of the state where the

court is located, but a federal statute governs to the extent it applies.

(2) *Obtaining Discovery.* In aid of the judgment or execution, the judgment creditor or a successor in interest whose interest appears of record may obtain discovery from any person—including the judgment debtor—as provided in these rules or by the procedure of the state where the court is located.

(b) Against Certain Public Officers. When a judgment has been entered against a revenue officer in the circumstances stated in 28 U.S.C. § 2006, or against an officer of Congress in the circumstances stated in 2 U.S.C. § 118,[1] the judgment must be satisfied as those statutes provide.

(Amended December 29, 1948, effective October 20, 1949; March 30, 1970, effective July 1, 1970; March 2, 1987 effective August 1, 1987; April 30, 2007, effective December 1, 2007.)

[1] Now editorially reclassified 2 U.S.C. § 5503.

RULE 70.   ENFORCING A JUDGMENT FOR A SPECIFIC ACT

(a) Party's Failure to Act; Ordering Another to Act. If a judgment requires a party to convey land, to deliver a deed or other document, or to perform any other specific act and the party fails to comply within the time specified, the court may order the act to be done—at the disobedient party's expense—by another person appointed by the court. When done, the act has the same effect as if done by the party.

(b) Vesting Title. If the real or personal property is within the district, the court—instead of ordering a conveyance—may enter a judgment divesting any party's title and vesting it in others. That judgment has the effect of a legally executed conveyance.

(c) Obtaining a Writ of Attachment or Sequestration. On application by a party entitled to performance of an act, the clerk must issue a writ of attachment or sequestration against the disobedient party's property to compel obedience.

(d) Obtaining a Writ of Execution or Assistance. On application by a party who obtains a judgment or order for possession, the clerk must issue a writ of execution or assistance.

(e) Holding in Contempt. The court may also hold the disobedient party in contempt.

(Amended April 30, 2007, effective December 1, 2007.)

RULE 71.   ENFORCING RELIEF FOR OR AGAINST A NONPARTY

When an order grants relief for a nonparty or may be enforced against a nonparty, the procedure for enforcing the order is the same as for a party.

(Amended March 2, 1987, effective August 1, 1987; April 30, 2007, effective December 1, 2007.)

TITLE IX. SPECIAL PROCEEDINGS

RULE 71.1. CONDEMNING REAL OR PERSONAL PROPERTY

(a) Applicability of Other Rules. These rules govern proceedings to condemn real and personal property by eminent domain, except as this rule provides otherwise.

(b) Joinder of Properties. The plaintiff may join separate pieces of property in a single action, no matter whether they are owned by the same persons or sought for the same use.

(c) Complaint.

(1) *Caption.* The complaint must contain a caption as provided in Rule 10(a). The plaintiff must, however, name as defendants both the property—designated generally by kind, quantity, and location—and at least one owner of some part of or interest in the property.

(2) *Contents.* The complaint must contain a short and plain statement of the following:

(A) the authority for the taking;

(B) the uses for which the property is to be taken;

(C) a description sufficient to identify the property;

(D) the interests to be acquired; and

(E) for each piece of property, a designation of each defendant who has been joined as an owner or owner of an interest in it.

(3) *Parties.* When the action commences, the plaintiff need join as defendants only those persons who have or claim an interest in the property and whose names are then known. But before any hearing on compensation, the plaintiff must add as defendants all those persons who have or claim an interest and whose names have become known or can be found by a reasonably diligent search of the records, considering both the property's character and value and the interests to be acquired. All others may be made defendants under the designation "Unknown Owners."

(4) *Procedure.* Notice must be served on all defendants as provided in Rule 71.1(d), whether they were named as defendants when the action commenced or were added later. A defendant may answer as provided in Rule 71.1(e). The court, meanwhile, may order any distribution of a deposit that the facts warrant.

(5) *Filing; Additional Copies.* In addition to filing the complaint, the plaintiff must give the clerk at least one copy for the defendants' use and additional copies at the request of the clerk or a defendant.

(d) Process.

(1) *Delivering Notice to the Clerk.* On filing a complaint, the plaintiff must promptly deliver to the clerk joint or several notices directed to the named defendants. When adding defendants, the plaintiff must deliver to the clerk additional notices directed to the new defendants.

(2) *Contents of the Notice.*

(A) *Main Contents.* Each notice must name the court, the title of the action, and the defendant to whom it is directed. It must describe the property sufficiently to identify it, but need not describe any property other than that to be taken from the named defendant. The notice must also state:

(i) that the action is to condemn property;

(ii) the interest to be taken;

(iii) the authority for the taking;

(iv) the uses for which the property is to be taken;

(v) that the defendant may serve an answer on the plaintiff's attorney within 21 days after being served with the notice;

(vi) that the failure to so serve an answer constitutes consent to the taking and to the court's authority to proceed with the action and fix the compensation; and

(vii) that a defendant who does not serve an answer may file a notice of appearance.

(B) *Conclusion.* The notice must conclude with the name, telephone number, and e-mail address of the plaintiff's attorney and an address within the district in which the action is brought where the attorney may be served.

(3) *Serving the Notice.*

(A) *Personal Service.* When a defendant whose address is known resides within the United States or a territory subject to the administrative or judicial jurisdiction of the United States, personal service of the notice (without a copy of the complaint) must be made in accordance with Rule 4.

(B) *Service by Publication.*

(i) A defendant may be served by publication only when the plaintiff's attorney files a certificate stating that the attorney believes the defendant cannot be personally served, because after diligent inquiry within the state where the complaint is filed, the defendant's place of residence is still unknown or, if known, that it is beyond the territorial limits of personal service. Service is then made by publishing the notice—once a week for at least 3 successive weeks—in a newspaper published in the county where the property is located or, if there is no such newspaper, in a newspaper with general circulation where the property is located. Before the last publication, a copy of the notice must also be mailed to every defendant who cannot be personally served but whose place of residence is then known. Unknown owners may be served by publication in the same manner by a notice addressed to "Unknown Owners."

(ii) Service by publication is complete on the date of the last publication. The plaintiff's attorney must prove publication and mailing by a certificate, attach a printed copy of the published notice, and mark on the copy the newspaper's name and the dates of publication.

(4) *Effect of Delivery and Service.* Delivering the notice to the clerk and serving it have the same effect as serving a summons under Rule 4.

(5) *Amending the Notice; Proof of Service and Amending the Proof.* Rule 4(a)(2) governs amending the notice. Rule 4(*l*) governs proof of service and amending it.

(e) Appearance or Answer.

(1) *Notice of Appearance.* A defendant that has no objection or defense to the taking of its property may serve a notice of appearance designating the property in which it claims an interest. The defendant must then be given notice of all later proceedings affecting the defendant.

(2) *Answer.* A defendant that has an objection or defense to the taking must serve an answer within 21 days after being served with the notice. The answer must:

(A) identify the property in which the defendant claims an interest;

(B) state the nature and extent of the interest; and

(C) state all the defendant's objections and defenses to the taking.

(3) *Waiver of Other Objections and Defenses; Evidence on Compensation.* A defendant waives all objections and defenses not stated in its answer. No other pleading or motion asserting an additional objection or defense is allowed. But at the trial on compensation, a defendant—whether or not it has previously appeared or answered—may present evidence on the amount of compensation to be paid and may share in the award.

(f) Amending Pleadings. Without leave of court, the plaintiff may—as often as it wants—amend the complaint at any time before the trial on compensation. But no amendment may be made if it would result in a dismissal inconsistent with Rule 71.1(i)(1) or (2). The plaintiff need not serve a copy of an amendment, but must serve notice of the filing, as provided in Rule 5(b), on every affected party who has appeared and, as provided in Rule 71.1(d), on every affected party who has not appeared. In addition, the plaintiff must give the clerk at least one copy of each amendment for the defendants' use, and additional copies at the request of the clerk or a defendant. A defendant may appear or answer in the time and manner and with the same effect as provided in Rule 71.1(e).

(g) Substituting Parties. If a defendant dies, becomes incompetent, or transfers an interest after being joined, the court may, on motion and notice of hearing, order that the proper party be substituted. Service of the motion and notice on a nonparty must be made as provided in Rule 71.1(d)(3).

(h) Trial of the Issues.

(1) *Issues Other Than Compensation; Compensation.* In an action involving eminent domain under federal law, the court tries all issues, including compensation, except when compensation must be determined:

(A) by any tribunal specially constituted by a federal statute to determine compensation; or

(B) if there is no such tribunal, by a jury when a party demands one within the time to answer or within any additional time the court sets, unless the court appoints a commission.

(2) *Appointing a Commission; Commission's Powers and Report.*

(A) *Reasons for Appointing.* If a party has demanded a jury, the court may instead appoint a three-person commission to determine compensation because of the character, location, or quantity of the property to be condemned or for other just reasons.

(B) *Alternate Commissioners.* The court may appoint up to two additional persons to serve as alternate commissioners to hear the case and replace commissioners who, before a decision is filed, the court finds unable or disqualified to perform their duties. Once the commission renders its final decision, the court must discharge any alternate who has not replaced a commissioner.

(C) *Examining the Prospective Commissioners.* Before making its appointments, the court must advise the parties of the identity and qualifications of each prospective commissioner and alternate, and may permit the parties to examine them. The parties may not suggest appointees, but for good cause may object to a prospective commissioner or alternate.

(D) *Commission's Powers and Report.* A commission has the powers of a master under Rule 53(c). Its action and report are determined by a majority. Rule 53(d), (e), and (f) apply to its action and report.

(i) Dismissal of the Action or a Defendant.

(1) *Dismissing the Action.*

(A) *By the Plaintiff.* If no compensation hearing on a piece of property has begun, and if the plaintiff has not acquired title or a lesser interest or taken possession, the plaintiff may, without a court order, dismiss the action as to that property by filing a notice of dismissal briefly describing the property.

(B) *By Stipulation.* Before a judgment is entered vesting the plaintiff with title or a lesser interest in or possession of property, the plaintiff and affected defendants may, without a court order, dismiss the action in whole or in part by filing a stipulation of dismissal. And if the parties so stipulate, the court may vacate a judgment already entered.

(C) *By Court Order.* At any time before compensation has been determined and paid, the court may, after a motion and hearing, dismiss the action as to a piece of property. But if the plaintiff has already taken title, a lesser interest, or possession as to any part of it, the court must award compensation for the title, lesser interest, or possession taken.

(2) *Dismissing a Defendant.* The court may at any time dismiss a defendant who was unnecessarily or improperly joined.

(3) *Effect.* A dismissal is without prejudice unless otherwise stated in the notice, stipulation, or court order.

(j) Deposit and Its Distribution.

(1) *Deposit.* The plaintiff must deposit with the court any money required by law as a condition to the exercise of eminent domain and may make a deposit when allowed by statute.

(2) *Distribution; Adjusting Distribution.* After a deposit, the court and attorneys must expedite the proceedings so as to distribute the deposit and to determine and pay compensation. If the compensation finally awarded to a defendant exceeds the amount distributed to that defendant, the court must enter judgment against the plaintiff for the deficiency. If the compensation awarded to a defendant is less than the amount distributed to that defendant, the court must enter judgment against that defendant for the over-payment.

(k) Condemnation Under a State's Power of Eminent Domain. This rule governs an action involving eminent domain under state law. But if state law provides for trying an issue by jury—or for trying the issue of compensation by jury or commission or both—that law governs.

(l) Costs. Costs are not subject to Rule 54(d).

(Adopted April 30, 1951, effective August 1, 1951; amended January 21, 1963, effective July 1, 1963; April 29, 1985, effective August 1, 1985; March 2, 1987, effective August 1, 1987; April 25, 1988, effective August 1, 1988; amended by Pub.L. 100–690, Title VII, § 7050, November 18, 1988, 102 Stat. 4401 (although amendment by Pub.L. 100–690 could not be executed due to prior amendment by Court order which made the same change effective August 1, 1988); amended April 22, 1993, effective December 1, 1993; March 27, 2003, effective December 1, 2003; April 30, 2007, effective December 1, 2007; March 26, 2009, effective December 1, 2009.)

RULE 72. MAGISTRATE JUDGES: PRETRIAL ORDER

(a) Nondispositive Matters. When a pretrial matter not dispositive of a party's claim or defense is referred to a magistrate judge to hear and decide, the magistrate judge must promptly conduct the required proceedings and, when appropriate, issue a written order stating the decision. A party may serve and file objections to the order within 14 days after being served with a copy. A party may not assign as error a defect in the order not timely objected to. The district judge in the case must consider timely objections and modify or set aside any part of the order that is clearly erroneous or is contrary to law.

(b) Dispositive Motions and Prisoner Petitions.

(1) *Findings and Recommendations.* A magistrate judge must promptly conduct the required proceedings when assigned, without the parties' consent, to hear a pretrial matter dispositive of a claim or defense or a prisoner petition challenging the conditions of confinement. A record must be made of all evidentiary proceedings and may, at the magistrate judge's discretion, be made of any other proceedings. The magistrate judge must enter a recommended disposition, including, if appropriate, proposed findings of fact. The clerk must promptly mail a copy to each party.

(2) *Objections.* Within 14 days after being served with a copy of the recommended disposition, a party may serve and file specific written objections to the proposed findings and recommendations. A party may respond to another party's objections within 14 days after being served with a copy. Unless the district judge orders otherwise, the objecting party must promptly arrange for transcribing the record, or whatever portions of it the parties agree to or the magistrate judge considers sufficient.

(3) *Resolving Objections.* The district judge must determine de novo any part of the magistrate judge's disposition that has been properly objected to. The district judge may accept, reject, or modify the recommended disposition; receive further evidence; or return the matter to the magistrate judge with instructions.

(Former Rule 72 abrogated December 4, 1967, effective July 1, 1968; new Rule 72 adopted April 28, 1983, effective August 1, 1983; amended April 30, 1991, effective December 1, 1991; April 22, 1993, effective December 1, 1993; April 30, 2007, effective December 1, 2007; March 26, 2009, effective December 1, 2009.)

RULE 73. MAGISTRATE JUDGES: TRIAL BY CONSENT; APPEAL

(a) Trial by Consent. When authorized under 28 U.S.C. § 636(c), a magistrate judge may, if all parties consent, conduct a civil action or proceeding, including a jury or nonjury trial. A record must be made in accordance with 28 U.S.C. § 636(c)(5).

(b) Consent Procedure.

(1) *In General.* When a magistrate judge has been designated to conduct civil actions or proceedings, the clerk must give the parties written notice of their opportunity to consent under 28 U.S.C. § 636(c). To signify their consent, the parties must jointly or separately file a statement consenting to the referral. A district judge or magistrate judge may be informed of a party's response to the clerk's notice only if all parties have consented to the referral.

(2) *Reminding the Parties About Consenting.* A district judge, magistrate judge, or other court official may remind the parties of the magistrate judge's availability, but must also advise them that they are free to withhold consent without adverse substantive consequences.

(3) *Vacating a Referral.* On its own for good cause—or when a party shows extraordinary circumstances—the district judge may vacate a referral to a magistrate judge under this rule.

(c) Appealing a Judgment. In accordance with 28 U.S.C. § 636(c)(3), an appeal from a judgment entered at a magistrate judge's direction may be taken to the court of appeals as would any other appeal from a district-court judgment.

(Former Rule 73 abrogated December 4, 1967, effective July 1, 1968; new Rule 73 adopted April 28, 1983, effective August 1, 1983; amended March 2, 1987, effective August 1, 1987; April 22, 1993, effective December 1, 1993; April 11, 1997, effective December 1, 1997; April 30, 2007, effective December 1, 2007.)

RULE 74. METHOD OF APPEAL FROM MAGISTRATE JUDGE TO DISTRICT JUDGE UNDER TITLE 28, U.S.C. § 636(c)(4) AND RULE 73(d) [ABROGATED]

(Former Rule 74 abrogated December 4, 1967, effective July 1, 1968; new Rule 74 adopted April 28, 1983, effective August 1, 1983; amended April 22, 1993, effective December 1, 1993; abrogated April 11, 1997, effective December 1, 1997; April 30, 2007, effective December 1, 2007.)

RULE 75. PROCEEDINGS ON APPEAL FROM MAGISTRATE JUDGE TO DISTRICT JUDGE UNDER RULE 73(d) [ABROGATED]

(Former Rule 75 abrogated December 4, 1967, effective July 1, 1968; new Rule 75 adopted April 28, 1983, effective August 1, 1983; amended March 2, 1987, effective August 1, 1987; April 22, 1993, effective December 1, 1993; abrogated April 11, 1997, effective December 1, 1997; April 30, 2007, effective December 1, 2007.)

RULE 76. JUDGMENT OF THE DISTRICT JUDGE ON THE APPEAL UNDER RULE 73(d) AND COSTS [ABROGATED]

(Former Rule 76 abrogated December 4, 1967, effective July 1, 1968; new Rule 76 adopted April 28, 1983, effective August 1, 1983; amended April 22, 1993, effective December 1, 1993; abrogated April 11, 1997, effective December 1, 1997; April 30, 2007, effective December 1, 2007.)

TITLE X. DISTRICT COURTS AND CLERKS: CONDUCTING BUSINESS; ISSUING ORDERS

RULE 77. CONDUCTING BUSINESS; CLERK'S AUTHORITY; NOTICE OF AN ORDER OR JUDGMENT

(a) When Court Is Open. Every district court is considered always open for filing any paper, issuing and returning process, making a motion, or entering an order.

(b) Place for Trial and Other Proceedings. Every trial on the merits must be conducted in open court and, so far as convenient, in a regular courtroom. Any other act or proceeding may be done or conducted by a judge in chambers, without the attendance of the clerk or other court official, and anywhere inside or outside the district. But no hearing—other than one ex parte—may be conducted outside the district unless all the affected parties consent.

(c) Clerk's Office Hours; Clerk's Orders.

(1) *Hours.* The clerk's office—with a clerk or deputy on duty—must be open during business hours every day except Saturdays, Sundays, and legal holidays. But a court may, by local rule or order, require that the office be open for specified hours on Saturday or a particular legal holiday other than one listed in Rule 6(a)(6)(A).

(2) *Orders.* Subject to the court's power to suspend, alter, or rescind the clerk's action for good cause, the clerk may:

(A) issue process;

(B) enter a default;

(C) enter a default judgment under Rule 55(b)(1); and

(D) act on any other matter that does not require the court's action.

(d) Serving Notice of an Order or Judgment.

(1) *Service.* Immediately after entering an order or judgment, the clerk must serve notice of the entry, as provided in Rule 5(b), on each party who is not in default for failing to appear. The clerk must record the service on the docket. A party also may serve notice of the entry as provided in Rule 5(b).

(2) *Time to Appeal Not Affected by Lack of Notice.* Lack of notice of the entry does not affect the time for appeal or relieve—or authorize the court to relieve—a party for failing to appeal within the time allowed, except as allowed by Federal Rule of Appellate Procedure (4)(a).

(Amended December 27, 1946, effective March 19, 1948; January 21, 1963, effective July 1, 1963; December 4, 1967, effective July 1, 1968; March 1, 1971, effective July 1, 1971; March 2, 1987, effective August 1, 1987; April 30, 1991, effective December 1, 1991; April 23, 2001, effective December 1, 2001; April 30, 2007, effective December 1, 2007; April 25, 2014, effective December 1, 2014.)

RULE 78. HEARING MOTIONS; SUBMISSION ON BRIEFS

(a) Providing a Regular Schedule for Oral Hearings. A court may establish regular times and places for oral hearings on motions.

(b) Providing for Submission on Briefs. By rule or order, the court may provide for submitting and determining motions on briefs, without oral hearings.

(Amended March 2, 1987, effective August 1, 1987; April 30, 2007, effective December 1, 2007.)

RULE 79. RECORDS KEPT BY THE CLERK

(a) Civil Docket.

(1) *In General.* The clerk must keep a record known as the "civil docket" in the form and manner prescribed by the Director of the Administrative Office of the United States Courts with the approval of the Judicial Conference of the United States. The clerk must enter each civil action in the docket. Actions must be assigned consecutive file numbers, which must be noted in the docket where the first entry of the action is made.

(2) *Items to be Entered.* The following items must be marked with the file number and entered chronologically in the docket:

(A) papers filed with the clerk;

(B) process issued, and proofs of service or other returns showing execution; and

(C) appearances, orders, verdicts, and judgments.

(3) *Contents of Entries; Jury Trial Demanded.* Each entry must briefly show the nature of the paper filed or writ issued, the substance of each proof of service or other return, and the substance and date of entry of each order and judgment. When a jury trial has been properly demanded or ordered, the clerk must enter the word "jury" in the docket.

(b) Civil Judgments and Orders. The clerk must keep a copy of every final judgment and appealable order; of every order affecting title to or a lien on real or personal property; and of any other order that the court directs to be kept. The clerk must keep these in the form and manner prescribed by the Director of the Administrative Office of the United States

Courts with the approval of the Judicial Conference of the United States.

(c) Indexes; Calendars. Under the court's direction, the clerk must:

(1) keep indexes of the docket and of the judgments and orders described in Rule 79(b); and

(2) prepare calendars of all actions ready for trial, distinguishing jury trials from nonjury trials.

(d) Other Records. The clerk must keep any other records required by the Director of the Administrative Office of the United States Courts with the approval of the Judicial Conference of the United States.

(Amended December 27, 1946, effective March 19, 1948; December 29, 1948, effective October 20, 1949; January 21, 1963, effective July 1, 1963; April 30, 2007, effective December 1, 2007.)

RULE 80. STENOGRAPHIC TRANSCRIPT AS EVIDENCE

If stenographically reported testimony at a hearing or trial is admissible in evidence at a later trial, the testimony may be proved by a transcript certified by the person who reported it.

(Amended December 27, 1946, effective March 19, 1948; April 30, 2007, effective December 1, 2007.)

TITLE XI. GENERAL PROVISIONS

RULE 81. APPLICABILITY OF THE RULES IN GENERAL; REMOVED ACTIONS

(a) Applicability to Particular Proceedings.

(1) *Prize Proceedings.* These rules do not apply to prize proceedings in admiralty governed by 10 U.S.C. §§ 7651–7681.

(2) *Bankruptcy.* These rules apply to bankruptcy proceedings to the extent provided by the Federal Rules of Bankruptcy Procedure.

(3) *Citizenship.* These rules apply to proceedings for admission to citizenship to the extent that the practice in those proceedings is not specified in federal statutes and has previously conformed to the practice in civil actions. The provisions of 8 U.S.C. § 1451 for service by publication and for answer apply in proceedings to cancel citizenship certificates.

(4) *Special Writs.* These rules apply to proceedings for habeas corpus and for quo warranto to the extent that the practice in those proceedings:

(A) is not specified in a federal statute, the Rules Governing Section 2254 Cases, or the Rules Governing Section 2255 Cases; and

(B) has previously conformed to the practice in civil actions.

(5) *Proceedings Involving a Subpoena.* These rules apply to proceedings to compel testimony or the production of documents through a subpoena issued by a United States officer or agency under a federal statute, except as other-

wise provided by statute, by local rule, or by court order in the proceedings.

(6) *Other Proceedings.* These rules, to the extent applicable, govern proceedings under the following laws, except as these laws provide other procedures:

(A) 7 U.S.C. §§ 292, 499g(c), for reviewing an order of the Secretary of Agriculture;

(B) 9 U.S.C., relating to arbitration;

(C) 15 U.S.C. § 522, for reviewing an order of the Secretary of the Interior;

(D) 15 U.S.C. § 715d(c), for reviewing an order denying a certificate of clearance;

(E) 29 U.S.C. §§ 159, 160, for enforcing an order of the National Labor Relations Board;

(F) 33 U.S.C. §§ 918, 921, for enforcing or reviewing a compensation order under the Longshore and Harbor Workers' Compensation Act; and

(G) 45 U.S.C. § 159, for reviewing an arbitration award in a railway-labor dispute.

(b) Scire Facias and Mandamus. The writs of scire facias and mandamus are abolished. Relief previously available through them may be obtained by appropriate action or motion under these rules.

(c) Removed Actions.

(1) *Applicability.* These rules apply to a civil action after it is removed from a state court.

(2) *Further Pleading.* After removal, repleading is unnecessary unless the court orders it. A defendant who did not answer before removal must answer or present other defenses or objections under these rules within the longest of these periods:

(A) 21 days after receiving—through service or otherwise—a copy of the initial pleading stating the claim for relief;

(B) 21 days after being served with the summons for an initial pleading on file at the time of service; or

(C) 7 days after the notice of removal is filed.

(3) *Demand for a Jury Trial.*

(A) *As Affected by State Law.* A party who, before removal, expressly demanded a jury trial in accordance with state law need not renew the demand after removal. If the state law did not require an express demand for a jury trial, a party need not make one after removal unless the court orders the parties to do so within a specified time. The court must so order at a party's request and may so order on its own. A party who fails to make a demand when so ordered waives a jury trial.

(B) *Under Rule 38.* If all necessary pleadings have been served at the time of removal, a party entitled to a jury trial under Rule 38 must be given one if the party serves a demand within 14 days after:

(i) it files a notice of removal; or

(ii) it is served with a notice of removal filed by another party.

(d) Law Applicable.

(1) *"State Law" Defined.* When these rules refer to state law, the term "law" includes the state's statutes and the state's judicial decisions.

(2) *"State" Defined.* The term "state" includes, where appropriate, the District of Columbia and any United States commonwealth or territory.

(3) *"Federal Statute" Defined in the District of Columbia.* In the United States District Court for the District of Columbia, the term "federal statute" includes any Act of Congress that applies locally to the District.

(Amended December 28, 1939, effective April 3, 1941; December 27, 1946, effective March 19, 1948; December 29, 1948, effective October 20, 1949; April 30, 1951, effective August 1, 1951; January 21, 1963, effective July 1, 1963; February 28, 1966, effective July 1, 1966; December 4, 1967, effective July 1, 1968; March 1, 1971, effective July 1, 1971; March 2, 1987, effective August 1, 1987; April 23, 2001, effective December 1, 2001; April 29, 2002, effective December 1, 2002; April 30, 2007, effective December 1, 2007; March 26, 2009, effective December 1, 2009.)

RULE 82.   JURISDICTION AND VENUE UNAFFECTED

These rules do not extend or limit the jurisdiction of the district courts or the venue of actions in those courts. An admiralty or maritime claim under Rule 9(h) is governed by 28 U.S.C. § 1390.

(Amended December 29, 1948, effective October 20, 1949; February 28, 1966, effective July 1, 1966; April 23, 2001, effective December 1, 2001; April 30, 2007, effective December 1, 2007; April 28, 2016, effective December 1, 2016.)

RULE 83.   RULES BY DISTRICT COURTS; JUDGE'S DIRECTIVES

(a) Local Rules.

(1) *In General.* After giving public notice and an opportunity for comment, a district court, acting by a majority of its district judges, may adopt and amend rules governing its practice. A local rule must be consistent with—but not duplicate—federal statutes and rules adopted under 28 U.S.C. §§ 2072 and 2075, and must conform to any uniform numbering system prescribed by the Judicial Conference of the United States. A local rule takes effect on the date specified by the district court and remains in effect unless amended by the court or abrogated by the judicial council of the circuit. Copies of rules and amendments must, on their adoption, be furnished to the judicial council and the Administrative Office of the United States Courts and be made available to the public.

(2) *Requirement of Form.* A local rule imposing a requirement of form must not be enforced in a way that causes a party to lose any right because of a nonwillful failure to comply.

(b) Procedure When There Is No Controlling Law. A judge may regulate practice in any manner consistent with federal law, rules adopted under 28 U.S.C. §§ 2072 and 2075, and the district's local rules. No sanction or other disadvantage may be imposed for noncompliance with any requirement not in federal law, federal rules, or the local rules unless the alleged violator has been furnished in the particular case with actual notice of the requirement.

(Amended April 29, 1985, effective August 1, 1985; April 27, 1995, effective December 1, 1995; April 30, 2007, effective December 1, 2007.)

RULE 84.   FORMS [ABROGATED]

(Amended December 27, 1946, effective March 19, 1948; April 30, 2007, effective December 1, 2007; abrogated April 29, 2015, effective December 1, 2015.)

RULE 85.   TITLE

These rules may be cited as the Federal Rules of Civil Procedure.

(Amended April 30, 2007, effective December 1, 2007.)

RULE 86.   EFFECTIVE DATES

(a) In General. These rules and any amendments take effect at the time specified by the Supreme Court, subject to 28 U.S.C. § 2074. They govern:

(1) proceedings in an action commenced after their effective date; and

(2) proceedings after that date in an action then pending unless:

    (A) the Supreme Court specifies otherwise; or

    (B) the court determines that applying them in a particular action would be infeasible or work an injustice.

(b) December 1, 2007 Amendments. If any provision in Rules 1–5.1, 6–73, or 77–86 conflicts with another law, priority in time for the purpose of 28 U.S.C. § 2072(b) is not affected by the amendments taking effect on December 1, 2007.

(Amended December 27, 1946, effective March 19, 1948; December 29, 1948, effective October 20, 1949; April 17, 1961, effective July 19, 1961; January 21, 1963, and March 18, 1963, effective July 1, 1963; April 30, 2007, effective December 1, 2007.)

APPENDIX OF FORMS [ABROGATED]

SUPPLEMENTAL RULES FOR ADMIRALTY OR MARITIME CLAIMS AND ASSET FORFEITURE ACTIONS

RULE A. SCOPE OF RULES

(1) These Supplemental Rules apply to:

(A) the procedure in admiralty and maritime claims within the meaning of Rule 9(h) with respect to the following remedies:

(i) maritime attachment and garnishment,

(ii) actions in rem,

(iii) possessory, petitory, and partition actions, and

(iv) actions for exoneration from or limitation of liability;

(B) forfeiture actions in rem arising from a federal statute; and

(C) the procedure in statutory condemnation proceedings analogous to maritime actions in rem, whether within the admiralty and maritime jurisdiction or not. Except as otherwise provided, references in these Supplemental Rules to actions in rem include such analogous statutory condemnation proceedings.

(2) The Federal Rules of Civil Procedure also apply to the foregoing proceedings except to the extent that they are inconsistent with these Supplemental Rules.

(Added Feb. 28, 1966, eff. July 1, 1966; amended Apr. 12, 2006, eff. Dec. 1, 2006.)

RULE B. IN PERSONAM ACTIONS: ATTACHMENT AND GARNISHMENT

(1) When Available; Complaint, Affidavit, Judicial Authorization, and Process. In an in personam action:

(a) If a defendant is not found within the district when a verified complaint praying for attachment and the affidavit required by Rule B(1)(b) are filed, a verified complaint may contain a prayer for process to attach the defendant's tangible or intangible personal property—up to the amount sued for—in the hands of garnishees named in the process.

(b) The plaintiff or the plaintiff's attorney must sign and file with the complaint an affidavit stating that, to the affiant's knowledge, or on information and belief, the defendant cannot be found within the district. The court must review the complaint and affidavit and, if the conditions of this Rule B appear to exist, enter an order so stating and authorizing process of attachment and garnishment. The clerk may issue supplemental process enforcing the court's order upon application without further court order.

(c) If the plaintiff or the plaintiff's attorney certifies that exigent circumstances make court review impracticable, the clerk must issue the summons and process of attachment and garnishment. The plaintiff has the burden in any post-attachment hearing under Rule E(4)(f) to show that exigent circumstances existed.

(d)(i) If the property is a vessel or tangible property on board a vessel, the summons, process, and any supplemental process must be delivered to the marshal for service.

(ii) If the property is other tangible or intangible property, the summons, process, and any supplemental process must be delivered to a person or organization authorized to serve it, who may be (A) a marshal; (B) someone under contract with the United States; (C) someone specially appointed by the court for that purpose; or, (D) in an action brought by the United States, any officer or employee of the United States.

(e) The plaintiff may invoke state-law remedies under Rule 64 for seizure of person or property for the purpose of securing satisfaction of the judgment.

(2) Notice to Defendant. No default judgment may be entered except upon proof—which may be by affidavit—that:

(a) the complaint, summons, and process of attachment or garnishment have been served on the defendant in a manner authorized by Rule 4;

(b) the plaintiff or the garnishee has mailed to the defendant the complaint, summons, and process of attachment or garnishment, using any form of mail requiring a return receipt; or

(c) the plaintiff or the garnishee has tried diligently to give notice of the action to the defendant but could not do so.

(3) Answer.

(a) By Garnishee. The garnishee shall serve an answer, together with answers to any interrogatories served with the complaint, within 21 days after service of process upon the garnishee. Interrogatories to the garnishee may be served with the complaint without leave of court. If the garnishee refuses or neglects to answer on oath as to the debts, credits, or effects of the defendant in the garnishee's hands, or any interrogatories concerning such debts, credits, and effects that may be propounded by the plaintiff, the court may award compulsory process against the garnishee. If the garnishee admits any debts, credits, or effects, they shall be held in the garnishee's hands or paid into the registry of the court, and shall be held in either case subject to the further order of the court.

(b) By Defendant. The defendant shall serve an answer within 30 days after process has been executed, whether by attachment of property or service on the garnishee.

(Added Feb. 28, 1966, eff. July 1, 1966; amended Apr. 29, 1985, eff. Aug. 1, 1985; Mar. 2, 1987, eff. Aug. 1, 1987; Apr. 17, 2000, eff. Dec. 1, 2000; Apr. 25, 2005, eff. Dec. 1, 2005; Mar. 26, 2009, eff. Dec. 1, 2009.)

RULE C. IN REM ACTIONS: SPECIAL PROVISIONS

(1) When Available. An action in rem may be brought:

(a) To enforce any maritime lien;

(b) Whenever a statute of the United States provides for a maritime action in rem or a proceeding analogous thereto.

Except as otherwise provided by law a party who may proceed in rem may also, or in the alternative, proceed in personam against any person who may be liable.

Statutory provisions exempting vessels or other property owned or possessed by or operated by or for the United States from arrest or seizure are not affected by this rule. When a statute so provides, an action against the United States or an instrumentality thereof may proceed on in rem principles.

(2) Complaint. In an action in rem the complaint must:

    (a) be verified;

    (b) describe with reasonable particularity the property that is the subject of the action; and

    (c) state that the property is within the district or will be within the district while the action is pending.

(3) Judicial Authorization and Process.

    (a) Arrest Warrant.

        (i) The court must review the complaint and any supporting papers. If the conditions for an in rem action appear to exist, the court must issue an order directing the clerk to issue a warrant for the arrest of the vessel or other property that is the subject of the action.

        (ii) If the plaintiff or the plaintiff's attorney certifies that exigent circumstances make court review impracticable, the clerk must promptly issue a summons and a warrant for the arrest of the vessel or other property that is the subject of the action. The plaintiff has the burden in any post-arrest hearing under Rule E(4)(f) to show that exigent circumstances existed.

    (b) Service.

        (i) If the property that is the subject of the action is a vessel or tangible property on board a vessel, the warrant and any supplemental process must be delivered to the marshal for service.

        (ii) If the property that is the subject of the action is other property, tangible or intangible, the warrant and any supplemental process must be delivered to a person or organization authorized to enforce it, who may be: (A) a marshal; (B) someone under contract with the United States; (C) someone specially appointed by the court for that purpose; or, (D) in an action brought by the United States, any officer or employee of the United States.

    (c) Deposit in Court. If the property that is the subject of the action consists in whole or in part of freight, the proceeds of property sold, or other intangible property, the clerk must issue—in addition to the warrant—a summons directing any person controlling the property to show cause why it should not be deposited in court to abide the judgment.

    (d) Supplemental Process. The clerk may upon application issue supplemental process to enforce the court's order without further court order.

(4) Notice. No notice other than execution of process is required when the property that is the subject of the action has been released under Rule E(5). If the property is not released within 14 days after execution, the plaintiff must promptly—or within the time that the court allows—give public notice of the action and arrest in a newspaper designated by court order and having general circulation in the district, but publication may be terminated if the property is released before publication is completed. The notice must specify the time under Rule C(6) to file a statement of interest in or right against the seized property and to answer. This rule does not affect the notice requirements in an action to foreclose a preferred ship mortgage under 46 U.S.C. §§ 31301 et seq., as amended.

(5) Ancillary Process. In any action in rem in which process has been served as provided by this rule, if any part of the property that is the subject of the action has not been brought within the control of the court because it has been removed or sold, or because it is intangible property in the hands of a person who has not been served with process, the court may, on motion, order any person having possession or control of such property or its proceeds to show cause why it should not be delivered into the custody of the marshal or other person or organization having a warrant for the arrest of the property, or paid into court to abide the judgment; and, after hearing, the court may enter such judgment as law and justice may require.

(6) Responsive Pleading; Interrogatories.

    (a) Statement of Interest; Answer. In an action in rem:

        (i) a person who asserts a right of possession or any ownership interest in the property that is the subject of the action must file a verified statement of right or interest:

            (A) within 14 days after the execution of process, or

            (B) within the time that the court allows;

        (ii) the statement of right or interest must describe the interest in the property that supports the person's demand for its restitution or right to defend the action;

        (iii) an agent, bailee, or attorney must state the authority to file a statement of right or interest on behalf of another; and

        (iv) a person who asserts a right of possession or any ownership interest must serve an answer within 21 days after filing the statement of interest or right.

    (b) Interrogatories. Interrogatories may be served with the complaint in an in rem action without leave of court. Answers to the interrogatories must be served with the answer to the complaint.

(Added Feb. 28, 1966, eff. July 1, 1966; amended Apr. 29, 1985, eff. Aug. 1, 1985; Mar. 2, 1987, eff. Aug. 1, 1987; Apr. 30, 1991, eff. Dec. 1, 1991; Apr. 17, 2000, eff. Dec. 1, 2000; Apr. 29, 2002, eff. Dec. 1, 2002; Apr. 25, 2005, eff. Dec. 1, 2005; Apr. 12, 2006, eff. Dec. 1, 2006; Apr. 23, 2008, eff. Dec. 1, 2008; Mar. 26, 2009, eff. Dec. 1, 2009.)

RULE D. POSSESSORY, PETITORY, AND PARTITION ACTIONS

In all actions for possession, partition, and to try title maintainable according to the course of the admiralty practice with respect to a vessel, in all actions so maintainable with respect to the possession of cargo or other maritime property, and in all actions by one or more part owners against the others to obtain security for the return of the vessel from any voyage undertaken without their consent, or by one or more part owners against the others to obtain possession of the vessel for any voyage on giving security for its safe return, the process shall be by a warrant of arrest of the vessel, cargo, or other property, and by notice in the manner provided by Rule B(2) to the adverse party or parties.

(Added Feb. 28, 1966, eff. July 1, 1966.)

RULE E. ACTIONS IN REM AND QUASI IN REM: GENERAL PROVISIONS

(1) Applicability. Except as otherwise provided, this rule applies to actions in personam with process of maritime attachment and garnishment, actions in rem, and petitory, possessory, and partition actions, supplementing Rules B, C, and D.

(2) Complaint; Security.

(a) Complaint. In actions to which this rule is applicable the complaint shall state the circumstances from which the claim arises with such particularity that the defendant or claimant will be able, without moving for a more definite statement, to commence an investigation of the facts and to frame a responsive pleading.

(b) Security for Costs. Subject to the provisions of Rule 54(d) and of relevant statutes, the court may, on the filing of the complaint or on the appearance of any defendant, claimant, or any other party, or at any later time, require the plaintiff, defendant, claimant, or other party to give security, or additional security, in such sum as the court shall direct to pay all costs and expenses that shall be awarded against the party by any interlocutory order or by the final judgment, or on appeal by any appellate court.

(3) Process.

(a) In admiralty and maritime proceedings process in rem or of maritime attachment and garnishment may be served only within the district.

(b) Issuance and Delivery. Issuance and delivery of process in rem, or of maritime attachment and garnishment, shall be held in abeyance if the plaintiff so requests.

(4) Execution of Process; Marshal's Return; Custody of Property; Procedures for Release.

(a) In General. Upon issuance and delivery of the process, or, in the case of summons with process of attachment and garnishment, when it appears that the defendant cannot be found within the district, the marshal or other person or organization having a warrant shall forthwith execute the process in accordance with this subdivision (4), making due and prompt return.

(b) Tangible Property. If tangible property is to be attached or arrested, the marshal or other person or organization having the warrant shall take it into the marshal's possession for safe custody. If the character or situation of the property is such that the taking of actual possession is impracticable, the marshal or other person executing the process shall affix a copy thereof to the property in a conspicuous place and leave a copy of the complaint and process with the person having possession or the person's agent. In furtherance of the marshal's custody of any vessel the marshal is authorized to make a written request to the collector of customs not to grant clearance to such vessel until notified by the marshal or deputy marshal or by the clerk that the vessel has been released in accordance with these rules.

(c) Intangible Property. If intangible property is to be attached or arrested the marshal or other person or organization having the warrant shall execute the process by leaving with the garnishee or other obligor a copy of the complaint and process requiring the garnishee or other obligor to answer as provided in Rules B(3)(a) and C(6); or the marshal may accept for payment into the registry of the court the amount owed to the extent of the amount claimed by the plaintiff with interest and costs, in which event the garnishee or other obligor shall not be required to answer unless alias process shall be served.

(d) Directions With Respect to Property in Custody. The marshal or other person or organization having the warrant may at any time apply to the court for directions with respect to property that has been attached or arrested, and shall give notice of such application to any or all of the parties as the court may direct.

(e) Expenses of Seizing and Keeping Property; Deposit. These rules do not alter the provisions of Title 28, U.S.C., § 1921, as amended, relative to the expenses of seizing and keeping property attached or arrested and to the requirement of deposits to cover such expenses.

(f) Procedure for Release From Arrest or Attachment. Whenever property is arrested or attached, any person claiming an interest in it shall be entitled to a prompt hearing at which the plaintiff shall be required to show why the arrest or attachment should not be vacated or other relief granted consistent with these rules. This subdivision shall have no application to suits for seamen's wages when process is issued upon a certification of sufficient cause filed pursuant to Title 46, U.S.C. §§ 603 and 604 [2] or to actions by the United States for forfeitures for violation of any statute of the United States.

(5) Release of Property.

(a) Special Bond. Whenever process of maritime attachment and garnishment or process in rem is issued the execution of such process shall be stayed, or the property released, on the giving of security, to be approved by the court or clerk, or by stipulation of the parties, conditioned to answer the judgment of the court or of any appellate court. The parties may stipulate the amount and nature of such security. In the event of the inability or refusal of the parties so to stipulate the court shall fix the principal sum of the bond or stipulation at an amount sufficient to cover the amount of the plaintiff's claim fairly stated with accrued interest and costs; but the principal sum shall in no event exceed (i) twice the amount of the plaintiff's claim or (ii) the value of the property on due appraisement, whichever is smaller. The bond or stipulation shall be conditioned for the payment of the principal sum and interest thereon at 6 per cent per annum.

(b) General Bond. The owner of any vessel may file a general bond or stipulation, with sufficient surety, to be approved by the court, conditioned to answer the judgment of such court in all or any actions that may be brought thereafter in such court in which the vessel is attached or arrested. Thereupon the execution of all such process against such vessel shall be stayed so long as the amount secured by such bond or stipulation is at least double the aggregate amount claimed by plaintiffs in all actions begun and pending in which such vessel has been attached or arrested. Judgments and remedies may be had on such bond or stipulation as if a special bond or stipulation had been filed in each of such actions. The district court may make necessary orders to carry this rule into effect, particularly as to the giving of proper notice of any action against or attachment of a vessel for which a general bond has been filed. Such bond or stipulation shall be indorsed by the clerk with a minute of the actions wherein process is so stayed. Further security may be required by the court at any time.

If a special bond or stipulation is given in a particular case, the liability on the general bond or stipulation shall cease as to that case.

(c) Release by Consent or Stipulation; Order of Court or Clerk; Costs. Any vessel, cargo, or other property in the custody of the marshal or other person or organization having the warrant may be released forthwith upon the marshal's acceptance and approval of a stipulation, bond, or other security, signed by the party on whose behalf the property is detained or the party's attorney and expressly authorizing such release, if all costs and charges of the court and its officers shall have first been paid. Otherwise no property in the custody of the marshal, other person or organization having the warrant, or other officer of the court shall be released without an order of the court; but such order may be entered as of course by the clerk, upon the giving of approved security as provided by law and these rules, or upon the dismissal or discontinuance of the action; but the marshal or other person or organization having the warrant shall not deliver any property so released until the costs and charges of the officers of the court shall first have been paid.

(d) Possessory, Petitory, and Partition Actions. The foregoing provisions of this subdivision (5) do not apply to petitory, possessory, and partition actions. In such cases the property arrested shall be released only by order of the court, on such terms and conditions and on the giving of such security as the court may require.

(6) Reduction or Impairment of Security. Whenever security is taken the court may, on motion and hearing, for good cause shown, reduce the amount of security given; and if the surety shall be or become insufficient, new or additional sureties may be required on motion and hearing.

(7) Security on Counterclaim.

(a) When a person who has given security for damages in the original action asserts a counterclaim that arises from the transaction or occurrence that is the subject of the original action, a plaintiff for whose benefit the security has been given must give security for damages demanded in the counterclaim unless the court, for cause shown, directs otherwise. Proceedings on the original claim must be stayed until this security is given unless the court directs otherwise.

(b) The plaintiff is required to give security under Rule E(7)(a) when the United States or its corporate instrumentality counterclaims and would have been required to give security to respond in damages if a private party but is relieved by law from giving security.

(8) Restricted Appearance. An appearance to defend against an admiralty and maritime claim with respect to which there has issued process in rem, or process of attachment and garnishment, may be expressly restricted to the defense of such claim, and in that event is not an appearance for the purposes of any other claim with respect to which such process is not available or has not been served.

(9) Disposition of Property; Sales.

(a) Interlocutory Sales; Delivery.

(i) On application of a party, the marshal, or other person having custody of the property, the court may order all or part of the property sold—with the sales proceeds, or as much of them as will satisfy the judgment, paid into court to await further orders of the court—if:

(A) the attached or arrested property is perishable, or liable to deterioration, decay, or injury by being detained in custody pending the action;

(B) the expense of keeping the property is excessive or disproportionate; or

(C) there is an unreasonable delay in securing release of the property.

(ii) In the circumstances described in Rule E(9)(a)(i), the court, on motion by a defendant or a person filing a statement of interest or right under Rule C(6), may order that the property, rather than being sold, be delivered to the movant upon giving security under these rules.

(b) Sales; Proceeds. All sales of property shall be made by the marshal or a deputy marshal, or by other person or organization having the warrant, or by any other person assigned by the court where the marshal or other person or organization having the warrant is a party in interest; and the proceeds of sale shall be forthwith paid into the registry of the court to be disposed of according to law.

(10) Preservation of Property. When the owner or another person remains in possession of property attached or arrested under the provisions of Rule E(4)(b) that permit execution of process without taking actual possession, the court, on a party's motion or on its own, may enter any order necessary to preserve the property and to prevent its removal.

(Added Feb. 28, 1966, eff. July 1, 1966; amended Apr. 29, 1985, eff. Aug. 1, 1985; Mar. 2, 1987, eff. Aug. 1, 1987; Apr. 30, 1991, eff. Dec. 1, 1991; Apr. 17, 2000, eff. Dec. 1, 2000; Apr. 12, 2006, eff. Dec. 1, 2006.)

2 Repealed by Pub. L. 98–89, § 4(b), Aug. 26, 1983, 97 Stat. 600, section 1 of which enacted Title 46, Shipping.

RULE F. LIMITATION OF LIABILITY

(1) **Time for Filing Complaint; Security.** Not later than six months after receipt of a claim in writing, any vessel owner may file a complaint in the appropriate district court, as provided in subdivision (9) of this rule, for limitation of liability pursuant to statute. The owner (a) shall deposit with the court, for the benefit of claimants, a sum equal to the amount or value of the owner's interest in the vessel and pending freight, or approved security therefor, and in addition such sums, or approved security therefor, as the court may from time to time fix as necessary to carry out the provisions of the statutes as amended; or (b) at the owner's option shall transfer to a trustee to be appointed by the court, for the benefit of claimants, the owner's interest in the vessel and pending freight, together with such sums, or approved security therefor, as the court may from time to time fix as necessary to carry out the provisions of the statutes as amended. The plaintiff shall also give security for costs and, if the plaintiff elects to give security, for interest at the rate of 6 percent per annum from the date of the security.

(2) **Complaint.** The complaint shall set forth the facts on the basis of which the right to limit liability is asserted and all facts necessary to enable the court to determine the amount to which the owner's liability shall be limited. The complaint may demand exoneration from as well as limitation of liability. It shall state the voyage if any, on which the demands sought to be limited arose, with the date and place of its termination; the amount of all demands including all unsatisfied liens or claims of lien, in contract or in tort or otherwise, arising on that voyage, so far as known to the plaintiff, and what actions and proceedings, if any, are pending thereon; whether the vessel was damaged, lost, or abandoned, and, if so, when and where; the value of the vessel at the close of the voyage or, in case of wreck, the value of her wreckage, strippings, or proceeds, if any, and where and in whose possession they are; and the amount of any pending freight recovered or recoverable. If the plaintiff elects to transfer the plaintiff's interest in the vessel to a trustee, the complaint must further show any prior paramount liens thereon, and what voyages or trips, if any, she has made since the voyage or trip on which the claims sought to be limited arose, and any existing liens arising upon any such subsequent voyage or trip, with the amounts and causes thereof, and the names and addresses of the lienors, so far as known; and whether the vessel sustained any injury upon or by reason of such subsequent voyage or trip.

(3) **Claims Against Owner; Injunction.** Upon compliance by the owner with the requirements of subdivision (1) of this rule all claims and proceedings against the owner or the owner's property with respect to the matter in question shall cease. On application of the plaintiff the court shall enjoin the further prosecution of any action or proceeding against the plaintiff or the plaintiff's property with respect to any claim subject to limitation in the action.

(4) **Notice to Claimants.** Upon the owner's compliance with subdivision (1) of this rule the court shall issue a notice to all persons asserting claims with respect to which the complaint seeks limitation, admonishing them to file their respective claims with the clerk of the court and to serve on the attorneys for the plaintiff a copy thereof on or before a date to be named in the notice. The date so fixed shall not be less than 30 days after issuance of the notice. For cause shown, the court may enlarge the time within which claims may be filed. The notice shall be published in such newspaper or newspapers as the court may direct once a week for four successive weeks prior to the date fixed for the filing of claims. The plaintiff not later than the day of second publication shall also mail a copy of the notice to every person known to have made any claim against the vessel or the plaintiff arising out of the voyage or trip on which the claims sought to be limited arose. In cases involving death a copy of such notice shall be mailed to the decedent at the decedent's last known address, and also to any person who shall be known to have made any claim on account of such death.

(5) **Claims and Answer.** Claims shall be filed and served on or before the date specified in the notice provided for in subdivision (4) of this rule. Each claim shall specify the facts upon which the claimant relies in support of the claim, the items thereof, and the dates on which the same accrued. If a claimant desires to contest either the right to exoneration from or the right to limitation of liability the claimant shall file and serve an answer to the complaint unless the claim has included an answer.

(6) **Information to be Given Claimants.** Within 30 days after the date specified in the notice for filing claims, or within such time as the court thereafter may allow, the plaintiff shall mail to the attorney for each claimant (or if the claimant has no attorney to the claimant) a list setting forth (a) the name of each claimant, (b) the name and address of the claimant's attorney (if the claimant is known to have one), (c) the nature of the claim, i.e., whether property loss, property damage, death, personal injury etc., and (d) the amount thereof.

(7) **Insufficiency of Fund or Security.** Any claimant may by motion demand that the funds deposited in court or the security given by the plaintiff be increased on the ground that they are less than the value of the plaintiff's interest in the vessel and pending freight. Thereupon the court shall cause due appraisement to be made of the value of the plaintiff's interest in the vessel and pending freight; and if the court finds that the deposit or security is either insufficient or excessive it shall order its increase or reduction. In like manner any claimant may demand that the deposit or security be increased on the ground that it is insufficient to carry out the provisions of the statutes relating to claims in respect of loss of life or bodily injury; and, after notice and hearing, the court may similarly order that the deposit or security be increased or reduced.

(8) **Objections to Claims: Distribution of Fund.** Any interested party may question or controvert any claim without filing an objection thereto. Upon determination of liability the fund deposited or secured, or the proceeds of the vessel and

pending freight, shall be divided pro rata, subject to all relevant provisions of law, among the several claimants in proportion to the amounts of their respective claims, duly proved, saving, however, to all parties any priority to which they may be legally entitled.

(9) Venue; Transfer. The complaint shall be filed in any district in which the vessel has been attached or arrested to answer for any claim with respect to which the plaintiff seeks to limit liability; or, if the vessel has not been attached or arrested, then in any district in which the owner has been sued with respect to any such claim. When the vessel has not been attached or arrested to answer the matters aforesaid, and suit has not been commenced against the owner, the proceedings may be had in the district in which the vessel may be, but if the vessel is not within any district and no suit has been commenced in any district, then the complaint may be filed in any district. For the convenience of parties and witnesses, in the interest of justice, the court may transfer the action to any district; if venue is wrongly laid the court shall dismiss or, if it be in the interest of justice, transfer the action to any district in which it could have been brought. If the vessel shall have been sold, the proceeds shall represent the vessel for the purposes of these rules.

(Added Feb. 28, 1966, eff. July 1, 1966; amended Mar. 2, 1987, eff. Aug. 1, 1987.)

RULE G. FORFEITURE ACTIONS IN REM

(1) Scope. This rule governs a forfeiture action in rem arising from a federal statute. To the extent that this rule does not address an issue, Supplemental Rules C and E and the Federal Rules of Civil Procedure also apply.

(2) Complaint. The complaint must:

(a) be verified;

(b) state the grounds for subject-matter jurisdiction, in rem jurisdiction over the defendant property, and venue;

(c) describe the property with reasonable particularity;

(d) if the property is tangible, state its location when any seizure occurred and—if different—its location when the action is filed;

(e) identify the statute under which the forfeiture action is brought; and

(f) state sufficiently detailed facts to support a reasonable belief that the government will be able to meet its burden of proof at trial.

(3) Judicial Authorization and Process.

(a) Real Property. If the defendant is real property, the government must proceed under 18 U.S.C. § 985.

(b) Other Property; Arrest Warrant. If the defendant is not real property:

(i) the clerk must issue a warrant to arrest the property if it is in the government's possession, custody, or control;

(ii) the court—on finding probable cause—must issue a warrant to arrest the property if it is not in the govern-

ment's possession, custody, or control and is not subject to a judicial restraining order; and

(iii) a warrant is not necessary if the property is subject to a judicial restraining order.

(c) Execution of Process.

(i) The warrant and any supplemental process must be delivered to a person or organization authorized to execute it, who may be: (A) a marshal or any other United States officer or employee; (B) someone under contract with the United States; or (C) someone specially appointed by the court for that purpose.

(ii) The authorized person or organization must execute the warrant and any supplemental process on property in the United States as soon as practicable unless:

(A) the property is in the government's possession, custody, or control; or

(B) the court orders a different time when the complaint is under seal, the action is stayed before the warrant and supplemental process are executed, or the court finds other good cause.

(iii) The warrant and any supplemental process may be executed within the district or, when authorized by statute, outside the district.

(iv) If executing a warrant on property outside the United States is required, the warrant may be transmitted to an appropriate authority for serving process where the property is located.

(4) Notice.

(a) Notice by Publication.

(i) When Publication Is Required. A judgment of forfeiture may be entered only if the government has published notice of the action within a reasonable time after filing the complaint or at a time the court orders. But notice need not be published if:

(A) the defendant property is worth less than $1,000 and direct notice is sent under Rule G(4)(b) to every person the government can reasonably identify as a potential claimant; or

(B) the court finds that the cost of publication exceeds the property's value and that other means of notice would satisfy due process.

(ii) Content of the Notice. Unless the court orders otherwise, the notice must:

(A) describe the property with reasonable particularity;

(B) state the times under Rule G(5) to file a claim and to answer; and

(C) name the government attorney to be served with the claim and answer.

(iii) Frequency of Publication. Published notice must appear:

(A) once a week for three consecutive weeks; or

(B) only once if, before the action was filed, notice of nonjudicial forfeiture of the same property was published on an official internet government forfeiture site for at least 30 consecutive days, or in a newspaper of general circulation for three consecutive weeks in a district where publication is authorized under Rule G(4)(a)(iv).

(iv) Means of Publication. The government should select from the following options a means of publication reasonably calculated to notify potential claimants of the action:

(A) if the property is in the United States, publication in a newspaper generally circulated in the district where the action is filed, where the property was seized, or where property that was not seized is located;

(B) if the property is outside the United States, publication in a newspaper generally circulated in a district where the action is filed, in a newspaper generally circulated in the country where the property is located, or in legal notices published and generally circulated in the country where the property is located; or

(C) instead of (A) or (B), posting a notice on an official internet government forfeiture site for at least 30 consecutive days.

(b) Notice to Known Potential Claimants.

(i) Direct Notice Required. The government must send notice of the action and a copy of the complaint to any person who reasonably appears to be a potential claimant on the facts known to the government before the end of the time for filing a claim under Rule G(5)(a)(ii)(B).

(ii) Content of the Notice. The notice must state:

(A) the date when the notice is sent;

(B) a deadline for filing a claim, at least 35 days after the notice is sent;

(C) that an answer or a motion under Rule 12 must be filed no later than 21 days after filing the claim; and

(D) the name of the government attorney to be served with the claim and answer.

(iii) Sending Notice.

(A) The notice must be sent by means reasonably calculated to reach the potential claimant.

(B) Notice may be sent to the potential claimant or to the attorney representing the potential claimant with respect to the seizure of the property or in a related investigation, administrative forfeiture proceeding, or criminal case.

(C) Notice sent to a potential claimant who is incarcerated must be sent to the place of incarceration.

(D) Notice to a person arrested in connection with an offense giving rise to the forfeiture who is not incarcerated when notice is sent may be sent to the address that person last gave to the agency that arrested or released the person.

(E) Notice to a person from whom the property was seized who is not incarcerated when notice is sent may be sent to the last address that person gave to the agency that seized the property.

(iv) When Notice Is Sent. Notice by the following means is sent on the date when it is placed in the mail, delivered to a commercial carrier, or sent by electronic mail.

(v) Actual Notice. A potential claimant who had actual notice of a forfeiture action may not oppose or seek relief from forfeiture because of the government's failure to send the required notice.

(5) Responsive Pleadings.

(a) Filing a Claim.

(i) A person who asserts an interest in the defendant property may contest the forfeiture by filing a claim in the court where the action is pending. The claim must:

(A) identify the specific property claimed;

(B) identify the claimant and state the claimant's interest in the property;

(C) be signed by the claimant under penalty of perjury; and

(D) be served on the government attorney designated under Rule G(4)(a)(ii)(C) or (b)(ii)(D).

(ii) Unless the court for good cause sets a different time, the claim must be filed:

(A) by the time stated in a direct notice sent under Rule G(4)(b);

(B) if notice was published but direct notice was not sent to the claimant or the claimant's attorney, no later than 30 days after final publication of newspaper notice or legal notice under Rule G(4)(a) or no later than 60 days after the first day of publication on an official internet government forfeiture site; or

(C) if notice was not published and direct notice was not sent to the claimant or the claimant's attorney:

(1) if the property was in the government's possession, custody, or control when the complaint was filed, no later than 60 days after the filing, not counting any time when the complaint was under seal or when the action was stayed before execution of a warrant issued under Rule G(3)(b); or

(2) if the property was not in the government's possession, custody, or control when the complaint was filed, no later than 60 days after the government complied with 18 U.S.C. § 985(c) as to real property, or 60 days after process was executed on the property under Rule G(3).

(iii) A claim filed by a person asserting an interest as a bailee must identify the bailor, and if filed on the bailor's behalf must state the authority to do so.

(b) Answer. A claimant must serve and file an answer to the complaint or a motion under Rule 12 within 21 days after filing the claim. A claimant waives an objection to in rem jurisdiction or to venue if the objection is not made by motion or stated in the answer.

(6) Special Interrogatories.

(a) Time and Scope. The government may serve special interrogatories limited to the claimant's identity and relationship to the defendant property without the court's leave at any time after the claim is filed and before discovery is closed. But if the claimant serves a motion to dismiss the action, the government must serve the interrogatories within 21 days after the motion is served.

(b) Answers or Objections. Answers or objections to these interrogatories must be served within 21 days after the interrogatories are served.

(c) Government's Response Deferred. The government need not respond to a claimant's motion to dismiss the action under Rule G(8)(b) until 21 days after the claimant has answered these interrogatories.

(7) Preserving, Preventing Criminal Use, and Disposing of Property; Sales.

(a) Preserving and Preventing Criminal Use of Property. When the government does not have actual possession of the defendant property the court, on motion or on its own, may enter any order necessary to preserve the property, to prevent its removal or encumbrance, or to prevent its use in a criminal offense.

(b) Interlocutory Sale or Delivery.

(i) Order to Sell. On motion by a party or a person having custody of the property, the court may order all or part of the property sold if:

(A) the property is perishable or at risk of deterioration, decay, or injury by being detained in custody pending the action;

(B) the expense of keeping the property is excessive or is disproportionate to its fair market value;

(C) the property is subject to a mortgage or to taxes on which the owner is in default; or

(D) the court finds other good cause.

(ii) Who Makes the Sale. A sale must be made by a United States agency that has authority to sell the property, by the agency's contractor, or by any person the court designates.

(iii) Sale Procedures. The sale is governed by 28 U.S.C. §§ 2001, 2002, and 2004, unless all parties, with the court's approval, agree to the sale, aspects of the sale, or different procedures.

(iv) Sale Proceeds. Sale proceeds are a substitute res subject to forfeiture in place of the property that was sold. The proceeds must be held in an interest-bearing account maintained by the United States pending the conclusion of the forfeiture action.

(v) Delivery on a Claimant's Motion. The court may order that the property be delivered to the claimant pending the conclusion of the action if the claimant shows circumstances that would permit sale under Rule G(7)(b)(i) and gives security under these rules.

(c) Disposing of Forfeited Property. Upon entry of a forfeiture judgment, the property or proceeds from selling the property must be disposed of as provided by law.

(8) Motions.

(a) Motion To Suppress Use of the Property as Evidence. If the defendant property was seized, a party with standing to contest the lawfulness of the seizure may move to suppress use of the property as evidence. Suppression does not affect forfeiture of the property based on independently derived evidence.

(b) Motion To Dismiss the Action.

(i) A claimant who establishes standing to contest forfeiture may move to dismiss the action under Rule 12(b).

(ii) In an action governed by 18 U.S.C. § 983(a)(3)(D) the complaint may not be dismissed on the ground that the government did not have adequate evidence at the time the complaint was filed to establish the forfeitability of the property. The sufficiency of the complaint is governed by Rule G(2).

(c) Motion To Strike a Claim or Answer.

(i) At any time before trial, the government may move to strike a claim or answer:

(A) for failing to comply with Rule G(5) or (6), or

(B) because the claimant lacks standing.

(ii) The motion:

(A) must be decided before any motion by the claimant to dismiss the action; and

(B) may be presented as a motion for judgment on the pleadings or as a motion to determine after a hearing or by summary judgment whether the claimant can carry the burden of establishing standing by a preponderance of the evidence.

(d) Petition To Release Property.

(i) If a United States agency or an agency's contractor holds property for judicial or nonjudicial forfeiture under a statute governed by 18 U.S.C. § 983(f), a person who has filed a claim to the property may petition for its release under § 983(f).

(ii) If a petition for release is filed before a judicial forfeiture action is filed against the property, the petition may be filed either in the district where the property was seized or in the district where a warrant to seize the property issued. If a judicial forfeiture action against the property is later filed in another district—or if the government shows that the action will be filed in another district—the petition may be transferred to that district under 28 U.S.C. § 1404.

(e) Excessive Fines. A claimant may seek to mitigate a forfeiture under the Excessive Fines Clause of the Eighth Amendment by motion for summary judgment or by motion made after entry of a forfeiture judgment if:

(i) the claimant has pleaded the defense under Rule 8; and

(ii) the parties have had the opportunity to conduct civil discovery on the defense.

(9) Trial. Trial is to the court unless any party demands trial by jury under Rule 38.

(Added Apr. 12, 2006, eff. Dec. 1, 2006; amended Mar. 26, 2009, eff. Dec. 1, 2009.)

INDEX TO
FEDERAL RULES OF CIVIL PROCEDURE

Habeas corpus, **FRCVP 81**

Harmless error, **FRCVP 61**

Hearings,
Admiralty, **FRCVP E, F**
Consolidation and merger, **FRCVP 42**
Depositions, motions, **FRCVP 32**
Discovery, **FRCVP 37**
Injunctions, **FRCVP 65**
Judges or justices, inability to proceed, **FRCVP 63**
New trial, **FRCVP 59**
Nonoral hearings, motions, **FRCVP 78**
Notice, **FRCVP 6**
Outside district, **FRCVP 77**
Preliminary hearings, **FRCVP 12**
Subpoenas, **FRCVP 45**
Successor judges, **FRCVP 63**
Temporary restraining orders, **FRCVP 65**
Voluntary dismissal, **FRCVP 41**

Holidays,
Clerks of courts, business hours, **FRCVP 77**
Definitions, **FRCVP 6**
Time, computation, **FRCVP 6**

Houses,
Pleading, service, **FRCVP 5**
Summons, service, **FRCVP 4**

Illegality, pleading, affirmative defenses, **FRCVP 8**

Illness, depositions, **FRCVP 32**

Immigration, privacy protection, **FRCVP 5.2**

Impeachment, depositions, **FRCVP 32**

Imprisonment, depositions, **FRCVP 32**

In forma pauperis, process, **FRCVP 4**

In personam actions, admiralty, **FRCVP B, C, E**

Inadvertence, judgments and decrees, **FRCVP 60**

Incompetency, **FRCVP 17**
Default judgments, **FRCVP 55**
Depositions, **FRCVP 27**
Substitution, **FRCVP 25**
Summons, **FRCVP 4**

Indexes, **FRCVP 79**

Indicative rulings, district courts, pending appeals, barred, **FRCVP 62.1**

Indorsement,
Admiralty, **FRCVP E**
Temporary restraining orders, **FRCVP 65**

Infirmities, depositions, **FRCVP 32**

Infringement, stay of proceedings, accounts and accounting, **FRCVP 62**

Initial discovery, **FRCVP 26**

Injunctions, **FRCVP 65**
Admiralty, **FRCVP F**
Appeal and review, **FRCVP 62**
Class actions, **FRCVP 23**

Inspection and inspectors,
Business records, **FRCVP 33**
Orders, **FRCVP 27**

Inspection and inspectors—Cont'd
Subpoenas, **FRCVP 45**

Instructions, jury, **FRCVP 49, 51**

Insular possessions, official record, authentication, **FRCVP 44**

Insurance, discovery, **FRCVP 26**

Intangible property, admiralty, **FRCVP C, E**

Intent, pleading, **FRCVP 9**

Interest, admiralty, **FRCVP F**

Interested parties,
Class actions, **FRCVP 23**
Depositions, **FRCVP 28**
Intervention, **FRCVP 24**
Joinder, **FRCVP 19**

Interlocutory proceedings,
Admiralty, **FRCVP E**
Injunctions, **FRCVP 52**

Internal Revenue Service, judgments and decrees, **FRCVP 69**

International agreements, summons, **FRCVP 4**

Interpleader, **FRCVP 22**
Injunctions, **FRCVP 65**

Interpreters, **FRCVP 43**

Interrogatories, **FRCVP 33**
Admiralty, **FRCVP B, C, G**
Alterations, **FRCVP 26**
Business records, **FRCVP 33**
Compelling answers, **FRCVP 37**
Electronically stored information, **FRCVP 33**
Evasive answers, **FRCVP 37**
Exceptions, **FRCVP 33**
Experts, **FRCVP 26**
General verdicts, **FRCVP 49**
Incomplete answers, **FRCVP 37**
Jury, **FRCVP 49**
Masters, **FRCVP 53**
Motions, **FRCVP 33 et seq.**
Objections and exceptions, **FRCVP 33**
Orders of court, **FRCVP 33, 37**
Sanctions, **FRCVP 37**
Service, **FRCVP 33**
Stipulations, **FRCVP 29**
Summary judgment, **FRCVP 56**
Supplementation, **FRCVP 26**
Time, **FRCVP 33**
Trial, **FRCVP 33**
Written interrogatories, **FRCVP 49**

Intervention, **FRCVP 24**
Constitutional challenges, statutes, **FRCVP 5.1**
Motions, **FRCVP 24**

Investigations,
Admiralty, **FRCVP E**
Foreign official records, **FRCVP 44**

Involuntary plaintiffs, joinder, **FRCVP 19**

Issues,
Court trial, **FRCVP 39**

FEDERAL RULES OF EVIDENCE

As Last Amended, Effective December 1, 2017

ARTICLE I. GENERAL PROVISIONS

RULE 101. SCOPE; DEFINITIONS

(a) **Scope.** These rules apply to proceedings in United States courts. The specific courts and proceedings to which the rules apply, along with exceptions, are set out in Rule 1101.

(b) **Definitions.** In these rules:

(1) "civil case" means a civil action or proceeding;

(2) "criminal case" includes a criminal proceeding;

(3) "public office" includes a public agency;

(4) "record" includes a memorandum, report, or data compilation;

(5) a "rule prescribed by the Supreme Court" means a rule adopted by the Supreme Court under statutory authority; and

(6) a reference to any kind of written material or any other medium includes electronically stored information.

(Pub.L. 93–595, § 1, Jan. 2, 1975, 88 Stat. 1929; Mar. 2, 1987, eff. Oct. 1, 1987; Apr. 25, 1988, eff. Nov. 1, 1988; Apr. 22, 1993, eff. Dec. 1, 1993; Apr. 26, 2011, eff. Dec. 1, 2011.)

RULE 102. PURPOSE

These rules should be construed so as to administer every proceeding fairly, eliminate unjustifiable expense and delay, and promote the development of evidence law, to the end of ascertaining the truth and securing a just determination.

(Pub.L. 93–595, § 1, Jan. 2, 1975, 88 Stat.1929; Apr. 26, 2011, eff. Dec. 1, 2011.)

RULE 103. RULINGS ON EVIDENCE

(a) **Preserving a Claim of Error.** A party may claim error in a ruling to admit or exclude evidence only if the error affects a substantial right of the party and:

(1) if the ruling admits evidence, a party, on the record:

(A) timely objects or moves to strike; and

(B) states the specific ground, unless it was apparent from the context; or

(2) if the ruling excludes evidence, a party informs the court of its substance by an offer of proof, unless the substance was apparent from the context.

(b) **Not Needing to Renew an Objection or Offer of Proof.** Once the court rules definitively on the record—either before or at trial—a party need not renew an objection or offer of proof to preserve a claim of error for appeal.

(c) **Court's Statement About the Ruling; Directing an Offer of Proof.** The court may make any statement about the character or form of the evidence, the objection made, and the ruling. The court may direct that an offer of proof be made in question-and-answer form.

(d) **Preventing the Jury from Hearing Inadmissible Evidence.** To the extent practicable, the court must conduct a jury trial so that inadmissible evidence is not suggested to the jury by any means.

(e) **Taking Notice of Plain Error.** A court may take notice of a plain error affecting a substantial right, even if the claim of error was not properly preserved.

(Pub.L. 93–595, § 1, Jan. 2, 1975, 88 Stat. 1929; Apr. 17, 2000, eff. Dec. 1, 2000; Apr. 26, 2011, eff. Dec. 1, 2011.)

RULE 104. PRELIMINARY QUESTIONS

(a) **In General.** The court must decide any preliminary question about whether a witness is qualified, a privilege exists, or evidence is admissible. In so deciding, the court is not bound by evidence rules, except those on privilege.

(b) **Relevance That Depends on a Fact.** When the relevance of evidence depends on whether a fact exists, proof must be introduced sufficient to support a finding that the fact does exist. The court may admit the proposed evidence on the condition that the proof be introduced later.

(c) **Conducting a Hearing So That the Jury Cannot Hear It.** The court must conduct any hearing on a preliminary question so that the jury cannot hear it if:

(1) the hearing involves the admissibility of a confession;

(2) a defendant in a criminal case is a witness and so requests; or

(3) justice so requires.

(d) **Cross–Examining a Defendant in a Criminal Case.** By testifying on a preliminary question, a defendant in a criminal case does not become subject to cross-examination on other issues in the case.

(e) **Evidence Relevant to Weight and Credibility.** This rule does not limit a party's right to introduce before the jury evidence that is relevant to the weight or credibility of other evidence. → sufficiency

(Pub.L. 93–595, § 1, Jan. 2, 1975, 88 Stat.1930; Mar. 2, 1987, eff. Oct. 1, 1987; Apr. 26, 2011, eff. Dec. 1, 2011.)

RULE 105. LIMITING EVIDENCE THAT IS NOT ADMISSIBLE AGAINST OTHER PARTIES OR FOR OTHER PURPOSES

If the court admits evidence that is admissible against a party or for a purpose—but not against another party or for another purpose—the court, on timely request, must restrict the evidence to its proper scope and instruct the jury accordingly.

(Pub.L. 93–595, § 1, Jan. 2, 1975, 88 Stat. 1930; Apr. 26, 2011, eff. Dec. 1, 2011.)

RULE 106. REMAINDER OF OR RELATED WRITINGS OR RECORDED STATEMENTS

If a party introduces all or part of a writing or recorded statement, an adverse party may require the introduction, at that time, of any other part—or any other writing or recorded statement—that in fairness ought to be considered at the same time.

(Pub.L. 93–595, § 1, Jan. 2, 1975, 88 Stat. 1930; Mar. 2, 1987, eff. Oct. 1, 1987; Apr. 26, 2011, eff. Dec. 1, 2011.)

ARTICLE II. JUDICIAL NOTICE

RULE 201. JUDICIAL NOTICE OF ADJUDICATIVE FACTS

(a) **Scope.** This rule governs judicial notice of an adjudicative fact only, not a legislative fact.

(b) **Kinds of Facts That May Be Judicially Noticed.** The court may judicially notice a fact that is not subject to reasonable dispute because it:

(1) is generally known within the trial court's territorial jurisdiction; or

(2) can be accurately and readily determined from sources whose accuracy cannot reasonably be questioned.

(c) **Taking Notice.** The court:

(1) may take judicial notice on its own; or

(2) must take judicial notice if a party requests it and the court is supplied with the necessary information.

(d) **Timing.** The court may take judicial notice at any stage of the proceeding.

(e) **Opportunity to Be Heard.** On timely request, a party is entitled to be heard on the propriety of taking judicial notice and the nature of the fact to be noticed. If the court takes judicial notice before notifying a party, the party, on request, is still entitled to be heard.

(f) **Instructing the Jury.** In a civil case, the court must instruct the jury to accept the noticed fact as conclusive. In a criminal case, the court must instruct the jury that it may or may not accept the noticed fact as conclusive.

(Pub.L. 93–595, § 1, Jan. 2, 1975, 88 Stat. 1930; Apr. 26, 2011, eff. Dec. 1, 2011.)

ARTICLE III. PRESUMPTIONS IN CIVIL CASES

RULE 301. PRESUMPTIONS IN CIVIL CASES GENERALLY

In a civil case, unless a federal statute or these rules provide otherwise, the party against whom a presumption is directed has the burden of producing evidence to rebut the presumption. But this rule does not shift the burden of persuasion, which remains on the party who had it originally.

(Pub.L. 93–595, § 1, Jan. 2, 1975, 88 Stat. 1931; Apr. 26, 2011, eff. Dec. 1, 2011.)

RULE 302. APPLYING STATE LAW TO PRESUMPTIONS IN CIVIL CASES

In a civil case, state law governs the effect of a presumption regarding a claim or defense for which state law supplies the rule of decision.

(Pub.L. 93–595, § 1, Jan. 2, 1975, 88 Stat. 1931; Apr. 26, 2011, eff. Dec. 1, 2011.)

ARTICLE IV. RELEVANCE AND ITS LIMITS

RULE 401. TEST FOR RELEVANT EVIDENCE

Evidence is relevant if:

(a) it has any tendency to make a fact more or less probable than it would be without the evidence; and

(b) the fact is of consequence in determining the action.

(Pub.L. 93–595, § 1, Jan. 2, 1975, 88 Stat.1931; Apr. 26, 2011, eff. Dec. 1, 2011.)

RULE 402. GENERAL ADMISSIBILITY OF RELEVANT EVIDENCE

Relevant evidence is admissible unless any of the following provides otherwise:

- the United States Constitution;
- a federal statute;
- these rules; or
- other rules prescribed by the Supreme Court.

Irrelevant evidence is not admissible.

(Pub.L. 93–595, § 1, Jan. 2, 1975, 88 Stat. 1931; Apr. 26, 2011, eff. Dec. 1, 2011.)

RULE 403. EXCLUDING RELEVANT EVIDENCE FOR PREJUDICE, CONFUSION, WASTE OF TIME, OR OTHER REASONS

The court may exclude relevant evidence if its probative value is substantially outweighed by a danger of one or more of the following: unfair prejudice, confusing the issues, misleading the jury, undue delay, wasting time, or needlessly presenting cumulative evidence.

(Pub.L. 93–595, § 1, Jan. 2, 1975, 88 Stat. 1932; Apr. 26, 2011, eff. Dec. 1, 2011.)

RULE 404. CHARACTER EVIDENCE; CRIMES OR OTHER ACTS

(a) Character Evidence.

(1) Prohibited Uses. Evidence of a person's character or character trait is not admissible to prove that on a particular occasion the person acted in accordance with the character or trait.

(2) Exceptions for a Defendant or Victim in a Criminal Case. The following exceptions apply in a criminal case:

(A) a defendant may offer evidence of the defendant's pertinent trait, and if the evidence is admitted, the prosecutor may offer evidence to rebut it;

(B) subject to the limitations in Rule 412, a defendant may offer evidence of an alleged victim's pertinent trait, and if the evidence is admitted, the prosecutor may:

(i) offer evidence to rebut it; and

(ii) offer evidence of the defendant's same trait; and

(C) in a homicide case, the prosecutor may offer evidence of the alleged victim's trait of peacefulness to rebut evidence that the victim was the first aggressor.

(3) Exceptions for a Witness. Evidence of a witness's character may be admitted under Rules 607, 608, and 609.

(b) Crimes, Wrongs, or Other Acts.

(1) Prohibited Uses. Evidence of a crime, wrong, or other act is not admissible to prove a person's character in order to show that on a particular occasion the person acted in accordance with the character.

(2) Permitted Uses; Notice in a Criminal Case. This evidence may be admissible for another purpose, such as proving motive, opportunity, intent, preparation, plan, knowledge, identity, absence of mistake, or lack of accident. On request by a defendant in a criminal case, the prosecutor must:

(A) provide reasonable notice of the general nature of any such evidence that the prosecutor intends to offer at trial; and

(B) do so before trial—or during trial if the court, for good cause, excuses lack of pretrial notice.

(Pub.L. 93–595, § 1, Jan. 2, 1975, 88 Stat.1932; Mar. 2, 1987, eff. Oct. 1, 1987; Apr. 30, 1991, eff. Dec. 1, 1991; Apr. 17, 2000, eff. Dec. 1, 2000; Apr. 12, 2006, eff. Dec. 1, 2006; Apr. 26, 2011, eff. Dec. 1, 2011.)

RULE 405. METHODS OF PROVING CHARACTER

(a) By Reputation or Opinion. When evidence of a person's character or character trait is admissible, it may be proved by testimony about the person's reputation or by testimony in the form of an opinion. On cross-examination of the character witness, the court may allow an inquiry into relevant specific instances of the person's conduct.

(b) By Specific Instances of Conduct. When a person's character or character trait is an essential element of a charge, claim, or defense, the character or trait may also be proved by relevant specific instances of the person's conduct.

(Pub.L. 93–595, § 1, Jan. 2, 1975, 88 Stat. 1932; Mar. 2, 1987, eff. Oct. 1, 1987; Apr. 26, 2011, eff. Dec. 1, 2011.)

RULE 406. HABIT; ROUTINE PRACTICE

Evidence of a person's habit or an organization's routine practice may be admitted to prove that on a particular occasion the person or organization acted in accordance with the habit or routine practice. The court may admit this evidence regardless of whether it is corroborated or whether there was an eyewitness.

(Pub.L. 93–595, § 1, Jan. 2, 1975, 88 Stat. 1932; Apr. 26, 2011, eff. Dec. 1, 2011.)

RULE 407. SUBSEQUENT REMEDIAL MEASURES

When measures are taken that would have made an earlier injury or harm less likely to occur, evidence of the subsequent measures is not admissible to prove:

- negligence;
- culpable conduct;
- a defect in a product or its design; or
- a need for a warning or instruction.

But the court may admit this evidence for another purpose, such as impeachment or—if disputed—proving ownership, control, or the feasibility of precautionary measures.

(Pub.L. 93–595, § 1, Jan. 2, 1975, 88 Stat. 1932; Apr. 11, 1997, eff. Dec. 1, 1997; Apr. 26, 2011, eff. Dec. 1, 2011.)

RULE 408. COMPROMISE OFFERS AND NEGOTIATIONS

(a) Prohibited Uses. Evidence of the following is not admissible—on behalf of any party—either to prove or disprove the validity or amount of a disputed claim or to impeach by a prior inconsistent statement or a contradiction:

(1) furnishing, promising, or offering—or accepting, promising to accept, or offering to accept—a valuable consideration in compromising or attempting to compromise the claim; and

(2) conduct or a statement made during compromise negotiations about the claim—except when offered in a criminal case and when the negotiations related to a claim by a public office in the exercise of its regulatory, investigative, or enforcement authority.

(b) Exceptions. The court may admit this evidence for another purpose, such as proving a witness's bias or prejudice, negating a contention of undue delay, or proving an effort to obstruct a criminal investigation or prosecution.

(Pub.L. 93–595, § 1, Jan. 2, 1975, 88 Stat. 1933; Apr. 12, 2006, eff. Dec. 1, 2006; Apr. 26, 2011, eff. Dec. 1, 2011.)

RULE 409. OFFERS TO PAY MEDICAL AND SIMILAR EXPENSES

Evidence of furnishing, promising to pay, or offering to pay medical, hospital, or similar expenses resulting from an injury is not admissible to prove liability for the injury.

(Pub.L. 93–595, § 1, Jan. 2, 1975, 88 Stat.1933; Apr. 26, 2011, eff. Dec. 1, 2011.)

RULE 410. PLEAS, PLEA DISCUSSIONS, AND RELATED STATEMENTS

(a) Prohibited Uses. In a civil or criminal case, evidence of the following is not admissible against the defendant who made the plea or participated in the plea discussions:

(1) a guilty plea that was later withdrawn;

(2) a nolo contendere plea;

(3) a statement made during a proceeding on either of those pleas under Federal Rule of Criminal Procedure 11 or a comparable state procedure; or

(4) a statement made during plea discussions with an attorney for the prosecuting authority if the discussions did not result in a guilty plea or they resulted in a later-withdrawn guilty plea.

(b) Exceptions. The court may admit a statement described in Rule 410(a)(3) or (4):

(1) in any proceeding in which another statement made during the same plea or plea discussions has been introduced, if in fairness the statements ought to be considered together; or

(2) in a criminal proceeding for perjury or false statement, if the defendant made the statement under oath, on the record, and with counsel present.

(Pub.L. 93–595, § 1, Jan. 2, 1975, 88 Stat. 1933; Pub.L. 94–149, § 1(9), Dec. 12, 1975, 89 Stat. 805; Apr. 30, 1979, eff. Dec. 1, 1980; Apr. 26, 2011, eff. Dec. 1, 2011.)

RULE 411. LIABILITY INSURANCE

Evidence that a person was or was not insured against liability is not admissible to prove whether the person acted negligently or otherwise wrongfully. But the court may admit this evidence for another purpose, such as proving a witness's bias or prejudice or proving agency, ownership, or control.

(Pub.L. 93–595, § 1, Jan. 2, 1975, 88 Stat.1933; Mar. 2, 1987, eff. Oct. 1, 1987; Apr. 26, 2011, eff. Dec. 1, 2011.)

RULE 412. SEX–OFFENSE CASES: THE VICTIM'S SEXUAL BEHAVIOR OR PREDISPOSITION

(a) Prohibited Uses. The following evidence is not admissible in a civil or criminal proceeding involving alleged sexual misconduct:

(1) evidence offered to prove that a victim engaged in other sexual behavior; or

(2) evidence offered to prove a victim's sexual predisposition.

(b) Exceptions.

(1) Criminal Cases. The court may admit the following evidence in a criminal case:

(A) evidence of specific instances of a victim's sexual behavior, if offered to prove that someone other than the defendant was the source of semen, injury, or other physical evidence;

(B) evidence of specific instances of a victim's sexual behavior with respect to the person accused of the sexual misconduct, if offered by the defendant to prove consent or if offered by the prosecutor; and

(C) evidence whose exclusion would violate the defendant's constitutional rights.

(2) Civil Cases. In a civil case, the court may admit evidence offered to prove a victim's sexual behavior or sexual predisposition if its probative value substantially outweighs the danger of harm to any victim and of unfair prejudice to any party. The court may admit evidence of a victim's reputation only if the victim has placed it in controversy.

(c) Procedure to Determine Admissibility.

(1) Motion. If a party intends to offer evidence under Rule 412(b), the party must:

(A) file a motion that specifically describes the evidence and states the purpose for which it is to be offered;

(B) do so at least 14 days before trial unless the court, for good cause, sets a different time;

(C) serve the motion on all parties; and

(D) notify the victim or, when appropriate, the victim's guardian or representative.

(2) Hearing. Before admitting evidence under this rule, the court must conduct an in camera hearing and give the victim and parties a right to attend and be heard. Unless the court orders otherwise, the motion, related materials, and the record of the hearing must be and remain sealed.

(d) Definition of "Victim." In this rule, "victim" includes an alleged victim.

(Added Pub.L. 95–540, § 2(a), Oct. 28, 1978, 92 Stat. 2046; amended Pub.L. 100–690, Title VII, § 7046(a), Nov. 18, 1988, 102 Stat. 4400; Apr. 29, 1994, eff. Dec. 1, 1994; Pub.L. 103–322, Title IV, § 40141(b), Sept. 13, 1994, 108 Stat. 1919; Apr. 26, 2011, eff. Dec. 1, 2011.)

RULE 413. SIMILAR CRIMES IN SEXUAL–ASSAULT CASES

(a) Permitted Uses. In a criminal case in which a defendant is accused of a sexual assault, the court may admit evidence that the defendant committed any other sexual assault. The evidence may be considered on any matter to which it is relevant.

(b) Disclosure to the Defendant. If the prosecutor intends to offer this evidence, the prosecutor must disclose it to the defendant, including witnesses' statements or a summary of the expected testimony. The prosecutor must do so at least 15 days before trial or at a later time that the court allows for good cause.

(c) Effect on Other Rules. This rule does not limit the admission or consideration of evidence under any other rule.

(d) Definition of "Sexual Assault." In this rule and Rule 415, "sexual assault" means a crime under federal law or under state law (as "state" is defined in 18 U.S.C. § 513) involving:

(1) any conduct prohibited by 18 U.S.C. chapter 109A;

(2) contact, without consent, between any part of the defendant's body—or an object—and another person's genitals or anus;

(3) contact, without consent, between the defendant's genitals or anus and any part of another person's body;

(4) deriving sexual pleasure or gratification from inflicting death, bodily injury, or physical pain on another person; or

(5) an attempt or conspiracy to engage in conduct described in subparagraphs (1)–(4).

(Added Pub.L. 103–322, Title XXXII, § 320935(a), Sept. 13, 1994, 108 Stat. 2136; Apr. 26, 2011, eff. Dec. 1, 2011.)

RULE 414. SIMILAR CRIMES IN CHILD– MOLESTATION CASES

(a) Permitted Uses. In a criminal case in which a defendant is accused of child molestation, the court may admit evidence that the defendant committed any other child molestation. The evidence may be considered on any matter to which it is relevant.

(b) Disclosure to the Defendant. If the prosecutor intends to offer this evidence, the prosecutor must disclose it to the defendant, including witnesses' statements or a summary of the expected testimony. The prosecutor must do so at least 15 days before trial or at a later time that the court allows for good cause.

(c) Effect on Other Rules. This rule does not limit the admission or consideration of evidence under any other rule.

(d) Definition of "Child" and "Child Molestation." In this rule and Rule 415:

(1) "child" means a person below the age of 14; and

(2) "child molestation" means a crime under federal law or under state law (as "state" is defined in 18 U.S.C. § 513) involving:

(A) any conduct prohibited by 18 U.S.C. chapter 109A and committed with a child;

(B) any conduct prohibited by 18 U.S.C. chapter 110;

(C) contact between any part of the defendant's body— or an object—and a child's genitals or anus;

(D) contact between the defendant's genitals or anus and any part of a child's body;

(E) deriving sexual pleasure or gratification from inflicting death, bodily injury, or physical pain on a child; or

(F) an attempt or conspiracy to engage in conduct described in subparagraphs (A)–(E).

(Added Pub.L. 103–322, Title XXXII, § 320935(a), Sept. 13, 1994, 108 Stat. 2136; Apr. 26, 2011, eff. Dec. 1, 2011.)

RULE 415. SIMILAR ACTS IN CIVIL CASES INVOLVING SEXUAL ASSAULT OR CHILD MOLESTATION

(a) Permitted Uses. In a civil case involving a claim for relief based on a party's alleged sexual assault or child molestation, the court may admit evidence that the party committed any other sexual assault or child molestation. The evidence may be considered as provided in Rules 413 and 414.

(b) Disclosure to the Opponent. If a party intends to offer this evidence, the party must disclose it to the party against whom it will be offered, including witnesses' statements or a summary of the expected testimony. The party must do so at least 15 days before trial or at a later time that the court allows for good cause.

(c) Effect on Other Rules. This rule does not limit the admission or consideration of evidence under any other rule.

(Added Pub.L. 103–322, Title XXXII, § 320935(a), Sept. 13, 1994, 108 Stat. 2137; Apr. 26, 2011, eff. Dec. 1, 2011.)

ARTICLE V. PRIVILEGES

RULE 501. PRIVILEGE IN GENERAL

The common law—as interpreted by United States courts in the light of reason and experience—governs a claim of privilege unless any of the following provides otherwise:

- the United States Constitution;
- a federal statute; or
- rules prescribed by the Supreme Court.

But in a civil case, state law governs privilege regarding a claim or defense for which state law supplies the rule of decision.

(Pub.L. 93–595, § 1, Jan. 2, 1975, 88 Stat. 1933; Apr. 26, 2011, eff. Dec. 1, 2011.)

RULE 502. ATTORNEY–CLIENT PRIVILEGE AND WORK PRODUCT; LIMITATIONS ON WAIVER

The following provisions apply, in the circumstances set out, to disclosure of a communication or information covered by the attorney-client privilege or work-product protection.

(a) Disclosure Made in a Federal Proceeding or to a Federal Office or Agency; Scope of a Waiver. When the disclosure is made in a federal proceeding or to a federal office or agency and waives the attorney-client privilege or work-product protection, the waiver extends to an undisclosed communication or information in a federal or state proceeding only if:

(1) the waiver is intentional;

(2) the disclosed and undisclosed communications or information concern the same subject matter; and

(3) they ought in fairness to be considered together.

(b) Inadvertent Disclosure. When made in a federal proceeding or to a federal office or agency, the disclosure does not operate as a waiver in a federal or state proceeding if:

(1) the disclosure is inadvertent;

(2) the holder of the privilege or protection took reasonable steps to prevent disclosure; and

(3) the holder promptly took reasonable steps to rectify the error, including (if applicable) following Federal Rule of Civil Procedure 26(b)(5)(B).

(c) Disclosure Made in a State Proceeding. When the disclosure is made in a state proceeding and is not the subject of a state-court order concerning waiver, the disclosure does not operate as a waiver in a federal proceeding if the disclosure:

(1) would not be a waiver under this rule if it had been made in a federal proceeding; or

(2) is not a waiver under the law of the state where the disclosure occurred.

(d) Controlling Effect of a Court Order. A federal court may order that the privilege or protection is not waived by disclosure connected with the litigation pending before the court—in which event the disclosure is also not a waiver in any other federal or state proceeding.

(e) Controlling Effect of a Party Agreement. An agreement on the effect of disclosure in a federal proceeding is binding only on the parties to the agreement, unless it is incorporated into a court order.

(f) Controlling Effect of This Rule. Notwithstanding Rules 101 and 1101, this rule applies to state proceedings and to federal court-annexed and federal court-mandated arbitration proceedings, in the circumstances set out in the rule. And notwithstanding Rule 501, this rule applies even if state law provides the rule of decision.

(g) Definitions. In this rule:

(1) "attorney-client privilege" means the protection that applicable law provides for confidential attorney-client communications; and

(2) "work-product protection" means the protection that applicable law provides for tangible material (or its intangible equivalent) prepared in anticipation of litigation or for trial.

(Pub.L. 110–322, § 1(a), Sept. 19, 2008, 122 Stat. 3537; Apr. 26, 2011, eff. Dec. 1, 2011.)

ARTICLE VI. WITNESSES

RULE 601. COMPETENCY TO TESTIFY IN GENERAL

Every person is competent to be a witness unless these rules provide otherwise. But in a civil case, state law governs the witness's competency regarding a claim or defense for which state law supplies the rule of decision. TX state law

(Pub.L. 93–595, § 1, Jan. 2, 1975, 88 Stat.1934; Apr. 26, 2011, eff. Dec. 1, 2011.)

RULE 602. NEED FOR PERSONAL KNOWLEDGE

A witness may testify to a matter only if evidence is introduced sufficient to support a finding that the witness has personal knowledge of the matter. Evidence to prove personal knowledge may consist of the witness's own testimony. This rule does not apply to a witness's expert testimony under Rule 703.

(Pub.L. 93–595, § 1, Jan. 2, 1975, 88 Stat. 1934; Mar. 2, 1987, eff. Oct. 1, 1987; Apr. 25, 1988, eff. Nov. 1, 1988; Apr. 26, 2011, eff. Dec. 1, 2011.)

RULE 603. OATH OR AFFIRMATION TO TESTIFY TRUTHFULLY

Before testifying, a witness must give an oath or affirmation to testify truthfully. It must be in a form designed to impress that duty on the witness's conscience.

(Pub.L. 93–595, § 1, Jan. 2, 1975, 88 Stat. 1934; Mar. 2, 1987, eff. Oct. 1, 1987; Apr. 26, 2011, eff. Dec. 1, 2011.)

RULE 604. INTERPRETER

An interpreter must be qualified and must give an oath or affirmation to make a true translation.

(Pub.L. 93–595, § 1, Jan. 2, 1975, 88 Stat. 1934; Mar. 2, 1987, eff. Oct. 1, 1987; Apr. 26, 2011, eff. Dec. 1, 2011.)

RULE 605. JUDGE'S COMPETENCY AS A WITNESS

The presiding judge may not testify as a witness at the trial. A party need not object to preserve the issue.

(Pub.L. 93–595, § 1, Jan. 2, 1975, 88 Stat. 1934; Apr. 26, 2011, eff. Dec. 1, 2011.)

RULE 606. JUROR'S COMPETENCY AS A WITNESS

(a) At the Trial. A juror may not testify as a witness before the other jurors at the trial. If a juror is called to testify, the court must give a party an opportunity to object outside the jury's presence.

(b) During an Inquiry Into the Validity of a Verdict or Indictment.

(1) **Prohibited Testimony or Other Evidence.** During an inquiry into the validity of a verdict or indictment, a juror may not testify about any statement made or incident that occurred during the jury's deliberations; the effect of anything on that juror's or another juror's vote; or any juror's

mental processes concerning the verdict or indictment. The court may not receive a juror's affidavit or evidence of a juror's statement on these matters.

(2) **Exceptions.** A juror may testify about whether:

(A) extraneous prejudicial information was improperly brought to the jury's attention;

(B) an outside influence was improperly brought to bear on any juror; or

(C) a mistake was made in entering the verdict on the verdict form.

(Pub.L. 93–595, § 1, Jan. 2, 1975, 88 Stat. 1934; Pub.L. 94–149, § 1(10), Dec. 12, 1975, 89 Stat. 805; Mar. 2, 1987, eff. Oct. 1, 1987; Apr. 12, 2006, eff. Dec. 1, 2006; Apr. 26, 2011, eff. Dec. 1, 2011.)

RULE 607. WHO MAY IMPEACH A WITNESS

Any party, including the party that called the witness, may attack the witness's credibility.

(Pub.L. 93–595, § 1, Jan. 2, 1975, 88 Stat.1934; Mar. 2, 1987, eff. Oct. 1, 1987; Apr. 26, 2011, eff. Dec. 1, 2011.)

RULE 608. A WITNESS'S CHARACTER FOR TRUTHFULNESS OR UNTRUTHFULNESS

(a) **Reputation or Opinion Evidence.** A witness's credibility may be attacked or supported by testimony about the witness's reputation for having a character for truthfulness or untruthfulness, or by testimony in the form of an opinion about that character. But evidence of truthful character is admissible only after the witness's character for truthfulness has been attacked.

(b) **Specific Instances of Conduct.** Except for a criminal conviction under Rule 609, extrinsic evidence is not admissible to prove specific instances of a witness's conduct in order to attack or support the witness's character for truthfulness. But the court may, on cross-examination, allow them to be inquired into if they are probative of the character for truthfulness or untruthfulness of:

(1) the witness; or

(2) another witness whose character the witness being cross-examined has testified about.

By testifying on another matter, a witness does not waive any privilege against self-incrimination for testimony that relates only to the witness's character for truthfulness.

(Pub.L. 93–595, § 1, Jan. 2, 1975, 88 Stat.1935; Mar. 2, 1987, eff. Oct. 1, 1987; Apr. 25, 1988, eff. Nov. 1, 1988; Mar. 27, 2003, eff. Dec. 1, 2003; Apr. 26, 2011, eff. Dec. 1, 2011.)

RULE 609. IMPEACHMENT BY EVIDENCE OF A CRIMINAL CONVICTION

(a) **In General.** The following rules apply to attacking a witness's character for truthfulness by evidence of a criminal conviction:

(1) for a crime that, in the convicting jurisdiction, was punishable by death or by imprisonment for more than one year, the evidence:

(A) must be admitted, subject to Rule 403, in a civil case or in a criminal case in which the witness is not a defendant; and

(B) must be admitted in a criminal case in which the witness is a defendant, if the probative value of the evidence outweighs its prejudicial effect to that defendant; and

(2) for any crime regardless of the punishment, the evidence must be admitted if the court can readily determine that establishing the elements of the crime required proving—or the witness's admitting—a dishonest act or false statement.

(b) **Limit on Using the Evidence After 10 Years.** This subdivision (b) applies if more than 10 years have passed since the witness's conviction or release from confinement for it, whichever is later. Evidence of the conviction is admissible only if:

(1) its probative value, supported by specific facts and circumstances, substantially outweighs its prejudicial effect; and

(2) the proponent gives an adverse party reasonable written notice of the intent to use it so that the party has a fair opportunity to contest its use.

(c) **Effect of a Pardon, Annulment, or Certificate of Rehabilitation.** Evidence of a conviction is not admissible if:

(1) the conviction has been the subject of a pardon, annulment, certificate of rehabilitation, or other equivalent procedure based on a finding that the person has been rehabilitated, and the person has not been convicted of a later crime punishable by death or by imprisonment for more than one year; or

(2) the conviction has been the subject of a pardon, annulment, or other equivalent procedure based on a finding of innocence.

(d) **Juvenile Adjudications.** Evidence of a juvenile adjudication is admissible under this rule only if:

(1) it is offered in a criminal case;

(2) the adjudication was of a witness other than the defendant;

(3) an adult's conviction for that offense would be admissible to attack the adult's credibility; and

(4) admitting the evidence is necessary to fairly determine guilt or innocence.

(e) **Pendency of an Appeal.** A conviction that satisfies this rule is admissible even if an appeal is pending. Evidence of the pendency is also admissible.

(Pub.L. 93–595, § 1, Jan. 2, 1975, 88 Stat.1935; Mar. 2, 1987, eff. Oct. 1, 1987; Jan. 26, 1990, eff. Dec. 1, 1990; Apr. 12, 2006, eff. Dec. 1, 2006; Apr. 26, 2011, eff. Dec. 1, 2011.)

RULE 610. RELIGIOUS BELIEFS OR OPINIONS

Evidence of a witness's religious beliefs or opinions is not admissible to attack or support the witness's credibility.

(Pub.L. 93–595, § 1, Jan. 2, 1975, 88 Stat.1936; Mar. 2, 1987, eff. Oct. 1, 1987; Apr. 26, 2011, eff. Dec. 1, 2011.)

RULE 611. MODE AND ORDER OF EXAMINING WITNESSES AND PRESENTING EVIDENCE

(a) Control by the Court; Purposes. The court should exercise reasonable control over the mode and order of examining witnesses and presenting evidence so as to:

(1) make those procedures effective for determining the truth;

(2) avoid wasting time; and

(3) protect witnesses from harassment or undue embarrassment.

(b) Scope of Cross–Examination. Cross-examination should not go beyond the subject matter of the direct examination and matters affecting the witness's credibility. The court may allow inquiry into additional matters as if on direct examination.

(c) Leading Questions. Leading questions should not be used on direct examination except as necessary to develop the witness's testimony. Ordinarily, the court should allow leading questions:

(1) on cross-examination; and

(2) when a party calls a hostile witness, an adverse party, or a witness identified with an adverse party.

(Pub.L. 93–595, § 1, Jan. 2, 1975, 88 Stat. 1936; Mar. 2, 1987, eff. Oct. 1, 1987; Apr. 26, 2011, eff. Dec. 1, 2011.)

RULE 612. WRITING USED TO REFRESH A WITNESS'S MEMORY

(a) Scope. This rule gives an adverse party certain options when a witness uses a writing to refresh memory:

(1) while testifying; or

(2) before testifying, if the court decides that justice requires the party to have those options.

(b) Adverse Party's Options; Deleting Unrelated Matter. Unless 18 U.S.C. § 3500 provides otherwise in a criminal case, an adverse party is entitled to have the writing produced at the hearing, to inspect it, to cross-examine the witness about it, and to introduce in evidence any portion that relates to the witness's testimony. If the producing party claims that the writing includes unrelated matter, the court must examine the writing in camera, delete any unrelated portion, and order that the rest be delivered to the adverse party. Any portion deleted over objection must be preserved for the record.

(c) Failure to Produce or Deliver the Writing. If a writing is not produced or is not delivered as ordered, the court may issue any appropriate order. But if the prosecution does not comply in a criminal case, the court must strike the witness's testimony or—if justice so requires—declare a mistrial.

(Pub.L. 93–595, § 1, Jan. 2, 1975, 88 Stat. 1936; Mar. 2, 1987, eff. Oct. 1, 1987; Apr. 26, 2011, eff. Dec. 1, 2011.)

RULE 613. WITNESS'S PRIOR STATEMENT

(a) Showing or Disclosing the Statement During Examination. When examining a witness about the witness's prior statement, a party need not show it or disclose its contents to the witness. But the party must, on request, show it or disclose its contents to an adverse party's attorney.

(b) Extrinsic Evidence of a Prior Inconsistent Statement. Extrinsic evidence of a witness's prior inconsistent statement is admissible only if the witness is given an opportunity to explain or deny the statement and an adverse party is given an opportunity to examine the witness about it, or if justice so requires. This subdivision (b) does not apply to an opposing party's statement under Rule 801(d)(2).

(Pub.L. 93–595, § 1, Jan. 2, 1975, 88 Stat.1936; Mar. 2, 1987, eff. Oct. 1, 1987; Apr. 25, 1988, eff. Nov. 1, 1988; Apr. 26, 2011, eff. Dec. 1, 2011.)

RULE 614. COURT'S CALLING OR EXAMINING A WITNESS

(a) Calling. The court may call a witness on its own or at a party's request. Each party is entitled to cross-examine the witness.

(b) Examining. The court may examine a witness regardless of who calls the witness.

(c) Objections. A party may object to the court's calling or examining a witness either at that time or at the next opportunity when the jury is not present.

(Pub.L. 93–595, § 1, Jan. 2, 1975, 88 Stat.1937; Apr. 26, 2011, eff. Dec. 1, 2011.)

RULE 615. EXCLUDING WITNESSES

At a party's request, the court must order witnesses excluded so that they cannot hear other witnesses' testimony. Or the court may do so on its own. But this rule does not authorize excluding:

(a) a party who is a natural person;

(b) an officer or employee of a party that is not a natural person, after being designated as the party's representative by its attorney;

(c) a person whose presence a party shows to be essential to presenting the party's claim or defense; or

(d) a person authorized by statute to be present.

(Pub.L. 93–595, § 1, Jan. 2, 1975, 88 Stat.1937; Mar. 2, 1987, eff. Oct. 1, 1987; Apr. 25, 1988, eff. Nov. 1, 1988; Pub.L. 100–690, Nov. 18, 1988, Title VII, § 7075(a), 102 Stat. 4405; Apr. 24, 1998, eff. Dec. 1, 1998; Apr. 26, 2011, eff. Dec. 1, 2011.)

ARTICLE VII. OPINIONS AND EXPERT TESTIMONY

RULE 701. OPINION TESTIMONY BY LAY WITNESSES

If a witness is not testifying as an expert, testimony in the form of an opinion is limited to one that is:

(a) rationally based on the witness's perception;

(b) helpful to clearly understanding the witness's testimony or to determining a fact in issue; and

(c) not based on scientific, technical, or other specialized knowledge within the scope of Rule 702.

(Pub.L. 93–595, § 1, Jan. 2, 1975, 88 Stat.1937; Mar. 2, 1987, eff. Oct. 1, 1987; Apr. 17, 2000, eff. Dec. 1, 2000; Apr. 26, 2011, eff. Dec. 1, 2011.)

RULE 702. TESTIMONY BY EXPERT WITNESSES

A witness who is qualified as an expert by knowledge, skill, experience, training, or education may testify in the form of an opinion or otherwise if:

(a) the expert's scientific, technical, or other specialized knowledge will help the trier of fact to understand the evidence or to determine a fact in issue;

(b) the testimony is based on sufficient facts or data;

(c) the testimony is the product of reliable principles and methods; and

(d) the expert has reliably applied the principles and methods to the facts of the case.

(Pub.L. 93–595, § 1, Jan. 2, 1975, 88 Stat. 1937; Apr. 17, 2000, eff. Dec. 1, 2000; Apr. 26, 2011, eff. Dec. 1, 2011.)

RULE 703. BASES OF AN EXPERT'S OPINION TESTIMONY

An expert may base an opinion on facts or data in the case that the expert has been made aware of or personally observed. If experts in the particular field would reasonably rely on those kinds of facts or data in forming an opinion on the subject, they need not be admissible for the opinion to be admitted. But if the facts or data would otherwise be inadmissible, the proponent of the opinion may disclose them to the jury only if their probative value in helping the jury evaluate the opinion substantially outweighs their prejudicial effect.

(Pub.L. 93–595, § 1, Jan. 2, 1975, 88 Stat.1937; Mar. 2, 1987, eff. Oct. 1, 1987; Apr. 17, 2000, eff. Dec. 1, 2000; Apr. 26, 2011, eff. Dec. 1, 2011.)

RULE 704. OPINION ON AN ULTIMATE ISSUE

(a) In General—Not Automatically Objectionable. An opinion is not objectionable just because it embraces an ultimate issue.

(b) Exception. In a criminal case, an expert witness must not state an opinion about whether the defendant did or did not have a mental state or condition that constitutes an element of the crime charged or of a defense. Those matters are for the trier of fact alone.

(Pub.L. 93–595, § 1, Jan. 2, 1975, 88 Stat. 1937; Pub.L. 98–473, Title II, § 406, Oct. 12, 1984, 98 Stat. 2067; Apr. 26, 2011, eff. Dec. 1, 2011.)

RULE 705. DISCLOSING THE FACTS OR DATA UNDERLYING AN EXPERT'S OPINION

Unless the court orders otherwise, an expert may state an opinion—and give the reasons for it—without first testifying to the underlying facts or data. But the expert may be required to disclose those facts or data on cross-examination.

(Pub.L. 93–595, § 1, Jan. 2, 1975, 88 Stat. 1938; Mar. 2, 1987, eff. Oct. 1, 1987; Apr. 22, 1993, eff. Dec. 1, 1993; Apr. 26, 2011, eff. Dec. 1, 2011.)

RULE 706. COURT–APPOINTED EXPERT WITNESSES

(a) Appointment Process. On a party's motion or on its own, the court may order the parties to show cause why expert witnesses should not be appointed and may ask the parties to submit nominations. The court may appoint any expert that the parties agree on and any of its own choosing. But the court may only appoint someone who consents to act.

(b) Expert's Role. The court must inform the expert of the expert's duties. The court may do so in writing and have a copy filed with the clerk or may do so orally at a conference in which the parties have an opportunity to participate. The expert:

(1) must advise the parties of any findings the expert makes;

(2) may be deposed by any party;

(3) may be called to testify by the court or any party; and

(4) may be cross-examined by any party, including the party that called the expert.

(c) Compensation. The expert is entitled to a reasonable compensation, as set by the court. The compensation is payable as follows:

(1) in a criminal case or in a civil case involving just compensation under the Fifth Amendment, from any funds that are provided by law; and

(2) in any other civil case, by the parties in the proportion and at the time that the court directs—and the compensation is then charged like other costs.

(d) Disclosing the Appointment to the Jury. The court may authorize disclosure to the jury that the court appointed the expert.

(e) Parties' Choice of Their Own Experts. This rule does not limit a party in calling its own experts.

(Pub.L. 93–595, § 1, Jan. 2, 1975, 88 Stat.1938; Mar. 2, 1987, eff. Oct. 1, 1987; Apr. 26, 2011, eff. Dec. 1, 2011.)

ARTICLE VIII. HEARSAY

RULE 801. DEFINITIONS THAT APPLY TO THIS ARTICLE; EXCLUSIONS FROM HEARSAY

(a) Statement. "Statement" means a person's oral assertion, written assertion, or nonverbal conduct, if the person intended it as an assertion.

(b) Declarant. "Declarant" means the person who made the statement.

(c) Hearsay. "Hearsay" means a statement that:

(1) the declarant does not make while testifying at the current trial or hearing; and

(2) a party offers in evidence to prove the truth of the matter asserted in the statement.

(d) Statements That Are Not Hearsay. A statement that meets the following conditions is not hearsay:

(1) **A Declarant–Witness's Prior Statement.** The declarant testifies and is subject to cross-examination about a prior statement, and the statement:

(A) is inconsistent with the declarant's testimony and was given under penalty of perjury at a trial, hearing, or other proceeding or in a deposition;

(B) is consistent with the declarant's testimony and is offered:

(i) to rebut an express or implied charge that the declarant recently fabricated it or acted from a recent improper influence or motive in so testifying; or

(ii) to rehabilitate the declarant's credibility as a witness when attacked on another ground; or

(C) identifies a person as someone the declarant perceived earlier.

(2) **An Opposing Party's Statement.** The statement is offered against an opposing party and:

(A) was made by the party in an individual or representative capacity;

(B) is one the party manifested that it adopted or believed to be true;

(C) was made by a person whom the party authorized to make a statement on the subject;

(D) was made by the party's agent or employee on a matter within the scope of that relationship and while it existed; or

(E) was made by the party's coconspirator during and in furtherance of the conspiracy.

The statement must be considered but does not by itself establish the declarant's authority under (C); the existence or scope of the relationship under (D); or the existence of the conspiracy or participation in it under (E).

(Pub.L. 93–595, § 1, Jan. 2, 1975, 88 Stat.1938; Pub.L. 94–113, § 1, Oct. 16, 1975, 89 Stat. 576; Mar. 2, 1987, eff. Oct. 1, 1987; Apr. 11, 1997, eff. Dec. 1, 1997; Apr. 26, 2011, eff. Dec. 1, 2011; Apr. 25, 2014, eff. Dec. 1, 2014.)

RULE 802. THE RULE AGAINST HEARSAY

Hearsay is not admissible unless any of the following provides otherwise:

- a federal statute;
- these rules; or
- other rules prescribed by the Supreme Court.

(Pub.L. 93–595, § 1, Jan. 2, 1975, 88 Stat. 1939; Apr. 26, 2011, eff. Dec. 1, 2011.)

RULE 803. EXCEPTIONS TO THE RULE AGAINST HEARSAY—REGARDLESS OF WHETHER THE DECLARANT IS AVAILABLE AS A WITNESS

The following are not excluded by the rule against hearsay, regardless of whether the declarant is available as a witness:

(1) **Present Sense Impression.** A statement describing or explaining an event or condition, made while or immediately after the declarant perceived it.

(2) **Excited Utterance.** A statement relating to a startling event or condition, made while the declarant was under the stress of excitement that it caused.

(3) **Then–Existing Mental, Emotional, or Physical Condition.** A statement of the declarant's then-existing state of mind (such as motive, intent, or plan) or emotional, sensory, or physical condition (such as mental feeling, pain, or bodily health), but not including a statement of memory or belief to prove the fact remembered or believed unless it relates to the validity or terms of the declarant's will.

(4) **Statement Made for Medical Diagnosis or Treatment.** A statement that:

(A) is made for—and is reasonably pertinent to—medical diagnosis or treatment; and

(B) describes medical history; past or present symptoms or sensations; their inception; or their general cause.

(5) **Recorded Recollection.** A record that:

(A) is on a matter the witness once knew about but now cannot recall well enough to testify fully and accurately;

(B) was made or adopted by the witness when the matter was fresh in the witness's memory; and

(C) accurately reflects the witness's knowledge.

If admitted, the record may be read into evidence but may be received as an exhibit only if offered by an adverse party.

(6) Records of a Regularly Conducted Activity. A record of an act, event, condition, opinion, or diagnosis if:

(A) the record was made at or near the time by—or from information transmitted by—someone with knowledge;

(B) the record was kept in the course of a regularly conducted activity of a business, organization, occupation, or calling, whether or not for profit;

(C) making the record was a regular practice of that activity;

(D) all these conditions are shown by the testimony of the custodian or another qualified witness, or by a certification that complies with Rule 902(11) or (12) or with a statute permitting certification; and

(E) the opponent does not show that the source of information or the method or circumstances of preparation indicate a lack of trustworthiness.

(7) Absence of a Record of a Regularly Conducted Activity. Evidence that a matter is not included in a record described in paragraph (6) if:

(A) the evidence is admitted to prove that the matter did not occur or exist;

(B) a record was regularly kept for a matter of that kind; and

(C) the opponent does not show that the possible source of the information or other circumstances indicate a lack of trustworthiness.

(8) Public Records. A record or statement of a public office if:

(A) it sets out:

(i) the office's activities;

(ii) a matter observed while under a legal duty to report, but not including, in a criminal case, a matter observed by law-enforcement personnel; or

(iii) in a civil case or against the government in a criminal case, factual findings from a legally authorized investigation; and

(B) the opponent does not show that the source of information or other circumstances indicate a lack of trustworthiness.

(9) Public Records of Vital Statistics. A record of a birth, death, or marriage, if reported to a public office in accordance with a legal duty.

(10) Absence of a Public Record. Testimony—or a certification under Rule 902—that a diligent search failed to disclose a public record or statement if:

(A) the testimony or certification is admitted to prove that

(i) the record or statement does not exist; or

(ii) a matter did not occur or exist, if a public office regularly kept a record or statement for a matter of that kind; and

(B) in a criminal case, a prosecutor who intends to offer a certification provides written notice of that intent at least 14 days before trial, and the defendant does not object in writing within 7 days of receiving the notice—unless the court sets a different time for the notice or the objection.

(11) Records of Religious Organizations Concerning Personal or Family History. A statement of birth, legitimacy, ancestry, marriage, divorce, death, relationship by blood or marriage, or similar facts of personal or family history, contained in a regularly kept record of a religious organization.

(12) Certificates of Marriage, Baptism, and Similar Ceremonies. A statement of fact contained in a certificate:

(A) made by a person who is authorized by a religious organization or by law to perform the act certified;

(B) attesting that the person performed a marriage or similar ceremony or administered a sacrament; and

(C) purporting to have been issued at the time of the act or within a reasonable time after it.

(13) Family Records. A statement of fact about personal or family history contained in a family record, such as a Bible, genealogy, chart, engraving on a ring, inscription on a portrait, or engraving on an urn or burial marker.

(14) Records of Documents That Affect an Interest in Property. The record of a document that purports to establish or affect an interest in property if:

(A) the record is admitted to prove the content of the original recorded document, along with its signing and its delivery by each person who purports to have signed it;

(B) the record is kept in a public office; and

(C) a statute authorizes recording documents of that kind in that office.

(15) Statements in Documents That Affect an Interest in Property. A statement contained in a document that purports to establish or affect an interest in property if the matter stated was relevant to the document's purpose—unless later dealings with the property are inconsistent with the truth of the statement or the purport of the document.

(16) Statements in Ancient Documents. A statement in a document that was prepared before January 1, 1998, and whose authenticity is established.

(17) Market Reports and Similar Commercial Publications. Market quotations, lists, directories, or other compilations that are generally relied on by the public or by persons in particular occupations.

(18) Statements in Learned Treatises, Periodicals, or Pamphlets. A statement contained in a treatise, periodical, or pamphlet if:

(A) the statement is called to the attention of an expert witness on cross-examination or relied on by the expert on direct examination; and

(B) the publication is established as a reliable authority by the expert's admission or testimony, by another expert's testimony, or by judicial notice.

If admitted, the statement may be read into evidence but not received as an exhibit.

(19) Reputation Concerning Personal or Family History. A reputation among a person's family by blood, adoption, or marriage—or among a person's associates or in the community—concerning the person's birth, adoption, legitimacy, ancestry, marriage, divorce, death, relationship by blood, adoption, or marriage, or similar facts of personal or family history.

(20) Reputation Concerning Boundaries or General History. A reputation in a community—arising before the controversy—concerning boundaries of land in the community or customs that affect the land, or concerning general historical events important to that community, state, or nation.

(21) Reputation Concerning Character. A reputation among a person's associates or in the community concerning the person's character.

(22) Judgment of a Previous Conviction. Evidence of a final judgment of conviction if:

(A) the judgment was entered after a trial or guilty plea, but not a nolo contendere plea;

(B) the conviction was for a crime punishable by death or by imprisonment for more than a year;

(C) the evidence is admitted to prove any fact essential to the judgment; and

(D) when offered by the prosecutor in a criminal case for a purpose other than impeachment, the judgment was against the defendant.

The pendency of an appeal may be shown but does not affect admissibility.

(23) Judgments Involving Personal, Family, or General History, or a Boundary. A judgment that is admitted to prove a matter of personal, family, or general history, or boundaries, if the matter:

(A) was essential to the judgment; and

(B) could be proved by evidence of reputation.

(24) [Other Exceptions.] [Transferred to Rule 807.]

(Pub.L. 93–595, § 1, Jan. 2, 1975, 88 Stat. 1939; Pub.L. 94–149, § 1(11), Dec. 12, 1975, 89 Stat. 805; Mar. 2, 1987, eff. Oct. 1, 1987; Apr. 11, 1997, eff. Dec. 1, 1997; Apr. 17, 2000, eff. Dec. 1, 2000; Apr. 26, 2011, eff. Dec. 1, 2011; Apr. 13, 2013, eff. Dec. 1, 2013; Apr. 25, 2014, eff. Dec. 1, 2014; Apr. 27, 2017, eff. Dec. 1, 2017.)

RULE 804. EXCEPTIONS TO THE RULE AGAINST HEARSAY—WHEN THE DECLARANT IS UNAVAILABLE AS A WITNESS

(a) Criteria for Being Unavailable. A declarant is considered to be unavailable as a witness if the declarant:

(1) is exempted from testifying about the subject matter of the declarant's statement because the court rules that a privilege applies;

(2) refuses to testify about the subject matter despite a court order to do so;

(3) testifies to not remembering the subject matter;

(4) cannot be present or testify at the trial or hearing because of death or a then-existing infirmity, physical illness, or mental illness; or

(5) is absent from the trial or hearing and the statement's proponent has not been able, by process or other reasonable means, to procure:

(A) the declarant's attendance, in the case of a hearsay exception under Rule 804(b)(1) or (6); or

(B) the declarant's attendance or testimony, in the case of a hearsay exception under Rule 804(b)(2), (3), or (4).

But this subdivision (a) does not apply if the statement's proponent procured or wrongfully caused the declarant's unavailability as a witness in order to prevent the declarant from attending or testifying.

(b) The Exceptions. The following are not excluded by the rule against hearsay if the declarant is unavailable as a witness:

(1) Former Testimony. Testimony that:

(A) was given as a witness at a trial, hearing, or lawful deposition, whether given during the current proceeding or a different one; and

(B) is now offered against a party who had—or, in a civil case, whose predecessor in interest had—an opportunity and similar motive to develop it by direct, cross-, or redirect examination.

(2) Statement Under the Belief of Imminent Death. In a prosecution for homicide or in a civil case, a statement that the declarant, while believing the declarant's death to be imminent, made about its cause or circumstances.

(3) Statement Against Interest. A statement that:

(A) a reasonable person in the declarant's position would have made only if the person believed it to be true because, when made, it was so contrary to the declarant's proprietary or pecuniary interest or had so great a tendency to invalidate the declarant's claim against someone else or to expose the declarant to civil or criminal liability; and

(B) is supported by corroborating circumstances that clearly indicate its trustworthiness, if it is offered in a criminal case as one that tends to expose the declarant to criminal liability.

(4) Statement of Personal or Family History. A statement about:

(A) the declarant's own birth, adoption, legitimacy, ancestry, marriage, divorce, relationship by blood, adoption, or marriage, or similar facts of personal or family history, even though the declarant had no way of acquiring personal knowledge about that fact; or

(B) another person concerning any of these facts, as well as death, if the declarant was related to the person by blood, adoption, or marriage or was so intimately associated with the person's family that the declarant's information is likely to be accurate.

(5) [**Other Exceptions.**] [Transferred to Rule 807.]

(6) Statement Offered Against a Party That Wrongfully Caused the Declarant's Unavailability. A statement offered against a party that wrongfully caused—or acquiesced in wrongfully causing—the declarant's unavailability as a witness, and did so intending that result.

(Pub.L. 93–595, § 1, Jan. 2, 1975, 88 Stat. 1942; Pub.L. 94–149, § 1(12), (13), Dec. 12, 1975, 89 Stat. 806; Mar. 2, 1987, eff. Oct. 1, 1987; Pub.L. 100–690, Title VII, § 7075(b), Nov. 18, 1988, 102 Stat. 4405; Apr. 11, 1997, eff. Dec. 1, 1997; Apr. 28, 2010, eff. Dec. 1, 2010; Apr. 26, 2011, eff. Dec. 1, 2011.)

RULE 805. HEARSAY WITHIN HEARSAY

Hearsay within hearsay is not excluded by the rule against hearsay if each part of the combined statements conforms with an exception to the rule.

(Pub.L. 93–595, § 1, Jan. 2, 1975, 88 Stat. 1943; Apr. 26, 2011, eff. Dec. 1, 2011.)

RULE 806. ATTACKING AND SUPPORTING THE DECLARANT'S CREDIBILITY

When a hearsay statement—or a statement described in Rule 801(d)(2)(C), (D), or (E)—has been admitted in evidence, the declarant's credibility may be attacked, and then supported, by any evidence that would be admissible for those purposes if the declarant had testified as a witness. The court

may admit evidence of the declarant's inconsistent statement or conduct, regardless of when it occurred or whether the declarant had an opportunity to explain or deny it. If the party against whom the statement was admitted calls the declarant as a witness, the party may examine the declarant on the statement as if on cross-examination.

(Pub.L. 93–595, § 1, Jan. 2, 1975, 88 Stat. 1943; Mar. 2, 1987, eff. Oct. 1, 1987; Apr. 11, 1997, eff. Dec. 1, 1997; Apr. 26, 2011, eff. Dec. 1, 2011.)

RULE 807. RESIDUAL EXCEPTION

(a) In General. Under the following circumstances, a hearsay statement is not excluded by the rule against hearsay even if the statement is not specifically covered by a hearsay exception in Rule 803 or 804:

(1) the statement has equivalent circumstantial guarantees of trustworthiness;

(2) it is offered as evidence of a material fact;

(3) it is more probative on the point for which it is offered than any other evidence that the proponent can obtain through reasonable efforts; and

(4) admitting it will best serve the purposes of these rules and the interests of justice.

(b) Notice. The statement is admissible only if, before the trial or hearing, the proponent gives an adverse party reasonable notice of the intent to offer the statement and its particulars, including the declarant's name and address, so that the party has a fair opportunity to meet it.

(Added Apr. 11, 1997, eff. Dec. 1, 1997; Apr. 26, 2011, eff. Dec. 1, 2011.)

ARTICLE IX. AUTHENTICATION AND IDENTIFICATION

RULE 901. AUTHENTICATING OR IDENTIFYING EVIDENCE

(a) In General. To satisfy the requirement of authenticating or identifying an item of evidence, the proponent must produce evidence sufficient to support a finding that the item is what the proponent claims it is.

(b) Examples. The following are examples only—not a complete list—of evidence that satisfies the requirement:

(1) Testimony of a Witness with Knowledge. Testimony that an item is what it is claimed to be.

(2) Nonexpert Opinion About Handwriting. A nonexpert's opinion that handwriting is genuine, based on a familiarity with it that was not acquired for the current litigation.

(3) Comparison by an Expert Witness or the Trier of Fact. A comparison with an authenticated specimen by an expert witness or the trier of fact.

(4) Distinctive Characteristics and the Like. The appearance, contents, substance, internal patterns, or other distinctive characteristics of the item, taken together with all the circumstances.

(5) Opinion About a Voice. An opinion identifying a person's voice—whether heard firsthand or through mechanical or electronic transmission or recording—based on hearing the voice at any time under circumstances that connect it with the alleged speaker.

(6) Evidence About a Telephone Conversation. For a telephone conversation, evidence that a call was made to the number assigned at the time to:

(A) a particular person, if circumstances, including self-identification, show that the person answering was the one called; or

(B) a particular business, if the call was made to a business and the call related to business reasonably transacted over the telephone.

(7) Evidence About Public Records. Evidence that:

(A) a document was recorded or filed in a public office as authorized by law; or

(B) a purported public record or statement is from the office where items of this kind are kept.

(8) Evidence About Ancient Documents or Data Compilations. For a document or data compilation, evidence that it:

   (A) is in a condition that creates no suspicion about its authenticity;

   (B) was in a place where, if authentic, it would likely be; and

   (C) is at least 20 years old when offered.

(9) Evidence About a Process or System. Evidence describing a process or system and showing that it produces an accurate result. → *necessary "machine" discussion*

(10) Methods Provided by a Statute or Rule. Any method of authentication or identification allowed by a federal statute or a rule prescribed by the Supreme Court.

(Pub.L. 93–595, § 1, Jan. 2, 1975, 88 Stat.1943; Apr. 26, 2011, eff. Dec. 1, 2011.)

RULE 902. EVIDENCE THAT IS SELF–AUTHENTICATING

The following items of evidence are self-authenticating; they require no extrinsic evidence of authenticity in order to be admitted:

(1) Domestic Public Documents That Are Sealed and Signed. A document that bears:

   (A) a seal purporting to be that of the United States; any state, district, commonwealth, territory, or insular possession of the United States; the former Panama Canal Zone; the Trust Territory of the Pacific Islands; a political subdivision of any of these entities; or a department, agency, or officer of any entity named above; and

   (B) a signature purporting to be an execution or attestation.

(2) Domestic Public Documents That Are Not Sealed but Are Signed and Certified. A document that bears no seal if:

   (A) it bears the signature of an officer or employee of an entity named in Rule 902(1)(A); and

   (B) another public officer who has a seal and official duties within that same entity certifies under seal—or its equivalent—that the signer has the official capacity and that the signature is genuine.

(3) Foreign Public Documents. A document that purports to be signed or attested by a person who is authorized by a foreign country's law to do so. The document must be accompanied by a final certification that certifies the genuineness of the signature and official position of the signer or attester—or of any foreign official whose certificate of genuineness relates to the signature or attestation or is in a chain of certificates of genuineness relating to the signature or attestation. The certification may be made by a secretary of a United States embassy or legation; by a consul general, vice consul, or consular agent of the United States; or by a diplomatic or consular official of the foreign country assigned or accredited to the United States. If all parties have been given a reasonable opportunity to investigate the document's authenticity and accuracy, the court may, for good cause, either:

   (A) order that it be treated as presumptively authentic without final certification; or

   (B) allow it to be evidenced by an attested summary with or without final certification.

(4) Certified Copies of Public Records. A copy of an official record—or a copy of a document that was recorded or filed in a public office as authorized by law—if the copy is certified as correct by:

   (A) the custodian or another person authorized to make the certification; or

   (B) a certificate that complies with Rule 902(1), (2), or (3), a federal statute, or a rule prescribed by the Supreme Court.

(5) Official Publications. A book, pamphlet, or other publication purporting to be issued by a public authority.

(6) Newspapers and Periodicals. Printed material purporting to be a newspaper or periodical.

(7) Trade Inscriptions and the Like. An inscription, sign, tag, or label purporting to have been affixed in the course of business and indicating origin, ownership, or control.

(8) Acknowledged Documents. A document accompanied by a certificate of acknowledgment that is lawfully executed by a notary public or another officer who is authorized to take acknowledgments.

(9) Commercial Paper and Related Documents. Commercial paper, a signature on it, and related documents, to the extent allowed by general commercial law.

(10) Presumptions Under a Federal Statute. A signature, document, or anything else that a federal statute declares to be presumptively or prima facie genuine or authentic.

(11) Certified Domestic Records of a Regularly Conducted Activity. The original or a copy of a domestic record that meets the requirements of Rule 803(6)(A)–(C), as shown by a certification of the custodian or another qualified person that complies with a federal statute or a rule prescribed by the Supreme Court. Before the trial or hearing, the proponent must give an adverse party reasonable written notice of the intent to offer the record—and must make the record and certification available for inspection—so that the party has a fair opportunity to challenge them.

(12) Certified Foreign Records of a Regularly Conducted Activity. In a civil case, the original or a copy of a foreign record that meets the requirements of Rule 902(11), modified as follows: the certification, rather than complying with a federal statute or Supreme Court rule, must be signed in a manner that, if falsely made, would subject the maker to a criminal penalty in the country where the certification is signed. The proponent must also meet the notice requirements of Rule 902(11).

(13) Certified Records Generated by an Electronic Process or System. A record generated by an electronic process or system that produces an accurate result, as shown by a certification of a qualified person that complies with the certification requirements of Rule 902(11) or (12).

The proponent must also meet the notice requirements of Rule 902(11).

(14) **Certified Data Copied from an Electronic Device, Storage Medium, or File.** Data copied from an electronic device, storage medium, or file, if authenticated by a process of digital identification, as shown by a certification of a qualified person that complies with the certification requirements of Rule 902(11) or (12). The proponent also must meet the notice requirements of Rule 902(11).

(Pub.L. 93–595, § 1, Jan. 2, 1975, 88 Stat. 1944; Mar. 2, 1987, eff. Oct. 1, 1987; Apr. 25, 1988, eff. Nov. 1, 1988; Apr. 17, 2000, eff. Dec. 1, 2000; Apr. 26, 2011, eff. Dec. 1, 2011; Apr. 27, 2017, eff. Dec. 1, 2017.)

ARTICLE X.   CONTENTS OF WRITINGS, RECORDINGS, AND PHOTOGRAPHS

RULE 1001. DEFINITIONS THAT APPLY TO THIS ARTICLE

In this article:

(a) A "writing" consists of letters, words, numbers, or their equivalent set down in any form.

(b) A "recording" consists of letters, words, numbers, or their equivalent recorded in any manner.

(c) A "photograph" means a photographic image or its equivalent stored in any form.

(d) An "original" of a writing or recording means the writing or recording itself or any counterpart intended to have the same effect by the person who executed or issued it. For electronically stored information, "original" means any printout—or other output readable by sight—if it accurately reflects the information. An "original" of a photograph includes the negative or a print from it.

(e) A "duplicate" means a counterpart produced by a mechanical, photographic, chemical, electronic, or other equivalent process or technique that accurately reproduces the original.

(Pub.L. 93–595, § 1, Jan. 2, 1975, 88 Stat. 1945; Apr. 26, 2011, eff. Dec. 1, 2011.)

RULE 1002. REQUIREMENT OF THE ORIGINAL

An original writing, recording, or photograph is required in order to prove its content unless these rules or a federal statute provides otherwise.

(Pub.L. 93–595, § 1, Jan. 2, 1975, 88 Stat. 1946; Apr. 26, 2011, eff. Dec. 1, 2011.)

RULE 1003. ADMISSIBILITY OF DUPLICATES

A duplicate is admissible to the same extent as the original unless a genuine question is raised about the original's authenticity or the circumstances make it unfair to admit the duplicate.

(Pub.L. 93–595, § 1, Jan. 2, 1975, 88 Stat. 1946; Apr. 26, 2011, eff. Dec. 1, 2011.)

RULE 903. SUBSCRIBING WITNESS'S TESTIMONY

A subscribing witness's testimony is necessary to authenticate a writing only if required by the law of the jurisdiction that governs its validity.

(Pub.L. 93–595, § 1, Jan. 2, 1975, 88 Stat.1945; Apr. 26, 2011, eff. Dec. 1, 2011.)

RULE 1004. ADMISSIBILITY OF OTHER EVIDENCE OF CONTENT

An original is not required and other evidence of the content of a writing, recording, or photograph is admissible if:

(a) all the originals are lost or destroyed, and not by the proponent acting in bad faith;

(b) an original cannot be obtained by any available judicial process;

(c) the party against whom the original would be offered had control of the original; was at that time put on notice, by pleadings or otherwise, that the original would be a subject of proof at the trial or hearing; and fails to produce it at the trial or hearing; or

(d) the writing, recording, or photograph is not closely related to a controlling issue.

(Pub.L. 93–595, § 1, Jan. 2, 1975, 88 Stat. 1946; Mar. 2, 1987, eff. Oct. 1, 1987; Apr. 26, 2011, eff. Dec. 1, 2011.)

RULE 1005. COPIES OF PUBLIC RECORDS TO PROVE CONTENT

The proponent may use a copy to prove the content of an official record—or of a document that was recorded or filed in a public office as authorized by law—if these conditions are met: the record or document is otherwise admissible; and the copy is certified as correct in accordance with Rule 902(4) or is testified to be correct by a witness who has compared it with the original. If no such copy can be obtained by reasonable diligence, then the proponent may use other evidence to prove the content.

(Pub.L. 93–595, § 1, Jan. 2, 1975, 88 Stat. 1946; Apr. 26, 2011, eff. Dec. 1, 2011.)

RULE 1006. SUMMARIES TO PROVE CONTENT

The proponent may use a summary, chart, or calculation to prove the content of voluminous writings, recordings, or photographs that cannot be conveniently examined in court. The proponent must make the originals or duplicates available for examination or copying, or both, by other parties at a reasonable time and place. And the court may order the proponent to produce them in court.

(Pub.L. 93–595, § 1, Jan. 2, 1975, 88 Stat. 1946; Apr. 26, 2011, eff. Dec. 1, 2011.)

RULE 1007. TESTIMONY OR STATEMENT OF A PARTY TO PROVE CONTENT

The proponent may prove the content of a writing, recording, or photograph by the testimony, deposition, or written statement of the party against whom the evidence is offered. The proponent need not account for the original.

(Pub.L. 93–595, § 1, Jan. 2, 1975, 88 Stat. 1947; Mar. 2, 1987, eff. Oct. 1, 1987; Apr. 26, 2011, eff. Dec. 1, 2011.)

RULE 1008. FUNCTIONS OF THE COURT AND JURY

Ordinarily, the court determines whether the proponent has fulfilled the factual conditions for admitting other evidence of the content of a writing, recording, or photograph under Rule 1004 or 1005. But in a jury trial, the jury determines—in accordance with Rule 104(b)—any issue about whether:

(a) an asserted writing, recording, or photograph ever existed;

(b) another one produced at the trial or hearing is the original; or

(c) other evidence of content accurately reflects the content.

(Pub.L. 93–595, § 1, Jan. 2, 1975, 88 Stat. 1947; Apr. 26, 2011, eff. Dec. 1, 2011.)

ARTICLE XI. MISCELLANEOUS RULES

RULE 1101. APPLICABILITY OF THE RULES

(a) To Courts and Judges. These rules apply to proceedings before:

- United States district courts;
- United States bankruptcy and magistrate judges;
- United States courts of appeals;
- the United States Court of Federal Claims; and
- the district courts of Guam, the Virgin Islands, and the Northern Mariana Islands.

(b) To Cases and Proceedings. These rules apply in:

- civil cases and proceedings, including bankruptcy, admiralty, and maritime cases;
- criminal cases and proceedings; and
- contempt proceedings, except those in which the court may act summarily.

(c) Rules on Privilege. The rules on privilege apply to all stages of a case or proceeding.

(d) Exceptions. These rules—except for those on privilege—do not apply to the following:

(1) the court's determination, under Rule 104(a), on a preliminary question of fact governing admissibility;

(2) grand-jury proceedings; and

(3) miscellaneous proceedings such as:

- extradition or rendition;

- issuing an arrest warrant, criminal summons, or search warrant;
- a preliminary examination in a criminal case;
- sentencing;
- granting or revoking probation or supervised release; and
- considering whether to release on bail or otherwise.

(e) Other Statutes and Rules. A federal statute or a rule prescribed by the Supreme Court may provide for admitting or excluding evidence independently from these rules.

(Pub.L. 93–595, § 1, Jan. 2, 1975, 88 Stat. 1947; Pub.L. 94–149, § 1(14), Dec. 12, 1975, 89 Stat. 806; Pub.L. 95–598, Title II, §§ 251, 252, Nov. 6, 1978, 92 Stat. 2673; Pub.L. 97–164, Title I, § 142, Apr. 2, 1982, 96 Stat. 45; Mar. 2, 1987, eff. Oct. 1, 1987; Apr. 25, 1988, eff. Nov. 1, 1988; Pub.L. 100–690, Title VII, § 7075(c), Nov. 18, 1988, 102 Stat. 4405; Apr. 22, 1993, eff. Dec. 1, 1993; Apr. 26, 2011, eff. Dec. 1, 2011.)

RULE 1102. AMENDMENTS

These rules may be amended as provided in 28 U.S.C. § 2072.

(Pub.L. 93–595, § 1, Jan. 2, 1975, 88 Stat.1948; Apr. 30, 1991, eff. Dec. 1, 1991; Apr. 26, 2011, eff. Dec. 1, 2011.)

RULE 1103. TITLE

These rules may be cited as the Federal Rules of Evidence.

(Pub.L. 93–595, § 1, Jan. 2, 1975, 88 Stat.1948; Apr. 26, 2011, eff. Dec. 1, 2011.)

INDEX TO
FEDERAL RULES OF EVIDENCE

FEDERAL RULES OF APPELLATE PROCEDURE

Including Amendments Effective December 1, 2018

TITLE I. APPLICABILITY OF RULES

RULE 1. SCOPE OF RULES; DEFINITION; TITLE

(a) Scope of Rules.

(1) These rules govern procedure in the United States courts of appeals.

(2) When these rules provide for filing a motion or other document in the district court, the procedure must comply with the practice of the district court.

(b) Definition. In these rules, "state" includes the District of Columbia and any United States commonwealth or territory.

(c) Title. These rules are to be known as the Federal Rules of Appellate Procedure.

(As amended Apr. 30, 1979, eff. Aug. 1, 1979; Apr. 25, 1989, eff. Dec. 1, 1989; Apr. 29, 1994, eff. Dec. 1, 1994; Apr. 24, 1998, eff. Dec. 1, 1998; Apr. 29, 2002, eff. Dec. 1, 2002; Apr. 28, 2010, eff. Dec. 1, 2010.)

RULE 2. SUSPENSION OF RULES

On its own or a party's motion, a court of appeals may—to expedite its decision or for other good cause—suspend any provision of these rules in a particular case and order proceedings as it directs, except as otherwise provided in Rule 26(b).

(As amended Apr. 24, 1998, eff. Dec. 1, 1998.)

TITLE II. APPEAL FROM A JUDGMENT OR ORDER OF A DISTRICT COURT

RULE 3. APPEAL AS OF RIGHT—HOW TAKEN

(a) Filing the Notice of Appeal.

(1) An appeal permitted by law as of right from a district court to a court of appeals may be taken only by filing a notice of appeal with the district clerk within the time allowed by Rule 4. At the time of filing, the appellant must furnish the clerk with enough copies of the notice to enable the clerk to comply with Rule 3(d).

(2) An appellant's failure to take any step other than the timely filing of a notice of appeal does not affect the validity of the appeal, but is ground only for the court of appeals to act as it considers appropriate, including dismissing the appeal.

(3) An appeal from a judgment by a magistrate judge in a civil case is taken in the same way as an appeal from any other district court judgment.

(4) An appeal by permission under 28 U.S.C. § 1292(b) or an appeal in a bankruptcy case may be taken only in the manner prescribed by Rules 5 and 6, respectively.

(b) Joint or Consolidated Appeals.

(1) When two or more parties are entitled to appeal from a district-court judgment or order, and their interests make joinder practicable, they may file a joint notice of appeal. They may then proceed on appeal as a single appellant.

(2) When the parties have filed separate timely notices of appeal, the appeals may be joined or consolidated by the court of appeals.

(c) Contents of the Notice of Appeal.

(1) The notice of appeal must:

(A) specify the party or parties taking the appeal by naming each one in the caption or body of the notice, but an attorney representing more than one party may describe those parties with such terms as "all plaintiffs," "the defendants," "the plaintiffs A, B, et al.," or "all defendants except X";

(B) designate the judgment, order, or part thereof being appealed; and

(C) name the court to which the appeal is taken.

(2) A pro se notice of appeal is considered filed on behalf of the signer and the signer's spouse and minor children (if they are parties), unless the notice clearly indicates otherwise.

(3) In a class action, whether or not the class has been certified, the notice of appeal is sufficient if it names one person qualified to bring the appeal as representative of the class.

(4) An appeal must not be dismissed for informality of form or title of the notice of appeal, or for failure to name a party whose intent to appeal is otherwise clear from the notice.

(5) Form 1 in the Appendix of Forms is a suggested form of a notice of appeal.

(d) Serving the Notice of Appeal.

(1) The district clerk must serve notice of the filing of a notice of appeal by mailing a copy to each party's counsel of record—excluding the appellant's—or, if a party is proceeding pro se, to the party's last known address. When a defendant in a criminal case appeals, the clerk must also serve a copy of the notice of appeal on the defendant, either by personal service or by mail addressed to the defendant. The clerk must promptly send a copy of the notice of appeal and of the docket entries—and any later docket entries—to the clerk of the court of appeals named in the notice. The district clerk must note, on each copy, the date when the notice of appeal was filed.

(2) If an inmate confined in an institution files a notice of appeal in the manner provided by Rule 4(c), the district clerk must also note the date when the clerk docketed the notice.

(3) The district clerk's failure to serve notice does not affect the validity of the appeal. The clerk must note on the docket the names of the parties to whom the clerk mails copies, with the date of mailing. Service is sufficient despite the death of a party or the party's counsel.

(e) Payment of Fees. Upon filing a notice of appeal, the appellant must pay the district clerk all required fees. The district clerk receives the appellate docket fee on behalf of the court of appeals.

(As amended Apr. 30, 1979, eff. Aug. 1, 1979; Mar. 10, 1986, eff. July 1, 1986; Apr. 25, 1989, eff. Dec. 1, 1989; Apr. 22, 1993, eff. Dec. 1, 1993; Apr. 29, 1994, eff. Dec. 1, 1994; Apr. 24, 1998, eff. Dec. 1, 1998.)

[RULE 3.1. APPEAL FROM A JUDGMENT OF A MAGISTRATE JUDGE IN A CIVIL CASE (ABROGATED APR. 24, 1998, EFF. DEC. 1, 1998)]

RULE 4. APPEAL AS OF RIGHT— WHEN TAKEN

(a) Appeal in a Civil Case.

(1) Time for Filing a Notice of Appeal.

(A) In a civil case, except as provided in Rules 4(a)(1)(B), 4(a)(4), and 4(c), the notice of appeal required by Rule 3 must be filed with the district clerk within 30 days after entry of the judgment or order appealed from.

(B) The notice of appeal may be filed by any party within 60 days after entry of the judgment or order appealed from if one of the parties is:

(i) the United States;

(ii) a United States agency;

(iii) a United States officer or employee sued in an official capacity; or

(iv) a current or former United States officer or employee sued in an individual capacity for an act or omission occurring in connection with duties performed on the United States' behalf—including all instances in which the United States represents that person when the judgment or order is entered or files the appeal for that person.

(C) An appeal from an order granting or denying an application for a writ of error coram nobis is an appeal in a civil case for purposes of Rule 4(a).

(2) Filing Before Entry of Judgment. A notice of appeal filed after the court announces a decision or order—but before the entry of the judgment or order—is treated as filed on the date of and after the entry.

(3) Multiple Appeals. If one party timely files a notice of appeal, any other party may file a notice of appeal within 14 days after the date when the first notice was filed, or within the time otherwise prescribed by this Rule 4(a), whichever period ends later.

(4) Effect of a Motion on a Notice of Appeal.

(A) If a party files in the district court any of the following motions under the Federal Rules of Civil Procedure—and does so within the time allowed by those rules—the time to file an appeal runs for all parties from the entry of the order disposing of the last such remaining motion:

(i) for judgment under Rule 50(b);

(ii) to amend or make additional factual findings under Rule 52(b), whether or not granting the motion would alter the judgment;

(iii) for attorney's fees under Rule 54 if the district court extends the time to appeal under Rule 58;

(iv) to alter or amend the judgment under Rule 59;

(v) for a new trial under Rule 59; or

(vi) for relief under Rule 60 if the motion is filed no later than 28 days after the judgment is entered.

(B)(i) If a party files a notice of appeal after the court announces or enters a judgment—but before it disposes of any motion listed in Rule 4(a)(4)(A)—the notice becomes effective to appeal a judgment or order, in whole or in part, when the order disposing of the last such remaining motion is entered.

(ii) A party intending to challenge an order disposing of any motion listed in Rule 4(a)(4)(A), or a judgment's alteration or amendment upon such a motion, must file a notice of appeal, or an amended notice of appeal—in compliance with Rule 3(c)—within the time prescribed by this Rule measured from the entry of the order disposing of the last such remaining motion.

(iii) No additional fee is required to file an amended notice.

(5) Motion for Extension of Time.

(A) The district court may extend the time to file a notice of appeal if:

(i) a party so moves no later than 30 days after the time prescribed by this Rule 4(a) expires; and

(ii) regardless of whether its motion is filed before or during the 30 days after the time prescribed by this Rule 4(a) expires, that party shows excusable neglect or good cause.

(B) A motion filed before the expiration of the time prescribed in Rule 4(a)(1) or (3) may be ex parte unless the court requires otherwise. If the motion is filed after the expiration of the prescribed time, notice must be given to the other parties in accordance with local rules.

(C) No extension under this Rule 4(a)(5) may exceed 30 days after the prescribed time or 14 days after the date when the order granting the motion is entered, whichever is later.

(6) Reopening the Time to File an Appeal. The district court may reopen the time to file an appeal for a period of 14 days after the date when its order to reopen is entered, but only if all the following conditions are satisfied:

(A) the court finds that the moving party did not receive notice under Federal Rule of Civil Procedure 77(d) of the entry of the judgment or order sought to be appealed within 21 days after entry;

(B) the motion is filed within 180 days after the judgment or order is entered or within 14 days after the moving party receives notice under Federal Rule of Civil Procedure 77(d) of the entry, whichever is earlier; and

(C) the court finds that no party would be prejudiced.

(7) Entry Defined.

(A) A judgment or order is entered for purposes of this Rule 4(a):

(i) if Federal Rule of Civil Procedure 58(a) does not require a separate document, when the judgment or order is entered in the civil docket under Federal Rule of Civil Procedure 79(a); or

(ii) if Federal Rule of Civil Procedure 58(a) requires a separate document, when the judgment or order is entered in the civil docket under Federal Rule of Civil Procedure 79(a) and when the earlier of these events occurs:

- the judgment or order is set forth on a separate document, or

- 150 days have run from entry of the judgment or order in the civil docket under Federal Rule of Civil Procedure 79(a).

(B) A failure to set forth a judgment or order on a separate document when required by Federal Rule of Civil Procedure 58(a) does not affect the validity of an appeal from that judgment or order.

(b) Appeal in a Criminal Case.

(1) Time for Filing a Notice of Appeal.

(A) In a criminal case, a defendant's notice of appeal must be filed in the district court within 14 days after the later of:

(i) the entry of either the judgment or the order being appealed; or

(ii) the filing of the government's notice of appeal.

(B) When the government is entitled to appeal, its notice of appeal must be filed in the district court within 30 days after the later of:

(i) the entry of the judgment or order being appealed; or

(ii) the filing of a notice of appeal by any defendant.

(2) Filing Before Entry of Judgment. A notice of appeal filed after the court announces a decision, sentence, or order—but before the entry of the judgment or order—is treated as filed on the date of and after the entry.

(3) Effect of a Motion on a Notice of Appeal.

(A) If a defendant timely makes any of the following motions under the Federal Rules of Criminal Procedure, the notice of appeal from a judgment of conviction must be filed within 14 days after the entry of the order

disposing of the last such remaining motion, or within 14 days after the entry of the judgment of conviction, whichever period ends later. This provision applies to a timely motion:

(i) for judgment of acquittal under Rule 29;

(ii) for a new trial under Rule 33, but if based on newly discovered evidence, only if the motion is made no later than 14 days after the entry of the judgment; or

(iii) for arrest of judgment under Rule 34.

(B) A notice of appeal filed after the court announces a decision, sentence, or order—but before it disposes of any of the motions referred to in Rule 4(b)(3)(A)—becomes effective upon the later of the following:

(i) the entry of the order disposing of the last such remaining motion; or

(ii) the entry of the judgment of conviction.

(C) A valid notice of appeal is effective—without amendment—to appeal from an order disposing of any of the motions referred to in Rule 4(b)(3)(A).

(4) Motion for Extension of Time. Upon a finding of excusable neglect or good cause, the district court may—before or after the time has expired, with or without motion and notice—extend the time to file a notice of appeal for a period not to exceed 30 days from the expiration of the time otherwise prescribed by this Rule 4(b).

(5) Jurisdiction. The filing of a notice of appeal under this Rule 4(b) does not divest a district court of jurisdiction to correct a sentence under Federal Rule of Criminal Procedure 35(a), nor does the filing of a motion under 35(a) affect the validity of a notice of appeal filed before entry of the order disposing of the motion. The filing of a motion under Federal Rule of Criminal Procedure 35(a) does not suspend the time for filing a notice of appeal from a judgment of conviction.

(6) Entry Defined. A judgment or order is entered for purposes of this Rule 4(b) when it is entered on the criminal docket.

(c) Appeal by an Inmate Confined in an Institution.

(1) If an institution has a system designed for legal mail, an inmate confined there must use that system to receive the benefit of this Rule 4(c)(1). If an inmate files a notice of appeal in either a civil or a criminal case, the notice is timely if it is deposited in the institution's internal mail system on or before the last day for filing and:

(A) it is accompanied by:

(i) a declaration in compliance with 28 U.S.C. § 1746—or a notarized statement—setting out the date of deposit and stating that first-class postage is being prepaid; or

(ii) evidence (such as a postmark or date stamp) showing that the notice was so deposited and that postage was prepaid; or

(B) the court of appeals exercises its discretion to permit the later filing of a declaration or notarized statement that satisfies Rule 4(c)(1)(A)(i).

(2) If an inmate files the first notice of appeal in a civil case under this Rule 4(c), the 14–day period provided in Rule 4(a)(3) for another party to file a notice of appeal runs from the date when the district court dockets the first notice.

(3) When a defendant in a criminal case files a notice of appeal under this Rule 4(c), the 30–day period for the government to file its notice of appeal runs from the entry of the judgment or order appealed from or from the district court's docketing of the defendant's notice of appeal, whichever is later.

(d) Mistaken Filing in the Court of Appeals. If a notice of appeal in either a civil or a criminal case is mistakenly filed in the court of appeals, the clerk of that court must note on the notice the date when it was received and send it to the district clerk. The notice is then considered filed in the district court on the date so noted.

(As amended Apr. 30, 1979, eff. Aug. 1, 1979; Nov. 18, 1988, Pub.L. 100–690, Title VII, § 7111, 102 Stat. 4419; Apr. 30, 1991, eff. Dec. 1, 1991; Apr. 22, 1993, eff. Dec. 1, 1993; Apr. 27, 1995, eff. Dec. 1, 1995; Apr. 24, 1998, eff. Dec. 1, 1998; Apr. 29, 2002, eff. Dec. 1, 2002; Apr. 25, 2005, eff. Dec. 1, 2005; Mar. 26, 2009, eff. Dec. 1, 2009; Apr. 28, 2010, eff. Dec. 1, 2010; Apr. 26, 2011, eff. Dec. 1, 2011; Apr. 28, 2016, eff. Dec. 1, 2016; Apr. 27, 2017, eff. Dec. 1, 2017.)

RULE 5.   APPEAL BY PERMISSION

(a) Petition for Permission to Appeal.

(1) To request permission to appeal when an appeal is within the court of appeals' discretion, a party must file a petition for permission to appeal. The petition must be filed with the circuit clerk with proof of service on all other parties to the district-court action.

(2) The petition must be filed within the time specified by the statute or rule authorizing the appeal or, if no such time is specified, within the time provided by Rule 4(a) for filing a notice of appeal.

(3) If a party cannot petition for appeal unless the district court first enters an order granting permission to do so or stating that the necessary conditions are met, the district court may amend its order, either on its own or in response to a party's motion, to include the required permission or statement. In that event, the time to petition runs from entry of the amended order.

(b) Contents of the Petition; Answer or Cross–Petition; Oral Argument.

(1) The petition must include the following:

(A) the facts necessary to understand the question presented;

(B) the question itself;

(C) the relief sought;

(D) the reasons why the appeal should be allowed and is authorized by a statute or rule; and

(E) an attached copy of:

(i) the order, decree, or judgment complained of and any related opinion or memorandum, and

(ii) any order stating the district court's permission to appeal or finding that the necessary conditions are met.

(2) A party may file an answer in opposition or a cross-petition within 10 days after the petition is served.

(3) The petition and answer will be submitted without oral argument unless the court of appeals orders otherwise.

(c) Form of Papers; Number of Copies; Length Limits. All papers must conform to Rule 32(c)(2). An original and 3 copies must be filed unless the court requires a different number by local rule or by order in a particular case. Except by the court's permission, and excluding the accompanying documents required by Rule 5(b)(1)(E):

(1) a paper produced using a computer must not exceed 5,200 words; and

(2) a handwritten or typewritten paper must not exceed 20 pages.

(d) Grant of Permission; Fees; Cost Bond; Filing the Record.

(1) Within 14 days after the entry of the order granting permission to appeal, the appellant must:

(A) pay the district clerk all required fees; and

(B) file a cost bond if required under Rule 7.

(2) A notice of appeal need not be filed. The date when the order granting permission to appeal is entered serves as the date of the notice of appeal for calculating time under these rules.

(3) The district clerk must notify the circuit clerk once the petitioner has paid the fees. Upon receiving this notice, the circuit clerk must enter the appeal on the docket. The record must be forwarded and filed in accordance with Rules 11 and 12(c).

(As amended Apr. 30, 1979, eff. Aug. 1, 1979; Apr. 29, 1994, eff. Dec. 1, 1994; Apr. 24, 1998, eff. Dec. 1, 1998; Apr. 29, 2002, eff. Dec. 1, 2002; Mar. 26, 2009, eff. Dec. 1, 2009; Apr. 28, 2016, eff. Dec. 1, 2016.)

[RULE 5.1.   APPEAL BY LEAVE UNDER 28 U.S.C. § 636 (c)(5) (ABROGATED APR. 24, 1998, EFF. DEC. 1, 1998)]

RULE 6.   APPEAL IN A BANKRUPTCY CASE

(a) Appeal From a Judgment, Order, or Decree of a District Court Exercising Original Jurisdiction in a Bankruptcy Case. An appeal to a court of appeals from a final judgment, order, or decree of a district court exercising jurisdiction under 28 U.S.C. § 1334 is taken as any other civil appeal under these rules.

(b) Appeal From a Judgment, Order, or Decree of a District Court or Bankruptcy Appellate Panel Exercising Appellate Jurisdiction in a Bankruptcy Case.

(1) Applicability of Other Rules. These rules apply to an appeal to a court of appeals under 28 U.S.C. § 158(d)(1) from a final judgment, order, or decree of a district court or bankruptcy appellate panel exercising appellate jurisdiction under 28 U.S.C. § 158(a) or (b), but with these qualifications:

(A) Rules 4(a)(4), 4(b), 9, 10, 11, 12(c), 13–20, 22–23, and 24(b) do not apply;

(B) the reference in Rule 3(c) to "Form 1 in the Appendix of Forms" must be read as a reference to Form 5;

(C) when the appeal is from a bankruptcy appellate panel, "district court," as used in any applicable rule, means "appellate panel"; and

(D) in Rule 12.1, "district court" includes a bankruptcy court or bankruptcy appellate panel.

(2) Additional Rules. In addition to the rules made applicable by Rule 6(b)(1), the following rules apply:

(A) Motion for Rehearing.

(i) If a timely motion for rehearing under Bankruptcy Rule 8022 is filed, the time to appeal for all parties runs from the entry of the order disposing of the motion. A notice of appeal filed after the district court or bankruptcy appellate panel announces or enters a judgment, order, or decree—but before disposition of the motion for rehearing—becomes effective when the order disposing of the motion for rehearing is entered.

(ii) If a party intends to challenge the order disposing of the motion—or the alteration or amendment of a judgment, order, or decree upon the motion—then the party, in compliance with Rules 3(c) and 6(b)(1)(B), must file a notice of appeal or amended notice of appeal. The notice or amended notice must be filed within the time prescribed by Rule 4—excluding Rules 4(a)(4) and 4(b)—measured from the entry of the order disposing of the motion.

(iii) No additional fee is required to file an amended notice.

(B) The Record on Appeal.

(i) Within 14 days after filing the notice of appeal, the appellant must file with the clerk possessing the record assembled in accordance with Bankruptcy Rule 8009—and serve on the appellee—a statement of the issues to be presented on appeal and a designation of the record to be certified and made available to the circuit clerk.

(ii) An appellee who believes that other parts of the record are necessary must, within 14 days after being served with the appellant's designation, file with the clerk and serve on the appellant a designation of additional parts to be included.

(iii) The record on appeal consists of:

• the redesignated record as provided above;

• the proceedings in the district court or bankruptcy appellate panel; and

• a certified copy of the docket entries prepared by the clerk under Rule 3(d).

(C) Making the Record Available.

(i) When the record is complete, the district clerk or bankruptcy-appellate-panel clerk must number the documents constituting the record and promptly make it available to the circuit clerk. If the clerk makes the record available in paper form, the clerk will not send documents of unusual bulk or weight, physical exhibits other than documents, or other parts of the record designated for omission by local rule of the court of appeals, unless directed to do so by a party or the circuit clerk. If unusually bulky or heavy exhibits are to be made available in paper form, a party must arrange with the clerks in advance for their transportation and receipt.

(ii) All parties must do whatever else is necessary to enable the clerk to assemble the record and make it available. When the record is made available in paper form, the court of appeals may provide by rule or order that a certified copy of the docket entries be made available in place of the redesignated record. But any party may request at any time during the pendency of the appeal that the redesignated record be made available.

(D) Filing the Record. When the district clerk or bankruptcy-appellate-panel clerk has made the record available, the circuit clerk must note that fact on the docket. The date noted on the docket serves as the filing date of the record. The circuit clerk must immediately notify all parties of the filing date.

(c) Direct Review by Permission Under 28 U.S.C. § 158(d)(2).

(1) Applicability of Other Rules. These rules apply to a direct appeal by permission under 28 U.S.C. § 158(d)(2), but with these qualifications:

(A) Rules 3–4, 5(a)(3), 6(a), 6(b), 8(a), 8(c), 9–12, 13–20, 22–23, and 24(b) do not apply;

(B) as used in any applicable rule, "district court" or "district clerk" includes—to the extent appropriate—a bankruptcy court or bankruptcy appellate panel or its clerk; and

(C) the reference to "Rules 11 and 12(c)" in Rule 5(d)(3) must be read as a reference to Rules 6(c)(2)(B) and (C).

(2) Additional Rules. In addition, the following rules apply:

(A) The Record on Appeal. Bankruptcy Rule 8009 governs the record on appeal.

(B) Making the Record Available. Bankruptcy Rule 8010 governs completing the record and making it available.

(C) Stays Pending Appeal. Bankruptcy Rule 8007 applies to stays pending appeal.

(D) Duties of the Circuit Clerk. When the bankruptcy clerk has made the record available, the circuit clerk must note that fact on the docket. The date noted on the docket serves as the filing date of the record. The circuit clerk must immediately notify all parties of the filing date.

(E) Filing a Representation Statement. Unless the court of appeals designates another time, within 14 days after entry of the order granting permission to appeal, the attorney who sought permission must file a statement with the circuit clerk naming the parties that the attorney represents on appeal.

(Added Apr. 25, 1989, eff. Dec. 1, 1989; amended Apr. 30, 1991, eff. Dec. 1, 1991; Apr. 22, 1993, eff. Dec. 1, 1993; Apr. 24, 1998, eff. Dec. 1, 1998; Mar. 26, 2009, eff. Dec. 1, 2009; Apr. 25, 2014, eff. Dec. 1, 2014.)

RULE 7. BOND FOR COSTS ON APPEAL IN A CIVIL CASE

In a civil case, the district court may require an appellant to file a bond or provide other security in any form and amount necessary to ensure payment of costs on appeal. Rule 8(b) applies to a surety on a bond given under this rule.

(As amended Apr. 30, 1979, eff. Aug. 1, 1979; Apr. 24, 1998, eff. Dec. 1, 1998.)

RULE 8. STAY OR INJUNCTION PENDING APPEAL

(a) Motion for Stay.

(1) Initial Motion in the District Court. A party must ordinarily move first in the district court for the following relief:

(A) a stay of the judgment or order of a district court pending appeal;

(B) approval of a bond or other security provided to obtain a stay of judgment; or

(C) an order suspending, modifying, restoring, or granting an injunction while an appeal is pending.

(2) Motion in the Court of Appeals; Conditions on Relief. A motion for the relief mentioned in Rule 8(a)(1) may be made to the court of appeals or to one of its judges.

(A) The motion must:

(i) show that moving first in the district court would be impracticable; or

(ii) state that, a motion having been made, the district court denied the motion or failed to afford the relief requested and state any reasons given by the district court for its action.

(B) The motion must also include:

(i) the reasons for granting the relief requested and the facts relied on;

(ii) originals or copies of affidavits or other sworn statements supporting facts subject to dispute; and

(iii) relevant parts of the record.

(C) The moving party must give reasonable notice of the motion to all parties.

(D) A motion under this Rule 8(a)(2) must be filed with the circuit clerk and normally will be considered by a panel of the court. But in an exceptional case in which time requirements make that procedure impracticable, the motion may be made to and considered by a single judge.

(E) The court may condition relief on a party's filing a bond or other security in the district court.

(b) Proceeding Against a Security Provider. If a party gives security with one or more security providers, each provider submits to the jurisdiction of the district court and irrevocably appoints the district clerk as its agent on whom any papers affecting its liability on the security may be served. On motion, a security provider's liability may be enforced in the district court without the necessity of an independent action. The motion and any notice that the district court prescribes may be served on the district clerk, who must promptly send a copy to each security provider whose address is known.

(c) Stay in a Criminal Case. Rule 38 of the Federal Rules of Criminal Procedure governs a stay in a criminal case.

(As amended Mar. 10, 1986, eff. July 1, 1986; Apr. 27, 1995, eff. Dec. 1, 1995; Apr. 24, 1998, eff. Dec. 1, 1998; Apr. 26, 2018, eff. Dec. 1, 2018.)

RULE 9. RELEASE IN A CRIMINAL CASE

(a) Release Before Judgment of Conviction.

(1) The district court must state in writing, or orally on the record, the reasons for an order regarding the release or detention of a defendant in a criminal case. A party appealing from the order must file with the court of appeals a copy of the district court's order and the court's statement of reasons as soon as practicable after filing the notice of appeal. An appellant who questions the factual basis for the district court's order must file a transcript of the release proceedings or an explanation of why a transcript was not obtained.

(2) After reasonable notice to the appellee, the court of appeals must promptly determine the appeal on the basis of the papers, affidavits, and parts of the record that the parties present or the court requires. Unless the court so orders, briefs need not be filed.

(3) The court of appeals or one of its judges may order the defendant's release pending the disposition of the appeal.

(b) Release After Judgment of Conviction. A party entitled to do so may obtain review of a district-court order regarding release after a judgment of conviction by filing a notice of appeal from that order in the district court, or by filing a motion in the court of appeals if the party has already filed a notice of appeal from the judgment of conviction. Both the order and the review are subject to Rule 9(a). The papers filed by the party seeking review must include a copy of the judgment of conviction.

(c) Criteria for Release. The court must make its decision regarding release in accordance with the applicable provisions of 18 U.S.C. §§ 3142, 3143, and 3145(c).

(As amended Apr. 24, 1972, eff. Oct. 1, 1972; Oct. 12, 1984, Pub.L. 98–473, Title II, § 210, 98 Stat. 1987; Apr. 29, 1994, eff. Dec. 1, 1994; Apr. 24, 1998, eff. Dec. 1, 1998.)

RULE 10. THE RECORD ON APPEAL

(a) Composition of the Record on Appeal. The following items constitute the record on appeal:

(1) the original papers and exhibits filed in the district court;

(2) the transcript of proceedings, if any; and

(3) a certified copy of the docket entries prepared by the district clerk.

(b) The Transcript of Proceedings.

(1) Appellant's Duty to Order. Within 14 days after filing the notice of appeal or entry of an order disposing of the last timely remaining motion of a type specified in Rule 4(a)(4)(A), whichever is later, the appellant must do either of the following:

(A) order from the reporter a transcript of such parts of the proceedings not already on file as the appellant considers necessary, subject to a local rule of the court of appeals and with the following qualifications:

(i) the order must be in writing;

(ii) if the cost of the transcript is to be paid by the United States under the Criminal Justice Act, the order must so state; and

(iii) the appellant must, within the same period, file a copy of the order with the district clerk; or

(B) file a certificate stating that no transcript will be ordered.

(2) Unsupported Finding or Conclusion. If the appellant intends to urge on appeal that a finding or conclusion is unsupported by the evidence or is contrary to the evidence, the appellant must include in the record a transcript of all evidence relevant to that finding or conclusion.

(3) Partial Transcript. Unless the entire transcript is ordered:

(A) the appellant must—within the 14 days provided in Rule 10(b)(1)—file a statement of the issues that the appellant intends to present on the appeal and must serve on the appellee a copy of both the order or certificate and the statement;

(B) if the appellee considers it necessary to have a transcript of other parts of the proceedings, the appellee must, within 14 days after the service of the order or certificate and the statement of the issues, file and serve on the appellant a designation of additional parts to be ordered; and

(C) unless within 14 days after service of that designation the appellant has ordered all such parts, and has so notified the appellee, the appellee may within the following 14 days either order the parts or move in the district court for an order requiring the appellant to do so.

(4) Payment. At the time of ordering, a party must make satisfactory arrangements with the reporter for paying the cost of the transcript.

(c) Statement of the Evidence When the Proceedings Were Not Recorded or When a Transcript Is Unavailable. If the transcript of a hearing or trial is unavailable, the appellant may prepare a statement of the evidence or proceedings from the best available means, including the appellant's recollection. The statement must be served on the appellee,

who may serve objections or proposed amendments within 14 days after being served. The statement and any objections or proposed amendments must then be submitted to the district court for settlement and approval. As settled and approved, the statement must be included by the district clerk in the record on appeal.

(d) Agreed Statement as the Record on Appeal. In place of the record on appeal as defined in Rule 10(a), the parties may prepare, sign, and submit to the district court a statement of the case showing how the issues presented by the appeal arose and were decided in the district court. The statement must set forth only those facts averred and proved or sought to be proved that are essential to the court's resolution of the issues. If the statement is truthful, it—together with any additions that the district court may consider necessary to a full presentation of the issues on appeal—must be approved by the district court and must then be certified to the court of appeals as the record on appeal. The district clerk must then send it to the circuit clerk within the time provided by Rule 11. A copy of the agreed statement may be filed in place of the appendix required by Rule 30.

(e) Correction or Modification of the Record.

(1) If any difference arises about whether the record truly discloses what occurred in the district court, the difference must be submitted to and settled by that court and the record conformed accordingly.

(2) If anything material to either party is omitted from or misstated in the record by error or accident, the omission or misstatement may be corrected and a supplemental record may be certified and forwarded:

(A) on stipulation of the parties;

(B) by the district court before or after the record has been forwarded; or

(C) by the court of appeals.

(3) All other questions as to the form and content of the record must be presented to the court of appeals.

(As amended Apr. 30, 1979, eff. Aug. 1, 1979; Mar. 10, 1986, eff. July 1, 1986; Apr. 30, 1991, eff. Dec. 1, 1991; Apr. 22, 1993, eff. Dec. 1, 1993; Apr. 27, 1995, eff. Dec. 1, 1995; Apr. 24, 1998, eff. Dec. 1, 1998; Mar. 26, 2009, eff. Dec. 1, 2009.)

RULE 11. FORWARDING THE RECORD

(a) Appellant's Duty. An appellant filing a notice of appeal must comply with Rule 10(b) and must do whatever else is necessary to enable the clerk to assemble and forward the record. If there are multiple appeals from a judgment or order, the clerk must forward a single record.

(b) Duties of Reporter and District Clerk.

(1) Reporter's Duty to Prepare and File a Transcript. The reporter must prepare and file a transcript as follows:

(A) Upon receiving an order for a transcript, the reporter must enter at the foot of the order the date of its receipt and the expected completion date and send a copy, so endorsed, to the circuit clerk.

(B) If the transcript cannot be completed within 30 days of the reporter's receipt of the order, the reporter may request the circuit clerk to grant additional time to complete it. The clerk must note on the docket the action taken and notify the parties.

(C) When a transcript is complete, the reporter must file it with the district clerk and notify the circuit clerk of the filing.

(D) If the reporter fails to file the transcript on time, the circuit clerk must notify the district judge and do whatever else the court of appeals directs.

(2) District Clerk's Duty to Forward. When the record is complete, the district clerk must number the documents constituting the record and send them promptly to the circuit clerk together with a list of the documents correspondingly numbered and reasonably identified. Unless directed to do so by a party or the circuit clerk, the district clerk will not send to the court of appeals documents of unusual bulk or weight, physical exhibits other than documents, or other parts of the record designated for omission by local rule of the court of appeals. If the exhibits are unusually bulky or heavy, a party must arrange with the clerks in advance for their transportation and receipt.

(c) Retaining the Record Temporarily in the District Court for Use in Preparing the Appeal. The parties may stipulate, or the district court on motion may order, that the district clerk retain the record temporarily for the parties to use in preparing the papers on appeal. In that event the district clerk must certify to the circuit clerk that the record on appeal is complete. Upon receipt of the appellee's brief, or earlier if the court orders or the parties agree, the appellant must request the district clerk to forward the record.

(d) [Abrogated.]

(e) Retaining the Record by Court Order.

(1) The court of appeals may, by order or local rule, provide that a certified copy of the docket entries be forwarded instead of the entire record. But a party may at any time during the appeal request that designated parts of the record be forwarded.

(2) The district court may order the record or some part of it retained if the court needs it while the appeal is pending, subject, however, to call by the court of appeals.

(3) If part or all of the record is ordered retained, the district clerk must send to the court of appeals a copy of the order and the docket entries together with the parts of the original record allowed by the district court and copies of any parts of the record designated by the parties.

(f) Retaining Parts of the Record in the District Court by Stipulation of the Parties. The parties may agree by written stipulation filed in the district court that designated parts of the record be retained in the district court subject to call by the court of appeals or request by a party. The parts of the record so designated remain a part of the record on appeal.

(g) Record for a Preliminary Motion in the Court of Appeals. If, before the record is forwarded, a party makes any of the following motions in the court of appeals:

- for dismissal;
- for release;
- for a stay pending appeal;
- for additional security on the bond on appeal or on a bond or other security provided to obtain a stay of judgment; or
- for any other intermediate order—

the district clerk must send the court of appeals any parts of the record designated by any party.

(As amended Apr. 30, 1979, eff. Aug. 1, 1979; Mar. 10, 1986, eff. July 1, 1986; Apr. 24, 1998, eff. Dec. 1, 1998; Apr. 26, 2018, eff. Dec. 1, 2018.)

RULE 12. DOCKETING THE APPEAL; FILING A REPRESENTATION STATEMENT; FILING THE RECORD

(a) Docketing the Appeal. Upon receiving the copy of the notice of appeal and the docket entries from the district clerk under Rule 3(d), the circuit clerk must docket the appeal under the title of the district-court action and must identify the appellant, adding the appellant's name if necessary.

(b) Filing a Representation Statement. Unless the court of appeals designates another time, the attorney who filed the notice of appeal must, within 14 days after filing the notice, file a statement with the circuit clerk naming the parties that the attorney represents on appeal.

(c) Filing the Record, Partial Record, or Certificate. Upon receiving the record, partial record, or district clerk's certificate as provided in Rule 11, the circuit clerk must file it and immediately notify all parties of the filing date.

(As amended Apr. 30, 1979, eff. Aug. 1, 1979; Mar. 10, 1986, eff. July 1, 1986; Apr. 22, 1993, eff. Dec. 1, 1993; Apr. 24, 1998, eff. Dec. 1, 1998; Mar. 26, 2009, eff. Dec. 1, 2009.)

RULE 12.1 REMAND AFTER AN INDICATIVE RULING BY THE DISTRICT COURT ON A MOTION FOR RELIEF THAT IS BARRED BY A PENDING APPEAL

(a) Notice to the Court of Appeals. If a timely motion is made in the district court for relief that it lacks authority to grant because of an appeal that has been docketed and is pending, the movant must promptly notify the circuit clerk if the district court states either that it would grant the motion or that the motion raises a substantial issue.

(b) Remand After an Indicative Ruling. If the district court states that it would grant the motion or that the motion raises a substantial issue, the court of appeals may remand for further proceedings but retains jurisdiction unless it expressly dismisses the appeal. If the court of appeals remands but retains jurisdiction, the parties must promptly notify the circuit clerk when the district court has decided the motion on remand.

(Added Mar. 26, 2009, eff. Dec. 1, 2009.)

TITLE III. APPEALS FROM THE UNITED STATES TAX COURT

RULE 13. APPEALS FROM THE TAX COURT

(a) Appeal as of Right.

(1) How Obtained; Time for Filing a Notice of Appeal.

(A) An appeal as of right from the United States Tax Court is commenced by filing a notice of appeal with the Tax Court clerk within 90 days after the entry of the Tax Court's decision. At the time of filing, the appellant must furnish the clerk with enough copies of the notice to enable the clerk to comply with Rule 3(d). If one party files a timely notice of appeal, any other party may file a notice of appeal within 120 days after the Tax Court's decision is entered.

(B) If, under Tax Court rules, a party makes a timely motion to vacate or revise the Tax Court's decision, the time to file a notice of appeal runs from the entry of the order disposing of the motion or from the entry of a new decision, whichever is later.

(2) Notice of Appeal; How Filed. The notice of appeal may be filed either at the Tax Court clerk's office in the District of Columbia or by mail addressed to the clerk. If sent by mail the notice is considered filed on the postmark date, subject to § 7502 of the Internal Revenue Code, as amended, and the applicable regulations.

(3) Contents of the Notice of Appeal; Service; Effect of Filing and Service. Rule 3 prescribes the contents of a notice of appeal, the manner of service, and the effect of its filing and service. Form 2 in the Appendix of Forms is a suggested form of a notice of appeal.

(4) The Record on Appeal; Forwarding; Filing.

(A) Except as otherwise provided under Tax Court rules for the transcript of proceedings, the appeal is governed by the parts of Rules 10, 11, and 12 regarding the record on appeal from a district court, the time and manner of forwarding and filing, and the docketing in the court of appeals.

(B) If an appeal is taken to more than one court of appeals, the original record must be sent to the court named in the first notice of appeal filed. In an appeal to any other court of appeals, the appellant must apply to that other court to make provision for the record.

(b) Appeal by Permission. An appeal by permission is governed by Rule 5.

(As amended Apr. 1, 1979, eff. Aug. 1, 1979; Apr. 29, 1994, eff. Dec. 1, 1994; Apr. 24, 1998, eff. Dec. 1, 1998; Apr. 16, 2013, eff. Dec. 1, 2013.)

RULE 14. APPLICABILITY OF OTHER RULES TO APPEALS FROM THE TAX COURT

All provisions of these rules, except Rules 4, 6–9, 15–20, and 22–23, apply to appeals from the Tax Court. References in any applicable rule (other than Rule 24(a)) to the district court and district clerk are to be read as referring to the Tax Court and its clerk.

(As amended Apr. 24, 1998, eff. Dec. 1, 1998; Apr. 16, 2013, eff. Dec. 1, 2013.)

TITLE IV. REVIEW OR ENFORCEMENT OF AN ORDER OF AN ADMINISTRATIVE AGENCY, BOARD, COMMISSION, OR OFFICER

RULE 15. REVIEW OR ENFORCEMENT OF AN AGENCY ORDER—HOW OBTAINED; INTERVENTION

(a) Petition for Review; Joint Petition.

(1) Review of an agency order is commenced by filing, within the time prescribed by law, a petition for review with the clerk of a court of appeals authorized to review the agency order. If their interests make joinder practicable, two or more persons may join in a petition to the same court to review the same order.

(2) The petition must:

(A) name each party seeking review either in the caption or the body of the petition—using such terms as "et al.," "petitioners," or "respondents" does not effectively name the parties;

(B) name the agency as a respondent (even though not named in the petition, the United States is a respondent if required by statute); and

(C) specify the order or part thereof to be reviewed.

(3) Form 3 in the Appendix of Forms is a suggested form of a petition for review.

(4) In this rule "agency" includes an agency, board, commission, or officer; "petition for review" includes a petition to enjoin, suspend, modify, or otherwise review, or a notice of appeal, whichever form is indicated by the applicable statute.

(b) Application or Cross-Application to Enforce an Order; Answer; Default.

(1) An application to enforce an agency order must be filed with the clerk of a court of appeals authorized to enforce the order. If a petition is filed to review an agency order that the court may enforce, a party opposing the petition may file a cross-application for enforcement.

(2) Within 21 days after the application for enforcement is filed, the respondent must serve on the applicant an answer to the application and file it with the clerk. If the respondent fails to answer in time, the court will enter judgment for the relief requested.

(3) The application must contain a concise statement of the proceedings in which the order was entered, the facts upon which venue is based, and the relief requested.

(c) Service of the Petition or Application. The circuit clerk must serve a copy of the petition for review, or an application or cross-application to enforce an agency order, on each respondent as prescribed by Rule 3(d), unless a different manner of service is prescribed by statute. At the time of filing, the petitioner must:

(1) serve, or have served, a copy on each party admitted to participate in the agency proceedings, except for the respondents;

(2) file with the clerk a list of those so served; and

(3) give the clerk enough copies of the petition or application to serve each respondent.

(d) Intervention. Unless a statute provides another method, a person who wants to intervene in a proceeding under this rule must file a motion for leave to intervene with the circuit clerk and serve a copy on all parties. The motion—or other notice of intervention authorized by statute—must be filed within 30 days after the petition for review is filed and must contain a concise statement of the interest of the moving party and the grounds for intervention.

(e) Payment of Fees. When filing any separate or joint petition for review in a court of appeals, the petitioner must pay the circuit clerk all required fees.

(As amended Apr. 22, 1993, eff. Dec. 1, 1993; Apr. 24, 1998, eff. Dec. 1, 1998; Mar. 26, 2009, eff. Dec. 1, 2009.)

RULE 15.1 BRIEFS AND ORAL ARGUMENT IN A NATIONAL LABOR RELATIONS BOARD PROCEEDING

In either an enforcement or a review proceeding, a party adverse to the National Labor Relations Board proceeds first on briefing and at oral argument, unless the court orders otherwise.

(Added Mar. 10, 1986, eff. July 1, 1986; amended Apr. 24, 1998, eff. Dec. 1, 1998.)

RULE 16. THE RECORD ON REVIEW OR ENFORCEMENT

(a) Composition of the Record. The record on review or enforcement of an agency order consists of:

(1) the order involved;

(2) any findings or report on which it is based; and

(3) the pleadings, evidence, and other parts of the proceedings before the agency.

(b) Omissions From or Misstatements in the Record. The parties may at any time, by stipulation, supply any omission from the record or correct a misstatement, or the court may so direct. If necessary, the court may direct that a supplemental record be prepared and filed.

(As amended Apr. 24, 1998, eff. Dec. 1, 1998.)

RULE 17. FILING THE RECORD

(a) Agency to File; Time for Filing; Notice of Filing. The agency must file the record with the circuit clerk within 40 days after being served with a petition for review, unless the statute authorizing review provides otherwise, or within 40 days after it files an application for enforcement unless the respondent fails to answer or the court orders otherwise. The court may shorten or extend the time to file the record. The clerk must notify all parties of the date when the record is filed.

(b) Filing—What Constitutes.

(1) The agency must file:

(A) the original or a certified copy of the entire record or parts designated by the parties; or

(B) a certified list adequately describing all documents, transcripts of testimony, exhibits, and other material constituting the record, or describing those parts designated by the parties.

(2) The parties may stipulate in writing that no record or certified list be filed. The date when the stipulation is filed with the circuit clerk is treated as the date when the record is filed.

(3) The agency must retain any portion of the record not filed with the clerk. All parts of the record retained by the agency are a part of the record on review for all purposes and, if the court or a party so requests, must be sent to the court regardless of any prior stipulation.

(As amended Apr. 24, 1998, eff. Dec. 1, 1998.)

RULE 18. STAY PENDING REVIEW

(a) Motion for a Stay.

(1) **Initial Motion Before the Agency.** A petitioner must ordinarily move first before the agency for a stay pending review of its decision or order.

(2) **Motion in the Court of Appeals.** A motion for a stay may be made to the court of appeals or one of its judges.

(A) The motion must:

(i) show that moving first before the agency would be impracticable; or

(ii) state that, a motion having been made, the agency denied the motion or failed to afford the relief requested and state any reasons given by the agency for its action.

(B) The motion must also include:

(i) the reasons for granting the relief requested and the facts relied on;

(ii) originals or copies of affidavits or other sworn statements supporting facts subject to dispute; and

(iii) relevant parts of the record.

(C) The moving party must give reasonable notice of the motion to all parties.

(D) The motion must be filed with the circuit clerk and normally will be considered by a panel of the court. But in an exceptional case in which time requirements make that procedure impracticable, the motion may be made to and considered by a single judge.

(b) Bond. The court may condition relief on the filing of a bond or other appropriate security.

(As amended Apr. 24, 1998, eff. Dec. 1, 1998.)

RULE 19. SETTLEMENT OF A JUDGMENT ENFORCING AN AGENCY ORDER IN PART

When the court files an opinion directing entry of judgment enforcing the agency's order in part, the agency must within 14 days file with the clerk and serve on each other party a proposed judgment conforming to the opinion. A party who disagrees with the agency's proposed judgment must within 10 days file with the clerk and serve the agency with a proposed judgment that the party believes conforms to the opinion. The court will settle the judgment and direct entry without further hearing or argument.

(As amended Mar. 10, 1986, eff. July 1, 1986; Apr. 24, 1998, eff. Dec. 1, 1998; Mar. 26, 2009, eff. Dec. 1, 2009.)

RULE 20. APPLICABILITY OF RULES TO THE REVIEW OR ENFORCEMENT OF AN AGENCY ORDER

All provisions of these rules, except Rules 3–14 and 22–23, apply to the review or enforcement of an agency order. In these rules, "appellant" includes a petitioner or applicant, and "appellee" includes a respondent.

(As amended Apr. 24, 1998, eff. Dec. 1, 1998.)

TITLE V. EXTRAORDINARY WRITS

RULE 21. WRITS OF MANDAMUS AND PROHIBITION, AND OTHER EXTRAORDINARY WRITS

(a) Mandamus or Prohibition to a Court: Petition, Filing, Service, and Docketing.

(1) A party petitioning for a writ of mandamus or prohibition directed to a court must file a petition with the circuit clerk with proof of service on all parties to the proceeding in the trial court. The party must also provide a copy to the trial-court judge. All parties to the proceeding in the trial court other than the petitioner are respondents for all purposes.

(2)(A) The petition must be titled "In re [name of petitioner]."

(B) The petition must state:

(i) the relief sought;

(ii) the issues presented;

(iii) the facts necessary to understand the issue presented by the petition; and

(iv) the reasons why the writ should issue.

(C) The petition must include a copy of any order or opinion or parts of the record that may be essential to understand the matters set forth in the petition.

(3) Upon receiving the prescribed docket fee, the clerk must docket the petition and submit it to the court.

(b) Denial; Order Directing Answer; Briefs; Precedence.

(1) The court may deny the petition without an answer. Otherwise, it must order the respondent, if any, to answer within a fixed time.

(2) The clerk must serve the order to respond on all persons directed to respond.

(3) Two or more respondents may answer jointly.

(4) The court of appeals may invite or order the trial-court judge to address the petition or may invite an amicus curiae to do so. The trial-court judge may request permission to address the petition but may not do so unless invited or ordered to do so by the court of appeals.

(5) If briefing or oral argument is required, the clerk must advise the parties, and when appropriate, the trial-court judge or amicus curiae.

(6) The proceeding must be given preference over ordinary civil cases.

(7) The circuit clerk must send a copy of the final disposition to the trial-court judge.

(c) Other Extraordinary Writs. An application for an extraordinary writ other than one provided for in Rule 21(a) must be made by filing a petition with the circuit clerk with proof of service on the respondents. Proceedings on the application must conform, so far as is practicable, to the procedures prescribed in Rule 21(a) and (b).

(d) Form of Papers; Number of Copies; Length Limits. All papers must conform to Rule 32(c)(2). An original and 3 copies must be filed unless the court requires the filing of a different number by local rule or by order in a particular case. Except by the court's permission, and excluding the accompanying documents required by Rule 21(a)(2)(C):

(1) a paper produced using a computer must not exceed 7,800 words; and

(2) a handwritten or typewritten paper must not exceed 30 pages.

(As amended Apr. 29, 1994, eff. Dec. 1, 1994; Apr. 23, 1996, eff. Dec. 1, 1996; Apr. 24, 1998, eff. Dec. 1, 1998; Apr. 29, 2002, eff. Dec. 1, 2002; Apr. 28, 2016, eff. Dec. 1, 2016.)

TITLE VI. HABEAS CORPUS; PROCEEDINGS IN FORMA PAUPERIS

RULE 22. HABEAS CORPUS AND SECTION 2255 PROCEEDINGS

(a) Application for the Original Writ. An application for a writ of habeas corpus must be made to the appropriate district court. If made to a circuit judge, the application must be transferred to the appropriate district court. If a district court denies an application made or transferred to it, renewal of the application before a circuit judge is not permitted. The applicant may, under 28 U.S.C. § 2253, appeal to the court of appeals from the district court's order denying the application.

(b) Certificate of Appealability.

(1) In a habeas corpus proceeding in which the detention complained of arises from process issued by a state court, or in a 28 U.S.C. § 2255 proceeding, the applicant cannot take an appeal unless a circuit justice or a circuit or district judge issues a certificate of appealability under 28 U.S.C. § 2253(c). If an applicant files a notice of appeal, the district clerk must send to the court of appeals the certificate (if any) and the statement described in Rule 11(a) of the Rules Governing Proceedings Under 28 U.S.C. § 2254 or § 2255 (if any), along with the notice of appeal and the file of the district-court proceedings. If the district judge has denied the certificate, the applicant may request a circuit judge to issue it.

(2) A request addressed to the court of appeals may be considered by a circuit judge or judges, as the court prescribes. If no express request for a certificate is filed, the notice of appeal constitutes a request addressed to the judges of the court of appeals.

(3) A certificate of appealability is not required when a state or its representative or the United States or its representative appeals.

(As amended Pub.L. 104–132, Title I, § 103, Apr. 24, 1996, 110 Stat. 1218; Apr. 24, 1998, eff. Dec. 1, 1998; Mar. 26, 2009, eff. Dec. 1, 2009.)

RULE 23. CUSTODY OR RELEASE OF A PRISONER IN A HABEAS CORPUS PROCEEDING

(a) Transfer of Custody Pending Review. Pending review of a decision in a habeas corpus proceeding commenced before a court, justice, or judge of the United States for the release of a prisoner, the person having custody of the prisoner must not transfer custody to another unless a transfer is directed in accordance with this rule. When, upon application, a custodian shows the need for a transfer, the court, justice, or judge rendering the decision under review may authorize the transfer and substitute the successor custodian as a party.

(b) Detention or Release Pending Review of Decision Not to Release. While a decision not to release a prisoner is under review, the court or judge rendering the decision, or the court of appeals, or the Supreme Court, or a judge or justice of either court, may order that the prisoner be:

(1) detained in the custody from which release is sought;

(2) detained in other appropriate custody; or

(3) released on personal recognizance, with or without surety.

(c) Release Pending Review of Decision Ordering Release. While a decision ordering the release of a prisoner is under review, the prisoner must—unless the court or judge rendering the decision, or the court of appeals, or the Supreme Court, or a judge or justice of either court orders otherwise—be released on personal recognizance, with or without surety.

(d) Modification of the Initial Order on Custody. An initial order governing the prisoner's custody or release, including any recognizance or surety, continues in effect pending review unless for special reasons shown to the court of appeals or the Supreme Court, or to a judge or justice of either court, the order is modified or an independent order regarding custody, release, or surety is issued.

(As amended Mar. 10, 1986, eff. July 1, 1986; Apr. 24, 1998, eff. Dec. 1, 1998.)

RULE 24. PROCEEDING IN FORMA PAUPERIS

(a) Leave to Proceed In Forma Pauperis.

(1) **Motion in the District Court.** Except as stated in Rule 24(a)(3), a party to a district-court action who desires to appeal in forma pauperis must file a motion in the district court. The party must attach an affidavit that:

(A) shows in the detail prescribed by Form 4 of the Appendix of Forms the party's inability to pay or to give security for fees and costs;

(B) claims an entitlement to redress; and

(C) states the issues that the party intends to present on appeal.

(2) **Action on the Motion.** If the district court grants the motion, the party may proceed on appeal without prepaying or giving security for fees and costs, unless a statute provides otherwise. If the district court denies the motion, it must state its reasons in writing.

(3) **Prior Approval.** A party who was permitted to proceed in forma pauperis in the district-court action, or who was determined to be financially unable to obtain an adequate defense in a criminal case, may proceed on appeal in forma pauperis without further authorization, unless:

(A) the district court—before or after the notice of appeal is filed—certifies that the appeal is not taken in good faith or finds that the party is not otherwise entitled to proceed in forma pauperis and states in writing its reasons for the certification or finding; or

(B) a statute provides otherwise.

(4) **Notice of District Court's Denial.** The district clerk must immediately notify the parties and the court of appeals when the district court does any of the following:

(A) denies a motion to proceed on appeal in forma pauperis;

(B) certifies that the appeal is not taken in good faith; or

(C) finds that the party is not otherwise entitled to proceed in forma pauperis.

(5) Motion in the Court of Appeals. A party may file a motion to proceed on appeal in forma pauperis in the court of appeals within 30 days after service of the notice prescribed in Rule 24(a)(4). The motion must include a copy of the affidavit filed in the district court and the district court's statement of reasons for its action. If no affidavit was filed in the district court, the party must include the affidavit prescribed by Rule 24(a)(1).

(b) Leave to Proceed In Forma Pauperis on Appeal from the United States Tax Court or on Appeal or Review of an Administrative–Agency Proceeding. A party may file in the court of appeals a motion for leave to proceed on appeal in forma pauperis with an affidavit prescribed by Rule 24(a)(1):

(1) in an appeal from the United States Tax Court; and

(2) when an appeal or review of a proceeding before an administrative agency, board, commission, or officer proceeds directly in the court of appeals.

(c) Leave to Use Original Record. A party allowed to proceed on appeal in forma pauperis may request that the appeal be heard on the original record without reproducing any part.

(As amended Apr. 1, 1979, eff. Aug. 1, 1979; Mar. 10, 1986, eff. July 1, 1986; Apr. 24, 1998, eff. Dec. 1, 1998; Apr. 29, 2002, eff. Dec. 1, 2002; Apr. 16, 2013, eff. Dec. 1, 2013.)

TITLE VII. GENERAL PROVISIONS

RULE 25. FILING AND SERVICE

(a) Filing.

(1) Filing with the Clerk. A paper required or permitted to be filed in a court of appeals must be filed with the clerk.

(2) Filing: Method and Timeliness.

(A) Nonelectronic Filing.

(i) In General. For a paper not filed electronically, filing may be accomplished by mail addressed to the clerk, but filing is not timely unless the clerk receives the papers within the time fixed for filing.

(ii) A Brief or Appendix. A brief or appendix not filed electronically is timely filed, however, if on or before the last day for filing, it is:

- mailed to the clerk by first-class mail, or other class of mail that is at least as expeditious, postage prepaid; or

- dispatched to a third-party commercial carrier for delivery to the clerk within 3 days.

(iii) Inmate Filing. If an institution has a system designed for legal mail, an inmate confined there must use that system to receive the benefit of this Rule 25(a)(2)(A)(iii). A paper not filed electronically by an inmate is timely if it is deposited in the institution's internal mail system on or before the last day for filing and:

- it is accompanied by: a declaration in compliance with 28 U.S.C. § 1746—or a notarized statement—setting out the date of deposit and stating that first-class postage is being prepaid; or evidence (such as a postmark or date stamp) showing that the paper was so deposited and that postage was prepaid; or

- the court of appeals exercises its discretion to permit the later filing of a declaration or notarized statement that satisfies Rule 25(a)(2)(A)(iii).

(B) Electronic Filing and Signing.

(i) By a Represented Person—Generally Required; Exceptions. A person represented by an attorney must file electronically, unless nonelectronic filing is allowed by the court for good cause or is allowed or required by local rule.

(ii) By an Unrepresented Person—When Allowed or Required. A person not represented by an attorney:

- may file electronically only if allowed by court order or by local rule; and

- may be required to file electronically only by court order, or by a local rule that includes reasonable exceptions.

(iii) Signing. A filing made through a person's electronic-filing account and authorized by that person, together with that person's name on a signature block, constitutes the person's signature.

(iv) Same as a Written Paper. A paper filed electronically is a written paper for purposes of these rules.

(3) Filing a Motion with a Judge. If a motion requests relief that may be granted by a single judge, the judge may permit the motion to be filed with the judge; the judge must note the filing date on the motion and give it to the clerk.

(4) Clerk's Refusal of Documents. The clerk must not refuse to accept for filing any paper presented for that purpose solely because it is not presented in proper form as required by these rules or by any local rule or practice.

(5) Privacy Protection. An appeal in a case whose privacy protection was governed by Federal Rule of Bankruptcy Procedure 9037, Federal Rule of Civil Procedure 5.2, or Federal Rule of Criminal Procedure 49.1 is governed by the same rule on appeal. In all other proceedings, privacy protection is governed by Federal Rule of Civil Procedure 5.2, except that Federal Rule of Criminal Procedure 49.1 governs when an extraordinary writ is sought in a criminal case.

(b) Service of All Papers Required. Unless a rule requires service by the clerk, a party must, at or before the time of filing a paper, serve a copy on the other parties to the appeal or review. Service on a party represented by counsel must be made on the party's counsel.

(c) Manner of Service.

(1) Nonelectronic service may be any of the following:

(A) personal, including delivery to a responsible person at the office of counsel;

(B) by mail; or

(C) by third-party commercial carrier for delivery within 3 days.

(2) Electronic service of a paper may be made (A) by sending it to a registered user by filing it with the court's electronic-filing system or (B) by sending it by other electronic means that the person to be served consented to in writing.

(3) When reasonable considering such factors as the immediacy of the relief sought, distance, and cost, service on a party must be by a manner at least as expeditious as the manner used to file the paper with the court.

(4) Service by mail or by commercial carrier is complete on mailing or delivery to the carrier. Service by electronic means is complete on filing or sending, unless the party making service is notified that the paper was not received by the party served.

(d) Proof of Service.

(1) A paper presented for filing must contain either of the following:

(A) an acknowledgment of service by the person served; or

(B) proof of service consisting of a statement by the person who made service certifying:

(i) the date and manner of service;

(ii) the names of the persons served; and

(iii) their mail or electronic addresses, facsimile numbers, or the addresses of the places of delivery, as appropriate for the manner of service.

(2) When a brief or appendix is filed by mailing or dispatch in accordance with Rule 25(a)(2)(A)(ii), the proof of service must also state the date and manner by which the document was mailed or dispatched to the clerk.

(3) Proof of service may appear on or be affixed to the papers filed.

(e) Number of Copies. When these rules require the filing or furnishing of a number of copies, a court may require a different number by local rule or by order in a particular case.

(As amended Mar. 10, 1986, eff. July 1, 1986; Apr. 30, 1991, eff. Dec. 1, 1991; Apr. 22, 1993, eff. Dec. 1, 1993; Apr. 29, 1994, eff. Dec. 1, 1994; Apr. 23, 1996, eff. Dec. 1, 1996; Apr. 24, 1998, eff. Dec. 1, 1998; Apr. 29, 2002, eff. Dec. 1, 2002; Apr. 12, 2006, eff. Dec. 1, 2006; Apr. 30, 2007, eff. Dec. 1, 2007; Mar. 26, 2009, eff. Dec. 1, 2009; Apr. 28, 2016, eff. Dec. 1, 2016; Apr. 26, 2018, eff. Dec. 1, 2018.)

RULE 26. COMPUTING AND EXTENDING TIME

(a) Computing Time. The following rules apply in computing any time period specified in these rules, in any local rule or court order, or in any statute that does not specify a method of computing time.

(1) Period Stated in Days or a Longer Unit. When the period is stated in days or a longer unit of time:

(A) exclude the day of the event that triggers the period;

(B) count every day, including intermediate Saturdays, Sundays, and legal holidays; and

(C) include the last day of the period, but if the last day is a Saturday, Sunday, or legal holiday, the period continues to run until the end of the next day that is not a Saturday, Sunday, or legal holiday.

(2) Period Stated in Hours. When the period is stated in hours:

(A) begin counting immediately on the occurrence of the event that triggers the period;

(B) count every hour, including hours during intermediate Saturdays, Sundays, and legal holidays; and

(C) if the period would end on a Saturday, Sunday, or legal holiday, the period continues to run until the same time on the next day that is not a Saturday, Sunday, or legal holiday.

(3) Inaccessibility of the Clerk's Office. Unless the court orders otherwise, if the clerk's office is inaccessible:

(A) on the last day for filing under Rule 26(a)(1), then the time for filing is extended to the first accessible day that is not a Saturday, Sunday, or legal holiday; or

(B) during the last hour for filing under Rule 26(a)(2), then the time for filing is extended to the same time on the first accessible day that is not a Saturday, Sunday, or legal holiday.

(4) "Last Day" Defined. Unless a different time is set by a statute, local rule, or court order, the last day ends:

(A) for electronic filing in the district court, at midnight in the court's time zone;

(B) for electronic filing in the court of appeals, at midnight in the time zone of the circuit clerk's principal office;

(C) for filing under Rules 4(c)(1), 25(a)(2)(A)(ii), and 25(a)(2)(A)(iii)—and filing by mail under Rule 13(a)(2)—at the latest time for the method chosen for delivery to the post office, third-party commercial carrier, or prison mailing system; and

(D) for filing by other means, when the clerk's office is scheduled to close.

(5) "Next Day" Defined. The "next day" is determined by continuing to count forward when the period is measured after an event and backward when measured before an event.

(6) "Legal Holiday" Defined. "Legal holiday" means:

(A) the day set aside by statute for observing New Year's Day, Martin Luther King Jr.'s Birthday, Washington's Birthday, Memorial Day, Independence Day, Labor Day, Columbus Day, Veterans' Day, Thanksgiving Day, or Christmas Day;

(B) any day declared a holiday by the President or Congress; and

(C) for periods that are measured after an event, any other day declared a holiday by the state where either of the following is located: the district court that rendered the challenged judgment or order, or the circuit clerk's principal office.

(b) Extending Time. For good cause, the court may extend the time prescribed by these rules or by its order to perform any act, or may permit an act to be done after that time expires. But the court may not extend the time to file:

(1) a notice of appeal (except as authorized in Rule 4) or a petition for permission to appeal; or

(2) a notice of appeal from or a petition to enjoin, set aside, suspend, modify, enforce, or otherwise review an order of an administrative agency, board, commission, or officer of the United States, unless specifically authorized by law.

(c) Additional Time after Certain Kinds of Service. When a party may or must act within a specified time after being served, 3 days are added after the period would otherwise expire under Rule 26(a), unless the paper is delivered on the date of service stated in the proof of service. For purposes of this Rule 26(c), a paper that is served electronically is treated as delivered on the date of service stated in the proof of service.

(As amended Mar. 1, 1971, eff. July 1, 1971; Mar. 10, 1986, eff. July 1, 1986; Apr. 25, 1989, eff. Dec. 1, 1989; Apr. 30, 1991, eff. Dec. 1, 1991; Apr. 23, 1996, eff. Dec. 1, 1996; Apr. 24, 1998, eff. Dec. 1, 1998; Apr. 29, 2002, eff. Dec. 1, 2002; Apr. 25, 2005, eff. Dec. 1, 2005; Mar. 26, 2009, eff. Dec. 1, 2009; Apr. 28, 2016, eff. Dec. 1, 2016; Apr. 26, 2018, eff. Dec. 1, 2018.)

RULE 26.1 CORPORATE DISCLOSURE STATEMENT

(a) Who Must File. Any nongovernmental corporate party to a proceeding in a court of appeals must file a statement that identifies any parent corporation and any publicly held corporation that owns 10% or more of its stock or states that there is no such corporation.

(b) Time for Filing; Supplemental Filing. A party must file the Rule 26.1(a) statement with the principal brief or upon filing a motion, response, petition, or answer in the court of appeals, whichever occurs first, unless a local rule requires earlier filing. Even if the statement has already been filed, the party's principal brief must include the statement before the table of contents. A party must supplement its statement whenever the information that must be disclosed under Rule 26.1(a) changes.

(c) Number of Copies. If the Rule 26.1(a) statement is filed before the principal brief, or if a supplemental statement is filed, the party must file an original and 3 copies unless the court requires a different number by local rule or by order in a particular case.

(Added Apr. 25, 1989, eff. Dec. 1, 1989; amended Apr. 30, 1991, eff. Dec. 1, 1991; Apr. 29, 1994, eff. Dec. 1, 1994; Apr. 24, 1998, eff. Dec. 1, 1998; Apr. 29, 2002, eff. Dec. 1, 2002.)

RULE 27. MOTIONS

(a) In General.

(1) Application for Relief. An application for an order or other relief is made by motion unless these rules prescribe another form. A motion must be in writing unless the court permits otherwise.

(2) Contents of a Motion.

(A) Grounds and relief sought. A motion must state with particularity the grounds for the motion, the relief sought, and the legal argument necessary to support it.

(B) Accompanying documents.

(i) Any affidavit or other paper necessary to support a motion must be served and filed with the motion.

(ii) An affidavit must contain only factual information, not legal argument.

(iii) A motion seeking substantive relief must include a copy of the trial court's opinion or agency's decision as a separate exhibit.

(C) Documents barred or not required.

(i) A separate brief supporting or responding to a motion must not be filed.

(ii) A notice of motion is not required.

(iii) A proposed order is not required.

(3) Response.

(A) Time to file. Any party may file a response to a motion; Rule 27(a)(2) governs its contents. The response must be filed within 10 days after service of the motion unless the court shortens or extends the time. A motion authorized by Rules 8, 9, 18, or 41 may be granted before the 10–day period runs only if the court gives reasonable notice to the parties that it intends to act sooner.

(B) Request for affirmative relief. A response may include a motion for affirmative relief. The time to respond to the new motion, and to reply to that response, are governed by Rule 27(a)(3)(A) and (a)(4). The title of the response must alert the court to the request for relief.

(4) Reply to Response. Any reply to a response must be filed within 7 days after service of the response. A reply must not present matters that do not relate to the response.

(b) Disposition of a Motion for a Procedural Order. The court may act on a motion for a procedural order—including a motion under Rule 26(b)—at any time without awaiting a response, and may, by rule or by order in a particular case, authorize its clerk to act on specified types of procedural motions. A party adversely affected by the court's, or the clerk's, action may file a motion to reconsider, vacate, or modify that action. Timely opposition filed after the motion is granted in whole or in part does not constitute a request to reconsider, vacate, or modify the disposition; a motion requesting that relief must be filed.

(c) Power of a Single Judge to Entertain a Motion. A circuit judge may act alone on any motion, but may not dismiss or otherwise determine an appeal or other proceeding. A court of appeals may provide by rule or by order in a particular case that only the court may act on any motion or class of motions. The court may review the action of a single judge.

(d) Form of Papers; Length Limits; Number of Copies.

(1) Format.

   (A) Reproduction. A motion, response, or reply may be reproduced by any process that yields a clear black image on light paper. The paper must be opaque and unglazed. Only one side of the paper may be used.

   (B) Cover. A cover is not required, but there must be a caption that includes the case number, the name of the court, the title of the case, and a brief descriptive title indicating the purpose of the motion and identifying the party or parties for whom it is filed. If a cover is used, it must be white.

   (C) Binding. The document must be bound in any manner that is secure, does not obscure the text, and permits the document to lie reasonably flat when open.

   (D) Paper size, line spacing, and margins. The document must be on 8½ by 11 inch paper. The text must be double-spaced, but quotations more than two lines long may be indented and single-spaced. Headings and footnotes may be single-spaced. Margins must be at least one inch on all four sides. Page numbers may be placed in the margins, but no text may appear there.

   (E) Typeface and type styles. The document must comply with the typeface requirements of Rule 32(a)(5) and the type-style requirements of Rule 32(a)(6).

(2) Length Limits. Except by the court's permission, and excluding the accompanying documents authorized by Rule 27(a)(2)(B):

   (A) a motion or response to a motion produced using a computer must not exceed 5,200 words;

   (B) a handwritten or typewritten motion or response to a motion must not exceed 20 pages;

   (C) a reply produced using a computer must not exceed 2,600 words; and

   (D) a handwritten or typewritten reply to a response must not exceed 10 pages.

(3) Number of Copies. An original and 3 copies must be filed unless the court requires a different number by local rule or by order in a particular case.

(e) Oral Argument. A motion will be decided without oral argument unless the court orders otherwise.

(As amended Apr. 1, 1979, eff. Aug. 1, 1979; Apr. 25, 1989, eff. Dec. 1, 1989; Apr. 29, 1994, eff. Dec. 1, 1994; Apr. 24, 1998, eff. Dec. 1, 1998; Apr. 29, 2002, eff. Dec. 1, 2002; Apr. 25, 2005, eff. Dec. 1, 2005; Mar. 26, 2009, eff. Dec. 1, 2009; Apr. 28, 2016, eff. Dec. 1, 2016.)

RULE 28. BRIEFS

(a) Appellant's Brief. The appellant's brief must contain, under appropriate headings and in the order indicated:

   (1) a corporate disclosure statement if required by Rule 26.1;

   (2) a table of contents, with page references;

   (3) a table of authorities—cases (alphabetically arranged), statutes, and other authorities—with references to the pages of the brief where they are cited;

   (4) a jurisdictional statement, including:

     (A) the basis for the district court's or agency's subject-matter jurisdiction, with citations to applicable statutory provisions and stating relevant facts establishing jurisdiction;

     (B) the basis for the court of appeals' jurisdiction, with citations to applicable statutory provisions and stating relevant facts establishing jurisdiction;

     (C) the filing dates establishing the timeliness of the appeal or petition for review; and

     (D) an assertion that the appeal is from a final order or judgment that disposes of all parties' claims, or information establishing the court of appeals' jurisdiction on some other basis;

   (5) a statement of the issues presented for review;

   (6) a concise statement of the case setting out the facts relevant to the issues submitted for review, describing the relevant procedural history, and identifying the rulings presented for review, with appropriate references to the record (see Rule 28(e));

   (7) a summary of the argument, which must contain a succinct, clear, and accurate statement of the arguments made in the body of the brief, and which must not merely repeat the argument headings;

   (8) the argument, which must contain:

     (A) appellant's contentions and the reasons for them, with citations to the authorities and parts of the record on which the appellant relies; and

     (B) for each issue, a concise statement of the applicable standard of review (which may appear in the discussion of the issue or under a separate heading placed before the discussion of the issues);

   (9) a short conclusion stating the precise relief sought; and

   (10) the certificate of compliance, if required by Rule 32(g)(1).

(b) Appellee's Brief. The appellee's brief must conform to the requirements of Rule 28(a)(1)–(8) and (10), except that none of the following need appear unless the appellee is dissatisfied with the appellant's statement:

   (1) the jurisdictional statement;

   (2) the statement of the issues;

   (3) the statement of the case; and

   (4) the statement of the standard of review.

(c) Reply Brief. The appellant may file a brief in reply to the appellee's brief. Unless the court permits, no further briefs may be filed. A reply brief must contain a table of contents, with page references, and a table of authorities—cases (alphabetically arranged), statutes, and other authorities—with references to the pages of the reply brief where they are cited.

(d) References to Parties. In briefs and at oral argument, counsel should minimize use of the terms "appellant" and "appellee." To make briefs clear, counsel should use the parties' actual names or the designations used in the lower court or agency proceeding, or such descriptive terms as "the employee," "the injured person," "the taxpayer," "the ship," "the stevedore."

(e) References to the Record. References to the parts of the record contained in the appendix filed with the appellant's brief must be to the pages of the appendix. If the appendix is prepared after the briefs are filed, a party referring to the record must follow one of the methods detailed in Rule 30(c). If the original record is used under Rule 30(f) and is not consecutively paginated, or if the brief refers to an unreproduced part of the record, any reference must be to the page of the original document. For example:

- Answer p. 7;
- Motion for Judgment p. 2;
- Transcript p. 231.

Only clear abbreviations may be used. A party referring to evidence whose admissibility is in controversy must cite the pages of the appendix or of the transcript at which the evidence was identified, offered, and received or rejected.

(f) Reproduction of Statutes, Rules, Regulations, etc. If the court's determination of the issues presented requires the study of statutes, rules, regulations, etc., the relevant parts must be set out in the brief or in an addendum at the end, or may be supplied to the court in pamphlet form.

(g) [Reserved]

(h) [Reserved]

(i) Briefs in a Case Involving Multiple Appellants or Appellees. In a case involving more than one appellant or appellee, including consolidated cases, any number of appellants or appellees may join in a brief, and any party may adopt by reference a part of another's brief. Parties may also join in reply briefs.

(j) Citation of Supplemental Authorities. If pertinent and significant authorities come to a party's attention after the party's brief has been filed—or after oral argument but before decision—a party may promptly advise the circuit clerk by letter, with a copy to all other parties, setting forth the citations. The letter must state the reasons for the supplemental citations, referring either to the page of the brief or to a point argued orally. The body of the letter must not exceed 350 words. Any response must be made promptly and must be similarly limited.

(As amended Apr. 30, 1979, eff. Aug. 1, 1979; Mar. 10, 1986, eff. July 1, 1986; Apr. 25, 1989, eff. Dec. 1, 1989; Apr. 30, 1991, eff. Dec. 1, 1991; Apr. 22, 1993, eff. Dec. 1, 1993; Apr. 29, 1994, eff. Dec. 1, 1994; Apr. 24, 1998, eff. Dec. 1, 1998; Apr. 29, 2002, eff. Dec. 1, 2002; Apr. 25, 2005, eff. Dec. 1, 2005; Apr. 16, 2013, eff. Dec. 1, 2013; Apr. 28, 2016, eff. Dec. 1, 2016.)

RULE 28.1 CROSS–APPEALS

(a) Applicability. This rule applies to a case in which a cross-appeal is filed. Rules 28(a)-(c), 31(a)(1), 32(a)(2), and 32(a)(7)(A)-(B) do not apply to such a case, except as otherwise provided in this rule.

(b) Designation of Appellant. The party who files a notice of appeal first is the appellant for the purposes of this rule and Rules 30 and 34. If notices are filed on the same day, the plaintiff in the proceeding below is the appellant. These designations may be modified by the parties' agreement or by court order.

(c) Briefs. In a case involving a cross-appeal:

(1) Appellant's Principal Brief. The appellant must file a principal brief in the appeal. That brief must comply with Rule 28(a).

(2) Appellee's Principal and Response Brief. The appellee must file a principal brief in the cross-appeal and must, in the same brief, respond to the principal brief in the appeal. That appellee's brief must comply with Rule 28(a), except that the brief need not include a statement of the case unless the appellee is dissatisfied with the appellant's statement.

(3) Appellant's Response and Reply Brief. The appellant must file a brief that responds to the principal brief in the cross-appeal and may, in the same brief, reply to the response in the appeal. That brief must comply with Rule 28(a)(2)–(8) and (10), except that none of the following need appear unless the appellant is dissatisfied with the appellee's statement in the cross-appeal:

(A) the jurisdictional statement;

(B) the statement of the issues;

(C) the statement of the case; and

(D) the statement of the standard of review.

(4) Appellee's Reply Brief. The appellee may file a brief in reply to the response in the cross-appeal. That brief must comply with Rule 28(a)(2)–(3) and (10) and must be limited to the issues presented by the cross-appeal.

(5) No Further Briefs. Unless the court permits, no further briefs may be filed in a case involving a cross-appeal.

(d) Cover. Except for filings by unrepresented parties, the cover of the appellant's principal brief must be blue; the appellee's principal and response brief, red; the appellant's response and reply brief, yellow; the appellee's reply brief, gray; and intervenor's or amicus curiae's brief, green; and any supplemental brief, tan. The front cover of a brief must contain the information required by Rule 32(a)(2).

(e) Length.

(1) Page Limitation. Unless it complies with Rule 28.1(e)(2), the appellant's principal brief must not exceed 30 pages; the appellee's principal and response brief, 35 pages; the appellant's response and reply brief, 30 pages; and the appellee's reply brief, 15 pages.

(2) Type-Volume Limitation.

(A) The appellant's principal brief or the appellant's response and reply brief is acceptable if it:

(i) contains no more than 13,000 words; or

(ii) uses a monospaced face and contains no more than 1,300 lines of text.

(B) The appellee's principal and response brief is acceptable if it:

(i) contains no more than 15,300 words; or

(ii) uses a monospaced face and contains no more than 1,500 lines of text.

(C) The appellee's reply brief is acceptable if it contains no more than half of the type volume specified in Rule 28.1(e)(2)(A).

(f) Time to Serve and File a Brief. Briefs must be served and filed as follows:

(1) the appellant's principal brief, within 40 days after the record is filed;

(2) the appellee's principal and response brief, within 30 days after the appellant's principal brief is served;

(3) the appellant's response and reply brief, within 30 days after the appellee's principal and response brief is served; and

(4) the appellee's reply brief, within 21 days after the appellant's response and reply brief is served, but at least 7 days before argument unless the court, for good cause, allows a later filing.

(As added April 25, 2005, eff. Dec. 1, 2005; amended Mar. 26, 2009, eff. Dec. 1, 2009; Apr. 16, 2013, eff. Dec. 1, 2013; Apr. 28, 2016, eff. Dec. 1, 2016; Apr. 26, 2018, eff. Dec. 1, 2018.)

RULE 29. BRIEF OF AN AMICUS CURIAE

(a) During Initial Consideration of a Case on the Merits.

(1) Applicability. This Rule 29(a) governs amicus filings during a court's initial consideration of a case on the merits.

(2) When Permitted. The United States or its officer or agency or a state may file an amicus brief without the consent of the parties or leave of court. Any other amicus curiae may file a brief only by leave of court or if the brief states that all parties have consented to its filing, but a court of appeals may prohibit the filing of or may strike an amicus brief that would result in a judge's disqualification.

(3) Motion for Leave to File. The motion must be accompanied by the proposed brief and state:

(A) the movant's interest; and

(B) the reason why an amicus brief is desirable and why the matters asserted are relevant to the disposition of the case.

(4) Contents and Form. An amicus brief must comply with Rule 32. In addition to the requirements of Rule 32, the cover must identify the party or parties supported and indicate whether the brief supports affirmance or reversal. An amicus brief need not comply with Rule 28, but must include the following:

(A) if the amicus curiae is a corporation, a disclosure statement like that required of parties by Rule 26.1;

(B) a table of contents, with page references;

(C) a table of authorities—cases (alphabetically arranged), statutes, and other authorities— with references to the pages of the brief where they are cited;

(D) a concise statement of the identity of the amicus curiae, its interest in the case, and the source of its authority to file;

(E) unless the amicus curiae is one listed in the first sentence of Rule 29(a)(2), a statement that indicates whether:

(i) a party's counsel authored the brief in whole or in part;

(ii) a party or a party's counsel contributed money that was intended to fund preparing or submitting the brief; and

(iii) a person—other than the amicus curiae, its members, or its counsel—contributed money that was intended to fund preparing or submitting the brief and, if so, identifies each such person;

(F) an argument, which may be preceded by a summary and which need not include a statement of the applicable standard of review; and

(G) a certificate of compliance under Rule 32(g)(1), if length is computed using a word or line limit.

(5) Length. Except by the court's permission, an amicus brief may be no more than one-half the maximum length authorized by these rules for a party's principal brief. If the court grants a party permission to file a longer brief, that extension does not affect the length of an amicus brief.

(6) Time for Filing. An amicus curiae must file its brief, accompanied by a motion for filing when necessary, no later than 7 days after the principal brief of the party being supported is filed. An amicus curiae that does not support either party must file its brief no later than 7 days after the appellant's or petitioner's principal brief is filed. A court may grant leave for later filing, specifying the time within which an opposing party may answer.

(7) Reply Brief. Except by the court's permission, an amicus curiae may not file a reply brief.

(8) Oral Argument. An amicus curiae may participate in oral argument only with the court's permission.

(b) During Consideration of Whether to Grant Rehearing.

(1) Applicability. This Rule 29(b) governs amicus filings during a court's consideration of whether to grant panel rehearing or rehearing en banc, unless a local rule or order in a case provides otherwise.

(2) When Permitted. The United States or its officer or agency or a state may file an amicus brief without the consent of the parties or leave of court. Any other amicus curiae may file a brief only by leave of court.

(3) Motion for Leave to File. Rule 29(a)(3) applies to a motion for leave.

(4) Contents, Form, and Length. Rule 29(a)(4) applies to the amicus brief. The brief must not exceed 2,600 words.

(5) Time for Filing. An amicus curiae supporting the petition for rehearing or supporting neither party must file its brief, accompanied by a motion for filing when necessary, no later than 7 days after the petition is filed. An amicus curiae opposing the petition must file its brief, accompanied by a motion for filing when necessary, no later than the date set by the court for the response.

(As amended Apr. 24, 1998, eff. Dec. 1, 1998; Apr. 28, 2010, eff. Dec. 1, 2010; Apr. 28, 2016, eff. Dec. 1, 2016; Apr. 26, 2018, eff. Dec. 1, 2018.)

RULE 30. APPENDIX TO THE BRIEFS

(a) Appellant's Responsibility.

(1) Contents of the Appendix. The appellant must prepare and file an appendix to the briefs containing:

(A) the relevant docket entries in the proceeding below;

(B) the relevant portions of the pleadings, charge, findings, or opinion;

(C) the judgment, order, or decision in question; and

(D) other parts of the record to which the parties wish to direct the court's attention.

(2) Excluded Material. Memoranda of law in the district court should not be included in the appendix unless they have independent relevance. Parts of the record may be relied on by the court or the parties even though not included in the appendix.

(3) Time to File; Number of Copies. Unless filing is deferred under Rule 30(c), the appellant must file 10 copies of the appendix with the brief and must serve one copy on counsel for each party separately represented. An unrepresented party proceeding in forma pauperis must file 4 legible copies with the clerk, and one copy must be served on counsel for each separately represented party. The court may by local rule or by order in a particular case require the filing or service of a different number.

(b) All Parties' Responsibilities.

(1) Determining the Contents of the Appendix. The parties are encouraged to agree on the contents of the appendix. In the absence of an agreement, the appellant must, within 14 days after the record is filed, serve on the appellee a designation of the parts of the record the appellant intends to include in the appendix and a statement of the issues the appellant intends to present for review. The appellee may, within 14 days after receiving the designation, serve on the appellant a designation of additional parts to which it wishes to direct the court's attention. The appellant must include the designated parts in the appendix. The parties must not engage in unnecessary designation of parts of the record, because the entire record is available to the court. This paragraph applies also to a cross-appellant and a cross-appellee.

(2) Costs of Appendix. Unless the parties agree otherwise, the appellant must pay the cost of the appendix. If the appellant considers parts of the record designated by the appellee to be unnecessary, the appellant may advise the appellee, who must then advance the cost of including those parts. The cost of the appendix is a taxable cost. But if any party causes unnecessary parts of the record to be included in the appendix, the court may impose the cost of those parts on that party. Each circuit must, by local rule, provide for sanctions against attorneys who unreasonably and vexatiously increase litigation costs by including unnecessary material in the appendix.

(c) Deferred Appendix.

(1) Deferral Until After Briefs Are Filed. The court may provide by rule for classes of cases or by order in a particular case that preparation of the appendix may be deferred until after the briefs have been filed and that the appendix may be filed 21 days after the appellee's brief is served. Even though the filing of the appendix may be deferred, Rule 30(b) applies; except that a party must designate the parts of the record it wants included in the appendix when it serves its brief, and need not include a statement of the issues presented.

(2) References to the Record.

(A) If the deferred appendix is used, the parties may cite in their briefs the pertinent pages of the record. When the appendix is prepared, the record pages cited in the briefs must be indicated by inserting record page numbers, in brackets, at places in the appendix where those pages of the record appear.

(B) A party who wants to refer directly to pages of the appendix may serve and file copies of the brief within the time required by Rule 31(a), containing appropriate references to pertinent pages of the record. In that event, within 14 days after the appendix is filed, the party must serve and file copies of the brief, containing references to the pages of the appendix in place of or in addition to the references to the pertinent pages of the record. Except for the correction of typographical errors, no other changes may be made to the brief.

(d) Format of the Appendix. The appendix must begin with a table of contents identifying the page at which each part begins. The relevant docket entries must follow the table of contents. Other parts of the record must follow chronologically. When pages from the transcript of proceedings are placed in the appendix, the transcript page numbers must be shown in brackets immediately before the included pages. Omissions in the text of papers or of the transcript must be indicated by asterisks. Immaterial formal matters (captions, subscriptions, acknowledgments, etc.) should be omitted.

(e) Reproduction of Exhibits. Exhibits designated for inclusion in the appendix may be reproduced in a separate volume, or volumes, suitably indexed. Four copies must be filed with the appendix, and one copy must be served on counsel for each separately represented party. If a transcript of a proceeding before an administrative agency, board, commission, or officer was used in a district-court action and has been designated for inclusion in the appendix, the transcript must be placed in the appendix as an exhibit.

(f) Appeal on the Original Record Without an Appendix. The court may, either by rule for all cases or classes of cases or by order in a particular case, dispense with the appendix and permit an appeal to proceed on the original record with any copies of the record, or relevant parts, that the court may order the parties to file.

(As amended Mar. 30, 1970, eff. July 1, 1970; Mar. 10, 1986, eff. July 1, 1986; Apr. 30, 1991, eff. Dec. 1, 1991; Apr. 29, 1994, eff. Dec. 1, 1994; Apr. 24, 1998, eff. Dec. 1, 1998; Mar. 26, 2009, eff. Dec. 1, 2009.)

RULE 31. SERVING AND FILING BRIEFS

(a) Time to Serve and File a Brief.

(1) The appellant must serve and file a brief within 40 days after the record is filed. The appellee must serve and file a brief within 30 days after the appellant's brief is served. The appellant may serve and file a reply brief within 21 days after service of the appellee's brief but a reply brief must be filed at least 7 days before argument, unless the court, for good cause, allows a later filing.

(2) A court of appeals that routinely considers cases on the merits promptly after the briefs are filed may shorten the time to serve and file briefs, either by local rule or by order in a particular case.

(b) Number of Copies. Twenty-five copies of each brief must be filed with the clerk and 2 copies must be served on each unrepresented party and on counsel for each separately represented party. An unrepresented party proceeding in forma pauperis must file 4 legible copies with the clerk, and one copy must be served on each unrepresented party and on counsel for each separately represented party. The court may by local rule or by order in a particular case require the filing or service of a different number.

(c) Consequence of Failure to File. If an appellant fails to file a brief within the time provided by this rule, or within an extended time, an appellee may move to dismiss the appeal. An appellee who fails to file a brief will not be heard at oral argument unless the court grants permission.

(As amended Mar. 30, 1970, eff. July 1, 1970; Mar. 10, 1986, eff. July 1, 1986; Apr. 29, 1994, eff. Dec. 1, 1994; Apr. 24, 1998, eff. Dec. 1, 1998; Apr. 29, 2002, eff. Dec. 1, 2002; Mar. 26, 2009, eff. Dec. 1, 2009; Apr. 26, 2018, eff. Dec. 1, 2018.)

RULE 32. FORM OF BRIEFS, APPENDICES, AND OTHER PAPERS

(a) Form of a Brief.

(1) Reproduction.

(A) A brief may be reproduced by any process that yields a clear black image on light paper. The paper must be opaque and unglazed. Only one side of the paper may be used.

(B) Text must be reproduced with a clarity that equals or exceeds the output of a laser printer.

(C) Photographs, illustrations, and tables may be reproduced by any method that results in a good copy of the original; a glossy finish is acceptable if the original is glossy.

(2) Cover. Except for filings by unrepresented parties, the cover of the appellant's brief must be blue; the appellee's, red; an intervenor's or amicus curiae's, green; any reply brief, gray; and any supplemental brief, tan. The front cover of a brief must contain:

(A) the number of the case centered at the top;

(B) the name of the court;

(C) the title of the case (see Rule 12(a));

(D) the nature of the proceeding (e.g., Appeal, Petition for Review) and the name of the court, agency, or board below;

(E) the title of the brief, identifying the party or parties for whom the brief is filed; and

(F) the name, office address, and telephone number of counsel representing the party for whom the brief is filed.

(3) Binding. The brief must be bound in any manner that is secure, does not obscure the text, and permits the brief to lie reasonably flat when open.

(4) Paper Size, Line Spacing, and Margins. The brief must be on 8½ by 11 inch paper. The text must be double-spaced, but quotations more than two lines long may be indented and single-spaced. Headings and footnotes may be single-spaced. Margins must be at least one inch on all four sides. Page numbers may be placed in the margins, but no text may appear there.

(5) Typeface. Either a proportionally spaced or a mono-spaced face may be used.

(A) A proportionally spaced face must include serifs, but sans-serif type may be used in headings and captions. A proportionally spaced face must be 14–point or larger.

(B) A monospaced face may not contain more than 10½ characters per inch.

(6) Type Styles. A brief must be set in a plain, roman style, although italics or boldface may be used for emphasis. Case names must be italicized or underlined.

(7) Length.

(A) Page Limitation. A principal brief may not exceed 30 pages, or a reply brief 15 pages, unless it complies with Rule 32(a)(7)(B).

(B) Type-Volume Limitation.

(i) A principal brief is acceptable if it:

● contains no more than 13,000 words; or

● uses a monospaced face and contains no more than 1,300 lines of text.

(ii) A reply brief is acceptable if it contains no more than half of the type volume specified in Rule 32(a)(7)(B)(i).

(b) Form of an Appendix. An appendix must comply with Rule 32(a)(1), (2), (3), and (4), with the following exceptions:

(1) The cover of a separately bound appendix must be white.

(2) An appendix may include a legible photocopy of any document found in the record or of a printed judicial or agency decision.

(3) When necessary to facilitate inclusion of odd-sized documents such as technical drawings, an appendix may be a size other than 8½ by 11 inches, and need not lie reasonably flat when opened.

(c) **Form of Other Papers.**

(1) **Motion.** The form of a motion is governed by Rule 27(d).

(2) **Other Papers.** Any other paper, including a petition for panel rehearing and a petition for hearing or rehearing en banc, and any response to such a petition, must be reproduced in the manner prescribed by Rule 32(a), with the following exceptions:

(A) A cover is not necessary if the caption and signature page of the paper together contain the information required by Rule 32(a)(2). If a cover is used, it must be white.

(B) Rule 32(a)(7) does not apply.

(d) **Signature.** Every brief, motion, or other paper filed with the court must be signed by the party filing the paper or, if the party is represented, by one of the party's attorneys.

(e) **Local Variation.** Every court of appeals must accept documents that comply with the form requirements of this rule and the length limits set by these rules. By local rule or order in a particular case, a court of appeals may accept documents that do not meet all the form requirements of this rule or the length limits set by these rules.

(f) **Items Excluded from Length.** In computing any length limit, headings, footnotes, and quotations count toward the limit but the following items do not:

- the cover page;
- a corporate disclosure statement;
- a table of contents;
- a table of citations;
- a statement regarding oral argument;
- an addendum containing statutes, rules, or regulations;
- certificates of counsel;
- the signature block;
- the proof of service; and
- any item specifically excluded by these rules or by local rule.

(g) **Certificate of Compliance.**

(1) **Briefs and Papers That Require a Certificate.** A brief submitted under Rules 28.1(e)(2), 29(b)(4), or 32(a)(7)(B)—and a paper submitted under Rules 5(c)(1), 21(d)(1), 27(d)(2)(A), 27(d)(2)(C), 35(b)(2)(A), or 40(b)(1)—must include a certificate by the attorney, or an unrepresented party, that the document complies with the type-volume limitation. The person preparing the certificate may rely on the word or line count of the word-processing system used to prepare the document. The certificate must

state the number of words—or the number of lines of monospaced type—in the document.

(2) **Acceptable Form.** Form 6 in the Appendix of Forms meets the requirements for a certificate of compliance.

(As amended Apr. 24, 1998, eff. Dec. 1, 1998; Apr. 29, 2002, eff. Dec. 1, 2002; Apr. 25, 2005, eff. Dec. 1, 2005; Apr. 28, 2016, eff. Dec. 1, 2016.)

RULE 32.1   CITING JUDICIAL DISPOSITIONS

(a) **Citation Permitted.** A court may not prohibit or restrict the citation of federal judicial opinions, orders, judgments, or other written dispositions that have been:

(i) designated as "unpublished," "not for publication," "non-precedential," "not precedent," or the like; and

(ii) issued on or after January 1, 2007.

(b) **Copies Required.** If a party cites a federal judicial opinion, order, judgment, or other written disposition that is not available in a publicly accessible electronic database, the party must file and serve a copy of that opinion, order, judgment, or disposition with the brief or other paper in which it is cited.

(Added Apr. 12, 2006, eff. Dec. 1, 2006.)

RULE 33.   APPEAL CONFERENCES

The court may direct the attorneys—and, when appropriate, the parties—to participate in one or more conferences to address any matter that may aid in disposing of the proceedings, including simplifying the issues and discussing settlement. A judge or other person designated by the court may preside over the conference, which may be conducted in person or by telephone. Before a settlement conference, the attorneys must consult with their clients and obtain as much authority as feasible to settle the case. The court may, as a result of the conference, enter an order controlling the course of the proceedings or implementing any settlement agreement.

(As amended Apr. 29, 1994, eff. Dec. 1, 1994; Apr. 24, 1998, eff. Dec. 1, 1998.)

RULE 34.   ORAL ARGUMENT

(a) **In General.**

(1) **Party's Statement.** Any party may file, or a court may require by local rule, a statement explaining why oral argument should, or need not, be permitted.

(2) **Standards.** Oral argument must be allowed in every case unless a panel of three judges who have examined the briefs and record unanimously agrees that oral argument is unnecessary for any of the following reasons:

(A) the appeal is frivolous;

(B) the dispositive issue or issues have been authoritatively decided; or

(C) the facts and legal arguments are adequately presented in the briefs and record, and the decisional process would not be significantly aided by oral argument.

(b) **Notice of Argument; Postponement.** The clerk must advise all parties whether oral argument will be scheduled, and, if so, the date, time, and place for it, and the time allowed for each side. A motion to postpone the argument or to allow longer argument must be filed reasonably in advance of the hearing date.

(c) Order and Contents of Argument. The appellant opens and concludes the argument. Counsel must not read at length from briefs, records, or authorities.

(d) Cross-Appeals and Separate Appeals. If there is a cross-appeal, Rule 28.1(b) determines which party is the appellant and which is the appellee for purposes of oral argument. Unless the court directs otherwise, a cross-appeal or separate appeal must be argued when the initial appeal is argued. Separate parties should avoid duplicative argument.

(e) Nonappearance of a Party. If the appellee fails to appear for argument, the court must hear appellant's argument. If the appellant fails to appear for argument, the court may hear the appellee's argument. If neither party appears, the case will be decided on the briefs, unless the court orders otherwise.

(f) Submission on Briefs. The parties may agree to submit a case for decision on the briefs, but the court may direct that the case be argued.

(g) Use of Physical Exhibits at Argument; Removal. Counsel intending to use physical exhibits other than documents at the argument must arrange to place them in the courtroom on the day of the argument before the court convenes. After the argument, counsel must remove the exhibits from the courtroom, unless the court directs otherwise. The clerk may destroy or dispose of the exhibits if counsel does not reclaim them within a reasonable time after the clerk gives notice to remove them.

(As amended Apr. 1, 1979, eff. Aug. 1, 1979; Mar. 10, 1986, eff. July 1, 1986; Apr. 30, 1991, eff. Dec. 1, 1991; Apr. 22, 1993, eff. Dec. 1, 1993; Apr. 24, 1998, eff. Dec. 1, 1998; Apr. 25, 2005, eff. Dec. 1, 2005.)

RULE 35.   EN BANC DETERMINATION

(a) When Hearing or Rehearing En Banc May Be Ordered. A majority of the circuit judges who are in regular active service and who are not disqualified may order that an appeal or other proceeding be heard or reheard by the court of appeals en banc. An en banc hearing or rehearing is not favored and ordinarily will not be ordered unless:

(1) en banc consideration is necessary to secure or maintain uniformity of the court's decisions; or

(2) the proceeding involves a question of exceptional importance.

(b) Petition for Hearing or Rehearing En Banc. A party may petition for a hearing or rehearing en banc.

(1) The petition must begin with a statement that either:

(A) the panel decision conflicts with a decision of the United States Supreme Court or of the court to which the petition is addressed (with citation to the conflicting case or cases) and consideration by the full court is therefore necessary to secure and maintain uniformity of the court's decisions; or

(B) the proceeding involves one or more questions of exceptional importance, each of which must be concisely stated; for example, a petition may assert that a proceeding presents a question of exceptional importance if it involves an issue on which the panel decision conflicts with the authoritative decisions of other United States Courts of Appeals that have addressed the issue.

(2) Except by the court's permission:

(A) a petition for an en banc hearing or rehearing produced using a computer must not exceed 3,900 words; and

(B) a handwritten or typewritten petition for an en banc hearing or rehearing must not exceed 15 pages.

(3) For purposes of the limits in Rule 35(b)(2), if a party files both a petition for panel rehearing and a petition for rehearing en banc, they are considered a single document even if they are filed separately, unless separate filing is required by local rule.

(c) Time for Petition for Hearing or Rehearing En Banc. A petition that an appeal be heard initially en banc must be filed by the date when the appellee's brief is due. A petition for a rehearing en banc must be filed within the time prescribed by Rule 40 for filing a petition for rehearing.

(d) Number of Copies. The number of copies to be filed must be prescribed by local rule and may be altered by order in a particular case.

(e) Response. No response may be filed to a petition for an en banc consideration unless the court orders a response.

(f) Call for a Vote. A vote need not be taken to determine whether the case will be heard or reheard en banc unless a judge calls for a vote.

(As amended Apr. 1, 1979, eff. Aug. 1, 1979; Apr. 29, 1994, eff. Dec. 1, 1994; Apr. 24, 1998, eff. Dec. 1, 1998; Apr. 25, 2005, eff. Dec. 1, 2005; Apr. 28, 2016, eff. Dec. 1, 2016.)

RULE 36.   ENTRY OF JUDGMENT; NOTICE

(a) Entry. A judgment is entered when it is noted on the docket. The clerk must prepare, sign, and enter the judgment:

(1) after receiving the court's opinion—but if settlement of the judgment's form is required, after final settlement; or

(2) if a judgment is rendered without an opinion, as the court instructs.

(b) Notice. On the date when judgment is entered, the clerk must serve on all parties a copy of the opinion—or the judgment, if no opinion was written—and a notice of the date when the judgment was entered.

(As amended Apr. 24, 1998, eff. Dec. 1, 1998; Apr. 29, 2002, eff. Dec. 1, 2002.)

RULE 37.   INTEREST ON JUDGMENT

(a) When the Court Affirms. Unless the law provides otherwise, if a money judgment in a civil case is affirmed, whatever interest is allowed by law is payable from the date when the district court's judgment was entered.

(b) When the Court Reverses. If the court modifies or reverses a judgment with a direction that a money judgment be entered in the district court, the mandate must contain instructions about the allowance of interest.

(As amended Apr. 24, 1998, eff. Dec. 1, 1998.)

RULE 38.　FRIVOLOUS APPEAL— DAMAGES AND COSTS

If a court of appeals determines that an appeal is frivolous, it may, after a separately filed motion or notice from the court and reasonable opportunity to respond, award just damages and single or double costs to the appellee.

(As amended Apr. 29, 1994, eff. Dec. 1, 1994; Apr. 24, 1998, eff. Dec. 1, 1998.)

RULE 39.　COSTS

(a) Against Whom Assessed. The following rules apply unless the law provides or the court orders otherwise:

(1) if an appeal is dismissed, costs are taxed against the appellant, unless the parties agree otherwise;

(2) if a judgment is affirmed, costs are taxed against the appellant;

(3) if a judgment is reversed, costs are taxed against the appellee;

(4) if a judgment is affirmed in part, reversed in part, modified, or vacated, costs are taxed only as the court orders.

(b) Costs For and Against the United States. Costs for or against the United States, its agency, or officer will be assessed under Rule 39(a) only if authorized by law.

(c) Costs of Copies. Each court of appeals must, by local rule, fix the maximum rate for taxing the cost of producing necessary copies of a brief or appendix, or copies of records authorized by Rule 30(f). The rate must not exceed that generally charged for such work in the area where the clerk's office is located and should encourage economical methods of copying.

(d) Bill of Costs: Objections; Insertion in Mandate.

(1) A party who wants costs taxed must—within 14 days after entry of judgment—file with the circuit clerk, with proof of service, an itemized and verified bill of costs.

(2) Objections must be filed within 14 days after service of the bill of costs, unless the court extends the time.

(3) The clerk must prepare and certify an itemized statement of costs for insertion in the mandate, but issuance of the mandate must not be delayed for taxing costs. If the mandate issues before costs are finally determined, the district clerk must—upon the circuit clerk's request—add the statement of costs, or any amendment of it, to the mandate.

(e) Costs on Appeal Taxable in the District Court. The following costs on appeal are taxable in the district court for the benefit of the party entitled to costs under this rule:

(1) the preparation and transmission of the record;

(2) the reporter's transcript, if needed to determine the appeal;

(3) premiums paid for a bond or other security to preserve rights pending appeal; and

(4) the fee for filing the notice of appeal.

(As amended Apr. 30, 1979, eff. Aug. 1, 1979; Mar. 10, 1986, eff. July 1, 1986; Apr. 24, 1998, eff. Dec. 1, 1998; Mar. 26, 2009, eff. Dec. 1, 2009; Apr. 26, 2018, eff. Dec. 1, 2018.)

RULE 40.　PETITION FOR PANEL REHEARING

(a) Time to File; Contents; Answer; Action by the Court if Granted.

(1) **Time.** Unless the time is shortened or extended by order or local rule, a petition for panel rehearing may be filed within 14 days after entry of judgment. But in a civil case, unless an order shortens or extends the time, the petition may be filed by any party within 45 days after entry of judgment if one of the parties is:

(A) the United States;

(B) a United States agency;

(C) a United States officer or employee sued in an official capacity; or

(D) a current or former United States officer or employee sued in an individual capacity for an act or omission occurring in connection with duties performed on the United States' behalf—including all instances in which the United States represents that person when the court of appeals' judgment is entered or files the petition for that person.

(2) **Contents.** The petition must state with particularity each point of law or fact that the petitioner believes the court has overlooked or misapprehended and must argue in support of the petition. Oral argument is not permitted.

(3) **Answer.** Unless the court requests, no answer to a petition for panel rehearing is permitted. But ordinarily rehearing will not be granted in the absence of such a request.

(4) **Action by the Court.** If a petition for panel rehearing is granted, the court may do any of the following:

(A) make a final disposition of the case without reargument;

(B) restore the case to the calendar for reargument or resubmission; or

(C) issue any other appropriate order.

(b) Form of Petition; Length. The petition must comply in form with Rule 32. Copies must be served and filed as Rule 31 prescribes. Except by the court's permission:

(1) a petition for panel rehearing produced using a computer must not exceed 3,900 words; and

(2) a handwritten or typewritten petition for panel rehearing must not exceed 15 pages.

(As amended Apr. 30, 1979, eff. Aug. 1, 1979; Apr. 29, 1994, eff. Dec. 1, 1994; Apr. 24, 1998, eff. Dec. 1, 1998; Apr. 26, 2011, eff. Dec. 1, 2011; Apr. 28, 2016, eff. Dec. 1, 2016.)

RULE 41.   MANDATE: CONTENTS; ISSUANCE AND EFFECTIVE DATE; STAY

(a) Contents. Unless the court directs that a formal mandate issue, the mandate consists of a certified copy of the judgment, a copy of the court's opinion, if any, and any direction about costs.

(b) When Issued. The court's mandate must issue 7 days after the time to file a petition for rehearing expires, or 7 days after entry of an order denying a timely petition for panel rehearing, petition for rehearing en banc, or motion for stay of mandate, whichever is later. The court may shorten or extend the time by order.

(c) Effective Date. The mandate is effective when issued.

(d) Staying the Mandate Pending a Petition for Certiorari.

(1) Motion to Stay. A party may move to stay the mandate pending the filing of a petition for a writ of certiorari in the Supreme Court. The motion must be served on all parties and must show that the petition would present a substantial question and that there is good cause for a stay.

(2) Duration of Stay; Extensions. The stay must not exceed 90 days, unless:

(A) the period is extended for good cause; or

(B) the party who obtained the stay notifies the circuit clerk in writing within the period of the stay:

(i) that the time for filing a petition has been extended, in which case the stay continues for the extended period; or

(ii) that the petition has been filed, in which case the stay continues until the Supreme Court's final disposition.

(3) Security. The court may require a bond or other security as a condition to granting or continuing a stay of the mandate.

(4) Issuance of Mandate. The court of appeals must issue the mandate immediately on receiving a copy of a Supreme Court order denying the petition, unless extraordinary circumstances exist.

(As amended Apr. 29, 1994, eff. Dec. 1, 1994; Apr. 24, 1998, eff. Dec. 1, 1998; Apr. 29, 2002, eff. Dec. 1, 2002; Mar. 26, 2009, eff. Dec. 1, 2009; Apr. 26, 2018, eff. Dec. 1, 2018.)

RULE 42.   VOLUNTARY DISMISSAL

(a) Dismissal in the District Court. Before an appeal has been docketed by the circuit clerk, the district court may dismiss the appeal on the filing of a stipulation signed by all parties or on the appellant's motion with notice to all parties.

(b) Dismissal in the Court of Appeals. The circuit clerk may dismiss a docketed appeal if the parties file a signed dismissal agreement specifying how costs are to be paid and pay any fees that are due. But no mandate or other process may issue without a court order. An appeal may be dismissed on the appellant's motion on terms agreed to by the parties or fixed by the court.

(As amended Apr. 24, 1998, eff. Dec. 1, 1998.)

RULE 43.   SUBSTITUTION OF PARTIES

(a) Death of a Party.

(1) After Notice of Appeal Is Filed. If a party dies after a notice of appeal has been filed or while a proceeding is pending in the court of appeals, the decedent's personal representative may be substituted as a party on motion filed with the circuit clerk by the representative or by any party. A party's motion must be served on the representative in accordance with Rule 25. If the decedent has no representative, any party may suggest the death on the record, and the court of appeals may then direct appropriate proceedings.

(2) Before Notice of Appeal Is Filed—Potential Appellant. If a party entitled to appeal dies before filing a notice of appeal, the decedent's personal representative—or, if there is no personal representative, the decedent's attorney of record—may file a notice of appeal within the time prescribed by these rules. After the notice of appeal is filed, substitution must be in accordance with Rule 43(a)(1).

(3) Before Notice of Appeal Is Filed—Potential Appellee. If a party against whom an appeal may be taken dies after entry of a judgment or order in the district court, but before a notice of appeal is filed, an appellant may proceed as if the death had not occurred. After the notice of appeal is filed, substitution must be in accordance with Rule 43(a)(1).

(b) Substitution for a Reason Other Than Death. If a party needs to be substituted for any reason other than death, the procedure prescribed in Rule 43(a) applies.

(c) Public Officer: Identification; Substitution.

(1) Identification of Party. A public officer who is a party to an appeal or other proceeding in an official capacity may be described as a party by the public officer's official title rather than by name. But the court may require the public officer's name to be added.

(2) Automatic Substitution of Officeholder. When a public officer who is a party to an appeal or other proceeding in an official capacity dies, resigns, or otherwise ceases to hold office, the action does not abate. The public officer's successor is automatically substituted as a party. Proceedings following the substitution are to be in the name of the substituted party, but any misnomer that does not affect the substantial rights of the parties may be disregarded. An order of substitution may be entered at any time, but failure to enter an order does not affect the substitution.

(As amended Mar. 10, 1986, eff. July 1, 1986; Apr. 24, 1998, eff. Dec. 1, 1998.)

RULE 44.   CASE INVOLVING A CONSTITUTIONAL QUESTION WHEN THE UNITED STATES OR THE RELEVANT STATE IS NOT A PARTY

(a) Constitutional Challenge to Federal Statute. If a party questions the constitutionality of an Act of Congress in a proceeding in which the United States or its agency, officer, or employee is not a party in an official capacity, the questioning party must give written notice to the circuit clerk immediately upon the filing of the record or as soon as the question is raised in the court of appeals. The clerk must then certify that fact to the Attorney General.

(b) Constitutional Challenge to State Statute. If a party questions the constitutionality of a statute of a State in a proceeding in which that State or its agency, officer, or employee is not a party in an official capacity, the questioning party must give written notice to the circuit clerk immediately upon the filing of the record or as soon as the question is raised in the court of appeals. The clerk must then certify that fact to the attorney general of the State.

(As amended Apr. 24, 1998, eff. Dec. 1, 1998; Apr. 29, 2002, eff. Dec. 1, 2002.)

RULE 45. CLERK'S DUTIES

(a) General Provisions.

(1) Qualifications. The circuit clerk must take the oath and post any bond required by law. Neither the clerk nor any deputy clerk may practice as an attorney or counselor in any court while in office.

(2) When Court Is Open. The court of appeals is always open for filing any paper, issuing and returning process, making a motion, and entering an order. The clerk's office with the clerk or a deputy in attendance must be open during business hours on all days except Saturdays, Sundays, and legal holidays. A court may provide by local rule or by order that the clerk's office be open for specified hours on Saturdays or on legal holidays other than New Year's Day, Martin Luther King, Jr.'s Birthday, Washington's Birthday, Memorial Day, Independence Day, Labor Day, Columbus Day, Veterans' Day, Thanksgiving Day, and Christmas Day.

(b) Records.

(1) The Docket. The circuit clerk must maintain a docket and an index of all docketed cases in the manner prescribed by the Director of the Administrative Office of the United States Courts. The clerk must record all papers filed with the clerk and all process, orders, and judgments.

(2) Calendar. Under the court's direction, the clerk must prepare a calendar of cases awaiting argument. In placing cases on the calendar for argument, the clerk must give preference to appeals in criminal cases and to other proceedings and appeals entitled to preference by law.

(3) Other Records. The clerk must keep other books and records required by the Director of the Administrative Office of the United States Courts, with the approval of the Judicial Conference of the United States, or by the court.

(c) Notice of an Order or Judgment. Upon the entry of an order or judgment, the circuit clerk must immediately serve a notice of entry on each party, with a copy of any opinion, and must note the date of service on the docket. Service on a party represented by counsel must be made on counsel.

(d) Custody of Records and Papers. The circuit clerk has custody of the court's records and papers. Unless the court

orders or instructs otherwise, the clerk must not permit an original record or paper to be taken from the clerk's office. Upon disposition of the case, original papers constituting the record on appeal or review must be returned to the court or agency from which they were received. The clerk must preserve a copy of any brief, appendix, or other paper that has been filed.

(As amended Mar. 1, 1971, eff. July 1, 1971; Mar. 10, 1986, eff. July 1, 1986; Apr. 24, 1998, eff. Dec. 1, 1998; Apr. 29, 2002, eff. Dec. 1, 2002; Apr. 25, 2005, eff. Dec. 1, 2005.)

RULE 46. ATTORNEYS

(a) Admission to the Bar.

(1) Eligibility. An attorney is eligible for admission to the bar of a court of appeals if that attorney is of good moral and professional character and is admitted to practice before the Supreme Court of the United States, the highest court of a state, another United States court of appeals, or a United States district court (including the district courts for Guam, the Northern Mariana Islands, and the Virgin Islands).

(2) Application. An applicant must file an application for admission, on a form approved by the court that contains the applicant's personal statement showing eligibility for membership. The applicant must subscribe to the following oath or affirmation:

"I, _____, do solemnly swear [or affirm] that I will conduct myself as an attorney and counselor of this court, uprightly and according to law; and that I will support the Constitution of the United States."

(3) Admission Procedures. On written or oral motion of a member of the court's bar, the court will act on the application. An applicant may be admitted by oral motion in open court. But, unless the court orders otherwise, an applicant need not appear before the court to be admitted. Upon admission, an applicant must pay the clerk the fee prescribed by local rule or court order.

(b) Suspension or Disbarment.

(1) Standard. A member of the court's bar is subject to suspension or disbarment by the court if the member:

(A) has been suspended or disbarred from practice in any other court; or

(B) is guilty of conduct unbecoming a member of the court's bar.

(2) Procedure. The member must be given an opportunity to show good cause, within the time prescribed by the court, why the member should not be suspended or disbarred.

(3) Order. The court must enter an appropriate order after the member responds and a hearing is held, if requested, or after the time prescribed for a response expires, if no response is made.

(c) Discipline. A court of appeals may discipline an attorney who practices before it for conduct unbecoming a member of the bar or for failure to comply with any court rule. First, however, the court must afford the attorney reasonable notice, an opportunity to show cause to the contrary, and, if requested, a hearing.

(As amended Mar. 10, 1986, eff. July 1, 1986; Apr. 24, 1998, eff. Dec. 1, 1998.)

RULE 47. LOCAL RULES BY COURTS OF APPEALS

(a) Local Rules.

(1) Each court of appeals acting by a majority of its judges in regular active service may, after giving appropriate public notice and opportunity for comment, make and amend rules governing its practice. A generally applicable direction to parties or lawyers regarding practice before a court must be in a local rule rather than an internal operating procedure or standing order. A local rule must be consistent with—but not duplicative of—Acts of Congress and rules adopted under 28 U.S.C. § 2072 and must conform to any uniform numbering system prescribed by the Judicial Conference of the United States. Each circuit clerk must send the Administrative Office of the United States Courts a copy of each local rule and internal operating procedure when it is promulgated or amended.

(2) A local rule imposing a requirement of form must not be enforced in a manner that causes a party to lose rights because of a nonwillful failure to comply with the requirement.

(b) Procedure When There Is No Controlling Law. A court of appeals may regulate practice in a particular case in any manner consistent with federal law, these rules, and local rules of the circuit. No sanction or other disadvantage may be imposed for noncompliance with any requirement not in federal law, federal rules, or the local circuit rules unless the alleged violator has been furnished in the particular case with actual notice of the requirement.

(As amended Apr. 27, 1995, eff. Dec. 1, 1995; Apr. 24, 1998, eff. Dec. 1, 1998.)

RULE 48. MASTERS

(a) Appointment; Powers. A court of appeals may appoint a special master to hold hearings, if necessary, and to recommend factual findings and disposition in matters ancillary to proceedings in the court. Unless the order referring a matter to a master specifies or limits the master's powers, those powers include, but are not limited to, the following:

(1) regulating all aspects of a hearing;

(2) taking all appropriate action for the efficient performance of the master's duties under the order;

(3) requiring the production of evidence on all matters embraced in the reference; and

(4) administering oaths and examining witnesses and parties.

(b) Compensation. If the master is not a judge or court employee, the court must determine the master's compensation and whether the cost is to be charged to any party.

(As amended Apr. 29, 1994, eff. Dec. 1, 1994; Apr. 24, 1998, eff. Dec. 1, 1998.)

APPENDIX OF FORMS

FORM 1. NOTICE OF APPEAL TO A COURT OF APPEALS FROM A JUDGMENT OR ORDER OF A DISTRICT COURT

United States District Court for the _____
District of _____
File Number _____

A.B., Plaintiff	)
	)
v.	) *Notice of Appeal*
	)
C.D., Defendant	)

Notice is hereby given that [____ (here name all parties taking the appeal)____ , (plaintiffs) (defendants) in the above named case,*] hereby appeal to the United States Court of Appeals for the _____ Circuit (from the final judgment) (from an order (describing it)) entered in this action on the _____ day of _____, 201___.

(s) _____
Attorney for [_____]
[Address:_____]

[Note to inmate filers: If you are an inmate confined in an institution and you seek the timing benefit of Fed. R. App. P. 4(c)(1), complete Form 7 (Declaration of Inmate Filing) and file that declaration along with this Notice of Appeal.]

* See Rule 3(c) for permissible ways of identifying appellants.

(As amended Apr. 22, 1993, eff. Dec. 1, 1993; Mar. 27, 2003, eff. Dec. 1, 2003; Apr. 28, 2016, eff. Dec. 1, 2016.)

FORM 2. NOTICE OF APPEAL TO A COURT OF APPEALS FROM A DECISION OF THE UNITED STATES TAX COURT

UNITED STATES TAX COURT

Washington, D.C.

A.B., *Petitioner*	)	
	)	
v.	)	Docket No. _____
	)	
Commissioner of Internal	)	
Revenue, *Respondent*	)	

Notice of Appeal

Notice is hereby given that [___here name all parties taking the appeal [1]___], hereby appeal to the United States Court of Appeals for the _____ Circuit from (that part of) the decision of this court entered in the above captioned proceeding on the _____ day of _____, 201__ (relating to _____).

        (s) _____
                       Counsel for [_____]
                       [Address:_____]

(As amended Apr. 22, 1993, eff. Dec. 1, 1993; Mar. 27, 2003, eff. Dec. 1, 2003.)

[1] See Rule 3(c) for permissible ways of identifying appellants.

FORM 3.   PETITION FOR REVIEW OF ORDER OF AN AGENCY, BOARD, COMMISSION OR OFFICER

United States Court of Appeals for the _____ Circuit

A.B., Petitioner   )
)
                    v.   )   Petition for Review
XYZ Commission, Respondent   )

[_____(here name all parties bringing the petition[1])_____] hereby petition the court for review of the Order of the XYZ Commission (describe the order) entered on _____, 201___.

                              [(s)] _____
                                      Attorney for Petitioners
                                      Address:_____

(As amended Apr. 22, 1993, eff. Dec. 1, 1993; Mar. 27, 2003, eff. Dec. 1, 2003.)

[1] See Rule 15.

FORM 4. AFFIDAVIT ACCOMPANYING MOTION FOR PERMISSION TO APPEAL IN FORMA PAUPERIS

UNITED STATES DISTRICT COURT
for the
<_____> DISTRICT OF <_____>

```
<Name(s) of plaintiff(s)>,        )
                                  )
        Plaintiff(s)              )
                                  )
v.                                )
                                  ) Case No. <Number>
<Name(s) of defendant(s)>,        )
                                  )
        Defendant(s)              )
                                  )
```

Affidavit in Support of Motion

I swear or affirm under penalty of perjury that, because of my poverty, I cannot prepay the docket fees of my appeal or post a bond for them. I believe I am entitled to redress. I swear or affirm under penalty of perjury under United States laws that my answers on this form are true and correct. (28 U.S.C. § 1746; 18 U.S.C. § 1621.)

Signed: _____

Instructions

Complete all questions in this application and then sign it. Do not leave any blanks: if the answer to a question is "0," "none," or "not applicable (N/A)," write in that response. If you need more space to answer a question or to explain your answer, attach a separate sheet of paper identified with your name, your case's docket number, and the question number.

Date: _____

My issues on appeal are:

1. *For both you and your spouse estimate the average amount of money received from each of the following sources during the past 12 months. Adjust any amount that was received weekly, biweekly, quarterly, semiannually, or annually to show the monthly rate. Use gross amounts, that is, amounts before any deductions for taxes or otherwise.*

Income source	Average monthly amount during the past 12 months		Amount expected next month	
	You	**Spouse**	**You**	**Spouse**
Employment	$_____	$_____	$_____	$_____
Self-employment	$_____	$_____	$_____	$_____
Income from real property (such as rental income)	$_____	$_____	$_____	$_____
Interest and dividends	$_____	$_____	$_____	$_____
Gifts	$_____	$_____	$_____	$_____
Alimony	$_____	$_____	$_____	$_____
Child support	$_____	$_____	$_____	$_____
Retirement (such as social security, pensions, annuities, insurance)	$_____	$_____	$_____	$_____
Disability (such as social security, insurance payments)	$_____	$_____	$_____	$_____
Unemployment payments	$_____	$_____	$_____	$_____
Public-assistance (such as welfare)	$_____	$_____	$_____	$_____

Other (specify): _____ $_____ $_____ $_____ $_____

Total monthly income: $_____ $_____ $_____ $_____

2. *List your employment history for the past two years, most recent employer first. (Gross monthly pay is before taxes or other deductions.)*

Employer	Address	Dates of employment	Gross monthly pay
_____	_____	_____	_____
_____	_____	_____	_____
_____	_____	_____	_____

3. *List your spouse's employment history for the past two years, most recent employer first. (Gross monthly pay is before taxes or other deductions.)*

Employer	Address	Dates of employment	Gross monthly pay
_____	_____	_____	_____
_____	_____	_____	_____
_____	_____	_____	_____

4. *How much cash do you and your spouse have?* $_____
Below, state any money you or your spouse have in bank accounts or in any other financial institution.

Financial institution	Type of account	Amount you have	Amount your spouse has
_____	_____	$_____	$_____
_____	_____	$_____	$_____
_____	_____	$_____	$_____

If you are a prisoner seeking to appeal a judgment in a civil action or proceeding, you must attach a statement certified by the appropriate institutional officer showing all receipts, expenditures, and balances during the last six months in your institutional accounts. If you have multiple accounts, perhaps because you have been in multiple institutions, attach one certified statement of each account.

5. *List the assets, and their values, which you own or your spouse owns. Do not list clothing and ordinary household furnishings.*

Home (Value)	**Other real estate** (Value)	**Motor vehicle #1** (Value)
_____	_____	Make & year: _____
_____	_____	Model: _____
_____	_____	Registration #: _____

Motor vehicle #2 (Value)	**Other assets** (Value)	**Other assets** (Value)
Make & year: _____	_____	_____
Model: _____	_____	_____
Registration #: _____	_____	_____

6. *State every person, business, or organization owing you or your spouse money, and the amount owed.*

Person owing you or your spouse money	Amount owed to you	Amount owed to your spouse
_____	_____	_____
_____	_____	_____
_____	_____	_____

7. *State the persons who rely on you or your spouse for support.*

Name [or, if under 18, initials only]	Relationship	Age
_____	_____	_____
_____	_____	_____

8. *Estimate the average monthly expenses of you and your family. Show separately the amounts paid by your spouse. Adjust any payments that are made weekly, biweekly, quarterly, semiannually, or annually to show the monthly rate.*

	You	**Your Spouse**
Rent or home-mortgage payment (include lot rented for mobile home)	$_____	$_____
Are real-estate taxes included? ☐ Yes ☐ No		
Is property insurance included? ☐ Yes ☐ No		
Utilities (electricity, heating fuel, water, sewer, and Telephone)	$_____	$_____
Home maintenance (repairs and upkeep)	$_____	$_____
Food	$_____	$_____
Clothing	$_____	$_____
Laundry and dry-cleaning	$_____	$_____
Medical and dental expenses	$_____	$_____
Transportation (not including motor vehicle payments)	$_____	$_____
Recreation, entertainment, newspapers, magazines, etc.	$_____	$_____
Insurance (not deducted from wages or included in mortgage payments)	$_____	$_____
Homeowner's or renter's:	$_____	$_____
Life:	$_____	$_____
Health:	$_____	$_____
Motor Vehicle:	$_____	$_____
Other: _____	$_____	$_____
Taxes (not deducted from wages or included in mortgage payments) (specify): __	$_____	$_____
Installment payments	$_____	$_____
Motor Vehicle:	$_____	$_____
Credit card (name): _____	$_____	$_____
Department store (name): _____	$_____	$_____
Other:	$_____	$_____
Alimony, maintenance, and support paid to others	$_____	$_____
Regular expenses for operation of business, profession, or farm (attach detailed statement)	$_____	$_____
Other (specify): _____	$_____	$_____
Total monthly expenses:	$_____	$_____

9. *Do you expect any major changes to your monthly income or expenses or in your assets or liabilities during the next 12 months?*
☐ Yes ☐ No   If yes, describe on an attached sheet.

10. *Have you spent—or will you be spending—any money for expenses or attorney fees in connection with this lawsuit?* ☐ Yes ☐ No
If yes, how much? $_____

11. *Provide any other information that will help explain why you cannot pay the docket fees for your appeal.*

12. *State the city and state of your legal residence.*
Your daytime phone number: (___) _____
Your age: _____ *Your years of schooling:* _____

(As amended Apr. 24, 1998, eff. Dec. 1, 1998; Apr. 28, 2010, eff. Dec. 1, 2010; Apr. 16, 2013, eff. Dec. 1, 2013; Apr. 26, 2018, eff. Dec. 1, 2018.)

FORM 5. NOTICE OF APPEAL TO A COURT OF APPEALS FROM A JUDGMENT OR ORDER OF A DISTRICT COURT OR A BANKRUPTCY APPELLATE PANEL

United States District Court for the ....
District of ....

In re	)
	)
....,	)
Debtor	) File No............
....,	)
Plaintiff	)
	)
v.	)
....,	)
Defendant	)

Notice of Appeal to
United States Court of Appeals
for the .... Circuit

........................., the plaintiff [or defendant or other party] appeals to the United States Court of Appeals for the .... Circuit from the final judgment [or order or decree] of the district court for the district of .... [or bankruptcy appellate panel of the .... circuit], entered in this case on ...., 20.... [here describe the judgment, order, or decree] ....

The parties to the judgment [or order or decree] appealed from and the names and addresses of their respective attorneys are as follows:

Dated ....
Signed ....
Attorney for Appellant

Address: ....
....

*[**Note to inmate filers:** If you are an inmate confined in an institution and you seek the timing benefit of Fed. R. App. P. 4(c)(1), complete Form 7 (Declaration of Inmate Filing) and file that declaration along with this Notice of Appeal.]*

(Added Apr. 25, 1989, eff. Dec. 1, 1989; amended Mar. 27, 2003, eff. Dec. 1, 2003; Apr. 28, 2016, eff. Dec. 1, 2016.)

FORM 6.   CERTIFICATE OF COMPLIANCE WITH TYPE–VOLUME LIMIT

Certificate of Compliance With Type-Volume Limit, Typeface
Requirements, and Type-Style Requirements

1.   This document complies with [the type-volume limit of Fed. R. App. P. [*insert Rule citation; e.g., 32(a)(7)(B)*]] [the word limit of Fed. R. App. P. [*insert Rule citation; e.g., 5(c)(1)*]] because, excluding the parts of the document exempted by Fed. R. App. P. 32(f) [and [*insert applicable Rule citation, if any*]]:

☐ this document contains [*state the number of*] words, **or**

☐ this brief uses a monospaced typeface and contains [*state the number of*] lines of text.

2.   This document complies with the typeface requirements of Fed. R. App. P. 32(a)(5) and the type-style requirements of Fed. R. App. P. 32(a)(6) because:

☐ this document has been prepared in a proportionally spaced typeface using [*state name and version of word-processing program*] in [*state font size and name of type style*], **or**

☐ this document has been prepared in a monospaced typeface using [*state name and version of word-processing program*] with [*state number of characters per inch and name of type style*].

(s)_____

Attorney for _____

Dated: _____

(Added Apr. 29, 2002, eff. Dec. 1, 2002; amended Apr. 28, 2016, eff. Dec. 1, 2016.)

FORM 7.   DECLARATION OF INMATE FILING

[insert name of court; for example,
United States District Court for the District of Minnesota]

A.B., Plaintiff

v.   Case No. _____

C.D., Defendant

I am an inmate confined in an institution.   Today, _____ *[insert date]*, I am depositing the _____ *[insert title of document; for example, "notice of appeal"]* in this case in the institution's internal mail system.   First–class postage is being prepaid either by me or by the institution on my behalf.

I declare under penalty of perjury that the foregoing is true and correct (see 28 U.S.C. § 1746; 18 U.S.C. § 1621).

Sign your name here _____

Signed on _____ *[insert date]*

*[**Note to inmate filers:** If your institution has a system designed for legal mail, you must use that system in order to receive the timing benefit of Fed. R. App. P. 4(c)(1) or Fed. R. App. P. 25(a)(2)(A)(iii).]*

(Added Apr. 28, 2016, eff. Dec. 1, 2016.   As amended Apr. 26, 2018, eff. Dec. 1, 2018.)

APPENDIX

This chart summarizes the length limits stated in the Federal Rules of Appellate Procedure. Please refer to the rules for precise requirements, and bear in mind the following:

- In computing these limits, you can exclude the items listed in Rule 32(f).

- If you use a word limit or a line limit (other than the word limit in Rule 28(j)), you must file the certificate required by Rule 32(g).

- For the limits in Rules 5, 21, 27, 35, and 40:

  - You must use the word limit if you produce your document on a computer; and

  - You must use the page limit if you handwrite your document or type it on a typewriter.

- For the limits in Rules 28.1, 29(a)(5), and 32:

  - You may use the word limit or page limit, regardless of how you produce the document; or

  - You may use the line limit if you type or print your document with a monospaced typeface. A typeface is monospaced when each character occupies the same amount of horizontal space.

	Rule	Document type	Word limit	Page limit	Line limit
Permission to appeal	5(c)	• Petition for permission to appeal • Answer in opposition • Cross–petition	5,200	20	Not applicable
Extraordinary writs	21(d)	• Petition for writ of mandamus or prohibition or other extraordinary writ • Answer	7,800	30	Not applicable
Motions	27(d)(2)	• Motion • Response to a motion	5,200	20	Not applicable
	27(d)(2)	• Reply to a response to a motion	2,600	10	Not applicable
Parties' briefs (where no cross–appeal)	32(a)(7)	• Principal brief	13,000	30	1,300
	32(a)(7)	• Reply brief	6,500	15	650
Parties' briefs (where cross–appeal)	28.1(e)	• Appellant's principal brief • Appellant's response and reply brief	13,000	30	1,300
	28.1(e)	• Appellee's principal and response brief	15,300	35	1,500
	28.1(e)	• Appellee's reply brief	6,500	15	650
Party's supplemental letter	28(j)	• Letter citing supplemental authorities	350	Not applicable	Not applicable

	Rule	Document type	Word limit	Page limit	Line limit
Amicus briefs	29(a)(5)	• Amicus brief during initial consideration of case on merits	One–half the length set by the Appellate Rules for a party's principal brief	One–half the length set by the Appellate Rules for a party's principal brief	One–half the length set by the Appellate Rules for a party's principal brief
	29(b)(4)	• Amicus brief during consideration of whether to grant rehearing	2,600	Not applicable	Not applicable
Rehearing and en banc filings	35(b)(2) & 40(b)	• Petition for hearing en banc • Petition for panel rehearing; petition for rehearing en banc	3,900	15	Not applicable

(Added Apr. 28, 2016, eff. Dec. 1, 2016.)

INDEX TO
FEDERAL RULES OF APPELLATE PROCEDURE

UNITED STATES COURT OF APPEALS
FOR THE
FIFTH CIRCUIT

Including Amendments Received Through
February 1, 2019

OTHER INTERNAL OPERATING PROCEDURES

APPENDIX OF FORMS

PLAN FOR REPRESENTATION ON APPEAL UNDER THE CRIMINAL JUSTICE ACT

PLAN FOR EXPEDITING CRIMINAL APPEALS

RULES FOR JUDICIAL–CONDUCT AND JUDICIAL– DISABILITY PROCEEDINGS

Preface [National Conduct Rules].
Preface [Fifth Circuit Conduct Rules].

ARTICLE I. GENERAL PROVISIONS

ARTICLE II. INITIATION OF A COMPLAINT

ARTICLE III. REVIEW OF COMPLAINT BY CHIEF JUDGE

ARTICLE IV. INVESTIGATION AND REPORT BY SPECIAL COMMITTEE

ARTICLE V. REVIEW BY JUDICIAL COUNCIL

ARTICLE VI. REVIEW BY COMMITTEE ON JUDICIAL CONDUCT AND DISABILITY

ARTICLE VII. MISCELLANEOUS RULES

TITLE I. APPLICABILITY OF RULES

FRAP 1. SCOPE OF RULES; DEFINITION; TITLE

[For text of rule, see the Federal Rules of Appellate Procedure]

FRAP 2. SUSPENSION OF RULES

[For text of rule, see the Federal Rules of Appellate Procedure]

TITLE II. APPEAL FROM A JUDGMENT OR ORDER OF A DISTRICT COURT

FRAP 3. APPEAL AS OF RIGHT—HOW TAKEN

[For text of rule, see the Federal Rules of Appellate Procedure]

RULE 3. FILING FEE

Filing Fee. When the notice of appeal is filed, the $505 fees established by 28 U.S.C. §§ 1913 and 1917 must be paid to the district court clerk. After the Fifth Circuit receives a duplicate copy of a notice of appeal, the clerk will send counsel or a party notice advising of other requirements of the rule. No additional fees are required. Failure to pay the fees does not prevent the appeal from being docketed, but is grounds for dismissal under 5th Cir. R. 42.

[Amended effective January 4, 1999; January 1, 2001; November 1, 2003; April 9, 2006.]

FRAP 3.1 APPEAL FROM A JUDGMENT OF A MAGISTRATE JUDGE IN A CIVIL CASE [ABROGATED]

[For text of rule, see the Federal Rules of Appellate Procedure]

FRAP 4. APPEAL AS OF RIGHT— WHEN TAKEN

[For text of rule, see the Federal Rules of Appellate Procedure]

FRAP 5. APPEAL BY PERMISSION

[For text of rule, see the Federal Rules of Appellate Procedure]

RULE 5. LENGTH OF PETITION

Length. The certificate of interested persons required by 5th Cir. R. 28.2.1 does not count toward the page limit.
[Added effective January 1, 2001. Amended effective December 1, 2002.]

FRAP 5.1 APPEAL BY LEAVE UNDER 28 U.S.C. § 636(c)(5) [ABROGATED]

[For text of rule, see the Federal Rules of Appellate Procedure]

FRAP 6. APPEAL IN A BANKRUPTCY CASE FROM A FINAL JUDGMENT, ORDER, OR DECREE OF A DISTRICT COURT OR BANKRUPTCY APPELLATE PANEL

[For text of rule, see the Federal Rules of Appellate Procedure]

FRAP 7. BOND FOR COSTS ON APPEAL IN A CIVIL CASE

[For text of rule, see the Federal Rules of Appellate Procedure]

FRAP 8. STAY OR INJUNCTION PENDING APPEAL

[For text of rule, see the Federal Rules of Appellate Procedure]

RULE 8. PROCEDURES IN DEATH PENALTY CASES INVOLVING APPLICATIONS FOR IMMEDIATE STAY OF EXECUTION AND APPEALS IN MATTERS IN WHICH THE DISTRICT COURT HAS EITHER ENTERED OR REFUSED TO ENTER A STAY

8.1 Documents Required. Non-death penalty cases will be handled as described in Fed. R. App. P. 8. Death penalty cases arising from actions brought under 28 U.S.C. §§ 2254 and 2255 will be processed under the procedures found in this rule. The appellant must file 4 copies of the motion for stay and attach, to each, legible copies of the documents listed below. If the appellant asserts there is insufficient time to file a written motion, the appellant must deliver to the clerk 4 legible copies of each of the listed documents as soon as possible. If the appellant cannot attach or deliver any listed document, a statement why it cannot be provided must be substituted. The documents required are:

(a) The complaint or petition to the district court;

(b) Each brief or memorandum of authorities filed by both parties in the district court;

(c) The opinion giving the district court's reasons for denying relief;

(d) The district court judgment denying relief;

(e) The application to the district court for a stay;

(f) The district court order granting or denying a stay, and the statement of reasons for its action;

(g) The certificate of appealability or, if there is none, the order denying a certificate of appealability;

(h) A copy of each state or federal court opinion or judgment involving any issue presented to this court or, if the ruling was not made in a written opinion or judgment, a copy of the relevant portions of the transcript.

8.1.1 If the state indicates that it does not oppose the stay, and the applicant states this fact in the application, these documents do not need to be filed with the application but must be filed within 14 days after the application is filed.

8.1.2 If the appellant raises an issue that was not raised before the district court or has not been exhausted in state court, the applicant must give the reasons why prior action was not taken and why a stay should be granted.

8.2 Panels. Death penalty case matters are handled by special panels selected in rotation from the court's regular screening panels. See 5th Cir. R. 27.2.3 for handling applications for certificates of appealability.

8.3 Motions to Vacate Stays. If the district court enters an order staying execution of a judgment, the party seeking to vacate the stay will attach 4 copies of each of the documents required by 5th Cir. R. 8.1 to the motion.

8.4 Emergency Motions. Emergency motions or applications, whether addressed to the court or to an individual judge, must be filed with the clerk rather than with an individual judge. If there is insufficient time to file a motion or application in person, by mail, or by fax, counsel may communicate with the clerk by telephone and thereafter must file the motion in writing with the clerk as soon as possible. The motion, application, or oral communication must contain a brief account of the prior actions of this or any other court or judge to which the motion or application, or a substantially similar or related petition for relief, was submitted.

8.5 Merits. The parties must address the merits of each issue presented by an application. The panel may allow additional time to permit the parties adequate opportunity to do so.

8.6 Consideration of Merits. If a certificate of appealability has been granted, the panel assigned to decide a motion for a stay of a state court judgment must, before denying a stay, consider and expressly rule on the merits of the appeal, unless the panel finds that the appeal is frivolous and entirely without merit.

8.7 Vacating Stays. The panel assigned to an appeal must consider the merits before vacating a stay of execution, unless the panel rules the appeal is frivolous and entirely without merit.

8.8 Mandate. The panel may order the mandate issued instantly or after such time as it may fix.

8.9 Stays of Execution Following Decision. Stays to permit the filing and consideration of a petition for a writ of certiorari ordinarily will not be granted. The court must determine whether there is a reasonable probability that 4 members of the Supreme Court would consider the underlying issues sufficiently meritorious for the grant of certiorari and whether there is a substantial possibility of reversal of its decision, in addition to a likelihood that irreparable harm will result if its decision is not stayed.

8.10 Time Requirements for Challenges to Death Sentences and/or Execution Procedures. Inmates sentenced to death who wish to appeal an adverse judgment by the district court on a first petition for writ of habeas corpus, who seek permission to file a successive petition, or who seek to challenge their convictions, sentences, or the execution procedures (including but not limited to a suit filed pursuant to 42 U.S.C. § 1983), must exercise reasonable diligence in moving for a certificate of appealability, for permission to file a second or successive habeas petition, or in filing a notice of appeal from an adverse judgment of the district court in any other type of proceeding, and a stay of execution with the clerk of this court at least 7 days before the scheduled execution. Counsel who seek a certificate of appealability, permission to file a successive petition, or an appeal from a district court judgment less than 7 days before the scheduled execution must attach to the proposed filing a detailed explanation stating under oath the reason for the delay. If the motions are filed less than 7 days before the scheduled execution, the court may direct counsel to show good cause for the late filing. If counsel cannot do so, counsel will be subject to sanctions.

If the state asks this court to vacate a district court order staying an execution, counsel for the state will file the state's appeal and application for relief from the stay as soon as practicable after the district court issues its order. Any unjustified delay by the state's counsel in seeking relief in this court will subject counsel to sanctions.

[Amended effective January 4, 1999; December 1, 2002; December 1, 2006; December 1, 2009.]

FRAP 9. RELEASE IN A CRIMINAL CASE

[For text of rule, see the Federal Rules of Appellate Procedure]

RULE 9. RELEASE IN A CRIMINAL CASE

9.1 Release Before Judgment of Conviction. The clerk's office will advise counsel of the requirements of this rule after receiving a copy of a notice of appeal from the district court from an order respecting release entered prior to a judgment of conviction (Fed. R. App. P. 9(a)), or on counsel's advice a notice of appeal has been or will be filed.

Four copies of a memorandum must be filed within 10 days of the filing of the notice of appeal, clearly setting out the nature and circumstances of the offense charged and why the order respecting release is unsupported by the district court proceedings.

9.2 Release After Judgment of Conviction. The original and 3 copies of an application regarding release pending appeal from a judgment of conviction (Fed. R. App. P. 9(b)) must be filed with the clerk of this court.

(a) The application for release must contain:

(1) The appellant's name;

(2) The district court docket number;

(3) The offense of which appellant was convicted; and

(4) The date and terms of sentence.

(b) The application must also contain:

(1) The legal basis for the contention that appellant is unlikely to flee or pose a danger to the safety of any other person or the community;

(2) An explanation why the district court's findings are clearly erroneous; and

(3) The issues to be raised on appeal that present substantial questions of law or fact likely to result in reversal or an order for a new trial on all counts of the indictment on which incarceration has been imposed, with pertinent legal argument establishing that the questions are substantial.

9.3 Required Documents. A copy of the district court's order respecting release pending trial or appeal, containing the written reasons for its ruling, must be appended to the memorandum or the application filed under 5th Cir. R. 9.1 or 9.2.

(a) If the appellant questions the factual basis of the order, a transcript of the district court proceedings on the motion for release must be filed with this court. If the transcript is not filed with the memorandum or application, the appellant must attach a court reporter's certificate verifying that the transcript has been ordered and that satisfactory financial arrangements have been made to pay for it, together with the transcript's estimated date of completion.

(b) If the appellant cannot obtain a transcript of the proceedings, the appellant must state in an affidavit the reasons why not.

9.4 Service. A copy of the memorandum or application filed under 5th Cir. R. 9.1 or 9.2 must be hand-delivered to government counsel or served by other expeditious method.

9.5 Response. The opposing party must file a written response to all requests for release within 10 days after service of the memorandum or application.

[Amended effective January 4, 1999; December 1, 2002; December 1, 2009.]

FRAP 10. THE RECORD ON APPEAL

[For text of rule, see the Federal Rules of Appellate Procedure]

RULE 10. THE RECORD ON APPEAL

10.1 Appellant's Duty to Order the Transcript. The appellant's order of the transcript of proceedings, or parts thereof, contemplated by Fed. R. App. P. 10(b), must be on a form prescribed by the clerk. Counsel will furnish a copy of the order form to the clerk and to the other parties set out in Fed. R. App. P. 10(b). If no transcript needs to be ordered, appellant must file with the clerk a copy of a certificate to that effect that counsel served on the parties under Fed. R. App. P. 10(b).

10.2 Form of Record. The district court must furnish the record on appeal to this court in paper form, and in electronic form whenever available. The paper and electronic records on appeal must be consecutively numbered and paginated. The paper record must be bound in a manner that facilitates reading.

I.O.P.—The district court will furnish a transcript order form, required by this court, when the notice of appeal is filed. Once counsel completes the transcript order, forwards it to the reporter, and makes adequate financial arrangements, counsel's responsibility under Fed. R. App. P. 10 and 11 is fulfilled.

[Amended effective January 4, 1999; December 1, 2005.]

FRAP 11. FORWARDING THE RECORD

[For text of rule, see the Federal Rules of Appellate Procedure]

RULE 11. TRANSMISSION OF THE RECORD

11.1 Duties of Court Reporters. In all cases where transcripts are ordered, the court reporter must use a form provided by the clerk of this court and:

(a) Acknowledge receiving the transcript order, and indicate the date of receipt;

(b) State whether adequate financial arrangements have been made under the CJA, or otherwise;

(c) Provide the number of trial or hearing days involved in the transcript, and estimate the total number of pages;

(d) Give an estimated date when the transcript will be finished; and

(e) Certify that he or she expects to file the transcript with the district court clerk within the time estimated.

11.2 Requests for Extensions of Time. Court reporters seeking extensions of the time for filing the transcript beyond the 30 day period fixed by Fed. R. App. P. 11(b) must file an extension request with the clerk of this court and must specify in detail:

(a) The amount of work accomplished on the transcript;

(b) A list of all outstanding transcripts due to this and other courts, including the due dates for filing; and

(c) A verification that the trial court judge who tried the case is aware of and approves the extension request.

If a court reporter's request for an extension of time is granted, he or she must promptly notify all counsel or unrepresented parties of the extended filing date and send a copy of the notification to this court.

11.3 Duty of the Clerk. The district court clerk is responsible for determining when the record on appeal is complete for purposes of the appeal. Unless the record on appeal is sent to this court within 15 days from the filing of the notice of appeal or 15 days after the filing of the transcript of any trial proceedings, whichever is later, the district court clerk must advise the clerk of this court of the reasons for delay and request an extension to file the record. The clerk of this court may grant an extension for no more than 45 days. Extensions beyond 45 days are referred to a single judge. When transmitting the record on appeal in a direct criminal appeal involving more than one defendant, the district court must separate and identify the pleadings and any transcripts of pre-trial, sentencing, and post-trial hearings that apply to fewer than all of the defendants. However, only one copy of the trial transcript is required. In an action involving more than one defendant at trial but where separate actions are filed under 28 U.S.C. § 2255, the district court must separate and identify the pleadings and transcripts of pre-trial, sentencing, and post-trial hearings that apply to less than all of the defendants. One copy of the trial transcript is required for each defendant filing a separate § 2255 action.

I.O.P.—The clerk will monitor all outstanding transcripts and delays.

On October 11, 1982, the Fifth Circuit Judicial Council adopted a resolution requiring each district court in the Fifth Circuit to develop a court reporter management plan providing for the day-to-day management and supervision of an efficient court reporting service within the district court. These plans must provide for the supervision of court reporters in their relations with litigants as specified in the Court Reporter Act, including fees charged for transcripts, adherence to transcript format prescriptions, and delivery schedules. The plans must also provide that a judge, the clerk, or some other person designated by the court supervises the court reporters.

[Amended effective January 4, 1999; January 1, 2001.]

FRAP 12. DOCKETING THE APPEAL; FILING A REPRESENTATION STATEMENT; FILING THE RECORD

[For text of rule, see the Federal Rules of Appellate Procedure]

RULE 12. REPRESENTATION STATEMENT

Counsel can satisfy the "representation statement" required by Fed. R. App. P. 12(b) by completing this court's "Notice of Appearance Form" and returning it to the clerk within 30 days of filing the notice of appeal.

[Amended effective January 4, 1999.]

FRAP 12.1 REMAND AFTER AN INDICATIVE RULING BY THE DISTRICT ON A MOTION FOR RELIEF THAT IS BARRED BY A PENDING APPEAL

[For text of rule, see the Federal Rules of Appellate Procedure]

TITLE III. APPEALS FROM THE UNITED STATES TAX COURT

FRAP 13. APPEALS FROM THE TAX COURT

[For text of rule, see the Federal Rules of Appellate Procedure]

FRAP 14. APPLICABILITY OF OTHER RULES TO APPEALS FROM THE TAX COURT

[For text of rule, see the Federal Rules of Appellate Procedure]

TITLE IV. REVIEW OR ENFORCEMENT OF AN ORDER OF AN ADMINISTRATIVE AGENCY, BOARD, COMMISSION, OR OFFICER

FRAP 15. REVIEW OR ENFORCEMENT OF AN AGENCY ORDER—HOW OBTAINED; INTERVENTION

[For text of rule, see the Federal Rules of Appellate Procedure]

RULE 15. REVIEW OR ENFORCEMENT OF AN AGENCY ORDER—HOW OBTAINED; INTERVENTION

15.1 Docketing Fee and Copy of Orders—Agency Review Proceedings. At the time a party files a petition for review under Fed. R. App. P. 15, the party must:

(a) Pay the filing fee to the clerk; and

(b) Attach a copy of the order or orders to be reviewed.

15.2 Proceedings for Enforcement of Orders of the National Labor Relations Board. In National Labor Relations Board enforcement proceedings under Fed. R. App. P. 15(b), the respondent is considered the petitioner, and the board the respondent, for briefing and oral argument purposes, unless otherwise ordered by the court.

15.3 Proceedings for Review of Orders of the Federal Energy Regulatory Commission.

15.3.1 *Petition for Review.* Every petition for review must specify in its caption the number, date, and identification of the order reviewed and append the service list required by Fed. R. App. P. 15(c). Counsel filing the petition must attach a certificate that the commission has posted, filed or entered the order being reviewed.

15.3.2 *Docketing.* All petitions for review and other documents concerning commission orders in the same number series (i.e., 699, 699A, 699B) are assigned to the same docket.

15.3.3 *Intervention.*

(a) Party. A party to a commission proceeding may intervene in a review of the proceeding in this court by filing a notice of intervention. The notice must state whether the intervenor is a petitioner who objects to the order or a respondent who supports the order. A notice of intervention confers petitioner or respondent status on the intervening party as to all proceedings.

(b) Nonparty. A person who is not a party to a commission proceeding desiring to intervene in a review of that proceeding must file with the clerk, and serve upon all parties to the proceeding, a motion for leave to intervene. The motion must contain a concise statement of the moving party's interest, the grounds upon which intervention is sought, and why the interest asserted is not adequately protected by existing parties. Oppositions to such motions must be filed within 14 days of service.

15.3.4 *Docketing Statement.* All parties filing petitions for review must file a joint docketing statement within 30 days of the filing of the initial petition for review, but not later than 14 days after the expiration of the period permitted for filing a petition for review. The docketing statement must:

(a) List each issue to be raised in the review;

(b) List any other pending review proceeding of the same order in any other court; and

(c) Attach copies of the order to be reviewed.

Every petitioner filing for review after filing a docketing statement must specify in the petition for review any exceptions taken or additions to the issues listed in the docketing statement. Every party who intervenes after the filing of the docketing statement must specify in the notice of intervention any exceptions taken to the issues listed in the docketing statement.

15.3.5 *Prehearing Conference.* The clerk may give notice of a prehearing conference 10 days after filing of a docketing statement, or 14 days after entry of an order by the court

deciding a venue issue, whichever is later. The prehearing conference will:

(a) Simplify and define issues;

(b) Agree on an appendix and record;

(c) Assign joint briefing responsibilities and schedule briefs; and

(d) Resolve any other matters aiding in the disposition of the proceeding.

Except for good cause, any party who petitions for review or intervenes after prehearing conference has been held is bound by the result of the prehearing conference.

15.3.6 *Severance.* Any petitioner or respondent may move to sever parties or issues by showing prejudice.

15.4 Proceedings for Review of Orders of the Benefits Review Board. In petitions filed by either the claimant or the employer under 33 U.S.C. § 921 to review orders of the Benefits Review Board, the Office of Workers Compensation of the United States Department of Labor, the nominal respondent, is aligned with the claimant for briefing and oral argument purposes, unless otherwise ordered by the court. Within 30 days of the filing of the petition for review of the board's decision, the petitioner must file a statement of the issues to be presented on appeal and serve them on the director and counsel for all parties so the appropriate alignment can be made.

15.5 Time for Filing Motion for Intervention. A motion to intervene under Fed. R. App. P. 15(d) should be filed promptly after the petition for review of the agency proceeding is filed, but not later than 14 days prior to the due date of the brief of the party supported by the intervenor.

[Amended effective January 4, 1999; December 1, 2002; December 1, 2009.]

FRAP 15.1 BRIEFS AND ORAL ARGUMENT IN A NATIONAL LABOR RELATIONS BOARD PROCEEDING

[For text of rule, see the Federal Rules of Appellate Procedure]

FRAP 16. THE RECORD ON REVIEW OR ENFORCEMENT

[For text of rule, see the Federal Rules of Appellate Procedure]

FRAP 17. FILING THE RECORD

[For text of rule, see the Federal Rules of Appellate Procedure]

RULE 17. FILING OF THE RECORD

Filing of the Record. Any agency failing to file the record within 40 days, must request an extension of time and provide specific reasons justifying the delay. The clerk may grant an extension for no more than 30 days. After such an extension expires, the court may order production of the record.

[Amended effective January 4, 1999.]

FRAP 18. STAY PENDING REVIEW

*[For text of rule, see the Federal Rules
of Appellate Procedure]*

FRAP 19. SETTLEMENT OF A JUDGMENT ENFORCING AN AGENCY ORDER IN PART

*[For text of rule, see the Federal Rules
of Appellate Procedure]*

FRAP 20. APPLICABILITY OF RULES TO THE REVIEW OR ENFORCEMENT OF AN AGENCY ORDER

*[For text of rule, see the Federal Rules
of Appellate Procedure]*

TITLE V. EXTRAORDINARY WRITS

FRAP 21. WRITS OF MANDAMUS AND PROHIBITION, AND OTHER EXTRAORDINARY WRITS

*[For text of rule, see the Federal Rules
of Appellate Procedure]*

RULE 21. WRITS OF MANDAMUS AND PROHIBITION, AND OTHER EXTRAORDINARY WRITS

Petition for Writ. The petition must contain a certificate of interested persons as described in 5th Cir. R. 28.2.1. The certificate of interested persons and the items required by 5th Cir. R. 21 do not count toward the page limit.

In addition to the items required by Fed. R. App. P. 21, the application must contain a copy of any memoranda or briefs filed in the district court supporting the application to that court for relief and any memoranda or briefs filed in opposi-

tion, as well as a transcript of any reasons the district court gave for its action.

I.O.P.—Mandamus Processing. If the petitioner does not accompany the petition with the requisite filing fee or motion to proceed IFP, the clerk will, by letter, notify the petitioner of the defect and set a correction deadline. If the petitioner fails to meet the deadline, the clerk will dismiss the petition 15 days after the deadline in accordance with our practices under 5th Cir. R. 42.3.1. If the petitioner accompanies the petition with the requisite filing fee or motion to proceed IFP, the clerk will docket the petition in accordance with Fed. R. App. 21(a)(3). With the exception of an emergency mandamus petition, which shall be handled in accordance with our existing rules for emergency motions, the clerk will forward all mandamus petitions to the jurisdictional review calendar or a screening panel for disposition.

[Amended effective January 4, 1999; January 1, 2001; December 1, 2002.]

TITLE VI. HABEAS CORPUS; PROCEEDINGS IN FORMA PAUPERIS

FRAP 22. HABEAS CORPUS AND SECTION 2255 PROCEEDINGS

*[For text of rule, see the Federal Rules
of Appellate Procedure]*

RULE 22. APPLICATIONS FOR CERTIFICATES OF APPEALABILITY AND MOTIONS FOR PERMISSION TO FILE SECOND OR SUCCESSIVE HABEAS CORPUS APPLICATIONS

Applications for certificates of appealability, motions for permission to file second or successive applications under 28 U.S.C. §§ 2254 and 2255, and any responses must conform to the format requirements and the length limitations of Fed. R. App. P. 32(a), and 5th Cir. R. 32 as applicable.

I.O.P.—See 5th Cir. R. 27.3 concerning emergency motions. Where the district court has granted a COA, the clerk shall include in the original briefing notice a deadline for any

application for COA on additional issues, and where feasible, shall make the deadline coextensive with the briefing deadline.

[Amended effective January 4, 1999; January 1, 2001; February 2011.]

FRAP 23. CUSTODY OR RELEASE OF A PRISONER IN A HABEAS CORPUS PROCEEDING

*[For text of rule, see the Federal Rules
of Appellate Procedure]*

I.O.P.—See 5th Cir. R. 9.2 for procedures governing applications for release.

FRAP 24. PROCEEDING IN FORMA PAUPERIS

*[For text of rule, see the Federal Rules
of Appellate Procedure]*

TITLE VII.   GENERAL PROVISIONS

FRAP 25.   FILING AND SERVICE

*[For text of rule, see the Federal Rules
of Appellate Procedure]*

RULE 25.   FILING AND SERVICE

25.1 Facsimile Filing. The clerk may accept, for filing, papers sent by facsimile in situations the clerk determines are emergencies or that present other compelling circumstances.

25.2 Electronic Case Filing Procedures.

25.2.1 *Electronic Filing.* At the court's direction, the clerk will set an implementation date for an initial period of voluntary, and a subsequent date for mandatory, use of the court's electronic filing system. Thereafter, all cases will be assigned to the court's electronic filing system. Counsel must register as Filing Users under Rule 25.2.3 and comply with the court's electronic filing standards, posted separately on the court's website, www.ca5.uscourts.gov, unless excused for good cause. Non-incarcerated pro se litigants may request the clerk's permission to register as a Filing User, in civil cases only, under such conditions as the clerk may authorize.

Except as authorized in the electronic filing rules and standards, Filing Users must submit all briefs, motions, petitions for rehearing in PDF text, (not scanned), format **and** in paper format as prescribed by the clerk, see 5th Cir. R. 30, 31, etc. Whenever possible, other documents, e.g., record excerpts, etc., should be in PDF text format, and in paper format as prescribed by the clerk. All paper filings **must** be identical to the electronic file(s). Upon the clerk's request, a Filing User must promptly provide an identical electronic version of any paper document previously filed in the same case.

25.2.2 *Filings in Original Proceedings.* Filing Users may be required to file case-initiating documents in original proceedings, e.g., mandamus, petitions for second and successive habeas corpus relief, petitions for review, etc., in paper format. Subsequent documents may be filed electronically and in paper format as prescribed by the clerk.

25.2.3 *Filing Users: Eligibility, Registration, Passwords.* All counsel not excused from filing electronically must register themselves, or any additional approved designee, as Filing Users of the court's electronic filing system. The clerk will define the registration requirements and continuing duty of counsel to keep their contact information current, see 5th Cir. R. 46.1, and will determine necessary training to receive Filing User registration.

Non-incarcerated pro se litigants granted Filing User status under Rule 25.2.1 will have Filing User status terminated as prescribed by the clerk, generally at the termination of the case. If a pro se party, permitted to register as a Filing User, retains an attorney, that counsel must advise the clerk.

A Filing User's registration constitutes consent to electronic service of all documents as provided in the Fed. R. App. P. and the 5th Cir. R.

Filing Users agree to protect the security of their passwords and immediately notify the PACER Service Center and the clerk if their password is compromised. Filing Users may be sanctioned for failure to comply with this provision.

Subject to a single judge's review, the clerk may terminate a Filing User's electronic filing privileges for abusing the system by an inordinate number of filings, filings of excessive size, or other failures to comply with the electronic filing rules and standards.

A Filing User may move to withdraw from participation in the electronic filing system for good cause shown.

25.2.4 *Consequences of Electronic Filing.* A Filing User's electronic transmission of a document to the electronic filing system consistent with these rules and the court's electronic filing standards, together with the court's transmission of a Notice of Docket Activity, constitutes filing of the document under the Fed. R. App. P. and 5th Cir. R., and constitutes entry of the document on the docket under Fed. R. App. P. 36 and 45(b). If a party must file a motion for leave to file, both the motion and document at issue must be submitted electronically and in identical paper form; the underlying document will be filed if the court so directs.

A Filing User must verify a document's legibility and completeness before filing it with the court. Except as authorized by the court's electronic filing rules and standards, documents the Filing User creates and files electronically must be in PDF text format. When a Filing User's document has been filed electronically, the official record is the electronic document stored by the court, and the filing party is bound by the document as filed. Except for documents first filed in paper form and subsequently submitted electronically under 5th Cir. R. 25.2.2, an electronically filed document is deemed filed at the date and time stated on the court's Notice of Docket Activity.

Filing must be completed by 11:59 p.m. Central Time to be considered timely filed that day.

25.2.5 *Service of Documents by Electronic Means.* The court's electronic Notice of Docket Activity constitutes service of the filed document on all Filing Users. Parties who are not Filing Users must be served with a copy of any document filed electronically in accordance with the Fed. R. App. P. 25 and 5th Cir. R. 25. If the document is not available electronically, the filer must use an alternative method of service.

The court's electronic Notice of Docket Activity does not replace the certificate of service required by Fed. R. App. P. 25(d).

25.2.6 *Entry of Court—Issued Documents.* Except as otherwise provided by rule or order, all of the court's orders, opinions, judgments, and proceedings relating to cases electronically filed will be filed in accordance with these rules, and will constitute entry on the docket under Fed. R. App. P. 36 and 45(b).

Any order or other court-issued document filed electronically does not require a signature of a judge or other court employee. An electronic order has the same force and effect as a paper copy of the order. Orders also may be entered as "text-only" entries on the docket, without an attached document. Such orders are official and binding.

25.2.7 *Attachments and Exhibits to Motions and Original Proceedings.* Filing Users must submit all documents referenced as exhibits or attachments, in electronic form within any file size limits the clerk may prescribe, as well as any paper copies the clerk specifies. A Filing User must submit as exhibits or attachments only those excerpts of the referenced documents that are directly germane to the matter under consideration by the court. Excerpted material must be clearly and prominently identified as such. The clerk may require parties to file additional excerpts or the complete document.

25.2.8 *Sealed Documents.* A Filing User may move to file documents under seal in electronic form if permitted by law, and as authorized in the court's electronic filing standards. The court's order authorizing or denying the electronic filing of documents under seal may be filed electronically. Documents ordered placed under seal may be filed traditionally in paper or electronically, as authorized by the court. If filed traditionally, a paper copy of the authorizing order must be attached to the documents under seal and delivered to the clerk.

25.2.9 *Retention Requirements.* The Filing User must maintain in paper form documents filed electronically and requiring original signatures, other than that of the Filing User, for 3 years after the mandate or order closing the case issues. On request of the court, the Filing User must provide original documents for review.

25.2.10 *Signatures.* The user log-in and password required to submit documents in electronic form serve as the Filing User's signature on all electronic documents filed with the court. They also serve as a signature for purposes of the Fed. R. App. P. 32(d) and 5th Cir. R. 28.5, and any other purpose for which a signature is required in connection with proceedings before the court.

The Filing User's name under whose log-in and password the document is submitted must be preceded by an "s/" and be typed in the space where the signature otherwise would appear.

No Filing User or other person may knowingly permit or cause to permit a Filing User's log-in and password to be used by anyone other than an authorized agent of the Filing User.

Documents which require more than one party's signature must be filed electronically by:

submitting a scanned document containing all necessary signatures;

showing the consent of the other parties on the document; or

any other manner approved by the court.

Electronically represented signatures of all parties and Filing Users described above are presumed valid. If any party, counsel of record, or Filing User objects to the representation of his or her signature on an electronic document as described above, he or she must file a notice within 10 days setting forth the basis of the objection.

25.2.11 *Notice of Court Orders and Judgment.* The clerk will transmit electronically a Notice of Docket Activity to Filing Users in the case when entering an order or judgment. This electronic transmission constitutes the notice and service of the opinion required by Fed. R. App. P. 36(b) and 45(c). The clerk must give notice in paper form in accordance with those rules to a person who has not consented to electronic service.

25.2.12 *Technical Failures.* A Filing User whose filing is made untimely as the result of a technical failure may seek appropriate relief from the court.

25.2.13 *Public Access/Redaction of Personal Identifiers.* Parties must refrain from including, or must partially redact where inclusion is necessary, certain personal data identifiers whether filed electronically or in paper form as prescribed in Fed. R. App. P. 25, Fed. R. Civ. P. 5.2(a), and Fed. R. Crim. P. 49.1. Responsibility for complying with the rules and redacting personal identifiers rests solely with counsel. The parties or their counsel may be required to certify compliance with these rules. The clerk will not review pleadings, and is not responsible for data redaction.

Parties wishing to file a document containing the personal data identifiers referenced above may:

file an un-redacted version of the document under seal, or

file a reference list under seal. The list must contain the complete personal data identifier(s) and the redacted identifier(s) used in its (their) place in the filing. All references in the case to the redacted identifiers included in the reference list will be construed to refer to the corresponding complete personal data identifier. The reference list must be filed under seal, and may be amended as of right.

The court will retain the un-redacted version of the document or the reference list as part of the record. The court may require the party to file a redacted copy for the public file.

25.2.14 *Hyperlinks.* Electronically filed documents may contain the following types of hyperlinks:

Hyperlinks to other portions of the same document;

Hyperlinks to PACER that contains a source document for a citation;

Hyperlinks to documents already filed in any CM/ECF database;

Hyperlinks between documents that will be filed together at the same time;

Hyperlinks that the clerk may approve in the future as technology advances.

Hyperlinks to cited authority may not replace standard citation format. Complete citations must be included in the text of the filed document. A hyperlink, or any site to which it refers, will not be considered part of the record. Hyperlinks are simply convenient mechanisms for accessing material cited in a filed document. The court accepts no responsibility for, and does not endorse, any product, organization, or content at any hyperlinked site, or at any site to which that site might be linked. The court accepts no responsibility for the availability or functionality of any hyperlink.

25.2.15 *Changes.* The clerk may make changes to the standards for electronic filing to adapt to changes in technology or to facilitate electronic filing. Changes to the court's electronic filing standards will be posted on the court's internet website.

I.O.P.—Limits on Recovery of Mailing or Commercial Carrier Delivery Costs. See 5th Cir. R. 39.2.

[Amended effective January 4, 1999; December 1, 2002; December 1, 2009.]

FRAP 26.   COMPUTING AND EXTENDING TIME

*[For text of rule, see the Federal Rules
of Appellate Procedure]*

RULE 26.   COMPUTATION AND EXTENSION OF TIME

26.1   Computing Time. Except for briefs and record excerpts, all other papers, including petitions for rehearing, are not timely unless the clerk actually receives them within the time fixed for filing. Briefs and record excerpts are deemed filed on the day sent to the clerk electronically where permitted by 5TH CIR. R. 30 and 31, by a third-party commercial carrier for delivery within 3 days, or on the day of mailing if the most expeditious form of delivery by mail is used. The additional 3 days after service by mail or after delivery to a commercial carrier for delivery within 3 days referred to in FED. R. APP. P. 26(c), applies only to matters served by a party and not to filings with the clerk of such matters as petitions for rehearing under FED. R. APP. P. 40, petitions for rehearing en banc under FED. R. APP. P. 35, and bills of costs under FED. R. APP. P. 39.

26.2   Extensions of Time. The court requires timely filing of all papers within the time period allowed by the rules, without extensions of time, except for good cause. Appeals which are not processed timely will be dismissed for want of prosecution without further notice under 5th Cir. R. 42. If the parties or counsel waive their right to file a reply brief, they must immediately notify the clerk to expedite submitting the case to the court.

[Amended effective January 4, 1999; December 1, 2002; December 1, 2009; December 1, 2016.]

FRAP 26.1   CORPORATE DISCLOSURE STATEMENT

*[For text of rule, see the Federal Rules
of Appellate Procedure]*

RULE 26.1   CORPORATE DISCLOSURE STATEMENT

26.1.1   Corporate Disclosure Statement. The court uses a "Certificate of Interested Persons" in lieu of a Corporate Disclosure Statement. See 5th Cir. R. 28.2.1.

FRAP 27.   MOTIONS

*[For text of rule, see the Federal Rules
of Appellate Procedure]*

RULE 27.   MOTIONS

27.1   Clerk May Rule on Certain Motions. Under Fed. R. App. P. 27(b), the clerk has discretion to act on, in accordance with the standards set forth in the applicable rules, or to refer to the court, the procedural motions listed below. The clerk's action is subject to review by a single judge upon a motion for reconsideration made within the 14 or 45 day period set by Fed. R. App. P. 40.

27.1.1 To extend the time for: filing answers or replies to pending motions; paying filing fees; filing motions to proceed in forma pauperis; filing petitions for panel rehearing and rehearing en banc, and for reconsideration of single judge orders, for not longer than 14 days, 30 days if the applicant for extension is a prisoner proceeding pro se; filing briefs as permitted by 5th Cir. R. 31.4; filing bills of costs; and filing applications under the Equal Access to Justice Act.

27.1.2 To rule on motions to file briefs out of time.

27.1.3 To stay further proceedings in appeals.

27.1.4 To correct briefs or pleadings filed in this court at counsel's request.

27.1.5 To stay the issuance of mandates pending certiorari in civil cases only, for no more than 30 days, provided the court has not ordered the mandate issued earlier.

27.1.6 To reinstate appeals dismissed by the clerk.

27.1.7 To enter and issue consent decrees in labor board and other government agency review cases.

27.1.8 To enter CJA Form 20 orders continuing trial court appointment of counsel on appeal for purposes of compensation.

27.1.9 To consolidate appeals.

27.1.10 To withdraw appearances.

27.1.11 To supplement or correct records.

27.1.12 To incorporate records or briefs on former appeals.

27.1.13 To file reply or supplemental briefs in addition to the single reply brief permitted by Fed. R. App. P. 28(c) prior to submission to the court.

27.1.14 To file an amicus curiae brief under Fed. R. App. P. 29 (see 5th Cir. R. 29.4).

27.1.15 To enlarge the number of pages of optional contents in record excerpts.

27.1.16 To extend the length limits for: briefs under Fed. R. App. P. 32(a)(7) and 5th Cir. R. 32; petitions for rehearing en banc and panel rehearing under Fed. R. App. P. 35(b)(2), and 40(b); certificates of appealability and motions for permission to file second or successive habeas corpus applications under 28 U.S.C. §§ 2254 and 2255, under 5th Cir. R. 22; petitions for permission to appeal under 5th Cir. R. 5; and petitions for mandamus and extraordinary writs under 5th Cir. R. 21.

27.1.17 To proceed in forma pauperis, see Fed. R. App. P. 24 and 28 U.S.C. § 1915;

27.1.18 To appoint counsel or to permit appointed counsel to withdraw;

27.1.19 To obtain transcripts at government expense.

27.1.20 To rule on an unopposed motion by the government or a defendant in a direct criminal appeal to gain access to matters sealed in the case and for the use in prosecution of its appeal.

27.2 Single Judge May Rule on Certain Motions. Pursuant to Fed. R. App. P. 27(c), any single judge of this court has discretion, subject to review by a panel upon a motion for reconsideration made within the 14 or 45 day period set forth in Fed. R. App. P. 40, to take appropriate action on the following procedural motions:

27.2.1 The motions listed in 5th Cir. R. 27.1 that have been referred to a single judge for initial action, or for single judge reconsideration of a ruling made by the clerk, but the judge is not limited to the time restrictions in 5th Cir. R. 27.1.1.

27.2.2 To permit interventions in agency proceedings pursuant to Fed. R. App. P. 15(d).

27.2.3 To act on applications for certificates of appealability under Fed. R. App. P. 22(b) and 28 U.S.C. § 2253 except for death penalty cases where a three judge panel must act.

27.2.4 To extend for good cause the times prescribed by the Federal Rules of Appellate Procedure or by the rules of this court except for enlarging the time for initiating an appeal, see Fed. R. App. P. 26(b).

27.2.5 To substitute parties under Fed. R. App. P. 43.

27.2.6 To exercise the power granted in Fed. R. App. P. 8 and 9, respecting stays, or injunctions, or releases in criminal cases pending appeal, and subject to the restrictions set out in those rules; and to exercise the power granted in Fed. R. App. P. 18, respecting stays pending review of agency decisions or orders, subject to the restrictions on the power of a single judge contained in that rule.

27.2.7 To stay the issuance of mandates or to recall same pending certiorari.

27.2.8 To expedite appeals.

27.2.9 To strike a nonconforming brief or record excerpts as provided in 5th Cir. R. 32.5 and to strike other papers not conforming to the Fed. R. App. P. and 5th Cir. R.

27.3 Emergency Motions in Cases Other Than Capital Cases. Parties should not file motions seeking emergency relief unless there is an emergency sufficient to justify disruption of the normal appellate process. In cases not governed by 5th Cir. R. 8.10, motions seeking relief before the expiration of 14 days after filing must, subject to the penalties of Fed. R. App. P. 46(c), be supported by good cause and must:

Be preceded by a telephone call to the clerk's office and to the offices of opposing counsel advising of the intent to file the emergency motion. If time does not permit the filing of the motion by hand delivery or by mail, the clerk may permit filing by facsimile or by other electronic means. In an extraordinary case, the clerk may permit the submission of an oral motion by telephone. If the motion is filed by means other than hand delivery or mail, counsel should also later file the motion by hand delivery or by mail.

Be labeled "Emergency Motion."

State the nature of the emergency and the irreparable harm the movant will suffer if the motion is not granted.

Certify that the facts supporting emergency consideration of the motion are true and complete.

Provide the date by which action is believed to be necessary.

Attach any relevant order or other ruling of the district court as well as copies of all relevant pleadings, briefs, memoranda, or other papers filed by all parties in the district court. If this cannot be done, counsel must state the reason that it cannot be done.

Be served on opposing counsel at the same time and, absent agreement to the contrary with opposing counsel, in the same manner as the emergency motion is filed with the court.

Be filed in the clerk's office by 2:00 p.m. on the day of filing.

27.3.1 Emergency Stays of Deportation. The court will give emergency consideration to stays of deportation **only** where the petitioner has a scheduled removal date and is in custody. Petitioners and counsel are responsible for obtaining accurate information about the custody status of their clients, as well as confirming the scheduled removal date. Emergency stays where petitioners have an imminent scheduled deportation date and are in custody will be processed in accordance with rule 27.3 above.

27.4 Form of Motions. Parties or counsel must comply with the requirements of Fed. R. App. P. 27 including the length limits of Fed. R. App. P. 27(d)(2). Except for purely procedural matters, motions must include a certificate of interested persons as described in 5th Cir. R. 28.2.1. Where a single judge or the clerk may act only an original and 1 copy need be filed. All motions requiring panel action require an original and 3 copies. **All motions must state that the movant has contacted or attempted to contact all other parties and must indicate whether an opposition will be filed.** Where a party's motion is not an Emergency Motion covered by 5th Cir. Rule 27.3, but the party has a serious need for the court to act within a specified time, the motion must state the time requirement and describe both the nature of the need and the facts that support it.

27.5 Motions to Expedite Appeal. Such motions are presented in the same manner as other motions. Only the court may expedite an appeal and only for good cause. If an appeal is expedited, the clerk will fix a briefing schedule unless a judge directs a specific date.

I.O.P.—General Standards for Ruling on Motions

5th Cir. R. 27 implements Fed. R. App. P. 27(b) and (c) and delegates to single judges and the clerk the authority to rule on specified motions, subject to review by the court. This I.O.P. provides the general sense of the court on the disposition of a variety of matters:

Briefs. The court expects that all briefs will be filed timely. Motions for extension of time to file briefs are disfavored and should be made only in exceptional instances where "good cause" exists. No extension is automatic. If an extension is granted, it will be for the very least amount of time necessary, and except in the most unusually compelling circumstances, will not exceed 30 days in a criminal case, or 40 days in a civil case.

Litigants seeking to file briefs after the due date set in the briefing letter should understand that the court generally will not permit the brief's filing "out of time". However even in the unusual case where out of time filing is authorized, a brief generally will not be filed out of time more than 30 days beyond the original due date in a criminal case, or 40 days in a civil case.

Motions for Extension of Time to File Answers, Replies to Pending Motions or to Pay Filing Fees. If such motions are granted, extensions generally will not exceed 30 days.

Reinstatement of Cases Dismissed by the Clerk. The court normally will not reinstate a case dismissed by the clerk under 5th Cir. R. 27.1.6 unless:

The deficiency which caused the dismissal has been remedied; and

The motion for reinstatement is made as soon as reasonably possible and in any event within 45 days of dismissal.

Motions Panels—Motions panels are drawn randomly from the active judges. These panels also operate as screening panels as discussed in the I.O.P. following 5th Cir. R. 34. The motions panels compositions are changed at the beginning of each court year to permit the judges to sit with other judges in screening and handling administrative motions.

DISTRIBUTION

To Judges—Motions requiring judges' consideration are assigned in rotation to all active judges on a routing log.

The clerk assembles a complete set of the motion papers, and any other necessary material and submits them with a routing form to the initiating judge. In single judge matters the judge acts on the motion and returns it to the clerk with an appropriate order. For motions requiring panel action, a single set of papers is prepared, but the initiating judge transmits the file to the next judge with a recommendation. The second judge sends it on to the third judge, who returns the file and an appropriate order to the clerk.

Emergency Motions—The clerk immediately assigns the matter to the next initiating judge in rotation on the administrative routing log and to the panel members. If the matter requires counsel to contact the initiating judge or panel members personally, the clerk will provide the names of the judges assigned the case, after getting approval from the initiating judge.

The motion papers are distributed as described above, except that a complete set, including any draft order, is forwarded to all members of the panel.

Motions After Assignment to Calendar—After cases are assigned to the oral argument calendar, motions are circulated to the hearing panel rather than to the standard motions panels. The senior active judge on the panel is considered the

initiating judge. The clerk enters orders responding to the motions on behalf of the panel until entry of the opinion.

POST–DECISION MOTIONS

Extension of Time to File Petition for Rehearing or Leave to File out of Time—The clerk may act on or refer to the court a timely motion for an extension of time to file a petition for panel rehearing or for rehearing en banc for a period not longer than 14 days, 30 days if the applicant is a prisoner proceeding pro se. Motions for additional time beyond 14 or 30 days, or to file out of time, are submitted to the writing judge, unless he or she is a visiting judge. In that event the matter is referred to the senior active judge on the panel. If the senior active judge dissented, the matter is referred to the other active judge on the panel.

Stay or Recall of Mandate—The clerk or a single judge, as appropriate, decides a motion for stay or recall of mandate pending action on a petition for writ of certiorari and routes and disposes of it in the same manner as in the preceding paragraph. (See 5th Cir. R. 27.1.5, 27.2.7, and 41.)

Motions to Amend, Correct, or Settle the Judgment— These motions are referred to the writing judge with copies to the panel members.

Remand From Supreme Court of the United States— Remands from the Supreme Court of the United States are sent to the original panel for disposition when the Supreme Court's judgment is received. Counsel does not need to file a formal motion.

[Amended effective January 4, 1999; January 1, 2001; December 1, 2002; November 1, 2004; December 1, 2005; April 1, 2008; December 1, 2009; May 25, 2016.]

FRAP 28. BRIEFS

*[For text of rule, see the Federal Rules
of Appellate Procedure]*

RULE 28. BRIEFS

28.1 Briefs—Technical Requirements. The technical requirements for permissible typefaces, paper size, line spacing, and length of briefs are found in Fed. R. App. P. and 5th Cir. R. 32.

28.2 Briefs—Contents.

28.2.1 *Certificate of Interested Persons.* The certificate of interested persons required by this rule is broader in scope than the corporate disclosure statement contemplated in Fed. R. App. P. 26.1. The certificate of interested persons provides the court with additional information concerning parties whose participation in a case may raise a recusal issue. A separate corporate disclosure statement is not required. Counsel and unrepresented parties will furnish a certificate for all private (non-governmental) parties, both appellants and appellees, which must be incorporated on the first page of each brief before the table of contents or index, and which must certify a complete list of all persons, associations of persons, firms, partnerships, corporations, guarantors, insurers, affiliates, parent corporations, or other legal entities who or which are financially interested in the outcome of the litigation. If a large group of persons or firms can be specified by a generic description, individual listing is not necessary. Each certificate must also list the names of opposing law firms and/or counsel in the case. The certificate must include all information called for by Fed. R. App. P. 26.1(a). Counsel and unrepresented parties must supplement their certificates of interested persons whenever the information that must be disclosed changes.

(a) Each certificate must list <u>all</u> persons known to counsel to be interested, on all sides of the case, whether or not represented by counsel furnishing the certificate. Counsel has the burden to ascertain and certify the true facts to the court.

(b) The certificate must be in the following form:

(1) Number and Style of Case;

(2) The undersigned counsel of record certifies that the following listed persons and entities as described in the fourth sentence of Rule 28.2.1 have an interest in the outcome of this case. These representations are made in order that the judges of this court may evaluate possible disqualification or recusal.

(Here list names of all such persons and entities and identify their connection and interest.)

Attorney of record for _____

28.2.2 *Record References.* Every assertion in briefs regarding matter in the record must be supported by a reference to the page number of the original record, whether in paper or electronic form, where the matter is found using the record citation form as directed by the Clerk of Court.

28.2.3 *Request for Oral Argument.* Counsel for appellant must include in a preamble to appellant's principal brief a short statement why oral argument would be helpful, or a statement that appellant waives oral argument. Appellee's counsel must likewise include in appellee's brief a statement why oral argument is or is not needed. The court will give these statements due, though not controlling, weight in determining whether to hold oral argument. See Fed. R. App. P. 34(a) and (f) and 5th Cir. R. 34.2.

28.3 **Brief—Order of Contents.** The order of the contents of the brief is governed by Fed. R. App. P. 28 and this rule and will be as follows:

(a) Certificate of interested persons required by 5th Cir. R. 28.2.1;

(b) Statement regarding oral argument required by 5th Cir. R. 28.2.3 (see Fed. R. App. P. 34(a)(1));

(c) A table of contents, with page references (see Fed. R. App. P. 28(a)(2));

(d) A table of authorities (see Fed. R. App. P. 28(a)(3));

(e) A jurisdictional statement as required by Fed. R. App. P. 28(a)(4)(A) through (D);

(f) A statement of issues presented for review (see Fed. R. App. P. 28(a)(5));

(g) A concise statement of the case setting out the facts relevant to the issues submitted for review (see Fed. R. App. P. 28(a)(6));

(h) A summary of the argument (see Fed. R. App. P. 28(a)(7));

(i) The argument (see Fed. R. App. P. 28(a)(8));

(j) A short conclusion stating the precise relief sought (see Fed. R. App. P. 28(a)(9));

(k) A signature of counsel or a party as required by Fed. R. App. P. 32(d);

(*l*) A certificate of service in the form required by Fed. R. App. P. 25;

(m) A certificate of compliance if required by FED. R. APP. P. 32(g)(1) and 5TH CIR. R. 32.3 (see FED. R. APP. P. 28(a)(10));

28.4 **Supplemental Briefs.** The rules do not permit the filing of supplemental briefs without leave of court, but there are some occasions, particularly after a case is orally argued or submitted on the summary calendar, where the court will call for supplemental briefs on particular issues. Also, where intervening decisions or new developments should be brought to the court's attention, counsel may direct a <u>letter</u>, not a supplemental brief, to the clerk with citations and succinct comment. See Fed. R. App. P. 28(j). If a new case is not reported, copies of the decision should be appended. The letter must be filed in 4 copies, and served on opposing counsel.

28.5 **Signing the Brief.** See Fed. R. App. P. 32(d). The signature requirement is interpreted broadly, and the attorney of record may designate another person to sign the brief for him or her. Where counsel for a particular party reside in different locations, it is not necessary to incur the expense of sending the brief from one person to another for multiple signatures.

28.6 **Pro Se Briefs.** Unless specifically directed by court order, pro se motions, briefs or correspondence will not be filed if the party is represented by counsel.

28.7 **Citation to Unpublished Opinions, Orders, etc.** Fed. R. App. P. 32.1(a) permits citation to unpublished judicial dispositions. Parties citing to such dispositions must comply with Fed. R. App. P. 32.1(b). If a party does not need to submit a copy of an unpublished disposition, the party must provide a citation to the disposition in a publicly accessible electronic database.

I.O.P.—Miscellaneous Brief Information

(a) **Acknowledgment of Briefs**—The clerk does not acknowledge the filing of briefs unless counsel or a party makes a special request.

(b) **Sample Briefs and Record Excerpts**—Upon request, the clerk may loan sample briefs and record excerpts to counsel and non-incarcerated pro se litigants. Because pro se prisoner briefs are not held to the same rigid standards as other briefs, copies of briefs are generally not sent to prisoners. Instead other informational material may be sent. Postage fees may be required before the materials are sent.

(c) Checklist Available—A copy of the checklist used by the clerk in examining briefs is available on request.

[Amended effective January 4, 1999; December 1, 2002; December 1, 2005; December 1, 2006; December 1, 2009; December 1, 2013; December 1, 2016.]

FRAP 28.1 CROSS–APPEALS

[For text of rule, see the Federal Rules of Appellate Procedure]

FRAP 29. BRIEF OF AN AMICUS CURIAE

[For text of rule, see the Federal Rules of Appellate Procedure]

RULE 29. BRIEF OF AN AMICUS CURIAE

29.1 Time for Filing Motion. Those wishing to file an amicus curiae brief should file a motion within 7 days after the filing of the principal brief of the party whose position the amicus brief will support.

29.2 Contents and Form. Briefs filed under this rule must comply with the applicable Fed. R. App. P. provisions and with 5th Cir. R. 31 and 32. The brief must include a supplemental statement of interested parties, if necessary to fully disclose all those with an interest in the amicus brief. The brief should avoid the repetition of facts or legal arguments contained in the principal brief and should focus on points either not made or not adequately discussed in those briefs. Any non-conforming brief may be stricken, on motion or sua sponte.

29.3 Length of Briefs. See FED. R. APP. P. 29(a)(5).

29.4 Denial of Amicus Curiae Status. After a panel opinion is issued, amicus curiae status will not be permitted if the allowance would result in the disqualification of any member of the panel or of the en banc court.

I.O.P.—See also 5th Cir. R. 31.2.

[Amended effective January 4, 1999; December 1, 2016.]

FRAP 30. APPENDIX TO THE BRIEFS

[For text of rule, see the Federal Rules of Appellate Procedure]

RULE 30. APPENDIX TO THE BRIEFS

30.1 Records on Appeal/Record Excerpts/Appendix—Appeals From District Courts, the Tax Court, and Agencies. Appeals from district courts and the Tax Court are decided on the original record on appeal (ROA). The clerk is authorized to require the party receiving the ROA to pay reasonable shipping costs as a condition of receiving the record. Moreover, counsel and unrepresented parties must review the ROA within 20 days of dispatch from the clerk's office and advise electronically or in writing both the appropriate District Court (or the Tax Court, if appropriate) and Fifth Circuit clerk's offices of any errors in, or omissions from, the ROA. Failure to comply may result in a denial of any requested extension of time to file a brief due to an alleged error in, or incomplete ROA. Record excerpts are filed in lieu of the appendix prescribed by Fed. R. App. P. 30. Petitions for review or enforcement of agency orders are governed by 5th Cir. R. 30.2, but parties may be required to pay reasonable shipping costs, and are responsible for timely review of the record and the notification requirements set out above.

30.1.1 *Purpose.* The record excerpts are intended primarily to assist the judges in making the screening decision on the need for oral argument and in preparing for oral argument. Counsel need excerpt only those parts of the record that will assist in these functions.

30.1.2 *Filing.* Four paper copies of excerpts of the district court record must accompany the appellant's brief, see 5th Cir. R. 30.1.4 and 30.1.5. If exempt from electronic filing under 5th Cir. R. 25.2, all appellants represented by counsel must file an electronic copy of the record excerpts on a CD, computer diskette, or such other electronic medium as the clerk may authorize. The electronic copy must be in a single Portable Document Format (PDF) file; contain nothing other than the record excerpts; and have as the first page of the electronic copy an index to the contents. If submitted on a CD, diskette, or other authorized physical media, the electronic version must have a label containing the case name and docket number and state "Record Excerpts." The appellant must serve a paper and electronic copy of the excerpts on counsel for each of the parties separately represented; a paper copy on any party proceeding pro se, and an electronic copy, if the pro se party is not an inmate confined in an institution. The appellee may similarly submit and serve additional record excerpts with the appellee's principal brief, with the required copies furnished to the clerk accompanying the appellee's brief.

30.1.3 *Prisoner Petitions Without Representation by Counsel.* Prisoners without counsel are not required to prepare and file record excerpts.

30.1.4 *Mandatory Contents.* The record excerpts must contain copies of the following portions of the district court record:

(a) The docket sheet;

(b) The notice of appeal;

(c) The indictment in criminal cases;

(d) The jury's verdict in all cases;

(e) The judgment or interlocutory order appealed;

(f) Any other orders or rulings sought to be reviewed;

(g) Any relevant magistrate judge's report and recommendation;

(h) Any supporting opinion or findings of fact and conclusions of law filed, or transcript pages of any such delivered orally; and

(i) A certificate of service complying with Fed. R. App. P. 25.

30.1.5 *Optional Contents.* The record excerpts may include those parts of the record, referred to in the briefs including:

(a) Essential pleadings or relevant portions thereof;

(b) The parts of the Fed. R. Civ. P. 16(e) pretrial order relevant to any issue on appeal;

(c) Any jury instruction given or refused that presents an issue on appeal, together with any objection and the court's ruling, and any other relevant part of the jury charge;

(d) Findings and conclusions of the administrative law judge, if the appeal is of a court order reviewing an administrative agency determination;

(e) A copy of the relevant pages of the transcript when the appeal challenges the admission or exclusion of evidence or any other interlocutory ruling or order; and

(f) The relevant parts of any written exhibit (including affidavits) that present an issue on appeal.

30.1.6 *Length.* The optional contents of the record excerpts must not exceed 40 pages unless authorized by the court.

30.1.7 *Form.* The record excerpts must:

(a) Have a numbered table of contents, with citation to the record, beginning with the lower court docket sheet;

(b) Be on letter-size, light paper, reproduced by any process that results in a clear black image. Care must be taken to reproduce fully the document filing date column on the docket sheet;

(c) Be tabbed to correspond to the numbers assigned in the table of contents;

(d) Be bound to expose fully the filing date columns and allow the document to lie reasonably flat when opened. The record excerpts must have a durable white cover conforming to Fed. R. App. P. 32(a)(2), except that it will be denominated "RECORD EXCERPTS."

The documents constituting the record excerpts do not need to be certified, but if the clerk's "filed" markings are either absent or not clearly legible, the accurate filing information must be typed or written thereon.

30.1.8 *Nonconforming Record Excerpts.* Record excerpts which do not conform to the requirements of this rule will be filed, but must be corrected within the time directed by the clerk. Failure to file corrected record excerpts may result in their being stricken and imposition of sanctions, under 5th Cir. R. 32.5.

30.2 Appendix—Agency Review Proceedings. Petitions for review or enforcement of orders of an administrative agency, board, commission or officer must proceed on the original record on review, without a Fed. R. App. P. 30 required appendix. If a party requests use of the original record, the clerk may require payment of reasonable shipping costs, and the party is responsible for timely review and notification to the agency and the Fifth Circuit clerk's office of any record deficiencies, see 5th Cir. R. 30.1.

(a) If a certified list of documents comprising the record is filed in lieu of the formal record, petitioner must prepare and file with the court and serve on the agency, board, or commission a copy of the portions of the record relied upon by the parties in their briefs. The list of documents must be suitably covered, numbered, and indexed and filed within 21 days of the filing of respondent's brief.

(b) Except in review proceedings covered by 5th Cir. R. 15.3, at the time of filing petitioner's brief, petitioner must file separately 4 copies of any order sought to be reviewed and any supporting opinion, findings of fact, or conclusions of law filed by the agency, board, commission, or officer.

[Amended effective January 4, 1999; December 1, 2002 November 1, 2004; December 1, 2009.]

FRAP 31. SERVING AND FILING BRIEFS

[For text of rule, see the Federal Rules of Appellate Procedure]

RULE 31. FILING AND SERVICE OF A BRIEF

31.1 Briefs—Number of Copies; Computer Generated Briefs. Only 7 paper copies of briefs need be filed. Where a party is represented by counsel who is exempt from electronic filing under 5th Cir. R. 25.2, and counsel generates his or her brief by computer, the party also must submit an electronic version of the brief to the court. The filing party must serve unrepresented parties and counsel for separately represented parties in accordance with Fed. R. App. P. 31(b), and also must serve an electronic version of the brief on each party separately represented. However, the parties may agree in writing to waive service of paper copies of the brief and to be served with an electronic copy only. Electronic service may be in a form agreed to in writing by the parties, or by the same means as submitted to the court. The electronic copy of the brief must be filed on a CD, computer diskette, or such other electronic medium as the clerk may authorize.

The electronic version must:

be prepared in a single Portable Document Format (PDF) file. (Briefs scanned into PDF are not acceptable);

contain nothing other than the brief;

have as the first page of the electronic file a brief cover page as required by Fed. R. App. P. 32(a)(2).

If submitted on a CD, diskette, or other authorized physical media, the electronic version must have a label containing the case name and docket number, and identifying the brief as the appellant's, appellee's, etc.

The proof of service must comply with Fed. R. App. P. 25(d)(1)(B) & (2).

31.2 Briefs—Time for Filing Briefs of Intervenors or Amicus Curiae. The time for filing the brief of the intervenor or amicus is extended until 7 days after the filing of the principal brief of the party supported by the intervenor or amicus.

31.3 Briefs—Time for Mailing or Delivery to a Commercial Carrier. The appellant must send his or her brief to the clerk not later than 40 days after the date of the briefing notice. Pursuant to FED. R. APP. P. 26(c), the appellee has 33 days from the appellant's date of the certificate of service to place the appellee's brief in the mail, file it with the clerk electronically where permitted, or to give it to a third-party commercial carrier for delivery within 3 days. This rule is effective ONLY when the appellant has effected service by mail or via delivery to a commercial carrier for delivery within

3 days and may not be combined with the additional time provisions of FED. R. APP. P. 26(c) to give the appellee 36 days to file a brief. The certificate of service required by FED. R. APP. P. 25(d) is placed in the brief as specified in 5TH CIR. R. 28.3, and must be dated. See 5TH CIR. R. 39.2 for limitations on recovery of certain mailing and commercial delivery costs.

31.4 Briefs—Time for Filing.

31.4.1 *General Provisions.* The court expects briefs to be filed timely and without extensions in the vast majority of cases. No extensions are automatic, even where the request is unopposed. Any requests for extensions should be made sparingly. No extension can be granted without good cause shown as required by Fed. R. App. P. 26(b), or without meeting the additional requirements contained in the 5th Cir. R.

(a) A request for extension should be made as soon as it is reasonably possible to foresee the need for the extension. The clerk must receive a request for extension at least 7 days before the due date, unless the movant demonstrates, in detail, that the facts that form the basis of the motion either did not exist earlier or were not and with due diligence could not have been known earlier.

(b) As specified in 5th Cir. R. 27.1, the movant must indicate that all other parties have been contacted and whether the motion is opposed. Movants should request only as much time as is absolutely needed. The pendency of a motion for extension does not toll the time for compliance.

31.4.2 *Grounds for Extensions.* As justification for extensions, generalities, such as that the purpose of the motion is not for delay or that counsel is too busy, are not sufficient. Grounds that may merit consideration for extensions are, without limitation, the following, which must be set forth if claimed as a reason in any motion for an extension beyond 30 days:

(a) Engagement of counsel in other litigation, provided such litigation is identified by caption, number, and court, and there is set forth:

(1) A description of any effort taken to defer the other litigation and of any ruling thereon;

(2) An explanation of why other litigation should receive priority over the case at hand; and

(3) Other relevant circumstances, including why other associated counsel cannot prepare the brief or relieve the movant's counsel of the other litigation.

(b) The matter is so complex that an adequate brief cannot reasonably be prepared when due.

(c) Extreme hardship will result unless an extension is granted, in which event the nature of the hardship must be set forth in detail.

31.4.3 *Levels of Extensions.* There are two levels of extensions: a Level 1 extension of 1–30 days from the original due date; and a Level 2 extension of more than 30 days from the original due date.

31.4.3.1 Level 1 Extensions. The clerk is authorized to act on or refer to the court Level 1 extensions. The court prefers that an unopposed request be made by telephone, but it may be by written motion or letter. When making the request, the movant must explain what good cause exists for the extension. If the extension is granted by telephone, the movant will immediately send a confirming letter to the clerk, with copies to all parties.

An opposed request for a Level 1 extension must be made by written motion setting forth why there is good cause. The motion must state the initial due date, whether any other extension has been granted, the length of the requested extension, and which parties have expressed opposition.

31.4.3.2 Level 2 Extensions. The clerk is authorized to act on or refer to the court Level 2 extensions. The request must be made by written motion, with copies to all parties, stating the initial due date, whether any other extension has been granted, the length of the requested extension, and whether the motion is opposed.

More than ordinary good cause is required for a Level 2 extension, and Level 2 extensions will be granted only under the most extraordinary of circumstances. The movant must demonstrate diligence and substantial need and must show in detail what special circumstances exist that make a Level 1 extension insufficient.

31.4.4 *Extensions for Reply Briefs.* The court greatly disfavors all extensions of time for filing reply briefs. The court assumes that the parties have had ample opportunity to present their arguments in their initial briefs and that extensions for reply briefs only delay submission of the case to the court.

I.O.P.—The court continues to receive a large number of motions requesting extensions of time to file briefs, or to file briefs out of time, which are considered extension requests. The majority of these motions were by counsel, and frequently were made in direct criminal appeals which have the longest average processing time from filing the notice of appeal to filing the last brief. To assure that this court decides cases more expeditiously, the court's goals are to: 1) reduce the number of motions to extend time to file briefs; and 2) to shorten the amount of time granted. In general and absent the most compelling of reasons, no more than 30 days extension of time will be granted in criminal cases and no more than 40 days extension of time will be granted in civil cases.

[Amended effective January 4, 1999; January 1, 2001; December 1, 2002; November 1, 2004; December 1, 2005; December 1, 2009; December 1, 2016.]

FRAP 32. FORM OF BRIEFS, APPENDICES, AND OTHER PAPERS

[For text of rule, see the Federal Rules of Appellate Procedure]

RULE 32. FORM OF BRIEFS, THE APPENDIX AND OTHER PAPERS

32.1 **Typeface.** Must comply with FED. R. APP. P. 32(a)(5), except that footnotes may be 12 point or larger in proportionally spaced typeface, or 12½ characters per inch or larger in monospaced typeface.

32.2 Type–Volume Limitations. See Fed. R. App. P. 32(f), and for cross-appeals, Fed. R. App. P. 28.1(e). The certificate of interested parties does not count toward the limitation.

32.3 Certificate of Compliance. See Form 6 in the Appendix of Forms to the Fed. R. App. P. A material misrepresentation in the certificate of compliance may result in striking the brief and in sanctions against the person signing the brief.

32.4 Motions for Extra–Length Briefs. A motion to file a brief in excess of the page length or word-volume limitations must be filed at least 10 days in advance of the brief's due date.

32.5 Rejection of Briefs and Record Excerpts. If all copies of briefs and record excerpts do not conform to 5th Cir. R. 28 and 30 and all provisions of Fed. R. App. P. 32, the clerk will file the briefs and record excerpts, but is authorized to return all nonconforming copies. An extension of 10 days is allowed for resubmission in a conforming format. The court may strike briefs and record excerpts if the party fails to submit conforming briefs or record excerpts within 14 days. If at any time the clerk believes the nonconformance is egregious or in bad faith, the clerk, in the alternative to filing the nonconforming matters, may submit them to a single judge, who can reject them and direct that they be returned unfiled. Failure to submit conforming briefs or record excerpts may result in imposition of sanctions.

I.O.P.—Form of Record Excerpts/Appendix—See 5th Cir. R. 30.

[Amended effective January 4, 1999; January 1, 2001; December 1, 2002; December 1, 2006; December 1, 2009; December 1, 2016; April 4, 2017.]

FRAP 32.1   CITING JUDICIAL DISPOSITIONS

[For text of rule, see the Federal Rules of Appellate Procedure]

FRAP 33.   APPEAL CONFERENCES

[For text of rule, see the Federal Rules of Appellate Procedure]

I.O.P.—Appeal Conferences—See 5th Cir. R. 15.3.5.

FRAP 34.   ORAL ARGUMENT

[For text of rule, see the Federal Rules of Appellate Procedure]

RULE 34.   ORAL ARGUMENT

34.1 Docket Control. In the interest of docket control, the chief judge may from time to time appoint a panel or panels to review pending cases for appropriate assignment or disposition under this rule or any other rule of this court.

34.2 Oral Arguments. Oral argument is governed by Fed. R. App. P. 34. Cases not set for oral argument are placed on the summary calendar for decision. The clerk will calendar the oral argument cases based upon the court's calendaring priorities. Counsel for each party must present oral argument unless excused by the court for good cause. The oral argument docket will show the time the court has allotted for each argument. If counsel for all parties indicate that oral argument is not necessary under paragraph .3 of this rule, the case will be governed by Fed. R. App. P. 34(f).

34.3 Submission Without Argument. A party desiring to waive oral argument in a case set for oral argument must file a motion to waive argument at least 7 days before the date set for hearing.

34.4 Number of Counsel to Be Heard. Not more than 2 counsel will be heard for each party on the argument of a case, and the time allowed may be apportioned between counsel in their discretion.

34.5 Expediting Appeals. The court may, on its own motion or for good cause on motion of either party, advance any case for hearing, and prescribe an abbreviated briefing schedule.

34.6 Continuance of Hearing. After a case has been set for hearing, the parties or counsel may not stipulate to delay the hearing. Only the court may delay argument for good cause shown. Engagement of counsel in other courts ordinarily is not considered good cause.

34.7 Recording of Oral Arguments. No cameras, tape recorders, or other equipment designed for the recording or transmission of visual images or sound may be used during oral argument without prior court approval. With the advance approval of the presiding judge, counsel may arrange, at their own expense, for a qualified court reporter to record and transcribe oral argument. If it is the court reporter's usual practice, the reporter may make and use a sound recording for the sole purpose of preparing an accurate transcript. The reporter may not make any recordings of the oral argument available to counsel, a party, or any other person until the court posts its recording of the oral argument on the court's Internet website.

34.8 Criminal Justice Act Cases. The court expects court-appointed counsel to present oral argument. An associate attorney not appointed under the act may present argument only under the most pressing and unusual circumstances, and upon the court's advance authorization.

34.9 Checking in With Clerk's Office. On the day of hearing counsel must check in with the clerk 30 minutes before court convenes to confirm the name of the attorney or attorneys who will present argument for each party and how the argument time will be divided between opening and rebuttal. All counsel in the fourth and fifth cases on the docket heard in New Orleans may check in by telephone, but must report in person to the clerk's office within one hour after court convenes. On the last day of a New Orleans session, all attorneys must report in person to the clerk's office 30 minutes before court convenes.

34.10 Submission Without Argument. When a case is placed on the oral argument calendar, a judge of the court has determined that oral argument would be helpful. Therefore, requests of the parties to waive oral argument are not looked upon with favor, and counsel may be excused only by the court for good cause. See 5th Cir. R. 34.3.

If appellant fails to appear in a criminal appeal from conviction, the court will not hear argument from the United States.

34.11 Time for Oral Argument. The time allowed for oral argument is indicated on the printed calendar. Most cases are allowed 20 minutes to the side. The word "side" refers to parties in their position on appeal. Where in doubt, consult the clerk's office.

34.12 Additional Time for Oral Argument. Additional time for oral argument is sparingly permitted. Requests for additional time should be set forth in a motion or letter to the clerk filed well in advance of the oral argument.

34.13 Calling the Calendar. The court usually does not call the calendar unless there are special problems requiring attention. The court hears the cases in the order they appear on the calendar.

I.O.P.—Screening—Screening is the name given to the method used by the court to determine whether cases should be argued orally or decided on briefs only. This is done under Fed. R. App. P. and 5th Cir. R. 34.

(a) The judges of the Court Screen Cases with Assistance from the Staff Attorney. When the last brief is filed, a case is generally sent to the staff Attorney for prescreening classification. If the staff attorney concludes that the case does not warrant oral argument, a brief memorandum may be prepared and the case returned to the clerk. The clerk then routes the case to 1 of the court's judges, selected in rotation. If that judge agrees that the case does not warrant oral argument, the briefs, together with a proposed opinion, are forwarded to the 2 other judges on the screening panel. If any party requests oral argument, all panel judges must concur that the case does not warrant oral argument, and also in the panel opinion as a proper disposition without any special concurrence or dissent. If no party requests oral argument, all panel judges must concur that the case does not warrant oral argument. However, absent a party's request for oral argument, summary disposition may include a concurrence or a dissent by panel members.

(b) If the staff attorney concludes that oral argument is required, the case is sent to an active judge for screening. If the screening judge agrees, the case is placed on the next appropriate calendar, consistent with the court's calendaring priorities. If the screening judge disagrees with the recommendation for oral argument, that judge's screening panel disposes of the case under the summary calendar procedure.

Decision Without Oral Argument—When all panel members agree that oral argument of a case is not needed, they advise the clerk the case has been placed on the summary calendar. The court's decision usually accompanies the notice to the clerk.

Court Year Schedule—The clerk prepares a proposed court schedule for an entire year which is approved by the scheduling proctor and chief judge of the court. The court schedule does not consider what specific cases are to be heard, but only sets the weeks of court in relation to the probable volume of cases and judge power availability for the year.

JUDGE ASSIGNMENTS

Panel Selection Procedure—Based on the number of weeks each active judge sits and the number of sittings available from the court's senior judges, and visiting circuit or district judges, the scheduling proctor and clerk create panels of judges for the sessions of the court for the entire court year. The judges are scheduled to avoid repetitive scheduling of panels composed of the same members.

Separation of Assignment of Judges and Calendaring of Cases—The judge assignments are made available only to the judges for their advance planning of their workload for the forthcoming court year. To insure complete objectivity in the assignment of judges and the calendaring of cases, the two functions of (1) judge assignments to panels and (2) calendaring of cases are carefully separated.

PREPARATION AND PUBLISHING CALENDARS

General—The clerk prepares calendars of cases under calendaring guidelines established by the court. Calendars are prepared for the number of sessions (usually between 3 and 5) scheduled for a month. Information about the names of the panel members is not disclosed within the clerk's office until the calendars of cases for the month are actually prepared so that briefs and other materials can be distributed.

Calendaring by Case Type—The clerk balances the calendars by dividing the cases evenly among the panels by case type so that each panel for a particular month has more or less an equal number of different types of litigation for consideration.

Preference Cases—The categories of cases listed in 5th Cir. R. 47.7 are given preference in processing and disposition. To assist the clerk in implementing this rule, any party to a civil appeal or review proceeding requiring priority status should notify the clerk and cite the statutory support for the preference.

Non–Preference Cases—All other cases are calendared for hearing in accordance with the court's "first-in first-out" rule. Unless the court assigns special priority the oldest cases in point of time of availability of briefs are ordinarily calendared first for hearing.

Calendaring for Convenience of Counsel—For the New Orleans sessions, cases with non-local lawyers are scheduled in the first positions on the calendar whenever possible for their convenience in making departure accommodations.

Number of Cases Assigned—Unless special provision is made, a regular session of a panel of the court will hear 5 cases per day for 4 days, Monday through Thursday.

Advance Notice—The court seeks to give counsel 60 days advance notice of cases set for oral argument.

Forwarding Briefs to Judges—Immediately after formally issuing the calendar the clerk sends the panel members copies of the briefs for the cases set on the calendar.

Pre–Argument Preparation—The judges invariably read all briefs prior to oral argument.

Identity of Panel—The clerk may not disclose the names of the panel members for a particular session until 1 week in advance of the session.

ORAL ARGUMENT

Presenting Argument—Counsel should prepare their oral arguments knowing the judges have already studied the briefs. Reading from briefs, decisions, or the record is not permitted except in unusual circumstances. Counsel should be prepared to answer the court's questions. The court will consider a motion to extend the time allotted for argument if the court's questions prevent completion of counsel's argument.

Lighting Signal Procedure—The courtroom deputy will keep track of the time using lighting signals:

(a) Appellant's Argument—A green light signals the beginning of the opening argument of appellant. Two minutes before expiration of the time allowed for opening argument, the green light goes off and a yellow light comes on. When the time reserved for opening argument expires, the yellow light goes off and a red light comes on. If counsel proceeds after the red light, time will be deducted from the rebuttal period.

(b) Appellee's Argument—The same procedure as outlined above is used.

(c) Appellant's Rebuttal—A green light signals commencement of time; a red light comes on when time expires. No yellow light is used.

Case Conferences and Designation of Writing Judge—The panel hearing the arguments usually confers on the cases at the conclusion of each day's arguments. A tentative decision is reached and the presiding judge assigns responsibility for opinion writing. There is no pre-argument assignment of opinion writing. Judges do not specialize. Assignments are made to equalize the workload of the entire session.

[Amended effective January 4, 1999; August 15, 2008; December 1, 2009; May 15, 2015.]

FRAP 35. EN BANC DETERMINATION

[For text of rule, see the Federal Rules of Appellate Procedure]

RULE 35. DETERMINATION OF CAUSES BY THE COURT EN BANC

35.1 Caution. Counsel are reminded that in every case the duty of counsel is fully discharged without filing a petition for rehearing en banc unless the case meets the rigid standards of Fed. R. App. P. 35(a). As is noted in Fed. R. App. P. 35, en banc hearing or rehearing is not favored. Among the reasons is that each request for en banc consideration must be studied by every active judge of the court and is a serious call on limited judicial resources. Counsel have a duty to the court commensurate with that owed their clients to read with attention and observe with restraint the standards of Fed. R. App. P. 35(b)(1). The court takes the view that, given the extraordinary nature of petitions for en banc consideration, it is fully justified in imposing sanctions on its own initiative under, inter alia, Fed. R. App. P. 38 and 28 U.S.C. § 1927, upon the person who signed the petitions, the represented party, or both, for manifest abuse of the procedure.

35.2 Form of Petition. Twenty copies of every petition for en banc consideration, whether upon initial hearing or rehearing, must be filed. The petition must not be incorporated in the petition for rehearing before the panel, if one is filed, but must be complete in itself. In no case will a petition for en banc consideration adopt by reference any matter from the petition for panel rehearing or from any other briefs or motions in the case. A petition for en banc consideration must contain the following items, in order:

35.2.1 Certificate of interested persons required for briefs by 5th Cir. R. 28.2.1.

35.2.2 If the party petitioning for en banc consideration is represented by counsel, a statement as set forth in Fed. R. App. P. 35(b)(1).

35.2.3 *Table of Contents and Authorities.*

35.2.4 Statement of the issue or issues asserted to merit en banc consideration. It will rarely occur that these will be the same as those appropriate for panel rehearing. A petition for en banc consideration must be limited to the circumstances enumerated in Fed. R. App. P. 35(a).

35.2.5 Statement of the course of proceedings and disposition of the case.

35.2.6 Statement of any facts necessary to the argument of the issues.

35.2.7 *Argument and Authorities.* These will concern only the issues required by paragraph (.2.4) hereof and shall address specifically, not only their merit, but why they are contended to be worthy of en banc consideration.

35.2.8 *Conclusion.*

35.2.9 *Certificate of Service.*

35.2.10 A copy of the opinion or order sought to be reviewed. The opinion or order will be bound with the petition and shall not be marked or annotated.

35.3 Response to Petition. No response to a petition for en banc consideration will be received unless requested by the court.

35.4 Time and Form—Extensions. Any petition for rehearing en banc must be received in the clerk's office within the time specified in Fed. R. App. P. 40. Counsel should not request extensions of time except for the most compelling reasons.

35.5 Length. See Fed. R. App. P. 35(b)(2). The statement required by Fed. R. App. P. 35(b)(1) is included in the limit and is not a "certificate[ ] of counsel" that is excluded by Fed. R. App P. 32(f).

35.6 Determination of Causes En Banc and Composition of En Banc Court. A cause will be heard or reheard en banc when it meets the criteria for en banc set out in Fed. R. App. P. 35(a).

The en banc court will be composed of all active judges of the court plus any senior judge of the court who participated in the panel decision who elects to participate in the en banc consideration. This election is to be communicated timely to the chief judge and clerk. Any judge participating in an en banc poll, hearing, or rehearing while in regular active service who subsequently takes senior status may elect to continue participating in the final resolution of the case.

I.O.P.—Petition for Rehearing En Banc

Extraordinary Nature of Petitions for Rehearing En Banc—A petition for rehearing en banc is an extraordinary procedure that is intended to bring to the attention of the entire court an error of exceptional public importance or an opinion that directly conflicts with prior Supreme Court, Fifth Circuit or state law precedent, subject to the following: Alleged errors in the facts of the case (including sufficiency of the evidence) or in the application of correct precedent to the facts of the case are generally matters for panel rehearing but not for rehearing en banc.

The Most Abused Prerogative—Petitions for rehearing en banc are the most abused prerogative of appellate advocates in the Fifth Circuit. Fewer than 1% of the cases decided by the court on the merits are reheard en banc; and frequently those rehearings granted result from a request for en banc reconsideration by a judge of the court rather than a petition by the parties.

Handling of Petition by the Judges

Panel Has Control—Although each panel judge and every active judge receives a copy of the petition for rehearing en banc, the filing of a petition for rehearing en banc does not take the case out of the control of the panel deciding the case. A petition for rehearing en banc is treated as a petition for rehearing by the panel if no petition is filed. The panel may grant rehearing without action by the full court.

Requesting a Poll—Within 10 days of the filing of the petition, any active judge of the court or any member of the panel rendering the decision, who desires that the case be reheard en banc, may notify the writing judge (the senior active Fifth Circuit judge if the writing judge is a non-active member) to this effect on or before the date shown on the clerk's form that transmits the petition. This notification is also notice that if the panel declines to grant rehearing, an en banc poll is desired.

If the panel decides not to grant the rehearing after such notice, it notifies the chief judge, who then polls the court by written ballot on whether en banc rehearing should be granted.

Requesting a Poll on Court's Own Motion—Any active member of the court or any member of the panel rendering the decision may request a poll of the active members of the court whether rehearing en banc should be granted, whether or not a party filed a petition for rehearing en banc. A requesting judge ordinarily sends a letter to the chief judge with copies to the other active judges of the court and any other panel member.

Polling the Court—When a request to poll the court is made, each active judge of the court casts a ballot and sends a copy to all other active judges of the court and any senior Fifth Circuit judge who is a panel member. The ballot indicates whether the judge voting desires oral argument if en banc is granted.

Negative Poll—If the vote is unfavorable to the grant of en banc consideration, the chief judge advises the writing judge. The panel originally hearing the case then enters an appropriate order.

Affirmative Poll—If a majority of the judges in active service who are not disqualified, vote for en banc hearing or rehearing, the chief judge instructs the clerk as to an appropriate order. The order indicates a rehearing en banc with or without oral argument has been granted, and specifies a briefing schedule for filing of additional briefs. The appellant's brief will have a blue cover; the appellee's will have a red cover.

Every party must then furnish to the clerk 20 additional copies of every brief the party previously filed.

No Poll Request—If the specified time for requesting a poll has expired and the writing judge of the panel has not received a request from any active member of the court, or other panel member, the judge may take such action deemed appropriate on the petition. However, in the order disposing of the case and the petition, the panel's order denying the petition for rehearing en banc must show no poll was requested.

Capital Cases—Consistent with long established legal principle and uniformly followed practice, the filing of a petition for rehearing (or hearing) en banc does not constitute or operate as a stay of execution and does not preclude carrying out an execution.

Timely petitions for rehearing (or hearing) en banc which are filed in a capital case while a scheduled execution date is pending and less than **22 days** before the scheduled date will be processed and distributed in the manner prescribed by the chief judge or delegee. The Chief Judge or delegee may order expedited consideration thereof and set a time limit for each judge eligible to vote thereon to advise the Chief Judge or delegee whether to call for a poll and whether (if a poll is or were to be timely requested by any judge) the judge would vote for or against rehearing (or hearing) en banc, and the petition for rehearing (or hearing) en banc will be disposed of accordingly. If no poll is timely requested, or if a poll results in no rehearing (or hearing) en banc, the panel may enter an order denying rehearing (or hearing) en banc. If a poll results in a grant of rehearing (or hearing) en banc, the Chief Judge, or delegee, will enter an order staying the execution pending further order of the court.

[Amended effective January 4, 1999; January 1, 2001; November 1, 2004; December 1, 2005; December 1, 2009; April 2, 2018.]

FRAP 36.   ENTRY OF JUDGMENT; NOTICE

[For text of rule, see the Federal Rules of Appellate Procedure]

FRAP 37. INTEREST ON JUDGMENT

*[For text of rule, see the Federal Rules
of Appellate Procedure]*

FRAP 38. FRIVOLOUS APPEAL— DAMAGES AND COSTS

*[For text of rule, see the Federal Rules
of Appellate Procedure]*

FRAP 39. COSTS

*[For text of rule, see the Federal Rules
of Appellate Procedure]*

RULE 39. COSTS

39.1 Taxable Rates. The cost of reproducing necessary copies of the briefs, appendices, or record excerpts shall be taxed at a rate of actual cost, or $.15 per page, whichever is less, including cover, index, and internal pages, for any form of reproduction costs. The cost of the binding required by 5th Cir. R. 32.2.3 that mandates that briefs must lie reasonably flat when open shall be a taxable cost but not limited to the foregoing rate. This rate is intended to approximate the current cost of the most economical acceptable method of reproduction generally available; and the clerk will, at reasonable intervals, examine and review it to reflect current rates. Taxable costs will be authorized for up to 15 copies for a brief and 10 copies of an appendix or record excerpts, unless the clerk gives advance approval for additional copies.

39.2 Nonrecovery of Mailing and Commercial Delivery Service Costs. Mailing and commercial delivery fees incurred in transmitting briefs are not recoverable as taxable costs.

39.3 Time for Filing Bills of Costs. The clerk must receive bills of costs and any objections within the times set forth in Fed. R. App. P. 39(d). See 5th Cir. R. 26.1.

[Amended effective January 4, 1999; December 1, 2009.]

FRAP 40. PETITION FOR PANEL REHEARING

*[For text of rule, see the Federal Rules
of Appellate Procedure]*

RULE 40. PETITION FOR REHEARING

40.1 Copies. Four copies of all petitions for rehearing will be filed. A party seeking panel rehearing must attach to the petition an unmarked copy of the opinion or order sought to be reviewed. If the party contemporaneously files a petition for rehearing en banc and attaches a copy of the opinion or order required by 5th Cir. R. 35.2.10, the party does not have to attach a copy to the petition for panel rehearing.

40.2 Limited Nature of Petition for Panel Rehearing. A petition for rehearing is intended to bring to the attention of the panel claimed errors of fact or law in the opinion. It is not used for reargument of the issue previously presented or to attack the court's well-settled summary calendar procedures.

Petitions for rehearing of panel decisions are reviewed by panel members only.

40.3 Length. See Fed. R. App. P. 40(b).

40.4 Time for Filing. The clerk must receive a petition for rehearing within the time prescribed in Fed. R. App. P. 40(a).

I.O.P.—Necessity for Filing—It is not necessary to file a petition for rehearing in the court of appeals as a prerequisite to filing a petition for certiorari in the Supreme Court of the United States.

Capital Cases—Consistent with long established legal principle and uniformly followed practice, the filing of a petition for rehearing does not constitute or operate as a stay of execution and does not preclude carrying out an execution.

[Amended effective January 4, 1999; November 1, 2004; December 1, 2005; December 1, 2009.]

FRAP 41. MANDATE: CONTENTS; ISSUANCE AND EFFECTIVE DATE; STAY

*[For text of rule, see the Federal Rules
of Appellate Procedure]*

RULE 41. ISSUANCE OF MANDATE; STAY OF MANDATE

41.1 Stay of Mandate—Criminal Appeals. A motion for a stay of the issuance of a mandate in a direct criminal appeal filed under Fed. R. App. P. 41 will not be granted simply upon request. Unless the petition sets forth good cause for stay or clearly demonstrates that a substantial question is to be presented to the Supreme Court, the motion shall be denied and the mandate thereafter issued forthwith.

41.2 Recall of Mandate. Once issued a mandate will not be recalled except to prevent injustice.

41.3 Effect of Granting Rehearing En Banc. Unless otherwise expressly provided, the granting of a rehearing en banc vacates the panel opinion and judgment of the court and stays the mandate. If, after voting a case en banc, the court lacks a quorum to act on the case for 30 consecutive days, the case is automatically returned to the panel, the panel opinion is reinstated as an unpublished (and hence nonprecedential) opinion, and the mandate is released. To act on a case, the en banc court must have a quorum consisting of a majority of the en banc court as defined in 28 U.S.C. § 46(c).

41.4 Issuance of Mandate in Expedited Appeals or Mandamus Actions. The clerk will issue the mandate forthwith in any expedited appeal of a criminal sentence and in actions denying mandamus relief, unless instructed otherwise by the court.

I.O.P.—Absent a motion for stay or a stay by operation of an order, rule, or procedure, mandates will issue promptly on the 8th day after the time for filing a petition for rehearing expires; or after entry of an order denying the petition. As an exception, and by court direction, the clerk will immediately issue the mandate when the court dismisses a case for failure to prosecute an appeal or for lack of jurisdiction, or in such other instances as the court may direct. The original record and any exhibits will be returned to the clerk of the district court with the mandate.

[Amended effective January 4, 1999; December 1, 2009; October 31, 2011.]

FRAP 42. VOLUNTARY DISMISSAL

*[For text of rule, see the Federal Rules
of Appellate Procedure]*

RULE 42. VOLUNTARY DISMISSAL

42.1 Dismissal by Appellant. In all cases where the appellant or petitioner files an unopposed motion to withdraw the appeal or agency review proceeding, the clerk will enter an order of dismissal and issue a copy of the order as the mandate.

42.2 Frivolous and Unmeritorious Appeals. If upon the hearing of any interlocutory motion or as a result of a review under 5th Cir. R. 34, it appears to the court that the appeal is frivolous and entirely without merit, the appeal will be dismissed.

42.3 Dismissal for Failure to Prosecute.

42.3.1 In direct criminal appeals proceeding in forma pauperis, the provisions of 5th Cir. R. 42.3.1.1 and 42.3.1.2 apply. In habeas cases, actions filed under 28 U.S.C. § 2255, and other prisoner matters proceeding in forma pauperis, the provisions of 5th Cir. R. 42.3.1.1 apply if the appellant is represented by counsel; prisoners proceeding pro se will be given an initial written deadline for filing a certificate of appealability, filing any briefs, for paying fees, or for complying with other directives of the court. If pro se prisoners do not meet the deadline established, or timely request an extension of time, the clerk will dismiss the appeal without further notice, 15 days after the deadline date.

42.3.1.1 Appeals With Counsel. If appellant is represented by appointed or retained counsel, the clerk will issue a notice to counsel that, upon expiration of 15 days from the date of the notice, the appeal may be dismissed for want of prosecution unless prior to that date the default is remedied, and must enter an order directing counsel to show cause within 15 days from the date of the order why disciplinary action should not be taken against counsel. If the default is remedied within that time, the clerk must not dismiss the appeal and may refer to the court the matter of disciplinary action against the attorney. If the default is not remedied within that time, the clerk may enter an order dismissing the appeal for want of prosecution or may refer to the court the question of dismissal. The clerk must refer to the court the matter of disciplinary action against the attorney. The court may refer the matter of disciplinary action to a special master including but not limited to a district or magistrate judge.

42.3.1.2 Appeals Without Counsel. The clerk must issue a notice to appellant that 15 days from the date of the notice the appeal will be dismissed for want of prosecution, unless the default is remedied before that date. If the default is

remedied within that time, the clerk must not dismiss the appeal.

42.3.2 In all other appeals when appellant fails to order the transcript, fails to file a brief, or otherwise fails to comply with the rules of the court, the clerk must dismiss the appeal for want of prosecution.

42.3.3 In all instances of failure to prosecute an appeal to hearing as required, the court may take such other action as it deems appropriate.

42.3.4 An order dismissing an appeal for want of prosecution must be issued to the clerk of the district court as the mandate.

42.4 Dismissals Without Prejudice. In acting on a motion under 5th Cir. R. 27.1.3 to stay further proceedings, the clerk may enter such appeals or agency review proceedings as dismissed without prejudice to the right of reinstatement of the appeal within 180 days from the date of dismissal. Any party desiring reinstatement, or an extension of the time to seek reinstatement, must notify the clerk in writing within the time period allowed for reinstatement. This procedure does not apply where the stay is sought pending a decision of this court in another case, a decision of the Supreme Court, or a stay on the court's own motion. If the appeal is not reinstated within the period fixed, the appeal is deemed dismissed with prejudice. However, an additional period of 180 days from the date of dismissal will be allowed for applying for relief from a dismissal with prejudice which resulted from mistake, inadvertence, or excusable neglect of counsel or a pro se litigant.

[Amended effective January 4, 1999; January 1, 2001; December 1, 2009.]

FRAP 43. SUBSTITUTION OF PARTIES

*[For text of rule, see the Federal Rules
of Appellate Procedure]*

FRAP 44. CASE INVOLVING A CONSTITUTIONAL QUESTION WHEN THE UNITED STATES OR THE RELEVANT STATE IS NOT A PARTY

*[For text of rule, see the Federal Rules
of Appellate Procedure]*

FRAP 45. CLERK'S DUTIES

*[For text of rule, see the Federal Rules
of Appellate Procedure]*

RULE 45. DUTIES OF CLERKS

45.1 Location. The clerk's office is maintained in the city of New Orleans, Louisiana.

45.2 Release of Original Papers. The clerk may release original records or papers without a court order for a limited time upon a party's or counsel's request, to facilitate preparation of a brief in a pending appeal.

45.3 Office to Be Open. The clerk's office is open for business on all days except Saturdays, Sundays, designated federal holidays, and Mardi Gras.

I.O.P.—Office hours are from 8:00 a.m. to 5:00 p.m. Central Time Monday Through Friday.

(a) The clerk's office welcomes telephone inquiries from counsel concerning rules and procedures. Telephone No. (504) 310–7700.

(b) In emergency situations after normal office hours, or on weekends, call the number shown above. An automated attendant provides an option connecting the caller to the emergency duty deputy.

[Amended effective January 4, 1999; December 1, 2002.]

FRAP 46. ATTORNEYS

*[For text of rule, see the Federal Rules
of Appellate Procedure]*

RULE 46. ATTORNEYS

46.1 Admission and Fees. Attorneys must have and maintain a valid underlying license to practice law issued by a governmental licensing authority listed in Fed. R. App. P. 46(a)(1) to be admitted and continue to practice before this court. Admission is governed by Fed. R. App. P. 46 and this rule. Attorneys admitted to this court must provide the clerk a valid e-mail and mailing address, as well as a working telephone number, and must provide updated information to the clerk when changes occur. Attorneys are admitted for a period of five years and must, after notice from the clerk, timely apply for readmission. To be admitted or readmitted, an attorney must pay the fee fixed by court order. No fee will be required of an attorney who otherwise has all qualifications for admission and is: appointed to represent an appellant in forma pauperis; appearing on behalf of the United States; or newly graduated from law school, licensed to practice in Louisiana, Mississippi, or Texas, and on orders for extended active duty in the Judge Advocate General's Corps.

46.2 Suspension or Disbarment. In addition to Fed. R. App. P. 46(b), attorneys may be suspended or removed from the roll of attorneys permitted to practice before this court if the appropriate law licensing authority withdraws or suspends the attorney's license to practice law, or the license to practice lapses.

46.3 Entry of Appearance. Attorneys admitted to the bar of this court must enter their appearance in each case in which they participate at the time the case is docketed or upon notice by the clerk. A form for entry of appearance is provided by the clerk. In addition to other pertinent information, the form requires counsel to cite all pending related cases and any cases on the docket of the Supreme Court, or this or any other United States Court of Appeals, which involve a similar issue or issues. Counsel must update such information at the time of briefing. Counsel must also indicate on the form whether the appeal is in a category of cases requiring preference in processing and disposition as set out in 5th Cir. R. 47.7.

I.O.P.—Disciplinary Action—Fed. R. App. P. 46(b) and (c) govern the procedures followed to invoke disciplinary action against any member of the bar of this court for failure to comply with the rules of this court, or for conduct unbecoming a member of the bar.

Duties of Court Appointed Counsel—The Judicial Council of the Fifth Circuit has adopted a plan under the Criminal Justice Act detailing the duties and responsibilities of court appointed counsel. A copy of this plan is available from the clerk.

An appointed counsel may claim compensation for services furnished by a partner or associate within the maximum compensation allowed by the act. However, the court expects court-appointed counsel to take the lead in preparing the brief and presenting oral argument, if argument is allowed. Claims by associate counsel for in-court services and travel expenses incurred in connection therewith are not allowed unless the partner or associate is appointed under the Criminal Justice Act on advance motion and approval by the court.

[Amended effective January 4, 1999; December 1, 2002; August 15, 2008; December 1, 2009.]

FRAP 47. LOCAL RULES BY COURTS OF APPEALS

*[For text of rule, see the Federal Rules
of Appellate Procedure]*

RULE 47. OTHER FIFTH CIRCUIT RULES

47.1 Name, Seal and Process.

(a) *Name.* The name of this court is "United States Court of Appeals for the Fifth Circuit."

(b) *Seal.* The seal of this court contains the American eagle encircled with the words "United States Court of Appeals" on the upper part of the outer edge; and the words "Fifth Circuit" on the lower part of the outer edge, running from left to right.

(c) *Writs and Process.* Writs and process of this court are under the seal of the court and signed by the clerk.

47.2 Sessions. Court sessions are held in each of the states constituting the circuit at least once each year. Sessions may be scheduled at any location having adequate facilities. On motion of a party or on the court's own motion, the court may change the hearing of any appeal to another location or time.

47.3 Circuit Executive, Library, and Staff Attorneys.

(a) *Circuit Executive.* The circuit executive's office is maintained at New Orleans, Louisiana. The circuit executive acts as Secretary of the Judicial Council of the Fifth Circuit, provides administrative support to the court, and performs such other duties as the judicial council or the chief judge assigns.

(b) *Library.* A public library is maintained at New Orleans, Louisiana, which is open during hours fixed by the court. Books and materials may not be removed from the library without permission of the librarian. Other libraries may be maintained at such places in the circuit as the court designates.

(c) *Staff Attorneys.* A central staff of attorneys is maintained at New Orleans, Louisiana, to perform such research and record analysis as the court directs.

47.4 Bankruptcy Appeals.

47.4.1 The Fed. R. App. P. and 5th Cir. R. apply to all appeals from United States Bankruptcy Courts to this court.

47.4.2 Appeals docketed in the district court or with the clerk of any authorized appellate panels, may not be transferred to this court unless the district judge or appellate panel approves the transfer in writing.

47.5 Publication of Opinions.

47.5.1 *Criteria for Publication.* The publication of opinions that merely decide particular cases on the basis of well-settled principles of law imposes needless expense on the public and burdens on the legal profession. However, opinions that may in any way interest persons other than the parties to a case should be published. Therefore, an opinion is published if it:

(a) Establishes a new rule of law, alters, or modifies an existing rule of law, or calls attention to an existing rule of law that appears to have been generally overlooked;

(b) Applies an established rule of law to facts significantly different from those in previous published opinions applying the rule;

(c) Explains, criticizes, or reviews the history of existing decisional or enacted law;

(d) Creates or resolves a conflict of authority either within the circuit or between this circuit and another;

(e) Concerns or discusses a factual or legal issue of significant public interest; or

(f) Is rendered in a case that has been reviewed previously and its merits addressed by an opinion of the United States Supreme Court.

An opinion may also be published if it:

Is accompanied by a concurring or dissenting opinion; or reverses the decision below or affirms it upon different grounds.

47.5.2 *Publication Decision.* An opinion will be published unless each member of the panel deciding the case determines that its publication is neither required nor justified under the criteria for publication. If any judge of the court or any party so requests the panel will reconsider its decision not to publish an opinion. The opinion will be published if, upon reconsideration, each member of the panel determines that it meets one or more of the criteria for publication or should be published for any other good reason, and the panel issues an order to publish the opinion.

47.5.3 *Unpublished Opinions Issued Before January 1, 1996.** Unpublished opinions issued before January 1, 1996,* are precedent. Although every opinion believed to have precedential value is published, an unpublished opinion may be cited pursuant to Fed. R. App. P. 32.1(a). The party citing to an unpublished judicial disposition must provide a citation to

the disposition in a publicly accessible electronic database. If the disposition is not available in an electronic database, a copy of any unpublished opinion cited in any document being submitted to the court, must be attached to each copy of the document, as required by Fed. R. App. P. 32.1(b).

47.5.4 *Unpublished Opinions Issued on or After January 1, 1996.** Unpublished opinions issued on or after January 1, 1996,* are not precedent, except under the doctrine of res judicata, collateral estoppel or law of the case (or similarly to show double jeopardy, notice, sanctionable conduct, entitlement to attorney's fees, or the like). An unpublished opinion may be cited pursuant to Fed. R. App. P. 32.1(a). The party citing to an unpublished judicial disposition should provide a citation to the disposition in a publicly accessible electronic database. If the disposition is not available in an electronic database, a copy of any unpublished opinion cited in any document being submitted to the court must be attached to each copy of the document, as required by Fed. R. App. P. 32.1(b). The first page of each unpublished opinion bears the following legend:

> Pursuant to 5th Circuit Rule 47.5, the court has determined that this opinion should not be published and is not precedent except under the limited circumstances set forth in 5th Circuit Rule 47.5.4.

47.5.5 *Definition of "Published."* An opinion is considered as "published" for purposes of this rule when the panel deciding the case determines, in accordance with 5th Cir. R. 47.5.2, that the opinion will be published and the opinion is issued.

* Effective date of amended Rule.

47.6 Affirmance Without Opinion. The judgment or order may be affirmed or enforced without opinion when the court determines that an opinion would have no precedential value and that any one or more of the following circumstances exists and is dispositive of a matter submitted for decision: (1) that a judgment of the district court is based on findings of fact that are not clearly erroneous; (2) that the evidence in support of a jury verdict is not insufficient; (3) that the order of an administrative agency is supported by substantial evidence on the record as a whole; (4) in the case of a summary judgment, that no genuine issue of material fact has been properly raised by the appellant; and (5) no reversible error of law appears. In such case, the court may, in its discretion, enter either of the following orders: "AFFIRMED. See 5th Cir. R. 47.6." or "ENFORCED. See 5th Cir. R. 47.6."

47.7 Calendaring Priorities. The following categories of cases are given preference in processing and disposition: (1) appeals in criminal cases, (2) habeas corpus petitions and motions attacking a federal sentence, (3) proceedings involving recalcitrant witnesses before federal courts or grand juries under 28 U.S.C. § 1826, (4) actions for temporary or preliminary injunctive relief, and (5) any other action if good cause therefor is shown. (Fed. R. App. P. 45(b) and 28 U.S.C. § 1657).

47.8 Attorney's Fees.

47.8.1 *Supporting Requirements.* Petitions or motions for the award of attorney's fees should always be supported by contemporaneous time records recording all work for which a fee is claimed and reflecting the hours or fractional hours of work done and the specific professional level of services performed by each lawyer seeking compensation. In the absence of such records, time expended will not be considered in setting the fee beyond the minimum amount necessary in the court's judgment for any lawyer to produce the work seen in court. Exceptions may be made only to avoid an unconscionable result.

The clerk will make reasonable efforts to advise counsel about this rule, but whether or not counsel has been advised, ignorance of this rule is not, standing alone, grounds for an exception. If the reasonableness of the hours claimed on the basis of time records becomes an issue, the applicant must make time records available for inspection by opposing counsel and, if a dispute is not resolved between them, by the court.

47.8.2 *Attorney's Fees and Expenses Under the Equal Access to Justice Act.* This rule implements the provisions of the Equal Access to Justice Act, Public Law No. 96–481, 94 Stat. 2325 (1980).

(a) Applications to the Court of Appeals. An application for an award of fees and expenses pursuant to 28 U.S.C. § 2412(d)(1)(B) must identify the applicant and the proceeding for which an award is sought. The application must show the nature and extent of services provided in this court and that the applicant has prevailed, and must identify the position of the United States or an agency thereof that the applicant alleges was not substantially justified.

(b) Petitions by Permission. A petition for leave to appeal pursuant to 5 U.S.C. § 504(c)(2) must be filed with the clerk of the court of appeals within 30 days after the entry of the agency's order, with proof of service on all other parties to the agency's proceedings.

(c) The petition must contain a copy of the order to be reviewed and any findings of fact, conclusions of law, and opinion relating thereto, a statement of the facts necessary to an understanding of the petition, and a memorandum showing why the petition for permission to appeal should be granted. An answer may be filed within 30 days after service of the petition, unless otherwise directed by the court. The application and any answer will be submitted without further briefing and oral argument unless otherwise ordered.

(d) An original and 3 copies must be filed with the court.

(e) Within 10 days after the entry of an order granting permission to appeal, the applicant must pay the clerk of this court the docket fee prescribed by the Judicial Conference of the United States. Upon receipt of the payment, the clerk will enter the appeal upon the docket. The record shall be transmitted and filed in accordance with Fed. R. App. P. 17. A notice of appeal need not be filed.

(f) Appeals/Petitions to Review. Appeals and petitions to review matters otherwise contemplated by the Equal Access to Justice Act may be filed pursuant to the applicable statutes and rules of the court.

47.9 Rules for the Conduct of Proceedings Under the Judicial Conduct and Disability Act, 28 U.S.C. §§ 351 et

seq. See separately published Judicial Council of the Fifth Circuit Rules for Judicial–Conduct or Judicial Disability effective May 4, 2008.

47.10 Rule Governing Appeals Raising Sentencing Guidelines Issues—18 U.S.C. § 3742.

47.10.1 *Scope of Rules.* These rules govern procedures in appeals raising sentencing issues pursuant to 18 U.S.C. § 3742(a) or (b). These cases will proceed in the same manner and under the general rules of court governing other appeals and will not be given special expedited treatment over other criminal cases, except as hereinafter specified.

47.10.2 *Motion to Expedite.* If the defendant is incarcerated for a period of 1 year or less pursuant to the sentence appealed, a party may file a motion to expedite the appeal upon a showing of irreparable harm. The motion must set out: (a) when the trial transcript can be prepared and made available; and, (b) how soon thereafter appellant can file a brief. The court disfavors bifurcation of issues concerning sentencing from those issues involving the conviction.

47.10.3 *The Appellate Record.*

(a) Oral Reasons for Imposition of Sentence. The oral statement of reasons of the district court for imposition of a sentence as required by 18 U.S.C. § 3553(c), as amended, must be reduced to writing, filed, and incorporated in the record on appeal.

(b) Transcript of Sentencing Proceedings. In addition to the requirements of Fed. R. App. P. 10(b) and 5th Cir. R. 10.1 for ordering the transcript of trial proceedings, appellant is required to order a transcript of the entire sentencing proceeding (excluding the oral statement of reasons for sentencing of the district court) if a sentencing issue under 18 U.S.C. § 3742 will be raised on appeal.

(c) Presentence Report. If a notice of appeal is filed as authorized by 18 U.S.C. § 3742(a) and (b) for review of a sentence, the clerk will transmit to this court the presentence report. The report is transmitted separately from other parts of the record on appeal and is labeled as a sealed record if sealed by the district court.

(d) Presentence reports filed in this court as part of a record on appeal are treated as matters of public record except where the report, or a portion thereof was sealed by order of the district court.

(e) Counsel wishing access to, or a copy of, sealed presentence reports, or portions of such reports, may request them from the clerk's office by such means as the clerk permits. Counsel must return the copy of the presentence report, without duplicating it. Counsel should avoid disclosure of confidential matters in their public filings.

[Amended effective January 4, 1999; December 1, 2002; July 15, 2003; November 1, 2005; December 1, 2006; December 1, 2009.]

FRAP 48. MASTERS

[For text of rule, see the Federal Rules of Appellate Procedure]

OTHER INTERNAL OPERATING PROCEDURES

Judicial Council. The judicial council established by 28 U.S.C. § 332 Is composed of 19 judges— the chief circuit judge, nine circuit judges, and nine district judges. The chief circuit judge and the active circuit judge next in seniority serve permanent terms. All other council members serve for staggered three-year terms. The council meets on call of the chief circuit judge pursuant to statute.

Judicial Conference. Pursuant to 28 U.S.C. § 333, the chief circuit judge may summon biennially or annually the federal judges of the circuit to a conference, at a designated time and place, for the purpose of considering the state of business of the courts and advising means of improving the administration of justice within the circuit. A copy of the court's rule for representation and active participation of the members of the bar of the circuit is available from the clerk or circuit executive.

Recusal or Disqualification of Judges.

(a) *Grounds.* Judges may recuse themselves under any circumstances considered sufficient to require such action. Judges must disqualify themselves under circumstances set forth in 28 U.S.C. § 455, or in accordance with Canon 3C, Code of Conduct for United States Judges as adopted by the Judicial Conference of the United States.

(b) *Procedure.*

(1) Administrative Motions. If an initiating judge recuses himself or herself from considering, or is disqualified to consider an administrative motion, he or she will notify the clerk, who will advise the recused judge of the next initiating judge and request that the file be sent to that judge.

(2) Summary Calendar Cases. The above procedure is followed, except that the substitute or backup judge is called because it is court practice that cases are not ordinarily disposed of on the merits by only 2 judges.

(3) Hearing Calendar Cases. Prior to the formal publication of the court calendar, each judge on the panel is furnished with a copy of the 5th Cir. R. 28.2.1 certificate of interested persons for the judge's study to determine whether recusal or disqualification is appropriate.

(c) If a judge recuses, or is disqualified, he or she immediately notifies the other members of the panel, and arrangements are made for a substitute judge.

SPECIAL PANELS AND CASES REQUIRING SPECIAL HANDLING

Corporate Reorganization—Chapter 11. The first appeal is handled in the usual manner. Counsel must state in their briefs whether the proceeding is likely to be complex and protracted so that the panel can determine whether it should enter an order directing that it will be the permanent panel for subsequent appeals in the same matter. If there are likely to be successive appeals, a single panel may thus become fully familiar with the case thus making the handling of future appeals more expeditious and economical for litigants, counsel and the court. (For the rule regarding direct appeals in bankruptcy matters see 5th Cir. R. 47.4).

Criminal Justice Act Plan. The court has adopted a plan and guidelines under the Criminal Justice Act. Copies are available from the clerk.

Certified Records for Supreme Court of the United States. The clerk's office does not prepare a certified record unless the Clerk of the United States Supreme Court so directs. (See generally Sup. Ct. R. 12.7, 16.2, and 19.4).

Building Security.

(a) *Reasons for Building Security.* These rules are to minimize interference with and disruptions of the court's business, to preserve decorum in conducting the court's business and to provide effective security in the John Minor Wisdom United States Court of Appeals Building and garage located at 600 Camp Street, and court occupied space at 600 S. Maestri Place, New Orleans, Louisiana. These entire premises are called The Buildings.

(b) *Security Personnel.* The term "Security Personnel" means the U.S. Marshal or Deputy Marshal, Court Security Officer, or a member of the Federal Protective Service Police.

(c) *Carrying of Parcels, Bags, and Other Objects.* Security Personnel shall inspect all objects carried by persons entering The Buildings. No one shall enter or remain in The Buildings without submitting to an inspection.

(d) *Search of Persons.* Security personnel may search any person entering The Buildings or any space in it. Anyone who refuses a search must be denied entry.

(e) *Unseemly Conduct.* No person shall:

(1) Loiter, sleep or conduct oneself in an unseemly or disorderly manner in The Buildings;

(2) Interfere with or disturb the conduct of the court's business in any manner;

(3) Eat or drink in the halls of The Buildings or in any courtrooms except at court approved social functions;

(4) Block any entrance to or exit from The Buildings or interfere in any person's entry into or exit from The Buildings.

(f) *Entering and Leaving.* All persons must enter and leave courtrooms only through such doorways and at such times as are designated by the Security Personnel.

(g) *Spectators.* The entrance and departure of spectators to or from courtrooms is subject to the presiding judge's directions. The U.S. Marshal may designate spectator seating in any courtroom. Spectators excluded because of lack of seating and spectators leaving the courtroom while court is in session or any recess shall not loiter or remain in the area adjacent to the courtroom.

(h) Cameras and recording devices are not permitted in the John Minor Wisdom United States Court of Appeals Building ("Building") without the court's permission. Laptops, tablets, cell phones, and other similar devices that contain cameras or recording functions are exempt from this subsection but are still subject to the following:

(1) After visual inspection and x-ray by a Court Security Officer, electronic devices may be admitted into the Building.

(2) Unless prior court permission is obtained, all electronic devices must be turned off (not "vibrate-only" mode or airplane mode) when inside a courtroom where a Fifth Circuit argument is being held. However, an attorney presenting argument or assisting at counsel table may use a laptop, tablet, or similar device. If the laptop, tablet, or similar device has a camera or recording device, those functions may not be used inside the courtroom. At no time may anyone use social media inside a courtroom.

(3) Under no circumstances will disruptive behavior be tolerated in any courtroom where a Fifth Circuit argument is being held. Violators will be promptly removed.

(i) *Weapons.* Except for Security Personnel, no person shall be admitted to or allowed to remain in The Buildings with any object that might be employed as a weapon unless authorized in writing by the court to do so.

(j) *Enforcement.* Security Personnel shall enforce these security provisions and any other provisions the court might implement. Attorneys and parties who violate these provisions are subject to, inter alia, contempt proceedings and sanctions.

[Amended effective January 4, 1999; April 7, 2015.]

APPENDIX OF FORMS

FORM 1. NOTICE OF APPEAL TO A COURT OF APPEALS FROM A JUDGMENT OR ORDER OF A DISTRICT COURT

[For text of form, see the Federal Rules of Appellate Procedure]

FORM 2. NOTICE OF APPEAL TO A COURT OF APPEALS FROM A DECISION OF THE UNITED STATES TAX COURT

[For text of form, see the Federal Rules of Appellate Procedure]

FORM 3. PETITION FOR REVIEW OF ORDER OF AN AGENCY, BOARD, COMMISSION OR OFFICER

[For text of form, see the Federal Rules of Appellate Procedure]

FORM 4. AFFIDAVIT ACCOMPANYING MOTION FOR PERMISSION TO APPEAL IN FORMA PAUPERIS

[For text of form, see the Federal Rules of Appellate Procedure]

FORM 5. NOTICE OF APPEAL TO A COURT OF APPEALS FROM A JUDGMENT OR ORDER OF A DISTRICT COURT OR A BANKRUPTCY APPELLATE PANEL

[For text of form, see the Federal Rules of Appellate Procedure]

FORM 6. CERTIFICATE OF COMPLIANCE WITH TYPE–VOLUME LIMIT

[For text of form, see the Federal Rules of Appellate Procedure]

FORM 7. DECLARATION OF INMATE FILING

[For text of form, see the Federal Rules of Appellate Procedure]

APPENDIX: LENGTH LIMITS STATED IN THE FEDERAL RULES OF APPELLATE PROCEDURE

[For text of appendix, see the Federal Rules of Appellate Procedure]

PLAN FOR REPRESENTATION ON APPEAL
UNDER THE CRIMINAL JUSTICE ACT

Section 1.   Purpose of the Plan

The Criminal Justice Act of 1964, 18 U.S.C. § 3006A, provides for representation of parties financially unable to pay for legal services. The Judicial Council of the Fifth Circuit hereby adopts this Plan to implement the Act's provisions in cases before the court. The plans adopted by the district courts within the Fifth Circuit apply on appeal to the extent they are consistent with this Plan.

Section 2.   Definitions

A.   **"The Act"** – the Criminal Justice Act of 1964, as amended.

B.   **"Death penalty proceedings"** – federal capital prosecutions under Title 18 or 21 of the United States Code, direct appeals in cases in which a death sentence was imposed, and collateral proceedings under 28 U.S.C. §§ 2254 and 2255 challenging a capital conviction and/or death sentence.

C.   **"This Plan" or "the Plan"** – Plan adopted by the Court of Appeals for the Fifth Circuit for representation under the Criminal Justice Act.

D.   **"Representation"** – includes counsel, investigators, experts, and other services necessary for adequate legal representation under the Plan.

Section 3.   Applicability

A.   Mandatory Appointment.   Any financially eligible person is entitled to appellate representation by appointed counsel if the district court appointed counsel pursuant to 18 U.S.C. § 3006A(a)(1) or (2), or if the district court appointed counsel for a financially eligible person seeking to set aside or vacate a death sentence under 28 U.S.C. § 2254 or 2255. The court of appeals shall appoint counsel for any financially eligible person in an appeal from any proceeding listed in section 3006A(a)(1)(a)–(j) who was not represented by appointed counsel in the district court and who requests appointment of counsel on appeal.

B.   Optional Appointment.   If the court of appeals determines that the interest of justice requires, the court may appoint counsel on appeal for a financially eligible person who has been convicted of a Class B or C misdemeanor or of an infraction for which a sentence to confinement has been imposed, or who is seeking relief from a sentence other than a death sentence under 28 U.S.C. § 2241, 2254, or 2255.

Section 4.   Eligibility for Representation

The court of appeals determines a person's eligibility for appellate representation under the Act based on his or her overall financial inability to hire an attorney, in keeping with Congress' intent in passing the Act. A person for whom counsel is appointed may have to pay a portion of the fees to the clerk of the court of appeals if the court determines he or she has sufficient resources to make a partial payment. The clerk will administer the funds according to the guidelines established by the Judicial Conference.

Section 5.   Appointment of Counsel

A.   Attorneys Eligible for Appointment.   The court of appeals will select counsel for appointment under this Plan from:

- panels of attorneys designated or approved by the district courts of the Fifth Circuit;

- a Federal Public Defender Organization;

- a Community Defender Organization approved by a district court plan and authorized to provide representation under the Act; or

- any other organized program the court of appeals has approved that provides attorneys to represent financially eligible persons on appeal.

Any judge of the court of appeals may appoint competent counsel not included in the above categories if the interest of justice requires.

In keeping with § (a)(3) of the Act and the directives of the Judicial Conference, at least 25% of all appointments must be to members of the private bar.

B. Continuation of District Court Appointment. Counsel appointed under the Act by the district court shall continue to provide representation on appeal unless relieved by court order. The court of appeals or the district court may relieve counsel of this obligation only by written order. The order must also appoint a substitute counsel, unless the party waives counsel and asks to proceed pro se. The court of appeals may make any appointment retroactive so that counsel's prior representation is included. Counsel shall be eligible to be compensated for such prior representation. If counsel appointed by the district court remains as counsel on appeal, the court of appeals will send a form continuing his or her representation.

If appointed counsel wishes to be relieved from further representation by the court of appeals, he or she must file with the clerk of the court of appeals four copies of a motion stating the reasons. Counsel must continue to represent the party on appeal until relieved by court order.

If a party represented by appointed counsel wishes the court of appeals to relieve counsel and appoint new counsel, he or she must file with the clerk a legible motion asking for that relief. The clerk will submit the motion to the court of appeals for ruling.

Counsel may be relieved upon a showing that there is a conflict of interest or other most pressing circumstances or that the interests of justice otherwise require relief of counsel.

C. Eligible Person Not Represented in District Court. The clerk of the court of appeals will notify a person who was not represented by counsel in the district court of the right to have an attorney appointed if the person is financially unable to hire one.

D. Determination of Financial Eligibility. The court of appeals may accept without further inquiry the district court's finding that the person is financially eligible for appointment of counsel. If a party moves for appointment of counsel under the Act for the first time on appeal, the clerk will direct the party to execute an affidavit demonstrating his or her financial inability to hire an attorney. After receiving the affidavit, the clerk will serve a copy on opposing counsel, who will have 15 days after receipt to furnish proof the affidavit is false. The court of appeals may grant a reasonable extension of time, if requested, for furnishing this proof. The clerk will then submit the papers and evidence to the court for appropriate action.

If the court of appeals finds, at any time, that a party who had retained counsel has become financially unable to pay the attorney, it may appoint counsel and authorize payment pursuant to §§ (b), (c), and (d) of the Act.

E. Cases With Multiple Parties. The court of appeals shall appoint separate counsel for persons having interests that cannot properly be represented by the same counsel, or when other good cause is shown.

F. Appointment of Multiple Counsel. In an extremely difficult case where the court of appeals finds it in the interest of justice, it may appoint an additional attorney for a party. Each attorney is eligible to receive the maximum compensation allowed under the Act. The court of appeals must include in its order of appointment the specific finding that the appointment of an additional attorney is necessary.

Section 6.   Duties of Appointed Counsel

In cases proceeding under the Act, appointed counsel must file CJA Form 24 with the district court to obtain the reporter's transcript of testimony at government expense.

If asked by his or her client in writing, appointed counsel must provide a copy of any motions or briefs filed on the client's behalf in the appeal. Counsel must also forward the client a copy of the court of appeals' decision when issued. The clerk will provide counsel an extra copy of the decision for that purpose.

Appointed counsel must appear for oral argument unless the court of appeals directs otherwise. An associate attorney, not appointed under the Act, may not present oral argument except in the most pressing and unusual circumstances.

Promptly after the court of appeals' decision issues, appointed counsel must advise the client in writing of the right to seek further review by filing a petition for writ of certiorari with the United States Supreme Court. If the client asks in writing that counsel file a petition, counsel must do so in a timely manner. If counsel believes filing a petition would be futile, he or she may move the court of appeals to be relieved of the obligation. The court of appeals also may act sua sponte to relieve counsel of any further representation.

Appointed counsel must inform the client of the right to appeal to the court of appeals and to seek certiorari review in the Supreme Court without prepayment of fees and costs, giving security, or filing the affidavit of financial inability specified by 28 U.S.C. § 1915(a).

Appointed counsel has a duty under Anders v. California, 386 U.S. 738 (1967), to advise the court of appeals if he or she concludes the appeal has no arguable merit, and to request to withdraw.

No one appointed under the Act may accept any payment from or on behalf of the person represented in the court of appeals without prior authorization by a judge of the court of appeals. All authorized payments are subject to the directions contained in the court of appeals' order and the provisions of § (f) of the Act.

Section 7.   Payment of Claims for Compensation and Expenses

A.   General Guidelines.   In all appeals under the Act, the court of appeals may authorize compensation for services and reimbursement for expenses reasonably incurred on appeal, within the limitations of the Act, by any person appointed under the Plan.   The court of appeals is cognizant that the hourly rates of compensation in the Act are intended as maximum, not standard, rates. Total compensation for representation on appeal may exceed the amount fixed in the statute or by the Judicial Conference only in cases involving extended or complex representation.   In such cases, the court of appeals must certify that the excess payment was necessary to provide fair compensation, and the chief judge must approve the excess payment.

B.   Compensation Limits.

1.   *Non–Death Penalty Cases.*   The Act sets the following limits for total compensation for services rendered, excluding approved expenses, for each attorney:

- Direct appeal in a felony or misdemeanor case or a habeas corpus appeal—$5,000

- Appeal from a proceeding before the U. S. Parole Commission under 18 U.S.C. § 4106A—$5,000

Appointed counsel may claim compensation for services furnished by a partner or an associate within the maximum compensation allowed by the Act, as long as appointed counsel takes the lead in preparation of the brief and presentation of oral argument, if allowed.   Only appointed counsel may claim compensation for in-court services and associated travel expenses.

If the court of appeals substitutes one attorney for another, the maximum compensation for both attorneys may not exceed the statutory maximum for one defendant.   The court of appeals may approve payment in excess of the statutory maximum if the case is complex or involves extended representation.   The court of appeals will not approve any payments in such cases until the conclusion of the appeal.

2.   *Death Penalty Proceedings.*   In death penalty proceedings, counsel requesting compensation shall file the request with the senior active member of the panel or that judge's designee who is an active member of the panel.   The maximum total compensation allowed for death penalty proceedings, including interim payments but excluding approved expenses, is as follows:

- $50,000 for representing one appellant in a capital murder direct appeal, or

- $15,000 for representing one petitioner or movant in a death penalty habeas case at the appellate level.

A request for compensation exceeding the above amounts, either in total amount claimed, hourly rate, or both, is presumptively excessive.   An attorney filing a presumptively excessive claim must justify the request in writing when submitting the voucher.   A judge who receives such a request will forward it along with a brief recommendation to the chief judge, or his or her designee, who will determine how much of the requested fees will be paid.

3.   *Maximum Hourly Rates.*   Pursuant to statute, the maximum hourly rates at which counsel may be compensated are set by the Judicial Conference of the United States.   For non-death penalty cases, the maximum hourly rate counsel may charge is $110 for in-court and out-of-court work.   For death penalty cases, the maximum hourly rate counsel may charge is $175.   Rates may be changed in the future by the Judicial Conference, and the schedule of applicable rates published by the Judicial Conference is incorporated herein by reference.

4.   *Vouchers in Excess of $800.*   Any claim exceeding $800 for out-of-court work must include an explanation of how counsel spent the time.

C.   Reimbursable Expenses.   The court of appeals will reimburse appointed counsel for the following expenses incurred in the course of providing representation under the Act:

1. *Travel Expenses.*

- Air Transportation—the court will arrange air transportation for counsel at government employee rates. The clerk's office provides the necessary information at the time the case is scheduled for oral argument. Accordingly, counsel does not incur any out-of-pocket expense. If counsel makes travel reservations personally, reimbursement will be only for the amount that could have been obtained at the government employee rate.

- Automobile—the rate per mile cannot exceed the current government authorized rate for official travel. The amount claimed cannot exceed that authorized for air fare at the government employee rate, except in an emergency or other unusual circumstance. In such a case, counsel must provide an explanation. Parking, ferry, bridge, road, and tunnel fees are reimbursable.

- Local Transportation—counsel must use the most economical means of local transportation possible (e.g., airport shuttle, if available) and may claim actual expenses.

- Meals and Lodging—counsel may claim the actual expenses incurred for meals and lodging. Expenses should be in line with the limits for federal employees, which can be obtained from the clerk. Counsel will be reimbursed for a maximum of one and one-half days for travel for oral argument.

2. *Miscellaneous Expenses.*

- Photocopying—counsel may claim actual expenses not to exceed $ .25 per page and must submit a copy of the bill. If counsel does photocopying in-house, he or she may claim actual expenses not to exceed $ .15 per page.

- Briefs—counsel may claim actual cost for preparing briefs, subject to the photocopying limits above. Reimbursement will be for a maximum of 15 copies, except if the case is heard en banc, where reimbursement will be for 23 copies.

- Courier and Other Special Service—counsel must attach an explanation for using services, except in capital cases. Briefs, motions, and other documents whose filing can be anticipated in advance should be prepared in time to permit the use of less expensive services, and excessive charges for shipping will not be reimbursed.

- Other Expenses—counsel may claim actual expenses for such things as postage, telephone calls, brief supplies, and the like. Counsel should use the least possible cost for such items.

3. *Petition for Writ of Certiorari.* If appointed counsel files a petition for writ of certiorari on behalf of the client, the time and expense are considered to be applicable to the case in the court of appeals. Counsel must attach a copy of the petition to the voucher.

D. Requesting Compensation. Counsel should file all voucher claims with the clerk not later than 30 days after completing representation. The clerk will refer all claims for compensation as directed by the court.

Section 8. Implementation

The court of appeals, by rule, internal operating procedure, or court policy, may delegate any of the duties set out in this Plan to a single judge, the clerk of court, or a deputy clerk.

This Plan becomes effective on April 1, 2009.

[Amended effective December 21, 1998; January 1, 2000; January 25, 2001; April 1, 2003; February 1, 2005; April 1, 2009.]

PLAN FOR EXPEDITING CRIMINAL APPEALS

1. Goal. The court desires to process criminal appeals at least within the federal appellate court median times from filing the notice of appeal to filing of the last brief, and from filing the notice of appeal to the court's decision.

2. Policy. Delays in deciding criminal cases are a matter of concern because by statute, criminal appeals must be expedited. The court grants extensions of briefing times only where the standards of the Federal Rules of Appellate Procedures are met. If extensions are permitted, they are subject to the guidelines in the Fifth Circuit Rules, and Internal Operating Procedures (I.O.P.s). Attorneys who violate the Federal, or Fifth Circuit Rules, or the court's I.O.P.s are subject to appropriate disciplinary sanctions. Court reporters must comply with the federal appellate and circuit rules governing the timely acknowledgment of transcript orders, and are directed to give precedence to transcribing criminal appeals before civil cases. District courts must meet the time limits established by the Fifth Circuit Rules and Court Reporter Management Plans, and must effectively manage their court reporters. Fifth Circuit judges are reminded of their obligations timely to screen and decide criminal appeals.

3. Procedures. *Criminal Appeals.* The Fifth Circuit clerk's office is responsible for: (a) communicating court policies concerning expediting criminal appeals; (b) supervising the processing of criminal cases; and (c) as requested, assembling data on reporters, clerks and counsel.

Filing of Reporters' Transcripts. District judges, clerks of court or court reporter coordinators are responsible for insuring court reporters give preference to filing transcripts in criminal cases before all other cases. Except in exceptional cases, criminal transcript should be filed within the 30–day period specified in Fed. R. App. P. 11(b). District judges, clerks of court, court reporter coordinators and court reporters are reminded of the requirements in 5th Cir. R. 11.2 governing requests for extension of time to file transcripts. Court reporters should neither request routine extensions of time to file criminal transcripts, nor expect them to be granted. Court reporters who ignore the requirements of this rule and fail to file transcripts timely risk the imposition of sanctions. 5th Cir. R. 11.2(c) requires district judges to verify the need for an extension and approve it before this court takes action. The district judges' careful review and adherence to this requirement will insure court reporters request extensions of time only where exceptional circumstances exist. District courts are responsible for overseeing the overall workload of their court reporters and for insuring that criminal transcripts are managed and prepared as quickly as possible.

Communications to Counsel and Reporters. The Fifth Circuit clerk's office will advise court reporters and attorneys representing defendants and the United States of the court's policy on expediting criminal appeals, the court's rule requirements, counsel's obligations, and establish due dates in accordance with the Federal and Fifth Circuit Rules, and I.O.P.s.

Notice to Counsel and Reporters. Fed. R. App. P. 10(b) requires appellant's counsel to order a transcript, or to certify no transcript will be ordered, within 10 days of filing the notice of appeal, or entry of an order disposing of certain motions in Fed. R. App. P. 4(a)(4)(A). Counsel must timely complete the transcript order form provided by the district court, make financial arrangements, and deliver the form to the court reporter by the most expeditious means. As soon as received, the reporter **immediately** must advise the court when a transcript has been ordered and payment arranged. The reporter also must give this court an expected completion date and an estimated number of pages for the transcript. Counsel and reporters may be sanctioned for failing to comply with the provisions of the Federal Rules and this court's implementing procedures.

Notice to U.S. Attorneys. When the clerk's office issues a briefing notice to appellant's counsel in direct criminal cases, it also will provide notice to the U.S. Attorney, advising of the court's rules and policies governing criminal appeals.

Extensions of Time to File Briefs. Counsel may request extensions only when absolutely necessary. The clerk or court will grant extensions sparingly and only as set forth in the rules and I.O.P.s. Extensions in criminal appeals will be for the minimum time needed, and if granted, will exceed 30 days only in exceptionally rare instances. Counsel are responsible for reviewing the record on appeal within 15 days of receipt. If there are omissions from the record, counsel must notify the district court and this court of any missing materials, particularly transcripts, and arrange immediately with the court reporter for any additional transcripts within this period. Counsel who fail to act promptly and to make arrangements for a complete record within this time period, cannot expect an extension of time to file the brief because their lack of diligence caused the record to be incomplete.

Screening and Calendaring Criminal Appeals. This court gives criminal appeals the highest priority in screening, calendaring and decision. Our circuit judges must meet expedited time lines for screening criminal cases, and the clerk's office must expedite calendaring of criminal appeals when oral argument is required. The clerk's office will monitor criminal appeals to reinforce the court's priorities in routing and return of cases for screening and in setting cases for oral argument when required. These procedures shall be reviewed and, if necessary, revised upon request from the court or Judicial Council.

Disposition. The priority given to criminal cases continues after oral hearing or submission on the record and briefs. By court policy, each judge must give direct criminal cases priority in the preparation and publication of opinions over all other cases except previously submitted direct criminal cases.

4. Disciplinary Action. For conduct unbecoming a member of the Bar, or for failure of counsel to comply with the applicable Federal and Fifth Circuit Rules, the court shall issue a show cause order as provided by Fed. R. App. P. 46(c), and 5th Cir. R. 42.3.1.1 and 42.3.3. Sanctions may be imposed upon delinquent counsel as may be individually appropriate, ranging from reprimand to fine, or Criminal Justice Act financial deduction or removal from the roll of attorneys permitted to practice before this court.

[Effective May 4, 2008.]

RULES FOR JUDICIAL–CONDUCT AND JUDICIAL–DISABILITY PROCEEDINGS

PREFACE [NATIONAL CONDUCT RULES]

These Rules were promulgated by the Judicial Conference of the United States, after public comment, pursuant to 28 U.S.C. §§ 331 and 358, to establish standards and procedures for addressing complaints filed by complainants or identified by chief judges, under the Judicial Conduct and Disability Act, 28 U.S.C. §§ 351–364.

[Adopted March 11, 2008, effective April 10, 2008. Amended effective April 12, 2018.]

Preface [Fifth Circuit Conduct Rules]

Fifth Circuit Rule 19 is taken from preexisting local Rule 7; it is not inconsistent with the rules promulgated by the Judicial Conference of the United States and remains in force as a result of the reaffirmation by the Judicial Council on May 4, 2008, of the order delegating petitions for review to five-judge panels. See rule 2(a).

The Fifth Circuit Comments and Procedures are adapted from the preexisting local rules not in conflict with the rules promulgated by the Judicial Conference of the United States. They are intended to provide additional information that may be useful to persons wishing to file complaints.

The former Fifth Circuit Rules Governing Complaints of Judicial Misconduct or Disability will hereinafter be cited as follows: 5th Cir. R. ___.

Delegations of authority approved by the Judicial Council are also appended to the respective rules to which they pertain.

ARTICLE I.   GENERAL PROVISIONS

RULE 1.   SCOPE

These Rules govern proceedings under the Judicial Conduct and Disability Act (the Act), 28 U.S.C. §§ 351–364, to determine whether a covered judge has engaged in conduct prejudicial to the effective and expeditious administration of the business of the courts or is unable to discharge the duties of office because of mental or physical disability.

[Adopted March 11, 2008, effective April 10, 2008. Amended effective September 17, 2015; April 12, 2018.]

Commentary on Rule 1

In September 2006, the Judicial Conduct and Disability Act Study Committee ("Breyer Committee"), appointed in 2004 by Chief Justice Rehnquist, presented a report ("Breyer Committee Report"), 239 F.R.D. 116 (Sept. 2006), to Chief Justice Roberts that evaluated implementation of the Judicial Conduct and Disability Act of 1980, 28 U.S.C. §§ 351–364. The Breyer Committee had been formed in response to criticism from the public and Congress regarding the effectiveness of the Act's implementation. The Executive Committee of the Judicial Conference directed its Committee on Judicial Conduct and Disability to consider the Breyer Committee's recommendations and to report on their implementation to the Conference.

The Breyer Committee found that it could not evaluate implementation of the Act without establishing interpretive standards, Breyer Committee Report, 239 F.R.D. at 132, and that a major problem faced by chief judges in implementing the Act was the lack of authoritative interpretive standards. *Id.* at 212–15. The Breyer Committee then established standards to guide its evaluation, some of which were new formulations and some of which were taken from the "Illustrative Rules Governing Complaints of Judicial Misconduct and Disability," discussed below. The principal standards used by the Breyer Committee are in Appendix E of its Report. *Id.* at 238.

Based on the Breyer Committee's findings, the Committee on Judicial Conduct and Disability concluded that there was a need for the Judicial Conference to exercise its power under Section 358 of the Act to fashion standards guiding the various officers and bodies that must exercise responsibility under the Act. To that end, the Committee on Judicial Conduct and Disability proposed rules that were based largely on Appendix E of the Breyer Committee Report and the Illustrative Rules.

The Illustrative Rules were originally prepared in 1986 by the Special Committee of the Conference of Chief Judges of the United States Courts of Appeals, and were subsequently revised and amended, most recently in 2000, by the predecessor to the Committee on Judicial Conduct and Disability. The Illustrative Rules were adopted, with minor variations, by circuit judicial councils, to govern complaints under the Judicial Conduct and Disability Act.

After being submitted for public comment pursuant to 28 U.S.C. § 358(c), the Judicial Conference promulgated the present Rules on March 11, 2008. They were amended on September 17, 2015.

RULE 2.   EFFECT AND CONSTRUCTION

(a) Generally. These Rules are mandatory; they supersede any conflicting judicial-council rules. Judicial councils may promulgate additional rules to implement the Act as long as those rules do not conflict with these Rules.

(b) Exception. A Rule will not apply if, when performing duties authorized by the Act, a chief judge, a special committee, a judicial council, the Committee on Judicial Conduct and Disability, or the Judicial Conference expressly finds that exceptional circumstances render application of that Rule in a particular proceeding manifestly unjust or contrary to the purposes of the Act or these Rules.

[Adopted March 11, 2008, effective April 10, 2008. Amended effective September 17, 2015; April 12, 2018.]

Commentary on Rule 2

Unlike the Illustrative Rules, these Rules provide mandatory and nationally uniform provisions governing the substantive and procedural aspects of misconduct and disability proceedings under the Act. The mandatory nature of these Rules is authorized by 28 U.S.C. §§ 358(a) and (c). Judicial councils retain the power to promulgate rules consistent with these Rules. For example, a local rule may authorize the electronic distribution of materials pursuant to Rule 8(b).

Rule 2(b) recognizes that unforeseen and exceptional circumstances may call for a different approach in particular cases.

RULE 3.   DEFINITIONS

(a) Chief Judge. "Chief judge" means the chief judge of a United States court of appeals, of the United States Court of International Trade, or of the United States Court of Federal Claims.

(b) Circuit Clerk. "Circuit clerk" means a clerk of a United States court of appeals, the clerk of the United States Court of International Trade, the clerk of the United States Court of Federal Claims, or the circuit executive of the United States Court of Appeals for the Federal Circuit.

(c) Complaint. A complaint is:

(1) a document that, in accordance with Rule 6, is filed by any person in his or her individual capacity or on behalf of a professional organization; or

(2) information from any source, other than a document described in (c)(1), that gives a chief judge probable cause to believe that a covered judge, as defined in Rule 4, has engaged in misconduct or may have a disability, whether or not the information is framed as or is intended to be an allegation of misconduct or disability.

(d) Court of Appeals, District Court, and District Judge. "Court of appeals," "district court," and "district judge," where appropriate, include the United States Court of Federal Claims, the United States Court of International Trade, and the judges thereof.

(e) Disability. "Disability" is a temporary or permanent impairment, physical or mental, rendering a judge unable to discharge the duties of the particular judicial office. Examples of disability include substance abuse, the inability to stay awake during court proceedings, or impairment of cognitive abilities that renders the judge unable to function effectively.

(f) Judicial Council and Circuit. "Judicial council" and "circuit," where appropriate, include any courts designated in 28 U.S.C. § 363.

(g) Magistrate Judge. "Magistrate judge," where appropriate, includes a special master appointed by the Court of Federal Claims under 42 U.S.C. § 300aa–12(c).

(h) Misconduct. Cognizable misconduct:

(1) is conduct prejudicial to the effective and expeditious administration of the business of the courts. Misconduct includes, but is not limited to:

(A) using the judge's office to obtain special treatment for friends or relatives;

(B) accepting bribes, gifts, or other personal favors related to the judicial office;

(C) having improper discussions with parties or counsel for one side in a case;

(D) treating litigants, attorneys, or others in a demonstrably egregious and hostile manner;

(E) engaging in partisan political activity or making inappropriately partisan statements;

(F) soliciting funds for organizations;

(G) retaliating against complainants, witnesses, or others for their participation in this complaint process;

(H) refusing, without good cause shown, to cooperate in the investigation of a complaint under these Rules; or

(I) violating other specific, mandatory standards of judicial conduct, such as those pertaining to restrictions on outside income and requirements for financial disclosure.

(2) is conduct occurring outside the performance of official duties if the conduct might have a prejudicial effect on the administration of the business of the courts, including a substantial and widespread lowering of public confidence in the courts among reasonable people.

(3) does not include:

(A) an allegation that is directly related to the merits of a decision or procedural ruling. An allegation that calls into question the correctness of a judge's ruling, including a failure to recuse, without more, is merits-related. If the decision or ruling is alleged to be the result of an improper motive, *e.g.*, a bribe, ex parte contact, racial or ethnic bias, or improper conduct in rendering a decision or ruling, such as personally derogatory remarks irrelevant to the issues, the complaint is not cognizable to the extent that it attacks the merits.

(B) an allegation about delay in rendering a decision or ruling, unless the allegation concerns an improper motive in delaying a particular decision or habitual delay in a significant number of unrelated cases.

(i) Subject Judge. "Subject judge" means any judge described in Rule 4 who is the subject of a complaint.

[Adopted March 11, 2008, effective April 10, 2008. Amended effective September 17, 2015; April 12, 2018.]

Commentary on Rule 3

Rule 3 is derived and adapted from the Breyer Committee Report and the Illustrative Rules.

Unless otherwise specified or the context otherwise indicates, the term "complaint" is used in these Rules to refer both to complaints identified by a chief judge under Rule 5 and to complaints filed by a complainant under Rule 6.

Under the Act, a "complaint" may be filed by "any person" or "identified" by a chief judge. *See* 28 U.S.C. §§ 351(a), (b). Under Rule 3(c)(1), complaints may be submitted by a person, in his or her individual capacity, or by a professional organization. Generally, the word "complaint" brings to mind the commencement of an adversary proceeding in which the contending parties are left to present the evidence and legal arguments, and judges play the role of an essentially passive arbiter. The Act, however, establishes an administrative, inquisitorial process. For example, even absent a complaint under Rule 6, chief judges are expected in some circumstances to trigger the process—"identify a complaint," *see* 28 U.S.C. § 351(b) and Rule 5—and conduct an investigation without becoming a party. *See* 28 U.S.C. § 352(a); Breyer Committee Report, 239 F.R.D. at 214; Illustrative Rule 2(j). Even when a complaint is filed by someone other than the chief judge, the complainant lacks many rights that a litigant would have, and the chief judge, instead of being limited to the "four corners of the complaint," must, under Rule 11, proceed as though misconduct or disability has been alleged where the complainant reveals information of misconduct or disability but does not claim it as such. *See* Breyer Committee Report, 239 F.R.D. at 183–84.

An allegation of misconduct or disability filed under Rule 6 is a "complaint," and the Rule so provides in subsection (c)(1). However, both the nature of the process and the use of the term "identify" suggest that the word "complaint" covers more than a document formally triggering the process. The process relies on chief judges considering known information and triggering the process when appropriate. "Identifying" a "complaint," therefore, is best understood as the chief judge's concluding that information known to the judge constitutes probable cause to believe that misconduct occurred or a disability exists, whether or not the information is framed as, or intended to be, an accusation. This definition is codified in subsection (c)(2).

Rule 3(e) relates to disability and provides only the most general definition, recognizing that a fact-specific approach is the only one available. A mental disability could involve cognitive impairment or any psychiatric or psychological condition that renders the judge unable to discharge the duties of office. Such duties may include those that are administrative. If, for example, the judge is a chief judge, the judicial council, fulfilling its obligation under 28 U.S.C. § 332(d)(1) to make "necessary and appropriate orders for the effective and expeditious administration of justice," may find, under 28 U.S.C. § 45(d) or § 136(e), that the judge is "temporarily unable to perform" his or her chief-judge duties. In that event, an appropriate remedy could involve, under Rule 20(b)(1)(D)(vii), temporary reassignment of chief-judge duties to the next judge statutorily eligible to perform them.

The phrase "prejudicial to the effective and expeditious administration of the business of the courts" is not subject to precise definition, and subsection (h)(1) therefore provides some specific examples. Although the Code of Conduct for United States Judges may be informative, its main precepts are highly general; the Code is in many potential applications aspirational rather than a set of disciplinary rules. Ultimately, the responsibility for determining what constitutes misconduct under the statute is the province of the judicial council of the circuit, subject to such review and limitations as are ordained by the statute and by these Rules.

Even where specific, mandatory rules exist—for example, governing the receipt of gifts by judges, outside earned income, and financial disclosure obligations—the distinction between the misconduct statute and these specific, mandatory rules must be borne in mind. For example, an inadvertent, minor violation of any one of these rules, promptly remedied when called to the attention of the judge, might still be a violation but might not rise to the level of misconduct under the statute. By contrast, a pattern of such violations of the Code might well rise to the level of misconduct.

Under Rule 3(h)(1)(G), a judge's efforts to retaliate against any person for his or her involvement in the complaint process may constitute cognizable misconduct. The Rule makes this explicit in the interest of public confidence in the complaint process.

Rule 3(h)(1)(H) provides that a judge's refusal, without good cause shown, to cooperate in the investigation of a complaint under these Rules may constitute cognizable misconduct. While the exercise of rights under the Fifth Amendment to the Constitution would constitute good cause under Rule 3(h)(1)(H), given the fact-specific nature of the inquiry, it is not possible to otherwise anticipate all circumstances that might also constitute good cause. The Commentary on Rule 13 provides additional discussion regarding Rule 3(h)(1)(H). The Rules contemplate that judicial councils will not consider commencing proceedings under Rule 3(h)(1)(H) except as necessary after other means to acquire the information have been tried or have proven futile.

Rule 3(h)(2) reflects that an allegation can meet the statutory standard even though the judge's alleged conduct did not occur in the course of the performance of official duties. And some conduct in the categories listed under subsection (h)(1), or in categories not listed, might, depending on the circumstances, amount to "misconduct" under

subsection (h)(2), or under both subsection (h)(1) and subsection (h)(2). Also, the Code of Conduct for United States Judges expressly covers a wide range of extra-official activities, and some of these activities may constitute misconduct. For example, allegations that a judge solicited funds for a charity or participated in a partisan political event are cognizable under the Act.

On the other hand, judges are entitled to some leeway in extra-official activities. For example, misconduct may not include a judge being repeatedly and publicly discourteous to a spouse (not including physical abuse) even though this might cause some reasonable people to have diminished confidence in the courts. Rule 3(h)(2) states that conduct of this sort is covered, for example, when it might lead to a "substantial and widespread" lowering of such confidence.

Rule 3(h)(3)(A) tracks the Act, 28 U.S.C. § 352(b)(1)(A)(ii), in excluding from the definition of misconduct allegations "[d]irectly related to the merits of a decision or procedural ruling." This exclusion preserves the independence of judges in the exercise of judicial power by ensuring that the complaint procedure is not used to collaterally attack the substance of a judge's ruling. Any allegation that calls into question the correctness of an official action of a judge—without more—is merits-related. The phrase "decision or procedural ruling" is not limited to rulings issued in deciding Article III cases or controversies. Thus, a complaint challenging the correctness of a chief judge's determination to dismiss a prior misconduct complaint would be properly dismissed as merits-related—in other words, as challenging the substance of the judge's administrative determination to dismiss the complaint—even though it does not concern the judge's rulings in Article III litigation. Similarly, an allegation that a judge had incorrectly declined to approve a Criminal Justice Act voucher is merits-related under this standard.

Conversely, an allegation—however unsupported—that a judge conspired with a prosecutor to make a particular ruling is not merits-related, even though it "relates" to a ruling in a colloquial sense. Such an allegation attacks the propriety of conspiring with the prosecutor and goes beyond a challenge to the correctness—"the merits"—of the ruling itself. An allegation that a judge ruled against the complainant because the complainant is a member of a particular racial or ethnic group, or because the judge dislikes the complainant personally, is also not merits-related. Such an allegation attacks the propriety of arriving at rulings with an illicit or improper motive. Similarly, an allegation that a judge used an inappropriate term to refer to a class of people is not merits-related even if the judge used it on the bench or in an opinion; the correctness of the judge's rulings is not at stake. An allegation that a judge treated litigants, attorneys, or others in a demonstrably egregious and hostile manner while on the bench is also not merits-related.

The existence of an appellate remedy is usually irrelevant to whether an allegation is merits-related. The merits-related ground for dismissal exists to protect judges' independence in making rulings, not to protect or promote the appellate process. A complaint alleging an incorrect ruling is merits-related even though the complainant has no recourse from that ruling. By the same token, an allegation that is otherwise cognizable under the Act should not be dismissed merely because an appellate remedy appears to exist (for example, vacating a ruling that resulted from an improper *ex parte* communication). However, there may be occasions when appellate and misconduct proceedings overlap, and consideration and disposition of a complaint under these Rules may be properly deferred by the chief judge until the appellate proceedings are concluded in order to avoid inconsistent decisions, among other things.

Because of the special need to protect judges' independence in deciding what to say in an opinion or ruling, a somewhat different standard applies to determine the merits-relatedness of a non-frivolous allegation that a judge's language in a ruling reflected an improper motive. If the judge's language was relevant to the case at hand—for example, a statement that a claim is legally or factually "frivolous"—

then the judge's choice of language is presumptively merits-related and excluded, absent evidence apart from the ruling itself suggesting an improper motive. If, on the other hand, the challenged language does not seem relevant on its face, then an additional inquiry under Rule 11 is necessary.

With regard to Rule 3(h)(3)(B), a complaint of delay in a single case is excluded as merits-related. Such an allegation may be said to challenge the correctness of an official action of the judge—in other words, assigning a low priority to deciding the particular case. But, by the same token, an allegation of a habitual pattern of delay in a significant number of unrelated cases, or an allegation of deliberate delay in a single case arising out of an illicit motive, is not merits-related.

The remaining subsections of Rule 3 provide technical definitions clarifying the application of the Rules to the various kinds of courts covered.

Rule 3.1   Basis for Complaints [Fifth Circuit Commentary 3.1]

The law authorizes complaints against United States circuit, district, bankruptcy, and magistrate judges who have "engaged in conduct prejudicial to the effective and expeditious administration of business of the courts", or who are "unable to discharge all the duties of office by reason of mental or physical disability." The conduct to which the law is addressed does not include making wrong decisions—even very wrong decisions—for a complaint may be dismissed if it is "directly related to the merits of a decision or procedural ruling." Disagreements with a judge's rulings should be raised through the normal appellate review process because these judicial misconduct procedures are not a substitute for or supplement to a proper appeal under the Federal Rules of Appellate Procedure. "Mental or physical disability" may include temporary conditions as well as permanent disability. (Former 5th Cir. R. 1(B))

Rule 3.2   Limitations on use of the Judicial Misconduct Procedures [Fifth Circuit Commentary 3.1]

The complaint procedures are not intended to provide a means of reviewing a judge's decision or ruling in a case. The judicial council of the circuit, the body which takes action under the complaint procedure, does not have the power to change a decision or ruling. Only a court can do that. More

specifically, the complaint procedures may not be ordinarily used to:

1. *Have a judge disqualified or recused from a case;*

2. *Transfer a pending case from one judge or court to another;*

3. *Compel a judge to make a ruling on a particular motion in a case;*

4. *Have money damages awarded;*

5. *Obtain release from custody.*

(Former 5th Cir. R. 1(E))

RULE 4.   COVERED JUDGES

A complaint under these Rules may concern the actions or capacity only of judges of United States courts of appeals, judges of United States district courts, judges of United States bankruptcy courts, United States magistrate judges, and judges of the courts specified in 28 U.S.C. § 363.

[Adopted March 11, 2008, effective April 10, 2008. Amended effective April 12, 2018.]

Commentary on Rule 4

This Rule tracks the Act. Rule 8(c) and (d) contain provisions as to the handling of complaints against persons not covered by the Act, such as other court personnel, or against both covered judges and noncovered persons.

Rule 4.   Judges Subject to the Procedure [Fifth Circuit Procedure 4]

(a) The judicial misconduct and disability complaint procedure applies to judges of the United States courts of appeals, district and bankruptcy courts, and magistrate judges of the Fifth Circuit. The rules therefore apply to judges of the Court of Appeals for the Fifth Circuit, district, bankruptcy, and magistrate judges of federal courts within the states of Texas, Louisiana, and Mississippi. (Former 5th Cir. R. 1(C)(1))

(b) Complaints against other federal court officials within the Fifth Circuit should be made to their supervisors. If the complaints cannot be resolved satisfactorily at lower levels, they may be referred to the chief judge of the employing court whose decision will be final, subject to review only as the judicial council may prescribe. (Former 5th Cir. R. 1(C)(2))

ARTICLE II.   INITIATION OF A COMPLAINT

RULE 5.   IDENTIFICATION OF COMPLAINT

(a) Identification. When a chief judge has information constituting reasonable grounds for inquiry into whether a covered judge has engaged in misconduct or has a disability, the chief judge may conduct an inquiry, as he or she deems appropriate, into the accuracy of the information even if no related complaint has been filed. A chief judge who finds probable cause to believe that misconduct has occurred or that a disability exists may seek an informal resolution that he or she finds satisfactory. If no informal resolution is achieved or

is feasible, the chief judge may identify a complaint and, by written order stating the reasons, begin the review provided in Rule 11. If the evidence of misconduct is clear and convincing and no informal resolution is achieved or is feasible, the chief judge must identify a complaint. A chief judge must not decline to identify a complaint merely because the person making the allegation has not filed a complaint under Rule 6. This Rule is subject to Rule 7.

(b) Submission Not Fully Complying with Rule 6. A legible submission in substantial but not full compliance with

Rule 6 must be considered as possible grounds for the identification of a complaint under Rule 5(a).

[Adopted March 11, 2008, effective April 10, 2008. Amended effective September 17, 2015; April 12, 2018.]

Commentary on Rule 5

This Rule is adapted from the Breyer Committee Report, 239 F.R.D. at 245–46.

The Act authorizes a chief judge, by written order stating reasons, to identify a complaint and thereby dispense with the filing of a written complaint. *See* 28 U.S.C. § 351(b). Under Rule 5, when a chief judge becomes aware of information constituting reasonable grounds to inquire into possible misconduct or disability on the part of a covered judge, and no formal complaint has been filed, the chief judge has the power in his or her discretion to begin an appropriate inquiry. A chief judge's decision whether to informally seek a resolution and/or to identify a complaint is guided by the results of that inquiry. If the chief judge concludes that there is probable cause to believe that misconduct has occurred or a disability exists, the chief judge may seek an informal resolution, if feasible, and if failing in that, may identify a complaint. Discretion is accorded largely for the reasons police officers and prosecutors have discretion in making arrests or bringing charges. The matter may be trivial and isolated, based on marginal evidence, or otherwise highly unlikely to lead to a misconduct or disability finding. On the other hand, if the inquiry leads the chief judge to conclude that there is clear and convincing evidence of misconduct or a disability, and no satisfactory informal resolution has been achieved or is feasible, the chief judge is required to identify a complaint.

An informal resolution is one agreed to by the subject judge and found satisfactory by the chief judge. Because an informal resolution under Rule 5 reached before a complaint is filed under Rule 6 will generally cause a subsequent Rule 6 complaint alleging the identical matter to be concluded, *see* Rule 11(d), the chief judge must be sure that the resolution is fully appropriate before endorsing it. In doing so, the chief judge must balance the seriousness of the matter against the particular judge's alacrity in addressing the issue. The availability of this procedure should encourage attempts at swift remedial action before a formal complaint is filed.

When a chief judge identifies a complaint, a written order stating the reasons for the identification must be provided; this begins the process articulated in Rule 11. Rule 11 provides that once a chief judge has identified a complaint, the chief judge, subject to the disqualification provisions of Rule 25, will perform, with respect to that complaint, all functions assigned to the chief judge for the determination of complaints filed by a complainant.

In high-visibility situations, it may be desirable for a chief judge to identify a complaint without first seeking an informal resolution (and then, if the circumstances warrant, dismiss or conclude the identified complaint without appointment of a special committee) in order to assure the public that the allegations have not been ignored.

A chief judge's decision not to identify a complaint under Rule 5 is not appealable and is subject to Rule 3(h)(3)(A), which excludes merits-related complaints from the definition of misconduct.

A chief judge may not decline to identify a complaint solely on the basis that the unfiled allegations could be raised by one or more persons in a filed complaint, but none of these persons has opted to do so.

Subsection (a) concludes by stating that this Rule is "subject to Rule 7." This is intended to establish that only (i) the chief judge of the home circuit of a potential subject judge, or (ii) the chief judge of a circuit in which misconduct is alleged to have occurred in the course of official business while the potential subject judge was sitting by designation, shall have the power or a duty under this Rule to identify a complaint.

Subsection (b) provides that submissions that do not comply with the requirements of Rule 6(d) must be considered under Rule 5(a). For instance, if a complaint has been filed but the form submitted is unsigned, or the truth of the statements therein are not verified in writing under penalty of perjury, then a chief judge must nevertheless consider the allegations as known information and as a possible basis for the identification of a complaint under the process described in Rule 5(a).

RULE 6. FILING OF COMPLAINT

(a) Form. A complainant may use the form reproduced in the appendix to these Rules or a form designated by the rules of the judicial council in the circuit in which the complaint is filed. A complaint form is also available on each court of appeals' website or may be obtained from the circuit clerk or any district court or bankruptcy court within the circuit. A form is not necessary to file a complaint, but the complaint must be written and must include the information described in (b).

(b) Brief Statement of Facts. A complaint must contain a concise statement that details the specific facts on which the claim of misconduct or disability is based. The statement of facts should include a description of:

(1) what happened;

(2) when and where the relevant events happened;

(3) any information that would help an investigator check the facts; and

(4) for an allegation of disability, any additional facts that form the basis of that allegation.

(c) Legibility. A complaint should be typewritten if possible. If not typewritten, it must be legible. An illegible complaint will be returned to the complainant with a request to resubmit it in legible form. If a resubmitted complaint is still illegible, it will not be accepted for filing.

(d) Complainant's Address and Signature; Verification. The complainant must provide a contact address and sign the complaint. The truth of the statements made in the complaint must be verified in writing under penalty of perjury. If any of these requirements are not met, the submission will be accepted, but it will be reviewed under only Rule 5(b).

(e) Number of Copies; Envelope Marking. The complainant shall provide the number of copies of the complaint required by local rule. Each copy should be in an envelope marked "Complaint of Misconduct" or "Complaint of Disability." The envelope must not show the name of any subject judge.

[Adopted March 11, 2008, effective April 10, 2008. Amended effective September 17, 2015; April 12, 2018.]

Commentary on Rule 6

The Rule is adapted from the Illustrative Rules and is self-explanatory.

Rule 6. Filing of Complaint [Fifth Circuit Procedure 6]

(a) Page Limit. The brief statement of facts should be limited to five single-sided and double-spaced pages on 8.5x11 inch paper, whether typed or handwritten. If a complainant believes that more than five pages are necessary for a "concise statement" of facts, the complainant may submit a proposed statement of facts to the Clerk, who will determine whether the over-length complaint will be accepted for filing as submitted. If the Clerk determines that the complaint should not be filed as submitted, the complainant will be given an opportunity to reduce the statement of facts to five pages.

(b) Exhibits. Documents referred to in the statement of facts may be filed with the complaint. Only documentation that is required to support the specific facts alleged should be submitted—excess or irrelevant documentation will be returned to the complainant only if the complainant provides a self-addressed envelope bearing sufficient postage.

(c) Supplements. Once a complaint is filed, it may not be supplemented by additional statements or documents except to correct inaccuracies in the original complaint. Supplements submitted after the complaint is filed will be returned to the complainant if they do not comply with this section.

(d) Number of Copies. Only an original of the complaint should be filed. (Former 5th Cir. R 2(E)).

Rule 6.1 Complainant's Address and Signature; Verification [Fifth Circuit Commentary 6.1]

If any of the requirements of Rule 6(d) are not met and the complaint is reviewed under Rule 5(b), the complainant will not be entitled to notice of any decision of the Chief Judge.

RULE 7. WHERE TO INITIATE COMPLAINTS

(a) Where to File. Except as provided in (b),

(1) a complaint against a judge of a United States court of appeals, a United States district court, a United States bankruptcy court, or a United States magistrate judge must be filed with the circuit clerk in the jurisdiction in which the subject judge holds office.

(2) a complaint against a judge of the United States Court of International Trade or the United States Court of Federal Claims must be filed with the respective clerk of that court.

(3) a complaint against a judge of the United States Court of Appeals for the Federal Circuit must be filed with the circuit executive of that court.

(b) Misconduct in Another Circuit; Transfer. If a complaint alleges misconduct in the course of official business while the subject judge was sitting on a court by designation under 28 U.S.C. §§ 291–293 and 294(d), the complaint may be filed or identified with the circuit clerk of that circuit or of the subject judge's home circuit. The proceeding will continue in the circuit of the first-filed or first-identified complaint. The judicial council of the circuit where the complaint was first filed or first identified may transfer the complaint to the subject judge's home circuit or to the circuit where the alleged misconduct occurred, as the case may be.

[Adopted March 11, 2008, effective April 10, 2008. Amended effective September 17, 2015; April 12, 2018.]

Commentary on Rule 7

Title 28 U.S.C. § 351 states that complaints are to be filed with "the clerk of the court of appeals for the circuit." However, in many circuits, this role is filled by circuit executives. Accordingly, the term "circuit clerk," as defined in Rule 3(b) and used throughout these Rules, applies to circuit executives.

Section 351 uses the term "the circuit" in a way that suggests that either the home circuit of the subject judge or the circuit in which misconduct is alleged to have occurred is the proper venue for complaints. With an exception for judges sitting by designation, the Rule requires the filing or identification of a misconduct or disability complaint in the circuit in which the judge holds office, largely based on the administrative perspective of the Act. Given the Act's emphasis on the future conduct of the business of the courts, the circuit in which the judge holds office is the appropriate forum because that circuit is likely best able to influence a judge's future behavior in constructive ways.

However, when judges sit by designation, the non-home circuit has a strong interest in redressing misconduct in the course of official business, and where allegations also involve a member of the bar—*ex parte* contact between an attorney and a judge, for example—it may often be desirable to have the judicial and bar misconduct proceedings take place in the same venue. Rule 7(b), therefore, allows transfer to, or filing or identification of a complaint in, the non-home circuit. The proceeding may be transferred by the judicial council of the filing or identified circuit to the other circuit.

Rule 7. Where to File [Fifth Circuit Procedure 7]

Complaints should be sent to the Clerk, United States Court of Appeals for the Fifth Circuit, 600 S. Maestri Place, New Orleans, LA 70130. The envelope should be marked "Complaint of Misconduct" or "Complaint of Disability." The name of the judge complained about should not appear on the envelope. (Former 5th Cir.R. 2(H))

RULE 8. ACTION BY CIRCUIT CLERK

(a) Receipt of Complaint. Upon receiving a complaint against a judge filed under Rule 6 or identified under Rule 5, the circuit clerk must open a file, assign a docket number according to a uniform numbering scheme promulgated by the Committee on Judicial Conduct and Disability, and acknowledge the complaint's receipt.

(b) Distribution of Copies. The circuit clerk must promptly send copies of a complaint filed under Rule 6 to the chief judge or the judge authorized to act as chief judge under Rule 25(f), and copies of complaints filed under Rule 6 or identified under Rule 5 to each subject judge. The circuit clerk must retain the original complaint. Any further distribution should be as provided by local rule.

(c) Complaint Against Noncovered Person. If the circuit clerk receives a complaint about a person not holding an office described in Rule 4, the clerk must not accept the complaint under these Rules.

(d) Complaint Against Judge and Another Noncovered Person. If the circuit clerk receives a complaint about a judge described in Rule 4 and a person not holding an office described in Rule 4, the clerk must accept the complaint under these Rules only with regard to the judge and must so inform the complainant.

[Adopted March 11, 2008, effective April 10, 2008. Amended effective September 17, 2015; April 12, 2018.]

Commentary on Rule 8

This Rule is adapted from the Illustrative Rules and is largely self-explanatory.

The uniform docketing scheme described in subsection (a) should take into account potential problems associated with a complaint that names multiple judges. One solution may be to provide separate docket numbers for each subject judge. Separate docket numbers would help avoid difficulties in tracking cases, particularly if a complaint is dismissed with respect to some, but not all of the named judges.

Complaints against noncovered persons are not to be accepted for processing under these Rules but may, of course, be accepted under other circuit rules or procedures for grievances.

Rule 8. Abatement [Fifth Circuit Procedure 8]

If a complaint raises issues which are also raised in pending litigation, the circuit clerk will advise the complainant that the complaint shall be (or is being) held in abeyance pending disposition of the litigation, including appeals, and that the complainant must advise the clerk in writing of the disposition of the litigation.

RULE 9. TIME FOR FILING OR IDENTIFYING COMPLAINT

A complaint may be filed or identified at any time. If the passage of time has made an accurate and fair investigation of a complaint impracticable, the complaint must be dismissed under Rule 11(c)(1)(E).

[Adopted March 11, 2008, effective April 10, 2008. Amended effective September 17, 2015; April 12, 2018.]

Commentary on Rule 9

This Rule is adapted from the Act, 28 U.S.C. §§ 351, 352(b)(1)(A)(iii), and the Illustrative Rules.

RULE 10. ABUSE OF COMPLAINT PROCEDURE

(a) Abusive Complaints. A complainant who has filed repetitive, harassing, or frivolous complaints, or has otherwise abused the complaint procedure, may be restricted from filing further complaints. After giving the complainant an opportunity to show cause in writing why his or her right to file further complaints should not be limited, the judicial council may prohibit, restrict, or impose conditions on the complainant's use of the complaint procedure. Upon written request of the complainant, the judicial council may revise or withdraw any prohibition, restriction, or condition previously imposed.

(b) Orchestrated Complaints. When many essentially identical complaints from different complainants are received and appear to be part of an orchestrated campaign, the chief judge may recommend that the judicial council issue a written order instructing the circuit clerk to accept only a certain number of such complaints for filing and to refuse to accept additional complaints. The circuit clerk must send a copy of any such order to anyone whose complaint was not accepted.

[Adopted March 11, 2008, effective April 10, 2008. Amended effective September 17, 2015; April 12, 2018.]

Commentary on Rule 10

This Rule is adapted from the Illustrative Rules.

Rule 10(a) provides a mechanism for a judicial council to restrict the filing of further complaints by a single complainant who has abused the complaint procedure. In some instances, however, the complaint procedure may be abused in a manner for which the remedy provided in Rule 10(a) may not be appropriate. For example, some circuits have been inundated with submissions of dozens or hundreds of essentially identical complaints against the same judge or judges, all submitted by different complainants. In many of these instances, persons with grievances against a particular judge or judges used the Internet or other technology to orchestrate mass complaint-filing campaigns against them. If each complaint submitted as part of such a campaign were accepted for filing and processed according to these Rules, there would be a serious drain on court resources without any benefit to the adjudication of the underlying merits.

A judicial council may, therefore, respond to such mass filings under Rule 10(b) by declining to accept repetitive complaints for filing, regardless of the fact that the complaints are nominally submitted by different complainants. When the first complaint or complaints have been dismissed on the merits, and when further, essentially identical submissions follow, the judicial council may issue a second order noting that these are identical or repetitive complaints, directing the circuit clerk not to accept these complaints or any further such complaints for filing, and directing the clerk to send each putative complainant copies of both orders.

This Rule is adapted from the Illustrative Rules.

Rule 10(a) provides a mechanism for a judicial council to restrict the filing of further complaints by a single complainant who has abused the complaint procedure. In some instances, however, the complaint procedure may be abused in a manner for which the remedy provided in Rule 10(a) may not be appropriate. For example, some circuits have been inundated with submissions of dozens or hundreds of essentially identical complaints against the same judge or judges, all submitted by different complainants. In many of these instances, persons with grievances against a particular judge or judges used the Internet or other technology to orchestrate mass complaint-filing campaigns against them. If each complaint submitted as part of such a campaign were accepted for filing and processed according to these Rules, there would be a serious drain on court resources without any benefit to the adjudication of the underlying merits.

A judicial council may, therefore, respond to such mass filings under Rule 10(b) by declining to accept repetitive complaints for filing, regardless of the fact that the complaints are nominally submitted by different complainants. When the first complaint or complaints have been dismissed on the merits, and when further, essentially identical submissions follow, the judicial council may issue a second order noting that these are identical or repetitive complaints, directing the circuit clerk not to accept these complaints or any further such complaints for filing, and directing the clerk to send each putative complainant copies of both orders.

Rule 10. [Fifth Circuit Commentary 10]

Fifth Circuit Commentary 10
THE JUDICIAL COUNCIL OF THE FIFTH CIRCUIT

In Re: Delegation to Chief Circuit Judge, or acting Judge Pursuant to rule 25(f) of the Rules For Judicial–Conduct and Judicial–Disability Proceedings

Before: JONES, Chief Judge, and Judges SMITH, KING, DAVIS, BARKSDALE, DENNIS, CLEMENT, OWEN, ELROD, SOUTHWICK, VANCE, BRADY, MELANCON, BIGGERS, GUIROLA, CUMMINGS, HEAD, HEARTFIELD, and BIERY.

Delegation

In order to effectuate Rule 10(a) of the Rules for Judicial–Conduct and Judicial Disability Proceedings (made effective April 10, 2008), the Judicial Council hereby delegates the following authority to the chief circuit judge or judge acting for the chief judge pursuant to rule 25(f) *When a complainant has filed repetitive, harassing or frivolous complaints, or has otherwise abused the complaint procedure, the order dismissing the complaint under Rule 11 (c) may include a provision suspending the right of the complainant to file further complaints without written permission from the chief judge or judge acting for him or her*

A complainant upon whom such a suspension is imposed may show cause, through a petition for review submitted pursuant to Rule 18, why his or her right to file further complaints should not be so limited. If, under Rule 19 (b) (1), the order of the chief judge is affirmed, the suspension shall become a permanent restriction prohibiting the filing of complaints, subject to its own terms and to the power of the Judicial Council under Rule 10(a) to revise or withdraw any prohibition, restriction or condition previously imposed.

FOR THE COUNCIL:

/s/Edith H. Jones

May 4, 2008

ARTICLE III. REVIEW OF COMPLAINT BY CHIEF JUDGE

RULE 11. CHIEF JUDGE'S REVIEW

(a) Purpose of Chief Judge's Review. When a complaint is identified by the chief judge or is filed, the chief judge must review it unless the chief judge is disqualified under Rule 25. If a complaint contains information constituting evidence of misconduct or disability, but the complainant does not claim it as such, the chief judge must treat the complaint as if it did allege misconduct or disability and give notice to the subject judge. After reviewing a complaint, the chief judge must determine whether it should be:

(1) dismissed;

(2) concluded on the ground that voluntary corrective action has been taken;

(3) concluded because intervening events have made action on the complaint no longer necessary; or

(4) referred to a special committee.

(b) Chief Judge's Inquiry. In determining what action to take under Rule 11(a), the chief judge may conduct a limited inquiry. The chief judge, or a designee, may communicate orally or in writing with the complainant, the subject judge, and any others who may have knowledge of the matter, and may obtain and review transcripts and other relevant documents. In conducting the inquiry, the chief judge must not determine any reasonably disputed issue. Any such determination must be left to a special committee appointed under Rule 11(f) and to the judicial council that considers the special committee's report.

(c) Dismissal.

(1) *Permissible Grounds.* A complaint must be dismissed in whole or in part to the extent that the chief judge concludes that the complaint:

  (A) alleges conduct that, even if true, is not prejudicial to the effective and expeditious administration of the business of the courts and does not indicate a mental or physical disability resulting in the inability to discharge the duties of judicial office;

  (B) is directly related to the merits of a decision or procedural ruling;

  (C) is frivolous;

  (D) is based on allegations lacking sufficient evidence to raise an inference that misconduct has occurred or that a disability exists;

  (E) is based on allegations that are incapable of being established through investigation;

  (F) has been filed in the wrong circuit under Rule 7; or

  (G) is otherwise not appropriate for consideration under the Act.

(2) *Impermissible Grounds.* A complaint must not be dismissed solely because it repeats allegations of a previously dismissed complaint if it also contains material information not previously considered and does not constitute harassment of the subject judge.

(d) Corrective Action. The chief judge may conclude a complaint proceeding in whole or in part if:

(1) an informal resolution under Rule 5 satisfactory to the chief judge was reached before the complaint was filed under Rule 6; or

(2) the chief judge determines that the subject judge has taken appropriate voluntary corrective action that acknowledges and remedies the problems raised by the complaint.

(e) Intervening Events. The chief judge may conclude a complaint proceeding in whole or in part upon determining that intervening events render some or all of the allegations moot or make remedial action impossible.

(f) Appointment of Special Committee. If some or all of a complaint is not dismissed or concluded, the chief judge must promptly appoint a special committee to investigate the complaint or any relevant portion of it and to make recommendations to the judicial council. Before appointing a special committee, the chief judge must invite the subject judge to respond to the complaint either orally or in writing if the judge was not given an opportunity during the limited inquiry. In the chief judge's discretion, separate complaints may be joined and assigned to a single special committee. Similarly, a single complaint about more than one judge may be severed and more than one special committee appointed.

(g) Notice of Chief Judge's Action; Petition for Review.

(1) *When Chief Judge Appoints Special Committee.* If the chief judge appoints a special committee, the chief judge must notify the complainant and the subject judge that the matter has been referred to a committee, notify the complainant of a complainant's rights under Rule 16, and identify the members of the committee. A copy of the order appointing the special committee must be sent to the Committee on Judicial Conduct and Disability.

(2) *When Chief Judge Disposes of Complaint Without Appointing Special Committee.* If the chief judge disposes of a complaint under Rule 11(c), (d), or (e), the chief judge must prepare a supporting memorandum that sets forth the reasons for the disposition. If the complaint was initiated by identification under Rule 5, the memorandum must so indicate. Except as authorized by 28 U.S.C. § 360, the memorandum must not include the name of the complainant or of the subject judge. The order and memoranda incorporated by reference in the order must be promptly sent to the complainant, the subject judge, and the Committee on Judicial Conduct and Disability.

(3) *Right to Petition for Review.* If the chief judge disposes of a complaint under Rule 11(c), (d), or (e), the complainant and the subject judge must be notified of the right to petition the judicial council for review of the disposition, as provided in Rule 18. If the chief judge so disposes of a complaint that was identified under Rule 5 or filed by its subject judge, the chief judge must transmit the order and memoranda incorporated by reference in the order to the judicial council for review in accordance with Rule 19. In the event of such a transmission, the subject judge may make a written submission to the judicial council but will have no further right of review except as allowed under Rule 21(b)(1)(B). When a disposition is to be reviewed by the judicial council, the chief judge must promptly transmit all materials obtained in connection with the inquiry under Rule 11(b) to the circuit clerk for transmittal to the council.

(h) Public Availability of Chief Judge's Decision. The
chief judge's decision must be made public to the extent, at the time, and in the manner provided in Rule 24.

[Adopted March 11, 2008, effective April 10, 2008. Amended effective September 17, 2015; April 12, 2018.]

Commentary on Rule 11

This Rule describes complaint-review actions available either to a chief judge or, where that judge is the subject judge or is otherwise disqualified under Rule 25, to the judge designated under Rule 25(f) to perform the chief judge's duties under these Rules. Subsection (a) of this Rule provides that where a complaint has been filed under Rule 6, the ordinary doctrines of waiver do not apply. The chief judge must identify as a complaint any misconduct or disability issues raised by the factual allegations of the complaint even if the complainant makes no such claim with regard to those issues. For example, an allegation limited to misconduct in fact-finding that mentions periods during a trial when the judge was asleep must be treated as a complaint regarding disability. Some formal order giving notice of the expanded scope of the proceeding must be given to the subject judge.

Subsection (b) describes the nature of the chief judge's inquiry. It is based largely on the Breyer Committee Report, 239 F.R.D. at 243–45. The Act states that dismissal is appropriate "when a limited inquiry ... demonstrates that the allegations in the complaint lack any factual foundation or are conclusively refuted by objective evidence." 28 U.S.C. § 352(b)(1)(B). At the same time, however, Section 352(a) states that "[t]he chief judge shall not undertake to make findings of fact about any matter that is reasonably in dispute." These two statutory standards should be read together, so that a matter is not "reasonably" in dispute if a limited inquiry shows that the allegations do not constitute misconduct or disability, that they lack any reliable factual foundation, or that they are conclusively refuted by objective evidence.

In conducting a limited inquiry under subsection (b), the chief judge must avoid determinations of reasonably disputed issues, including reasonably disputed issues as to whether the facts alleged constitute misconduct or disability, which are ordinarily left to the judicial council and its special committee. An allegation of fact is ordinarily not "refuted" simply because the subject judge denies it. The limited inquiry must reveal something more in the way of refutation before it is appropriate to dismiss a complaint that is otherwise cognizable. If it is the complainant's word against the subject judge's—in other words, there is simply no other significant evidence of what happened or of the complainant's unreliability—then there must be a special-committee investigation. Such a credibility issue is a matter "reasonably in dispute" within the meaning of the Act.

However, dismissal following a limited inquiry may occur when a complaint refers to transcripts or to witnesses and the chief judge determines that the transcripts and witnesses all support the subject judge. Breyer Committee Report, 239 F.R.D. at 243. For example, consider a complaint alleging that the subject judge said X, and the complaint mentions, or it is independently clear, that five people may have heard what the judge said. *Id.* The chief judge is told by the subject judge and one witness that the judge did not say X, and the chief judge dismisses the complaint without questioning the other four possible witnesses. *Id.* In this example, the matter remains reasonably in dispute. If all five witnesses say the subject judge did not say X, dismissal is appropriate, but if potential witnesses who are reasonably accessible have not been questioned, then the matter remains reasonably in dispute. *Id.*

Similarly, under subsection (c)(1)(A), if it is clear that the conduct or disability alleged, even if true, is not cognizable under these Rules, the complaint should be dismissed. If that issue is reasonably in dispute, however, dismissal under subsection (c)(1)(A) is inappropriate.

Essentially, the standard articulated in subsection (b) is that used to decide motions for summary judgment pursuant to Fed. R. Civ. P. 56. Genuine issues of material fact are not resolved at the summary judgment stage. A material fact is one that "might affect the outcome of the suit under the governing law," and a dispute is "genuine" if "the evidence is such that a reasonable jury could return a verdict for the nonmoving party." *Anderson v. Liberty Lobby*, 477 U.S. 242, 248 (1986). Similarly, the chief judge may not resolve a genuine issue concerning a material fact or the existence of misconduct or a disability when conducting a limited inquiry pursuant to subsection (b).

Subsection (c) describes the grounds on which a complaint may be dismissed. These are adapted from the Act, 28 U.S.C. § 352(b), and the Breyer Committee Report, 239 F.R.D. at 239–45. Subsection (c)(1)(A) permits dismissal of an allegation that, even if true, does not constitute misconduct or disability under the statutory standard. The proper standards are set out in Rule 3 and discussed in the Commentary on that Rule. Subsection (c)(1)(B) permits dismissal of complaints related to the merits of a decision by a subject judge; this standard is also governed by Rule 3 and its accompanying Commentary.

Subsections (c)(1)(C)–(E) implement the statute by allowing dismissal of complaints that are "frivolous, lacking sufficient evidence to raise an inference that misconduct has occurred, or containing allegations which are incapable of being established through investigation." 28 U.S.C. § 352(b)(1)(A)(iii).

Dismissal of a complaint as "frivolous" under Rule 11(c)(1)(C) will generally occur without any inquiry beyond the face of the complaint. For instance, when the allegations are facially incredible or so lacking in indicia of reliability that no further inquiry is warranted, dismissal under this subsection is appropriate.

A complaint warranting dismissal under Rule 11(c)(1)(D) is illustrated by the following example. Consider a complainant who alleges an impropriety and asserts that he knows of it because it was observed and reported to him by a person who is identified. The subject judge denies that the event occurred. When contacted, the source also denies it. In such a case, the chief judge's proper course of action may turn on whether the source had any role in the allegedly improper conduct. If the complaint was based on a lawyer's statement that he or she had an improper *ex parte* contact with a judge, the lawyer's denial of the impropriety might not be taken as wholly persuasive, and it would be appropriate to conclude that a real factual issue is raised. On the other hand, if the complaint quoted a disinterested third party and that disinterested party denied that the statement had been made, there would be no value in opening a formal investigation. In such a case, it would be appropriate to dismiss the complaint under Rule 11(c)(1)(D).

Rule 11(c)(1)(E) is intended, among other things, to cover situations when no evidence is offered or identified, or when the only identified source is unavailable. Breyer Committee Report, 239 F.R.D. at 243. For example, a complaint alleges that an unnamed attorney told the complainant that the subject judge did X. *Id.* The subject judge denies it. The chief judge requests that the complainant (who does not purport to have observed the subject judge do X) identify the unnamed witness, or that the unnamed witness come forward so that the chief judge can learn the unnamed witness's account. *Id.* The complainant responds that he has spoken with the unnamed witness, that the unnamed witness is an attorney who practices in federal court, and that the unnamed witness is unwilling to be identified or to come forward. *Id.* at 243–44. The allegation is then properly dismissed as containing allegations that are incapable of being established through investigation. *Id.*

If, however, the situation involves a reasonable dispute over credibility, the matter should proceed. For example, the complainant alleges an impropriety and alleges that he or she observed it and that there were no other witnesses; the subject judge denies that the event occurred. Unless the complainant's allegations are facially incredible or so lacking indicia of reliability as to warrant dismissal under Rule 11(c)(1)(C), a special committee must be appointed because there is a material factual question that is reasonably in dispute.

Dismissal is also appropriate when a complaint is filed so long after an alleged event that memory loss, death, or changes to unknown residences prevent a proper investigation.

Subsection (c)(2) indicates that the investigative nature of the process prevents the application of claim preclusion principles where new and material evidence becomes available. However, it also recognizes that at some point a renewed investigation may constitute harassment of the subject judge and should not be undertaken, depending of course on the seriousness of the issues and the weight of the new evidence.

Rule 11(d) implements the Act's provision for dismissal if voluntary appropriate corrective action has been taken. It is largely adapted from the Breyer Committee Report, 239 F.R.D. at 244–45. The Act authorizes the chief judge to conclude the complaint proceedings if "appropriate corrective action has been taken." 28 U.S.C. § 352(b)(2). Under the Rule, action taken after a complaint is filed is "appropriate"

when it acknowledges and remedies the problem raised by the complaint. Breyer Committee Report, 239 F.R.D. at 244. Because the Act deals with the conduct of judges, the emphasis is on correction of the judicial conduct that was the subject of the complaint. *Id.* Terminating a complaint based on corrective action is premised on the implicit understanding that voluntary self-correction or redress of misconduct or a disability is preferable to sanctions. *Id.* The chief judge may facilitate this process by giving the subject judge an objective view of the appearance of the judicial conduct in question and by suggesting appropriate corrective measures. *Id.* Moreover, when corrective action is taken under Rule 5 satisfactory to the chief judge before a complaint is filed, that informal resolution will be sufficient to conclude a subsequent complaint based on identical conduct.

"Corrective action" must be voluntary action taken by the subject judge. Breyer Committee Report, 239 F.R.D. at 244. A remedial action directed by the chief judge or by an appellate court without the participation of the subject judge in formulating the directive or without the subject judge's subsequent agreement to such action does not constitute the requisite voluntary corrective action. *Id.* Neither the chief judge nor an appellate court has authority under the Act to impose a formal remedy or sanction; only the judicial council can impose a formal remedy or sanction under 28 U.S.C. § 354(a)(2). *Id.* Compliance with a previous judicial-council order may serve as corrective action allowing conclusion of a later complaint about the same behavior. *Id.*

Where a subject judge's conduct has resulted in identifiable, particularized harm to the complainant or another individual, appropriate corrective action should include steps taken by that judge to acknowledge and redress the harm, if possible, such as by an apology, recusal from a case, or a pledge to refrain from similar conduct in the future. *Id.* While the Act is generally forward-looking, any corrective action should, to the extent possible, serve to correct a specific harm to an individual, if such harm can reasonably be remedied. *Id.* In some cases, corrective action may not be "appropriate" to justify conclusion of a complaint unless the complainant or other individual harmed is meaningfully apprised of the nature of the corrective action in the chief judge's order, in a direct communication from the subject judge, or otherwise. *Id.*

Voluntary corrective action should be proportionate to any plausible allegations of misconduct in a complaint. The form of corrective action should also be proportionate to any sanctions that the judicial council might impose under Rule 20(b), such as a private or public reprimand or a change in case assignments. Breyer Committee Report, 239 F.R.D at 244–45. In other words, minor corrective action will not suffice to dispose of a serious matter. *Id.*

Rule 11(e) implements Section 352(b)(2) of the Act, which permits the chief judge to "conclude the proceeding" if "action on the complaint is no longer necessary because of intervening events," such as a resignation from judicial office. Ordinarily, however, stepping down from an administrative post such as chief judge, judicial-council member, or court-committee chair does not constitute an event rendering unnecessary any further action on a complaint alleging judicial misconduct. Breyer Committee Report, 239 F.R.D. at 245. As long as the subject of a complaint performs judicial duties, a complaint alleging judicial misconduct must be addressed. *Id.*

If a complaint is not disposed of pursuant to Rule 11(c), (d), or (e), a special committee must be appointed. Rule 11(f) states that a subject judge must be invited to respond to the complaint before a special committee is appointed, if no earlier response was invited.

Subject judges, of course, receive copies of complaints at the same time that they are referred to the chief judge, and they are free to volunteer responses to them. Under Rule 11(b), the chief judge may request a response if it is thought necessary. However, many complaints are clear candidates for dismissal even if their allegations are accepted as true, and there is no need for the subject judge to devote time to a defense.

The Act requires that the order dismissing a complaint or concluding a proceeding contain a statement of reasons and that a copy of the order be sent to the complainant. 28 U.S.C. § 352(b). Rule 24, dealing with availability of information to the public, contemplates that the order will be made public, usually without disclosing the names of the complainant or the subject judge. If desired for administrative purposes, more identifying information can be included in a non-public version of the order.

When a complaint is disposed of by the chief judge, the statutory purposes are best served by providing the complainant with a full, particularized, but concise explanation, giving reasons for the conclu-sions reached. *See also* Commentary on Rule 24 (dealing with public availability).

Rule 11(g) provides that the complainant and the subject judge must be notified, in the case of a disposition by the chief judge, of the right to petition the judicial council for review. Because an identified complaint has no "complainant" to petition for review, the chief judge's dispositive order on such a complaint will be transmitted to the judicial council for review. The same will apply where a complaint was filed by its subject judge. A copy of the chief judge's order, and memoranda incorporated by reference in the order, disposing of a complaint must be sent by the circuit clerk to the Committee on Judicial Conduct and Disability.

ARTICLE IV. INVESTIGATION AND REPORT BY SPECIAL COMMITTEE

RULE 12. SPECIAL COMMITTEE'S COMPOSITION

(a) Membership. Except as provided in (e), a special committee appointed under Rule 11(f) must consist of the chief judge and equal numbers of circuit and district judges. These judges may include senior judges. If the complaint is about a district judge, bankruptcy judge, or magistrate judge, then, when possible, the district-judge members of the special committee must be from districts other than the district of the subject judge. For the courts named in 28 U.S.C. § 363, the special committee must be selected from the judges serving on the subject judge's court.

(b) Presiding Officer. When appointing the special committee, the chief judge may serve as the presiding officer or else must designate a committee member as the presiding officer.

(c) Bankruptcy Judge or Magistrate Judge as Adviser. If the subject judge is a bankruptcy judge or magistrate judge, he or she may, within 14 days after being notified of the special committee's appointment, ask the chief judge to designate as a committee adviser another bankruptcy judge or magistrate judge, as the case may be. The chief judge must grant such a request but may otherwise use discretion in naming the adviser. Unless the adviser is a Court of Federal Claims special master appointed under 42 U.S.C. § 300aa–12(c), the adviser must be from a district other than the district of the subject bankruptcy judge or subject magistrate judge. The adviser cannot vote but has the other privileges of a special-committee member.

(d) Provision of Documents. The chief judge must certify to each other member of the special committee and to any adviser copies of the complaint and statement of facts, in whole or relevant part, and any other relevant documents on file.

(e) Continuing Qualification of Special–Committee Member. A member of a special committee may continue to serve on the committee even though the member relinquishes the position of chief judge, active circuit judge, or active district judge, as the case may be, but only if the member continues to hold office under Article III, Section 1, of the Constitution of the United States, or under 28 U.S.C. § 171.

(f) Inability of Special–Committee Member to Complete Service. If a member of a special committee can no longer serve because of death, disability, disqualification, resignation, retirement from office, or other reason, the chief judge must decide whether to appoint a replacement member, either a circuit or district judge as needed under (a). No special committee appointed under these Rules may function with only a single member, and the votes of a two-member committee must be unanimous.

(g) Voting. All actions by a special committee must be by vote of a majority of all members of the committee.

[Adopted March 11, 2008, effective April 10, 2008. Amended effective September 17, 2015; April 12, 2018.]

Commentary on Rule 12

This Rule is adapted from the Act and the Illustrative Rules.

Rule 12 leaves the size of a special committee flexible, to be determined on a case-by-case basis. The question of the size of a special committee is one that should be weighed with care in view of the potential for consuming the members' time; a large committee should be appointed only if there is a special reason to do so. Rule 12(a) acknowledges the common practice of including senior judges in the membership of a special committee.

Although the Act requires that the chief judge be a member of each special committee, 28 U.S.C. § 353(a)(1), it does not require that the chief judge preside. Accordingly, Rule 12(b) provides that if the chief judge does not preside, he or she must designate another member of the special committee as the presiding officer.

Rule 12(c) provides that the chief judge must appoint a bankruptcy judge or magistrate judge as an adviser to a special committee at the request of a bankruptcy or magistrate subject judge. Subsection (c) also provides that the adviser will have all the privileges of a member of the special committee except a vote. The adviser, therefore, may participate in all deliberations of the special committee, question witnesses at hearings, and write a separate statement to accompany the committee's report to the judicial council.

Rule 12(e) provides that a member of a special committee who remains an Article III judge may continue to serve on the committee even though the member's status otherwise changes. Thus, a special committee that originally consisted of the chief judge and an equal number of circuit and district judges, as required by the law, may continue to function even though changes of status alter that composition. This provision reflects the belief that stability of membership will contribute to the quality of the work of such committees.

Stability of membership is also the principal concern animating Rule 12(f), which deals with the case in which a special committee loses a member before its work is complete. The Rule permits the chief judge to determine whether a replacement member should be appointed. Generally, appointment of a replacement member is desirable in these situations unless the special committee has conducted evidentiary hearings before the vacancy occurs. However, cases may arise in which a special committee is in the late stages of its work, and in which it would be difficult for a new member to play a meaningful role. The Rule also preserves the collegial character of the special-committee process by prohibiting a single surviving member from serving as a committee and by providing that a committee of two surviving members will, in essence, operate under a unanimity rule.

Rule 12(g) provides that actions of a special committee must be by vote of a majority of all the members. All the members of a special committee should participate in committee decisions. In that circumstance, it seems reasonable to require that special-committee decisions be made by a majority of the membership, rather than a majority of some smaller quorum.

RULE 13. CONDUCT OF SPECIAL–COMMITTEE INVESTIGATION

(a) Extent and Methods of Special–Committee Investigation. A special committee should determine the appropriate extent and methods of its investigation in light of the allegations of the complaint and its preliminary inquiry. The investigation may include use of appropriate experts or other professionals. If, in the course of the investigation, the special committee has cause to believe that the subject judge may have engaged in misconduct or has a disability that is beyond the scope of the complaint, the committee must refer the new matter to the chief judge for a determination of whether action under Rule 5 or Rule 11 is necessary before the committee's investigation is expanded to include the new matter.

(b) Criminal Conduct. If the special committee's investigation concerns conduct that may be a crime, the committee must consult with the appropriate prosecutorial authorities to the extent permitted by the Act to avoid compromising any criminal investigation. The special committee has final authority over the timing and extent of its investigation and the formulation of its recommendations.

(c) Staff. The special committee may arrange for staff assistance to conduct the investigation. It may use existing staff of the Judiciary or may hire special staff through the Director of the Administrative Office of the United States Courts.

(d) Delegation of Subpoena Power; Contempt. The chief judge may delegate the authority to exercise the subpoena powers of the special committee. The judicial council or special committee may institute a contempt proceeding under 28 U.S.C. § 332(d) against anyone who fails to comply with a subpoena.

[Adopted March 11, 2008, effective April 10, 2008. Amended effective September 17, 2015; April 12, 2018.]

Commentary on Rule 13

This Rule is adapted from the Illustrative Rules.

Rule 13, as well as Rules 14, 15, and 16, are concerned with the way in which the special committee carries out its mission. They reflect the view that the special committee has two roles that are separated in ordinary litigation. First, the special committee has an investigative role of the kind that is characteristically left to executive branch agencies or discovery by civil litigants. 28 U.S.C. § 353(c). Second, it has a formalized fact-finding and recommendation-of-disposition role that is characteristically left to juries, judges, or arbitrators. *Id.* Rule 13 generally governs the investigative stage. Even though the same body has responsibility for both roles under the Act, it is important to distinguish between them in order to ensure that appropriate rights are afforded at appropriate times to the subject judge.

Rule 13(a) includes a provision making clear that a special committee may choose to consult appropriate experts or other professionals if it determines that such a consultation is warranted. If, for example, the special committee has cause to believe that the subject judge may be unable to discharge all of the duties of office by reason of mental or physical disability, the committee could ask the subject judge to respond to inquiries and, if necessary, request the judge to undergo a medical or psychological examination. In advance of any such examination, the special committee may enter into an agreement with the subject judge as to the scope and use that may be made of the examination results. In addition or in the alternative, the special committee may ask to review existing records, including medical records.

The extent of the subject judge's cooperation in the investigation may be taken into account in the consideration of the underlying complaint. If, for example, the subject judge impedes reasonable efforts to confirm or disconfirm the presence of a disability, the special committee may still consider whether the conduct alleged in the complaint and confirmed in the investigation constitutes disability. The same would be true of a complaint alleging misconduct.

The special committee may also consider whether such a judge might be in violation of his or her duty to cooperate in an investigation under these Rules, a duty rooted not only in the Act's definition of misconduct but also in the Code of Conduct for United States Judges, which emphasizes the need to maintain public confidence in the Judiciary, *see* Canon 2(A) and Canon 1 cmt., and requires judges to "facilitate the performance of the administrative responsibilities of other judges and court personnel," Canon 3(B)(1). If the special committee finds a breach of the duty to cooperate and believes that the breach may amount to misconduct under Rule 3(h)(1)(H), it should determine, under the final sentence of Rule 13(a), whether that possibility should be referred to the chief judge for consideration of action under Rule 5 or Rule 11. *See also* Commentary on Rule 3.

One of the difficult questions that can arise is the relationship between proceedings under the Act and criminal investigations. Rule 13(b) assigns responsibility for coordination to the special committee in cases in which criminal conduct is suspected, but gives the committee the authority to determine the appropriate pace of its activity in light of any criminal investigation.

Title 28 U.S.C. § 356(a) provides that a special committee will have full subpoena powers as provided in 28 U.S.C. § 332(d). Section 332(d)(1) provides that subpoenas will be issued on behalf of a judicial council by the circuit clerk "at the direction of the chief judge of the circuit or his designee." Rule 13(d) contemplates that, where the chief judge designates someone else as presiding officer of the special committee, the presiding officer also be delegated the authority to direct the circuit clerk to issue subpoenas related to committee proceedings. That is not intended to imply, however, that the decision to use the subpoena power is exercisable by the presiding officer alone. *See* Rule 12(g).

RULE 14. CONDUCT OF SPECIAL–COMMITTEE HEARINGS

(a) Purpose of Hearings. The special committee may hold hearings to take testimony and receive other evidence, to hear argument, or both. If the special committee is investigating allegations against more than one judge, it may hold joint or separate hearings.

(b) Special–Committee Evidence. Subject to Rule 15, the special committee must obtain material, nonredundant evidence in the form it considers appropriate. In the special committee's discretion, evidence may be obtained by committee members, staff, or both. Witnesses offering testimonial evidence may include the complainant and the subject judge.

(c) Counsel for Witnesses. The subject judge has the right to counsel. The special committee has discretion to decide whether other witnesses may have counsel present when they testify.

(d) Witness Fees. Witness fees must be paid as provided in 28 U.S.C. § 1821.

(e) Oath. All testimony taken at a hearing must be given under oath or affirmation.

(f) Rules of Evidence. The Federal Rules of Evidence do not apply to special-committee hearings.

(g) Record and Transcript. A record and transcript must be made of all hearings.

[Adopted March 11, 2008, effective April 10, 2008. Amended effective September 17, 2015; April 12, 2018.]

Commentary on Rule 14

This Rule is adapted from the Act, 28 U.S.C. § 353, and the Illustrative Rules.

Rule 14 is concerned with the conduct of fact-finding hearings. Special-committee hearings will normally be held only after the investigative work has been completed and the committee has concluded that there is sufficient evidence to warrant a formal fact-finding proceeding. Special-committee proceedings are primarily inquisitorial rather than adversarial. Accordingly, the Federal Rules of Evidence do not apply to such hearings. Inevitably, a hearing will have something of an adversary character. Nevertheless, that tendency should be moderated to the extent possible. Even though a proceeding will commonly have investigative and hearing stages, special-committee members should not regard themselves as prosecutors one day and judges the next. Their duty—and that of their staff—is at all times to be impartial seekers of the truth.

Rule 14(b) contemplates that material evidence will be obtained by the special committee and presented in the form of affidavits, live testimony, etc. Staff or others who are organizing the hearings should regard it as their role to present evidence representing the entire picture. With respect to testimonial evidence, the subject judge should normally be called as a special-committee witness. Cases may arise in which the subject judge will not testify voluntarily. In such cases, subpoena powers are available, subject to the normal testimonial privileges. Although Rule 15(c) recognizes the subject judge's statutory right to call witnesses on his or her own behalf, exercise of this right should not usually be necessary.

RULE 15. SUBJECT JUDGE'S RIGHTS

(a) Notice.

(1) *Generally.* The subject judge must receive written notice of:

(A) the appointment of a special committee under Rule 11(f);

(B) the expansion of the scope of an investigation under Rule 13(a);

(C) any hearing under Rule 14, including its purposes, the names of any witnesses the special committee intends to call, and the text of any statements that have been taken from those witnesses.

(2) *Suggestion of Additional Witnesses.* The subject judge may suggest additional witnesses to the special committee.

(b) Special–Committee Report. The subject judge must be sent a copy of the special committee's report when it is filed with the judicial council.

(c) Presentation of Evidence. At any hearing held under Rule 14, the subject judge has the right to present evidence, to compel the attendance of witnesses, and to compel the production of documents. At the request of the subject judge, the chief judge or the judge's designee must direct the circuit clerk to issue a subpoena to a witness under 28 U.S.C. § 332(d)(1). The subject judge must be given the opportunity to cross-examine special-committee witnesses, in person or by counsel.

(d) Presentation of Argument. The subject judge may submit written argument to the special committee and must be given a reasonable opportunity to present oral argument at an appropriate stage of the investigation.

(e) Attendance at Hearings. The subject judge has the right to attend any hearing held under Rule 14 and to receive copies of the transcript, of any documents introduced, and of any written arguments submitted by the complainant to the special committee.

(f) Representation by Counsel. The subject judge may choose to be represented by counsel in the exercise of any right enumerated in this Rule. As provided in Rule 20(e), the United States may bear the costs of the representation.

[Adopted March 11, 2008, effective April 10, 2008. Amended effective September 17, 2015; April 12, 2018.]

Commentary on Rule 15

This Rule is adapted from the Act and the Illustrative Rules.

The Act states that these Rules must contain provisions requiring that "the judge whose conduct is the subject of a complaint . . . be afforded an opportunity to appear (in person or by counsel) at proceedings conducted by the investigating panel, to present oral and documentary evidence, to compel the attendance of witnesses or the production of documents, to cross-examine witnesses, and to present argument orally or in writing." 28 U.S.C. § 358(b)(2). To implement this provision, Rule 15(e) gives the subject judge the right to attend any hearing held for the purpose of receiving evidence of record or hearing argument under Rule 14.

The Act does not require that the subject judge be permitted to attend all proceedings of the special committee. Accordingly, the Rules do not give a right to attend other proceedings—for example, meetings at which the special committee is engaged in investigative activity, such as interviewing persons to learn whether they ought to be called as witnesses or examining for relevance purposes documents delivered pursuant to a subpoena duces tecum, or meetings in which the committee is deliberating on the evidence or its recommendations.

RULE 16. COMPLAINANT'S RIGHTS IN INVESTIGATION

(a) Notice. The complainant must receive written notice of the investigation as provided in Rule 11(g)(1). When the special committee's report to the judicial council is filed, the complainant must be notified of the filing. The judicial council may, in its discretion, provide a copy of the report of a special committee to the complainant.

(b) Opportunity to Provide Evidence. If the complainant knows of relevant evidence not already before the special committee, the complainant may briefly explain in writing the basis of that knowledge and the nature of that evidence. If the special committee determines that the complainant has information not already known to the committee that would assist in the committee's investigation, a representative of the committee must interview the complainant.

(c) Presentation of Argument. The complainant may submit written argument to the special committee. In its discretion, the special committee may permit the complainant to offer oral argument.

(d) Representation by Counsel. A complainant may submit written argument through counsel and, if permitted to offer oral argument, may do so through counsel.

(e) Cooperation. In exercising its discretion under this Rule, the special committee may take into account the degree of the complainant's cooperation in preserving the confidentiality of the proceedings, including the identity of the subject judge.

[Adopted March 11, 2008, effective April 10, 2008. Amended effective September 17, 2015; April 12, 2018.]

Commentary on Rule 16

This Rule is adapted from the Act and the Illustrative Rules.

In accordance with the view of the process as fundamentally administrative and inquisitorial, these Rules do not give the complainant the rights of a party to litigation and leave the complainant's role largely to the discretion of the special committee. However, Rule 16(b) gives the complainant the prerogative to make a brief written submission showing that he or she is aware of relevant evidence not already known to the special committee. (Such a submission may precede any written or oral argument the complainant provides under Rule 16(c), or it may accompany that argument.) If the special committee determines, independently or from the complainant's submission, that

the complainant has information that would assist the committee in its investigation, the complainant must be interviewed by a representative of the committee. Such an interview may be in person or by telephone, and the representative of the special committee may be either a member or staff.

Rule 16 does not contemplate that the complainant will ordinarily be permitted to attend proceedings of the special committee except when testifying or presenting oral argument. A special committee may exercise its discretion to permit the complainant to be present at its proceedings, or to permit the complainant, individually or through counsel, to participate in the examination or cross-examination of witnesses.

The Act authorizes an exception to the normal confidentiality provisions where the judicial council in its discretion provides a copy of the report of the special committee to the complainant and to the subject judge. 28 U.S.C. § 360(a)(1). However, the Rules do not entitle the complainant to a copy of the special committee's report.

In exercising their discretion regarding the role of the complainant, the special committee and the judicial council should protect the confidentiality of the complaint process. As a consequence, subsection (e) provides that the special committee may consider the degree to which a complainant has cooperated in preserving the confidentiality of the proceedings in determining what role beyond the minimum required by these Rules should be given to that complainant.

RULE 17. SPECIAL–COMMITTEE REPORT

The special committee must file with the judicial council a comprehensive report of its investigation, including findings and recommendations for council action. The report must be accompanied by a statement of the vote by which it was adopted, any separate or dissenting statements of special-committee members, and the record of any hearings held under Rule 14. In addition to being sent to the subject judge under Rule 15(b), a copy of the report and any accompanying statements and documents must be sent to the Committee on Judicial Conduct and Disability.

[Adopted March 11, 2008, effective April 10, 2008. Amended effective September 17, 2015; April 12, 2018.]

Commentary on Rule 17

This Rule is adapted from the Illustrative Rules and is self-explanatory. The provision for sending a copy of the special-committee report and accompanying statements and documents to the Committee on Judicial Conduct and Disability is new.

ARTICLE V. REVIEW BY JUDICIAL COUNCIL

RULE 18. PETITIONS FOR REVIEW OF CHIEF–JUDGE DISPOSITION UNDER RULE 11(c), (d), or (e)

(a) Petition for Review. After the chief judge issues an order under Rule 11(c), (d), or (e), the complainant or the subject judge may petition the judicial council of the circuit to review the order. By rules promulgated under 28 U.S.C. § 358, the judicial council may refer a petition for review filed under this Rule to a panel of no fewer than five members of the council, at least two of whom must be district judges.

(b) When to File; Form; Where to File. A petition for review must be filed in the office of the circuit clerk within 42

days after the date of the chief judge's order. The petition for review should be in letter form, addressed to the circuit clerk, and in an envelope marked "Misconduct Petition" or "Disability Petition." The name of the subject judge must not be shown on the envelope. The petition for review should be typewritten or otherwise legible. It should begin with "I hereby petition the judicial council for review of . . ." and state the reasons why the petition should be granted. It must be signed.

(c) Receipt and Distribution of Petition. A circuit clerk who receives a petition for review filed in accordance with this Rule must:

(1) acknowledge its receipt and send a copy to the complainant or subject judge, as the case may be;

(2) promptly distribute to each member of the judicial council, or its relevant panel, except for any member disqualified under Rule 25, or make available in the manner provided by local rule, the following materials:

(A) copies of the complaint;

(B) all materials obtained by the chief judge in connection with the inquiry;

(C) the chief judge's order disposing of the complaint;

(D) any memorandum in support of the chief judge's order;

(E) the petition for review; and

(F) an appropriate ballot; and

(3) send the petition for review to the Committee on Judicial Conduct and Disability. Unless the Committee on Judicial Conduct and Disability requests them, the circuit clerk will not send copies of the materials obtained by the chief judge.

(d) Untimely Petition. The circuit clerk must refuse to accept a petition that is received after the time allowed in (b).

(e) Timely Petition Not in Proper Form. When the circuit clerk receives a petition for review filed within the time allowed but in a form that is improper to a degree that would substantially impair its consideration by the judicial council—such as a document that is ambiguous about whether it is intended to be a petition for review—the circuit clerk must acknowledge its receipt, call the filer's attention to the deficiencies, and give the filer the opportunity to correct the deficiencies within the original time allowed for filing the petition or within 21 days after the date on which a notice of the deficiencies was sent to the complainant, whichever is later. If the deficiencies are corrected within the time allowed, the circuit clerk will proceed according to paragraphs (a) and (c) of this Rule. If the deficiencies are not corrected, the circuit clerk must reject the petition.

[Adopted March 11, 2008, effective April 10, 2008. Amended effective September 17, 2015; April 12, 2018.]

Commentary on Rule 18

Rule 18 is adapted largely from the Illustrative Rules.

Subsection (a) permits the subject judge, as well as the complainant, to petition for review of the chief judge's order dismissing a complaint under Rule 11(c), or concluding that appropriate corrective action or intervening events have remedied or mooted the problems raised by the complaint pursuant to Rule 11(d) or (e). Although the subject judge may ostensibly be vindicated by the dismissal or conclusion of a complaint, the chief judge's order may include language disagreeable to the subject judge. For example, an order may dismiss a complaint, but state that the subject judge did in fact engage in misconduct. Accordingly, a subject judge may wish to object to the content of the order and is given the opportunity to petition the judicial council of the circuit for review.

Subsection (b) contains a time limit of 42 days to file a petition for review. It is important to establish a time limit on petitions for review of chief judges' dispositions in order to provide finality to the process. If the complaint requires an investigation, the investigation should proceed; if it does not, the subject judge should know that the matter is closed.

The standards for timely filing under the Federal Rules of Appellate Procedure should be applied to petitions for review. *See* Fed. R. App. P. 25(a)(2)(A), (C).

Rule 18(e) provides for an automatic extension of the time limit imposed under subsection (b) if a person files a petition that is rejected for failure to comply with formal requirements.

Rule 18. *Petitions for Review [Fifth Circuit Procedure 18]*

(a) Substance. Petitions may but need not include supporting argument. Review by the Judicial Council is limited to facts set forth in the complaint, and supplemental allegations and information will not be considered.

(b) Page Limit. Petitions should not exceed five single-sided and double-spaced pages on 8.5x11 inch paper, whether typed or handwritten, and should not include attachments.

(c) Supplements. Once a petition is filed, it may not be supplemented by additional statements or documents except to correct inaccuracies in the original petition. Supplements submitted after the petition is filed will be returned to the complainant if they do not comply with this section.

(d) Extensions. Extensions to the time to file a petition for review will be considered only in the most compelling circumstances.

(e) Where to File. Petitions should be sent to the Clerk, United States Court of Appeals for the Fifth Circuit, 600 S. Maestri Place, New Orleans, LA 70130. The envelope should be marked "Misconduct Petition" or "Disability Petition." The name of the judge complained about should <u>not</u> appear on the envelope. (Former 5th Cir. R. 5 (H))

RULE 19. JUDICIAL–COUNCIL DISPOSITION OF PETITION FOR REVIEW

(a) Rights of Subject Judge. At any time after a complainant files a petition for review, the subject judge may file a written response with the circuit clerk. The circuit clerk must promptly distribute copies of the response to each member of the judicial council or of the relevant panel, unless that member is disqualified under Rule 25. Copies must also be distributed to the chief judge, to the complainant, and to the Committee on Judicial Conduct and Disability. The subject judge must not otherwise communicate with individual judicial-council members about the matter. The subject judge must be given copies of any communications to the judicial council from the complainant.

(b) Judicial–Council Action. After considering a petition for review and the materials before it, the judicial council may:

(1) affirm the chief judge's disposition by denying the petition;

(2) return the matter to the chief judge with directions to conduct a further inquiry under Rule 11(b) or to identify a complaint under Rule 5;

(3) return the matter to the chief judge with directions to appoint a special committee under Rule 11(f); or

(4) in exceptional circumstances, take other appropriate action.

(c) Notice of Judicial–Council Decision. Copies of the judicial council's order, together with memoranda incorporated by reference in the order and separate concurring or dissenting statements, must be given to the complainant, the subject judge, and the Committee on Judicial Conduct and Disability.

(d) Memorandum of Judicial–Council Decision. If the judicial council's order affirms the chief judge's disposition, a supporting memorandum must be prepared only if the council concludes that there is a need to supplement the chief judge's explanation. A memorandum supporting a judicial-council order must not include the name of the complainant or the subject judge.

(e) Review of Judicial–Council Decision. If the judicial council's decision is adverse to the petitioner, and if no member of the council dissented, the complainant must be notified that he or she has no right to seek review of the decision. If there was a dissent, the petitioner must be informed that he or she can file a petition for review under Rule 21(b).

(f) Public Availability of Judicial–Council Decision. Materials related to the judicial council's decision must be made public to the extent, at the time, and in the manner set forth in Rule 24.

[Adopted March 11, 2008, effective April 10, 2008. Amended effective September 17, 2015; April 12, 2018.]

Commentary on Rule 19

This Rule is adapted largely from the Act and is self-explanatory.

The judicial council should ordinarily review the decision of the chief judge on the merits, treating the petition for review for all practical purposes as an appeal. The judicial council may respond to a petition for review by affirming the chief judge's order, remanding the matter, or, in exceptional cases, taking other appropriate action. A petition for review of a judicial council's decision may be filed under Rule 21(b) in any matter in which one or more members of the council dissented from the order.

Rule 19. Review by the Judicial Council [Fifth Circuit Rule 19]

The judicial council may, consistent with 28 U.S.C. § 352(d), delegate the review process to rotating panels drawn at random with power to act on behalf of the full council. (Former 5th Cir. R. 7)

RULE 20. JUDICIAL–COUNCIL ACTION FOLLOWING APPOINTMENT OF SPECIAL COMMITTEE

(a) Subject Judge's Rights. Within 21 days after the filing of the report of a special committee, the subject judge may send a written response to the members of the judicial council. The subject judge must also be given an opportunity to present argument, personally or through counsel, written or oral, as determined by the judicial council. The subject judge must not otherwise communicate with judicial-council members about the matter.

(b) Judicial–Council Action.

(1) *Discretionary Actions.* Subject to the subject judge's rights set forth in subsection (a), the judicial council may:

(A) dismiss the complaint because:

(i) even if the claim is true, the claimed conduct is not conduct prejudicial to the effective and expeditious administration of the business of the courts and does not indicate a mental or physical disability resulting in inability to discharge the duties of office;

(ii) the complaint is directly related to the merits of a decision or procedural ruling;

(iii) the facts on which the complaint is based have not been established; or

(iv) the complaint is otherwise not appropriate for consideration under 28 U.S.C. §§ 351–364.

(B) conclude the proceeding because appropriate corrective action has been taken or intervening events have made the proceeding unnecessary.

(C) refer the complaint to the Judicial Conference with the judicial council's recommendations for action.

(D) take remedial action to ensure the effective and expeditious administration of the business of the courts, including:

(i) censuring or reprimanding the subject judge, either by private communication or by public announcement;

(ii) ordering that no new cases be assigned to the subject judge for a limited, fixed period;

(iii) in the case of a magistrate judge, ordering the chief judge of the district court to take action specified by the council, including the initiation of removal proceedings under 28 U.S.C. § 631(i) or 42 U.S.C. § 300aa–12(c)(2);

(iv) in the case of a bankruptcy judge, removing the judge from office under 28 U.S.C. § 152(e);

(v) in the case of a circuit or district judge, requesting the judge to retire voluntarily with the provision (if necessary) that ordinary length-of-service requirements be waived;

(vi) in the case of a circuit or district judge who is eligible to retire but does not do so, certifying the disability of the judge under 28 U.S.C. § 372(b) so that an additional judge may be appointed; and

(vii) in the case of a circuit chief judge or district chief judge, finding that the judge is temporarily unable to perform chief-judge duties, with the result that those duties devolve to the next eligible judge in accordance with 28 U.S.C. § 45(d) or § 136(e).

(E) take any combination of actions described in (b)(1)(A)–(D) of this Rule that is within its power.

(2) *Mandatory Actions.* A judicial council must refer a complaint to the Judicial Conference if the council determines that a circuit judge or district judge may have engaged in conduct that:

(A) might constitute ground for impeachment; or

(B) in the interest of justice, is not amenable to resolution by the judicial council.

(c) Inadequate Basis for Decision. If the judicial council finds that a special committee's report, recommendations, and record provide an inadequate basis for decision, it may return the matter to the committee for further investigation and a new report, or it may conduct further investigation. If the judicial council decides to conduct further investigation, the subject judge must be given adequate prior notice in writing of that decision and of the general scope and purpose of the additional investigation. The judicial council's conduct of the additional investigation must generally accord with the procedures and powers set forth in Rules 13 through 16 for the conduct of an investigation by a special committee.

(d) Judicial–Council Vote. Judicial–council action must be taken by a majority of those members of the council who are not disqualified. A decision to remove a bankruptcy judge from office requires a majority vote of all the members of the judicial council.

(e) Recommendation for Fee Reimbursement. If the complaint has been finally dismissed or concluded under (b)(1)(A) or (B) of this Rule, and if the subject judge so requests, the judicial council may recommend that the Director of the Administrative Office use funds appropriated to the Judiciary to reimburse the judge for reasonable expenses incurred during the investigation, when those expenses would not have been incurred but for the requirements of the Act and these Rules. Reasonable expenses include attorneys' fees and expenses related to a successful defense or prosecution of a proceeding under Rule 21(a) or (b).

(f) Judicial–Council Order. Judicial–council action must be by written order. Unless the judicial council finds that extraordinary reasons would make it contrary to the interests of justice, the order must be accompanied by a memorandum setting forth the factual determinations on which it is based and the reasons for the council action. Such a memorandum may incorporate all or part of any underlying special-committee report. If the complaint was initiated by identification under Rule 5, the memorandum must so indicate. The order and memoranda incorporated by reference in the order must be provided to the complainant, the subject judge, and the Committee on Judicial Conduct and Disability. The complainant and the subject judge must be notified of any right to review of the judicial council's decision as provided in Rule 21(b). If the complaint was identified under Rule 5 or filed by its subject judge, the judicial council must transmit the order and memoranda incorporated by reference in the order to the Committee on Judicial Conduct and Disability for review in accordance with Rule 21. In the event of such a transmission, the subject judge may make a written submission to the Committee on Judicial Conduct and Disability but will have no further right of review.

[Adopted March 11, 2008, effective April 10, 2008. Amended effective September 17, 2015; April 12, 2018.]

Commentary on Rule 20

This Rule is largely adapted from the Illustrative Rules.

Rule 20(a) provides that within 21 days after the filing of the report of a special committee, the subject judge may address a written response to all of the members of the judicial council. The subject judge must also be given an opportunity to present argument to the judicial council, personally or through counsel, or both, at the direction of the council. Whether that argument is written or oral would be for the judicial council to determine. The subject judge may not otherwise communicate with judicial-council members about the matter.

Rule 20(b)(1)(D) recites the remedial actions enumerated in 28 U.S.C. § 354(a)(2) while making clear that this list is not exhaustive. A judicial council may consider lesser remedies. Some remedies may be unique to senior judges, whose caseloads can be modified by agreement or through statutory designation and certification processes.

Under 28 U.S.C. §§ 45(d) and 136(e), which provide for succession where "a chief judge is temporarily unable to perform his duties as such," the determination whether such an inability exists is not expressly reserved to the chief judge. Nor, indeed, is it assigned to any particular judge or court-governance body. Clearly, however, a chief judge's inability to function as chief could implicate "the effective and expeditious administration of justice," which the judicial council of the circuit must, under 28 U.S.C. § 332(d)(1), "make all necessary and appropriate orders" to secure. For this reason, such reassignment is among a judicial council's remedial options, as subsection (b)(1)(D)(vii) makes clear. Consistent with 28 U.S.C. §§ 45(d) and 136(e), however, any reassignment of chief-judge duties must not outlast the subject judge's inability to perform them. Nor can such reassignment result in any extension of the subject judge's term as chief judge.

Rule 20(c) provides that if the judicial council decides to conduct an additional investigation, the subject judge must be given adequate prior notice in writing of that decision and of the general scope and purpose of the additional investigation. The conduct of the investigation will be generally in accordance with the procedures set forth in Rules 13 through 16 for the conduct of an investigation by a special committee. However, if hearings are held, the judicial council may limit testimony or the presentation of evidence to avoid unnecessary repetition of testimony and evidence before the special committee.

Rule 20(d) provides that judicial-council action must be taken by a majority of those members of the council who are not disqualified, except that a decision to remove a bankruptcy judge from office requires a majority of all the members of the council as required by 28 U.S.C. § 152(e). However, it is inappropriate to apply a similar rule to the less severe actions that a judicial council may take under the Act. If some members of the judicial council are disqualified in the matter, their disqualification should not be given the effect of a vote against council action.

With regard to Rule 20(e), the judicial council, on the request of the subject judge, may recommend to the Director of the Administrative Office that the subject judge be reimbursed for reasonable expenses incurred, including attorneys' fees. The judicial council has the authority to recommend such reimbursement where, after investigation by a special committee, the complaint has been finally dismissed or concluded under subsection (b)(1)(A) or (B) of this Rule. It is contemplated that such reimbursement may be provided for the successful prosecution or defense of a proceeding under Rule 21(a) or (b), in other words, one that results in a Rule 20(b)(1)(A) or (B) dismissal or conclusion.

Rule 20(f) requires that judicial-council action be by order and, normally, that it be supported with a memorandum of factual determinations and reasons. Notice of the action must be given to the complainant and the subject judge, and must include notice of any right to petition for review of the judicial council's decision under Rule 21(b). Because an identified complaint has no "complainant" to petition for review, a judicial council's dispositive order on an identified complaint on which a special committee has been appointed must be transmitted to the Committee on Judicial Conduct and Disability for review. The same will apply where a complaint was filed by its subject judge.

ARTICLE VI.   REVIEW BY COMMITTEE ON JUDICIAL CONDUCT AND DISABILITY

RULE 21.   COMMITTEE ON JUDICIAL CONDUCT AND DISABILITY

(a) Committee Review. The Committee on Judicial Conduct and Disability, consisting of seven members, considers and disposes of all petitions for review under (b) of this Rule, in conformity with the Committee's jurisdictional statement. Its review of judicial-council orders is for errors of law, clear errors of fact, or abuse of discretion. Its disposition of petitions for review is ordinarily final. The Judicial Conference may, in its sole discretion, review any such Committee decision, but a complainant or subject judge does not have a right to this review.

(b) Reviewable Matters.

(1) *Upon Petition.* A complainant or subject judge may petition the Committee for review of a judicial-council order entered in accordance with:

(A) Rule 20(b)(1)(A), (B), (D), or (E); or

(B) Rule 19(b)(1) or (4) if one or more members of the judicial council dissented from the order.

(2) *Upon Committee's Initiative.* At its initiative and in its sole discretion, the Committee may review any judicial-council order entered under Rule 19(b)(1) or (4), but only to determine whether a special committee should be appointed. Before undertaking the review, the Committee must invite that judicial council to explain why it believes the appointment of a special committee is unnecessary, unless the reasons are clearly stated in the council's order denying the petition for review. If the Committee believes that it would benefit from a submission by the subject judge, it may issue an appropriate request. If the Committee determines that a special committee should be appointed, the Committee must issue a written decision giving its reasons.

(c) Committee Vote. Any member of the Committee from the same circuit as the subject judge is disqualified from considering or voting on a petition for review related to that subject judge. Committee decisions under (b) of this Rule must be by majority vote of the qualified Committee members. Those members hearing the petition for review should serve in that capacity until final disposition of the petition, whether or not their term of Committee membership has ended. If only six members are qualified to consider a petition for review, the Chief Justice shall select an additional judge to join the qualified members to consider the petition. If four or fewer members are qualified to consider a petition for review, the Chief Justice shall select a panel of five judges, including the qualified Committee members, to consider it.

(d) Additional Investigation. Except in extraordinary circumstances, the Committee will not conduct an additional investigation. The Committee may return the matter to the judicial council with directions to undertake an additional investigation. If the Committee conducts an additional investigation, it will exercise the powers of the Judicial Conference under 28 U.S.C. § 331.

(e) Oral Argument; Personal Appearance. There is ordinarily no oral argument or personal appearance before the Committee. In its discretion, the Committee may permit written submissions.

(f) Committee Decision. A Committee decision under this Rule must be transmitted promptly to the Judicial Conference. Other distribution will be by the Administrative Office at the direction of the Committee chair.

(g) Finality. All orders of the Judicial Conference or of the Committee (when the Conference does not exercise its power of review) are final.

[Adopted March 11, 2008, effective April 10, 2008. Amended effective September 17, 2015; April 12, 2018.]

Commentary on Rule 21

This Rule is largely self-explanatory.

Rule 21(a) is intended to clarify that the delegation of power to the Committee on Judicial Conduct and Disability to dispose of petitions for review does not preclude review of such dispositions by the Judicial Conference. However, there is no right to such review in any party.

Rules 21(b)(1)(B) and (b)(2) are intended to fill a jurisdictional gap as to review of a dismissal or a conclusion of a complaint under Rule 19(b)(1) or (4). Where one or more members of a judicial council reviewing a petition have dissented, the complainant or the subject judge has the right to petition for review by the Committee. Under Rule 21(b)(2), the Committee may review such a dismissal or conclusion in its sole discretion, whether or not a dissent occurred, and only as to the appointment of a special committee. Any review under Rule 21(b)(2) will be conducted as soon as practicable after the dismissal or conclusion at issue. No party has a right to such review, and such review will be rare.

Rule 21(c) provides for review only by Committee members from circuits other than that of the subject judge. The Rule provides that every petition for review must be considered and voted on by at least five, and if possible by seven, qualified Committee members to avoid the possibility of tie votes. If six, or four or fewer, members are qualified, the Chief Justice shall appoint other judges to join the qualified members to consider the petition for review. To the extent possible, the judges whom the Chief Justice selects to join the qualified members should be drawn from among former members of the Committee.

Under this Rule, all Committee decisions are final in that they are unreviewable unless the Judicial Conference, in its discretion, decides to review a decision. Committee decisions, however, do not necessarily constitute final action on a complaint for purposes of Rule 24.

RULE 22.   PROCEDURES FOR REVIEW

(a) Filing Petition for Review. A petition for review of a judicial-council decision on a complaint referred to a special committee may be filed by sending a brief written statement to the Committee on Judicial Conduct and Disability at JCD_PetitionforReview@ao.uscourts.gov or to:

Judicial Conference Committee on Judicial Conduct and Disability
Attn: Office of General Counsel
Administrative Office of the United States Courts

One Columbus Circle, NE
Washington, D.C. 20544

The Administrative Office will send a copy of the petition for review to the complainant or subject judge, as the case may be.

(b) Form and Contents of Petition. No particular form is required. The petition for review must contain a short statement of the basic facts underlying the complaint, the history of its consideration before the appropriate judicial council, a copy of the council's decision, and the grounds on which the petitioner seeks review. The petition for review must specify the date and docket number of the judicial council order for which review is sought. The petitioner may attach any documents or correspondence arising in the course of the proceeding before the judicial council or its special committee. A petition for review should not normally exceed 20 pages plus necessary attachments. A petition for review must be signed by the petitioner or his or her attorney.

(c) Time. A petition for review must be submitted within 42 days after the date of the order for which review is sought.

(d) Action on Receipt of Petition. When a petition for review of a judicial-council decision on a complaint referred to a special committee is submitted in accordance with this Rule, the Administrative Office shall acknowledge its receipt, notify the chair of the Committee on Judicial Conduct and Disability, and distribute the petition to the members of the Committee for their deliberation.

[Adopted March 11, 2008, effective April 10, 2008. Amended effective September 17, 2015; April 12, 2018.]

Commentary on Rule 22

Rule 22 is self-explanatory.

ARTICLE VII. MISCELLANEOUS RULES

RULE 23. CONFIDENTIALITY

(a) General Rule. The consideration of a complaint by a chief judge, a special committee, a judicial council, or the Committee on Judicial Conduct and Disability is confidential. Information about this consideration must not be disclosed by any judge or employee of the Judiciary or by any person who records or transcribes testimony except as allowed by these Rules. A chief judge may disclose the existence of a proceeding under these Rules when necessary or appropriate to maintain public confidence in the Judiciary's ability to redress misconduct or disability.

(b) Files. All files related to a complaint must be separately maintained with appropriate security precautions to ensure confidentiality.

(c) Disclosure in Decisions. Except as otherwise provided in Rule 24, written decisions of a chief judge, a judicial council, or the Committee on Judicial Conduct and Disability, and dissenting opinions or separate statements of members of a council or the Committee may contain information and exhibits that the authors consider appropriate for inclusion, and the information and exhibits may be made public.

(d) Availability to Judicial Conference. On request of the Judicial Conference or its Committee on Judicial Conduct and Disability, the circuit clerk must furnish any requested records related to a complaint. For auditing purposes, the circuit clerk must provide access to the Committee on Judicial Conduct and Disability to records of proceedings under the Act at the site where the records are kept.

(e) Availability to District Court. If the judicial council directs the initiation of proceedings for removal of a magistrate judge under Rule 20(b)(1)(D)(iii), the circuit clerk must provide to the chief judge of the district court copies of the report of the special committee and any other documents and records that were before the council at the time of its decision. On request of the chief judge of the district court, the judicial council may authorize release to that chief judge of any other records relating to the investigation.

(f) Impeachment Proceedings. If the Judicial Conference determines that consideration of impeachment may be warranted, it must transmit the record of all relevant proceedings to the Speaker of the House of Representatives.

(g) Subject Judge's Consent. If both the subject judge and the chief judge consent in writing, any materials from the files may be disclosed to any person. In any such disclosure, the chief judge may require that the identity of the complainant, or of witnesses in an investigation conducted under these Rules, not be revealed.

(h) Disclosure in Special Circumstances. The Judicial Conference, its Committee on Judicial Conduct and Disability, or a judicial council may authorize disclosure of information about the consideration of a complaint, including the papers, documents, and transcripts relating to the investigation, to the extent that disclosure is justified by special circumstances and is not prohibited by the Act. Disclosure may be made to judicial researchers engaged in the study or evaluation of experience under the Act and related modes of judicial discipline, but only where the study or evaluation has been specifically approved by the Judicial Conference or by the Committee on Judicial Conduct and Disability. Appropriate steps must be taken to protect the identities of the subject judge, the complainant, and witnesses from public disclosure. Other appropriate safeguards to protect against the dissemination of confidential information may be imposed.

(i) Disclosure of Identity by Subject Judge. Nothing in this Rule precludes the subject judge from acknowledging that he or she is the judge referred to in documents made public under Rule 24.

(j) Assistance and Consultation. Nothing in this Rule prohibits a chief judge, a special committee, a judicial council, or the Judicial Conference or its Committee on Judicial Conduct and Disability, in the performance of any function authorized under the Act or these Rules, from seeking the help of qualified staff or experts or from consulting other judges who may be helpful regarding the performance of that function.

[Adopted March 11, 2008, effective April 10, 2008. Amended effective September 17, 2015; April 12, 2018.]

Commentary on Rule 23

Rule 23 was adapted from the Illustrative Rules.

The Act applies a rule of confidentiality to "papers, documents, and records of proceedings related to investigations conducted under this chapter" and states that they may not be disclosed "by any person in any proceeding," with enumerated exceptions. 28 U.S.C. § 360(a). Three questions arise: Who is bound by the confidentiality rule, what proceedings are subject to the rule, and who is within the circle of people who may have access to information without breaching the rule?

With regard to the first question, Rule 23(a) provides that judges, employees of the Judiciary, and those persons involved in recording proceedings and preparing transcripts are obliged to respect the confidentiality requirement. This of course includes subject judges who do not consent to identification under Rule 23(i).

With regard to the second question, Rule 23(a) applies the rule of confidentiality broadly to consideration of a complaint at any stage.

With regard to the third question, there is no barrier of confidentiality among a chief judge, a judicial council, the Judicial Conference, and the Committee on Judicial Conduct and Disability. Each may have access to any of the confidential records for use in their consideration of a referred matter, a petition for review, or monitoring the administration of the Act. A district court may have similar access if the judicial council orders the district court to initiate proceedings to remove a magistrate judge from office, and Rule 23(e) so provides.

In extraordinary circumstances, a chief judge may disclose the existence of a proceeding under these Rules. The disclosure of such information in high-visibility or controversial cases is to reassure the public that the Judiciary is capable of redressing judicial misconduct or disability. Moreover, the confidentiality requirement does not prevent the chief judge from "communicat[ing] orally or in writing with . . . [persons] who may have knowledge of the matter" as part of a limited inquiry conducted by the chief judge under Rule 11(b).

Rule 23 recognizes that there must be some exceptions to the Act's confidentiality requirement. For example, the Act requires that certain orders and the reasons for them must be made public. 28 U.S.C. § 360(b). Rule 23(c) makes it explicit that written decisions, as well as dissenting opinions and separate statements, may contain references to information that would otherwise be confidential and that such information may be made public. However, subsection (c) is subject to Rule 24(a), which provides the general rule regarding the public availability of decisions. For example, the name of a subject judge cannot be made public in a decision if disclosure of the name is prohibited by that Rule.

The Act makes clear that there is a barrier of confidentiality between the judicial branch and the legislative branch. It provides that material may be disclosed to Congress only if it is believed necessary to an impeachment investigation or trial of a judge. 28 U.S.C. § 360(a)(2). Accordingly, Section 355(b) of the Act requires the Judicial Conference to transmit the record of a proceeding to the House of Representatives if the Conference believes that impeachment of a subject judge may be appropriate. Rule 23(f) implements this requirement.

The Act provides that confidential materials may be disclosed if authorized in writing by the subject judge and by the chief judge. 28 U.S.C. § 360(a)(3). Rule 23(g) implements this requirement. Once the subject judge has consented to the disclosure of confidential materials related to a complaint, the chief judge ordinarily will refuse consent only to the extent necessary to protect the confidentiality interests of the complainant or of witnesses who have testified in investigatory proceedings or who have provided information in response to a limited inquiry undertaken pursuant to Rule 11. It will generally be necessary, therefore, for the chief judge to require that the identities of the complainant or of such witnesses, as well as any

identifying information, be shielded in any materials disclosed, except insofar as the chief judge has secured the consent of the complainant or of a particular witness to disclosure, or there is a demonstrated need for disclosure of the information that, in the judgment of the chief judge, outweighs the confidentiality interest of the complainant or of a particular witness (as may be the case where the complainant is delusional or where the complainant or a particular witness has already demonstrated a lack of concern about maintaining the confidentiality of the proceedings).

Rule 23(h) permits disclosure of additional information in circumstances not enumerated. For example, disclosure may be appropriate to permit a prosecution for perjury based on testimony given before a special committee. Another example might involve evidence of criminal conduct by a judge discovered by a special committee.

Subsection (h) also permits the authorization of disclosure of information about the consideration of a complaint, including the papers, documents, and transcripts relating to the investigation, to judicial researchers engaged in the study or evaluation of experience under the Act and related modes of judicial discipline. The Rule envisions disclosure of information from the official record of a complaint proceeding to a limited category of persons for appropriately authorized research purposes only, and with appropriate safeguards to protect individual identities in any published research results. In authorizing disclosure, a judicial council may refuse to release particular materials when such release would be contrary to the interests of justice, or when those materials constitute purely internal communications. The Rule does not envision disclosure of purely internal communications between judges and their colleagues and staff.

Under Rule 23(j), any of the specified judges or entities performing a function authorized under these Rules may seek expert or staff assistance or may consult with other judges who may be helpful regarding performance of that function; the confidentiality requirement does not preclude this. A chief judge, for example, may properly seek the advice and assistance of another judge who the chief judge deems to be in the best position to communicate with the subject judge in an attempt to bring about corrective action. As another example, a new chief judge may wish to confer with a predecessor to learn how similar complaints have been handled. In consulting with other judges, of course, a chief judge should disclose information regarding the complaint only to the extent the chief judge deems necessary under the circumstances.

RULE 24.   PUBLIC AVAILABILITY OF DECISIONS

(a) General Rule; Specific Cases. When final action has been taken on a complaint and it is no longer subject to review, all orders entered by the chief judge and judicial council, including memoranda incorporated by reference in those orders and any dissenting opinions or separate statements by members of the judicial council, but excluding any orders under Rule 5 or 11(f), must be made public, with the following exceptions:

(1) if the complaint is finally dismissed under Rule 11(c) without the appointment of a special committee, or if it is concluded under Rule 11(d) because of voluntary corrective action, the publicly available materials must not disclose the name of the subject judge without his or her consent.

(2) if the complaint is concluded because of intervening events, or dismissed at any time after a special committee is appointed, the judicial council must determine whether the name of the subject judge should be disclosed.

(3) if the complaint is finally disposed of by a privately communicated censure or reprimand, the publicly available materials must not disclose either the name of the subject judge or the text of the reprimand.

(4) if the complaint is finally disposed of under Rule 20(b)(1)(D) by any action other than private censure or reprimand, the text of the dispositive order must be included in the materials made public, and the name of the subject judge must be disclosed.

(5) the name of the complainant must not be disclosed in materials made public under this Rule unless the chief judge orders disclosure.

(b) Manner of Making Public. The orders described in (a) must be made public by placing them in a publicly accessible file in the office of the circuit clerk and by placing the orders on the court's public website. If the orders appear to have precedential value, the chief judge may cause them to be published. In addition, the Committee on Judicial Conduct and Disability will make available on the Judiciary's website, www.uscourts.gov, selected illustrative orders described in paragraph (a), appropriately redacted, to provide additional information to the public on how complaints are addressed under the Act.

(c) Orders of Committee on Judicial Conduct and Disability. Orders of the Committee on Judicial Conduct and Disability constituting final action in a complaint proceeding arising from a particular circuit will be made available to the public in the office of the circuit clerk of the relevant court of appeals. The Committee on Judicial Conduct and Disability will also make such orders available on the Judiciary's website, www.uscourts.gov. When authorized by the Committee on Judicial Conduct and Disability, other orders related to complaint proceedings will similarly be made available.

(d) Complaint Referred to Judicial Conference. If a complaint is referred to the Judicial Conference under Rule 20(b)(1)(C) or 20(b)(2), materials relating to the complaint will be made public only if ordered by the Judicial Conference.

[Adopted March 11, 2008, effective April 10, 2008. Amended effective September 17, 2015; April 12, 2018.]

Commentary on Rule 24

Rule 24 is adapted from the Illustrative Rules and the recommendations of the Breyer Committee.

The Act requires the circuits to make available only written orders of a judicial council or the Judicial Conference imposing some form of sanction. 28 U.S.C. § 360(b). The Judicial Conference, however, has long recognized the desirability of public availability of a broader range of orders and other materials. In 1994, the Judicial Conference "urge[d] all circuits and courts covered by the Act to submit to the West Publishing Company, for publication in Federal Reporter 3d, and to Lexis all orders issued pursuant to [the Act] that are deemed by the issuing circuit or court to have significant precedential value to other circuits and courts covered by the Act." Report of the Proceedings of the Judicial Conference of the United States, Mar. 1994, at 28. Following this recommendation, the 2000 revision of the Illustrative Rules contained a public availability provision very similar to Rule 24. In 2002, the Judicial Conference again voted to encourage the circuits "to submit non-routine public orders disposing of complaints of judicial misconduct or disability for publication by on-line and print services." Report of the Proceedings of the Judicial Conference of the United

States, Sept. 2002, at 58. The Breyer Committee Report further emphasized that "[p]osting such orders on the judicial branch's public website would not only benefit judges directly, it would also encourage scholarly commentary and analysis of the orders." Breyer Committee Report, 239 F.R.D. at 216. With these considerations in mind, Rule 24 provides for public availability of a wide range of materials.

Rule 24 provides for public availability of orders of a chief judge, a judicial council, and the Committee on Judicial Conduct and Disability, as well as the texts of memoranda incorporated by reference in those orders, together with any dissenting opinions or separate statements by members of the judicial council. No memoranda other than those incorporated by reference in those orders shall be disclosed. However, these orders and memoranda are to be made public only when final action on the complaint has been taken and any right of review has been exhausted. The provision that decisions will be made public only after final action has been taken is designed in part to avoid public disclosure of the existence of pending proceedings. Whether the name of the subject judge is disclosed will then depend on the nature of the final action. If the final action is an order predicated on a finding of misconduct or disability (other than a privately communicated censure or reprimand) the name of the subject judge must be made public. If the final action is dismissal of the complaint, the name of the subject judge must not be disclosed. Rule 24(a)(1) provides that where a proceeding is concluded under Rule 11(d) by the chief judge on the basis of voluntary corrective action, the name of the subject judge must not be disclosed. Shielding the name of the subject judge in this circumstance should encourage informal disposition.

If a complaint is dismissed as moot, or because intervening events have made action on the complaint unnecessary, after appointment of a special committee, Rule 24(a)(2) allows the judicial council to determine whether the subject judge will be identified. In such a case, no final decision has been rendered on the merits, but it may be in the public interest—particularly if a judicial officer resigns in the course of an investigation—to make the identity of the subject judge known.

Once a special committee has been appointed, and a proceeding is concluded by the full judicial council on the basis of a remedial order of the council, Rule 24(a)(4) provides for disclosure of the name of the subject judge.

Rule 24(a)(5) provides that the identity of the complainant will be disclosed only if the chief judge so orders. Identifying the complainant when the subject judge is not identified would increase the likelihood that the identity of the subject judge would become publicly known, thus circumventing the policy of nondisclosure. It may not always be practicable to shield the complainant's identity while making public disclosure of the judicial council's order and supporting memoranda; in some circumstances, moreover, the complainant may consent to public identification.

Rule 24(b) makes clear that circuits must post on their external websites all orders required to be made public under Rule 24(a).

Matters involving orders issued following a special-committee investigation often involve highly sensitive situations, and it is important that judicial councils have every opportunity to reach a correct and just outcome. This would include the ability to reach informal resolution before a subject judge's identity must be released. But there must also come a point of procedural finality. The date of finality—and thus the time at which other safeguards and rules such as the publication requirement are triggered—is the date on which the judicial council issues a Final Order. *See In re Complaint of Judicial Misconduct*, 751 F.3d 611, 617 (2014) (requiring publication of a judicial-council order "[e]ven though the period for review had not yet elapsed" and concluding that "the order was a final decision because the Council had adjudicated the matter on the merits after having received a report from a special investigating committee"). As determined in the cited case, modifications of this kind to a final order are subject to review by the Committee on Judicial Conduct and Disability.

RULE 25.   DISQUALIFICATION

(a) **General Rule.** Any judge is disqualified from participating in any proceeding under these Rules if the judge, in his or her discretion, concludes that circumstances warrant disqualification. If a complaint is filed by a judge, that judge is disqualified from participating in any consideration of the complaint except to the extent that these Rules provide for a complainant's participation. A chief judge who has identified a complaint under Rule 5 is not automatically disqualified from considering the complaint.

(b) **Subject Judge.** A subject judge is disqualified from considering a complaint except to the extent that these Rules provide for participation by a subject judge.

(c) **Chief Judge Disqualified from Considering Petition for Review of Chief Judge's Order.** If a petition for review of the chief judge's order entered under Rule 11(c), (d), or (e) is filed with the judicial council in accordance with Rule 18, the chief judge is disqualified from participating in the council's consideration of the petition.

(d) **Member of Special Committee Not Disqualified.** A member of the judicial council who serves on a special committee, including the chief judge, is not disqualified from participating in council consideration of the committee's report.

(e) **Subject Judge's Disqualification.** After Appointment of Special Committee. Upon appointment of a special committee, the subject judge is disqualified from participating in the identification or consideration of any complaint, related or unrelated to the pending matter, under the Act or these Rules. The disqualification continues until all proceedings on the complaint against the subject judge are finally terminated with no further right of review.

(f) **Substitute for Disqualified Chief Judge.** If the chief judge is disqualified from performing duties that the Act and these Rules assign to a chief judge, those duties must be assigned to the most-senior active circuit judge not disqualified. If all circuit judges in regular active service are disqualified, the judicial council may determine whether to request a transfer under Rule 26, or, in the interest of sound judicial administration, to permit the chief judge to dispose of the complaint on the merits. Members of the judicial council who are named in the complaint may participate in this determination if necessary to obtain a quorum of the council.

(g) **Judicial–Council Action When Multiple Judges Disqualified.** Notwithstanding any other provision in these Rules to the contrary,

(1) a member of the judicial council who is a subject judge may participate in its disposition if:

(A) participation by one or more subject judges is necessary to obtain a quorum of the judicial council;

(B) the judicial council finds that the lack of a quorum is due to the naming of one or more judges in the complaint for the purpose of disqualifying that judge or those judges, or to the naming of one or more judges based on their

participation in a decision excluded from the definition of misconduct under Rule 3(h)(3); and

(C) the judicial council votes that it is necessary, appropriate, and in the interest of sound judicial administration that one or more subject judges be eligible to act.

(2) otherwise disqualified members may participate in votes taken under (g)(1)(B) and (g)(1)(C).

(h) **Disqualification of Members of Committee on Judicial Conduct and Disability.** No member of the Committee on Judicial Conduct and Disability is disqualified from participating in any proceeding under the Act or these Rules because of consultations with a chief judge, a member of a special committee, or a member of a judicial council about the interpretation or application of the Act or these Rules, unless the member believes that the consultation would prevent fair-minded participation.

[Adopted March 11, 2008, effective April 10, 2008. Amended effective September 17, 2015; April 12, 2018.]

Commentary on Rule 25

Rule 25 is adapted from the Illustrative Rules.

Subsection (a) provides the general rule for disqualification. Of course, a judge is not disqualified simply because the subject judge is on the same court. However, this subsection recognizes that there may be cases in which an appearance of bias or prejudice is created by circumstances other than an association with the subject judge as a colleague. For example, a judge may have a familial relationship with a complainant or subject judge. When such circumstances exist, a judge may, in his or her discretion, conclude that disqualification is warranted.

Subsection (e) makes it clear that the disqualification of the subject judge relates only to the subject judge's participation in any proceeding arising under the Act or these Rules. For example, the subject judge cannot initiate complaints by identification, conduct limited inquiries, or choose between dismissal and special-committee investigation as the threshold disposition of a complaint. Likewise, the subject judge cannot participate in any proceeding arising under the Act or these Rules as a member of any special committee, the judicial council of the circuit, the Judicial Conference, or the Committee on Judicial Conduct and Disability. The Illustrative Rule, based on Section 359(a) of the Act, is ambiguous and could be read to disqualify a subject judge from service of any kind on each of the bodies mentioned. This is undoubtedly not the intent of the Act; such a disqualification would be anomalous in light of the Act's allowing a subject judge to continue to decide cases and to continue to exercise the powers of chief circuit or district judge. It would also create a substantial deterrence to the appointment of special committees, particularly where a special committee is needed solely because the chief judge may not decide matters of credibility in his or her review under Rule 11.

While a subject judge is barred by Rule 25(b) from participating in the disposition of the complaint in which he or she is named, Rule 25(e) recognizes that participation in proceedings arising under the Act or these Rules by a judge who is the subject of a special committee investigation may lead to an appearance of self-interest in creating substantive and procedural precedents governing such proceedings. Rule 25(e) bars such participation.

Under the Act, a complaint against the chief judge is to be handled by "that circuit judge in regular active service next senior in date of commission." 28 U.S.C. § 351(c). The Rules do not purport to prescribe who is to preside over meetings of the judicial council. Consequently, where the presiding member of the judicial council is disqualified from participating under these Rules, the order of precedence prescribed by Rule 25(f) for performing "the duties and responsibilities of the chief circuit judge under these Rules" does not apply to determine the acting presiding member of the council. That is a matter left to the internal rules or operating practices of each judicial council. In most cases the most senior active circuit judge who is a member of the judicial council and who is not disqualified will preside.

Sometimes a single complaint is filed against a large group of judges. If the normal disqualification rules are observed in such a case, no court of appeals judge can serve as acting chief judge of the circuit, and the judicial council will be without appellate members. Where the complaint is against all circuit and district judges, under normal rules no member of the judicial council can perform the duties assigned to the council under the statute.

A similar problem is created by successive complaints arising out of the same underlying grievance. For example, a complainant files a complaint against a district judge based on alleged misconduct, and the complaint is dismissed by the chief judge under the statute. The complainant may then file a complaint against the chief judge for dismissing the first complaint, and when that complaint is dismissed by the next senior judge, still a third complaint may be filed. The threat is that the complainant will bump down the seniority ladder until, once again, there is no member of the court of appeals who can serve as acting chief judge for the purpose of the next complaint. Similarly, complaints involving the merits of litigation may involve a series of decisions in which many judges participated or in which a rehearing en banc was denied by the court of appeals, and the complaint may name a majority of the judicial council as subject judges.

In recognition that these multiple-judge complaints are virtually always meritless, the judicial council is given discretion to determine: (1) whether it is necessary, appropriate, and in the interest of sound judicial administration to permit the chief judge to dispose of a complaint where it would otherwise be impossible for any active circuit judge in the circuit to act, and (2) whether it is necessary, appropriate, and in the interest of sound judicial administration, after appropriate findings as to need and justification are made, to permit subject judges of the judicial council to participate in the disposition of a petition for review where it would otherwise be impossible to obtain a quorum.

Applying a rule of necessity in these situations is consistent with the appearance of justice. See, e.g., In re Complaint of Doe, 2 F.3d 308 (8th Cir. Jud. Council 1993) (invoking the rule of necessity); In re Complaint of Judicial Misconduct, No. 91–80464 (9th Cir. Jud. Council 1992) (same). There is no unfairness in permitting the chief judge to dispose of a patently insubstantial complaint that names all active circuit judges in the circuit.

Similarly, there is no unfairness in permitting subject judges, in these circumstances, to participate in the review of the chief judge's dismissal of an insubstantial complaint. The remaining option is to assign the matter to another body. Among other alternatives, the judicial council may request a transfer of the petition under Rule 26. Given the administrative inconvenience and delay involved in these alternatives, it is desirable to request a transfer only if the judicial council determines that the petition for review is substantial enough to warrant such action.

In the unlikely event that a quorum of the judicial council cannot be obtained to consider the report of a special committee, it would normally be necessary to request a transfer under Rule 26.

Rule 25(h) recognizes that the jurisdictional statement of the Committee on Judicial Conduct and Disability contemplates consultation between members of the Committee and judicial participants in proceedings under the Act and these Rules. Such consultation should not automatically preclude participation by a member in that proceeding.

RULE 26. TRANSFER TO ANOTHER JUDICIAL COUNCIL

In exceptional circumstances, the chief judge or the judicial council may ask the Chief Justice to transfer a proceeding based on a complaint identified under Rule 5 or filed under Rule 6 to the judicial council of another circuit. The request for a transfer may be made at any stage of the proceeding before a reference to the Judicial Conference under Rule 20(b)(1)(C) or 20(b)(2) or a petition for review is filed under Rule 22. Upon receiving such a request, the Chief Justice may refuse the request or select the transferee judicial council, which may then exercise the powers of a judicial council under these Rules.

[Adopted March 11, 2008, effective April 10, 2008. Amended effective September 17, 2015; April 12, 2018.]

Commentary on Rule 26

Rule 26 is new; it implements the Breyer Committee's recommended use of transfers. Breyer Committee Report, 239 F.R.D. at 214–15.

Rule 26 authorizes the transfer of a complaint proceeding to another judicial council selected by the Chief Justice. Such transfers may be appropriate, for example, in the case of a serious complaint where there are multiple disqualifications among the original judicial council, where the issues are highly visible and a local disposition may weaken public confidence in the process, where internal tensions arising in the council as a result of the complaint render disposition by a less involved council appropriate, or where a complaint calls into question policies or governance of the home court of appeals. The power to effect a transfer is lodged in the Chief Justice to avoid disputes in a judicial council over where to transfer a sensitive matter and to ensure that the transferee council accepts the matter.

Upon receipt of a transferred proceeding, the transferee judicial council shall determine the proper stage at which to begin consideration of the complaint—for example, reference to the transferee chief judge, appointment of a special committee, etc.

RULE 27. WITHDRAWAL OF COMPLAINT OR PETITION FOR REVIEW

(a) Complaint Pending Before Chief Judge. With the chief judge's consent, the complainant may withdraw a complaint that is before the chief judge for a decision under Rule 11. The withdrawal of a complaint will not prevent the chief judge from identifying or having to identify a complaint under Rule 5 based on the withdrawn complaint.

(b) Complaint Pending Before Special Committee or Judicial Council. After a complaint has been referred to the special committee for investigation and before the committee files its report, the complainant may withdraw the complaint only with the consent of both the subject judge and either the special committee or the judicial council.

(c) Petition for Review. A petition for review addressed to the judicial council under Rule 18, or the Committee on Judicial Conduct and Disability under Rule 22, may be withdrawn if no action on the petition has been taken.

[Adopted March 11, 2008, effective April 10, 2008. Amended effective September 17, 2015; April 12, 2018.]

Commentary on Rule 27

Rule 27 is adapted from the Illustrative Rules and treats the complaint proceeding, once begun, as a matter of public business rather than as the property of the complainant. Accordingly, the chief judge or the judicial council remains responsible for addressing any complaint under the Act, even a complaint that has been formally withdrawn by the complainant.

Under subsection (a), a complaint pending before the chief judge may be withdrawn if the chief judge consents. Where the complaint clearly lacked merit, the chief judge may accordingly be saved the burden of preparing a formal order and supporting memorandum. However, the chief judge may, or be obligated under Rule 5, to identify a complaint based on allegations in a withdrawn complaint.

If the chief judge appoints a special committee, Rule 27(b) provides that the complaint may be withdrawn only with the consent of both the body before which it is pending (the special committee or the judicial council) and the subject judge. Once a complaint has reached the stage of appointment of a special committee, a resolution of the issues may be necessary to preserve public confidence. Moreover, the subject judge is given the right to insist that the matter be resolved on the merits, thereby eliminating any ambiguity that might remain if the proceeding were terminated by withdrawal of the complaint.

With regard to all petitions for review, Rule 27(c) grants the petitioner unrestricted authority to withdraw the petition. It is thought that the public's interest in the proceeding is adequately protected, because there will necessarily have been a decision by the chief judge and often by the judicial council as well in such a case.

RULE 28.   AVAILABILITY OF RULES AND FORMS

These Rules and copies of the complaint form as provided in Rule 6(a) must be available without charge in the office of the circuit clerk of each court of appeals, district court, bankruptcy court, or other federal court whose judges are subject to the Act. Each court must also make these Rules, the complaint form, and complaint-filing instructions available on the court's website, or provide an Internet link to these items on the appropriate court of appeals website or on www.uscourts.gov.

[Adopted March 11, 2008, effective April 10, 2008. Amended effective September 17, 2015; April 12, 2018.]

RULE 29.   EFFECTIVE DATE

These Rules will become effective 30 days after promulgation by the Judicial Conference of the United States.

[Adopted March 11, 2008, effective April 10, 2008. Amended effective April 12, 2018.]

APPENDIX

Complaint of Judicial Misconduct or Disability

To begin the complaint process, complete this form and prepare the brief statement of facts described in item 4 (below). The RULES FOR JUDICIAL-CONDUCT AND JUDICIAL-DISABILITY PROCEEDINGS, adopted by the Judicial Conference of the United States, contain information on what to include in a complaint (Rule 6), where to file a complaint (Rule 7), and other important matters. Requests for copies of the rules should be directed to: Clerk, United States Court of Appeals for the Fifth Circuit, 600 S. Maestri Place, New Orleans, LA 70130. The rules are also available at www.ca5.uscourts.gov.

Your complaint (this form and the statement of facts) should be typewritten and must be legible. Only an original of the complaint must be filed. Enclose the copy of the complaint in an envelope marked "COMPLAINT OF MISCONDUCT" or "COMPLAINT OF DISABILITY" and submit it to: Clerk, United States Court of Appeals for the Fifth Circuit, 600 S. Maestri Place, New Orleans, LA 70130. **Do <u>not</u> put the name of any judge on the envelope.**

1. Name of Complainant:

Contact Address:

Daytime telephone: (   )

2. Name(s) of Judge(s):

Court:

3. Does this complaint concern the behavior of the judge(s) in a particular lawsuit or lawsuits?

         [   ] Yes   [   ] No

If "yes," give the following information about each lawsuit:

Court:

Case Number:

Docket number of any appeal to the 5th Circuit: _____

Are (were) you a party or lawyer in the lawsuit?

         [   ] Party   [   ] Lawyer   [   ] Neither

If you are (were) a party and have (had) a lawyer, give the lawyer's name, address, and telephone number:

4. **Brief Statement of Facts.** Attach a brief statement of the specific facts on which the claim of judicial misconduct or disability is based. Include what happened, when and where it happened, and any information that would help an investigator check the facts. If the complaint alleges judicial disability, also include any additional facts that form the basis of that allegation.

5. **Declaration and signature:** I declare under penalty of perjury that the statements made in this complaint are true and correct to the best of my knowledge.

(Signature) _____ (Date) _____

[Adopted March 11, 2008, effective April 10, 2008. Amended effective September 17, 2015; April 12, 2018.]

SELECTED ORDERS
GENERAL ORDER GOVERNING THE CIRCUIT MEDIATION PROGRAM

1. Pursuant to Federal Rule of Appellate Procedure 33, it is hereby ORDERED that, in matters selected for participation in the court's circuit mediation program, or referred to the program by the court, proceedings shall be conducted in accordance with the provisions of this General Order.

2. Counsel will be notified by electronic mail of the date and time scheduled for the initial conference. Conferences may be conducted by telephone or in person at the option of the circuit mediator, or upon request of all parties. Conferences will be scheduled and adjourned at the circuit mediator's discretion, with due regard for the availability and convenience of counsel.

3. The principal purpose of the program is to explore the possibility of settlement and to facilitate settlement discussions. Conferences may also entail consideration of simplification, clarification, and reduction of issues, and any other matters relating to the efficient management and disposition of the appeal.

4. Counsel's participation is required at any scheduled conference. The circuit mediator may also require attendance by the parties in person or through appropriate corporate representatives or representatives of insurers providing a defense. After a case has been assigned to the program, any party may submit to the circuit mediator a request not to participate in or to terminate settlement discussions. In cases selected for the program by the circuit mediator, such a request will be honored, and any further proceedings will be restricted to the other purposes of the program. In cases referred to the program by the court, the request will be submitted to the court, and proceedings will be held in abeyance pending further directions from the court.

5. The circuit mediator may require counsel to provide pertinent written information or materials, including position statements, lists of issues, outlines of arguments or other documents that the circuit mediator believes may be helpful in accomplishing the purposes of conferences under Rule 33.

6. Counsel should not send the Clerk of Court copies of materials or documents requested by the circuit mediator or otherwise prepared specifically for the program. Documents created for the program and furnished to the circuit mediator will not be included in the court's file.

7. The time allowed for filing of briefs will not be tolled automatically by proceedings pursuant to this order. If the parties are engaged in settlement discussions, the circuit mediator may recommend a resetting of the briefing schedule. The circuit mediator may also recommend the entry of other orders controlling the course of proceedings, including orders altering the page and type-volume limitations for briefs and record excerpts.

8. All statements made by the parties or their counsel in the course of proceedings pursuant to this order, and all documents specifically prepared for use in such proceedings, shall be without prejudice, and, apart from any settlement agreement reached, shall not be binding on the parties. Such statements and documents shall not be quoted, cited, referred to or otherwise used by the parties or their counsel in the course of the appeal or in any other proceeding, except as they may be admissible in a proceeding to enforce a settlement agreement. Such statements and documents shall be privileged from discovery by the parties except in such a proceeding.

9. Confidentiality is required with respect to all settlement discussions conducted under program auspices. Information concerning such discussions shall neither be made known to the court nor voluntarily disclosed to anyone not involved in circuit mediation proceedings (or entitled to be kept informed of such proceedings), by either the circuit mediator, the parties or their counsel, except insofar as such information may be admissible in a proceeding to enforce a settlement agreement and except as provided below.

10. Information about the assignment of particular cases to the program shall not be made public either by the staff of the program or by the Clerk. For good cause (and in the absence of an explicit agreement to the contrary) the fact that a case has been assigned to the program may be disclosed by any party as long as substantive information about settlement discussions is not revealed, and the disclosure is not purposely used in an effort to gain an advantage over another party. Any such improper disclosure will result in the release of the case from the program. The identity of cases assigned to the program may in any event be provided to the court in statistical reports, in response to inquiries and in connection with recommendations about procedural orders.

11. Once all briefs have been filed, or when a motion is under submission to the court, the circuit mediator may report to the court whether active settlement discussions are under way in order to assist the court in scheduling. Such reports may include information about the likelihood and timing of settlement, but information about the parties' respective positions or other substantive aspects of settlement discussions will not be revealed to the court except upon the joint request of all parties.

12. The confidentiality provisions of this order shall extend to discussions occurring in the course of preliminary contacts between the circuit mediator and counsel about the possibility of settlement, whether or not the case is eventually assigned to the program. These provisions shall also be binding on non-parties (such as insurers or parties to related disputes) who accept invitations to participate in mediation program proceedings. For the purposes of this order these participants shall be treated as parties, and participation in settlement discussions under the auspices of the program shall be deemed to constitute an agreement to be bound by the confidentiality provisions of this order.

13. Counsel for each party shall be responsible for providing a copy of this order to all persons participating in mediation program proceedings on behalf of that party. In addition, before disclosing any information about settlement discussions conducted under program auspices to any other person whose position or relationship with a party requires such disclosure, counsel shall provide such person with a copy of this order and obtain such person's agreement to be bound as a party would be bound by its provisions requiring confidentiality.

14. If a party is subject to obligations of disclosure to the public or to persons from whom such agreement cannot be obtained, counsel shall inform the circuit mediator and counsel for the other party or parties. Settlement discussions may then be conducted under program auspices only if all parties agree to proceed. This order is not intended of its own force to prevent disclosure required under applicable law, but parties subject to such requirements must make every effort to maintain, to the extent permitted by such provisions of law, the confidentiality of such settlement discussions.

15. The confidentiality of any settlement agreement will be governed by the terms of that agreement and the law otherwise applicable thereto,

16. This General Order supersedes the prior General Order issued March 27, 2000, which shall nevertheless continue to be effective for cases assigned to the program before the date hereof.

[Dated: October 13, 2016.]

CITATIONS TO RECORDS ON APPEAL IN THE FIFTH CIRCUIT

Prior to 2013, the paper record on appeal (ROA) prepared by the district court was the official record on appeal. Paper ROA contained Bates stamped pagination that included "USCA5" on each page. Supplemental records (if any) in paper record cases restarted pagination at page one, rather than continuing the pagination from the original record. Parties cited to the paper record using the USCA5 page number (and when necessary, to the supplemental volume number).

In 2013, the court adopted the Electronic Record on Appeal (EROA) as the official record on appeal. The EROA also uses Bates stamped pagination, but one that includes the Fifth Circuit appeal number, followed by a period, followed by the page number (for example, "13–12345.123"). When there are supplemental proceedings in an EROA record, the pagination continues from the last page of the original EROA.

At present, appeals in the Fifth Circuit may include cases in which the paper ROA is the official record on appeal, cases in which the EROA is the official record, or appeals with a combination of a paper ROA and a supplemental EROA.

Parties should cite to the record using the following rules:

—If the official record contains USCA5 pagination, cite to the USCA5 page number. If the record in that appeal contains a supplemental record, then cite to the volume and page of the supplemental record, as appropriate.

—If the official record is the EROA, cite with the format "ROA," followed by a period, followed by the page number (e.g., ROA.123) if the appeal involves only one record. If the appeal is consolidated with other appeals, and hence there are multiple records, cite using the format "ROA," followed by a period, by the Fifth Circuit's case number of the record you reference, followed by another period, and then the page number (e.g., ROA.13–12345.123).

—For any appeal that contains both a paper record (paginated with "USCA5") and an electronic record (with the actual case number, such as 13–12345) cite using the rules set out above for the type of record referenced.

These formats comply with the 2014 amendment to Fifth Circuit Rule 28.2.2, and permit a court developed computer program to insert hyperlinks into pleadings, providing judges a link to the actual page of the EROA cited by parties.

Never use the "ROA" shorthand citation when referring to records with USCA5 pagination, as the program will not properly hyperlink those records.

[Dated: July 18, 2014.]

INDEX TO UNITED STATES COURT OF APPEALS
FOR THE FIFTH CIRCUIT

UNITED STATES DISTRICT COURT FOR THE NORTHERN DISTRICT OF TEXAS

Including Amendments Received Through
February 1, 2019

LOCAL CIVIL RULES

LOCAL CIVIL RULES

LR 1.1 DEFINITIONS

Unless the context indicates a contrary intention, the following definitions apply in these rules:

(a) Court. The word "court" means the district judges of the United States District Court for the Northern District of Texas, as a collective body.

(b) Presiding Judge. The term "presiding judge" means the judge to whom a case is assigned. The word "judge" includes district judges and magistrate judges.

(c) Attorney. The word "attorney" means either:

(1) a person licensed to practice law by the highest court of any state or the District of Columbia; or

(2) a party proceeding pro se in any civil action.

(d) Clerk. The word "clerk" means the clerk of this court.

(e) Discovery Materials. The term "discovery materials" means notices of and depositions upon oral examination or written questions, interrogatories, requests for documents and things, requests for inspection or to permit entry upon land, requests for admission, and answers and responses thereto, and disclosures made in compliance with Fed. R. Civ. P. 26(a)(1) or (2).

(f) ECF. The term "ECF" means electronic case filing and refers to the court's web-based document filing system that allows a document to be transmitted, signed, or verified by electronic means in a manner that is consistent with technical standards established by the Judicial Conference of the United States.

(g) Judge's Copy. The term "judge's copy" means a paper copy of an original pleading, motion, or other paper that is submitted for use by the presiding judge.

[Effective April 15, 1997. Amended effective December 1, 2000; September 1, 2006; September 1, 2008.]

LR 3.1 FILING COMPLAINT BY ELECTRONIC MEANS

A plaintiff may file a complaint by electronic means by following the procedures set forth in the ECF Administrative Procedures Manual. The complaint must be accompanied by:

(a) a civil cover sheet;

(b) the required filing fee or the appropriate application to proceed without prepayment of fees; and

(c) a separately signed certificate of interested persons—in a form approved by the clerk—that contains—in addition to the information required by Fed. R. Civ. P. 7.1(a)—a complete list of all persons, associations of persons, firms, partnerships, corporations, guarantors, insurers, affiliates, parent or subsidiary corporations, or other legal entities that are financially interested in the outcome of the case. If a large group of persons or firms can be specified by a generic description, individual listing is not necessary.

[Effective April 15, 1997. Amended effective September 1, 2000; September 1, 2008.]

LR 3.2 FILING COMPLAINT ON PAPER

To file a complaint on paper, a plaintiff must provide the clerk:

(a) an original of the complaint;

(b) a copy of the complaint and a completed civil summons form for each defendant to be served;

(c) a civil cover sheet;

(d) the required filing fee or the appropriate application to proceed without prepayment of fees; and

(e) a separately signed certificate of interested persons—in a form approved by the clerk—that contains—in addition to the information required by Fed. R. Civ. P. 7.1(a)—a complete list of all persons, associations of persons, firms, partnerships, corporations, guarantors, insurers, affiliates, parent or subsidiary corporations, or other legal entities that are financially interested in the outcome of the case. If a large group of persons or firms can be specified by a generic description, individual listing is not necessary.

[Effective September 1, 2008.]

LR 3.3 FILING COMPLAINT IN RELATED CASE; NOTICE OF RELATED CASE

(a) Notice Requirement. When a plaintiff files a complaint and there is a related case, as defined by LR 3.3(b)(1), (b)(2), or (b)(3), the complaint must be accompanied by a notice of related case. The notice must state the style and civil action number of the related case, the name of the presiding judge, whether the case is pending, and, if the case has been dismissed or remanded, the date of the final judgment or order remanding the case.

(b) Related Case Defined. A "related case" is any civil action

(1) that the plaintiff dismissed with the intent or for the purpose of obtaining a different assigned presiding judge and that is being refiled through the complaint;

(2) that the plaintiff dismissed under Fed. R. Civ. P. 41(a)(1) by notice of dismissal, and that is being refiled through the complaint without changing the parties, or after adding or omitting one or more parties;

(3) that—to the best of the plaintiff's or removing party's knowledge, information, and belief, formed after an inquiry reasonable under the circumstances—arises from a common nucleus of operative fact with the case being filed or removed, regardless whether the related case is a pending case; or

(4) that was remanded and, regardless whether one or more parties or one or more claims or defenses have changed, is being removed again.

(c) Effect of Failure to File Notice of Related Case. A plaintiff who does not file a notice of related case under LR 3.3(a), and a removing party who does not file a notice of related case under LR 81.1(a)(3), certifies that there is no related case, as defined in LR 3.3(b), to the case being filed or removed.

[Effective September 1, 2010.]

LR 4.1 PROOF OF SERVICE OR OF WAIVER OF SERVICE

Proof of service or of waiver of service must be made by filing with the clerk the summons and any supporting documentation required or allowed by Fed. R. Civ. P. 4, or an executed waiver.

[Effective April 15, 1997. Amended effective September 1, 2006; September 1, 2008.]

LR 4.2 MARSHAL'S FEES [REPEALED EFFECTIVE SEPTEMBER 1, 2004]

LR 5.1 FILING AND SERVING PLEADINGS, MOTIONS, OR OTHER PAPERS

(a) Filing With the Clerk. A pleading, motion, or other paper that the Federal Rules of Civil Procedure permit or require to be filed, or that the court orders to be filed, that is submitted on paper, must be filed with the clerk's office for the appropriate division. Unless the presiding judge agrees to accept it for filing, the pleading, motion, or other paper must not be sent directly to the presiding judge.

(b) Original and Judge's Copy Required. An original and one judge's copy of each pleading, motion, or other paper that is submitted on paper must be filed with the clerk. If a pleading, motion, or other paper is filed by electronic means, the judge's copy must be submitted following procedures set forth in the ECF Administrative Procedures Manual.

(c) Document Containing More Than One Pleading, Motion, or Other Paper. Except for a proposed order or judgment, a document may contain more than one pleading, motion, or other paper. Any such document must clearly identify each included pleading, motion, or other paper in its title.

(d) Serving by Electronic Means. Delivery of the notice of electronic filing that is automatically generated by ECF constitutes service under Fed. R. Civ. P. 5(b)(2)(E) on each party who is a registered user of ECF.

(e) Electronic Filing Required. Unless the presiding judge otherwise directs, an attorney—other than a prisoner pro se party—must file any pleading (except a complaint), motion, or other paper by electronic means, subject to the restrictions and requirements of the ECF Administrative Procedures Manual. A party may, for cause, move to be excused from the requirement of electronic filing.

(f) Registration as an ECF User Required. Unless excused for cause, an attorney—other than a prisoner pro se party— must register as an ECF user within 14 days of the date the attorney appears in a case, following the registration procedures set forth in the ECF Administrative Procedures Manual.

[Effective April 15, 1997. Amended effective December 1, 2000; September 1, 2006; September 1, 2008; September 1, 2009; December 1, 2009.]

LR 5.2 FILING DISCOVERY MATERIALS

(a) Discovery Materials Not to Be Filed. [Repealed 12/1/2000]

(b) Deposition Notices Not to Be Filed. [Repealed 12/1/2000]

(c) Filing Discovery Materials for Use in Discovery Proceedings. A motion that relates to a discovery proceeding must only contain the portions of the discovery materials in dispute.

(d) Filing Discovery Materials for Use in Pretrial Motions. When discovery materials are necessary for consideration of a pretrial motion, a party shall file only the portions of discovery on which that party relies to support or oppose the motion.

[Effective April 15, 1997. Amended effective December 1, 2000.]

LR 5.3 PRISONER'S CIVIL RIGHTS COMPLAINTS

A prisoner's complaint alleging violations of civil rights under 28 U.S.C. § 1331 or § 1343 must be filed in accordance with the current miscellaneous order establishing procedures for such actions.

[Effective April 15, 1997.]

LR 5.4 POST–CONVICTION RELIEF

A prisoner application, motion, or petition filed under 28 U.S.C. § 2241, § 2254, or § 2255 must be filed in accordance with the current miscellaneous order establishing procedures for such applications, motions, or petitions.

[Effective April 15, 1997. Amended effective September 1, 2016.]

LR 6.1 TIME DEEMED FILED

A pleading, motion, or other paper that is filed by electronic means before midnight central time of any day will be deemed filed on that day. A pleading, motion, or other paper that is filed on paper before the clerk's office is scheduled to close on any day will be deemed filed on that day.

[Effective September 1, 2008. Amended effective December 1, 2009.]

LR 7.1   MOTION PRACTICE

Unless otherwise directed by the presiding judge, motion practice is controlled by subsection (h) of this rule. In addition, the parties must comply with the following:

(a) Conference. Before filing a motion, an attorney for the moving party must confer with an attorney for each party affected by the requested relief to determine whether the motion is opposed. Conferences are not required for motions to dismiss, motions for judgment on the pleadings, motions for summary judgment, motions for new trial, or when a conference is not possible.

(b) Certificate of Conference.

(1) Each motion for which a conference is required must include a certificate of conference indicating that the motion is unopposed or opposed.

(2) If a motion is opposed, the certificate must state that a conference was held, indicate the date of conference and the identities of the attorneys conferring, and explain why agreement could not be reached.

(3) If a conference was not held, the certificate must explain why it was not possible to confer, in which event the motion will be presumed to be opposed.

(c) Proposed Order. Except for an opposed motion that is submitted on paper, each motion must be accompanied by a proposed order that is set forth separately. An agreed proposed order must be signed by the attorneys or parties.

(d) Brief. An opposed motion must be accompanied by a brief that sets forth the moving party's contentions of fact and/or law, and argument and authorities, unless a brief is not required by subsection (h) of this rule. A response to an opposed motion must be accompanied by a brief that sets forth the responding party's contentions of fact and/or law, and argument and authorities. A responding party is not required to file a brief in opposition to a motion for which a brief is not required by subsection (h) of this rule.

(e) Time for Response and Brief. A response and brief to an opposed motion must be filed within 21 days from the date the motion is filed.

(f) Time for Reply Briefs. Unless otherwise directed by the presiding judge, a party who has filed an opposed motion may file a reply brief within 14 days from the date the response is filed.

(g) No Oral Argument. Unless otherwise directed by the presiding judge, oral argument on a motion will not be held.

(h) Uniform Requirements on Motion Practice.

B—Brief required (not required with agreed motion)
C—Certificate of conference required

MOTION (to/for)	B	C
AMEND		X
CHANGE OF VENUE	X	X
COMPEL	X	X
CONSOLIDATION	X	X
CONTINUANCE		X
DISMISS	X	
EXTEND TIME		X
INTERVENE	X	X
JUDGMENT AS A MATTER OF LAW	X	
JUDGMENT ON PLEADINGS	X	
LEAVE TO FILE	X	X
LIMINE	X	X
MORE DEFINITE STATEMENT	X	X
NEW TRIAL	X	
PRELIMINARY INJUNCTION	X	X
PRODUCE DOCUMENTS	X	X
PROTECTIVE ORDER	X	X
QUASH	X	X
REMAND	X	X
SANCTIONS	X	X
STAY	X	X
STRIKE	X	X
SUBSTITUTE COUNSEL		X
SUMMARY JUDGMENT	X	

NOTE: If a motion is not listed, a brief and certificate of conference are required.

(i) Requirement of Appendix; Appendix Requirements.

(1) A party who relies on materials—including depositions, documents, electronically stored information, affidavits, declarations, stipulations, admissions, interrogatory answers, or other materials—to support or oppose a motion must include the materials in an appendix.

(2) The appendix must be assembled as a self-contained document, separate from the motion, response, reply, and brief.

(3) Each page of the appendix must measure $8\frac{1}{2} \times 11$ inches. Non-documentary materials (*e.g.*, videotapes and other physical materials) and oversized materials (*e.g.*, maps and schematic drawings) that are included in the appendix must be placed in an envelope that measures 9×12 inches.

(4) Each page of the appendix must be numbered legibly in the lower, right-hand corner. The first page must be numbered as "1," and succeeding pages must be numbered sequentially through the last page of the entire appendix (*i.e.*, the numbering system must not re-start with each succeeding document in the appendix). An envelope that contains a non-documentary or oversized materials must be numbered as if it were a single page.

[Effective April 15, 1997. Amended effective April 15, 1998; September 1, 1999; September 1, 2004; September 1, 2006; September 1, 2007; December 1, 2009; September 1, 2011.]

LR 7.2   BRIEFS

(a) General Form. A brief must be printed, typewritten, or presented in some other legible form.

(b) Amicus Briefs. An amicus brief may not be filed without leave of the presiding judge. The brief must specifically set forth the interest of the amicus curiae in the outcome of the litigation.

(c) Length. A brief must not exceed 25 pages (excluding the table of contents and table of authorities). A reply brief must not exceed 10 pages. Permission to file a brief in excess of these page limitations will be granted by the presiding judge only for extraordinary and compelling reasons.

(d) Tables of Contents and Authorities. A brief in excess of 10 pages must contain:

(1) a table of contents with page references; and

(2) an alphabetically arranged table of cases, statutes, and other authorities cited, with page references to the location of all citations.

(e) Citations to Appendix. If a party's motion or response is accompanied by an appendix, the party's brief must include citations to each page of the appendix that supports each assertion that the party makes concerning any documentary or non-documentary materials on which the party relies to support or oppose the motion.

[Effective April 15, 1997. Amended effective September 1, 1999; September 1, 2011.]

LR 7.3   CONFIRMATION OF INFORMAL LEAVE OF COURT

When a presiding judge informally grants leave, such as an extension of time to file a response, an attorney for the party to whom leave is granted must file a document confirming the leave and must serve the document on all other parties.

[Effective April 15, 1997.]

LR 7.4   CERTIFICATE OF INTERESTED PERSONS

The initial responsive pleading that a defendant files in a civil action must be accompanied by a separately signed certificate of interested persons that complies with LR 3.1(c) or 3.2(e). If the defendant concurs in the accuracy of another party's previously-filed certificate, the defendant may adopt that certificate.

[Effective September 1, 2000. Amended effective September 1, 2008.]

LR 7.5   PAGE LIMITS IN DEATH PENALTY HABEAS CASES

In any post-conviction proceeding seeking to vacate or set aside a death sentence, the following page limits (excluding pages that contain a table of contents and table of authorities) apply:

(a) the application, motion, or petition, and any supporting brief or memorandum (whether filed contemporaneously with—or after—the application, motion, or petition), must not exceed 100 pages in total;

(b) the answer to the application, motion, or petition, and any supporting brief or memorandum (whether filed contemporaneously with, or after, the answer), must not exceed 100 pages in total; and

(c) the reply, and any supporting brief or memorandum (whether filed contemporaneously with, or after, the reply), must not exceed 25 pages in total.

[Effective September 1, 2016.]

LR 9.1   SOCIAL SECURITY AND BLACK LUNG CASES

(a) Form of Complaint. A complaint filed pursuant to Section 205(g) of the Social Security Act, 42 U.S.C. § 405(g), for benefits under Titles II, XVI, or XVIII of the Social Security Act, or Part B, Title VI, of the Federal Coal Mine Health and Safety Act, must contain, in the first paragraph of the complaint, the last four digits of the social security number of:

(1) the worker on whose wage record the application for benefits is filed, regardless whether the worker is the plaintiff; and

(2) the plaintiff.

On the defendant's request, the plaintiff must separately disclose the complete social security number of the worker or the plaintiff, but the defendant must not disclose or otherwise use the complete number except by leave of court or in accordance with law.

(b) Summary Judgment Motions Required. Unless otherwise directed by the presiding judge, all parties to actions filed under 42 U.S.C. § 405(g) must file motions for summary judgment within 30 days after the answer is filed.

[Effective April 15, 1997. Amended effective September 1, 2004.]

LR 10.1   REQUIRED FORM

In addition to the requirements of the Federal Rules of Civil Procedure, each pleading, motion, or other paper must:

(a) contain on its face a title clearly identifying each included pleading, motion, or other paper;

(b) contain a signature block that sets forth the attorney's bar number for the jurisdiction in which the attorney is admitted to practice, and a facsimile number and e–mail address where information may be sent to the attorney;

(c) use a page size of 8½ x 11 inches;

(d) be typed, printed, or legibly handwritten on numbered pages; and

(e) when submitted on paper, unless otherwise provided by the local civil rules or order of the presiding judge, be two-hole punched at the top and either stapled in the upper, left-hand corner or secured with a durable fastener at the top.

[Effective April 15, 1997. Amended effective April 15, 1998; September 1, 2006.]

LR 11.1   ELECTRONIC SIGNATURE

(a) What Constitutes Electronic Signature. The signature of an attorney who submits a pleading, motion, or other paper for filing by electronic means is the login and password issued to the attorney by the clerk.

(b) Requirements for Electronic Signature. An attorney who submits a document for filing by electronic means must place on the document an "s/" and the typed name of the attorney, or a graphical signature, in the space where the attorney's signature would have appeared had the document been submitted on paper.

(c) Certification of Signature of Another Person. By submitting a document by electronic means and representing the consent of another person on the document, an attorney who submits the document certifies that the document has been properly signed.

(d) Requirements for Another Person's Electronic Signature. An attorney who submits a document by electronic means that is signed by another person—including by a moving party under LR 40.1—must:

(1) include a scanned image of the other person's signature, or represent the consent of the other person in a manner permitted or required by the presiding judge; and

(2) maintain the signed paper copy of the document for one year after final disposition of the case.

[Effective September 1, 2006. Amended effective September 1, 2008.]

LR 12.1 MOTION FOR MORE DEFINITE STATEMENT [REPEALED EFFECTIVE SEPTEMBER 1, 2006]

LR 15.1 MOTIONS TO AMEND

(a) When Filed on Paper. When a party files a motion for leave to file an amended pleading that, if leave is granted, will be filed on paper, the party must attach a copy of the proposed amended pleading as an exhibit to the motion. The party must also submit with the motion an original and a judge's copy of the proposed pleading. The original and judge's copy must neither be physically attached to the motion nor made exhibits to the motion. The original of the proposed pleading must contain the original signature of the signing attorney. If leave is granted, the clerk will file the original of the amended pleading.

(b) When Filed by Electronic Means. When a party files by electronic means a motion for leave to file an amended pleading, the party must attach the proposed amended pleading to the motion as an exhibit. If leave is granted, the amended pleading will be deemed filed as of the date of the order granting leave, or as otherwise specified by the presiding judge, and the clerk will file a copy of the amended pleading.

[Effective April 15, 1997. Amended effective September 1, 1999; September 1, 2006; September 1, 2008; September 2, 2014.]

LR 16.1 EXEMPTIONS FROM PRETRIAL SCHEDULING AND MANAGEMENT

The following categories of cases are exempt from the scheduling and planning requirements of Fed. R. Civ. P. 16(b):

(a) actions for social security benefits, including appeals from decisions of the Secretary of Health and Human Services, and black lung cases subject to LR 9.1;

(b) prisoner civil rights complaints filed pursuant to 42 U.S.C. § 1981, et seq.;

(c) forfeiture actions;

(d) cases filed by the United States Attorney for collection of promissory notes payable to the United States or any government agency;

(e) bankruptcy appeals;

(f) cases involving pro se plaintiffs;

(g) habeas corpus complaints filed pursuant to 28 U.S.C. § 2254 or § 2255;

(h) petitions for enforcement of an Internal Revenue Service summons;

(i) actions for review of the administrative action of any federal agency; and

(j) all cases not reported by the clerk for statistical purposes as filed cases.

[Effective April 15, 1997. Amended effective December 1, 2000.]

LR 16.2 AUTHORITY OF MAGISTRATE JUDGES AS TO SCHEDULING ORDERS

Unless the presiding judge otherwise directs, a magistrate judge shall have the authority under Fed.R.Civ.P. 16(b) to enter and modify scheduling orders.

[Effective April 15, 1997.]

LR 16.3 SETTLEMENT

(a) Settlement Negotiations. Parties in a civil action must make good-faith efforts to settle. Settlement negotiations must begin at the earliest possible time, well in advance of any pretrial conference.

(b) Settlement Conferences. A judge will be available for settlement discussions. In nonjury cases the presiding judge will not discuss settlement figures unless requested to do so by all concerned parties.

[Effective April 15, 1997.]

LR 16.4 PRETRIAL ORDER

Unless otherwise directed by the presiding judge, a pretrial order must be submitted to the presiding judge at least 14 days before the scheduled date for trial. All attorneys are responsible for preparing the pretrial order, which must contain the following:

(a) a summary of the claims and defenses of each party;

(b) a statement of stipulated facts;

(c) a list of contested issues of fact;

(d) a list of contested issues of law;

(e) an estimate of the length of trial;

(f) a list of any additional matters that might aid in the disposition of the case;

(g) the signature of each attorney; and

(h) a place for the date and the signature of the presiding judge.

[Effective April 15, 1997. Amended effective December 1, 2009.]

LR 23.1   COMPLAINT

A complaint alleging a class action must bear in its title the designation "COMPLAINT—CLASS ACTION," and must contain a separate heading entitled "Class Action Allegations."

[Effective April 15, 1997.]

LR 23.2   MOTION FOR CERTIFICATION; BRIEFS

Within 90 days of filing a class action complaint, or at such other time as the presiding judge by order directs, an attorney for the plaintiff must move for certification. A brief must accompany the motion for certification and must specifically set out the following:

(a) the appropriate sections of Fed.R.Civ.P. 23 under which the suit is properly maintainable as a class action;

(b) specific factual allegations concerning the alleged class, including:

(1) the approximate number of class members;

(2) the definition of the class and any subclasses;

(3) the distinguishing and common characteristics of class members, such as geography, time, and common financial incentives;

(4) questions of law and fact that are common to the class; and

(5) in actions asserting a class under Fed.R.Civ.P. 23(b)(3), allegations concerning the findings required by that section;

(c) the basis of the named plaintiff's claim to be an adequate representative of the class, including financial responsibility to fund the action;

(d) the basis for determining any required jurisdictional amount;

(e) the type and estimated expense of notice to be given to class members, and the source of funds from which notice costs will be paid;

(f) the discovery necessary for a class certification hearing and the estimated time necessary for such discovery; and

(g) all arrangements for payment of plaintiffs' attorney's fees.

[Effective April 15, 1997. Amended effective September 1, 2002.]

LR 23.3   CLASS NOTICE RESPONSES

(a) Once a case is conditionally certified as a class action and the presiding judge requires that notice be given to potential class members, the following rules apply:

(1) if there are fewer than 1,000 potential class members, the presiding judge may require that notification responses be sent directly to the clerk; but

(2) if there are 1,000 or more potential class members, the presiding judge may require that notification responses be sent to a United States Postal Service box in the name of the clerk. Plaintiff must pay the fees for the box, but such fees will be taxed as costs.

(b) The presiding judge may name an individual to collect, account for, and tabulate notice responses. Plaintiff must pay such individual a reasonable fee for these services, as determined by the presiding judge, but such fee will be taxed as costs.

[Effective April 15, 1997.]

LR 26.1   INITIAL DISCLOSURES NOT REQUIRED [REPEALED EFFECTIVE DECEMBER 1, 2000]

LR 26.2   EXCHANGING EXHIBITS, EXHIBIT LISTS, AND WITNESS LISTS; DESIGNATING DEPOSITION EXCERPTS

(a) **Exchanging Exhibits.** All exhibits that a party intends to offer at trial, except those offered solely for impeachment, must be marked with gummed labels or tags that identify them by the exhibit number under which they will be offered at trial, and must be exchanged with opposing parties at least 14 days before the scheduled date for trial. When practicable, a copy of such exhibits must be furnished to the presiding judge at a time and in a manner prescribed by the presiding judge.

(b) **Exchanging Exhibit and Witness Lists.** At least 14 days before the scheduled trial date, the parties must file with the clerk and deliver to opposing parties and the court reporter, separate lists of exhibits and witnesses, except those offered solely for impeachment.

(c) **Designating Deposition Excerpts.** The parties must designate, in lists delivered to opposing parties and filed with the clerk at least 14 days before the scheduled trial date, the portions of any depositions to be offered at trial.

[Effective April 15, 1997. Amended effective April 15, 1998; December 1, 2009.]

LR 40.1   MOTIONS FOR CONTINUANCE

A motion for continuance of a trial setting must be signed by the moving party as well as by the party's attorney of record. Unless the presiding judge orders otherwise, the granting of a motion for continuance will not extend or revive any deadline that has already expired in a case.

[Effective April 15, 1997.]

LR 41.1   ORDER OF DISMISSAL [REPEALED EFFECTIVE SEPTEMBER 1, 2007]

LR 42.1   MOTIONS TO CONSOLIDATE

Motions to consolidate civil actions, and all briefs and other papers concerning consolidation, must be served on an attorney for each party in each case sought to be consolidated.

After consolidation, all pleadings, motions, or other papers must only bear the caption of the first case filed. All post-consolidation filings must also bear the legend "(Consolidated with [giving the docket numbers of all the other cases])."

[Effective April 15, 1997.]

LR 47.1 CONTACT WITH JURORS

A party, attorney, or representative of a party or attorney, shall not, before or after trial, contact any juror, prospective juror, or the relatives, friends, or associates of a juror or prospective juror, unless explicitly permitted to do so by the presiding judge.

[Effective April 15, 1997.]

LR 51.1 REQUESTED JURY CHARGE [REPEALED EFFECTIVE DECEMBER 1, 2003]

LR 52.1 PROPOSED FINDINGS IN NONJURY CASES

Unless otherwise directed by the presiding judge, at least 14 days before trial in all nonjury cases, each party must file with the clerk and serve on opposing parties proposed findings of fact and conclusions of law. The parties must submit such amendments to the proposed findings of fact and conclusions of law as the presiding judge directs.

[Effective April 15, 1997. Amended effective December 1, 2009.]

LR 53.1 BRIEFING PRACTICE FOR OBJECTIONS AND MOTIONS CONCERNING ORDERS, REPORTS, AND RECOMMENDATIONS OF MASTERS

(a) **Brief.** Objections or a motion filed under Fed. R. Civ. P. 53(f)(2) must be accompanied by a brief that sets forth the party's contentions of fact and/or law, and argument and authorities, and complies with LR 7.2.

(b) **Response Brief.** A response brief to objections or a motion filed under Fed. R. Civ. P. 53(f)(2) must comply with LR 7.2 and be filed within 21 days from the date the objections or motion is filed.

(c) **Reply Brief.** Unless otherwise directed by the presiding judge, a party who files objections or a motion under Fed. R. Civ. P. 53(f)(2) may file a reply brief within 14 days from the date the response brief is filed. The brief must comply with LR 7.2.

(d) **Appendix Required.** A party who relies on materials—including depositions, documents, electronically stored information, affidavits, declarations, stipulations, admissions, interrogatory answers, or other materials—to support or oppose objections or a motion filed under Fed. R. Civ. P. 53(f)(2) must include the materials in an appendix that complies with LR 7.1(i)(2)–(4).

(e) **Preparing the Record.** A party who files objections or a motion under Fed. R. Civ. P. 53(f)(2) is responsible for preparing the record and—if necessary for disposition of the

objections or motion—obtaining a hearing transcript. Unless otherwise directed by the presiding judge, the transcript must be filed contemporaneously with the objections or motion.

[Effective September 1, 2005. Amended effective September 1, 2008; December 1, 2009; September 1, 2011.]

LR 54.1 TIME FOR FILING BILL OF COSTS

A party awarded costs by final judgment or by judgment that a presiding judge directs be entered as final under Fed. R. Civ. P. 54(b) must apply to the clerk for taxation of such costs by filing a bill of costs in a form approved by the clerk. Unless otherwise provided by statute or by order of the presiding judge, the bill of costs must be filed with the clerk and served on any party entitled to such service no later than 14 days after the clerk enters the judgment on the docket.

[Effective September 1, 2002.]

LR 55.1 FAILURE TO OBTAIN DEFAULT JUDGMENT

If a defendant has been in default for 90 days, the presiding judge may require the plaintiff to move for entry of a default and a default judgment. If the plaintiff fails to do so within the prescribed time, the presiding judge will dismiss the action, without prejudice, as to that defendant.

[Effective April 15, 1997.]

LR 55.2 DEFAULT JUDGMENTS BY THE UNITED STATES [REPEALED EFFECTIVE SEPTEMBER 1, 2011]

LR 55.3 REQUEST FOR ENTRY OF DEFAULT BY CLERK

Before the clerk is required to enter a default, the party requesting such entry must file with the clerk a written request for entry of default, submit a proposed form of entry of default, and file any other materials required by Fed. R. Civ. P. 55(a).

[Effective September 1, 1999.]

LR 56.1 MOTION PRACTICE NOT MODIFIED GENERALLY

Except as expressly modified, the motion practice prescribed by LR 7.1–7.3 is not affected by LR 56.2–56.7.

[Effective April 15, 1997. Amended effective April 15, 1998.]

LR 56.2 LIMITS ON TIME FOR FILING AND NUMBER OF MOTIONS

(a) **Time for Filing.** Unless otherwise directed by the presiding judge, no motion for summary judgment may be filed within 90 days of the trial setting.

(b) Number. Unless otherwise directed by the presiding judge, or permitted by law, a party may file no more than one motion for summary judgment.

[Effective April 15, 1998. Amended effective September 1, 2002.]

LR 56.3 CONTENT OF MOTION

(a) Except as provided in subsection (b) of this rule, a motion for summary judgment must, in addition to the contents required by Fed. R. Civ. P. 56(a),

(1) on the first page, under the heading "summary," state concisely the elements of each claim or defense as to which summary judgment is sought, and

(2) if the motion is accompanied by an appendix and it is necessary to cite support for an assertion about the absence or presence of a genuine dispute of fact, comply with LR 56.5(c).

(b) A moving party may satisfy the requirements of subsection (a) of this rule by stating in its motion that each of the required matters will be set forth in the party's brief.

(c) If a moving party seeks summary judgment on fewer than all claims or defenses, the motion must be styled as a motion for partial summary judgment.

(d) A motion for summary judgment must not contain argument and authorities.

[Effective April 15, 1998. Amended effective December 1, 2010; September 1, 2011.]

LR 56.4 CONTENT OF RESPONSE

(a) Except as provided in subsection (b) of this rule, a response to a motion for summary judgment must

(1) state in reasonably concise terms why the responding party opposes the motion, and

(2) if the response is accompanied by an appendix and it is necessary to cite support for an assertion about the absence or presence of a genuine dispute of fact, comply with LR 56.5(c).

(b) A responding party may satisfy the requirements of subsection (a) of this rule by stating in its response that each of the required matters will be set forth in the party's brief.

(c) A response to a motion for summary judgment must not contain argument and authorities.

[Effective April 15, 1998. Amended effective December 1, 2010; September 1, 2011.]

LR 56.5 REQUIREMENT OF BRIEF; BRIEFING REQUIREMENTS

(a) Brief Required. A summary judgment motion and a response must be accompanied by a brief that sets forth the argument and authorities on which the party relies in support of or opposition to a motion, and must contain the matters required by LR 56.3(a) or LR 56.4(a) if the party has opted to comply with those rules by including the required matters in its brief. Notwithstanding LR 5.1(c), the brief must be filed as a separate document from the motion or response that it supports.

(b) Length of Briefs. The requirements of LR 7.2 apply to briefs filed pursuant to LR 56.5(a), except that, excluding the table of contents and table of authorities, the length of a principal brief must not exceed 50 pages and a reply brief must not exceed 25 pages. The presiding judge, by order or other appropriate notice issued in a civil action, may restrict the length of briefs to fewer pages than are permitted by this rule.

(c) Citations to Appendix. When citing materials in the record, as required by Fed. R. Civ. P. 56(c)(1)(A) or (B), a party must support each assertion by citing each relevant page of its own or the opposing party's appendix.

[Effective April 15, 1998. Amended effective December 1, 2010; September 1, 2011.]

LR 56.6 REQUIREMENT OF APPENDIX; APPENDIX REQUIREMENTS

(a) Appendix Required. A party who relies on materials in the record—including depositions, documents, electronically stored information, affidavits, declarations, stipulations, admissions, interrogatory answers, or other materials—to support or oppose a motion for summary judgment must include the materials in an appendix.

(b) Appendix Requirements.

(1) The appendix must be assembled as a self-contained document, separate from the motion and brief or response and brief.

(2) Each page of the appendix must measure 8½ × 11 inches. Non-documentary materials (*e.g.*, videotapes and other physical materials) and oversized materials (*e.g.*, maps and schematic drawings) that are included in the appendix must be placed in an envelope that measures 9 × 12 inches.

(3) Each page of the appendix must be numbered legibly in the lower, right-hand corner. The first page must be numbered as "1," and succeeding pages must be numbered sequentially through the last page of the entire appendix (*i.e.*, the numbering system must not re-start with each succeeding document in the appendix). An envelope that contains non-documentary or oversized materials must be numbered as if it were a single page.

[Effective April 15, 1998. Amended effective September 1, 2004; September 1, 2006; December 1, 2010; September 1, 2011.]

LR 56.7 LIMIT ON SUPPLEMENTAL MATERIALS

Except for the motions, responses, replies, briefs, and appendixes required by these rules, a party may not, without the permission of the presiding judge, file supplemental pleadings, briefs, authorities, or evidence.

[Effective April 15, 1998.]

LR 58.1 PROPOSED JUDGMENTS

Each proposed judgment must be set forth on a separate document.

[Effective April 15, 1997.]

LR 62.1 SUPERSEDEAS BOND

Unless otherwise ordered by the presiding judge, a supersedeas bond staying execution of a money judgment shall be in the amount of the judgment, plus 20% of that amount to cover interest and any award of damages for delay, plus $250.00 to cover costs. The parties may waive the requirement of a supersedeas bond by stipulation.

[Effective April 15, 1997.]

LR 67.1 DEPOSIT OF MONEY IN COURT REGISTRY [VACATED EFFECTIVE SEPTEMBER 2, 2014]

LR 71A.1 CONDEMNATION OF PROPERTY

Where the United States files separate condemnation actions and a single declaration of taking relating to the separate actions, the clerk may establish a master file for the declaration of taking. The single declaration in such master file shall constitute a filing of the declaration in each individual action to which it relates.

[Effective April 15, 1997.]

LR 72.1 BRIEFING PRACTICE CONCERNING OBJECTIONS TO MAGISTRATE JUDGE ORDERS IN NONDISPOSITIVE MATTERS

(a) **Brief.** Objections filed under Fed. R. Civ. P. 72(a) must be accompanied by a brief that sets forth the party's contentions of fact and/or law, and argument and authorities, and complies with LR 7.2.

(b) **Response Brief.** A response brief to objections filed under Fed. R. Civ. P. 72(a) must comply with LR 7.2 and be filed within 21 days from the date the objections are filed.

(c) **Reply Brief.** Unless otherwise directed by the presiding judge, a party who files objections under Fed. R. Civ. P. 72(a) may file a reply brief within 14 days from the date the response brief is filed. The brief must comply with LR 7.2.

(d) **Appendix Required.** A party who relies on materials—including depositions, documents, electronically stored information, affidavits, declarations, stipulations, admissions, interrogatory answers, or other materials—to support or oppose objections filed under Fed. R. Civ. P. 72(a) must include the materials in an appendix that complies with LR 7.1(i)(2)–(4).

(e) **Preparing the Record.** A party who files objections under Fed. R. Civ. P. 72(a) is responsible for preparing the record and—if necessary for disposition of the objections—obtaining a hearing transcript. Unless otherwise directed by the presiding judge, the transcript must be filed contemporaneously with the objections.

[Effective September 1, 2005. Amended effective December 1, 2009; September 1, 2011.]

LR 72.2 BRIEFING PRACTICE CONCERNING OBJECTIONS TO MAGISTRATE JUDGE RECOMMENDATIONS ON DISPOSITIVE MOTIONS AND PRISONER PETITIONS

(a) **Brief.** Objections filed under Fed. R. Civ. P. 72(b)(2) must be accompanied by a brief that sets forth the party's contentions of fact and/or law, and argument and authorities, and complies with LR 7.2.

(b) **Response Brief.** A response brief to objections filed under Fed. R. Civ. P. 72(b)(2) must comply with LR 7.2.

(c) **Reply Brief.** Unless otherwise directed by the presiding judge, a party who files objections under Fed. R. Civ. P. 72(b)(2) may file a reply brief within 14 days from the date the response brief is filed. The brief must comply with LR 7.2.

(d) **Appendix Required.** A party who relies on materials—including depositions, documents, electronically stored information, affidavits, declarations, stipulations, admissions, interrogatory answers, or other materials—to support or oppose objections filed under Fed. R. Civ. P. 72(b)(2) must include the materials in an appendix that complies with LR 7.1(i)(2)–(4).

(e) **Preparing the Record.** A party who files objections under Fed. R. Civ. P. 72(b)(2) is responsible for preparing the record and—if necessary for disposition of the objections—obtaining a hearing transcript. Unless otherwise directed by the presiding judge, the transcript must be filed contemporaneously with the objections.

[Effective September 1, 2005. Amended effective September 1, 2008; December 1, 2009; September 1, 2011.]

LR 77.1 NOTICE OF ORDERS AND JUDGMENTS

(a) **Furnishing Copies of Orders and Judgments.** Unless the presiding judge otherwise directs, the clerk shall furnish a copy of each order and judgment to counsel of record by first class mail or by electronic transmission. Where a party is represented by more than one attorney of record, the attorney designated in accordance with LR 77.1(b) or (c) shall receive copies of orders and judgments and distribute them to co-counsel for the same party who have not received a notice of electronic filing from ECF.

(b) **Designation of Counsel to Receive Orders and Judgments.** The clerk shall designate an attorney to receive copies of orders and judgments, in the following manner:

(1) the first attorney to sign a plaintiff's complaint;

(2) the first attorney to sign a defendant's initial responsive pleading;

(3) the first attorney to sign a removing party's notice of removal, and the first attorney listed on the civil cover sheet and/or supplemental civil cover sheet for the remaining parties; and

(4) the first attorney listed on the bankruptcy docket sheet for each party in a bankruptcy withdrawal or bankruptcy appeal.

(c) Change in Designation of Counsel. If the attorney designated to receive orders and judgments desires that another attorney be substituted for this purpose, the attorney must request substitution in the manner prescribed by the clerk.

[Effective April 15, 1997. Amended effective September 1, 2006; September 1, 2008.]

LR 79.1 CASE FILES

(a) Official Record. The electronic version of a document maintained on ECF, or the paper version of a document not so maintained, is the official record of the court.

(b) Inspection of Files. Except as otherwise limited by rule or by court order, the electronic portion of an original file in a pending or closed case shall be available for public inspection in the clerk's office. The paper portion of an original file shall be available in the division where the case is filed, unless the file has been removed to a federal records center. The clerk shall not release the paper portion of a file from the clerk's custody without the permission of the presiding judge, or except as permitted by subsection (d) of this rule.

(c) Inspection of Closed Files. [Repealed September 1, 2006.]

(d) Copies of Files. Upon request, the clerk shall provide copies of the contents of case files, including transcripts of oral depositions and court proceedings. The clerk shall charge the fee established by the court for this service. When large numbers of copies are requested, the clerk is authorized to release the file to a commercial copying service, and to direct that the copy fee be paid directly to the service by the requesting party.

[Effective April 15, 1997. Amended effective September 1, 2006; September 1, 2008.]

LR 79.2 DISPOSITION OF EXHIBITS

(a) Release While Case Pending. Without an order from the presiding judge, no exhibit in the custody of the court may be removed from the clerk's office while the case is pending.

(b) Removal or Destruction After Final Disposition of Case. All exhibits in the custody of the court must be removed from the clerk's office within 60 days after final disposition of a case. The attorney who introduced the exhibits shall be responsible for their removal. Any exhibit not removed within the 60-day period may be destroyed or otherwise disposed of by the clerk.

[Effective April 15, 1997.]

LR 79.3 SEALED DOCUMENTS

(a) A party may file under seal any document that a statute or rule requires or permits to be so filed. The term "document," as used in this rule, means any pleading, motion, other paper, or physical item that the Federal Rules of Civil Procedure permit or require to be filed.

(b) If no statute or rule requires or permits a document to be filed under seal, a party may file a document under seal only on motion and by permission of the presiding judge.

(1) When a party files on paper a motion for leave to file a document under seal, the clerk must file the motion under seal. The party must attach as an exhibit to the motion a copy of the document to be filed under seal. The party must also submit with the motion the original and a judge's copy of the document to be filed under seal. The original of the document must neither be physically attached to the motion nor made an exhibit to the motion. If leave to file the document under seal is granted, the clerk must file the original of the document under seal.

(2) When a party files by electronic means a motion for leave to file a document under seal, the party may file the motion under seal and must attach the proposed sealed document as an exhibit. If leave is granted, the sealed document will be deemed filed as of the date of the order granting leave, or as otherwise specified by the presiding judge, and the clerk will file a copy of the sealed document.

[Effective April 15, 1998. Amended effective September 1, 2008; September 2, 2014.]

LR 79.4 DISPOSITION OF SEALED DOCUMENTS

Unless the presiding judge otherwise directs, all sealed documents maintained on paper will be deemed unsealed 60 days after final disposition of a case. A party that desires that such a document remain sealed must move for this relief before the expiration of the 60-day period. The clerk may store, transfer, or otherwise dispose of unsealed documents according to the procedure that governs publicly available court records.

[Effective April 15, 1998. Amended effective September 1, 2008.]

LR 80.1 COURT REPORTER'S FEES [REPEALED EFFECTIVE SEPTEMBER 1, 2004]

LR 81.1 REQUIRED FORM OF DOCUMENTS TO BE FILED UPON REMOVAL

(a) The party or parties that remove a civil action from state court must provide the following to the clerk for filing:

(1) a completed civil cover sheet;

(2) a supplemental civil cover sheet; and

(3) if there is a "related case," as defined by LR 3.3(b)(3) or (b)(4), a notice of related case that complies with LR 3.3(a); and

(4) a notice of removal with a copy of each of the following attached to both the original and the judge's copy—

(A) an index of all documents that clearly identifies each document and indicates the date the document was filed in state court;

(B) a copy of the docket sheet in the state court action;

(C) each document filed in the state court action, except discovery material (if filed on paper, each document must be individually tabbed and arranged in chronological order according to the state court file date; if filed by electronic means, each document must be filed as a separate attachment); and

(D) a separately signed certificate of interested persons that complies with LR 3.1(c) or 3.2(e).

(b) If the documents listed in subsection (a) of this rule are filed on paper, they must be two-hole punched at the top, and either stapled in the upper, left-hand corner or secured at the top with durable fasteners if too thick to staple. If these documents are too voluminous to be filed as a single unit, each unit must be secured in the manner required by this subsection (b) and must contain a cover sheet that identifies the case by its caption and by the civil action number assigned by the clerk.

[Effective April 15, 1998. Amended effective September 1, 2000; September 1, 2007; September 1, 2008; September 1, 2010.]

LR 81.2 CERTIFICATE OF INTERESTED PERSONS

Within 21 days after the notice of removal is filed, the plaintiff shall file a separately signed certificate of interested persons that complies with LR 3.1(c) or 3.2(e). If the plaintiff concurs in the accuracy of another party's previously-filed certificate, the plaintiff may adopt that certificate.

[Effective September 1, 2000. Amended effective September 1, 2008; December 1, 2009.]

LR 83.1 APPLICATION OF RULES BY A PRESIDING JUDGE

Notwithstanding the local civil rules, a presiding judge may direct the parties to proceed in any manner that the judge deems just and expeditious.

[Effective April 15, 1997.]

LR 83.2 MISCELLANEOUS AND SPECIAL ORDERS

The clerk shall maintain in each division a copy of all miscellaneous and special orders adopted by the court, and shall make these orders available for inspection and copying.

[Effective April 15, 1997.]

LR 83.3 ASSIGNMENT OF CASES

The district judges shall determine the method by which all cases are assigned to individual judges.

[Effective April 15, 1997.]

LR 83.4 CONDUCT OF ATTORNEYS AT TRIAL OR HEARING

Unless the presiding judge otherwise directs, during a trial or hearing, attorneys must:

(a) stand when making objections or otherwise addressing the presiding judge;

(b) use the lectern while examining or cross-examining witnesses;

(c) when examining a witness, refrain from making statements, comments, or remarks before or after asking a question;

(d) limit to one attorney for each party the examination or cross-examination of a witness; and

(e) in making an objection, state plainly and briefly the grounds for objecting and not offer argument unless requested by the presiding judge.

[Effective April 15, 1997.]

LR 83.5 CLERK'S FEES [REPEALED EFFECTIVE SEPTEMBER 1, 2004]

LR 83.6 APPLICATIONS TO PROCEED IN FORMA PAUPERIS

A party desiring to proceed without prepayment of fees or costs must complete the appropriate form and file it with the clerk.

[Effective April 15, 1997.]

LR 83.7 ADMISSION OF ATTORNEYS

Attorneys must fulfill the following requirements to be admitted to practice in this court:

(a) Eligibility for Admission. Any attorney licensed to practice law by the Supreme Court of Texas, or by the highest court of any state or the District of Columbia, may be admitted to the bar of this court if the attorney is of good personal and professional character and is a member in good standing of the bar where the attorney is licensed.

(b) Procedure for Admission. Attorneys desiring admission to the bar of this court must complete an application for admission, to be approved by a district judge, and except as provided in subsection (c) of this rule, be introduced by a member in good standing of the bar of this court, and take the required oath or affirmation before a judge of this court. After the oath or affirmation is administered, and the applicant has paid the appropriate fee, the clerk shall issue a certificate stating that the attorney is admitted to practice before this court.

(c) Admission Before Judges of Other Districts. Any nonresident attorney who has completed all requirements for admission to the bar of this court may, with the approval of a district judge of the division where the application is pending, have the oath of admission administered by a judge in another district. The nonresident attorney must file the oath with the clerk and pay the appropriate fee before the attorney's name will be added to the roll of attorneys for this district.

(d) Admission is Discretionary. All admissions to practice before this court shall be discretionary with the district judge reviewing the application for admission.

[Effective April 15, 1997. Amended effective September 1, 2002.]

LR 83.8 LOSS OF MEMBERSHIP AND DISCIPLINE OF ATTORNEYS

(a) Loss of Membership. A member of the bar of this court is subject to suspension or disbarment by the court under the following circumstances:

(1) if for any reason other than nonpayment of dues, failure to meet continuing legal education requirements, or voluntary resignation unrelated to a disciplinary proceeding or problem, an attorney loses, either temporarily or permanently, the right to practice law before:

(A) the courts of the State of Texas;

(B) the highest court of any other state or the District of Columbia; or

(C) any federal court; or

(2) if an attorney fails to maintain the right to practice law before the highest court of at least one state or the District of Columbia, unless the member's failure to maintain such right results from nonpayment of dues or failure to meet continuing legal education requirements.

(b) Grounds for Disciplinary Action. A presiding judge, after giving opportunity to show cause to the contrary, may take any appropriate disciplinary action against a member of the bar for:

(1) conduct unbecoming a member of the bar;

(2) failure to comply with any rule or order of this court;

(3) unethical behavior;

(4) inability to conduct litigation properly;

(5) conviction by any court of a felony or crime involving dishonesty or false statement; or

(6) having been publicly or privately disciplined by any court, bar, court agency or committee.

(c) Appeal of Disciplinary Action. [Repealed].

(d) Reporting by Members. Any member of the bar of this court who has:

(1) lost or relinquished, temporarily or permanently, the right to practice in any court of record;

(2) been disciplined, publicly or privately, by any court, bar, court agency, or committee; or

(3) been convicted of a felony or crime involving dishonesty or false statement,

shall promptly report such fact in writing to the clerk, supplying full details and copies of all pertinent documents reflecting, or explaining, such action.

(e) Unethical Behavior. The term "unethical behavior," as used in this rule, means conduct undertaken in or related to a civil action in this court that violates the Texas Disciplinary Rules of Professional Conduct.

(f) Readmission. An attorney applying for readmission to the bar of this court must submit an application for readmission, together with the following materials:

(1) a full disclosure concerning the attorney's loss or relinquishment of membership in the bar of this court; and

(2) all information required by subsection (d) of this rule concerning facts that occurred prior to the date of application for readmission.

(g) Appointment of Counsel. A presiding judge shall have the right to appoint any member of the court's bar to assist in the handling of any proceeding contemplated by or resulting from this rule. An attorney appointed under this rule shall perform as requested unless relieved from doing so. An attorney desiring relief from appointment must move for such relief, which will be granted only upon a showing of good cause.

(h) Reciprocal Discipline.

i. A member of the bar who is subject to suspension or disbarment under LR 83.8(a) must be given written notice by the chief judge, or by a district judge designated by the chief judge, that the court intends to suspend or disbar the member. The notice must identify the ground for imposing reciprocal discipline and provide the member an opportunity to show cause, within the time prescribed by the notice, why the member should not be suspended or disbarred.

ii. If the member does not respond to the notice, or responds but does not oppose reciprocal discipline, the chief judge or a designee district judge may enter an appropriate order after the prescribed time for a response expires or the response is received.

iii. If the member responds and, in whole or in part, opposes reciprocal discipline, the chief judge, or a district judge designated by the chief judge, must designate three district judges to hear the matter. The decision of a majority of the three-judge panel concerning the appropriate discipline shall be the final ruling of this court.

[Effective April 15, 1997. Amended effective September 1, 2002; September 1, 2004.]

LR 83.9 ATTORNEYS NOT ADMITTED TO PRACTICE BEFORE THIS COURT

(a) Eligibility to Appear. An attorney who is licensed to practice law by the highest court of any state or the District of Columbia, but who is not admitted to practice before this court, may represent a party in proceedings in this court only by permission of the presiding judge.

(b) Application to Appear. Unless exempted by LR 83.11, an attorney who is not admitted to practice in this court, who desires to appear as counsel in a case, and who is eligible pursuant to subsection (a) of this rule to appear, shall apply for admission pro hac vice on a court-approved form and pay the applicable fee to the clerk.

(c) Regulation of Attorneys Admitted Pro Hac Vice. By appearing in any case, an attorney becomes subject to the rules of this court.

[Effective April 15, 1997. Amended effective September 1, 1999.]

LR 83.10 REQUIREMENT OF LOCAL COUNSEL

(a) Local Counsel Required. Unless exempted by LR 83.11, local counsel is required in all cases where an attorney appearing in a case does not reside or maintain the attorney's principal office in this district. "Local counsel" means a member of the bar of this court who resides or maintains the attorney's principal office in this district and whose residence or principal office is located within 50 miles of the courthouse in the division in which the case is pending. Attorneys desiring to proceed without local counsel must obtain leave from the presiding judge. If the request for leave is denied, written designation of local counsel must be filed within 14 days of the denial.

(b) Duties of Local Counsel. Local counsel must be authorized to present and argue a party's position at any hearing called by the presiding judge. Local counsel must also be able to perform, on behalf of the party represented, any other duty required by the presiding judge or the local rules of this court.

[Effective April 15, 1997. Amended effective December 1, 2009; September 4, 2012.]

LR 83.11 EXEMPTION FROM ADMISSION TO PRACTICE, AND FROM REQUIREMENT OF LOCAL COUNSEL, FOR ATTORNEYS APPEARING ON BEHALF OF THE UNITED STATES JUSTICE DEPARTMENT OR THE ATTORNEY GENERAL OF THE STATE OF TEXAS

Unless the presiding judge otherwise directs, an attorney appearing on behalf of the United States Justice Department or the Attorney General of the State of Texas, and who is eligible pursuant to LR 83.9(a) to appear in this court, shall be exempt from the requirements of LR 83.9(b) and 83.10, but shall otherwise be subject to all requirements applicable to attorneys who have been granted leave to appear pro hac vice.

[Effective April 15, 1997.]

LR 83.12 WITHDRAWAL OF ATTORNEY

(a) Except as provided in subsection (b) or (c) of this rule, an attorney desiring to withdraw in any case must file a motion to withdraw. This motion must, in addition to the matters required by LR 7.1, specify the reasons requiring withdrawal and provide the name and address of the succeeding attorney. If the succeeding attorney is not known, the motion must set forth the name, address, and telephone number of the client and either bear the client's signature approving withdrawal or state specifically why, after due diligence, the attorney was unable to obtain the client's signature.

(b) When an Assistant United States Attorney enters an appearance in a case, another Assistant United States Attorney may replace the attorney by filing a notice of substitution that identifies the attorney being replaced. Unless the presiding judge otherwise directs, the notice effects the withdrawal of the attorney being replaced.

(c) When the Federal Public Defender is appointed to represent a party and an Assistant Federal Public Defender enters an appearance in the case, another Assistant Federal Public Defender may replace the attorney who has entered an appearance by filing a notice of substitution that identifies the attorney being replaced. Unless the presiding judge other-

wise directs, the notice effects the withdrawal of the attorney being replaced.

[Effective April 15, 1997. Amended effective September 1, 2002; September 1, 2009.]

LR 83.13 CHANGE OF CONTACT INFORMATION OR NAME

(a) Attorney Who Is Not a Registered User of ECF. When an attorney who is not a registered user of ECF changes the attorney's business address, e-mail address, telephone number, facsimile number, or name, the attorney must promptly notify the clerk, using the approved method, and the presiding judge, in writing, in each pending case.

(b) Attorney Who Is a Registered User of ECF. When an attorney who is a registered user of ECF changes the attorney's business address, e-mail address, telephone number, facsimile number, or name, the attorney must promptly change this information in ECF, following procedures set forth in the ECF Administrative Procedures Manual.

[Effective April 15, 1997. Amended effective September 1, 2006; September 1, 2008.]

LR 83.14 PARTIES PROCEEDING PRO SE

Any party proceeding on the party's own behalf is considered pro se. Pro se parties must read and follow the local civil rules of this court and the Federal Rules of Civil Procedure.

[Effective April 15, 1997.]

LR 83.15 ATTORNEY AS A WITNESS [REPEALED EFFECTIVE SEPTEMBER 1, 2004]

LR 83.16 DRESS AND CONDUCT

All persons present in a courtroom where a trial, hearing, or other proceeding is in progress must dress and conduct themselves in a manner demonstrating respect for the court. The presiding judge shall have the discretion to establish appropriate standards of dress and conduct.

[Effective April 15, 1997.]

LR 83.17 WEAPONS FORBIDDEN

Firearms and other weapons are prohibited in areas of buildings designated for court use. Such weapons may be carried by the United States Marshal, the marshal's deputies, courtroom security personnel, and other persons to whom a presiding judge has given approval.

[Effective April 15, 1997.]

LR 83.18 PHOTOGRAPHS, BROADCASTING, RECORDING, AND TELEVISION FORBIDDEN

No person may photograph, electronically record, televise, or broadcast a judicial proceeding. This rule shall not apply to ceremonial proceedings or electronic recordings by an official court reporter or other authorized court personnel.

[Effective April 15, 1997. Amended effective September 1, 2007.]

LOCAL CRIMINAL RULES

LCrR 1.1 DEFINITIONS

Unless the context indicates a contrary intention, the following definitions apply in these rules:

(a) Court. The word "court" means the district judges of the United States District Court for the Northern District of Texas, as a collective body.

(b) Presiding Judge. The term "presiding judge" means the judge to whom a case is assigned. The word "judge" includes district judges and magistrate judges.

(c) Attorney. The word "attorney" means either:

(1) a person licensed to practice law by the highest court of any state or the District of Columbia; or

(2) a party proceeding pro se in any criminal action.

(d) Clerk. The word "clerk" means the clerk of this court.

(e) ECF. The term "ECF" means electronic case filing and refers to the court's web-based document filing system that allows a document to be transmitted, signed, or verified by electronic means in a manner that is consistent with technical standards established by the Judicial Conference of the United States.

(f) Judge's Copy. The term "judge's copy" means a paper copy of an original pleading, motion, or other paper that is submitted for use by the presiding judge.

[Effective April 15, 1997. Amended effective September 1, 2006; September 1, 2008.]

LCrR 16.1 EXCHANGING EXHIBITS, EXHIBIT LISTS, AND WITNESS LISTS

(a) Exchanging Exhibits. All exhibits, except those offered solely for impeachment, that a party intends to offer at trial, must be marked with gummed labels or tags that identify them by the exhibit number under which they will be offered at trial, and must be exchanged with opposing parties at least 14 days before the scheduled date for trial. When practicable, a copy of such exhibits must be furnished to the presiding judge.

(b) Exchanging Exhibit and Witness Lists. At least 14 days before the scheduled date for trial, the parties must file with the clerk and deliver to opposing parties and the court reporter, separate lists of exhibits and witnesses, except those offered solely for impeachment.

[Effective April 15, 1997. Amended effective December 1, 2009.]

LCrR 23.1 PROPOSED FINDINGS IN NONJURY CASES

Unless otherwise directed by the presiding judge, at least 14 days before trial in all nonjury cases, parties must file with the clerk and serve on opposing parties proposed findings of fact and conclusions of law. The parties must submit such amendments to the proposed findings of fact and conclusions of law as the presiding judge directs.

[Effective April 15, 1997. Amended effective December 1, 2009.]

LCrR 24.1 CONTACT WITH JURORS

A party, attorney, or representative of a party or attorney, shall not, before or after trial, contact any juror, prospective juror, or the relatives, friends, or associates of a juror or prospective juror, unless explicitly permitted to do so by the presiding judge.

[Effective April 15, 1997.]

LCrR 30.1 REQUESTED JURY CHARGE

Unless otherwise directed by the presiding judge, at least 14 days before trial, each party must file with the clerk and serve on opposing parties the requested jury charge, including instructions. The requested instructions should cite the authorities relied on.

[Effective April 15, 1997. Amended effective December 1, 2009.]

LCrR 32.1 NONDISCLOSURE OF RECOMMENDATION

A probation officer shall not disclose any recommendation regarding the sentence.

[Effective April 15, 1997.]

LCrR 45.1 TIME DEEMED FILED

A pleading, motion, or other paper that is filed by electronic means before midnight central time of any day will be deemed filed on that day. A pleading, motion, or other paper that is filed on paper before the clerk's office is scheduled to close on any day will be deemed filed on that day.

[Effective September 1, 2008. Amended effective December 1, 2009.]

LCrR 47.1 MOTION PRACTICE

Unless otherwise directed by the presiding judge, motion practice is controlled by subsection (h) of this rule. In addition, the parties must comply with the following:

(a) Conference. Before filing a motion, an attorney for the moving party must confer with an attorney for each party affected by the requested relief to determine whether the motion is opposed. Conferences are not required for motions to dismiss the entire action or indictment, or when a conference is not possible.

(b) Certificate of Conference.

(1) Each motion for which a conference is required must include a certificate of conference indicating that the motion is unopposed or opposed.

(2) If a motion is opposed, the certificate must state that a conference was held, indicate the date of conference and the

identities of the attorneys conferring, and explain why agreement could not be reached.

(3) If a conference was not held, the certificate must explain why it was not possible to confer, in which event the motion will be presumed to be opposed.

(c) Proposed Order. An unopposed motion must be accompanied by an agreed proposed order, signed by the attorneys or parties. An opposed motion that is submitted on paper must be accompanied by a proposed order, set forth on a separate document, unless an order is not required by subsection (h) of this rule.

(d) Brief. An opposed motion must be accompanied by a brief that sets forth the moving party's contentions of fact and/or law, and argument and authorities, unless a brief is not required by subsection (h) of this rule. A response to an opposed motion must be accompanied by a brief that sets forth the responding party's contentions of fact and/or law, and argument and authorities. A responding party is not required to file a brief in opposition to a motion for which a brief is not required by subsection (h) of this rule.

(e) Time for Response and Brief. A response and brief to an opposed motion must be filed within 14 days from the date the motion is filed.

(f) Reply Brief. Reply briefs may not be filed unless the moving party requests, and the presiding judge grants, leave to do so. If leave is granted, the reply brief shall be filed no later than the deadline set by the presiding judge.

(g) No Oral Argument. Unless otherwise directed by the presiding judge, oral argument on a motion will not be held.

(h) Uniform Requirements on Motion Practice.

B—Brief required (not required with agreed motion)
C—Certificate of conference required
O—Order required

MOTION (to/for)	B	C	O
CHANGE OF VENUE	X	X	X
COMPEL	X	X	X
CONSOLIDATION	X	X	X
CONTINUANCE		X	X
DISMISS	X		
EXTEND TIME		X	X
JUDGMENT OF ACQUITTAL	X		X
LEAVE TO FILE	X	X	X
LIMINE	X	X	X
NEW TRIAL	X		
PRODUCE DOCUMENTS	X	X	X
PROTECTIVE ORDER	X	X	X
QUASH	X	X	X
SANCTIONS	X	X	X
SUBSTITUTE COUNSEL		X	X
TRANSFER		X	X
WITHDRAW		X	X

NOTE: If a motion is not listed, a brief, certificate of conference, and an order are required.

[Effective April 15, 1997. Amended effective April 15, 1998; September 1, 2000; September 1, 2006; December 1, 2009; September 1, 2015.]

LCrR 47.2   BRIEFS

(a) General Form. A brief must be printed, typewritten, or presented in some other legible form.

(b) Amicus Briefs. An amicus brief may not be filed without leave of the presiding judge. The brief must specifically set forth the interest of the amicus curiae in the outcome of the litigation.

(c) Length. A brief must not exceed 25 pages (excluding the table of contents and table of authorities). A reply brief must not exceed 10 pages. Permission to file a brief in excess of these page limitations will be granted by the presiding judge only for extraordinary and compelling reasons.

(d) Tables of Contents and Authorities. A brief in excess of 10 pages must contain:

(1) a table of contents with page references; and

(2) an alphabetically arranged table of cases, statutes, and other authorities cited, with page references to the location of all citations.

[Effective April 15, 1997.]

LCrR 47.3   CONFIRMATION OF INFORMAL LEAVE OF COURT

When a presiding judge informally grants leave, such as an extension of time to file a response, an attorney for the party to whom leave is granted must file a document confirming the leave and must serve the document on all other parties.

[Effective April 15, 1997.]

LCrR 47.4   MOTION PRACTICE IN CASES SEEKING POST–CONVICTION RELIEF

Motion practice in a prisoner application, motion, or petition filed under 28 U.S.C. § 2241, § 2254, or § 2255 is governed by the local civil rules.

[Effective September 1, 2016.]

LCrR 49.1   FILING CRIMINAL CASES

When a criminal case is filed, the United States must also submit, for each defendant, a completed criminal-case cover sheet, in the approved form.

[Effective April 15, 1997. Amended effective September 1, 2008.]

LCrR 49.2   FILING AND SERVING PLEADINGS, MOTIONS, OR OTHER PAPERS

(a) Filing With the Clerk. Except for discovery material, a pleading, motion, or other paper that the Federal Rules of Criminal Procedure permit or require to be filed, that is submitted on paper, must be filed with the clerk's office for the appropriate division. Such pleading, motion, or other paper must not be sent directly to the presiding judge.

(b) Original and Judge's Copy Required. An original and one judge's copy of each pleading, motion, or other paper that is submitted on paper must be filed with the clerk. If a pleading, motion, or other paper is filed by electronic means, the judge's copy must be submitted following procedures set forth in the ECF Administrative Procedures Manual.

(c) Document Containing More Than One Pleading, Motion, or Other Paper. Except for a proposed order, a document may contain more than one pleading, motion, or other paper. Any such document must clearly identify in the title each included pleading, motion, or other paper.

(d) Certificate of Service. All pleadings, motions, notices, and similar papers that Fed. R. Crim. P. 49 or a court order requires or permits be served must contain a certificate of service.

(e) Serving by Electronic Means. Delivery of the notice of electronic filing that is automatically generated by ECF constitutes service under Fed. R. Crim. P. 49(b) on each party who is a registered user of ECF.

(f) Electronic Filing Required. Unless the presiding judge otherwise directs, an attorney—other than a prisoner pro se party—must file any pleading (except an indictment or information), motion, or other paper by electronic means, subject to the restrictions and requirements of the ECF Administrative Procedures Manual. A party may, for cause, move to be excused from the requirement of electronic filing.

(g) Registration as an ECF User Required. Unless excused for cause, an attorney—other than a prisoner pro se party—must register as an ECF user within 14 days of the date the attorney appears in a case, following the registration procedures set forth in the ECF Administrative Procedures Manual.

[Effective April 15, 1997. Amended effective September 1, 2000; September 1, 2006; September 1, 2008; December 1, 2009.]

LCrR 49.3   REQUIRED FORM

In addition to the requirements of the Federal Rules of Criminal Procedure, each pleading, motion, or other paper must:

(a) contain on its face a title clearly identifying each included pleading, motion, or other paper;

(b) contain a signature block that sets forth the attorney's bar number for the jurisdiction in which the attorney is admitted to practice, and a facsimile number and e-mail address where information may be sent to the attorney;

(c) use a page size of 8½ × 11 inches;

(d) be typed, printed, or legibly handwritten on numbered pages; and

(e) when submitted on paper, unless otherwise provided by the local criminal rules or order of the presiding judge, be two-

hole punched at the top and either stapled in the upper, left-hand corner or secured with a durable fastener at the top.

[Effective April 15, 1997. Amended effective April 15, 1998; September 1, 2006.]

LCrR 49.4   NOTICE OF ORDERS AND JUDGMENTS

(a) Furnishing Copies of Orders and Judgments. Unless the presiding judge otherwise directs, the clerk shall furnish a copy of each order and judgment to counsel of record by first class mail or, where the clerk has the capability to do so, by electronic transmission. To receive orders and judgments by electronic transmission, the attorney of record must sign an agreement form provided by the clerk, and must comply with the applicable procedures established by the clerk. Where a party is represented by more than one attorney of record, the attorney designated in accordance with LCrR 49.4(b) or (c) shall receive copies of orders and judgments and distribute them to co-counsel for the same party who have not received a notice of electronic filing from ECF.

(b) Designation of Counsel to Receive Orders and Judgments. The clerk shall designate an attorney to receive copies of orders and judgments, in the following manner:

(1) the first attorney to sign an indictment; and

(2) the attorney appointed or retained to represent a defendant, or, when a defendant is represented by more than one attorney, the attorney who appears to be acting as lead counsel.

(c) Change in Designation of Counsel. If the attorney designated to receive orders and judgments desires that another attorney be substituted for this purpose, the attorney must request substitution in the manner prescribed by the clerk.

[Effective April 15, 1997. Amended effective September 1, 2006.]

LCrR 49.5   ELECTRONIC SIGNATURE

(a) What Constitutes Electronic Signature. The signature of an attorney who submits a pleading, motion, or other paper for filing by electronic means is the login and password issued to the attorney by the clerk.

(b) Requirements for Electronic Signature. An attorney who submits a document for filing by electronic means must place on the document an "s/" and the typed name of the attorney, or a graphical signature, in the space where the attorney's signature would have appeared had the document been submitted on paper.

(c) Certification of Signature of Another Person. By submitting a document by electronic means and representing the consent of another person on the document, an attorney who submits the document certifies that the document has been properly signed.

(d) Requirements for Another Person's Electronic Signature. An attorney who submits a document by electronic means that is signed by another person—other than a charging document or a document signed by a defendant—must:

(1) include a scanned image of the other person's signature, or represent the consent of the other person in a manner permitted or required by the presiding judge; and

(2) maintain the signed paper copy of the document for one year after final disposition of the case.

[Effective September 1, 2006. Amended effective September 1, 2008.]

LCrR 49.6   REQUIREMENT OF PAPER COPIES OF CERTAIN ELECTRONICALLY–FILED DOCUMENTS

When a charging document—including a complaint, information, indictment, or superseding indictment—or any document signed by a criminal defendant is submitted by electronic means, the attorney who submitted the document must deliver an original, signed paper document to the clerk within 7 days.

[Effective September 1, 2006. Amended effective December 1, 2009.]

LCrR 53.1   PHOTOGRAPHS, BROADCASTING, RECORDING, AND TELEVISION FORBIDDEN

No person may photograph, electronically record, televise, or broadcast a judicial proceeding. This rule shall not apply to ceremonial proceedings or electronic recordings by an official court reporter or other authorized court personnel.

[Effective April 15, 1997. Amended effective September 1, 2007.]

LCrR 53.2   DRESS AND CONDUCT

All persons present in a courtroom where a trial, hearing, or other proceeding is in progress must dress and conduct themselves in a manner demonstrating respect for the court. The presiding judge shall have the discretion to establish appropriate standards of dress and conduct.

[Effective April 15, 1997.]

LCrR 53.3   WEAPONS FORBIDDEN

Firearms and other weapons are prohibited in areas of buildings designated for court use. Such weapons may be carried by the United States Marshal, the marshal's deputies, courtroom security personnel, and other persons to whom a presiding judge has given approval.

[Effective April 15, 1997.]

LCrR 55.1   CASE FILES

(a) **Official Record.** The electronic version of a document maintained on ECF, or the paper version of a document not so maintained, is the official record of the court.

(b) **Inspection of Files.** Except as otherwise limited by rule or by court order, the electronic portion of an original file in a pending or closed case shall be available for public inspection in the clerk's office. The paper portion of an original file shall be available in the division where the case is filed, unless the file has been removed to a federal records center. The clerk shall not release the paper portion of a file from the clerk's custody without the permission of the presiding judge, or except as permitted by subsection (d) of this rule.

(c) **Inspection of Closed Files.** [Repealed September 1, 2006.]

(d) **Copies of Files.** Upon request, the clerk shall provide copies of the contents of case files, including transcripts of oral depositions and court proceedings. The clerk shall charge the fee established by the court for this service. When large numbers of copies are requested, the clerk is authorized to release the file to a commercial copying service, and to direct that the fee charged be paid directly to the service.

[Effective April 15, 1997. Amended effective September 1, 2006; September 1, 2008.]

LCrR 55.2   DISPOSITION OF EXHIBITS

(a) **Release While Case Pending.** Without an order from the presiding judge, no exhibit in the custody of the court may be removed from the clerk's office while the case is pending.

(b) **Removal or Destruction After Final Disposition of Case.** All exhibits in the custody of the court must be removed from the clerk's office within 60 days after final disposition of a case. The attorney who introduced the exhibits shall be responsible for their removal. Any exhibit not removed within the 60–day period may be destroyed or otherwise disposed of by the clerk.

[Effective April 15, 1997.]

LCrR 55.3   SEALED DOCUMENTS

(a) A party may file under seal any document that a statute or rule requires or permits to be so filed. The term "document," as used in this rule, means any pleading, motion, other paper, or physical item that the Federal Rules of Criminal Procedure permit or require to be filed.

(b) If no statute or rule requires or permits a document to be filed under seal, a party may file a document under seal only on motion and by permission of the presiding judge.

(1) When a party files on paper a motion for leave to file a document under seal, the clerk must file the motion under seal. The party must attach as an exhibit to the motion a copy of the document to be filed under seal. The party must also submit with the motion the original and a judge's copy of the document to be filed under seal. The original of the document must neither be physically attached to the motion nor made an exhibit to the motion. If leave to file the document under seal is granted, the clerk must file the original of the document under seal.

(2) When a party files by electronic means a motion for leave to file a document under seal, the party may file the motion under seal and must attach the proposed sealed document as an exhibit. If leave is granted, the sealed document will be deemed filed as of the date of the order granting leave, or as otherwise specified by the presiding judge, and the clerk will file a copy of the sealed document.

[Effective April 15, 1998. Amended effective September 1, 2008; September 2, 2014.]

LCrR 55.4 DISPOSITION OF SEALED DOCUMENTS

Unless the presiding judge otherwise directs, all sealed documents maintained on paper will be deemed unsealed 60 days after final disposition of a case. A party that desires that such a document remain sealed must move for this relief before the expiration of the 60–day period. The clerk may store, transfer, or otherwise dispose of unsealed documents according to the procedure that governs publicly available court records.

[Effective April 15, 1998. Amended effective September 1, 2008.]

LCrR 57.1 APPLICATION OF RULES BY A PRESIDING JUDGE

Notwithstanding the local criminal rules, a presiding judge may direct the parties to proceed in any manner that the judge deems just and expeditious.

[Effective April 15, 1997.]

LCrR 57.2 MISCELLANEOUS AND SPECIAL ORDERS

The clerk shall maintain in each division a copy of all miscellaneous and special orders adopted by the court, and shall make these orders available for inspection and copying.

[Effective April 15, 1997.]

LCrR 57.3 ASSIGNMENT AND TRANSFER OF CASES

(a) Assignment of Cases. The district judges shall determine the method by which all cases are assigned to individual judges.

(b) Transfer of Cases. A party desiring to transfer a case from the assigned presiding judge to another judge of this court must file a motion to transfer.

[Effective April 15, 1997. Amended effective September 1, 2015.]

LCrR 57.4 CONDUCT OF ATTORNEYS AT TRIAL OR HEARING

Unless the presiding judge otherwise directs, during a trial or hearing, attorneys must:

(a) stand when making objections or otherwise addressing the presiding judge;

(b) use the lectern while examining or cross-examining witnesses;

(c) when examining a witness, refrain from making statements, comments, or remarks before or after asking a question;

(d) limit to one attorney for each party the examination or cross-examination of a witness; and

(e) in making an objection, state plainly and briefly the grounds for objecting and not offer argument unless requested by the presiding judge.

[Effective April 15, 1997.]

LCrR 57.5 CLERK'S FEES [REPEALED EFFECTIVE SEPTEMBER 1, 2004]

LCrR 57.6 COURT REPORTER'S FEES [REPEALED EFFECTIVE SEPTEMBER 1, 2004]

LCrR 57.7 ADMISSION OF ATTORNEYS

Attorneys must fulfill the following requirements to be admitted to practice in this court:

(a) Eligibility for Admission. Any attorney licensed to practice law by the Supreme Court of Texas, or by the highest court of any state or the District of Columbia, may be admitted to the bar of this court if the attorney is of good personal and professional character and is a member in good standing of the bar where the attorney is licensed.

(b) Procedure for Admission. Attorneys desiring admission to the bar of this court must complete an application for admission, to be approved by a district judge, and, except as provided in subsection (c) of this rule, be introduced by a member in good standing of the bar of this court, and take the required oath or affirmation before a judge of this court. After the oath or affirmation is administered, and the applicant has paid the appropriate fee, the clerk shall issue a certificate stating that the attorney is admitted to practice before this court.

(c) Admission Before Judges of Other Districts. Any nonresident attorney who has completed all requirements for admission to the bar of this court may, with the approval of a district judge of the division where the application is pending, have the oath of admission administered by a judge in another district. The nonresident attorney must file the oath with the clerk and pay the appropriate fee before the attorney's name will be added to the roll of attorneys for this district.

(d) Admission Is Discretionary. All admissions to practice before this court shall be discretionary with the district judge reviewing the application for admission.

[Effective April 15, 1997. Amended effective September 1, 2002.]

LCrR 57.8 LOSS OF MEMBERSHIP AND DISCIPLINE OF ATTORNEYS

(a) Loss of Membership. A member of the bar of this court is subject to suspension or disbarment by the court under the following circumstances:

(1) if for any reason other than nonpayment of dues, failure to meet continuing legal education requirements, or voluntary resignation unrelated to a disciplinary proceeding or problem, an attorney loses, either temporarily or permanently, the right to practice law before:

(A) the courts of the State of Texas;

(B) the highest court of any other state or the District of Columbia; or

(C) any federal court; or

(2) if an attorney fails to maintain the right to practice law before the highest court of at least one state or the District of Columbia, unless the member's failure to maintain such right results from nonpayment of dues or failure to meet continuing legal education requirements.

(b) Grounds for Disciplinary Action. A presiding judge, after giving opportunity to show cause to the contrary, may take any appropriate disciplinary action against a member of the bar for:

(1) conduct unbecoming a member of the bar;

(2) failure to comply with any rule or order of this court;

(3) unethical behavior;

(4) inability to conduct litigation properly;

(5) conviction by any court of a felony or crime involving dishonesty or false statement; or

(6) having been publicly or privately disciplined by any court, bar, court agency or committee.

(c) Appeal of Disciplinary Action. [Repealed.]

(d) Reporting by Members. Any member of the bar of this court who has:

(1) lost or relinquished, temporarily or permanently, the right to practice in any court of record;

(2) been disciplined, publicly or privately, by any court, bar, court agency, or committee; or

(3) been convicted of a felony or crime involving dishonesty or false statement,

shall promptly report such fact in writing to the clerk, supplying full details and copies of all pertinent documents reflecting, or explaining, such action.

(e) Unethical Behavior. The term "unethical behavior," as used in this rule, means conduct undertaken in or related to a criminal proceeding in this court that violates the Texas Disciplinary Rules of Professional Conduct.

(f) Readmission. An attorney applying for readmission to the bar of this court must submit an application for readmission, together with the following materials:

(1) a full disclosure concerning the attorney's loss or relinquishment of membership in the bar of this court; and

(2) all information required by subsection (d) of this rule concerning facts that occurred prior to the date of application for readmission.

(g) Appointment of Counsel. The judge reviewing an application for admission shall have the right to appoint any member of the court's bar to assist in the handling of any proceeding contemplated by or resulting from this rule. An attorney appointed under this rule shall perform as requested unless relieved from doing so. An attorney desiring relief from appointment must move for such relief, which will be granted only upon a showing of good cause.

(h) Reciprocal Discipline.

(1) A member of the bar who is subject to suspension or disbarment under LCrR 57.8(a) must be given written notice by the chief judge, or by a district judge designated by the chief judge, that the court intends to suspend or disbar the member. The notice must identify the ground for imposing reciprocal discipline and provide the member an opportunity to show cause, within the time prescribed by the notice, why the member should not be suspended or disbarred.

(2) If the member does not respond to the notice, or responds but does not oppose reciprocal discipline, the chief judge or a designee district judge may enter an appropriate order after the prescribed time for a response expires or the response is received.

(3) If the member responds and, in whole or in part, opposes reciprocal discipline, the chief judge, or a district judge designated by the chief judge, must designate three district judges to hear the matter. The decision of a majority of the three-judge panel concerning the appropriate discipline shall be the final ruling of this court.

[Effective April 15, 1997. Amended effective September 1, 2002; September 1, 2004.]

LCrR 57.9 ATTORNEYS NOT ADMITTED TO PRACTICE BEFORE THIS COURT

(a) Eligibility to Appear. An attorney who is licensed to practice law by the highest court of any state or the District of Columbia, but who is not admitted to practice before this court, may represent a party in proceedings in this court only by permission of the presiding judge.

(b) Application to Appear. Unless exempted by LCrR 57.11, an attorney who is not admitted to practice in this court, who desires to represent a party in a proceeding, and who is eligible pursuant to subsection (a) of this rule to appear, shall apply for admission pro hac vice on a court-approved form and pay the applicable fee to the clerk.

(c) Regulation of Attorneys Admitted Pro Hac Vice. By appearing in any case, an attorney becomes subject to the rules of this court.

[Effective April 15, 1997. Amended effective September 1, 1999.]

LCrR 57.10 REQUIREMENT OF LOCAL COUNSEL

(a) Local Counsel Required. Unless exempted by LCrR 57.11, local counsel is required in all cases where an attorney appearing in a case does not reside or maintain the attorney's principal office in this district. "Local counsel" means a member of the bar of this court who resides or maintains the attorney's principal office in this district and whose residence or principal office is located within 50 miles of the courthouse in the division in which the case is pending. Attorneys desiring to proceed without local counsel must obtain leave from the presiding judge. If the request for leave is denied, written designation of local counsel must be filed within 14 days of the denial.

(b) Duties of Local Counsel. Local counsel must be authorized to present and argue a party's position at any hearing called by the presiding judge. Local counsel must also be able to perform, on behalf of the party represented, any other duty required by the presiding judge or the local criminal rules of this court.

[Effective April 15, 1997. Amended effective December 1, 2009; September 4, 2012.]

LCrR 57.11 EXEMPTION FROM ADMISSION TO PRACTICE, AND FROM REQUIREMENT OF LOCAL COUNSEL, FOR ATTORNEYS APPEARING ON BEHALF OF THE UNITED STATES JUSTICE DEPARTMENT OR THE ATTORNEY GENERAL OF THE STATE OF TEXAS

Unless the presiding judge otherwise directs, an attorney appearing on behalf of the United States Justice Department or the Attorney General of the State of Texas, and who is eligible pursuant to LCrR 57.9(a) to appear in this court, shall be exempt from the requirements of LCrR 57.9(b) and 57.10, but shall otherwise be subject to all requirements applicable to attorneys who have been granted leave to appear pro hac vice.

[Effective April 15, 1997.]

LCrR 57.12 WITHDRAWAL OF ATTORNEY

(a) Except as provided in subsection (b) or (c) of this rule, an attorney desiring to withdraw in any case must file a motion to withdraw. This motion must, in addition to the matters required by LCrR 47.1, specify the reasons requiring withdrawal and provide the name and address of the succeeding attorney. If the succeeding attorney is not known, the motion must set forth the name, address, and telephone number of the client and either bear the client's signature approving withdrawal or state specifically why, after due diligence, the attorney was unable to obtain the client's signature.

(b) When an Assistant United States Attorney enters an appearance in a case, another Assistant United States Attorney may replace the attorney by filing a notice of substitution that identifies the attorney being replaced. Unless the presiding judge otherwise directs, the notice effects the withdrawal of the attorney being replaced.

(c) When the Federal Public Defender is appointed to represent a party and an Assistant Federal Public Defender enters an appearance in the case, another Assistant Federal Public Defender may replace the attorney who has entered an appearance by filing a notice of substitution that identifies the attorney being replaced. Unless the presiding judge otherwise directs, the notice effects the withdrawal of the attorney being replaced.

[Effective April 15, 1997. Amended effective September 1, 2002; September 1, 2009.]

LCrR 57.13 CHANGE OF CONTACT INFORMATION OR NAME

(a) Attorney Who Is Not a Registered User of ECF. When an attorney who is not a registered user of ECF changes the attorney's business address, e-mail address, telephone number, facsimile number, or name, the attorney must promptly notify the clerk, using the approved method, and the presiding judge, in writing, in each pending case.

(b) Attorney Who Is a Registered User of ECF. When an attorney who is a registered user of ECF changes the attorney's business address, e-mail address, telephone number, facsimile number, or name, the attorney must promptly change this information in ECF, following procedures set forth in the ECF Administrative Procedures Manual.

[Effective April 15, 1997. Amended effective September 1, 2006; September 1, 2008.]

LCrR 57.14 PARTIES PROCEEDING PRO SE

Any party proceeding on the party's own behalf is considered pro se. Pro se parties must read and follow the local criminal rules of this court and the Federal Rules of Criminal Procedure.

[Effective April 15, 1997.]

LCrR 57.15 ATTORNEY AS A WITNESS [REPEALED EFFECTIVE SEPTEMBER 1, 2004]

LCrR 58.1 PROCEDURE GOVERNED BY MISCELLANEOUS ORDER

The procedures for conducting proceedings involving minor criminal offenses, as defined by 18 U.S.C. § 3401, shall be governed by the current miscellaneous order establishing such procedures.

[Effective April 15, 1997.]

LCrR 59.1 BRIEFING PRACTICE CONCERNING OBJECTIONS TO MAGISTRATE JUDGE ORDERS IN NONDISPOSITIVE MATTERS

(a) Brief. Objections filed under Fed. R. Crim. P. 59(a) must be accompanied by a brief that sets forth the party's contentions of fact and/or law, and argument and authorities, and complies with LCrR 47.2.

(b) Response Brief. A response brief to objections filed under Fed. R. Crim. P. 59(a) must comply with LCrR 47.2 and be filed within 14 days from the date the objections are filed.

(c) Reply Brief. Reply briefs may not be filed unless the moving party requests, and the presiding judge grants, leave to do so. If leave is granted, the reply brief shall be filed no later than the deadline set by the presiding judge and comply with LCrR 47.2.

(d) Preparing the Record. A party who files objections under Fed. R. Crim. P. 59(a) is responsible for preparing the record and—if necessary for disposition of the objections—obtaining a hearing transcript. Unless otherwise directed by the presiding judge, the transcript must be filed contemporaneously with the objections.

[Effective December 1, 2005. Amended effective December 1, 2009.]

LCrR 59.2   BRIEFING PRACTICE CONCERNING OBJECTIONS TO MAGISTRATE JUDGE RECOMMENDATIONS ON DISPOSITIVE MOTIONS

(a) **Brief.** Objections filed under Fed. R. Crim. P. 59(b)(2) must be accompanied by a brief that sets forth the party's contentions of fact and/or law, and argument and authorities, and complies with LCrR 47.2.

(b) **Response Brief.** A response brief to objections filed under Fed. R. Crim. P. 59(b)(2) must comply with LCrR 47.2 and be filed within 14 days from the date the objections are filed.

(c) **Reply Brief.** Reply briefs may not be filed unless the moving party requests, and the presiding judge grants, leave to do so. If leave is granted, the reply brief shall be filed no later than the deadline set by the presiding judge and comply with LCrR 47.2.

[Effective December 1, 2005. Amended effective December 1, 2009.]

LOCAL BANKRUPTCY RULES

LBR 8005.1 PROCEDURE FOR PRESENTING MOTION [REPEALED EFFECTIVE SEPTEMBER 1, 2015]

LBR 8006.2 DUTY OF PARTIES TO PROVIDE COPIES OF ITEMS FOR INCLUSION IN THE RECORD [REPEALED EFFECTIVE SEPTEMBER 1, 2015]

LBR 8006.3 DUTY OF BANKRUPTCY CLERK WHEN PARTY FAILS TO PROVIDE COPIES OF DESIGNATED ITEMS; PREPAYMENT REQUIREMENT [REPEALED EFFECTIVE SEPTEMBER 1, 2015]

LBR 8006.6 RELEASE, CIRCULATION, AND RETURN OF RECORD ON APPEAL [REPEALED EFFECTIVE SEPTEMBER 1, 2015]

LBR 8009.1 DUTY OF BANKRUPTCY CLERK TO INDEX THE RECORD ON APPEAL

When the bankruptcy clerk prepares the record on appeal, the clerk shall include as the first document an index that notes the page numbers in the record where (1) the notice of appeal, (2) the judgment, order, or decree appealed from, (3) any opinion, findings of fact, and conclusions of law of the bankruptcy court, (4) the bankruptcy court docket sheet; and (5) the parties' designated items can be found.

[Former LBR 8006.5 effective September 1, 1999. Renumbered LBR 8009.1 and amended effective September 1, 2015.]

LBR 8009.2 DUTY OF BANKRUPTCY CLERK TO ORGANIZE ITEMS IN THE RECORD ON APPEAL

When the bankruptcy clerk prepares the record on appeal, the following items shall be included after the index required by LBR 8009.1, in this order: (1) the notice of appeal, (2) the judgment, order, or decree appealed from, (3) any opinion, findings of fact, and conclusions of law of the bankruptcy court, and (4) the bankruptcy court docket sheet.

The bankruptcy clerk shall otherwise prepare the record on appeal as required or permitted by the Federal Rules of Bankruptcy Procedure, the local bankruptcy rules of this court, and any applicable administrative procedures that conform to Fed. R. Bankr. P. 8026.

[Former LBR 8006.1 effective September 1, 1999. Renumbered LBR 8009.2 and amended effective September 1, 2015.]

LBR 8009.3 DUTY OF BANKRUPTCY CLERK TO NUMBER THE RECORD ON APPEAL

The bankruptcy clerk shall consecutively number each page of the record on appeal.

[Former LBR 8006.4 effective September 1, 1999. Renumbered LBR 8009.3 and amended effective September 1, 2015.]

LBR 8010.3 LENGTH OF BRIEFS [REPEALED EFFECTIVE SEPTEMBER 1, 2015]

LBR 8010.4 CITATION OF SUPPLEMENTAL AUTHORITIES [REPEALED EFFECTIVE SEPTEMBER 1, 2015]

LBR 8012.1 CERTIFICATE OF INTERESTED PERSONS

(a) The appellant and the appellee must file a "Certificate of Interested Persons," certifying a complete list of all persons, associations of persons, firms, partnerships, corporations, guarantors, insurers, affiliates, parent corporations, or other legal entities who or which are financially interested in the outcome of the appeal. If a large group of persons or firms can be specified by a generic description, individual listing is not necessary. Each such certificate shall also list the names of opposing law firms and/or counsel in the case.

(b) The appellant must file a Certificate of Interested Persons no later than 7 days, and the appellee must file a certificate no later than 14 days, after the district clerk dockets the appeal under Fed. R. Bankr. P. 8003(d)(2) or 8004(c)(2).

[Former LBR 8010.1 effective September 1, 1999. Renumbered LBR 8012.1 and amended effective September 1, 2015.]

LBR 8014.1 CITATIONS TO THE RECORD

The requirement of Fed. R. Bankr. P. 8014(a)(8) and 8014(b) that the argument contain citations to the parts of the record relied on must be satisfied by citing the record page number assigned by the bankruptcy clerk pursuant to LBR 8009.3 (*e.g.*, R. 105). The brief must not cite a transcript or document only by its own page (*e.g.*, Hearing Tr. 10 or Contract p. 7), but may contain such a citation if the specific record page is cited first (*e.g.*, R. 105, Hearing Tr. 10).

[Former LBR 8010.2 effective September 1, 1999. Renumbered LBR 8014.1 and amended effective September 1, 2015.]

APPENDICES

APPENDIX I. INFORMATION ABOUT CASES AND FORMS

A. Information About Current Status Of Cases, Settings, Etc. (Judges' Letter Designation Before Name). Information concerning the status of cases, motion settings, pretrial settings, trial settings or other scheduling information is kept by either the courtroom deputy or the judge's secretary. This information may be obtained by calling:

(M)	Chief Judge Barbara M.G. **LYNN**	214–753–2420
(D)	Judge Sidney A. **FITZWATER**	214–753–2333
(A)	Judge John H. **McBRYDE**	817–850–6650
(L)	Judge Sam A. **LINDSAY**	214–753–2365
(N)	Judge David C. **GODBEY**	214–753–2700
(K)	Judge Ed **KINKEADE**	214–753–2720
(B)	Judge Jane J. **BOYLE**	214–753–2740
(O)	Judge Reed **O'CONNOR**	817–850–6788
(S)	Judge Karen **GREN–SCHOLER**	214–753–2342
(G)	Senior Judge A. Joe **FISH**	214–753–2310
(C)	Senior Judge Sam R. **CUMMINGS**	806–472–1922
(Y)	Senior Judge Terry R. **MEANS**	817–850–6670

B. Information About Entry of Legal Documents and Orders. Each civil case is assigned to a judge by random draw. For information about what legal documents have actually been filed and entered on the official docket sheet, go to the Electronic Case Files system on the court's website at www.txnd.uscourts.gov or call:

Dallas Division

214–753–2633
866–243–2866

Abilene Division

325–677–6311

Amarillo Division

806–468–3805

Fort Worth Division

817–850–6733
800–240–7240

Lubbock Division

806–472–1905

San Angelo Division

325–655–4506

Wichita Falls Division

940–767–1902

C. Summons in a Civil Action.

D. Civil Cover Sheet.

[Amended effective September 1, 2016; September 1, 2018.]

APPENDIX II. TABLE OF DIVISIONS

The following table sets forth the official number and name of each Division of the Northern District of Texas, the counties that each Division encompasses, and the name, mailing address, and telephone number of the Clerk, the District Judges, the Magistrate, and the Bankruptcy Judges for each Division.

1. Abilene Division. Comprises the counties of Callahan, Eastland, Fisher, Haskell, Howard, Jones, Mitchell, Nolan, Shackelford, Stephens, Stonewall, Taylor, and Throckmorton.

Ms. Misti **GRANT**, Deputy–in–Charge 325–677–3971
341 Pine Street, Room 2008
Abilene, Texas 79601–5928

Magistrate Judge E. Scott **FROST** 325–676–4582
341 Pine Street, Room 2313
Abilene, Texas 79601

Bankruptcy Judge Robert L. **JONES** 806–472–5020
1205 Texas Avenue, Room 312
Lubbock, Texas 79401

2. Amarillo Division. Comprises the counties of Armstrong, Briscoe, Carson, Castro, Childress, Collingsworth, Dallam, Deaf Smith, Donley, Gray, Hall, Hansford, Hartley, Hemphill, Hutchinson, Lipscomb, Moore, Ochiltree, Oldham, Parmer, Potter, Randall, Roberts, Sherman, Swisher, and Wheeler.

Ms. Delynda **SMITH**, Deputy–in–Charge 806–468–3831
205 E. Fifth Street, Room 103
Amarillo, Texas 79101–1559

AMARILLO DIVISION 806–468–3822
205 E. Fifth Street, Room 226
Amarillo, Texas 79101

Judge Sidney A. **FITZWATER** 214–753–2333
1100 Commerce Street, Room 1528
Dallas, Texas 75242–9970

Magistrate Judge Lee Ann **RENO** 806–468–3832
205 E. Fifth Street, Room 321
Amarillo, Texas 79101

3. Dallas Division. Comprises the counties of Dallas, Ellis, Hunt, Johnson, Kaufman, Navarro, and Rockwall.

Ms. Karen **MITCHELL**, Clerk of Court ....   for recorded information: 214–753–2200
1100 Commerce Street, Room 1452   for assistance: 214–753–2201
Dallas, Texas 75242–1495

Chief Judge Barbara M.G. **LYNN** 214–753–2420
1100 Commerce Street, Room 1572
Dallas, Texas 75242

Judge Sidney A. **FITZWATER** 214–753–2333
1100 Commerce Street, Room 1528
Dallas, Texas 75242–9970

Judge Sam A. **LINDSAY** 214–753–2365
L2–31100 Commerce Street, Room 1544
Dallas, Texas 75242

Judge David C. **GODBEY** 214–753–2700
1100 Commerce Street, Room 1504
Dallas, Texas 75242

Judge Ed **KINKEADE** 214–753–2720
1100 Commerce Street, Room 1625
Dallas, Texas 75242

Judge Jane J. **BOYLE** 214–753–2740
L2–31100 Commerce Street, Room 1358
Dallas, Texas 75242

Judge Karen **GREN–SCHOLER** 214–753–2342
1100 Commerce Street, Room 1654
Dallas, Texas 75242

Senior Judge A. Joe **FISH** 214–753–2310
1100 Commerce Street, Room 1404
Dallas, Texas 75242–1597

Senior Judge Sam R. **CUMMINGS** 806–472–1922
1205 Texas Avenue, Room C–210
Lubbock, Texas 79401

Magistrate Judge Irma C. **RAMIREZ** 214–753–2393
1100 Commerce Street, Room 1567
Dallas, Texas 75242

Magistrate Judge Renée Harris **TOLIVER** 214–753–2385
1100 Commerce Street, Room 1611
Dallas, Texas 75242

Magistrate Judge David L. **HORAN** 214–753–2400
1100 Commerce Street, Room 1549
Dallas, Texas 75242

Magistrate Judge Rebecca **RUTHERFORD** 214–753–2410
1100 Commerce Street, Room 1312
Dallas, Texas 75242

Chief Bankruptcy Judge Barbara J. **HOUSER** 214–753–2055
1100 Commerce Street, Room 1424
Dallas, Texas 75242

Bankruptcy Judge Harlin D. **HALE** 214–753–2016
1100 Commerce Street, Room 1420
Dallas, Texas 75242

Bankruptcy Judge Stacey G.C. **JERNIGAN** 214–753–2040
1100 Commerce Street, Room 1428
Dallas, Texas 75242

4. Fort Worth Division. Comprises the counties of Comanche, Erath, Hood, Jack, Palo Pinto, Parker, Tarrant, and Wise.

Mr. Brian **REBECEK**, Manager 817–850–6613
501 West 10th Street, Room 310
Fort Worth, Texas 76102

Judge John H. **McBRYDE** 817–850–6650
501 West 10th Street, Room 401
Fort Worth, Texas 76102

Judge Reed **O'CONNOR** 817–850–6788
501 West 10th Street, Room 201
Fort Worth, Texas 76102

Senior Judge Terry R. **MEANS** 817–850–6670
501 West 10th Street, Room 502
Fort Worth, Texas 76102

Magistrate Judge Jeffrey L. **CURETON** 817–850–6690
501 West 10th Street, Room 520
Fort Worth, Texas 76102

Bankruptcy Judge Russell F. **NELMS** 817–333–6025
501 West 10th Street, Room 206
Fort Worth, Texas 76102

Bankruptcy Judge Mark X. **MULLIN** 817–333–6020
501 West 10th Street, Room 128
Fort Worth, Texas 76102

5. Lubbock Division. Comprises the counties of Bailey, Borden, Cochran, Crosby, Dawson, Dickens, Floyd, Gaines, Garza, Hale, Hockley, Kent, Lamb, Lubbock, Lynn, Motley, Scurry, Terry, and Yoakum.

Mr. Erik **PALTROW**, Deputy–in–Charge 806–472–1900
1205 Texas Avenue, Room 209
Lubbock, Texas 79401

Senior Judge Sam R. **CUMMINGS** 806–472–1922
1205 Texas Avenue, Room C–210
Lubbock, Texas 79401

Magistrate Judge D. Gordon **BRYANT, JR.** 806–472–1963
1205 Texas Avenue, Room 211
Lubbock, Texas 79401

Bankruptcy Judge Robert L. **JONES** 806–472–5020
1205 Texas Avenue, Room 312
Lubbock, Texas 79401

6. San Angelo Division. Comprises the counties of Brown, Coke, Coleman, Concho, Crocket, Glasscock, Irion, Menard, Mills, Reagan, Runnels, Schleicher, Sterling, Sutton, and Tom Green.

Mr. Erik **PALTROW**, Deputy–in–Charge 806–472–1900
33 E. Twohig Street, Room 202 325–655–4506
San Angelo, Texas 76903

Senior Judge Sam R. **CUMMINGS**   806–472–1922
1205 Texas Ave., Room C–210
Lubbock, Texas 79401

Magistrate Judge E. Scott **FROST** 325–676–4582
341 Pine Street, Room 2313
San Angelo, Texas 76901

Bankruptcy Judge Robert L. **JONES** 806–472–5020
1205 Texas Avenue, Rm 312
Lubbock, Texas 79401

7. Wichita Falls Division. Comprises the counties of Archer, Baylor, Clay, Cottle, Foard, Hardeman, King, Knox, Montague, Wichita, Wilbarger, and Young.

Ms. Teena **TIMMONS**, Deputy–In–Charge 940–767–2525
1000 Lamar Street, Room 203
Wichita Falls, Texas 76301

Judge Reed **O'CONNOR** 817–850–6788
501 W. 10th Street, Room 310
Fort Worth, Texas 76102

Magistrate Judge Hal R. **RAY, JR.** 940–767–2726
1000 Lamar Street, Room 203
Wichita Falls, Texas 76301

Bankruptcy Judge Harlin D. **HALE** 817–333–6020
501 West 10th Street, Room 20
Fort Worth, Texas 76102

[Effective September 4, 2012. Amended effective September 1, 2015; September 1, 2016; September 1, 2018.]

APPENDIX III. INDEX OF MISCELLANEOUS ORDERS*

1. Order Establishing the Procedure for Issuance of Orders for Entry on Premises to Effect Levy by Internal Revenue Service *(Adopted 9–26–77; Amended 2–16–79).*

2. Standing Order on Probation Conditions *(Adopted 8–28–64).*

3. Order Adopting the Plan for Representation of Defendants Under the Criminal Justice Act of 1964 *(Adopted 8–20–65; Amended 12–30–93; Amended 9–19–00).*

4. Standing Order Establishing Reporters' Rates for Transcripts *(Adopted 11–7–66; Amended 10–23–07).*

5. Order Relating to the Selection of Grand and Petit Jurors in the Northern District of Texas *(Adopted 9–13–68; Amended 5–14–98; Amended 1–12–09).*

6. Order for the Adoption of Rules for the Exercise of Powers and Performance of Duties by United States Magistrates *(Adopted 1–20–71; Amended 5–05–05; Amended 7–29–09)* [See Appendix V].

7. Order Relating to the Disposition of Minor Offenses *(Adopted 3–15–71; Amended 5–5–93; Amended 1–22–13)* [See LCrR 58.1].

8. Order Adopting the Plan for Achieving Prompt Disposition of Criminal Cases *(Adopted 3–6–73; Amended 6–23–80).*

9. Order on Payment of Fees for Attorneys Appointed Under the Criminal Justice Act of 1964 *(Adopted 3–26–73; Amended 4–14–87).*

10. Order Requiring Civil Cover Sheet for All Cases Filed as Civil Actions *(Adopted 8–15–73)* [See LR 3.1 and Appendix I–D].

11. Standing Orders Relating to Bankruptcy Matters *(Adopted 7–28–75; Amended 9–30–79)* [Historical Only].

12. Order Providing for the Fixing of Conditions of Release *(Adopted 2–27–76)* [Historical Only].

13. Order Establishing Procedures for Handling Petitions and/or Motions for Post Conviction Relief Under 28 U.S.C. 2254 and 2255 *(Adopted 3–18–77; Amended 11–18–99; Amended 5–22–03; Amended 10–15–10)* [See LR 5.4].

14. Order Establishing Procedure for Handling Prisoner Civil Rights Actions *(Adopted 12–16–77; Amended 10–8–97)* [See LR 5.3].

15. Order Governing Applications to Proceed *In Forma Pauperis (Adopted 12–16–77; Amended 10–15–10)* [See LR 83.6].

16. Order Establishing Procedure for Admission to Practice in the United States District Court for the Northern District of Texas *(Adopted 12–16–77; Amended 8–15–07)* [See LR 83.7 and LCrR 57.7].

17. Order Adopting Local Rules of Practice *(Adopted 12–16–77; Amended 7–1–85)* [Now Special Order 2–1].

18. Order Establishing Special Miscellaneous Order Files and Repealing Previously Existing Local Rules and Miscellaneous Orders *(Adopted 12–16–77)* [See LR 83.2 and LCrR 57.2].

19. Order Sealing All Notifications of Disclosure of Grand Jury Material Pursuant to Rule 6(e)(2)(A)(ii) and Rule 6(e)(2)(B), Federal Rules of Criminal Procedure *(Adopted 12–5–77)* [Now Special Order 5–1].

20. Order Establishing the Procedure for Service of Civil Process and Central Violation Summons *(Adopted 3–2–78, Repealed by Miscellaneous Order No. 30 4–1–81)* [Historical Only].

21. Order Concerning Civil Jury Composition *(Adopted 4–7–78; Amended 5–29–80)* [Historical Only] [Not adopted as a Local Rule].

22. Order Concerning the Creation of Three New District Judgeships in the Northern District of Texas and the Orderly Assignment of Cases Pending on the Docket *(Adopted 10–27–78; Amended 5–13–82)* [Now Special Order 3–1].

23. Order Establishing the Procedure for Issuance of Inspection Warrants for Entry on Premises by Compliance Officers of the Occupational Safety and Health Administration, U.S. Department of Labor *(Adopted 12–4–78)*.

24. Order Adopting the Model Federal Rules of Disciplinary Enforcement *(Adopted 12–7–78; Repealed 3–25–87)* [See LR 83.8 and LCrR 57.8].

25. Order Establishing Simplified Procedures for the United States of America to Take Money Judgment by Default *(Adopted 4–3–79)*.

26. Order Regarding Petition for Disclosure of Pre-sentence or Probation Records *(Adopted 6–18–79; Amended 6–1–90)*.

27. Order Amending Rule 11.3 of the Local Rules of Practice Before the United States District Court for the Northern District of Texas *(Adopted 7–9–80)* [Historical Only] [See LR 79.2 and LCrR 55.2].

28. Order Adopting Affirmative Action Plan for the United States District Court for the Northern District of Texas *(Adopted 7–11–80; Amended 5–18–93)* [Now Special Order No. 17].

29. Order Amending Local Rules 2.2 and 6.1(b) *(Adopted 10–24–80; Amended 6–24–83; Amended 6–24–85)* [Historical Only] [See LR 5.2].

30. Order Establishing Procedures for Service of Civil Process—Repealing Miscellaneous Order No. 20 *(Adopted 4–1–81; Amended 7–28–81)* [Historical Only].

31. Order Relating to Persons Detained/Incarcerated for Attendance at Criminal Trial as Witness *(Adopted 4–15–81)*.

32. Order Establishing Procedures Following Appeal in Criminal Cases *(Adopted 10–21–81)*.

33. Order Pertaining to Bankruptcy Judges Authority *(Adopted 10–4–82; Amended 12–19–84)*.

34. Order Adopting the Plan for the Management of Court Reporting for the Northern District of Texas *(Adopted 2–1–83; Amended 7–12–04)*.

35. Order Exempting Cases From Schedule and Planning Mandates of Rule 16(b), Federal Rules of Civil Procedure *(Adopted 9–16–83; Amended 1–16–84)* [See LR 16.1].

36. Order Establishing Procedures for Seeking Stay of Enforcement of State Court Judgment or Order *(Adopted 12–5–83)*.

37. Order Amending Local Rule 5.1(e) Responding to Motions, Time for Responses, Provision for Reply; New Local Rule 8.1(c) Designation of Expert Witnesses; New Local Rule 12.2 Request for Attorney's Fees *(Adopted 1–16–84)* [Historical Only] [See LR 7.1, LR 26.2, LCrR 16.1, and LCrR 47.1].

38. Order Concerning the Requirement and Need for United States Marshals in All Criminal Proceedings in the Northern District of Texas *(Adopted 12–17–84)* [Now Special Order 6–1].

39. Order Pertaining to Interim Appointment of United States Attorney for the Northern District of Texas *(Adopted 6–17–85)* [Historical Only].

40. Order Pertaining to Firearms Policy for the United States Probation Office, Northern District of Texas *(Adopted 12–16–85; Amended 2/21/97)* [Now Special Order 7–1].

41. Order Pertaining to Clerk Accepting and Disbursing All Restitution Payments Other Than Those Payable to the United States, for Offenses Committed On or After January 1, 1985 *(Adopted 1–27–86)* [Now Special Order 10–1].

42. Order Pertaining to the Schedule Adopted for the Supervision of Grand Jury Proceedings by the United States District Judges of the Dallas Division of the Northern District of Texas *(Adopted 4–14–86; Amended 1–26–87)* [Now Special Order 5–2].

43. Order Pertaining to the Criminal Docket in the Dallas Division and the Assignment of Cases on Such Docket To Include the Name of the Honorable Sidney A. Fitzwater *(Adopted 4–17–86)* [Now Special Order 3–2].

44. Order Establishing Length of Briefs and Requiring Table of Contents and Table of Authorities in Briefs Which Exceed Ten Pages in Length *(Adopted 12–23–88)* [See LR 7.2 and LCrR 47.2].

45. Order Regarding Deposit in Court Pursuant to Rule 67 of the Civil Rules *(Adopted 6–23–89; Amended 10–7–97; Amended 5–6–11; Amended 3–7–14 (45–7))*.

46. Civil Justice Expense and Delay Reduction Plan *(Adopted 3–22–93; Amended 5–21–02)*.

47. Order Adopting Rules Governing Practice Before this Court by Law Students and Unlicensed Law Graduates *(Adopted 10–27–93)*.

48. Order Enforcing Sanctions Imposed by Another Federal Court in Texas *(Adopted 11–15–93)*.

49. Order Regarding Matters Pertaining to Court Interpreters *(Adopted 8–16–93; Amended 8–30–93)*.

50. Order Closing Abilene Courtroom for Renovations *[Adopted 4–18–95]*.

51. Order Providing for Disposition of Passports Surrendered *(Adopted 1–9–96; Amended 2–1–06)*.

52. Order for Probation Form 12 Procedures *(Adopted 7–9–96)*.

53. Amendment to Special Order No. 7–27 Firearms Policy for U.S. Probation Office *(Adopted 8–16–96; Amended 4–26–06)*.

54. Approval of Oleoresin Capsicum (OC) a Personal Defense Spray for Duty for use by U.S. Probation and Pretrial Officers in the Northern District of Texas *(Adopted 11–4–96)*.

55. Prisoner In Forma Pauperis Proceedings *(Adopted 2/26/97; Amended 5–26–98)*.

56. Petition for Actions on Conditions of Pretrial release and Order for Warrant Shall be Presented to the Court in Envelope Marked "SEALED" *(Adopted 2/18/97)*.

57. Order Establishing Disclosure of Information to State/Local Authorities for Sex Offender Registration/Notification *(Adopted 1–21–99; Amended 7–21–00)*.

58. Order Requiring Counsel to Notify the Presiding Judge of Any Proposed Change to Scheduled Arraignment or Rearraignment in the Dallas Division *(Adopted 2–23–00)*.

59. Order allowing probation officers to transport non-governmental personnel in GSA vehicles and persons under supervision in officers' privately owned vehicles where circumstances justify doing so *(Adopted 7–9–01)*.

60. Order authorizing Probation and Pretrial Services offices to establish and operate an on-site drug testing laboratory to better serve the court, defendants, and offenders in the Northern District of Texas *(Adopted 10–15–01)*.

61. Order adopting procedures to control electronic case filing (ECF) in the Northern District of Texas as defined in this order and in the clerk's office ECF User's Manual *(Adopted 2–21–03; Amended 5–28–08; Amended 10–21–08)*.

62. Order adopting procedures to control management of Dallas division patent cases in the Northern District of Texas as defined in this Order *(Adopted 4–2–07; Amended 11–17–09)*.

63. Order adopting procedures to control management of electronic communication devices, including, but not limited to, cellular telephones, pagers, personal digital assistants, laptop computers, and tape recorders, onto any court floor within the Northern District of Texas *(Adopted 4–2–07; Amended 11–17–10)*.

[Effective September 4, 2012. Amended effective September 1, 2015; September 1, 2016.]

* Dates of amendments reflect most recent amendment for each miscellaneous order.

APPENDIX IV. INDEX OF SPECIAL ORDERS

Special Order No. 20:	Orders regarding Jury Utilization Management Plan as a guideline for judges and court personnel to encourage efficient juror utilization
Special Order No. 21:	Orders regarding authorization of Court Security Officers to carry personal handguns onto federal property
Special Order No. 22:	Orders regarding magistrate judge appointments, reappointments, verification proceedings, and appointment of magistrate judge merit selection panels
Special Order No. 23:	Orders regarding Pretrial Diversion Agreement ("PS4 form") submitted to the Court by and through the United States Attorney's Office that is not associated with a criminal case. Each such PS4 form will remain under seal unless otherwise ordered by a judge

[Amended effective September 1, 2015; September 1, 2016.]

APPENDIX V. MISCELLANEOUS ORDER NO. 6
Rule 1

Powers and Duties of Magistrates under 28 U.S.C. § 636(a)

A magistrate judge appointed to serve in the United States District Court for the Northern District of Texas is hereby granted authority and is specially designated to perform all duties that may be performed by a United States magistrate judge under law. A magistrate judge has all power necessary to perform such duties except as otherwise limited by law. Nothing in this Miscellaneous Order should be construed as limiting the powers of the district judge to perform all such duties, except as otherwise limited by law.

Rule 2

Additional Powers and Duties of Magistrate Judges under 28 U.S.C. § 636(b)

a. Unless otherwise directed by the presiding district judge, a magistrate judge serving within the Northern District of Texas is authorized, without further order of the court, to perform the following duties in all actions filed by prisoners, persons proceeding *pro se*, or persons seeking leave to proceed *in forma pauperis*:

(1) Review and construe papers presented to the clerk and direct the clerk as to whether and in what manner said papers will be accepted, if appropriate, for filing or other disposition by the court;

(2) Direct a litigant to resubmit pleadings or other filings on forms approved by the court, or to provide a more definite statement or amended pleadings, and to issue notices of deficiency as authorized by the rules and orders of this court;

(3) Order that the matter be transferred to another district or division if venue is not properly laid in the Northern District of Texas or the particular division in which the action was filed, or when venue is more appropriate in another district or division;

(4) Determine whether leave to proceed *in forma pauperis* should be granted unconditionally or provisionally, and to

(a)(i) enter orders permitting a *pro se* litigant to proceed *in forma pauperis*; (ii) grant leave to proceed *in forma pauperis* to a person seeking relief pursuant to 28 U.S.C. Sections 2241 and 2254, if the average six month balance of the person's inmate trust account and other financial resources are less than Fifty Dollars; and (iii) enter orders to assess and collect filing fees pursuant to the Prison Litigation Reform Act of 1996; or

(b) in the event that the magistrate judge determines that a person is not entitled to proceed *in forma pauperis*, file a recommendation setting out the reasons for the determination pursuant to 28 U.S.C. § 636(b)(1)(B);

(5) Direct litigants seeking leave to proceed *in forma pauperis* to provide additional financial information necessary to determine whether leave should be granted and to take appropriate steps or make appropriate recommendations in the event that the litigant does not provide the information;

(6) Conduct such proceedings and enter such orders as are necessary to screen matters pursuant to 28 U.S.C. § 1915, 28 U.S.C. § 1915A, 42 U.S.C. § 1997e or other provision of applicable law, including but not limited to the issuance of questionnaires, orders requiring further or more definite statement, and hearings;

(7) After screening, make all necessary and appropriate reports and recommendations if the magistrate judge determines that claims or cases are subject to dismissal under 28 U.S.C. § 1915, 28 U.S.C. § 1915A, 42 U.S.C. § 1997e or other applicable law;

(8) After screening, make all necessary orders for issuance and service of process if leave to proceed *in forma pauperis* is granted;

(9) Make appropriate orders or reports and recommendations in proceedings brought pursuant to 28 U.S.C. Sections 2241, 2254 and 2255;

(10) Upon an order of transfer from the presiding district judge, exercise jurisdiction under 28 U.S.C. § 636(c) if, prior to service of process, the parties to the action consent to proceed before the magistrate judge; and

(11) Make appropriate orders or reports and recommendations on motions for certificates of appealability.

b. A magistrate judge performing any duties under this Rule shall have all powers necessary to perform such duties except as otherwise limited by law.

Rule 3

Assignments to Magistrate Judges

In a division with more than one magistrate judge, the clerk will select a magistrate judge in accordance with the court's random assignment procedure from among all magistrate judges in that division for any matters referred or transferred pursuant to 28 U.S.C. § 636(c) by the presiding district judge. This method of assignment does not limit the district-wide jurisdiction of a magistrate judge.

Rule 4

Consent to Exercise of Jurisdiction by a Magistrate Judge

a. At the time any action that may be tried by consent before a magistrate judge pursuant to 28 U.S.C. § 636(c)(1) is filed or as soon thereafter as is practicable, the clerk will provide plaintiff or plaintiff's representative an approved notice and consent form, along with a sufficient number of copies for the plaintiff to attach to the complaint and summons, when served. The plaintiff, or the defendant if the plaintiff is acting *pro se*, will be primarily responsible for securing the execution of a consent form by the parties and for filing such form with the clerk.

b. If, after the clerk has notified the parties of the availability of a magistrate judge to exercise jurisdiction, and that such consent is wholly voluntary and without any adverse consequences if a party chooses not to consent, and upon the written consents of all parties and upon an order of transfer from the presiding district judge, the clerk will reassign the case to the designated magistrate judge for all further proceedings as provided for in 28 U.S.C. § 636(c). A part-time magistrate judge may exercise consent jurisdiction when the chief judge of the court certifies that a full-time magistrate judge is not reasonably available in accordance with guidelines established by the judicial council of the Fifth Circuit.

c. Upon the death, retirement, disqualification or resignation of a magistrate judge exercising jurisdiction under this Rule, the case will be reassigned to another magistrate judge, unless a party consented to a specific magistrate judge.

[Amended effective May 5, 2005; September 1, 2015.]

CIVIL JUSTICE EXPENSE AND DELAY REDUCTION PLAN

I. INTRODUCTION

In consultation with its Civil Justice Reform Act (CJRA) Advisory Committee, the Court developed this Plan, pursuant to the Civil Justice Reform Act of 1990, 28 U.S.C. §§ 471–82. The Plan is based on consideration of the following:

- recommendations in the Report of the Advisory Committee as required by 28 U.S.C. § 472(a);

- suggestions of the judges and magistrate judges in this District, and review of the Court's existing practices and rules;

- the Model Plan provided by the Administrative Office, plans from Early Implementation Districts and Pilot Districts, and plans from other districts throughout the country; and

- the purposes set forth in 28 U.S.C. § 471, the principles and guidelines set out in 28 U.S.C. § 473(a), and the techniques set out in 28 U.S.C. § 473(b).

The Court determined that the chief reasons for delay in the civil docket in the Northern District are threefold: (1) the constant and substantial increase in recent years in the number of criminal cases (an increase of 18% in 1992 over 1991) and multi-defendant criminal cases (an increase of 37% in the number of criminal defendants in 1992 over 1991); (2) the shortage of judges for several years, until recently; and (3) the increase in the amount of trial time required for criminal trials (during the period 1986–90 the percentage of total trial time devoted to criminal cases doubled, from 25% to 50%; in 1992 criminal cases accounted for 57% of the District's trials).

The judges of this Court are committed to providing a "hands-on" approach to civil cases. The judges are aware, however, that too many conferences and procedures can increase costs and delay and confuse attorneys and litigants. The judges will continue to try to simplify procedures and minimize the number of conferences. The judges realize that each case must be considered individually. Many cases need only minimal court supervision; others need extensive court supervision.

A credible, firm trial date is the sine qua non of reducing excessive costs and delay. The Court faces the challenge of harmonizing that preeminent principle of litigation management with the urgent demands of a steadily increasing criminal docket.

II. DISCOVERY

Excessive discovery is perceived as the principal reason for excessive costs in litigation. The Court recognizes that discovery serves the beneficial purposes of reducing unfair surprise in litigation, streamlining the presentation of pertinent evidence, and promoting pretrial resolution of cases by counsel who by discovery obtain a better knowledge of the positions of the parties. In some cases, however, the costs of conducting discovery outweigh the returns that may reasonably be expected. Where feasible, litigants should mutually agree to forgo or significantly curtail formal discovery. A judge may impose limits on discovery at any time.

The Court also recognizes that firm deadlines for completion of discovery can promote reductions in costs and delay. Unless the presiding judge otherwise directs, a firm date for completion of discovery will be fixed at an early stage of the litigation. The continuance of the trial of a case will not extend the date for completion of discovery unless ordered by the presiding judge.

In every case determined by the presiding judge to be complex, an early conference will be set with the judge or a magistrate judge for development of a discovery scheduling order. At the conference, the parties must be prepared to identify and exchange core information relevant to the case, including names and addresses of persons with information relevant to claims and defenses as well as the location and custodians of relevant documents. The parties will be encouraged (and directed, if necessary) to produce and exchange documents upon informal requests. The judge or magistrate judge will also determine at the conference whether some discovery relating to the nature and extent of damages should be scheduled early in the litigation.

A discovery scheduling conference and order may be established in any case, at a judge's discretion.

In discovery, and in all other aspects of litigation, the Court will insist upon adherence to the principles of Dondi Properties Corp. v. Commerce Sav. & Loan Ass'n., 121 F.R.D. 284 (N.D. Tex. 1988)(en banc).

At the discretion of the presiding judge, discovery disputes may be referred to a magistrate judge for hearing and determination. A magistrate judge may be authorized to monitor all aspects of discovery in a case.

[Amended effective May 20, 2002.]

III. ALTERNATIVE DISPUTE RESOLUTION (ADR)

The Court endorses Alternative Dispute Resolution (ADR) programs as effective in bringing about settlement or narrowing of issues in civil actions. The Clerk's Office will provide to counsel for all litigants and to pro se parties a pamphlet describing the ADR methods, their use by the Court, and their potential advantages. The following policy regarding ADR is adopted:

A. ADR Referral. The Court requires that litigants in all civil cases, except those set out in local civil rule 16.1, consider the use of an alternative dispute resolution process at an appropriate stage in the litigation. A judge may refer a case to ADR on the motion of any party, on the agreement of the parties, or on the judge's own motion. The judge will respect the parties' agreement unless the judge believes another ADR method or provider is better suited to the case and parties. The authority to refer a case to ADR does not preclude a judge from suggesting or requiring other settlement procedures.

B. Opposition to ADR Referral. A party opposing either the ADR referral or the appointed provider must file written objections within ten days of entry of the order of referral, explaining the reason(s) for any opposition.

C. ADR Methods. The Court recognizes the following ADR methods: mediation, mini-trial, summary jury trial, and early neutral evaluation. A judge may approve the ADR method the parties suggest or any other method the judge believes is suited to the litigation. A judge may not require any alternative dispute resolution process except mediation and early neutral evaluation.

D. Attendance. Subject to the provisions of 28 U.S.C. § 473(c), in addition to counsel, party representatives with the authority to negotiate a settlement, and all other persons necessary to negotiate a settlement, including insurance carriers, must attend the ADR sessions.

E. Binding Nature. The results of ADR are non-binding, unless the parties agree otherwise.

F. Confidentiality; Privileges and Immunities. All communications made during ADR procedures are confidential and protected from disclosure and do not constitute a waiver of any existing privileges and immunities.

G. Administration. At the conclusion of each ADR proceeding the provider will complete and file with the District Clerk a form supplied by the Clerk that will include:

1. The style and civil action number of the case;

2. A list of those in attendance;

3. The names, addresses, and telephone numbers of counsel;

4. The type of case;

5. The method of ADR proceeding;

6. Whether or not the case settled; and

7. The provider's fee.

The District Clerk annually shall tabulate, analyze and report on the disposition of ADR proceedings.

H. Neutrals. The Court will adopt appropriate processes for making neutrals available for use by the parties for each category of process offered, and promulgate procedures and criteria for the selection of neutrals on its panels. A person designated as a neutral in a case must request to be excused from the designation in such circumstances as 28 U.S.C. § 455 would disqualify a justice, judge, or magistrate judge of the United States, or other applicable or professional responsibility standards so require.

I. ADR Provider Fees. Fees charged by ADR providers, whether selected by agreement of the parties or by appointment of the court, shall be in amounts that are reasonable and customary in the division in which the case is filed or in which the ADR service is provided. No ADR provider shall charge a contingent fee.

[Amended effective January 20, 1999; May 20, 2002.]

IV. SETTLEMENT CONFERENCES

The Court strongly favors early settlement discussions. The parties in every civil action must make a good faith effort to settle; settlement discussions must be entered into at the earliest possible time, well in advance of any pretrial conference. The presiding judge will be available for settlement conferences, and may require, and establish procedures for, such conferences. In non-jury cases, a judge will not discuss settlement figures unless requested by the parties.

V. MOTIONS

The Court will continue to insist on proper motion practice as an effective means of reducing costs and delay. Local Civil Rules 7.1 and 56.1–56.7 govern motion practice. Inter alia, Rule 7.1(b) requires certificates of conference on most motions and Rules 7.1(e) and 7.1(f) set deadlines for responses to motions and for replies to responses. Local Civil Rules 7.2(c) and 56.5(b) limit the length of briefs. Other Local Civil Rules provide for the form and content of certain motions (e.g., Local Civil Rules 56.1–56.7 regulate motions for summary judgment).

Motions for continuance must be signed by the party as well as by the attorney of record. The granting of a motion for continuance will not extend or revive any deadlines that have already passed in a case unless ordered by the presiding judge. See Local Civil Rule 40.1.

[Amended effective March 20, 2002.]

VI. PRETRIAL PROCEDURES

The Court recognizes the importance of scheduling orders in reducing delay and containing costs. A scheduling order will be issued in each case within 90 days after issue is joined. Unless changed by the presiding judge, the scheduling order will set a trial date, and deadlines for the following:

- completion of discovery;
- motions to join other parties;
- motions to amend the pleadings;
- motions for summary judgment and other dispositive motions;
- reports on the status of settlement negotiations, and counsel's respective attitudes concerning referring the case to mediation or to a magistrate judge for trial by consent per 28 U.S.C. Section 636(c);
- a joint pretrial order, including the contents of such order;
- exchange of witness lists, exhibit lists and deposition designations, and objections thereto;
- designation of expert witnesses; and
- any additional matter that the presiding judge deems appropriate.

Scheduling orders are not required in exempt cases (see section IX, infra) or where the presiding judge deems that a scheduling order is unnecessary.

[Amended effective March 20, 2002; May 20, 2002.]

VII. TRIAL

The presiding judge may limit the length of trial, the number of witnesses each party may present for its case, the number of exhibits each party may have admitted into evidence, and the amount of time each party may have to examine witnesses. The conduct of counsel at trial will continue to be governed by Local Civil Rule 83.4.

[Amended effective March 20, 2002; May 20, 2002.]

VIII. ATTORNEYS

The Court has always had detailed requirements governing the admission and discipline of attorneys. See Local Civil Rules 83.7 and 83.8. The Court will continue to stress adherence to the principles of Dondi Properties Corp. v. Commerce Sav. & Loan Ass'n., 121 F.R.D. 284 (N.D. Tex. 1988)(en banc).

Any out-of-district attorney applying for pro hac vice status must affirm in writing that he/she has read and will comply with Dondi and the Local Civil Rules. The presiding judge may revoke pro hac vice status for failure to observe the Local Civil Rules or for failure to comply with the Dondi standards.

[Amended effective March 20, 2002; May 20, 2002.]

IX. MAGISTRATE JUDGES AND SPECIAL MASTERS

The Court has experienced, competent and hard-working magistrate judges who are available to try jury and non-jury civil cases pursuant to 28 U.S.C. § 636(c). The Court will increase its emphasis on encouraging parties to consent to trial before a magistrate judge.

The Court encourages the use of special masters consistent with the provisions of Fed.R.Civ.P. 53. The presiding judge may appoint a special master on her or his own motion or on the motion of a party.

X. SPECIAL CATEGORIES OF CASES

The Court will continue to exempt certain categories of cases from the requirements for scheduling orders and pretrial orders, unless the presiding judge otherwise orders. See Local Civil Rule 9.1 (regarding social security and black lung cases), and the case categories referred to in Local Civil Rule 16.1, as follows:

- actions filed by incarcerated persons pursuant to the Civil Rights Acts, 42 U.S.C. §§ 1981, et seq.;
- actions for forfeiture;
- cases filed by the United States Attorney for collection of promissory notes payable to the United States of America or any government agency;
- appeals from the Bankruptcy Court; and
- cases involving pro se plaintiffs.

[Amended effective March 20, 2002.]

XI. CONTINUATION OF OTHER EXISTING POLICIES AND PRACTICES THAT CONTRIBUTE TO REDUCING COSTS AND DELAY

1. Each judge currently designates at least one staff member to coordinate scheduling. The District Clerk will provide whatever additional training is needed for case management.

2. Each judge will continue to give priority to the monitoring and resolution of pending motions.

3. The Court will endeavor to stay informed of the latest technological advances regarding information, management and office efficiency, and will utilize these advances where and when appropriate.

4. The Court will continue to conduct a regular review of its Local Rules.

5. The Court will continue to try civil cases as promptly as it can judiciously do so, consistent with the demands of its criminal docket.

6. Each judge will endeavor to improve ease of communications between the Court and counsel in order to reduce costs and delay.

7. The Court will impose sanctions as needed to control litigation abuses.

8. The judges will endeavor to improve the exchange of information concerning practices and procedures designed to reduce costs and delay. Judges and their staffs in each division will meet together at least once a year, and if possible, more often, for the purpose of comparing their differing practices and exchanging ideas about reduction of costs and delay.

9. The judges will endeavor to release cases scheduled for trial when it appears certain that such cases will not be reached for trial. The judges will be sensitive to lawyers and litigants in cases involving particular complexity or expense in trial preparation which might have to be duplicated if the cases were continued too soon before the scheduled trial date.

XII. IMPLEMENTATION

The Court may consult an Advisory Committee to develop criteria by which to measure the Court's success in reducing costs and delay. The Court will expect the Advisory Committee to monitor such success and to advise the Court regarding its findings and recommendations.

This Plan is adopted as Miscellaneous Order No. 46, and is effective as a Local Civil Rule and will be construed as such. This Plan is intended to supplement, but not to supersede, any other Local Civil Rule; however, in the event of an inconsistency between a provision of this Plan and another Local Civil Rule, the presiding judge will determine which will govern.

This Plan applies to all cases filed on or after July 1, 1993. In the discretion of the presiding judge the Plan may be applied to any case filed before the effective date.

[Dated March 22, 1993 and effective July 1, 1993. Amended effective March 20, 2002; May 20, 2002.]

STANDARDS OF PRACTICE TO BE OBSERVED BY ATTORNEYS APPEARING IN CIVIL ACTIONS

Adopted in *Dondi Properties Corp. v. Commerce Sav. and Loan Ass'n*,
121 F.R.D. 284 (N.D.Tex., July 14, 1988)

(A) In fulfilling his or her primary duty to the client, a lawyer must be ever conscious of the broader duty to the judicial system that serves both attorney and client.

(B) A lawyer owes, to the judiciary, candor, diligence and utmost respect.

(C) A lawyer owes, to opposing counsel, a duty of courtesy and cooperation, the observance of which is necessary for the efficient administration of our system of justice and the respect of the public it serves.

(D) A lawyer unquestionably owes, to the administration of justice, the fundamental duties of personal dignity and professional integrity.

(E) Lawyers should treat each other, the opposing party, the court, and members of the court staff with courtesy and civility and conduct themselves in a professional manner at all times.

(F) A client has no right to demand that counsel abuse the opposite party or indulge in offensive conduct. A lawyer shall always treat adverse witnesses and suitors with fairness and due consideration.

(G) In adversary proceedings, clients are litigants and though ill feeling may exist between clients, such ill feeling should not influence a lawyer's conduct, attitude, or demeanor towards opposing lawyers.

(H) A lawyer should not use any form of discovery, or the scheduling of discovery, as a means of harassing opposing counsel or counsel's client.

(I) Lawyers will be punctual in communications with others and in honoring scheduled appearances, and will recognize that neglect and tardiness are demeaning to the lawyer and to the judicial system.

(J) If a fellow member of the Bar makes a just request for cooperation, or seeks scheduling accommodation, a lawyer will not arbitrarily or unreasonably withhold consent.

(K) Effective advocacy does not require antagonistic or obnoxious behavior and members of the Bar will adhere to the higher standard of conduct which judges, lawyers, clients, and the public may rightfully expect.

ELECTRONIC CASE FILING PROCEDURES
MISCELLANEOUS ORDER NO. 61

This order supersedes all previous orders designated as "Miscellaneous Order No. 61."

I. Public Access; Attorney Responsibility to Redact

The Judicial Conference of the United States has adopted a policy regarding the electronic availability of transcripts of court proceedings. *See* Attachment 1. Under the policy, transcripts are now available electronically to anyone holding a login and password to the judiciary's public access to electronic records system ("PACER") and to anyone using a public terminal in the clerk's office. Therefore, attorneys must take specific steps to keep personal data identifiers out of transcripts.

To implement the Judicial Conference policy, this court has adopted the following procedures that apply to all transcripts filed on or after May 28, 2008.

A. Once a transcript has been ordered by an attorney and produced by a court reporter, the court reporter will electronically file the transcript with the clerk's office, and the clerk's office will notify all attorneys in the case of the filing.

B. An electronically filed transcript will immediately be available for viewing at public terminals in the clerk's office. The transcript cannot be copied or reproduced in the clerk's office until 90 calendar days have elapsed from the date of filing.

C. Each attorney in the case must review the electronically filed transcript and determine if any personal data identifier listed in the Judicial Conference policy is included in the transcript. An attorney is generally only responsible for reviewing and indicating redactions in the testimony of the witnesses called on behalf of the party represented by the attorney and in the opening statement and closing argument made on behalf of the party; however, both the attorney for the government and attorney for the defendant must review the entire transcript of a sentencing proceeding.

D. If an attorney determines that a transcript contains a Social Security number, taxpayer identification number, birth date, the name of an individual known to be a minor, financial account number, or (in a criminal case) a home address, the attorney must file a "Redaction Request" with the clerk's office on the approved form. *See* Attachment 2. This form must be filed within 21 calendar days of the date the transcript was filed. If the attorney wants information other than these personal identifiers to be redacted from a transcript, the attorney must file a motion seeking this relief from the court.

E. A court reporter must redact each personal data identifier, as requested by an attorney, and must electronically file a redacted transcript within 31 calendar days after the filing of the transcript.

F. Restrictions on an electronically filed transcript, or a redacted version of the transcript if a redaction request was filed, will be removed 90 calendar days after the filing of the transcript unless a redaction request is still pending or the presiding judge otherwise directs. The transcript will then be available remotely to view, download, or print from PACER or CM/ECF, or to obtain from the clerk's office.

II. Delegation of Authority to Clerk to Refund an Erroneous Electronically Paid Fee and to Forgo Collection of Fee for an Erroneous Filing

The court delegates to the clerk the authority to refund a fee paid by an ECF user who has used ECF to pay a fee and the fee was paid erroneously because the payment was:

A. a duplicate fee payment related to the submission of a single document (including a single document erroneously submitted two or more times); or

B. a fee payment when no fee was due (e.g., when no document was attached to a submission, or the submission did not require payment of a fee).

To obtain a refund, an ECF user must make a written request to the clerk.

If an ECF user continues (or ECF users from the same law firm continue) to make repeated mistakes when submitting fees electronically, the court may consider remedial action, such as issuing an order to show cause why further requests for refunds should be considered.

III. Administrative Procedures

The clerk is authorized to establish administrative procedures regarding access and use of the ECF system.

Attachment 1

Judicial Conference Policy on Privacy and Public Access to Electronic Case Files

Amendments to the Appellate, Bankruptcy, Civil, and Criminal Rules to implement the requirements of the E–Government Act of 2002 took effect on December 1, 2007. The new rules codify, to a large extent, the 2001 Judicial Conference privacy policy, as revised in 2003, requiring redaction of personal identifier information from filings.[1] The personal identifiers to be redacted are Social Security numbers, names of minor children, financial account numbers, dates of birth, and, in criminal cases, home addresses.[2]

Because of the enactment of the rules, the previous policy is no longer operative except for two portions of the earlier privacy policy that remain in force, separate from the new rules. They are listed below.

I. Documents in criminal case files for which public access should not be provided

The following documents in a criminal case shall not be included in the public case file and should not be made available to the public at the courthouse or via remote electronic access:

- unexecuted summonses or warrants of any kind (e.g., search warrants, arrest warrants);
- pretrial bail or presentence investigation reports;
- statements of reasons in the judgment of conviction;
- juvenile records;
- documents containing identifying information about jurors or potential jurors;
- financial affidavits filed in seeking representation pursuant to the Criminal Justice Act;
- ex parte requests for authorization of investigative, expert or other services pursuant to the Criminal Justice Act; and
- sealed documents (e.g., motions for downward departure for substantial assistance, plea agreements indicating cooperation or victim statements).

II. The redaction of electronic transcripts of court proceedings

Courts making electronic documents remotely available to the public shall make electronic transcripts of proceedings remotely available to the public if such transcripts are prepared. Prior to being made electronically available from a remote location, however, the transcripts must conform to Fed. R. Civ. P. 5.2(a), Fed. R. Crim. P. 49.1(a), or Fed. R. Bankr. P. 9037(a).

Once a prepared transcript is delivered to the clerk's office pursuant to 28 U.S.C. § 753, the attorneys in the case are (or, where there is a self-represented party, the party is) responsible for reviewing it for the personal data identifiers required by the federal rules to be redacted, and providing the court reporter or transcriber with a statement of the redactions to be made to comply with the rules. Unless otherwise ordered by the court, the attorney must review the following portions of the transcript:

(a) opening and closing statements made on the party's behalf;

(b) statements of the party;

(c) the testimony of any witnesses called by the party;

(d) sentencing proceedings; and

(e) any other portion of the transcript as ordered by the court.

Within seven calendar days of the delivery by the court reporter or transcriber of the official transcript to the clerk's office, each attorney must inform the court, by filing a notice of redaction with the clerk, of his or her intent to direct the redaction of personal data identifiers from the electronic transcript of the court proceeding. If no such notice is filed within the allotted time, the court will assume redaction of personal data identifiers from the transcript is not necessary.

An attorney serving as "standby" counsel appointed to be available to assist a pro se defendant in his or her defense in a criminal case must review the same portions of the transcript as if the pro se defendant were his or her client. If the transcript relates to a panel attorney representation pursuant to the Criminal Justice Act (CJA), including serving as standby counsel, the attorney conducting the review is entitled to compensation under the CJA for functions reasonably performed to fulfill the redaction obligation and for reimbursement for related reasonable expenses.

A party is to submit to the court reporter or transcriber, within 21 calendar days of the transcript's delivery to the clerk, or longer if a court so orders, a statement indicating where the personal data identifiers to be redacted appear in the transcript. The court reporter or transcriber must redact the identifiers as directed by the party.

These procedures are limited to the redaction of the specific personal data identifiers listed in the rules. During the 21-day period, or longer if the court so orders, an attorney may move the court for additional redactions to the transcript. The transcript shall not be made available on the internet until the court has ruled upon any such motion.

The court reporter or transcriber must, within 31 calendar days of the delivery of the transcript to the clerk of court, or longer if the court so orders, perform the requested redactions, and file a redacted version of the transcript with the clerk of court. The original unredacted electronic transcript should be retained by the clerk of court.

Policy Note

This policy applies to transcripts made available via CM/ECF, WEBPACER, PACER, RACER or a non-court related electronic depository (e.g., Exemplaris). It does not affect in any way the obligation of the court reporter or transcriber, pursuant to Judicial Conference policy, to promptly deliver to the clerk of court the court reporter's or transcriber's original records of a proceeding or the inclusion of a transcript with the records of the court.

If a party desires to respond to a motion for additional redaction, the court may establish a briefing schedule.

Nothing in this policy creates a private right of action.

Nothing in this policy changes any rules or policies with respect to sealing or redaction of court records for any other purpose.

This policy does not affect or limit the right of any party (or any other person or entity) to order production of a transcript on an expedited basis. This policy does not affect any court rules or ruling requiring the sealing of materials or the protection of sealed materials.

An attorney appointed pursuant to the Criminal Justice Act (CJA) is entitled to compensation under the CJA for functions performed to fulfill his or her obligations under the policy, including the following: (1) traveling to gain access to the transcript, if needed; (2) reviewing a transcript to determine whether to file notice of intent to redact; (3) filing a notice of intent to redact or a motion for an extension of time; (4) reviewing a transcript to determine the location of information to be requested to be redacted or whether to file a motion for additional redaction; (5) preparing and filing a redaction request or motion; and (6) other actions (including creating pleadings, attending hearings or other follow-up). The attorney is also entitled to reimbursement under the CJA for the costs of obtaining a transcript for purposes of review. If a case involving a CJA representation has already been closed and the original attorney is no longer available, or if standby counsel is no longer available, new counsel may be appointed under the CJA and compensated as outlined above. In the event that the original appointed counsel is still available, but has filed a final voucher for the underlying case, the attorney shall be permitted to file a supplemental voucher for compensation.

Extensions of time to comply with the deadlines set forth in these procedures should not be routinely granted, due to the potential for delay of court of appeals proceedings in the event redaction procedures extend beyond 31 days.

Attachment 2

UNITED STATES DISTRICT COURT
FOR THE NORTHERN DISTRICT OF TEXAS

_____ Division

_____	§	
Plaintiff	§	
	§	
v.	§	
	§	_____
	§	Civil/Criminal Action No.
_____	§	
Defendant	§	

REDACTION REQUEST—TRANSCRIPT

Pursuant to Judicial Conference policy, ___(Plaintiff/Defendant Name)___ requests redaction of transcript(s) on file in this case:

(Please list the document, page, and line number and a redacted identifier for each redaction necessary; *e.g.*, Doc. No. 15, Page 12, Line 9, Social Security No. to read xxx–xx–6130.)

Document No. of Transcript	Page No.	Line No(s).	Redacted Identifier

The undersigned understands that redaction of information other than personal identifiers listed below requires an order of the court.

Social Security or taxpayer-identification number to the last four digits
Date of birth to the year
Name of an individual known to be a minor to the initials
Financial account number to the last four digits
Home address to the city and state (in a criminal case)

Date:_____   s/ Typed Name or Graphical Signature of Attorney

Bar Number: _____

Address: _____

_____

_____

Telephone: _____

Fax: _____

E-mail: _____

CERTIFICATE OF SERVICE

I hereby certify that on ___(Date)___, I electronically filed the foregoing with the clerk of court for the U.S. District Court, Northern District of Texas, using the CM/ECF system which will send notification to case participants registered for electronic notice. I further certify that I have served all case participants not registered for electronic notice by another manner authorized by Federal Rule of Civil Procedure 5(b)(2).

s/ Typed Name or Graphical Signature
of Attorney

NOTE: To electronically file this document, you will find the event in our Case Management (CM/ECF) system, under Civil or Criminal/Other Filings/Other Documents/Redaction Request—Transcript.

[Effective February 21, 2004. Amended effective March 8, 2006; August 30, 2006; May 28, 2008; October 21, 2008.]

1 JCUS–SEP/OCT 01, pp. 48–50 and JCUS–SEP 03, pp. 15–16.

2 Fed. R. App. P. 25(a), Fed. R. Bankr. P. 9037, Fed. R. Civ. P. 5.2, and Fed. R. Crim. P. 49.1.

ECF ADMINISTRATIVE PROCEDURES
I. THE ELECTRONIC CASE FILING SYSTEM ("ECF")

A. Introduction. Under LR 5.1(e) and LCrR 49.2(f), unless the presiding judge otherwise directs, you must file any pleading (except a complaint in a civil case, or an indictment or information in a criminal case), motion, or other paper by electronic means. Under LR 3.1, you are permitted, but not required, to file a complaint by electronic means.

You may, for cause, move to be excused from the requirement of electronic filing. See LR 5.1(e), and LCrR 49.2(f).

B. Registration as an ECF User Required. Registration is required within 14 days of the date you appear in a case. See LR 5.1(f) and LCrR 49.2(g). To register, follow the procedure on the court's website on the ECF Registration page.

To maintain your login and password and the contact information covered by LR 83.13(b) or LCrR 57.13(b)—your business address, e-mail address, telephone number, facsimile number, or name—follow the procedure on the court's website under Maintaining Your Account.

Please protect the security of your login and password. If you believe your password has been compromised, you should change it immediately. You may use the Forgot Your ECF Password? link to reset your password.

C. Registration as a PACER User Required. You must have a PACER account to use the "Query" and "Report" menus of the ECF system and to view electronically stored document images. To obtain a PACER login, register online at http://pacer.psc.uscourts.gov or contact the PACER Service Center at (800) 676–6856.

D. Portable Document Format (PDF) Required. Except for proposed orders, documents must be filed in Portable Document Format (PDF). When using a PDF fillable form, you must "flatten" the document after completing the form fields to ensure it can be viewed on all devices. Follow the procedures on the court's website for Flattening a PDF.

E. Accessing the ECF System and Menu Features. You may connect to ECF at https://ecf.txnd.uscourts.gov. The options in the blue menu bar at the top of the opening screen provide the functionality noted below:

- Civil – To electronically file civil documents;

- Criminal – To electronically file criminal documents;

- Query – To obtain specific case information and view or print docket sheets or previously filed documents;

- Reports – To obtain cases-filed reports and docket sheets;

- Utilities –   To view your personal transaction log and maintain personal account information;

- Search –   To search by keyword for the most applicable event for the document you intend to file; and

- Logout –   To exit the system after completing your transactions.

II. ELECTRONIC CASE FILING AND SERVICE OF DOCUMENTS

A. Filing a Civil or Miscellaneous Case. To file a civil case, follow the procedure on the court's website under Opening a Civil Case/Filing a Complaint.

To file a miscellaneous case, follow the procedure on the court's website under Opening a Miscellaneous Case.

B. Filing a Pleading, Motion, or Other Paper. To file a pleading, motion, or other paper, follow the procedure on the court's website under Filing a Pleading, Motion, or Other Paper. ECF will e-mail a Notice of Electronic Filing to each registered user in the case (including a non-prisoner *pro se* party) at the user's primary and secondary e-mail addresses, as maintained within the ECF system. Review the Notice of Electronic Filing to determine who received electronic service and who you must serve by other means.

Note: A certificate of service is required even though you file a pleading, motion, or other paper electronically. Sample language may be found on the court's website under Certificate of Service.

C. Judge's Copy. A "judge's copy" is a paper copy of an original pleading, motion, or other paper submitted for use by the presiding judge. To comply with LR 5.1(b) and LCrR 49.2(b), you must provide the judge's copy according to the requirements on the court's website under Judges' Copy Requirements.

D. Signature. An example of a signature block that complies with Fed. R. Civ. P. 5(d)(3)(c) is:

s/ John Doe
John Doe
Bar Number: 12345
123 Main Street
Dallas, TX 75201
E-mail: john_doe@lawfirm.com
Telephone: (214) 123–4567
Fax: (214) 123–4567

E. Fee Payable to the Clerk. To pay a filing fee by credit card or debit card, follow the procedure on the court's website under Online Filing Fee Payment Guide.

F. Proposed Order. To satisfy the requirement of LR 7.1(c) or LCrR 47.1(c), you must use the "Proposed Orders" event and submit the proposed order in a word-processing format (e.g., Word or WordPerfect, not PDF). To serve a copy, you may attach a PDF version as an exhibit to the motion, but this does **not** satisfy the requirement to submit a proposed order to the judge.

G. Selecting an Event Consistent With the Title of the Document. When you file a pleading, motion or other paper, you must select the appropriate category (e.g., "Initial Pleadings and Service," "Motions and Related Filings," "Other Filings"), and then the event most consistent with the title of your document (e.g., Motions, Notices, ADR Documents). Use the "Search" feature from the main menu to search by keyword.

H. When ECF is Down and Other Technical Failures. If you are at risk of missing a deadline because ECF is down, follow the procedures on the court's website under Emergency Filing Information (if our system is down). If you are at risk of missing a deadline because your system is down, follow the procedures under Emergency Filing Information (if your system is down).

III. FILING OF DOCUMENTS WITH SPECIAL CONSIDERATIONS

A. Document to Be Filed Under Seal and/or Ex Parte. To file a pleading, motion, or other paper under seal, except a document related to a Presentence Report, follow the applicable procedure on the court's website under Filing a Sealed and/or Ex Parte Document in a Civil Case or Filing a Sealed and/or Ex Parte Document in a Criminal Case. Access to the document will be immediately restricted consistent with the choices you make when filing the document.

Access to this restricted entry is granted via the ECF Filer login of the filing attorney. To access a restricted document, follow the procedure on the court's website under Accessing Restricted Documents.

B. Document Related to a Presentence Report. To submit a document related to a Presentence Report, follow the procedure on the court's website under Using ECF to Electronically Submit Documents Related to the Presentence Report. A Notice of Electronic Filing will be sent only to the Assistant U.S. Attorney, the attorney(s) for the related defendant (not to any co-defendant's attorney), and the U.S. Probation Office. The original must be received by the presiding judge on or before the date the document is submitted using ECF.

Access to these restricted documents is granted via the ECF Filer login of the attorney for the applicable defendant or the government. To access a restricted document, follow the procedure on the court's website under Accessing Restricted Documents.

C. Document Granted Leave to File. If you are granted leave to file a document that is available in the Court's record (e.g., attached as an exhibit to your motion for leave to file), the clerk will file the document as of the date of the order granting leave. If the document is not available in the court's record because you have not submitted it yet, you must electronically file the document upon receipt of the order granting leave.

D. Non–Documentary or Oversized Object. If you are unable to electronically file a non-documentary or oversized object because of its physical size or character, submit it to the clerk's office for filing. The clerk will docket a text-only event, generating a Notice of Electronic Filing, that describes the non-documentary or oversized object filed.

E. Document Larger Than the Electronic File Size Limit. The maximum size for any file is thirty five megabytes. To file a pleading, motion, or other paper that is larger than thirty five megabytes, follow the procedure on the court's website under Filing Large Documents and Adding Attachments.

F. Document to Be Issued by the Clerk. To request the clerk to tax costs, use the "Bill of Costs" event. To request the clerk to issue any other type of document (*e.g.*, Clerk's Entry of Default, abstract of judgment, etc.), use the "Request for Clerk to Issue Document" event.

G. Consent to Proceed Before a United States Magistrate Judge. To consent to the disposition of a civil case by a United States Magistrate Judge, complete the "Consent to Proceed Before U.S. Magistrate Judge" event. Each party will receive a Notice of Electronic Filing, but the information will not be displayed on the docket sheet unless the presiding judge reassigns the case.

IV. AMENDMENT OF THIS MANUAL

The clerk's office may amend this ECF Administrative Procedures Manual, which includes by reference, all of the linked procedures, at any time, without prior notice.

V. ECF HELP DESK

For assistance, please contact your local clerk's office or ECF Help Desk at:

Amarillo—(800) 596–9414
Dallas/Abilene—(866) 243–2866
Fort Worth/Wichita Falls—(800) 240–7240
Lubbock/San Angelo—(806) 472–1905.

[Effective April 1, 2004. Amended effective September 1, 2006; November 1, 2006; June 1 2007; October 2008; November 9, 2009; July 1, 2010; January 18, 2011; May 9, 2011; February 4, 2013; September 2, 2014; March 9, 2015; July 16, 2015; August 10, 2016; November 7, 2016; January 18, 2017; August 16, 2017; December 1, 2018.]

JUDICIAL CONFERENCE POLICY ON PRIVACY AND PUBLIC ACCESS TO ELECTRONIC CASE FILES

Amendments to the Appellate, Bankruptcy, Civil, and Criminal Rules to implement the requirements of the E–Government Act of 2002 took effect on December 1, 2007. The new rules codify, to a large extent, the 2001 Judicial Conference privacy policy, as revised in 2003, requiring redaction of personal identifier information from filings.[1] The personal identifiers to be redacted are Social Security numbers, names of minor children, financial account numbers, dates of birth, and, in criminal cases, home addresses.[2]

Because of the enactment of the rules, the previous policy is no longer operative except for two portions of the earlier privacy policy that remain in force, separate from the new rules. They are listed below.

I. Documents in criminal case files for which public access should not be provided

The following documents in a criminal case shall not be included in the public case file and should not be made available to the public at the courthouse or via remote electronic access:

- unexecuted summonses or warrants of any kind (e.g., search warrants, arrest warrants);
- pretrial bail or presentence investigation reports;
- statements of reasons in the judgment of conviction;
- juvenile records;
- documents containing identifying information about jurors or potential jurors;
- financial affidavits filed in seeking representation pursuant to the Criminal Justice Act;
- ex parte requests for authorization of investigative, expert or other services pursuant to the Criminal Justice Act; and
- sealed documents (e.g., motions for downward departure for substantial assistance, plea agreements indicating cooperation or victim statements).

II. The redaction of electronic transcripts of court proceedings

Courts making electronic documents remotely available to the public shall make electronic transcripts of proceedings remotely available to the public if such transcripts are prepared. Prior to being made electronically available from a remote location, however, the transcripts must conform to Fed. R. Civ. P. 5.2(a), Fed. R. Crim. P. 49.1(a), or Fed. R. Bankr. P. 9037(a).

Once a prepared transcript is delivered to the clerk's office pursuant to 28 U.S.C. § 753, the attorneys in the case are (or, where there is a self-represented party, the party is) responsible for reviewing it for the personal data identifiers required by the federal rules to be redacted, and providing the court reporter or transcriber with a statement of the redactions to be made to comply with the rules. Unless otherwise ordered by the court, the attorney must review the following portions of the transcript:

- (a) opening and closing statements made on the party's behalf;
- (b) statements of the party;
- (c) the testimony of any witnesses called by the party;
- (d) sentencing proceedings; and
- (e) any other portion of the transcript as ordered by the court.

Within seven calendar days of the delivery by the court reporter or transcriber of the official transcript to the clerk's office, each attorney must inform the court, by filing a notice of redaction with the clerk, of his or her intent to direct the redaction of personal data identifiers from the electronic transcript of the court proceeding. If no such notice is filed within the allotted time, the court will assume redaction of personal data identifiers from the transcript is not necessary.

An attorney serving as "standby" counsel appointed to be available to assist a pro se defendant in his or her defense in a criminal case must review the same portions of the transcript as if the pro se defendant were his or her client. If the transcript relates to a panel attorney representation pursuant to the Criminal Justice Act (CJA), including serving as standby counsel, the attorney conducting the review is entitled to compensation under the CJA for functions reasonably performed to fulfill the redaction obligation and for reimbursement for related reasonable expenses.

A party is to submit to the court reporter or transcriber, within 21 calendar days of the transcript's delivery to the clerk, or longer if a court so orders, a statement indicating where the personal data identifiers to be redacted appear in the transcript. The court reporter or transcriber must redact the identifiers as directed by the party.

These procedures are limited to the redaction of the specific personal data identifiers listed in the rules. During the 21–day period, or longer if the court so orders, an attorney may move the court for additional redactions to the transcript. The transcript shall not be made available on the internet until the court has ruled upon any such motion.

The court reporter or transcriber must, within 31 calendar days of the delivery of the transcript to the clerk of court, or longer if the court so orders, perform the requested redactions, and file a redacted version of the transcript with the clerk of court. The original unredacted electronic transcript should be retained by the clerk of court.

Policy Note

This policy applies to transcripts made available via CM/ECF, WEBPACER, PACER, RACER or a non-court related electronic depository (e.g., Exemplaris). It does not affect in any way the obligation of the court reporter or transcriber, pursuant to Judicial Conference policy, to promptly deliver to the clerk of court the court reporter's or transcriber's original records of a proceeding or the inclusion of a transcript with the records of the court.

If a party desires to respond to a motion for additional redaction, the court may establish a briefing schedule.

Nothing in this policy creates a private right of action.

Nothing in this policy changes any rules or policies with respect to sealing or redaction of court records for any other purpose.

This policy does not affect or limit the right of any party (or any other person or entity) to order production of a transcript on an expedited basis. This policy does not affect any court rules or ruling requiring the sealing of materials or the protection of sealed materials.

An attorney appointed pursuant to the Criminal Justice Act (CJA) is entitled to compensation under the CJA for functions performed to fulfill his or her obligations under the policy, including the following: (1) traveling to gain access to the transcript, if needed; (2) reviewing a transcript to determine whether to file notice of intent to redact; (3) filing a notice of intent to redact or a motion for an extension of time; (4) reviewing a transcript to determine the location of information to be requested to be redacted or whether to file a motion for additional redaction; (5) preparing and filing a redaction request or motion; and (6) other actions (including creating pleadings, attending hearings or other follow-up). The attorney is also entitled to reimbursement under the CJA for the costs of obtaining a transcript for purposes of review. If a case involving a CJA representation has already been closed and the original attorney is no longer available, or if standby counsel is no longer available, new counsel may be appointed under the CJA and compensated as outlined above. In the event that the original appointed counsel is still available, but has filed a final voucher for the underlying case, the attorney shall be permitted to file a supplemental voucher for compensation.

Extensions of time to comply with the deadlines set forth in these procedures should not be routinely granted, due to the potential for delay of court of appeals proceedings in the event redaction procedures extend beyond 31 days.

[March 2008.]

1 JCUS–SEP/OCT 01, pp. 48–50 and JCUS–SEP 03, pp. 15–16.

2 Fed. R. App. P. 25(a), Fed. R. Bankr. P. 9037, Fed. R. Civ. P. 5.2, and Fed. R. Crim. P. 49.1.

JURY PLAN

MISCELLANEOUS ORDER NO. 5

CURRENT PLAN FOR THE SELECTION OF GRAND AND PETIT JURORS IN ALL DIVISIONS OF THE NORTHERN DISTRICT OF TEXAS ADOPTED PURSUANT TO THE JURY SELECTION AND SERVICE ACT OF 1968, SECTION 1861, ET SEQ., TITLE 28, UNITED STATES CODE

I. PURPOSE

This plan implements the policies of the Jury Selection and Service Act of 1968 (28 U.S.C. § 1861, et seq.) to the effect that:

A. All litigants in federal courts entitled to trial by jury will have the right to grand and petit juries selected at random from a fair cross section of the community in the district or division wherein the court convenes;

B. All citizens will have the opportunity to be considered for service on grand and petit juries in the district courts of the United States, and no citizen shall be excluded from service as a grand or petit juror in the district courts of the United States on account of race, color, religion, sex, national origin, or economic status; and

C. All citizens will have an obligation to serve as jurors when summoned for that purpose.

II. DEFINITIONS

A. "Court" means the District Judges of the United States District Court of the Northern District of Texas, as a collective body.

B. "Chief Judge" means the Chief Judge of the Northern District of Texas or, in the event of the Chief Judge's absence or inability to act, the next available active District Judge in the Northern District of Texas who has been in service for the greatest length of time.

C. "Duty Judge" means the District Judge assigned to a division. In a division having more than one District Judge, the word "Duty Judge" means the Chief Judge or other District Judge who, by agreement or designation, is responsible for overseeing jury matters in that division.

D. "Presiding Judge" means the Judge to whom a case is assigned. The word "Judge" includes District and Magistrate Judges.

E. "Clerk" means the Clerk of the United States District Court for the Northern District of Texas, any Deputy Clerk authorized by the Clerk, and any other person authorized by the Court to assist the Clerk in the performance of functions under this plan.

F. "Division" means one of the statutory divisions in the Northern District of Texas as provided in 28 U.S.C. § 124.

G. "General Election Voter Registration Lists" means the official records maintained by state or local election officials of persons registered to vote in either the most recent state or the most recent federal general election. The term also includes the list of eligible voters maintained by any federal examiner pursuant to the Voting Rights of 1965 where the names on such list have not been included on the official registration lists or other official lists maintained by the appropriate state or local officials.

H. "Jury wheel" means a properly programmed electronic data processing system for pure randomized selection of grand or petit jurors.

I. "Juror qualification form" means a form prescribed by the Administrative Office of the United States Courts and approved by the Judicial Conference of the United States, in accordance with 28 U.S.C. § 1869(h).

J. "Lists of licensed drivers" means official lists of licensed drivers and state identification card holders maintained by appropriate officials of the State of Texas as such records are prepared according to the state licensing cycle.

K. "Publicly draw" means to draw by electronic means in a place open to the public at large under supervision of the Clerk as required by the Judicial Conference of the United States. The place of the drawing may be an electronic data processing center located in or out of the district after reasonable notice is given in the district.

III. APPLICABILITY OF PLAN

This plan will be applicable to each division of this Court as established by 28 U.S.C. § 124. A master and qualified jury wheel will be maintained for each division. The counties comprising each division are as follows:

A. The Abilene Division comprises the counties of Callahan, Eastland, Fisher, Haskell, Howard, Jones, Mitchell, Nolan, Shackelford, Stephens, Stonewall, Taylor, and Throckmorton. Court for the Abilene Division will be held at Abilene.

B. The Amarillo Division comprises the counties of Armstrong, Brisco, Carson, Castro, Childress, Collingsworth, Dallam, Deaf Smith, Donley, Gray, Hall, Hansford, Hartley, Hemphill, Hutchinson, Lipscomb, Moore, Ochiltree, Oldham, Parmer, Potter, Randall, Roberts, Sherman, Swisher, and Wheeler. Court for the Amarillo Division will be held at Amarillo.

C. The Dallas Division comprises the counties of Dallas, Ellis, Hunt, Johnson, Kaufman, Navarro, and Rockwall. Court for the Dallas Division will be held at Dallas.

D. The Fort Worth Division comprises the counties of Comanche, Erath, Hood, Jack, Palo Pinto, Parker, Tarrant, and Wise. Court for the Fort Worth Division will be held at Fort Worth.

E. The Lubbock Division comprises the counties of Bailey, Borden, Cochran, Crosby, Dawson, Dickens, Floyd, Gaines, Garza, Hale, Hockley, Kent, Lamb, Lubbock, Lynn, Motley, Scurry, Terry, and Yoakum. Court for the Lubbock Division will be held at Lubbock.

F. The San Angelo Division comprises the counties of Brown, Coke, Coleman, Concho, Crockett, Glasscock, Irion, Menard, Mills, Reagan, Runnels, Schleicher, Sterling, Sutton, and Tom Green. Court for the San Angelo Division will be held at San Angelo.

G. The Wichita Falls Division comprises the counties of Archer, Baylor, Clay, Cottle, Foard, Hardeman, King, Knox, Montague, Wichita, Wilbarger, and Young. Court for the Wichita Falls Division will be held at Wichita Falls.

IV. STATUTORY PROVISIONS INCORPORATED HEREIN

There is incorporated herein by reference all provisions of Chapter 121, sections 1861, et seq., Title 28, United States Code, and all amendments thereto, and other laws that may hereafter be enacted relating to juries and trial by jury.

V. MANAGEMENT OF THE JURY SELECTION PROCESS

The Clerk is responsible for managing the jury selection process under the general direction of the Duty Judge.

The Court has determined that electronic data processing methods can be advantageously used for managing this plan. Therefore, a properly programmed electronic data processing system or a combination system employing both manual and electronic machine methods may be used to select master wheel names, select names of persons to be sent questionnaires, select names of persons to be summoned, and to perform other clerical and record keeping functions as determined by the Clerk. Non-court personnel are authorized to assist the Clerk with electronic data processing to comply with the random selection of prospective jurors.

VI. JURY SELECTION SOURCES

The source from which the names of petit and grand jurors will be selected at random will be the General Election Voter Registration Lists from all counties within the relevant division. While such lists represent a fair cross-section of the community in this district, it is necessary to foster the statutory policy of 28 U.S.C. §§ 1861 and 1862 to supplement such lists in accordance with 28 U.S.C. § 1862(b)(2) with lists of licensed drivers from all counties within each division using an automated system that will eliminate, as reasonably as possible, any name duplications. The list or lists used to select names for the master jury wheel will hereafter be referred to as the "source list."

VII. MASTER JURY WHEEL

For each division, the Clerk will provide a master jury wheel into which the names and/or identifying numbers of those selected at random from the source list for that division will be placed. The total number of names initially added will be determined by the Chief Judge on recommendation of the Clerk based on the Clerk's estimate of the number needed for a period of two years. This number must be at least one-half of one percent of the total number of persons on the voter registration lists in each division, and not less than 1,000. The Clerk will refill the master jury wheel every two years between January 1 and September 1, or at more frequent intervals as determined by the Chief Judge on recommendation of the Clerk. The number of names selected from each county will be in the same ratio to the total number of names to be selected as the number of registered voters in that county bears to the total number of registered voters in the division. Additional names may be placed in the master jury wheel from time to time as may be necessary as determined by the Clerk.

For the purpose of calculating from the voter registration list the total number of registered voters within a respective division within the district, the Clerk will add together the totals contained from each county. The number taken as the total for each county may be based, at the Clerk's option, upon either a manual or a mechanized count of the names on the voter registration list. After first determining the total number of names needed for the master wheel and then the proportionate shares of names to be drawn from the source list of each particular county, the Clerk will proceed, either manually or through a combination of manual and computer methods, to make the selection of names from the source list of each county.

The selection of names from the source list may be accomplished by a purely randomized process through a properly programmed electronic data processing system. The selection process must ensure that each county within a jury division is substantially proportionally represented in the master wheel in accordance with 28 U.S.C. § 1863(b)(3). The selection of names from the source list must also ensure that the mathematical odds of any single name being picked are substantially equal.

VIII. DRAWING NAMES FROM THE MASTER WHEEL AND COMPLETION OF JUROR QUALIFICATION FORMS

At periodic intervals, the Clerk will publicly draw at random from the master jury wheels the names of as many persons as may be required to maintain an adequate number of names in the qualified jury wheels. This may be accomplished using a properly programmed electronic data processing system for pure randomized selection.

The Clerk will mail to each person whose name is drawn a juror qualification form prescribed by the Administrative Office of the United States Courts and approved by the Judicial Conference of the United States, together with an appropriate letter of instruction directing the completion and return by mail or on-line within ten days. Each person will be admonished on transmittal of the questionnaire that failure to complete and return this questionnaire form, or any wilful misrepresentation of any material fact requested by it for the purpose of avoiding or securing jury service, may subject such person to criminal penalties.

IX. QUALIFICATIONS, EXEMPTIONS, AND EXCUSES FROM JURY SERVICE

Under the supervision of the Duty Judge, the Clerk will determine, solely on the basis of information provided on the juror qualification form and other competent evidence, whether a person is qualified for, unqualified for, exempt from, or eligible for excuse from jury service under subparagraphs A, B, and C below. The determination will be noted on the juror qualification form or on supporting documentation and recorded in automated records of the master jury wheel. The method used for this determination may be either electronic, manual, or a combination of both.

A. Qualifications. Every person will be deemed qualified to serve on grand and petit juries in this district, unless he or she:

276

1. is not a citizen of the United States, at least 18 years old, who has resided for a period of one year within the judicial district;

2. is unable to read, write, and understand the English language with a degree of proficiency sufficient to fill out satisfactorily the jury qualification form;

3. is unable to speak the English language;

4. is incapable, by reason of mental or physical infirmity, to render satisfactory jury service; or

5. has a charge pending against him or her for the commission of, or has been convicted in a state or federal court of record of, a crime punishable by imprisonment for more than one year and his or her civil rights have not been restored.

B. Exemptions. The following persons are exempt from jury service under 28 U.S.C. § 1863(b)(6):

1. members in active service in the Armed Forces of the United States;

2. members of the fire or police departments of any state, district, territory, possession, or subdivision thereof; and

3. public officers in the executive, legislative, or judicial branches of the government of the United States, or any state, district, territory, or possession or subdivision thereof, who are actively engaged in the performance of official duties.

C. Automatic Excuses on Individual Request. The Court has determined that jury service by the following occupational classes or groups of persons would entail undue hardship or extreme inconvenience to the members thereof, and the excuse of such members will not be inconsistent with 28 U.S.C. §§ 1861 and 1862, and will be granted upon individual request.

1. a person who is over the age of 70 years;

2. a person who serves in an official capacity without compensation as a firefighter or member of a rescue squad or ambulance crew for a public agency in accordance with 28 U.S.C. § 1863(b)(5)(B); and

3. a person who has served on a federal grand or petit jury panel within the past two years.

X. QUALIFIED JURY WHEEL

The Clerk will place the name of each person drawn from the master jury wheel who is determined to be qualified as a juror and not exempt or excused under paragraph IX in the qualified jury wheel for the division in which that person resides. The qualified jury wheel in each division will be emptied and refilled within six months after refilling the corresponding master jury wheel, but not later than October 1 of the refill year. A minimum of 300 names must be maintained in the qualified jury wheel in each division.

XI. SUMMONING OF JURORS

When the Duty Judge orders a grand or petit jury to be drawn, the Clerk will publicly draw at random the names of persons in the number required for service from the qualified wheel using a properly programmed electronic data system for pure randomized selection. The Clerk will issue summons for persons randomly chosen by this process in accordance with 28 U.S.C. § 1866(b).

Thereafter, the persons summoned will be gathered in the designated central jury room for selection to grand and petit jury panels using lists of names randomly drawn from the names of those who have been summoned.

The Court has determined that the composition of persons summoned to serve on any grand jury convened in any of the seven divisions identified in this plan also represents a fair cross section of the entire population of the district. Therefore, grand jury sessions may be held at any of the seven divisions and grand jurors may be drawn from the qualified jury wheel for a single division or a combination of some or all divisions. If a grand jury is drawn from the qualified jury wheel of more than one division, the names will be drawn in essentially the same proportion that the number of names on the voter registration lists in each division bears to the total number of names on all of the voter registration lists of the combined divisions.

XII. FURTHER EXCUSES AND EXCLUSIONS AFTER SUMMONS

Except as provided in paragraph IX above, no person will be disqualified, excluded, excused, or exempt from service as a juror, provided that any person summoned for jury service may be excused by a Judge or by the Clerk under the supervision of the Duty Judge upon a showing of undue hardship or extreme inconvenience, for such period as deemed necessary. The Clerk will make arrangements as to any juror who has been excused temporarily based on undue hardship or extreme inconvenience for deferral of the juror's service to the specific future date ordered by the Judge granting the excuse, or if the juror is excused indefinitely for such a reason the Clerk will return the juror's name to the qualified wheel.

The Court has determined that service by the following groups of persons and occupational classes of persons would entail undue hardship or extreme inconvenience to the members thereof and that excuse from jury service of the members thereof on individual request after summons would not be inconsistent with 28 U.S.C. §§ 1861 and 1862:

A. a person licensed to and actively practicing medicine in the state;

B. a person who actively cares for a child or children under ten years of age whose service on a jury would require leaving the child or children without adequate supervision;

C. a person essential to care for an aged or infirm person; or

D. a full-time student of a public or private secondary school or an accredited college or university.

XIII. SELECTION OF JURORS IN CASES OF UNANTICIPATED SHORTAGE

When there is an unanticipated shortage of available petit jurors drawn from any division's qualified jury wheel, the Duty Judge may require the marshal to summon a sufficient number of additional petit jurors selected at random from the qualified jury wheel of that division.

XIV. FAILURE TO APPEAR AS SUMMONED

Any person summoned for jury service who fails to appear as directed may be ordered by the Presiding Judge to appear forthwith and show cause for the person's failure to comply with the summons. Any person who fails to show good cause for non-compliance with a summons may be fined and/or imprisoned as allowed by law.

XV. CHALLENGING COMPLIANCE WITH SELECTION PROCEDURE

In civil cases and in criminal cases, the exclusive method of challenging any jury on the ground that such jury was not selected in conformity with the provisions of Chapter 121 of Title 28, United States Code, will be that provided by any existing statute and rule of criminal and civil procedure, including but not limited to 28 U.S.C. § 1867.

XVI. DISCLOSURE OF RECORDS

Disclosure of the contents of any jury records and papers used by the Clerk in connection with the jury selection process is not permitted except as provided by 28 U.S.C. § 1867(f) or on order of the Duty Judge. Parties requesting access to these records must submit the request in writing to the Clerk setting forth the reasons for requesting access.

The clerk will not disclose the names of jurors drawn from the qualified wheel for service on a grand jury panel. These names will be kept confidential except as otherwise authorized by order of the Duty Judge.

The Clerk will not disclose the names of jurors drawn from the qualified wheel for service on a petit jury panel in a case—unless otherwise ordered by the Presiding Judge—until the first day of the jurors' term of service, at which time the names will be disclosed only as necessary for voir dire proceedings. The Clerk will not disclose the juror names to the media or public except on order of the Presiding Judge.

XVII. MAINTENANCE OF RECORDS

After any master jury wheel is emptied and refilled as provided in this plan and after all persons selected to serve as jurors prior to emptying of the master jury wheel have completed such service, all papers and records compiled and maintained by the Clerk prior to emptying of the master jury wheel will be preserved in the custody of the Clerk for four years, or for such longer period as may be ordered by the Duty Judge.

XVIII. REPORTING STATEMENT

This plan is based on the conclusion and judgment that the policy, purpose, and intent of the Jury Selection and Service Act of 1968 will be fully accomplished and implemented by the use of voter registration lists, as supplemented by the inclusion of subsequent registrants to the latest practicable date and lists of licensed drivers, as the source of an at-random selection of prospective grand and petit jurors who represent a fair cross section of the community. As required by the Judicial Conference of the United States, a report will be made within six months after each periodic refilling of the master wheel on forms approved by the Judicial Conference giving general data relating to the master wheel, the time and manner of name selection, an analysis of the race, ethnicity and sex of prospective jurors based on returns from a statistically reliable sample of persons chosen at random from the master jury wheel to whom juror qualification forms have been sent, and an analysis by race, ethnicity, and sex of all persons who have actually been qualified for jury service during the period covered by the report.

XIX. EFFECTIVE DATE

Provisions of the plan now in effect are superseded and this plan as amended will take effect when approved by a reviewing panel of the Judicial Council of the United States Court of Appeals for the Fifth Circuit, as provided in 28 U.S.C. § 1863.

[Dated: June 12, 2008. Approved by the Judicial Council for the Fifth Circuit December 31, 2008.]

CRIMINAL JUSTICE ACT PLAN

I. Authority

Under the Criminal Justice Act (CJA) of 1964, as amended, 18 U.S.C. § 3006A, and *Guide to Judiciary Policy (Guide)*, Volume 7A, the judges of the United States District Court for the Northern District of Texas adopt this Plan, as approved by the circuit, for furnishing representation in federal court for any person financially unable to obtain adequate representation in accordance with the CJA.

II. Statement of Policy

A. Objectives. The objectives of this Plan are:

1. to attain the goal of equal justice under the law for all persons;

2. to provide all eligible persons with timely appointed counsel services that are consistent with the best practices of the legal profession, are cost-effective, and protect the independence of the defense function so that the rights of individual defendants are safeguarded and enforced; and

3. to particularize the requirements of the CJA, the USA Patriot Improvement and Reauthorization Act of 2005 (recodified at 18 U.S.C. § 3599), and *Guide*, Vol. 7A, in a way that meets the needs of this district.

This Plan must therefore be administered so that those accused of a crime, or otherwise eligible for services under the CJA, will not be deprived of the right to counsel, or any element of representation necessary to an effective defense, due to lack of financial resources.

B. Compliance.

1. This Plan is intended to be consistent with applicable law and Judicial Conference policy and to provide guidance to the court, its clerk, the federal public defender and attorneys appointed under the CJA.

2. The court will ensure that a current copy of the Plan is made available on the court's website, and provided to CJA counsel on request.

III. Definitions

A. Representation. "Representation" includes counsel and investigative, expert, and other services.

B. Appointed Attorney. "Appointed attorney" is an attorney designated to represent a financially eligible person under the CJA and this Plan. Such attorneys include private attorneys and the federal public defender and staff attorneys of the federal public defender organization.

IV. Determination of Eligibility for CJA Representation

A. Subject Matter Eligibility.

1. *Mandatory.* Representation must be provided for any financially eligible person who:

a. is charged with a felony or with a Class A misdemeanor;

b. is a juvenile alleged to have committed an act of juvenile delinquency as defined in 18 U.S.C. § 5031;

c. is charged with a violation of probation, or faces a change of a term or condition of probation (unless the modification sought is favorable to the probationer and the government has not objected to the proposed change);

d. is under arrest, when such representation is required by law;

e. is entitled to appointment of counsel in parole proceedings;

f. is charged with a violation of supervised release or faces modification, reduction, or enlargement of a condition, or extension or revocation of a term of supervised release;

g. is subject to a mental condition hearing under 18 U.S.C. chapter 313;

h. is in custody as a material witness;

i. is seeking to set aside or vacate a death sentence under 28 U.S.C. § 2254 or § 2255;

j. is entitled to appointment of counsel in verification of consent proceedings in connection with a transfer of an offender to or from the United States for the execution of a penal sentence under 18 U.S.C. § 4109;

k. is entitled to appointment of counsel under the Sixth Amendment to the Constitution; or

l. faces loss of liberty in a case and federal law requires the appointment of counsel.

2. *Discretionary.* Whenever a district judge or magistrate judge determines that the interests of justice so require, representation may be provided for any financially eligible person who:

a. is charged with a petty offense (Class B or C misdemeanor, or an infraction) for which a sentence to confinement is authorized;

b. is seeking relief (other than to set aside or vacate a death sentence) under 28 U.S.C. § 2241, 2254, or 2255;

c. is charged with civil or criminal contempt and faces loss of liberty;

d. has been called as a witness before a grand jury, a court, the Congress, or a federal agency or commission which has the power to compel testimony, and there is reason to believe, either prior to or during testimony, that the witness could be subject to a criminal prosecution, a civil or criminal contempt proceeding, or face loss of liberty;

e. has been advised by the United States attorney or a law enforcement officer that they are the target of a grand jury investigation;

f. is proposed by the United States attorney for processing under a pretrial diversion program; or

g. is held for international extradition under 18 U.S.C. chapter 209.

3. *Ancillary Matters.* Representation may also be provided for financially eligible persons in ancillary matters appropriate to the criminal proceedings under 18 U.S.C. § 3006A(c). In determining whether representation in an ancillary matter is appropriate to the criminal proceedings, the court should consider whether such representation is reasonably necessary:

a. to protect a constitutional right;

b. to contribute in some significant way to the defense of the principal criminal charge;

c. to aid in preparation for the trial or disposition of the principal criminal charge;

d. to enforce the terms of a plea agreement in the principal criminal charge;

e. to preserve the claim of the CJA client to an interest in real or personal property subject to civil forfeiture proceeding under 18 U.S.C. § 983, 19 U.S.C. § 1602, 21 U.S.C. § 881, or similar statutes, which property, if recovered by the client, may be considered for reimbursement under 18. U.S.C. § 3006A(f); or

f. effectuate the return of real or personal property belonging to the CJA client, which may be subject to a motion for return of property under Fed. R. Crim. P. 41(g), which property, if recovered by the client, may be considered for reimbursement under 18 U.S.C. § 3006A(f).

B. Financial Eligibility.

1. *Presentation of Accused for Financial Eligibility Determination.*

a. Duties of Law Enforcement.

(i) Upon arrest, and where the defendant has not retained or waived counsel, federal law enforcement officials must promptly notify, telephonically or electronically, the appropriate court personnel, who in turn will notify the federal public defender of the arrest of an individual in connection with a federal criminal charge.

(ii) Employees of law enforcement agencies should not participate in the completion of the financial affidavit or seek to obtain information concerning financial eligibility from a person requesting the appointment of counsel.

b. Duties of United States Attorney's Office.

(i) Upon the return or unsealing of an indictment or the filing of a criminal information, and where the defendant has not retained or waived counsel, the United States attorney or their delegate will promptly notify, telephonically or electronically, appropriate court personnel, who in turn will notify the federal public defender.

(ii) Upon issuance of a target letter, and where the individual has not retained or waived counsel, the United States attorney or their delegate must promptly notify, telephonically or electronically, the appropriate court personnel, who in turn will notify the federal public defender, unless the United States Attorney's Office is aware of an actual or potential conflict with the target and the federal public defender, in which case they must promptly notify the court.

(iii) Employees of the United States Attorney's Office should not participate in the completion of the financial affidavit or seek to obtain information concerning financial eligibility from a person requesting the appointment of counsel.

c. Duties of Federal Public Defender's Office.

(i) In cases in which the federal public defender may be appointed, the office will:

● immediately investigate and determine whether an actual or potential conflict exists; and

● in the event of an actual or potential conflict, promptly notify the court to facilitate the timely appointment of other counsel.

(ii) When practicable, the federal public defender will discuss with the person who indicates that he or she is not financially able to secure representation the right to appointed counsel and, if appointment of counsel seems likely, assist in the completion of a financial affidavit (Form CJA 23) and arrange to have the person promptly presented before a magistrate judge or district judge of this court for determination of financial eligibility and appointment of counsel.

d. Duties of Probation/Pretrial Services Office.

(i) When practicable, a pretrial services officer will not conduct the pretrial service interview of a financially eligible defendant without the presence of counsel unless the defendant waives the right to counsel or consents to a pretrial service interview without counsel.

(ii) When counsel has been appointed, the pretrial services officer will provide counsel notice and a reasonable opportunity to attend any interview of the defendant by the pretrial services officer prior to the initial pretrial release or detention hearing.

2. *Factual Determination of Financial Eligibility.*

a. In every case where appointment of counsel is authorized under 18 U.S.C. § 3006A(a) and related statutes, the court must advise the person that he or she has a right to be represented by counsel throughout the case and that, if so desired, counsel will be appointed to represent the person if he or she is financially unable to obtain counsel.

b. The determination of eligibility for representation under the CJA is a judicial function to be performed by the court after making appropriate inquiries concerning the person's financial eligibility. Other employees of the court may be designated to obtain or verify the facts relevant to the financial eligibility determination.

c. In determining whether a person is "financially unable to obtain counsel," consideration should be given to the cost of providing the person and his or her dependents with the necessities of life, the cost of securing pretrial release, asset encumbrance, and the likely cost of retained counsel.

d. Except to the extent consistent with the community property laws of Texas, determination of eligibility must be made without regard to the financial ability of the person's family to retain counsel unless their family indicates willingness and ability to do so promptly.

e. Any doubts about a person's eligibility should be resolved in the person's favor; erroneous determinations of eligibility may be corrected at a later time.

f. Relevant information bearing on the person's financial eligibility should be reflected on a financial eligibility affidavit (Form CJA 23).

g. If at any time after the appointment of counsel a judge finds that a person provided representation is financially able to obtain counsel or make partial payment for the representation, the judge may terminate the appointment of counsel or direct that any funds available to the defendant be paid as provided in 18 U.S.C. § 3006A(f).

h. If at any stage of the proceedings a judge finds that a person is no longer financially able to pay retained counsel, counsel may be appointed in accordance with the general provisions set forth in this Plan.

V. Timely Appointment of Counsel

A. Timing of Appointment. Counsel must be provided to eligible persons as soon as feasible in the following circumstances, whichever occurs earliest:

1. after they are taken into custody;

2. when they appear before a magistrate or district court judge;

3. when they are formally charged or notified of charges if formal charges are sealed; or

4. when a magistrate or district court judge otherwise considers appointment of counsel appropriate under the CJA and related statutes.

B. Retroactive Appointment of Counsel. Appointment of counsel may be made retroactively to include representation provided prior to appointment.

VI. Provision of Representational Services

A. Federal Public Defender and Private Counsel. This Plan provides for representational services by the federal public defender organization and for the appointment and compensation of private counsel from a CJA Panel list maintained by the court in cases authorized under the CJA and related statutes.

B. Administration. Administration of each CJA Panel is the responsibility of the court.

C. Apportionment of Cases. Where practical and cost effective, private attorneys will be appointed in a substantial proportion of the cases in which the accused is determined to be financially eligible for representation under the CJA. "Substantial" will usually be defined as a minimum of twenty-five percent (25%) of the annual CJA appointments.

D. Number of Counsel. More than one attorney may be appointed in any case determined by the presiding judge to be extremely difficult.

E. Capital Cases. Procedures for appointment of counsel in cases where the defendant is charged with a crime that may be punishable by death, or is seeking to vacate or set aside a death sentence in proceedings under 28 U.S.C. §§ 2254 or 2255, are set forth in section XIV of this Plan.

VII. Federal Public Defender Organization

A. Establishment. The Federal Public Defender's Office of the Northern District of Texas (FPD) is established in this district under the CJA as the federal public defender organization. The FPD is responsible for rendering defense services, on appointment, throughout this district. When appointment of counsel is mandatory under Part XIV. E and F, *infra*, a judge in any federal district court in Texas may appoint the FPD to represent an eligible person, if such representation will not compromise the ability of the FPD to carry out its duties in this district.

B. Standards. The FPD must provide high quality representation consistent with the best practices of the legal profession and commensurate with those services rendered when counsel is privately retained.

C. Workload. The FPD will continually monitor the workloads of its staff to ensure high quality representation for all clients.

D. Professional Conduct. The FPD must conform to the highest standards of professional conduct, including, but not limited to, the Texas Disciplinary Rules of Professional Conduct, the Code of Conduct for Federal Public Defender Employees, and requirements of the court's local rules.

E. Private Practice of Law. Neither the federal public defender nor any defender employee may engage in the private practice of law except as authorized by Judicial Conference policy.

F. Supervision of Defender Organization. The federal public defender will be responsible for the supervision and management of the FPD. Accordingly, the federal public defender will be appointed in all cases assigned to that organization for subsequent assignment to staff attorneys at the discretion of the federal public defender.

G. Training. The federal public defender will assess the training needs of FPD staff and, in coordination with the CJA Panel Attorney District Representative,[1] the training needs of the local CJA Panel attorneys, and provide training opportunities and other educational resources.

VIII. CJA Panels of Private Attorneys

A. Recognition of the Existing CJA Panel Advisory Committee.

1. The CJA Panel Advisory Committee ("CJA Committee") established by the court is hereby recognized. Members are appointed to the CJA Committee by the chief judge in consultation with the federal public defender. The CJA Committee consists of one district court judge, one magistrate judge, the CJA Panel Attorney District Representative (PADR), at least two other criminal defense attorneys who practice regularly in the district, the federal public defender, and the clerk of court. The latter two members shall serve ex officio.

2. The district's PADR, federal public defender, and the clerk of court are permanent members of the CJA Committee.

3. The term of membership on the CJA Committee will be determined by the CJA Committee chair, in consultation with the chief judge.

4. The CJA Committee will meet at least once a year and at any time the court asks the Committee to consider an issue.

B. Duties of the CJA Committee. The CJA Committee is available to serve as a resource for each division of the court. However, given the differences among the divisions of the court, the responsibilities of the CJA Committee will vary as determined by the presiding judges in each division.

Responsibilities of the CJA Committee may include any of the following:

1. *Membership.* Examine the qualifications of applicants for membership on a CJA Panel and recommend the approval of those attorneys who are deemed qualified and the rejection of the applications of those attorneys deemed unqualified.

2. *Recruitment.* Engage in recruitment efforts to establish a diverse CJA Panel and ensure that all qualified attorneys are encouraged to participate in the furnishing of representation in CJA cases.

3. *Annual Report.* Review the operation and administration of each CJA Panel over the preceding year, and recommend any necessary or appropriate changes to the chief judge concerning:

    a. the size of a CJA Panel;

    b. the recruitment of qualified and diverse attorneys as required and set forth in this plan; and

    c. recurring issues or difficulties encountered by CJA Panel members or their CJA clients.

4. *Removal.* Recommend the removal of any CJA Panel member who:

    a. fails to satisfactorily fulfill the requirements of CJA Panel membership during their term of service, including the failure to provide high quality representation to CJA clients, or

    b. has engaged in other conduct such that his or her continued service on a CJA Panel is inappropriate.

5. *Training.* Assist the FPD in providing training for CJA Panel members on substantive and procedural legal matters affecting representation of CJA clients.

6. *Voucher Review.* At the request of the presiding judge, review and make recommendations on the processing and payment of CJA vouchers.

7. *Mentoring.* Create and administer a mentoring program designed to identify and help prepare viable candidates to qualify for consideration for appointment to a CJA Panel. Experienced members of the criminal defense bar who have practiced extensively in the federal courts will be selected to serve as mentors. The CJA Committee will review the mentee applications, make recommendations concerning their participation in the mentoring program, identify appropriate cases for the mentoring program, evaluate the success of the mentoring program, and provide guidance to the mentors.

IX. Establishment of a CJA Panel

A. Approval of CJA Panel.

1. The existing, previously established panels of attorneys who are eligible and willing to be appointed to provide representation under the CJA is hereby recognized. A magistrate judge in each division serves as CJA Panel coordinator.

2. The judge(s) in each division of the court will approve attorneys for membership on the CJA Panel that serves their division after receiving recommendations from the magistrate judge CJA Panel coordinator.

B. Size of CJA Panel.

1. The size of each CJA Panel will be determined by each division of the court.

2. A CJA Panel must be large enough to provide a sufficient number of experienced attorneys to handle the CJA caseload, yet small enough so that CJA Panel members will receive an adequate number of appointments to maintain their proficiency in federal criminal defense work enabling them to provide high quality representation consistent with the best practices of the legal profession and commensurate with those services rendered when counsel is privately retained.

C. Qualifications and Membership on a CJA Panel.

1. *Application.* Application forms for membership on a CJA Panel are available from the clerk's office.

2. *Equal Opportunity.* All qualified attorneys are encouraged to participate in furnishing representation in CJA cases.

3. *Eligibility.*

   a. An applicant for a CJA Panel must be a member in good standing of the federal bar of this district and the Fifth Circuit Court of Appeals. An applicant must have practiced law for at least four years unless the applicant has sufficient trial or other relevant experience that might warrant a waiver of this requirement.

   b. An applicant must maintain a principal office in this district in a city and county that is in close proximity to the county in which court is held.

   c. An applicant must possess strong litigation skills and demonstrate proficiency with the federal sentencing guidelines, federal sentencing procedures, the Bail Reform Act, the Federal Rules of Criminal Procedure, and the Federal Rules of Evidence.

   d. An applicant must have significant experience including federal experience, representing persons charged with serious criminal offenses and demonstrate a commitment to the defense of people who lack the financial means to hire an attorney.

   e. An attorney who does not possess the experience set forth above but has equivalent other experience is encouraged to apply and set forth in writing the details of that experience for the court's consideration.

4. *Removal from a CJA Panel.*

   a. Mandatory Removal. Service on a CJA Panel is a privilege and not a right. Any member of a CJA Panel who is suspended or disbarred from the practice of law by the state court before whom such member is admitted, or who is suspended or disbarred from this court or any federal court, will be removed from a CJA Panel immediately. Additionally, any district judge may, for good cause, remove the name of an attorney from a CJA Panel.

   b. Removal by Request. A CJA Panel member should submit a written request to the court using an approved form to be removed from the Panel.

X. CJA Panel Attorney Appointment in Non–Capital Cases

A. Appointment List. The clerk of court will maintain a current list of all attorneys included on each CJA Panel, with current office addresses, email addresses, and telephone numbers, as well as a statement of qualifications and experience.

B. Appointment Procedures.

1. The court is responsible for overseeing the appointment of cases to CJA Panel attorneys. The clerk of court will maintain a record of CJA Panel attorney appointments and, when appropriate, data reflecting the apportionment of appointments between attorneys from the FPD and CJA Panel attorneys.

2. Appointment of cases to CJA Panel members will ordinarily be made on a rotational basis. In a complex or otherwise difficult case, a judge may appoint counsel outside of the normal rotation to ensure the defendant has sufficiently experienced counsel.

3. Under special circumstances a judge may appoint a member of the bar of the court who is not a member of a CJA Panel. Such special circumstances may include cases in which the court determines that the appointment of a particular attorney is in the interests of justice, judicial economy, or continuity of representation, or for any other compelling reason. It is not anticipated that special circumstances will arise often, and the procedures set forth in the Plan are presumed to be sufficient in the vast majority of cases in which counsel are to be appointed.

XI. Duties of CJA Panel Members

A. Standards and Professional Conduct.

1. CJA Panel members must provide high quality representation consistent with the best practices of the legal profession and commensurate with those services rendered when counsel is privately retained.

Attorneys appointed under the CJA must conform to the highest standards of professional conduct, including but not limited to, the Texas Disciplinary Rules of Professional Conduct and requirements of the court's local rules.

2. CJA Panel members must promptly notify the court in writing through the clerk of court when any licensing authority, grievance committee, or administrative body has taken action against them, or when a finding of contempt, sanction, or reprimand has been issued against the CJA Panel member by any state or federal court. (See LCrR 57.8(d).)

B. Training and Continuing Legal Education.

1. Attorneys on a CJA Panel are expected to remain current with developments in federal criminal defense law, practice, and procedure, including the Recommendation for Electronically Stored Information (ESI) Discovery Production in Federal Criminal Cases.[2]

2. CJA Panel members are expected to attend continuing legal education hours relevant to federal criminal practice annually.

3. Failure to comply with these training and legal education requirements may be grounds for removal from a CJA Panel.

C. Facilities and Technology Requirements.

1. CJA Panel attorneys must have facilities, resources, and technological capability to effectively and efficiently manage assigned cases.

2. CJA Panel attorneys must comply with the requirements of electronic filing and eVoucher.

3. CJA Panel attorneys must know and abide by procedures related to requests for investigative, expert, and other services.

D. Continuing Representation. Once counsel is appointed under the CJA, counsel will continue the representation until the matter, including appeals (unless provided otherwise by the Fifth Circuit's CJA plan) or review by certiorari, is closed; or until substitute counsel has filed a notice of appearance; or until an order is entered allowing or requiring the person represented to proceed pro se; or until the appointment is terminated by court order.

E. Miscellaneous.

1. *Case Budgeting.* In non-capital representations of unusual complexity that are likely to become extraordinary in terms of cost, the court may require development of a case budget consistent with *Guide*, Vol. 7A, Ch. 2, §§ 230.26.10–20.

2. *No Receipt of Other Payment.* Appointed counsel may not require, request, or accept any payment or promise of payment or any other valuable consideration for representation under the CJA, unless such payment is approved by order of the court.

3. *Redetermination of Need.* If at any time after appointment, counsel has reason to believe that a party is financially able to obtain counsel, or make partial payment for counsel, and the source of counsel's information is not protected as a privileged communication, counsel will advise the court.

XII.   Compensation of CJA Panel Attorneys

A.   Policy of the Court Regarding Compensation. Providing fair compensation to appointed counsel is a critical component of the administration of justice. CJA Panel attorneys must be compensated for time expended in court and time reasonably expended out of court, and reimbursed for expenses reasonably incurred.

B.   Payment Procedures.

1. Claims for compensation must be submitted on the appropriate CJA form through the court's eVoucher system.

2. An appointed attorney may not claim compensation for services furnished by another attorney, including a partner or associate, without prior authorization by the presiding judge. A judge may retroactively approve services by a partner or associate.

3. Claims for compensation should be submitted no later than 45 days after final disposition of the case, unless good cause is shown.

4. The clerk of court or the clerk's designee will review the claim for mathematical and technical accuracy and for conformity with *Guide*, Vol. 7A and, if correct, will forward the claim for consideration and action by the presiding judge.

5. Absent extraordinary circumstances, the court should act on CJA compensation claims within 30 days of submission, and vouchers should not be delayed or reduced for the purpose of diminishing Defender Services program costs in response to adverse financial circumstances.

6. Under 18 U.S.C. § 3006A(d)(5), and in accordance with the provisions of *Guide*, Vol. 7A, Ch. 2, § 230.36, the presiding judge will fix the compensation and reimbursement to be paid to the attorney.

XIII.   Investigative, Expert, and Other Services

A.   Financial Eligibility. Counsel for a person who is financially unable to obtain investigative, expert, or other services necessary for an adequate defense may request such services in an application to the court as provided in 18 U.S.C. § 3006A(e)(1), regardless of whether counsel is appointed under the CJA. Upon finding that the services are necessary and that the person is financially unable to obtain them, the court must authorize counsel to obtain the services.[3]

B.   Applications. Requests for authorization of funds for investigative, expert, and other services should be submitted in an ex parte application to the court and should not be disclosed except with the consent of the person represented or as required by law or Judicial Conference policy.

C.   Compliance. Counsel must comply with Judicial Conference policies set forth in *Guide*, Vol. 7A, Ch. 3.

XIV.   Appointment of Counsel and Case Management in CJA Capital Cases

A.   Applicable Legal Authority. The appointment and compensation of counsel in capital cases and the authorization and payment of persons providing investigative, expert, and other services are governed by 18 U.S.C. §§ 3005, 3006A, and 3599, *Guide*, Vol. 7A, Ch. 6, and the Special Procedures for Reviewing Attorney Compensation Requests in Death Penalty Cases promulgated by the Judicial Council of the Fifth Circuit.[4] Nothing in this section is intended to diminish the discretion of a presiding judge to appoint counsel under the law as the judge deems just and expeditious.

B. General Applicability and Appointment of Counsel Requirements.

1. Unless otherwise specified, the provisions set forth in this section apply to all capital proceedings in the federal courts, whether those matters originated in a district court (federal capital trials) or in a state court (habeas proceedings under 28 U.S.C. § 2254). Such matters include those in which the death penalty may be or is being sought by the prosecution, motions for a new trial, direct appeal, applications for a writ of certiorari to the Supreme Court of the United States, all post-conviction proceedings under 28 U.S.C. §§ 2254 or 2255 seeking to vacate or set aside a death sentence, applications for stays of execution, competency proceedings, proceedings for executive or other clemency, and other appropriate motions and proceedings.

2. Any person charged with a crime that may be punishable by death who is or becomes financially unable to obtain representation is entitled to the assistance of appointed counsel throughout every stage of available judicial proceedings, including pretrial proceedings, trial, sentencing, motions for new trial, appeals, applications for writ of certiorari to the Supreme Court of the United States, and all available post-conviction processes, together with applications for stays of execution and other appropriate motions and procedures, competency proceedings, and proceedings for executive or other clemency as may be available to the defendant. See 18 U.S.C. § 3599(e).

3. Qualified counsel must be appointed in capital cases at the earliest possible opportunity.

4. Given the complex and demanding nature of capital cases, where appropriate, the court may wish to utilize the expert services available through the Administrative Office of the United States Courts (AO), Defender Services Death Penalty Resource Counsel projects ("Resource Counsel projects") which include: (1) Federal Death Penalty Resource Counsel and Capital Resource Counsel Projects (for federal capital trials), (2) Federal Capital Appellate Resource Counsel Project, (3) Federal Capital Habeas § 2255 Project, and (4) National and Regional Habeas Assistance and Training Counsel Projects (§ 2254). These counsel are death penalty experts who may be relied upon by the court for assistance with selection and appointment of counsel, case budgeting, and legal, practical, and other matters arising in federal capital cases.

5. The presiding judge may appoint an attorney furnished by a state or local public defender organization or legal aid agency or other private, non-profit organization to represent a person charged with a capital crime or seeking federal death penalty habeas corpus relief provided that the attorney is fully qualified. Such appointments may be in place of, or in addition to, the appointment of a federal defender organization or a CJA Panel attorney or an attorney appointed pro hac vice. See 18 U.S.C. § 3006A(a)(3).

C. Appointment of Trial Counsel in Federal Death–Eligible Cases.[5]

1. *General Requirements.*

a. Appointment of qualified capital trial counsel must occur when a defendant is formally charged with a federal criminal offense where the penalty of death is possible, or earlier. See 18 U.S.C. § 3005.

b. To protect the rights of an individual who, although uncharged, is the subject of an investigation in a federal death-eligible case, the court may appoint capitally-qualified counsel upon request, consistent with Sections C.1, 2, and 3 of these provisions.

c. At the outset of every capital case, the court must appoint two attorneys, at least one of whom meets the qualifications for "learned counsel" as described below. If necessary for adequate representation, a judge may appoint more than two attorneys to represent a defendant in a capital case. See 18 U.S.C. § 3005.

d. When appointing counsel, the judge shall consider the recommendation of the federal public defender, who may consult with Federal Death Penalty Resource Counsel to recommend qualified counsel. See 18 U.S.C. § 3005.

e. To effectuate the intent of 18 U.S.C. § 3005 that the federal public defender's recommendation be provided to the court, the judge should ensure the federal public defender has been notified of the need to appoint capitally-qualified counsel.

f. Reliance on a list for appointment of capital counsel is not recommended because selection of trial counsel should account for the particular needs of the case and the defendant, and be based on individualized recommendations from the federal public defender.

g. Out–of–district counsel, including federal defender organization staff, who possess the requisite expertise may be considered for appointment in capital trials to achieve high quality representation together with cost and other efficiencies.

h. In evaluating the qualifications of proposed trial counsel, consideration should be given to their current caseload, including other capital cases, and their willingness to effectively represent the interests of the client.

2. *Qualifications of Learned Counsel.*

a. Learned counsel must either be a member of this district's bar or be eligible for admission pro hac vice based on his or her qualifications. Appointment of counsel from outside the jurisdiction is common in federal capital cases to achieve cost and other efficiencies together with high quality representation.

b. Learned counsel must meet the minimum experience standards set forth in 18 U.S.C. §§ 3005 and 3599.

c. Learned counsel should have distinguished prior experience in the trial, appeal, or post-conviction review of federal death penalty cases, or distinguished prior experience in state death penalty trials, appeals, or post-conviction review that, in combination with co-counsel, will assure high quality representation.

d. "Distinguished prior experience" contemplates excellence, not simply prior experience. Counsel with distinguished prior experience should be appointed even if meeting this standard requires appointing counsel from outside the district where the matter arises.

e. The suitability of learned counsel should be assessed with respect to the particular demands of the case, the stage of the litigation, and the defendant.

f. Learned counsel must be willing and able to adjust other caseload demands to accommodate the extraordinary time required by the capital representation.

g. Learned counsel should satisfy the qualification standards endorsed by bar associations and other legal organizations regarding the quality of representation in capital cases.

3. *Qualifications of Second and Additional Counsel.*

a. Second and additional counsel may, but are not required to, satisfy the qualifications for learned counsel, as set forth above.

b. Second and additional counsel must be well qualified, by virtue of their distinguished prior criminal defense experience, training, and commitment to serve as counsel in this highly specialized and demanding litigation.

c. Second and additional counsel must be willing and able to adjust other caseload demands to accommodate the extraordinary time required by the capital representation.

d. The suitability of second and additional counsel should be assessed with respect to the demands of the individual case, the stage of the litigation, and the defendant.

D. Appointment and Qualifications of Direct Appeal Counsel in Federal Death Penalty Cases.

1. When appointing appellate counsel, the judge shall consider the recommendation of the federal public defender, who may consult with Federal Capital Appellate Resource Counsel to recommend qualified counsel.

2. Counsel appointed to represent a death-sentenced federal appellant should include at least one attorney who did not represent the appellant at trial.

3. Each trial counsel who withdraws should be replaced with similarly qualified counsel to represent the defendant on appeal.

4. Out–of–district counsel, including federal defender organization staff, who possess the requisite expertise may be considered for appointment in capital appeals to achieve high quality representation together with cost and other efficiencies.

5. Appellate counsel, between them, should have distinguished prior experience in federal criminal appeals and capital appeals.

6. At least one of the attorneys appointed as appellate counsel must have the requisite background, knowledge, and experience required by 18 U.S.C. § 3599(c) or (d).

7.   In evaluating the qualifications of proposed appellate counsel, the judge may consider the qualification standards endorsed by bar associations and other legal organizations regarding the quality of legal representation in capital cases.

8.   In evaluating the qualifications of proposed appellate counsel, consideration should be given to their current caseload, including other capital cases, and their willingness to effectively represent the interests of the client.

E.   Appointment and Qualifications of Post–Conviction Counsel in Federal Death Penalty Cases (28 U.S.C. § 2255).

1.   A financially eligible person seeking to vacate or set aside a death sentence in proceedings under 28 U.S.C. § 2255 is entitled to appointment of fully qualified counsel.   See 18 U.S.C. § 3599(a)(2).

2.   A judge should appoint the FPD, consistent with funding and staffing levels of the FPD related to these types of cases, when no conflict of interest exists.   If the FPD has already been appointed to the maximum number of cases, as determined by the Committee on Defender Services of the Judicial Conference of the United States, and has not agreed to an excess appointment or is otherwise prevented from accepting the appointment, the judge should appoint other fully qualified counsel.

3.   Due to the complex, demanding, and protracted nature of death penalty proceedings, the court should consider appointing at least two attorneys.

4.   In light of the accelerated timeline applicable to capital § 2255 proceedings, prompt appointment of counsel is essential.   Wherever possible, appointment should take place prior to the denial of certiorari on direct appeal by the United States Supreme Court.

5.   When appointing counsel in a capital § 2255 matter, the judge should consider the recommendation of the federal public defender, who may consult with the Federal Capital Habeas § 2255 Project.

6.   Out–of–district counsel, including federal defender organization staff, who possess the requisite expertise may be considered for appointment in capital § 2255 cases to achieve high quality representation together with cost and other efficiencies.

7.   Counsel in § 2255 cases should have distinguished prior experience in the area of federal post-conviction proceedings and in capital post-conviction proceedings.

8.   When possible, post-conviction counsel should have distinguished prior experience in capital § 2255 representations.

9.   In evaluating the qualifications of proposed post-conviction counsel, the judge may consider the qualification standards endorsed by bar associations and other legal organizations regarding the quality of legal representation in capital cases.

10.   In evaluating the qualifications of proposed post-conviction § 2255 counsel, consideration should be given to their current caseload, including other capital cases, and their willingness to effectively represent the interests of the client.

F.   Appointment and Qualifications of Counsel in Federal Capital Habeas Corpus Proceedings (28 U.S.C. § 2254).

1.   A financially eligible person seeking to vacate or set aside a death sentence in proceedings under 28 U.S.C. § 2254 is entitled to the appointment of qualified counsel.   See 18 U.S.C. § 3599(a)(2).

2.   A judge should appoint the FPD, consistent with funding and staffing levels of the FPD related to these types of cases, when no conflict of interest exists.   If the FPD has already been appointed to the maximum number of cases, as determined by the Committee on Defender Services of the Judicial Conference of the United States, and has not agreed to an excess appointment or is otherwise prevented from accepting the appointment, the judge should appoint other fully qualified counsel.

3.   Due to the complex, demanding, and protracted nature of death penalty proceedings, the judge should consider appointing at least two attorneys.

4.   When appointing counsel in a capital § 2254 matter, the judge may consider the recommendation of the federal public defender who may consult with the National or Regional Habeas Assistance and Training Counsel projects.

5.   Out–of–district counsel, including federal defender organization staff, who possess the requisite expertise may be considered for appointment in capital § 2254 cases to achieve cost and other efficiencies together with high quality representation.

6.   Unless precluded by a conflict of interest, or replaced by similarly qualified counsel upon motion by the attorney or motion by the defendant, capital § 2254 counsel must represent the defendant throughout every subsequent stage of available judicial proceedings and all available post-conviction processes, together with applications for stays of execution and other appropriate motions and procedures, and must also represent the defendant in such competency proceedings and proceedings for executive or other clemency as may be available to the defendant. See 18 U.S.C. § 3599(e).

7.   Counsel in capital § 2254 cases should have distinguished prior experience in the area of federal post-conviction proceedings and in capital post-conviction proceedings.

8.   When possible, capital § 2254 counsel should have distinguished prior experience in capital § 2254 representations.

9.   In evaluating the qualifications of proposed capital § 2254 counsel, the judge may consider the qualification standards endorsed by bar associations and other legal organizations regarding the quality of legal representation in capital cases.

10.   In evaluating the qualifications of proposed capital § 2254 counsel, consideration should be given to proposed counsel's current caseload, including other capital cases, and their willingness to represent effectively the interests of the client.

[Adopted effective July, 2018, approved by the Judicial Council of the Fifth Circuit on December 12, 2018.]

[1] The CJA Panel Attorney District Representative (PADR) is a member of the district's CJA Panel who is selected by the local federal public defender, with acquiescence from the chief judge, to serve as the representative of the district's CJA Panel for the national Defender Services CJA PADR program and local CJA committees.

[2] The ESI paper is available on the court's website at www.txnd.uscourts.gov under CJA Attorney Information, Links and Resources.

[3] Requests and authorizations for investigative, expert, or other services in capital cases are controlled by 18 U.S.C. § 3599(f), which provides that requests may not be submitted ex parte except on a showing of the need for confidentiality.

[4] As to investigative, expert, and other services, Section 3599(f) provides:

Upon a finding that investigative, expert, or other services are reasonably necessary for the representation of the defendant, whether in connection with issues relating to guilt or the sentence, the court may authorize the defendant's attorneys to obtain such services on behalf of the defendant and, if so authorized, shall order the payment of fees and expenses therefor under subsection (g). No ex parte proceeding, communication, or request may be considered pursuant to this section unless a proper showing is made concerning the need for confidentiality. Any such proceeding, communication, or request shall be transcribed and made a part of the record available for appellate review.

[5] The Judicial Conference adopted detailed recommendations on the appointment and compensation of counsel in federal death penalty cases in 1998 (JCUS–SEP 98, p. 22). In September 2010, the Defender Services Committee endorsed revised commentary to the Judicial Conference's 1998 recommendations. CJA Guidelines, Vol. 7A, Appx. 6A (Recommendations and Commentary Concerning the Cost and Quality of Defense Representation (Updated Spencer Report, September 2010)) ("Appx. 6A") is available on the judiciary's website.

SELECTED ORDERS

SPECIAL ORDER 2–46. PROCEDURES FOR CONSIDERATION AND ADOPTING MODIFICATIONS TO THE LOCAL CIVIL, CRIMINAL, AND BANKRUPTCY RULES

By vote of the district judges of this court, the following procedures are implemented for considering and adopting modifications to the local civil, criminal, and bankruptcy rules.

1.   Except when the court is required to act in an emergency, to comply with an Act of Congress, or to conform to the provisions of a national rule, the local civil, criminal, and bankruptcy rules will be modified no more than once each year, and any modifications will take effect on September 1 of the year in which they are adopted.

2.   November 1 is established as the deadline to submit proposals for local rules modifications that are to take effect on September 1 of the following year. Proposals must be submitted to:

Clerk of Court
United States District Court for the Northern District of Texas
Attention: Proposed Local Rules Modifications
1100 Commerce Street, Room 14A20
Dallas, Texas 75242–1495

3.   Local Rules modifications that are to take effect on September 1 will be adopted and distributed for public comment no later than April 1. Public comment must be submitted no later than June 1.

4.   Subject to changes made following receipt of public comment, the court will formally adopt no later than July 1 the local rules modifications that are to take effect on September 1.

5.   If a date specified in this order falls on a Saturday, Sunday, legal holiday, or date on which the clerk's office is closed by direction of the court or is otherwise inaccessible, the deadline is the next day that is not one of the aforementioned days.

This order shall not apply to rules changes that took effect prior to April 16, 1998.

The clerk of court shall disseminate this order to the Bar and to the public by appropriate means.

[Dated: April 14, 1998.]

SECOND AMENDED SPECIAL ORDER 19–1. PUBLIC ACCESS TO CERTAIN DOCUMENTS

Unless otherwise directed by the presiding judge, the clerk of court will ensure that there no public access, either in paper or electronic form, to the following documents:

1.   criminal complaints, supporting affidavits, and related papers, until each named defendant has been arrested or has made an appearance in federal court;

2.   search and seizure applications, warrants, and related papers, until ordered unsealed;

3.   unexecuted summonses and unexecuted warrants of any kind;

4.   pretrial bail or presentence investigation reports;

5.   statements of reasons in a judgment of conviction;

6.   juvenile records;

7.   documents containing identifying information about jurors or potential jurors;

8.   financial affidavits or target letters filed in seeking representation pursuant to the Criminal Justice Act;

9.   ex parte requests for authorization of investigative, expert, or other services pursuant to the Criminal Justice Act;

10.   plea agreement supplements;

11.   motions filed for downward departure under United States Sentencing Commission, Guidelines Manual § 5K1.1; and

12.   motions filed for a reduction of sentence under Rule 35(b) of the Federal Rules of Criminal Procedure.

Attorneys for the government and criminal defense attorneys must take reasonable steps to ensure that cooperator information does not become part of the public record in any case. In particular, both prosecutors and defense attorneys must review each transcript before the transcript becomes publicly available to identify information that would convey cooperation with the government and must request that the information be redacted or that relevant portions of the transcript be sealed.

[Dated: January 17, 2017.]

AMENDED SPECIAL ORDER 3–250.   ESTABLISHED PROCEDURES FOR THE DIRECT ASSIGNMENT OF CASES

With the consent of the district judges of this Court, this order governs the direct assignment of cases in the Dallas and Fort Worth divisions.

1.   An incoming transfer of probation jurisdiction case will be directly assigned to the judge in the division who previously presided over a criminal case involving the defendant, if any, and, if there is no such judge in the division, then to the judge who signed the transfer order.

2.   An incoming case involving a transfer for plea and sentence under Fed.R.Crim.P. 20 will be directly assigned to the judge assigned to any prior criminal case involving the same defendant.

3.   A petition for a writ of habeas corpus under 28 U.S.C. § 2241 will be directly assigned to the judge in the division who previously presided over a criminal case involving the defendant, if any.

4.   A successive petition for writ of habeas corpus challenging a sentence of death or an action seeking to stay execution related to a prior petition for writ of habeas corpus challenging a sentence of death will be directly assigned to the judge in the division who previously presided over a case that challenged the same sentence of death, if any.

5.   A motion filed under 28 U.S.C. § 2255 will be directly assigned to the sentencing judge.

6.   A pre-judgment writ of garnishment will be directly assigned to the judge in the division assigned to the case to which the pre-judgment writ of garnishment relates, if any.

7.   If a case is severed, any new case will be directly assigned to the judge who severed the case (absent a contrary direction in the order severing).

8.   In the Dallas division, when a new case is directly assigned or transferred to a judge because the judge was assigned to a prior case, and a magistrate judge was also assigned to the prior case, the new case will also be directly assigned to the magistrate judge assigned to the prior case.

9.   If this order provides for a case to be directly assigned to a judge or magistrate judge who is no longer accepting new cases, or if the case is of a type that the judge or magistrate judge is no longer accepting, the case will be randomly assigned.

10.   If the United States Judicial Panel on Multidistrict Litigation transfers a case to this court, or a party files a notice of related case under LR 3.3(a) or LR 81.1(a)(3) identifying a case as related to a Multidistrict Litigation (MDL) case pending in this court, the case will be directly assigned to the judge assigned to the MDL case. A magistrate judge will not be assigned to an MDL case unless the judge assigned to the MDL case otherwise directs. The chief judge, after consulting the judge assigned the MDL case and other affected judges, will determine whether to adjust the number of cases assigned to the judge assigned to the MDL case from the regular civil deck based on the number of transferred or "tag along" cases and will instruct the clerk accordingly.

11.   Absent a written order to directly assign the case, any other case will be randomly assigned.

[Dated: August 24, 2011.]

MISCELLANEOUS ORDER 16.   ADMINISTRATION OF NON–APPROPRIATED FUND; REIMBURSEMENT OF ATTORNEY EXPENSES IN CIVIL CASES
Plan for the Administration of the Non–Appropriated Fund

The judges of the United States District Court for the Northern District of Texas hereby adopt this Plan for the Administration of the Non-Appropriated Fund. This Plan supersedes all prior Plans for the Administration of the Non-Appropriated Fund.

I. Administration of Non-Appropriated Fund.

A. *Advisory Committee.* The members of the Non-Appropriated Fund Advisory Committee shall include the Chief Judge as Chairman; a District Judge to be appointed by the Chief Judge for a term of six years; a Magistrate Judge to be appointed by the Chief Judge for a term of six years; a member of the bar admitted to this district in the Dallas division to be appointed by the Chief Judge for a term of two years; a member of the bar admitted to this district in another division to be appointed by the Chief Judge for a term of two years; and the Clerk of Court. Members of this Committee shall serve without compensation. The Committee will:

1. Advise the court and its Custodian on matters of policy in the administration of the Fund;

2. Authorize expenditures when determined by the Committee that said disbursements are appropriate and will be of benefit to the bench and bar in the administration of justice;

3. Review the quarterly financial statements prepared by the Custodian and thereby confirm the adequate safeguarding and investment of the Fund or advise the Custodian of any inadequacy of financial accounting methods, records, or reports.

B. *Custodian/Trustee.* The Clerk of Court will serve as the Custodian/Trustee of the Non-Appropriated Fund for this court. The Custodian/Trustee will:

1. Receive, safeguard, deposit, disburse, invest and account for all monies in the Fund in accordance with the direction of the Advisory Committee and applicable guidelines and statutes;

2. Secure a bond, to be paid for from assets of the Fund, if required by the Court;

3. Establish an accounting system for the Fund and maintain proper records and receipts of all Fund activity;

4. Prepare and submit to the Advisory Committee a quarterly report of Fund activity, specifying the balance, receipts, disbursements, investments, estimated earnings, and any other information that the Advisory Committee may require;

5. Attest to the financial status of the Fund by signing financial statements and reports, thereby certifying the accuracy of said statements;

6. Perform such other functions as the Advisory Committee may direct.

C. *Successor Custodian.* Upon appointment by the Advisory Committee of a Successor Custodian, the Advisory Committee will designate or retain a disinterested party to conduct an exit audit. The results of this audit shall be reported to the Advisory Committee by the auditor in a report which includes:

1. A statement of assets and liabilities of the Fund;

2. A statement of operations or of receipts and disbursements covering the period since the preceding statement of operations and net worth, up to the date of transfer of responsibility to the Successor Custodian;

3. A statement of the balance in any Fund accounts and investments as of the date of transfer of responsibility to the Successor Custodian.

The Successor Custodian shall execute a receipt for all funds after being satisfied as to the accuracy and completeness of the statements and records provided by the auditor. Acceptance may be conditioned upon audit and verification by a disinterested person, when the circumstances so warrant.

II. Financial Guidelines.

A. *Receipt of Funds.* Each divisional office within the Northern District of Texas will collect a fee for each attorney admission and pro hac vice admission in the amount prescribed by the Judicial Conference, plus a $25.00 district fee. On receipt of the fee, the financial deputy in each division will issue a receipt and place the General Fund portion of the admission fee in Fund 085000, the Judiciary Fund portion of the admission fee in Fund 510000, and the Non-Appropriated Fund portion of the admission fee in Fund 6855XX. All Non-Appropriated Fund monies will be deposited into an account segregated from all other monies in the custody of the Court.

B. *Establishment of Checking Account.* An account shall be established in the name of the Fund with the Custodian as Trustee. All accounts will be established at federally insured banks or savings institutions.

The check issued each month by the Dallas financial officer to the Custodian shall be deposited to the checking account for the Fund. The balance shall be maintained at the minimum required to avoid bank service fees.

C. *Investment of Funds.* Any amount on deposit at the end of the month which exceeds the established maximum checking balance shall be disbursed by the Custodian by check and deposited into an interest-bearing account, government security, or money market fund invested in government obligations to the credit of the Custodian as Trustee for the Fund.

The Custodian shall submit recommendations as to the investment of the funds to the Advisory Committee for its approval. The Advisory Committee shall inform the Custodian how the funds are to be invested.

The Custodian shall apprise the Advisory Committee of each reinvestment of the funds.

D. *Disbursements.* All requests for expenditure of Non-Appropriated Funds shall be submitted to the Custodian in writing. The Custodian will forward the request to the Chairperson of the Advisory Committee. The Custodian will make any approved disbursements in accordance with the decision and instructions of the Advisory Committee.

The Custodian is authorized to make individual disbursements, without prior approval, of up to $100, provided the expenditure clearly belongs to one of the categories on the approved list of appropriate uses for the Fund and is duly reported to the Advisory Committee at the next meeting of said Committee.

No countersignature shall be required for expenditure of funds.

E. *Audits.* The Advisory Committee may appoint or retain a disinterested party or an auditor to conduct an annual audit as well as those audits required by this plan, i.e., upon the appointment of a Successor Trustee and upon the dissolution of the Fund.

The results of any audit shall be provided to the Advisory Committee. Compensation may be provided to the auditor or inspector from Fund assets if said auditor or inspector is not a government employee acting in an official capacity.

F. *Dissolution of Fund.* Courts may dissolve these non-appropriated funds which they have created; in addition, the Advisory Committee may recommend to the Court that the Fund be dissolved. In the event the Fund is ordered dissolved:

    1. The Custodian shall ensure that all outstanding obligations are liquidated prior to dissolution, including expenses associated with the final required audit;

    2. A terminal audit shall be conducted by a disinterested person appointed by the Court;

    3. The auditor shall file with the Court the results of the terminal audit of the Fund.

G. *Exemption from Payment of Fees for Federal Government Attorneys.* Under Judicial Conference Policy no fee for attorney admission, certificate of admission, duplicate certificate of admission, or certificate of good standing is to be charged to a federal government attorney. Therefore the clerk will not collect the $25.00 district fee for an attorney admission or pro hac vice admission of an attorney employed by the federal government.

III. Guidelines for Disbursement of Funds.

Monies derived from Attorney Admission fees and accumulated within the Non-Appropriated Fund are to be used for the joint benefit of the bench and the bar in the administration of justice. Non-Appropriated Funds may not be used to supplement appropriated funds or to pay for materials or services available from statutory appropriations.

Approved uses of the Non-Appropriated Fund include, but are not limited to, the following:

    1. purchase of periodicals, publications, and library material of mutual access and benefit to the bench and bar;

    2. establishment and maintenance of attorney admission and disciplinary programs;

    3. enforcement and implementation of the local rules;

    4. enhancement of juror comfort and convenience;

    5. establishment and maintenance of attorney lounge facilities;

6. acquisition of a surety bond for the Custodian of the fund, in an amount covering only those monies in the Fund;

7. payment of fees for services associated with auditing the Fund;

8. purchase of charts, stands, equipment, and materials to assist attorneys in the courtroom;

9. support of the annual law clerk orientation;

10. payment of expenses for printing court rules, manuals on practice and procedures, or other documents related to court operations;

11. payment of expenses in connection with court memorial and commendation services or events;

12. funding of court projects, programs, or acquisitions which interest or benefit the bar or which enhance the quality of advocacy in the court;

13. funding of the collection and preservation of court records of historical value;

14. payment of expenses for representation of indigents in cases where compensation is not otherwise available;

15. funding of projects designed to educate or train court personnel on matters which enhance their understanding of judicial history and procedure or their abilities to serve the public and the bar; and

16. establishment of a Judicial Portrait fund.

IV. Reimbursement of Attorney Expenses in Civil Cases.

The Plan for Reimbursement of Attorney Expenses in Civil Cases attached to this Order is hereby adopted. It supersedes all prior Plans for Reimbursement of Attorney Expenses in Civil Cases and applies to all cases hereafter commenced and, insofar as just and practicable, to all cases now pending.

[Dated: March 8, 2006.]

PLAN FOR REIMBURSEMENT OF
ATTORNEY FEES AND EXPENSES IN CIVIL CASES
I. Overview of the Program

It is the policy of this Court to encourage members of the bar to represent parties who cannot afford counsel. To further this policy, the Court adopts this Plan for Reimbursement of Attorney Fees and Expenses in Civil Cases ("Plan") and the attached Appointment of Pro Bono Counsel form ("PBP 20") for use in appointing counsel under this Plan.

When an attorney has been appointed to represent an indigent party in a civil matter, that attorney will be allowed to petition the Court for fees and reimbursement of certain expenses. Fees and expenses must be incurred in the preparation and presentation of the case. The maximum amount that may be reimbursed for all expenses in a case is $3,500, and the maximum amount that may be paid for all fees in a case is $1,000. The Non-Appropriated Fund Committee has the authority to grant exceptions to the maximums established for fees and expenses. Funding for this program comes from this Court's Non-Appropriated Fund.

II. Restrictions

1. Any fees and expenses that are either waived or recoverable under the provisions of Title 18, U.S.C. or Title 28, U.S.C. or that have been recovered under any other plan of reimbursement may not be reimbursed from the Non-Appropriated Fund.

2. An attorney appointed to a case under this Plan who has been awarded fees and/or expenses in the case is not eligible for fees and/or reimbursement of expenses from the Non-Appropriated Fund.

3. Only those fees and expenses associated with the preparation or presentation of a civil action in the United States District Court for the Northern District of Texas may be approved for payment. No fees or expenses associated with the preparation or presentation of an appeal to the U.S. Court of Appeals or the U.S. Supreme Court will be reimbursed from the Non–Appropriated Fund.

III. Procedure for Requesting Fees and/or Expenses

All requests for fees and/or reimbursement of expenses in civil cases must be filed within thirty days of the entry of judgment. No interim payments will be made.

The appointed attorney must file with the Clerk's Office a request for fees and/or reimbursement of expenses on a PBP 20 form that has been approved and signed by the presiding judge. The form must be accompanied by an itemized statement and receipts to substantiate the request. The clerk will forward the PBP 20 form and attachments to the Non–Appropriated Fund Committee Chairperson for final approval.

If an appointed attorney has withdrawn or has been dismissed prior to the entry of judgment, that attorney must file a request for fees and/or expenses within thirty days of withdrawal or dismissal. Any work product or services for which reimbursement is requested from the Non–Appropriated Fund must subsequently be provided to newly-appointed counsel or, if no new counsel is appointed, to the party.

IV. Allowable Expenses

Appointed attorneys may request reimbursement under this Plan for the following expenses:

1. **Depositions and Transcripts.** Appointed counsel may order transcripts or depositions necessary in the preparation of the case. The cost of such transcripts may not exceed the page rate for ordinary copy established in the Northern District of Texas. Only the cost of one original of any transcript will be allowed; the cost of additional copies will not be reimbursed. In the interest of efficiency and cost-effectiveness, appointed attorneys are encouraged to use audio tapes for depositions. If audio tape depositions are used, transcription of the depositions may be reimbursed at the ordinary page rate established in the Northern District of Texas.

2. **Investigative or Expert Services.** Counsel may request investigative or expert services necessary for the adequate preparation of a matter. Such services must have prior court approval by the judge to whom the case is assigned to be approved for reimbursement.

Approval for investigative or expert services is not automatic. Therefore, attorneys should be prepared to explain why the services are necessary.

3. **Travel Expenses.** Travel by privately-owned car for trips in excess of thirty miles (each way) may be claimed at the current mileage rate authorized for federal employees. In addition, out-of-pocket expenses for parking may also be reimbursed.

4. **Fees for Service of Process.** Fees for service of papers and the appearance of witnesses not otherwise voided, waived or recovered may be reimbursed.

5. **Interpreter Services.** Costs of interpreter services not otherwise voided, waived, or recoverable may be reimbursed.

6. **Photocopying, Telephone Calls, etc.** Actual expenses incurred for such items as photocopying, photographs used in the case, toll calls, and the like may be reimbursed. Such expenses must be unavoidable in preparation of the case.

IV. Non–Allowable Expenses.

The following expenses will not be reimbursed under this Plan:

1. General office expenses, including office overhead, payroll costs, equipment depreciation, basic telephone service, and the like will not be reimbursable under this Plan.

2. Any expense not properly documented with receipts or other proof may be disallowed by the judge or the Non–Appropriated Fund Committee.

3. Expenses that may be statutorily recovered or costs or fees taxed against a party or appointed counsel will not be reimbursed by this Plan.

UNITED STATES DISTRICT COURT NORTHERN DISTRICT OF TEXAS
_____ DIVISION

```
                          )
                          )
                          )        CIVIL ACTION NO.
                          )
                          )
```

CLAIM FOR REIMBURSEMENT OF ATTORNEY EXPENSES

Pursuant to the Plan for Reimbursement of Attorney Expenses in Civil Cases, I was appointed by the Honorable _____ on _____ to represent _____ in the above captioned case. Final judgment was entered on _____ or I withdrew/was dismissed from the case prior to entry of a judgment on _____. (Strike out inapplicable wording.)

Under the provisions of the Plan, I request reimbursement for the following expenses:

Expense	Amount
a. Depositions and Transcripts	$ _____
b. Investigative or Expert Services (prior court approval was granted on _____)	$ _____
c. Travel Expenses:	
Mileage _____ @ _____ ¢ per mile	$ _____
Parking	$ _____
d. Fees for Service of Process	$ _____
e. Interpreter Services	$ _____
f. Other:	
Photocopying	$ _____
Photographs	$ _____
Telephone Toll Calls	$ _____
_____	$ _____
_____	$ _____

TOTAL AMOUNT CLAIMED $ _____

I certify the above expenses were incurred in the preparation and presentation of this case; that these expenses do not include any costs either waived or recoverable under the provisions of Title 18, U.S.C. or Title 28, U.S.C., or which have been recovered under any other plan; and no costs and/or fees were awarded pursuant to a judgment before this Court.

Receipts for the above expenses are attached in support of my claim for reimbursement.

_____

Attorney

_____

Date

The above claim for reimbursement is APPROVED/DENIED in the amount of $ _____.

_____
United States District Judge

_____
Date

Payment _____ APPROVED   _____ DENIED

_____
Chairman,
Non-Appropriated Fund Committee

_____
Date

[Dated: October 18, 2011.]

AMENDED MISCELLANEOUS ORDER 62. PILOT PROJECT FOR THE EFFICIENT AND EFFECTIVE MANAGEMENT OF PATENT CASES [DALLAS DIVISION][1]

The Dallas division of the Northern District of Texas is participating in a pilot project for the efficient and effective management of patent cases.[2] Unless otherwise directed by the presiding judge in an individual case, this Order will control the management of patent cases as defined below in paragraph 1–2.

1. SCOPE.

1–1. Title. This Order should be cited as "Miscellaneous Order No. 62," followed by the applicable paragraph number.

1–2. Scope and Construction. This Order applies to all civil actions filed in or transferred to the Dallas division of the Northern District of Texas that allege infringement of a utility patent in a complaint, counterclaim, cross-claim, or third party claim or seek a declaratory judgment that a utility patent is not infringed, is invalid, or is unenforceable. The presiding judge may accelerate, extend, eliminate, or modify the obligations or deadlines established in this Order based on the circumstances of any particular patent case, including, without limitation, the complexity of the case or the number of patents, claims, products, or parties involved. If any motion filed prior to the claim construction hearing provided for in paragraph 4–6 raises claim construction issues, the presiding judge may, for good cause shown, defer the motion until after completion of the disclosures, filings, or ruling following the claim construction hearing. The local civil rules of this court apply to these actions except to the extent they are inconsistent with this Order.

1–3. Effective Date. This Order will take effect on May 1, 2007, and will apply to any Dallas division patent case filed on or after that date. It will also apply to any pending Dallas division patent case in which, on the date this Order takes effect, more than 9 days remain before the initial disclosure of asserted claims and preliminary infringement contentions required by paragraph 3–1 is due.

The parties to any other pending Dallas division patent case must meet and confer promptly after May 1, 2007, to determine whether any provision in this Order should be made applicable to that case. No later than 7 days after the parties meet and confer, the parties must file a stipulation setting forth a proposed order that relates to the application of this Order. Unless and until the presiding judge enters an order applying this Order, the rules of practice previously applicable to these other pending Dallas division patent cases will govern.

2. GENERAL PROVISIONS

2–1. Governing Procedure.

(a) *Initial Case Management Conference.* Parties conferring with each other under Fed. R. Civ. P. 26(f) may attend the initial case management conference either in person or by telephone. In the case management statement filed under Fed. R. Civ. P. 26(f), the parties must address the matters required to be covered by Fed. R. Civ. P. 26, and the following additional matters:

(1) Proposed modification of the deadlines provided for in this Order, and the effect of any such modification on the date and time of the claim construction hearing, if any;

(2) Electronic discovery plan;

(3) The need for presenting technical tutorials to the presiding judge and the mode for presenting same;

(4) Deviations from and additions to the protective order (see Appendix A);

(5) Whether either party desires the presiding judge to hear live testimony at the claim construction hearing;

(6) The need for and any specific limits on discovery relating to claim construction, including depositions of witnesses, including expert witnesses;

(7) The order of presentation at the claim construction hearing;

(8) The scheduling of a claim construction prehearing conference between attorneys to be held after the filing of the joint claim construction and prehearing statement required by paragraph 4–3;

(9) Whether the presiding judge should authorize the filing under seal of any documents containing confidential information; and

(10) The need for any deviation from the ordinary practice of early and late mediations, as well as the potential dates for early and late mediations.

(b) *Further Case Management Conferences.* To the extent that some or all of the matters provided for in paragraph 2–1(a)(1)–(10) are not discussed by the parties at the initial case management conference, the parties must propose dates for further case management conferences so that all matters required to be discussed are addressed in the case management statement.

2–2. Confidentiality.
All documents or information produced under this Order will be governed by the terms and conditions of the protective order (see Appendix A). The protective order will be deemed automatically entered upon the filing or transfer of any civil action to which this Order applies, unless the protective order is modified by agreement of the parties or by order of the presiding judge.

2–3. Certification of Initial Disclosures.
Each statement, disclosure, or chart filed or served in accordance with this Order must be dated and signed by the attorney of record. An attorney's signature constitutes a certification that to the best of the attorney's knowledge, information, and belief, formed after an inquiry that is reasonable under the circumstances, the information contained in the statement, disclosure, or chart is complete and correct at the time it is made.

2–4. Admissibility of Disclosures.
Statements, disclosures, or charts governed by this Order are admissible to the extent permitted by the Federal Rules of Evidence or Civil Procedure. However, the statements or disclosures provided for in paragraph 4–1 and 4–2 are not admissible for any purpose other than in connection with motions seeking an extension or modification of the time periods within which actions contemplated by this Order must be taken.

2–5. Relationship to Federal Rules of Civil Procedure.

(a) Unless the presiding judge otherwise directs, the scope of discovery is not limited to the preliminary infringement contentions or preliminary invalidity contentions but is governed by the Federal Rules of Civil Procedure. Except as provided in this paragraph or as otherwise directed by the presiding judge, it will not be a legitimate ground for objecting to an opposing party's discovery request (e.g., interrogatory, document request, request for admission, deposition question) or declining to provide information otherwise required to be disclosed under Fed. R. Civ. P. 26(a)(1) that the discovery request or disclosure requirement is premature in light of, or otherwise conflicts with, this Order. A party may object to the following categories of discovery requests (or may decline to provide information in its initial disclosures under Fed. R. Civ. P. 26(a)(1)) on the ground that they are premature in light of the timetable provided in this Order:

(1) Requests seeking to elicit a party's claim construction position;

(2) Requests seeking to elicit from the patent claimant a comparison of the asserted claims and the accused apparatus, product, device, process, method, act, or other instrumentality;

(3) Requests seeking to elicit from an accused infringer a comparison of the asserted claims and the prior art; and

(4) Requests seeking to elicit from an accused infringer the identification of any opinions of an attorney, and related documents, that it intends to rely upon as a defense to an allegation of willful infringement.

(b) When a party properly objects to a discovery request (or declines to provide information in its initial disclosures under Fed. R. Civ. P. 26(a)(1)) as set forth above, that party must provide the requested information on the date it is required to provide the requested information to an opposing party under this Order, unless there exists another legitimate ground for objection.

3. PATENT INITIAL DISCLOSURES

3–1. Disclosure of Asserted Claims and Preliminary Infringement Contentions.

(a) Not later than 14 days after the initial case management conference, a party claiming patent infringement must serve on each opposing party a disclosure of asserted claims and preliminary infringement contentions and file notice of such service with the clerk. The disclosure of asserted claims and preliminary infringement contentions must contain, separately for each opposing party, the following information:

(1) Each claim of each patent in suit that is allegedly infringed by each opposing Party;

(2) Separately for each asserted claim, each accused apparatus, product, device, process, method, act, or other instrumentality ("accused instrumentality") of each opposing party of which the party is aware. This identification must be as specific as possible. Each product, device, and apparatus must be identified by name or model number, if known. Each method or process must be identified by name, if known, or by any product, device, or apparatus that, when used, allegedly results in the practice of the claimed method or process;

(3) A chart identifying specifically and in detail where each element of each asserted claim is found within each accused instrumentality, including for each element that such party contends is governed by 35 U.S.C. § 112(6), the identity of each structure, act, or material in the accused instrumentality that performs the claimed function;

(4) Whether each element of each asserted claim is claimed to be literally present or present under the doctrine of equivalents in the accused instrumentality;

(5) For any patent that claims priority to an earlier application, the priority date to which each asserted claim allegedly is entitled; and

(6) If a party claiming patent infringement wishes to preserve the right to rely, for any purpose, on the assertion that its own apparatus, product, device, process, method, act, or other instrumentality practices the claimed invention, the party must identify, separately for each asserted claim, each such apparatus, product, device, process, method, act, or other instrumentality that incorporates or reflects that particular claim.

(b) Failure to comply with the requirements of this paragraph, including the requirement of specificity and detail in contending infringement, may result in appropriate sanctions, including dismissal.

3–2. Document Production Accompanying Disclosure.

(a) In addition to serving the disclosure of asserted claims and preliminary infringement contentions, the party claiming patent infringement must produce or make available for inspection and copying to each opposing party:

(1) Documents (e.g., contracts, purchase orders, invoices, advertisements, marketing materials, offer letters, beta site testing agreements, and third party or joint development agreements) sufficient to evidence each discussion with, disclosure to, or other manner of providing to a third party, or sale of or offer to sell, the claimed invention prior to the date of application for the patent in suit. A party's production of a document as required by this paragraph does not constitute an admission that the document evidences or is prior art under 35 U.S.C. § 102;

(2) All documents evidencing the conception, reduction to practice, design, and development of each claimed invention, that were created on or before the date of application for the patent in suit or the priority date identified under paragraph 3–1(a)(5), whichever is earlier; and

(3) A copy of the file history for each patent in suit.

(b) The producing party must separately identify by production number which documents correspond to each category.

3–3. Preliminary Invalidity Contentions.

(a) Within 45 days from the date the party claiming patent infringement serves the disclosure of asserted claims and preliminary infringement contentions on all opposing parties, each party opposing a claim of patent infringement must serve on all other parties its preliminary invalidity contentions and file notice of such service with the clerk. The preliminary invalidity contentions must contain the following information:

(1) The identity of each item of prior art that allegedly anticipates each asserted claim or renders it obvious. Each prior art patent must be identified by its number, country of origin, and date of issue. Each prior art publication must be identified by its title, date of publication, and, when feasible, author and publisher. Prior art under 35 U.S.C. § 102(b) must be identified by specifying the item offered for sale or publicly used or known, the date the offer or use took place or the information became known, and the identity of the person or entity that made the use or made and received the offer, or the person or entity that made the information known or to whom it was made known. Prior art under 35 U.S.C. § 102(f) must be identified by providing the name of each person from whom and the circumstances under which the invention or any part of it was derived. Prior art under 35 U.S.C. § 102(g) must be identified by providing the identity of each person or entity involved in and the circumstances surrounding the making of the invention before the patent applicant;

(2) Whether each item of prior art anticipates each asserted claim or renders it obvious. If a combination of items of prior art makes a claim obvious, each such combination, and the motivation to combine such items, must be identified;

(3) A chart identifying where specifically and in detail in each alleged item of prior art each element of each asserted claim is found, including for each element that the party contends is governed by 35 U.S.C. § 112(6), the identity of the structure, act, or material in each item of prior art that performs the claimed function; and

(4) Any grounds of invalidity based on indefiniteness under 35 U.S.C. § 112(2), or enablement or written description under 35 U.S.C. § 112(1), of any of the asserted claims.

(b) Failure to comply with the requirements of this paragraph, including the requirement of specificity and detail, may result in appropriate sanctions.

3–4. Document Production Accompanying Preliminary Invalidity Contentions.

At the time the preliminary invalidity contentions are served on all opposing parties, the party opposing a claim of patent infringement must also produce or make available for inspection and copying to all opposing parties:

(a) Source code, specifications, schematics, flow charts, artwork, formulas, or other documentation sufficient to show the operation of any aspects or elements of an accused instrumentality identified by the patent claimant in its paragraph 3–1(a)(3) chart; and

(b) A copy of each item of prior art identified under paragraph 3–3(a)(1) that does not appear in the file history of each patent at issue. To the extent any such item is not in English, an English translation of each portion relied upon must be produced.

3–5. Disclosure Requirement in Patent Cases for Declaratory Judgment.

(a) *Invalidity Contentions If No Claim of Infringement.* In all cases in which a party files a complaint or other pleading seeking a declaratory judgment that a patent is not infringed, is invalid, or is unenforceable, paragraph 3–1 and 3–2 will not apply unless and until a claim for patent infringement is made by a party. If the defendant does not assert a claim for patent infringement in its answer to the complaint, then no later than 14 days after the defendant files its answer, or 14 days after the initial case management conference, whichever is later, the party seeking a declaratory judgment must serve upon each opposing party its preliminary invalidity contentions that conform to paragraph 3–3 and produce or make available for inspection and copying by all opposing parties the documentation described in paragraph 3–4. The parties must meet and confer within 14 days of the service of the preliminary invalidity contentions for the purpose of determining the date the plaintiff will file its final invalidity contentions, which must be filed within 50 days from the date the presiding judge's claim construction ruling is filed.

(b) *Application of Rules When No Specified Triggering Event.* If the filings or actions in a Dallas division patent case do not trigger the application of this Order, then as soon as this is known, the parties to the patent case must meet and confer for the purpose of agreeing on the application of this Order to the patent case.

(c) *Inapplicability.* This paragraph does not apply to a Dallas division patent case in which a request for a declaratory judgment that a patent is not infringed, is invalid, or is unenforceable is filed in response to a complaint for infringement of the same patent.

3–6. Final Contentions. Each party's preliminary infringement contentions and preliminary invalidity contentions will be deemed to be that party's final contentions, except as set forth below.

(a) If a party claiming patent infringement believes in good faith that the presiding judge's claim construction ruling so requires, that party may serve final infringement contentions without leave of court that amend the party's preliminary infringement contentions with respect to the information required by paragraph 3–1(a)(3) and (4) within 30 days from the date the presiding judge's claim construction ruling is filed.

(b) Within 50 days from the date the presiding judge's claim construction ruling is filed, each party opposing a claim of patent infringement may serve its final invalidity contentions without leave of court that amend its preliminary invalidity contentions with respect to the information required by paragraph 3–3 if:

(1) a party claiming patent infringement has served its final infringement contentions under paragraph 3–6(a), or

(2) the party opposing a claim of patent infringement believes in good faith that the presiding judge's claim construction ruling so requires.

3–7. Amendment to Contentions. Amendment of the preliminary or final infringement contentions or the preliminary or final invalidity contentions, other than as expressly permitted in paragraph 3–6, may be made only by order of the presiding judge upon a showing of good cause. Good cause for the purposes of this paragraph may include newly discovered accused instrumentalities, newly discovered bases for claiming infringement, or newly discovered prior art references. A party seeking amendment of the preliminary or final infringement contentions or the preliminary or final invalidity contentions must include in its motion to amend a statement that the newly discovered accused instrumentalities, newly discovered bases for claiming infringement, or newly discovered prior art references were not known to that party prior to the motion despite diligence in seeking out same.

3–8. Willfulness.

(a) By the date established in the scheduling order, each party opposing a claim of patent infringement that will rely on an opinion of an attorney as part of a defense to a claim of willful infringement must:

(1) Produce or make available for inspection and copying each opinion and any other documents relating to the opinion as to which the party agrees the attorney-client or work product protection has been waived; and

(2) Serve a privilege log identifying any other documents, except those authored by an attorney acting solely as trial counsel, relating to the subject matter of the opinion the party is withholding on the grounds of attorney-client privilege or work product protection.

(b) A party opposing a claim of patent infringement who does not comply with the requirements of this paragraph will not be permitted to rely on an opinion of an attorney as part of a defense to willful infringement absent a stipulation of all parties or by order of the presiding judge upon a showing of good cause.

4. CLAIM CONSTRUCTION PROCEEDINGS

4–1. Exchange of Proposed Terms and Claim Elements for Construction.

(a) Not later than 14 days after service of the preliminary invalidity contentions under paragraph 3–3, each party must simultaneously exchange a list of claim terms, phrases, or clauses that the party contends should be construed by the presiding judge, and any claim element that the party contends should be governed by 35 U.S.C. § 112(6).

(b) After exchanging this list, the parties must meet and confer for the purposes of finalizing a combined list, narrowing or resolving differences, and facilitating the ultimate preparation of a joint claim construction and prehearing statement.

4–2. Exchange of Preliminary Claim Constructions and Extrinsic Evidence.

(a) Not later than 21 days after the exchange of lists under paragraph 4–1(a), the parties must simultaneously exchange a preliminary proposed construction of each claim term, phrase, or clause that the parties collectively have identified for claim construction purposes, and must also identify each structure, act, or material corresponding to each claim element that the parties collectively contend is governed by 35 U.S.C. § 112(6).

(b) At the same time the parties exchange their respective preliminary claim constructions, they must each also exchange a preliminary identification of extrinsic evidence, including, without limitation, dictionary definitions, citations to learned treatises and prior art, and testimony of percipient and expert witnesses they contend support their respective claim constructions. The parties must identify each item of extrinsic evidence by production number or produce a copy of any such item not previously produced. With respect to any percipient or expert witness, the parties must also provide a brief description of the substance of that witness' proposed testimony.

(c) The parties must thereafter meet and confer for the purposes of narrowing the issues and finalizing preparation of a joint claim construction and prehearing statement.

4–3. Joint Claim Construction and Prehearing Statement.
Not later than 60 days after service of the preliminary invalidity contentions, the parties must complete and file a joint claim construction and prehearing statement that contains the following information:

(a) The construction of those claim terms, phrases, or clauses on which the parties agree;

(b) Each party's proposed construction of each disputed claim term, phrase, or clause, together with an identification of all references from the specification or prosecution history that support that construction, and an identification of any extrinsic evidence known to the party on which the party intends to rely, either to support its proposed construction of the claim or to oppose any other party's proposed construction of the claim, including, but not limited to, as permitted by law, dictionary definitions, citations to learned treatises and prior art, and testimony of percipient and expert witnesses;

(c) The anticipated length of time necessary for the claim construction hearing;

(d) Whether any party proposes to call one or more witnesses, including experts, at the claim construction hearing, the identity of each witness, and, for each expert, a summary of each opinion to be offered in sufficient detail to permit a meaningful deposition of that expert; and

(e) A list of any other issues that might appropriately be taken up at a prehearing conference prior to the claim construction hearing, and, if not previously set, proposed dates for any such prehearing conference.

4–4. Completion of Claim Construction Discovery.
Within 30 days from the date the joint claim construction and prehearing statement is filed, the parties must complete all discovery relating to claim construction, including any depositions with respect to claim construction of any witnesses, including experts, identified in the joint claim construction and prehearing statement.

4–5. Claim Construction Briefs.

(a) Within 45 days from the date the joint claim construction and prehearing statement is filed, each party must serve and file a claim construction brief and any evidence supporting its claim construction. The requirements of LR 7.2 apply to such briefs, except that, excluding the table of contents and table of authorities, the length of a brief must not exceed 30 pages. By order or other appropriate notice issued in the case, the presiding judge may restrict the length of a brief to fewer than 30 pages, or, for good cause, may enlarge the length of a brief.

(b) Each party may serve and file a responsive brief and supporting evidence within 14 days from the date the opposing party's claim construction brief is filed. The requirements of LR 7.2 apply to such briefs, except that, excluding the table of contents and table of authorities, the length of a brief must not exceed 30 pages. By order or other appropriate notice issued in the case, the presiding judge may restrict the length of a brief to fewer than 30 pages, or, for good cause, may enlarge the length of a brief. Unless the presiding judge otherwise directs, no further claim construction briefing will be permitted.

(c) Within 10 days[3] of the claim construction hearing scheduled under paragraph 4–6, the parties must jointly submit a claim construction chart on computer disk in WordPerfect format or in such other format as the presiding judge may direct.

(1) The claim construction chart must have a column listing the complete language of disputed claims with disputed terms in bold type and separate columns for each party's proposed construction of each disputed term. The chart must also include a fourth column entitled "Judge's Construction," that is otherwise left blank. Additionally, the chart must direct the presiding judge's attention to each patent and claim number where a disputed term appears.

(2) The parties may also include constructions for claim terms to which they have agreed. If the parties choose to include agreed constructions, each party's proposed construction columns must state "[AGREED]," and the agreed construction must be inserted in the "Judge's Construction" column.

(3) The purpose of this claim construction chart is to assist the presiding judge and the parties in tracking and resolving disputed terms. Accordingly, aside from the requirements set forth in this Order, the parties are afforded substantial latitude in the chart's format so that they may fashion a chart that most clearly and efficiently outlines the disputed terms and proposed constructions. Appendices to the presiding judge's prior published and unpublished claim construction opinions may provide helpful guidelines for parties fashioning claim construction charts.

4–6. Claim Construction Hearing. Subject to the convenience of the presiding judge's calendar, two weeks after the responsive briefs under paragraph 4–5(b) have been filed, the presiding judge will conduct a claim construction hearing, to the extent the parties or the presiding judge believe a claim construction hearing is necessary for construction of the claims at issue.

The clerk is directed to make appropriate distribution of this Order.

APPENDIX A

IN THE UNITED STATES DISTRICT COURT FOR THE
NORTHERN DISTRICT OF TEXAS

Plaintiff, v. Defendant.)) Civil Action No.

PROTECTIVE ORDER

Proceedings and Information Governed.

1. This Order ("Protective Order") is made under Fed. R. Civ. P. 26(c). It governs any document, information, or other thing furnished by any party to any other party, and it includes any non-party who receives a subpoena in connection with this action. The information protected includes, but is not limited to: answers to interrogatories; answers to requests for admission; responses to requests for production of documents; deposition transcripts and videotapes; deposition exhibits; and other writings or things produced, given or filed in this action that are designated by a party as "Confidential Information" or "Confidential Attorney Eyes Only Information" in accordance with the terms of this Protective Order, as well as to any copies, excerpts, abstracts, analyses, summaries, descriptions, or other forms of recorded information containing, reflecting, or disclosing such information.

Designation and Maintenance of Information.

2. For purposes of this Protective Order, (a) the "Confidential Information" designation means that the document is comprised of trade secrets or commercial information that is not publicly known and is of technical or commercial advantage to its possessor, in accordance with Fed. R. Civ. P. 26(c)(7), or other information required by law or agreement to be kept confidential and (b) the "Confidential Attorney Eyes Only" designation means that the document is comprised of information that the producing party deems especially sensitive, which may include, but is not limited to, confidential research and development, financial, technical, marketing, any other sensitive trade secret information, or information capable of being utilized for the preparation or prosecution of a patent application dealing with such subject matter. Confidential Information and Confidential

Attorney Eyes Only Information does not include, and this Protective Order does not apply to, information that is already in the knowledge or possession of the party to whom disclosure is made unless that party is already bound by agreement not to disclose such information, or information that has been disclosed to the public or third persons in a manner making such information no longer confidential.

3. Documents and things produced during the course of this litigation within the scope of paragraph 2(a) above, may be designated by the producing party as containing Confidential Information by placing on each page and each thing a legend substantially as follows:

CONFIDENTIAL INFORMATION
SUBJECT TO PROTECTIVE ORDER

Documents and things produced during the course of this litigation within the scope of paragraph 2(b) above may be designated by the producing party as containing Confidential Attorney Eyes Only Information by placing on each page and each thing a legend substantially as follows:

CONFIDENTIAL ATTORNEY EYES ONLY INFORMATION
SUBJECT TO PROTECTIVE ORDER

A party may designate information disclosed at a deposition as Confidential Information or Confidential Attorney Eyes Only Information by requesting the reporter to so designate the transcript or any portion of the transcript at the time of the deposition. If no such designation is made at the time of the deposition, any party will have fourteen (14) calendar days after the date of the deposition to designate, in writing to the other parties and to the court reporter, whether the transcript is to be designated as Confidential Information or Confidential Attorneys Eyes Only Information. If no such designation is made at the deposition or within this fourteen (14) calendar day period (during which period, the transcript must be treated as Confidential Attorneys Eyes Only Information, unless the disclosing party consents to less confidential treatment of the information), the entire deposition will be considered devoid of Confidential Information or Confidential Attorneys Eyes Only Information. Each party and the court reporter must attach a copy of any final and timely written designation notice to the transcript and each copy of the transcript in its possession, custody or control, and the portions designated in such notice must thereafter be treated in accordance with this Protective Order. It is the responsibility of counsel for each party to maintain materials containing Confidential Information or Confidential Attorney Eyes Only Information in a secure manner and appropriately identified so as to allow access to such information only to such persons and under such terms as is permitted under this Protective Order.

Inadvertent Failure to Designate.

4. The inadvertent failure to designate or withhold any information as confidential or privileged will not be deemed to waive a later claim as to its confidential or privileged nature, or to stop the producing party from designating such information as confidential at a later date in writing and with particularity. The information must be treated by the receiving party as confidential from the time the receiving party is notified in writing of the change in the designation.

Challenge to Designations.

5. A receiving party may challenge a producing party's designation at any time. Any receiving party disagreeing with a designation may request in writing that the producing party change the designation. The producing party will then have ten (10) business days after receipt of a challenge notice to advise the receiving party whether or not it will change the designation. If the parties are unable to reach agreement after the expiration of this ten (10) business day time-frame, and after the conference required under LR 7.1(a), the receiving party may at any time thereafter seek an order to alter the confidential status of the designated information. Until any dispute under this paragraph is ruled upon by the presiding judge, the designation will remain in full force and effect, and the information will continue to be accorded the confidential treatment required by this Protective Order.

Disclosure and Use of Confidential Information.

6. Information designated as Confidential Information or Confidential Attorney Eyes Only Information may only be used for purposes of preparation, trial, and appeal of this action.

Confidential Information or Confidential Attorney Eyes Only Information may not be used under any circumstances for prosecuting any patent application, for patent licensing, or for any other purpose.

7.   Subject to paragraph 9 below, Confidential Information may be disclosed by the receiving party only to the following individuals, provided that such individuals are informed of the terms of this Protective Order: (a) two (2) employees of the receiving party who are required in good faith to provide assistance in the conduct of this litigation, including any settlement discussions, and who are identified as such in writing to counsel for the designating party in advance of the disclosure; (b) two (2) in-house counsel who are identified by the receiving party; (c) outside counsel for the receiving party; (d) supporting personnel employed by (b) and (c), such as paralegals, legal secretaries, data entry clerks, legal clerks, and private photocopying services; (e) experts or consultants; and (f) any persons requested by counsel to furnish services such as document coding, image scanning, mock trial, jury profiling, translation services, court reporting services, demonstrative exhibit preparation, or the creation of any computer database from documents.

8.   Subject to paragraph 9 below, Confidential Attorney Eyes Only Information may be disclosed by the receiving party only to the following individuals, provided that such individuals are informed of the terms of this Protective Order: (a) outside counsel for the receiving party; (b) supporting personnel employed by outside counsel, such as paralegals, legal secretaries, data entry clerks, legal clerks, private photocopying services; (c) experts or consultants; and (d) those individuals designated in paragraph 11(c).

9.   Further, prior to disclosing Confidential Information or Confidential Attorney Eyes Only Information to a receiving party's proposed expert, consultant, or employees, the receiving party must provide to the producing party a signed Confidentiality Agreement in the form attached as Exhibit A, the resume or curriculum vitae of the proposed expert or consultant, the expert or consultant's business affiliation, and any current and past consulting relationships in the industry. The producing party will thereafter have ten (10) business days from receipt of the Confidentiality Agreement to object to any proposed individual, The objection must be made for good cause and in writing, stating with particularity the reasons for the objection. Failure to object within ten (10) business days constitutes approval. If the parties are unable to resolve any objection, the receiving party may apply to the presiding judge to resolve the matter. There will be no disclosure to any proposed individual during the ten (10) business day objection period, unless that period is waived by the producing party, or if any objection is made, until the parties have resolved the objection, or the presiding judge has ruled upon any resultant motion.

10.   Counsel is responsible for the adherence by third-party vendors to the terms and conditions of this Protective Order. Counsel may fulfill this obligation by obtaining a signed Confidentiality Agreement in the form attached as Exhibit B.

11.   Confidential Information or Confidential Attorney Eyes Only Information may be disclosed to a person who is not already allowed access to such information under this Protective Order if:

(a) the information was previously received or authored by the person or was authored or received by a director, officer, employee or agent of the company for which the person is testifying as a designee under Fed. R. Civ. P. 30(b)(6);

(b) the designating party is the person or is a party for whom the person is a director, officer, employee, consultant or agent; or

(c) counsel for the party designating the material agrees that the material may be disclosed to the person.

In the event of disclosure under this paragraph, only the reporter, the person, his or her counsel, the presiding judge, and persons to whom disclosure may be made and who are bound by this Protective Order, may be present during the disclosure or discussion of Confidential Information. Disclosure of material pursuant to this paragraph does not constitute a waiver of the confidential status of the material so disclosed.

Non Party Information.

12.   The existence of this Protective Order must be disclosed to any person producing documents, tangible things, or testimony in this action who may reasonably be expected to desire confidential treatment for such documents, tangible things or testimony. Any such person may designate documents, tangible things, or testimony confidential pursuant to this Protective Order.

Filing Documents With the Court.

13. If any party wishes to submit Confidential Information to the court, the submission must be filed only in a sealed envelope bearing the caption of this action and a notice in the following form:

CONFIDENTIAL INFORMATION

[caption]

This envelope, which is being filed under seal,
contains documents that are subject to a Protective
Order governing the use of confidential discovery material.

No Prejudice.

14. Producing or receiving confidential information, or otherwise complying with the terms of this Protective Order, will not (a) operate as an admission by any party that any particular Confidential Information contains or reflects trade secrets or any other type of confidential or proprietary information; (b) prejudice the rights of a party to object to the production of information or material that the party does not consider to be within the scope of discovery; (c) prejudice the rights of a party to seek a determination by the presiding judge that particular materials be produced; (d) prejudice the rights of a party to apply to the presiding judge for further protective orders; or (e) prevent the parties from agreeing in writing to alter or waive the provisions or protections provided for in this Protective Order with respect to any particular information or material.

Conclusion of Litigation.

15. Within sixty (60) calendar days after final judgment in this action, including the exhaustion of all appeals, or within sixty (60) calendar days after dismissal pursuant to a settlement agreement, each party or other person subject to the terms of this Protective Order is under an obligation to destroy or return to the producing party all materials and documents containing Confidential Information or Confidential Attorney Eyes Only Information, and to certify to the producing party that this destruction or return has been done. However, outside counsel for any party is entitled to retain all court papers, trial transcripts, exhibits, and attorney work provided that any such materials are maintained and protected in accordance with the terms of this Protective Order.

Other Proceedings.

16. By entering this Protective Order and limiting the disclosure of information in this case, the presiding judge does not intend to preclude another court from finding that information may be relevant and subject to disclosure in another case. Any person or party subject to this Protective Order who may be subject to a motion to disclose another party's information designated Confidential pursuant to this Protective Order must promptly notify that party of the motion so that the party may have an opportunity to appear and be heard on whether that information should be disclosed.

Remedies.

17. It is Ordered that this Protective Order will be enforced by the sanctions set forth in Fed. R. Civ. P. 37(b) and any other sanctions as may be available to the presiding judge, including the power to hold parties or other violators of this Protective Order in contempt. All other remedies available to any person injured by a violation of this Protective Order are fully reserved.

18. Any party may petition the presiding judge for good cause shown if the party desires relief from a term or condition of this Protective Order.

Exhibit A

IN THE UNITED STATES DISTRICT COURT FOR
THE NORTHERN DISTRICT OF TEXAS

Plaintiff, v. Defendant.)) Civil Action No.

**CONFIDENTIALITY AGREEMENT FOR EXPERT,
CONSULTANT OR EMPLOYEES OF ANY PARTY**

I hereby affirm that:

Information, including documents and things, designated as "Confidential Information," or "Confidential Attorney Eyes Only Information," as defined in the Protective Order entered in the above-captioned action ("Protective Order"), is being provided to me pursuant to the terms and restrictions of the Protective Order.

I have been given a copy of and have read the Protective Order.

I am familiar with the terms of the Protective Order and I agree to comply with and to be bound by its terms.

I submit to the jurisdiction of this Court for enforcement of the Protective Order.

I agree not to use any Confidential Information or Confidential Attorney Eyes Only Information disclosed to me pursuant to the Protective Order except for purposes of the above-captioned litigation and not to disclose any of this information to persons other than those specifically authorized by the Protective Order, without the express written consent of the party who designated the information as confidential or by order of the presiding judge. I also agree to notify any stenographic, clerical or technical personnel who are required to assist me of the terms of this Protective Order and of its binding effect on them and me.

I understand that I am to retain all documents or materials designated as or containing Confidential Information or Confidential Attorney Eyes Only Information in a secure manner, and that all such documents and materials are to remain in my personal custody until the completion of my assigned duties in this matter, whereupon all such documents and materials, including all copies thereof, and any writings prepared by me containing any Confidential Information or Confidential Attorney Eyes Only Information are to be returned to counsel who provided me with such documents and materials.

Exhibit B

IN THE UNITED STATES DISTRICT COURT FOR
THE NORTHERN DISTRICT OF TEXAS

Plaintiff, v. Defendant.)) Civil Action No.

CONFIDENTIALITY AGREEMENT FOR THIRD–PARTY VENDORS

I hereby affirm that:

Information, including documents and things, designated as "Confidential Information," or "Confidential Attorney Eyes Only Information," as defined in the Protective Order entered in the above-captioned action ("Protective Order"), is being provided to me pursuant to the terms and restrictions of the Protective Order.

I have been given a copy of and have read the Protective Order.

I am familiar with the terms of the Protective Order and I agree to comply with and to be bound by its terms.

I submit to the jurisdiction of this Court for enforcement of the Protective Order.

I agree not to use any Confidential Information or Confidential Attorney Eyes Only Information disclosed to me pursuant to the Protective Order except for purposes of the above-captioned litigation and not to disclose any of this information to persons other than those specifically authorized by the Protective Order, without the express written consent of the party who designated the information as confidential or by order of the presiding judge.

[Dated: November 16, 2009.]

1 Amended Miscellaneous Order No. 62 takes effect on December 1, 2009, notwithstanding the references to May 1, 2007 (the effective date of the order when originally adopted). The amended order contains changes that bring the original order into conformity with the time-computation amendments to the Federal Rules of Civil Procedure and the local civil rules of this court that also take effect on December 1, 2009.

2 The rules of practice established by this Order will be carefully reviewed for editorial and substantive revisions and will be renumbered in accordance with Judicial Conference policy if later considered for adoption as local civil rules of this court.

3 The decision to retain this 10–day deadline in the amended order is intentional.

MISCELLANEOUS ORDER 63.   ELECTRONIC DEVICES IN COURT FACILITIES

No electronic communication devices, including, but not limited to, cellular telephones, pagers, personal digital assistants, laptop computers, and tape recorders, may be brought onto any court floor within the Northern District of Texas, with the following exceptions:

1. Employees of the United States Marshals Service, court security officers, other law enforcement personnel upon production of proper identification, and employees of the Texas Department of Criminal Justice who have transported state prisoners to court may possess electronic communication devices on a court floor, unless otherwise directed by a judge.

2. Employees of the federal judiciary may possess electronic communication devices on a court floor unless otherwise directed by a judge as to the judge's physical area of responsibility and control or by the clerk as to the clerk's physical area of responsibility and control.

3. Additional division-specific exceptions are identified on the chart attached to this order.

Electronic communication devices allowed on a court floor may only be used in a courtroom with the explicit permission of the presiding judge and may not be used to photograph, record, televise or broadcast court proceedings by audio, visual, or other means. The presiding judge may impose additional restrictions on the use of any such equipment in the courtroom to ensure that its use is consistent with the rights of the parties, will not unduly distract participants in the proceeding, and will not otherwise interfere with the administration of justice.

This order restates and replaces the order entered on August 17, 2007.

[Dated: August 24, 2007.]

MISCELLANEOUS ORDER NO. 63 ATTACHMENT

Divisional Office	Additional Exceptions
Abilene	Electronic communication devices may be used by any person having business with the court in the hallway outside of the courtroom, but they may not be brought into the courtroom.
Amarillo District Court	No exceptions.
Amarillo Bankruptcy Court Only (624 S. Polk Street)	Electronic communication devices may be used by any person having business with the court in the hallway outside of the courtroom, but they may not be brought into the courtroom.
Dallas	The following are authorized to bring electronic communication devices onto court floors in the Dallas division: 1. any person who produces a written authorization signed by a judge or the judge's designee and verified as authentic by a court security officer; 2. an attorney with a valid bar identification card having business within the court facility; or 3. a petit juror; however, a juror must turn in the juror's electronic communication devices to a courtroom deputy, court security officer, or other designated person during jury deliberations.
Forth Worth	The following are authorized to bring electronic communication devices onto the first, second third and fifth floors of the courthouse in the Fort Worth division:

Divisional Office	Additional Exceptions
	1. any person who produces a written authorization signed by Judge Means, Bankruptcy Judge Lynn or Bankruptcy Judge Nelms; or
	2. an attorney with a valid bar identification card who has business in the chambers or courtroom of District Judge Means, Magistrate Judge Bleil, Bankruptcy Judge Lynn, or Bankruptcy Judge Nelms.
Lubbock	Electronic communication devices may be used by any person having business with the court in the hallway outside of the courtroom, but they may not be brought into the courtroom.
San Angelo	Electronic communication devices may be used by any person having business with the court in the hallway outside of the courtroom, but they may not be brought into the courtroom.
Wichita Falls	Electronic communication devices may be used by any person having business with the court in the hallway outside of the courtroom, but they may not be brought into the courtroom.

[Effective September 1, 2007.]

UNITED STATES BANKRUPTCY COURT FOR THE NORTHERN DISTRICT OF TEXAS

Including Amendments Received Through
February 1, 2019

APPENDICES

ECF PROCEDURES

SELECTED ORDERS AND NOTICES

PART I. COMMENCEMENT OF CASE; PROCEEDINGS RELATING TO PETITION AND ORDER FOR RELIEF

L.B.R. 1001–1. SHORT TITLE AND SCOPE

(a) **Short Title.** Any citation referencing these rules shall be made as N.D. Tex. L.B.R. and the number of the pertinent rule.

(b) **Scope.**

(1) The Local Bankruptcy Rules govern procedure in the United States Bankruptcy Court for the Northern District of Texas in cases under title 11 of the United States Code (the "Bankruptcy Code"). The Local Bankruptcy Rules supplement, but do not replace the Federal Rules of Bankruptcy Procedure, and shall be construed consistently with those rules to secure the just, expeditious and economical administration and determination of every case and proceeding under the Bankruptcy Code.

(2) In addition to these Local Bankruptcy Rules, the Administrative Procedures for CM/ECF, Procedures for Complex Chapter 11 Cases, and the standing and general orders of the Bankruptcy Court govern practice.

(3) Notwithstanding these Local Bankruptcy Rules, the Presiding Judge may direct the parties to proceed in any manner that the judge deems just and expeditious and may suspend or modify any Local Bankruptcy Rule in a particular case.

(4) Any appendix to these Local Bankruptcy Rules may be modified by the Bankruptcy Court without the necessity of a formal amendment to these Local Bankruptcy Rules.

[Effective September 1, 2010.]

L.B.R. 1002–2. COMMENCEMENT OF CASE WITHOUT COUNSEL

(a) **Individual Filers.** Only an individual may file a voluntary bankruptcy petition or appear in court without being represented by a licensed attorney. All other entities, including partnerships, corporations and trusts may not, without counsel, appear in court or sign pleadings, including the petition. If a debtor that is not an individual files a petition without legal counsel, the Presiding Judge may dismiss the case without notice, either sua sponte, or on motion of a party in interest.

(b) **Responsibility of Pro Se Individuals.** Any individual proceeding on the individual's own behalf is considered pro se. Individuals proceeding pro se must read and follow the Local

Bankruptcy Rules, the Federal Rules of Bankruptcy Procedure, and the Bankruptcy Code.

[Effective September 1, 2010.]

L.B.R. 1006–1. FILING FEES—INSTALLMENT PAYMENTS

(a) Application to Pay in Installments. An application to pay a filing fee in installments by an individual shall be filed contemporaneously with the petition and be accompanied by an initial installment payment as follows:

(1) in Chapter 7, 12 and 13 cases, $50.00.

(2) in any other case, $100.00.

(b) Applications Filed Without Initial Installment Payment. Any application to pay a filing fee in installments which is presented without the initial installment payment set forth in subsection (a) shall be denied.

[Effective September 1, 2010.]

L.B.R. 1006–2. FILING FEES— FORM OF PAYMENT

(a) Payment of Filing Fee. Acceptable methods of payment include cash, check, money order, cashier check and debit or credit card. Only attorney filers may pay filing fees by check, debit or credit card.

(b) Payment by Check. Payment by check is permitted only if drawn on the account of the attorney for the debtor or another party, or on the account of a law firm of which the attorney is a member, partner, or associate. Checks shall be payable to "Clerk, U.S. Bankruptcy Court." The check is accepted subject to collection.

[Effective September 1, 2010.]

L.B.R. 1007–1. LISTS, SCHEDULES AND STATEMENTS

(a) Mailing List. A mailing list containing the name and address of each entity included or to be included on Schedules D, E, F, G and H shall be filed contemporaneously with every voluntary petition and within 7 days of the entry of an order for relief in an involuntary case. The mailing list shall be submitted in accordance with the Court's Administrative Procedures for Electronic Filing, and shall include those agencies and offices of the United States required to receive notice pursuant to Bankruptcy Rule 2002(j). The mailing list shall be filed by the debtor or party responsible for filing the schedules and statements of affairs. Failure to file the mailing list as prescribed in this rule is cause for summary dismissal of the case.

(b) Extension of Time to File. Before filing a motion for extension, counsel for the debtor shall confer with the Office of the United States Trustee, any committee, trustee, examiner or the standing chapter 12 or 13 trustee (if applicable) to determine whether or not the requested extension will be opposed. If unopposed, the motion for extension shall be accompanied by a certificate of conference certifying that the motion is unopposed. If opposed, the debtor shall request a

hearing; however, any hearing on the motion will only be held at the discretion of the Presiding Judge.

(c) Exclusion From Means Testing—Statement of Current Monthly Income Not Required.

(1) An individual debtor in a chapter 7 case is not required to file a Statement of Current Monthly Income, as provided in Bankruptcy Rule 1007(b)(4), if:

(A) § 707(b)(2)(D)(i) applies, or

(B) § 707(b)(2)(D)(ii) applies and the exclusion from means testing granted therein extends beyond the period specified by Bankruptcy Rule 1017(e).

(2) An individual debtor who is temporarily excluded from means testing pursuant to subsection (c)(1)(B) of this rule shall file any statement and calculations required by Bankruptcy Rule 1007(b)(4) no later than 14 days after the expiration of the temporary exclusion if the expiration occurs within the time specified by Bankruptcy Rule 1017(e).

(3) If the temporary exclusion from means testing under § 707(b)(2)(D)(ii) terminates due to the circumstances specified in subsection (c)(2) of this rule, and if the debtor has not previously filed a statement and calculations required by Bankruptcy Rule 1007(b)(4), the Bankruptcy Clerk shall promptly notify the debtor that the required statement and calculations must be filed within the time specified in subsection (c)(2).

(d) Privacy Provisions.

(1) *Redaction of Personal Identifiers.* Parties shall refrain from including, or shall partially redact where inclusion is necessary, the following personal data identifiers from all documents and pleadings filed with the court, including exhibits thereto, whether filed electronically or in paper, unless otherwise ordered by the court:

(A) Social Security Numbers. If an individual's social security numbers must be included in a pleading, only the last four digits of that number should be used;

(B) Names of Minor Children. If the involvement of a minor child must be mentioned, only the initials of that child should be used. On Schedule I of Official Bankruptcy Form 106, list relationship and age of a debtor's dependents (i.e., son, age 6);

(C) Dates of Birth. If an individual's date of birth must be included in a pleading, only the year should be used.

(D) Financial Account Numbers. If the financial account numbers are relevant, only the last four digits of these numbers should be used. On Schedules D, E, and F of Official Bankruptcy Forms 106 and 206, debtors, if they so choose, may include their full account numbers to assist the trustee and creditors.

(2) *Responsible Party.* The responsibility for redacting these personal identifiers rests solely with counsel and the parties. The Bankruptcy Clerk will not review each document and pleading for compliance with this rule. Any party wishing to file a document containing the personal data identifiers listed above may file an unredacted document under seal. This document shall be retained by the court as part of the

record. The Bankruptcy Court may, however, still require the party to file a redacted copy for the public file.

(3) *Statement of Social Security Number.* Unless otherwise ordered by the Bankruptcy Court, individual debtors must complete and file electronically an Official Bankruptcy Form 121 *Your Statement About Your Social Security Numbers.*

[Effective September 1, 2010.]

L.B.R. 1009–1.   AMENDMENTS TO LISTS & SCHEDULES

(a) **Amendments to Mailing Lists.** Whenever schedules or amendments add new entities or make corrections to mailing addresses, including the debtor's mailing address, the debtor shall file with the document an amendment to the mailing list which shall include only the names and addresses of entities to be added or corrected. A verification of mailing list shall also be filed with the amendment, and as provided on the form, shall indicate that the amendment to the mailing list adds new entities, or corrects addresses of entities appearing on a previously filed mailing list. It is the debtor's responsibility to comply with 11 U.S.C. § 342(e).

(b) **Amendments to Schedules.** When creditors are added by amendment to the schedules, the debtor's attorney (or debtor, if pro se) shall give notice to each such creditor of the filing of the bankruptcy and all applicable bar dates and deadlines if these bar dates and deadlines have been set at the time of the amendment, including notice of the meeting of creditors pursuant to 11 U.S.C. § 341(a), and any continued or rescheduled meeting of creditors.

(c) **Amendments to Schedule of Exemptions.** If a debtor's schedule of exemptions is amended, the person filing the amendment shall, within 2 days of such amendment, serve notice of such amendment to all creditors and to any trustee appointed in the case and file a certificate of service with the Bankruptcy Clerk.

(d) **Amendments to Schedules I and J.** A debtor in an individual chapter 11, 12 or 13 case shall file amended Schedules I and J if there is any material change in income or expenses prior to plan confirmation. Within 2 days of such amendment, the debtor shall serve notice of such amendment to all creditors and to any trustee appointed in the case and file a certificate of service with the Bankruptcy Clerk.

[Effective September 1, 2010.]

L.B.R. 1010–1.   PETITION—INVOLUNTARY

Counsel for an alleged debtor shall file with the Bankruptcy Clerk a notice of appearance in an involuntary case promptly upon employment.

[Effective September 1, 2010.]

L.B.R. 1015–1.   JOINT ADMINISTRATION

(a) **Motions for Joint Administration.** When a case is filed for or against a debtor related to a debtor with a case pending in the Bankruptcy Court, a party in interest may file a motion for joint administration in each case. Motions for joint administration will be assigned for determination to the bankruptcy judge presiding over the first related case filed in this district, regardless of the division in which the case is filed.

(b) **Joint Petition.** The filing of a joint petition shall be deemed an order directing joint administration for the purpose of Bankruptcy Rule 1015, unless the court orders otherwise.

[Effective September 1, 2010.]

L.B.R. 1019–1.   CONVERSION—PROCEDURE FOLLOWING

(a) **To Chapter 7.** Within 14 days after the entry of an order converting a case to chapter 7, the debtor shall file a schedule of those assets remaining in the possession of the debtor as of the date of conversion, a list of abandoned property and property against which the automatic stay of lien enforcement terminated during the case, a schedule of assets and unpaid post-petition obligations or expenses, if any, and if the debtor is an individual, a statement of current monthly income and means test calculation (Official Bankruptcy Form 122A). The schedule shall be signed by the debtor under penalty of perjury certifying that the schedule and any attachments have been read and that they are true and correct to the best of the debtor's knowledge, information and belief. With respect to unpaid post-petition obligations or expenses, the debtor shall prepare and file a supplemental mailing matrix.

(b) **To Chapter 12 or 13.** Within 14 days after the entry of order converting a chapter 11 case to a case under chapter 12 or 13, the debtor shall serve, in electronic format, the standing chapter 12 or 13 trustee with a copy of the original petition, schedules and statements, and any amendments thereto filed in the superseded case; and where the case is converted to a case under chapter 13, a Statement of Current Monthly Income And Calculation of Commitment Period and Disposable Income (Official Bankruptcy Forms 122C–1 and 122C–2).

[Effective September 1, 2010.]

PART II.   OFFICERS AND ADMINISTRATION; NOTICES; MEETINGS; EXAMINATIONS; ELECTIONS; ATTORNEYS AND ACCOUNTANTS

L.B.R. 2002–1.   NOTICE TO CREDITORS & OTHER INTERESTED PARTIES

(a) **Twenty–One Day Notices to Parties in Interest.**

(1) Notice of the meeting of creditors pursuant to 11 U.S.C. § 341 shall be served by the Bankruptcy Clerk in all cases under chapters 7, 12 and 13, and by the debtor in possession or the trustee in all cases under chapter 11.

(2) Notice of a proposed use, sale, or lease of property of the estate, other than in the ordinary course of business, shall be prepared and served by the proponent of such use, sale, or lease.

(3) Notice of the hearing on approval of a compromise or settlement of a controversy shall be served by one of the parties proposing the compromise.

(4) In a chapter 7 liquidation, notice of the hearing on the dismissal or conversion of a case to another chapter shall be served by the Bankruptcy Clerk. In a chapter 11 reorganization, notice of the hearing on the dismissal or conversion of a case to another chapter shall be served by the movant. When the United States Trustee is the movant, notice of the hearing on the dismissal or conversion of a chapter 11 case shall be served by the Bankruptcy Clerk. In a chapter 12 or 13 debt adjustment, notice of the hearing on the dismissal or conversion of a case to another chapter shall be served by the standing trustee.

(5) Notice of the time fixed to accept or reject a proposed modification of a plan shall be prepared and served by the proponent of the modification.

(6) Notice of hearings on all applications for compensation or reimbursement of expenses totaling in excess of $1,000.00, except those to be heard in connection with a chapter 7 Trustee's Final Report, shall be prepared and served by the applicant.

(7) Unless otherwise ordered by the court, notice of the time fixed or "bar date" for filing proofs of claim or interest in chapter 11 cases pursuant to Bankruptcy Rule 3003(c)(3), either specifically set by the court, or as set by Local Bankruptcy Rule 3003–1, shall be served by the trustee or debtor in possession.

(8) Notice of the time fixed for filing objections and the hearing to consider confirmation of a chapter 12 plan shall be generated by the standing trustee and served by the debtor.

(9) Notice of the time fixed for filing proofs of claim in a chapter 7, 12 or 13 case pursuant to Bankruptcy Rule 3002(c), shall be served by the Bankruptcy Clerk and shall be combined with the meeting of creditors notice included in Official Bankruptcy Forms 309A–I; and

(10) Notice of the time fixed for filing objections to a chapter 13 plan shall be served by the standing trustee.

(b) Twenty–Eight Day Notices to Parties in Interest. The notices required by Bankruptcy Rule 2002(b)(1) and (b)(2) shall be served by the party whose disclosure statement is being considered or by the proponent of the plan, as the case may be. With respect to the hearing to consider confirmation of chapter 13 plan, notice shall be given by the standing trustee.

(c) Notice to Equity Security Holders. Unless otherwise ordered by the court, notice of the order for relief and of any meeting of equity security holders ordered by the court pursuant to 11 U.S.C. § 341, shall be served by the debtor in possession or trustee in all cases under chapter 11. The notices required by subdivisions (d)(3), (4), (5), (6), and (7) of Bankruptcy Rule 2002 shall be served in accordance with (a)(2), (4), (5) and (b) of this Rule.

(d) Other Notices.

(1) The notices required by subdivisions (f)(1), (3), (4), and (5) of Bankruptcy Rule 2002 shall be served by the party responsible for serving notice of the § 341 meeting of creditors as provided in subdivision (a)(1) of this rule.

(2) Notice of the dismissal of a case under chapter 7 or 11 shall be served by the Bankruptcy Clerk, provided that the debtor in possession shall serve such notice if the order was entered on motion of the debtor in possession. Notice of the dismissal of a chapter 12 or 13 case shall be served by the standing trustee.

(3) The notices required by subdivisions (f)(6), (8), (9), (10) and (11) of Bankruptcy Rule 2002 shall be served by the Bankruptcy Clerk.

(4) The notice required by subdivision (f)(7) of Bankruptcy Rule 2002 shall be served by the proponent of the confirmed plan.

(e) Debtor to Provide Notice. Whenever notice is required to be served under this Rule by the Bankruptcy Clerk or a party other than the debtor in possession, such debtor in possession shall serve the notice if the mailing list required by Local Bankruptcy Rule 1007–1(a) has not been filed.

(f) Notices to Creditors Whose Claims are Filed. In a chapter 7 case, after the expiration of time to file a claim under Bankruptcy Rule 3002(c), all notices required by subdivision (a) of this rule may be mailed only to creditors whose claims have been filed, and parties who have filed a request for notices with the Bankruptcy Clerk.

(g) Certificate of Service When Notice Served by Party. When a party other than the Bankruptcy Clerk is required by this rule to serve notice, such party shall file a copy of the notice with a certificate of service evidencing the names and addresses of the parties served and the date and manner of service.

(h) Other Parties. The Bankruptcy Court may require notices to be served by the parties other than those specified in these Local Bankruptcy Rules.

(i) Notice of an Extension to File Schedules. Notice of an extension of time to file schedules and statements shall be given by the debtor to any committee, trustee, examiner, the United States Trustee, standing chapter 12 or 13 trustee, indenture trustees or labor unions (if applicable), and to any other party as the Bankruptcy Court may direct.

(j) Parties Requesting Notice. Pursuant to Bankruptcy Rule 2002(m), the Bankruptcy Court orders that any party in interest may file a notice of appearance and request for notice in a case and shall thereafter be served with all notices in that case.

[Effective September 1, 2010. Amended effective December 1, 2017.]

L.B.R. 2004–1. EXAMINATIONS

(a) Motions for Examination. Before filing a motion for examination under Bankruptcy Rule 2004, counsel for the moving party shall confer with the proposed examinee or the examinee's counsel (if represented by counsel) to arrange for a mutually agreeable date, place and time for the examination.

All motions for examination shall include either: (1) a certificate which states that a conference was held as required and that all parties have agreed to the date, time and place of examination; (2) a certificate explaining why it was not possible for the required conference to be held; or (3) a certificate which states that a conference was held as required, that no agreement could be reached and that the motion is presented to the Bankruptcy Court for determination.

(b) Exemption. If a contested matter or an adversary proceeding is pending, the adversary discovery rules (Bankruptcy Rules 7027–7036), not Bankruptcy Rule 2004 and Local Bankruptcy Rule 2004–1, govern discovery pertaining to such contested matter or adversary proceeding.

[Effective September 1, 2010.]

L.B.R. 2007.1–1. EXAMINERS—CHAPTER 11

Upon approval of the appointment of an examiner in a chapter 11 case, the examiner shall be given all notices required to be mailed to committees under Bankruptcy Rule 2002(i).

[Effective September 1, 2010.]

L.B.R. 2014–1. EMPLOYMENT OF PROFESSIONALS

(a) Statement Required by § 329 and Rule 2016(b). A motion for employment by an attorney for the debtor or a motion for substitution of counsel for the debtor shall have attached the statement required by Bankruptcy Rule 2016(b) and 11 U.S.C. § 329.

(b) Retroactive Employment.

(1) If a motion for approval of the employment of a professional is made within 30 days of the commencement of that professional's provision of services, it is deemed contemporaneous.

(2) If a motion for the approval of the employment of a professional is made more than 30 days after that professional commences provision of services and the motion seeks to make the authority retroactive to the commencement, the motion shall include:

(A) an explanation of why the motion was not filed earlier;

(B) an explanation why the order authorizing retroactive employment is required; and

(C) an explanation, to the best of the applicant's knowledge, as to how approval of the motion may prejudice any parties-in-interest.

(3) Motions to approve the retroactive employment of professionals shall be approved only on notice and opportunity for hearing. Unless the court orders otherwise, all creditors in the case shall be served with notice of the motion.

[Effective September 1, 2010.]

L.B.R. 2015–1. TRUSTEES—GENERAL

In any chapter 7 case where the trustee has not been authorized to conduct the business of the debtor, the trustee may advance from estate funds only the following without further order: (1) expenses payable to unrelated third parties, subject to the subsequent court approval for reasonableness after notice and hearing, provided that no single such expense exceeds $200.00 and the aggregate amount of such expenses does not exceed $1,000.00; (2) adversary filing fees; and (3) payment of bond premiums as authorized by the United States Trustee.

[Effective September 1, 2010.]

L.B.R. 2016–1. COMPENSATION OF PROFESSIONALS

(a) Statement Required by § 329 and Rule 2016(b). The statement required by 11 U.S.C. § 329 and Bankruptcy Rule 2016(b) shall be filed by the attorney for the debtor within 14 days after the order for relief, whether or not the attorney seeks to be employed or compensated by the estate.

(b) Retainer Funds. In chapter 9, 11, 12 and 13 cases, all attorneys and accountants employed by a debtor shall deposit retainer funds, whether received from the debtor or an insider of the debtor (as defined in 11 U.S.C. § 101(31)), in a trust account. Any withdrawal in a chapter 13 case from a retainer, other than for payment of filing fees, one credit report and fees paid for credit counseling required by 11 U.S.C. § 109(h)(1), to the extent that the attorney has incurred these charges, may not be made on an amount that exceeds $3,000.00, in an individual case or $3,500.00 in a business case, except after approval of a formal fee application. A retainer in a chapter 9, 11 or 12 case may be withdrawn provided the attorney or accountant complies with the following procedure:

(1) A motion for distribution of retainer shall be filed with the Bankruptcy Clerk, and a copy shall be served on:

(A) The debtor, and, if the debtor is represented by an attorney, the attorney;

(B) Any attorney for a committee appointed or elected in the case, or if no attorney has been employed to represent the committee, through service on its members; and if no committee has been appointed in a chapter 9 or 11 case, the creditors included on the list filed pursuant to Bankruptcy Rule 1007(d);

(C) The United States Trustee;

(D) Any trustee appointed in the case; and

(E) All parties requesting notice pursuant to Local Bankruptcy Rule 2002–1(j);

(2) At a minimum, the motion for distribution of retainer shall contain a Fee Application Cover Sheet, a description of services rendered, including the time spent, hourly rates charged and the name of the attorney, accountant, other professional or paraprofessional performing the work;

(3) For the purpose of distribution of retainer, this motion shall be deemed an application within the provisions of Bankruptcy Rule 2016, with the final compensation of counsel to be

determined at a subsequent hearing before the court as required by Bankruptcy Rule 2016; and

(4) If no objection is filed within 14 days of the mailing thereof, said professional may withdraw funds as described in the proposal in the amounts set forth as interim allowances. Motions for distribution may not be filed more frequently than monthly, without leave of court. If an objection is received, the affected professional shall request a hearing before the court. Said hearing shall be held pursuant to Bankruptcy Rule 2017(a), and will not require preparation of a formal fee application.

(c) **Fee Application Form.** At a minimum, an application for compensation shall:

(1) include a Fee Application Cover Sheet;

(2) comply with the Court's Guidelines For Compensation and Expense Reimbursement of Professionals; and

(3) comply with any other applicable guidelines and court orders.

[Effective September 1, 2010.]

L.B.R. 2020–1. UNITED STATES TRUSTEE—GUIDELINES FOR CHAPTER 11 CASES

The United States Trustee may from time to time publish and file with the Bankruptcy Clerk guidelines on matters such as insurance, operating reports, bank accounts and money of estates and other subjects pertaining to the administration of chapter 11 cases. Failure to comply with the requirements of these guidelines may constitute cause justifying the appointment of a trustee, or dismissal or conversion of the case pursuant to 11 U.S.C. § 1112(b).

[Effective September 1, 2010.]

L.B.R. 2090–1. ATTORNEYS—ADMISSION TO PRACTICE

(a) **Eligibility for Admission.** Any attorney licensed to practice law by the Supreme Court of Texas, or by the highest court of any state or the District of Columbia, may be admitted to the bar of this court if the attorney is of good personal and professional character and is a member in good standing of the bar where the attorney is licensed.

(b) **Procedure for Admission.** Attorneys desiring admission to the bar of this court must complete an application for admission, to be approved by a district judge, and except as provided in subsection (c) of this rule, be introduced by a member in good standing of the bar of this court, and take the required oath or affirmation before a judge of this court. After the oath or affirmation is administered, and the applicant has paid the appropriate fee, the District Clerk shall issue a certificate stating that the attorney is admitted to practice before this court.

(c) **Admission Before Judges of Other Districts.** Any nonresident attorney who has completed all requirements for admission to the bar of this court may, with the approval of a district judge of the division where the application is pending, have the oath of admission administered by a judge in another district. The nonresident attorney must file the oath with the District Clerk and pay the appropriate fee before the attorney's name will be added to the roll of attorneys for this district.

(d) **Admission is Discretionary.** All admissions to practice before this court shall be discretionary with the judge reviewing the application for admission.

(e) **Conduct of Attorneys at Trial or Hearing.** Unless the Presiding Judge otherwise directs, during a trial or hearing, attorneys must:

(1) stand when making objections or otherwise addressing the Presiding Judge;

(2) use the lectern while examining or cross-examining witnesses;

(3) when examining a witness, refrain from making statements, comments, or remarks before or after asking a question;

(4) limit to one attorney for each party the examination or cross-examination of a witness; and

(5) in making an objection, state plainly and briefly the grounds for objecting and not offer argument unless requested by the Presiding Judge.

(f) **Exemption From Admission to Practice, and From Requirement of Local Counsel, for Attorneys Appearing on Behalf of the United States Justice Department or Any State Attorney General's Office.** Unless the Presiding Judge otherwise directs, an attorney appearing on behalf of the United States Justice Department or the Attorney General's Office of any state, and who is eligible pursuant to Local Bankruptcy Rule 2090–1(a) to appear in this court, shall be exempt from the requirements of Local Bankruptcy Rule 2090–1(b), 2090–4 and 2091–1, but shall otherwise be subject to all requirements applicable to attorneys who have been granted leave to appear pro hac vice.

[Effective September 1, 2010.]

L.B.R. 2090–2. ATTORNEYS—DISCIPLINE AND DISBARMENT

(a) **Loss of Membership.** A member of the bar of this court is subject to suspension or disbarment by the court under the following circumstances:

(1) if for any reason other than nonpayment of dues, failure to meet continuing legal education requirements, or voluntary resignation unrelated to a disciplinary proceeding or problem, an attorney loses, either temporarily or permanently, the right to practice law before:

(i) the courts of the State of Texas;

(ii) the highest court of any other state or the District of Columbia; or

(iii) any federal court; or

(2) if an attorney fails to maintain the right to practice law before the highest court of at least one state or the District of Columbia, unless the member's failure to maintain such right results from nonpayment of dues or failure to meet continuing legal education requirements.

(b) Grounds for Disciplinary Action. A Presiding Judge, after giving opportunity to show cause to the contrary, may take any appropriate disciplinary action against a member of the bar for:

(1) conduct unbecoming a member of the bar;

(2) failure to comply with any rule or order of the Bankruptcy Court;

(3) unethical behavior;

(4) inability to conduct litigation properly;

(5) conviction by any court of a felony or crime involving dishonesty or false statement; or

(6) having been publicly or privately disciplined by any court, bar, court agency or committee.

(c) Reporting by Members. Any member of the bar of this court who has:

(1) lost or relinquished, temporarily or permanently, the right to practice in any court of record;

(2) been disciplined, publicly or privately, by any court, bar, court agency, or committee; or

(3) been convicted of a felony or crime involving dishonesty or false statement, shall promptly report such fact in writing to the District Clerk, supplying full details and copies of all pertinent documents reflecting, or explaining, such action.

(d) Unethical Behavior. The term "unethical behavior," as used in this rule, means conduct undertaken in or related to a case or proceeding in this court that violates the Texas Disciplinary Rules of Professional Conduct.

(f) Re-Admission. An attorney applying for re-admission to the bar of this court must submit an application for re-admission, together with the following materials:

(1) a full disclosure concerning the attorney's loss or relinquishment of membership in the bar of this court; and

(2) all information required by subsection (c) of this rule concerning facts that occurred prior to the date of application for re-admission.

(g) Appointment of Counsel. A Presiding Judge shall have the right to appoint any member of the court's bar to assist in the handling of any proceeding contemplated by or resulting from this rule. An attorney appointed under this rule shall perform as requested unless relieved from doing so. An attorney desiring relief from appointment must move for such relief, which will be granted only upon a showing of good cause.

(h) Reciprocal Discipline.

(1) A member of the bar who is subject to suspension or disbarment under 2090–2(a) must be given written notice by the chief judge of the District Court, or by a district judge designated by the chief judge, that the court intends to suspend or disbar the member. The notice must identify the ground for imposing reciprocal discipline and provide the member an opportunity to show cause, within the time prescribed by the notice, why the member should not be suspended or disbarred.

(2) If the member does not respond to the notice, or responds but does not oppose reciprocal discipline, the chief judge of the District Court or a designee district judge may enter an appropriate order after the prescribed time for a response expires or the response is received.

(3) If the member responds and, in whole or in part, opposes reciprocal discipline, the chief judge of the District Court, or a designee district judge, must designate three judges to hear the matter. The decision of a majority of the three-judge panel concerning the appropriate discipline shall be the final ruling of the court.

[Effective September 1, 2010.]

L.B.R. 2090–3. ATTORNEYS—NOT ADMITTED TO PRACTICE BEFORE THIS COURT

(a) Eligibility to Appear. An attorney who is licensed to practice law by the highest court of any state or the District of Columbia, but who is not admitted to practice before this court, may represent a party in proceedings in this court only by permission of the Presiding Judge.

(b) Application to Appear. Unless exempted by Local Bankruptcy Rule 2090–1(f), an attorney who is not admitted to practice in this court, who desires to appear as counsel in a case, and who is eligible pursuant to subsection (a) of this rule to appear, shall apply for admission pro hac vice on a Bankruptcy Court-approved form and pay the applicable fee to the Bankruptcy Clerk.

(c) Regulation of Attorneys Admitted Pro Hac Vice. By appearing in any case, an attorney becomes subject to the rules of the Bankruptcy Court.

[Effective September 1, 2010.]

L.B.R. 2090–4. ATTORNEYS—REQUIREMENT OF LOCAL COUNSEL

(a) Local Counsel Required. Unless exempted by Local Bankruptcy Rule 2090–1(f), Local Counsel is required in all cases where an attorney appearing in a case does not reside or maintain an office in this district. "Local Counsel" means a member of the bar of this court who resides or maintains an office within 50 miles of the division in which the case is pending. Attorneys desiring to proceed without Local Counsel must obtain leave from the Presiding Judge. If the request for leave is denied, written designation of Local Counsel must be filed within 14 days of the denial.

(b) Duties of Local Counsel. Local Counsel must be authorized to present and argue a party's position at any hearing called by the Presiding Judge on short notice. Local Counsel must also be able to perform, on behalf of the party represented, any other duty required by the Presiding Judge or the Local Bankruptcy Rules.

[Effective September 1, 2010.]

L.B.R. 2091–1. ATTORNEYS—WITHDRAWALS

An attorney desiring to withdraw in any case must file a motion to withdraw. This motion must, in addition to the matters required by Local Bankruptcy Rule 7007–1, specify the reasons requiring withdrawal and provide the name and address of the succeeding attorney. If the succeeding attorney is not known, the motion must set forth the name, address, and telephone number of the client and either bear the client's signature approving withdrawal or state specifically why, after due diligence, the attorney was unable to obtain the client's signature.

[Effective September 1, 2010.]

L.B.R. 2091–2. ATTORNEYS—CHANGE OF CONTACT INFORMATION OR NAME

(a) **Attorney Who Is Not a Registered User of ECF.** When an attorney who is not a registered user of ECF changes the attorney's business address, e-mail address, telephone number, facsimile number, or name, the attorney must promptly notify the Bankruptcy Clerk, in writing, in each pending case.

(b) **Attorney Who Is a Registered User of ECF.** When an attorney who is a registered user of ECF changes the attorney's business address, e-mail address, telephone number, facsimile number, or name, the attorney must promptly change this information in ECF, following the procedures set forth in the ECF Administrative Procedures Manual.

[Effective September 1, 2010.]

PART III. CLAIMS AND DISTRIBUTION TO CREDITORS AND EQUITY INTEREST HOLDERS; PLANS

L.B.R. 3001–1. PROOF OF CLAIM ATTACHMENT REQUIRED FOR CLAIMS SECURED BY SECURITY INTEREST IN THE DEBTOR'S PRINCIPAL RESIDENCE

(a) **In General.** This rule applies in all cases and with regard to claims that are secured by a security interest in the individual debtor's principal residence. For chapter 13 cases, this rule applies in addition to the requirements of Rules 3002 and 3002.1.

(b) **Mortgage Proof of Claim Attachment.** The holder of a claim secured by a security interest in the debtor's principal residence shall attach to its proof of claim an exhibit reflecting at least the following details regarding the prepetition claim being asserted: (a) all prepetition interest amounts due and owing, itemized such that the applicable interest rate is shown, as well as the start and end dates for accrual of interest at such interest rate; (b) all prepetition fees, expenses, and charges due and owing, itemized to show specific categories (*e.g.*, appraisals, foreclosure expenses, *etc.*) and the dates incurred; (c) any escrow amount included in the monthly payment and, if there is an escrow account, a supplemental attachment of an escrow statement prepared as of the petition date; and (d) a statement reflecting the total amount necessary to cure any default as of the petition date (which statement must show (i) the number of missed payments, (ii) plus the aggregate amount of any fees, expenses, and charges due and owing, (iii) less any funds the creditor has received but not yet applied).

(c) **Form and Content.** The proof of claim attachment described in this rule shall be prepared as prescribed by Official Bankruptcy Form 410A.

[Effective April 1, 2012.]

L.B.R. 3002.1–1 MID–CASE AUDIT PROCEDURES WITH REGARD TO CLAIMS SECURED BY SECURITY INTEREST IN THE DEBTOR'S PRINCIPAL RESIDENCE

(a) **In General.** This rule applies in a chapter 13 case to claims that are (1) secured by a security interest in the debtor's principal residence, and (2) provided for under § 1322(b)(5) of the Code in the debtor's plan. This rule is in addition to the requirements of Rule 3002.1.

(b) **Mid–Case Notice by Chapter 13 Trustee.** The Mid-Case Notice described in this paragraph will not be required in any conduit case, but may be filed in the Trustee's sole discretion. For all other cases filed on or after December 1, 2011, the Chapter 13 Trustee shall (during the periods month 18 to month 22, and month 42 to month 46 of the case) file and serve on the holder of the claim and its counsel and the debtor and debtor's counsel a "Notice to Deem Mortgage Current," or alternatively, a "Notice of Amount Deemed Necessary to Cure," ("Mortgage Notice") stating whether or not, to the trustee's knowledge, the debtor is current on his plan and mortgage, and, if not, the amount believed necessary to cure any default on the plan and mortgage claim. The Mortgage Notice shall also contain negative notice language.

(c) **Response to Mid–Case Notice.** Within 60 days after the filing of a Mortgage Notice the holder shall file and serve on the debtor, debtor's counsel, and the trustee a response indicating whether it disputes the information in such notice. The response shall itemize any cure amounts or postpetition arrearages that the holder contends exist as of the date of the response. The Debtor may file a reply within 90 days after the date of the filing of a Mortgage Notice.

(d) **Determination of Mid–Case Notice by Court.** Whenever there is a response and/or reply to a Mortgage Notice, as set forth in subdivisions (b) and (c) above, the court shall, after notice and hearing, determine whether or not the debtor is current on all required postpetition amounts. If the holder of a claim fails to respond and/or the debtor fails to reply, the court may make this determination by default. An order shall be issued reflecting any determination by the court.

(e) **Effect of Order on Mid–Case Notice.** Any order issued on a Mortgage Notice, (whether by default or after a response, and/or reply) shall preclude the holder and the debtor from contesting the amounts set forth in the order in any contested matter or adversary proceeding in this case, or in any other matter, manner, or forum after a discharge in this case, unless the court determines, after notice and a hearing, that the failure to respond and/or reply was substantially justified or is harmless.

(f) Reconciliation of This Rule With National Bankruptcy Rule 3002.1. Nothing in this Local Bankruptcy Rule shall be interpreted to conflict with National Bankruptcy Rule 3002.1. For example, the requirement that the holder of a claim secured by a security interest in the debtor's principal residence file a Notice of Postpetition Mortgage Fees, Expenses and Charges (Official Bankruptcy Form 410S–2), to reflect postpetition charges, pursuant to National Bankruptcy Rules 3002.1(c) and (d), is not superseded by this rule, nor is the procedure and timing for a debtor or trustee to file a motion pursuant to subsection (e) of that rule, to challenge the propriety of amounts set forth in such Notice, superseded. This local rule is intended to provide an additional mechanism for parties to identify and resolve disputes regarding postpetition mortgage arrearages (including alleged missed payments of postpetition principal and interest, as well as asserted postpetition fees and charges) at different checkpoints during a Chapter 13 case.

[Former Rule 3002–2, effective April 1, 2012. Renumbered and amended effective December 1, 2016. Amended effective December 1, 2017.]

L.B.R. 3003–1. FILING PROOFS OF CLAIM OR INTEREST IN A CHAPTER 9 OR 11 CASE

In a chapter 9 or 11 case, where no bar date has otherwise been specifically set, an unsecured creditor or equity security holder whose claim or interest is not scheduled or is scheduled as disputed, contingent, or unliquidated, has a proof of claim timely filed if it is filed not later than 90 days after the first date set for the meeting of creditors pursuant to 11 U.S.C. § 341, except that a proof of claim filed by a governmental unit is timely filed if it is filed not later than 180 days after the date of the order for relief.

[Effective September 1, 2010.]

L.B.R. 3007–1. CLAIM OBJECTIONS

(a) Contents of the Objection. Every objection to claim shall identify the claim by claim number, claimant and date filed. If the amount or classification of the claim is being disputed, the objection to claim shall state the amount of the claim, if any, that is not in dispute and the classification considered proper by the objecting party. The objection shall state with particularity the basis for the objection.

(b) Service. At a minimum, the objecting party shall serve any claim objection and the notice of hearing thereon, if applicable, on the claimant as provided in Rule 3007(a)(2), and if applicable, on the claimant's attorney. Pursuant to Bankruptcy Rule 7005, the objecting party shall file with the Bankruptcy Clerk a certificate of service, attached to the objection, evidencing the date and mode of service and the names and addresses of the parties served.

[Effective September 1, 2010. Amended effective December 1, 2017.]

L.B.R. 3007–2. OMNIBUS CLAIM OBJECTIONS

(a) Omnibus Claim Objection Procedures. When making an omnibus claim objection, the following procedures shall be followed:

(1) The objector shall object to no more than 100 proofs of claim in one pleading;

(2) Copies of the claims need not be attached to the omnibus claim objection. However, the objector shall notify the claimant that a copy of the claim may be obtained from the objector upon request;

(3) The notice of hearing and objection shall be served on the person whose name appears in the signature block on the proof of claim and in accordance with Bankruptcy Rule 7004;

(4) A hearing on each objection shall be held at least 40 days after service of the objection, and the date of such hearing, as well as whether the objector intends for the court to conduct an evidentiary hearing or a status conference, shall be clearly set forth in the notice of hearing. The objector is permitted to file a reply, including evidence, to any response at least 3 days prior to a hearing on the objection; and

(5) After the hearing on each omnibus claim objection, the objector may submit to the court a form order sustaining each objection as to which the claimant has defaulted.

(b) Omnibus Claim Objection Hearings. All pending objections to claims included in an omnibus objection shall follow the same hearing schedule, unless otherwise ordered by the court. When multiple claims subject to an omnibus claim objection are reset, all claims from that objection shall be reset to the same hearing date. A party resetting a hearing on an omnibus claim objection shall provide to the court, no fewer than 2 days prior to the reset hearing date, a list or chart setting forth the claim objections which remain to be determined on the reset hearing date, specifying which of those the party believes will be defaulted or settled.

[Effective September 1, 2010.]

L.B.R. 3007–3. RESPONSE TO CLAIM OBJECTIONS

As indicated in L.B.R. 9007–1(c) and (g)(5), except in chapter 7, 12 and 13 cases, where a claim objection may be served subject to negative notice language, no response is required to a claim objection. Nevertheless, the Presiding Judge may order otherwise, in other cases, on request of a party.

[Effective September 1, 2010.]

L.B.R. 3007–4. ESTIMATION OF CLAIMS

(a) If a claim is objected to or is filed in an unliquidated amount, the objecting party, the claimant, the trustee, the debtor in possession or any plan proponent may file a motion requesting that the claim be estimated in accordance with 11 U.S.C. § 502(c). Filing a motion to estimate commences a contested matter.

(b) The motion to estimate shall include those purposes (e.g., voting, allowance, etc.) for which estimation is sought, and an explanation of why estimation, as opposed to full trial of the claim objection, is appropriate. The movant, as soon as practicable following filing of the motion to estimate, shall consult with the claimant and the objecting party to determine whether either opposes the motion.

(c) If the movant, the claimant and the objecting party agree that the claim should be estimated, they shall attempt to agree upon and submit to the court procedures applicable to estimation of the claim. If they are unable to agree upon procedures, each party may submit proposed procedures. Proposed procedures shall be filed with the court at least 4 days prior to the hearing on the motion to estimate.

(d) If the claimant or the objecting party contests the motion to estimate, such entity shall file a response to the motion at least 4 days prior to the hearing on the motion.

(e) If the motion to estimate is granted, following such additional steps as the Presiding Judge may direct, the Presiding Judge shall enter such orders as are appropriate establishing procedures and schedules for estimating the claim.

[Effective September 1, 2010.]

L.B.R. 3015–3. CHAPTER 13—CONFIRMATION

Unless the court orders otherwise, an objection to confirmation shall be filed no later than 7 days prior to the date set for the pre-hearing conference on confirmation of the plan.

[Effective September 1, 2010.]

L.B.R. 3015–4. CHAPTER 12—CONFIRMATION

(a) Objections. Unless the court orders otherwise, an objection to confirmation shall be filed no later than 7 days prior to the date set for hearing on confirmation of the plan.

(b) General Provisions Applicable in Chapter 12 Plans.

(1) *Settlement Conference.* Unless the court orders otherwise, prior to the confirmation hearing, debtor's attorney, the standing chapter 12 trustee, and any party who has filed written objections to the debtor's plan shall appear at a pre-confirmation settlement conference to be held at a time and place specified by the standing chapter 12 trustee. Any party objecting to the plan shall be represented at the conference by a person with full authority to settle. If no written objections to the confirmation of the debtor's plan are filed within the time prescribed by the court, then the conference need not be held.

(2) *Hearing.* After notice, the court shall conduct a hearing on confirmation of the chapter 12 plan. The court may accept the standing chapter 12 trustee's report.

(3) *Notice.* When a chapter 12 plan is filed, the debtor's attorney shall give the standing chapter 12 trustee, all creditors, and all parties in interest notice of the time fixed for filing objections to the debtor's plan, the date, time and place of the pre-confirmation conference and of the confirmation hearing. The debtor's attorney shall give notice by a form of notice promulgated by the standing chapter 12 trustee.

[Effective September 1, 2010.]

L.B.R. 3016–1. CHAPTER 11—PLAN

(a) Extension of Exclusivity Period. If the debtor desires an extension of the exclusive period for filing a plan of reorganization, the debtor shall file a motion requesting the extension that includes a statement of the reasons why a plan has not been filed and a detailed timetable of the steps to be taken in order to file a plan. No order extending the periods of exclusivity as provided in 11 U.S.C. § 1121(b) or (e) shall be entered in the absence of such information.

(b) Small Business Cases. If the debtor desires an extension of the periods provided for filing or confirming a plan of reorganization in a small business case, as provided in 11 U.S.C. § 1121(e)(3), then the debtor shall file and serve a motion requesting the extension, as described in subsection (a), on all parties in interest. The motion should be filed sufficiently in advance of the expiration of the time periods provided in § 1121(e) to provide at least 21 days' notice of the hearing and for the order extending time to be signed before the existing deadline has expired. Expedited or emergency hearings will be granted only in exceptional circumstances.

(c) Report Required for Plans Not Filed Within Initial Exclusivity Period. Whenever a plan has not been filed within the exclusive period for filing a plan of reorganization as set forth in 11 U.S.C. § 1121(b) or (e), or upon the expiration of any extension or reduction of exclusivity, the debtor shall file either: (1) a report stating the reasons why a plan has not been filed and a detailed timetable of the steps to be taken in order to file a plan; or (2) a recommendation that the case either be dismissed or converted.

[Effective September 1, 2010.]

L.B.R. 3017–1. DISCLOSURE STATEMENT—APPROVAL

The transmission and notice required by subsection (d) of Bankruptcy Rule 3017 shall be mailed by the proponent of the plan.

[Effective September 1, 2010.]

L.B.R. 3017–2. DISCLOSURE STATEMENT—SMALL BUSINESS CASES

(a) Procedure for Conditional Approval Under Bankruptcy Rule 3017.1. A plan proponent in a small business case may seek conditional approval of a disclosure statement, subject to final approval after notice and hearing, by filing a motion with the Court contemporaneously with the filing of the proposed plan of reorganization. Such motion shall contain a certificate of service evidencing service upon the parties designated by Local Bankruptcy Rule 9007–1(b) and shall be accompanied by a proposed order. The motion may be presented to the Court for immediate consideration upon notice to the United States Trustee and any case trustee.

(b) Waiver. A plan proponent in a small business case may seek to waive the requirement of a disclosure statement because the proposed plan of reorganization itself provides adequate information. Such waiver may be sought by motion to be filed contemporaneously with the proposed plan of reorganization. Such motion shall be served upon the parties designated by Local Bankruptcy Rule 9007–1(b) and may contain 14–day negative notice language.

[Effective September 1, 2010.]

L.B.R. 3018–1. BALLOTS—VOTING ON PLANS

Unless the court orders otherwise, at least one day prior to the hearing on confirmation, the proponent of a plan or other party who receives the acceptances or rejections shall file a ballot certification which identifies the amount and number of allowed claims of each class accepting or rejecting the plan and the amount of allowed interests of each class accepting or rejecting the plan. A copy of the certification shall be served on the debtor, case trustee, if any, United States Trustee and any committee appointed or elected in the case. On the basis of the certification, the Presiding Judge may find that the plan has been accepted or rejected.

[Effective September 1, 2010.]

L.B.R. 3020–1. CHAPTER 11—CONFIRMATION

Unless the court orders otherwise, an objection to confirmation shall be filed and served no later than 4 days prior to the date set for hearing on confirmation of the plan.

[Effective September 1, 2010.]

L.B.R. 3022–1. CHAPTER 11—FINAL DECREE

A Post–Confirmation Report and Application for Final Decree (Local Form BTXN–078) shall be filed by the proponent(s) of the Plan. The application for final decree shall either be set for hearing or contain the required negative notice language set forth in Local Bankruptcy Rule 9007–1(c). The application shall be served on the United States Trustee and all creditors and other parties in interest.

[Effective September 1, 2010.]

PART IV. THE DEBTOR: DUTIES AND BENEFITS

L.B.R. 4001–1. AUTOMATIC STAY—RELIEF FROM

(a) Motions; Service. No summons is required. The movant shall file with the Bankruptcy Clerk a certificate of service attached to the motion, evidencing the mode of service and the names and addresses of the parties served, and a certificate of conference evidencing compliance with Local Bankruptcy Rule 9014–1(d)(1). The motion shall contain a notice of the requirement of the filing of a response to the motion as set forth in subdivision (b) of this rule. A motion for relief from the automatic stay shall be served on the following parties:

(1) The debtor, and, if the debtor is represented by an attorney, the attorney;

(2) Any attorney for a committee appointed or elected in the case, or if no attorney has been employed to represent the committee, through service on its members; and if no committee has been appointed in a chapter 9 or 11 case, the creditors included on the list filed pursuant to Bankruptcy Rule 1007(d);

(3) Any party scheduled in the case as holding a lien, with respect to a motion seeking relief from the stay of an act against property;

(4) The United States Trustee;

(5) Any trustee or examiner appointed in the case; and

(6) All parties requesting notice pursuant to Local Bankruptcy Rule 2002–1(j).

(b) Response Required. Any party opposing the motion for relief from stay shall file a response within 14 days from the date of service of the motion. Such response shall include a detailed and comprehensive statement as to how the movant can be "adequately protected" if the stay is to be continued. If no response is filed, the allegations in the motion may be deemed admitted, and an order granting the relief sought may be entered by default. The motion for relief shall contain a statement in substantially the following form:

PURSUANT TO LOCAL BANKRUPTCY RULE 4001–1(b), A RESPONSE IS REQUIRED TO THIS MOTION, OR THE ALLEGATIONS IN THE MOTION MAY BE DEEMED ADMITTED, AND AN ORDER GRANTING THE RELIEF SOUGHT MAY BE ENTERED BY DEFAULT.

ANY RESPONSE SHALL BE IN WRITING AND FILED WITH THE CLERK OF THE UNITED STATES BANKRUPTCY COURT AT (ADDRESS OF CLERK'S OFFICE) BEFORE CLOSE OF BUSINESS ON (MONTH) (DAY), (YEAR), WHICH IS AT LEAST 14 DAYS FROM THE DATE OF SERVICE HEREOF. A COPY SHALL BE SERVED UPON COUNSEL FOR THE MOVING PARTY AND ANY TRUSTEE OR EXAMINER APPOINTED IN THE CASE. ANY RESPONSE SHALL INCLUDE A DETAILED AND COMPREHENSIVE STATEMENT AS TO HOW THE MOVANT CAN BE "ADEQUATELY PROTECTED" IF THE STAY IS TO BE CONTINUED.

(c) Discovery. The time within which responses to discovery requests on automatic stay issues are due under Bankruptcy Rules 7028–7036 is shortened from 30 to 14 days. Similarly, depositions on automatic stay issues may be taken commencing at the expiration of 14 days after service of the motion for relief from the automatic stay.

(d) Attorney Certification. In any evidentiary hearing conducted on a motion for relief from the automatic stay, all counsel shall certify before the presentation of evidence: (1) that good faith settlement discussions have been held or why they were not held; (2) that all exhibits, appraisals and lists of witnesses (it is presumed that the debtor(s) will testify) have been exchanged at least 2 days in advance of the hearing date; and (3) the anticipated length of the hearing. Exhibits shall be marked in advance of the hearing and two bound, marked sets of exhibits shall be presented to the court prior to the commencement of the hearing.

(e) Preliminary Hearings and Affidavits.

(1) *Preliminary Hearings and Affidavits, Generally.* Absent compelling circumstances warranting an alternative procedure, evidence presented at preliminary hearings in the Dallas and Fort Worth Divisions on motions for relief from the automatic stay will be by affidavit only. Except as set forth below (with regard to a motion filed by the holder of claim secured by a security interest in the debtor's principal residence, and with regard to requests for expedited settings), the party requesting the hearing shall serve evidentiary affidavits at least 7 days in advance of such hearing; the responding party shall serve evidentiary affidavits at least 2 days in advance of such hearing; the party requesting the hearing must give notice to all other affected parties of the requirement of this rule. The failure of a respondent to file an evidentiary affidavit, or the failure of an attorney to attend a scheduled and noticed preliminary hearing, shall be grounds for granting the relief, regardless of the filing of a response to the motion.

(2) *Special Affidavits and Proof Requirements for Holders of Mortgages on a Debtor's Principal Residence (Applicable in all Chapter Cases).* Whenever a motion for relief from automatic stay or whenever a motion for approval of an agreement regarding automatic stay is filed regarding a security interest in the debtor's principal residence, an affidavit in support of the motion shall be filed and served on the debtor, debtor's counsel, trustee, United States Trustee, and any other affected party within 7 days of the filing of the motion-regardless of the hearing date and regardless of whether any opposition is expected. The affidavit must be signed and certified under penalty of perjury by a person with knowledge of the facts, and must include: (a) a copy of the note or other debt instrument and any and all assignments thereof to substantiate proof of holder status; (b) a copy of the deed of trust showing the date, volume, page and county of recordation; and (c) in the event of alleged delinquent payments as a "cause" for relief from stay, a chronological payment history for the debtor showing, on a month-by-month basis, beginning with the first payment alleged to be delinquent, the date payment was due, the amount due, the date payment was received (if applicable), the amount received (if applicable), how any received payments were applied (*e.g.,* applied to balance, put in suspense, put in escrow, *etc.*), and also indicating any other types of defaults alleged including escrow shortages, such as for payments for insurance premiums or ad valorem tax payments made by the creditor. The affidavit shall clearly reflect all amounts received by the movant since the debtor allegedly first became delinquent, and whether such amounts were applied to indebtedness, put in suspense, or otherwise dealt with. The response deadline for motions for relief from automatic stay or for a motion for approval of an agreement regarding automatic stay regarding security interests in the debtor's principal residence, as well as the affidavit deadline for any responders, is the same as set forth in subdivisions (b) and (e)(1) of this L.B.R. 4001–1. No Order will be entered on a motion for relief from automatic stay or on a motion for approval of an agreement regarding a security interest in the debtor's principal residence unless an affidavit complying with this subdivision is filed and properly served (regardless of

whether there is any pending opposition to the motion by any party).

(3) *Time for Filing Affidavit in the Event of a Request for an Expedited Hearing.* Notwithstanding the foregoing, whenever a party seeks an expedited setting on a motion for relief from automatic stay, an affidavit in support of such motion shall be filed at the time of the filing of the motion.

(4) *Motions to Extend Time to File Affidavits/Dismissal of Stay Motions.* In the event that an Affidavit is not timely filed by a holder of a security interest in the debtor's principal residence, as set forth in subsection (e)(2) above, the underlying motion may be sua sponte dismissed by the court. A holder of a security interest in the debtor's principal residence may move for an extension of time to file the required affidavit, but (a) extensions shall be granted only in exceptional circumstances; and (b) in the event of an extension, the preliminary hearing will be continued out to a date that is at least as many days long as the extended time to file the affidavit. By seeking such an extension, the holder of a security interest in the debtor's principal residence waives the time periods provided by Section 362(e).

(5) *Application of Rule of Divisions.* Subsections (2) through (4) of this Rule 4001–1(e), describing the specific affidavit requirements in connection with stay motions involving a debtor's principal residence, apply in all Divisions of the Northern District of Texas. Subsection (1) of this Rule 4001–1(e), which more generally refers to there being preliminary hearings on motions to lift stay, applies only in the Dallas and Fort Worth Divisions.

(f) Continuation or Imposition of Automatic Stay.

(1) *Motion Required.* Any party that seeks a continuation or imposition of the automatic stay under 11 U.S.C. §§ 362(c)(3)(B) or –(c)(4)(B) shall file a motion with the court, and shall set the motion for hearing on notice to all parties against whom the movant seeks to continue or impose the stay.

(2) *Filing, Service and Setting.* The motion shall be filed and served promptly upon the filing of a petition for relief under the Bankruptcy Code so that it may be heard by the court within 30 days of the date of the filing of the petition, and so that parties may be given at least 21 days' notice of the hearing without the need for an expedited or emergency hearing, which will be granted only in exceptional circumstances. A copy of the motion and notice of hearing shall be served on all parties against whom the debtor seeks to continue or impose the stay, and proof of such service shall be filed within 2 days after service of the motion.

(3) *Content of Motion.* The motion shall:

(A) specifically allege the identity of the creditor(s) as to which the movant seeks to continue or impose the stay;

(B) identify, by case number, any and all prior bankruptcy filings by the debtor;

(C) state whether the debtor has had more than one previous case pending within the preceding year;

(D) state whether any previous case was dismissed within the preceding year after the debtor failed to perform any of the acts set forth in 11 U.S.C. § 362(c)(3)(C)(i)(II);

(E) state whether there has been a substantial change in the financial or personal affairs of the debtor and, if so, support the statement with specific factual allegations;

(F) state whether any creditor moved for relief from the automatic stay in a previous case and, if so, the disposition of that motion; and

(G) allege specific facts entitling the movant to relief.

(4) *Evidence Presented at Hearing.* At the hearing on the motion, the movant shall present evidence demonstrating that the new case is filed in good faith as to the creditor(s) to be stayed. The movant shall be present at the hearing to testify.
[Effective September 1, 2010. Amended effective April 1, 2012.]

PART V. COURTS AND CLERKS

L.B.R. 5003–1. BANKRUPTCY CLERK— GENERAL AUTHORITY

(a) Bankruptcy Clerk Authorized to Amend Form of Mailing List. The Bankruptcy Clerk shall be authorized to change the form of the mailing list required by Local Bankruptcy Rule 1007–1(a) to meet requirements of any automated case management system hereafter employed by the Bankruptcy Clerk. The Bankruptcy Clerk shall give appropriate notice to the bar of any such change in form.

(b) Bankruptcy Clerk Authorized to Refuse Certain Forms of Payment. The Bankruptcy Clerk shall maintain a list of all attorneys and law firms whose checks or credit or debit cards have been dishonored. The Bankruptcy Clerk may refuse future check, credit or debit card payments from such attorneys or firms and require an alternative form of payment.
[Effective September 1, 2010.]

L.B.R. 5004–1. DISQUALIFICATION—RECUSAL

A Presiding Judge, upon recusal in any case, shall request that the chief bankruptcy judge or the Bankruptcy Clerk reassign the case.
[Effective September 1, 2010.]

L.B.R. 5005–1. FILING PAPERS— REQUIREMENTS

(a) Filing the Petition. The petition shall be filed in the office of the Bankruptcy Clerk responsible for the division in which the case is to be filed.

(b) Signature Block. The signature block of every pleading shall include the name, state bar number, if applicable, address, telephone number and email address, if applicable, of the party or attorney filing the pleading. In the case of an attorney, the attorney's firm name and the name of the party represented shall also be included.

(c) Attorney Name and Address. The attorney's name, state bar number, mailing address, telephone number, email address, if applicable, and the name of the party represented shall appear on the upper-left corner of the first page of every pleading, except on proposed orders.

(d) Form of Pleadings.

(1) The heading, style and caption shall appear beneath the name of the attorney.

(2) The case number, including the initials of the Presiding Judge, shall appear on the right side of the page across from the style, with the adversary number, if applicable, below the case number.

(3) The nature of the hearing and the hearing date and time shall appear below the case or adversary number(s).
[Effective September 1, 2010.]

L.B.R. 5005–4. ELECTRONIC FILING

The Bankruptcy Clerk is authorized to accept documents for filing, issue notices and serve orders and judgments electronically, and to specify practices in electronic case management, subject to the procedures approved by the Bankruptcy Court and consistent with technical standards, if any, that the Judicial Conference of the United States establishes, and to the extent permitted by applicable rules.
[Effective September 1, 2010.]

L.B.R. 5011–1. WITHDRAWAL OF REFERENCE

(a) Procedure. A motion to withdraw the reference of a case or a proceeding in a case shall be directed to the district court, but shall be filed with the Bankruptcy Clerk. A status conference on the motion shall be held by the bankruptcy judge with notice to all parties involved in a contested matter or adversary proceeding of which the reference is proposed to be withdrawn. At the status conference, the bankruptcy judge shall consider and determine the following:

(1) whether any response to the motion to withdraw the reference was filed;

(2) whether a motion to stay the proceeding pending the district court's decision on the motion to withdraw the reference has been filed, in which court the motion was filed, and the status (pending, granted or denied) of the motion;

(3) whether the proceeding is core or non-core, or both and with regard to the non-core and mixed issues, whether the parties consent to entry of a final order by the bankruptcy judge;

(4) whether a jury trial has been timely requested, and if so, whether the parties consent to the bankruptcy judge conducting a jury trial, and whether the district court is requested to designate the bankruptcy judge to conduct a jury trial;

(5) if a jury trial has not been timely requested or if the proceeding does not involve a right to jury trial;

(6) whether a scheduling order has been entered in the proceeding;

(7) whether the parties are ready for trial;

(8) whether the bankruptcy judge recommends that

  (A) the motion be granted,

  (B) the motion be granted upon certification by the bankruptcy judge that the parties are ready for trial,

  (C) the motion be granted but that pre-trial matters be referred to the bankruptcy judge, or

  (D) the motion be denied; and

(9) any other matters relevant to the decision to withdraw the reference.

(b) Report to the District Court. Following the completion of the status conference the bankruptcy judge will prepare a report to the district court that contains the above findings and recommendation and any scheduling order that has been entered by the bankruptcy court in the proceeding. A copy of the report and recommendation shall be entered on the docket by the Bankruptcy Clerk and noticed in the same manner as the entry of an order, and the original shall be transmitted to the District Clerk.

[Effective September 1, 2010.]

L.B.R. 5072-1.   COURT DECORUM

All persons present in a courtroom where a trial, hearing, or other proceeding is in progress must dress and conduct themselves in a manner demonstrating respect for the court. The Presiding Judge shall have the discretion to establish appropriate standards of dress and conduct.

[Effective September 1, 2010.]

L.B.R. 5072-2.   COURT SECURITY

Firearms and other weapons are prohibited in areas of buildings designated for court use. Such weapons may be carried by the United States Marshal, the marshal's deputies, courtroom security personnel, and other persons to whom a Presiding Judge has given approval.

[Effective September 1, 2010.]

L.B.R. 5073-1.   PHOTOGRAPHY, BROADCASTING, RECORDING AND TELEVISING

No person may photograph, electronically record, televise, or broadcast a judicial proceeding. This rule shall not apply to ceremonial proceedings or electronic recordings by an official court reporter or other authorized court personnel.

[Effective September 1, 2010.]

L.B.R. 5075-1.   BANKRUPTCY CLERK— DELEGATED FUNCTIONS

(a) Authority to Sign Notices and Orders. Pursuant to 28 U.S.C. §§ 157(b) and 956, The Bankruptcy Court authorizes the Bankruptcy Clerk to sign and enter the following Notices and Orders for the Bankruptcy Court:

(1) Notices which require appearances at meetings, hearings, conferences or trials;

(2) Notices to trustees of status conferences;

(3) Notices of the filing of the Trustee's Final Report, Application for Compensation, Proposed Distribution and Deadline for Filing Objections;

(4) Orders discharging trustee, terminating liability on bond, and closing or converting chapter 12 and chapter 13 cases;

(5) Orders accepting trustee's report and closing estate in no-asset chapter 7 cases, where the debtor has been discharged or the case has been dismissed;

(6) Orders to show cause, except those involving contempt or sanctions;

(7) Orders granting applications to pay filing fees in installments;

(8) Standing Scheduling Orders in adversary proceedings;

(9) Standing Scheduling Orders in involuntary cases;

(10) The Chapter 13 Order Discharging Debtor Upon Completion of Plan (after trustee's final report and account);

(11) Orders discharging the trustee and closing the estate in chapter 7 asset cases after the Trustee's Final Report and Account is filed and all disbursements made;

(12) Orders administratively closing chapter 13 cases where more than 180 days have passed since the entry of the discharge and no Final Report has been filed by the standing trustee;

(13) Orders converting cases (upon conversion of chapter 12 and 13 cases to chapter 7);

(14) Orders directing payment of unclaimed funds of $1,000.00 or less into the Unclaimed Funds Registry of the Bankruptcy Court;

(15) Orders withdrawing motions to dismiss case filed by the Chapter 13 Trustee; and

(16) Other orders as the Bankruptcy Court may designate by standing order.

(b) Deputy Clerks. The Bankruptcy Clerk is authorized to delegate this authority to any deputy clerk. On any order or notice signed by the Bankruptcy Clerk or on behalf of the Bankruptcy Clerk, there shall appear the legend "FOR THE COURT" above the signature line.

[Effective September 1, 2010.]

PART VI.   COLLECTION AND LIQUIDATION OF THE ESTATE

L.B.R. 6070–1.   TAX RETURNS & TAX REFUNDS—CHAPTER 12 AND 13 CASES

The standing chapter 12 and 13 trustees are authorized to endorse on behalf of any chapter 12 or 13 debtor for deposit to the chapter 12 or 13 trustee's trust fund account, any and all federal income tax refunds payable to the debtor. A standing chapter 12 trustee may apply the refunds to any delinquent payments under the confirmed chapter 12 plan or any modifi-cation thereof. Consistent with the Bankruptcy Court's Standing Order Concerning All Chapter 13 Cases, a standing chapter 13 trustee, may apply up to $2,000.00 of the refund to delinquent plan payments or any modification thereof. The standing chapter 12 or 13 trustee shall give notice of the deposit and application to the debtor at the address last shown in the records of the office of the standing chapter 12 or 13 trustee, and to the debtor's attorney of record.

[Effective September 1, 2010.]

PART VII.   ADVERSARY PROCEEDINGS

L.B.R. 7001–1.   ADVERSARY PROCEEDINGS—GENERAL

An adversary complaint shall be filed in the division in which the related chapter case is pending, if such chapter case is pending in this district, except as otherwise required by 28 U.S.C. § 1409.

[Effective September 1, 2010.]

L.B.R. 7003–1.   COVER SHEET

Every adversary proceeding filed in this district shall be accompanied by an adversary proceeding cover sheet.

[Effective September 1, 2010.]

L.B.R. 7004–2.   SERVICE OF SUMMONS

If the plaintiff consents to such delivery, an electronic version of the summons containing the Bankruptcy Court's seal may be sent to the plaintiff. The plaintiff is then respon-sible for opening the link, receiving the electronic summons, and serving the summons on all opposing parties in accordance with Bankruptcy Rule 7004.

[Effective September 1, 2010.]

L.B.R. 7005–1.   SERVICE OF PLEADINGS AND OTHER PAPERS BY ELECTRONIC MEANS

Subject to the administrative procedures approved by the Bankruptcy Court and consistent with technical standards, if any, that the Judicial Conference of the United States estab-lishes, parties are permitted to make service through the Bankruptcy Court's transmission facilities, as permitted by Federal Rule of Civil Procedure 5(b)(2)(E). This rule is not applicable to the service of process of a summons and com-plaint, which must be served in accordance with Bankruptcy Rule 7004.

[Effective September 1, 2010.]

L.B.R. 7007–1.   MOTION PRACTICE

Unless otherwise directed by the Presiding Judge, motion practice is controlled by subsection (f) of this rule. In addi-tion, the parties shall comply with the following:

(a) Conference. Before filing a motion, an attorney for the moving party shall confer with an attorney for each party affected by the requested relief to determine whether the motion is opposed. Conferences are not required for motions to dismiss, motions for judgment on the pleadings, motions for summary judgment, motions for new trial, or when a confer-ence is not possible or practicable.

(b) Certificate of Conference.

(1) Each motion for which a conference is required shall include a certificate of conference indicating that the motion is unopposed or opposed.

(2) If a motion is opposed, the certificate shall state that a conference was held, indicate the date of conference and the identities of the attorneys conferring, and explain why agree-ment could not be reached.

(3) If a conference was not held, the certificate shall explain why it was not possible or practicable to confer, in which event the motion will be presumed to be opposed.

(c) Proposed Order. Each motion shall be accompanied by a proposed order that is set forth separately as an exhibit to the motion. An agreed proposed order shall be signed by the attorneys or parties to the agreement.

(d) Brief. An opposed motion shall be accompanied by a brief that sets forth the moving party's contentions of fact or law, and argument and authorities, unless a brief is not required by subsection (h) of this rule. A response to an opposed motion shall be accompanied by a brief that sets forth the responding party's contentions of fact or law, and argu-ment and authorities. A responding party is not required to file a brief in opposition to a motion for which a brief is not required by subsection (h) of this rule. A brief of less than 10 pages may be included in the same document as the motion, otherwise briefs shall be filed separately.

(e) Time for Response and Brief. A response and brief to an opposed motion shall be filed within 21 days from the date the motion is filed.

(f) Uniform Requirements on Motion Practice.

B—Brief required (not required with agreed motion)
C—Certificate of Conference required*

MOTION (to/for):	B	C
AMEND	X	

MOTION (to/for):	B	C
CHANGE OF VENUE	X	X
COMPEL	X	X
CONSOLIDATION	X	X
CONTINUANCE		X
DISMISS	X	
EXTEND TIME TO ANSWER		X
INTERVENE	X	X
JUDGMENT AS MATTER OF LAW	X	X
JUDGMENT ON PLEADINGS	X	
LEAVE TO FILE	X	X
LIMINE	X	X
MORE DEFINITE STATEMENT	X	X
NEW TRIAL	X	
PRELIMINARY INJUNCTION	X	X
PRODUCE DOCUMENTS	X	X
PROTECTIVE ORDER	X	X
QUASH	X	X
REINSTATE		
REMAND	X	X
SANCTIONS	X	X
STAY PENDING APPEAL	X	X
STRIKE	X	X
SUBSTITUTE COUNSEL		X
SUMMARY JUDGMENT	X	
WITHDRAW AS ATTY. OF RECORD		X

* NOTE: If your motion is not listed above, then a brief and a certificate of conference is required.

(g) Appendix Requirements.

(1) A party who relies on documentary (including an affidavit, declaration, deposition, answer to interrogatory, or admission) or non-documentary evidence (including videotapes and other physical exhibits) to support or oppose a motion shall include such evidence in an appendix.

(2) The appendix shall be separate from the motion, response, reply, or brief.

(3) The appendix shall be submitted in accordance with the Court's Administrative Procedures for Electronic Filing; however, non-documentary exhibits and oversized exhibits that cannot be scanned electronically shall be placed in an envelope that measures 9 × 12 inches and filed separately.

(4) Each page of the appendix shall be numbered legibly in the lower, right hand corner. The first page shall be numbered as "1," and succeeding pages shall be numbered sequentially through the last page of the entire appendix (i.e., the numbering system shall not re-start with each succeeding document in the appendix). Any envelope that contains a non-documentary or oversized exhibit shall be numbered as if it were a single page.

[Effective September 1, 2010.]

L.B.R. 7007–2.   BRIEFS

(a) General Form. A brief shall be printed, typewritten, or presented in some other legible form.

(b) Amicus Briefs. An amicus brief may not be filed without leave of the Presiding Judge. The brief shall specifically set forth the interest of the amicus curiae in the outcome of the litigation.

(c) Length. A brief shall not exceed 25 pages (excluding the table of contents and table of authorities). A reply brief shall not exceed 10 pages. Permission to file a brief in excess of these page limitations will be granted by the Presiding Judge only for extraordinary and compelling reasons.

(d) Tables of Contents and Authorities. A brief in excess of 10 pages shall contain:

(1) a table of contents with page references; and

(2) an alphabetically arranged table of cases, statutes, and other authorities cited, with page references to the location of all citations.

(e) Citations to Appendix. If a party's motion or response is accompanied by an appendix, the party's brief shall include citations to each page of the appendix that supports each assertion that the party makes concerning any documentary or non-documentary evidence on which the party relies to support or oppose the motion.

[Effective September 1, 2010.]

L.B.R. 7007–3.   CONFIRMATION OF INFORMAL LEAVE OF COURT

When a Presiding Judge informally grants leave, such as an extension of time to file a response or brief, an attorney for the party to whom leave is granted shall file a document confirming the leave and shall serve the document on all other parties.

[Effective September 1, 2010.]

L.B.R. 7016–1.   PRETRIAL PROCEDURES

(a) Joint Pretrial Order. Unless otherwise directed by the Presiding Judge, a joint pretrial order shall be uploaded to the Presiding Judge at least 7 days prior to trial docket call. All attorneys are responsible for preparing the pretrial order, which shall contain the following:

(1) a summary of the claims and defenses of each party;

(2) a statement of stipulated facts;

(3) a list of contested issues of fact;

(4) a list of contested issues of law;

(5) an estimate of the length of trial;

(6) a list of any additional matters that might aid in the disposition of the case; and

(7) the signature of each attorney.

(b) Proposed Findings and Conclusions. Proposed findings of fact and conclusions of law shall be filed at least 7 days prior to trial docket call, and shall be emailed to the Presiding Judge's courtroom deputy in word processing format upon filing with the court.

(c) Conflict Between Scheduling Order and Local Rule. In any conflict between a scheduling order entered in an adversary proceeding and these Local Bankruptcy Rules, the scheduling order controls.

[Effective September 1, 2010.]

L.B.R. 7026–1. DISCOVERY

(a) Filing Discovery Materials.

(1) *For Use in Discovery Proceedings.* A motion that relates to a discovery proceeding may only contain the portions of the discovery materials in dispute.

(2) *For Use in Pretrial Motions.* When discovery materials are necessary for consideration of a pretrial motion, a party shall file only the portions of the discovery on which that party relies to support or oppose the motion.

(b) Depositions Used at Trial. When a deposition is reasonably expected to be used at trial, it shall be pre-marked for identification as a trial exhibit and exchanged pursuant to the scheduling order.

[Effective September 1, 2010.]

L.B.R. 7040–1. ASSIGNMENT OF ADVERSARY PROCEEDINGS

(a) Adversary Proceeding Related to a Case in This District. Except where considerations for equalization of the docket otherwise dictate, adversary proceedings will be assigned to the bankruptcy judge to whom the related chapter proceeding is assigned.

(b) Adversary Proceeding Related to a Case in Another District. Whenever an adversary proceeding which is related to a chapter case pending in another district is filed in a division of this court served by more than one bankruptcy judge, the Bankruptcy Clerk shall randomly assign proceedings among the bankruptcy judges in a proportion determined by the Bankruptcy Court.

[Effective September 1, 2010.]

L.B.R. 7042–1. CONSOLIDATION OF ADVERSARY PROCEEDINGS— SEPARATE TRIALS

Motions to consolidate adversary proceedings, and all briefs and other papers concerning consolidation, shall be served on an attorney for each party in each case sought to be consolidated. After consolidation, all pleadings, motions, or other papers shall only bear the caption of the first case filed. All post-consolidation filings shall also bear the legend "(Consolidated with [giving the docket numbers of all the other cases])."

[Effective September 1, 2010.]

L.B.R. 7055–1. DEFAULT JUDGMENT

(a) Failure to Obtain Default Judgment. If a defendant has been in default for 90 days, the Presiding Judge may require the plaintiff to move for entry of a default and a default judgment. If the plaintiff fails to do so within the prescribed time, the Presiding Judge may dismiss the proceeding, without prejudice, as to that defendant.

(b) Request for Entry of Default by Bankruptcy Clerk. Before the Bankruptcy Clerk is required to enter a default, the party requesting such entry shall file with the Bankruptcy Clerk a written request for entry of default, submit a proposed form of entry of default, and file any other materials required by Fed. R. Civ. P. 55(a).

[Effective September 1, 2010.]

L.B.R. 7056–1. SUMMARY JUDGMENT

(a) Motion Practice Not Modified Generally. Except as expressly modified, the motion practice prescribed by Local Bankruptcy Rules 7007.1–7007.3 is not affected by this rule.

(b) Limits on Time for Filing and Number of Motions.

(1) *Time for Filing.* Unless otherwise directed by the Presiding Judge, no motion for summary judgment may be filed within 45 days of the docket call setting.

(2) *Number.* Unless otherwise directed by the Presiding Judge, or permitted by law, a party may file no more than one motion for summary judgment.

(c) Content of Motion.

(1) Except as provided in subsection (2) of this rule, a motion for summary judgment shall:

(A) on the first page, under the heading "summary," contain a concise statement that identifies the elements of each claim or defense as to which summary judgment is sought,

(B) contain the legal or factual grounds on which the moving party relies, and

(C) if the motion is accompanied by an appendix, include citations to each page of the appendix that supports each assertion that the party makes concerning the summary judgment evidence.

(2) A moving party may satisfy the requirements of subsection (1) of this rule by stating in its motion that each of the required matters will be set forth in the party's brief.

(3) If a moving party seeks summary judgment on fewer than all claims or defenses, the motion shall be styled as a motion for partial summary judgment.

(4) A motion for summary judgment shall not contain argument and authorities.

(d) Content of Response.

(1) Except as provided in subsection (2) of this rule, a response to a motion for summary judgment shall contain the legal or factual grounds on which the responding party relies in opposition to the motion.

(2) A responding party may satisfy the requirement of subsection (1) of this rule by stating in its response that each of the required matters will be set forth in the party's brief.

(3) A response to a motion for summary judgment shall not contain argument and authorities, which will be set forth in the contemporaneously filed brief.

(e) Briefing Requirements.

(1) *Brief Required.* A summary judgment motion or a response shall be accompanied by a brief that sets forth the argument and authorities on which the party relies in support of or opposition to a motion, and shall contain the matters required by subsections (c)(1) or (d)(1) of this rule if the party has opted to comply with those subsections by including the required matters in its brief. The brief shall be filed as a separate document from the motion or response that it supports.

(2) *Length of Briefs.* The requirements of Local Bankruptcy Rule 7007–2 apply to briefs filed pursuant to this rule, except that, excluding the table of contents and table of authorities, the length of a principal brief may not exceed 50 pages and a reply brief may not exceed 25 pages. The Presiding Judge, by order or other appropriate notice, may restrict or expand the length of briefs permitted by this rule.

(3) *Citations to Appendix.* A party whose motion or response is accompanied by an appendix shall include in its brief citations to each page of the appendix that supports each assertion that the party makes concerning the summary judgment evidence.

(f) Appendix Requirements.

(1) *Appendix Required.* A party who relies on affidavits, depositions, answers to interrogatories, or admissions on file to support or oppose a motion for summary judgment shall include such evidence in an appendix.

(2) *Appendix Format.*

(A) The appendix shall be assembled as a self-contained document, separate from the motion and brief or response and brief.

(B) Each page of the appendix shall measure 8½ × 11 inches. Non–documentary exhibits and oversized exhibits that are included in the appendix shall be placed in an envelope that measures 9 × 12 inches.

(C) Each page of the appendix shall be numbered legibly in the lower, right hand corner. The first page shall be numbered as "1," and succeeding pages shall be numbered sequentially through the last page of the entire appendix (i.e., the numbering system shall not re-start with each succeeding document in the appendix). An envelope that contains a non-documentary or oversized exhibit shall be numbered as if it were a single page.

(g) Limit on Supplemental Materials. Except for the motions, responses, replies, briefs, and appendixes required by these rules, a party may not, without the permission of the Presiding Judge, file supplemental pleadings, briefs, authorities, or evidence.

[Effective September 1, 2010.]

L.B.R. 7067–1. REGISTRY FUND

(a) Deposit. The deposit of any money into the registry of the Bankruptcy Court shall be as directed by written order of the court. Funds so deposited shall be invested by the Bankruptcy Clerk in accordance with the terms of the order, if included, otherwise such funds will be invested at the discretion of the Bankruptcy Clerk. Negotiable instruments tendered for deposit shall be made payable to "Clerk, U.S. Bankruptcy Court" and are accepted subject to collection.

(b) Withdrawal. The withdrawal of funds in the registry shall be in accordance with a written order of the court. The disbursement of accrued interest shall only be made if the order so provides. Any order for the distribution of less than all funds and accrued interest on deposit with the court shall be denominated "Order for Partial Distribution from the Registry of the Court," otherwise the order shall be treated as an Order for Final Distribution. Whenever an Order for Final Distribution from the registry of the court does not provide for the distribution of all funds or interest on deposit, the Bankruptcy Clerk shall pay such funds into the Treasury of the United States. This rule applies to both adversary proceedings and bankruptcy cases.

(c) Statement of Payee's Name, Address and Tax Identification Number. All orders authorizing disbursement from the registry shall state the payee's name, address, tax I.D. number and the dollar amount to be paid. Prior to receiving any disbursement from the registry, each payee shall deliver to the Bankruptcy Clerk an executed IRS Form W–9.

[Effective September 1, 2010.]

PART IX. GENERAL PROVISIONS*

* **[Publisher's Note:** So in original. No Part VIII promulgated by this Court. *See* the Local Bankruptcy Rules of the U.S. District Court for the Northern District of Texas, *ante.*]

L.B.R. 9001–1. DEFINITIONS

(a) "Bankruptcy Rule(s)" means the Federal Rule(s) of Bankruptcy Procedure currently in effect, and as thereafter amended.

(b) "Bankruptcy Court" means the bankruptcy judges of the United States Bankruptcy Court for the Northern District of Texas, as a collective body.

(c) "Bankruptcy Clerk" means Clerk of the Bankruptcy Court for the Northern District of Texas.

(d) "District Clerk" means Clerk of the District Court for the Northern District of Texas.

(e) "District Court Local Civil Rule(s)" means the Local Rules of the United States District Court for the Northern District of Texas, effective September 1, 2009, and as thereafter amended.

(f) "Local Bankruptcy Rules" means these Local Bankruptcy Rules of the United States Bankruptcy Court for the Northern District of Texas, as hereafter may be amended.

(g) "Presiding Judge" means the bankruptcy judge to whom the case, adversary proceeding, or contested matter is assigned.

(h) The phrase "small business case" means a case filed under chapter 11 of the Bankruptcy Code in which the debtor is a small business debtor, as defined in 11 U.S.C. § 101(51D).

[Effective September 1, 2010.]

L.B.R. 9007–1. GENERAL AUTHORITY TO REGULATE NOTICES

(a) Negative Notice Procedure Authorized. When authority to act or relief is sought which can only be authorized or granted upon notice or "after notice and hearing" as defined in 11 U.S.C. § 102, subject to Local Bankruptcy Rule 9014–1 and Local Bankruptcy Rule 3007–1, the party may, with respect to both motions under Bankruptcy Rule 9013 and contested matters under Bankruptcy Rule 9014, serve notice of the relief sought, and unless impracticable, any underlying motion, as follows using the "negative notice" procedure as set forth in this rule, except as provided in subsection (h) hereof. When this procedure is used with respect to a contested matter, no summons is required but service shall otherwise comply with the Federal Rules of Bankruptcy Procedure.

(b) Minimum Service Requirement. At a minimum, the pleading or notice shall be served upon the following parties in interest:

(1) The debtor, and, if the debtor is represented by an attorney, the attorney;

(2) Any attorney for a committee appointed or elected in the case, or if no attorney has been employed to represent the committee, through service on its members; and if no committee has been appointed in a chapter 9 or 11 case, the creditors included on the list filed pursuant to Bankruptcy Rule 1007(d);

(3) The United States Trustee;

(4) Any trustee appointed in the case; and

(5) All parties requesting notice pursuant to Local Bankruptcy Rule 2002–1(j); and

(6) Any entity required to be served by any applicable Bankruptcy Rule.

(c) Notice of Hearing Requirement. The pleading or notice served shall contain a statement in substantially the following form:

NO HEARING WILL BE CONDUCTED HEREON UNLESS A WRITTEN RESPONSE IS FILED WITH THE CLERK OF THE UNITED STATES BANKRUPTCY COURT AT (ADDRESS OF CLERK'S OFFICE) BEFORE CLOSE OF BUSINESS ON (MONTH) (DAY), (YEAR), WHICH IS AT LEAST 21 DAYS FROM THE DATE OF SERVICE HEREOF.

ANY RESPONSE SHALL BE IN WRITING AND FILED WITH THE CLERK, AND A COPY SHALL BE SERVED UPON COUNSEL FOR THE MOVING PARTY PRIOR TO THE DATE AND TIME SET FORTH HEREIN. IF A RESPONSE IS FILED A HEARING MAY BE HELD WITH NOTICE ONLY TO THE OBJECTING PARTY.

IF NO HEARING ON SUCH NOTICE OR MOTION IS TIMELY REQUESTED, THE RELIEF REQUESTED SHALL BE DEEMED TO BE UNOPPOSED, AND THE COURT MAY ENTER AN ORDER GRANTING THE RELIEF SOUGHT OR THE NOTICED ACTION MAY BE TAKEN.

Where sales free and clear are involved, Bankruptcy Rule 6004 shall be complied with by changing the first paragraph above to read substantially as follows:

HEARING DATE ON SUCH SALE IS SET FOR (MONTH, DAY, YEAR), WHICH IS AT LEAST 21 DAYS FROM THE DATE OF SERVICE HEREOF. NO OBJECTION TO SUCH SALE WILL BE CONSIDERED UNLESS A WRITTEN RESPONSE IS FILED WITH THE CLERK OF THE UNITED STATES BANKRUPTCY COURT AT (ADDRESS OF CLERK'S OFFICE) AT LEAST 4 DAYS IN ADVANCE OF SUCH HEARING DATE.

Where objections to claims in chapter 7, 12 and 13 cases are involved, the first paragraph of the notice shall be modified to provide:

NO HEARING WILL BE CONDUCTED ON THIS OBJECTION TO CLAIM UNLESS A WRITTEN RESPONSE IS FILED WITH THE CLERK OF THE UNITED STATES BANKRUPTCY COURT AT (ADDRESS OF CLERK'S OFFICE) BEFORE CLOSE OF BUSINESS ON (MONTH, DAY, YEAR), WHICH IS AT LEAST 30 DAYS FROM THE DATE OF SERVICE HEREOF.

(d) Statement of Relief Sought. Any notice shall state what authority to act or relief is sought by the moving party with sufficient particularity to apprise noticed parties of the subject matter of the notice or motion by reference to the pleadings delivered and shall not just refer to a pleading on file with the court. The court may deny any relief not sufficiently described so as to give general notice of the relevant factors to parties in interest.

(e) Certificate of Service. The movant shall file with the Bankruptcy Clerk a certificate of service, evidencing the date and mode of service and the names and addresses of the parties served.

(f) Certificate of Conference. A certificate of conference indicating whether or not a conference was held prior to filing the motion is required. The certificate shall indicate the date of conference and the identities of the attorneys conferring, and explain why agreement could not be reached. If a conference was not held, the certificate shall explain why it was not possible or practicable to confer. A conference is not required to be held when it is reasonably anticipated that the number of responding parties may be too numerous to contact prior to filing the motion.

(g) Certificate of No Objections. If no response and request for a hearing has been timely filed following service of notice in accordance with this rule, the moving party shall file a certificate with the court after the expiration of the applicable notice period stating that no objections have been timely served upon the moving party. In the event that the court has entered an order limiting the parties to whom notice shall be given or copies shall be sent, or limiting the time to respond, the certificate also shall state the date and substance of such order so that the existence of and compliance with such order may be determined from such certificate.

(h) Exceptions. This procedure may not be used for the following requests for relief, which shall be set for hearing:

(1) motions to dismiss or convert filed by a party in interest other than the debtor;

(2) motions for relief from the automatic stay, which are governed by Local Bankruptcy Rule 4001–1;

(3) motions to extend or impose the automatic stay;

(4) motions for use of cash collateral or for financing authority;

(5) objections to claims, other than in chapter 7, 12 and 13 cases;

(6) motions to assume, or to assume and assign, executory contracts or unexpired leases;

(7) motions to extend exclusivity or the time to confirm a plan of reorganization;

(8) motions for substantive consolidation;

(9) confirmation of a plan in a chapter 9, 11 or 12 case, or approval of a disclosure statement, other than pursuant to Local Bankruptcy Rule 3017–2(a); and

(10) any motion for which the Bankruptcy Rules specifically require a hearing.

[Effective September 1, 2010.]

L.B.R. 9013–1. MOTION PRACTICE

(a) Application of Local Adversary Rules. Local Bankruptcy Rules 7007–1(a)–(c) and 7007–3 apply to motion practice before the Bankruptcy Court.

(b) Paper Copies. Unless otherwise ordered by the Presiding Judge, a complete paper copy of the following pleadings, including all attachments thereto and any related briefs and appendices, should be delivered within 24 hours of the electronic filing of the following documents to the Bankruptcy Clerk:

(1) Chapter 9 or Chapter 11 Plan of Reorganization;

(2) Disclosure Statement;

(3) Motion for Summary Judgment;

(4) Application for Compensation and/or Reimbursement of Expenses; and

(5) Motion to Dismiss pursuant to Fed. R. Bankr. P. 7012.

[Effective September 1, 2010.]

L.B.R. 9014–1. CONTESTED MATTERS

(a) Response Required. Except as set forth in subparagraphs (f) and (h) hereof, and subject to the requirement that a movant provide proof in support of a motion, a response is required with respect to a contested matter. This rule shall constitute the Bankruptcy Court's direction requiring a response under Bankruptcy Rule 9014. A response is not required to a Chapter 13 Trustee's Notice of Intent to Dismiss, or an objection to confirmation of a chapter 13 plan.

(b) Service and Conference. The movant shall serve the motion electronically, or by mail, in the manner provided by Bankruptcy Rule 7004. No summons is required. Following service of the motion, pursuant to Bankruptcy Rule 7005, movant shall file with the Bankruptcy Clerk a certificate of service, attached to the motion, evidencing the date and mode of service and the names and addresses of the parties served, and where reasonably feasible, a certificate of conference evidencing compliance with Local Bankruptcy Rules 7007–1(a) and 9014–1(d)(1). A certificate of conference will not be required when it is reasonably anticipated that the number of opposing parties may be too numerous to contact prior to the filing of the motion.

(c) Exchanging Exhibits, Lists, and Designating Deposition Excerpts.

(1) *Exchanging Exhibits.* All exhibits that a party intends to offer at the hearing, except those to be offered solely for impeachment, shall be marked with gummed labels or tags that identify them by the party's initials or name, followed by the exhibit number or letter under which they will be offered, and shall be exchanged with opposing parties at least 3 days before the scheduled hearing date. Two bound copies of such exhibits shall be furnished to the Presiding Judge prior to the beginning of the hearing.

(2) *Exchanging Exhibit and Witness Lists.* At least 3 days before the scheduled hearing date, the parties shall file with the Bankruptcy Clerk and deliver to opposing parties, separate lists of exhibits and witnesses, except those to be offered solely for impeachment. One copy of the exhibit and witness list shall be presented to the court reporter at the beginning of the hearing. It is assumed that the debtor(s) will testify.

(3) *Designating Deposition Excerpts.* The parties shall designate, in lists delivered to opposing parties and filed with the Bankruptcy Clerk at least 3 days before the scheduled hearing date, the portions of any depositions to be offered at the hearing.

(d) Certification of Counsel at Evidentiary Hearing. In any evidentiary hearing, all counsel shall certify before the presentation of evidence:

(1) that good faith settlement discussions have been held or why they were not held,

(2) that all exhibits (except for those used solely for impeachment), lists of witnesses, and appraisals (if applicable) have been exchanged at least 3 days in advance of the hearing date. In any conflict between a scheduling order entered in a contested matter and these Local Bankruptcy Rules, the scheduling order controls.

(e) Motions to Lift Stay. Motions to lift the automatic stay pursuant 11 U.S.C. § 362(d) are governed by Local Bankruptcy Rule 4001–1.

(f) Objections to Claims. Objections to claims do not require a written response unless the party filing the objection has used the negative notice procedure set forth in Local Bankruptcy Rule 9007–1.

(g) Expedited Motions. Where a party has obtained a hearing on an expedited motion, the Court may waive the response requirement.

[Effective September 1, 2010. Amended effective April 1, 2012.]

L.B.R. 9019–1. MOTIONS TO COMPROMISE

(a) Filing.

(1) A motion to compromise an adversary proceeding shall be filed in the main bankruptcy case, not in the adversary proceeding. It shall bear the style of the main bankruptcy case, not the adversary proceeding.

(2) A motion to compromise an adversary proceeding shall, within the body of the motion, set out the style and number of the adversary proceeding.

(3) No motion to compromise an adversary proceeding need be filed in order to settle a proceeding filed pursuant to 11 U.S.C. §§ 523 or 524.

(b) Notice.

(1) Motions to compromise adversary proceedings are governed by Local Bankruptcy Rule 9007–1, and may include negative notice language.

(2) Motions to compromise and motions that contemplate a dismissal of an objection to discharge under 11 U.S.C. § 727 shall identify the cause of action and any consideration paid or agreed to be paid and shall be served on all creditors and parties in interest.

(c) Order and Judgment. A motion to compromise an adversary proceeding shall be accompanied by two forms of proposed order. The first form of proposed order shall be one to approve the motion to compromise, bearing the style of the main bankruptcy case. The second form of proposed order shall be a proposed agreed judgment or order of dismissal, bearing the style of the adversary proceeding, for entry in the underlying adversary proceeding.

[Effective September 1, 2010.]

L.B.R. 9019–2. ALTERNATIVE DISPUTE RESOLUTION (ADR)

(a) Referral of a Case or Proceeding to Mediation. The Presiding Judge, either sua sponte or upon the motion of any party or party in interest, may order parties to participate in mediation and may order the parties to bear expenses in such proportion as the Presiding Judge finds appropriate.

(b) Other ADR Methods. Upon motion and agreement of the parties, the Presiding Judge may submit a case or proceeding to binding arbitration, early neutral evaluation or mini-trial.

[Effective September 1, 2010.]

L.B.R. 9027–1. REMOVAL

(a) Filing. A removed claim or cause of action related to a bankruptcy case shall be filed in the bankruptcy court as an adversary proceeding and assigned directly to a bankruptcy judge. The filing shall contain a completed Adversary Proceeding Cover Sheet.

(b) Filing Fee. The adversary proceeding filing fee is due upon the filing of the notice of removal. A fee is not required if the party removing the case is the debtor, or child support creditor. If the party removing the case is the trustee or debtor in possession, a motion to defer filing fee may be filed along with a proposed order.

(c) Attachments. A notice of removal shall include a copy of the docket sheet, and shall be accompanied by a copy of all pleadings from the court from which the claim or cause of action is removed. The plaintiff(s) and defendant(s) shall be identical to the plaintiff(s) and defendant(s) in the court from which the claim or cause of action is removed.

[Effective September 1, 2010.]

L.B.R. 9029–3. LOCAL RULES—DISTRICT COURT

(a) Applicability of District Court Local Civil Rules. Other than the District Court Local Civil Rules adopted specifically in these Local Bankruptcy Rules or adopted in a separate order of the Bankruptcy Court, and District Court Local Civil Rules 8005.1 through 8010.4 regarding bankruptcy appeals, the District Court Local Civil Rules do not apply in the Bankruptcy Court.

(b) Attorney Admission and Conduct. The District Court Local Civil Rules that govern attorney admission, conduct, suspension, and disbarment control in this district and apply in bankruptcy cases and proceedings. They have generally been adopted as stated in Local Bankruptcy Rules 2090–1, through 2091–2; however, certain terms have been modified where appropriate to distinguish where "judge," "court," or "clerk" means either Presiding Judge, Bankruptcy Court or Bankruptcy Clerk; or district judge, District Court or District Clerk.

[Effective September 1, 2010.]

L.B.R. 9036–1. NOTICE BY ELECTRONIC TRANSMISSION

Subject to the administrative procedures approved by the Bankruptcy Court and consistent with technical standards, if any, that the Judicial Conference of the United States establishes, parties are authorized to serve notices under Bankruptcy Rule 9036 through the Bankruptcy Court's transmission facilities.

[Effective September 1, 2010.]

L.B.R. 9070–1. EXHIBITS

(a) Release While Case Pending. Without an order from the Presiding Judge, no exhibit in the custody of the Bankruptcy Clerk may be removed from the Bankruptcy Clerk's Office while the case is pending.

(b) Removal or Destruction After Final Disposition of Case. All exhibits in the custody of the Bankruptcy Clerk shall be removed from the Bankruptcy Clerk's office within 60 days after final disposition of a case. The attorney who introduced the exhibits shall be responsible for their removal. Any exhibit not removed within the 60–day period may be destroyed or otherwise disposed of by the Bankruptcy Clerk.

[Effective September 1, 2010.]

L.B.R. 9076–1. ELECTRONIC SERVICE

Subject to the administrative procedures approved by the Bankruptcy Court and consistent with technical standards, if any, that the Judicial Conference of the United States establishes, parties are authorized to serve pleadings and other papers through the Bankruptcy Court's electronic transmission facilities. However, neither the service of process of a summons and complaint in an adversary proceeding under Bankruptcy Rule 7004, nor the service of a subpoena under Bankruptcy Rule 9016 may be made by electronic transmission.

[Effective September 1, 2010.]

L.B.R. 9077–1. SEALED DOCUMENTS

(a) Permitted or Required by Statute or Rule. A party may file under seal any document that a statute or rule requires or permits to be so filed. The term "document," as used in this rule, means any pleading, motion, other paper, or physical item that the Federal Rules of Bankruptcy Procedure permit or require to be filed.

(b) Motions to File Documents Under Seal. If no statute or rule requires or permits a document to be filed under seal, a party may file a document under seal only on motion and by permission of the Presiding Judge.

(c) Procedure. When a party files a document under seal or a motion for leave to file a document under seal, the party must submit with the motion the original and a judge's copy of the document to be filed under seal, along with an electronic copy of the document on electronic media. The original of the document must be referenced as an exhibit to the motion. If leave to file the document under seal is granted, the Bankruptcy Clerk must file the original of the document under seal.

[Effective September 1, 2010.]

L.B.R. 9077–2. DISPOSITION OF SEALED DOCUMENTS

Unless the Presiding Judge otherwise directs, all sealed documents maintained on paper will be deemed unsealed 60 days after final disposition of a case or proceeding. A party that desires that such a document remain sealed must move for this relief before the expiration of the 60–day period. The Bankruptcy Clerk may store, transfer, or otherwise dispose of unsealed documents according to the procedure that governs publicly available court records.

[Effective September 1, 2010.]

L.B.R. 9078–1. SUBMISSION OF FILES TO THE DISTRICT COURT

After the expiration of the time for filing objections under Bankruptcy Rule 9033, or upon receipt of an order by a district judge withdrawing the reference pursuant to 28 U.S.C. § 157(d) and Bankruptcy Rule 5011, or upon the docketing of an appeal in the district court, the Bankruptcy Clerk shall submit the record of the case, proceeding or appeal to the District Clerk.

[Effective September 1, 2010.]

APPENDICES

APPENDIX A.   ORDER OF REFERENCE OF BANKRUPTCY CASES AND PROCEEDINGS NUNC PRO TUNC

UNITED STATES DISTRICT COURT
NORTHERN DISTRICT OF TEXAS

MISCELLANEOUS RULE NO. 33

Pursuant to Section 104 of the Bankruptcy Amendments and Federal Judgeship Act of 1984, 28 U.S.C. Section 157, it is hereby

ORDERED nunc pro tunc as of June 27, 1984 that any or all cases under Title 11 and any or all proceedings arising under Title 11 or arising in or related to a case under Title 11 which were pending in the Bankruptcy Court of the Northern District of Texas on June 27, 1984, which have been filed in this district since that date and which may be filed herein hereafter (except those cases and proceedings now pending on appeal) be and they hereby are referred to the Bankruptcy Judges of this district for consideration and resolution consistent with law.

It is further ORDERED that the Bankruptcy Judges for the Northern District of Texas be, and they hereby are, directed to exercise the authority and responsibilities conferred upon them as Bankruptcy Judges by the Bankruptcy Amendments and Federal Judgeship Act of 1984 and this court's order of reference, as to all cases and proceedings covered by this order from and after June 27, 1984.

In accordance with 28 U.S.C. Section 157(b)(5), it is further ORDERED that all personal injury tort and wrongful death claims arising in or related to a case under Title 11 pending in this court shall be tried in, or as determined by, this court and shall not be referred by this order.

[Effective August 3, 1984.]

APPENDIX B. FEE APPLICATION COVER SHEET

Interim / Final Fee Application of: _____

Capacity: _____ **Time Period:** _____

Bankruptcy Petition Filed on: _____

Date of Entry of Retention Order: _____ **Status of Case:** _____

Amount Requested:		**Reductions:**	
Fees:	$ _____	Voluntary fee reductions:	$ _____
Expenses:	$ _____	Expense reductions:	$ _____
Other:	$ _____	**Total Reductions:**	$ _____
Total:	$ _____		

Draw Down Request:		**Expense Detail:**	
Retainer Received:	$ _____	Copies—per page cost and total:	$ _____
Previous Draw Down(s):	$ _____	Fax—per page cost and total:	$ _____
Remaining Retainer (now):	$ _____	Computer Research:	$ _____
Requested Draw Down:	$ _____	Other:	$ _____
Retainer Remaining (after):	$ _____	Other:	$ _____

Hourly Rates	**Attorney/Accountant**	**Paralegal/Clerical**
Highest Billed Rate:	$ _____	$ _____
Total Hours Billed:	_____	_____
Blended Rate:	$ _____	$ _____

[Effective September 1, 2010.]

APPENDIX C. FREQUENTLY USED ADDRESSES OF GOVERNMENTAL AGENCIES AND STANDING CHAPTER 12 AND CHAPTER 13 TRUSTEE ADDRESSES

FEDERAL

UNITED STATES TRUSTEE
Office of the United States Trustee
1100 Commerce Street, Room 976
Dallas, TX 75242–1699

INTERNAL REVENUE SERVICE
Internal Revenue Service *(eff. 1/1/2011)*
Special Procedures—Insolvency
P.O. Box 7346 (replaces P.O. Box 21126)
Philadelphia, PA 19101–7346

UNITED STATES ATTORNEY
Office of the United States Attorney
3rd Floor, 1100 Commerce Street
Dallas, Texas 75242–1699

ATTORNEY GENERAL OF THE UNITED STATES
Office of the Attorney General
Main Justice Building, Room 5111
10th & Constitution Avenue, N.W.
Washington, D.C. 20530

DEPARTMENT OF AGRICULTURE
For farm loans, farm programs and Commodity Credit Corporation:
Farm Service Agency, USDA
2405 Texas Ave. South
College Station, Texas 77840

For house loans:
Rural Housing Service, USDA
Centralized Servicing Center
P.O. Box 66879
St. Louis, MO 63166–6879

For apartment loans:
Rural Housing Service, USDA
Rural Development State Office
Attn: Multi–Family Housing Section
101 South Main Street
Temple, Texas 76501

DEPARTMENT OF HOUSING AND URBAN DEVELOPMENT

Dallas and Fort Worth Divisions:
HUD
1600 Throckmorton
Fort Worth, Texas 76113

Lubbock and Amarillo Divisions:
HUD
1205 Texas Avenue
Lubbock, Texas 79401

SMALL BUSINESS ADMINISTRATION
Dallas and Fort Worth Divisions:
Small Business Administration
4300 Amon Carter Blvd. Suite 114
Fort Worth, Texas 76155

Lubbock and Amarillo Divisions:
Small Business Administration
1205 Texas Avenue, Room 408
Lubbock, Texas 79401–2693

DEPARTMENT OF VETERAN'S AFFAIRS
Department of Veteran's Affairs
Regional Office
Finance Section (24)
One Veterans plaza
701 Clay Avenue
Waco, Texas 76799

UNITED STATES POSTAL SERVICE

United States Postal Service
Law Department, Southwest Field
Office
P.O. Box 227078
Dallas, Texas 75222–7078

STATE OF TEXAS

ATTORNEY GENERAL

For notices other than in child support matters:
Texas Attorney General's Office
Bankruptcy—Collections Division
P.O. Box 12548
Austin, Texas 78711–2548

Notices involving child support matters should be sent to the Child Support Division Branch Office handling the individual debtor's case.

COMPTROLLER OF PUBLIC ACCOUNTS

State Comptroller of Public Accounts
Revenue Accounting Division–
Bankruptcy Section
P.O. Box 13528
Austin, Texas 78711

TEXAS WORKFORCE COMMISSION

Texas Workforce Commission
TEC Building—Bankruptcy
101 East 15th Street
Austin, Texas 78778

TEXAS ALCOHOL BEVERAGE COMMISSION

Texas Alcohol Beverage Commission
License and Permits Division
P.O. Box 13127
Austin, Texas 7871–3127

CITY OF DALLAS

Dallas City Secretary's Office
1500 Marilla Street, Suite 5DS
Dallas, TX 75201
citysecretary@dallascityhall.com

[Effective April 15, 1997. Revised July 1, 2002; March 27, 2012.]

APPENDIX D.   DIVISIONAL LISTING OF COUNTIES

The following listing of counties by division is adapted from 28 U.S.C. § 124:

1) The Abilene Division includes the following counties:

Callahan	Howard	Nolan	Stonewall
Eastland	Jones	Shackleford	Taylor
Fisher Mitchell	Stephens	Throckmorton	
Haskell			

2) The Amarillo Division includes the following counties:

Armstrong	Deaf Smith	Hutchinson	Potter
Brisco Donley	Lipscomb	Randall	
Carson Gray	Moore	Roberts	
Castro Hall	Ochiltree	Sherman	
Childress	Hansford	Oldham	Swisher
Collingsworth	Hartley	Parmer	Wheeler
Dallam Hemphill			

3) The Dallas Division includes the following counties:

Dallas Hunt	Kaufman	Rockwall
Ellis Johnson	Navarro	

4) The Fort Worth Division includes the following counties:

Comanche	Hood	Palo Pinto	Tarrant
Erath Jack	Parker	Wise	

5) The Lubbock Division includes the following counties:

Bailey Dickens	Hockley	Motley	
Borden Floyd	Kent	Scurry	
Cochran	Gaines	Lamb	Terry
Crosby Garza	Lubbock	Yoakum	
Dawson	Hale	Lynn	

6) The San Angelo Division includes the following counties:

Brown Crockett	Mills	Sterling	
Coke Glasscock	Reagan	Sutton	
Coleman	Irion	Runnels	Tom Green
Concho Menard	Schleicher		

7) The Wichita Falls Division includes the following counties:

Archer Cottle	King	Wichita
Baylor Foard	Knox	Wilbarger
Clay Hardeman	Montague	Young

[Effective April 15, 1997.]

APPENDIX E. PROCEDURES FOR COMPLEX CHAPTER 11 CASES

The following procedures shall be implemented in complex Chapter 11 cases.

1. "A complex Chapter 11 case" is defined as a case filed in this district under Chapter 11 of the Bankruptcy Code that requires special scheduling and other procedures because of a combination of the following factors:

   a. The size of the case (usually total debt of more than $10 million);

   b. The large number of parties in interest in the case (usually more than 50 parties in interest in the case);

   c. The fact that claims against the debtor and/or equity interests in the debtor are publicly traded (with some creditors possibly being represented by indenture trustees); or

   d. Any other circumstances justifying complex case treatment.

2. "Expedited" means a matter which, for cause shown, should be heard on less than 23 days' notice. "Emergency" means a matter which, for cause shown, should be heard on less than 7 day's notice.

3. If any party filing a Chapter 11 bankruptcy petition believes that the case should be classified as a complex Chapter 11 case, the party shall file with the bankruptcy petition a Notice of Designation as Complex Chapter 11 Case in the form.

4. If a party has "First Day" matters requiring emergency consideration by the court, it should submit a Request for Emergency Consideration of Certain "First Day" Matters.

5. Each judge shall arrange the judge's calendar so that "first day" emergency hearings, as requested in the court-approved form entitled Request for Emergency Consideration of Certain First Day Matters, can be conducted consistent with the Bankruptcy Code and Rules, including Rule 4001, as required by the circumstances, but not more than 2 days after the request for emergency "first day" hearings.

6. When a party has filed a Chapter 11 case and filed a Notice of Designation as Complex Chapter 11 Case, the Clerk of Court shall:

   a. Generally assign the case to a judge in accordance with the usual procedures and general orders of the district or division;

   b. Immediately confer with the court about designating the case as a complex Chapter 11 case and about setting hearings on emergency or first day motions. If the court determines that the case does not qualify as a complex Chapter 11 case, the court shall issue an Order Denying Complex Case Treatment. If the court determines that the case appears to be a complex Chapter 11 case, the court shall issue an Order Granting Complex Chapter 11 Case Treatment; and

   c. Notify and serve counsel for the debtor with the order entered by the court relating to the complex case treatment and notify counsel for the debtor regarding the hearing settings for emergency first day matters.

2.* Counsel for the debtor, upon receipt of notice of entry of an order regarding complex Chapter 11 case treatment, shall,

   a. Serve the order granting or denying complex Chapter 11 case on all parties in interest within 7 days.

   b. Provide notice of the first day emergency hearings in accordance with the Procedures for Obtaining Hearings in Complex Chapter 11 Cases.

3.** Counsel shall follow the Agenda Guidelines for Hearings in Complex Chapter 11 Cases and the Guidelines For Mailing Matrices and Shortened Service Lists.

PROCEDURES FOR OBTAINING HEARINGS IN COMPLEX CHAPTER 11 CASES

I. Hearing on First Day Matters: Official Forms for Request for Expedited Consideration of Certain First Day Matters.

Upon the filing of a complex Chapter 11 case, if the debtor has matters that require expedited consideration ("first day" or "near first day" relief), the debtor should file a "Request for

Expedited Consideration of Certain 'First Day' Matters" using the form of Exhibit B to the Procedures for Complex Chapter 11 Cases ("First Day Hearing Request"). The first day hearing request will be immediately forwarded by the clerk of court to the judge who has been assigned the complex Chapter 11 case (or if there are multiple, related debtor cases, to the judge assigned to the first-filed case). The court will hold a hearing within 2 days of the time requested by the debtor's counsel and the courtroom deputy will notify counsel for the debtor of the time of the setting. If the judge assigned to the complex Chapter 11 case is not available to hold the hearing within 2 days of the time requested by the debtor's counsel, an available judge will hold a hearing within 2 days of the time requested by the debtor's counsel and the courtroom deputy will notify counsel for the debtor of the time of the setting. The debtor's counsel should (1) serve by fax and electronically, if the email address is available, (or by immediate hand–delivery) a copy of the first day hearing request on all affected parties, including the U.S. Trustee, simultaneously with its filing; and (2) notify by fax and electronically, if the email address is available, or telephonically (or by immediate hand delivery) all affected parties of the hearing time on first day matters as soon as possible after debtor's counsel has received confirmation from the court. The court will allow parties in interest to participate telephonically at the hearing on first day matters whenever (and to the extent) practicable, and debtor's counsel will be responsible for the coordination of the telephonic participation.

II. Pre–Set Hearing Dates.

The debtor may request (as one of its first day matters or otherwise) that the court establish in a complex Chapter 11 case a weekly/bi–monthly/monthly setting time ("Pre–Set Hearing Dates") for hearings in the complex Chapter 11 case (e.g., every Wednesday at 1:30 p.m.). The court will accommodate this request for pre-set hearing dates in a complex Chapter 11 case if it appears justified. After pre-set hearing dates are established, all matters in the complex Chapter 11 case (whether initiated by a motion of the debtor or by another party in interest) will be set upon approval by the courtroom deputy on the first pre-set hearing date that is at least 23 days after the filing/service of a particular motion (unless otherwise requested by a party or ordered by the court) and the movant shall indicate the hearing date and time on the face of the pleading.

II.*** Notice of Hearing.

Notice of hearing of matters scheduled for pre-set hearing dates shall be accomplished in the following manner in each district:

Northern District: By the moving party, who shall file a notice of hearing with a certificate of service that proper notice has been accomplished in accordance with these procedures.

Western District: By the moving party, who shall file a certificate that the notice has been accomplished in accordance with these procedures.

Southern District: See Southern District of Texas procedures.

Eastern District: By the moving party, who shall file a certificate that the notice has been accomplished in accordance with these procedures.

IV. Case Emergencies (Other than the First Day Matters).

If a party in interest has an emergency or other situation that it believes requires consideration on less than 23–days' notice, the party should file and serve, a separate, written motion for expedited hearing, in respect of the underlying motion, and may present the motion for an expedited hearing either (a) ex parte at a regular docket call of the presiding judge, or (b) at the next available pre-set hearing date. The court will rule on the motion for expedited hearing within 24 hours of the time it is presented. If the court grants the motion for expedited hearing, the underlying motion will be set by the courtroom deputy at the next available pre-set hearing date or at some other appropriate shortened date approved by the court. Motions for expedited hearings will only be granted under emergency or exigent circumstances.

AGENDA GUIDELINES FOR HEARINGS IN COMPLEX CHAPTER 11 CASES

In complex Chapter 11 cases where five or more matters are noticed for the same hearing date, counsel for the debtor-in-possession, the party requesting the hearings, or trustee shall file and serve an agenda describing the nature of the items set for hearing.

1. **Timing of Filing.** Counsel shall file an agenda at least 24 hours prior to the date and time of the hearing. At the same time, counsel shall also serve the agenda (or confirm electronic service has

been effectuated) upon all attorneys who have filed papers with respect to the matters scheduled and upon the service list.

2. Sequence of Items on Agenda. Uncontested matters should be listed ahead of contested matters. Contested matters should be listed in the order in which they appear on the court's docket.

3. Status Information. For each motion filed in the complex Chapter 11 case, each motion filed in an adversary proceeding concerning the Chapter 11 case, each objection to claim, or application concerning the case, the agenda shall indicate the moving party, the nature of the motion, the docket number of the pleadings, if known, the response deadline, and the status of the matter. The status description should indicate whether the motion is settled, going forward, whether a continuance is requested (and any opposition to the continuance, if known) and any other pertinent information.

4. Information for Motions in the Case. For each motion that is going forward, or where a continuance request is not consensual, the agenda shall also list all pleadings in support of the motion, and any objections or responses. Each pleading listed shall identify the entity that filed the pleading and the docket number of the pleading, if known. If any entity has not filed a responsive pleading, but has engaged in written or oral communications with the debtor, that fact should be indicated on the agenda, as well as the status or outcome of those communications. For an omnibus objection to claims, responses to the objection which have been continued by consent may be listed collectively (e.g., "the following responses have been continued by consent:").

5. Changes in Agenda Information. After the filing of the agenda, counsel shall notify judge's chambers by phone or letter of additional related pleadings that have been filed, and changes in the status of any agenda matter.

6. The requirements listed above should not be construed to prohibit other information of a procedural nature that counsel thinks would be helpful to the court.

ALL MOTIONS AND PLEADINGS SHALL CONTAIN THE HEARING DATE AND TIME BELOW THE CASE/ADVERSARY NUMBER

GUIDELINES FOR MAILING MATRICES AND SHORTENED SERVICE LISTS IN COMPLEX CHAPTER 11 CASES

I. Mailing List or Matrix (a/k/a the Rule 2002 Notice List)

A. Helpful Hints Regarding Whom to Include on the Mailing Matrix in a Complex Chapter 11 Case.

There are certain events and deadlines that occur in a Chapter 11 case which Bankruptcy Rule 2002 requires be broadly noticed to all creditors, indenture trustees, equity interest holders, and other parties in interest ("Rule 2002 notice list"). To facilitate this, Local Bankruptcy Rule 1007–2 requires a debtor to file a mailing list or matrix at the commencement of any case. This list must include all creditors, equity interest holders, and certain other parties in interest (who might be impacted by any relief granted in the bankruptcy case), in order to ensure that parties receive reasonable and adequate notice and are insured due process. When preparing the mailing matrix and after consultation with the clerk of court, debtor's counsel shall evaluate and consider whether the following people are required to be included:

1. Creditors (whether a creditor's claim is disputed, undisputed, contingent, non-contingent, liquidated, unliquidated, matured, unmatured, fixed, legal, equitable, secured or unsecured);

2. Indenture trustees:

3. Financial institutions at which the debtor has maintained accounts (regardless of whether such institutions are creditors);

4. Vendors with whom the debtor has dealt, even if the debtor's records currently indicate no amount is owed;

5. Parties to contracts, executory contracts or leases with the debtor;

6. All federal, state, or local taxing authorities with which the debtor deals, including taxing authorities in every county in which the debtor owns real or personal property with regard to which ad valorem taxes might be owed;

7. All governmental entities with which the debtor might interact (including, but not limited to, the U.S. Trustee and the SEC);

8. Any party who might allege a lien on property of the debtor;

9. Parties to litigation involving the debtor;

10. Parties with which the debtor might be engaged in some sort of dispute, whether or not a claim has formally been made against the debtor;

11. Tort claimants or accident victims;

12. Insurance companies with whom the debtor deals or has policies;

13. Active and retired employees of the debtor;

14. Officers or directors of the debtor;

15. Customers who are owed deposits, refunds, or store credit;

16. Utilities;

17. Shareholders (preferred and common), holders of options, warrants or other rights or equitable interests in the debtor;

18. Miscellaneous others who, in debtor's counsel's judgment, might be entitled to "party in interest" status or who have requested notice.

B. Flexible ("User–Friendly") Format Rules for Mailing Matrix in a Complex Chapter 11 Case in Which Debtor's Counsel Serves Notices.

In a complex Chapter 11 case, where the mailing matrix is likely to be very lengthy, the following special format rules will apply, in lieu of Local Bankruptcy Rule 1007–2, whenever it is the debtor's responsibility to serve notices in the case. The debtor (since it will typically be the party serving all notices in the Chapter 11 case rather than the clerk of court) may create the mailing matrix in whatever format it finds convenient so long as it is neatly typed in upper and lower case letter-quality characters (in no smaller than 10 point and no greater than 14 point type, in either Courier, Times Roman, Helvetica or Orator font) on 8–1/2 × 11 inch blank, unlined, standard white paper. The mailing matrix, if lengthy, should ideally include separate subheadings throughout, to help identify categories of parties in interest. By way of example the following subheadings (among others) might be used:

Debtor and its Professionals

Secured Creditors

Indenture Trustees

Unsecured Creditors

Governmental Entities

Current and Retired Employees

Officers and Directors

Tort Claimants

Parties to Executory Contracts

Equity Interest Holders

Etc.

Parties in interest within each category/subheading should be listed alphabetically. Also, the mailing matrix may be filed in separate volumes, for the separate categories of parties of interest, if the mailing matrix is voluminous (e.g., Volume 2: Unsecured Creditors). Finally, if there are multiple, related debtors and the debtors intend to promptly move for joint administration of their cases, the debtors may file a consolidated mailing matrix, subject to later being required to file separate mailing matrices if joint administration is not permitted.

C. When Inclusion of Certain Parties in Interest on a Mailing Matrix is Burdensome.

If inclusion of certain categories of parties in interest on the mailing matrix would be extremely impracticable, burdensome and costly to the estate, the debtor may file a motion, pursuant to Bankruptcy Rule 2002(1), requesting authority to provide notice by publication in lieu of mailing certain notices to certain categories of parties in interest and may forego including those categories of parties in interest on the mailing matrix in the court grants the motion.

II. Shortened Service List Procedure in a Complex Chapter 11 Case.

   A. Procedures/Contents/Presumptions.

If the court has entered an order granting complex Chapter 11 case treatment, the debtor shall provide service as required by ¶1 of that order. If the court has not entered such an order, the debtor may move to limit notice—that is, for approval of a shortened service list—that will be acceptable for noticing most events in the bankruptcy case, other than those events/deadlines that Bankruptcy Rule 2002 contemplates be served on all creditors and equity interest holders. At a minimum, the shortened list should include the debtor and its professionals, the secured creditors, the 20 largest unsecured creditors, any official committees and the professional for same, the U.S. Trustee, the IRS and other relevant governmental entities, and all parties who have requested notice. Upon the court's approval of a shortened service list in a complex Chapter 11 case, notice in any particular situation during a case shall be presumed adequate if there has been service on (1) the most current service list on file in the case; plus (2) any other party directly affected by the relief requested and not otherwise included on the service list.

B. Obligation to Update, File and Serve Service List

The debtor must update the service list as parties request to be added to it or as circumstances otherwise require. To be added to the list, a party should file a notice of appearance and request for service and serve the notice on debtor's counsel. Parties should include fax or email transmission information if they wish to receive expedited service of process during the case. Additionally, the debtor should file an updated service list and should serve a clean and redlined copy of the updated service list on all parties on the service list weekly for the first month after filing, then bi-monthly for the next 60 days, then monthly thereafter during the pendency of the case. If, in a particular month, there are no changes to the service list, the debtor should simply file a notice with the court so stating.

[Effective September 1, 2010.]

  * [**Publisher's Note:** So in original. Probably should be 7.]

 ** [**Publisher's Note:** So in original. Probably should be 8.]

*** [**Publisher's Note:** So in original. Probably should be III.]

APPENDIX F. GUIDELINES FOR COMPENSATION AND REIMBURSEMENT OF PROFESSIONALS IN CHAPTER 11 CASES

NOTICE

The following are guidelines governing the most significant issues related to applications for compensation and expense reimbursement. The guidelines cover the narrative portion of an application, time records, and expenses. It applies to all professionals with the exception of chapter 7 and chapter 13 trustees, but is not intended to cover every situation. All professionals are required to exercise reasonable billing judgment, notwithstanding total hours spent.

If, in a chapter 11 case, a professional to be employed pursuant to section 327 or 1103 of the Bankruptcy Code desires to have the terms of its compensation approved pursuant to section 328(a) of the Bankruptcy Code at the time of such professional's retention, then the application seeking such approval should so indicate and the Court will consider such request after an evidentiary hearing on notice to be held after the United States trustee has had an opportunity to form a statutory committee of creditors pursuant to section 1102 of the Bankruptcy Code and the debtor and such committee have had an opportunity to review and comment on such application. At a hearing to consider whether a professional's compensation arrangement should be approved pursuant to section 328(a), such professional should be prepared to produce evidence that the terms of compensation for which approval under section 328(a) is sought comply with the certification requirements of section I.G(3) of these guidelines.

I. NARRATIVE

A. Employment and Prior Compensation

The application should disclose the date of the order approving applicant's employment and contain a clear statement itemizing the date of each prior request for compensation, the amount requested, the amount approved, and the amount paid.

B. Case Status

With respect to interim requests, the application should briefly explain the history and the present posture of the case, including a description of the status of pending litigation and the amount of recovery sought for the estate.

In chapter 11 cases, the information furnished should describe the general operations of the debtor; whether the business of the debtor, if any, is being operated at a profit or loss; the debtor's cash flow; whether a plan has been filed, and if not, what the prospects are for reorganization and when it is anticipated that a plan will be filed and a hearing set on the disclosure statement.

In chapter 7 cases, the application should contain a report of the administration of the case including the disposition of property of the estate; when property remains to be disposed of: why the estate is not in a position to be closed; and whether it is feasible to pay an interim dividend to creditors.

In both chapter 7 and chapter 11 cases, the application should state the amount of money on hand in the estate and the estimated amount of other accrued expenses of administration. On applications for interim fees, the applicant should orally supplement the application at the hearing to inform the Court of any changes in the current financial status of the debtor's estate since the filing of the application. All retainers, previous draw downs, and fee applications and orders should be listed specifying the date of the event and the amounts involved and drawn down or allowed.

With respect to final requests, applications should meet the same criteria except where a chapter 7 trustee's final account is being heard at the same time, the financial information in final account need not be repeated.

Fee applications submitted by special counsel seeking compensation from a fund generated directly by their efforts, auctioneers, real estate brokers, or appraisers do not have to comply with the above. For all other application, when more than one application is noticed for the same hearing, they may, to the extent appropriate, incorporate by reference the narrative history furnished in a contemporaneous application.

C. Project Billing

This is required in all cases where the applicant's professional fee is expected to exceed $10,000.00. The narrative should be categorized by subject matter, and separately discuss each professional project or task. All work for which compensation is requested should be in a category. Miscellaneous items may be included in a category such as "Case Administration." The professional may use reasonable discretion in defining projects for this purpose, provided that the application provides meaningful guidance to the Court as to the complexity and difficulty of the task, the professional's efficiency, and the results achieved. With respect to each project or task, the number of hours spent and the amount of compensation and expenses requested should be set forth at the conclusion of the discussion of that project or task. In larger cases with multiple professionals, efforts should be made by the professionals for standard categorization.

D. Billing Summary

Hours and total compensation requested in each application should be aggregated and itemized as to each professional and paraprofessional who provided compensable services. Dates of changes in rates should be itemized as well as reasons for said changes.

E. Paraprofessionals

Fees may be sought for paralegals, professional assistants and law clerks only if identified as such and if the application includes a resume or summary of the paraprofessional's qualifications.

F. Preparation of Application

Reasonable fees for preparation of a fee application and responding to objections thereto may be requested. The aggregate number of hours spent, the amount requested, and the percentage of the total request which the amount represents must be disclosed. If the actual time spent will be reflected and charged in a future fee application, this fact should be stated, but an estimate provided, nevertheless.

G. Certification

Each application for compensation and expense reimbursement must contain a certification by the professional designated by the applicant with the responsibility in the particular case for compliance with these guidelines ("Certifying Professional") that 1) the Certifying Professional has read the application: 2) to the best of the Certifying Professional's knowledge, information and belief, formed after reasonable inquiry, the compensation and expense reimbursement sought is in conformity with these guidelines, except as specifically noted in the application; and 3) the compensation and expense reimbursement requested are billed at rates, in accordance with practices, no less favorable than those customarily employed by the applicant and generally accepted by the applicant's clients.

H. Interim Compensation Arrangements in Complex Cases

In a complex case, the Court may, upon request, consider at the outset of the case approval of an interim compensation mechanism for estate professionals that would enable professionals on a monthly basis to be paid up to 80% of their compensation for services rendered and reimbursed up to 100% of their actual and necessary out of pocket expenses. In connection with such a procedure, if approved in a particular complex case, professionals shall be required to circulate monthly billing statements to the U.S. Trustee and other primary parties in interest, and the Debtor in Possession or Trustee will be authorized to pay the applicable percentage of such bill not disputed or contested by a party in interest.

II. TIME RECORDS

A. Time Records Required

All professionals, except auctioneers, real estate brokers, and appraisers must keep accurate contemporaneous time records.

B. Increments

Professionals are required to keep time records in minimum increments no greater than six minutes. Professionals who utilize a minimum billing increment greater than 1 hour are subject to a substantial reduction of their requests.

C. Descriptions

At a minimum, the time entries should identify the person performing the service, the date(s) performed, what was done, and the subject involved. Mere notations of telephone calls, conferences, research, drafting, etc., without identifying the matter involved, may result in disallowance of the time covered by the entries.

D. Grouping of Tasks

If a number of separate tasks are performed on a single day, the fee application should disclose the time spent for each such task, i.e., no "grouping" or "clumping." Minor administrative matters may be lumped together where the aggregate time attributed thereto is relatively minor. A rule of reason applies as to how specific and detailed the breakdown needs to be. For grouped entries, the applicant must accept the Court inferences therefrom.

E. Conferences

Professionals should be prepared to explain time spent in conferences with other professionals or paraprofessionals in the same firm. Relevant explanation would include complexity of issues involved and the necessity of more individuals' involvement. Failure to justify this time may result in disallowance of all, or a portion of, fees related to such conferences.

F. Multiple Professionals

Professional should be prepared to explain the need for more than one professional or paraprofessional from the same firm at the same court hearing, deposition, or meeting. Failure to justify this time may result in compensation for only the person with the lowest billing rate. The Court acknowledges, however, that in complex chapter 11 cases the need for multiple professionals' involvement will e more common and that in hearings involving multiple or complex issues, a law firm may justifiably be required to utilize multiple attorneys as the circumstances of the case require.

G. Travel Time

Travel time is compensable at one-half rates, but work actually done during travel time is fully compensable.

H. Administrative Tasks

Time spent in addressing, stamping and stuffing envelopes, filing, photocopying or "supervising" any of the foregoing is generally not compensable, whether performed by a professional, paraprofessional, or secretary.

III. EXPENSES

A. Firm Practice

The Court will considered the customary practice of the firm in charging or not charging non-bankruptcy/insolvency clients for particular expense items. Where any other clients, with the exception of pro-bono clients, are not billed for a particular expense, the estate should not be billed. Where expenses are billed to all other clients, reimbursement should be sought at the least expensive rate the firm or professional charges to any client for comparable services or expenses. It is recognized that there will be differences in billing practices among professionals.

B. Actual Cost

This is defined as the amount paid to a third party provider of goods or services without enhancement for handling or other administrative charge.

C. Documentation

This must be retained and made available upon request for all expenditures in excess of $50.00. Where possible, receipts should be obtained for all expenditures.

D. Office Overhead

This is not reimbursable. Overhead includes: secretarial time, secretarial overtime (where clear necessity for same has not been shown), word processing time, charges for after-hour and weekend air conditioning and other utilities, and cost of meals, or transportation provided to professionals and staff who work late or on weekends.

E. Word Processing

This is not reimbursable.

F. Computerized Research

This is reimbursable at actual cost. For large amounts billed to computerized research, significant explanatory detail should be furnished.

G. Paraprofessional Services

These services may be compensated as a paraprofessional under § 330, but not charged or reimbursed as an expense.

H. Professional Services

A professional employed under § 327 may not employ, and charge as an expense, another professional (e.g., special litigation counsel employing an expert witness) unless the employment of the second professional is approved by the Court prior to the rendering of service.

I. Photocopies (Internal)

Charges must be disclosed on an aggregate and per-page basis. If the per-page cost exceeds $.20, the professional must demonstrate to the satisfaction of the Court, with data, that the per-page cost represents a good faith estimate of the actual cost of the copies, based upon the purchase or lease cost of the copy machine and supplies therefor, including the space occupied by the machine, but not including time spent in operating the machine.

J. Photocopies (Outside)

This item is reimbursable at actual cost.

K. Postage

This is reimbursable at actual cost.

L. Overnight Delivery

This is reimbursable at actual cost where it is shown to be necessary. The court acknowledges that in complex chapter 11 cases overnight delivery or messenger services may often be appropriate, particularly when shortened notice of a hearing has been requested.

M. Messenger Service

This is reimbursable at actual cost where it is shown to be necessary. An in-house messenger service is reimbursable, but the estate cannot be charged more than the cost of comparable services available outside the firm.

N. Facsimile Transmissions

The actual cost of telephone charges for outgoing transmissions is reimbursable. Transmissions received are reimbursable on a per-page basis. If the per-page cost exceeds $.20, the professional must demonstrate, with data, to the satisfaction of the Court, that the per-page cost represents a good faith estimate of the actual cost of the copies, based upon the purchase or lease cost of the facsimile machine and supplies therefor, including the space occupied by the machine, but not including time spent in operating the machine.

O. Long Distance Telephone

This is reimbursable at actual cost.

P. Parking

This is reimbursable at actual cost.

Q. Air Transportation

Air travel is expected to be at regular coach fare for all flights.

R. Hotels

Due to wide variation in hotel costs in various cities, it is not possible to establish a single guideline for this type of expense. All persons will be required to exercise reasonable discretion and prudence in connection with hotel expenditures.

S. Meals (Travel)

Reimbursement may be sought for the reasonable cost of breakfast, lunch and dinner while traveling.

T. Meals (Working)

Working meals at restaurants or private clubs are not reimbursable. Reasonable reimbursement may be sought for working meals only where food is catered to the professional's office in the course of a meeting with clients, such as a Creditors' Committee, for the purpose of allowing the meeting to continue through a normal meal period.

U. Amenities

Charges for entertainment, alcoholic beverages, newspapers, dry cleaning, shoe shines, etc. are not reimbursable.

V. Filing Fees

These are reimbursable at actual cost.

W. Court Reporter Fees

These are reimbursable at actual cost.

X. Witness Fees

These are reimbursable at actual cost.

Y. Process Service

This is reimbursable at actual cost.

Z. UCC Searches

These are reimbursable at actual cost.

[Effective September 1, 2010.]

APPENDIX G. GUIDELINES FOR EARLY DISPOSITION OF ASSETS IN CHAPTER 11 CASES, THE SALE OF SUBSTANTIALLY ALL ASSETS UNDER 11 U.S.C. § 363 AND OVERBID AND TOPPING FEES

The following guidelines are promulgated as a result of the increasing use of pre-negotiated or pre-packaged plans and 11 U.S.C. § 363 sales to dispose of substantially all assets of a Chapter 11 debtor shortly after the filing of the petition. The guidelines recognize that parties in interest perceive the need at times to act expeditiously on such matters. In addition, the guidelines are written to provide procedural protection to the parties in interest. The court will consider requests to modify the guidelines to fit the circumstances of a particular case.

OVERBIDS AND TOPPING FEES

1. Topping Fees and Break-up Fees. Any request for the approval of a topping fee or break-up fee provision shall be supported by a statement of the precise conditions under which the topping fee or break-up fee would be payable and the factual basis on which the seller determined the provision was reasonable. The request shall also disclose the identities of other potential purchasers, the offers made by them (if any), and the nature of the offer, including, without limitation, any disclosure of their plans as it relates to retention of debtor's employees.

2. Topping fees, break-up fees, overbid amounts and other buyer protection provisions will be reviewed on a case by case basis and approved if supported by evidence and case law. Case law may not support buyer protection provisions for readily marketable assets.

3. In connection with a request to sell substantially all assets under § 363 within 60 days of the filing of the petition, buyer protections may be considered upon motion, on an expedited basis.

THE SALE OF SUBSTANTIALLY ALL ASSETS UNDER SECTION 363 WITHIN 60 DAYS OF THE FILING OF THE PETITION

1. The Motion to Sell. In connection with any hearing to approve the sale of substantially all assets at any time before 60 days after the filing of the petition, a motion for an order authorizing a sale procedure and hearing or the sale motion itself when regularly noticed, should include factual information on the following points:

   a. Creditors' Committee. If a creditors' committee existed pre-petition, indicate the date and manner in which the committee was formed, as well as the identity of the members of the committee and the companies with which they are affiliated.

   b. Counsel for Committee. If the pre-petition creditors' committee retained counsel, indicate the date counsel was engaged and the selection process, as well as the identify of committee counsel.

   c. Sale Contingencies. Statement of all contingencies to the sale agreement, together with a copy of the agreement.

   d. Creditor Contact List. If no committee has been formed, a list of contact persons, together with fax and phone numbers for each of the largest 20 unsecured creditors.

   e. Administrative Expenses. Assuming the sale is approved, an itemization and an estimate of administrative expenses relating to the sale to be incurred prior to closing and the source of payment for those expenses.

   f. Proceeds of Sale. An estimate of the gross proceeds anticipated from the sale, together with an estimate of the new proceeds coming to the estate with an explanation of the items making up the difference. Itemize all deductions that are to be made from gross sale proceeds and include a brief description of the basis for any such deductions.

   g. Debt Structure of Debtor. A brief description of the debtor's debt structure, including the amount of the debtor's secured debt, priority claims and general unsecured claims.

   h. Need for Quick Sale. An extensive description of why the assets of the estate must be sold on an expedited basis. Include a discussion of alternatives to the sale.

   i. Negotiating Background. A description of the length of time spent in negotiating the sale, and which parties in interest were involved in the negotiation, along with a description of the details of any other offers to purchase, including, without limitation, the potential purchaser's plans in connection with retention of the debtor's employees.

j. Marketing of Assets. A description of the manner in which the assets were marketed for sale, including the period of time involved and the results achieved.

k. Decision to Sell. The date on which the debtor accepted the offer to purchase the assets.

l. Relationship of Buyer. A statement identifying the buyer and setting forth all of the buyer's (including its officers, directors and shareholders) connections with the debtor, creditors, any other party in interest, their respective attorneys, accountants, the U.S. Trustee or any person employed in the office of the U.S. Trustee.

m. Post Sale Relationship with Debtor. A statement setting forth any relationship or connection the debtor (including its officers, directors, shareholders and employees) will have with the buyer after the consummation of the sale, assuming it is approved.

n. Relationship with Secured Creditors. If the sale involves the payment of all or a portion of secured debt(s), a statement of all connections between debtor's officers, directors, employees or other insiders and each secured creditor involved (for example, release of insider's guaranty).

o. Insider Compensation. Disclosure of current compensation received by officers, directors, key employees or other insiders pending approval of the sale.

p. Notice Timing. Notice of the hearing on the motion to approve the motion to sell will be provided as is necessary under the circumstances.

2. Proposed Order Approving Sale. A proposed order approving the sale must be included with the motion or the notice of hearing. A proposed final order and redlined version of the order approving the sale should be provided to chambers twenty-four hours prior to the hearing.

3. Good Faith Finding. There must be an evidentiary basis for a finding of good faith under 11 U.S.C. § 363(m).

4. Competing Bids. Unless the court orders otherwise, competing bids may be presented at the time of the hearing. The motion to sell and the notice of hearing should so provide.

5. Financial Ability to Close. Unless the court orders otherwise, any bidder must be prepared to demonstrate to the satisfaction of the court, through an evidentiary hearing, its ability to consummate the transaction if it is the successful bidder, along with evidence regarding any financial contingencies to closing the transaction.

6. Hearing and Notice Regarding Sale. Unless the court orders otherwise, all sales governed by these guidelines, including auctions or the presentation of competing bids, will occur at the hearing before the court. The court may, for cause, including the need to maximize and preserve asset value, expedite a hearing on a motion to sell substantially all assets under § 363.

[Effective September 1, 2010.]

APPENDIX H. CHECKLIST FORM AND COMMENTS FOR MOTIONS AND ORDERS PERTAINING TO THE USE OF CASH COLLATERAL AND POST–PETITION FINANCING

IN THE UNITED STATES BANKRUPTCY COURT
FOR THE NORTHERN DISTRICT OF TEXAS
_____ DIVISION

IN RE: §

                                     §
_____   §   CASE NO. _____
         DEBTOR.   §
                                     §   HEARING: _____
                                     §

ATTORNEY CHECKLIST CONCERNING MOTIONS AND ORDERS
PERTAINING TO USE OF CASH COLLATERAL AND
POST–PETITION FINANCING
(WHICH ARE IN EXCESS OF TEN (10) PAGES)

Motions and orders pertaining to cash collateral and post-petition financing matters tend to be lengthy and complicated. Although the Court intends to read such motions and orders carefully, it will assist the Court if counsel will complete this checklist. All references are to the Bankruptcy Code (§) or Rules (R). PLEASE NOTE:

* Means generally <u>not</u> favored by Bankruptcy Courts in this District.

** Means generally <u>not</u> favored by Bankruptcy Courts in this District without a reason and a time period for objections.

If your motion or order makes provision for any of the following, so indicate in the space provided:

CERTIFICATE BY COUNSEL

This is to certify that the following checklist fully responds to the Court's inquiry concerning material terms of the motion and/or proposed order:

Yes, at Page/Exhibit
Y means yes; N means no
N/A means not applicable
(Page Listing Optional)

1. Identification of Proceeding:

    (a) Preliminary or final motion/order (circle one) .... _____
    (b) Continuing use of cash collateral (§ 363) .... _____
    (c) New financing (§ 364) .... _____
    (d) Combination of §§ 363 and 364 financing .... _____
    (e) Emergency hearing (immediate and irreparable harm) .... _____

2. Stipulations:

    (a) Brief history of debtor's businesses and status of debtor's prior relationships with lender .... _____
    (b) Brief statement of purpose and necessity of financing .... _____
    (c) Brief statement of type of financing (i.e.) accounts receivable, inventory)... _____

**   (d)   Are lender's pre-petition security interest(s) and liens deemed valid, fully perfected and non–avoidable? .... _____

         (i)   Are there provisions to allow for objections to above? .... _____

    (e)   Is there a post-petition financing agreement between lender and debtor? .... _____

         (i)   If so, is agreement attached? .... _____

**   (f)   If there is an agreement, are lender's post-petition security interests and liens deemed valid, fully perfected and non–avoidable? .... _____

    (g)   Is lender under secured or oversecured? (circle one) .... _____

    (h)   Has lender's non-cash collateral been appraised? .... _____

         Insert date of latest appraisal .... _____

    (i)   Is debtor's proposed budget attached? .... _____

    (j)   Are all pre-petition loan documents identified? .... _____

    (k)   Are pre-petition liens on single or multiple assets? (circle one) .... _____

    (l)   Are there pre-petition guaranties of debt? .... _____

         (i)   Limited or unlimited (circle one) .... _____

3.   Grant of Liens.

*   (a)   Do post-petition liens secure pre-petition debts? .... _____

*   (b)   Is there cross-collaterization? .... _____

**   (c)   Is the priority of post-petition liens equal to or higher than existing liens? .... _____

**   (d)   Do post-petition liens have retroactive effect? .... _____

    (e)   Are there restrictions on granting further liens or liens of equal or higher priority? .... _____

*   (f)   Is lender given liens on claims under §§ 506(c), 544–50 and §§ 522? .. _____

**   (i)   Are lender's attorneys fees to be paid? .... _____

*   (ii)   Are debtor's attorneys fees excepted from § 506(c)? .... _____

*   (g)   Is lender given liens upon proceeds of causes of action under §§ 544, 547, and 548? .... _____

4.   Administrative Priority Claims:

    (a)   Is lender given an administrative priority? .... _____

    (b)   Is administrative priority higher than § 507(a)? .... _____

    (c)   Is there a conversion of pre-petition secured claim to post-petition administrative claim by virtue of use of existing collateral? .... _____

5.   Adequate Protection (§ 361):

    (a)   Is there post-petition debt service? .... _____

    (b)   Is there a replacement/additional 361(1) lien? (circle one or both). .... _____

**   (c)   Is the lender's claim given super–priority? .... _____
        (§ 364(c) or (d)) [designate] .... _____

    (d)   Are there guaranties? .... _____

    (e)   Is there adequate insurance coverage? .... _____

    (f)   Other? _____ _____

6. Waiver/Release Claims v. Lender

** (a) Debtor waives or releases claims against lender, including, but not
        limited to, claims under §§ 506(c), 544–550, 552, and 553 of
        the Code? . . . . _____
** (b) Does the debtor waive defenses to claim or liens of lender? . . . . _____

7. Source of Post–Petition Financing (§ 364 Financing):

    (a) Is the proposed lender also the pre-petition lender? . . . . _____
    (b) New post-petition lender? . . . . _____
    (c) Is the lender an insider? . . . . _____

8. Modification of Stay:

** (a) Is any modified lift of stay allowed? . . . . _____
** (b) Will the automatic stay be lifted to permit lender to exercise self-help
        upon default without further order? . . . . _____
    (c) Are there any other remedies exercisable without further order of
        court? . . . . _____
    (d) Is there a provision that any future modification of order shall not
        affect status of debtor's post-petition obligations to lender? . . . . _____

9. Creditors' Committee:

    (a) Has creditors' committee been appointed? . . . . _____
    (b) Does creditors' committee approve of proposed financing? . . . . _____

10. Restrictions on Parties in Interest

** (a) Is a plan proponent restricted in any manner, concerning modification
        of lender's rights, liens and/or causes? . . . . _____
** (b) Is the debtor prohibited from seeking to enjoin the lender in pursuit
        of rights? . . . . _____
** (c) Is any party in interest prohibited from seeking to modify this
        order? . . . . _____
    (d) Is the entry of any order conditioned upon payment of debt to
        lender? . . . . _____
    (e) Is the order binding on subsequent trustee on conversion? . . . . _____

11. Nunc Pro Tunc.

** (a) Does any provision have retroactive effect? . . . . _____

12. Notice and Other Procedures.

    (a) Is shortened notice requested? . . . . _____
    (b) Is notice requested to shortened list? . . . . _____
    (c) Is time to respond to be shortened? . . . . _____
    (d) If final order sought, have 15 days elapsed since service of motion
        pursuant to Rule 4001(b)(2)? . . . . _____
    (e) If preliminary order sought, is cash collateral necessary to avoid
        immediate and irreparable harm to the estate pending a final
        hearing? . . . . _____
    (f) Is a Certificate of Conference included? . . . . _____
    (g) Is a Certificate of Service included? . . . . _____
    (h) Is there verification of transmittal to U.S. Trustee included pursuant
        to Rule 9034? . . . . _____
    (i) Has an agreement been reached subsequent to filing motion? . . . . _____

        (i) If so, has notice of the agreement been served pursuant to Rule
            4001(d)(1)? . . . . _____

    (ii) Is the agreement in settlement of motion pursuant to Rule 4001(d)(4)? .... _____

    (iii) Does the motion afford reasonable notice of material provisions of agreement pursuant to Rule 4001(d)(4)? .... _____

    (iv) Does the motion provide for opportunity for hearing pursuant to Rule 9014? .... _____

SIGNED this the _____ day of _____, 20 ___.

[Firm Name]

By: _____

        [Attorney's Name]
        [Texas Bar No.]

        [Address]
        [Telephone Number]
        [Email Address]
        [Identification of role in case]

COMMENTS TO CASH COLLATERAL AND DIP FINANCING CHECKLIST

1. Interim vs. Final Orders

  a. Stipulations in preliminary or interim orders should be minimized. Notice is generally not adequate to test the validity of stipulations, and they should be avoided to the extent not absolutely necessary to the interim approval process.

  b. Simply state the nature of notice given; do not recite notice was "sufficient and adequate" since that is usually not the case particularly on the first day. The order should simply note that the financing is being approved pursuant to Bankruptcy Rule 4001(c)(2) authorizing such financing to avoid immediate and irreparable harm.

  c. Adequate protection for the use of pre-petition cash collateral may be granted to the extent of a diminution of collateral. The court will not approve on an interim basis language that adequate protection is granted in the form of replacement liens on post-petition assets based on stipulations that use of cash collateral shall be deemed a dollar for dollar decrease in the value of the pre-petition collateral." At the final hearing, the court will consider evidence to determine the extent to which the lender's pre-petition collateral has or is likely to diminish in value. That evidence will inform the extent to which adequate protection will be granted.

  d. The court expects that other parties in interest will be involved in the process of developing an interim cash collateral order to the extent practicable. If the court finds that the debtor and lender have not made reasonable efforts to afford the best notice possible, preliminary relief will not be granted until parties in interest have had a reasonable opportunity to review and comment on any proposed interim order.

  e. Bankruptcy Rule 4001(b) and (c) limit the extent to which the court may grant relief on less than 15 days' notice. The debtor and the lender must negotiate interim orders within the confines of that authority. Interim orders shall be expressly without prejudice to the rights of parties in interest at a final hearing.

2. Stipulations

  a. The lender may request a stipulation as to the amount, validity, priority and extent of the pre-petition documents. The stipulation will only be approved if the order provides the stipulation is binding on other parties in interest only after the passage of an appropriate period of time (customarily 90 days) during which the parties in interest will have the opportunity to test the validity of the lien and the allowance of the claim.

3. Grant of Liens

  a. Liens granted in the cash collateral and DIP financing orders may not secure pre-petition debts. Financing orders should not be used to elevate a pre-petition lender's collateral inadequacy to a fully secured status.

b. Avoidance actions are frequently one of the few sources of recovery for creditors other than secured lenders. Orders granting liens on these unencumbered assets for the benefit of the lender will require a showing of extraordinary circumstances. In most cases the adequate protection grant will protect the lender since the lender will have a super priority under § 507(b) that will give the lender who suffers a failure of adequate protection a first right to payment out of the proceeds from such actions before payment of any other expenses of the Chapter 11 case. Avoidance actions in the event of a conversion to Chapter 7 may be the only assets available to fund the trustee's discharge of his or her statutory duties.

c. Similarly, limitations on the surcharge of the lender's collateral under § 506(c) are disfavored. The secured creditor may be the principal beneficiary of the proceedings in Chapter 11. Since the burden to surcharge requires a showing of direct benefit to the lender's collateral, lenders are not unreasonably exposed to surcharges of their collateral. And in light of the decision in Hartford Underwriter's Insurance Co. v. Union Planters Bank N.A. (In re Hen House Interstate Inc.), 530 U.S. 1, 120 S.Ct. 1942 (2000), only the DIP or the trustee may recover under § 506(c).

4. Modification of Stay

a. Authority for unilateral action by lender without necessity to return to court to establish post-petition default or breach or at least a notice to parties in interest will not be approved. If the cash collateral or financing order provides for a termination of the automatic stay in the event of a default, parties in interest must have an opportunity to be heard before the stay lifts.

5. Restrictions on Plan Process

a. The court will not approve cash collateral orders (or post-petition financing orders that are in substance cash collateral orders that have the effect of converting all the pre-petition liens and claims to post-petition liabilities under the guise of collecting pre-petition accounts and re-advancing them post–petition) that have the effect of converting pre-petition secured debt into post-petition administrative claims that must be paid in full in order to confirm a plan. That type of provision unfairly limits the ability and flexibility of the debtor and other parties in interest to formulate a plan. That type of provision, granted at the outset of a case, effectively compels the debtor to pay off the secured lender in full on the effective date and has the consequence of eviscerating § 1129(b).

b. On the other hand, persons who are advancing new money to the debtor post-petition may include in financing orders provisions that the post-petition loans have a § 364(c)(1) super-super priority.

6. Loan Agreements

a. If there will be a loan agreement, the language of the financing order does not need to restate all of the terms of the loan agreement. The financing motion should, however, summarize the essential elements of the proposed borrowing or use of cash collateral, such as, amount of loan facility, sublimits on availability, borrowing base formula, conditions to new advances, interest rate, maturity, events of default, limitation on use of funds and description of collateral.

7. Professional Fees

a. To the extent consistent with the market for similar financings, the lender may request reimbursement of reasonable professional fees. The lender should provide reasonably detailed invoices to the debtor and the committees so a proper assessment of reasonableness can be made.

b. The parties may agree on carve-outs for estate professionals. Lenders may exclude from the carve-out payment of professional fees for litigation of the extent, validity or perfection of the lender's claim as well as prosecution of lender liability suits. The carve-out should not, however, exclude the due diligence work by the committee or its professionals to determine whether a challenge to the lender is justified.

8. Work Fees/Loan Fees

a. Underwriting a substantial DIP loan may involve both direct out-of-pocket expenses and, at times, a certain lost opportunity cost. The debtor may move for the reimbursement of its lender's direct out-of-pocket expenses. The debtor and lender must be prepared to establish actual out-of-pocket costs, the reasonableness of the costs, and that the type of costs are actually paid in the market. On a case-by-case basis, the court will consider on an expedited basis the debtor's request to pay a reasonable up-front fee to a prospective DIP lender to reimburse it for direct out-of-pocket costs. In addition, in connection with approving a DIP loan facility, on motion of the debtor, the court will consider evidence of market rates and pricing for comparable loans in determining whether commitment fees, facility or availability fees, and other up-front or periodic loan charges are appropriate. The lender must provide evidence that it actually has provided or will provide the services customarily associated with these fees.

[Effective September 1, 2010.]

ECF PROCEDURES
NOTICE: MANDATORY ELECTRONIC FILING

Effective October 1, 2003, the court will no longer accept paper documents for filing. All documents submitted to the court must be submitted electronically through the court's electronic filing system (CM/ECF). Filers who have not yet received their ECF login should sign up for the appropriate training to become an electronic filing user. Until you receive your login, you must submit all documents on a 3.5–inch diskette or CD–ROM pursuant to General Order 2003–04. See attached exhibit for additional instructions.

EXHIBIT

1. Documents, orders, and claims not filed electronically must be submitted on a 3.5–inch diskette or CD–ROM in PDF format, except for matrices (in text format) and orders (in word processing format).

2. Diskettes will be submitted with a label that contains the case number, case name, document description(s), and related document number, if any. One diskette may contain multiple documents for the same case. Each case will require a separate diskette.

3. Documents should be saved on diskette or CD–ROM using the following file-naming format:

A. For new bankruptcy cases or related documents where no case number has been assigned (such as petition, schedules, plan, APD, etc.), the filename should contain the debtor(s) name and description of the document being filed. For example:

john_doe_petition.pdf
john_doe_mat rix.txt
john_doe_schedules.pdf
john_do e_plan.pdf

B. For existing case filings (where a case number has been assigned), the filename should contain the case number along with a description of the document being filed. For example:

02_39456_motion.pdf
02_39456_order .wpd
02_39456_response.pdf

C. For new adversary filings, the filename should contain the plaintiff's name and a description of the document. For example:

sam_jones_complaint.pdf

D. If the cover sheet is not included with the complaint, then the adversary cover sheet should be named. For example:

sam_jones_adv_cover.pdf

E. For answer(s) to the complaint or related documents in an existing adversary proceeding, the filename should contain the adversary case number and a description of the document. For example:

03_3001_answer.pdf

4. If the filer would like to receive a file-stamped copy of the document being filed, a paper copy of the document(s) should be submitted along with the diskette.

5. For chapter 11 cases and adversary proceeding documents, a judicial courtesy copy should be submitted to the clerk's office.

6. Motions that require a hearing should be filed with a separate notice of hearing and certificate of service to ensure the hearing will be set on the court's calendar.

7. Orders should be submitted in the specified format outlined in the Administrative Procedures, which are available on the web site at www.txnb.uscourts.gov.

8. For motions with negative notice language, the order should be submitted after the objection deadline has expired if no objections were filed.

9. For motions that may be considered by the court without a hearing (without negative notice language), the order should be submitted with the motion. These documents may be submitted on the same diskette or CD–ROM provided the motion is in PDF format and the order is in word processing format.

10. For motions that require a hearing, the order should be submitted after the court's ruling.

11. For motions that have agreed orders, the order should be submitted timely after the agreement is reached.

[Effective October 1, 2003.]

GENERAL ORDER 2004–06. REGARDING ADMINISTRATIVE PROCEDURES FOR ELECTRONIC FILING

By General Order Nos. 2003–01.2 and 2003–01, the court adopted Administrative Procedures for Electronic Case Filing. The court provided that the procedures may be amended from time to time by order of the court. In coordination with the United States Bankruptcy Courts for the Southern, Eastern and Western Districts of Texas, the court has determined to issue revised procedures. Accordingly,

IT IS ORDERED that the court adopts the attached Administrative Procedures for the Filing, Signing and Verifying of Documents by Electronic Means in Texas Bankruptcy Courts, effective December 1, 2004.

IT IS FURTHER ORDERED that the Administrative Procedures for the Filing, Signing and Verifying of Documents by Electronic Means in Texas Bankruptcy Courts supercede the procedures adopted by General Order No. 2003–01.2.

IT IS FURTHER ORDERED that the Administrative Procedures for the Filing, Signing and Verifying of Documents by Electronic Means in Texas Bankruptcy Courts may be amended from time to time by order of the court.

The court has authorized the Chief Bankruptcy Judge of the district to enter this order on behalf of the court.

[Effective November 30, 2004.]

ADMINISTRATIVE PROCEDURES FOR THE FILING, SIGNING, AND VERIFYING OF DOCUMENTS BY ELECTRONIC MEANS IN TEXAS BANKRUPTCY COURTS

I. THE ELECTRONIC CASE FILING SYSTEM

A. Statewide ECF Administrative Procedures. The United States Bankruptcy Courts for the Northern, Southern, Eastern, and Western Districts of Texas (collectively, the "Texas Bankruptcy Courts") have each authorized the filing, signing and verification of documents by electronic means. The precise scope of documents authorized or required to be filed in an electronic format varies by district.[1] The purpose of this Appendix is to provide attorneys and other parties who seek to file documents by electronic means a convenient means by which to ascertain the appropriate electronic filing procedures for a particular Texas Bankruptcy Court (hereafter referenced as the "Authorizing Court").

B. Participation in the Electronic Filing Program.

1. *Registration Requirement.* An approved participant (an "Electronic Filer"), including any attorney admitted to practice before the Authorizing Court, must register for an authorization through which such person can accomplish the electronic filing of documents with such Authorizing Court.[2]

2. *Authorization.* An approved participant (an "Electronic Filer") will be assigned a login and password combination with which to access the Electronic Filing System (the "System") for a particular Authorizing Court.

C. Electronic Filing by Creditors and Agents for Creditors. A creditor or an agent for a creditor (including an attorney-agent not admitted to practice before the Authorizing Court) may also become an Electronic Filer for the purpose of filing by electronic means proofs of claim and a limited range of claim-related documents with the Authorizing Court. Each Authorizing Court shall determine the precise scope of documents which may be filed through a creditor authorization. Any creditor who routinely files claims and other documents in any Authorizing Court may be required to become an Electronic Filer.

D. Electronic Filing by Other Persons. Documents to be filed by any person who is not an Electronic Filer may be filed by electronic means at any office of the Clerk of the Authorizing Court. Each Authorizing Court shall determine the precise methodologies and procedures to accomplish such filings.

II. REGISTRATION AND TRAINING

A. Registration.

1. *Registration Forms.* Registration forms are available from the Clerk of each Authorizing Court for which electronic filing registration is sought or through the Authorizing Court's website:

Northern District:	**www.txnb.uscourts.gov**
Southern District:	**www.txs.uscourts.gov**
Eastern District:	**www.txeb.uscourts.gov**
Western District:	**www.txwb.uscourts.gov**

The completed application must be returned to the applicable Clerk as follows:

Northern District: Clerk, United States Bankruptcy Court
Attn: Electronic Filing Registration
1100 Commerce Street, Suite 1254
Dallas, TX 75242.
Phone: (214) 753–2600

Southern District: Electronic Registration
United States District Court
515 Rusk Avenue
P.O. Box 61010
Houston, TX 77208–1010
Phone: (866) 358–6201

Eastern District: ECF HelpDesk
United States Bankruptcy Court
Plaza Tower
110 N. College, Ninth Floor
Tyler, TX 75702.
Phone: (903) 590–3233

Western District: ECF HelpDesk
United States Bankruptcy Court
615 E. Houston St.
San Antonio, TX
Phone: (210) 472–6720 ext. 5170

[or if mailed]:   P.O. Box 1439
San Antonio, TX 78295–1439

A separate registration form must be submitted for each attorney within a particular law firm.

2. *Login/Password Assignments.* An approved participant (an "Electronic Filer") will be assigned a login and password combination with which to access the Electronic Filing System (the "System") for a particular Authorizing Court. Additional login/password combinations may be authorized by the Clerk of the Authorizing Court. Only the Electronic Filer, or an authorized representative, may receive the electronic notice of the assigned login and password combination(s).

Unless the Clerk of the Authorizing Court grants a request for delivery of the login/password assignment by first class mail or through some other approved means, the Electronic Filer shall receive notice of such assignments by electronic mail. Each Authorizing Court reserves the right to revoke or to change any assigned login and/or password from time to time as may become necessary.

3. *System Access.* The assignment of a login and password combination will initially be utilized for training purposes only and such combination will not be activated for use on the "live" System until such time as the Electronic Filer has successfully completed all training requirements imposed by the Authorizing Court and has received full authorization from that Court to utilize its System.

4. *Consent to Electronic Notice from Court.* By accepting a login and password from the Authorizing Court, an Electronic Filer consents, in lieu of any right to receive notice by first class mail, including notice issued pursuant to Fed. R. Bankr. P. 2002(a) and 9022, to the receipt of notice by electronic means from the Authorizing Court or from the Bankruptcy Noticing Center.

5. *Consent to Electronic Notice from Parties.* By accepting a login and password from the Authorizing Court, an Electronic Filer consents, in lieu of any right to service of any document by personal service or by first class mail from interested parties, to accept service from such parties by electronic means through the transmission facilities of the Authorizing Court, excepting the service of process of a summons and complaint in an adversary proceeding under Fed. R. Bank. P. 7004, or the service of a subpoena under Fed. R. Bankr. P. 9016.

6. *Password Security.* An Electronic Filer may find it desirable to change his/her password periodically. This may be accomplished through procedures set forth in the User's Manual available on the website of the Authorizing Court. In the event that an Electronic Filer believes that the security of an existing password has been compromised, the Electronic Filer shall give immediate notice to the Clerk of the Authorizing Court in order to prevent access to the System by the use of that password. Such notice may be given in the manner set forth in the User's Manual issued by the Authorizing Court.

7. *Change of Address.* In the event of a change in any registration information (e.g., mailing address, e-mail address, etc.), an Electronic Filer assumes sole responsibility for updating such registration information with the Authorizing Court through the Utilities section of the System.

B. Training.

1. *Prerequisite to Live Access.* An Electronic Filer must demonstrate the ability to docket pleadings satisfactorily to the Authorizing Court's training system as a prerequisite to obtaining access to such Court's "live" System.

2. *Training Sessions.* To assist prospective Electronic Filers in fulfilling the above prerequisite, each Authorizing Court shall conduct classroom training sessions as needed to train prospective Electronic Filers and shall reserve the right to organize such training sessions according to party-type (e.g., trustees, debtor attorneys, creditor attorneys, etc.). Staff members associated with prospective Electronic Filers, such as paralegals and legal assistants, are strongly encouraged to attend these sessions.

3. *Reciprocity.* Attorneys who are admitted to practice before an Authorizing Court and who have been authorized to file documents by electronic means in another federal district may become an Electronic Filer in the Authorizing Court upon a demonstration of the ability to docket pleadings successfully to that Court's training system. Such reciprocity requests should be presented to the Clerk of the Authorizing Court who shall exercise sole discretion as to whether such reciprocity request should be granted or whether additional training requirements should be imposed.

4. *Telephonic Training.* Certain Electronic Filers who require only limited access to electronic document filing, such as for proofs of claim only, may not be required to attend classroom training, but instead may receive training assistance by telephone. However, each Authorizing Court reserves the right to require classroom training for any prospective Electronic Filer and those trained via telephone shall still be required to demonstrate the ability to docket pleadings satisfactorily to the Court's training system prior to gaining access to the "live" system of the Authorizing Court.

III. ELECTRONIC FILING AND SERVICE OF DOCUMENTS

A. Filing.

1. *Scope.* Except as stated otherwise below, any petition, complaint, motion, answer, objection, comment, response, memorandum of law, proof of claim, or other document in connection with a case

may be filed by electronic means. Such document must be in a portable document format ("PDF") at the time of submission to the System.

2. *Methodology.* Any such document, together with any pleading attachments thereto, shall be electronically filed under one docket entry and the Electronic Filer will be responsible for designating an appropriate title for the document by utilizing one of the docket event categories authorized by the System.

3. *Certificate of Service.* Any required certificate of service shall be included in the main document.

   [Exception (Southern District): Certificates of service may also be filed separately.]

4. *Proposed Orders Due Upon Filing.* See Section IV of this Appendix for specific instructions for the submission of proposed orders in each particular district.

5. *Pleading Attachments.* See Section III(C) of this Appendix for specific instructions regarding the filing of any document in conjunction with any pleading or proof of claim.

6. *PDF File Limitations.* No single PDF file, whether containing a document or an attachment, may exceed forty (40) pages in length. Documents and/or attachments in excess of forty pages must be divided into multiple PDF files and accurately described to the Authorizing Court. If a document, together with any attachments thereto, exceeds one hundred (100) pages in length, please call the Clerk of the Authorizing Court for guidance prior to filing such document by electronic means.

7. *Motion for Leave.* A motion for leave of court to file a document must be filed by electronic means. The document for which such leave is sought shall be submitted for review as a pleading attachment to the main document. Upon receipt of an order granting leave, an Electronic Filer shall file the authorized document by electronic means.

8. *Motion to File Document Under Seal.* A motion to file a document under seal shall be filed electronically *without* attachment of the subject document(s) for which protection is sought. The Authorizing Court may require the submission of paper copies of the subject document(s) in a sealed envelope prior to the issuance of any ruling on the motion. Upon the granting of the motion, and only if paper copies of the protected subject document(s) have not previously been provided, the Electronic Filer shall file paper copies of the protected document(s) in a sealed envelope, with a copy of the order authorizing the filing of the documents under seal affixed to such envelope.

9. *Adversary Complaint and Summons.* A complaint, with a proposed summons as an attachment, must be filed electronically with the Court. Because service of the summons by electronic means is currently precluded under the Federal Rules of Civil Procedure, the Court will print the proposed summons, affix the appropriate signature and seal upon it, and issue the executed original to the filing party by mail.

   [Exception (Southern District): The filing party must deliver the summons form in paper format to the Clerk's office for execution.]

10. *Emergency and Expedited Hearing Requests.* Upon the filing of documents which require the immediate attention of the Authorizing Court, such as requests for emergency or expedited hearings, an Electronic Filer shall immediately notify the applicable Courtroom Deputy or Case Manager by telephone or by e-mail. Telephone and e-mail information for each of the Texas Bankruptcy Courts are as follows:

   (a) Northern District:

Hon. Steven Felsenthal:	Traci Davis, Courtroom Deputy Phone: (214) 753–2046 Email: **saf_settings@txnb.uscourts.gov**
Hon. Harlin Hale:	Flo Coleman, Courtroom Deputy Phone: (214) 753–2060 Email: **hdh_settings@txnb.uscourts.gov**
Hon. Barbara Houser:	Viola Salcido, Courtroom Deputy Phone: (214) 753–2059 Email: **bjh_settings@txnb.uscourts.gov**
Hon. Robert Jones:	Julie Combs, Courtroom Deputy Phone: (806) 472–5006

Email: **rlj_settings@txnb.uscourts.gov**

Hon. Michael Lynn:

Sandy Chonody, Courtroom Deputy
Phone: (817) 333–6016
Email: **dml_settings@txnb.uscourts.gov**

Hon. Russell Nelms

Jana McCrory, Courtroom Deputy
Phone: (817) 333–6036
Email: **rfn_settings@txnb.uscourts.gov**

(b) Southern District:

Hon. Jeff Bohm:

Robin Stennis, Case Manager
Phone: (713) 250–5405
Email: **cmA420@www.txs.uscourts.gov**

Hon. Karen Brown:

Maureen Bryan, Case Manager
Phone: (713) 250–5445
Email: **cmA487@www.txs.uscourts.gov**

Hon. Letitia Clark:

Maria Rodriguez, Case Manager
Phone: (713) 250–5410 **(preferred)**
Email: **cmA330@www.txs.uscourts.gov**

Hon. Marvin Isgur:

Anita Ainsworth, Case Manager
Phone: (713) 250–5421
Email: **cmA671@www.txs.uscourts.gov**

Hon. Richard Schmidt:

Letitia Garza, Case Manager
Phone: (361) 888–3452 **(preferred)**
Email: **cmA417@www.txs.uscourts.gov**

Hon. Wesley Steen:

Jean Kell, Case Manager
Phone: (713) 250–5779 **(preferred)**
Email: **cmA580@www.txs.uscourts.gov**

(c) Eastern District:

Hon. Bill Parker:
(Tyler & Marshall Divisions)

Chasha Traylor, Courtroom Deputy
Phone: (903) 590–3237
Email: **Chasha_Traylor@txeb.uscourts.gov**

Hon. Bill Parker:
(Beaumont & Lufkin Divisions)

Debra Theriot, Courtroom Deputy
Phone: (409) 839–2617, ext. 225
Email: **Debra_Theriot@txeb.uscourts.gov**

Hon. Brenda Rhoades:

Shirley Rasco, Courtroom Deputy
Phone: (972) 509–1240, ext. 226
Email: **Shirley_Rasco@txeb.uscourts.gov**.

(d) Western District:

Hon. Tony M. Davis:

Jennifer Lopez, Courtroom Deputy Phone:
(512) 916–5237, ext. 2711
Email: **jennifer_lopez@txwb.uscourts.gov**

Hon. Craig A. Gargotta:

Lisa Elizondo, Courtroom Deputy Phone:
(210) 472–6720, ext. 5736
Email: **lisa_elizondo@txwb.uscourts.gov**

Hon. Ronald B. King:

Deanna Castleberry, Courtroom Deputy
Phone: (210) 472–6720, ext. 5735
Email: **deanna_castleberry@txwb.uscourts.gov**

Hon. H. Christopher Mott:

Ronda Farrar, Courtroom Deputy
Phone: (512) 916–5237, ext. 2712
Email: **ronda_farrar@txwb.uscourts.gov**

11. *Designation of Appellate Record.* A designation of the items to be included in the record on appeal pursuant to Fed. R. Bankr. P. 8009 must be filed by electronic means. However, copies of the designated documents to be delivered to the Clerk of the Authorizing Court pursuant to the applicable local rule shall be delivered in a paper format, with the format of all subsequent filings to be determined by the appropriate District Court.

12. *Unavailability of System.* If there is a technical failure of the Court's System which renders it inaccessible to an Electronic Filer on the last day prescribed under any applicable rule or court order for the timely filing of a document, such prescribed period shall be extended until the end of the next business day after access to the System has been restored.

> *Practice Note: Parties should be aware that the Authorizing Court may lack authority to relieve a party from the operation of any applicable statute of limitations based upon the unavailability of the Court's System. In such event, alternative filing means should be utilized in a timely manner.*

B. Signatures.

1. *Signature Requirement.* A document filed by electronic means shall either:

(a) contain a scanned image of any manual signature or an electronic signature affixed thereto; or

(b) display an "/s/" with the name typed in the location at which the signature would otherwise appear such as:

/s/ Jane Doe; OR

/s/ Jane Doe, Notary Public;[3] OR

/s/ Jane Doe, President, ABC Corporation.

2. *Consequence of Login/Password Usage.* Without relieving an Electronic Filer of the duty to comply with the signature requirement outlined above in Section III(B)(1), the filing of any document using a login/password combination issued by the Authorizing Court shall constitute an Electronic Filer's signature for purposes of signing the document under Fed. R. Bankr. P. 9011 or any other signature requirement imposed by the Bankruptcy Code, the Federal Rules of Bankruptcy Procedure, or any local rule of the Authorizing Court. No person shall knowingly utilize or cause another person to utilize the password of an Electronic Filer unless such a person is an authorized agent of the Electronic Filer.

3. *Declarations for Electronic Filing.* Within five (5) business days of the filing by electronic means of a bankruptcy petition, list, schedule, or statement that requires verification or an unsworn declaration under Fed. R. Bankr. P. 1008, the Electronic Filer shall tender to the Court in paper format the appropriate "Declaration for Electronic Filing," substantially conforming either to Exhibit "B–1," "B–2," or "B–3," which has been executed by any individual debtor or by the authorized representative of any corporate or partnership debtor. Such Declaration shall be thereafter maintained by the Clerk of the Authorizing Court in paper format.

4. *Retention of Documents With Third–Party Signatures.* Except as otherwise set forth in this Appendix, or as otherwise ordered by the Authorizing Court, documents which contain the original signature of any party other than the Electronic Filer, other than a Declaration for Electronic Filing as referenced above, shall be retained by the Electronic Filer for a period of not less than five (5) years after the case or adversary proceeding is closed and, upon request, such original document must be provided to the Court or other parties for review.

C. Pleading Attachments.

1. *Definition.* A "pleading attachment" is any document filed in support of, or in conjunction with, any pleading or proof of claim filed with the Authorizing Court. A pleading attachment shall be submitted as a PDF attachment to (and docketed with) the main document.

> *Exception[1]: Memorandum of Law. A memorandum of law pertaining to a pleading must be filed separately and linked as a related document to such pleading.*
> *Exception[2]: Trial Exhibits. No trial exhibit shall be filed by electronic means.*

2. *Summary or Excerpt Required.* Except as stated below or otherwise authorized by separate court order, no document in excess of forty (40) pages shall be filed as a pleading attachment. In lieu thereof, the Electronic Filer shall either create and thereafter file as the pleading attachment:

(a) an accurate summary of such document; or

(b) an excerpt of such portion of such document as may be directly germane to the issue being presented to the Court provided; however, that the excerpted material is clearly and prominently identified as such.

3. *Service of Complete Copy Upon Request.* If a summary or excerpt is filed with the Court as a pleading attachment, any party entitled to service of the pleading under the Federal Rules of Bankruptcy Procedure, the Local Rules of any Authorizing Court or any court order has a right to request service of a complete copy of the source document for which the summary or excerpt is submitted and the filing party shall immediately comply with such request at no charge to the requesting party. A complete copy of the source document must also be available for distribution to the Court and opposing parties at any scheduled hearing pertaining to the matter.

4. *Exceptions to the Summary/Excerpt Requirement.* Pleading attachments to the following pleadings are excepted from the summary/excerpt requirement expressed above and shall instead be filed in their entirety by electronic means, subject to the PDF file limitations imposed by Section III(A)(6) of this Appendix:

(a) Chapter 9 or Chapter 11 Plan of Reorganization;

(b) Disclosure Statement;

(c) Application for Compensation and/or Reimbursement of Expenses;

(d) Applications to Employ pursuant to Fed. R. Bankr. P. 2014;

(e) Motion to Dismiss pursuant to Fed. R. Bankr. P. 7012;

(f) Motion for Summary Judgment pursuant to Fed. R. Bankr. P. 7056;

(g) Motion for TRO/Injunctive Relief pursuant to Fed. R. Bankr. P. 7065;

(h) Motion for New Trial or to Alter/Amend Judgment pursuant to Fed. R. Bankr. P. 9023;

(i) Motion for Relief from Judgment/Order pursuant to Fed. R. Bankr. P. 9024;

(j) Motion for Remand pursuant to Fed. R. Bankr. P. 9027;

(k) Trustee's Final Report and Account (in all chapters);

(*l*) Any documents containing affidavits or verified statements; and

(m) Proofs of Claim.

5. *Paper Copy for Chambers Required.* Unless otherwise ordered, a complete paper copy of the following pleadings, including all attachments thereto, should be delivered within 24 hours of the electronic filing to the Clerk of the Authorizing Court for use by the assigned judge. Such pleadings are designated below according to district:

(a) Northern District:

    (1) Chapter 9 or Chapter 11 Plan of Reorganization;

    (2) Disclosure Statement;

    (3) Motion for Summary Judgment;

    (4) Application for Compensation and/or Reimbursement of Expenses; and

    (5) Motion to Dismiss pursuant to Fed. R. Bankr. P. 7012.

(b) Southern District:

    (1) Chapter 9 or Chapter 11 Plan of Reorganization;

    (2) Disclosure Statement;

    (3) Any motion or application filed under Fed. R. Bankr. P. 2014, 7012, 7056, 7065, 9023 or 9024;

    (4) Trustee's Final Report and Account (in all chapters); and

    (5) Any documents containing affidavits or verified statements.

(c) Eastern District:

    (1) Chapter 9 or Chapter 11 Plan of Reorganization;

    (2) Disclosure Statement;

(3) Motion for Summary Judgment;

(4) Application for Compensation and/or Reimbursement of Expenses (only when fee exhibit exceeds 25 pages); and

(5) Motion to Dismiss pursuant to Fed. R. Bankr. P. 7012 (if over 25 pages).

(d) Western District: None at this time.

6. *Affidavits.* The digital representation of an affidavit filed pursuant to the directives of this Section shall be construed as a valid affidavit upon which the Authorizing Court shall be entitled to rely. At the request of the Court or upon any dispute regarding the validity of the underlying affidavit, the Electronic Filer shall produce the originally-executed affidavit at any scheduled hearing pertaining to the matter.

7. *Trial Exhibits.* No trial exhibit shall be filed by electronic means.

D. Special Instructions Regarding Fees.

1. *Northern District:* Please consult the ECF On–Line Credit Card Payment Guide which is available at: http://www.txnb.uscourts.gov/ecf/cc_attorney_guide.pdf. Electronic Filers who choose to pay filing fees for multiple filings in a single payment or those using a "quick filing" or "flash filing" feature offered in certain bankruptcy filing software must settle their accounts by the close of business each day.

2. *Southern District:* None at this time.

3. *Eastern District:* Please consult the ECF On–Line Credit Card Payment Guide which is available at http://www.txeb.uscourts.gov/Finance/Internet Credit Card Manual.pdf. Electronic Filers may elect to pay the required filing fee after each transaction or make a single payment for all accumulated filing fees.

4. *Western District:* None at this time.

E. Service.

1. *Notice of Electronic Filing.* Whenever a document is filed by electronic means in accordance with these procedures, the System will automatically generate for the Electronic Filer a "Notice of Electronic Filing" at the time of docketing in a format substantially conforming to Exhibit "A."

2. *Fulfillment of Service Requirements.* The System will serve either the "Notice of Electronic Filing" or, if so elected by the recipient, a "Daily Summary Report of Bankruptcy Filings" containing notice of the electronic filing of the document, upon all parties who have consented to electronic service. The service of the "Notice of Electronic Filing" or the "Daily Summary Report of Bankruptcy Filings" upon such parties is the equivalent of service of the document upon such parties by the Electronic Filer.

3. *Service of Paper Documents.* The Electronic Filer must serve the document in paper format upon the debtor(s), if required, as well as upon any party entitled to service who is not registered for electronic service and is not, therefore, listed as a recipient of electronic notice on the Notice of Electronic Filing. Any supplemental certification regarding the service of paper documents must be filed by electronic means.

4. *Electronic Service of Summons/Complaint/Subpoena Prohibited.* Service of a summons and complaint under Fed. R. Bankr. P. 7004 or of a subpoena under Fed. R. Bankr. P. 9016 by electronic means is prohibited by the Federal Rules of Civil Procedure.

5. *Miscellaneous Service Provisions.*

(a) Northern District:

(1) Notice of Hearing Required. A Notice of Hearing must be filed and served by the movant for all matters requiring a hearing, and for all subsequent continuances of that matter. When the movant is given a hearing date and time for a matter by the Court, it is the movant's responsibility to file and serve the Notice of Hearing.

(b) Southern District:

(1) Service of Paper Documents. A debtor must serve manually signed paper copies of required schedules and statements upon the case trustee.

(c) Eastern District: None at this time.

(d) Western District: None at this time.

F. Consequences of Electronic Filing. When a document has been transmitted to the System in a manner consistent with these Procedures and the System has generated to the Electronic Filer a responsive "Notice of Electronic Filing," the document is filed as of the date and time noted on such Notice. A document is filed on a particular day if the transmission of the document is completed prior to midnight in the Central time zone.

IV. SUBMISSION OF ORDERS

A. General Provisions.

1. *Cover Sheet Not Required.* A cover sheet is not required for any order submitted by electronic means.

2. *Restrictions on Fonts.* The proper processing of orders through the Bankruptcy Noticing Center requires the use of designated fonts in any proposed order. The fonts used with Adobe Acrobat Writer version 3 or 4 must be Courier, Helvetica, or Times New Roman (regular, bold, italic, and bold italic). The fonts used with Adobe Acrobat Writer version 5 must be Arial, Courier, or Times New Roman (regular, bold, italic, and bold italic).

3. *Affixing Signatures.* Required signatures of parties or their respective attorneys on any agreed order or judgment may be documented through any means authorized under Section III(B) of this Appendix.

B. Specific Directives on Orders: Northern District.

1. *Submission of Proposed Order Upon Filing.* If a proposed order is required to be submitted to the Court, an Electronic Filer in the Northern District of Texas must submit the proposed order in either WordPerfect or Microsoft Word format using the Court's order processing system and may separately submit the order in PDF format. The User's Manual explains this requirement.

2. *Submission of Court–Directed Orders and Judgments.* When directed by the Court to submit a proposed order or judgment, the proposed order or judgment shall be submitted using the Court's order processing system.

3. *Specifications.* All orders submitted by electronic means in the Northern District of Texas must conform to the following specifications:

(a) The top margin on the FIRST PAGE must be four (4) inches. All other pages of the order will have a top margin of one (1) inch.

(b) To assist the Court in verifying that the "entire" body of the submitted order has been properly transmitted, the LAST LINE in the order must consist of "# # # END OF ORDER # # #" which is centered in the middle of the page to indicate that the order is completed. Any signatures and/or attachments will be placed below this line.

(c) A line for the date and a signature line for the judge is to be omitted. All orders will be signed electronically by the judge in the space provided at the top of the first page.

(d) All orders prepared by legal counsel shall indicate the name of the law firm, the signature of the attorney responsible for the order, the mailing address and phone number for the firm and the fax number and/or e-mail address, if applicable, below the "# # # END OF ORDER # # #" line.

(e) If the submitting party wishes to indicate to whom copies of the signed order should be sent, those parties' names and addresses shall be included on the order below the "# # # END OF ORDER # # #" line.

C. Specific Directives on Orders: Southern District.

1. *Submission of Proposed Order Upon Filing.* If a proposed order is required to be submitted to the Court, an Electronic Filer in the Southern District of Texas must submit the proposed order as an attachment to the main document at the time of filing.

2. *Submission of Agreed and Court–Directed Orders and Judgments ("Greensheet Orders").* Unless otherwise ordered by the Court, the submission of orders and judgments to the Court, whether by agreement of the parties prior to a scheduled hearing or trial, or pursuant to a directive of the Court issued at the conclusion of a hearing or trial, shall be accomplished by electronic means through the selection of the following event: *"proposed order submission after hearing (greensheet)."*

D. Specific Directives on Orders: Eastern District.

1. *Submission of Proposed Order Upon Filing.* If a proposed order is required to be submitted to the Court, an Electronic Filer in the Eastern District of Texas must submit the proposed order as an attachment to the main document at the time of filing.

2. *Submission of Agreed and Court–Directed Orders and Judgments.* The submission of orders and judgments to the Court, whether by agreement of the parties prior to a scheduled hearing or trial, or pursuant to a directive of the Court issued at the conclusion of a hearing or trial, shall be accomplished by electronic means:

(a) For orders pertaining to contested matters, the "Upload for Agreed and Court–Directed Orders" link in the "Bankruptcy Event" section of the System should be used.

(b) For judgments or orders pertaining to adversary proceedings, the "Upload for Agreed and Court–Directed Orders and Judgments" link in the "Adversary Event" section of the System should be used.

3. *Submission Prior to Hearing.* If an agreed order or judgment which completely resolves all matters in dispute is submitted to the Court by electronic means at any time prior to a scheduled hearing or trial, the scheduled hearing or trial shall be canceled and the attendance of the parties at that scheduled hearing or trial shall be excused.

4. *Specifications.* Any type of order or judgment submitted by electronic means in the Eastern District shall be submitted in a traditional format, concluding with an open space of not less than 1.5 inches in length for the affixing of the judge's signature. This space shall be in lieu of the traditional dateline and signature block.

E. Specific Directives on Orders: Western District.

1. *Submission of Proposed Order Upon Filing.* For all motions, applications, objections to claims, and other requests for relief, including those with "negative notice language" (bankruptcy case or adversary proceeding) filed in the Western District of Texas, the Electronic Filer at the time of filing must separately submit a proposed order by electronic means using the Court's Order Upload feature in the System. The proposed order must also be attached as an exhibit to the motion. See L.R. 9013(b).

> *Exception[1]: Orders Pertaining to Wage Withholding and Filing Fee Installments. Requests for entry of order to pay wages and applications to pay filing fee in installments are considered administrative orders and proposed orders regarding these two pleadings shall be submitted as an attachment to the main document upon filing*

2. *Submission of Agreed and Court–Directed Orders and Judgments.* The submission of orders and judgments to the Court, whether by agreement of the parties prior to a scheduled hearing or trial, or pursuant to a directive of the Court issued at the conclusion of a hearing or trial, shall be accomplished by electronic means using the Court's Order Upload feature in the System.

3. *Specifications.* Except as otherwise directed below, all orders submitted by electronic means in the Western District of Texas must conform to the following specifications:

(a) The top margin on the FIRST PAGE must be four (4) inches. All other pages of the order will have a top margin of one (1) inch.

(b) To assist the Court in verifying that the "entire" body of the submitted order has been properly transmitted, the LAST LINE in the order must consist of three (3) pound symbols (# # #) which is centered in the middle of the page to indicate that the order is completed.

(c) A line for the date and a signature line for the judge is to be omitted. All orders will be signed electronically by the judge in the space provided by the top margin on the first page.

(d) All orders prepared by legal counsel shall indicate the name of the law firm, the name of the attorney responsible for the order, the mailing address and phone number for the firm and, if desirable, the fax number and/or e-mail address. This information shall be included on the order, after the line containing the three (3) pound symbols.

(e) If the submitting party wishes to indicate to whom copies of the signed order should be sent, those parties' names and addresses shall be included on the order, after the line containing the three (3) pound symbols.

V. PUBLIC ACCESS TO THE DOCKET

A. Internet Access.

1. *Access Through Websites.* Any person may obtain access to the documents and dockets maintained by the Texas Bankruptcy Courts through their respective websites:

Northern District:	**www.txnb.uscourts.gov**
Southern District:	**www.txs.uscourts.gov**
Eastern District:	**www.txeb.uscourts.gov**
Western District:	**www.txwb.uscourts.gov**

Such Internet access requires registration with the PACER Service Center at www.pacer.psc. uscourts.gov. (or 1–800–676–6856) and, in accordance with the mandate of the Judicial Conference of the United States, a user fee will be charged, except that parties who are served with a document through the use of the "Notice of Electronic Filing" generated by the Court's transmission facilities have one opportunity to view, save, or print that document without charge by utilizing the hyperlink which will appear in that Notice.

2. *Protective Orders.* Any person may move the Authorizing Court for an order limiting electronic access to, or prohibiting the electronic filing of, specifically identified materials upon the grounds that the utilization of electronic access or electronic filing is likely to prejudice the privacy interests of an affected party.

B. Public Access at the Court.

Public access to the information maintained in an electronic format by the Texas Bankruptcy Courts may be obtained without charge in each divisional office of the Clerk during regular business hours, excluding federal holidays and extraordinary circumstances (i.e. delayed openings due to inclement weather).

C. Conventional Copies and Certified Copies.

Conventional copies and certified copies of documents maintained in an electronic format may be purchased in each divisional office of the Clerk during business hours. The fee for copying and certification is prescribed by 28 U.S.C. § 1930.

Exhibit A: Sample Notice of Electronic Filing

U.S.B.C. Western District of Texas (TRAINING)   Page 1 of 1

File a Motion:
03-70029-rbk Alexander Jones Washington and Mary Lynn Washington

U.S. Bankruptcy Court

Western District of Texas

Notice of Electronic Filing

The following transaction was received from Sugarplum, Loretta A. entered on 11/29/2004 at 2:41 PM
CST and filed on 11/29/2004
Case Name: Alexander Jones Washington and Mary Lynn Washington
Case Number: 03-70029-rbk
Document Number: 9

Docket Text:
Motion to Avoid Lien with Sears *(20 Day Objection Language)* filed by Loretta A. Sugarplum for
Debtors Alexander Jones Washington, Mary Lynn Washington (Sugarplum, Loretta)

The following document(s) are associated with this transaction:

Document description: Main Document
Original filename:C:\cmecf\amd_claim_0404.pdf
Electronic document Stamp:
[STAMP bkecfStamp_ID=988230274 [Date=11/29/2004] [FileNumber=84067-0]
[15bceabcbe4c41bd54b7d962cb3247a0fda4e620970f3cd14ceace3db2f877a2a8c86
7143392a252e31e6d86dcf876703c5b06a133fe6fcb9d0237a2451458af]]

03-70029-rbk Notice will be electronically mailed to:

David H. Williams   david_h_williams@txwb.uscourts.gov

03-70029-rbk Notice will not be electronically mailed to:

Christy Carouth
406 Oak Glen
San Angelo, TX 76909

Janet S Casciato-Northrup
4615 SW Freeway #410
Houston, TX 77027

Exhibit B-1 to Appendix 5005: If filing petition and all schedules/statements simultaneously

IN THE UNITED STATES BANKRUPTCY COURT
FOR THE *[insert]* DISTRICT OF TEXAS

IN RE:

§
§
_____ §   Case No. _____
§
§
          Debtor(s)   §   Chapter _____

DECLARATION FOR ELECTRONIC FILING OF BANKRUPTCY
PETITION, LISTS, STATEMENTS, AND SCHEDULES

PART I: DECLARATION OF PETITIONER:

As an individual debtor in this case, or as the individual authorized to act on behalf of the corporation, partnership, or limited liability company seeking bankruptcy relief in this case, I hereby request relief as, or on behalf of, the debtor in accordance with the chapter of title 11, United States Code, specified in the petition to be filed electronically in this case. I have read the information provided in the petition, lists, statements, and schedules to be filed electronically in this case and *I hereby declare under penalty of perjury* that the information provided therein, as well as the social security information disclosed in this document, is true and correct. I understand that this Declaration is to be filed with the Bankruptcy Court within five (5) business days after the petition, lists, statements, and schedules have been filed electronically. I understand that a failure to file the signed original of this Declaration will result in the dismissal of my case.

☐   *[Only include for Chapter 7 individual petitioners whose debts are primarily consumer debts]* –
I am an individual whose debts are primarily consumer debts and who has chosen to file under chapter 7. I am aware that I may proceed under chapter 7, 11, 12, or 13 of title 11, United States Code, understand the relief available under each chapter, and choose to proceed under chapter 7.

☐   *[Only include if petitioner is a corporation, partnership or limited liability company]* –
I hereby further declare under penalty of perjury that I have been authorized to file the petition, lists, statements, and schedules on behalf of the debtor in this case.

Date: _____.

_____   _____
John Doe, Debtor   Jane Doe, Joint Debtor
Soc. Sec. No. _____   **Soc. Sec. No.** _____
           OR
John Doe, Position/Capacity

PART II: DECLARATION OF ATTORNEY:

I declare *under penalty of perjury* that: (1) I will give the debtor(s) a copy of all documents referenced by Part I herein which are filed with the United States Bankruptcy Court; and (2) I have informed the debtor(s), if an individual with primarily consumer debts, that he or she may proceed under chapter 7, 11, 12, or 13 of title 11, United States Code, and have explained the relief available under each such chapter.

Date: _____.

_____
A. Lawyer, Attorney for Debtor

Exhibit B-2 to Appendix 5005: If filing "bare-bones" petition, matrix, & 20 largest unsecured list.

IN THE UNITED STATES BANKRUPTCY COURT
FOR THE *[insert]* DISTRICT OF TEXAS

IN RE: §
§
_____ §   Case No. _____
§
§
Debtor(s) §   Chapter _____

DECLARATION FOR ELECTRONIC FILING OF
BANKRUPTCY PETITION AND MASTER MAILING LIST (MATRIX)

PART I: DECLARATION OF PETITIONER:

As an individual debtor in this case, or as the individual authorized to act on behalf of the corporation, partnership, or limited liability company seeking bankruptcy relief in this case, I hereby request relief as, or on behalf of, the debtor in accordance with the chapter of title 11, United States Code, specified in the petition to be filed electronically in this case. I have read the information provided in the petition and in the lists of creditors to be filed electronically in this case and *I hereby declare under penalty of perjury* that the information provided therein, as well as the social security information disclosed in this document, is true and correct. I understand that this Declaration is to be filed with the Bankruptcy Court within five (5) business days after the petition and lists of creditors have been filed electronically. I understand that a failure to file the signed original of this Declaration will result in the dismissal of my case.

☐ *[Only include for Chapter 7 individual petitioners whose debts are primarily consumer debts]* –
I am an individual whose debts are primarily consumer debts and who has chosen to file under chapter 7. I am aware that I may proceed under chapter 7, 11, 12, or 13 of title 11, United States Code, understand the relief available under each chapter, and choose to proceed under chapter 7.

☐ *[Only include if petitioner is a corporation, partnership or limited liability company]* –
I hereby further declare under penalty of perjury that I have been authorized to file the petition and lists of creditors on behalf of the debtor in this case.

Date: _____.

_____   _____
John Doe, Debtor   Jane Doe, Joint Debtor
Soc. Sec. No. _____   **Soc. Sec. No.** _____
OR
John Doe, Position/Capacity

PART II: DECLARATION OF ATTORNEY:

I declare *under penalty of perjury* that: (1) I will give the debtor(s) a copy of all documents referenced by Part I herein which are filed with the United States Bankruptcy Court; and (2) I have informed the debtor(s), if an individual with primarily consumer debts, that he or she may proceed under chapter 7, 11, 12, or 13 of title 11, United States Code, and have explained the relief available under each such chapter.

Date: _____.

_____
A. Lawyer, Attorney for Debtor

*Exhibit B-3 to Appendix 5005: If filing schedules/statements subsequent to petition date or
amendments of petition, matrix, schedules or statements.*

IN THE UNITED STATES BANKRUPTCY COURT
FOR THE *[insert]* DISTRICT OF TEXAS

IN RE: §
                                          §
                                          §   Case No. _____
_____   §
                                          §
          Debtor(s)   §   Chapter _____

DECLARATION FOR ELECTRONIC FILING OF AMENDED PETITION, ORIGINAL/AMENDED BANKRUPTCY STATEMENTS AND SCHEDULES, AND/OR AMENDED MASTER MAILING LIST (MATRIX)

As an individual debtor in this case, or as the individual authorized to act on behalf of the corporation, partnership, or limited liability company named as the debtor in this case, *I hereby declare under penalty of perjury* that I have read

☐   the original statements and schedules to be filed electronically in this case

☐   the voluntary petition as amended on the date indicated below and to be filed electronically in this case

☐   the statements and schedules as amended on the date indicated below and to be filed electronically in this case

☐   the master mailing list (matrix) as amended on the date indicated below and to be filed electronically in this case

and that the information provided therein is true and correct. I understand that this Declaration is to be filed with the Bankruptcy Court within five (5) business days after such statements, schedules, and/or amended petition or matrix have been filed electronically. I understand that a failure to file the signed original of this Declaration as to any original statements and schedules will result in the dismissal of my case and that, as to any amended petition, statement, schedule or matrix, such failure may result in the striking of the amendment(s).

☐   *[Only include if petitioner is a corporation, partnership or limited liability company]* –
       I hereby further declare under penalty of perjury that I have been authorized to file the statements, schedules, and/or amended petition or amended matrix on behalf of the debtor in this case.

Date: _____.

_____   _____
John Doe, Debtor   Jane Doe, Joint Debtor
OR
John Doe, Position/Capacity

[Effective September 1, 2010. Amended effective September 20, 2013; December 1, 2013; January 16, 2014; March 11, 2015; December 1, 2016; February 1, 2019.]

1 Though permissive language is utilized in this Appendix, please consult the electronic filing information provided on the Internet homepage of each particular Texas Bankruptcy Court to determine whether the filing of documents by electronic means is required. Those websites are identified in Sections II(A)(1) and VI(A)(1) of this Appendix.

2 In the Northern District, this includes government attorneys exempted from admission requirements under LR 83.11.

3 If the "/s/" signature option is utilized for a notary public, the commission date for such notary public should be typed on the electronically-submitted document.

SELECTED ORDERS AND NOTICES

GENERAL PROCEDURES ORDER 2000–03. COURT ELECTRONIC NOTICING PROCEDURES

THIS MATTER arises sua sponte upon the need to for the Court to announce its procedures for obtaining notices electronically. Pursuant to Bankruptcy Rule 9036—Notice by Electronic Transmission, the court may direct notice by electronic transmission if the entity entitled to receive the bankruptcy notice requests in writing that the notice be transmitted electronically. This written request requirement is fulfilled through an electronic noticing agreement.

Accordingly, it is ORDERED that the Court will provide electronic noticing agreements through the judiciary's Bankruptcy Noticing Center to any entity requesting this service. The terms and procedures for electronic noticing are detailed in the court's noticing agreement provided by the Bankruptcy Noticing Center.

[Dated: June 19, 2000.]

STANDING ORDER 2000–04. IN RE: STANDING ORDER CONCERNING VIDEO HEARINGS

Absent compelling circumstances, the following rules will apply to video hearings before the Bankruptcy Court in the following Divisions of the Northern District of Texas: [Abilene, Amarillo, Dallas, Fort Worth, Lubbock, San Angelo, and Wichita Falls]. These rules do not replace the Local Rules or any Scheduling Order. The intent of this order is not to additionally burden counsel, but to attempt to assist counsel and the Court in dealing with video hearings.

It is hereby ORDERED that the following procedures apply to video hearings on contested matters:

A. Under Local Bankruptcy Rules 9014.1(c)(2) and 4001.1(d), when an exhibit or appraisal is furnished to an opponent, it shall be mailed to the presiding judge of the hearing within the same time parameters of the local rules, together with time estimates for the hearing. If a party anticipates using impeachment exhibits not normally required to be revealed in advance of the hearing, the impeachment exhibits must be furnished to the presiding judge at least two days before the hearing in a sealed envelope containing the following legend

[Number and style of case, nature of hearing, hearing date and time].

"Impeachment exhibits of [PARTY NAME]. Only to be opened by the presiding judge at such bearing, if offered into evidence at such bearing." [Attorney's name, address and telephone number].

The clerk is to date stamp the envelope "Received" and deliver it to the presiding judge, who will destroy it if the exhibits are not offered into evidence at the hearing.

B. On preliminary stay hearings, regardless of which Division is hearing the matter, Local Bankruptcy Rule 4001.1(e) will govern the conduct of the hearing and any evidentiary affidavits referred to in Local Bankruptcy Rule 4001.1(e) must be filed with the Clerk's Office, and copies mailed to the judge presiding over such hearing at or about the time they are to be served on an opponent, together with time estimates of the hearing.

It is further ORDERED that the following procedures apply in video trials of adversary proceedings: At least seven days in advance of trial, copies of all exhibits, except those for impeachment purposes, are to be exchanged between counsel and mailed to the presiding judge, together with the time estimates of the trial. If a party anticipates using impeachment exhibits not normally required to be revealed in advance of trial, the impeachment exhibits are to be furnished to the presiding judge at least two days before the trial in a scaled envelope containing the following legend:

[Number and style of case, trial date and time]. "Impeachment exhibits of [PARTY NAME]. Only to be opened by the presiding judge at trial, if offered into evidence at trial." [Attorney's name, address and telephone number].

The clerk is to date stamp the envelope "Received" and deliver it to the presiding judge, who will destroy the envelope if the exhibits are not offered into evidence at trial.

[Dated: September 29, 2000.]

GENERAL ORDER 2000–07. IN RE: STANDING ORDER CONCERNING GUIDELINES FOR COMPENSATION AND EXPENSE REIMBURSEMENT OF PROFESSIONALS, FOR EARLY DISPOSITION OF ASSETS IN CHAPTER 11 CASES, AND FOR MOTIONS AND ORDERS PERTAINING TO USE OF CASH COLLATERAL AND POST–PETITION FINANCING

The Court having previously adopted the attached Guidelines for compensation and Expense Reimbursement of Professionals, Guideline for Early Disposition of Assets in Chapter 11 Cases, and Attorney Checklist Concerning Motions and Order Pertaining to Use of Cash Collateral and Post–Petition Financing,

IT IS HEREBY ORDERED that the attached guidelines* are applicable in accordance with their terms to compensation and expenses reimbursement of professionals, to procedures for the early disposition of assets in Chapter 11 cases, and to motions and orders pertaining to the use of cash collateral and post-petition financing.

*[**Publisher's Note:** For the Guidelines for Compensation and Expense Reimbursement of Professionals, see Appendix F, *ante*.]

[Dated: December 21, 2000.]

GUIDELINES FOR EARLY DISPOSITION OF ASSETS IN CHAPTER 11 CASES THE SALE OF SUBSTANTIALLY ALL ASSETS UNDER SECTION 363 AND OVERBID AND TOPPING FEES

The following guidelines are promulgated as a result of the increasing use of pre-negotiated or prepackaged plans and 11 U.S.C. § 363 sales to dispose of substantially all assets of a Chapter 11 debtor shortly after the filing of the petition. The guidelines recognize that parties in interest perceive the need at times to act expeditiously on such matters. In addition, the guidelines are written to provide procedural protection to the parties in interest. The court will consider requests to modify the guidelines to fit the circumstances of a particular case.

OVERBIDS & TOPPING FEES

1. Topping Fees and Break-up Fees. Any request for the approval of a topping fee or break-up fee provision shall be supported by a statement of the precise conditions under which the topping fee or break-up fee would be payable and the factual basis on which the seller determined the provision was reasonable. The request shall also disclose the identities of other potential purchasers, the offers made by them (if any), and the nature of the offer, including, without limitation, any disclosure of their plans as it relates to retention of debtor's employees.

2. Topping fees, break-up fees, overbid amounts and other buyer protection provisions will be reviewed on a case by case basis and approved if supported by evidence and case law. Case law may not support buyer protection provisions for readily marketable assets.

3. In connection with a request to sell substantially all assets under § 363 within 60 days of the filing of the petition, buyer protections may be considered upon motion, on an expedited basis.

THE SALE OF SUBSTANTIALLY ALL ASSETS UNDER SECTION 363 WITHIN 60 DAYS OF THE FILING OF THE PETITION

1. The Motion to Sell. In connection with any hearing to approve the sale of substantially all assets at any time before 60 days after the filing of the petition, a motion for an order authorizing a sale procedure and hearing or the sale motion itself when regularly noticed, should include factual information on the following points:

a. Creditors' Committee. If a creditors' committee existed pre-petition, indicate the date and manner in which the committee was formed, as well as the identity of the members of the committee and the companies with which they are affiliated.

b. Counsel for Committee. If the pre-petition creditors' committee retained counsel, indicate the date counsel was engaged and the selection process, as well as the identity of committee counsel.

c. Sale Contingencies. Statement of all contingencies to the sale agreement, together with a copy of the agreement.

d. Creditor Contact List. If no committee has been formed, a list of contact persons, together with fax and phone numbers for each of the largest 20 unsecured creditors.

e. Administrative Expenses. Assuming the sale is approved, an itemization and an estimate of administrative expenses relating to the sale to be incurred prior to closing and the source of payment for those expenses.

f. Proceeds of Sale. An estimate of the gross proceeds anticipated from the sale, together with an estimate of the net proceeds coming to the estate with an explanation of the items making up the difference. Itemize all deductions that are to be made from gross sale proceeds and include a brief description of the basis for any such deductions.

g. Debt Structure of Debtor. A brief description of the debtor's debt structure, including the amount of the debtor's secured debt, priority claims and general unsecured claims.

h. Need for Quick Sale. An extensive description of why the assets of the estate must be sold on an expedited basis. Include a discussion of alternatives to the sale.

i. Negotiating Background. A description of the length of time spent in negotiating the sale, and which parties in interest were involved in the negotiation, along with a description of the details of any other offers to purchase, including, without limitation, the potential purchaser's plans in connection with retention of the debtor's employees.

j. Marketing of Assets. A description of the manner in which the assets were marketed for sale, including the period of time involved and the results achieved.

k. Decision to Sell. The date on which the debtor accepted the offer to purchase the assets.

l. Relationship of Buyer. A statement identifying the buyer and setting forth all of the buyer's (including its officers, directors and shareholders) connections with the debtor, creditors, any other party in interest, their respective attorneys, accountants, the United States Trustee or any person employed in the office of the United States Trustee.

n.* Post Sale Relationship with Debtor. A statement setting forth any relationship or connection the debtor (including its officers, directors, shareholders and employees) will have with the buyer after the consummation of the sale, assuming it is approved.

o. Relationship with Secured Creditors. If the sale involves the payment of all or a portion of secured debt(s), a statement of all connections between debtor's officers, directors, employees or other insiders and each secured creditor involved (for example, release of insider's guaranty).

p. Insider Compensation. Disclosure of current compensation received by officers, directors, key employees or other insiders pending approval of the sale.

q. Notice Timing. Notice of the hearing on the motion to approve the motion to sell will be provided as is necessary under the circumstances.

2. Proposed Order Approving Sale. A proposed order approving the sale must be included with the motion or the notice of hearing. A proposed final order and redlined version of the order approving the sale should be provided to chambers twenty-four hours prior to the hearing.

3. Good Faith Finding. There must be an evidentiary basis for a finding of good faith under 11 U.S.C. § 363(m).

4. Competing Bids. Unless the court orders otherwise, competing bids may be presented at the time of the hearing. The motion to sell and the notice of hearing should so provide.

5. Financial Ability to Close. Unless the court orders otherwise, any bidder must be prepared to demonstrate to the satisfaction of the court, through an evidentiary hearing, its ability to consummate the transaction if it is the successful bidder, along with evidence regarding any financial contingencies to closing the transaction.

6.   Hearing and Notice Regarding Sale. Unless the court orders otherwise, all sales governed by these guidelines, including auctions or the presentation of competing bids, will occur at the hearing before the court. The court may, for cause, including the need to maximize and preserve asset value, expedite a hearing on a motion to sell substantially all assets under § 363.

———————

[Enter: Attorney's Name]

[Enter: Texas Bar No.]

[Enter: Firm Name]

[Enter: Address]

[Enter: Telephone Number]

[Enter: Identification Role in Case]

IN THE UNITED STATES BANKRUPTCY COURT
FOR THE NORTHERN DISTRICT OF TEXAS
DALLAS DIVISION

IN RE:)
)
)
_____   )   CASE NO. _____
)
)
            DEBTOR   )   HEARING: _____

ATTORNEY CHECKLIST CONCERNING MOTIONS AND ORDERS PERTAINING
TO USE OF CASH COLLATERAL AND PORT–PETITION FINANCING
(WHICH ARE IN EXCESS OF TEN (10) PAGES)

Motions and orders pertaining to cash collateral and post-petition financing matters tend to be lengthy and complicated. Although the Court intends to read such motions and orders carefully, it will assist the Court if counsel will complete this checklist. All references are to the Bankruptcy Code (§) or Rules (R). PLEASE NOTE:

   * Means generally not favored by Bankruptcy Courts in this District.

   ** Means generally not favored by Bankruptcy Courts in this District without a reason and a time period for objections.

If your motion or order makes provision for any of the following, so indicate in the space provided:

CERTIFICATE BY COUNSEL

This is to certify that the following checklist fully responds to the Court's inquiry concerning material terms of the motion and/or proposed order:

                                                 Yes, at Page/Exhibit
                                                 Y means yes; N means no
                                                 N/A means not applicable
                                                 (Page Listing Optional)

1.   Identification of Proceedings:
     (a) Preliminary or final motion/order (circle one) . . . . _____
     (b) Continuing use of cash collateral (§ 363) . . . . _____
     (c) New financing (§ 364) . . . . _____
     (d) Combination of §§ 363 and 364 financing . . . . _____
     (e) Emergency hearing (immediate and irreparable harm) . . . . _____
2.   Stipulations:

Yes, at Page/Exhibit
Y means yes; N means no
N/A means not applicable
(Page Listing Optional)

(a) Brief history of debtor's businesses and status of debtor's prior relationships with lender . . . . _____

(b) Brief statement of purpose and necessity of financing . . . . _____

(c) Brief statement of type of financing (i.e., accounts receivable, inventory) . . . . _____

** (d) Are lender's pre-petition security interest(s) and liens deemed valid, fully perfected and non-avoidable . . . . _____

    (i) Are there provisions to allow for objections to above? . . . . _____

(e) Is there a post-petition financing agreement between lender and debtor? . . . . _____

    (i) If so, is agreement attached? . . . . _____

** (f) If there is an agreement are lender's post-petition security interests and liens deemed valid, fully perfected and non-avoidable? . . . . _____

(g) Is lender undersecured or oversecured? (circle one) . . . . _____

(h) Has lender's non-cash collateral been appraised? . . . . _____

    (i) Insert date of latest appraisal . . . . _____

(i) Is debtor's proposed budget attached? . . . . _____

(j) Are all pre-petition loan documents identified? . . . . _____

(k) Are pre-petition liens on single or multiple assets? (circle one) . . . . . . _____

(l) Are there pre-petition guaranties of debt? . . . . _____

    (i) Limited or unlimited? (circle one) . . . . _____

3. Grant of Liens:

* (a) Do post-petition liens secure pre-petition debts? . . . . _____

* (b) Is there cross-collaterization? . . . . _____

** (c) Is the priority of post-petition liens equal to or higher than existing liens? . . . . _____

** (d) Do post-petition Liens have retroactive effect? . . . . _____

(e) Are there restrictions on granting further liens or liens of equal or higher priority? . . . . _____

* (f) Is lender given liens on claims under §§ 506(c), 544–50 and §§ 522? . . . . _____

**   (i) Are lender's attorneys fees to be paid? . . . . _____

    (ii) Are debtor's attorneys fees excepted from § 506(c) . . . . _____

* (g) Is lender given liens upon proceeds of causes of action under §§ 544, 547 and 548? . . . . _____

4. Administrative priority Claims:

(a) Is lender given an administrative priority? . . . . _____

(b) Is administrative priority higher than § 507(a)? . . . . _____

(c) Is there a conversion of pre-petition secured claim to post-petition administrative claim by virtue of use of existing collateral? . . . . _____

5. Adequate Protection (§ 361):

(a) Is there post-petition debt service? . . . . _____

(b) Is there a replacement/addition 361(l) lien? (circle one or both) . . . . _____

** (c) Is the lender's claim given super-priority? (§ 364(c) or (d)) [designate] . . . . _____

(d) Are there guaranties? . . . . _____

(e) Is there adequate Insurance coverage? . . . . _____

(f) Other? . . . . _____

6. Waiver/Release Claims v. Lender:

** (a) Debtor waives or release claims against lender, including, but not limited to, claims under §§ 506(c), 544–550, 552, and 553 of the Code? . . . . _____

** (b) Does the debtor waive defenses to claim or liens of lender? . . . . _____

7. Source of Post–Petition Financing (§ 364 Financing):

(a) Is the proposed lender also the pre-petition lender? . . . . _____

Yes, at Page/Exhibit
Y means yes; N means no
N/A means not applicable
(Page Listing Optional)

     (b) New post-petition lender? .... _____

     (c) Is the lender an insider? .... _____

8.   Modification of Stay:

**   (a) Is any modified lift of stay allowed? .... _____

**   (b) Will the automatic stay be lifted to permit lender to exercise self-help upon default without further order? .... _____

     (c) Are there any other remedies exercisable without further order of court? .... _____

     (d) Is there a provision that any future modification of order shall not affect status of debtor's post-petition obligations to lender?.... _____

9.   Creditors' Committee:

     (a) Has creditors' committee been appointed? .... _____

     (b) Does creditors' committee approve of proposed financing? .... _____

10. Restrictions on Parties in Interest:

**   (a) Is a plan proponent restricted in any manner, concerning modification of lender's rights, liens and/or causes? .... _____

**   (b) Is the debtor prohibited from seeking to enjoin the lender in pursuant of rights? .... _____

**   (c) Is any party in interest prohibited from seeking to modify this order? .... _____

     (d) Is the entry of any order conditioned upon payment of debt to lender? .... _____

     (e) Is the order binding on subsequent trustee on conversion? .... _____

11. Nunc Pro Tunc:

     (a) Does any provision have retroactive effect? .... _____

12. Notice and Other Procedures:

     (a) Is shortened notice requested? .... _____

     (b) Is notice requested to shortened list .... _____

     (c) Is time to respond to be shortened? .... _____

     (d) If final order sought, have 15 days elapsed since service of motion pursuant to Rule 4001(b)(2)? .... _____

     (e) If preliminary order sought, is cash collateral necessary to avoid immediate and irreparable harm to the estate pending a final hearing? .... _____

     (f) Is a Certificate of Conference included? .... _____

     (g) Is a Certificate of Service included? .... _____

     (h) Is there verification of transmittal to U.S. Trustee included pursuant to Rule 9034? .... _____

     (i) Has an agreement been reached subsequent to filing motion? .... _____

        (i) If so, has notice of the agreement been served pursuant to Rule 4001(d)(l) .... _____

       (ii) Is the agreement in settlement of motion pursuant to Rule 4001(d)(4)? .... _____

     (iii) Does the motion afford reasonable notice of material provisions of agreement pursuant to Rule 4001(d)(4)? .... _____

     (iv) Does the motion provide for opportunity for hearing pursuant to Rule 9014? .... _____

SIGNED this the _____ day of _____, 2001.

[Enter: Firm Name]

By: _____

[Enter: Attorney's Name]

[Enter: Texas Bar No.]

[Enter: Address]

[Enter: Telephone Number]

[Enter: Identification Role in Case]

COMMENTS TO CASH COLLATERAL AND DIP FINANCING CHECKLIST

1. Interim vs. Final Orders

a. Stipulations in preliminary or interim orders should be minimized. Notice is generally not adequate to test the validity of stipulations, and they should be avoided to the extent not absolutely necessary to the interim approval process.

b. Simply state the nature of notice given; do not recite notice was "sufficient and adequate" since that is usually not the case particularly on the first day. The order should simply note that the financing is being approved pursuant to Bankruptcy Rule 4001(c)(2) authorizing such financing to avoid immediate and irreparable harm.

c. Adequate protection for the use of pre-petition cash collateral may be granted to the extent of a diminution of collateral. The court will not approve on an interim basis language that adequate protection is granted in the form of replacement liens on post-petition assets based on stipulations that "use of cash collateral shall be deemed a dollar for dollar decrease in the value of the pre-petition collateral." At the final hearing the court will consider evidence to determine the extent to which the lender's pre-petition collateral has or is likely to diminish in value. That evidence will inform the extent to which adequate protection will be granted.

d. The court expects that other parties in interest will be involved in the process of developing an interim cash collateral order to the extent practicable. If the court finds that the debtor and lender have not made reasonable efforts to afford the best notice possible, preliminary relief will not be granted until parties in interest have had a reasonable opportunity to review and comment on any proposed interim order.

e. Bankruptcy Rule 4001(b) and (c) limit the extent to which the court may grant relief on less than 15 days' notice. The debtor and the lender must negotiate interim orders within the confines of that authority. Interim orders shall be expressly without prejudice to the rights of parties in interest at a final hearing.

2. Stipulations

a. The lender may request a stipulation as to the amount, validity, priority and extent of the pre-petition documents. The stipulation will only be approved if the order provides the stipulation is binding on other parties in interest only after the passage of an appropriate period of time (customarily 90 days) during which the parties in interest will have the opportunity to test the validity of the lien and the allowance of the claim.

3. Grant of Liens

a. Liens granted in the cash collateral and DIP financing orders may not secure prepetition debts. Financing orders should not be used to elevate a pre-petition lender's collateral inadequacy to a fully secured status.

b. Avoidance actions are frequently one of the few sources of recovery for creditors other than secured lenders. Orders granting liens on these unencumbered assets for the benefit of the lender will require a showing of extraordinary circumstances. In most cases the adequate protection grant will protect the lender since the lender will have a superpriority under § 507(b) that will give the lender who suffers a failure of adequate protection a first right to payment out of the proceeds from such actions before payment of any other expenses of the Chapter 11 case. Avoidance actions in the event of a conversion to Chapter 7 may be the only assets available to fund the trustee's discharge of his or her statutory duties.

c. Similarly, limitations on the surcharge of the lender's collateral under § 506(c) are disfavored. The secured creditor may be the principal beneficiary of the proceedings in Chapter 11. Since the burden to surcharge requires a showing of direct benefit to the lender's collateral, lenders are not unreasonably exposed to surcharges of their collateral. And in light of the decision in Hartford Underwriter's Insurance Co. v. Union Planters Bank N.A. (In re Hen House Interstate Inc.), ___ U.S. ___, 120 S.Ct. 1942 (2000), only the DIP or the trustee may recover under § 506(c).

4. Modification of Stay

a. Authority for unilateral action by lender without necessity to return to court to establish post-petition default or breach or at least a notice to parties in interest will not be approved. If the cash collateral or financing order provides for a termination of the automatic stay in the event of a default, parties in interest must have an opportunity to be heard before the stay lifts.

5. Restrictions on Plan Process

a. The court will not approve cash collateral orders (or post-petition financing orders that are in substance cash collateral orders that have the effect of converting all the pre-petition liens and claims to post-petition liabilities under the guise of collecting pre-petition accounts and readvancing them post-petition) that have the effect of converting pre-petition secured debt into post-petition administrative claims that must be paid in full in order to confirm a plan. That type of provision unfairly limits the ability and flexibility of the debtor and other parties in interest to formulate a plan. That type of provision, granted at the outset of a case, effectively compels the debtor to pay off the secured lender in full on the effective date and has the consequence of eviscerating § 1129(b).

b. On the other hand, persons who are advancing new money to the debtor postpetition may include in financing orders provisions that the post-petition loans have a § 364(c)(1) super-super priority.

6. Loan Agreements

a. If there will be a loan agreement, the language of the financing order does not need to restate all of the terms of the loan agreement. The financing motion should, however, summarize the essential elements of the proposed borrowing or use of cash collateral, such as, amount of loan facility, sublimits on availability, borrowing base formula, conditions to new advances, interest rate, maturity, events of default, limitation on use of funds and description of collateral.

7. Professional Fees

a. To the extent consistent with the market for similar financings, the lender may request reimbursement of reasonable professional fees. The lender should provide reasonably detailed invoices to the debtor and the committees so a proper assessment of reasonableness can be made.

b. The parties may agree on carve-outs for estate professionals. Lenders may exclude from the carve-out payment of professional fees for litigation of the extent, validity or perfection of the lender's claim as well as prosecution of lender liability suits. The carve-out should not, however, exclude the due diligence work by the committee or its professionals to determine whether a challenge to the lender is justified.

8. Work Fees/Loan Fees

a. Underwriting a substantial DIP loan may involve both direct out-of-pocket expenses and, at times, a certain lost opportunity cost. The debtor may move for the reimbursement of its lender's direct out-of-pocket expenses. The debtor and lender must be prepared to establish actual out-of-pocket costs, the reasonableness of the costs, and that the type of costs are actually paid in the market. On a case-by-case basis, the court will consider on an expedited basis the debtor's request to pay a reasonable up-front fee to a prospective DIP lender to reimburse it for direct out-of-pocket costs. In addition, in connection with approving a DIP loan facility, on motion of the debtor, the court will consider evidence of market rates and pricing for comparable loans in determining whether commitment fees, facility or availability fees, and other up-front or periodic loan charges are appropriate. The lender must provide evidence that it actually has provided or will provide the services customarily associated with these fees.

[Dated: December 21, 2000.]

* [**Publisher's Note:** So in original. No subsec. m. promulgated.]

GENERAL ORDER 2003–04. THE MATTER OF THE FILING OF PLEADINGS AND EXHIBITS AND ATTACHMENTS TO PLEADINGS AND PROOF(S) OF CLAIM BY PERSONS NOT REGISTERED AS ELECTRONIC FILING USERS

General Order No. 2003–01 mandates that all cases filed in the Bankruptcy Court for the Northern District of Texas be filed electronically in the court's Electronic Filing System. The court directs that persons accessing the court become registered as a Filing User eligible to file documents in the Electronic Filing System as expeditiously as possible. In recognition of the transition period for persons accessing the court to be registered as a Filing User eligible to file documents in the Electronic Filing System, the following order shall govern the filing of pleadings and the submission of exhibits and attachments to pleadings by persons not yet authorized to be a Filing User.

Pleadings and Other Documents

All pleadings and other documents to be filed with the court by persons not registered to be Electronic Filing Users pursuant to General Order 2003–01 shall be submitted with a diskette containing the pleading or other document in an electronic format that may be uploaded by the court into the Electronic Filing System.

Exhibits and Attachments to Pleadings and Proofs of Claim

1. With regard to the following:

    a. A Plan of Reorganization and Disclosure Statement;

    b. Motions filed pursuant to Fed. R. Bankr. P. 7012, 7056, 7065, 9023, and 9024;

    c. Applications for compensation and reimbursement of expenses;

    d. Trustee's final report and account; and

    e. Any filed document which requires an affidavit to be attached (e.g., application for temporary order) but not including a motion under 11 U.S.C. § 362;

all required exhibits and attachments must be included with the document that is filed with the court and submitted on a diskette. If the exhibit or attachment has been prepared in electronic format, it must be tendered to the court on a diskette. An exhibit or attachment not originally prepared in electronic format must be converted by the filer into an electronic format and submitted to the court for filing on a diskette. The court will upload the entire document with the exhibits and attachments into the Electronic Filing System. An exhibit or attachment not originally prepared in electronic format will not be scanned by the court into the Electronic Filing System.

2. With regard to all other pleadings, if an exhibit or attachment has not been prepared originally in electronic format, the filer must either electronically submit on a diskette an excerpt of the referenced documents that are directly germane to the matter under consideration by the court or a summary of the exhibit. The filer shall clearly and prominently identify excerpted material. The filer may timely submit in electronic format on a diskette additional excerpts or summaries. Responding parties, if they are not Filing Users registered on the Court's Electronic Filing System, may timely electronically submit on a diskette additional excerpts or summaries that they believe are directly germane to the matter under consideration. The complete exhibit or attachment must be served on opposing counsel and, if requested, provided to the court, and must be available in the courtroom at any hearing pertaining to the matter.

3. Exhibits must be available in the courtroom at any hearing pertaining to the filed pleading or document.

Format

The court requests that pleadings, exhibits and attachments be submitted on the required diskette in PDF format as described in the Court's Mandatory Electronic Case Filing Notice. The court will accept other electronic formats, including word processing, provided that the contents may be uploaded by the court into the Electronic Filing System.

[Dated: September 4, 2003.]

GENERAL ORDER 2004–02. IN THE MATTER
OF CHAPTER 7 TRUSTEE EXPENSES
GENERAL ORDER AUTHORIZING CHAPTER 7 TRUSTEES TO PAY EXPENSES

By Standing Order No. 94–1, the court authorized Chapter 7 trustees to advance from bankruptcy estate funds expenses payable to unrelated third parties, subject to subsequent court approval for reasonableness after notice and hearing, provided no single expense exceeded $100, and the aggregate amount of expenses did not exceed $500. The court also authorized the Chapter 7 trustees to advance from estate funds adversary proceeding filing fees.

The court recognized that relatively de minimis expenses should be paid by the Chapter 7 estate without the necessity of notice and hearing in advance of payment. A Chapter 7 trustee who has not been authorized to operate the business of a debtor pursuant to 11 U.S.C. § 721 may incur expenses in the administration of an estate. Under 11 U.S.C. §§ 330 and 331, the court may award the trustee reimbursement for actual, necessary expenses after notice and hearing. The guidelines of the Office of the United States Trustee do not permit a trustee to pay any expenses of administration from the funds of an estate without prior court approval. Standing Order No. 94–1 authorized the trustees to pay the de minimis expenses of administration of an estate without the necessity of notice and hearing in advance of payments.

The court reaffirms the authorization for the Chapter 7 trustees to pay de minimis expenses without the necessity of notice and hearing in advance of payments. Recognizing the impact of inflation since the court entered Standing Order No. 94–1, the court has increased the authorized limits.

IT IS THEREFORE ORDERED that the Chapter 7 trustees are authorized to pay from bankruptcy estate funds:

1.   Expenses to unrelated third parties, subject to subsequent court approval for reasonableness after notice and hearing, provided no single expense exceeds $200, and the aggregate amount of expenses does not exceed $1,000; and

2.   Adversary proceeding filing fees.

IT IS FURTHER ORDERED that this order is effective upon entry and supercedes Standing Order No. 94–1.

The court has authorized the Chief Bankruptcy Judge of the district to enter this order on behalf of the court.

[Dated: May 3, 2004.]

GENERAL ORDER 2005–06. IMPLEMENTATION OF NOTICE OF
PREFERRED ADDRESSES UNDER 11 U.S.C. § 342(e) AND (f)
AND NATIONAL CREDITOR REGISTRATION SERVICE

IT IS HEREBY ORDERED:

1.   An entity and a notice provider may agree that when the notice provider is directed by the Court to give a notice to that entity, the notice provider shall give the notice to the entity in the manner agreed to and at the address or addresses the entity supplies to the notice provider. That address is conclusively presumed to be a proper address for notice. The notice provider's failure to use the supplied address does not invalidate any notice that is otherwise effective under applicable law.

2.   The filing of a notice of preferred address pursuant to 11 U.S.C. § 342(f) by a creditor directly with the agency or agencies that provide noticing services for the Bankruptcy Court will constitute the filing of such a notice with the Court.

3.   Registration with the National Creditor Registration Service must be accomplished through the agency that provides noticing services for the Bankruptcy Court. Forms and registration information are available at www.ncrsuscourts.com.

[Dated: October 20, 2005.]

GENERAL ORDER 2006–02.   IN THE MATTER OF PROCEDURES FOR COMPLEX CHAPTER 11 CASES

By General Order Nos. 2000–06, 2002–05, and 2004–03, the court adopted Procedures for Complex Chapter 11 Cases. The court provided that the procedures would be reviewed from time to time and amended by order of the court. In coordination with the United States Bankruptcy Courts for the Eastern, Southern and Western Districts of Texas, the court has determined to issue revised procedures. Accordingly,

IT IS ORDERED that the court adopts the attached Procedures for Complex Chapter 11 Cases, effective February 01, 2006.

IT IS FURTHER ORDERED that these Procedures For Complex Chapter 11 Cases supersede the procedures adopted by General Order Nos. 2000–06, 2002–05, and 2004–03.

IT IS FURTHER ORDERED that these Procedures For Complex Chapter 11 Cases may be amended from time to time by order of the court.

The court has authorized the Chief Bankruptcy Judge of the district to enter this order on behalf of the court.

PROCEDURES FOR COMPLEX CHAPTER 11 CASES

[**Publisher's Note:** For the Procedures for Complex Chapter 11 Cases, see Appendix E, *ante*.]

EXHIBIT A.   NOTICE OF DESIGNATION AS COMPLEX CHAPTER 11 BANKRUPTCY CASE

IN THE UNITED STATES BANKRUPTCY COURT
FOR THE NORTHERN DISTRICT OF TEXAS

_____ DIVISION

IN RE: §
                         §
                         §   CASE NO. _____
                         §
DEBTOR.   §

NOTICE OF DESIGNATION AS COMPLEX
CHAPTER 11 BANKRUPTCY CASE

This bankruptcy case was filed on _____, 200 ___. The undersigned party in interest believes that this case qualifies as a complex Chapter 11 case because:

☐ The debtor has total debt of more than $10 million;

☐ There are more than 50 parties in interest in this case;

☐ Claims against the debtor are publicly traded;

☐ Other (Substantial explanation is required. Attach additional sheets if necessary.)

_____, 200 ___

Name

Address

Telephone, Fax Numbers, and Email

**EXHIBIT B.   REQUEST FOR EMERGENCY CONSIDERATION
OF CERTAIN "FIRST DAY" MATTERS**

**IN THE UNITED STATES BANKRUPTCY
COURT FOR THE NORTHERN DISTRICT OF TEXAS**

———————— DIVISION

IN RE: §
                                        §
                                        §   CASE NO. ———————————
                                        §
DEBTOR.   §

**REQUEST FOR EMERGENCY CONSIDERATION
OF CERTAIN "FIRST DAY" MATTERS**

On ————, ————————————— filed a petition for relief under Chapter 11 of the Bankruptcy Code. Counsel for the debtor believes that the case qualifies as a "Complex Chapter 11 Case." The debtor needs emergency consideration of the following initial case matters (check those that apply):

☐ JOINT MOTION FOR JOINT ADMINISTRATION

☐ MOTION FOR ORDER EXTENDING TIME TO FILE SCHEDULES AND STATEMENT OF FINANCIAL AFFAIRS

☐ MOTION RE MAINTENANCE OF BANK ACCOUNTS AND EXISTING CASH MANAGEMENT, ATTACHING NOTICE OF CONFERENCE WITH U.S. TRUSTEE

☐ MOTION TO PAY PRE–PETITION WAGES, SALARIES, *ET AL.*, ATTACHING NOTICE OF CONFERENCE WITH U.S. TRUSTEE AND DETAILED EXHIBIT SHOWING WHO DEBTOR PROPOSES TO PAY AND AMOUNTS

☐ MOTION FOR ENTRY OF INTERIM ORDER AUTHORIZING USE OF CASH COLLATERAL

☐ MOTION FOR INTERIM APPROVAL OF POST–PETITION SECURED AND SUPER PRIORITY FINANCING PURSUANT TO SECTION 364(c) OF THE BANKRUPTCY CODE

☐ MOTION PURSUANT TO 11 U.S.C. § 366, FOR ENTRY OF INTERIM ORDER (1) DETERMINING ADEQUATE ASSURANCE OF PAYMENT FOR FUTURE UTILITY SERVICES AND (2) RESTRAINING UTILITY COMPANIES FROM DISCONTINUING, ALTERING, OR REFUSING SERVICE

☐ MOTION TO ESTABLISH INTERIM NOTICE PROCEDURES

☐ MOTION FOR ORDER APPROVING INTERIM RETENTION OF PROFESSIONALS

☐ MOTION FOR ORDER APPROVING PAYMENT OF PRE–PETITION CLAIMS OF CERTAIN CRITICAL VENDORS

☐ OTHERS (LIST):

————————, 200 ——————————————

Name

Address

Telephone, Fax Numbers and Email

* NOTE: The court expects the parties to exercise judgment regarding which motions are applicable.

EXHIBIT C.　ORDER DENYING COMPLEX CASE TREATMENT

**IN THE UNITED STATES BANKRUPTCY COURT
FOR THE NORTHERN DISTRICT OF TEXAS**

_____ DIVISION

IN RE:　　　　　　　　　§
　　　　　　　　　　　　§
　　　　　　　　　　　　§　　CASE NO. _____
　　　　　　　　　　　　§
DEBTOR.　　　　　　　§

**ORDER DENYING COMPLEX
CASE TREATMENT**

This bankruptcy case was filed on _____, 200 ___. A Notice of Designation as Complex Chapter 11 Case was filed. After review of the initial pleadings filed in this case, the court concludes that the case does not appear to qualify as a complex Chapter 11 case. Therefore, the case will proceed under the local bankruptcy rules and procedures generally applicable to bankruptcy cases without special scheduling orders. The court may reconsider this determination on motion, after hearing.

EXHIBIT D. ORDER GRANTING COMPLEX CHAPTER 11 BANKRUPTCY CASE TREATMENT

IN THE UNITED STATES BANKRUPTCY COURT FOR THE NORTHERN DISTRICT OF TEXAS

_____ DIVISION

IN RE:	§	
	§	
	§	CASE NO. _____
	§	
	§	
DEBTOR.	§	

ORDER GRANTING COMPLEX CHAPTER 11 BANKRUPTCY CASE TREATMENT

This bankruptcy case was filed on _____, 2000 ___. A Notice of Designation as Complex Chapter 11 Case was filed. After review of the initial pleadings filed in this case, the court concludes that this case appears to be a complex Chapter 11 case. Accordingly, unless the court orders otherwise,

IT IS ORDERED:

1.   The debtor shall maintain a service list identifying the parties that must be served whenever a motion or other pleading requires notice. Unless otherwise required by the Bankruptcy Code or Rules, notices of motions and other matters will be limited to the parties on the service list.

   a.   The service list shall initially include the debtor, debtor's counsel, counsel for the unsecured creditors' committee, the U.S. Trustee, all secured creditors, the 20 largest unsecured creditors of each debtor, any indenture trustee, and any party that requests notice;

   b.   Any party in interest that wishes to receive notice, other than as listed on the service list, shall be added to the service list by filing and serving the debtor and debtor's counsel with a notice of appearance and request for service.

   c.   Parties on the service list, who have not otherwise consented to service by e-mail, through the act of becoming a registered e-filer in this district, are encouraged to provide an e-mail address for service of process and to authorize service by e-mail; consent to e-mail service may be included in the party's notice of appearance and request for service; in the event a party has not consented to e-mail service, a "hard copy" shall be served by fax or by regular mail.

   d.   The initial service list shall be filed within 3 days after entry of this order. A revised list shall be filed 7 days after the initial service list is filed. The debtor shall update the service list, and shall file a copy of the updated service list, (i) at least every 7 days during the first 30 days of the case; (ii) at least every 15 days during the next 60 days of the case; and (iii) at least every 30 days thereafter throughout the case.

2.   [The court sets _____ of [each week] [every other week, commencing [Month and Day] [each month] at _____ am/pm as the pre-set hearing day and time for hearing all motions and other matters in these cases.].   The court sets the following dates and times for the next two months as the pre-set hearing date and time for hearing all motions and other matters in these cases [insert dates and times]. Settings for the following months will be published by the court no later than 30 days prior to the first hearing date in the said following months. (There may be exceptions; those exceptions will be noted on the court's internet schedule, available at www.txnb.uscourts.gov.)

   a.   All motions and other matters requiring hearing, but not requiring expedited or emergency hearing, shall be noticed for hearing, on the next hearing day that is at least 23 days after the notice is mailed. As a preface to each pleading, just below the case caption, [in lieu of the language required by any Local Bankruptcy Rule] the pleading shall state:

A HEARING WILL BE CONDUCTED ON THIS MATTER ON _____ AT _____ AM/PM IN COURTROOM ___, [COURTHOUSE NAME & ADDRESS], _____, TEXAS. In addition, if the relief sought in the pleading may be urged subject to negative notice, as permitted by Local Bankruptcy Rules 9007.1 and 9014.1 and General Order 2005–01, the pleading may further state:

IF YOU OBJECT TO THE RELIEF REQUESTED, YOU MUST RESPOND IN WRITING, SPECIFICALLY ANSWERING EACH PARAGRAPH OF THIS PLEADING. UNLESS OTHERWISE DIRECTED BY THE COURT, YOU MUST FILE YOUR RESPONSE WITH THE CLERK OF THE BANKRUPTCY COURT WITHIN TWENTY–THREE DAYS FROM THE DATE YOU WERE SERVED WITH THIS PLEADING. YOU MUST SERVE A COPY OF YOUR RESPONSE ON THE PERSON WHO SENT YOU THE NOTICE; OTHERWISE, THE COURT MAY TREAT THE PLEADING AS UNOPPOSED AND GRANT THE RE-LIEF REQUESTED.

b. All motions and other matters requiring expedited or emergency hearing shall comply with the usual court requirements for explanation and verification of the need for emergency or expedited hearing. Specifically, if a party in interest has a situation that it believes requires consideration on less than 23–days' notice, or an emergency that it believes requires consideration on less than 5 business days' notice, then the party should file and serve a separate, written motion for expedited hearing, with respect to the underlying motion. The court will make its best effort to rule on the motion for expedited or emergency hearing within 24 hours of the time it is presented. If the court grants the motion for expedited or emergency hearing, the underlying motion will be set by the courtroom deputy at the next available pre-set hearing day or at some other appropriate shortened date approved by the court. The party requesting the hearing shall be responsible for providing proper notice in accordance with this order and the Bankruptcy Code and Rules.

3. Emergency and expedited hearings (and other hearings in limited circumstances) in this case may be conducted by telephone or, where available, video. Parties must request permission to participate by telephone by calling the courtroom deputy, _____, at _____.

4. If a matter is properly noticed for hearing and the parties reach a settlement of the dispute prior to the final hearing, the parties may announce the settlement at the scheduled hearing. If the court determines that the notice of the dispute and the hearing is adequate notice of the effects of the settlement, (i.e., that the terms of the settlement are not materially different from what parties in interest could have expected if the dispute were fully litigated), the court may approve the settlement at the hearing without further notice of the terms of the settlement.

5. The debtor shall give notice of this order to all parties in interest within 7 days. If any party in interest, at any time, objects to the provisions of this order, that party shall file a motion articulating the objection and the relief requested. After hearing the objection and any responses the court may reconsider any part of this order and may grant relief, if appropriate.

EXHIBIT E.   PROCEDURES FOR OBTAINING HEARINGS
IN COMPLEX CHAPTER 11 CASES

1.   Hearing on First Day Matters: Official Form for Request for Expedited Consideration of Certain First Day Matters.   Upon the filing of a complex Chapter 11 case, if the debtor has matters that require immediate emergency consideration ("first day" or "near first day" relief), the debtor should file a "Request for Emergency Consideration of Certain 'First Day' Matters" using the form of Exhibit B to the Procedures for Complex Chapter 11 Cases ("First Day Hearing Request").   The first day hearing request will be immediately forwarded by the clerk of court to the judge who has been assigned the complex Chapter 11 case (or if there are multiple, related debtor cases, to the judge assigned to the first-filed case).   The court will hold a hearing within 2 business days for the time requested by the debtor's counsel and the courtroom deputy will notify counsel for the debtor of the time of the setting.   If the judge assigned to the complex Chapter 11 case is not available to hold the hearing within 2 business days of the time requested by the debtor's counsel, an available judge will hold a hearing within 2 business days of the time requested by the debtor's counsel and the courtroom deputy will notify counsel for the debtor of the time of the setting.   If no judge is available to hold a hearing within 2 business days, then a hearing date will be scheduled at the earliest possible date that a judge is available.   The debtor's counsel should (1) serve electronically, if the e-mail address is available (or by facsimile or immediate hand-delivery), a copy of the first day hearing request on all affected parties, including the U.S. Trustee, simultaneously with its filing; and (2) notify electronically, if the e-mail address is available, or by fax or telephonically (or by immediate hand-delivery), all affected parties of the hearing time on first day matters as soon as possible after debtor's counsel has received confirmation from the court.   The court will allow parties in interest to participate telephonically at the hearing on first day matters whenever (and to the extent) practicable, and debtor's counsel will be responsible for the coordination of the telephonic participation.

2.   Pre–Set Hearing Dates.   The debtor may request (as one of its first day matters or otherwise) that the court establish in a complex Chapter 11 case a weekly/bi-monthly/monthly setting time ("Pre–Set Hearing Dates") for hearings in the complex Chapter 11 case (*e.g.*, every Wednesday at 1:30 p.m.).   The court will accommodate this request for pre-set hearing dates in a complex Chapter 11 case if it appears justified.   After pre-set hearing dates are established, all matters in the complex Chapter 11 case (whether initiated by a motion of the debtor or by another party in interest) will be set on pre-set hearing dates that are at least 23 days after the filing/service of a particular motion (unless otherwise requested by a party or ordered by the court) and the movant shall indicate the hearing date and time on the face of the pleading.   Movant shall advise the courtroom deputy of all such settings prior to filing, and the courtroom deputy will advise the movant whether there is enough time on the docket that day to accommodate the matter.

3.   Notice of Hearing.   Notice of hearing of matters scheduled for pre-set hearing dates shall be accomplished in the following manner in each district:

Northern District: By the moving party, who shall file a notice of hearing with a certificate of service that proper notice has been accomplished in accordance with these procedures.

Western District: By the moving party, who shall file a certificate that the notice has been accomplished in accordance with these procedures.

Southern District: See Southern District of Texas procedures.

Eastern District: By the moving party, who shall file a certificate that the notice has been accomplished in accordance with these procedures.

4.   Case Emergencies (Other Than the First–Day Matters).   If a party in interest has an expedited or emergency situation that it believes requires consideration on less than 23–days' notice, the party must file and serve a separate, written motion for expedited or emergency hearing, with respect to the underlying motion, which must comply with the usual court requirements for explanation and verification of the need for expedited or emergency hearing.   The court will make its best effort to rule on the motion for expedited or emergency hearing within 24 hours of the time it is presented.   If the court grants the motion for expedited or emergency hearing, the underlying motion will be set by the courtroom deputy at the next available pre-set hearing date or at some other appropriate shortened date approved by the court.   Motions for expedited and emergency hearings will only be granted for clear cause shown and presented with particularity in the body of the motion.

EXHIBIT F.   AGENDA GUIDELINES FOR HEARINGS IN COMPLEX CHAPTER 11 CASES

In complex Chapter 11 cases where five or more matters are noticed for the same hearing date, counsel for the debtor-in-possession, the party requesting the hearings, or trustee shall file and serve an agenda describing the nature of the items set for hearing.

1. **Timing of Filing.** Counsel shall file an agenda at least 24 hours prior to the date and time of the hearing. At the same time, counsel shall also serve the agenda (or confirm electronic service has been effectuated) upon all attorneys who have filed papers with respect to the matters scheduled and upon the service list.

2. **Sequence of Items on Agenda.** Uncontested matters should be listed ahead of contested matters. Contested matters should be listed in the order in which they appear on the court's docket.

3. **Status Information.** For each motion filed in the complex Chapter 11 case, each motion filed in an adversary proceeding concerning the Chapter 11 case, each objection to claim, or application concerning the case, the agenda shall indicate the moving party, the nature of the motion, the docket number of the pleadings, if known, the response deadline, and the status of the matter. The status description should indicate whether the motion is settled, going forward, whether a continuance is requested (and any opposition to the continuance, if known) and any other pertinent information.

4. **Information for Motions in the Case.** For each motion that is going forward, or where a continuance request is not consensual, the agenda shall also list all pleadings in support of the motion, and any objections or responses. Each pleading listed shall identify the entity that filed the pleading and the docket number of the pleading, if known. If any entity has not filed a responsive pleading, but has engaged in written or oral communications with the debtor, that fact should be indicated on the agenda, as well as the status or outcome of those communications. For an omnibus objection to claims, responses to the objection which have been continued by consent may be listed collectively (e.g., "the following responses have been continued by consent:").

5. **Changes in Agenda Information.** After the filing of the agenda, counsel shall notify judge's chambers by phone or letter of additional related pleadings that have been filed, and changes in the status of any agenda matter.

6. The requirements listed above should not be construed to prohibit other information of a procedural nature that counsel thinks would be helpful to the court.

ALL MOTIONS AND PLEADINGS SHALL CONTAIN THE HEARING DATE AND TIME BELOW THE CASE/ADVERSARY NUMBER.

EXHIBIT G.   GUIDELINES FOR SERVICE LISTS AND SHORTENED SERVICE LISTS IN COMPLEX CHAPTER 11 CASES

I.   Bankruptcy Rule 2002 Notice/Service List

A.   Helpful Hints Regarding Whom to Include on the Service List in a Complex Chapter 11 Case. There are certain events and deadlines that occur in a Chapter 11 case which Federal Rules of Bankruptcy Procedure 2002 requires be broadly noticed to all creditors, indenture trustees, equity interest holders, and other parties in interest ("Rule 2002 notice list"). To facilitate this, debtor's counsel shall evaluate and consider whether the following persons and entities need to be included on the Rule 2002 notice list:

1.   creditors (whether a creditor's claim is disputed, undisputed, contingent, non-contingent, liquidated, unliquidated, matured, unmatured, fixed, legal, equitable, secured or unsecured);

2.   indenture trustees;

3.   financial institutions at which the debtor has maintained accounts (regardless of whether such institutions are creditors);

4.   vendors with whom the debtor has dealt, even if the debtor's records currently indicate no amount is owed;

5.   parties to contracts, executory contracts or leases with the debtor;

6.   federal, state, or local taxing authorities with which the debtor deals, including taxing authorities in every county in which the debtor owns real or personal property with regard to which ad valorem taxes might be owed;

7.   governmental entities with which the debtor might interact (including, but not limited to, the U.S. Trustee and the SEC);

8.   any party who might assert a lien against property of the debtor;

9.   parties to litigation involving the debtor;

10.   parties with which the debtor might be engaged in some sort of dispute, whether or not a claim has formally been made against the debtor;

11.   tort claimants or accident victims;

12.   insurance companies with whom the debtor deals or has policies;

13.   active and retired employees of the debtor;

14.   officers or directors of the debtor;

15.   customers who are owed deposits, refunds, or store credit;

16.   utilities;

17.   shareholders (preferred and common), holders of options, warrants or other rights or equitable interests in the debtor;

18.   miscellaneous others who, in debtor counsel's judgment, might be entitled to "party in interest" status or who have requested notice.

B.   Flexible ("User Friendly") Format Rules for Mailing Matrix or Creditor List in a Complex Debtor 11 Case in Which Debtor's Counsel Serves Notices. In a complex Chapter 11 case, where the mailing matrix (or creditor list) is likely to be very lengthy, the following special format rules will apply, [in lieu of any applicable local bankruptcy rule, save and except the Administrative Procedures for the Filing, Signing and Verifying of Documents by Electronic Means in Texas Bankruptcy Courts, adopted by local rule or general order in all federal districts in Texas] whenever it is the debtor's responsibility to serve notices in the case. The debtor (since it will typically be the party serving all notices in the Chapter 11 case rather than the clerk of court) may create the mailing matrix or creditor list in whatever format it finds convenient so long as it is neatly typed in upper and lower case letter-quality characters (in no smaller than 10 point and no greater than 14 point type, in either Courier, Times Roman, Helvetica or Orator font) in a format equivalent to 8 ½ inch by 11 inch blank, unlined, standard white paper. The mailing matrix or creditor list, if lengthy, should ideally include separate subheadings throughout, to help identify categories of parties in interest. By way of example, the following subheadings (among others) might be used:

Debtor and its Professionals

Secured Creditors
Indenture Trustees
Unsecured Creditors
Governmental Entities
Current and Retired Employees
Officers and Directors
Tort Claimants
Parties to Executory Contracts
Equity Interest Holders
Other

Parties in interest within each category/subheading should be listed alphabetically.

Also, the mailing matrix or creditor list may be filed in separate volumes, for the separate categories of parties in interest, if the mailing matrix or creditor list is voluminous. Finally, if there are multiple, related debtors and the debtors intend to promptly move for joint administration of their cases, the debtors may file a consolidated mailing matrix or creditor list, subject to later being required to file separate mailing matrices if joint administration is not permitted.

C. When Inclusion of Certain Parties in Interest on a Mailing Matrix is Burdensome. If inclusion of certain categories of parties in interest on the mailing matrix or creditor list would be extremely impracticable, burdensome and costly to the estate, the debtor may file a motion, pursuant to FRBP 2002(l), and on notice to the affected categories of parties in interest, requesting authority to provide notices to certain categories of parties in interest and may forego including those categories of parties in interest on the mailing matrix if the court grants the motion.

II. Shortened Service List Procedure in a Complex Chapter 11 Case

A. Procedures/Contents/Presumptions. If the court has entered an order granting complex Chapter 11 case treatment, the debtor shall provide service as required by paragraph 1 of that order. If the court has not entered such an order, the debtor may move to limit notice—that is, for approval of a shortened service list—that will be acceptable for noticing most events in the bankruptcy case, other than those events/deadlines that Federal Rules of Bankruptcy Procedure 2002 contemplates be served on all creditors and equity interest holders. At a minimum, the shortened list should include the debtor and its professionals, the secured creditors, the 20 largest unsecured creditors, any official committees and the professionals for same, the U.S. Trustee, the IRS and other relevant governmental entities, and all parties who have requested notice. Upon the court's approval of a shortened service list in a complex Chapter 11 case, notice in any particular situation during a case shall be presumed adequate if there has been service on (1) the most current service list on file in the case; plus (2) any other party directly affected by the relief requested and not otherwise included on the service list.

B. Obligation to Update, File and Serve Service List. The debtor must update the service list as parties request to be added to it or as circumstances otherwise require. To be added to the list, a party must file a notice of appearance and request for service and serve the notice on debtor's counsel. Parties should include e-mail transmission information if they wish to receive expedited service of process during the case. Additionally, the debtor must file an updated service list and must serve a clean and redlined copy of the updated service list on all parties on the service list weekly for the first month after filing, then bi-monthly for the next 60 days, then monthly thereafter during the pendency of the case. If, in a particular month, there are no changes to the service list, the debtor must file a notice with the court so stating.

EXHIBIT H.   GUIDELINES FOR COMPENSATION AND EXPENSE REIMBURSEMENT OF PROFESSIONALS IN COMPLEX CHAPTER 11 CASES*

[The following order is an exemplar of the type of order that a district may enter if it chooses to implement the guidelines which follow.   It is recommended that each such district do so, as achieving uniformity in the handling of professional compensation is an important component of the administration of complex chapter 11 cases.]

* [Publisher's Note: *See* also Appendix F, *ante*.]

STANDING ORDER CONCERNING GUIDELINES FOR COMPENSATION AND EXPENSE REIMBURSEMENT OF PROFESSIONALS, FOR EARLY DISPOSITION OF ASSETS IN CHAPTER 11 CASES, AND FOR MOTIONS AND ORDERS PERTAINING TO USE OF CASH COLLATERAL AND POST–PETITION FINANCING

ORDER

The Court having previously adopted the attached Guidelines for compensation and Expense Reimbursement of Professionals, Guideline for Early Disposition of Assets in Chapter 11 Cases, and Attorney Checklist Concerning Motions and Order Pertaining to Use of Cash Collateral and Post–Petition Financing,

IT IS HEREBY ORDERED that the attached guidelines are applicable in accordance with their terms to compensation and expenses reimbursement of professionals, to procedures for the early disposition of assets in Chapter 11 cases, and to motions and orders pertaining to the use of cash collateral and post-petition financing.

SO ORDERED.

GUIDELINES FOR COMPENSATION AND EXPENSE REIMBURSEMENT OF PROFESSIONALS

The following are guidelines govern the most significant issues relating to applications for compensation and expense reimbursement.   The guidelines cover the narrative portion of an application, time records, and expenses.   It applies to all professionals, but is not intended to cover every situation.   All professionals are required to exercise reasonable billing judgment, notwithstanding total hours spent.

If, in a chapter 11 case, a professional to be employed pursuant to section 327 or 1103 of the Bankruptcy Code desires to have the terms of its compensation approved pursuant to section 328(a) of the Bankruptcy Code at the time of such professional's retention, then the application seeking such approval should so indicate and the Court will consider such request after an evidentiary hearing on notice to be held after the United States trustee has had an opportunity to form a statutory committee of creditors pursuant to section 1102 of the Bankruptcy Code and the debtor had such committee have had an opportunity to review and comment on such application.   At a hearing to consider whether a professional's compensation arrangement should be approved pursuant to section 328(a), such professional should be prepared to produce evidence that the terms of compensation for which approval under section 328(a) is sought comply with the certification requirements of section I.G(3) of these guidelines.

I. NARRATIVE

A.   Employment and Prior Compensation. The application should disclose the date of the order approving applicant's employment and contain a clear statement itemizing the date of each prior request for compensation, the amount requested, the amount approved, and the amount paid.

B.   Case Status. With respect to interim requests, the application should briefly explain the history and the present posture of the case, including a description of the status of pending litigation and the amount of recovery sought for the estate.

In chapter 11 cases, the information furnished should describe the general operations of the debtor; whether the business of the debtor, if any, is being operated at a profit or loss; the debtor's cash flow; whether a plan has been filed, and if not, what the prospects are for reorganization and when it is anticipated that a plan will be filed and a hearing set on the disclosure statement.

In chapter 7 cases, the application should contain a report of the administration of the case including the disposition of property of the estate; what property remains to be disposed of; why the estate is not in a position to be closed; and whether it is feasible to pay an interim dividend to creditors.

In both chapter 7 and chapter 11 cases, the application should state the amount of money on hand in the estate and the estimated amount of other accrued expenses of administration. On applications for interim fees, the applicant should orally supplement the application at the hearing to inform the Court of any changes in the current financial status of the debtor's estate since the filing of the application. All retainers, previous draw downs, and fee applications and orders should be listed specifying the date of the event and the amounts involved and drawn down or allowed.

With respect to final requests, applications should meet the same criteria except where a chapter 7 trustee's final account if being heard at the same time, the financial information in the final account need not be repeated.

Fee applications submitted by special counsel seeking compensation from a fund generated directly by their efforts, auctioneers, real estate brokers, or appraisers do not have to comply with the above. For all other applications, when more than one application is noticed for the same hearing, they may, to the extent appropriate, incorporate by reference the narrative history furnished in a contemporaneous application.

C. **Project Billing.** This is required in all cases where the applicant's professional fee is expected to exceed $10,000.00. The narrative should be categorized by subject matter, and separately discuss each professional project or task. All work for which compensation is requested should be in a category. Miscellaneous items may be included in a category such as "Case Administration." The professional may use reasonable discretion in defining projects for this purpose, provided that the application provides meaningful guidance to the Court as to the complexity and difficulty of the task, the professional's efficiency, and the results achieved. With respect to each project or task, the number of hours spent and the amount of compensation and expenses requested should be set forth at the conclusion of the discussion of that project or task. In larger cases with multiple professionals, efforts should be made by the professionals for standard categorization.

D. **Billing Summary.** Hours and total compensation requested in each application should be aggregate and itemized as to each professional and paraprofessional who provided compensable services. Dates of changes in rates should be itemized as well as reasons for said changes.

E. **Paraprofessionals.** Fees may be sought for paralegals, professional assistants and law clerks only if identified as such and if the application includes a resume or summary of the paraprofessional's qualifications.

F. **Preparation of Application.** Reasonable fees for preparation of a fee application and responding to objections thereto may be requested. The aggregate number of hours spent, the amount requested, and the percentage of the total request which the amount represents must be disclosed. If the actual time spent will be reflected and charged in a future fee application, this fact should be stated, but an estimate provided, nevertheless.

G. **Certification.** Each application for compensation and expense reimbursement must contain a certification by the professional designated by the applicant with the responsibility in the particular case for compliance with these guidelines ("Certifying Professional") that 1) the Certifying Professional has read the application; 2) to the best of the Certifying Professional's knowledge, information and belief, formed after reasonable inquiry, the compensation and expense reimbursement sought is in conformity with these guidelines, except as specifically noted in the application; and 3) the compensation and expenses reimbursement requested are billed at rates, in accordance with practices, no less favorable than those customarily employed by the applicant and generally accepted by the applicant's clients.

H. **Interim Compensation Arrangements in Complex Cases.** In a complex case, the Court may, upon request, consider at the outset of the case approval of an interim compensation mechanism for estate professionals that would enable professionals on a monthly basis to be paid up to 80% of their compensation for services rendered and reimbursed up to 100% of their actual and necessary out of pocket expenses. In connection with such a procedure, if approved in a particular complex case, professionals shall be required to circulate monthly billing statements to the US Trustee and other primary parties in interest, and the Debtor in Possession or Trustee will be authorized to pay the applicable percentage of such bill not disputed or contested by a party in interest.

II. TIME RECORDS

A. Time Records Required. All professionals, except auctioneers, real estate brokers, and appraisers must keep accurate contemporaneous time records.

B. Increments. Professionals are required to keep time records in minimum increments no greater than six minutes. Professionals who utilize a minimum billing increment greater than .1 hour are subject to a substantial reduction of their requests.

C. Descriptions. At a minimum, the time entries should identify the person performing the service, the date(s) performed, what was done, and the subject involved. Mere notations of telephone calls, conferences, research, drafting, etc., without identifying the matter involved, may result in disallowance of the time covered by the entries.

D. Grouping of Tasks. If a number of separate tasks are performed on a single day, the fee application should disclose the time spent for each such task, i.e., no "grouping" or "clumping." Minor administrative matters may be lumped together where the aggregate time attributed thereto is relatively minor. A rule of reason applies as to how specific and detailed the breakdown needs to be. For grouped entries, the applicant must accept the Court inferences therefrom.

E. Conferences. Professionals should be prepared to explain time spent in conferences with other professionals or paraprofessionals in the same firm. Relevant explanation would include complexity of issues involved and the necessity of more individuals' involvement. Failure to justify this time may result in disallowance of all, or a portion of, fees related to such conferences.

F. Multiple Professionals. Professionals should be prepared to explain the need for more than one professional or paraprofessional from the same firm at the same court hearing, deposition, or meeting. Failure to justify this time may result in compensation for only the person with the lowest billing rate. The Court acknowledges, however, that in complex chapter 11 cases the need for multiple professionals' involvement will be more common and that in hearings involving multiple or complex issues a law firm may justifiably be required to utilize multiple attorneys as the circumstances of the case require.

G. Travel Time. Travel time is compensable at one-half rates, but work actually done during travel is fully compensable.

H. Administrative Tasks. Time spent in addressing, stamping and stuffing envelopes, filing, photocopying or "supervising" any of the foregoing is generally not compensable, whether performed by a professional, paraprofessional, or secretary.

III. EXPENSES

A. Firm Practice. The Court will consider the customary practice of the firm in charging or not charging non-bankruptcy/insolvency clients for particular expense items. Where any other clients, with the exception of pro-bono clients, are not billed for a particular expense, the estate should not be billed. Where expenses are billed to all other clients, reimbursement should be sought at the least expensive rate the firm or professional charges to any client for comparable services or expenses. It is recognized that there will be differences in billing practices among professionals.

B. Actual Cost. This is defined as the amount paid to a third party provider of goods or services without enhancement for handling or other administrative charge.

C. Documentation. This must be retained and made available upon request for all expenditures in excess of $50.00. Where possible, receipts should be obtained for all expenditures.

D. Office Overhead. This is not reimbursable. Overhead includes: secretarial time, secretarial overtime (where clear necessity for same has not been shown), word processing time, charges for after-hour and weekend air conditioning and other utilities, and cost of meals or transportation provided to professionals and staff who work late or on weekends.

E. Word Processing. This is not reimbursable.

F. Computerized Research. This is reimbursable at actual cost. For large amounts billed to computerized research, significant explanatory detail should be furnished.

G. Paraprofessional Services. These services may be compensated as a paraprofessional under § 330, but not charged or reimbursed as an expense.

H. Professional Services. A professional employed under § 327, may not employ, and charge as an expense, another professional (e.g., special litigation counsel employing an expert witness) unless the employment of the second professional is approved by the Court prior to the rendering of service.

I. Photocopies (Internal). Charges must be disclosed on an aggregate and per-page basis. If the per-page cost exceeds $.20, the professional must demonstrate to the satisfaction of the Court, with data, that the per-page cost represents a good faith estimate of the actual cost of the copies, based upon the purchase or lease cost of the copy machine and supplies therefor, including the space occupied by the machine, but not including time spent in operating the machine.

J. Photocopies (Outside). This item is reimbursable at actual cost.

K. Postage. This is reimbursable at actual cost.

L. Overnight Delivery. This is reimbursable at actual cost where it is shown to be necessary. The court acknowledges that in complex chapter 11 cases overnight delivery or messenger services may often be appropriate, particularly when shortened notice of a hearing has been requested.

M. Messenger Service. This is reimbursable at actual cost where it is shown to be necessary. An in-house messenger service is reimbursable, but the estate cannot be charged more than the cost of comparable services available outside the firm.

N. Facsimile Transmission. The actual cost of telephone charges for outgoing transmissions is reimbursable. Transmissions received are reimbursable on a per-page basis. If the per-page cost exceeds $.20, the professional must demonstrate, with data, to the satisfaction of the Court, that the per-page cost represents a good faith estimate of the actual cost of the copies, based upon the purchase or lease cost of the facsimile machine and supplies therefor, including the space occupied by the machine, but not including time spent in operating the machine.

O. Long Distance Telephone. This is reimbursable at actual cost.

P. Parking. This is reimbursable at actual cost.

Q. Air Transportation. Air travel is expected to be at regular coach fare for all flights.

R. Hotels. Due to wide variation in hotel costs in various cities, it is not possible to establish a single guideline for this type of expense. All persons will be required to exercise reasonable discretion and prudence in connection with hotel expenditures.

S. Meals (Travel). Reimbursement may be sought for the reasonable cost of breakfast, lunch and dinner while traveling.

T. Meals (Working). Working meals at restaurants or private clubs are not reimbursable. Reasonable reimbursement may be sought for working meals only where food is catered to the professional's office in the course of a meeting with clients, such as a Creditors' Committee, for the purpose of allowing the meeting to continue through a normal meal period.

U. Amenities. Charges for entertainment, alcoholic beverages, newspapers, dry cleaning, shoe shines, etc. are not reimbursable.

V. Filing Fees. These are reimbursable at actual cost.

W. Court Reporter Fees. These are reimbursable at actual cost.

X. Witness Fees. These are reimbursable at actual cost.

Y. Process Service. This is reimbursable at actual cost.

Z. UCC Searches. These are reimbursable at actual cost.

[Dated: January 13, 2006.]

CLERK'S NOTICE 07–04. ELECTRONIC COMMUNICATION DEVICES ON COURT FLOORS

On August 27, 2007, the United States District Court for the Northern District of Texas entered Miscellaneous Order No. 63* regarding use of electronic communication devices, including but not limited to, cellular telephones, pagers, personal digital assistants, and laptop computers, on court floors within the Northern District of Texas. The order is **effective September 1, 2007,** and provides for division-specific exceptions which include exceptions for the bankruptcy court as follows:

Abilene Bankruptcy Court—Electronic communication devices may be used by any person having business with the court in the hallway outside of the courtroom, but they may not be brought into the courtroom.

Amarillo Bankruptcy Court—Electronic communication devices may be used by any person having business with the court in the hallway outside of the courtroom, but they may not be brought into the courtroom.

Dallas Bankruptcy Court—Electronic communication devices may be used by any person who produces a written authorization signed by a judge or the judge's designee; or an attorney with a valid bar identification card having business in the chambers or courtroom of Chief Judge Houser, Judge Hale, or Judge Jernigan may bring electronic communication devices onto the 14th floor.

Fort Worth Bankruptcy Court—Electronic communication devices may be used by any person who produces a written authorization signed by Judge Lynn or Judge Nelms; or an attorney with a valid bar identification card who has business in the chambers or courtroom of Judge Lynn or Judge Nelms may bring electronic communication devices onto the **first and second floor.**

Lubbock Bankruptcy Court—Electronic communication devices may be used by any person having business with the court in the hallway outside of the courtroom, but they may not be brought into the courtroom.

San Angelo Bankruptcy Court—Electronic communication devices may be used by any person having business with the court in the hallway outside of the courtroom, but they may not be brought into the courtroom.

Wichita Falls Bankruptcy Court—Electronic communication devices may be used by any person having business with the court in the hallway outside of the courtroom, but they may not be brought into the courtroom.

Please direct any questions you may have regarding the use of electronic devices on bankruptcy court floors to the appropriate divisional manager. For a complete copy of Miscellaneous Order No. 63, please visit www.txnd.uscourts.gov.

[Dated: August 30, 2007.]

*[**Publisher's Note:** For the text of Miscellaneous Order No. 63, *see* the Selected Orders of the United States District Court the for the Northern District of Texas, *ante*.]

GENERAL ORDER 2008–01. IN THE MATTER OF VACATING GENERAL ORDERS 2005–04 AND 2006–07

When the Bankruptcy Abuse Prevention and Consumer Protection Act of 2005 (the "Act") was enacted into law, this court adopted Interim Bankruptcy Rules approved by the Judicial Conference in General Orders 2005–04 and 2006–07.

New rules and amendments to the Federal Rules of Bankruptcy Procedure will take effect on December 1, 2008, unless Congress acts to the contrary, and will supersede the Interim Bankruptcy Rules adopted by the Court with the exception of Interim Rule 5012 (Communication of and Cooperation with Foreign Courts and Foreign Representatives). Accordingly, General Orders 2005–04 and 2006–07 are vacated as of December 1, 2008.

[Dated: November 25, 2008.]

[**Publisher's Note:** The text of Interim Bankruptcy Rule 5012 is reproduced below:

Rule 5012. Communication and Cooperation With Foreign Courts and Foreign Representatives. Except for communications for scheduling and administrative purposes, the court in any case commenced by a foreign representative shall give at least 20 days' notice of its intent to communicate with a foreign court or a foreign representative. The notice shall identify the subject of the anticipated communication and shall be given in the manner provided by Rule 2002(q). Any entity that wishes to participate in the communication shall notify the court of its intention not later than 5 days before the scheduled communication.]

GENERAL ORDER 2016–03. IN THE MATTER OF INVESTMENT OF REGISTRY FUNDS
ORDER REGARDING DEPOSIT AND INVESTMENT OF REGISTRY FUNDS

The Court, having determined that it is necessary to adopt local procedures to ensure uniformity in the deposit, investment, and tax administration of funds in the Court's Registry,

IT IS ORDERED that the following shall govern the receipt, deposit, and investment of registry funds:

I. Receipt of Funds.

A. No money shall be sent to the Court or its officers for deposit in the Court's registry without a court order signed by the presiding judge in the case or proceeding.

B. The party making the deposit or transferring funds to the Court's registry shall serve the order permitting the deposit or transfer on the Clerk of Court.

C. Unless provided for elsewhere in this Order, all monies ordered to be paid to the Court or received by its officers in any case pending or adjudicated shall be deposited with the Treasurer of the United States in the name and to the credit of this Court pursuant to 28 U.S.C. § 2041 through depositories designated by the Treasury to accept such deposit on its behalf.

II. Investment of Registry Funds.

A. Where, by order of the Court, funds on deposit with the Court are to be placed in some form of interest-bearing account or invested in a court-approved, interest-bearing instrument in accordance with Rule 67 of the Federal Rules of Civil Procedure, the Court Registry Investment System ("CRIS"), administered by the Administrative Office of the United States Courts under 28 U.S.C. § 2045, shall be the only investment mechanism authorized.

B. Interpleader funds deposited under 28 U.S.C. § 1335 meet the IRS definition of a "Disputed Ownership Fund" (DOF), a taxable entity that requires tax administration. Unless otherwise ordered by the court, interpleader funds shall be deposited in the DOF established within the CRIS and administered by the Administrative Office of the United States Courts, which shall be responsible for meeting all DOF tax administration requirements.

C. The Director of Administrative Office of the United States Courts is designated as custodian for all CRIS funds. The Director or the Director's designee shall perform the duties of custodian. Funds held in the CRIS remain subject to the control and jurisdiction of the Court.

D. Money from each case deposited in the CRIS shall be "pooled" together with those on deposit with Treasury to the credit of other courts in the CRIS and used to purchase Government Account Series securities through the Bureau of Public Debt, which will be held at Treasury, in an account in the name and to the credit of the Director of Administrative Office of the United States Courts. The pooled funds will be invested in accordance with the principles of the CRIS Investment Policy as approved by the Registry Monitoring Group.

E. An account will be established in the CRIS Liquidity Fund titled in the name of the case giving rise to the deposit invested in the fund. Income generated from fund investments will be distributed to each case based on the ratio each account's principal and earnings has to the aggregate principal and income total in the fund after the CRIS fee has been applied. Reports showing the interest earned and the principal amounts contributed in each case will be prepared and distributed to each court participating in the CRIS and made available to litigants and/or their counsel.

F. For each interpleader case, an account shall be established in the CRIS Disputed Ownership Fund, titled in the name of the case giving rise to the deposit invested in the fund. Income generated from fund investments will be distributed to each case after the DOF fee has been applied and tax withholdings have been deducted from the fund. Reports showing the interest earned and the principal amounts contributed in each case will be available through the FedInvest/CMS application for each court participating in the CRIS and made available to litigants and/or their counsel. On appointment of an administrator authorized to incur expenses on behalf of the DOF in a case, the case DOF funds should be transferred to another investment account as directed by court order.

III. Fees and Taxes.

A. The custodian is authorized and directed by this Order to deduct the CRIS fee of an annualized 10 basis points on assets on deposit for all CRIS funds, excluding the case funds held in the DOF, for the management of investments in the CRIS. According to the Court's Miscellaneous Fee Schedule, the CRIS fee is assessed from interest earnings to the pool before a pro rata distribution of earnings is made to court cases.

B. The custodian is authorized and directed by this Order to deduct the DOF fee of an annualized 20 basis points on assets on deposit in the DOF for management of investments and tax administration. According to the Court's Miscellaneous Fee Schedule, the DOF fee is assessed from interest earnings to the pool before a pro rata distribution of earnings is made to court cases. The custodian is further authorized and directed by this Order to withhold and pay federal taxes due on behalf of the DOF.

IV. Transition From Former Investment Procedure.

A. The Clerk of Court is further directed to develop a systematic method of redemption of all existing investments and their transfer to the CRIS.

B. Deposits to the CRIS DOF will not be transferred from any existing CRIS Funds. Only new deposits pursuant to 28 U.S.C. § 1335 from the effective date of April 1, 2017 will be placed in the CRIS DOF.

C. Parties not wishing to transfer certain existing registry deposits into the CRIS may seek leave to transfer them to the litigants or their designees on proper motion and approval of the judge assigned to the specific case.

D. This Order supersedes and abrogates all prior orders of this Court regarding the deposit and investment of registry funds.

[Dated: November 17, 2016.]

GENERAL ORDER 2017–01. IN RE: STANDING ORDER CONCERNING ALL CHAPTER 13 CASES

STANDING ORDER CONCERNING ALL CHAPTER 13 CASES

IT IS HEREBY ORDERED:

1. **Effective Date.** Unless otherwise ordered by the Court in a given Case or Cases, this General Order shall be effective as of July 1, 2017. This General Order governs and supersedes General Orders 2010–01, 2013–01, 2014–03, 2016–01 and it applies in all Chapter 13 Cases filed on, filed after, or pending as of or after the Effective Date in all Divisions of the United States Bankruptcy Court for the Northern District of Texas. Each Chapter 13 Trustee shall place a copy of this General Order on the Trustee's website and, upon request, shall furnish a copy of it to any party in interest in any pending Case.

2. **Definitions.** The following definitions shall apply to and are provisions of this General Order[1]
—

AAPD—An Authorization for Adequate Protection Disbursements that is filed with the Court.

Base Amount—The sum of the total payments required to be made to the Trustee pursuant to the Debtor's confirmed Plan; a Court approved Plan Modification; any Notice of Payment Change; any allowed Notice of Fees, Expenses, and Charges; any order entered by the Court; and any other provision of this General Order.

Case—A Chapter 13 bankruptcy case pending in the Northern District of Texas.

Claims Bar Date—The date set for the filing of claims pursuant to the Bankruptcy Rules and 11 U.S.C. §§ 502(a)(9) and 1308.

Collateral—The property securing a claim.

Conduit Case—A Case in which the Debtor is required to or elects to pay all Mortgage Arrearage(s), the Current Post–Petition Mortgage Payment(s), and any Mortgage Fees owed to the Mortgage Lender through disbursements by the Trustee.

Conduit Debtor—Any Debtor required by the provisions of this General Order to participate in the Conduit Program or any Debtor that elects to be a Conduit Debtor.

Conduit Program—The process by which all Mortgage Arrearage(s), the Current Post-petition Mortgage Payment(s), and any Mortgage Fees owed to the Mortgage Lender are disbursed by the Trustee.

Conversion Date—The date of the conversion of a pending bankruptcy case to a Chapter 13 Case.

Converted Case—A bankruptcy case originally filed under Chapter 7, 11, or 12 and then converted to a Chapter 13 Case.

Current Post–Petition Mortgage Payment(s)—The ongoing, periodic mortgage payments, including all escrow amounts, owed by Debtors to their Mortgage Lenders.

Debtor—Any individual with a pending Case as of or after the Effective Date. Such term shall include a Conduit Debtor.

Debtor's Counsel—The attorney(s) representing the Debtor and, with regard to *pro se* Debtors, the Debtor, individually.

Mortgage Arrearage—Any pre- or post-petition past due payments or any other charges owed to the Mortgage Lender, other than Mortgage Fees.

Mortgage Fees—Any post-petition fees, expenses, and charges that are allowed following the filing by the Mortgage Lender of a proper and timely Notice of Fees, Expenses, and Charges pursuant to Bankruptcy Rule 3002.1(c).

Mortgage Lender—Any lender secured by a security interest in the Debtor's principal residence or homestead property or any agent of such lender.

Mortgage Loan—Any loan secured by a lien on the Debtor's principal residence or homestead property.

Nonstandard Provision—a provision not otherwise included in the Trustee's approved Plan form or which deviates from the Trustee's approved Plan form.

Notice of Fees, Expenses, and Charges—The notice required pursuant to Bankruptcy Rule 3002.1(c) which notice complies with the provisions of that Rule and any applicable Local Bankruptcy Rules.

Notice of Payment Change by Mortgage Lender—The notice required pursuant to Bankruptcy Rule 3002.1(b) which notice complies with the provisions of that Rule and any applicable Local Bankruptcy Rules.

Notice of Plan Payment Adjustment—The notice sent by the Trustee to the Conduit Debtor, Debtor's Counsel, and the Mortgage Lender, notifying the Conduit Debtor of an adjustment to the monthly Plan Payment to be paid to the Trustee.

Notice to Reserve Funds—A notice filed with the Court by any party-in-interest requesting that the Trustee reserve funds received from the Conduit Debtor which would otherwise be disbursed by the Trustee to the Mortgage Lender or, if filed by the Trustee, notifying parties that the Trustee will reserve funds as described therein.

Petition Date—The date the Case is filed.

Plan—The document required to be filed by the Debtor in compliance with the applicable provisions of the Bankruptcy Code and Bankruptcy Rules and any pre-confirmation amendment thereto which shall be filed using a form approved by the Trustee and containing all information required in the Trustee's approved form. Any Nonstandard Provision shall be set out in Section III of the Chapter 13 Plan form in the designated area for same. Any changes to the Trustee's approved Plan form that do not conform to the preceding sentence or any Nonstandard Provision set out elsewhere in the Plan are ineffective and will not be considered a part of the Plan confirmed by the Court.

Plan Modification—Any modification of the Plan filed with the Court post-confirmation pursuant to 11 U.S.C. § 1329.

Plan Payment(s)—The monthly payment amount which the Debtor is required to pay to the Trustee pursuant to the AAPD, the Plan, any Plan Modification, any Notice of Plan Payment Adjustment, or any order of the Court. A Plan Payment may be for the purposes of a pre-confirmation or post-confirmation disbursement, may include payments for leases of personal property that become due after the Petition Date or Conversion Date in accordance with Section 1326(a)(1)(B) of the Bankruptcy Code, and/or adequate protection payments in accordance with Section 1326(a)(1)(C) of the Bankruptcy Code, to the extent the Trustee is to disburse such payments.

Service—Service on parties in interest is governed by the applicable provisions of the Bankruptcy Code, the Bankruptcy Rules, all Local Rules applicable in bankruptcy cases, and General Order 2004–06, as they may be amended or superseded from time to time. When a Debtor is represented by an attorney, Service shall be on both the Debtor and Debtor's Counsel.

Surrendered Collateral—The Collateral to be surrendered under the Plan or allowed to be surrendered in any Plan Modification.

Trustee—The Trustee appointed in the Case by the United States Trustee, including the Standing Chapter 13 Trustee or the United States Trustee if serving as Trustee in the Case.

Trustee's Percentage Fee—That fee which may be collected by the Trustee as set out in 28 U.S.C. § 586(e).

3. Dismissal Without Further Notice. A Case may be dismissed without prejudice and without further notice after 14 days (as to subsections (d)(5) and (e) deficiencies) or 7 days (as to subsections (a), (b), (c), (d)(1), (d)(2), (d)(3), or (d)(4) deficiencies) if a prior written Notice of Intent to Dismiss ("NOI") is filed with the Court and served on the Debtor and Debtor's Counsel unless any default or deficiency is cured prior to the expiration of such period. The Clerk is authorized to enter an Order of Dismissal upon certification by the Trustee, or such other authority ordered by the Court or allowed by law, that—

(a) The Debtor did not file all of the documents required by Sections 521(a)(1) and 521(b) of the Bankruptcy Code within 14 days of the Petition Date or Conversion Date, unless within such time, the Debtor filed a motion to extend such time or, if an extension of time is granted, such documents are not filed within the extended time; or

(b) The Debtor did not file with the petition or serve on all scheduled creditors (or to be scheduled creditors if the Schedules have not been filed) a Plan as required by Section 1321 of the Bankruptcy Code and Bankruptcy Rule 3015(b), and an AAPD as required herein, on forms prescribed by the Trustee, within 14 days of the Petition Date or Conversion Date unless within such time(s), the Debtor filed with the Clerk and served on all scheduled creditors (or to be scheduled creditors) a motion to extend such time(s) or, if an extension of time is granted, such documents are not filed within the extended time; or

(c) The Debtor did not pay the first Plan Payment to the Trustee within 30 days after the Petition Date or the Conversion Date as required by Section 1326(a)(1) of the Bankruptcy Code; or

(d) *The Debtor failed to*—

(1) Attend the Section 341 Meeting of Creditors as required by Section 343 of the Bankruptcy Code (the "Section 341 Meeting") or any continued Section 341 Meeting which the Trustee required the Debtor to attend, without the agreement of the Trustee to continue the Section 341 Meeting;

(2) Provide to the Trustee, not later than 7 days before the date first set for the Section 341 Meeting, a copy of the Federal Income Tax Return or a transcript for the most recent tax year ending immediately before the Petition Date or Conversion Date for which a return was filed, as required by Section 521(e)(2)(A)(I) of the Bankruptcy Code, or the Debtor failed to timely file, with the appropriate taxing authorities, the tax returns required by Section 1308 of the Bankruptcy Code, unless the Trustee agrees to hold open the Section 341 Meeting (up to 120 days) as provided in Section 1308(b)(1) of the Bankruptcy Code, or unless extended by the Court as provided in Section 1308(b)(2) of the Bankruptcy Code. In the event the Trustee agrees to hold open the Section 341 Meeting, the Trustee shall nevertheless file a report of the initial meeting indicating that the meeting is being held open;

(3) Timely file with the Court, upon a written request filed with the Court and served on the Debtor and Debtor's Counsel, tax returns or transcripts as required by Sections 521(f) and 521(g)(2) of the Bankruptcy Code; PROVIDED, HOWEVER, that pursuant to Bankruptcy Rule 4002(b)(5) and the Interim Guidance Regarding Tax Information established by the Director of the

Administrative Office of the United States Courts, the United States Trustee, the Trustee, or any party in interest that desires to obtain access to the Debtor's tax information must file and serve upon the Debtor and Debtor's Counsel, a motion which should include (i) a description of the movant's status in the Case to allow the Court to ascertain whether the movant may properly be given access to the requested tax information, (ii) a description of the specific tax information sought, (iii) a statement indicating that the information cannot be obtained by the movant from any other sources, and (iv) a statement showing a demonstrated need for the tax information. Access to the Debtor's tax information will only be permitted after the Court approves the request;

(4) Timely provide to the Trustee documents that establish the identity of the Debtor, including a driver's license, passport, or other document that contains a photograph of the Debtor as required by Section 521(h) of the Bankruptcy Code; or

(5) Cooperate with the Trustee as necessary to enable the Trustee to perform the Trustee's duties under the Bankruptcy Code as required by Section 521(a)(3) of the Bankruptcy Code. Any such notice shall state specifically what the Debtor did or did not do constituting such failure to cooperate.

(e) The Debtor did not pay to the Trustee when due, any Plan Payment (except the first Plan Payment[2]) specified in the Plan; PROVIDED, HOWEVER, that—

(1) The NOI shall specify the exact dollar amount due to bring all Payments completely current as of the 14th day after the date of the NOI;

(2) No Order of Dismissal shall be submitted or requested by the Trustee with regard to a subparagraph "(e)" deficiency if an Interlocutory Order ("I/O") satisfactory to the Trustee has been approved by the Debtor or Debtor's Counsel and delivered to the Trustee as of the 14th day after the date of the NOI; and

(3) No Order of Dismissal shall be submitted or requested by the Trustee if, prior to the expiration of the NOI period, a response is filed and served by the Debtor, set by Debtor on the Court's next available Chapter 13 docket after the expiration of 14 days and notice of such setting is filed and served by the Debtor at least 14 days prior to such setting.

4. Mandatory Wage Directive. Unless the Court orders otherwise, the Trustee may require a Debtor who is a wage or salaried employee to complete and deliver to the Trustee, not later than the initial setting for the Section 341 Meeting, the information necessary for the submission of a wage directive by the Trustee to such Debtor's employer. Unless otherwise ordered by the Court, such directive may be terminated by the Trustee.

5. Other Required Documents and Information.

(a) Within three business days of the Petition Date or Conversion Date, every Debtor, whether a Conduit Debtor or not, shall submit to the Trustee a completed and signed "Mortgage Information Sheet" and a completed and signed "Authorization to Release Information to the Trustee Regarding Secured Claim." Additionally, the Debtor shall attach a copy of the current mortgage statement or a written explanation of why such statement is not available to the Mortgage Information Sheet. Copies of these forms are attached to this General Order. If the Debtor is represented by an attorney and the attorney timely submits to the Trustee a complete and correct (1) Mortgage Information Sheet with a current mortgage statement or a written explanation of why such statement is not available attached and (2) Authorization to Release Information to the Trustee Regarding Secured Claim, the attorney for the Debtor is entitled to an additional $200 as part of the Standard Fee described in paragraph 21 herein.

(b) A Debtor with domestic support obligations shall provide the Trustee with the name, address, and telephone number of the domestic support claimant, if known, at or before the Section 341 Meeting.

6. Good Funds. The Trustee is not required to disburse any funds to any party in interest unless the Trustee is satisfied, within the Trustee's sole discretion, that good funds have been received by the Trustee.

7. Adequate Protection Disbursements.

(a) *Debtor Shall Authorize Adequate Protection Disbursements by the Trustee.* Unless otherwise ordered by the Court, within 14 days of the Petition Date or Conversion Date, the Debtor shall file and serve on all scheduled creditors (unless Service is made by the Clerk), an AAPD in a form prescribed by the Trustee. Any amendment to the AAPD shall—(1) be filed with the Court, (2) be served on all affected creditors and on the creditors' counsel, if a Notice of Appearance has been filed and served on Debtor's Counsel by creditor's counsel, and (3) contain a Certificate of Service reflecting this service. Protection concerning motor vehicles shall be presumed adequate if in a monthly amount equal to 1.25% of the value of the motor vehicle determined by averaging the wholesale and retail values contained in the most recent NADA publication for a comparable motor vehicle. In the Case of a Conduit Debtor, the amount of the Current Post–Petition Mortgage Payment(s) must be included in the AAPD.

(b) *Trustee Shall Disburse Adequate Protection Payments.* Pre-confirmation, the Trustee will disburse Plan Payments received by the Trustee to the appropriate parties according to the AAPD in the next regularly scheduled monthly disbursement, subject to normal operating procedures. Unless otherwise ordered by the Court, the Trustee may disburse adequate protection payments monthly as provided in the AAPD, whether or not a proof of claim has been filed, to the category of claimants described and in the order set out in the AAPD under "Order of Payment." If funds received by the Trustee are insufficient to pay a full monthly payment to any specified category cumulatively, payments shall be made pro rata within such category.

(c) *Use of Interest.* Any interest received by the Trustee as a result of Plan Payments shall be paid into the Trustee's expense account and used exclusively to pay the compensation and reasonable and necessary expenses of the Trustee, as may be approved by the United States Trustee. Any Plan Payments may be held by the Trustee in a non-interest bearing account.

(d) *Payments Made for Adequate Protection Disbursement Considered Payments.* Payments made by a Debtor to the Trustee for an adequate protection disbursement shall be considered Plan Payments pursuant to 11 U.S.C. § 1326(a) and 28 U.S.C. § 586(e)(2).

(e) Adequate protection disbursements may include the Trustee's Noticing Fees, Filing Fees, Payments on Secured Claims including applicable Current Post–Petition Mortgage Payments, priority claims, and fees for Debtor's Counsel, unless the Debtor is *pro se*.

(f) *Adequate Protection to Vehicle Lenders.* In addition to the AAPD required herein, in each Case, the Debtor's use of vehicles under Section 363 of the Bankruptcy Code is authorized only if the Debtor (i) maintains insurance on the vehicles in the amount required by the Debtor's pre-petition contract; (ii) provides proof of insurance to the lien holder upon request; and (iii) provides the Trustee with all necessary information for a wage directive not later than the date of the initial Section 341 Meeting (if the Debtor is a wage or salaried employee and the Court has not ordered otherwise).

8. **Surrendered Collateral and the Lifting of the Automatic Stay.** The Plan or any Plan Modification (if surrender is allowed) shall describe any Collateral to be surrendered. This will be construed by the Court as a request that the stay be terminated as to the Surrendered Collateral, and THE AUTOMATIC STAY SHALL BE TERMINATED and the Trustee shall cease disbursements on any secured claim which is secured by the Surrendered Collateral without further order of the Court on the 7th day after the date the Plan or Plan Modification providing for the surrender is filed. In such event, the Trustee shall reserve the funds that would otherwise be disbursed to the creditor until the Plan is confirmed or the Plan Modification is approved or an order of the Court regarding the disbursement of such funds by the Trustee is entered. PROVIDED, HOWEVER, that the stay shall not be terminated if the Trustee or affected secured lender files with the Court and serves on the Debtor, Debtor's Counsel, and the party to whom the Collateral is proposed to be surrendered (and/or for whose benefit the Collateral is proposed to be surrendered), an objection to the proposed surrender within 7 days of the filing of the Plan or the Plan Modification. If such an objection is filed and served, the automatic stay shall remain in effect until the objection is disposed of by an order of the Bankruptcy Court. Upon the lifting of the Automatic Stay for any other reason, and upon the filing of a notice of termination of the automatic stay by the secured creditor, the Debtor, or on other notice acceptable to the Trustee, all future disbursements by the Trustee to the secured creditor with regard to the collateral securing the indebtedness will cease, and may only be resumed by order of the Bankruptcy Court.

9. **Trustee's Percentage Fee and Noticing Fee.**

(a) Pursuant to 28 U.S.C. § 586(e), the Trustee is authorized to collect the Trustee's Percentage Fee at the time of the receipt of any funds paid by or on behalf of the Debtor to the Trustee or recovered by the Trustee from any source, including, but not limited to, the receipt of any funds that the Trustee will disburse on any Mortgage Arrearage(s), Current Post–Petition Mortgage Payment(s), Mortgage Fees, and/or adequate protection payments.

(b) The Trustee may charge, in addition to the percentage fee fixed pursuant to 28 U.S.C. § 586(e)(1)(B), noticing fees in each Case administered by the respective Trustee equal to $.50, plus postage per envelope.

(c) The Trustee may collect noticing fees, in advance or otherwise, for the Service of notices, reports or orders, including, but not limited to: Notice of Deadline For Objecting to Confirmation, Trustee's Pre–Hearing Conference and Confirmation Hearing; Trustee's Recommendation Concerning Claims, Objection to Claims and Plan Modification (if required) and the Notice of Hearing and Pre–Hearing Conference with regard to same; Notice or Order of Dismissal or Conversion; Notice or Order of Debtor Discharge; Chapter 13 Trustee's Final Report and Account and/or Notice of Filing of Final Report and Account by Trustee; Notice of Final Cure; Mid–Case Notice of Amount Deemed Necessary to Cure Mortgage Arrearage; and/or Notices required under 11 U.S.C. § 1302(d) regarding domestic support obligations. It is hereby found and determined that said fees are reasonable and appropriate to defray the actual, necessary costs and expenses reasonably attributable to the giving of said notices. Subject to United States Trustee's approval, the Trustee may choose to reduce the number of notices for which noticing fees are collected. The Trustee shall be entitled to collect noticing fees authorized hereby from the first and any subsequent monies received from the Debtor, whether before or after confirmation.

10. Creditor's Certificate of Conference on § 362 Motions and Objections to Confirmation and Requirement to Provide Limited Payment History, Evidence of Debt, and Perfection of Lien Regarding Real Property.

(a) A Creditor shall include a Certificate of Conference with Debtor's Counsel on any Section 362 motion to modify stay or any objection to confirmation. The Certificate of Conference shall state that the creditor or its counsel made a good faith effort to negotiate a settlement of the dispute with Debtor's Counsel or that Debtor's Counsel failed to respond to the creditor's communication (made during regular business hours) by the same time on the 2nd business day after such communication. The Certificate of Conference shall evidence that the creditor or creditor's counsel attempted at least once to contact Debtor's Counsel by telephone, e-mail, fax or in person. The Court reserves the right to sanction parties and/or counsel who fail to confer in good faith prior to the filing of such motions and/or objections.

(b) Notwithstanding L.B.R. 4001.1(e), if a Mortgage Lender files a § 362 motion to terminate, annul, modify or condition the automatic stay, within 7 days, the creditor shall file a sworn affidavit detailing any alleged payment delinquency and providing a current chronological payment history beginning with the first payment alleged to be delinquent.

11. Confirmation Hearing and Trustee's Pre–Hearing Conference Regarding Confirmation.

(a) The Debtor will be responsible for serving the Plan or summary thereof on all parties in interest on the date the Plan is filed, notifying such parties that the Plan has been filed.

(b) The confirmation hearing shall be set and commenced at the last available date the Court has scheduled confirmation hearings that is not more than 45 days after the Section 341 Meeting. The Trustee will be responsible for mailing a Notice of the date, place, and deadline for objecting to confirmation, as well as the date, place and time of the Trustee's pre-hearing conference and the Confirmation hearing to all parties in interest.

(c) Unless the Court orders otherwise, the hearing on Section 506 valuations, interest rate, and treatment under the Plan will occur at the confirmation hearing. Claim amount and classification will be determined by the TRCC as described herein or other order of the Court.

(d) Objections to confirmation of the Plan by the Trustee or any creditors shall be in writing and filed and served on the Debtor, Debtor's Counsel, and the Trustee no later than 7 days prior to the Trustee's pre-hearing conference (the "Objection Deadline"), or be deemed waived.

(e) After the Objection Deadline and before the confirmation hearing, the Trustee shall conduct a Trustee's pre-hearing conference regarding confirmation (on the date and at the time and place designated by the Trustee). Any matter resolved at the Trustee's pre-hearing conference may be contained in an agreed Confirmation Order that the Trustee may submit to the Court for entry without the need for any amendment to the Plan or further notice to parties in interest, PROVIDED that no party not a party to the agreement is materially adversely affected by the agreement.

(f) Any objections to confirmation of the Plan or valuation disputes not resolved at or before the Trustee's pre-hearing conference shall be heard by the Court at the confirmation hearing.

(g) All objections to confirmation of the Plan and/or the motion for valuation shall be deemed waived—

(1) if not timely filed and served as provided above; or

(2) if the proponent of any objection or motion fails to attend the Trustee's pre-hearing conference or give the Trustee prior written notice that a hearing is necessary.

(h) If the confirmation hearing is continued by the Court, the Trustee shall file a notice of continued confirmation hearing.

(i) *Domestic Support Obligations and Tax Returns.*

(1) No more than 14 days before the Trustee's pre-hearing conference concerning confirmation, a Debtor with domestic support obligations shall file a certificate pursuant to Section 1325(a)(8) of the Bankruptcy Code with the Court.

(2) Prior to confirmation, pursuant to Section 1325(a)(9) of the Bankruptcy Code, a Debtor shall file with the Court a certificate verifying the filing of all applicable Federal, State, and local tax returns as required by Section 1308 of the Bankruptcy Code on a form that substantially conforms to the Debtor's(s') Certificate That All Tax Returns Have Been Filed, a copy of which form is attached to this General Order.

12. The Trustee's Pre–Hearing Conference. The Trustee may assign matters to a pre-hearing conference docket (see www.13network.com for pre-hearing conference dates/times) including, but not limited to—

(a) Motions to dismiss or convert filed by a party in interest other than the Debtor;

(b) Motions for use of cash collateral or for financing authority;

(c) Objections to claims;

(d) Motions to assume, or to assume and assign, executory contracts or unexpired leases;

(e) Motions for substantive consolidation;

(f) Confirmation of a Plan;

(g) Any Plan Modification;

(h) Motions to Sell pursuant to 11 U.S.C. § 363;

(i) Motions to Incur Debt/Obtain Credit;

(j) Motions to Modify Home Mortgage Loans; and

(k) Any Motion for which the Bankruptcy Rules, the Local Bankruptcy Rules for the Northern District of Texas and/or this General Order require a hearing, except as otherwise provided herein.

13. Trustee's Review and Approval of all Agreed Orders. In the event the Debtor and creditor reach an agreement with respect to a motion to modify stay or objection to confirmation, or any other contested matter between a Debtor and a creditor, the Trustee shall be permitted, if required by the Trustee, 7 days to review the agreed Order prior to its presentation to the Court, without prejudice to the Trustee's right to object to the agreed Order prior to it becoming a final order.

14. Who Is Required to Be a Conduit Debtor. Unless otherwise ordered by the Court following a motion by a party in interest in a specific Case, any Debtor meeting the following criteria is required to participate in the Conduit Program and is designated as a Conduit Debtor:

(a) Any Debtor that is the monetary equivalent of two full months or more in arrears to a Mortgage Lender as of the Petition Date or Conversion Date;

(b) Any Debtor that defaults on payments to a Mortgage Lender during the pendency of the Case such that the Debtor is the monetary equivalent of two full months or more in arrears on Current Post–Petition Mortgage Payments to the Mortgage Lender, except that in a Case within twelve months of completion, the Trustee may elect not to require the Debtor to participate in the Conduit Program; or

(c) Any Debtor who elects to participate in the Conduit Program by including the Current Post–Petition Mortgage Payment in the Plan Payments and the Base Amount and (1) Section I, D.(2) of the Plan or (2) in a Plan Modification.

Once designated as a Conduit Debtor, the Debtor shall remain a Conduit Debtor until the payment in full of the Base Amount (even if the Mortgage Loan is modified), or until the Case is converted or dismissed, unless otherwise ordered by the Court.

15. Provisions Regarding the Conduit Program. Unless otherwise ordered by the Court, the following provisions shall apply in the Case of a Conduit Debtor—

(a) *Additional Responsibilities of the Conduit Debtor*—In addition to all other responsibilities, duties, and obligations of the Debtor required by applicable law and rules, and this General Order—

(1) The Conduit Debtor shall include any Mortgage Arrearage(s), the Current Post–Petition Mortgage Payment(s) and any Mortgage Fees, plus the Trustee's Percentage Fee, in the calculation of the Plan Payment, and such amounts shall be included in the calculation of the Base Amount.

(2) The Conduit Debtor shall file an AAPD authorizing the Trustee to disburse the Current Post–Petition Mortgage Payments to the Mortgage Lender prior to confirmation.

(3) The Conduit Debtor is responsible for responding to and defending all motions for relief from the automatic stay. The Conduit Debtor is responsible for objecting to any proof of claim or any amended proof of claim filed by a Mortgage Lender, as well as any Notice of Payment Change by Mortgage Lender and/or any Notice of Fees, Expenses, and Charges. The Trustee is not obligated to but, within the Trustee's sole discretion, may object to any proof of claim or amended proof of claim filed by or on behalf of a Mortgage Lender and may file a response to any motion for relief from the automatic stay, Notice of Payment Change by Mortgage Lender and/or any Notice of Fees, Expenses, and Charges.

(b) *Additional Responsibilities of the Mortgage Lender*—In addition to all other responsibilities, duties, and obligations of the Mortgage Lender required by applicable law and rules and this General Order—

(1) If the Mortgage Lender files a Notice of Fees, Expenses, and Charges and does not attach legible copies of any unpaid invoices to such Notice to substantiate the fees, expenses and charges requested, the Trustee or the Debtor may object to such Notice for that reason. Upon the earlier of (i) the expiration of the period of time for filing an objection to the Notice of Fees, Expenses, and Charges or (ii) the entry of a Final Order allowing such fees, expenses and charges in whole or in part, the Trustee is authorized to pay them in full as a secured claim with no interest.

(2) If the Mortgage Lender files a proof of claim or amended proof of claim which includes pre-petition fees, expenses, or other charges as part of the claim amount and does not attach legible copies of any unpaid invoices substantiating same, the Trustee or the Debtor may object to the proof of claim or amended proof of claim for that reason.

(3) In the event there is a change in the name of the Mortgage Lender and/or the servicer for the Mortgage Lender and/or the address to which disbursements to the Mortgage Lender are to be sent, the Mortgage Lender shall file with the Court and serve on the Trustee, the Conduit Debtor and the Debtor's Counsel a notice substantively conforming with the Notice of Transfer of Servicing or Change of Address attached to this General Order. If the Notice of Transfer of Servicing or Change of Address is not received by the Trustee at least twenty-one (21) days prior to the Trustee's next disbursement date (but not including the disbursement date), the Trustee shall have no obligation or liability for recovering or requesting the refund of any funds disbursed within that twenty-one (21) day period. The Debtor shall receive full credit for any such payment disbursed by the Trustee to or on behalf of the Mortgage Lender. All disbursements made more than twenty-one (21) days after a Notice of Transfer of Servicing or Change of Address is filed shall be made in the name of and to the address set forth in such Notice if it conforms with the Notice of Transfer of Servicing or Change of Address attached to this General Order.

(c) *Other Applicable Provisions*—

(1) In the event the Current Post–Petition Mortgage Payment changes during the term of the Plan or Plan Modification, the Mortgage Lender shall file a Notice of Payment Change by Mortgage Lender. After receiving same, the Trustee may send a Notice of Plan Payment Adjustment to the Conduit Debtor, Debtor's Counsel and the Mortgage Lender. If the Notice of Payment Change by Mortgage Lender is timely and properly filed by the Mortgage Lender and indicates it was properly served, the Trustee shall disburse the Current Post–Petition Mortgage Payment(s) consistent with the Notice of Payment Change by Mortgage Lender as of the effective date of the change set out therein, assuming there are available funds in the Case to do so.

(2) If the Mortgage Lender files a proof of claim or an amended proof of claim that sets out a Mortgage Arrearage, a Mortgage Fee, or a Current Post–Petition Mortgage Payment in an amount different than the amount used to calculate the Plan Payment, the Trustee may serve a Notice of Plan Payment Adjustment.

(3) In the event of an adjustment to the monthly Plan Payment or the Base Amount due to the Trustee as a result of (i) the filing of a proof of claim or amended proof of claim by the Mortgage Lender, (ii) the filing of a Notice of Payment Change by Mortgage Lender, (iii) the filing of a Notice of Fees, Expenses, and Charges, (iv) an insufficiency in the Base Amount necessary to disburse a full, final Current Post–Petition Mortgage Payment, and/or (v) the entry of an order of the Court, the monthly Plan Payment and/or the Base Amount may be automatically adjusted by the Trustee by the amount of the required payment adjustment, plus the Trustee's Percentage Fee, without the necessity of filing an amended AAPD, an amended Plan or a Plan Modification to effectuate the adjustment of the Plan Payment. The Trustee will notify the Debtor of any change in the Plan Payment by serving a Notice of Plan Payment Adjustment. Unless otherwise ordered by the Court, the amount set out in the Notice of Plan Payment Adjustment is the Plan Payment as of the effective date contained therein and the amount due to the Mortgage Lender set out in the Notice of Plan Payment Adjustment is the amount the Trustee shall disburse to the Mortgage Lender from available funds in the Case.

(4) Unless otherwise ordered by the Court, and subject to Bankruptcy Rule 3002.1(f)–(h), if the Conduit Debtor is current on Plan Payments or the payments due pursuant to any wage directive, the Mortgage Loan shall be deemed current post-petition.

(5) Pre-confirmation, the Trustee may make Current Post–Petition Mortgage Payments to the Mortgage Lender, as identified by the Conduit Debtor, at the address provided by the Conduit Debtor, in the amount stated by the Conduit Debtor and utilizing the account number provided by the Conduit Debtor, pursuant to an AAPD authorizing such payments, without the necessity of the Mortgage Lender filing a proof of claim or having a proof of claim filed on its behalf.

(6) Following the entry of an order confirming the Plan, the Trustee shall make Current Post–Petition Mortgage Payments to the Mortgage Lender only if a proof of claim is filed and has not been disallowed. However, the Trustee will reserve the Current Post–Petition Mortgage Payments received until either (a) the date the Mortgage Lender's proof of claim is timely filed as set out in Rule 3002(c) of the Bankruptcy Rules of Procedure or (b) the expiration of the extended Claims Bar Date set out in Rules 3004 and 3005 of the Bankruptcy Rules of Procedure. In the event no proof of claim is filed by or on behalf of the Mortgage Lender within the time periods set out above, the reserve will be removed and the Trustee may disburse any reserved funds to other claimants.

(7) Notice To Reserve Funds—

(A) Any party in interest may file and serve a Notice to Reserve Funds if, and only if, the following is filed: (i) an objection to a Notice of Payment Change by Mortgage Lender; (ii) an objection to a Notice of Fees, Expenses, and Charges; (iii) an objection to a proof of claim or amended proof of claim filed by or on behalf of the Mortgage Lender; and/or (iv) an adversary disputing the validity, priority, and extent of the lien asserted by the Mortgage Lender. The Trustee is not obligated to but may, in the Trustee's sole discretion, file a Notice to Reserve Funds. A form of this Notice to be used by parties other than the Trustee is attached as an exhibit to this General Order. Such Notice may be filed only as permitted in this General Order and parties other than the Trustee must use the attached form of the Notice to Reserve Funds.

(B) The Notice to Reserve Funds must be filed with the Court in the Case (as opposed to an ancillary proceeding) and served on the Mortgage Lender, the Conduit Debtor, the Debtor's Counsel and the Trustee and, if filed by a party other than the Trustee, must be received by the Trustee no less than five business days prior to the Trustee's scheduled disbursement date. If a Notice to Reserve Funds is filed, the Trustee will reserve funds specified in the Notice which would otherwise be disbursed to the Mortgage Lender until an order of the Court is entered instructing the Trustee how to disburse the funds.

(C) A Notice to Reserve Funds is without prejudice to the rights of any party in interest to request other and further relief from the Court, including, but not limited to, an order of the Court to authorize or compel the Trustee to disburse any reserved funds.

(8) If any party in interest files a proceeding described in Section 15(c)(7)(A) of this General Order, the Conduit Debtor shall continue remitting the Plan Payment to the Trustee and the

Trustee shall continue disbursements to the Mortgage Lender, unless a Notice to Reserve Funds is filed or unless otherwise ordered by the Court. In the event a party in interest is successful with regard to such proceeding but no Notice to Reserve Funds is filed, the Trustee may, but is not obligated to, request or obtain a refund of any payments to the Mortgage Lender disbursed by the Trustee prior to the resolution of the filed objection or lien avoidance adversary.

(9) Each Trustee shall develop the internal procedures for the administration of the Conduit Program which will be applicable to all Conduit Cases administered by the Trustee, unless otherwise ordered by the Court.

16. Trustee's Recommendation Concerning Claims and Plan Modification, if Required.

(a) As soon as practicable after the governmental Claims Bar Date, the Trustee may prepare and serve on Debtor, Debtor's Counsel, all creditors who were scheduled, all creditors who filed claims, and any party that has filed a Notice of Appearance, a Trustee's Recommendation Concerning Claims, Objection to Claims and Plan Modification (the "TRCC") and a Notice of Hearing and Pre-Hearing Conference thereon. The TRCC may be deemed in part to be an objection to claims pursuant to Bankruptcy Rule 3007(d) and (e). Service of the TRCC on any agency or office of the United States of America will comply with the provisions of Rule 7004 of the Bankruptcy Rules of Procedure.

(b) The TRCC may list and propose disallowance of any claims scheduled but not filed.

(c) Objections to the TRCC shall be filed within thirty (30) days from the date of Service of the TRCC.

(d) The TRCC may contain a proposed Plan Modification.

(e) Unless an objection is timely filed as to the amount or classification of any claim or to any Plan Modification, the claim or Plan Modification will be allowed or approved as described in the TRCC, and such amount and classification will be final and binding on all parties without further order of the Court.

(f) The TRCC shall include a notice of the time, date, and location of the court hearing on any objection, as well as the time, date, and location of the Trustee's pre-hearing conference thereon. If no objection is timely filed, no Trustee's pre-hearing conference or Court hearing will be held. Matters resolved at or before the pre-hearing conference may be presented to the Court by the Trustee in the form of an agreed Order prior to or at the scheduled court hearing.

(g) All unresolved objections to the TRCC shall be deemed waived—

(1) if not timely filed and served as provided above; or

(2) if the proponent of any such objection fails to attend the Trustee's pre-hearing conference or give the Trustee prior written notice that a hearing is necessary.

(h) The TRCC will not affect value of Collateral, treatment under the Plan unless modified, or interest rate determined at confirmation, but may show these for information only.

(i) To the extent secured and/or priority claims being paid through the Plan by the Trustee are allowed for amounts in excess of the amounts provided for in the Plan, the Plan will be promptly modified to provide for full payment of the allowed amount except as otherwise provided in this General Order or by order of the court.

(j) After the order approving the TRCC becomes final, if the Plan becomes infeasible and/or insufficient, it shall constitute cause to dismiss the Case.

17. Mid–Case Audit.

The procedures for the service and resolution of the Mid–Case Notice of Amount Deemed Necessary to Cure Mortgage Arrearage are set out in L.B.R. 3002.1–1 and General Order 2017–02 which is entitled "Standing Scheduling Order Concerning Mid–Case Audits in Chapter 13 Cases," as it may be amended or superseded. The Mid–Case Notice described in this paragraph will not be required in any Conduit Case although the Trustee, within the Trustee's sole discretion, may continue to file the Mid–Case Notice in any Conduit Case.

18. Disbursement by the Trustee Upon Dismissal or Conversion.

(a) If the Case is dismissed pre-confirmation, any balance on hand shall be disbursed by the Trustee as provided in the AAPD for one disbursement cycle or as otherwise ordered by the Court, and any remaining balance shall be refunded to the Debtor. If a Case is dismissed after confirmation, the Trustee shall disburse any balance on hand as provided in the confirmed Plan or court approved Plan Modification for one disbursement cycle and then refund the remaining balance to the Debtor.

(b) In the Case of a Conduit Debtor, if a Case is dismissed and there is a balance on hand in any amount that is less than one full Current Post–Petition Mortgage Payment, the Trustee may, but is not required to, disburse those funds to claimants other than the Mortgage Lender.

(c) If the Case converts to another Chapter of the Bankruptcy Code, any balance on hand will be disbursed by the Trustee in accordance with applicable law.

19. Obligation to Notify. Debtor must notify the Chapter 13 Trustee of any material increase in the Debtor's personal or household income and of the acquisition of any property of the estate with a value exceeding the Trustee's guidelines, the sale of any property post-petition, and/or of the receipt of any life, auto, or home owner's insurance proceeds in an amount that exceeds the Trustee's guidelines.

20. IRS Refunds.

(a) *See* **Section 362(b)(26) of the Bankruptcy Code for setoff rights by the IRS.**

(b) Each year, upon filing, the Debtor shall remit to the Chapter 13 Trustee a completed copy of any tax return filed with the Internal Revenue Service during the bankruptcy proceeding.

(c) If the Debtor receives a tax refund, after any allowable IRS offset or offset under the Treasury Offset Program, any amount in excess of $2000 shall be deemed as "the excess tax refund."

(d) The Trustee may file a Plan Modification to increase the Base Amount by the excess tax refund for the benefit of the allowed general unsecured creditors.

(e) If the Debtor files an objection to the Trustee's Plan Modification, at least three business days prior to any hearing on the Plan Modification, the Debtor shall provide to the Trustee—

(1) A detailed written narrative by the Debtor or the attorney for the Debtor explaining the Debtor's need for the excess tax refund and, if required by the Trustee, an affidavit or other sworn statement signed by the Debtor attesting to such need; and

(2) Supplemental documentation to support the Debtor's written narrative, sworn statement or affidavit including, but not limited to, receipts, bids, and proof of any payments made with the tax refund.

21. Compensation and Expense Reimbursement to Debtor's Counsel in Chapter 13 Cases.

(a) Unless otherwise ordered by the Court, this General Order governs the compensation of Debtor's Counsel and reimbursement of expenses in Cases pending on or after the Effective Date.

(b) The Debtor's Counsel shall be the attorney of record from the filing of the petition for relief under Chapter 13 (if signed by the attorney), from the filing of a notice of appearance on behalf of the Debtor (if the Debtor filed the Case *pro se*), or from the date of the substitution of counsel (if the Debtor filed the Case with other counsel) until the close or dismissal of the Case (including disposition of motion(s) to reinstate), unless relieved of representation by order of the Court in accordance with L.B.R. 2091–1.

(c) In an individual, non-business Case, the Court deems $3,500 (the "Standard Fee") as reasonable compensation and reimbursement of expenses for an attorney representing the Debtor in accordance with 11 U.S.C. § 330(a)(3)(B). The Court will therefore allow the Standard Fee, plus bankruptcy clerk filing fees and the cost of a credit report for each Debtor (collectively, the "Costs"), in an individual, non-business Case, without the requirement of an application for compensation under 11 U.S.C. § 330 and Bankruptcy Rule 2016(a). PROVIDED, HOWEVER, that an attorney may request attorney's fees and expenses exceeding the Standard Fee and Costs upon (i) formal application under Rule 2016(a) and Section 21(i) of this General Order, with notice and hearing, for all fees and expenses; (ii) formal application under Section 21(j) of this General Order for fees and expenses exceeding the Standard Fee and Costs; or (iii) a motion under Section 21(k) of this General Order for matters designated therein. Allowance of fees and expenses greater than the Standard Fee and Costs shall be by separate order of the Court.

(d) An attorney may not receive a post-petition retainer or payment from the Debtor other than as specified in this General Order without leave of Court.

(e) As guidelines, the Court contemplates that the following matters will be included in the Standard Fee—

(1) All conferences with the Debtor, including timely responses to Debtor inquiries, whether by telephone or in writing;

(2) Preparation of the bankruptcy petition, including emergency petitions, Schedules, Statement of Financial Affairs, Chapter 13 Statement of Your Current Monthly Income and Calculation of Commitment Period (Official Form 122C–1), Chapter 13 Calculation of Your Disposable Income (Official Form 122C–2), Plan, and AAPD;

(3) Preparation of, and representation of the Debtor on, a motion to continue or impose the stay;

(4) Representation of the Debtor at the Section 341 Meeting and any continued meeting;

(5) Representation of the Debtor at the pre-hearing conference and confirmation hearing;

(6) Representation of the Debtor in connection with two motions under 11 U.S.C. § 362, but not including an evidentiary final hearing;

(7) Representation of the Debtor on motions to dismiss, including Trustee motions to dismiss (with or without prejudice);

(8) Preparation of, and representation of the Debtor on, motions to avoid liens and judgments;

(9) Preparation of, and representation of the Debtor on, one motion to reinstate the Case;

(10) Preparation of, and representation of the Debtor on, motions to except the Debtor from the mandatory wage directive provisions of this General Order;

(11) Preparation of documents and notices, including submissions for Trustee recommendation, and attendance at all hearings and/or pre-hearing conferences, including—

(A) Suggestion(s) of bankruptcy or other similar notification and filing same in the appropriate courts;

(B) Requests for Plan Payment deferrals;

(C) Motions for emergency refund of Plan Payments;

(D) Objections to claims and/or the TRCC, after appropriate review;

(E) The Plan and Plan documents;

(F) The AAPD;

(G) Notices to creditors, where appropriate, explaining the automatic stay;

(H) Communications and negotiations with the Internal Revenue Service;

(I) Communications to the Debtor explaining the Trustee's annual or semi-annual report, a Mid–Case Notice of Amount Deemed Necessary to Cure Mortgage Arrearage, and Notice of Final Cure;

(J) Motions to extend the time to file paperwork;

(K) Requests to the Trustee to reset the Section 341 Meeting;

(L) Amendments of Schedules and/or Statement of Financial Affairs;

(M) All Case-related correspondence;

(N) Notices or motions, if necessary, to convert the Case;

(O) Motions to dismiss the Case;

(P) Motions regarding the manner of the Debtor's attendance at the Section 341 Meeting;

(Q) Interlocutory orders;

(R) Notice to Reserve Funds; and/or

(S) Mortgage Information Sheet and Authorization to Release Information to the Trustee Regarding Secured Claim, except as set out in Section 5(a)(1) of this General Order, supra.

(12) Wage order review;

(13) Budget consultations;

(14) Making and performing, or assisting the Debtor in making or performing, the disclosures and duties required by 11 U.S.C. §§ 521, 527, 528, and 1308;

(15) Taking all steps reasonably necessary to insure that the Debtor receives a discharge in the Case; and

(16) Other miscellaneous normal, customary services, including correspondence to clients and review of correspondence from clients, communication with the Trustee and the Trustee's office, and communication with the Clerk.

(f) The guidelines assume two lift stay motions and one motion to reinstate the Case, all of which typically occur in the life of a Chapter 13 case. The guidelines assume the resolution of lift stay motions at preliminary hearings, or by agreement (at either preliminary or final hearings), and a typical hearing of 10 to 20 minutes on other contested matters routinely heard at a Chapter 13 Standing Trustee docket. The guidelines do not contemplate that the Standard Fee would include an evidentiary final hearing on a motion to lift stay, or an evidentiary hearing of more than 30 minutes on a motion to dismiss, objection to exemption, confirmation hearing, claims objection, or other contested matters, or would include representation of the Debtor in an adversary proceeding.

(g) Other than Section 21(b), this General Order does not apply to a Chapter 13 Case converted to a case under Chapter 7 of the Bankruptcy Code. Upon entry of an order converting a Case to Chapter 7, the amount and manner of payment of compensation for an attorney for Chapter 7 related services is a matter between the Debtor and his or her attorney.

(h) In a Level 2 business Case, the Court deems $4,000 as reasonable compensation and reimbursement of expenses for an attorney under 11 U.S.C. § 330(a)(3)(B) (the "Business Standard Fee"). The Court will therefore allow the Business Standard Fee, plus bankruptcy clerk filing fees, in a Level 2 business Case without the requirement of an application for compensation under 11 U.S.C. § 330 and Rule 2016(a). A Level 2 business Case is when (1) the Debtor's monthly gross receipts (or the monthly gross receipts of any corporation, partnership, LLC, etc. controlled by the Debtor) are $10,000 or more, (2) the Debtor incurs trade credit in the production of income that is not paid in full every month, (3) the business has any employees other than family, (4) the business has a liquor license, or (5) any other reason that in the opinion of the Trustee justifies a more thorough investigation than is possible at a 341 docket.

(i) In any Case, the Debtor's Counsel may elect to apply for all compensation and expenses based solely on a lodestar analysis, with notice and hearing. The application must comply with 11 U.S.C. § 330, Rule 2016(a) and the Court's Guidelines for Compensation and Expense Reimbursement of Professionals effective January 1, 2001. The application must include time records for all work performed on the Case. For lodestar applications, the Court will not approve a fee over $700 for the preparation of the fee application.

(j) For applications requesting compensation and expenses for particular matters not included in the Standard Fee or the Business Standard Fee under this General Order, e.g., a final evidentiary hearing on a motion to lift stay, the attorney must include time records for the particular matter. For those matters, the Debtor's Counsel must use the lodestar analysis and comply with 11 U.S.C. § 330, Rule 2016(a), and the Court's Guidelines for Compensation and Expense Reimbursement of Professionals effective January 1, 2001. For lodestar applications for particular matters, the Court will not approve a fee over $400 for the preparation of the fee application.

(k) As set out in paragraph 5(a), if the Debtor is represented by an attorney and the attorney timely submits to the Trustee a complete and correct (1) Mortgage Information Sheet with a current mortgage statement or a written explanation of why such statement is not available attached and (2) Authorization to Release Information to the Trustee Regarding Secured Claim, the attorney for the Debtor is entitled to an additional $200 as part of the Standard Fee or Business Standard Fee described in this paragraph.

(l) Provided the Debtor agrees, and notwithstanding any other provision of this General Order, for certain matters not within the guidelines for the Standard Fee or the Business Standard Fee, and to encourage uniformity and consistency and to minimize the expense of the fee application process, the Court will approve, upon motion, and waive the application requirement, for the following fees:

(1) For a Plan Modification, $350, plus expenses not to exceed $50.

(2) For a motion to sell property, $350, plus expenses not to exceed $50.

(3) For a motion to incur debt, $350, plus expenses not to exceed $50.

(4) For defending a motion to lift stay (after the two motions to lift stay included within the Standard Fee or the Business Standard Fee), $350, plus expenses not to exceed $50.

(5) For an objection/response to a Plan Modification proposed by the Trustee to increase the Base Amount by the amount of the excess tax refund, a responsive pleading to a Trustee motion to

compel with regard to a tax return and/or tax refund, or a similar pleading addressing tax refunds and who is entitled to same, $350, plus expenses not to exceed $50.

(6) For modification of the Debtor's mortgage, $200, plus expenses not to exceed $50, and up to an additional $500 if the application includes a certification that the Debtor's attorney has been significantly involved in the process to modify the Debtor's mortgage.

(m) A motion under this paragraph may request that the Court authorize the Debtor to pay these fees or expenses directly to his or her attorney.

(n) This General Order amends all previous standing orders regarding the setting of attorney's fees in Chapter 13 Cases.

22. Compensation and Expense Reimbursement to Creditor Attorneys in Chapter 13 Cases. The Court deems the lesser of (1) $700 and (2) the actual amount paid or to be paid by the creditor to its attorney as fees and expenses to be reasonable compensation to a creditor's attorney who is entitled to compensation from a Debtor's estate under 11 U.S.C § 506(b) and applicable non-bankruptcy law in any Case, without prejudice to a party contesting entitlement to fees, or the reasonableness of the amount or mode of payment of fees and expenses. Allowance of fees and/or expenses in a greater amount shall be by separate order of the Court after a hearing on a properly noticed application or motion. Effective February 1, 2007, the submission of an agreed Order containing a provision providing for the recovery of attorney's fees in a pending bankruptcy Case shall constitute an affirmative representation to the judges of this Court by all signatories to the agreed Order that there is objective evidence supporting a finding that the creditor has a properly perfected lien and is oversecured or is otherwise legally entitled to recover such fees. Upon the entry of this Order, such submission shall also constitute an affirmative representation by the creditor and its counsel that the attorney's fees provided for in the Order do not exceed the amount of the fees actually paid or to be paid.

23. Monthly Statements Will Not Violate the Automatic Stay. Unless the Debtor or Debtor's Counsel has notified the creditor to discontinue sending post-petition statements, a creditor will be deemed not to have violated the automatic stay by voluntarily continuing to send the Debtor the usual and customary monthly statements concerning the Debtor's accounts. A creditor claiming a lien on real property and whose lien is provided for with "direct" payments in the Plan shall continue to send the Debtor regular payment statements, invoices, or other memoranda of regular payments due after the Petition Date or Conversion Date, if it was the practice of the creditor to send the Debtor such statements before the Petition Date or Conversion Date, and the continued sending of these payment statements, invoices, or other memoranda of regular payments will be deemed not to violate the automatic stay.

24. Chapter 13 Discharge.

(a) When a Debtor completes all payments to the Trustee required by the Plan, the Trustee will file a Notice of Completion with the Court. No Order of discharge will be submitted by the Trustee until the Debtor has filed Debtor(s) Certification and Motion for Entry of Chapter 13 Discharge Pursuant to 11 U.S.C. § 1328(a)[3] (hereinafter "Certification and Motion") and the 21–day time for any objection has expired with no objection having been filed. If the Certification and Motion is not filed, no Discharge Order will be submitted by the Trustee. If the 21 days has passed and the Debtor has not filed the Certification and Motion, and the Case is ready to be closed otherwise, the clerk's office will close the Case without a discharge. If the Debtor wishes to receive a discharge after the Case has been closed, he/she will be required to reopen the Case and pay the required filing fee to reopen the Case and timely file the Certification and Motion for a Chapter 13 Discharge.

(b) In a Conduit Case, except as provided in Rule 3002.1 (f)–(h) of the Bankruptcy Rules of Procedure, when the Conduit Debtor completes all the payments required by the Plan and has paid the Base Amount in full, and an order of discharge is entered, the Conduit Debtor shall be deemed current on all payments of any kind due to the Mortgage Lender up through and including the date specified by the Trustee's records as the date through which the Trustee made the last Current Post–Petition Mortgage Payment to the Mortgage Lender and, as of that payment date, it shall be deemed that there are no payments owed to the Mortgage Lender, including, but not limited to, escrow shortages, late charges, attorney's fees, or other charges or costs.

Conduit Debtor 1 name: _____   Case number: _____

Conduit Debtor 2 name: _____

MORTGAGE INFORMATION SHEET

SUBMIT TO THE TRUSTEE ONLY—DO NOT FILE WITH THE COURT

Within three (3) business days following the Petition Date or the date the bankruptcy case is converted to a Chapter 13 proceeding, whichever is later, please provide the Trustee with this information:

___ Conduit Debtor rents/leases.

___ The Conduit Debtor(s) is/are current on all home mortgage payments and shall continue to pay the regular monthly payments directly to the creditor listed below.

___ The Conduit Debtor(s) is/are _____ months in arrears on payments to the Mortgage Lender, pre-petition.

___ Other (reverse mortgage, paid in full, etc.). _____

A copy of current mortgage statement or a written explanation of why such statement is not available is attached.

Amount of mortgage payment and date due: $ _____ Date _____

Amount of pre-petition arrearage, if any: $ _____

Complete name of mortgage creditor/servicer: _____

Correspondence address: _____

_____

Payment address: _____

_____

Telephone number: ( ) _____

Name of legal representative: _____

Address of legal representative: _____

_____

_____

_____

Telephone number: ( ) _____

Complete account number (not redacted):   _____

Are insurance and taxes escrowed?   _____ (Yes) _____ (No)

_____   _____
Debtor or Debtor Attorney Signature   Date
Date

AUTHORIZATION TO RELEASE INFORMATION
TO THE TRUSTEE REGARDING SECURED CLAIMS

**SUBMIT TO THE TRUSTEE ONLY
DO NOT FILE WITH THE COURT**

Debtor 1 name: Case number:

Debtor 2 name: Division:

The Debtor(s) in the above captioned bankruptcy case do hereby authorize any and all holder(s) of a lien on real and/or personal property of the bankruptcy estate or of the Debtor(s), or servicers of said lienholders, to release information to the Standing Chapter 13 Trustee in this bankruptcy case and/or to his or her staff.

The information to be released includes, but is not limited to, the amount of the post-petition monthly installment payment, amount of any pre-petition or post-petition arrearage, the interest rate and its type, the loan balance, impound accounts, amount of any contractual late charges, and the mailing address for payments. This information will be used by the Trustee and his or her staff only for the purpose of the administration of the bankruptcy estate and case, and may be included in pleadings filed with the Court.

_____   Date: _____

Signature of Debtor 1
Printed or Typed Name: _____

_____   Date: _____

Signature of Debtor 2
Printed or Typed Name: _____

IN THE UNITED STATES BANKRUPTCY COURT
FOR THE NORTHERN DISTRICT OF TEXAS

IN RE: §
                                   §
                                   §   CASE NO. _____

(NAME OF DEBTOR(S)),   §

DEBTOR(S).   §   CHAPTER 13
                                   §

DEBTOR'S(S') CERTIFICATE THAT ALL TAX RETURNS HAVE BEEN FILED

Pursuant to General Order 2017–01, paragraph 11(i)(2) (and as the General Order may be amended) and 11 U.S.C. § 1325(a)(9), the Debtor(s) certifies/certify as follows:

I/WE HAVE FILED all federal income tax returns with the Internal Revenue Service (IRS) for the following 4–year period ending immediately prior to my bankruptcy petition date, those being the returns for tax years: 20   , 20   , 20   , and 20   .

In addition, **I/WE HAVE FILED** any other Federal, State and local tax returns required under applicable bankruptcy law and as required by 11 U.S.C. § 1308 for all taxable periods ending during the 4–year period ending immediately prior to my bankruptcy petition date, those being described as follows (identify the type of tax and period):

_____

_____

I/WE ACKNOWLEDGE that the failure to file any tax return required by 11 U.S.C. § 1308 may result in dismissal or conversion of my/our bankruptcy case under 11 U.S.C. § 1307(e).

I/WE DECLARE under penalty of perjury that the foregoing information is true and correct.

DATED: _____   _____
                                          DEBTOR

                                 _____
                                       JOINT DEBTOR

IN THE UNITED STATES BANKRUPTCY COURT
FOR THE NORTHERN DISTRICT OF TEXAS

IN RE:	§	
	§	CASE NO. _____
(NAME OF DEBTOR(S)),	§	
DEBTOR(S).	§	CHAPTER 13
	§	

NOTICE TO RESERVE FUNDS

TO THE HONORABLE JUDGE OF SAID COURT:

COMES NOW [Name of moving party] and notifies the Court and all parties in interest, including [insert name of Mortgage Lender] ("Mortgage Lender") as follows:

The following pleading(s) have been filed (must select at least one):

[ ] An objection to proof of claim number [insert number here], filed by the Mortgage Lender;

[ ] An adversary disputing the validity, priority, and extent of the lien asserted by Mortgage Lender, Adversary Proceeding Number [insert number];

[ ] A response and objection filed by [insert name of responding/objecting party] to the Notice of Payment Change filed by the Mortgage Lender; and/or

[ ] A response and objection filed by [insert name of responding/objecting party] to the Notice of Fees, Expenses and Charges filed by the Mortgage Lender.

In the event that an objection to a proof of claim or an adversary disputing the validity, priority, and extent of the lien has been filed, the Trustee is notified to reserve and place a hold on all funds that otherwise would be disbursed to Mortgage Lender until otherwise ordered by the Court. In the event of a response and objection to a Notice of Payment Change by Mortgage Lender or a Notice of Fees, Expenses and Charges, the Trustee is notified to reserve and place a hold on funds in the amount specified herein that otherwise would be disbursed to Mortgage Lender but for the filing of said Notice until otherwise ordered by the Court. The amount specified for the Trustee to reserve is $ _____ per month.

This Notice to Reserve Funds is without prejudice to the rights of any party in interest to request other and further relief from the Court, including, but not limited to, requesting an order of the Court to authorize or compel the Trustee to disburse any reserved funds.

Respectfully submitted,

_____

Movant's Attorney

Address

Phone Number

Email address

CERTIFICATE OF SERVICE

I, the undersigned, hereby certify that I served the foregoing Notice to Reserve Funds on the following entities in the method described below on the _____ day of _____, 20:

Debtor(s) (specifying the name and address of the Debtor(s)) by (method of service)

Debtor's(s') attorney, if any, (specifying the name and address of the Debtor's(s') attorney) by (method of service)

Mortgage Lender (specifying the name and address of the Mortgage Lender) by (method of service)

Attorney for Mortgage Lender, if known (specifying the name and address of the Attorney for the Mortgage Lender) by (method of service)

Chapter 13 Trustee (specifying the name and address of the Trustee) by (method of service)

_____

Authorized signature

IN THE UNITED STATES BANKRUPTCY COURT
FOR THE NORTHERN DISTRICT OF TEXAS

IN RE: §
§   CASE NO. _____
(NAME OF DEBTOR(S)),   §
DEBTOR(S).   §   CHAPTER 13
§

NOTICE OF TRANSFER OF SERVICING OR NAME CHANGE OR
CHANGE OF ADDRESS

PLEASE TAKE NOTICE that the servicing of the Mortgage Loan as set out in Proof of Claim No. ___ filed on _____ in the amount of $ _____ by _____ ("Transferor"), with the address of _____ has been transferred OR the name of the Mortgage Lender has changed OR the address for payment has been changed. The new information is set out below:

Servicer Name (if changed): _____

Address: _____

Contact Person: _____

Telephone Number: _____ Fax Number: _____

E–mail: _____

Effective Date: _____

[Name of Mortgage Lender]   Date: _____
[Mortgage Lender's address]
[Mortgage Lender's Phone and Fax numbers]
By: _____
[signature of authorized individual]
Its: _____
[title of authorized individual]

[Dated: July 1, 2017.]

1 All references in this General Order to the Bankruptcy Code or Sections thereof are references to the United States Bankruptcy Code and all references to the Bankruptcy Rules are references to the Federal Rules of Bankruptcy Procedure, sometimes referred to as "Fed. R. Bankr. P." or "Rule," unless otherwise noted.

2 See subpart (c) of this paragraph regarding the first Plan Payment.

3 See Clerk's Notice 07–06 dated November 5, 2007.

GENERAL ORDER 2017–02. IN RE: STANDING SCHEDULING ORDER
CONCERNING MID–CASE AUDITS IN CHAPTER 13 CASES

This General Order amends and supersedes General Order 2014–02 and applies to all Chapter 13 Cases. In order to provide a consistent method for resolving disputes arising from the Mid–Case Audit Procedures found in Local Bankruptcy Rule 3002.1–1. It is

ORDERED that the attached Standing Scheduling Order Regarding Mid–Case Audit (the "Scheduling Order") is approved by the United States Bankruptcy Court for the Northern District of Texas; and it is further

ORDERED that the Scheduling Order shall be entered by the Clerk of the Court in every Chapter 13 case concurrently with any Notice to Deem Mortgage Current or Notice of Amount Deemed Necessary to Cure filed by a Chapter 13 Trustee.

IN THE UNITED STATES BANKRUPTCY COURT
NORTHERN DISTRICT OF TEXAS

In re:

Debtor's Name   Case No. _____

Debtor.

Scheduling Order Regarding Mid–Case
Notice of Amount Deemed Necessary to Cure Mortgage Arrearage

On **[insert date of notice]**, the chapter 13 trustee filed and served a Notice of Amount Deemed Necessary to Cure Mortgage Arrearage (the **Mortgage Notice**). This scheduling order shall govern any disputes over the Mortgage Notice.

THE FOLLOWING DEADLINES APPLY IN THIS CASE:

The Mortgage Notice is set for a pre-hearing conference on **[insert date and time]** at **[insert location]**. The trustee is not required to send a separate notice of the pre-hearing conference to any party.

If the lender disputes the information in the Mortgage Notice, the lender must file a response (the **Lender's Response**) on or before **[insert date 60 days from the date of the Mortgage Notice]**. The Lender's Response must be served on the chapter 13 trustee, the debtor and the debtor's counsel, if the debtor has counsel. The Lender's Response must include an itemization of any cure amounts or post-petition arrearages as of the date of the Lender's Response. If the lender fails to respond by the deadline provided herein, or files a response stating that the lender agrees with the Mortgage Notice, and the debtor does not timely file a Debtor's Reply, as described herein, neither the lender, nor the debtor is required to attend the pre-hearing conference and the Court will enter an order approving the amounts asserted in the Mortgage Notice.

If the debtor disputes the information in the Mortgage Notice or the Lender's Response, the debtor must file a reply (the **Debtor's Reply**) on or before **[insert date 90 days from the date of the Mortgage Notice]** and must appear at the pre-hearing conference. The Debtor's Reply must admit or deny whether any pre- or post-petition delinquency exists and must provide specific information to contest any delinquency asserted by the trustee in the Mortgage Notice and/or the lender in the Lender's Response. If the debtor denies any asserted delinquency, a general denial will not suffice; rather, the Debtor's Reply must provide specific facts in support of the denial, such as the date and amount of any payment the debtor made that supports the debtor's denial of delinquency. If the Debtor's Reply does not contain such specific information, the trustee may grant the debtor an additional 14 days to provide specific information. If the debtor fails to provide the specific information within the 14–day period, the trustee may deem the Debtor's Reply to be a default under the terms of this order. The Debtor's Reply must be served on the chapter 13 trustee, the lender and the lender's counsel, if the lender has counsel.

If the debtor fails to respond by the deadline provided herein, or files a response stating that the debtor agrees with the Mortgage Notice and/or the Lender's Response (if any), the debtor is not required to attend the pre-hearing conference and the Court will enter an order approving the amounts asserted in the Mortgage Notice or Lender's Response, as follows: (1) in a non-conduit case, if a timely filed Lender's Response asserts a different post-petition arrearage than that asserted in the Mortgage Notice, then the post-petition arrearage in the Lender's Response shall control and be set forth in the order regarding the Mortgage Notice; (2) in a conduit case, if a timely filed Lender's Response asserts a different post-petition arrearage than that asserted in the Mortgage Notice, then the lender must appear at the pre-hearing conference to attempt to resolve the discrepancy; or (3) in either case, if the Lender's Response states that the lender agrees with the Mortgage Notice, then the Court will enter an order approving the amounts asserted in the Mortgage Notice.

If the matter is not resolved as of the time of the pre-hearing conference, the trustee shall either set the matter on the Court's next regularly scheduled chapter 13 docket, or at the trustee's option, contact the courtroom deputy and obtain a special setting for an evidentiary hearing. The Court will use its best efforts to provide an evidentiary hearing within 30 to 45 days after the pre-hearing conference. All witness and exhibit lists must be filed and exhibits must be exchanged at least three business days before the evidentiary hearing date.

Once the Court enters an order on the Mortgage Notice, the debtor and the lender will be barred from contesting the amounts set out in the order in any contested matter or adversary proceeding in this case, or in any other matter, manner or forum after a discharge in the case, unless the Court determines, after notice and hearing, that the failure to respond, reply, and/or to attend the pre-hearing conference was substantially justified or is harmless.

[Dated: June 24, 2017.]

GENERAL ORDER 2018–02. IN RE: GENERAL ORDER ADOPTING BANKRUPTCY LOAN MODIFICATION PROGRAM FOR CHAPTER 13 CASES IN THE NORTHERN DISTRICT OF TEXAS

This General Order adopts the attached Loan Modification Program for Chapter 13 Cases in the Northern District of Texas ("Loan Modification Program") developed by the Bankruptcy Law Section of the State Bar of Texas. A copy of the attached Loan Modification Program and all Mandatory Forms (BTXN Forms 300—312) will be posted on the Court's website and may also be posted on the websites maintained by the Chapter 13 Standing Trustees for the Northern District of Texas.

Effective October 1, 2018, the Loan Modification Program shall apply to all active Chapter 13 Cases pending in the Northern District of Texas. The Court may modify the terms of the Loan Modification Program and the Mandatory Forms from time to time. Any amended documents will be posted on the Court's website.

It is **SO ORDERED**.

The Chief Bankruptcy Judge has been authorized to enter this Order on behalf of the Court.

BANKRUPTCY LOAN MODIFICATION PROGRAM FOR CHAPTER 13 DEBTORS IN THE NORTHERN DISTRICT OF TEXAS

1. Purpose. This Loan Modification Program (also "LMP") is adopted to provide a uniform procedure to allow Chapter 13 Debtors, Lenders, and other parties to negotiate a potential modification of an Eligible Loan. The goal of the Loan Modification Program is to facilitate communication between the parties; provide for the confidential exchange of information and documents; and to encourage the parties to finalize a feasible, consensual, and beneficial loan modification.

2. Effective Date. This Loan Modification Program shall apply to all active Chapter 13 Cases pending in the Northern District of Texas on or after October 1, 2018.

3. Court Discretion. All provisions set forth herein shall apply to every Loan Modification Matter (also "LMM") unless otherwise ordered by the Court in any specific Case. Any request for a variance shall be made by a motion served on all LMM Parties and the Chapter 13 Trustee or on those parties as directed by the Court. Such parties shall have fourteen (14)days from the date of service to object and request a hearing. If an objection to such motion is not timely filed, the Court may enter an order approving the relief sought without conducting a hearing.

4. Definitions and General Provisions. In this Loan Modification Program, the following definitions and general provisions shall apply. Defined terms used in this LMP are capitalized. **Read this section carefully since these definitions and provisions apply throughout this Loan Modification Program:**

Additional Parties—Any non-Debtor entity whose participation in the LMM may be necessary or desirable, including any non-Debtor co-obligor or co-borrower on the Eligible Loan; any non–Debtor entity with an ownership interest in the Eligible Property; any creditor with a lien on the Eligible Property, other than the Lender; and any other third party.

Auditor—The person appointed by the Program Manager who may complete a review of the LMM, as described herein.

Case—A Chapter 13 bankruptcy case pending in the Court.

Certification of Document Preparation—The Certification obtained by the Debtor upon completion of the Document Preparation Software and payment of the Document Preparation Software Fee. The Certification of Document Preparation must be attached to the filed *Initial Notice of Loan Modification Matter*. The Certificate is generated by the Document Preparation Software.

Conduit Program—The process by which all mortgage arrears, the periodic post-petition mortgage payments, and any mortgage fees, expenses and charges owed to a mortgage lender are disbursed by the Trustee. This includes any Trial Period Payments and payments pursuant to a Loan Modification Agreement.

Court—The United States Bankruptcy Court in which the Case is pending.

Debtor—Any individual with a pending Case as of or after the Effective Date, including a *pro se* Debtor. The term includes joint debtors.

Direct Pay—Disbursements by the Debtor directly to the Lender on an Eligible Loan, as opposed to disbursements by the Trustee to the Lender.

Document Preparation Software—The secure online program, maintained and operated by the Portal Provider, which facilitates the preparation of the Initial LMM Package by (1) populating the Initial Documents and (2) by generating a customized checklist of the required additional forms and supporting documents required by the Lender.

Document Preparation Software Fee—A non-refundable fee to be paid by the Debtor to the Portal Provider. The fee is $40.00 as of the Effective Date. This fee is in addition to the LMM Portal Submission Fee. A separate Document Preparation Software Fee shall be collected by the Portal Provider for each Eligible Loan submitted to the Loan Modification Program. If the Debtor is authorized to initiate more than one LMM on any Eligible Loan, a separate Document Preparation Software Fee shall be collected by the Portal Provider each time an LMM is initiated.

Eligible Loan—Any loan, extension of money or credit, or any repayment obligation which is secured by Eligible Property. This term includes, without limitation, subprime or non-traditional loans; loans in foreclosure prior to the filing of the Case; loans secured by a first or junior deed of trust or lien on Eligible Property; and/or a loan that has been pooled, securitized, or assigned to a creditor or trustee.

Eligible Property—Real property in which the Debtor has an ownership interest, including an ownership interest in the Debtor's principal residence and/or homestead property, secondary property, or commercial property.

Final LMM Report—The report to be filed with the Court by the Debtor or the Program Manager at the conclusion of the LMM.

Initial Documents—Collectively, this includes those documents generally required by a Lender to initiate the review of Debtor's LMM, which documents are included in the Document Preparation Software.

Initial LMM Package—All Initial Documents and, additionally, any other forms and supporting documents required by the Lender, as reported by the Lender to the Portal Provider, in order to commence the assessment of a Debtor's LMM.

Initial Notice of Loan Modification Matter—The Mandatory Form filed by the Debtor which states that the Debtor has completed all required procedures to commence the LMM.

Lender—The owner, holder, servicer or assignee of the Loan as well as any Successor Lender. Use of this term in this LMP neither establishes nor modifies the legal relationship of the parties.

Loan Modification Agreement—The written agreement to be signed by all LMM Parties which sets out the basic terms agreed to by the LMM Parties, if an agreement is reached. The Loan Modification Agreement must be attached as an exhibit to the *Motion to Approve Loan Modification Agreement*.

Loan Modification Matter or LMM—A request for a modification of the repayment terms of an Eligible Loan from Lender or for any other Loss Mitigation solution. Debtor must commence a separate LMM for each Eligible Loan.

Loan Modification Program or LMP—The procedures, obligations, duties and deadlines set out herein.

LMM Objection Period—The fourteen (14) day period following the service of the *Initial Notice of Loan Modification Matter* during which any LMM Party or Party–in–Interest may file a written objection if such party objects to the proposed LMM.

LMM Party or Parties—This term includes (1) the Debtor and the Lender, (2) any Additional Party that has been ordered by the Court or has agreed to or requested to participate in the LMM or (3) any of them.

LMM Portal Submission Fee—A non-refundable fee to be paid by the Debtor to the Portal Provider. The fee is $40.00 as of the Effective Date. This fee is in addition to the Document Preparation Software Fee. A separate LMM Portal Submission Fee shall be collected by the Portal Provider for each Eligible Loan submitted to the LMP. If the Debtor is authorized to initiate more than one LMM on any Eligible Loan, a separate Portal Submission Fee shall be collected by the Portal Provider each time an LMM is initiated.

Loss Mitigation—This term includes the full range of solutions that may prevent (1) the loss of Eligible Property through foreclosure and/or (2) an increase in costs to the Lender. This term includes, without limitation, a loan modification, loan refinance, forbearance, short sale, or surrender of the Eligible Property in full or partial satisfaction of the Eligible Loan.

Mandatory Forms—The forms adopted by the Court for use in the LMP. A list of Mandatory Forms is attached. If the title of a form is italicized in this LMP, it is a Mandatory Form.

Original Term—The initial duration of the LMM which is one hundred and fifty (150) days from the filing of the *Initial Notice of Loan Modification Matter* or the entry of a Court order authorizing the Debtor to proceed with the LMM, whichever date is later.

Party–in–Interest or Parties–in–Interest—Any party in a Case entitled to be served with a Chapter 13 Plan pursuant to the Rules and Procedures.

Plan—The document filed by the Debtor in compliance with the applicable provisions of the Bankruptcy Code and any applicable Rules and Procedures as well as any pre-confirmation amendment of same and any post-confirmation modification of the Plan.

Portal—The secure online service maintained and operated by the Portal Provider which allows documents, information, and communications to be submitted, retrieved and tracked by the LMM Parties and the Trustee. All LMM Parties must register to obtain access to the Portal (see paragraph 5E for information on Portal registration).

Portal Provider—An independent third-party approved by the Court to assist in the management of this LMP. As of the Effective Date, the Portal Provider is Default Mitigation Management, LLC ("DMM"). The Court may, in its sole discretion, select different or additional Portal Providers.

Program Manager Fee—The non-refundable payment to the Portal Provider for (1) compensation of the Program Manager, and (2) the compensation of the Auditor (if required). The fee is $600.00 as of the Effective Date and shall be paid $300.00 by the Debtor and $300.00 by the Lender at the times specified in this LMP. A separate Portal Provider's Fee shall be collected by the Portal Provider for each Eligible Loan submitted to the LMP. If the Debtor is authorized to initiate more than one LMM on any Eligible Loan, a separate Program Manager Fee shall be collected by the Portal Provider each time an LMM is initiated.

Program Manager—Collectively, any individual assigned to an LMM by the Portal Provider and the software used by the Portal Provider to monitor and administer the LMM.

Reserved Funds—The difference, if any, between the regular periodic payments on an Eligible Loan and the Trial Period Payments. When the Debtor is in a Conduit Program, the Reserved Funds may be retained by the Trustee and, if retained, will be disbursed as set out in this LMP.

Rules and Procedures—Collectively, the Federal Rules of Bankruptcy Procedure and any applicable Local Rules, General Orders, administrative orders, established procedures of the Court, or Trustee's procedures.

Successor Lender—Any entity to which the Lender transfers the Eligible Loan or the servicing of the Eligible Loan during the pendency of the LMM. Use of this term in this LMP neither establishes nor modifies the legal relationship of the parties.

Trial Period Payments—Payments required by the Lender prior to a final determination regarding permanent modification of the repayment obligation on an Eligible Loan.

Trustee or Chapter 13 Trustee—The bankruptcy trustee appointed in the Case.

5. Filing, Submission, Uploading, the Mandatory Use of Forms and Other Provisions.

A. Any reference to filing a document or to a document being filed refers to the filing of that document with the Court.

B. Any reference to a submission or upload of a document refers to posting that document on the Portal.

C. All Mandatory Forms must be used, without alternation, by all LMM Parties, the Portal Provider and the Program Manager. Use of a nonstandard form shall have no effect. Failure to complete a Mandatory Form properly may result in the LMM being terminated.

D. When service of a document is required, that service shall be made in compliance with the Rules and Procedures.

E. LMM Parties must register on the Portal as described in this LMP. Registration on the Portal is free and is a onetime event. The instructions for registration on the Portal may be found at www.dmmportal.com.

6. Eligibility. An LMM may be commenced with regard to any Eligible Loan.

7. General Provisions Regarding the Portal Provider, Program Manager and Auditor.

A. The Portal Provider shall have extensive knowledge of (1) the forms and supporting documents required by a Lender to complete an Initial LMM Package, (2) the various programs for the modification of the terms of an Eligible Loan offered by the Lender, and (3) other available Loss Mitigation remedies.

B. The Portal Provider shall be approved by the Court and must provide a Portal for the use of the LMM Parties, the Program Manager, the Auditor (if any), and the Trustee.

C. The Portal Provider must provide access to the Document Preparation Software and the Portal and is responsible for maintaining both in good working order. The Portal and the Document Preparation Software can be accessed at www.dmmportal.com.

D. The Portal Provider shall be responsible for making the Document Preparation Software available on the Portal. The Document Preparation Software should (1) ensure that the submission by the Debtor to the Lender is as complete and accurate as possible, (2) expedite the Lender's review of the submissions, and (3) protect all confidential information.

E. The Portal Provider and the Program Manager shall be familiar with the rules and procedures of the LMP and be able to advise the LMM Parties about their responsibilities and the basic procedures for participation in an LMM, including, without limitation, directing users to the relevant provisions of the LMP and to required forms and documents.

F. The Portal Provider, upon request, shall provide free training on the use of the Document Preparation Software and the Portal to any LMM Party or Trustee personnel.

G. The Program Manager shall monitor all communications on the Portal between the LMM Parties and shall ensure that each LMM Party is performing its/their obligations and duties as required herein, including, without limitation: (1) confirming that the Debtor has uploaded a complete Initial LMM Package; (2) facilitating the exchange of information and documents among the LMM Parties; (3) ensuring that the Loss Mitigation review proceeds according to the terms and within the required deadlines of the LMP; (4) tracking and monitoring deadlines for each LMM Party; (5) preparing for, scheduling, and conducting any conferences; and (6) reporting any unresolved noncompliance of an LMM Party to the Court by filing a *Notice of Non–Compliance* which shall include the details of the non-compliance.

H. All requests by the Portal Provider, the Program Manager, or the Auditor for information or the submission of documents shall be made through the Portal.

I. The Program Manager shall assist with any out–of–Court resolution of all allegations by an LMM Party that any other party has failed to comply with any of the provisions of this LMP.

J. The Portal Provider may retain outside parties, at no additional cost to the LMM Parties, to assist it in its duties, provided such parties have the necessary skill, experience, and knowledge base in Loss Mitigation as determined by the Portal Provider.

K. The Portal Provider, Program Manager, and Auditor are subject to the jurisdiction of the Court and will promptly answer all inquiries from the Court, the Trustee and LMM Parties regarding the status of the LMM.

8. General Provisions Regarding LMM Parties. The following is applicable to all LMM Parties, in addition to the specific duties and responsibilities for each type of LMM Party as set out in this LMP:

A. All LMM Parties shall act in good faith throughout the entirety of the LMM, including, without limitation, promptly responding to all inquiries made through the Portal and providing all requested documentation and information promptly and timely.

B. All LMM Parties shall be bound by the provisions of this LMP.

C. All LMM Parties shall comply with the deadlines set out herein, subject to any permitted extension of those deadlines by the agreement of the LMM Parties or by Court order.

D. During the LMM, all material communications and requests for documents and information by and between the LMM Parties shall be conducted exclusively through the Portal, provided however, that any litigated matters between the LMM Parties shall be considered as separate matters and not subject to this requirement. By way of example, communications regarding an adversary proceeding, a contested matter, or a discovery dispute are not subject to this requirement.

E. On behalf of each LMM Party, a person (1) with complete knowledge of the Eligible Loan; (2) who is reasonably capable of answering questions posed by the Court, any other LMM Party or the Trustee; and (3) with full authority to enter a binding settlement agreement, shall participate in the LMM, including, without limitation, all conferences, and shall attend any LMM related hearings, unless such attendance is excused. Any LMM Party may appear at hearings through counsel unless the Court orders otherwise in a specific LMM.

F. The pendency of an LMM does not relieve any LMM Party from full compliance with any (1) orders of the Court or (2) applicable provisions of or deadlines established by the United States Bankruptcy Code or the Rules and Procedures.

G. Any LMM Party who requires (1) a foreign language interpreter or (2) an interpreter because of a hearing impairment in order to participate in any part of the LMM shall provide such interpreter at that LMM Party's sole expense.

H. If the Case is dismissed, converted, or venue of the Case is transferred to a Court without an LMP prior to the completion of the LMM, the LMM will immediately terminate. LMM Parties will be relieved of all LMP requirements.

I. If the Case is otherwise eligible to be closed, the Case shall remain open during the pendency of the LMM.

J. All communications and information exchanged on the Portal during the LMM are privileged and confidential. They are inadmissible in any subsequent proceeding to the extent provided by any applicable Rules and Procedures or the Federal Rules of Evidence.

K. During the pendency of the LMM, nothing herein precludes the LMM Parties from negotiating Loss Mitigation solutions other than a modification of the repayment terms of the Eligible Loan, provided such negotiations are conducted through the Portal.

L. If any LMM Party fails to comply with any of the provisions of this LMP, the other LMM Parties must attempt to resolve the issues through communication on the Portal, requesting assistance from the Program Manager, if needed. If a resolution cannot be reached, any LMM Party may file a *Motion to Terminate Loan Modification Matter*, detailing the basis for the relief sought.

M. The Trustee may establish procedures which are not inconsistent with the provisions of this LMP for the administration of Cases involved in the LMM. Such procedures must be in writing and include an effective date. Such procedures shall be posted on the Trustee's website. All LMM Parties must comply with the Trustee's procedures. The Trustee, in his/her sole discretion, may revise the Trustee's procedures. Revised Trustee procedures, if any, shall be posted on the Trustee's website and must include the effective date of the revisions.

N. The Court may set status conferences to monitor the progress of any LMM.

9. Provisions Regarding the Debtor.

A. All *pro-se* Debtors shall have the same duties and responsibilities as a Debtor represented by an attorney and shall comply with all provisions of the LMP.

B. Debtor shall comply with all requirements necessary to commence an LMM and timely file and serve the *Initial Notice of Loan Modification Matter,* as well as upload a copy to the Portal. The *Initial Notice of Loan Modification Matter* shall be served in compliance with the Rules and Procedures on any Party–in–Interest and any person filing a Notice of Appearance in the Case.

C. A separate LMM must be commenced for each Eligible Loan.

D. Within seven (7) days of the filing of the *Initial Notice of Loan Modification Matter* or the Lender's registration on the Portal, whichever occurs later, the Debtor shall complete the upload of all documents known to be part of the Lender's Initial LMM Package to the Portal.

E. If the Debtor contemplates initiating an LMM, the Debtor shall include language in any Plan filed by the Debtor stating that the Debtor intends to commence an LMM. Such provision shall be included in the section of the Plan reserved for nonstandard language. The following mandatory language must be used:

The Debtor may enter the Loan Modification Program adopted by this Court which could result in a modification of a loan secured by real property in which the Debtor owns an interest or in other loss mitigation solutions, including, without limitation, loan refinance, forbearance, short sale, or surrender of the real property in full or partial satisfaction of the debt secured by the real property. Such loan modification or other loss mitigation solution may be approved by the Court without further notice to parties-in-interest and without modification of the Chapter 13 Plan if the loan modification or loss mitigation solution does not create a material adverse impact on the treatment of creditor's claims under this Plan, other than the Lender's; does not render the Plan unfeasible or insufficient; and does not increase or decrease the Plan payment to the Trustee.

F. Debtor shall remain current on all payments required to be paid pursuant to the Plan during the pendency of the LMM, including, without limitation, payments disbursed by Direct Pay.

G. A Debtor in a Conduit Program is required make all payments on an Eligible Loan through the Trustee including ongoing periodic post-petition mortgage payments; Trial Period Payments; all payments pursuant to any Loan Modification Agreement; all mortgage arrears; and all post-petition fees, expenses and charges pursuant to Rule 3002.1 of the Federal Rules of Bankruptcy Procedure.

H. If the Court has not adopted a Conduit Program, the Debtor shall disburse any periodic post-petition mortgage payments owed on the Eligible Loan by Direct Pay, including Trial Period Payments. Debtor may propose a Plan which defers the payment of any pre-petition or post-petition arrears for a reasonable period of time. Any payment required pursuant to a Notice of Fees, Expenses, and Charges filed pursuant to Rule 3002.1 of the Federal Bankruptcy Rules of Procedure will be paid in accordance with the existing procedures established by the Court, including disbursement by Direct Pay.

I. If the Court has adopted a Conduit Program, the Debtor shall make monthly Plan payments to the Trustee which are sufficient to pay any periodic post-petition mortgage payments owed on the Eligible Loan including Trial Period Payments. Debtor may propose a Plan which defers the payment of any pre-petition or post-petition arrears for a reasonable period of time. Any payment required pursuant to a Notice of Fees, Expenses, and Charges filed pursuant to Rule 3002.1 of the Federal Bankruptcy Rules of Procedure will be paid in accordance with the existing procedures of the applicable Conduit Program. Any payments pursuant to a permanent loan modification shall be disbursed by the Trustee in accordance with the Loan Modification Agreement.

J. Debtor shall promptly answer any questions from and shall provide additional documentation and information to the Lender, the Portal Provider and/or the Program Manager through the Portal. All questions and requests for additional documentation and information must be reasonable.

K. Within seven (7) days of the earlier of (1) the conclusion of the Original Term, including any extension thereof, or (2) the date the Lender reports its final decision on the Portal regarding the LMM request, the Debtor shall prepare the Final LMM Report on the Portal and file and serve it on all LMM Parties and the Trustee. The Final LMM Report will be completed in accordance with the instructions provided on the Portal and shall state whether: (1) the Eligible Loan will be modified, (2) the loan modification request was denied, or (3) another Loss Mitigation solution was agreed upon. A printout of the current and complete Portal history shall be attached to the Final LMM Report. In the event the Debtor fails to prepare, file, and serve the Final LMM Report, the Program Manager may do so.

10. Provisions Regarding Lender.

A. If the Lender is not previously registered on the Portal and does not timely file a written objection to participating in the LMM, the Lender shall register on the Portal within fourteen (14) days of the filing of the *Initial Notice of Loan Modification Matter*. If the Lender files a written objection to participating in the LMM, the Lender is required to register on the Portal within seven (7) days of the entry of an order requiring the Lender to participate in the LMM. If Lender's counsel is not registered on the Portal, counsel is subject to the same requirements set out herein.

B. If the Lender does not file a written objection to participating in the LMM within the LMM Objection Period, the Lender shall provide the Portal Provider with Lender's most current Initial LMM Package as part of Lender's registration on the Portal. If the Lender is already registered on the Portal, Lender will provide any updates to Lender's Initial LMM Package within fourteen (14) days of the filing of the *Initial Notice of Loan Modification Matter*. If the Lender files a written objection to participating in the LMM, the Lender is required to provide the Portal Provider with Lender's most current Initial LMM Package within seven (7) days of the entry of any order requiring the Lender to participate in the LMM. Lender is responsible for providing any updates to its Initial LMM Package to the Portal Provider, if necessary.

C. Within seven (7) days after the Debtor submits the completed Initial LMM Package on the Portal, Lender shall, on the Portal: (1) acknowledge receipt of Debtor's completed Initial LMM Package and (2) designate Lender's single point of contact and Lender's counsel, if any. The designated single point of contact must have all requisite authority, within the investor's guidelines, to settle any and all issues that arise during the LMM. Legal counsel may be granted such requisite authority by the Lender.

D. Within seven (7) days of the Lender's receipt of the Debtor's Initial LMM Package on the Portal, Lender shall pay one-half of the Program Manager's Fee directly to the Portal Provider.

E. Upon receipt of the completed Initial LMM Package, Lender shall promptly review the package to determine Debtor's eligibility for any Loss Mitigation solutions, including modification of the repayment terms of the Eligible Loan.

F. No more than thirty (30) days after the submission of the Initial LMM Package, if the Lender requires additional or corrected documentation or information to complete its review of the Initial LMM Package, Lender shall notify the appropriate LMM Party through the Portal of such requirements and shall promptly acknowledge the submission of the additional or corrected documentation or information. If no request for additional documents or information is timely made by the Lender, the submissions made in the LMM shall be deemed complete. Lender shall not request that any information be provided on a specific form—i.e., if the Debtor provided the Lender with information on a standard government form, Lender shall use reasonable diligence in reviewing the information provided by the Debtor.

G. Lender shall promptly review all documents and information submitted by any LMM Party through the Portal and shall promptly respond to any inquiries made by any LMM Party or the Program Manager.

H. Lender shall attend and participate in any conferences regarding the LMM, unless the Lender's attendance is excused by the Program Manager or Auditor.

I. Lender shall have no more than thirty (30) days after the submissions made in the LMM are deemed complete to state its decision on the Portal regarding the request to modify an Eligible Loan or any other Loss Mitigation solution. The Lender's decision includes (1) denial of the loan modification request, (2) approval of the loan modification request, (3) requiring Trial Period Payments and the satisfaction of any other terms and conditions set out in the *Notice of Trial Period Payments*, or (4) acceptance of any other Loss Mitigation solution.

J. Lender shall promptly notify any Successor Lender of the pendency of the LMM and shall provide the Successor Lender with a copy of the *Initial Notice of Loan Modification Matter* and any orders entered by the Court which are relevant to the LMM. The Successor Lender is obligated to comply with all terms of any entered order and all terms of this LMP. Without limiting the foregoing, the Successor Lender is required to accept all documents and information submitted by any LMM Party which was previously accepted by the Lender. In the event there is a change in ownership of the Eligible Loan, the parties shall comply with the Rules and Procedures regarding a transferred claim. In the event there is a change in the servicer for the Eligible Loan, Lender shall file a *Notice Substituting Servicer* and shall transfer the submissions on the Portal to the Successor Lender, provided, however, that nothing herein shall preclude the Debtor or Program Manager from transferring such submissions. If the Successor Lender is not registered on the Portal, the

Successor Lender shall register within fourteen (14) days of the filing of the *Notice Substituting Servicer.*

11. Commencement of LMM and Opportunity to Object.

A. The Debtor may commence an LMM at any time after the filing of the Case. Only the Debtor may commence an LMM.

B. To commence the LMM, the Debtor shall complete all of the following steps:

1. Register on the Portal;

2. Complete the Document Preparation Software and pay the Document Preparation Software Fee;

3. Review the Initial LMM Package prepared on the Document Preparation Software and be prepared to execute all required forms and upload all required documents to the Portal upon the expiration of the LMM Objection Period;

4. File the *Initial Notice of Loan Modification Matter*, together with the Certification of Document Preparation;

5. If Bankruptcy Schedules I and J were filed by the Debtor more than six (6) months prior to the filing of the *Initial Notice of Loan Modification Matter*, the Debtor must either (1) sign and file amended Schedules I and J pursuant to the Official Bankruptcy Forms prior to filing the *Initial Notice of Loan Modification Matter* or (2) state in the *Initial Notice of Loan Modification Matter* that Bankruptcy Schedules I and J as filed correctly state the Debtor's current income and expenses.

6. If no objection to the LMM is filed, then within seven (7) days after the expiration of the LMM Objection Period, Debtor shall submit the Initial LMM Package to the Portal, together with a file-stamped copy of the *Initial Notice of Loan Modification Matter*. As part of the Portal submission, Debtor will pay the LMM Portal Submission Fee as well as the Debtor's share of the Program Manager Fee;

7. If an objection to the LMM is filed, then within seven (7) days after a court order is entered directing the parties to proceed with the LMM, Debtor shall submit the Initial LMM Package to the Portal, together with a copy of said Order. As part of the Portal submission, Debtor will pay the LMM Portal Submission Fee as well as the Debtor's share of the Program Manager Fee.

C. During the LMM Objection Period, any LMM Party or Party–in–Interest may file a written objection to the *Initial Notice of Loan Modification Matter* if such party objects to the LMM or to participating in the LMM. Any written objection shall clearly state the reasons for objecting to the LMM or to participating in the LMM. If a written objection is not filed, each non-objecting party shall be deemed to have waived its objection to the Debtor initiating an LMM and/or to participating in the LMM. No Court order commencing the LMM is required if no objection is filed. If an objection is filed, the Court will determine, after notice and hearing, whether the Debtor may proceed with the LMM. If the Court authorizes the Debtor to proceed with the LMM, the objecting party shall be deemed to be an LMM Party, if appropriate.

D. If any entity objects to the LMM or to participating in the LMM, all deadlines set forth in this LMP shall be suspended pending the resolution of the objection.

12. Provisions Regarding Additional Parties.

A. Any LMM Party may request and the Court may order that a specific Additional Party be required to participate in the LMM, to the extent that the Court has jurisdiction over the Additional Party. Any such request shall be made by filing a *Motion to Add an Additional Party to Loan Modification Matter*. If an objection is not timely filed, the Additional Party shall be deemed to have consented to participate in the LMM and the Court may enter an order requiring the participation of the Additional Party without conducting a hearing. Any Additional Party ordered by the Court to participate in the LMM shall be deemed to be an LMM Party.

B. An Additional Party may consent to participate in the LMM by signing and filing a *Consent to Participate in Loan Modification Matter by Additional Party*. Upon the filing of this consent, the Additional Party shall be deemed an LMM Party.

C. Any LMM Party may file a motion to request that the Court determine whether the LMM can proceed without the inclusion and participation of a specific Additional Party.

13. Trustee. The Trustee, in his/her sole discretion, may, but is not required to, participate in the LMM.

14. Duration.

A. The LMM Parties may extend the Original Term by agreement by filing a *Notice of Extension of Loan Modification Matter*. The LMM Parties may not extend the duration of the LMM for more than a total of ninety (90) days beyond the Original Term by agreement. A Court order is necessary for a longer extension of time and may be sought by filing a *Motion to Extend the Duration of Loan Modification Matter.*

B. If an agreement to extend the Original Term cannot be reached, any LMM Party may file a *Motion to Extend the Duration of Loan Modification Matter* detailing the basis for the extension which shall be served on all LMM Parties and the Trustee. The Portal history must be attached to this motion. The deadline for objecting to such motion is seven (7) days from the date of service of same. If an objection is not filed, each non-objecting party shall be deemed to have waived its objection to the extension of the Original Term. If an objection is timely filed, the Court may schedule a hearing to determine whether an extension of the Original Term should be granted or may rule without a hearing.

C. The Debtor or Program Manager shall report any extension of the Original Term on the Portal.

D. Notwithstanding the other provision of this LMP, if the LMM Parties agree to the payment of Trial Period Payments, as evidenced by the filing of *Notice of Trial Period Payments*, the duration of the LMM shall be extended, without Court order, to allow the Debtor to complete the Trial Period Payments plus an additional sixty (60) days to allow for the approval of any Loan Modification Agreement.

E. If any LMM Party wishes to terminate the LMM prior to the expiration of the Original Term or any extension thereof, that party shall file a *Motion to Terminate Loan Modification Matter* detailing the basis for such termination request. The motion must be served on all LMM Parties and the Trustee. The Portal history must be attached to this motion. The deadline for objecting to termination of the LMM is fourteen (14) days from the date of service of such motion. If an objection is not filed, each non-objecting party shall be deemed to have waived its objection and the Court may terminate the LMM without a further hearing. If an objection is timely filed, the Court may schedule a hearing to determine whether to terminate the LMM or may rule without a hearing.

15. Conferences.

A. There is no requirement that a conference must be scheduled in an LMM. Conferences should be requested by the LMM Parties or scheduled by the Program Manager only if needed to accomplish the purpose of the LMP.

B. All conferences shall be telephonic. All LMM Parties shall participate in the conference unless excused by the other LMM Parties or the Program Manager. No telephonic conference shall be recorded. The only parties who may participate in the telephonic conference are (1) the Program Manager and (2) the LMM Parties and their attorneys.

C. A conference may be scheduled by the Program Manager upon the request of any LMM Party and as deemed necessary by the Program Manager, acting reasonably. After consultation with all LMM Parties and their attorneys (if any), the Program Manager shall fix a reasonable date and time for such conference and notify all LMM Parties and their attorneys (if any) thereof. The Program Manager shall include a call-in number for the conference as part of the notice.

D. Each LMM Party may request one (1) conference. The Program Manager, in his/her sole discretion, may schedule more than one conference.

E. The Program Manager shall report the scheduling of the conference on the Portal. The Program Manager shall participate in all conferences.

F. No LMM Party is required to participate in conferences for more than a total of two (2) hours during the pendency of the LMM.

G. All LMM Parties participating in the conference must either personally be or must appoint a representative who is ready, willing and able to sign a binding settlement agreement during the conference and must have the ability to scan, send and receive documents by facsimile, email or other electronic means during the conference.

H. If an LMM Party that is required to appear at a conference fails to appear, the Program Manager may file a *Notice of Non–Compliance*.

16. Trial Period Payments and Loan Modification Approval Process.

A. If the Lender decides to offer a trial modification of the repayment terms of the Eligible Loan, the Debtor or the Lender shall file a *Notice of Trial Period Payments* which shall be served only on the LMM Parties and the Trustee. The *Notice* shall be uploaded to the Portal by the filing party. The *Notice* must be signed by the Lender and by the Debtor, by and through the Debtor's attorney, if any. All LMM Parties and the Trustee will have fourteen (14) days following the service of the *Notice* to file a written objection to the Trial Period Payments. Any written objection shall clearly state the basis for objecting to the Trial Period Payments. If no written objection is filed, any objection to the Trial Period Payments shall be deemed waived by the non-objecting party and the Trustee, if the Debtor is in a Conduit Program, or the Debtor, if the Debtor is not in a Conduit Program, is authorized to disburse the Trial Period Payments to the Lender and to retain Reserved Funds as set out in the *Notice*. If an objection to the *Notice* is filed, the Court will determine, after notice and hearing, whether the Trial Period Payments are approved. If so, the Court will enter an *Order Approving Trial Period Payments* and the Trustee, if the Debtor is in a Conduit Program, or the Debtor, if the Debtor is not in a Conduit Program, is authorized to disburse the Trial Period Payments and to retain Reserved Funds as set out in the *Order*. The Lender is not required to file a Notice of Payment Changes pursuant to Rule 3002.1 with regard to the Trial Period Payments.

B. In the event a Debtor makes all Trial Period Payments and satisfies any other terms and conditions required by the Lender which are set out in the *Notice of Trial Period Payments*, Debtor shall be entitled to a permanent and binding modification of the repayment terms of the Eligible Loan. The full agreement between the parties shall be reduced to writing and executed by all necessary parties. The Debtor or the Lender shall file a *Motion to Approve Loan Modification Agreement* which shall be served on the LMM Parties and the Trustee. The *Motion* shall be uploaded to the Portal by the filing party. A copy of the completed and signed Loan Modification Agreement and any related documents must be attached to the *Motion*. All LMM Parties and the Trustee will have fourteen (14) days following the service of the *Motion* to file a written objection. Any written objection shall clearly state the basis for objecting to the approval of the Loan Modification Agreement. If no written objection is filed, any objection to the approval of the Loan Modification Agreement shall be deemed waived by the non-objecting party. If no objection is filed, the Court may enter an *Order Approving Loan Modification Agreement*. If an objection is filed, the Court will determine, after notice and hearing, whether the Loan Modification Agreement should be approved. If so, the Court will enter an *Order Approving Loan Modification Agreement*.

C. Dismissal or conversion of the Case shall not be a permissible condition of any agreement regarding Trial Period Payments or any Loan Modification Agreement and may not be included in either as a term or condition.

D. The Court may require pro-se Debtors to personally appear prior to approving the Trial Period Payments or any Loan Modification Agreement.

E. The Trustee may be heard at any hearing regarding the approval of any Trial Period Payments or any *Motion to Approve Loan Modification Agreement*, but is not required to participate in such hearings.

F. If the Court enters an *Order Approving Loan Modification Agreement*, the Trustee, if the Debtor is in a Conduit Program, or the Debtor, if the Debtor is not in a Conduit Program, is authorized to make disbursements to the Lender as set out in the *Motion to Approve Loan Modification Agreement* without any further modification of the Plan. Any arrearage or any other obligations owed to the Lender, whether pre- or post- petition, shall be paid pursuant to the terms set out in the *Motion to Approve Loan Modification Agreement* and/or the Loan Modification Agreement. Unless otherwise required by the terms of any applicable Conduit Program, if the Plan is not modified, the Plan payment will not be adjusted and any funds paid to the Trustee which the Trustee does not disburse to the Lender may be disbursed by the Trustee to satisfy the claims of other creditors. Additionally, any Reserved Funds shall be disbursed by the Trustee to the Debtor's attorney until the outstanding balance of any attorney's fees is paid in full and, thereafter, shall disburse any remaining Reserved Funds to satisfy the claims of other creditors. The Trustee shall make all disbursements in accordance with the provisions of the Plan and all applicable Rules and Procedures.

G. If the Lender or any other LMM Party is to receive payment of or reimbursement for any fee, cost or charge that arose from or during the LMM process, all such fees, costs and charges shall be disclosed in the *Motion to Approve Loan Modification Agreement*. If the Lender fails to disclose such fees, costs and charges as described herein, the Lender shall have waived its right to collect such fee, costs and charges.

H. If the *Motion to Approve Loan Modification Agreement* is granted by the Court, any proof of claim filed by the Lender shall be deemed amended by the terms set out in the *Motion to Approve Loan Modification Agreement* and the Lender will not be required to file an amended proof of claim. Additionally, the Lender will not be required to file any Notice of Payment Change or any Notice of Fees, Expenses, and Charges pursuant to Rule 3002.1 of the Federal Rules of Bankruptcy Procedure with regard to any payment obligation disclosed in the *Motion to Approve Loan Modification Agreement*. The Chapter 13 Trustee is authorized to make disbursements in accordance with the terms set out in the *Motion to Approve Loan Modification Agreement* and/or the *Order Approving Loan Modification Agreement*, including discontinuing disbursements on an arrearage claim provided for in the Plan, if that is consistent with the terms set out in the *Motion to Approve Loan Modification Agreement* and/or the *Order Approving Loan Modification Agreement*. All disbursements to the Lender will be made in accordance with the procedures established by the Court for the payment of such claims.

I. Unless otherwise ordered by the Court, and subject to Bankruptcy Rule 3002.1(f)–(h), if a Debtor in a Conduit Program is current on Plan payments or the payments due pursuant to any wage directive, the Trial Period Payments or any other payment that the Trustee is directed to disburse to the Lender pursuant to a *Notice of Trial Period Payments*, an *Order Approving Trial Period Payments, a Motion to Approve Loan Modification Agreement* and/or the Loan Modification Agreement shall be deemed current, even if not yet disbursed by the Trustee to the Lender.

J. All LMM Parties shall execute and deliver any and all documents, in addition to the Loan Modification Agreement, which are reasonably necessary to effectuate the agreement between the parties only if such documents are described as required documents in the *Motion to Approve Loan Modification Agreement*. The pleading shall also e uploaded to the Portal.

J.* The LMM Parties may also file a motion or other appropriate pleading to have the Court approve any other Loss Mitigation solution of the LMM. Any such pleading must be served on all LMM Parties and the Trustee and provide each party with no less than fourteen days to object to the relief sought.

17. Denial.

A. In the event the Lender denies the request for a modification of the repayment terms of an Eligible Loan and the Debtor requests an audit of the LMM, the Program Manager will appoint an Auditor from its list of approved Auditors to review the LMM for the purpose of determining whether the Lender considered all possible loan modification programs available to the Debtor and considered all relevant information in making its decision on the requested loan modification. The Auditor will also discuss the reasons for the denial with the Debtor.

B. If a plan modification is required following the denial, that plan modification shall be filed no later than thirty (30) days from the date the Lender posts the denial on the Portal.

C. In the event the Court enters an order denying the *Motion to Approve Loan Modification Agreement*, the Court shall enter an *Order Denying Approval of Loan Modification Agreement*.

D. Following a denial by the Lender which is posted on the Portal or the entry of a Court order denying the *Motion to Approve Loan Modification Agreement*, the Trustee shall disburse any Reserved Funds to the Lender.

18. Plan modification.

A. A Plan modification is not required if the loan modification or Loss Mitigation solution does not create a material adverse impact on the treatment of any creditor's claims under this Plan, other than the Lender's; does not render the Plan unfeasible or insufficient; and does not increase or decrease the Plan payment to the Trustee.

B. If a plan modification is required, the Debtor shall file a Plan modification which shall be served on any Party–in–Interest pursuant to the Rules and Procedures. The Plan modification shall be filed and served within thirty (30) days of the entry of an order granting the *Motion to Approve Loan Modification Agreement* or approving another Loss Mitigation solution.

C. The Trustee may move to modify the Debtor's Plan if, in the discretion of the Trustee, such modification is warranted.

19. Attorney Fees.

A. *No Look Standard Fee*—The standard, "presumed reasonable and necessary" fee for counsel for the Debtor for representation of the Debtor in an LMM is $2500.00 plus $100.00 in costs, in addition to the fees and costs incurred in the representation of the Debtor in the Case. Such fees and costs shall be disclosed in the *Initial Notice of Loan Modification Matter*, which disclosure shall be deemed to fulfill the requirements of Rule 2016 of the Federal Rules of Bankruptcy Procedure. The following will be included in the standard "no-look" fee:

1. Determining the Debtor's eligibility to participate in the LMP;

2. Preparing the Initial LMM Package for the Debtor through the Document Preparation Software;

3. Filing amended Schedules I and J, if required;

4. Preparing, filing, and serving the *Initial Notice of Loan Modification Matter*;

5. Assisting the Debtor in completing any forms or providing any other information or counsel in connection with the LMM;

6. Submitting all required documents and information through the Portal;

7. Filing all required pleadings;

8. Preparation of proposed orders and settlement documents;

9. Communicating with other LMM Parties and the Portal Provider, Program Manager and/or Auditor, as required;

10. Participating in any LMM conferences and/or Court hearings;

11. Reviewing all documents regarding a modification of the repayment terms of the Eligible Loan or other Loss Mitigation solution.

B. The standard "no-look" fee does not include preparation of or representation of the Debtor regarding the modification of the Plan.

C. Debtor's counsel may elect to file a fee application for reasonable compensation in connection with an LMM, including costs, rather than accept the standard "no-look" fee. If Debtor's counsel files a fee application, it shall be served pursuant to the Rules and Procedures.

D. The Trustee and any other Party–in–Interest retain their rights to object to any request by Debtor's counsel for the payment of any fees or the reimbursement of any costs.

E. Any attorney's fees and costs payable to the Debtor's counsel will be paid in accordance with the procedures established by the Court for the payment of compensation and the reimbursement of costs to Debtor's counsel.

20. No Prohibition.

The pendency of an LMM shall not prohibit or preclude any LMM Party from taking whatever lawful action that party deems necessary to protect its interests during the pendency of the LMM, including moving for relief from the automatic stay, moving for the dismissal of the Case, objecting to confirmation of a Plan or any similar pleading, objecting to a proof of claim, or filing an adversary proceeding which names any LMM Party as a plaintiff or defendant.

21. Remedies.

A. Any LMM Party may file a *Motion to Terminate Loan Modification Matter* which must detail the basis for the requested termination and must be served on all LMM Parties and the Trustee and uploaded to the Portal. All LMM Parties shall have fourteen (14) days following the service of the motion to file a written objection. Each non-objection party shall be deemed to have waived its objection to the relief sought and the Court may enter an order awarding appropriate relief without a hearing. If a written objection is filed, the motion will be set on the Court's docket for hearing. The filing party is responsible for filing and serving a notice of the hearing on all other LMM Parties and the Trustee.

B. The Court may order any appropriate remedy, including sanctions, dismissal of the LMM, or any other remedy that the Court deems appropriate to protect the interests and rights of the LMM Parties.

22. Venue and Choice of Law.

All disputes in connection with the LMM shall be governed by the provisions of the United States Bankruptcy Code; the law of the state of Texas, irrespective of the conflict of law principles of that state; the Rules and Procedures; and this LMP. Any action or proceeding arising from a dispute concerning a LMM or this LMP shall be brought in the Court.

LIST OF MANDATORY FORMS

BTXN 300   *Initial Notice of Loan Modification Matter*

BTXN 301   *Motion to Add an Additional Party to Loan Modification Matter*

BTXN 302   *Consent to Participate in Loan Modification Matter by Additional Party*

BTXN 303   *Notice of Extension of Loan Modification Matter*

BTXN 304   *Motion to Extend the Duration of Loan Modification Matter*

BTXN 305   *Motion to Terminate Loan Modification Matter*

BTXN 306   *Notice of Non–Compliance*

BTXN 307   *Notice Substituting Servicer*

BTXN 308   *Notice of Trial Period Payments*

BTXN 309   *Order Approving Trial Period Payments*

BTXN 310   *Motion to Approve Loan Modification Agreement*

BTXN 311   *Order Approving Loan Modification Agreement*

BTXN 312   *Order Denying Approval of Loan Modification Agreement*

[Dated: October 1, 2018.]

* [**Publisher's Note:** So in original.]

UNITED STATES DISTRICT COURT FOR THE SOUTHERN DISTRICT OF TEXAS

Including Amendments Received Through
February 1, 2019

2014–6. In Re: Admission of Attorneys and Electronic Filing Registration.

SPEEDY TRIAL PLAN

JURY SELECTION PLAN

2013–6. In the Matter of Revised Order Establishing a Plan for Jury Selection for the Southern District of Texas.

CRIMINAL JUSTICE ACT PLAN

SELECTED ORDERS

91–26. In the Matter of Guidelines for Coordination of Criminal Procedures.

2001–7. In re Guidelines for Professional Conduct.

2002–13. In the Matter of Jurisdiction and Procedures for Duties Assigned to United States Magistrate Judges in This District.

2004–11. In the Matter of Protecting Personal Privacy in Public Case Files.

2007–12. In the Matter of Transcript Fees.

2011–04. In the Matter of Deposit and Investment of Registry Funds.

2011–12. In the Matter of Bankruptcy Jurisdiction.

2012–6. In re: Order of Reference to Bankruptcy Judges.

2016–14. In the Matter of Deposit and Investment of Registry Funds.

CIVIL RULES

LR 3. COMMENCEMENT OF ACTION

Parties represented by counsel must file a civil action cover sheet (Form JS44c) with all original pleadings.

[Effective May 1, 2000.]

LR 4. SUMMONS

Parties other than prisoners must provide completed summons forms for issuance by the clerk.

[Effective May 1, 2000.]

LR 5. FILING REQUIREMENTS

LR5.1 Electronic Filing. Except as expressly provided or unless permitted by the presiding Judge, the Court requires documents being filed to be submitted, signed or verified by electronic means that comply with the procedures established by the Court. The notice of electronic filing that is automatically generated by the Court's electronic filing system constitutes service of the document on those registered as filing users of the system.

LR5.2 Related Litigation Policy. The parties must advise the Court of related current or recent litigation and of directly affected non-parties.

LR5.3 Certificate of Service. Papers must have at the end a certificate reflecting how and when service has been made or why service is not required. Federal Rule of Civil Procedure 5(b).

LR5.4 Discovery Not Filed. Depositions, interrogatories, answers to interrogatories, requests for admission, production, or inspection, responses to those requests, and other discovery material shall not be filed with the clerk.

LR5.5 Service of Pleadings and Other Papers. All motions must be served on all parties. Motions for default judgment must be served on the defendant-respondent by certified mail (return receipt requested).

[Effective May 1, 2000. Amended effective September 7, 2004; March 12, 2007.]

LR 7. CIVIL PRETRIAL MOTION PRACTICE

LR7.1 Form. Opposed motions shall

A. Be in writing;

B. Include or be accompanied by authority;

C. Be accompanied by a separate proposed order granting the relief requested and setting forth information sufficient to communicate the nature of the relief granted;

D. Except for motions under Federal Rules of Civil Procedure 12(b), (c), (e), or (f) and 56, contain an averment that

(1) The movant has conferred with the respondent and

(2) Counsel cannot agree about the disposition of the motion.

LR7.2 Unopposed Motions. Motions without opposition and their proposed orders must bear in their caption "unopposed." They will be considered as soon as it is practicable.

LR7.3 Submission. Opposed motions will be submitted to the judge 21 days from filing without notice from the clerk and without appearance by counsel.

LR7.4 Responses and Replies. Failure to respond to a motion will be taken as a representation of no opposition. Responses to motions

A. Must be filed by the submission day;

B. Must be written;

C. Must include or be accompanied by authority; and

D. Must be accompanied by a separate form order denying the relief sought.

E. *Replies.* Unless otherwise directed by the presiding judge, a party who has filed an opposed motion may file a brief within 7 days from the date the response is filed.

LR7.5 Oral Submission.

7.5.A *By Request.* If a party views oral argument as helpful to the Court, the motion or response may include a request for it. If it is granted, the parties will be notified by the clerk.

7.5.B *By Order.* When oral presentation is required by the Court, counsel will be notified by the clerk of a date for oral presentation irrespective of any submission day.

LR7.6 Consolidation. A motion to consolidate cases will—

A.   Contain in the caption of the motion:

(1) The case numbers;

(2) Full styles; and

(3) Judge to whom each of the cases is assigned.

B.   Be filed only in the oldest case with a courtesy copy furnished to the other affected courts.

C.   Be heard by the judge to whom the oldest case is assigned.

D.   The term "oldest case," as used in this Rule, means the case filed first in any court, state or federal, including cases removed or transferred to this Court.

LR7.7 Supporting Material. If a motion or response requires consideration of facts not appearing of record, proof by affidavit or other documentary evidence must be filed with the motion or response.

LR7.8 Hearing. The Court may in its discretion, on its own motion or upon application, entertain and decide any motion, shorten or extend time periods, and request or permit additional authority or supporting material.

[Effective May 1, 2000. Amended effective December 1, 2009; November 26, 2018.]

LR 10.   FORM OF PLEADINGS

LR10.1 Caption. Papers must have a caption, including the name and party designation of the party filing it and a statement of its character, like "Defendant John Doe's Motion for Partial Summary Judgment." Federal Rule of Civil Procedure 10(a).

LR10.2 Format. Papers offered for filing may not be in covers. They must be on 8½″ x 11″ paper, stapled at the top only, punched at the top with two holes, double spaced, and paginated.

[Effective May 1, 2000.]

LR 11.   SIGNING OF PLEADINGS, MOTIONS AND OTHER PAPERS BY ATTORNEY IN CHARGE

LR11.1 Designation. On first appearance through counsel, each party shall designate an attorney-in charge. Signing the pleading effects designation.

LR11.2 Responsibility. The attorney-in-charge is responsible in that action for the party. That individual attorney shall attend all court proceedings or send a fully informed attorney with authority to bind the client.

LR11.3 Signing of Pleadings. Every document filed must be signed by, or by permission of, the attorney-in-charge.

11.3.A *Required Information.* Under the signature shall appear:

(1) attorney's individual name,

(2) designation "attorney-in-charge,"

(3) State bar number,

(4) Southern District of Texas bar number,

(5) office address including zip code, and

(6) telephone and facsimile numbers with area codes.

11.3.B *Allowed Information.* Names of firms and associate counsel may appear with the designation "of counsel."

LR11.4 Sanctions. A paper that does not conform to the local or federal rules or that is otherwise objectionable may be struck on the motion of a party or by the Court.

[Effective May 1, 2000.]

LR 16.   CIVIL PRETRIAL PROCEEDINGS

LR16.1 Civil Initial Pretrial Conference; Scheduling Order. Within 140 days after the filing of a complaint or notice of removal, the judge will conduct an initial pretrial conference under Federal Rule of Civil Procedure 16 and enter a scheduling order, except in these types of cases: (a) prisoner civil rights; (b) state and federal habeas corpus; (c) student and veteran loan; (d) social security appeals; (e) bankruptcy appeals; and (f) forfeiture of seized assets.

A judge may conduct an initial pretrial conference and enter a scheduling order in any of the types of cases excepted.

A scheduling order setting cut-off dates for new parties, motions, expert witnesses and discovery, setting a trial date, and establishing a time framework for disposition of motions will be entered at the conference. Should there be an earlier Rule 26(f) discovery conference, the scheduling order may be entered at that conference.

Additional pretrial/settlement/discovery conferences may be scheduled by the Court as the need is identified.

By individual notice, the Court will require attendance at conferences "by an attorney who has the authority to bind that party regarding all matters . . .", 28 U.S.C. § 473(b)(2).

LR16.2 Pretrial Order. The form of the pretrial order in Appendix B is acceptable to the judges who require one.

LR16.3 Notice of Settlement. Counsel shall notify the Court immediately of settlements that obviate court settings. Unnecessarily summoned veniremen or disrupted court schedules resulting from an unexcusable failure to notify may be the predicate for sanctions.

LR16.4. Alternative Dispute Resolution. Pursuant to 28 U.S.C. § 652 (1998) and to facilitate the settlement or narrowing of issues in civil actions, the Court adopts the following Alternative Dispute Resolution Program:

16.4.A. *ADR Methods Available.* The Court approves the use of the following ADR methods in civil cases pending before district, magistrate, and bankruptcy judges: mediation, early neutral evaluation, mini-trial, summary jury trial, and, if the parties consent, non-binding arbitration pursuant to 28 U.S.C. § 654 (1998) (collectively, "ADR"). A judge may approve any other ADR method the parties suggest and the judge finds appropriate for a case.

16.4.B. *Timing of ADR Decision.*

(1) Before the initial conference in a case, counsel are required to discuss with their clients and with opposing counsel the appropriateness of ADR in the case.

(2) At the initial pretrial conference the parties shall advise the judge of the results of their discussions concerning ADR. At that time and at other conferences, if necessary, the judge shall explore with the parties the possibility of using ADR. The judge may require the use of mediation, early neutral evaluation, and, if the parties consent, non-binding arbitration pursuant to 28 U.S.C. § 654 (1998).

16.4.C. *ADR Referral.* A judge may refer any civil case to ADR on motion of any party, on the agreement of the parties, or on its own motion. If the parties agree upon an ADR method or provider, the judge will respect the parties' agreement unless the judge believes another ADR method or provider is better suited to the case and parties. The authority to refer a case to ADR does not preclude the judge from suggesting or requiring other settlement initiatives.

16.4.D. *Opposition to ADR Referral, ADR Method or ADR Provider.* A party opposing in a particular case either the ADR referral, ADR method, or the appointed ADR provider must file written objections within 14 days of entry of the order for ADR, and must explain the reasons for any opposition. The objections and related submissions shall be filed with the judge presiding over the case.

16.4.E. *Standing Panel, ADR Administrator and List of Providers.*

(1) Standing Panel. The Court shall maintain a Standing Panel on ADR Providers ("Panel") to oversee implementation, administration, and evaluation of the Court's ADR program. The Chief Judge of the District will appoint three members, one of whom shall be a district judge who shall serve as chairperson. Each Panel member shall be appointed for a three year term. The Panel shall review applications from prospective ADR providers and annually shall prepare an ADR List of those qualified under the criteria contained in this rule.

(2) ADR Administrator. The Court shall designate a person in the Court clerk's office as ADR Administrator to assist the Panel with its responsibilities and to serve as the primary contact for public inquiries regarding the Court's ADR Program.

(3) ADR Provider List.

a. Copies of the ADR Provider List shall be available to the public in the clerk's office and on the District's website.

b. To be eligible for initial listing as an ADR provider, the applicant must meet the following minimum qualifications: (i) membership in the bar of the United States District Court for the Southern District of Texas; (ii) licensed to practice law for at least ten years; and (iii) completion of at least forty hours training in dispute resolution techniques in an alternative dispute resolution course approved by the State Bar of Texas Minimum Continuing Legal Education department.

c. Each applicant for the ADR Provider List shall submit a completed application in December or January for consideration for the next ADR Provider List. The applicant must use the form available in the clerk's office or on the District's website. The application shall contain: (i) the ADR method(s) for which the applicant seeks to be listed; (ii) a concise summary of the applicant's training, experience, and qualifications for the ADR method(s) for which the applicant seeks to be listed; (iii) the subject matter area(s) in which the applicant has particular expertise (*e.g.*, the concentration of non-ADR practice, board certification); (iv) the applicant's fee schedule; and (v) a commitment to accept some cases for no fee or a reduced fee.

d. To maintain the listing, an ADR Provider annually, between January 1 and January 31, must file a certification with the ADR Administrator that the provider has completed five hours of ADR training during the previous calendar year. Self-study of court decisions on ADR and authoritative writings on ADR techniques and/or ADR ethics may be used to satisfy this requirement, if the provider identifies the materials studied and the dates of study in the annual certificate.

e. Each ADR provider shall remain on the ADR Provider List for five years, provided the requirements of subparagraph E(3)(d) are met. After a five-year term, the ADR provider may apply for re-listing.

f. An applicant denied listing may request a review of that decision by sending a letter to the Chief Judge of the District. The Chief Judge shall have final decision-making authority on the matter.

g. In any particular case, a judge may approve any ADR provider on which the parties agree, even if the provider is not listed on the ADR Provider List or does not satisfy the criteria for eligibility for the list.

16.4.F. *Attendance; Authority to Settle.* Party representatives (in addition to litigation counsel) with authority to settle and all other persons necessary to negotiate a settlement, such as insurance carriers, must attend the ADR proceeding.

16.4.G. *Fees.* The provider and the parties generally will determine the fees for each ADR proceeding. However, the judge presiding over a case has the right to review the reasonableness of fees and to adjust them as appropriate. A judge also may at any time request a provider on the ADR Provider List or any other person to conduct an ADR proceeding pro bono or for a reduced fee.

16.4.H. *Binding Nature.* The results of all ADR proceedings approved by this rule are non-binding unless the parties agree otherwise in a written agreement or by announcement in open court.

16.4.I. *Confidentiality, Privileges and Immunities.* All communications made during ADR proceedings (other than communications concerning scheduling, a final agreement, or ADR provider fees) are confidential, are protected from disclosure, and may not be disclosed to anyone, including the Court, by the provider or the parties. Communications made during ADR proceedings do not constitute a waiver of any existing privileges and immunities. The ADR provider may not testify about statements made by participants or negotiations that occurred during the ADR proceedings. This provision does not modify the requirements of 28 U.S.C. § 657 (1998) applicable to non-binding arbitrations.

16.4.J. *Standards of Professional Conduct and Disqualification of ADR Providers.*

(1) All providers are subject to disqualification pursuant to standards consistent with those set forth in 28 U.S.C. § 455 (1988). In addition, all ADR providers are required to comply with the State Bar of Texas Alternative Dispute Resolution Section's Ethical Guidelines for Mediators, the Code of Ethics for Arbitrators in Commercial Disputes promulgated by the American Arbitration Association, and the American Bar Association and such other rules and guidelines as the Panel specifies.

(2) Issues concerning potential ADR provider conflicts shall be raised with the judge presiding in the case relating to the ADR proceeding.

16.4.K. *Conclusion of ADR Proceedings.* After each ADR proceeding the provider, the parties, and the Court will take the following actions:

(1) Within 14 days of completion of the proceeding, the parties jointly must file a memorandum in the case stating the style and civil action number of the case; the names, addresses, and telephone numbers of counsel and party representatives in attendance; the type of case; the name of the ADR Provider, the ADR method used; whether the case settled; and the fees paid to the ADR provider. This reporting provision does not apply to non-binding arbitrations conducted pursuant to 28 U.S.C. § 654.

(2) Within 14 days of completion of the proceeding, the ADR provider must file a report in the case disclosing only the information listed in subparagraph K.1.

(3) Thereafter, the ADR Administrator shall submit a questionnaire evaluating the ADR provider and proceeding to the parties and counsel; counsel and the parties must complete and return the questionnaires by mail to the ADR Administrator. The Court, attorneys, and the public may review the questionnaires in the clerk's office. Data in the questionnaires shall be compiled by the ADR Administrator each calendar year. The questionnaires shall be retained by the clerk's office for at least three years.

16.4.L. *Evaluations.* The Court annually shall evaluate and issue a public report on the use of ADR in the district, dispositions of ADR proceedings, and other matters the Panel requires.

16.4.M. *Sanctions.* Fed. R. Civ. P. 16(f) sanctions apply to violations of this rule.

[Effective May 1, 2000. Amended effective December 1, 2009; October 18, 2012.]

LR 26. DISCOVERY

LR26.1 Use of Discovery. When a discovery document is needed in a pretrial procedure, the required portions may be filed as an exhibit to a motion or response. Discovery material needed at trial or hearing may be introduced in open court under the Federal Rules of Evidence.

LR26.2 Placement of Discovery. Every answer, objection, or other response to any interrogatory, request for admission, or to produce shall be preceded by the question or request to which the response pertains.

[Effective May 1, 2000.]

LR 30. DEPOSITIONS

LR30.1 Video–Taped Depositions. By this rule, leave of Court is granted, in civil cases, for video-taped depositions without contemporaneous stenographic recordation. The notice or subpoena must indicate that the deposition is to be by video-tape to allow anyone desiring stenographic recordation to arrange for it.

[Effective May 1, 2000.]

LR 33. INTERROGATORIES

LR33.1 Limitation of Interrogatories. No more than twenty-five interrogatories (counting sub-parts) may be served without leave of Court.

[Effective May 1, 2000.]

LR 38. JURY TRIALS

LR38.1 Jury Demand. Pleadings in which a jury is demanded shall bear the word "jury" at the top, immediately below the case number.

[Effective May 1, 2000.]

LR 44. PROOF OF OFFICIAL RECORD

LR44.1 Authentication of Exhibits. A party requiring authentication of an exhibit must notify the offering party in writing within 7 days after the exhibit is listed and made available. Failure to object in advance of the trial in writing concedes authenticity.

[Effective May 1, 2000. Amended effective December 1, 2009.]

LR 46. OBJECTIONS TO EXHIBITS

Objections to admissibility of exhibits must be made at least 7 days before trial by notifying the Court in writing of the disputes, with copies of the disputed exhibit and authority.

[Effective May 1, 2000. Amended effective December 1, 2009.]

LR 47. JUROR CONTACT

Except with leave of Court, no attorney, party, nor agent of either of them may communicate with a former juror to obtain evidence of misconduct in the jury's deliberations.

[Effective May 1, 2000.]

LR 54. COSTS

LR54.1 Deposit for Costs.

A. The clerk will not be required to perform any service requiring a payment unless

(1) The payment is deposited with the clerk;

(2) A law excuses the payment or the deposit in advance; or

(3) Leave to proceed in forma pauperis has been granted. 28 U.S.C. § 1915.

B. The U.S. Marshal may require a deposit to cover fees and expenses. 28 U.S.C. § 1921(d).

LR54.2 Bill of Costs. The parties must maintain their own record of taxable costs. The clerk does not record taxable costs. An application for costs shall be made by filing a bill of costs within 14 days of the entry of a final judgment. When attorney's fees are taxable as costs, an application for them must be made with the application for other costs. Objections to allowance of the bill, the attorney's fees, or both must be filed within 7 days of the bill's filing. Rule 54(d). 28 U.S.C. § 1920.

[Effective May 1, 2000. Amended effective December 1, 2009.]

LR 65. BOND PROCEDURE

LR65.1 Sureties. No employee of the United States Courts or of the United States Marshal's Service will be accepted as surety on any bond or undertaking in any proceeding.

LR65.2 Non-Assignability of Receipts. A clerk's receipt or the claim for the refund of a deposit is not assignable.

[Effective May 1, 2000.]

LR 72. UNITED STATES MAGISTRATE JUDGES

The magistrate judges of this District are authorized to perform all of the duties allowed by law, including the provisions of 28 U.S.C. § 636, and General Order 2001–6. These rules apply to proceedings before a magistrate judge.

[Effective June 25, 2001.]

LR 79. BOOKS AND RECORDS KEPT BY THE CLERK

LR79.1 Withdrawal of Instruments. No filed instrument shall be removed from the clerk's custody without an order.

LR79.2 Disposition of Exhibits.

A. Exhibits that are not easily stored in a file folder (like posters, parts, or models) must be withdrawn within 7 days after the completion of the trial and reduced reproductions or photographs substituted.

B. If there is no appeal, exhibits will be removed by the offering party within thirty days after disposition of the case. When there is an appeal, exhibits returned by the court of appeals will be removed by the offering party within 14 days after written notice from the clerk. Exhibits not removed will be disposed of by the clerk, and the expenses incurred will be taxed against the offering party.

Effective May 1, 2000. Amended effective December 1, 2009.]

LR 81. REMOVAL

Notices for removal shall have attached only the following documents:

1. All executed process in the case;

2. Pleadings asserting causes of action, e.g., petitions, counterclaims, cross actions, third-party actions, interventions and all answers to such pleadings;

3. All orders signed by the state judge;

4. The docket sheet;

5. An index of matters being filed; and

6. A list of all counsel of record, including addresses, telephone numbers and parties represented.

[Effective May 1, 2000.]

LR 83. MISCELLANEOUS LOCAL RULES

LR 83.1. Admission to Practice.

A. *Eligibility.* A lawyer applying for admission to the bar of this court must be licensed to practice law by the licensing authority of one of the fifty states, the District of Columbia, or a Territory of the United States. If licensed by a licensing authority other than the State of Texas, then an attorney must also be a member in good standing of a United States District Court. Attorneys employed by the Department of Justice or the Federal Public Defender are exempt from the requirement of good standing in another United States District Court.

B. *Division.* Lawyers who reside in the district must apply in the division where the lawyer resides. Applicants who do not reside in the district may apply for admission in any division.

C. *Application.* The lawyer shall file an application on a form prescribed by the Court.

D. *Committee on Admissions.* The district shall have one committee on admissions comprised of five attorney members chosen by the Chief Judge and who shall serve staggered three-year terms. The participation of three members, either in person or by electronic means, shall constitute a quorum.

E. *Action on the Application.* After a review of the application, the Court will admit or deny admission. A person not admitted may request a hearing to show why the application should be granted. The hearing will be conducted under the procedures for disciplinary matters.

F. *Uncompensated Assignments.* The pro bono representation of indigent clients is encouraged by this Court. It is hoped that as a matter of public service a member of the Bar of the Southern District of Texas will accept an uncompensated assignment to an indigent's civil matter as often as every twelve months.

G. *Workshop.* An approved applicant must attend a workshop held by the Court before being admitted, unless the applicant either is over seventy years old or resides out of the district and is a member of the bar of another United States District Court. Former Circuit, District, Bankruptcy and Magistrate Judges are exempt from attending the workshop.

(1) On approval of an application, the clerk will notify the applicant, giving the locations and dates of the next workshops.

(2) Applicants who reside in the Houston or Galveston Divisions must attend the workshop in Houston.

(3) Applicants for admission in the Brownsville, Corpus Christi, Laredo, McAllen and Victoria Divisions may attend a workshop in any division.

H. *Expiration.* Members of the bar must reapply every five years from the date of admission by filing a new application and paying the fee. If a member fails to reapply before the expiration of the term, a later application will be treated as an original application, requiring reapproval and attendance at a workshop.

I. *Oath.* On admission, the lawyer will take this oath before any judicial officer of the United States:

I do solemnly swear [affirm] that I will discharge the duties of attorney and counselor of this court faithfully, that I will demean myself uprightly under the law and the highest ethics of our profession, and that I will support and defend the Constitution of the United States.

J. *Fee.* The applicant will pay the fee set by order. Should an applicant scheduled to take the oath unreasonably fail to notify the clerk that he will not appear as scheduled, the applicant forfeits the fee.

K. *Practice Without Admission.* A lawyer who is not admitted to practice before this Court may appear as attorney-in-charge for a party in a case in this Court with the permission of the judge before whom the case is pending. When a lawyer who is not a member of the bar of this Court first appears in a case, the lawyer shall move for leave to appear as attorney-in-charge for the client.

L. *Conduct of Attorneys.* The Rules of Discipline in Appendix A govern membership in the bar of the United States District Court for the Southern District of Texas.

LR 83.2. Withdrawal of Counsel. Although no delay will be countenanced because of a change in counsel, withdrawal of counsel-in-charge may be effected by motion and order, under conditions imposed by the Court.

LR 83.3. Notices. All communications about an action will be sent to the attorney-in-charge who is responsible for notifying associate counsel.

LR 83.4. Change of Address. Notices will be sent only to the address on file. A lawyer or pro se litigant is responsible for keeping the clerk advised in writing of the current address. Counsel of record and pro se litigants must include in this advice the case numbers of all pending cases in which they are participants in this district.

LR 83.5. Parties' Agreement. Agreements among the parties are enforceable by the Court only if they are announced in open court or reduced to writing and signed. Nevertheless, agreements of the parties are not binding on the Court.

LR 83.6. Preserving Confidentiality.

83.6.A. *Civil Actions.* On the filing of a civil action that the party desires be sealed, the party shall present an application to the clerk attaching the complaint and accompanying materials in a sealed envelope marked "sealed exhibit." A miscellaneous case number will be assigned and the case file presented to the miscellaneous judge. Once that judge has ruled on the application, the case file and order will be returned immediately to the clerk for the drawing of a civil action number and random assignment to a judge.

83.6.B. *Jurors' Names.* The trial judge may hold the names of petit jurors confidential. Names of jurors held confidential shall not be disclosed other than to employees of the judiciary of the United States in their official duties.

LR 83.7. Electro–Mechanical Devices. Except by leave of the presiding judge, no photo- or electro-mechanical means of recordation or transmission of court proceedings is permitted in the courthouse.

LR 83.8. Courtroom Behavior. Traditional, formal courtroom etiquette is required of all who appear in court as specified in Appendix C.

[Effective May 1, 2000. Amended effective March 22, 2018.]

SUPPLEMENTAL ADMIRALTY RULES

A. DESIGNATION AS "ADMIRALTY CASE"

Papers in cases arising within the admiralty or maritime jurisdiction shall bear the word "admiralty" at the top, immediately below the case number.

[Effective May 1, 2000.]

E. ADMIRALTY SALES

In the absence of conflicting requirements in the order of sale, these are the procedures for sales of property under marshal's seizure in admiralty actions:

E.1 Notice. The notice of sale shall be published in a daily newspaper of general circulation in the division of the seizure on at least four days, between three and thirty-one days before the sale date.

E.2 Payment.

A. Payment to the marshal shall be by cash, cashier's check, or certified check; acceptance of cashiers' checks is conditioned on their payment.

B. Accepted bids of less than $1,000 shall be paid to the marshal on their acceptance.

C. For accepted bids of $1,000 and more, the higher of ten percent of the bid or $1,000 shall be deposited immediately and be paid in full within 7 days of the sale. If an objection is filed within the 7 days, the buyer may defer payment of the balance until the sale is confirmed.

E.3 Default. If the buyer does not pay the bid on time, (1) the deposit is forfeited to the action, applied to costs, then paid to the registry; and (2) the Court may accept the second bid or order a new sale.

E.4 Objections.

E.4.1 *Time.* Objections must be written and filed with the marshal within 7 days of the sale date.

E.4.2 *Deposit.* Objections shall be accompanied by a cost deposit of seven days of estimated expenses of custody.

E.4.3 *Disposition.*

A. If sustained, the deposits by the bidder and objector will be refunded immediately.

B. If overruled, the balance of the objector's deposit that remains after deduction of the expenses of custody from the day of the objection until the day of the confirmation will be paid to the objector.

[Effective May 1, 2000. Amended effective December 1, 2009.]

SUPPLEMENTAL HABEAS CORPUS RULES

1. STAYS OF EXECUTION

A. Application Requirements. A party who seeks to stay the execution of a Texas death warrant shall include in the application:

(1) A copy of each state court opinion and judgment in the matter;

(2) A description of the relief sought from any United States Court, including action number and court name;

(3) The reasons for denying relief given by the courts that have considered the matter, by written opinion or portions of the transcript; and

(4) An explanation why issues urged in the application have not been raised or exhausted in state court.

B. Appeal. If a certificate of appealability is issued, the stay of execution will continue until the court of appeals acts.

C. Successive Applications. All applications for relief from state orders in a single matter will be assigned to the judge to whom the first application was assigned. All applications for relief from state orders after the first will be strictly and promptly considered.

[Effective May 1, 2000.]

CRIMINAL RULES

CrLR 6. GRAND JURY WITNESSES

Names of witnesses appearing before a grand jury may be sealed for cause.

[Effective May 1, 2000.]

CrLR 12. CRIMINAL PRETRIAL MOTION PRACTICE

CrLR12.1   Implementation. Federal Rule of Criminal Procedure 12 and this rule are to be followed to ensure consistent and efficient practice before this Court. Motions and responses that do not comply with these rules are waived.

CrLR12.2   Form. A pretrial motion shall be in writing and state specifically the basis for the motion. The motion shall be supported by a statement of authority. It shall also be accompanied by a separate order granting the relief requested and by an averment that the movant has conferred with the respondent, but that an agreement cannot be reached on the disposition of the motion. If the motion presents issues of fact, it shall be supported by affidavit or declaration which sets forth with particularity the material facts at issue. An unopposed motion and its order must bear in the captions "unopposed."

CrLR12.3   Responses. If the respondent contests the motion, the response must be in writing, accompanied by authority and controverting affidavit or declaration of material facts, together with a separate order denying the relief sought.

CrLR12.4   Service. All motions must be served on all parties and contain a certificate of service.

CrLR12.5   Submission. At the time of arraignment the judicial officer shall set the time for pretrial motions and for any responses to the motions.

[Effective May 1, 2000.]

CrLR 23.   TRIAL

CrLR23.1   Free Press–Fair Trial Guidelines. The Free Press–Fair Trial Guidelines of the Judicial Conference of the United States shall apply to all criminal proceedings in this district. 87 F.R.D. 519, 525 (1980).

CrLR23.2   Electro Mechanical Devices. Except by leave of the presiding judge, no photo- or electro-mechanical means of recordation or transmission of court proceedings is permitted in the courthouse.

[Effective May 1, 2000.]

CrLR 24.   JURIES

CrLR24.1   Juror Contact. Except with leave of Court, no attorney, party, nor agent of either of them may communicate with a former juror to obtain evidence of misconduct in the jury's deliberations.

CrLR24.2   Jurors' Names.

A.   The names of grand jurors shall be held confidential.

B.   The trial judge may hold the names of petit jurors confidential.

C.   Names of jurors held confidential shall not be disclosed other than to employees of the judiciary of the United States in their official duties.

[Effective May 1, 2000.]

CrLR 32.   SENTENCING PROCEDURES

CrLR32.1   Waiver of the Presentence Investigation. A presentence investigation will be prepared and submitted to the Court unless the Court finds that information in the record enables it to exercise its sentencing authority under 18 U.S.C. § 3553 and explains this finding on the record.

A.   On motion filed before rearraignment, the Court will consider waiving the preparation of the presentence investigation. The motion shall contain:

(1) a factual summary of the defendant's relevant conduct in committing the offense;

(2) a listing of the defendant's criminal history, including dates of conviction, dispositions, and representation by counsel;

(3) guideline calculations leading to the establishment of the total offense level and criminal history category;

(4) a statement reflecting the resulting imprisonment, fine and supervised release ranges, as well as any factors that may warrant a departure from these ranges;

(5) a statement as to the identity and address of any victim(s) and the amount of restitution due to any victim. In the case of any identified victim where no restitution or only partial restitution is being recommended, the motion shall include a statement justifying the recommendation.

CrLR32.2   Order of Presentence Investigation and Initial Disclosure Date. At the time of determination of guilt, the Court will fix the date by which the initial presentence report shall be disclosed to counsel. The normal schedule for investigation, preparation, and completion of the initial report will be 35 days. In addition, unless waived by the defendant, the presentence report shall be disclosed not less than 35 days before the sentencing date.

CrLR32.3   Presence of Counsel. On request, defense counsel is entitled to notice and a reasonable opportunity to attend any interview of the defendant by a probation officer in the course of a presentence investigation.

A.   A request to be present at interviews conducted by the probation officer must be made to the probation office immediately after the determination of guilt, followed by written notice to the probation office within 7 days. (Amended by General Order 2009–17, effective 12/1/09)

B.   The term "interview" applies to communications initiated by the probation officer for purposes of developing information which will be used in preparation of the presentence investigation. Spontaneous or unplanned encounters between the defendant and probation officer would not normally fall within the purview of this rule.

C. Having received notice, defense counsel, or his/her designee, is responsible for being present at the interview(s) to enable timely completion of the presentence report.

CrLR32.4 Delivery. Presentence reports and related documents are filed under seal by the probation office electronically in the Court's Electronic Filing System (CM/ECF). The Notice of Electronic Filing (NEF) automatically generated by the Court's Electronic Filing System notifies counsel their copy of the report can be retrieved utilizing their Filing User log-in and password issued upon admittance to the bar of this Court. (See Administrative Procedures for Electronic Filing in Civil and Criminal Cases). In extenuating circumstances, paper copies may be requested from the probation office by counsel. Counsel will then be responsible for obtaining the paper copy of the report at the probation office in the city of the sentencing court, or making arrangements with the probation office for alternative delivery, at counsel's expense. These arrangements should be confirmed in writing with the probation office. Delivery via facsimile is not authorized. Alternative delivery extends no time limits.

CrLR32.5 Counsel's Duty. Defense counsel shall disclose every report to the client.

CrLR32.6 Objections.

A. Within 14 days after disclosure of the initial report, counsel shall deliver objections to the report in writing to the probation office. Objections to the report shall include proposed changes to the facts of the offense as reported and to the interpretation and application of the sentencing guidelines.

B. A party not objecting must deliver a statement of non-opposition to the probation office.

C. All papers must contain a certificate of service on all counsel. A copy of the instrument and certificate shall be filed with the district clerk.

CrLR32.7 Final Report.

A. After the time for objections, the probation office shall promptly investigate and revise the initial report, as required. The probation office may require counsel to meet the officer to discuss disputed factual and legal issues.

B. Within 14 days after the time for objections but in no event later than 7 days before sentencing, the probation office shall submit to the sentencing judge the final report, with an addendum of unresolved objections and the officer's comments on them. The final report shall contain a certificate that it has been disclosed to all counsel and that a copy has been filed under seal with the district clerk.

CrLR32.8 Availability. The initial report may be obtained on the disclosure date established by the Court. The final report (if different from the initial report) and addendum may be obtained as soon as counsel are notified that the report is available. Notification will be accomplished via a Notice of Electronic Filing issued by the Court's Electronic Filing System (CM/ECF).

CrLR32.9 Effect. Except for objections in the addendum, the Court may accept the final report as accurate. Absent a clear demonstration of good cause, no party shall be allowed at the time of sentencing to present other objections.

CrLR32.10 Sentencing Date. Unless waived by the defendant, the sentencing date shall be at least 7 days after the final report is delivered to the Court.

CrLR32.11 Limitation. This rule does not require disclosure of portions of the report not disclosable under Federal Rule of Criminal Procedure 32. The probation officer's recommendation on the sentence shall not be disclosed unless so ordered by the sentencing judge.

[Effective May 1, 2000. Amended effective December 1, 2009; January 31, 2014.]

CrLR 46. BOND PROCEDURE

CrLR46.1 Sureties and Non–Assignability of Receipts. No employee of the United States Courts or of the United States Marshal's Service will be accepted as surety on any bond or undertaking in any proceeding. A clerk's receipt or the claim for the refund of a deposit is not assignable.

CrLR46.2 Return of Criminal Bond Deposits. When a depositor is entitled to a refund of the deposit, the clerk will submit the request for the refund to the United States Attorney who will certify that the defendant has met the obligations of the bond fully and that the United States Attorney consents to the return.

[Effective May 1, 2000.]

CrLR 49. FILING REQUIREMENTS

The provisions of LR5 with respect to electronic filing and service in civil cases are applicable to criminal cases.

[Effective May 1, 2000. Amended effective April 6, 2005.]

CrLR 55. RECORDS

CrLR55.1 Withdrawal of Instruments. No filed instrument shall be removed from the clerk's custody without an order.

CrLR55.2 Exhibits at Criminal Trials.

A. *Authentication of Exhibits.* A party requiring authentication of an exhibit must notify the offering party in writing within 7 days after the exhibit is listed and made available. Failure to object in advance of the trial in writing concedes authenticity.

B. *Objections to Exhibits.* Objections to admissibility of exhibits must be made at least 7 days before trial by notifying the Court in writing of the disputes, with copies of the disputed exhibit and authority.

C. *Disposition of Exhibits.*

(1) Exhibits that are not easily stored in a file folder (like posters, parts, or models) must be withdrawn within 7 days after the completion of the trial and reduced reproductions or photographs substituted.

(2) If there is no appeal, exhibits will be removed by the offering party within thirty days after disposition of the case. When there is an appeal, exhibits returned by the

court of appeals will be removed by the offering party within 14 days after written notice from the clerk. Exhibits not removed will be disposed of by the clerk, and the expenses incurred will be taxed against the offering party.

[Effective May 1, 2000.   Amended effective December 1, 2009.]

CrLR 57.   MISCELLANEOUS

CrLR57.1   Magistrate Judges. The magistrate judges of this District are authorized to perform all of the duties allowed by law, including the provisions of 28 U.S.C. § 636, General Order No. 2001–6, and General Order 91–26. These local rules apply to proceedings before a magistrate judge.

CrLR57.2   Courtroom Behavior. Traditional, formal courtroom etiquette is required of all who appear in court as specified in Appendix C.

CrLR57.3.   Admission to Practice. The provisions of LR83.1 with respect to admission to practice are applicable to criminal cases.

[Effective May 1, 2000.   Amended effective June 25, 2001;   October 18, 2012.]

CrLR 58.   PROCEDURE FOR MISDEMEANORS AND OTHER PETTY OFFENSES

CrLR58.1   Forfeiture of Collateral in Lieu of Appearance.

A.   A person or organization charged with a misdemeanor or a petty offense as defined in Title 18, United States Code, Section 19, for which there is a published schedule providing for forfeiture of collateral may, in lieu of appearance, post collateral in the amount indicated for the offense, waive appearance before the United States District or Magistrate Judge, and consent to forfeiture of collateral.

B.   The Court has adopted forfeiture schedules and may from time to time modify and change these schedules by general order of the court without notice or comment.

C.   If a person or organization charged with an offense under Section A of this Rule fails to post and forfeit collateral, any punishment, including fine, imprisonment, or probation, may be imposed within the limits established by law upon conviction by plea or after trial.

D.   A person or organization charged with a misdemeanor or petty offense for which there is not a published schedule providing for forfeiture of collateral must appear before a United States District or Magistrate Judge.

E.   Of the total collateral amount paid, the sum of five dollars is designated as the special assessment required by Title 18, United States Code, Section 3013.

[Effective May 3, 2001.]

APPENDICES

APPENDIX A. RULES OF DISCIPLINE UNITED STATES DISTRICT COURT SOUTHERN DISTRICT OF TEXAS

RULE 1. STANDARDS OF CONDUCT

A. Lawyers who practice before this court are required to act as mature and responsible professionals, and the minimum standard of practice shall be the Texas Disciplinary Rules of Professional Conduct.

B. Violation of the Texas Disciplinary Rules of Professional Conduct shall be grounds for disciplinary action, but the court is not limited by that code.

[Effective October 10, 1996. Amended effective June 19, 2007.]

RULE 2. CONVICTION OF CRIME

A. A lawyer convicted of a felony or a misdemeanor involving moral turpitude or controlled substance shall promptly notify this court in writing and furnish to the clerk of court a certified copy of the judgment of conviction. A lawyer convicted of a felony shall immediately cease practicing before this court pending further action by the court.

B. After the court has notice that a lawyer practicing before it has a conviction described in Rule 2(A), it will follow the due process procedure in these rules to determine whether discipline should be imposed on the lawyer.

[Effective October 10, 1996. Amended effective June 19, 2007.]

RULE 3. DISCIPLINE BY ANOTHER COURT

A. A lawyer disciplined by another court in the United States shall promptly notify this court in writing and furnish to the clerk of the court a certified copy of the order of discipline. A lawyer suspended or disbarred by another court in the United States shall immediately cease to practice before this court. A lawyer subjected to a reprimand may continue to practice, pending review by this court.

B. A final adjudication in another court that the lawyer has been guilty of an offense leading to the action referred to in Rule 3A shall establish conclusively the conduct for the purposes of proceeding in this court unless the lawyer requests a hearing and carries the burden of showing that such prior action lacked due process.

[Effective October 10, 1996. Amended effective June 19, 2007.]

RULE 4. DISBARMENT BY CONSENT OR RESIGNATION IN OTHER COURTS

A. A lawyer who is disbarred or suspended by consent or agreement or who resigns from the bar of another court in the United States to avoid further discipline must advise this court in writing and immediately cease to practice before this court. The lawyer shall furnish a certified copy of the disciplinary order or letter of resignation to the clerk.

B. Upon request by the lawyer, the court will follow the due process procedure in these rules to determine under what conditions the lawyer might continue to practice in this court.

[Effective October 10, 1996. Amended effective June 19, 2007.]

RULE 5. CHARGES OF MISCONDUCT WARRANTING DISCIPLINE

A. Charges that any lawyer of this bar has engaged in conduct which might warrant disciplinary action shall be brought to the attention of the court by a writing addressed to the chief judge with a copy to the clerk of court.

B. Upon receipt of a charge that is not frivolous, the chief judge shall order the clerk to file the charge and randomly assign it to a district judge for review to determine whether further disciplinary proceedings should be held. The reviewing judge shall notify the charged lawyer of the charges made and give that lawyer an opportunity to respond. If the charge is made by a bankruptcy judge or is one occurring in bankruptcy court, the clerk may assign the charge to a bankruptcy judge, who may serve as reviewing judge. The chief judge may elect to forego the review procedures of this paragraph if, in the judgment of the chief judge, the information provided to the chief judge with the charge is sufficiently clear to warrant further disciplinary proceedings of paragraph 5(C), et seq.

C. After review, the judge will, by written report, recommend to the chief judge whether further disciplinary proceedings should be heard and the charges to be heard. If further proceedings are recommended, the chief judge shall order further hearings to be held before a district judge, who may have been the reviewing judge.

D. The hearing judge will give at least 14 days notice to the charged lawyer of the time of the hearing, the charges and the right to counsel at the hearing. The hearing shall be held on the record in open court as a miscellaneous proceeding. Rule 1101(d)(3), Federal Rules of Evidence applies, and all witnesses shall be sworn.

E. In the hearing of charges before the hearing judge, the prosecution shall be by an attorney specially appointed by the hearing judge. Costs of the prosecutor and fees allowed by the hearing judge may be paid from the Attorney Admissions Fund.

F. The hearing judge shall file his judgment, providing a copy to the chief judge and the lawyer. If the hearing judge determines that disciplinary action should be taken, the judge shall make findings of violations and order either permanent disbarment, a suspension, a written or oral reprimand and whether such should be public or private with such conditions as the judge may order.

G. The decision of the hearing judge is final, except that, within 14 days, the lawyer may appeal the judgment by filing a notice of appeal. A panel of three district judges of the court, randomly assigned, will hear the appeal. The appeal shall be on the record developed at the hearing. Facts found by the hearing judge are not reviewable unless clearly erroneous. The law determined by the hearing judge is reviewable de novo. The decision of the panel is final. There is no en banc review.

H. If the membership in the Southern District Bar of the lawyer being disciplined was not current at the time of the court order imposing discipline, the order may include that the lawyer shall not reapply for admission except under such conditions as the court may impose.

[Effective October 10, 1996. Amended effective June 19, 2007; December 1, 2009.]

RULE 6. REINSTATEMENT

A. A suspended or disbarred lawyer must apply to this court for reinstatement before resuming practice before this court. A lawyer who has been suspended may apply for reinstatement before or after the end of his term of suspension. The term of suspension includes all conditions and periods of suspension, including probated and inactive suspension. A lawyer who has been disbarred may apply for reinstatement but not before five years from the effective date of the disbarment.

B. All petitions for reinstatement shall be filed with the clerk of the court who will promptly refer the petition to the Attorney Admissions Committee for its recommendation on the petition to the chief judge. The chief judge may make the final decision of the court on the petition.

C. Petitions for reinstatement shall be accompanied by an advance cost deposit in an amount to be set by the court to cover anticipated costs of the proceeding.

D. No petition for reinstatement may be filed within one year following an adverse ruling on a previous petition.

[Effective October 10, 1996. Amended effective June 19, 2007.]

RULE 7. LAWYERS SPECIALLY ADMITTED

An appearance by a lawyer before the court, by writing, or in person, confers disciplinary jurisdiction upon the court under these rules.

[Effective October 10, 1996.]

RULE 8. SERVICE OF PAPERS

Service of papers under these rules shall be by personal service or by first class mail addressed to the respondent or respondent's attorney.

[Effective October 10, 1996.]

RULE 9. SPECIAL DUTIES OF THE CLERK

A. In addition to all other duties assigned, the clerk shall collect advance cost deposits and place them in the Attorney Admissions Fund. These sums shall be maintained by the clerk as trustee and administered by the court for expenses incurred under these rules and not on behalf of the United States.

B. Upon final disciplinary action by the court, the clerk shall send certified copies of the court's order to the State Bar of Texas.

[Effective October 10, 1996.]

RULE 10. INHERENT POWER OF JUDGES

The existence of these rules shall not limit the power of district judges to exercise their inherent powers over lawyers who practice before them, and the chief judge shall have the right to designate another district judge, to serve under these rules in the place of the chief judge.

[Effective October 10, 1996.]

RULE 11. EFFECTIVE DATE

These rules are effective immediately; all pending disciplinary matters will be concluded under these rules; and the rules effective October 10, 1996 are superseded by them.

[Effective October 10, 1996.]

APPENDIX B. JOINT PRETRIAL ORDER

UNITED STATES DISTRICT COURT
SOUTHERN DISTRICT OF TEXAS

_____,	§	
Plaintiffs	§	
	§	
vs.	§	CIVIL ACTION NO.
	§	
_____,	§	
Defendants	§	

JOINT PRETRIAL ORDER

1. APPEARANCE OF COUNSEL

List each party, its counsel, and counsel's address and telephone number in separate paragraphs.

2. STATEMENT OF THE CASE

Give a brief statement of the case, one that the judge could read to the jury panel for an introduction to the facts and parties; include names, dates, and places.

3. JURISDICTION

Briefly specify the jurisdiction of the subject matter and the parties. If there is an unresolved jurisdictional question, state it.

4. MOTIONS

List pending motions.

5. CONTENTIONS OF THE PARTIES

State concisely in separate paragraphs each party's claims.

6. ADMISSIONS OF FACT

List all facts that require no proof.

7. CONTESTED ISSUES OF FACT

List all material facts in controversy.

8. AGREED PROPOSITIONS OF LAW

List the legal propositions that are not in dispute.

9. CONTESTED PROPOSITIONS OF LAW

State briefly the unresolved questions of law, with authorities to support each.

10. EXHIBITS

A. On a form similar to the one provided by the clerk, each party will attach two lists of all exhibits expected to be offered and will make the exhibits available for examination by opposing counsel. All documentary exhibits must be exchanged before trial, except for rebuttal exhibits or those whose use cannot be anticipated.

B. A party requiring authentication of an exhibit must notify the offering counsel in writing within 7 days after the exhibit is listed and made available; failure to object in advance of the trial in writing concedes authenticity.

C. Within reason, other objections to admissibility of exhibits must be made at least 7 days before trial; the Court will be notified in writing of disputes, with copies of the disputed exhibit and authority.

D. Parties must mark their exhibits to include the date and case number on each.

E. At the trial, the first step will be the offer and receipt in evidence of exhibits.

11. WITNESSES

A. List the names and addresses of witnesses who may be called with a brief statement of the nature of their testimony. Include the qualifications of expert witnesses; these will be used to qualify the expert at trial.

B. Include:

"If other witnesses to be called at the trial become known, their names, addresses, and subject of their testimony will be reported to opposing counsel in writing as soon as they are known; this does not apply to rebuttal or impeachment witnesses."

12. SETTLEMENT

State that all settlement efforts have been exhausted, that the case cannot be settled, and that it will have to be tried.

13. TRIAL

A. Probable length of trial; and

B. Logistical problems, including availability of witnesses, out-of-state people, bulky exhibits, and demonstrations.

14. ATTACHMENTS

Include these required attachments:

A. For a jury trial:

(1) Proposed questions for the voir dire examination.

(2) Proposed charge, including instructions, definitions, and special interrogatories, with authority.

B. For a nonjury trial:

(1) Proposed findings of fact (without repeating uncontested facts) and

(2) Conclusions of law, with authority.

Date: _____

UNITED STATES DISTRICT JUDGE

Approved:

Date: _____

_____
Attorney-in-Charge, Plaintiff

Date: _____

_____
Attorney-in-Charge, Defendant

[Amended effective December 1, 2009.]

APPENDIX C.   COURTROOM ETIQUETTE

People who appear in court must observe these and other conventions of courteous, orderly behavior.

A.   Be punctual.

B.   Remain in attendance until excused. All persons sitting before the bar shall remain there during each session and return after recess. Parties and counsel must remain in attendance during jury deliberations; absence waives the right to attend the return of the verdict.

C.   Dress with dignity.

D.   Address others only by their titles and surnames, including lawyers, witnesses, and court personnel.

E.   Stand when the Court speaks to you; stand when you speak to the Court. Speak only to the Court, except for questioning witnesses and, in opening and closing, addressing the jury.

F.   Avoid approaching the bench. Counsel should anticipate the necessity for rulings and discuss them when the jury is not seated. When a bench conference is unavoidable, get permission first.

G.   Hand to the clerk, not the judge or reporter, all things for examination by the judge.

H.   Stand when the judge or jury enters or leaves the courtroom.

I.   Contact with the law clerks is ex parte contact with the Court. Contact must be through the case manager.

J.   Assist the summoning of witnesses from outside the courtroom. Furnish the clerk and marshal with a list of witnesses showing the order they are likely to be called.

K.   Question witnesses while seated at counsel table or standing at the lectern. When it is necessary to question a witness about an exhibit, ask permission to approach the witness.

L.   Conduct no experiment or demonstration without permission.

M.   Do not participate in a trial as an attorney if you expect you may be called as a material witness.

N.   Avoid disparaging remarks and acrimony toward counsel, and discourage ill will between the litigants. Counsel must abstain from unnecessary references to opposing counsel, especially peculiarities.

O.   Make no side-bar remarks.

P.   Counsel are responsible for advising their clients, witnesses, and associate counsel about proper courtroom behavior.

Q.   Request the use of easels, light boxes, and other equipment well in advance so that they may be set up while the Court is not in session.

APPENDIX D. GUIDELINES FOR PROFESSIONAL CONDUCT

A. In fulfilling his or her primary duty to the client, a lawyer must be ever conscious of the broader duty to the judicial system that serves both attorney and client.

B. A lawyer owes, to the judiciary, candor, diligence and utmost respect.

C. A lawyer owes, to opposing counsel, a duty of courtesy and cooperation, the observance of which is necessary for the efficient administration of our system of justice and the respect of the public it serves.

D. A lawyer unquestionably owes, to the administration of justice, the fundamental duties of personal dignity and professional integrity.

E. Lawyers should treat each other, the opposing party, the court, and members of the court staff with courtesy and civility and conduct themselves in a professional manner at all times.

F. A client has no right to demand that counsel abuse the opposite party or indulge in offensive conduct. A lawyer shall always treat adverse witnesses and suitors with fairness and due consideration.

G. In adversary proceedings, clients are litigants and though ill feeling may exist between clients, such ill feeling should not influence a lawyer's conduct, attitude, or demeanor towards opposing lawyers.

H. A lawyer should not use any form of discovery, or the scheduling of discovery, as a means of harassing opposing counsel or counsel's client.

I. Lawyers will be punctual in communications with others and in honoring scheduled appearances, and will recognize that neglect and tardiness are demeaning to the lawyer and to the judicial system.

J. If a fellow member of the Bar makes a just request for cooperation, or seeks scheduling accommodation, a lawyer will not arbitrarily or unreasonably withhold consent.

K. Effective advocacy does not require antagonistic or obnoxious behavior and members of the Bar will adhere to the higher standard of conduct which judges, lawyers, clients, and the public may rightfully expect.

[Dated: May 8, 2001.]

LOCAL RULES OF PRACTICE FOR PATENT CASES

1. SCOPE OF RULES

1–1. TITLE

These are the Rules of Practice for Patent Cases before the United States District Court for the Southern District of Texas ("Patent Rules," to be cited as "P. R. ___").

[Effective January 1, 2008.]

1–2. SCOPE AND CONSTRUCTION

(a) These Patent Rules apply to all civil actions filed in or transferred to the Southern District of Texas that allege claims for patent infringement in a complaint, counterclaim, cross-claim or third-party claim, or seek a declaratory judgment that a patent is not infringed, is invalid, or is unenforceable (a "patent claim").

(b) The presiding judge may accelerate, extend, eliminate, or modify the obligations or deadlines established in these Patent Rules based on the circumstances of a particular case, including, without limitation, its complexity or the number of patents, claims, products, or parties involved.

(c) If any motion filed before the Claim Construction Hearing (*see* P.R. 4–6) raises claim construction issues, the presiding judge may, for good cause, defer the motion until after the parties' disclosures or filings for the Claim Construction Hearing.

(d) The Local Civil Rules of the Southern District of Texas apply to patent cases except to the extent that the Local Civil Rules are inconsistent with these Patent Rules.

[Effective January 1, 2008.]

1–3. EFFECTIVE DATE

These Patent Rules will become effective January 1, 2008, and apply to all cases involving a patent claim filed thereafter, unless otherwise ordered by the presiding judge. The parties in each case involving a patent claim pending on the effective date of these Patent Rules must confer and, to the extent possible, submit an agreed scheduling order consistent with these Patent Rules. The parties must use the Scheduling Order Template available at the Southern District of Texas Court website (www.txs.uscourts.gov). To the extent the parties cannot agree, they must notify the presiding judge, who will resolve the issues.

[Effective January 1, 2008.]

2. GENERAL PROVISIONS

2–1. PROCEDURE

(a) Parties' Preparation for Initial Case Management Conference. In addition to the matters covered by Fed. R. Civ. P. 26, the parties must confer and address in their Joint Case Management Report the following topics:

(1) any proposed modification of the schedule provided in the Scheduling Order Template, which is available at the District's website;

(2) a plan for completing electronic discovery;

(3) the need for presenting technical tutorials to the presiding judge and the mode for such presentations (*i.e.*, live testimony, video presentations) at or before the claim construction hearing;

(4) any deviations from and additions to the form protective order (available at the District's website);

(5) whether any party desires to present live testimony at the claim construction hearing;

(6) the need for and any specific limits on discovery relating to claim construction, including depositions of fact and expert witnesses;

(7) the order of presentation at the claim construction hearing;

(8) the scheduling of a claim construction prehearing conference after the "Joint Claim Construction and Prehearing Statement" provided in P.R. 4–3 has been filed; and

(9) whether the presiding judge should authorize the filing under seal of any documents containing confidential information,

(b) Insufficient Information. If warranted by the patent(s) and/or products in issue, the party claiming patent infringement ("claimant") may include in the Joint Case Management Report a statement that the claimant in good faith lacks sufficient information concerning the opponent's products or processes to provide the necessary specificity for the Preliminary Infringement Contentions (*see* P.R. 3–1). If the presiding judge orders, the opponent within twenty* 21 days must produce to the claimant sufficient information concerning each product or process of the type or class specified by the claimant in its statement to enable the claimant to determine whether to claim that the product or process infringes. Neither the claimant's statement nor the opponent's production will be an admission or evidence of infringement or noninfringement. These steps are solely to determine what is alleged to be infringing.

(c) Case Management Conference and Scheduling Order. At the initial case management conference, after considering the parties' Joint Case Management Report, the presiding judge will enter a Case Management Scheduling Order ("Scheduling Order").

(d) Further Case Management Conferences. If some or all of the matters provided under P.R. 2–1(a) are not resolved or decided at the initial case management conference, the parties must propose dates for further case management conferences.

[Effective January 1, 2008. Amended effective December 1, 2009.]

* [Publisher's Note: So in original.]

2–2. CONFIDENTIALITY AND PROPOSED PROTECTIVE ORDER

Documents and information produced in cases governed by these Patent Rules will be governed by the form protective order available at the District's website, www.txs.uscourts.gov, unless the presiding judge otherwise orders. If the parties seek to modify the form protective order, they must submit to the presiding judge, with the Joint Case Management Report, the protective order they propose and must identify proposed variations to the form protective order.

[Effective January 1, 2008.]

2–3. CERTIFICATION OF INITIAL DISCLOSURES AND ENGLISH TRANSLATIONS

(a) All statements, disclosures, or charts filed or served in accordance with these Patent Rules must comply with the Federal Rules of Civil Procedure and the Administrative Procedures for Electronic Filing of Documents in Civil and Criminal Cases issued by the United States District Court for the Southern District of Texas.

(b) To the extent any document or disclosure is not in English, an English translation of the portion(s) relied on must be produced.

[Effective January 1, 2008.]

2–4. ADMISSIBILITY

Statements, disclosures, or charts governed by these Patent Rules are admissible in evidence to the extent permitted by the Federal Rules of Evidence or the Federal Rules of Civil Procedure. However, the statements or disclosures provided for in P.R. 4–1 and 4–2 are not admissible for any purpose other than in connection with motions seeking an extension or modification of the deadlines set out in these Patent Rules.

[Effective January 1, 2008.]

2–5. RELATIONSHIP TO FEDERAL RULES OF CIVIL PROCEDURE

(a) Unless the presiding judge otherwise directs, the scope of discovery is not limited to the preliminary infringement contentions or preliminary invalidity contentions, but is governed by the Federal Rules of Civil Procedure.

(b) Except as provided in this paragraph or as otherwise ordered, it is not a legitimate ground for objecting to an opposing party's discovery request or declining to disclose information under Fed. R. Civ. P. 26(a)(1) that the discovery request or disclosure requirement is premature or otherwise conflicts with these Patent Rules. A party may object to certain categories of discovery requests or may decline to disclose information under Fed. R. Civ. P. 26(a)(1) on the ground that the request or disclosure is premature in light of the timetable provided in the Patent Rules. The categories are:

(1) requests seeking to elicit a party's claim construction position;

(2) requests seeking to elicit from the patent claimant a comparison of the asserted claims and the accused apparatus, product, device, process, method, act, or other instrumentality;

(3) requests seeking to elicit from an accused infringer a comparison of the asserted claims and the prior art; and

(4) requests seeking to elicit from an accused infringer the identification of any opinions of counsel and related documents that it intends to rely upon as a defense to a willful infringement allegation; however, a party may not assert a prematurity objection to a request for nonprivileged information identifying the existence of such opinions of counsel.

(c) When a party properly objects to a discovery request, or declines to provide information in its initial disclosures under Fed. R. Civ. P. 26(a)(1), as set forth above, that party must provide the requested information on the date it is required to provide the requested information to an opposing party under these Patent Rules, unless there is another legitimate ground for objection.

[Effective January 1, 2008.]

3. PATENT INITIAL DISCLOSURES

3–1. DISCLOSURE OF ASSERTED CLAIMS AND PRELIMINARY INFRINGEMENT CONTENTIONS

As provided in the Scheduling Order issued by the presiding judge at the initial scheduling conference, a party claiming patent infringement must serve on all parties a "Disclosure of Asserted Claims and Preliminary Infringement Contentions," which must contain the following information:

(a) each claim of each patent-in-suit that is allegedly infringed by an opposing party;

(b) for each asserted claim, a specific and separate identification of each accused apparatus, product, device, process, method, act, or other instrumentality ("Accused Instrumentality") of each opposing party, including where possible:

(1) each product, device, and apparatus identified by name or model number, and

(2) each method or process identified by name, any product, device, or apparatus that, when used, allegedly results in the practice of the claimed method or process;

(c) a chart identifying specifically where each element of each asserted claim is found within each Accused Instrumentality, including for each element that is allegedly governed by 35 U.S.C. § 112, ¶ 6, the identity of the structures, acts, or materials in the Accused Instrumentality that performs the claimed function;

(d) for each Accused Instrumentality and each element of each asserted claim, identification of whether the element is claimed to be literally present or present under the doctrine of equivalents;

(e) for any patent that claims priority to an earlier application, the priority date to which each asserted claim allegedly is entitled; and

(f) if a party claiming patent infringement wishes to preserve the right to rely, for any purpose, on the assertion that its own apparatus, product, device, process, method, act, or other instrumentality practices the claimed invention, the party must identify, separately for each asserted claim, each such apparatus, product, device, process, method, act, or other instrumentality that incorporates or reflects that particular claim.

[Effective January 1, 2008.]

3–2. DOCUMENT PRODUCTION ACCOMPANYING DISCLOSURE

(a) With the "Disclosure of Asserted Claims and Preliminary Infringement Contentions," the party claiming patent infringement must produce to each opposing party or make available for inspection and copying, the following:

(1) documents (*e.g.*, contracts, purchase orders, invoices, advertisements, marketing materials, offer letters, beta site testing agreements, and third-party or joint development agreements) sufficient to show each discussion with, disclosure to, or other manner of providing to a third-party, or sale of or offer to sell, the claimed invention before the application date for the patent-in-suit;

(2) documents evidencing the conception, reduction to practice, design, and development of each claimed invention, which were created on or before the application date for the patent-in-suit or the priority date identified under P.R. 3–1(e), whichever is earlier;

(3) a copy of the file history for each patent-in-suit; and

(4) license agreements for the patents-in-suit.

(b) The producing party must separately identify by production number which documents correspond to each category.

(c) A party's production of a document as required by this paragraph is not an admission that the document is evidence of or is prior art under 35 U.S.C. § 102.

[Effective January 1, 2008.]

3–3. PRELIMINARY INVALIDITY CONTENTIONS

After service upon it of the "Disclosure of Asserted Claims and Preliminary Infringement Contentions," each party opposing a patent infringement claim must serve on all parties, by the deadline set forth in the Scheduling Order, "Preliminary Invalidity Contentions" containing the following information:

(a) the identity of each item of prior art that allegedly anticipates each asserted claim or renders it obvious, including:

(1) each prior art patent identified by its number, country of origin, and date of issue;

(2) each prior art publication identified by its title, date of publication, and, author and publisher when feasible;

(3) prior art under 35 U.S.C. § 102(b) identified by the item offered for sale or publicly used or known; the date the offer or use took place or the information became known; and the identity of the person or entity that made the use or that made and received the offer, or the person or entity that made the information known or to whom it was made known;

(4) prior art under 35 U.S.C. § 102(f) identified by the name of the person(s) from whom and the circumstances under which the invention or any part of it was derived; and

(5) prior art under 35 U.S.C. § 102(g) identified by the identities of the person(s) or entities involved in and the circumstances surrounding the making of the invention prior to the patent applicant(s);

(b) whether each item of prior art anticipates each asserted claim or renders it obvious and, if the latter, the detailed bases for these contentions;

(c) a chart identifying where specifically in each alleged item of prior art each element of each asserted claim is found, including for each element that such party contends is governed by 35 U.S.C. § 112, ¶ 6, the identity of the structure(s), act(s), or material(s) in each item of prior art that performs the claimed function; and

(d) any other invalidity grounds including, but not limited to indefiniteness under 35 U.S.C. § 112, ¶ 2, or lack of enablement or written description under 35 U.S.C. § 112, ¶ 1, of any of the asserted claims, including the detailed basis for these contentions.

[Effective January 1, 2008.]

3–4. PRODUCTION ACCOMPANYING PRELIMINARY INVALIDITY CONTENTIONS

With the "Preliminary Invalidity Contentions," the party opposing a claim of patent infringement must produce or make available for inspection and copying:

(a) documents and information sufficient to show the operation of any aspects or elements of an Accused Instrumentality identified by the patent claimant in its P.R. 3–1(c) chart (*e.g.*, source code, specifications, schematics, flow charts, artwork, or formulas);

(b) a copy of each item of prior art identified under P.R. 3–3(a) that does not appear in the file history of the patent(s) at issue; and

(c) documents and information, including summaries when reasonably available, sufficient to show the amount sold, revenues, costs, and profits of each Accused Instrumentality identified under P.R. 3–1(b) since the issuance of the patents-in-suit.

[Effective January 1, 2008.]

3–5. DISCLOSURE REQUIREMENT IN PATENT CASES SEEKING DECLARATORY JUDGMENT

(a) Invalidity Contentions if No Infringement Claim. In all cases in which a party seeks a declaratory judgment ("declaratory plaintiff") that a patent is not infringed, is invalid, or is unenforceable, P.R. 3–1 and 3–2 do not apply unless and until a party makes a patent infringement claim. If the declaratory defendant does not assert a patent infringement claim in its response to the claim, then, by the deadline set in the Scheduling Order, the declaratory plaintiff must serve on each opposing party its Preliminary Invalidity Contentions conforming to P.R. 3–3 and must produce or make available for inspection and copying the documents and information described in P.R. 3–4. The declaratory plaintiff will file its Final Invalidity Contentions by the deadline in the Scheduling Order.

(b) Application of Rules When No Specified Triggering Event. If the pleadings in a case do not initially trigger the application of these Patent Rules, but later filings reveal that patent claims or issues are involved, the parties, as soon as practicable, must confer about whether these Patent Rules should be applied to the case and notify the presiding judge of the issue.

(c) Inapplicability. P.R. 3–5 does not apply to cases in which a request for a declaratory judgment that a patent is not infringed, is invalid, or is unenforceable is filed in response to a complaint alleging infringement of the same patent.

[Effective January 1, 2008.]

3–6. AMENDED AND FINAL CONTENTIONS— LEAVE OF COURT NOT REQUIRED

Each party's "Preliminary Infringement Contentions" and "Preliminary Invalidity Contentions" will be that party's final contentions, *except* as set forth below.

(a) If a party claiming patent infringement has good cause to believe that the material produced by an opposing party under P.R. 3–4 requires amendment of its "Preliminary Infringement Contentions" with respect to the information required by P.R. 3–1(c) and (d), leave of court is not required. These amended contentions must be served within a reasonable time after the opposing party's document production.

(b) If a party claiming patent infringement has good cause to believe that the Court's Claim Construction Ruling requires "Final Infringement Contentions" amending its "Preliminary Infringement Contentions" with respect to the information required by P.R. 3–1(c) and (d), leave of court is not required.

These Final Infringement Contentions must be served by the deadline set in the Scheduling Order.

(c) By the deadline set in the Scheduling Order, each party opposing a claim of patent infringement may serve, without leave of court, "Final Invalidity Contentions" that amend that party's "Preliminary Invalidity Contentions" with respect to the information required by P.R. 3–3, *if either*:

(1) a party claiming patent infringement has served amended infringement contentions under P.R. 3–6(a) or "Final Infringement Contentions" under P.R. 3–6(b), *or*

(2) the party opposing a patent infringement claim has good cause to believe that the Court's Claim Construction Ruling requires the amendment.

[Effective January 1, 2008.]

3–7. AMENDMENTS TO CONTENTIONS BY LEAVE OF COURT

(a) Amendment or modification of the Preliminary or Final Infringement Contentions or the Preliminary or Final Invalidity Contentions, other than expressly permitted in P.R. 3–6, may be made only if the presiding judge finds there is good cause for the requested changes.

(b) Good cause may include, but is not limited to, newly discovered **(1)** accused instrumentalities, **(2)** bases for claiming infringement, or **(3)** prior art references, provided that good cause may be found only if the party seeking leave to amend shows that it exercised diligence in seeking the newly discovered information or documents.

[Effective January 1, 2008.]

3–8. WILLFULNESS

(a) If a party opposing a patent infringement claim will rely on an opinion of counsel as part of a defense to a claim of willful infringement, that party must by the date(s) set in the Scheduling Order:

(1) produce or make available for inspection and copying each opinion and documents relating to the opinion as to which that party agrees the attorney-client privilege or work-product protection has been waived; and

(2) serve a privilege log identifying any other documents, except those authored by counsel acting solely as litigation counsel, relating to the subject matter of the opinion and withheld based on attorney-client privilege or work product protection claims.

(b) If a party opposing a patent infringement claim does not comply with the requirements of P.R. 3–8, that party may not rely on an opinion of counsel as part of a defense to willful infringement unless all parties agree or the presiding judge permits the defense based on a good cause showing.

[Effective January 1, 2008.]

4. CLAIM CONSTRUCTION PROCEEDINGS

4–1. EXCHANGE OF PROPOSED TERMS AND CLAIM ELEMENTS FOR CONSTRUCTION

(a) By the deadline set in the Scheduling Order, each party must simultaneously exchange a list of claim terms, phrases, or clauses that the party contends should be construed by the presiding judge and must identify any claim element that the party contends should be governed by 35 U.S.C. § 112, ¶ 6.

(b) The parties must then meet and confer for the purposes of finalizing this list, resolving or narrowing differences, and facilitating the preparation of a Joint Claim Construction and Prehearing Statement.

[Effective January 1, 2008.]

4–2. EXCHANGE OF PRELIMINARY CLAIM CONSTRUCTIONS AND EXTRINSIC EVIDENCE

(a) By the deadline set in the Scheduling Order, the parties must simultaneously exchange a proposed "Preliminary Claim Construction" of each element of each claim term, phrase, or clause in issue. Each "Preliminary Claim Construction" must also identify the structures, acts, or materials corresponding to each claim element governed by 35 U.S.C. § 112, ¶ 6.

(b) At the same time the parties exchange their respective "Preliminary Claim Constructions," they must also exchange a preliminary identification of extrinsic evidence they contend supports their respective claim constructions, such as dictionary definitions, citations to learned treatises and prior art, and testimony of fact and expert witnesses. The parties must identify each item of extrinsic evidence by production number or produce a copy of any such item not previously produced. With respect to each fact or expert witness a party intends to rely on for claim construction, the party must also provide a brief description of the substance of that witness's proposed testimony.

(c) The parties must then meet and confer for the purposes of narrowing the issues and finalizing preparation of a Joint Claim Construction and Prehearing Statement.

[Effective January 1, 2008.]

4–3. JOINT CLAIM CONSTRUCTION AND PREHEARING STATEMENT

(a) By the deadline set in the Scheduling Order, the parties must file a Joint Claim Construction and Prehearing Statement that contains the following information:

(1) the construction of those claim terms, phrases, or clauses on which the parties agree;

(2) each party's proposed construction of each disputed element of a claim, together with an identification of all references from the specification or prosecution history that support that claim construction, and an identification of extrinsic evidence known to the party on which it intends to rely either to support its proposed claim construction or to oppose any other party's proposed claim construction, such as dictio-

nary definitions, citations to learned treatises and prior art, and fact and expert witnesses;

(3) the anticipated time necessary for the claim construction hearing;

(4) whether any party proposes to call one or more witnesses at that hearing, the identity of each witness and, for each such expert witness, a summary of the witness's anticipated testimony; and

(5) a list of any other issues that might appropriately be taken up at a prehearing conference before the Claim Construction Hearing, and proposed dates, if not previously set, for any such prehearing conference.

(b) At the time of filing the Joint Claim Construction Statement, for each expert witness a party discloses in response to P.R. 4–3(a)(4), that party must provide to the opposing parties the materials required by Fed. R. Civ. P. 26(a)(2).

[Effective January 1, 2008.]

4–4. COMPLETION OF CLAIM CONSTRUCTION DISCOVERY

The parties must complete by the deadline in the Scheduling Order all discovery relating to claim construction identified in the Joint Claim Construction and Prehearing Statement.

[Effective January 1, 2008.]

4–5. CLAIM CONSTRUCTION BRIEFS AND CHARTS

(a) By the deadlines set in the Scheduling Order:

(1) the party claiming patent infringement must serve and file an opening brief and any evidence supporting its claim construction;

(2) each opposing party must serve and file its responsive brief and supporting evidence;

(3) the party claiming patent infringement must serve and file its reply brief and any evidence directly rebutting the supporting evidence contained in an opposing party's response; and

(4) the parties must submit the Joint Claim Construction Chart (*see* P.R. 4–5(b)) on electronic media in WordPerfect format or in such other format as the presiding judge directs.

(b) The Joint Claim Construction Chart must contain:

(1) a column listing in separate rows the complete language of each disputed claim, with disputed terms in bold type;

(2) separate columns for each party's proposed construction of each disputed term;

(3) a column entitled "Court's Construction" and otherwise left blank; and

(4) the patent and claim numbers where the disputed terms appears.

(c) The parties may also list agreed claim terms in the Joint Claim Construction Chart. If included, the agreed terms must be marked "[**AGREED**]" and state in the "Court's Construction" column the parties' agreed construction.

(**d**) The purpose of the Joint Claim Construction Chart is to assist the presiding judge and the parties in tracking and resolving disputed terms. Accordingly, aside from the requirements of this rule, the parties are afforded substantial latitude to fashion a chart in a format that most clearly and efficiently outlines the disputed terms and proposed constructions.

[Effective January 1, 2008.]

4–6. CLAIM CONSTRUCTION HEARING

The presiding judge will determine if an evidentiary or other form of claim construction hearing is necessary. The hearing will be conducted on the date set in the Scheduling Order, unless otherwise reset by the judge.

[Effective January 1, 2008.]

ORDER SETTING SCHEDULING CONFERENCE, PROPOSED SCHEDULING ORDER, SCOPE OF PERMISSIBLE DISCOVERY AND DIRECTIVE TO CONFER IN PATENT CASES

IN THE UNITED STATES DISTRICT COURT
FOR THE SOUTHERN DISTRICT OF TEXAS

HOUSTON DIVISION

_____,	§	
Plaintiff,	§	
	§	
v.	§	CIVIL ACTION NO. H-_____
	§	
_____,	§	
Defendant.	§	

ORDER SETTING SCHEDULING CONFERENCE, PROPOSED SCHEDULING ORDER, SCOPE OF PERMISSIBLE DISCOVERY AND DIRECTIVE TO CONFER IN PATENT CASES

The Court issues this Order in preparation for the _____, 200 ___, Initial Case Management Conference in this patent infringement case. The following are hereby **ORDERED.**

PROPOSED DATES FOR SCHEDULING ORDER

Proposed dates for the Scheduling Order in this case will be discussed at the conference. The parties are directed to meet and confer in accordance with FED. R. CIV. P. 26(f) and Rule 2–1 of the Rules of Practice for Patent Cases in the Houston Division of the Southern District of Texas ("P.R.", available at United States District Court for the Southern District of Texas Court website **www.txs. uscourts.gov**) no later than **14 days** before the conference. The parties must file no later than **7 days** before the conference a "Joint Case Management Plan" setting forth the information required in P.R. 2–1 and, in brief, their disagreements, if any, on the schedule and procedures to govern this case. The parties also must submit with the Plan a draft Scheduling Order using the template for patent cases on the District's website.

DISCOVERY ORDER

At the Scheduling Conference, the parties may make requests and/or suggestions to the Court regarding discovery. In the interim, after a review of the pleaded claims and defenses in this action and in furtherance of the management of the Court's docket under FED. R. CIV. P. 16, the Court issues the following **DISCOVERY ORDER:**

1. **Disclosures.** In conjunction with disclosures under FED. R. CIV. P. 26(a), and without awaiting a discovery request, each party must disclose to every other party the following information:

   (a) the correct names of the parties to the lawsuit;

   (b) the name, address, and telephone number of any potential parties;

   (c) the legal theories and, in general, the factual bases of the disclosing party's claims or defenses (the disclosing party need not marshal all evidence that may be offered at trial);

   (d) the name, address, and telephone number of persons having knowledge of relevant facts, a brief statement of each identified person's connection with the case, and a brief, fair summary of the substance of the information known by such person;

   (e) any indemnity and insuring agreements under which any person or entity may be liable to satisfy part or all of a judgment entered in this action or to indemnify or reimburse for payments made to satisfy the judgment;

(f) any settlement agreements relevant to the subject matter of this action;

(g) any statement of any party to the litigation;

2. Additional Disclosures.

(a) Each party must provide to every other party the following information:

(i) the disclosures required by the Court's Patent Rules in accordance with the deadlines set forth in said rules;

(ii) to the extent that any party pleads a claim for relief or defensive matter other than those addressed in the Patent Rules, within forty-five (45) days after the Scheduling Conference or the date the Scheduling Order is issued by the Court, and without awaiting a discovery request, a copy of all documents, data compilations and tangible things in the possession, custody, or control of the party that are relevant to those additionally pleaded claims or defenses involved in this action; and

(iii) within forty-five (45) days after the production of information under P.R. 3–4(c), a complete computation of any category of damages claimed by any party to the action, making available for inspection and copying, the documents or other evidentiary materials on which such computation is based, including materials bearing on the nature and extent of injuries suffered; and authorizations necessary to obtain from third parties documents on which the calculations are founded.

(b) If feasible, counsel must meet to exchange these and any other disclosures required by this Order; otherwise, such disclosures must be served as provided by FED. R. CIV. P. 5.

(c) By written agreement of all parties, alternative forms of disclosure may be provided in lieu of paper copies. For example, the parties may agree to exchange images of documents electronically or by means of computer disk; or the parties may agree to review and copy disclosure materials at the offices of the attorneys representing the parties instead of requiring each side to furnish paper copies of the disclosure materials.

(d) Notification of the Court. The parties must promptly file a notice with the Court that the disclosures required under this order have taken place, but no detail is required.

3. Testifying Experts. By the date(s) provided in the Scheduling Order, in addition to the information provided in the Patent Rules, each party shall disclose to the other parties for each testifying expert:

(a) the expert's name, address, and telephone number;

(b) the subject matter on which the expert will testify;

(c) the general substance of the expert's mental impressions and opinions and a brief summary of the basis for them, or if the expert is not retained by, employed by, or otherwise subject to the control of the disclosing party, documents reflecting information such as:

(i) whether the expert is retained by, employed by, or otherwise subject to the control of the disclosing party;

(ii) all documents, tangible things, reports, models, or data compilations that have been provided to, reviewed by, or prepared by or for the expert in anticipation of the expert's testimony; and

(iii) the expert's current resume and bibliography.

4. Discovery Limitations. Discovery is limited in this case to the disclosures described in Paragraphs 1-3 together with 60 interrogatories; 60 requests for admissions; a reasonable number of requests for production or inspection not duplicative of the Patent Rules disclosures; depositions of the parties; depositions on written questions of custodians of business records for third parties; and depositions of three expert witnesses per side. "Side" means a party or a group of parties with a common interest. If parties seek depositions of third-party witnesses or additional experts, the parties either must agree or raise the issue with the Court.

5. Privileged Information. There is no duty to disclose privileged documents or information. However, the parties are directed to meet and confer concerning privileged documents or information after the Scheduling Conference.

(a) By the date provided in the Scheduling Order, the parties must exchange privilege logs identifying the documents or information and the basis for any disputed claim of privilege in a manner that, without revealing information itself privileged or protected, will enable the other parties to assess the applicability of the privilege or protection.

(b) If the parties have no disputes concerning privileged documents or information, then the parties must inform the Court of that fact by the date provided in the Scheduling Order.

(c) A party may move the Court for an order compelling the production of any privileged documents or information identified on any other party's privilege log. If such a motion is made, the party asserting the privilege must file with the Court within thirty (30) days of the filing of the motion to compel proof in the form of declarations or affidavits to support their assertions of privilege, along with the documents over which privilege is asserted for in camera inspection.

6. **Pretrial Order and Accompanying Disclosures.** By the date provided in the Scheduling Order, each party must provide to every other party the materials and disclosures regarding the evidence that the disclosing party intends to present at trial as required by the form Pretrial Order (Appendix B to the Local Rules of the Southern District of Texas), which information must include but not be limited to the following:

(a) Witness Lists: The name and, if not previously provided, the address and telephone number, of each witness, separately identifying those whom the party expects to present at trial and those whom the party may call if the need arises.

(b) Deposition Designations: The designation of those witnesses whose testimony is expected to be presented by means of a deposition, with designations to the transcripts.

(c) Exhibit Lists and Copies: All exhibits must be pre-marked separately identifying those which the party expects to offer in its case in chief and those which the party may offer if the need arises.

(d) Objections, together with the grounds therefor, to live witnesses and deposition designations by another party under subparagraph (b) above. Objections not so disclosed are deemed waived unless excused by the Court for good cause shown.

(e) Objections, together with the grounds therefor, to authentication and/or admissibility of exhibits identified under subparagraph (c) above. Objections not so disclosed are deemed waived unless excused by the Court for good cause shown.

(f) **Legal Memoranda and Related Material:**

(i) Bench trials: proposed findings of fact and conclusions of law with citation to authority;

(ii) Jury trials: joint proposed jury instructions with citation to authority, and proposed verdict form.

7. **Signatures.** The disclosures required by this Order must be made electronically or in writing and signed by the party making the disclosures. **NOTE:** Signatures by the party or counsel constitute a certification that, to the best of the signer's knowledge, information and belief, such disclosure is complete and correct as of the time it is made.

8. **Protective Orders.** The parties may submit a proposed protective order, preferably using the form Protective Order for use in patent cases (available at the District's website), to ensure the confidentiality of parties' materials is maintained during this case to the extent feasible. To propose modifications to the form, *see* P.R. 2–2.

9. **Rules of Practice.** The Federal Rules of Civil Procedure, the District's Local Rules, and the District's Local Patent Rules apply in this case, unless otherwise ordered. The District Local Rules and the Local Patent Rules are available at the District's website.

10. **Discovery Disputes.** Counsel are directed to adhere to procedures of the presiding judge for bringing discovery disputes to the Court's attention.

11. **No Excuses.** A party is not excused from the requirements of this Discovery Order because it has not fully completed its investigation of the case, or because it challenges the sufficiency of another party's disclosures, or because another party has not made its disclosures. Absent court order to the contrary, a party is not excused from disclosure because there are pending motions to dismiss, to remand or to change venue. Parties asserting the defense of qualified immunity may submit a motion to limit disclosure to those materials necessary to decide the issue of qualified immunity.

12. **E–Filing.** Except for good cause shown or as provided in the Local Rules, all documents (with the exception of correspondence and those documents referenced in the District's Local Rules)

in cases pending in this Court must be filed electronically. The file in each case is maintained electronically. Neither the Clerk's Office nor the Court will maintain a paper file except as provided in the District's Local Rules.

When filing electronically, the Court prefers:

(a) that documents be published to *PDF* and then filed with the Court, rather than filing scanned documents; and

(b) proposed orders be included as attachments to motions, not incorporated within the filed motion and not filed as a separate docket entry.

13. Duty to Supplement. After disclosure is made pursuant to this Order, each party is under a duty to supplement or correct its disclosures immediately if the party obtains information on the basis of which it knows that the information disclosed was either incomplete or incorrect when made, or is no longer complete or true.

14. Courtesy Paper Copies. The parties must comply with the presiding judge's procedures for courtesy copies.

15. Hearing Notebooks. Unless a different time or method is provided by the presiding judge or in the Scheduling Order in this case, the movant is to provide the Court, no later than 14 days before any motion hearing, an original and one copy of a hearing notebook containing all motion papers with the corresponding docket numbers on each and all pleadings and exhibits appropriately tabbed.

16. Sealed Documents. The filing of sealed documents is disfavored. The Court will not seal a document *unless* the movant shows the document contains genuinely confidential or proprietary material, and otherwise meets the requirements for sealing filed documents.

SIGNED at Houston, Texas, this ___ day of _____, 200 ___.

_____

[JUDGE'S NAME]
UNITED STATES DISTRICT JUDGE

[Effective January 1, 2008. Revised December 1, 2009.]

PROPOSED PATENT CASE—SCHEDULING ORDER

[INSERT—CASE CAPTION]

It is hereby **ORDERED**, after consultation with the parties, that the following schedule will apply in this case:

0	1/1/05 [sample date: chosen for illustration]	**Scheduling Conference** (*see* # 32 re: **MEDIATION**)
1	[2 weeks after Scheduling Conf.] 1/15/05	**Comply with P.R. 3–1 and P.R. 3–2: Parties to make disclosure of asserted claims and preliminary infringement contentions & make document production.** *After this date*, it is necessary to obtain leave of court to add and/or amend infringement contentions, pursuant to Patent Rule (P.R.) 3–7. **Join additional parties.** It is not necessary to file a motion to join additional parties before this date. Thereafter, it is necessary to obtain leave of court to join additional parties. **Add new patents and/or claims** for patents-in-suit. It is not necessary to file a motion to add additional patents or claims before this date. Thereafter, it is necessary to obtain leave of court to add patents or claims.
2	[6 weeks after # 1] 2/26/05	Comply with P.R. 3–3 and 3–4: **Parties to serve preliminary invalidity contentions** and make document production. Thereafter, it is necessary to obtain leave of Court to add and/or amend invalidity contentions, pursuant to P.R. 3–7. Add any **inequitable conduct allegations** to pleadings. Before this date, it is not necessary to file a motion for leave to add inequitable conduct allegations to pleadings. Thereafter, it is necessary to obtain leave of court to add inequitable conduct allegations to pleadings.
3	[2 weeks after # 2] 3/12/05	Comply with P.R. 4–1: **Parties' exchange of proposed terms and claim elements needing construction.**
4	[3 weeks after # 3] 4/2/05	Comply with P.R. 4–2: **Parties' exchange of preliminary claim constructions and extrinsic evidence.** **Privilege Logs** to be exchanged by parties (or a letter to the Court stating that there are no disputes as to claims of privileged documents).
5	[9 weeks after # 2; 17 weeks after Conf.] 4/30/05	Deadline to comply with P.R. 4–3: **Filing of joint claim construction and pre-hearing statement.** **Disclosure of parties' claim construction experts** & service of FED. R. CIV. P. 26(a)(2) materials
6	[matches # 5] 4/30/05	**Deadline for all parties to file amended pleadings (pre-claim construction).** It is not necessary to file a Motion for Leave to Amend before the deadline to amend pleadings. (It will be necessary to file a Motion for Leave to Amend after this deadline.) **NOTE:** If the amendment would affect preliminary infringement contentions or preliminary invalidity contentions, a motion must be made pursuant to P.R. 3–7 irrespective of whether the amendment is made prior to this deadline.
7	[22 weeks after Scheduling Conf.] 6/4/05	Each party to provide name, address, phone number, and curriculum vitae for up to three (3) candidates for a **court-appointed special master** (*see* FED. R. CIV. P. 53) **or court-appointed expert** (*see* FED. R. EV. 706), with information regarding the nominee's availability for *Markman* hearing or other assignments as deemed necessary by the court. The parties shall indicate if they agree on any of the nominees.
8	[22 weeks after Scheduling Conf.; generally matches # 7] 6/4/05	Deadline for parties (optional) to provide Court with **written tutorials concerning technology involved in patent in issue.** If a special master or court-appoint-

ed expert is hereafter selected, the parties will provide
each tutorial to the master or expert.

9	[2 weeks after # 6; generally 19 weeks after Scheduling Conf.] 5/14/05	**Responses to amended pleadings due.**
10	[2 weeks after # 9; 21 weeks after Scheduling Conf.] 5/28/05	**Discovery deadline on claim construction issues** (*see* P.R. 4–4)
11	[7 weeks after # 5; 3 weeks after # 10; generally 24 weeks after Scheduling Conf.] 6/18/05	Comply with P.R. 4–5(a): **the party claiming patent infringement** must serve and file a **Claim Construction Opening Brief** with its supporting evidence. The moving party is to provide the Court with 2 copies of the binders containing their Opening Brief and exhibits. If a special master or court-appointed expert has been appointed, the moving party must provide the Opening Brief on disk or CD along with a hard copy, tabbed and bound in notebook format with exhibits, to the special master or court-appointed expert.
12	[2 weeks after # 11] 7/2/05	Comply with P.R. 4–5(b): **Responsive Brief and supporting evidence due to party claiming patent infringement.** The moving party is to provide the Court with two (2) courtesy copies of the Responsive Brief and exhibits. If a special master or court-appointed expert has been appointed, the nonmoving party must supply a copy of its Response on disk or CD along with a hard copy, tabbed and bound in notebook format with exhibits, to the special master or court-appointed expert.
13	[1 week after # 12] 7/9/05	Comply with P.R. 4–5(c): **Party claiming infringement shall file a Reply Brief and supporting evidence on claim construction.** The moving party is to provide the Court with two (2) copies of the Reply Brief and exhibits. If a special master or court-appointed expert has been appointed, the moving party must provide the Reply Brief on disk or CD along with a hard copy, tabbed and bound in notebook format with exhibits, to the special master or court-appointed expert. Parties to file a **notice** with the Court stating the **estimated amount of time** requested for the Claim Construction (*Markman*) Hearing. The Court will notify the parties if it is unable to accommodate this request.
14	[1 week *before Markman* Hearing] 8/6/05	Parties to submit **Claim Construction Chart** in WordPerfect 8.0 (or higher) format in compliance with P.R. 4–5(d).
15	[approx. 15 weeks after # 5; approx. 5 weeks after # 13; 32 weeks after Scheduling Hrg.] 8/13/05	**Claim Construction (*Markman*) Hearing at _____ ____.m. at the United States District Court, 515 Rusk Street, Courtroom 9–F, Houston, Texas**
16	[*Markman* ruling within 6 weeks after *Markman* hearing] 9/24/05	**Court's Decision on Claim Construction** (*Markman* Ruling) *(If ruling is late, parties may seek amendment of remaining dates in Scheduling Order.)*
17	[4 weeks after *Markman* Ruling (# 16)] 10/22/05	**Deadline for final infringement contentions and to amend pleadings on infringement claims** NOTE: Except as provided in P.R. 3–6, if the amendment would affect preliminary or final infringement contentions, a motion must be made under P.R. 3–7 irrespective of whether the amendment is made before this deadline.
18	[6 weeks after *Markman* Ruling (# 16); 2 weeks after # 17] 11/5/05	**Deadline for final invalidity contentions and to amend pleadings on invalidity claims.** NOTE: Except as provided in P.R. 3–6, if the amendment would affect preliminary or final invalidity contentions, a motion must be made under P.R. 3–7 irrespective of whether the amendment is made before this deadline.
19	[matches # 17; ~ 10.5 mos. after Scheduling Conf.] 10/22/05	Comply with P.R. 3–8. **All parties furnish** documents and privilege logs **pertaining to willful infringement.**
20	[4 weeks after # 19] [~ 8 weeks after *Markman* Ruling (# 16) and ~ 11.5 mos. after Scheduling Conf.]	Date for **designation of expert witnesses on non-construction issues on which the party has the burden of proof ("BOP")** and **service of expert witness reports.**

	11/19/05	[Refer to Fed. Rules of Civil Proc. for information required.]
21	[4 weeks after # 20] 12/17/05	**Date for designation of responsive expert witnesses on non-claim construction issues on which party does *not* have BOP, and service of responsive expert witness reports.** [Refer to Fed. Rules of Civil Proc. for information required.]
22	[8 weeks after # 21, ~ 5 mos. after *Markman* Ruling (# 16), and ~ 14.5 mos. after Sched. Conf.] 2/11/06	**Discovery Deadline on all issues.** *(If ruling is late, parties may seek amendment of remaining dates in Scheduling Order.)*
23	Motions due: 3/11/06 [4+ weeks after # 22] Responsive Briefs due (3 wks): 4/1/06 Reply Briefs due (1 wk): 4/8/06	**Dispositive and Non–Dispositive Motions and Briefing deadlines**
24	[~ 8 weeks after motions in # 23 filed; ~ 17 mos. from Sched'g Conf.] 5/6/06	**Court's ruling on all pending motions**
25	[4 weeks after # 24; at least 2 weeks before Docket Call] 6/3/06	**Joint Pretrial Order** due including **all components** required by Local Rules and this Court's Procedures (such as witness lists, exhibit lists and copies of exhibits (*see* # 29 below), and (a) in bench trials, proposed findings of fact and conclusions of law with citation to authority and (b) for jury trials, joint proposed jury instructions with citation to authority, and proposed verdict form). **Statement of Expected Length of Trial:** ___ days (—6 hours with jury per day).
26	[same day as JPTO (# 25)—but filed separately] 6/3/06	**Written notice due for request for daily transcript or real time reporting of trial proceedings.**
27	[Same day as JPTO (# 25)] 6/3/06	**Video and Deposition Designations** due. Each party who proposes to offer a deposition by video must file a disclosure identifying the line and page numbers to be offered. All other parties will have **1 week** to file a response requesting **cross designation** line and page numbers to be included. Each party is responsible for **preparation of the final edited video** in accordance with their parties' designations and the Court's rulings on objections.
28	[same day as JPTO (# 25)] 6/3/06	**Motions in Limine due.**
29	[1 week after JPTO filed (# 25)] 6/10/06	**Objections** to opponents' proposed witnesses, proposed exhibits, designated deposition testimony, and any other matters due.
30	[1 day before Docket Call—3 p.m.] 6/17/06	The **parties** are directed to confer and **advise the Court** about (a) which limine requests the parties agree to.
31	[18.5 mos. after Scheduling Conf.; ~ 20 mos. after case filed] 6/18/06	9:00 a.m. **Docket Call/ Final Pretrial Conference** at the United States District Court, 515 Rusk Street, Houston, Texas.
32	**MEDIATION is required prior to Docket Call** 6/17/06	*The Court refers most patent cases to mediation. The parties should discuss proposed mediators and timing of mediation prior to the Scheduling Conference and be prepared with recommendations for the Court.* **Mediation to be completed by this date.** The parties must select a mediator for this case. The parties and mediator must comply with S.D. TEXAS LOCAL RULE 16.
33	[generally, the first day of jury trial] ~ **July, 2006**	9:00 a.m. **JURY SELECTION** at the United States District Court
34	[Generally same date as jury selection # 33] ~ July, 2006	**JURY TRIAL** (9:30 a.m.) commences, subject to Court's criminal docket

OTHER REQUIREMENTS and LIMITATIONS:

(a) **All depositions** to be read into evidence as part of the parties' case-in-chief must be **EDITED** (*with* notice to opposing parties) to exclude all unnecessary, repetitious, and irrelevant testimony. **ONLY** those portions relevant to the issues in controversy may be read into evidence.

(b) The Court will refuse to entertain any **motion to compel discovery** filed after the date of this Order unless the movant advises the Court within the body of the motion that counsel for the parties have first conferred in a good faith attempt to resolve the matter. See Southern District of Texas Local Rules 7.1, 7.2.

(c) The following **excuses will neither warrant a continuance** nor justify a failure to comply with the discovery deadline:

(i) the fact that there are motions for summary judgment or motions to dismiss pending;

(ii) the fact that one or more of the attorneys is set for trial in another court on the same day, unless the other setting was made prior to the date of this order or was made as a special provision for the parties in the other case;

(iii) the failure to complete discovery prior to trial, unless the parties can demonstrate that it was impossible to complete discovery despite their good faith effort to do so.

(d) **Exhibits**

(i) Each party must provide the Court with a courtesy copy of exhibits and exhibit lists. The presiding judge's preferred format for Exhibit Lists is available on the Court's website at www.txs.uscourts.gov under **Court Procedures.**

(ii) If exhibits are voluminous, provide only specific pages that pertain to the issues on the two courtesy copies. The original exhibits that are agreed upon by the parties, should be ready to be tendered to the Clerk of the Court at the beginning of trial. Other exhibits that are admitted during trial should be tendered to the Clerk of the Court immediately after admission.

(iii) The parties are to label all proposed exhibits with the following information on each label: Designation of Plaintiff's or Defendant's Exhibit Number and Case Number. For example:

Plaintiff's Exhibit	**Defendant's Exhibit**
Exhibit No. _____	Exhibit No. _____
Case No. _____	Case No. _____

SIGNED at Houston, Texas, this ____ day of _____, 200 ____.

_____
[JUDGE'S NAME]
UNITED STATES DISTRICT JUDGE

[Effective January 1, 2008.]

PROTECTIVE ORDER

IN THE UNITED STATES DISTRICT COURT
FOR THE SOUTHERN DISTRICT OF TEXAS

HOUSTON DIVISION

————————————————,	§	
Plaintiff,	§	
	§	
v.	§	CIVIL CASE NO. H-_____
	§	
	§	
————————————————,	§	
Defendant.	§	

PROTECTIVE ORDER

1. Proceedings and Information Governed. This Order ("Protective Order") is made under Rule 26(c) of the Federal Rules of Civil Procedure ("FED. R. CIV. P.").

This Protective Order applies to any document, information, or other tangible or intangible thing (collectively, "documents") furnished by a party to any other party, as well as documents furnished by non-parties who receive subpoenas in connection with this action, if and when the documents are designated by a party or non-party as "Confidential Information" or "Highly Confidential Information" in accordance with the terms of this Protective Order. This Protective Order also applies to copies, excerpts, abstracts, analyses, summaries, descriptions, or other forms of recorded information or data containing, reflecting, or disclosing all or parts of designated documents.

2. Designation and Maintenance of Documents and Information.

A. "Confidential Information" designation means that the document contains trade secrets or commercial information not publicly known, which trade secrets or commercial information is of technical or commercial advantage to its possessor, in accordance with FED. R. CIV. P. 26(c)(7), or other information required by law or agreement to be kept confidential.

B. The "Highly Confidential Information" designation means that the document contains information that the producing party deems especially sensitive, which may include, but is not limited to, confidential research and development, financial, technical, marketing, any other sensitive trade secret information, or information capable of being utilized for the preparation or prosecution of a patent application dealing with such subject matter.

C. "Confidential Information" and "Highly Confidential Information" does not include, and this Protective Order does not apply to, documents already in the knowledge or possession of the party to whom disclosure is made unless that party is already bound by an agreement not to disclose such information, or information that has been disclosed to the public or third persons in a manner making such information no longer confidential.

3. Documents Produced in Discovery and Depositions.

A. Documents and things produced during the course of this litigation within the scope of paragraph 2(A) or 2(B) above, may be designated by the producing party as containing "Confidential Information" by placing on each page and each thing a legend substantially as follows:

CONFIDENTIAL INFORMATION

SUBJECT TO PROTECTIVE ORDER

Documents and things produced during the course of this litigation within the scope of paragraph 2(A) above may be designated by the producing party as containing "Highly Confidential Information" by placing on each page and each thing a legend substantially as follows:

HIGHLY CONFIDENTIAL INFORMATION
SUBJECT TO PROTECTIVE ORDER

B. Depositions

(i) For deposition testimony or exhibits to be entitled to protection under this Order, a party must designate the testimony and exhibits disclosed at a deposition as "Confidential Information" or "Highly Confidential Information" by requesting the reporter to so designate the transcript or any portion of the transcript at the time of the deposition.

(ii) If no such designation is made at the time of the deposition, any party has fourteen (14) days after delivery by the court reporter of the transcript of the deposition session to designate, in writing to the other parties and to the court reporter, what portions of the transcript and which exhibits the party designates as "Confidential Information" and "Highly Confidential Information."

(iii) During the transcription and following fourteen (14) day period after a deposition session, the transcript and exhibits must be treated as Highly Confidential Information, unless the disclosing party consents to less confidential treatment of the information.

(iv) Each party and the court reporter must attach a copy of any final and timely written designation notice to the transcript and each copy of the transcript in its possession, custody or control, and the portions designated in such notice must thereafter be treated in accordance with this Protective Order. It is the responsibility of counsel for each party to maintain materials containing Confidential Information or Highly Confidential Information in a secure manner and appropriately identified so as to allow access to such information only to such persons and under such terms as is permitted under this Protective Order.

(v) If no such designation is made at the deposition or within the fourteen (14) day period following delivery of the transcript, then the entire deposition will be considered devoid of Confidential Information or Highly Confidential Information.

4. Inadvertent Failure to Designate.

A. The inadvertent failure to designate a documents as "Confidential Information" or "Highly Confidential Information" will not be a waiver of a claim that the document contains confidential information, and will not prevent the producing party from designating such information as confidential at a later date in writing, so long as the designation is done with particularity.

B. In the event a producing party late designates a document as "Confidential Information" or "Highly Confidential Information," the document must be treated by the receiving party as confidential from the time of receipt of the notice of the "Confidential Information" or "Highly Confidential Information" designation.

5. Challenges to Designations.

A party's designation of documents "Confidential Information" or "Highly Confidential Information" is not binding if the procedures below are followed:

A. A receiving party may challenge a producing party's designation at any time. Any receiving party may request in writing that the producing party change the designation. The producing party within fourteen (14) days after receipt of a written challenge, must advise the receiving party whether or not it will change the designation.

B. If the parties are unable to reach agreement after the expiration of this fourteen (14) day period, they shall confer. If they cannot resolve the issue, the receiving party may seek an order to alter the confidential status of the designated information.

C. Until the presiding judge has ruled on a dispute under this paragraph, the "Confidential Information" or "Highly Confidential Information" designation will remain in full force and effect, and the document continues to be protected by this Protective Order.

6. Disclosure and Use of Confidential Information.

A. Information designated as "Confidential Information" or "Highly Confidential Information" may only be used for purposes of preparation, trial, and appeal of this action. "Confidential Information" or "Highly Confidential Information" may not be used under any circumstances for prosecuting any patent application, for patent licensing, or for any other purpose.

B. Subject to paragraph 9 below, "Confidential Information" may be disclosed by the receiving party only to the following individuals, provided that such individuals are informed of the terms of this Protective Order: **(a)** two employees of the receiving party who are required in good faith to provide assistance in the conduct of this litigation, including any settlement discussions, and who are identified as such in writing to counsel for the designating party in advance of the disclosure; **(b)** two in-house counsel who are identified by the receiving party; **(c)** outside counsel of record for the receiving party; **(d)** supporting personnel employed by (b) and (c), such as paralegals, legal secretaries, data entry clerks, legal clerks, and private photocopying services; **(e)** experts or consultants; and **(f)** any persons requested by counsel to furnish services such as document coding, image scanning, mock trial, jury profiling, translation services, court reporting services, demonstrative exhibit preparation, or the creation of any computer database from documents.

C. Subject to paragraph 9 below, "Highly Confidential Information" may be disclosed by the receiving party only to the following individuals, provided that such individuals are informed of the terms of this Protective Order: **(a)** outside counsel of record for the receiving party; **(b)** supporting personnel employed by outside counsel, such as paralegals, legal secretaries, data entry clerks, legal clerks, private photocopying services; **(c)** experts or consultants; and **(d)** those individuals designated in paragraph 6(F)(c) below.

D. Further, prior to disclosing "Confidential Information" or "Highly Confidential Information" to a receiving party's proposed expert, consultant, or employees, the receiving party must provide to the producing party a signed Confidentiality Agreement in the form attached as Exhibit A, the resume or curriculum vitae of the proposed expert or consultant, the expert or consultant's business affiliation, and any current and past consulting relationships in the industry. The producing party will thereafter have fourteen (14) days from receipt of the Confidentiality Agreement to object to any proposed individual. The objection must be made for good cause and in writing, stating with particularity the reasons for the objection. Failure to object within fourteen (14) days constitutes approval. If the parties are unable to resolve any objection, the receiving party may apply to the presiding judge to resolve the matter. There will be no disclosure to any proposed individual during the fourteen (14) day objection period, unless that period is waived by the producing party, or if any objection is made, until the parties have resolved the objection, or the presiding judge has ruled upon any resultant motion.

E. Counsel is responsible for the adherence by third-party vendors to the terms and conditions of this Protective Order. Counsel may fulfill this obligation by obtaining a signed Confidentiality Agreement in the form attached as Exhibit B.

F. "Confidential Information" or "Highly Confidential Information" may be disclosed to a person who is not already allowed access to such information under this Protective Order *if*: **(a)** the information was previously received or authored by the person or was authored or received by a director, officer, employee or agent of the company for which the person is testifying as a designee under FED. R. CIV. P. 30(b)(6); **(b)** the designating party is the person or is a party for whom the person is a director, officer, employee, consultant or agent; or **(c)** counsel for the party designating the material agrees that the material may be disclosed to the person.

In the event of disclosure under this section 6(F), only the reporter, the person, his or her counsel, the presiding judge, and persons to whom disclosure may be made and who are bound by this Protective Order, may be present during the disclosure or discussion of Confidential Information.

Disclosure of material pursuant to this section 6(F) does not constitute a waiver of the confidential status of the material so disclosed.

7. Non–Party Information.

The existence of this Protective Order must be disclosed to any person producing documents, tangible things, or testimony in this action who may reasonably be expected to desire confidential treatment for such documents, tangible things or testimony. Any such person may designate documents, tangible things, or testimony confidential pursuant to this Protective Order.

8. Filing Documents With the Court.

Any party may submit Confidential Information to the court under seal by designating the document "sealed" in the CM/ECF system of the court or may deliver the document for filing by the Clerk's Office. If a party delivers a copy to the court, the document must be in a sealed envelope bearing the caption of this action and a label containing the following:

CONFIDENTIAL INFORMATION

[case caption]

**This envelope, which is being filed under seal,
contains documents that are subject to a Protective Order
governing the use of confidential discovery material.**

9. No Prejudice.

Producing or receiving "Confidential Information" or "Highly Confidential Information," or otherwise complying with the terms of this Protective Order, will ***not***: **(a)** operate as an admission by any party that any particular "Confidential Information" or "Highly Confidential Information" contains or reflects trade secrets or any other type of confidential or proprietary information; **(b)** prejudice the rights of a party to object to the production of information or material that the party does not consider to be within the scope of discovery; **(c)** prejudice the rights of a party to seek a determination by the presiding judge that particular materials be produced; **(d)** prejudice the rights of a party to apply to the presiding judge for further protective orders; or **(e)** prevent the parties from agreeing in writing to alter or waive the provisions or protections provided for in this Protective Order with respect to any particular information or material.

10. Conclusion of Litigation.

Within sixty (60) days after final judgment in this action, including the exhaustion of all appeals, or within sixty (60) days after dismissal pursuant to a settlement agreement, each party or other person subject to the terms of this Protective Order is under an obligation to destroy or return to the producing party all materials and documents containing "Confidential Information" or "Highly Confidential Information," and to certify to the producing party that this destruction or return has been done. However, outside counsel for any party is entitled to retain all court papers, trial transcripts, exhibits, and attorney work provided that any such materials are maintained and protected in accordance with the terms of this Protective Order.

11. Other Proceedings.

By entering this Protective Order and limiting the disclosure of information in this case, the presiding judge does not intend to preclude another court from finding that information may be relevant and subject to disclosure in another case. Any person or party subject to this Protective Order who may be subject to a motion to disclose another party's information designated "Confidential" or "Highly Confidential" pursuant to this Protective Order must promptly notify that party of the motion so that the party may have an opportunity to appear and be heard on whether that information should be disclosed.

12. Remedies.

It is **ORDERED** that this Protective Order will be enforced by the sanctions set forth in FED. R. CIV. P. 37(a) and any other sanctions as may be available to the presiding judge, including the power to hold parties or other violators of this Protective Order in contempt. All other remedies available to any person injured by a violation of this Protective Order are fully reserved.

13. Relief from Protective Order.

Any party may petition the presiding judge for good cause shown if the party desires relief from a term or condition of this Protective Order.

Signed at Houston, Texas, this ___ day of _____, 20 ___.

_____

[Judge's Name]
United States District Judge

Exhibit A

[CAPTION]

CONFIDENTIALITY AGREEMENT FOR EXPERT, CONSULTANT OR EMPLOYEES OF ANY PARTY

I, _____, under penalty of perjury, 28 U.S.C. § 1746, that:

1. Information, including documents and things, designated as "Confidential Information" or "Highly Confidential Information," as defined in the Protective Order entered in the above-captioned action ("Protective Order"), is being provided to me pursuant to the terms and restrictions of the Protective Order.

2. I have been given a copy of and have read the Protective Order.

3. I am familiar with the terms of the Protective Order and I agree to comply with and to be bound by its terms.

4. I submit to the jurisdiction of the United States District Court for the Southern District of Texas for enforcement of the Protective Order.

5. I agree not to use any "Confidential Information" or "Highly Confidential Information" disclosed to me pursuant to the Protective Order except for purposes of the above-captioned litigation and not to disclose any of this information to persons other than those specifically authorized by the Protective Order, without the express written consent of the party who designated the information as confidential or by order of the presiding judge.

6. I also agree to notify any stenographic, clerical or technical personnel who are required to assist me of the terms of this Protective Order and of its binding effect on them and me.

7. I understand that I am to retain all documents or materials designated as or containing "Confidential Information" or "Highly Confidential Information" in a secure manner, and that all such documents and materials are to remain in my personal custody until the completion of my assigned duties in this matter, whereupon all such documents and materials, including all copies thereof, and any writings prepared by me containing any "Confidential Information" or "Highly Confidential Information" are to be returned to counsel who provided me with such documents and materials.

Signed at _____, _____, this _____, day of _____, 20 ___.

_____
Signature

Exhibit B

[CAPTION]

CONFIDENTIALITY AGREEMENT FOR THIRD–PARTY VENDORS

I, _____, under penalty of perjury, 28 U.S.C. § 1746, that:

1. Information, including documents and things, designated as "Confidential Information" or "Highly Confidential Information" as defined in the Protective Order entered in the above-captioned action ("Protective Order"), is being provided to me pursuant to the terms and restrictions of the Protective Order.

2. I have been given a copy of and have read the Protective Order.

3. I am familiar with the terms of the Protective Order and I agree to comply with and to be bound by its terms.

4. I submit to the jurisdiction of the United States District Court for the Southern District of Texas for enforcement of the Protective Order.

5. I agree not to use any Confidential Information or Highly Confidential Information disclosed to me pursuant to the Protective Order except for purposes of the above-captioned litigation and not to disclose any of this information to persons other than those specifically authorized by the Protective Order, without the express written consent of the party who designated the information as confidential or by order of the presiding judge.

Signed at _____, _____, this _____ day of _____, 20 ___.

_____
Signature

[Effective January 1, 2008. Revised December 1, 2009.]

ELECTRONIC FILING
ADMINISTRATIVE PROCEDURES FOR ELECTRONIC FILING IN CIVIL AND CRIMINAL CASES

1. Scope of Electronic Filing.

A. These procedures are intended to facilitate electronic filing and do not supersede any federal or local rules of procedure.

B. All civil, criminal, and miscellaneous cases are covered by the Electronic Filing System.

(1). Civil Cases. Except as expressly provided or unless permitted by the presiding Judge, a Filing User is required to file electronically all complaints, initial papers, petitions, motions, memoranda of law, briefs, and other pleadings and documents filed with the court in connection with a civil case.

(2). Criminal Cases. Except as expressly provided or unless permitted by the presiding Judge, a Filing User is required to file electronically all petitions, motions, memoranda of law, briefs, and other pleadings and documents filed with the court in connection with a criminal case. However, the following items shall be filed in conventional paper form unless otherwise directed by the presiding judge: the charging documents, including the complaint, information, or indictment; documents relating to requests for search warrants, wire interceptions, pen registers, and other tracking devices; grand jury proceedings; documents pertaining to eligibility for release under the Bail Reform Act.

C. A Filing User filing an imaged document must verify the legibility of the document.

D. A non-Filing User is not required to electronically file pleadings and other papers in a case.

E. Pleadings and other papers not electronically filed (conventional filings) will be imaged by the Clerk's Office and will become part of the electronic record. However, the Clerk may determine that documents too voluminous to be imaged, such as the records of proceedings in state court or social security appeals, or any other documents or thing not capable of being imaged will be filed and maintained in the conventional manner. After imaging conventional filings, the Clerk will retain them in one master file by date of filing for one (1) year, at which time they will be destroyed.

2. Eligibility, Registration, Passwords.

A. Attorneys admitted to the bar of this Court, as well as those admitted pro hac vice, are required to register as Filing Users of the Court's Electronic Filing System. The registration form prescribed by the Clerk requires the Filing User's name, address, telephone number, internet e-mail address, and a declaration that the attorney is admitted to the bar of this Court or admitted pro hac vice. Registration as a Filing User constitutes consent to electronic service of all documents as provided in these procedures and in accordance with Rule Fed. R. Civ. P. 5(b)(2)(D) and Fed. R. Crim. P. 49(b).

B. Once registration is completed, the Filing User will receive notification of the user log-in and password. Filing Users agree to protect the security of their passwords and must **immediately** notify the Clerk if their password has been compromised. Users may be subject to sanctions for failure to comply with this provision.

C. An attorney may seek from the presiding Judge an exemption from being a Filing User upon a finding of exceptional circumstances.

3. Consequences of Electronic Filing.

A. Electronic transmission of a document to the Electronic Filing System consistent with these procedures, together with the transmission of a Notice of Electronic Filing issued by the Court, constitutes filing of the document for all purposes of the Federal Rules of Civil and Criminal Procedure and the Local Rules of this Court, and constitutes entry of the document on the docket kept by the Clerk of Court under Fed. R. Civ. P. 58 and 79, and Fed. R. Crim. P. 49 and 55.

B. When a document has been filed electronically, the official record is the electronic recording of the document as stored by the Court, and the filing party is bound by the document as filed. A document filed electronically is deemed filed at the date and time stated on the Notice of Electronic Filing issued by the Court.

C.   Filing a document electronically does not alter the filing deadline for that document.   Filing must be completed before midnight, Central Time Zone, in order to be considered timely filed that day, unless otherwise ordered.

4.   Entry of Court–Issued Documents.

A.   All orders, decrees, judgments, and proceedings of the Court will be filed in accordance with these procedures and will constitute entry on the docket kept by the Clerk of Court under Fed. R. Civ. P. 58 and 79, and Fed. R. Crim. P. 49 and 55.   All signed orders will be filed electronically.   Any order or other court-issued document filed with an electronic or digital signature of a Judge or Court Employee has the same force and effect as if the Judge or Court Employee physically signed a paper copy.

B.   A civil case summons may be signed, sealed and issued electronically, although a party may not serve any summons electronically.   The Court may issue a criminal case warrant or summons electronically, but it must be served in accordance with Fed. R. Crim. P. 4(c).

C.   A proposed order for electronically filed motions must be filed as an electronic attachment to the motion, unless otherwise directed by the presiding Judge.

D.   Transcripts of court proceedings will be filed electronically by court reporters and transcribers.   Transcripts of sealed proceedings must be filed under seal.

5.   Attachments and Exhibits.   Filing Users must submit in electronic form all documents referenced as exhibits or attachments, unless the presiding Judge permits conventional filing.   A Filing User may submit as exhibits or attachments only those excerpts of the referenced documents that are material to the matter under consideration.   The source and page numbers of excerpted material must be clearly and prominently identified, and the length of the full source document must be disclosed.   Responding parties may timely file such additional excerpts or complete documents as they believe are material.   The presiding Judge also may require parties to file additional excerpts or the complete document.   Non-documentary exhibits to instruments should be filed conventionally and also electronically, if they can be converted to a format capable of electronic filing such as a photograph.

6.   Sealed Documents.

A.   Filing Users must submit in conventional form all requests for in camera proceedings.

B.   *Civil Cases:*

(1).   Under L.R. 83.6, Filing Users must ask the Court's permission to file a civil case under seal.   Filing Users must electronically file the request as a miscellaneous case, attaching to it a motion to seal the complaint and the proposed sealed complaint.

(2).   In unsealed civil cases, Filing Users may electronically file any document under seal, subject to paragraph 6.E.

C.   *Criminal or miscellaneous cases:*

(1).   Filing users must electronically file the following documents under seal:

a.   Documents related to pre-sentence reports

b.   Requests to Debrief

c.   Motions for downward departure, including motions under Fed R. Crim. P. 35(b)

d.   Requests for continuances or other relief for cooperating Defendants

e.   Psychiatric reports

f.   Ex Parte requests or advisories to the Court

g.   Victim statements and other crime victim information.

h.   Financial information regarding a Defendant

(2).   Filing Users may electronically file other documents under seal, subject to paragraph 6.E.

D.   Documents filed under seal will be kept by the Court in electronic form, but will not be viewable by Filing Users or the public.   Accordingly, any document filed under seal must be conventionally served on all parties, except Ex Parte requests.

E.   The presiding Judge may order the sealing or unsealing of any document

7. Document Format and Size Limitations.

A. Parties are strongly encouraged to file text-only documents in electronically created format, not in imaged form.

B. The current size limitation for electronically filed documents, including exhibits or attachments, is 5 megabytes. While this limit will not likely affect electronically created documents, in the case of imaged documents it would be the equivalent of approximately 75 pages. Larger imaged documents must be separated into 5 megabyte sections. As technology develops in the future, the Court periodically will publish technical instructions governing the electronic filing of unusually voluminous pleadings, attachments, and exhibits.

C. Any Filing User encountering technical difficulties electronically filing voluminous documents may choose to file them conventionally.

8. Signatures and Retention Requirements.

A. The user log-in and password required to submit documents to the Electronic Filing System serve as the Filing User's signature on all electronic documents filed with the Court. They also serve as a signature for purposes of Fed. R. Civ. P. 11, the Federal Rules of Criminal Procedure, the Local Rules of this Court, and any other purpose for which a signature is required in connection with court proceedings. Electronically filed documents must include a signature block in compliance with Local Rule 11.3.A. The Filing User under whose log-in and password the document is submitted must include an "s/" and the Filing User's typed name in the space where the signature would otherwise appear.

B. Each password is personal to the Filing User, who shall not permit that password to be used by anyone, including other attorneys, other than an authorized agent of the Filing User.

C. Documents containing multiple persons' signatures.

(1). A Filing User who electronically files any document requiring the signature of another individual must either (a) submit an imaged document containing all the necessary signatures inserted by hand; or (b) indicate all persons' signatures on the original document by including on the filed document the designation "s/" followed by each other individual's typed name.

(2). A document containing the signature of a defendant in a criminal case must be filed in an imaged format that contains an image of the defendant's signature.

(3). Original documents containing original signatures of persons other than the Filing User must be retained by the Filing Users until expiration of three years after the time for all appeals in the case.

(4). A designation on a document that one person has affixed another person's signature "by permission" may be used under circumstances when signing by permission would be acceptable on a conventionally filed document.

9. Service of Documents by Electronic Means.

A. The Notice of Electronic Filing that is automatically generated by the Court's Electronic Filing System constitutes service of the filed document on Filing Users. A Filing User may also notify another Filing User of electronically filed documents by other means (*e.g.*, fax, mail, personal delivery), but the service date will still be determined by the Notice of Electronic Filing. Parties who are not Filing Users must be served with a paper copy of any electronically filed document in accordance with the Federal Rules of Civil and Criminal Procedure, and the Local Rules of this Court.

B. A certificate of service must be included with all documents filed electronically, reflecting that service on known Filing Users will be automatically accomplished through the Notice of Electronic Filing and indicating how service was accomplished on any party or counsel who is not a Filing User.

C. If the Court's Electronic Filing System indicates that a Notice of Electronic Filing has not been successfully transmitted to an intended recipient, the Clerk will promptly notify the Filing User who originated the filing so that other service must be attempted. *See* Fed. R. Civ. P. 5(b)(3); Fed. R. Crim. P. 49(b).

10. Notice of Court Orders and Judgments.

A. Immediately upon the entry of an order or judgment in an action assigned to the Electronic Filing System, the Clerk will transmit to Filing Users in the case, in electronic form, a Notice of Electronic Filing.

B. Electronic transmission of the Notice of Electronic Filing constitutes the notice required by Fed. R. Civ. P. 77(d) and Fed. R. Crim. P. 49(c). The Clerk will give notice of orders and judgments by first-class mail to unrepresented persons and to attorneys who are not registered as Filing Users in accordance with the Federal Rules of Civil and Criminal Procedure, and the Local Rules of this Court.

11. Technical Failures. A Filing User whose electronic filing is or would be made untimely as the result of a technical failure may seek appropriate relief from the presiding Judge in the case.

12. Public Access and Confidentiality.

A. A person may review at the Clerk's Office filings that have not been sealed by the Court. A person also may access the Electronic Filing System at the Court's internet site, www.txs.uscourts.gov, by obtaining a PACER log-in and password. A person who has PACER access may retrieve docket sheets and documents; however, some restrictions may apply to certain types of cases or records.

B. Anyone may purchase paper copies, including certified and exemplified copies of electronically filed documents from the Clerk by requesting the copy in person or mailing the request to the Clerk. Each request must designate the case number and document by title or docket entry number. Requests submitted by mail must include a self-addressed, stamped return envelope and the applicable fee provided in 28 U.S.C. § 1914.

C. Transcripts will be electronically available on PACER to the public 90 days after their filing with the court. To comply with the privacy requirements of Fed. R. Civ. P. 5.2 and Fed. R. Crim. P. 49.1, parties must ensure that certain protected information is redacted from transcripts prior to their availability on PACER. During this 90 day period, transcripts will be available for review at the public access terminals in the clerk's office.

D. Under Fed. R. Civ. P. 5.2 and Fed. R. Crim. P. 49.1, effective December 1, 2007, all filers must refrain from including or, where inclusion is necessary, partially redact the following personal identifiers from electronic and conventional filings with the Court:

(1) Social Security Numbers. If an individual's social security number must be included in a pleading, only the last four digits of that number may be used.

(2) Names of Minor Children. If the name of a minor must be mentioned, only the initials of that child may be used.

(3) Dates of Birth. If an individual's date of birth must be included in a pleading, only the year may be used.

(4) Financial Account Numbers. If financial account numbers are relevant, only the last four digits of these numbers may be used.

(5) Home Addresses to the City and State. If a home address must be included, only the city and state may be listed (only applicable to pleadings filed in criminal cases).

[Dated: July 18, 2013.]

GENERAL ORDER NO. 2014–6. IN RE: ADMISSION OF ATTORNEYS AND ELECTRONIC FILING REGISTRATION
SPECIAL ORDER CONCERNING ADMISSION OF ATTORNEYS AND ELECTRONIC FILING TRAINING CLASS

On this date, the undersigned considered the proposal of the Texas Young Lawyers Association concerning the admission of attorneys to practice before this Court and the certification class required to be taken before use of the court's Electronic Filing System. It appearing to be in the best interest of the administration of justice that this proposal be adopted,

It is hereby ORDERED that any approved applicant for admission to this Court who attends the entire 2014 Federal Court Practice Course sponsored by the Texas Young Lawyers Association and TexasBarCLE, to be presented on May 16 and June 20, 2014 and thereafter online at www.TexasBarCLE.com, shall be deemed to have fulfilled the:

(1) Educational requirements for admission set forth in S.D. Tex. L.R. 83.1(G); and

(2) The Court's Electronic Filing System certification class requisite to receiving electronic filing privileges, which addresses signature and notice issues, reviews the Administrative Procedures for Electronic Filing and provides a demonstration of the system.

It is further ORDERED that proof of full attendance at the Course may be evidenced by the applicants' submission of a "Certificate of Attendance" which TexasBarCLE shall provide to applicants who attend the entire course as described above.

[Dated: May 8, 2014.]

SPEEDY TRIAL PLAN

I. INTRODUCTORY MATERIAL

A. This Plan was adopted by the court on the 9th day of May, 1980, to become effective on July 1, 1980.

B. The members of the District Planning Group are:

Chief Judge John V. Singleton
United States District Court
Southern District of Texas
United States Courthouse, Room 11144
515 Rusk
Houston, Texas 77002

Mr. Jesse E. Clark United States District Clerk Southern District of Texas Post Office Box 61010 Houston, Texas 77208	Mr. James McCullough Designee of the Clerk Post Office Box 61010 Houston, Texas 77208
Mr. J. A. "Tony" Canales United States Attorney Post Office Box 61129 Houston, Texas 77208	Mr. Lawrence E. Higgins Chief Probation Officer Post Office Box 61207 Houston, Texas 77208
Mr. Roland E. Dahlin, II Federal Public Defender Post Office Box 61508 Houston, Texas 77208 Houston, Texas 77208	The Honorable H. Lingo Platter United States Magistrate Post Office Box 61408 Houston, Texas 77208
Mr. W. James Kronzer Attorney at Law 800 Commerce Street Houston, Texas 77002	Mr. James A. Schlecht Chief Deputy U. S. Marshal Post Office Box 61608 Houston, Texas 77208
The Honorable William M. Mallet United States Magistrate Post Office Box 1633 Brownsville, Texas 78520	Mr. Morton L. Susman Attorney at Law 2290 Two Shell Plaza Houston, Texas 77002

Reporter
Professor Thomas Black
St. Mary's University Law School
One Camino Santa Maria
San Antonio, Texas 78284

C. Copies of this Plan will be available for public inspection in the office of the United States District Clerk in each division of this district.

[Dated: May 9, 1980.]

II. STATEMENT OF TIME LIMITS AND PROCEDURES FOR ACHIEVING PROMPT DISPOSITION OF CRIMINAL CASES

A. Pursuant to the requirements of Rule 50(b) of the Federal Rules of Criminal Procedure, the Speedy Trial Act of 1974 (18 U.S.C. Chapter 208), the Speedy Trial Act Amendments Act of 1979 (Pub. L. No. 96–43, 93 Stat. 327), and the Federal Juvenile Delinquency Act (18 U.S.C. §§ 5036,

5037), the judges of the United States District Court for the Southern District of Texas have adopted the following time limits and procedures to minimize undue delay and to further the prompt disposition of criminal cases and certain juvenile proceedings.

1. *Applicability.*

a. Offenses. The time limits set forth herein are applicable to all criminal offenses triable in this **court,** * including cases triable by United States Magistrates, except for petty offenses as defined in 18 U.S.C. § 1(3). Except as specifically provided, they are not applicable to proceedings under the Federal Juvenile Delinquency Act. [§ 3172]

* 18 U.S.C. § 3172 defines offense as "any Federal criminal offense which is in violation of any Act of Congress . . ."

b. Persons. The time limits are applicable to persons accused who have not been indicted or informed against as well as those who have, and the word "defendant" includes such persons unless the context indicates otherwise.

2. *Priorities in Scheduling Criminal Cases.* Preference shall be given to criminal proceedings as far as practicable as required by Rule 50(a) of the Federal Rules of Criminal Procedure. The trial of defendants in custody solely because they are awaiting trial and of high-risk defendants as defined in section 5 should be given preference over other criminal cases. [§ 3164(a)]

3. *Time Within Which an Indictment or Information Must be Filed.*

a. Time Limits. If an individual is arrested or served with a summons and the complaint charges an offense to be prosecuted in this district, any indictment or information subsequently filed in connection with such charge shall be filed within 30 days of arrest or service. [§ 3161(b)]

b. Grand Jury Not in Session. If the defendant is charged with a felony to be prosecuted in this district, and no grand jury in the district has been in session during the 30–day period prescribed in subsection (a), such period shall be extended an additional 30 days. [§ 3161(b)]

c. Measurement of Time Periods. If a person has not been arrested or served with a summons on a federal charge, an arrest will be deemed to have been made at such time as the person (i) is held in custody solely for the purpose of responding to a federal charge; (ii) is delivered to the custody of a federal official in connection with a federal charge; or (iii) appears before a judicial officer in connection with a federal charge.

d. Related Procedures.

(1) At the time of the earliest appearance before a judicial officer of a person who has been arrested for an offense not charged in an indictment or information, the judicial officer shall establish for the record the date on which the arrest took place.

(2) In the absence of a showing to the contrary. a summons shall be considered to have been served on the date of service shown on the return thereof.

4. *Time Within Which Trial Must Commence.*

a. Time Limits. The trial of a defendant shall commence not later than 70 days after the last to occur of the following dates:

(1) the date on which an indictment or information is filed in this district;

(2) the date on which a sealed indictment or information is unsealed; or

(3) the date of the defendant's first appearance before a judicial officer of this district. [§ 3161(c)(1)]

b. Retrial; Trial After Reinstatement of an Indictment or Information. The retrial of a defendant shall commence within 70 days from the date the order occasioning the retrial becomes final, as shall the trial of a defendant upon an indictment or information dismissed by a trial court and reinstated following an appeal. If the retrial or trial follows an appeal or collateral attack, the court may extend the period if unavailability of witnesses or other factors resulting from passage of time make trial within 70 days impractical. The extended period shall not exceed 180 days. [§ 3161(d)(2), (e)]

c. Withdrawal of Plea. If a defendant enters a plea of guilty or nolo contendere to any or all charges in an indictment or information and is subsequently permitted to withdraw it, the time limit shall be determined for all counts as if the indictment or information were filed on the day the order permitting withdrawal of the plea became final. [§ 3161(i)]

d. Superseding Charges. If, after an indictment or information has been filed, a complaint, indictment, or information is filed which charges the defendant with the same offense or with an offense required to be joined with that offense, the time limit applicable to the subsequent charge will be determined as follows:

(1) If the original indictment or information was dismissed on motion of the defendant before the filing of the subsequent charge, the time limit shall be determined without regard to the existence of the original charge. [§ 3161(d)(1)]

(2) If the original indictment or information is pending at the time the subsequent charge is filed, the trial shall commence within the time limit for commencement of trial on the original indictment or information. [§ 3161(h)(6)]

(3) If the original indictment or information was dismissed on motion of the United States Attorney before the filing of the subsequent charge, the trial shall commence within the time limit for commencement of trial on the original indictment or information, but the period during which the defendant was not under charges shall be excluded from the computations. Such period is the period between the dismissal of the original indictment or information and the date the time would have commenced to run on the subsequent charge had there been no previous charge. *[§ 3161(h)(6)] If the subsequent charge is contained in a complaint, the formal time limit within which an indictment or information must be obtained on the charge shall be determined without regard to the existence of the original indictment or information, but earlier action may in fact be required if the time limit for commencement of trial is to be satisfied.

*Under the rule of this paragraph, if an indictment was dismissed on May 1, with 20 days remaining within which trial must be commenced, and the defendant was arrested on a new complaint on June 1, the time remaining for trial would be 20 days from June 1: the time limit would be based on the original indictment, but the period from the dismissal to the new arrest would not count.

e. Measurement of Time Periods. For the purposes of this section:

(1) If a defendant signs a written consent to be tried before a magistrate and no indictment or information charging the offense has been filed, the time limit shall run from the date of such consent.

(2) In the event of a transfer to this district under Rule 20 of the Federal Rules of Criminal Procedure, the indictment or information shall be deemed filed in this district when the papers in the proceeding or certified copies thereof are received by the clerk.

(3) A trial in a jury case shall be deemed to commence at the beginning of voir dire.

(4) A trial in a nonjury case shall be deemed to commence on the day the case is called, provided that some step in the trial procedure immediately follows.

f. Related Procedures.

(1) At the time of the defendant's earliest appearance before a judicial officer of this district, the officer will take appropriate steps to assure that the defendant is represented by counsel and shall appoint counsel where appropriate under the Criminal Justice Act and Rule 44 of the Federal Rules of Criminal Procedure.

(2) The court shall have sole responsibility for setting cases for trial after consultation with counsel. Where the same counsel has cases before more than one judge of this court, the judges of the court shall, wherever possible, avoid conflicts so that said counsel can appear in all of his cases so as to avoid, if possible, other counsel having to appear for any defendant, if this can be accomplished without doing violence to the limits set in this Plan. At the time of arraignment or as soon thereafter as is practicable, each case will be set for trial on a day certain or listed for trial on a weekly or other short-term calendar. [§ 3161(a)]

(3) Individual calendars shall be managed so that it will be reasonably anticipated that every criminal case set for trial will be reached during the week of original setting. A conflict in schedules of Assistant United States Attorneys or defense counsel will be ground for a continuance or delayed setting only if approved by the court and called to the court's attention at the earliest practicable time.

(4) In the event that a complaint, indictment, or information is filed against a defendant charged in a pending indictment or information or in an indictment or information dismissed on motion of the United States Attorney, the trial on the new charge shall commence within the time limit for commencement of trial on the original indictment or information unless the court

finds that the new charge is not for the same offense charged in the original indictment or information or an offense required to be joined therewith.

(5) At the time of the filing of a complaint, indictment, or information described in paragraph (4), the United States Attorney shall give written notice to the court and the clerk of that circumstance and of his position with respect to the computation of the time limits.

(6) All pretrial hearings shall be conducted as soon after the arraignment as possible, consistent with the priorities of other matters on the court's criminal docket and with the need of counsel to complete discovery and prepare pretrial motions.

5. *Defendants in Custody and High–Risk Defendants.**

*If a defendant's presence has been obtained through the filing of a detainer with state authorities, the Interstate Agreement on Detainers, 18 U.S.C., Appendix, may require that trial commence before the deadline established by the Speedy Trial Act. See United States v. Mauro, 436 U.S. 340, 356–57 n.24 (1978).

a.   Time Limits.   Notwithstanding any longer time periods that may be permitted under sections 3 and 4, the following time limits will also be applicable to defendants in custody and high-risk defendants as herein defined:

(1) The trial of a defendant held in custody solely for the purpose of trial on a federal charge shall commence within 90 days following the beginning of continuous custody.

(2) The trial of a high-risk defendant shall commence within 90 days of the designation as high-risk. [§ 3164(b)]

b.   Definition of "High–Risk Defendant."   A high-risk defendant is one reasonably designated by the United States Attorney as posing a danger to himself or any other person or to the community.

c.   Measurement of Time Periods.   For the purposes of this section:

(1) A defendant is deemed to be in detention awaiting trial when he is arrested on a federal charge or otherwise held for the purpose of responding to a federal charge.   Detention is deemed to be solely because the defendant is awaiting trial unless the person exercising custodial authority has an independent basis (not including a detainer) for continuing to hold the defendant.

(2) If a case is transferred pursuant to Rule 20 of the Federal Rules of Criminal Procedure and the defendant subsequently rejects disposition under Rule 20 or the court declines to accept the plea, a new period of continuous detention awaiting trial will begin at that time.

(3) A trial shall be deemed to commence as provided in sections 4(e)(3) and 4(e)(4).

d.   Related Procedures.

(1) If a defendant is being held in custody solely for the purpose of awaiting trial, the United States Attorney shall advise the court at the earliest practicable time of the date of the beginning of such custody.

(2) The United States Attorney shall advise the court at the earliest practicable time (usually at the hearing with respect to bail) if the defendant is considered by him to be high risk.

(3) If the court finds that the filing of a "high-risk" designation as a public record may result in prejudice to the defendant, it may order the designation sealed for such period as is necessary to protect the defendant's right to a fair trial, but not beyond the time that the court's judgment in the case becomes final.   During the time the designation is under seal, it shall be made known to the defendant and his counsel but shall not be made known to other persons without the permission of the court.

6. *Exclusion of Time From Computations.*

a.   Applicability.   The periods of delay set forth in 18 U.S.C. § 3161(h) shall apply in computing the time limits for sections 3, 4, and 5.   Such periods of delay shall be included in computing the minimum period for commencement of trial under section 7.

b.   Records of Excludable Time.   The clerk of the court shall enter on the docket, in the form prescribed by the Administrative office of the United States Courts information with respect to excludable periods of time for each criminal defendant.   With respect to proceedings prior to the filing of an indictment or information, excludable time shall be reported to the clerk by the United States Attorney.

c. Stipulations.

(1) The attorney for the government and the attorney for the defendant may at any time enter into stipulations with respect to the accuracy of the docket entries recording excludable time.

(2) To the extent that the amount of time stipulated by the parties does not exceed the amount recorded on the docket for any excludable Period of delay, the stipulation shall be conclusive as between the parties unless it has no basis in fact or law. It shall similarly be conclusive as to a codefendant for the limited purpose of determining, under 18 U.S.C. § 3161(h)(7), whether time has run against the defendant entering into the stipulation.

(3) To the extent that the amount of time stipulated exceeds the amount recorded on the docket, the stipulation shall have no effect unless approved by the court.

d. Preindictment Procedures.

(1) In the event that the United States Attorney anticipates that an indictment or information will not be filed within the time limit set forth in section 3, he may file a written motion with the court for a determination of excludable time. In the event that the United States Attorney seeks a continuance under 18 U.S.C. § 3161(h)(8), he shall file a written motion with the court requesting such a continuance.

(2) The motion of the United States Attorney shall state (i) the period of time proposed for exclusion, and (ii) the basis of the proposed exclusion. If the motion is for a continuance under 18 U.S.C. § 3161(h)(8), it shall also state whether or not the defendant is being held in custody on the basis of the complaint. In appropriate circumstances, the motion may include a request that some or all of the supporting material be considered ex parte and in camera.

(3) The court may grant a continuance under 18 U.S.C. § 3161(h)(8) for either a specific of time or a period to be determined by reference to an event (such as recovery from illness) not within the control of the government. If the continuance is to a date not certain, the court shall require one or both parties to inform the court promptly when and if the circumstances that justify the continuance no longer exist. In addition, the court shall require one or both parties to file periodic reports bearing on the continued existence of such circumstances. The court shall determine the frequency of such reports in the light of the facts of the particular case.

e. Postindictment Procedures.

(1) At each appearance of counsel before the court, counsel shall examine the clerk's records of excludable time for completeness and accuracy and shall bring to the court's immediate attention any claim that the clerk's record is in any way incorrect.

(2) In the event that the court continues a trial beyond the time limit set forth in sections 4 or 5, the court shall determine whether the limit may be recomputed by excluding time pursuant to 18 U.S.C. § 3161(h).

(3) If it is determined that a continuance is justified, the court shall set forth its findings in the record, either orally or in writing. If the continuance is granted under 18 U.S.C. § 3161(h)(8), the court shall also set forth its reasons for finding that the ends of justice served by granting the continuance outweigh the best interests of the public and the defendant in a speedy trial. If the continuance is to a date not certain, the court shall require one or both parties to inform the court promptly when and if the circumstances that justify the continuance no longer exist. In addition, the court shall require one or both parties to file periodic reports bearing on the continued existence of such circumstances. The court shall determine the frequency of such reports in the light of the facts of the particular case.

(4) In the event that either the United States Attorney or counsel for the defendant seeks a continuance under 18 U.S.C. § 3161(h)(8), he shall file a written motion with the court. The motion shall state (i) whether or not the defendant is being held in custody on the basis of the complaint, (ii) the period of time proposed for exclusion, and (iii) the basis of the proposed exclusion. In appropriate circumstances, it may include a request that some or all of the supporting material be considered ex parte and in camera.

7. *Minimum Period for Defense Preparation.* Unless the defendant consents in writing to the contrary, the trial shall not commence earlier than 30 days from the date on which the indictment or information is filed or, if later, from the date on which counsel first enters an appearance or on which the defendant expressly waives counsel and elects to proceed pro se. In circumstances in which the 70–day time limit for commencing trial on a charge in an indictment or information is determined by reference to an earlier indictment or information pursuant to section 4(d), the 30–day minimum

period shall also be determined by reference to the earlier indictment or information. When prosecution is resumed on an original indictment or information following a mistrial, appeal, or withdrawal of a guilty plea, a new 30–day minimum period will not begin to run. The court will in all cases schedule trials so as to permit defense counsel adequate preparation time in the light of all the circumstances. [§ 3161(c)(2)]

8. *Time Within Which Defendant Should be Sentenced.*

a. Time Limit. A defendant shall ordinarily be sentenced within [45] days of the date of his conviction or plea of guilty or nolo contendere.

b. Related Procedures. If the defendant and his counsel consent thereto, a presentence investigation may be commenced prior to a plea of guilty or nolo contendere or a conviction.

9. *Juvenile Proceedings.*

a. Time Within Which Trial Must Commence. An alleged delinquent who is in detention pending trial shall be brought to trial within 30 days of the date on which such detention was begun, as provided in 18 U.S.C. § 5036.

b. Time of Dispositional Hearing. If a juvenile is adjudicated delinquent, a separate dispositional hearing shall be held no later than 20 court days after trial, unless the court has ordered further study of the juvenile in accordance with 18 U.S.C. § 5037(c).

10. *Sanctions.*

a. Dismissal or Release From Custody. Failure to comply with the requirements of Title I of the Speedy Trial Act may entitle the defendant to dismissal of the charges against him or to release from pretrial custody. Nothing in this Plan shall be construed to require that a case be dismissed or a defendant be released from custody in circumstances in which such action would not be required by 18 U.S.C. §§ 3162 and 3164.*

*Dismissal may also be required in some cases under the Interstate Agreement on Detainers, 18 U.S.C., Appendix.

b. High–Risk Defendants. A high-risk defendant whose trial has not commenced within the time limit set forth in 18 U.S.C. § 3164(b) shall, if the failure to commence trial was through no fault of the attorney for the government, have his release conditions automatically reviewed. A high-risk defendant who is found by the court to have intentionally delayed the trial of his case shall be subject to an order of the court modifying his nonfinancial conditions of release under chapter 207 of title 18 of the United States Code to ensure that he shall appear at trial as required. [§ 3164(c)]

c. Discipline of Attorneys. In a case in which counsel (i) knowingly allows the case to be set for trial without disclosing the fact that a necessary witness would be unavailable for trial, (ii) files a motion solely for the purpose of delay which he knows is frivolous and without merit, (iii) makes a statement for the purpose of obtaining a continuance which he knows to be false and which is material to the granting of the continuance, or (iv) otherwise willfully fails to proceed to trial without justification consistent with 18 U.S.C. § 3161, the court may punish such counsel as provided in 18 U.S.C. § 3162 (b)–(c).

d. Alleged Juvenile Delinquents. An alleged delinquent in custody whose trial has not commenced within the time limit set forth in 18 U.S.C. § 5036 shall be entitled to dismissal of his case pursuant to that section unless the Attorney General shows that the delay was consented to or caused by the juvenile or his counsel, or would be in the interest of justice in the particular case.

11. *Persons Serving Terms of Imprisonment.* If the United States Attorney knows that a person charged with an offense is serving a term of imprisonment in any penal institution, he shall promptly seek to obtain the presence of the prisoner for trial, or cause a detainer to be filed, in accordance with the provisions of 18 U.S.C. § 3161(j).

12. *Effective Dates.*

a. The amendments to the Speedy Trial Act made by Pub. L. No. 96–43 became effective August 2, 1979. To the extent that this revision of the district's Plan does more than merely reflect the amendments, the revised Plan shall take effect upon approval of the reviewing panel designated in accordance with 18 U.S.C. § 3165(c). However, the dismissal sanction and the sanctions against attorneys authorized by 18 U.S.C. § 3162 and reflected in sections 10(a) and (c) of this Plan shall apply only to defendants whose cases are commenced by arrest or summons on or after July 1, 1980, and to indictments and informations filed on or after that date.

b. If a defendant was arrested or served with a summons before July 1, 1980, the time within which an information or indictment must be filed shall be determined under the Plan that was in effect at the time of such arrest or service.

c. If a defendant was arraigned before August 2, 1979, the time within which the trial must commence shall be determined under the Plan that was in effect at the time of such arraignment.

d. If a defendant was in custody on August 2, 1979, solely because he was awaiting trial, the 90–day period under section 5 shall be computed from that date.

III. SUMMARY OF EXPERIENCE UNDER THE ACT WITHIN THE DISTRICT

A. Progress Toward Meeting the Permanent Time Limits. The statistical tables attached hereto indicate a steady progress during the preceding years toward compliance with the ultimate speedy trial time limits. Current performance statistics indicate substantial compliance with most of the time limits by most of the courts and agencies involved, and it is the consensus of the members of the Planning Group, based upon their observations and experience, that full compliance can be accomplished.

B. Problems Encountered.

1. The United States Attorney has encountered problems in the form of delays in obtaining reports from law enforcement agencies which are necessary to make effective presentations to a grand jury preparatory to indictment. This, of course, will affect compliance with the 30–day time limit from arrest to indictment.

2. The absence of a full-time speedy trial monitor in multidivision districts has proved to be a problem causing inefficient reporting and ineffective control. This problem is expected to be resolved or at least eased by the use of Courtran computer reporting throughout the district.

3. The communication from district to district has been poor and without uniform standard. There is a need for standardized notification on out-of-district arrests, in order that proper calendaring and notification within speedy trial limits may be made.

4. The burden is on the defendant's counsel to prepare for trial within the 70–day limit in complex or multiple-count criminal cases.

C. Incidence of, and Reasons for, Requests for Allowances of Extension of Time Beyond the District Standards [18 U.S.C. § 3166(b)(1)-(4)]. No known requests or allowances to date.

D. If There Have Been Cases Not in Compliance With the Time Limits for Indictment and Commencement of Trial Under 18 U.S.C. § 3161(b) and (c), the Reasons Why the Exclusions Were Inadequate to Accommodate Reasonable Periods of Delay [18 U.S.C. § 3167(b)]. No reasons.

E. The Effect on Criminal Justice Administration of the Prevailing Time Limits [18 U.S.C. § 3166(b)(5)]. The administration of criminal justice has progressed steadily toward the ultimate goals of the Act. The resulting effect has been prompt and efficient movement of criminal dockets as reflected by the attached tables.

F. Effect of Compliance With the Time Limits on the Civil Calendar [18 U.S.C. § 3166(b)(9)]. A by-product has been the negative effect on the civil dockets in the various divisions of this district. Regular civil dockets and the orderly scheduling of civil cases have often been difficult. On occasions civil cases have had to be postponed or tried on a haphazard basis when time becomes available.

G. Frequency of Use of Sanctions Under the "Interim" Time Limits [18 U.S.C. § 3166(b)(3)]. During the administration of the Speedy Trial Act, the exercise of sanctions as provided by 18 U.S.C. § 3166(b)(3) has not been utilized.

IV. STATEMENT OF PROCEDURES AND INNOVATIONS THAT HAVE BEEN OR WILL BE ADOPTED BY THE DISTRICT COURT TO EXPEDITE THE DISPOSITION OF CRIMINAL CASES IN ACCORDANCE WITH THE SPEEDY TRIAL ACT [18 U.S.C. § 3167(b)]

A. Site of Grand Jury, Arraignment, and Trial. (Modified September 1997)

Because of the limited criminal business of the division of this court at Galveston, the judges of this court approve the consolidation of the Galveston and Houston Divisions of our court, for the purpose of indictment and arraignment. Continuing the practice in effect since July 1, 1976, grand juries sitting in Houston shall be composed of members residing in the Houston and Galveston Divisions. While defendants accused of committing crimes in either the Houston or Galveston Divisions of our court will be indicted by a grand jury from both divisions while sitting in Houston, for the purpose of arraignment, defendants accused of committing criminal acts in the Galveston Divisions will be arraigned in the Houston Division. Those accused of committing criminal acts in the Galveston Division of this court will be tried, if necessary, in the Galveston Division, unless such defendants waive this right in writing.

B. Scheduling of Grand Juries. (Modified September 1997)

Grand juries will be scheduled to meet at least once each thirty days in every division, and more often as required. The United States Attorney must be informed immediately of all arrests by complaint by the arresting agency so that indictments may be sought within thirty days. It is the recommendation of the Planning Group that grand juries meet on a Tuesday and that arraignments be scheduled on a regular basis on Friday of the following week. This will assist the clerk in sending out arraignment notices.

C. Submission of Offense Reports. Law enforcement agencies should accelerate the submission of case reports to the United States Attorney in order to comply with the time limit from arrest to indictment.

D. Notice of Actions. Since the clerk of the court will have the responsibility of keeping the courts informed of all defendants awaiting trial and seeing that the time limits under the Act and this adopted Plan are not violated, it is essential that the clerk receive prompt reporting at all stages beginning with the arrest. In this connection, the magistrates, the United States Attorney, and the United States Marshal are requested to inform the clerk of all actions that they take in connection with any defendant as soon as the action occurs, including the addresses of the defendant and of counsel and other pertinent information, as well as any changes that may occur.

With respect to defendants against whom complaints have already been filed, the United States Attorney, whenever possible, will provide the clerk with a list of those defendants whose names will be brought before a grand jury, so that the clerk can prepare in advance notices of arraignment to be mailed out to those defendants who are in fact indicted. The list furnished by the United States Attorney shall not be filed, and it shall be kept confidential by the clerk. A copy of the grand jury assignment sheet shall be delivered to the Criminal Section of the Clerk's Office upon the concurrence of the grand jury to indict or true bill.

E. Court Calendars. The Planning Group recommends that court calendars be provided to the office of the United States Marshal at least 24 hours before scheduled court appearances. Court calendars should not be changed within 24 hours of scheduled court appearances except in unusual circumstances.

F. Representation by Counsel. The Planning Group recommends that in each case as soon after arrest as possible, a determination be made as to whether the defendant has counsel. If a defendant indicates he does not have and cannot retain counsel, he should be taken before a United States Magistrate for a determination of his eligibility for appointed counsel. If a defendant is eligible for appointed counsel, counsel should be appointed immediately. If possible, defendants should be represented by counsel at the initial appearance.

G. Master Docket Control Sheet. The Planning Group recommends that the United States District Clerk use a master docket control sheet for multiple-defendant cases at both the magistrate and district court level.

H. Court Settings. The Planning Group recommends that the court consult with counsel for the defendant and with counsel for the government before scheduling court appearances and further recommends that counsel be given the maximum time feasible after arraignment for the submission of pretrial motions.

I. Continuances. The Planning Group recommends that the court exercise the discretion granted by 18 U.S.C.A. § 3161(h)(8) to grant continuances where the facts indicate that the ends of justice will thereby be served. The Planning Group further recommends that there be a presumption that the ends of justice served by granting a continuance outweigh the best interests of the public and the defendant in a speedy trial in (i) tax and other types of fraud cases, (ii) complex multi-defendant conspiracy cases, (iii) cases with out-of-town witnesses, (iv) cases in which the evidence includes audio tapes recorded as a result of wiretap, (v) cases with multiple defendants and multiple counts, and (vi) cases involving white-collar crime, so long as the motion for continuance is filed at least 20 days before the expiration of the time limit.

J. Waiver. The Planning Group recommends that a policy be uniformly applied throughout the district permitting a defendant to waive, in writing and with the concurrence of the United States Attorney, his right to be tried within the Speedy Trial Act time limits.

K. The United States Attorney has adopted a practice of indicting before arrest so as to eliminate problems with the 30-day time interval whenever feasible.

L. Civil Docket. In all divisions of the district, the court should hold regular civil dockets and try civil cases to the fullest extent possible between priority criminal trials.

V. STATEMENT OF ADDITIONAL RESOURCES NEEDED TO ACHIEVE COMPLIANCE WITH THE ACT [18 U.S.C. § 3166(d)]

A. Magistrates. There is an immediate need for an additional magistrate in the Houston Division of our court and for making the part-time magistrate in McAllen, Texas, a full-time position.

B. United States Attorney.

1. Three additional Assistant United States Attorneys are needed. Additional attorneys are needed to comply with the Speedy Trial Act and to avoid the need for restricting the number of cases handled by the United States Attorney or the need to defer cases to state prosecution.

2. One additional person with either legal, paralegal, or specialized clinical training, to be located in Houston, Texas, is needed to monitor the status of all defendants in the district, to make certain that the time limits are not running out with respect to any defendant, and to assist in the reports that the United States Attorney must make to the United States District Clerk.

C. United States District Clerk.

1. *Personnel.* Five additional deputies are needed. One deputy clerk is needed in the Houston Division, to act as speedy trial monitor on a district-wide basis. One deputy clerk is needed to coordinate the Courtran program throughout the district and to train other deputies in the operation of Courtran terminals. One deputy clerk is needed as a Courtran terminal operator in each of the division offices in Brownsville, Corpus Christi, and Laredo.

2. *Computer Access.* The United States District Clerk needs to have district-wide access to the national Courtran system. Four Courtran terminals are needed: one in each current division except Victoria and Galveston. Access to the Courtran system is necessary in order to have sufficient timely information to manage the criminal case load in compliance with Speedy Trial Act time limits.

D. United States Marshal.

1. At least five additional operation deputies are needed in the Houston Division to replace deputies reassigned from Houston to Corpus Christi, Galveston, and McAllen.

2. Since the institution of the Speedy Trial Act, the United States Marshal has found that their overtime payment for salary has increased by 30 percent. The Speedy Trial Act has compelled the United States Marshal to keep deputies in courts during the workweek on a daily basis. This circumstance is forcing the marshal's service to serve process after working hours and to transport prisoners to institutions and provide in-district movement on weekends to keep current and fulfill their mission.

E. Other. Undoubtedly, the several federal law enforcement agencies will need additional secretarial help in order to prepare their case reports in time for prompt presentation to grand juries. Now, as during the transition period to date, the slowness in obtaining complete offense reports impedes compliance with Speedy Trial Act time limits.

VI. RECOMMENDATIONS FOR CHANGES IN STATUTES, RULES OR ADMINISTRATIVE PROCEDURES [18 U.S.C. § 3166(b)(7), (d)(3)]

A. Speedy Trial Act.

1. The Planning Group recommends that the Speedy Trial Act be amended to provide longer time limits for the following types or classes of cases: (i) tax and other types of fraud cases; (ii) complex

multi-defendant cases; (iii) cases with out-of-town witnesses; (iv) cases in which the evidence consists primarily of audio tapes recorded as a result of a wiretap; (v) cases with multiple defendants and multiple counts; and (vi) cases involving white-collar crime.

2. The Planning Group recommends that the Speedy Trial Act be amended to allow for excludable time when, in a pending case, the ultimate legal issue involved is pending in another case before the appellate courts and the defendant has no objection to delaying his trial until the issue is determined in the former proceeding.

3. The Planning Group recommends that the Speedy Trial Act be amended to allow a more realistic exclusion of time when a defendant is out of state and must be transported into the district for trial. Time taken by the United States Marshal to bring a defendant before a judicial officer of the district where the defendant will be tried should be excluded, and the limits of the act should not apply until a defendant is available to the court in the district where the trial will be held.

4. Reasons supporting proposed amendments:

a. The members of the Planning Group favor the amendments proposed above as a result of their collective experience in trying to discharge their respective responsibilities and comply with the Speedy Trial Act during the interim period.

b. The Speedy Trial Act requires that local plans accelerate the disposition of criminal cases consistent with objectives of effective law enforcement and also consistent with fairness to accused persons. It is the experience of defense counsel that they cannot discharge their duties to represent their clients zealously within the bounds of the law and conduct the investigation, preparation, and legal research that representation entails within the stringent time limitations required by the final phase of the Act.

c. After indictment and arraignment in a case that is set for trial, it is difficult for defense counsel to complete discovery in time to file meaningful pretrial motions. It is difficult for the United States Attorney to respond to defense counsel's pretrial motions within the current limits of the act. This lack of response time is especially aggravated in multiple-defendant cases where the United States Attorney must respond in a limited time to many motions submitted by numerous defense counsel.

B. Other Statutes. Congress should assure that all law enforcement agencies have the necessary personnel in order to perform their duties and to submit complete and accurate case reports promptly to the United States Attorney for prompt presentation of cases to a grand jury.

C. Forms and Reporting Procedures.

1. *Forms.* The criminal docket packet used in conjunction with speedy trial reporting is designed for individual defendants. For effective docketing in multi-defendant cases, there should be an adoption of a master docket format. This would aid not only the docket clerk but also the appeals clerk if/when more than one defendant appeals. Communication between districts indicates that fragmented and individual initiative has been used to overcome this problem. Certainly, it would appear more realistic to develop a national standardized master docket.

2. *Reporting Procedures.* Reporting procedures on a national level are adequate, but in local reporting, adequate monitoring of each judge's case load is difficult. Some thought should be given to the immediate use of Courtran in multi-judge and division districts. Immediate response to judicial inquiry could be met, thus eliminating time-consuming individual audits and preparation of intradistrict reports. Also, it would be more effective in allowing immediate and informational review of pending case loads. Additionally, composite reporting from the Administrative Office has frequently been in error, resulting in confusion, delay, and frustration.

VII. INCIDENCE AND LENGTH OF, REASONS FOR, AND REMEDIES FOR DETENTION PRIOR TO TRIAL (18 U.S.C. § 3166(b)(6)]

In our district, a significant number of defendants are detained prior to trial. The number of detainees decrease markedly after the tenth day after initial appearance before the magistrate. These facts are reflected by Table 3 of the statistical tables in section VIII of the Plan.

The reason for this high initial incidence of detained defendants is inherent in the geographic location of our district. The southern boundary of our district is also the border between the United States and Mexico. Since many of our defendants are aliens here and citizens of a close foreign county, if released before trial they can easily flee the country and the jurisdiction of the court. As indicated by Table 3, however, the cases of these defendants are still being handled within Speedy Trial Act time limits.

Remedy: none.

FOR ATTACHMENTS, PLEASE SEE ORIGINAL GENERAL ORDER ON FILE IN THE CLERK'S OFFICE.

[Adopted May 9, 1980, approved by the Judicial Council of the Fifth Circuit, June 10, 1980. Amended August 28, 1997, approved by the Judicial Council of the Fifth Circuit, October 20, 1997.]

JURY SELECTION PLAN

GENERAL ORDER NO. 2013–6. IN THE MATTER OF REVISED ORDER ESTABLISHING A PLAN FOR JURY SELECTION FOR THE SOUTHERN DISTRICT OF TEXAS

It appearing to the court that the order establishing the method for the selection of grand and petit jurors in this district adopted July 31, 1968, to comply with the Jury Selection and Service Act of 1968 (Pub. L. No. 90–274, 28 U.S.C.A. § 1861 et seq.), as amended through October 13, 2008 should be modified;

And it being the policy of the United States, as enunciated by the above-named statute, (a) that all litigants entitled to trial by jury shall have the right to grand and petit juries selected at random from a fair cross section of the community in the district or division wherein the court convenes; (b) that all citizens shall have the opportunity to be considered for service on grand and petit juries in the United States District Courts and shall have an obligation to serve when summoned for that purpose; and (c) that no citizen shall be excluded from service as a grand or petit juror on account of race, color, religion, sex, national origin, or economic status;

IT IS THEREFORE ORDERED:

1. This Plan shall apply and pertain to the entire Southern District of Texas, and to each of the divisions thereof. This district, as provided by 28 U.S.C.A. § 124, is composed of seven divisions, each being comprised of the counties as follows:

Brownsville Division—counties of Cameron and Willacy.

Corpus Christi Division-counties of Aransas, Bee, Brooks, Duval, Jim Wells, Kenedy, Kleburg, Live Oak, Nueces and San Patricio.

Galveston Division-counties of Brazoria, Chambers, Galveston, and Matagorda.

Houston Division-counties of Austin, Brazos, Colorado, Fayette, Fort Bend, Grimes, Harris, Madison, Montgomery, San Jacinto, Walker, Waller, and Wharton.

Laredo Division-counties of Jim Hogg, La Salle, McMullen, Webb, and Zapata.

McAllen Division-counties of Hidalgo and Starr.

Victoria Division—counties of Calhoun, DeWitt, Goliad, Jackson, Lavaca, Refugio, and Victoria.

2. **Management of Jury Selection Process.** The Clerk of Court is authorized to manage the jury selection process, acting under the supervision and control of the Chief Judge of this court. In the event of absence or disability of the Chief Judge, the judge in active service and senior in commission shall serve. The judges to whom the work of a division of this court is assigned by the Chief Judge by general order shall be in charge of the day-to-day operation of the jury selection process in that division (i.e. such judges shall, as needed, order the addition of names to the wheel, the drawing of names therefrom, the granting of temporary excuses, etc.).

Pursuant to 28 U.S.C. § 1861, all litigants "have the right to grand and petit jurors selected at random from a fair cross section of the community." The court uses a two-step process to select jurors: a qualifying step, followed by a summoning step. A master jury wheel is created by selecting names at random from the voter registration lists. Then, names are randomly drawn periodically from the master jury wheel to receive juror qualification questionnaires. Individuals' answers to these questionnaires determine whether they are legally qualified to serve. If so, the names of those persons are put on a second wheel, a qualified jury wheel. As prospective jurors are needed for a specific trial or grand jury, juror summonses are sent to persons randomly selected from the qualified wheel. All of these selections are carried out through a properly programmed electronic data processing system for pure randomized selection. The pure randomized process ensures that the mathematical odds of any single name being picked are substantially equal.

3. **Source of Names.** It is the considered judgment of this court that voter registration lists from each county do and will furnish a fair cross section of the community of this district, and of each division thereof, and such voter registration lists shall be the exclusive source of names of prospective jurors to be chosen as hereinafter provided.

4. **Authorization for Electronic Data Processing System.** This court finds it advantageous to use a properly programmed electronic data processing system to maintain the master jury wheel and perform other clerical services related to the jury system. Accordingly, the Clerk is authorized to

make such arrangements and procure such assistance as necessary to establish an electronic data system, or a combination manual and electronic records system, to perform the duties of the Clerk as hereinafter designated in a manner to achieve the same results as the following manual selection procedure.

This district will utilize the automated data processing equipment furnished by a contractor and in compliance with resolution by the Judicial Conference of the United States, to select the names from complete source list databases in electronic media for the master jury wheel. This process will be accomplished by a purely randomized process through a properly programmed electronic data processing system, as more fully described in Section 9.

5. The Master Jury Wheel and Selection of Names Therefor. Names of prospective jurors to serve on grand and petit juries shall be selected at random, in the manner hereinafter set out, from the voter registration lists of the various counties comprising each division.

6. The voter registration lists referred to shall be those compiled and maintained by the County Tax Assessor–Collector of each county showing the names of those persons registered to vote in the last general election as supplemented by the inclusion of subsequent registrants to the latest practicable date.

7. Such voter registration information is supplied by the Tax Assessor–Collector of each county from voter registration lists for each precinct within such county to the Office of the Secretary of State in Austin, Texas. It is the judgment of this court that the voter registration data used to construct the Master Jury Wheel may be acquired either directly from the County Tax Assessor–Collector of each county or from the Office of the Secretary of State in Austin, Texas, provided the data acquired from either source is the most current information available and has been updated to the last practicable date.

8. Having secured such lists as to each precinct in each county, the lists for a given county shall be placed in numerical order (i.e. the list for Precinct No. 1, followed by the list for Precinct No. 2, followed by the list for Precinct No. 3, etc.), which shall constitute the voter registration list for that county. Following the alphabetical order of the names of the counties, the lists from the several counties in a division will be assembled, and collectively will constitute the voter registration list for that division.

Such lists for each of the divisions of this court shall be kept and maintained by the Clerk in each such division, or may be kept either jointly or severally in a duly authorized data processing center.

9. In each division the Clerk shall maintain a master jury wheel for that division, into which the names, or the identifying numbers, of those selected at random from the voter registration lists for that division shall be placed.

The court will by order indicate from time to time the number of names to be placed in the master wheel. The Clerk will select names from complete source list databases in electronic media for the master jury wheel by a purely randomized process through a properly programmed electronic data processing system. Such random selections of names from the source lists for inclusion in the master wheel by data computer personnel must insure that each county within the jury division is substantially proportionally represented in the master jury wheel in accordance with 28 U.S.C. § 1863(b)(3). The selections of names from the source list must also insure that the mathematical odds of any single name being picked are substantially equal.

10. The court may order additional names to be placed in the master jury wheel from time to time as necessary.

11. On the initial refilling of the master wheel in each division, not less than one percent (1%) of the total number of names appearing on the voter registration lists for that division shall be placed in such wheel.

12. The master wheel of each division shall be emptied and refilled no later than October 1 of the year following a presidential general election. Each master jury wheel shall be emptied and refilled periodically every four years.

13. Drawing from the Master Jury Wheel. From time to time as directed by the court, the Clerk shall draw at random from the master jury wheel the names of as many persons as may be required by court order for jury service, The clerk shall post a general notice in the form of Section 2, paragraph 2 for public review in the clerk's office and on the court's website explaining the process by which names are periodically and randomly drawn. A properly programmed electronic data processing system for pure randomized selection will be used to select names from the master wheel provided that the system insures that the mathematical odds of any single name being picked are substantially equal. The Clerk shall mail to every person whose name is drawn from the master wheel a juror qualification form (as furnished by the Administrative Office of the United States Courts and as approved by the Judicial Conference of the United States), accompanied by instructions to fill out and return the form, duly signed and sworn, to the Clerk by mail or to submit the information required by the form through the court's website within ten (10) days. If the person is unable to fill out the form, another shall do it for him and shall indicate that he has done so and the reason therefor. In any case in which it appears that there is an omission, ambiguity, or error in a form, the Clerk shall return the form with instructions to the person to make such additions or corrections as may be necessary and to return the form to the Clerk within ten (10) days. Any person who fails to return a completed juror qualification form as instructed may be summoned by the Clerk forthwith to appear before the Clerk to fill out a juror qualification form.

14. Persons Exempt from Jury Service and Excuses on Individual Request.

(a) *Persons Exempt.* The court finds that exemption of the following groups of persons or occupational classes is in the public interest and would not be inconsistent with the Act; accordingly, members of such groups are barred from jury service.

(1) Members in active service in the Armed Forces of the United States.

(2) Members of the fire or police departments of any state, city, municipality, district, territory, possession, or subdivision thereof.

(3) Public Officers in the executive, legislative, or judicial branches of the government of the United States, or of any state, district, territory, possession, or subdivision thereof, who are actively engaged in the performance of official duties. ("Public Officer" shall mean a person who is either elected to public office or who is directly appointed by a person elected to public office.)

(b) *Excuses on Individual Request.* The court hereby finds that jury service by members of the following occupational classes or groups of persons would entail undue hardship or extreme inconvenience to the members thereof, and the excuse of such members will not be inconsistent with the Act, and shall be granted upon individual request:

(1) Persons having active care and custody of a child or children under the age of ten (10) years whose health and/or safety would be jeopardized by their absence for jury service; or a person who is essential to the care of the aged or infirm persons and who is not employed outside of the home.

(2) Persons who have served as a grand or petit juror in federal court within the past two years. In this connection, in any two-year period, no person shall be required to

(i) serve or attend court for prospective service as a petit juror for a total of more than thirty days, except when necessary to complete service in a particular case, or

(ii) serve on more than one grand jury, or

(iii) serve as both a grand and petit juror.

(3) Persons over seventy (70) years of age.

(4) Members of federal law enforcement agencies (i.e., FBI agents, postal inspectors, customs agents, etc.).

(5) Members of volunteer safety organizations who work in an official capacity, without compensation, as fire fighters, members of a rescue squad or members of an ambulance crew.

15. Determination of Qualifications, Excuses, and Exemptions.

(a) The court upon its own initiative or upon recommendation of the Clerk, or the Clerk under supervision of the court, shall determine solely on the basis of information provided on the juror qualification form and other competent evidence whether a person is unqualified for, exempt, or to be excused from jury service. The Clerk shall enter such determination in the space provided on the juror qualification form and on any alphabetical list of names drawn from the master jury wheel. If a person did not appear in response to a summons, such fact shall be noted on said list.

(b) In making such determination, the court or Clerk under supervision of the court, shall deem any person qualified to serve on grand and petit juries in the district unless he:

(1) is not a citizen of the United States eighteen years old who has resided for a period of one year within the judicial district;

(2) is unable to read, write and understand the English language with a degree of proficiency sufficient to fill out satisfactorily the juror qualification form;

(3) is unable to speak the English language;

(4) is incapable, by reason of mental or physical infirmity, to render satisfactory jury service, or

(5) has a charge pending against him for the commission of, or has been convicted in a state or federal court of record of, a crime punishable by imprisonment for more than one year and his civil rights have not been restored.

(c) The court shall have the authority to transmit to the Office of the Secretary of State in Austin, Texas the names of those individuals who are deemed disqualified under section 15 (b)l for claiming non-citizenship in the United States.

16. Qualified Jury Wheel. The Clerk shall maintain separate qualified jury wheels for each division in the district, and shall place in such wheel the names of all persons drawn from the master jury wheel who are not disqualified, exempt, or excused pursuant to this Plan. The Clerk shall insure that at all times at least 300 names are contained in each division's qualified wheel. The qualified jury wheel in each division shall be emptied and refilled effective October 1 of each year in which the master jury wheel is emptied and refilled, pursuant to Section 12 of this Plan. The qualified wheel shall then be periodically supplemented with the names of additional qualified persons from time to time as the need should occur during the life of the master jury wheel.

17. Drawing of Names From the Qualified Wheel. In each division, the names of persons for service as grand or petit jurors shall be drawn by the Clerk at random from the qualified wheel at such times and in such numbers as shall be ordered by the court. The clerk shall post a general notice in the form of Section 2, paragraph 2 for public review in the clerk's office and on the court's website explaining the process by which names are periodically and randomly drawn. A properly programmed electronic data processing system for pure randomized selection will be used to select names from the qualified wheel provided such system insures that the mathematical odds of any single name being picked are substantially equal. Such names shall form a pool from which both grand and petit jurors may be summoned. The Clerk shall use the following procedure for insuring the privacy of those people whose names are selected.

(a) The names so drawn shall not be disclosed to any person other than employees of the United States in the performance of their official duties, until after such jurors have been qualified and sworn by a judge or officer of the Court. The court may direct an earlier disclosure of the names drawn from the qualified jury wheel when the interests of justice require, and shall do so when required by statute (see, e.g., 18 U.S.C.A. § 3432). Unless ordered by the court, the names of jurors summoned for service shall not be disclosed except as provided in subsections (b) and (c) of this section.

(1) In each division, the Clerk shall prepare a list of names of persons drawn from the qualified wheel for grand or petit juror service. The Clerk shall issue or cause to be issued summons directed to the persons so drawn by use of first-class mail. In the event of an unanticipated shortage of available petit jurors, additional names may be drawn from the qualified wheel on order of the court.

(2) In the Galveston and Houston divisions, all grand juries shall sit in the Houston division, with members summoned from among those qualified for service in the Galveston or Houston division. The Clerk shall prepare a list of names of persons drawn from the qualified wheel of each division in a proportion equal to the proportion of registered voters between the two divisions. He shall issue or cause to be issued summons directed to the persons so drawn by use of first-class mail, requiring that such persons report for service to the Houston divisional office.

(b) After petit jurors have been qualified and sworn by a judge or officer of the Court, the names of such petit jurors who will proceed through voir dire in open court shall be made available to those parties and attorneys participating in the trial. The presiding judge may order that the names remain undisclosed when it is in the interests of justice to do so. Upon completion of voir dire, all papers on which juror names appear shall be collected. Copies of the strike list and other papers associated with voir dire will be filed by the Clerk for maintenance according to Section 21 of this Plan.

(c) The names of those selected for grand jury service shall not be maintained in any public record or otherwise disclosed to any person other than employees of the United States in the performance of their official duties, except upon written motion for good cause, and in the public interest. Such motion shall be presented to the Chief Judge or, in his absence, to the judge next senior in commission. In connection with such disclosure, certain United States statutes, such as 18 U.S.C.A. § 3432, require disclosure.

18. **Disqualification, Exemption, and Excuse After Summons.** Except as herein above provided, no person or class of persons shall be disqualified, excluded, excused, or exempt from jury service, provided, that any person summoned for jury service may be:

(a) Excused by the Court, or by the Clerk under supervision of the Court, upon a showing of undue hardship or extreme inconvenience for such period as the court deems necessary. Jurors so excused shall be subject to subsequent jury service, unless the judge granting the excuse should otherwise rule at the time of the excuse.

Any person appearing pursuant to summons and then requesting to be excused for reasons that could readily have been presented prior to his appearance, shall not receive attendance or mileage fees. When there is an excess of jurors present (e.g., grand jury) and their presence is required for only one day, the court shall, in its discretion, upon excusing excess jurors, inform them that they are subject to subsequent jury service.

(b) Excluded by the court on the ground that such person may be unable to render impartial jury service or that his service as a juror would be likely to disrupt the proceedings;

(c) Excluded upon peremptory challenge as provided by law;

(d) Excluded pursuant to the procedure specified by law upon a challenge by any party for good cause shown;

(e) Excluded upon determination by the court that his service as a juror would be likely to threaten the secrecy of the proceedings, or otherwise adversely affect the integrity of jury deliberations.

No person shall be excluded under clause (e), above, unless the judge, in open court, determines that such is warranted and that exclusion of the person will not be inconsistent with 28 U.S.C. §§ 1861 and 1862. The number of persons excluded under clause (e), above, shall not exceed one percent of the number of persons who return executed juror qualification forms during the period, specified in the Plan, between two consecutive fillings of the master jury wheel. The names of persons excluded under clause (e), above, together with detailed explanations for the exclusions, shall be forwarded immediately to the Judicial Council of the circuit, which shall have the power to make any appropriate order, prospective, or retroactive, to redress any misapplication of clause (e), but otherwise exclusions effectuated under such clause shall not be subject to challenge under the provisions of Title 28 of the United States Code. Any person excluded from a particular jury under clause (b), (c), or (d), above, shall be eligible to sit on another jury if the basis for his initial exclusion would not be relevant to his ability to serve on such other jury.

19. **Utilization of Petit Jurors Among Various Judges in the Same Division.** It shall be the policy of this court to utilize the services of all qualified jurors summoned as fully and as efficiently as circumstances permit. To that end, it is contemplated that the judges of this court will coordinate their jury settings to permit the same pool of petit jurors to serve more than one judge. Jurors summoned for service shall appear as instructed in the summons. The names of those appearing shall be listed in computerized database records. In choosing a panel to serve in a particular judge's courtroom for a given period of time, or for the trial of a particular case or cases, the panel shall be chosen by shuffling or thoroughly mixing database records of all jurors in the jury pool then available for such service; and the requisite number to compose such panel shall be taken in order from such commingled database records. On completion of such service, the jurors composing such panel may be returned to the pool for further service in the same or another courtroom.

20. **Challenging Compliance With Selection Procedures.** The procedures prescribed by 28 U.S.C.A. § 1867 shall be the exclusive means of challenging any jury on the ground that such jury was not selected in conformity with the provisions of Chapter 121 of Title 28 of the United States Code Annotated.

21. **Maintenance of Records.** After any master jury wheel is emptied and refilled as provided above, and after all persons selected to serve as jurors before such master wheel was emptied have completed their service, all papers and records compiled and maintained by the Clerk before the master wheel was emptied shall be preserved in the custody of the Clerk for four (4) years and shall be available for inspection as ordered by the court for the purpose of determining the validity of the

selection of any jury. At the conclusion of such four-year period, such records and papers shall be destroyed.

22. This plan is based on the conclusion and judgment that the policy, purpose, and intent of the Jury Selection and Service Act of 1968 will be fully accomplished and implemented by the use of voter registration lists, as supplemented by the inclusion of subsequent registrants to the latest practicable date, as the source of an at random selection of prospective grand and petit jurors who represent a fair cross section of the community. This determination is supported by all the information this court has been able to obtain after diligent effort on its part and after full consultation with the Fifth Circuit Jury Working Committee and the Judicial Council of the Fifth Circuit. In order to assure the continuous implementation of the policy, purpose and intent of the Jury Selection and Service Act, as required by the Judicial Conference of the United States, a report will be made to the U. S. District Court, Southern District of Texas within six months following each periodic refilling of the master jury wheel, on forms approved by the Judicial Conference, giving general data relating to the master jury wheel, the time and manner of name selection, the source and number of names placed in the wheel and related information, and an analysis of the race and sex of prospective jurors based on returns of juror qualification forms mailed to a statistically reliable sample of persons chosen at random from the master jury wheel.

[Adopted July 21, 2005, approved by the Judicial Council of the Fifth Circuit, October 26, 2005. Amended May 7, 2013, approved by the Judicial Council of the Fifth Circuit, July 1, 2013.]

CRIMINAL JUSTICE ACT PLAN

I. AUTHORITY

Under the Criminal Justice Act (CJA) of 1964, as amended, 18 U.S.C. § 3006A, and Guide to Judiciary Policy (Guide), Volume 7A, the judges of the United States District Court for the Southern District of Texas adopt this Plan, as approved by the Fifth Circuit Court of Appeals, for furnishing representation in federal court for any person financially unable to obtain adequate representation in accordance with the CJA.

II. STATEMENT OF POLICY

A. Objectives. The objectives of this Plan are:

1. to attain the goal of equal justice under the law for all persons;

2. to provide all eligible persons with timely appointed counsel services that are consistent with the best practices of the legal profession, are cost-effective, and protect the independence of the defense function so that the rights of individual defendants are safeguarded and enforced; and

3. to implement the requirements of the CJA, the USA Patriot Improvement and Reauthorization Act of 2005 (recodified at 18 U.S.C. § 3599), and Guide, Vol. 7A, in a way that meets the needs of this district.

This Plan must be administered so that individuals accused of a crime, or who are otherwise eligible for services under the CJA, will not be deprived of the right to counsel, or any element of representation necessary to an effective defense, due to lack of financial resources.

B. Compliance.

1. The Court, its Clerk, the Federal Public Defender's office, and private attorneys appointed under the CJA must comply with Guide, Vol. 7A, approved by the Judicial Conference of the United States or its Committee on Defender Services, and with this Plan.

2. The Court will ensure that a current copy of the CJA Plan is made available on the Court's website, and provided to CJA counsel upon the attorney's designation as a member of the CJA panel of private attorneys (CJA Panel).

3. Nothing in this District CJA Plan should be interpreted as limiting or preventing each Division CJA Committee from establishing policies that reflect the unique needs of the Division that do not conflict with the District CJA Plan and the Criminal Justice Act. Any procedures established or implemented by a division must first be approved by the District and subsequently be approved by the Judicial Council of the Fifth Circuit.

III. DEFINITIONS

A. Representation. Representation includes counsel and investigative, expert, and related services.

B. Appointed Attorney. Appointed attorney means an attorney ordered by the Court to represent a financially eligible person under the CJA and this Plan. Such attorneys include the Federal Public Defender, staff attorneys of the Federal Public Defender, private attorneys on the CJA Panel, and other attorneys appointed by the Court.

IV. DETERMINATION OF ELIGIBILITY FOR CJA REPRESENTATION

A. Subject Matter Eligibility.

1. *Mandatory.* Representation must be provided for any financially eligible person who:

  a. is charged with a felony or with a Class A misdemeanor;

  b. is a juvenile alleged to have committed an act of juvenile delinquency as defined in 18 U.S.C. § 5031;

c. is charged with a violation of probation, or faces a change of a term or condition of probation (unless the modification sought is favorable to the probationer and the government has not objected to the proposed change);

d. is under arrest, when such representation is required by law;

e. is entitled to appointment of counsel in parole proceedings;

f. is charged with a violation of supervised release or faces modification, reduction, or enlargement of a condition, or extension or revocation of a term of supervised release;

g. is subject to a mental condition hearing under 18 U.S.C. § § 4241, et seq;

h. has been designated by the Court as a material witness;

i. is seeking to set aside or vacate a death sentence under 28 U.S.C. § 2254 or § 2255;

j. is entitled to appointment of counsel in verification of consent proceedings in connection with a transfer of an offender to or from the United States for the execution of a penal sentence under 18 U.S.C. § 4109;

k. is entitled to appointment of counsel under the Sixth Amendment to the Constitution; or

l. faces loss of liberty in a case and federal law requires the appointment of counsel.

2. *Discretionary.* Whenever a district or magistrate judge determines that the interests of justice so require, representation may be provided for any financially eligible person who:

a. is charged with a petty offense (Class B or C misdemeanor, or an infraction) for which a sentence to confinement is authorized;

b. is seeking relief under 28 U.S.C. §§ 2241, 2254, or 2255 other than to set aside or vacate a death sentence;

c. is charged with civil or criminal contempt and faces loss of liberty;

d. has been called as a witness before a grand jury, a court, the Congress, or a federal agency or commission that has the power to compel testimony, and there is reason to believe, either prior to or during testimony, that the witness could be subject to a criminal prosecution, a civil or criminal contempt proceeding, or a loss of liberty;

e. has been advised by the United States attorney or a law enforcement officer that he or she is the target of a grand jury investigation;

f. is proposed by the United States attorney for processing under a pretrial diversion program; or

g. is held for international extradition under 18 U.S.C. Chapter 209.

3. *Ancillary Matters.* Representation may also be provided for financially eligible persons in ancillary matters appropriate to a proceeding under 18 U.S.C. § 3006A(c). In determining whether representation in an ancillary matter is appropriate to a proceeding, the Court should consider whether such representation is reasonably necessary:

a. to protect a constitutional right;

b. to contribute in a significant way to the defense of a principal criminal charge;

c. to aid in preparation for the trial or disposition of a principal criminal charge;

d. to enforce the terms of a plea agreement in a principal criminal charge;

e. to preserve the claim of the CJA client to an interest in real or personal property subject to civil forfeiture proceeding under 18 U.S.C. § 983, 19 U.S.C. § 1602, 21 U.S.C. § 881, or similar statutes, which property, if recovered by the client, may be considered for reimbursement under 18 U.S.C. § 3006A(f); or

f. effectuate the return of real or personal property belonging to a CJA client, which may be subject to a motion for return of property under Fed. R. Crim. P. 41(g), which property, if recovered by the client, may be considered for reimbursement under 18 U.S.C. § 3006A(f).

B. Financial Eligibility.

1. *Presentation of Accused for Financial Eligibility Determination.*

a. Duties of Law Enforcement

(i) Upon arrest, and when the defendant has not retained counsel, federal law enforcement officials must as soon as feasible notify—telephonically or electronically—the appropriate Court personnel, who in turn will appoint counsel under this Plan.

(ii) Employees of law enforcement agencies must not participate in the completion of the financial affidavit or seek to obtain information concerning financial eligibility from a person requesting the appointment of counsel.

b.   Duties of United States Attorney's Office.

(i) Upon the return or unsealing of an indictment or the filing of a criminal information, and when the defendant has not retained counsel, the United States Attorney (or his or her delegate) must as soon as feasible notify—telephonically or electronically—appropriate Court personnel, who in turn will appoint counsel under this Plan.

(ii) Upon issuance of a target letter, and where the individual has not retained counsel, the United States Attorney (or his or her delegate) must as soon as feasible notify-telephonically or electronically—the appropriate Court personnel, who in turn will appoint counsel under this Plan.

(iii) Employees of the United States Attorney's Office must not participate in the completion of the financial affidavit or seek to obtain information concerning financial eligibility from a person requesting the appointment of counsel.

c.   Duties of the Federal Public Defender's Office

(i) In cases in which the Federal Public Defender is appointed, the office will:

 - promptly investigate and determine whether an actual or potential conflict exists; and

 - in the event of an actual or potential conflict, promptly notify the Court to facilitate the timely appointment of other counsel.

(ii) When practicable, the Federal Public Defender will discuss with the person who indicates that he or she is not financially able to secure representation the right to appointed counsel and, if appointment of counsel seems likely, assist in the completion of a financial affidavit (Form CJA 23) and arrange to have the person promptly presented before a magistrate judge or district judge of this Court for determination of financial eligibility and appointment of counsel.

d.   Duties of Pretrial Services Office.

(i) The pretrial services officer will not conduct the pretrial service interview of a financially eligible defendant until counsel has been appointed, unless the right to counsel is waived or the defendant otherwise consents to a pretrial service interview without counsel. The pretrial services officer must inform the defendant of his or her right and obtain a waiver. *See* Attachment "A".

(ii) When counsel has been appointed, the pretrial services officer will provide counsel notice and a reasonable opportunity to attend any interview of the defendant by the pretrial services officer before the initial pretrial release or detention hearing.

2.   *Factual Determination of Financial Eligibility.*

a.   In every case where appointment of counsel is authorized under 18 U.S.C. § 3006A(a) or other statutes, the Court must advise the person that he or she has a right to be represented by counsel throughout the case and that, if so desired, counsel will be appointed to represent the person if he or she is financially unable to obtain counsel.

b.   The determination of eligibility for representation under the CJA is a judicial function to be performed by the Court after making appropriate inquiries concerning the person's financial eligibility. Other employees of the Court may be designated to obtain or verify the facts relevant to the financial eligibility determination.

c.   In determining whether a person is financially unable to obtain counsel, consideration should be given to the cost of providing the person and his or her dependents with the necessities of life, the cost of securing pretrial release, asset encumbrance, and the likely cost of retained counsel.

d.   The initial determination of eligibility must be made without regard to the financial ability of the person's family to retain counsel unless their family indicates willingness and ability to do so promptly.

e. Any doubts about a person's eligibility should be resolved in the person's favor; erroneous determinations of eligibility may be corrected at a later time.

f. Relevant information bearing on the person's financial eligibility should be reflected on a financial eligibility affidavit (Form CJA 23).

g. If at any time after the appointment of counsel, a judge finds that a person provided representation is financially able to obtain counsel or make partial payment for the representation, the judge may terminate the appointment of counsel or direct that any funds available to the defendant be paid as provided in 18 U.S.C. § 3006A(f).

h. If at any stage of the proceedings a judge finds that a person is no longer financially able to pay retained counsel, counsel may be appointed under the provisions of this Plan.

V. TIMELY APPOINTMENT OF COUNSEL

A. Timing of Appointment. Counsel must be provided to eligible persons as soon as feasible in the following circumstances, whichever occurs earliest:

1. after they are taken into custody;

2. when they appear before a magistrate or district court judge;

3. when they are formally charged or notified of charges if formal charges are sealed; or

4. when a magistrate or district court judge otherwise considers appointment of counsel appropriate under the CJA or other statutes.

B. Court's Responsibility. The Court, in cooperation with the Federal Public Defender and the United States Attorney and the CJA Panel, will make the arrangements with federal, state, and local investigative and police agencies that will ensure timely appointment of counsel.

C. Pretrial Service Interview. Unless the right to counsel is waived or the defendant otherwise consents to a pretrial service interview without counsel, financially eligible defendants will be provided appointed counsel before being interviewed by a pretrial services officer.

D. Retroactive Appointment of Counsel. Appointment of counsel may be made retroactive to include representation provided before appointment.

VI. PROVISION OF REPRESENTATIONAL SERVICES

A. Federal Public Defender and Private Counsel. This Plan provides for representational services by the Federal Public Defender and for the appointment and compensation of private counsel from a CJA Panel list maintained by the Court in cases authorized under the CJA and other statutes.

B. Administration. Administration of the CJA Panel, as set forth in this Plan, is delegated and assigned to the Court.

C. Apportionment of Cases. Where practical and cost effective, private attorneys from the CJA Panel will be appointed in a substantial proportion of the cases in which the accused is determined to be financially eligible for representation under the CJA. "Substantial" will usually be defined as a minimum of twenty-five percent (25%) of the annual CJA appointments.

D. Number of Counsel. More than one attorney may be appointed in any case under the Court's discretion.

E. Capital Cases. Procedures for appointment of counsel in cases where the defendant is charged with a crime that may be punishable by death, or is seeking to vacate or set aside a death sentence in proceedings under 28 U.S.C. §§ 2254 or 2255, are set forth in section XIV of this Plan.

VII. FEDERAL PUBLIC DEFENDER OFFICE

A. Establishment. The Federal Public Defender is established in this district under the CJA and is responsible for rendering defense services on appointment throughout this district.

B. Standards. The Federal Public Defender must provide high quality representation consistent with the best practices of the legal profession and commensurate with those services rendered when counsel is privately retained. See Polk County v. Dodson, 454 U.S. 312, 318 (1981). ("Once a lawyer has undertaken the representation of an accused, the duties and obligations are the same whether the lawyer is privately retained, appointed, or serving in a legal aid or defender program." (quoting ABA Standards for Criminal Justice section 43.9 (2d ed. 1980))).

C. Workload. The Federal Public Defender will continually monitor the workloads of its staff to ensure high quality representation for all clients.

D. Professional Conduct. The Federal Public Defender must conform to the highest standards of professional conduct, including but not limited to the American Bar Association's Model Rules of Professional Conduct; American Bar Association's Model Code of Professional Conduct; Code of Conduct for Federal Public Defender Employees; Model Code of Conduct for Federal Community Defender Employees; the Texas Disciplinary Rules of Professional Conduct; and other standards for professional conduct adopted by the Court.

E. Private Practice of Law. Neither the Federal Public Defender nor any defender employee may engage in the private practice of law except as authorized by the Federal Public Defender Code of Conduct.

F. Supervision of Defender Organization. The Federal Public Defender will be responsible for the supervision and management of the Federal Public Defender Office. Accordingly, the Federal Public Defender will be appointed in all cases assigned to that office for subsequent assignment to staff attorneys at the discretion of the Federal Public Defender.

G. Training. The Federal Public Defender will assess the training needs of Federal Public Defender staff and, in coordination with the CJA Panel Attorney District Representative,[1] the training needs of the local panel attorneys, and provide training opportunities and other educational resources.

VIII. CJA COMMITTEES FOR PANEL ATTORNEYS

A. Establishment of the CJA Ad Hoc Panel Committee.

1. A CJA Panel Committee (Ad Hoc CJA Committee) will be established by the Court in consultation with the Federal Public Defender. The CJA Committee will consist of one district court judge, at least one magistrate judge, the Federal Public Defender, the CJA Panel Attorney District Representative (PADR), and at least one criminal defense attorney who practices regularly in the district and who is a CJA panel member. The Committee is an Ad Hoc Committee appointed by and serves at the pleasure of the Chief Judge.

2. The PADR is selected by the Chief Judge after conferring with the FPD and serves all District and Division CJA Panels for the National Defender Services CJA PADR program and local CJA Committees.

3. The Federal Public Defender and the office of the district PADR are permanent members of the CJA Committee.

Each Division or combination of Divisions will establish a Division CJA Committee in consultation with the Federal Public Defender and the District Representative. The Division Committee consists of a district judge appointed by the Chief Judge, a magistrate judge, the Federal Public Defender or representative, a Division Representative and at least one criminal defense attorney who practices regularly in the Division and who is a CJA Panel member. The district judge or his or her designee will appoint a magistrate judge, a Division Representative and any criminal defense attorney(s) in consultation from the Division Judges.

Membership on the Division CJA Committee will otherwise be for a term of three years and may be extended for an additional three years. Members' terms will be staggered to ensure continuity.

4. The Division CJA Committees will meet at least once per year and at any time the Court asks the Committee to consider an issue.

B. Duties of the CJA Committee.

1. *Membership.* The Committee examines the qualifications of applicants for membership on the CJA Panel and votes to recommend to the Court the approval of attorneys who are deemed qualified or the rejection or removal of attorneys deemed unqualified after receiving comments concerning eligibility from magistrate and district judges.

2. *Recruitment.* The Committee will engage in recruitment efforts to establish a diverse panel and ensure that all qualified attorneys are encouraged to participate in the furnishing of representation in CJA cases.

3. *Annual Review and (Optional) Report.* Each Division CJA Committee will review the operation and administration of the CJA Panel over the preceding year, and make necessary changes, and report to the full Court concerning:

    a. the size of the CJA Panel;

    b. the recruitment of qualified and diverse attorneys as required and set forth in this plan; and

    c. recurring issues or difficulties encountered by panel members, their CJA clients, or the bar at large.

4. *Removal.* Any member of the Committee may recommend the removal of any CJA panel member who:

    a. fails to satisfactorily fulfill the requirements of CJA panel membership during his or her term of service, including the failure to provide high quality representation to CJA clients, or

    b. has engaged in other conduct such that his or her continued service on the CJA Panel is inappropriate.

    c. *See also* Section IX.C.(7).

5. *Training.* The Committee may assist the Federal Public Defender's Office in providing training for the CJA Panel on substantive and procedural legal matters affecting representation of CJA clients.

IX. ESTABLISHMENT OF A DIVISION CJA PANEL

A. Approval of the Division CJA Panel.

1. The existing, previously established panel of attorneys who are eligible and willing to be appointed to provide representation under the CJA is hereby recognized.

2. Each Division will have a CJA Committee that will review attorney applications, reapplications, and continued membership on the Division's CJA Panel.

3. The Division CJA Committee will recommend to the Court qualified attorneys for membership on the CJA Panel after receiving recommendations from the members of the Committee or the Court.

B. Size of CJA Panel.

1. The size of the CJA Panel will be determined by the Division CJA Committee based on the caseload and activity of the panel members, subject to review by the Court.

2. The CJA Panel must be large enough to provide enough experienced attorneys to handle the CJA caseload, yet small enough so that CJA panel members will receive enough appointments to maintain their proficiency in federal criminal defense work, enabling them to provide high quality representation consistent with the best practices of the legal profession and commensurate with legal services provided when counsel is privately retained.

C. Qualifications and Membership on the CJA Panel.

1. *Application.* Application forms for membership on the CJA Panel are available on the Court's website.

2. *Equal Opportunity.* All qualified attorneys are encouraged to apply for the CJA Panel.

3. *Eligibility.*

    a. Applicants for the CJA Panel must be members in good standing of the federal bar of this District.

    b. Applicants must maintain a primary, satellite, or shared office in this District.

    c. Applicants must possess strong litigation skills and demonstrate proficiency with the federal sentencing guidelines, federal sentencing procedures, the Bail Reform Act, the Federal Rules of Criminal Procedure, and the Federal Rules of Evidence.

d. Applicants must have significant experience representing persons charged with serious criminal offenses and demonstrate a commitment to the defense of people who lack the financial means to hire an attorney.

e. Attorneys who do not possess the experience set forth above but believe they have equivalent other experience are encouraged to apply and set forth in writing the details of that experience for the Division CJA Committee's consideration.

4. *Appointment to CJA Panel.* After a review of the applications and comments from the Court and members of the Division CJA Committee, the Committee will recommend to the Court the appointment or reappointment of attorneys to the Division CJA Panel. An appointment to the Panel is no guarantee of reappointment or appointment as counsel in any particular Court proceeding. Due to the highly complex and demanding nature of capital and habeas corpus cases, special procedures will be followed for the eligibility and appointment of counsel in such cases. See Section XIV of this Plan.

5. *Terms of CJA Panel Members.* To establish staggered CJA membership terms, the Division CJA Panel will be divided into three groups, approximately equal in number. Attorneys admitted to membership on the CJA Panel will each serve for a term of at least three years, subject to the reappointment procedures set forth in this plan.

6. *Reappointment of Division CJA Panel Members.*

a. The Court will notify CJA panel members, before their current term expires, of the need to apply for reappointment to the Division CJA Panel.

b. A member of the CJA Panel who wishes to be considered for reappointment must apply for an additional term no later than the deadline set by the Court. Application forms for reappointment are available on the Court's website.

c. The Division CJA Committee will solicit input concerning the quality of representation provided by lawyers seeking reappointment.

d. The Division CJA Committee will consider, among other things, how many cases the Division CJA panel member has accepted and declined during the review period, whether the member has participated in training opportunities, whether the member has been the subject of any complaints, and whether the member continues to meet the prerequisites and obligations of a Division CJA panel members as set forth in this Plan.

7. *Removal from the CJA Panel.*

a. Mandatory Removal. Any member of the Division CJA Panel who is suspended or disbarred from the practice of law by the state court before whom such member is admitted, or who is suspended or disbarred from this Court or any federal court, will be removed from the Division CJA Panel immediately.

b. Automatic Review. The Division CJA Committee will conduct an automatic review of any Division CJA panel member against whom any licensing authority, grievance committee, or administrative body has taken action, or when there has been a finding of probable cause, contempt, sanction, or reprimand against the panel member by any state or federal court. Nevertheless, all panel attorneys serve on the CJA Panel at the pleasure of the Court

X. CJA PANEL ATTORNEY APPOINTMENT IN NON–CAPITAL CASES

A. Appointment List. The Court will maintain a current list of all attorneys included on the CJA Panel, with current office addresses, email addresses, and telephone numbers. The list may include a statement of qualifications and experience.

B. Appointment Procedures.

1. The Court is responsible for overseeing the appointment of cases to panel attorneys. The Court will maintain a record of panel attorney appointments and, when appropriate, data reflecting the apportionment of appointments between attorneys from the Federal Public Defender Office and Panel attorneys.

2. Appointment of cases to Division CJA panel members will be at the Court's discretion. The Court will consider the nature of the case, the characteristics of the defendant, and the background

and experience of the potential appointed attorneys in order to ensure effective assistance of counsel is provided.

3. Under special circumstances, a judge may find it necessary to appoint a member of the bar of the Court who is not a member of the Division CJA Panel. These circumstances may include cases in which the judge determines that the appointment of a particular attorney is in the interests of justice, judicial economy, or continuity of representation, or for any other compelling reason. It is not anticipated that special circumstances will arise often, and the procedures set forth in the Plan are presumed to be sufficient in the majority of cases in which counsel are to be appointed. Appointments made under this section will be reported to the CJA Committee by the appointing judge.

XI. DUTIES OF DIVISION CJA PANEL MEMBERS

A. Standards and Professional Conduct.

1. Division CJA Panel members must provide high quality representation consistent with the best practices of the legal profession and commensurate with those services rendered when counsel is privately retained. See Polk County v. Dodson, 454 U.S. 312, 318 (1981) ("Once a lawyer has undertaken the representation of an accused, the duties and obligations are the same whether the lawyer is privately retained, appointed, or serving in a legal aid or defender program." (quoting ABA Standards for Criminal Justice section 4–3.9 (2d ed. 1980))).

2. Attorneys appointed under the CJA must conform to the highest standards of professional conduct, including the American Bar Association's Model Rules of Professional Conduct, the American Bar Association's Model Code of Professional Conduct, the Texas Disciplinary Rules of Professional Conduct, and other standards for professional conduct adopted by the Court.

3. Each Division CJA Panel member must notify within 10 days the chair of the Division CJA Committee after: 1) being notified that a complaint has been filed against the Panel member with any licensing authority, grievance committee, or administrative body; 2) being notified that any authority, committee or body has taken action against the Panel member, or 3) being notified when a finding of contempt, sanction, or reprimand has been issued against the Panel member by any court.

B. Training and Continuing Legal Education.

1. Attorneys on the Division CJA Panel are expected to remain current with developments in federal criminal defense law, practice, and procedure.

2. Attorneys on the Division CJA Panel are expected to attend seminars sponsored by the Federal Public Defender.

3. Attorneys on the Division CJA Panel will be guided in their practice by the Federal Adaptation of the National Legal Aid and Defender Association Performance Guidelines for Criminal Defense Representations.

4. CJA panel members must annually attend continuing legal education relevant to federal criminal practice and report any such attendance to the Committee.

5. Failure to comply with these training and legal education requirements may be grounds for removal from the CJA Panel.

C. Facilities and Technology Requirements.

1. CJA Panel attorneys must have the facilities, resources, and technological capability to effectively and efficiently manage assigned cases.

2. CJA Panel attorneys must comply with the requirements of electronic filing and eVoucher.

3. CJA Panel attorneys must know and abide by procedures related to requests for investigative, expert, and other services.

D. Continuing Representation.
Once appointed under the CJA, counsel will continue the representation until: the matter, including appeals or review by certiorari, is closed; substitute counsel has filed a notice of appearance; an order is entered allowing or requiring the person represented to proceed pro se; or until the appointment is terminated by Court order.

E. Miscellaneous.

1. *Case Budgeting.* In complex non-capital representations that are likely to become unusual in terms of cost, the Court may require development of a case budget consistent with Guide, Vol. 7A, Ch. 2, §§ 230.26.10 and 20.

2. *No Receipt of Other Payment.* Appointed counsel may not require, request, or accept any payment, promise of payment, or any other valuable consideration for representation under the CJA, unless the payment is approved by order of the Court.

3. *Redetermination of Need.* If at any time after appointment, counsel has reason to believe that a party is financially able to obtain counsel, or to make partial payment for counsel, and the source of counsel's information is not protected as a privileged communication, counsel will advise the Court.

4. The Court appoints all counsel with the expectation that counsel will perform all tasks required of an attorney. None of these tasks should be delegated to another person or attorney without notice to or permission of the Court.

XII. COMPENSATION OF CJA PANEL ATTORNEYS

A. Policy of the Court Regarding Compensation. Providing fair compensation to appointed counsel is a critical component of the administration of justice. CJA Panel attorneys must be compensated for time expended in Court and time reasonably expended out of Court, and reimbursed for expenses reasonably incurred.

B. Payment Procedures.

1. Claims for compensation must be submitted on the appropriate CJA form through the Court's eVoucher system.

2. Claims for compensation should be submitted no later than 45 days after final disposition of the case, unless good cause is shown.

3. The clerk will review the claims for mathematical and technical accuracy and for conformity with Guide, Vol. 7A and, if correct, will forward them for consideration and action by Court.

4. Absent extraordinary circumstances, the Court should act on CJA compensation claims within 30 days of submission, and vouchers should not be delayed or reduced for the purpose of diminishing Defender Services program costs generally or in response to adverse financial circumstances.

5. In cases when the voucher for compensation submitted for services should, in the Judge's opinion, be reduced (except for mathematical corrections), the Division CJA attorney will receive notice from an eVoucher clerk indicating that the claim has been rejected or reduced. The Judge who reduced the voucher should indicate or describe the reductions, in order that counsel may supplement his or her claim with additional supporting documentation.

6. The Court, when contemplating reducing a CJA voucher for other than mathematical reasons, may refer the voucher to the Division CJA Committee for review and recommendation before final action on the claim is taken. See Section VIII of this Plan.

7. Notwithstanding the procedure described above, the Court may, in the first instance, contact appointed counsel to raise questions or concerns with a claim for compensation.

XIII. INVESTIGATIVE, EXPERT, AND OTHER SERVICES

A. Financial Eligibility. Counsel for a person who is financially unable to obtain investigative, expert, or other services necessary for an adequate defense may request these services in a sealed, ex parte application to the Court as provided in 18 U.S.C. § 3006A(e)(1), regardless of whether counsel is appointed under the CJA. Upon finding that the services are necessary, and that the person is financially unable to obtain them, the Court must authorize counsel to obtain the services.

B. Applications. In non-capital cases, requests for authorization of funds for investigative, expert, and other services must be submitted in a sealed, ex parte application to the Court in advance of any commitment. The requests must not be publicly disclosed except with the consent of the person represented or as required by law or Judicial Conference policy.

C. Compliance. Counsel must comply with Judicial Conference policies set forth in Guide, Vol. 7A, Ch. 3.

XIV. APPOINTMENT OF COUNSEL AND CASE MANAGEMENT IN CJA CAPITAL CASES

A. Applicable Legal Authority. The appointment and compensation of counsel in capital cases and the authorization and payment of persons providing investigative, expert, and other services are governed by 18 U.S.C. §§ 3005, 3006A, and 3599,[2] and Guide, Vol. 7A, Ch. 6, and the Special Procedures for Reviewing Attorney Compensation Requests in Death Penalty Cases promulgated by the Judicial Council of the Fifth Circuit..

B. General Applicability and Appointment of Counsel Requirements.

1. Unless otherwise specified, the provisions set forth in this section apply to all capital proceedings in the federal courts, whether they originated in a district court (federal capital trials) or in a state court (habeas proceedings under 28 U.S.C. § 2254). The proceedings include those in which the death penalty may be or is being sought by the prosecution, motions for a new trial, direct appeal, applications for a writ of certiorari to the Supreme Court of the United States, all post-conviction proceedings under 28 U.S.C. §§ 2254 or 2255 seeking to vacate or set aside a death sentence, applications for stays of execution, competency proceedings, proceedings for executive or other clemency, and other related motions and proceedings.

2. Any person charged with a crime that may be punishable by death who is or becomes financially unable to obtain representation is entitled to the assistance of appointed counsel throughout every stage of available judicial proceedings, including pretrial proceedings, trial, sentencing, motions for new trial, appeals, applications for writ of certiorari to the Supreme Court of the United States, and all available post-conviction processes, together with applications for stays of execution and other appropriate motions and procedures, competency proceedings, and proceedings for executive or other clemency as may be available to the defendant. See 18 U.S.C. § 3599(e).

3. Qualified counsel must be appointed in capital cases at the earliest possible opportunity. The Court should consult with the Federal Public Defender about potential counsel to be appointed in CJA capital matters.

4. Given the complex and demanding nature of capital cases, where appropriate, the Court will use the expert services available through the Administrative Office of the United States Courts (AO), Defender Services Death Penalty Resource Counsel projects (Resource Counsel projects), which include: (1) the Federal Death Penalty Resource Counsel and Capital Resource Counsel Projects (for federal capital trials); (2) the Federal Capital Appellate Resource Counsel Project; (3) the Federal Capital Habeas § 2255 Project; and (4) the National and Regional Habeas Assistance and Training Counsel Projects (§ 2254). These counsel are death penalty experts who the Court may rely on for assistance with selecting and appointing counsel, case budgeting, and handling the legal, practical, and other matters arising in federal capital cases.

5. The Federal Public Defender should promptly notify and consult with the appropriate Resource Counsel projects about potential and actual federal capital trial, appellate, and habeas corpus cases, and consider their recommendations for appointment of counsel.

6. The presiding judge may appoint an attorney furnished by a state or local public defender organization or legal aid agency or other private, non-profit organization to represent a person charged with a capital crime or seeking federal death penalty habeas corpus relief provided that the attorney is fully qualified. The appointments may be in place of, or in addition to, the appointment of the Federal Public Defender or a CJA panel attorney or an attorney appointed pro hac vice. See 18 U.S.C. § 3006A(a)(3).

7. All attorneys appointed in federal capital cases must be well qualified by training, commitment, and distinguished prior capital defense experience at the relevant stage of the proceeding, to serve as counsel in this highly specialized and demanding litigation.

8. All attorneys appointed in federal capital cases must have sufficient time and resources to devote to the representation, taking into account their current caseloads and the extraordinary demands of federal capital cases.

9. All attorneys appointed in federal capital cases must comply with the American Bar Association's 2003 Guidelines for the Appointment and Performance of Defense Counsel in Death Penalty Cases (Guidelines 1.1 and 10.2 et seq.), and the 2008 Supplementary Guidelines for the Mitigation Function of Defense Teams in Death Penalty Cases.

10. All attorneys appointed in federal capital cases should consult regularly with the appropriate Resource Counsel projects.

11. Questions about the appointment and compensation of counsel and the authorization and payment of investigative, expert, and other service providers in federal capital cases should be directed to the AO Defender Services Office, Legal and Policy Division Duty Attorney at 202–502–3030 or via email at ods_lpb@ao.uscourts.gov. The Fifth Circuit Budgeting Attorney and Administrative Attorney can also be contacted at 504–310–7799 for guidance.

C. Appointment of Trial Counsel in Federal Death–Eligible Cases.[3]

1. *General Requirements.*

a. Appointment of qualified capital trial counsel must occur no later than when a defendant is charged with a federal criminal offense for which the penalty of death is possible. See 18 U.S.C. § 3005.

b. To protect the rights of an individual who, although uncharged, is the subject of an investigation in a federal death-eligible case, the Court may appoint capital-qualified counsel upon request, consistent with Sections C.1, 2, and 3 of these provisions.

c. At the outset of every capital case, the Court must appoint two attorneys, at least one of whom meets the qualifications for "learned counsel." as described below. If necessary for adequate representation, more than two attorneys may be appointed to represent a defendant in a capital case. See 18 U.S.C. § 3005.

d. When appointing counsel, the Court must consider the recommendation of the Federal Public Defender, who will consult with Federal Death Penalty Resource Counsel to recommend qualified counsel. See 18 U.S.C. § 3005.

e. To effectuate the intent of 18 U.S.C. § 3005 that the Federal Public Defender's recommendation be provided to the Court, the judge should ensure that the Federal Public Defender has been notified of the need to appoint capital-qualified counsel.

f. Total reliance on a list for appointment of capital counsel is not recommended because selection of trial counsel should account for the particular needs of the case and the defendant, and should be based on individualized recommendations from the Federal Public Defender in conjunction with the Federal Death Penalty Resource Counsel and Capital Resource Counsel projects.

g. Out–of–district counsel who have the requisite expertise may be considered for appointment in capital trials to achieve high quality representation together with cost and other efficiencies.

h. In evaluating the qualifications of proposed trial counsel, consideration should be given to their commitment to the defense of capital cases, their current caseload including other capital cases, and their willingness to effectively represent the interests of the client.

2. *Qualifications of Learned Counsel.*

a. Learned counsel must either be a member of this district's bar or be eligible for admission pro hac vice based on his or her qualifications.

b. Learned counsel must meet the minimum experience standards set forth in 18 U.S.C. §§ 3005 and 3599.

c. Learned counsel should have distinguished prior experience in the trial, appeal, or post-conviction review of federal death penalty cases, or distinguished prior experience in state death penalty trials, appeals, or post-conviction review that, in combination with co-counsel, will assure high quality representation.

d. Distinguished prior experience contemplates excellence, not simply prior experience. Counsel with distinguished prior experience should be appointed even if meeting this standard requires appointing counsel from outside the district where the matter arises.

e. The suitability of learned counsel should be assessed with respect to the particular demands of the case, the stage of the litigation, and the defendant.

f. Learned counsel must be willing and able to adjust other caseload demands to accommodate the extraordinary time required by the capital representation.

g. Learned counsel must satisfy the qualification standards endorsed by bar associations and other legal organizations regarding the quality of representation in capital cases.

3. *Qualifications of Second and Additional Counsel.*

a. Second and additional counsel may, but are not required to, satisfy the qualifications for learned counsel, as set forth above.

b. Second and additional counsel must be well qualified, by distinguished prior criminal defense experience, training and commitment, to serve as counsel in this highly specialized and demanding litigation.

c. Second and additional counsel must be willing and able to adjust other caseload demands to accommodate the extraordinary time required by the capital representation.

d. The suitability of second and additional counsel should be assessed with respect to the demands of the individual case, the stage of the litigation, and the defendant.

D. Appointment and Qualifications of Direct Appeal Counsel in Federal Death Penalty Cases.

1. When appointing appellate counsel, the Court must consider the recommendation of the Federal Public Defender, who will consult with Federal Capital Appellate Resource Counsel to recommend qualified counsel.

2. Counsel appointed to represent a death-sentenced federal appellant should include at least one attorney who did not represent the appellant at trial.

3. Each trial counsel who withdraws should be replaced with similarly qualified counsel to represent the defendant on appeal.

4. Out-of-district counsel, including Federal Public Defender staff, who have the requisite expertise, may be considered for appointment in capital appeals to achieve high quality representation together with cost and other efficiencies.

5. Appellate counsel, between them, should have distinguished prior experience in federal criminal appeals and capital appeals.

6. At least one of the attorneys appointed as appellate counsel must have the requisite background, knowledge, and experience required by 18 U.S.C.§ 3599(c) or (d).

7. In evaluating the qualifications of proposed appellate counsel, consideration should be given to the qualification standards endorsed by bar associations and other legal organizations regarding the quality of legal representation in capital cases.

8. In evaluating the qualifications of proposed appellate counsel, consideration should be given to their commitment to the defense of capital cases, their current caseload including other capital cases, and their willingness to effectively represent the interests of the client.

E. Appointment and Qualifications of Post-Conviction Counsel in Federal Death Penalty Cases (28 U.S.C. § 2255).

1. A financially eligible person seeking to vacate or set aside a death sentence in proceedings under 28 U.S.C. § 2255 is entitled to appointment of fully qualified counsel. See 18 U.S.C. § 3599(a)(2).

2. Due to the complex, demanding, and protracted nature of death penalty proceedings, the Court should consider appointing at least two attorneys.

3. In light of the accelerated timeline applicable to capital § 2255 proceedings, prompt appointment of counsel is essential. Wherever possible, appointment should take place prior to the denial of certiorari on direct appeal by the United States Supreme Court.

4. When appointing counsel in a capital § 2255 matter, the Court should consider the recommendation of the Federal Public Defender, who will consult with the Federal Capital Habeas § 2255 Project.

5. Out-of-district counsel, including Federal Public Defender staff, who have the requisite expertise, may be considered for appointment in capital § 2255 cases to achieve high quality representation together with cost and other efficiencies.

6. Counsel in § 2255 cases should have distinguished prior experience in the area of federal post-conviction proceedings and in capital post-conviction proceedings.

7. When possible, post-conviction counsel should have distinguished prior experience in capital § 2255 representations.

8. In evaluating the qualifications of proposed post-conviction counsel, consideration should be given to the qualification standards endorsed by bar associations and other legal organizations regarding the quality of legal representation in capital cases.

9. In evaluating the qualifications of proposed post-conviction § 2255 counsel, consideration should be given to their commitment to the defense of capital cases, their current caseload including other capital cases, and their willingness to effectively represent the interests of the client.

F. Appointment and Qualifications of Counsel in Federal Capital Habeas Corpus Proceedings (28 U.S.C. § 2254).

1. A financially eligible person seeking to vacate or set aside a death sentence in proceedings under 28 U.S.C. § 2254 is entitled to the appointment of qualified counsel. See 18 U.S.C. § 3599(a)(2).

2. Due to the complex, demanding, and protracted nature of death penalty proceedings, the Court should consider appointing at least two attorneys.

3. When appointing counsel in a capital § 2254 matter, the appointing authority should consider the recommendation of the Federal Public Defender who will consult with the National or Regional Habeas Assistance and Training Counsel projects.

4. Out-of-district counsel, including Federal Public Defender staff, who possess the requisite expertise may be considered for appointment in capital § 2254 cases to achieve cost and other efficiencies together with high quality representation.

5. In order for federal counsel to avail themselves of the full statute of limitations period to prepare a petition, the Court should appoint counsel and provide appropriate litigation resources at the earliest possible time permissible by law, preferably no later than the conclusion of the state direct appeal.

6. Unless precluded by a conflict of interest, or replaced by similarly qualified counsel upon motion by the attorney or motion by the defendant, capital § 2254 counsel must represent the defendant throughout every subsequent stage of available judicial proceedings and all available postconviction processes, together with applications for stays of execution and other appropriate motions and procedures, and must also represent the defendant in competency proceedings and proceedings for executive or other clemency as may be available to the defendant. See 18 U.S.C. § 3599(e).

7. Counsel in capital § 2254 cases should have distinguished prior experience in the area of federal post-conviction proceedings and in capital post-conviction proceedings.

8. When possible, capital § 2254 counsel should have distinguished prior experience in capital § 2254 representations.

9. In evaluating the qualifications of proposed capital § 2254 counsel, consideration should be given to the qualification standards endorsed by bar associations and other legal organizations regarding the quality of legal representation in capital cases.

10. In evaluating the qualifications of proposed capital § 2254 counsel, consideration should be given to proposed counsel's commitment to the defense of capital cases, their current caseload including other capital cases, and their willingness to represent effectively the interests of the client.

XV. EFFECTIVE DATE

This Plan will become effective when approved by the Judicial Council of the Fifth Circuit.

[Amended December 15, 2005, approved by the Judicial Council of the Fifth Circuit, April 7, 2006; Amended and approved by the Judicial Council of the Fifth Circuit December 12, 2018.]

1 The CJA Panel Attorney District Representative (PADR) is a member of the district's CJA Panel who is selected by the Chief Judge, after conferring with the FPD, to serve as the representative of the district's CJA Panel for the national Defender Services CJA PADR program and local CJA committees.

2 As to investigative, expert, and other services, Section 3599(f) provides:

Upon a finding that investigative, expert, or other services are reasonably necessary for the representation of the defendant, whether in connection with issues relating to guilt or the sentence, the court may authorize the defendant's attorneys to obtain such services on behalf of the defendant and, if so authorized, shall order the payment of fees and expenses therefor under subsection (g). No ex parte proceeding, communication, or request may be considered pursuant to this section unless a proper showing is made concerning the need for confidentiality. Any such proceeding, communication, or request shall be transcribed and made a part of the record available for appellate review.

3 The Judicial Conference adopted detailed recommendations on the appointment and compensation of counsel in federal death penalty cases in 1998 (JCUS–SEP 98, p. 22). In September 2010, the Defender Services Committee endorsed revised commentary to the Judicial Conference's 1998 recommendations. CJA Guidelines, Vol. 7A, Appx. 6A (Recommendations and

Commentary Concerning the Cost and Quality of Defense Representation (Updated Spencer Report, September 2010)) (Appx. 6A is available on the judiciary's website.

SELECTED ORDERS

ORDER 91–26. IN THE MATTER OF GUIDELINES FOR COORDINATION OF CRIMINAL PROCEDURES

Since December, 1983, criminal procedures in the Houston Division involving this Court, the U.S. Attorney, the Pretrial Services Agency and the Federal Law Enforcement Agencies have been coordinated by guidelines issued by the U.S. Magistrate Judges. The existing guidelines have been revised, and "Guidelines for Coordination of Criminal Procedures", in the form attached to this Order, are **ADOPTED** by the Court.

One of the objectives of the guidelines has been to establish procedures to insure that a person, when arrested, is taken without unnecessary delay before the nearest available federal magistrate judge, as provided by Rule 5(a), Federal Rules of Criminal Procedure. The Pretrial Services Agency coordinates the appearance of the defendant before the magistrate judge and obtains and verifies information pertaining to pretrial release for reporting to the Court at the initial hearing.

It is ORDERED that an arresting agency, or a receiving agency if the defendant surrenders, shall give prompt notice to the Pretrial Services Agency, as provided in the Guidelines for Coordination of Criminal Procedures, of the arrest or surrender of the defendant, his location, and his availability for interview and initial appearance in court.

[Dated: November 25, 1991.]

GUIDELINES FOR COORDINATION OF CRIMINAL PROCEDURES U.S. MAGISTRATE JUDGES, U.S. ATTORNEY, PRETRIAL SERVICES AGENCY & FEDERAL AGENCIES SOUTHERN DISTRICT OF TEXAS, HOUSTON DIVISION

I. PROCEDURE

Regular court hearings on criminal matters are docketed before the duty magistrate judge at 10 a.m. and 2 p.m. each day. Special hearings at other times may be scheduled by the duty magistrate judge upon advance request. Each magistrate judge has a calendar criminal duty month, alternating each fourth month. Agencies will present matters to the duty magistrate judge or in his absence to the designated substitute magistrate judge.

A. Documents.

1. Since the U.S. Attorney is responsible for prosecuting federal offenses, every criminal proceeding must have his prior authorization. His "approval" herein includes authorization, review, revision and final approval of the complaint, warrant or any other form of pleading to be presented by an agent. The authorizing AUSA will initial the pleading to indicate approval. The judicial branch, including magistrates judges and court staff, is not permitted to draft, prepare, revise or type criminal pleadings. Each agency should maintain a supply of current printed criminal forms.

2. Advance planning must be made to present papers at the U.S. Courthouse (515 Rusk) during normal business hours; processing must be performed there. When an agency presents papers outside the Courthouse, there must be appropriate quantities for execution and distribution. The magistrate judge will retain the documents and deliver them to the Case Manager for docketing and distribution.

3. If possible, advance notice should be given to the duty magistrate judge and Case Manager when matters are anticipated after normal business hours or outside the Courthouse. Estimated time of presentation should be established, with follow-up notifications of any changes.

B. Arrest Without Warrant.

1. During regular business hours—refer to C. and E. below.

2. After regular business hours

   a. Agent prepares complaint for approval by Assistant United States Attorney.

   b. Following immediately upon completion of the administrative procedures incident to arrest, the arresting agent will turn arrestee over to United States Marshal for custody.

c.   Agent contacts duty magistrate judge or state magistrate if applicable for presentation of complaint and determination of probable cause during daytime hours.

d.   Magistrate judge will indicate on complaint time and date accepted by him or her, as well as an express statement whether or not probable cause is found.

e.   Arrestee will be brought before the duty magistrate judge for initial appearance at the 10 a.m. setting on the first business day after arrest. Refer to E.(3) below.

C.   Complaint.

1.   Preparation by agency and approval by U.S. Attorney, Criminal Division.

2.   Submit all documents to Case Manager of duty magistrate judge for processing:

a.   Assign docket number and prepare docket sheet.

b.   Review forms for approval, content and sufficiency of copies.

c.   If Case Manager of duty magistrate judge not available, processing by another deputy clerk.

3.   Case Manager will accompany agent to magistrate judge for verification, execution and sealing.

4.   Case manager will retain original complaint and warrant and copies for distribution; other copies returned to agent.

D.   Indictment or Information

1.   U.S. Attorney prepares order for issuance of bench warrant or summons, with suggested conditions of release; execution by duty magistrate judge.

2.   Original order to Criminal Clerk for issuance of warrant or summons; copy to Pretrial Services Agency (PSA), with copy of indictment or information.

3.   U.S. Marshal serves summons or executes warrant.

4.   Criminal Clerk refers case file to Case Manager of duty magistrate judge.

E.   Arrest and Initial Appearance of Defendant. Initial appearance of defendant before the duty magistrate judge should be made at either of the regular hearings scheduled daily at 10 a.m. and 2 p.m.

1.   The arresting or receiving agency will give prompt notice to the Pretrial Services Agency (PSA) of the detention and location of the defendant, and will have the defendant available for interview by PSA in sufficient time before next regular hearing before the magistrate judge. The agency is responsible for detention and presentation of defendant until transferred to custody of U.S. Marshal at or prior to the initial appearance.

a.   PSA will interview defendant and confer with U.S. Attorney and agency to collect and verify information to be considered for pretrial release. Where charges originate outside this division, PSA will consult with Pretrial Services Agency in the charging district to determine setting or recommendation of detention or conditions of release.

b.   If defendant requests counsel and is indigent, PSA will provide financial affidavit for execution by defendant and will notify Federal Public Defender of request for representation.

c.   PSA will notify Case Manager of duty magistrate judge to schedule appearance of defendant. If arrested on warrant, Case Manager must prepare papers for initial appearance; if arrest without warrant, complaint must be executed and filed (see C above), and papers must be prepared.

d.   PSA will advise the duty magistrate judge verbally, by written report, or personally at the initial appearance, of information regarding defendant and PSA's recommendation for conditions of release.

e.   Where defendant surrenders voluntarily or in response to summons, PSA will proceed as outline in Subsections (a)-(d) above.

2.   *Untimely Presentation or Notification.*

a.   Agency and PSA processing are encouraged to be planned so defendant will appear at a scheduled docket.

b.   Without advance notice and agreement, U.S. Marshal (USM) is not available to take custody of defendant from the arresting agent after the last trip of prisoners to jail facility, usually departing from the Courthouse at 4:00 p.m.

3. *Late Afternoon, Weekend and Holiday Arrests.*

   a. For late afternoon arrests, near or after U.S. Marshals deadline, arresting agent should transport defendant to jail facility and return him for the next docket appearance. If defendant is to be released, advise Case Manager, USM and PSA in advance for special appearance before magistrate judge.

   b. A defendant arrested after 4:00 p.m. on the last working day before a weekend or a holiday will be taken by the arresting agent directly to the jail facility. The arresting agency will give prompt notice to the Pretrial Services Agency (PSA) of the arrest and location of the defendant. Similar notice will be given for a defendant who surrenders. PSA will initiate and coordinate internal procedures to schedule the initial appearance of the defendant before the duty magistrate judge.

   c. On warrantless arrests, the agent will prepare the complaint for presentation to magistrate judge in accordance with I.B. above.

F. Search Warrant or Seizure Warrant.

1. Approval by U.S. Attorney; request and order if affidavit and warrant to be sealed.

2. Process and execution—same as C, 2–4 above; original warrant returned to agent.

3. Advance notification if telephonic search warrant is anticipated.

4. Within the period prescribed therein, the original warrant, whether executed or not, will be delivered by the agent to the Case Manager for completion of return before the magistrate judge.

G. Electronic Surveillance or Tracking Device Warrant.

1. Approval by U.S. Attorney; request and order if affidavit and warrant to be sealed.

2. Process and execution—same procedures as C, 2–4 above; original warrant returned to agent.

3. Renewal or extension—same procedures as C, 2–4 above.

4. Normally no return is required.

H. Pen Register, Trap and Trace, Telephone Toll Records or Bank Records Orders.

1. Approval by U.S. Attorney; request and order if application and order to be sealed.

2. Process and execution—same procedures as C, 2–4 above; original order returned to agent.

3. Renewal or extension—same procedures as C, 2–4 above.

4. Normally no return is required.

I. OSHA Warrant.

1. Preparation by OSHA.

2. Process and execution—same procedures as C, 2–4 above; original warrant returned to agent.

3. Normally no return is required.

J. IRS Warrant or Summons (Will Have Miscellaneous Docket Number).

1. Approval by U.S. Attorney, Civil Division.

2. Process and execution—same procedures as C, 2–4 above; original warrant or summons returned to agent.

3. Normally no return is required.

K. Writ of Habeas Corpus Ad Prosequendum/Testificandum.

1. Preparation by U.S. Attorney

2. Submit application and writ to Case Manager.

3. Case Manager will present documents to magistrate judge for execution.

4. Case Manager will retain original application and copy of writ; original and true copy of writ delivered to U.S. Marshal.

II. EMERGENCY, CRITICAL AND NON–ROUTINE REQUIREMENTS

Emergency critical or non-routine matters may develop which require special hearings. Normally these proceedings will be conducted in the same manner as regular docketed hearings and will require full court and support personnel. Advance planning must be made to arrange the presence of personnel.

III. U.S. DISTRICT JUDGES

U.S. District Judges inherently have the powers to perform all the acts outlined above for magistrate judges, as well as exclusive powers, such as authorization of telephonic wire-taps. Inquiries regarding presentations to District Judges should be directed to the Clerk of the District Court.

IV. EFFECTIVE DATE

These guidelines have been modified and adopted by the United States District Court, Southern District of Texas, as the official operational policy for the Houston Division, effective November 21, 1991 (superseding the guidelines as revised June 1, 1988).

GENERAL ORDER 2001–7.   IN RE GUIDELINES FOR PROFESSIONAL CONDUCT

The Judges of this Court, meeting on April 30, 2001, decided by majority vote to adopt the attached Guidelines for Professional Conduct, to be observed by all attorneys appearing before any district judge, bankruptcy judge, or magistrate judge presiding in the Southern District of Texas. These guidelines are derived from the decision in *Dondi Properties Corp. v. Commerce Savings and Loan Ass'n.*, 121 F.R.D. 284 (N.D. Tex. 1988). These Guidelines shall be attached as Appendix D to the Local Rules of this Court.

[Dated: May 8, 2001.]

GUIDELINES FOR PROFESSIONAL CONDUCT

(A) In fulfilling his or her primary duty to the client, a lawyer must be ever conscious of the broader duty to the judicial system that serves both attorney and client.

(B) A lawyer owes, to the judiciary, candor, diligence and utmost respect.

(C) A lawyer owes, to opposing counsel, a duty of courtesy and cooperation, the observance of which is necessary for the efficient administration of our system of justice and the respect of the public it serves.

(D) A lawyer unquestionably owes, to the administration of justice, the fundamental duties of personal dignity and professional integrity.

(E) Lawyers should treat each other, the opposing party, the court, and members of the court staff with courtesy and civility and conduct themselves in a professional manner at all times.

(F) A client has no right to demand that counsel abuse the opposite party or indulge in offensive conduct. A lawyer shall always treat adverse witnesses and suitors with fairness and due consideration.

(G) In adversary proceedings, clients are litigants and though ill feeling may exist between clients, such ill feeling should not influence a lawyer's conduct, attitude, or demeanor towards opposing lawyers.

(H) A lawyer should not use any form of discovery, or the scheduling of discovery, as a means of harassing opposing counsel or counsel's client.

(I) Lawyers will be punctual in communications with others and in honoring scheduled appearances, and will recognize that neglect and tardiness are demeaning to the lawyer and to the judicial system.

(J) If a fellow member of the Bar makes a just request for cooperation, or seeks scheduling accommodation, a lawyer will not arbitrarily or unreasonably withhold consent.

(K) Effective advocacy does not require antagonistic or obnoxious behavior and members of the Bar will adhere to the higher standard of conduct which judges, lawyers, clients, and the public may rightfully expect.

GENERAL ORDER 2002–13. IN THE MATTER OF JURISDICTION AND PROCEDURES FOR DUTIES ASSIGNED TO UNITED STATES MAGISTRATE JUDGES IN THIS DISTRICT

ARTICLE I. AUTHORITY OF MAGISTRATE JUDGES

A. General Designation. A magistrate judge of this district is designated to perform, and may be assigned, any duty allowed by 28 U.S.C. § 636 or any other law. In performing any duty, a magistrate judge may determine preliminary matters; require parties, attorneys, and witnesses to appear; require briefs, proofs. and argument; and conduct any hearing, conference, or other proceeding the magistrate judge deems appropriate. Duties which may be performed by a magistrate judge include:

1. Conducting arraignments in criminal cases not triable by a magistrate judge and taking not guilty pleas in such cases;

2. Receiving grand jury returns in accordance with Rule 6(f), Federal Rules of Criminal Procedure;

3. Accepting waivers of indictment, pursuant to Rule 7(b), Federal Rules of Criminal Procedure;

4. Conducting voir dire and selecting petit juries for the district court, to the extent allowed by law;

5. Accepting petit jury verdicts in civil cases in the absence of a district judge;

6. Conducting necessary proceedings leading to the potential revocation of probation;

7. Ordering the exoneration of forfeiture bonds;

8. Issuing subpoenas, writs of habeas corpus ad testificandum or habeas corpus ad prosequendum, or other orders necessary to obtain the presence of parties, witnesses or evidence needed for court proceedings;

9. Conducting proceedings under Rules Governing § 2254 Cases and § 2255 Proceedings;

10. Conducting examinations of judgment debtors in accordance with Rule 69, Federal Rules of Civil Procedure;

11. Performing the functions specified in 18 U.S.C. §§ 4107, 4108, and 4109 regarding proceedings for verification of consent by offenders to transfer to or from the United States and the appointment of counsel therein;

12. Performing any other duties not inconsistent with the Constitution and the laws of the United States.

B. Special Designation to Exercise Civil Consent Authority (28 U.S.C. § 636(c)). Upon the consent of the parties, a district judge may assign a full-time magistrate judge to conduct any or all proceedings in any jury or nonjury civil matter and order the entry of judgment in the case.

C. Special Designation to Conduct Misdemeanor Trials (18 U.S.C. § 3401). A magistrate judge may try persons accused of misdemeanor offenses and sentence persons convicted of misdemeanor offenses.

D. Special Designation to Handle Extradition Matters (18 U.S.C. § 3184). A magistrate judge is authorized to handle all matters pertaining to extradition complaints filed pursuant to 18 U.S.C. § 3184.

ARTICLE II. ASSIGNMENT OF MATTERS TO MAGISTRATE JUDGES

A. Criminal Cases.

1. *Misdemeanor Cases.* Upon the of an information, complaint or violation notice or the return of an indictment, all misdemeanor cases shall generally be assigned to a magistrate judge, who shall proceed in accordance with the provisions of 18 U.S.C. § 3401 and Rule 58, Federal Rules of Criminal Procedure. Unless the assignment procedure is modified by the district judges in a

particular division, misdemeanor cases shall be assigned to the duty magistrate judges in each division.

    2. *Felony Cases.* Upon the return of an indictment or the filing of an information, all felony cases shall be assigned initially by the clerk of the court to a magistrate judge for the conducting of the initial appearance and arraignment. Thereafter, the district judge to whom the case is assigned may refer the case to a magistrate judge for such pretrial conferences as necessary, and for the hearing and determination or recommendation as to all pretrial procedural and discovery motions.

    B.   Civil Cases. A district judge may refer any civil case to a magistrate judge for the conduct of conferences, hearings and other proceedings, and for the hearing and determination of all pretrial procedural and discovery motions. Where the parties consent to trial and disposition of a case by a magistrate judge under Subsection B of Article 1, above, such case shall, upon the approval of the district judge to whom it is assigned, be reassigned to a magistrate judge for the conduct of all further proceedings and the entry of judgment.

    C.   Reservation. Nothing in this order shall preclude any district judge from reserving any proceeding for conduct by a district judge, rather than a magistrate judge.

ARTICLE III.   PROCEDURES FOR CIVIL CONSENT CASES—28 U.S.C. § 636(c); Rule 73, Fed.R.Civ.P.

    A.   Notice of Consent Option. Upon the filing or removal of a complaint in a civil case, the clerk of court will plaintiff, plaintiff's counsel, or counsel for the removing party a court-approved notice informing the parties that they may consent to have a magistrate judge conduct all further proceedings in the case and order the entry of final judgment. Such notice shall be given to the other parties as attachments to copies of the complaint and summons, when served. Additional notices may be furnished to the parties at later stages of the proceedings, and may be included with Pretrial notices and instructions,

    B.   Execution of Consent. The plaintiff or removing party, or their counsel, shall be responsible for securing the execution of a consent form by the parties and for filing such form with the clerk of court. The parties may file joint or separate consent forms. A district judge or magistrate judge may inform the parties, at any time, that they have the option of referring a case to a magistrate judge, but in doing so, the judge shall also advise the parties that they are free to withhold consent without adverse substantive consequences.

    C.   Reference. After the consent form has been executed and filed, the clerk shall transmit it to the district judge to whom the case has been assigned for approval and referral of the case to a magistrate judge. If the district judge refers the case to a magistrate judge, the magistrate judge shall have authority to conduct any and all proceedings to which the parties have consented and to direct the clerk of court to enter a final judgment in the same manner as if a district judge had presided.

    D.   Party Added After Consent Occurs. A party added to a civil case after reference of the cast to a magistrate judge on consent will be given an opportunity to consent to the continued exercise of case-dispositive authority by the magistrate judge. The clerk shall give the added party an unexecuted copy of the notice described in Subsection A, above. If the party chooses to consent, it must, within 14 days of its appearance, file with the clerk the notice denoting its consent signed by the party or its attorney. Should the party not file a notice of consent, the case will be returned to the assigned district judge for all further proceedings.

ARTICLE IV. APPEAL OF MAGISTRATE JUDGE RULINGS

    Appeals of magistrate judge rulings are governed by Rules 72 and 73, Fed.R.Civ.P. and 28 U.S.C. § 636. Appeal of a special master report filed by a magistrate judge is governed by the applicable rule in the Federal Rules of Civil Procedure. Appeal of a judgment of conviction by a magistrate judge in a misdemeanor case shall be in accordance with the provisions of Rule 58(g), Federal Rules of Criminal Procedure.

This General Order supersedes General Order No. 2001–6 and is adopted by the Judges of this Court, effective the 13th day of December, 2002.

[Dated: December 13, 2002.]

GENERAL ORDER 2004–11.   IN THE MATTER OF PROTECTING
PERSONAL PRIVACY IN PUBLIC CASE FILES

This Order amends General Order No. 2003–4, dated August 24, 2003. It is issued in compliance with the policy of the Judicial Conference of the United States and also Sec. 205 of the E-Government Act of 2002 (Pub. L. No. 107–347), as amended.

In order to promote electronic access to case files while also protecting personal privacy and other legitimate interests, it is ORDERED that parties shall refrain from including, or shall partially redact where inclusion is necessary, the following personal data identifiers from all pleadings filed with the court, including exhibits thereto, whether filed electronically or in paper, unless otherwise ordered by the Court:

   a.   **Social Security Numbers.** If an individual's social security number must be included in a pleading, only the last four digits of that number should be used.

   b.   **Names of Minor Children.** If the involvement of a minor must be mentioned, only the initials of that child should be used.

   c.   **Dates of Birth.** If an individual's date of birth must be included in a pleading, only the year should be used.

   d.   **Financial Account Numbers.** If financial account numbers are relevant, only the last four digits of these numbers should be used.

   e.   **Home Addresses.** If a home address must be included, only the city and state should be listed.

Effective November 1, 2004, images of documents in criminal cases which are scanned will be electronically available to the public at the courthouse or through subscription to PACER. When electronic filing is authorized in criminal cases, those documents filed electronically will also be electronically available the public at the courthouse or through subscription to PACER. Documents that have been sealed or otherwise restricted by the court will not be electronically available.

For filings in Bankruptcy Court because of conflicting bankruptcy statutes and rules, this Order shall apply only to personal identifiers b and c, pertaining to names of minor children and dates of birth. The Order does not apply to social security and financial account numbers in Bankruptcy Court filings. Also, this Order does not apply to any cases brought pursuant to Section 205(g) of the Social Security Act, 42 U.S.C. § 405(g), since remote electronic availability of documents in those cases is restricted to parties only.

Because of remote electronic availability, caution should be exercised and the necessity to seal considered when filing documents that contain any of the following information:

   a. any personal identifying number, such as driver's license number;

   b. medical records, treatment and diagnosis;

   c. employment history;

   d. individual financial information;

   e. proprietary or trade secret information;

   f. information regarding an individual's cooperation with the government;

   g. information regarding the victim of any criminal activity;

   h. national security information; and

   i. sensitive security information as described in 49 U.S.C. § 114(s).

Notwithstanding any foregoing provision, however, and in compliance with the E–Government Act, any party wishing to file a document containing the personal data identifiers listed above may:

   a. file an unredacted version of the document under seal which shall be retained by the court as part of the record, or

   b. file a reference list under seal. The reference list shall contain the complete personal data identifier(s) and the redacted identifier(s) used in its (their) place in the filing. All references in the case to the redacted identifiers included in the reference list will be construed to refer to the corresponding complete identifier. The reference list must be filed under seal, and may be amended as a matter of right. It shall be retained by the court as part of the record.

The court may, however, still require the party to file a redacted copy for the public file.

The following documents shall not be included in the public case file and should not be made available to the public at the courthouse or via remote electronic access:

    a. unexecuted summonses or warrants of any kind (e.g., search warrants, arrest warrants);

    b. pretrial bail or presentence investigation reports;

    c. statements of reasons in the judgment of conviction;

    d. juvenile records;

    e. documents containing identifying information about jurors or potential jurors;

    f. financial affidavits filed in seeking representation pursuant to the Criminal Justice Act;

    g. ex parte requests (e.g., authorization of investigative, expert or other services pursuant to the Criminal Justice Act); and

    h. sealed documents (e.g., motions for downward departure for substantial assistance, plea agreements indicating cooperation).

The responsibility for redacting personal identifiers and properly filing documents to be sealed rests solely with counsel and the parties. The Clerk will not review each pleading for compliance with this rule.

[Dated: October 18, 2004.]

GENERAL ORDER 2007–12.   IN THE MATTER OF TRANSCRIPT FEES

Attached are the maximum transcript rates per page for all transcripts ordered on or after November 1, 2007, prepared by official court reporters and official transcribing services throughout the Southern District of Texas, whether privately paid or government paid, whether in district court or bankruptcy court.

These rates do not alter the Judicial Conference rates to be paid from Criminal Justice Act funds for more than one copy of a transcript of the same proceeding ordered in multi-defendant cases.

Attachment

Maximum Transcript Fee Rates—All Parties Per Page

	Original	First Copy to Each Party	Each Add'l Copy to the Same Party
Ordinary Transcript (30 day) A transcript to be delivered within thirty (30) calendar days after receipt of an Order	$3.65	$ .90	$ .60
14–Day Transcript A transcript to be delivered within fourteen (14) calendar days after receipt of an order	$4.25	$ .90	$ .60
Expedited Transcript (7 day) A transcript to be delivered within seven (7) calendar days after receipt of an order.	$4.85	$ .90	$ .60
Daily Transcript A transcript to be delivered following adjournment and prior to the normal opening hour of the court on the following morning whether or not it actually is a court day.	$6.05	$1.20	$ .90

	Original	First Copy to Each Party	Each Add'l Copy to the Same Party
Hourly Transcript A transcript of proceedings ordered under unusual circumstances to be delivered within two (2) hours.	$7.25	$1.20	$ .90
Realtime Transcript A draft unedited transcript produced by a certified realtime reporter as a byproduct of realtime to be delivered electronically during proceedings or immediately following adjournment.	$3.05	$1.20	

[Dated: November 1, 2007.]

GENERAL ORDER 2011–04. IN THE MATTER OF DEPOSIT AND INVESTMENT OF REGISTRY FUNDS

The Court, having determined that it is necessary to amend local procedures to reflect the transition of accountability and administration of the Court Registry Investment System ("CRIS") from the United States District Court for the Southern District of Texas to the Administrative Office of the United States Courts pursuant to this Order, as well as ensure the continued uniformity in the deposit and investment of funds in the Court's Registry,

IT IS ORDERED that the following shall govern the transfer, receipt, deposit and investment of registry funds:

I. Transfer of Funds

All funds existing in the Court Registry which are on deposit and invested in CRIS administered by the United States District Court for the Southern District of Texas shall be transferred to the custody and control of CRIS administered by the Administrative Office of the United States Courts, and be subject to the investment and fee deduction provisions of Paragraphs III and IV of this Order. Each deposit transferred will relate back to its original date of deposit in CRIS administered by the United States District Court for the Southern District of Texas.

II. Receipt of Funds

A. No money shall be sent to the Court or its officers for deposit in the Court's registry without a court order signed by the presiding judge in the case or proceeding.

B. Unless provided for elsewhere in this Order, all monies ordered to be paid to the Court or received by its officers in any case pending or adjudicated shall be deposited with the Treasurer of the United States in the name and to the credit of this Court pursuant to 28 U.S.C. § 2041 through depositories designated by the Treasury to accept such deposit on its behalf.

C. The party making the deposit or transferring funds to the Court's registry shall serve the order permitting the deposit or transfer on the Clerk of Court.

III. Investment of Registry Funds

A. Where, by order of the Court, funds on deposit with the Court are to be placed in some form of interest-bearing account, CRIS, administered by the Administrative Office of the United States Courts, shall be the only investment mechanism authorized.

B. Money from each case deposited in CRIS shall be "pooled" together with those on deposit with Treasury to the credit of other courts in CRIS and used to purchase Government Account Series securities through the Bureau of Public Debt, which will be held at Treasury, in an account in the name and to the credit of the Director of Administrative Office of the United States Courts, hereby designated as custodian for CRIS.

C.   An account for each case will be established in CRIS titled in the name of the case giving rise to the investment in the fund.   Income generated from fund investments will be distributed to each case based on the ratio each account's principal and earnings has to the aggregate principal and income total in the fund.   Reports showing the interest earned and the principal amounts contributed in each case will be prepared and distributed to each court participating in CRIS and made available to litigants and/or their counsel.

IV.   Deductions of Fees

A.   The custodian is authorized and directed by this Order to deduct the registry fee for maintaining accounts in CRIS and the investment services fee for the management of investments. The proper registry fee is to be determined on the basis of the rates published by the Director of the Administrative Office of United States Courts as approved by the Judicial Conference.   The investment services fee is assessed from interest earnings according to the Court's Miscellaneous Fee Schedule.

B.   If registry fees were assessed against the case under the old 45–day requirement prior to deposit in CRIS, no additional registry fee will be assessed.

V.   Transition From Former Investment Procedure

A.   The Clerk of Court is directed to develop a systematic method of redemption of all existing Treasury Securities held in CRIS and the transfer of "pooled" funds to the custody of the Administrative Office of the United States Courts for investment in Government Account Series securities.

B.   This Order shall become effective May 19, 2011, and supercedes and abrogates all prior orders of this Court regarding the deposit and investment of registry funds, with the exception of District Court Miscellaneous Order entered March 5, 1986 directing the consolidation of all Bankruptcy Court registry funds with the District Court registry funds for the purpose of control, audit and disbursement.

[Dated: May 19, 2011.]

GENERAL ORDER 2011–12.   IN THE MATTER OF BANKRUPTCY JURISDICTION

AUTHORITY OF BANKRUPTCY JUDGES
TO ENTER FINAL ORDERS

By vote of members of the Court, the following Order is entered:

1.   In an adversary proceeding, a party should move to withdraw the reference within 90 days of the complaint or notice of removal.

2.   In a contested matter, a party should move to withdraw the reference within 21 days of the pleading initiating the contested matter.

3.   Motions to withdraw the reference must be first submitted to the bankruptcy judge for a recommendation to the district court.

4.   Before the bankruptcy judge, on appeal, or both, a party may challenge the bankruptcy judge's authority at any time.   A party's not having moved to withdraw the reference within these times does not waive a party's right to challenge the bankruptcy judge's authority.

5.   The general right of a party in interest to move to withdraw an adversary proceeding or contested matter to the district court remains.

6.   The bankruptcy judge or district judge may raise the issue of the bankruptcy judge's authority at any time and on their own initiative.

[Dated: November 29, 2011.]

GENERAL ORDER 2012–6.   IN RE: ORDER OF REFERENCE TO BANKRUPTCY JUDGES

1.   Bankruptcy cases and proceedings arising under Title 11 or arising in or related to a case under Title 11 of the United States Code are automatically referred to the bankruptcy judges of this district, except:

A.   Civil actions pending before the United States District Court for the Southern District of Texas before a related bankruptcy petition is filed.   With respect to these:

(1)   The automatic stay applies until it is modified by an order; and

(2)   The district judge may refer these to the Bankruptcy Court.

B.   Civil actions, bankruptcy cases and proceedings specifically withdrawn from the general reference to the Bankruptcy Court.

C.   Appeals from the Bankruptcy Court.

2.   In civil actions, bankruptcy cases and proceedings referred to them, the bankruptcy judges may exercise the full authority allowed them by law.

3.   Cases related to a bankruptcy may be *removed* only from state court to the United States District Court and not from other federal courts.

4.   If a bankruptcy judge or district judge determines that entry of a final order or judgment by a bankruptcy judge would not be consistent with Article III of the United States Constitution in a particular proceeding referred under this order and determines that proceeding to be a core matter, the bankruptcy judge shall, unless otherwise ordered by the District Court, hear the proceeding and submit proposed findings of fact and conclusions of law to the District Court.   The District Court may treat any order of the Bankruptcy Court as proposed findings of fact and conclusions of law if the District Court concludes that the bankruptcy judge could not have entered a final order or judgment consistent with Article III of the United States Constitution.

5.   This order supersedes General Order 2005–6.

[Dated: May 24, 2012.]

GENERAL ORDER 2016–14.   IN THE MATTER OF DEPOSIT AND INVESTMENT OF REGISTRY FUNDS

ORDER REGARDING DEPOSIT AND INVESTMENT OF REGISTRY FUNDS

The Court, having determined that it is necessary to adopt local procedures to ensure uniformity in the deposit, investment, and tax administration of funds in the Court's Registry,

IT IS ORDERED that the following shall govern the receipt, deposit, and investment of registry funds:

I.   Receipt of Funds

A.   No money shall be sent to the Court or its officers for deposit in the Court's registry without a court order signed by the presiding judge in the case or proceeding.

B.   The party making the deposit or transferring funds to the Court's registry shall serve the order permitting the deposit or transfer on the Clerk of Court.

C.   Unless provided for elsewhere in this Order, all monies ordered to be paid to the Court or received by its officers in any case pending or adjudicated shall be deposited with the Treasurer of the United States in the name and to the credit of this Court pursuant to 28 U.S.C. § 2041 through depositories designated by the Treasury to accept such deposit on its behalf.

II.   Investment of Registry Funds

A.   Where, by order of the Court, funds on deposit with the Court are to be placed in some form of interest-bearing account or invested in a court-approved, interest-bearing instrument in accordance with Rule 67 of the Federal Rules of Civil Procedure, the Court Registry Investment System (CRIS), administered by the Administrative Office of the United States Courts under 28 U.S.C. § 2045, shall be the only investment mechanism authorized.

B.   Interpleader funds deposited under 28 U.S.C. § 1335 meet the IRS definition of a "Disputed Ownership Fund" (DOF), a taxable entity that requires tax administration.   Unless otherwise ordered by the court, interpleader funds shall be deposited in the DOF established within the CRIS and administered by the Administrative Office of the United States Courts, which shall be responsible for meeting all DOF tax administration requirements.

C.   The Director of the Administrative Office of the United States Courts is designated as custodian for all CRIS funds.   The Director or the Director's designee shall perform the duties of custodian.   Funds held in the CRIS remain subject to the control and jurisdiction of the Court.

D.   Money from each case deposited in the CRIS shall be "pooled" together with those on deposit with Treasury to the credit of other courts in the CRIS and used to purchase Government Account Series securities through the Bureau of Public Debt, which will be held at Treasury, in an account in the name and to the credit of the Director of Administrative Office of the United States Courts.   The pooled funds will be invested in accordance with the principles of the CRIS Investment Policy as approved by the Registry Monitoring Group.

E.   An account will be established in the CRIS Liquidity Fund titled in the name of the case giving rise to the deposit invested in the fund.   Income generated from fund investments will be distributed to each case based on the ratio each account's principal and earnings has to the aggregate principal and income total in the fund after the CRIS fee has been applied.   Reports showing the interest earned and the principal amounts contributed in each case will be prepared and distributed to each court participating in the CRIS and made available to litigants and/or their counsel.

F.   For each interpleader case, an account shall be established in the CRIS Disputed Ownership Fund, titled in the name of the case giving rise to the deposit invested in the fund.   Income generated from fund investments will be distributed to each case after the DOF fee has been applied and tax withholdings have been deducted from the fund.   Reports showing the interest earned and the principal amounts contributed in each case will be available through the FedInvest/CMS application for each court participating in the CRIS and made available to litigants and/or their counsel.

III.   Fees and Taxes

A.   The custodian is authorized and directed by this Order to deduct the CRIS fee according to the Judicial Conference Schedule of Fees promulgated under 28 U.S.C. §§ 1914, 1930, for the management of registry funds invested in the CRIS, excluding the case funds held in the DOF.

B.   The custodian is authorized and directed by this Order to deduct the DOF fee according to the Judicial Conference Schedule of Fees promulgated under 28 U.S.C. §§ 1914, 1930, for the management and tax administration of funds invested in the DOF.   The custodian is further authorized and directed by this Order to withhold and pay federal taxes due on behalf of the DOF.

IV.   Transition from Former Investment Procedure

A.   Deposits to the CRIS DOF will not be transferred from any existing CRIS Funds.   Only new deposits pursuant to 28 U.S.C. § 1335 from the effective date of this order will be placed in the CRIS DOF.

B.   This Order supersedes and abrogates all prior orders of this Court regarding the deposit and investment of registry fluids, with the exception of District Court Miscellaneous Order entered March 5, 1986, directing the consolidation of all Bankruptcy Court registry funds with the District Court registry funds for the purpose of control, audit and disbursement.

[Dated: December 5, 2016.]

UNITED STATES BANKRUPTCY COURT FOR THE SOUTHERN DISTRICT OF TEXAS

Including Amendments Received Through
February 1, 2019

APPENDICES

ECF PROCEDURES

SELECTED ORDERS AND PROCEDURES

LOCAL RULE 1001–1. GENERAL

(a) These rules may be cited as the "Bankruptcy Local Rules" or "BLR".

(b) In addition to these rules, the Local Rules of the District Court, the Administrative Procedures for CM/ECF, and the standing and general orders govern practice in the bankruptcy court.

(c) The court's website, www.txs.uscourts.gov contains:

(1) Judges' schedules

(2) Dates for setting hearings

(3) Forms referenced in these rules

(4) Judges' individual court procedures

(5) Rules for chapter 11 cases designated as complex cases

(6) General and standing orders

(d) A judge may modify the application of the rules in any case.

(e) The forms referenced in these rules are on the court's website (www.txs.uscourts.gov). "Official Forms" referenced in these rules are nationally promulgated forms and may be found via a link on the court's website.

(f) All citations to statutory sections are to Title 11 of the United States Code (i.e, the Bankruptcy Code) unless otherwise specified.

[Effective December 1, 2009.]

LOCAL RULE 1002–1. COMMENCEMENT OF CASE

(a) Corporate or partnership parties must be represented by counsel at all times.

(b) Cases should be filed in the division of the debtor's "principal location", as defined in subparagraphs (c) and (d). Absent good cause, cases filed outside of the debtor's principal location will be transferred by the court sua sponte or on motion of a party.

(c) For an individual debtor, the debtor's principal location is the county of the debtor's principal residence or domicile for the longest portion of the 180 days preceding the date of the petition. If an individual debtor did not have a principal residence or domicile within the Southern District of Texas for at least 91 days before the filing of the petition, the individual debtor's principal location is the county of the debtor's principal assets within the Southern District of Texas.

(d) For a debtor that is not an individual, the debtor's principal location is the county of the debtor's principal executive offices or principal assets, if either has been located within the Southern District of Texas for at least 91 days prior to the filing of the petition.

[Effective December 1, 2009.]

LOCAL RULE 1007–1. SUPPORTING DOCUMENTS

(a) On schedules D and E/F of Official Form 106, creditors must be in alphabetical order.

(b) Official Form 121 must be submitted to the clerk with conventionally filed petitions and must be submitted to the clerk within 7 days of electronically filed petitions.

(c) In all Chapter 13 Cases, the debtor must file with the plan:

(1) If the debtor is a wage or salary employee, the debtor must file a wage order with service on the Trustee; or

(2) If the debtor is not a wage or salary employee, the debtor must file on the forms promulgated from time to time by the Court:

(A) a proposed Order For EFT Payments (Online Banking) and Debtor's Certification; or

(B) a proposed Order For ACH Payments and Debtor's Certification.

(3) If there are extraordinary circumstances justifying an exception to (1) or (2) above, the debtor may file a motion to allow direct payment of funds to the Trustee.

[Effective December 1, 2009. Amended effective December 15, 2011. December 1, 2015.]

LOCAL RULE 1009–1. AMENDMENTS OF VOLUNTARY PETITIONS AND THEIR SUPPORTING DOCUMENTS

(a) If an amendment or supplement is filed to add a creditor or to change the status, classification, or amount owed a creditor, no later than two days after the filing, the debtor must:

(1) Serve the amendment by first class mail, postage prepaid, on the trustee, U.S. trustee, and all creditors affected by the amendment,

(2) File a certificate of service,

(3) File an amended mailing list in the form directed by the clerk, and

(4) Pay the filing fee.

(b) Amendments to schedules must be marked to identify added, deleted or changed information.

(c) If it appears to the court or trustee that the supporting documents need to be amended, the court or trustee may notify the debtor, specifying the items, documents, and time for amendment.

(d) If the debtor moves to correct an erroneous social security number, the debtor must serve all parties in interest. The proposed form of order must extend the deadline for objecting to exemptions and discharge if necessary.

[Effective December 1, 2009. Amended effective January 24, 2011; July 20, 2012.]

LOCAL RULE 1014–1. INTRADISTRICT TRANSFER

On motion of a party in interest or on its own motion, the judge may transfer a case, an adversary proceeding, or a contested proceeding to another judge or division in this district. This rule does not apply to the reassignment of a judge following a recusal.

[Effective December 1, 2009.]

LOCAL RULE 1015–1. JOINT ADMINISTRATION

(a) Motions and proposed orders for joint administration should itemize the requested relief. The motion and order must be in the form published on the court's website.

(b) A motion for joint administration must be made to the judge with the lowest case number.

[Effective December 1, 2009.]

LOCAL RULE 1017–2. DISMISSALS

(a) Among the reasons a case may be dismissed for want of prosecution under Fed. R. Bankr. P. 1017 are:

(1) Incomplete or late schedules filed by the debtor;

(2) The failure of a non-individual debtor to act through counsel in the filing of a bankruptcy petition or the prosecution of a case;

(3) Unpaid or late filing fees by the debtor;

(4) Failure by the debtor to timely file mailing lists of creditors in the prescribed format;

(5) Failure by the debtor to include the required creditors list with the petition;

(6) Failure by the debtor to timely file the forms required by BLR 1007–1;

(7) The debtor's lack of diligent, prompt prosecution through filing of a plan late, missing or incomplete disclosure statement or other document required by the code, rules, or orders;

(8) The debtor's failure to attend the § 341 creditors meeting;

(9) The debtor's failure to timely amend schedules requested by the trustee or the U.S. trustee; and

(10) Unpaid U.S. trustee quarterly fees.

(b) Chapter 13 trustees may file motions to dismiss for nonpayment, in the exercise of their discretion, at any time. Chapter 13 trustees must timely file motions to dismiss if the debtor is two monthly payments behind. The hearing must be set at the first panel following the expiration of 28 days after the motion is filed. The form of motion shall be in a form promulgated from time-to-time by the Bankruptcy Court. Responses and requests for hearings on motions to dismiss must be filed not later than 21 days after service. If no timely response is filed, the Court may dismiss the case without a hearing, at its discretion.

(c) In chapter 13 cases, federal tax issues will be governed by the following procedures:

(1) At or before 7 days before the date first set for the first § 341 meeting of creditors, the Internal Revenue Service must send a tax transcript to the chapter 13 trustee, the debtor and debtor's counsel.

(2) Within 7 days after the § 341 meeting of creditors, the trustee must file a motion to dismiss any chapter 13 case in which the IRS transcript reflects a delinquent return for a period in which taxes would be entitled to a priority. The motion shall be in a form published from time-to-time on the Court's website.

(3) Within 21 days after the chapter 13 trustee has filed a motion to dismiss a case based on delinquent tax returns, the debtor must file a response to the motion.

(4) If all tax returns that are the subject of a motion under BLR 1017–2(b) have not been filed, the plan will not be confirmed. If all tax returns have been filed, the court may confirm the plan or may deny confirmation based on an estimate of the IRS's claim pursuant to § 502(c). The order confirming the plan will provide that the plan has been confirmed based on an estimate of the debtor's tax liability and that the actual amount payable by the debtor in order to discharge the tax liability will be the actual amount determined based on the allowance of the tax claim, without regard for any provision in the plan to the contrary.

(5) The proposed order dismissing for failure to file tax returns will provide for dismissal with prejudice until all delinquent returns have been filed and must be in the form published from time-to-time on the Court's website.

[Effective December 1, 2009.]

LOCAL RULE 1019–1. SUPPLEMENTAL SCHEDULES IN CONVERTED CASES

Within 14 days after entry of an order converting a case from one chapter to another, the debtor must file: (1) supplemental schedules itemizing changes from the original schedules in property of the estate and in creditor lists, or (2) a statement that there are no changes.

[Effective December 1, 2009.]

LOCAL RULE 1075–1. COMPLEX CASES

Procedures for the administration of complex cases are governed by the Procedures for Complex Cases as posted on the Court's website. Those procedures govern the extent to which the Texas Procedures for complex Chapter 11 Cases (also posted on the Court's website) apply.

[Effective December 1, 2009.]

LOCAL RULE 2002–1. NOTICES TO CREDITORS, EQUITY SECURITY HOLDERS, AND THE UNITED STATES

Notices given under Bankruptcy Rule 2002 must be given as ordered by the Court. If the Court does not enter a separate order directing the method of notice:

(a) Under Bankruptcy Rule 2002(a), the Court directs that notices that are governed by that rule must be given:

(1) With respect to the matters in Bankruptcy Rule 2002(a)(1), notice will be given by the clerk.

(2) With respect to the matters in Bankruptcy Rule 2002(a)(2), notice must be given by the proponent of the proposed use, sale, or lease of property.

(3) With respect to the matters in Bankruptcy Rule 2002(a)(3), notice must be given:

(A) In a chapter 7 case with a compromise involving exempt property, by the Debtor(s); in all other chapter 7 matters, by the trustee.

(B) In a chapter 11 case with Debtor(s) in possession, by the Debtor(s) in possession; in a chapter 11 case with a trustee, by the trustee.

(C) In a chapter 13 case when the proponent of the compromise is the chapter 13 trustee, by the chapter 13 trustee; in all other chapter 13 matters, by the Debtor(s).

(4) With respect to the matters in Bankruptcy Rule 2002(a)(4), notice must be given by the proponent of the dismissal or conversion.

(5) With respect to the matters in Bankruptcy Rule 2002(a)(5), notice must be given by the proponent of the proposed plan modification.

(6) With respect to the matters in Bankruptcy Rule 2002(a)(6), notice must be given by the applicant.

(7) With respect to the matters in Bankruptcy Rule 2002(a)(7), notice must be given by the clerk if the notice is sent with the notice of the initial meeting of creditors under § 341. All other notices for matters in Bankruptcy Rule 2002(a)(7) must be given by the party requesting a bar date.

(8) With respect to the matters set forth in Bankruptcy Rule 2002(a)(8), notice must be given by the proponent of the proposed plan.

(b) With respect to the matters in Bankruptcy Rule 2002(b), notices must be given by the proponent of a proposed plan under chapters 9 and 11. With respect to a chapter 13 plan, notice must be given by the clerk as set forth in BLR 2002–1(c).

(c) The clerk must send a notice promptly after a chapter 13 case is filed. The notice must:

(1) Set the initial meeting of creditors under § 341 (the "§ 341 Meeting").

(2) Set the initial confirmation date for the Debtor(s)' proposed plan and a hearing on § 506 valuations on the last available date that is not more than 45 days after the § 341 meeting. If the plan is filed on the petition date, the notice shall include a copy of the plan.

[Effective December 1, 2009. Amended effective January 24, 2011; December 1, 2017.]

LOCAL RULE 2003–1. SECTION 341 MEETINGS OF CREDITORS OR EQUITY SECURITY HOLDERS

(a) The debtor must attend creditors' meetings unless excused by the court from attendance.

(b) With trustee's consent, a debtor may participate at the creditors meeting by telephone in accordance with procedures established by the U.S. trustee. Any other requested participation requires a court order. The U.S. trustee's procedures are available on the Court's website.

(c) The chapter 13 trustee will file a recommendation regarding confirmation of the debtor's proposed plan at the conclusion of the debtor's § 341 meeting. If no timely confirmation objection is filed and the trustee recommends confirmation, then the judge may confirm the plan without a hearing or conduct a hearing on confirmation of the plan.

The trustee may withdraw a recommendation in favor of confirmation at any time. If the trustee withdraws the confirmation recommendation less than 7 days before confirmation, the confirmation hearing will be rescheduled.

[Effective December 1, 2009. Amended effective January 24, 2011.]

LOCAL RULE 2004–1. EXAMINATION

(a) The purpose of this rule is to avoid a motion and court order for a 2004 examination unless an objection is filed and to encourage agreements on an examination schedule.

(b) A written agreement between the proponent, opposing counsel, and the person or entity to be examined of date, time, and place of a 2004 examination is enforceable by a motion to compel or for sanctions without necessity of court order or subpoena.

(c) Conferences to arrange for an agreeable examination schedule are required. Failure to confer is grounds for a motion to quash and sanctions.

(d) Not fewer than 14 days written notice of a proposed examination must be given to the person or entity to be examined, its counsel, and to affected parties under BLR 9013–1(a). The notice must apprise the party of the scope of the examination and categories of documents to be produced. The notice must be filed.

(e) If no response is served, the notice to conduct an examination under this rule is deemed ordered, without requiring the entry of an order.

(f) If a party to be examined has objections, that party has the burden to seek relief from the court by filing a motion to quash or for a protective order. The motion must comply with BLR 9013–1. The entity to be examined and affected parties have 7 days to respond or object to the proposed examination.

(g) If anyone has been unreasonable in seeking or resisting discovery under Fed. R. Bankr. P. 2004, the court may impose sanctions.

[Effective December 1, 2009.]

LOCAL RULE 2006–1.   TRUSTEE ELECTION

A party seeking to conduct an election of a trustee must give written notice to the U.S. trustee not later than 7 days before the commencement of the § 341 meeting of creditors.

[Effective December 1, 2009.]

LOCAL RULE 2014–1.   EMPLOYMENT OF PROFESSIONALS

(a) An application for employment by an attorney for the debtor or a motion for substitution of counsel for the debtor must have attached the statement required by FED. R. BANKR. P. 2016(b) and § 329 of the Bankruptcy Code.

(b) Nunc Pro Tunc Application.

(1) If an application for approval of the employment of a professional is made within 30 days of the commencement of that professional's provision of services, it is deemed contemporaneous.

(2) If an application for the approval of the employment of a professional is made more than 30 days after that professional commences provision of services and the application seeks to make the authority retroactive to the commencement, the application must include:

(A) An explanation of why the application was not filed earlier;

(B) An explanation why the order authorizing employment is required nunc pro tunc;

(C) An explanation, to the best of the applicant's knowledge, how approval of the application may prejudice any parties-in-interest.

(3) Applications to approve the employment of professionals nunc pro tunc shall be approved only on notice and opportunity for hearing. All creditors in the case must be served with notice of the application. The notice must include the negative notice language of BLR 9013–1(b).

(c) An ex parte application to employ accountant combined with application to pay compensation may be allowed without further application or notice and hearing, under this rule, when the compensation will not exceed $300 per annum and employment will not exceed three years.

(1) In chapter 7 cases, the trustee may make an ex parte application to employ combined with application to compensate an accountant for the estate for the purpose of tax preparation and accounting services, without further notice or hearing if it limits payment to less than $300 per year for each year's tax returns payable at the completion of a return, and which employment shall be for no longer than three years;

(2) This ex parte procedure is available only where no earlier application to employ an accountant has been made and no later applications are contemplated by the trustee;

(3) The trustee must indicate to the court that the administration of the estate is expected to be completed within three years; and

(4) Employment beyond tax preparation and attendant accounting services where compensation in excess of $300 per year or a duration longer than three years is sought requires separate applications to employ and for compensation with notice to all creditors and other parties in interest under FED. R. BANKR. P. 2016 and BLR 2016–1.

(d) Applications to retain special counsel in an individual chapter 7, 11, 12 or 13 case for the purpose of prosecuting a tort claim must be filed in a form as published on the Court's website. The proposed form of order must also be on a form as published on the Court's website. Leave from this BLR 2014–1(d) must be sought by a separate motion.

(e) Service of applications to employ professionals is governed by BLR 9003–1.

[Effective December 1, 2009.   Amended effective April 12, 2012.]

LOCAL RULE 2015–3.   REPORTS

Periodic reports required by Fed. R. Bankr. P. 2015 must be filed monthly.

[Effective December 1, 2009.]

LOCAL RULE 2016–1.   PROFESSIONAL FEES

(a) Each judge's web page contains fee application procedures.

(b) In chapter 11 cases, retainers may be deposited with attorneys or accountants only (i) prior to the filing of the petition; or (ii) pursuant to a Court order, if paid after the filing of the petition.

(c) In chapter 11 cases, attorneys and accountants must deposit retainer funds in trust accounts, whether the retainer is received from the debtor or from anyone else. A retainer may be applied to fees and expenses only if no objection has been filed and 21 days have elapsed from the filing and service of a notice for the distribution of a retainer. The notice must describe the services rendered, time spent, hourly rates charged, and the name of the professional or paraprofessional doing the work. A notice of distribution may not be filed more frequently than once a month. Compensation withdrawn under this rule is interim until a final fee application is approved.

(d) Chapter 13 debtor's attorneys may seek attorneys' fees on a fixed fee basis or a lodestar basis as follows:

(1) Fixed fee agreements must be filed within 21 days of the petition date and be in the form promulgated from time-to-time by the Bankruptcy Court.

(2) Lodestar applications must include (A) a cover sheet in the form promulgated from time-to-time by the Bankruptcy Court, (B) attached, detailed, contemporaneous time records; (C) a statement setting forth the basis of the retention (i.e., whether the retention was on a fixed or hourly fee basis and any other pertinent details); and (D) a narrative description setting forth any unique, unusual or time consuming issues particular to the chapter 13 case. A copy of the lodestar fee application, with required attachments, must be sent to the court's case manager.

(e) A chapter 7 trustee is authorized to pay, without prior Court approval, administrative expenses from funds of the estate for:

(1) filing fees for adversary proceedings;

(2) bond premiums as authorized by the United States Trustee;

(3) reasonable and necessary bank charges;

(4) additional routine administrative expenses incurred in the administration of the estate for the preservation of estate assets, such as locksmith charges and storage rental expenses payable to unrelated third party vendors, in amounts not exceeding an aggregate of $2,000.00 to any single entity.

Payments made pursuant to subsection 2016–1(e)(4) must be itemized and described in the Trustee's Request for Fees and Expenses and are subject to Court approval after notice and hearing. This Rule does not (x) apply to payments advanced by professionals retained by the estate; or (y) limit amounts that may be paid by a chapter 7 trustee who is authorized to operate the business of a debtor pursuant to § 721 of the Code.

[Effective December 1, 2009. Amended effective May 20, 2010; September 26, 2011.]

LOCAL RULE 3001–1. PROOFS OF CLAIM ON HOME MORTGAGES

Nothing in these Rules or the Federal Rules of Bankruptcy Procedure precludes the Court from requiring additional disclosures or the production of supporting documents to verify the validity or amount of a claim.

[Effective April 1, 2010. Amended effective December 1, 2015.]

LOCAL RULE 3003–1. DEADLINE FOR FILING PROOFS OF CLAIM AND PROOFS OF INTEREST IN CHAPTER 9 AND CHAPTER 11 CASES

(a) In chapter 9 and chapter 11 cases, unless otherwise ordered by the court or governed by BLR 3003–1(b), proofs of claim and proofs of interest must be filed within 90 days after the first date set for the meeting of creditors under section 341(a), except that a proof of claim filed by a governmental unit must be filed within 180 days after the order for relief.

(b) BLR 3003–1(a) does not apply to chapter 11 cases that (1) are ordered treated as complex cases, or (2) transferred from another judicial district.

[Effective December 1, 2009.]

LOCAL RULE 3007–1. OBJECTIONS TO CLAIMS

(a) An objection to claim must list the claimant, the date the proof of claim was filed, the amount of the claim, and the classification of the claim as secured, priority unsecured or general unsecured. The legal and factual basis for the objection must be clear from the face of the pleading. The objection must include an affidavit signed by a person with personal knowledge supporting the objection.

(b) An objection to claim may be filed without a hearing date. Objections to claims filed in accordance with this Rule, and to which no reply has been filed, may be considered without a hearing. If an objection to claim is filed without a

hearing date, the objection must state in bold print immediately below the title:

This is an objection to your claim. This objection asks the Court to disallow the claim that you filed in this bankruptcy case. If you do not file a response within 30 days after the objection was served on you, your claim may be disallowed without a hearing.

(c) An objection to claim may include an initial hearing date obtained from the judge's web page or case manager. If an initial hearing date is scheduled, the objection must state in bold print immediately below the title:

This is an objection to your claim. This objection asks the Court to disallow the claim that you filed in this bankruptcy case. If you do not file a response within 30 days after the objection was served on you, your claim may be disallowed without a hearing.

A hearing has been set on this matter on [date] at [time] in Courtroom _____, address].

(d) Unless otherwise ordered by the Court or by consent of the parties, the initial hearing will be non-evidentiary and used as a scheduling conference. The parties should confer prior to the initial hearing regarding any required discovery and other issues necessary for a trial on the merits. Notwithstanding the foregoing, the failure of either party to appear at the initial hearing may result in the summary disposition of the objection. Agreed orders may be presented at the initial hearing or filed prior to the initial hearing.

[Effective December 1, 2009. Amended effective October 7, 2013; December 1, 2017.]

LOCAL RULE 3010–1. DATE OF DISTRIBUTION IN DISMISSED CHAPTER 13 CASES

Distributions in dismissed cases should be made by the chapter 13 trustee at the earliest practicable date following the disposition of all motions for administrative expenses that are timely filed or that are deemed allowed pursuant to BLR 4001–1. Timely filed motions for administrative expenses will be those filed within 21 days of the dismissal order.

[Effective December 1, 2009.]

LOCAL RULE 3011–1. NOTICE OF APPLICATION FOR WITHDRAWAL OF UNCLAIMED FUNDS FROM REGISTRY OF THE COURT

Applications to withdraw unclaimed funds that were deposited into the registry of the court by a trustee under 11 U.S.C. § 347(a) must be served on the United States Attorney for the Southern District of Texas and on the United States trustee.

[Effective December 1, 2009.]

LOCAL RULE 3015–1. CONFIRMATION OF CHAPTER 13 PLANS AND RULE 3015.1 OPT–OUT

(a) **Uniform Plan and Motion for Valuation of Collateral.** Pursuant to FED. R. BANKR. P. 3015.1, the Court requires that a Local Form Plan must be used instead of the Official

Form Plan. The Local Form Plan is posted on the Court's website.

(b) Mortgage Payments Through the Chapter 13 Trustee. Home mortgage payments will be made through the chapter 13 trustee, in accordance with Chapter 13 Trustee Procedures for Administration of Home Mortgage Payments ("Home Mortgage Payment Procedures"). The Home Mortgage Payment Procedures adopted by the Court are posted on the Court's website.

(c) Plan Modifications. To obtain a modification of a confirmed chapter 13 plan:

(1) The party seeking to modify the plan must file (i) a proposed modified plan and a proposed modified plan summary, each utilizing the official forms posted on the Court's website; and (ii) a proposed amended wage order or electronic payment mechanism consistent with the proposed modification.

(2) The proposed modified plan must be self-calendared for a hearing on the next available date as scheduled on the Chapter 13 Trustee's website.

(3) If the proposed modified plan is filed by the Debtor(s), the Debtor(s) must simultaneously file amended schedules I and J.

[Effective December 1, 2009. Amended effective January 24, 2011; December 1, 2017.]

LOCAL RULE 3016–1. CHAPTER 11 PLANS

(a) If a proponent of a plan seeks to impose an injunction of the type referenced in FED. R. BANKR. P. 3016(c), the proponent must orally notify the court at the disclosure statement hearing of the proponent's intent to seek the injunctive relief.

(b) In chapter 11 cases in which a debtor is an individual, the form of the chapter 11 plan must either

(1) Be in the form as published on the Court's website and state in the title of the Plan that the Plan is a "Uniform Individual Chapter 11 Plan"; or

(2) State in the title of the Plan that the Plan is a "Non–Uniform Individual Chapter 11 Plan."

[Effective December 1, 2009. Amended effective April 12, 2012.]

LOCAL RULE 3021–1. PAYMENTS BY CHAPTER 13 TRUSTEE

(a) Chapter 13 trustees must make payments in accordance with confirmed plans.

(b) Payment of Debtor(s)' attorneys' fees shall be made only after entry of an order allowing the fees. Under fixed fee agreements, attorneys' fees are allowed on entry of the order approving the fixed fee agreement.

(c) The priority of payments to be made under a plan is established by the confirmed plan.

(d) Each chapter 13 trustee will place information on the chapter 13 trustee's website regarding all payments made under Plans.

[Effective December 1, 2009. Amended effective April 12, 2012; December 1, 2017.]

LOCAL RULE 4001–1. RELIEF FROM AUTOMATIC STAY

(a) Motions for relief from stay:

(1) Motions for relief from the stay must contain a certificate that the movant has conferred with opposing counsel (or, in the event of pro se parties, opposing parties) and been unable to reach an agreement on the requested relief. If no conference has been conducted, movant must certify the dates and times on which movant has attempted to confer. Notwithstanding the foregoing, no conference is required if the movant files a certification that a confirmed plan provides for the surrender of the collateral that is the subject of the motion.

(2) A motion for relief from stay must include a hearing date from the judge's web page. Failure to obtain a hearing date from the judge's web page and to include the notice in BLR 4001–1(a)(3) is a waiver of the automatic termination of the automatic stay under 11 U.S.C. § 362(e) or 1301(d).

(3) The motion must state immediately below the title:

This is a motion for relief from the automatic stay. If it is granted, the movant may act outside of the bankruptcy process. If you do not want the stay lifted, immediately contact the moving party to settle. If you cannot settle, you must file a response and send a copy to the moving party at least 7 days before the hearing. If you cannot settle, you must attend the hearing. Evidence may be offered at the hearing and the court may rule.

Represented parties should act through their attorney.

There will be a hearing on this matter on [date] at [time] in courtroom ___, [address].

(4) In addition to service as required by FED. R. BANKR. P. 4001(a)(1), on the same day that it is filed, the motion must be served on debtor, debtor's attorney, parties requesting notice, parties with an interest in collateral that is the subject of the requested relief, co-debtors under 11 U.S.C. § 1301, parties who are identified as a party against whom relief is sought in the motion, and the trustee.

(5) If the moving party schedules a hearing on a motion for relief from stay or agrees to continue the hearing to a date more than thirty (30) days after the date the motion was filed (21 days for motions to lift the co-debtor stay), the party shall be deemed to have waived the automatic termination under 11 U.S.C. § 362(e) and/or 1301(d).

(6) All motions to lift stay that request foreclosure on improved real property must be accompanied by documents evidencing the debt and lien perfection, and a payment history, including an explanation of transaction codes. Responses disputing the payment history must specify payments made that are not reflected in the payment history, the dates of payment, the amounts, and the mode. Evidence not accompanying the motion or response may be inadmissible in an evidentiary hearing.

(7) Failure of the movant to prosecute the motion at a preliminary hearing may result in dismissal of the motion for want of prosecution unless there is (i) an order continuing the hearing and waiving the 30–day requirement; (ii) a stipulation of the parties to continue the hearing and waive the 30–day

requirement; or (iii) an agreed order resolving the motion that is entered prior to or is signed at the hearing.

(8) Motions for relief from the stay may never be combined with a request for other relief.

(9) In addition to other procedures applicable to motions for relief from the stay, a chapter 13 debtor must timely respond to motions for relief from the stay. A timely response includes the filing of an agreed order, a denial that conforms with FED. R. BANKR. P. 7008, a statement of non-opposition, or another accurate statement reflecting the current status of the motion. If no timely response is filed, the court may grant the motion for relief from the stay with or without a hearing, at its discretion.

(10) Responses should state the efforts of respondent to reach an agreement with movant and either (i) itemize each disputed issue of law or fact; or (ii) comply with FED. R. CIV. P. 8 as applied by FED. R. BANKR. P. 7008.

(11) In any evidentiary hearing conducted on a motion for relief from the automatic stay, all counsel shall certify before the presentation of evidence (1) that good faith settlement discussions have been held or why they have not been held; (2) that counsel has complied with Local Rule 9013–2 (except that the debtor is presumed to be a witness and need not be identified); and (3) the anticipated length of the hearing.

(b) Motions filed under BR 4001(b), 4001(c), or 4001(d) for the use of cash collateral, obtaining credit, or for approval of agreements on BR 4001 matters, must state immediately below the title:

This motion seeks an order that may adversely affect you. If you oppose the motion, you should immediately contact the moving party to resolve the dispute. If you and the moving party cannot agree, you must file a response and send a copy to the moving party. You must file and serve your response within 14 days of the date this was served on you. Your response must state why the motion should not be granted. If you do not file a timely response, the relief may be granted without further notice to you. If you oppose the motion and have not reached an agreement, you must attend the hearing. Unless the parties agree otherwise, the court may consider evidence at the hearing and may decide the motion at the hearing.

Represented parties should act through their attorney.

If a hearing has been set on the motion, this language must be added at the end of the notice:

There will be a hearing on this motion on [date] at [time] in courtroom ___, [address].

(c) Motions to approve agreements governed by Bankruptcy Rule 4001(d) must be served:

(1) If the agreement is in an individual chapter 7 case or a chapter 13 case and concerns consumer goods, the debtor's homestead or a non-business-use vehicle, notice should be given to the chapter 13 trustee, the debtor, any co-obligor, and any party with an interest in the collateral.

(2) Motions to approve all other agreements governed by Bankruptcy Rule 4001(d) shall be served under BLR 2002–1(a)(3).

(d) Attorneys' fees will be awarded to creditors for filing motions for relief from the stay as follows:

(1) Undersecured creditors will not be awarded attorneys' fees for the filing of a motion for relief from the stay in a chapter 13 bankruptcy case.

(2) With respect to motions by oversecured creditors or by home lenders filing post-confirmation motions governed by § 1322(b)(2), the court will approve agreed orders (i) providing for attorneys' fees and costs not to exceed $500.00 plus statutory filing fees; and (ii) providing for attorneys' fees and costs exceeding that sum only upon a submission of fee statements reflecting actual time incurred. All requests for attorneys' fees must (i) include a certification that the amount requested is less than or equal to the amount that will be paid by the holder of the lien to the holder's counsel; and (ii) be reasonable under the facts and circumstances.

(3) Attorneys' fees in matters not resolved by agreed orders will be considered on an evidentiary basis.

(e) In each chapter 13 case, the Court will issue an order that authorizes the use of estate vehicles under § 363 and provides adequate protection to the holders of liens on the vehicles.

(1) The adequate protection order will require the debtor to (i) maintain insurance on the vehicle in the amount required by the debtor(s) prepetition contract; (ii) provide proof of insurance to the lien holder; and (iii) enter into a wage order or EFT Order not later than 14 days after the petition date.

(2) As additional adequate protection, the lien holder will be given an administrative claim, with priority under § 507(b), in an amount equal to 1.25% of the value of the vehicle for each 30 days that elapses from the date of the adequate protection order. For example, if the vehicle is valued at $10,000, a § 507(b) adequate protection claim in the amount of $125 will accrue each month. In the event of a dismissal or conversion of the chapter 13 case, the trustee will distribute the proceeds in accordance with § 1326(a)(2). This will result, in most cases, in payments being made in the following order of priority:

(A) First, to the vehicle lien holders in the amount of the adequate protection reserve;

(B) Second, to debtor's counsel for unpaid fees for which an application is filed on or before 21 days after entry of the order of dismissal and that have been allowed by court order;

(C) Third, to the debtor (directly and not through counsel).

(D) Payments under paragraph "1" shall be made following the expiration of 14 days of entry of the dismissal order, unless the dismissal order is stayed.

(3) The debtor or any other party in interest may object to the adequate protection order not later than 30 days after entry of the court's order. The objecting party must state the date that the hearing will be conducted, which date will be the next chapter 13 panel after the expiration of 14 days from the date of the objection. The objection must be served on the debtor, the debtor's counsel, the chapter 13 trustee, and any party holding security interest in the vehicle. The objecting

party must attend the hearing and present evidence in support of the objection.

(4) For purposes of valuation in the absence of any objection, the vehicle value will be determined as of the date of the filing of the chapter 13 petition and will be equal to the average wholesale and retail value listed by NADA (without options or mileage adjustments). In determining the principal amount due to the lien holder under the plan, the § 507(b) payments will be (i) deducted from the value of the vehicle, if the value of the vehicle is less than the lien; and (ii) applied to interest if the value of the vehicle is greater than the lien. If the value of the vehicle is less than the lien, interest will begin to accrue on the confirmation date.

(5) The adequate protection order will not provide protection to a vehicle lender if the debtor voluntarily surrenders the vehicle by delivering the vehicle to the vehicle lender within 28 days of the petition date.

(6) If a debtor proposes to make direct, post-petition payments to a lender on a vehicle loan that was not in default as of the petition date, no additional adequate protection payments are required, unless otherwise ordered by the Court. If a debtor defaults on direct payments, the debtor must make a cash payment to the lien holder at or before the time of any plan modification. The cash payment must equal or exceed 1.25% of the vehicle's value (determined in the manner set forth in paragraph 4 above) for each one month of missed direct payments.

(f) Motions for relief from the automatic stay that pertain to exempt residences or exempt vehicles ("Consumer Lift Stay Motions") are governed by this BLR 4001–1(f).

(1) Parties who file motions for relief from the stay on exempt residences or exempt vehicles in chapter 7 and chapter 13 cases must comply with this BLR 4001–1(f) and must use the forms promulgated by the court from time to time.

(2) Variance from this rule is allowed, if exceptional circumstances exist.

(A) Exceptional circumstances include:

(1) A motion for relief from the stay filed against a repeat bankruptcy case filer for which the movant seeks relief other than a routine termination of the stay; or

(2) A motion for relief from the stay on which there are disputes regarding the extent, validity, or priority of liens on the collateral that is the subject of the motion.

(B) A party believing that are other exceptional circumstances justifying exemption from this rule must allege the exceptional circumstances with particularity in the motion.

(3) Variance from this rule is allowed, if exceptional circumstances exist. When exceptional circumstances are alleged, the court may conduct an evidentiary hearing at which time the exceptional circumstances must be demonstrated by a preponderance of the evidence.

(4) Prior to filing a Consumer Lift Stay Motion, the movant must attempt to contact the debtor(s)' counsel to discuss whether an agreement can be reached utilizing the court's a agreed order forms. If such an agreement can be reached, the parties may submit a Motion for Entry of Agreed Order

under FRBP 4001. Conferences may be attempted by telephone or by e-mail. In all conferences, movant's counsel must provide a contact person with a direct telephone number for future discussions. The motion may be filed by the movant in accordance with the following table:

Day of Initial Attempt to Confer	When Motion May be Filed
Monday	5:00 p.m. on Wednesday
Tuesday	5:00 p.m. on Thursday
Wednesday	5:00 p.m. on Friday
Thursday	5:00 p.m. on the following Monday
Friday	5:00 p.m. on the following Tuesday

(5) If the parties cannot reach agreement to submit an agreed order in the court's format, the party seeking relief from the stay may file a Consumer Lift Stay Motion in the court's format along with a proposed order, also in the court's format. Responses by the debtor must be one of the following and must be filed at least 7 days before the hearing:

(A) Submission of an agreed order terminating the stay utilizing a form from the court's website. If an agreed order is filed in accordance with these procedures, the court usually will issue the order prior to the hearing. Attendance at the originally scheduled hearing is not necessary, by either party. If the court declines to issue the order, the court will issue an order for further proceedings.

(B) Submission of an agreed order conditioning the stay utilizing a form from the court's website. If an agreed order is filed in accordance with these procedures, the court will usually issue the order prior to the hearing. Attendance at the originally scheduled hearing is not necessary, by either party. If the court declines to issue the order, the court will issue an order for further proceedings.

(C) Filing an answer or other response. Answers must comply with FRBP 9011. Responses must be based on reasonable investigation and must not be filed for delay or other improper purpose. A response stating that the debtor(s)' attorney has not been able to contact the debtor(s) or a general denial not based on reasonable investigation may not be sufficient to prevent default relief. If a timely response is filed, attendance at the hearing by both parties is required.

(6) If a sufficient response has not been timely filed, the movant must submit a proposed form of default order with a certification of default. The proposed form of default order and certification must comply with the court's form as promulgated from time to time. The court may issue a default order if an adequate response is not filed at least 7 days before the hearing. If the court issues a default order prior to the hearing, counsel need not appear at the hearing. If the court has not issued a default order and a party who has failed to respond appears at the hearing, the court may nevertheless grant default relief or may set a date for an evidentiary hearing.

[Effective December 1, 2009. Amended effective January 24, 2011; July 20, 2012.]

LOCAL RULE 4002–1. DUTIES OF DEBTOR–IN–POSSESSION

(a) A debtor in possession is responsible for strict compliance with the Bankruptcy Code, Federal Rules of Bankruptcy Procedure, and standing orders. Counsel for the debtor-in-possession is responsible for instructing the debtor about the U.S. trustee guidelines for a debtor-in-possession and insuring compliance with those guidelines.

(b) The debtor, its officers, and agents hold and manage the debtor's assets as fiduciaries for the estate; they must strictly comply with court orders and Bankruptcy Code §§ 363 and 1107. The debtor must prevent the depletion of the assets of the business during the proceedings, and it must notify its counsel immediately of a depletion or potential depletion.

(c) If the debtor becomes aware of facts indicating that the continued operation of its business may not be in the best interest of the creditors or of the estate, it must immediately notify its counsel, who may immediately notify the court and recommend a solution.

(d) The debtor may not use property of the estate to pay any prepetition unsecured obligation except on order.

(e) The debtor must not transfer (sell, give, move, encumber) an asset outside of the ordinary course of business except on order.

(f) The debtor must not incur administrative and priority expenses unless funds are reasonably expected to be generated to pay them.

(g) The debtor must comply fully with Title 11's tax provisions, with the deposit requirements of the Internal Revenue Code and Regulations, and with all state tax laws.

(h) The debtor must pay on a current basis all obligations incurred by it in operating its business.

(i) The debtor must not use cash collateral without prior written consent of the secured creditor or an order.

(j) This list of duties is not exclusive, and it does not exclude unenumerated obligations imposed by law. Counsel for the debtor-in-possession is responsible to instruct the debtor of this rule immediately on filing the case.

(k) Counsel may advise the court of any knowing violation by debtor.

[Effective December 1, 2009.]

LOCAL RULE 4003–1. EXEMPTIONS

(a) If an amendment or supplement to the list of exemptions is filed after the § 341(a) meeting of creditors, it must be served by the party claiming the exemption under BLR 9013–1.

(b) When a hearing date on an objection to an amended or supplemented list of exemptions is established, the objector must give notice as if the objection were a motion with service under BLR 9013–1.

[Effective December 1, 2009.]

LOCAL RULE 4008–1. REAFFIRMATION AGREEMENTS

The filing of a reaffirmation agreement will be a request for a hearing if the reaffirmation agreement is not accompanied by a § 524(c)(3) declaration or affidavit of debtor's counsel. No motion is required to invoke the reaffirmation procedures of § 524(c).

[Effective December 1, 2009.]

LOCAL RULE 5005–1. FILING OF PAPERS

(a) The Texas statewide procedures for electronic filing are adopted by this court and are published on the Court's website.

(b) Except as expressly provided or unless permitted by the presiding Judge, the Court requires documents being filed to be submitted, signed or verified by electronic means that comply with the procedures established by the Court. The notice of electronic filing that is automatically generated by the Court's electronic filing system constitutes service of the document on those registered as filing users of the system.

(c) Depositions, interrogatories, answers to interrogatories, requests for production or inspection, responses to those requests, and other discovery material may not be filed. When a discovery document is needed in a pretrial proceeding, those portions that are needed will be an exhibit to it. When this material is needed at trial, it may be introduced under the Federal Rules of Evidence.

[Effective December 1, 2009.]

LOCAL RULE 5011–1. WITHDRAWAL OF REFERENCE

A motion to withdraw a case, contested matter, or adversary proceeding to the district court must be filed with the clerk. Unless the district court orders otherwise, the matter will first be presented to the bankruptcy judge for recommendation.

[Effective December 1, 2009.]

LOCAL RULE 5074–1. COMMUNICATION AND COOPERATION WITH FOREIGN COURTS AND FOREIGN REPRESENTATIVES

Except for communications for scheduling and administrative purposes, the court in any case commenced by a foreign representative shall give at least 21 days' notice of its intent to communicate with a foreign court or a foreign representative. The notice shall identify the subject of the anticipated communication and shall be given in the manner provided by Rule 2002(q). Any entity that wishes to participate in the communication shall notify the court of its intention not later than 7 days before the scheduled communication.

[Effective December 1, 2009.]

LOCAL RULE 6007–1. SURRENDER OF COLLATERAL IN CHAPTER 13 CASES

(a) If a chapter 13 plan[1] requires the surrender of collateral that is subject to a debtor's possession or control, this Rule governs the implementation of the surrender, unless the Court orders otherwise.

(b) Debtors and holders of security interests may enter into written agreements (including agreements made by email) providing for the orderly surrender of collateral under a confirmed plan. No agreement may impose personal liability on a debtor or limit a debtor's discharge. If a written agreement is made, the Court will enforce it according to its terms unless the agreement contravenes applicable law. The balance of this Rule governs the method of surrender under a confirmed plan when there is not a written agreement.

(c) The procedures for the surrender of collateral made pursuant to Paragraph 7 of the plan must commence not later than 7 days following entry of the order approving the plan.

(d) The procedures for the surrender of collateral made pursuant to Paragraph 20 of a confirmed plan must commence no earlier than 21 days nor later than 28 days after a Surrender Notice is filed.

(e) This subsection applies to the surrender of real property and for which no written agreement has been made under BLR 6007–1(b).

i. The Debtor(s) must send a letter, substantially in the form set forth on the Court's website, offering immediate possession of the real property to each holder of a security interest on the real property that is listed as a secured creditor on the Debtor's Schedule D or that has filed a proof of claim asserting a secured claim in the real property to be surrendered.

ii. The letter must be sent by prepaid United States Mail to (i) the last known address of the security interest holder; and if a proof of claim has been filed, to the address for notices set forth on the proof of claim; or (ii) if the security interest holder has appeared through counsel in the case, to the counsel who has appeared.

iii. If there is more than one security interest holder and a dispute arises between the security interest holders as to the disposition of the property, the security interest holders must promptly notify the Debtor(s). In the event of such a dispute, the Debtor(s) must vacate the property within 14 days of receipt of the notice.

iv. If a security interest holder requests possession of the property, the Debtor(s) must fully cooperate in vacating the premises. This includes, without limitation, complying with a written request from the security interest holder to deliver all keys, garage door openers, alarm codes, and other information that will allow the security interest holder unfettered access to the property in a prepaid package supplied by the holder of the security interest holder. The premises must be vacated not later than the date set forth in writing by the security interest holder, which date may not be sooner than 14 days following delivery of the request. Any request must be (i) sent by email to the Debtor's counsel (if any), and (ii) served on the Debtor in accordance with Fed. R. Bankr. P. 7004. Subject to FED. R. BANKR. P. 9006(f), delivery of the request will be deemed to occur when the requirements of the preceding sentence have been satisfied.

v. The procedures set forth in subparagraphs (iii) and (iv) of this subparagraph may be implemented by a holder of a security interest immediately following the 7–day period set forth in subparagraph (c) of this Rule and without waiting for the sending or receipt of the letter required by subparagraph (e)(1) of this Rule.

vi. If a document is required to be sent under this Rule to the United States or its agencies, the document must additionally be sent (i) to the United States Attorney at 1000 Louisiana Street, Suite 2300, Houston, Texas 77002 (attention: Civil Process Clerk); or (ii) in accordance with Bankruptcy Rule 7004.

(f) This subsection applies to the surrender of a vehicle that is permitted to operate on public roads and for which no written agreement has been made under BLR 6007–1(b).

i. The holder of a security interest must file a Delivery Notice. The Delivery Notice must instruct the Debtor(s) (i) to deliver the vehicle to a specific location; and (ii) as to the disposition of the keys to the vehicle at the time of delivery. The Delivery Notice must be served by United States mail on the Debtor(s) at their address as listed on the docket sheet. The Debtor(s) must deliver the vehicle within 14 days of the filing of the Delivery Notice.

ii. The specific location in the Delivery Notice must be within 25 driving miles of the Debtor(s)' home, as listed on the docket sheet.

A. If the specific location is a public street address, the Debtor(s) must park the vehicle on the designated public street and within 2 city blocks of the address. No public street address may be designated by the security interest holder unless free parking is available on the public street. When the Debtor(s) park the vehicle, the Debtor(s) must photograph the exterior and interior of the vehicle. The exterior must be photographed such that the location is visible from the photograph. The car must be locked.

B. After the vehicle is parked in accordance with this Rule, the security interest holder will have the sole risk of loss as to the vehicle, and will be responsible for the payment of any traffic fines or other penalties arising out of compliance with the instructions in the Delivery Notice.

C. If the specified location is not an address on a public street, the location must be available for delivery of the vehicle and staffed with at least one person (i) not less than 4 days per week; (ii) at least one weekend day each week; (iii) by 7:00 a.m. on at least one day each week; and (iv) until at least 7:00 p.m. on at least one day each week. Upon delivery:

1. the staff person at the delivery location must execute and deliver a receipt to the Debtor(s), which receipt will reflect that the vehicle was delivered. The receipt will not be an acknowledgement that the vehicle was received in any particular condition.

2. the Debtor(s) and the staff person at the delivery location must each take pictures of the interior and exterior of the vehicle. The pictures will be taken after delivery, but prior to the execution of the receipt.

D. If the holder of the security interest has not been provided with a current certificate of insurance, the vehicle is not operable, or the vehicle is not in the Debtor(s)' possession or control, the holder of the security interest may repossess the vehicle in accordance with applicable non-bankruptcy law. Additionally, the Debtor(s) must:

1. Within 7 days of the filing of a Delivery Notice, notify the security interest holder in writing of the circumstances that preclude the Debtor(s) from delivering the vehicle. The notification must inform the security interest holder of the location of the vehicle if known. Notices to the security interest holder must be sent to (i) the last known address of the security interest holder; and if a proof of claim has been filed, to the address for notices set forth on the proof of claim; or (ii) if the security interest holder has appeared through counsel in the case, to the counsel who has appeared;

2. Fully cooperate in allowing the security interest holder to retrieve the vehicle, including agreeing to meet the security interest holder at a specific date and time to allow the retrieval of the vehicle; and,

3. Not drive a vehicle that is uninsured.

(g) The surrender of any other property is governed by this Rule and by applicable non-bankruptcy law. The holder of a security interest must make reasonable efforts to take possession of the surrendered property before the expiration of 28 days following (i) the confirmation of a plan that provides for the surrender or collateral under paragraph 7 of a confirmed plan; or (ii) the filing of a Surrender Notice under paragraph 20 of a confirmed plan.

(h) If the Debtor(s) fail to comply with the provisions of this Rule, the holder of the security interest may seek (i) to compel compliance by the Debtor(s); and (ii) to recover from the Debtor(s) the holder's reasonable costs and attorney's fees as an administrative expense to be paid under the confirmed plan; provided, there shall be no liability for the failure to take photographs as required by this Rule. The failure to take photographs as required by his Rule may result in an adverse evidentiary inference.

(i) If a holder of a security interest, secured by personal property, fails to comply with the provisions of this Rule, the Debtor(s) may (i) seek to compel compliance by the holder; and (ii) impose a monthly storage fee, secured by a first priority lien on the holder's collateral, equal to 0.5% of the fair market value of the collateral for every day that the collateral is held by the Debtor(s) after the expiration of 28 days following (i) the confirmation of a plan that provides for the surrender or collateral under paragraph 7 of a confirmed plan; or (ii) the filing of a Surrender Notice under paragraph 20 of a confirmed plan. If the holder retrieves the collateral after the 28 day period, the security interest lien holder must pay cash to the Debtor(s) in the amount of all accrued storage fees. The Debtor(s)' rights created by the lien under this subpara-

graph may be enforced through the Bankruptcy Court or any other court of competent jurisdiction.

(j) Subject to subparagraph (f) of this Rule, the Debtors may use any collateral pending the retrieval by the lien holder.

(k) If a writing is required by this Rule, the writing may include an email communication, a facsimile signature, or a paper document.

(*l*) This Rule applies only in Chapter 13 cases.

[Former Rule 6007–2, effective December 1, 2017. Renumbered effective January 11, 2018.]

    1 This rule applies equally to modified plans.

LOCAL RULE 6007–2. ABANDONMENT OF PROPERTY IN CHAPTER 7 CASES

Upon the filing by the chapter 7 trustee of a Notice of Proposed Abandonment and Report of No Distribution, the clerk shall promptly send the Notice to all persons listed on the CM/ECF list of creditors. If no objection is filed within 14 days of the sending of the notice by the clerk, property scheduled by the Debtor(s) is abandoned without further Court order.

[Former Rule 6007–1, effective December 1, 2017. Renumbered effective January 11, 2018.]

LOCAL RULE 7007–1. MOTIONS IN ADVERSARY PROCEEDINGS

Motion practice in adversary proceedings is governed by BLR 9013–1.

[Effective December 1, 2009.]

LOCAL RULE 7008–1. STATEMENT REGARDING CONSENT TO ENTRY OF ORDERS OR JUDGMENT IN CORE PROCEEDING

In an adversary proceeding before a bankruptcy judge, in addition to statements required by Rule 7008(a) of the Federal Rules of Bankruptcy Procedure, if the complaint, counterclaim, crossclaim, or third-party complaint contains a statement that the proceeding or any part of it is core, it shall contain a statement that the pleader does or does not consent to the entry of final orders or judgment by the bankruptcy judge if it is determined that the bankruptcy judge, absent consent of the parties, cannot enter final orders or judgment consistent with Article III of the United States Constitution.

[Effective July 20, 2012.]

LOCAL RULE 7012–1. STATEMENT IN RESPONSIVE PLEADING REGARDING CONSENT TO ENTRY OF ORDERS OR JUDGMENT IN CORE PROCEEDING

In addition to statements required by Rule 7012(b) of the Federal Rules of Bankruptcy Procedure, if a responsive pleading contains a statement that the proceeding or any part of it is core, it shall contain a statement that the pleader does or does not consent to the entry of final orders or judgment by the bankruptcy judge if it is determined that the bankruptcy judge, absent consent of the parties, cannot enter final orders or judgment consistent with Article III of the United States Constitution.

[Effective July 20, 2012.]

LOCAL RULE 7016–1. PRETRIAL ADVERSARY PROCEEDING CASE MANAGEMENT

Parties must comply with pretrial procedures on the website of the judge to whom the adversary proceeding has been assigned.

[Effective December 1, 2009.]

LOCAL RULE 7041–1. SETTLEMENT

When a motion to approve a compromise of controversy is required, the motion must be filed in the main case, accompanied by a proposed order in the main case and by a proposed final judgment in the adversary proceeding.

[Effective December 1, 2009.]

LOCAL RULE 7067–1. REGISTRY OF THE COURT AND COSTS

A proposed order for the deposit or withdrawal of funds from the court registry must contain the approval stamp of the Finance Department of the Office of the Clerk of Court. Unless the court orders otherwise, a motion to deposit funds will be considered ex parte.

[Effective December 1, 2009.]

LOCAL RULE 9003–1. MATTERS HEARD EX PARTE

Motions for admission pro hac vice may be considered ex parte. Applications to retain general counsel or accountants need be served only on the U.S. trustee or as ordered. Applications to retain special counsel pursuant to § 327(e) must be served under BLR 9013–1 or as ordered.

[Effective December 1, 2009.]

LOCAL RULE 9013–1. PLEADINGS, HEARINGS, AND SERVICE

(a) Pleadings must include a title that identifies the party filing the pleading and a brief description of the nature of the pleading. Example: XYZ Finance Company Motion for Relief From the Stay for 2003 Ford Explorer. Responses, other pleadings, and proposed orders filed after the initial motion should state the title and the docket number of the motion to which it applies. Example: Joe Debtor Response to XYZ Finance Company Motion for Relief from the Stay for 2003 Ford Explorer (docket 17).

(b) Except as noted in (e), each pleading seeking an order must include this immediately below the title:

This motion seeks an order that may adversely affect you. If you oppose the motion, you should immediately contact the moving party to resolve the dispute. If you and the moving party cannot agree, you must file a response and

send a copy to the moving party. You must file and serve your response within 21 days of the date this was served on you. Your response must state why the motion should not be granted. If you do not file a timely response, the relief may be granted without further notice to you. If you oppose the motion and have not reached an agreement, you must attend the hearing. Unless the parties agree otherwise, the court may consider evidence at the hearing and may decide the motion at the hearing.

Represented parties should act through their attorney.

(c) Movants should check the individual judge's web page to determine whether the motion may be self calendared. If the motion may be self-calendared, this language must be added at the end of the notice:

There will be a hearing on this motion on [date] at [time] in courtroom ____, [address].

(d) In addition to service required by the FED. R. BANKR. P., and except as noted in (e), the movant must serve the entities with pleadings requesting an order, notices, and hearing settings:

Main case

Party against whom relief is sought and its counsel, if known;

Debtors;

Debtors' counsel;

Trustee, if one has been appointed;

Examiner, if one has been appointed;

Committees, if any have been appointed;

Parties who have filed a notice of appearance;

Twenty largest unsecured creditors;

Parties claiming an interest in any property that is affected by the motion;

Parties claiming a lien on any property that is affected by the motion;

United States trustee;

Parties on whom the court has ordered notice.

Adversary Proceedings

Parties to the proceeding.

(e) The notice language, hearing settings, and service requirements for the following matters are governed by the rules noted, instead of BLR 9013–1(a–d):

Claim Objections, Rule 3007

Motions for Relief from Stay, Rule 4001

Employment Applications, Rule 2014 and Rule 9003

Pro Hac Vice Applications, Rule 9003

(f) Whenever service of a pleading, notice, or other document is required under these rules or the Federal Rules of Bankruptcy Procedure, the serving party must serve it no later than the next day after the pleading is filed. The serving party must file a certificate of service including the name and address of those served.

(g) Responses to Motions.

(1) Responses to motions to lift the automatic stay are governed by BLR 4001–1. Responses to all other motions are governed by FED. R. BANKR. P. 7008. Prior to filing a response, counsel (or unrepresented parties) shall confer with movant to attempt to resolve the relief requested in the motion

without the necessity of a hearing. Responses must include a certificate either that (i) a conference was held and that the parties were unable to resolve the matter; or (ii) the specific dates that the respondent attempted to contact the movant and the reason why no conference was held.

(2) If no timely response is filed, the court may grant the motion without a hearing.

(h) Each motion, application, objection, and response filed with the court must be accompanied by a proposed order.

(i) Some judges allow self-calendaring of emergency motions through the judge's web page. If self-calendaring is not authorized, requests for emergency hearings may be made in the pleading requesting the relief. No separate motion requesting an emergency hearing is required. The emergency motion must contain the word "Emergency" in the title of the motion. The motion must include a detailed statement why an emergency exists and the date relief is needed to avoid the consequences of the emergency. The motion seeking an emergency hearing must be certified for its accuracy by the party seeking the emergency relief or by its counsel.

In addition to the notice required by BLR 9013–1(b), the movant must include the following paragraph:

Emergency relief has been requested. If the Court considers the motion on an emergency basis, then you will have less than 21 days to answer. If you object to the requested relief or if you believe that the emergency consideration is not warranted, you should file an immediate response.

[Effective December 1, 2009. Amended effective January 24, 2011; July 20, 2012.]

LOCAL RULE 9013–2. EXCHANGE OF EXHIBITS, EXHIBIT LISTS AND WITNESS LISTS IN ALL CONTESTED MATTERS AND ADVERSARY PROCEEDINGS

(a) Unless otherwise directed by the Court, this rule shall apply to all contested matters and adversary proceedings in which a response is filed except for (i) hearings held during a chapter 13 panel, such as hearings on motions to dismiss chapter 13 cases; (ii) motions to modify the automatic stay in chapter 13 cases and individual chapter 7 cases to allow the foreclosure of liens on the debtor's principal residence or vehicle(s); (iii) objections to claims to which no response has been filed; or (iv) contested matters and trials covered by a separate scheduling order that specifically provides alternative deadlines for the exchange of exhibits, exhibit lists and witness list.

(b) Counsel for each party shall exchange exhibits by noon on the Day of Exchange in accordance with Table 1.

(c) Counsel for each party shall also exchange and file exhibit and witness lists with the Clerk of the Court by noon on the Day of Exchange in accordance with Table 1. Witness lists must identify whether each witness is to be called as a fact witness or as an expert. If no delineation is made, the witness will only be allowed to testify as a fact witness unless otherwise ordered by the Court, or the witness is an owner of the property at issue opining as to value.

(d) If counsel intends to use only hard copy exhibits at the hearing or trial, then counsel must deliver either (i) a hard copy of the exhibits to opposing counsel; or (ii) a copy of the exhibits by electronic mail to opposing counsel and, if requested in writing from opposing counsel, a hard copy of the exhibits within 24 hours of receiving the written request. If no written request is made, counsel shall provide a hard copy of the exhibits to opposing counsel at the hearing or trial. If counsel intends to use technology in the courtroom by putting the exhibits on an electronic media so that exhibits may be shown on the screens in the courtroom, then counsel must deliver an electronic copy of the exhibits to opposing counsel and, if requested in writing, a hard copy of the exhibits within 24 hours of receiving the request. The electronic copy must contain the exhibits in the same order as they are contained on the electronic media to be used in the courtroom. Alternatively, the parties may agree in writing to a different manner of exchange, i.e., exchange by electronic mail, facsimile, Dropbox (or other form of internet-based distribution service), etc. Any party agreeing in writing to a different manner of exchange under this paragraph waives the right to object to the admission of any exhibit for non-compliance with this rule and to receive a hard copy of the exhibits under this paragraph.

(e) All hard copy exhibits should be clearly marked, tabbed and bound in a 3–ring notebook or utilizing another binding method that allows the exhibit book to open and lay flat on an even surface.

(f) For exhibits that are more than 10 pages in length, each page of that exhibit must be numbered or bates labeled.

(g) If counsel has identified expert witnesses on the witness list, then counsel must ensure that the written reports of the expert witnesses are timely provided to opposing counsel. Expert reports shall be delivered to opposing counsel by noon on the Day of Exchange in accordance with Table 1. Notwithstanding the foregoing, no expert reports shall be required for (i) owners of property opining on the value of the property; and (ii) attorneys providing expert testimony regarding the reasonableness and amount of attorney's fees.

(h) **Emergency Hearings.** If a hearing is scheduled on an emergency basis and unless a specific order is otherwise issued, all of the above referenced procedures shall apply except that counsel must (i) exchange exhibits, exhibit and witness lists; and (ii) file exhibit and witness lists with the Clerk of the Court by noon of the Day of Exchange in accordance with Table 2. An emergency hearing is a hearing set (i) by order that expressly states that the hearing is an emergency hearing; or (ii) a hearing set by docket entry on less than 72 hours' notice. If a hearing is set on less than two (2) days' notice, then the exhibits must be exchanged at the earliest practicable time.

(i) **Contested Hearings in Chapter 13 and 7 Cases Involving Less Than Ten Exhibits.** In other contested matters in chapter 13 and 7 cases where a party intends to offer ten or fewer exhibits, counsel are not required to provide bound exhibits and may exchange exhibits with opposing counsel by electronic mail. <u>All other requirements and deadlines will apply.</u>

(j) Contested Hearings in Complex Chapter 11 Cases. In contested matters in complex chapter 11 cases, counsel may deliver exhibits via an internet-based distribution service that does not assess a charge to the party performing the download. The website address along with instructions for downloading the exhibits shall be made available in accordance with Table 1 or Table 2 as appropriate. If a party elects to deliver exhibits in accordance with this paragraph, counsel are not required to provide bound exhibits to counsel. All other requirements and deadlines will apply.

(k) The failure to timely comply with this rule may be grounds for the denial of the admission of any or all exhibits and the exclusion of witness testimony.

(l) Regardless of the manner of exchange between counsel and unless otherwise instructed by the Court, counsel shall bring three hard copies of the exhibits to the scheduled hearing or trial—one for the court; one for the courtroom deputy; and one for witnesses.

(m) Table 1.

Scheduled Day for Hearing or Trial	Day of Exchange
Monday	Previous Thursday
Tuesday	Previous Friday
Wednesday	Previous Monday
Thursday	Previous Tuesday
Friday	Previous Wednesday

If the Day of Exchange is a legal holiday, the Day of Exchange would be the preceding Day of Exchange. For example, if the Scheduled Day for Hearing or Trial was a Wednesday and the Previous Monday was a legal holiday, the Day of Exchange would be the Previous Friday.

(n) Table 2.

Scheduled Day for Emergency Hearing	Day of Exchange
Monday	Previous Friday
Tuesday	Previous Monday
Wednesday	Previous Tuesday
Thursday	Previous Wednesday
Friday	Previous Thursday

If the Day of Exchange is a legal holiday, the Day of Exchange would be the preceding Day of Exchange. For example, if the Scheduled Day for Emergency Hearing was a Wednesday and the Previous Tuesday was a legal holiday, the Day of Exchange would be the Previous Monday.

[Effective April 12, 2012. Amended effective July 20, 2012; March 11, 2015.]

LOCAL RULE 9027–1. REMOVAL

(a) A party removing a civil action to the bankruptcy court must comply with Fed. R. Bankr. P. 9027 and must (i) list all names and addresses of the parties, (ii) designate on which parties service of process has been accomplished, and (iii) list the name, address, and telephone number of the counsel for every party.

(b) The notice of removal must be accompanied by copies of all papers that have been filed in the court from which the case is removed.

(c) Removals under 28 U.S.C. § 1452 must contain this caption:

IN THE UNITED STATES
BANKRUPTCY COURT
FOR THE SOUTHERN DISTRICT OF TEXAS
_____ DIVISION

[Effective December 1, 2009.]

LOCAL RULE 9027–2. STATEMENT IN NOTICE OF REMOVAL REGARDING CONSENT TO ENTRY OF ORDERS OR JUDGMENT IN CORE PROCEEDING

If, pursuant to Rule 9027(a)(1) of the Federal Rules of Bankruptcy Procedure, a notice of removal states that upon removal of the claim or cause of action the proceeding or any part of it is core, the notice shall also state that the party removing the proceeding does or does not consent to the entry of final orders or judgment by the bankruptcy judge if it is determined that the bankruptcy judge, absent consent of the parties, cannot enter final orders or judgment consistent with Article III of the United States Constitution.

[Effective July 20, 2012.]

LOCAL RULE 9027–3. STATEMENT REGARDING CONSENT TO ENTRY OF ORDERS OR JUDGMENT IN CORE PROCEEDING

If a statement filed pursuant to Rule 9027(e)(3) by a party who filed a pleading in connection with a removed claim or cause of action, other than the party filing the notice of removal, states that the proceeding or any part of it is core, the party shall also state that the party does or does not consent to the entry of final orders or judgment by the bankruptcy judge if it is determined that the bankruptcy judge, absent consent of the parties, cannot enter final orders or judgment consistent with Article III of the United States Constitution.

[Effective July 20, 2012.]

LOCAL RULE 9033–1. PROPOSED FINDINGS AND CONCLUSIONS IN CERTAIN CORE PROCEEDINGS

If the Court determines that it cannot enter a final order or judgment consistent with Article III of the United States Constitution in a particular proceeding referred to the Court and designated as core under section 157(b) of title 28, and the Court hears the proceeding, Rule 9033(a), (b), and (c) of the Federal Rules of Bankruptcy Procedure shall apply as if it is a non-core proceeding.

[Effective July 20, 2012.]

LOCAL RULE 9037–1.   SEALED DOCUMENTS

(a) The sealing of documents is discouraged.

(b) Certain documents are routinely redacted to remove personal identifying information or other content that is not relevant to a decision by the Court. In those instances, (i) the document may be filed in redacted form only; (ii) no document should be filed that contains the redacted information; and (iii) the balance of this Rule 5003–1 does not apply.

(c) A motion, reply or other document may initially be filed under seal if the filing party simultaneously files a motion requesting that the document be maintained under seal. The document must be filed using the correct CM/ECF code for the filing of a sealed document. The filing party should notify the Case Manager if a motion to seal is filed.

(d) In some instances, it may be practicable to redact relevant confidential information from a document, and to file the redacted document in the public record. In those instances, (i) a redacted document should be filed, not under seal; and (ii) the unredacted document should simultaneously be filed, under seal.

(e) A document filed under seal will be kept by the clerk in electronic form, but will be viewable only by the bankruptcy judges and staff.

(f) Documents filed under seal must be served by the filing party by e-mail and conventional means on parties-in-interest entitled to receive the sealed document.

(g) A motion to seal the document must be filed in the public record and served as any other motion. The motion to seal must state whether a redacted version of the document has been filed.

(h) Instructions for filing documents under seal are on the Court's web site.

(i) After reviewing the motion to seal, the Court may order appropriate relief, including the unsealing of the document.

[Effective December 1, 2015.]

APPENDICES
APPENDIX A. COURTROOM ETIQUETTE

People who appear in court must observe these and other conventions of courteous, orderly behavior.

1. Be punctual.

2. Remain in attendance until excused. All persons sitting before the bar shall remain there during each session and return after recess.

3. Wear attire that is appropriate for a federal courtroom.

4. Address witnesses only by their titles and surnames. Refer to others in the same way.

5. Stand when the court speaks to you; stand when you speak to the court, unless otherwise excused or directed. Speak only to the court, except for questioning witnesses and, in opening and closing.

6. Avoid approaching the bench. Counsel should anticipate the necessity for rulings and discuss them before court is in session. When a bench conference is unavoidable, get permission first.

7. Hand to the clerk, not the judge or reporter, all things for examination by the judge.

8. Stand when the judge enters or leaves the courtroom.

9. Contact with the court must be through the case manager. Do not initiate calls to the Court's law clerks.

10. Assist the summoning of witnesses from outside the courtroom. Furnish the clerk and Electronic Court Recorder (ERO) with a list of witnesses showing the order they are likely to be called.

11. Question witnesses while seated at counsel table or standing at the lectern. When it is necessary to question a witness about an exhibit, ask permission to approach the witness.

12. Conduct no experiment or demonstration without permission.

13. Do not participate in a trial as an attorney if you expect you may be called as a material witness.

14. Avoid disparaging remarks and acrimony towards anyone, especially adverse parties and counsel, and discourage ill-will between the litigants. Counsel must abstain from unnecessary references to opposing counsel, especially peculiarities.

15. Make no side-bar remark.

16. Counsel are responsible for advising their clients, witnesses, and associate counsel about proper courtroom behavior.

17. Request the use of easels, light boxes, and other equipment well in advance so that they may be set up while court is not in session.

[Effective January 1, 1993.]

APPENDIX B. ORDER FOR JOINT ADMINISTRATION

UNITED STATES BANKRUPTCY COURT
SOUTHERN DISTRICT OF TEXAS
HOUSTON DIVISION

IN RE:
)
) BANKRUPTCY NUMBER

DEBTOR,   ) [*lower number*]
)

and   )
)
) BANKRUPTCY NUMBER

DEBTOR.   ) [*higher number*]

ORDER FOR JOINT ADMINISTRATION
AND/OR TRANSFER OF CASES

On the motion for joint administration of these cases under Bankruptcy Rule 1015, the Court orders that the above referenced cases are jointly administered. Additionally, the following checked items are ordered:

1. ____ One disclosure statement and plan of reorganization may be filed for both cases by any plan proponent.

2. ____ Case No. _____ (higher case number) shall be transferred to Judge _____, who has the lower numbered case.

3. ____ Parties may request joint hearings on matters pending in any of the jointly administered cases.

4. ____ Other: _____
_____
_____

Only the lines checked are ordered.

Dated: _____ _____

United States Bankruptcy Judge

[Effective January 1, 1993.]

APPENDIX C. STANDARD JOINT PRETRIAL STATEMENT
UNITED STATES BANKRUPTCY COURT
SOUTHERN DISTRICT OF TEXAS
HOUSTON DIVISION

IN RE:	)	
	)	
DEBTOR.	) CASE NO.	
	)	
	)	
PLAINTIFF,	) ADVERSARY NO.	
versus	)	
	)	
	)	
DEFENDANT.	)	

STANDARD JOINT PRETRIAL STATEMENT

Under Local Bankruptcy Rule 7016 and Rule 6 of the Local Rules of the District Court, counsel shall file a joint pretrial statement setting forth these matters. Plaintiff is responsible for filing the jointly prepared pretrial statement. All counsel shall cooperate in its preparation.

1. **Statement of the Case.** Concise statement of the case for the convenience of the court.

2. **Jurisdiction.** Indicate any jurisdictional questions; state if core or noncore. If noncore, the parties must all state whether they consent to entry of final orders or judgment by the bankruptcy judge.

3. **Motions.** List all pending motions.

4. **Contentions of Parties.** State concisely in short separate paragraphs what each party claims.

5. **Admissions of Fact.** List all facts which have been stipulated or otherwise require no proof.

6. **Contested Issues of Fact.** List all facts in controversy that are necessary to the final disposition of this case.

7. **Agreed Applicable Propositions of Law.** List the legal propositions not in dispute.

8. **Contested Issue of Law.** State briefly the issues of law in dispute. Memoranda of authorities on each shall be filed by litigants with the joint pretrial order.

9. **Exhibits.** An Exhibit List numbering and briefly describing all exhibits to be offered in evidence or referred to in trial shall be attached to the joint pretrial statement. To the greatest extent possible, exhibits at trial should be bound with the exhibit list as in inside cover sheet. All exhibits must be marked by the parties for identification before trial, designating such exhibits by the name of the offering party, followed by an exhibit number. (For example, "Plaintiff's Exhibit 1"). ALL EXHIBITS WILL BE ADMITTED INTO EVIDENCE BY AGREEMENT OF COUNSEL AS THE FIRST ITEM OF BUSINESS AT TRIAL. Counsel for all parties are ordered to confer at their earliest convenience for the purpose of arriving at all possible stipulations and for the exchange of documents which will be offered in evidence at the trial. Documents or physical evidence not listed in the joint pretrial statement or produced to opposing counsel before the pretrial conference date will be inadmissible for any purpose during trial, except upon motion and leave. This shall not apply to rebuttal exhibits which cannot be anticipated. Objections to admissibility will be taken up at the pretrial conference. Supporting legal authorities and copies of exhibits in dispute shall be submitted to the court at least three business days before the pretrial conference. Counsel is encouraged to utilize the Court's electronics systems for the presentation of exhibits.

10. **Witnesses.** Each party should list the names and addresses of all witnesses expected to be called during trial with a brief statement of the facts expected to be proved by each witness. Counsel are expected to stipulate to the qualifications of experts. Inability to stipulate must be in the pretrial statement and specifically brought to the court's attention for resolution prior to trial. The proponent of a witness must state the amount of courtroom time needed for direct examination. The opponent must state the amount of courtroom time needed for cross examination of that witness.

Failure to provide any of this information may result in counsel's inability to call or examine that witness for testimony at trial. This does not apply to rebuttal or impeachment witnesses.

11. Settlement. Report prospects of settlement.

Counsel are expected to provide the Court with an analysis of those areas in dispute continuing to exist.

12. Estimated Trial Time. A statement of the estimated time to try the proceedings, and a statement as to availability of witnesses, including out of state witnesses.

13. Attachments. Include these required attachments for each party:

A. Proposed findings of fact and conclusions of law, with supporting authorities in a memorandum of law;

B. Exhibit Lists:

 i. 5 paper copies if exhibits will not be electronically presented; or

 ii. 1 paper copy for Court if exhibits will be electronically presented.

C. Objections to Exhibits (2 copies); and

D. Witness Lists (2 copies).

_____	_____
Counsel for Plaintiff	Counsel for Defendant

[Effective January 1, 1993.]

APPENDIX D. WITNESS AND EXHIBIT LIST

UNITED STATES BANKRUPTCY COURT
SOUTHERN DISTRICT OF TEXAS
HOUSTON DIVISION

Main Case No.	Name of Debtor:
Adversary No:	Style of Adversary:

Witnesses:

Judge:
Courtroom Deputy:
Hearing Date:
Hearing Time:
Party's Name:
Attorney's Name:
Attorney's Phone:
Nature of Proceeding:

EXHIBITS

Ex. #	Description	Offered	Objection	Admitted/ Not Admitted	Disposition

NOTE: This exhibit list is to be prepared in advance of the date of trial by counsel to parties and furnished to the court in triplicate and served on the opposing parties.

[Effective January 1, 1993.]

APPENDIX E.   COMPREHENSIVE SCHEDULING, PRE–TRIAL AND TRIAL ORDER

UNITED STATES BANKRUPTCY COURT
SOUTHERN DISTRICT OF TEXAS
HOUSTON DIVISION

In Re:	)
	)
Debtor.	) Case No.
	)
	)
Plaintiff,	) Adversary No.
versus	)
	)
	)
Defendant.	)

COMPREHENSIVE SCHEDULING, PRE–TRIAL AND TRIAL ORDER

A pretrial conference was held on _____. The parties submitted a Rule 26 Report:

   A. _____ which is attached and is accepted by the Court except as modified by this order; or

   B. _____ which is filed at docket # ____ and is accepted by the Court except as modified by this order.

Under authority of Fed.R.Bankr.P. 7016 and Fed.R.Civ.P. 16, it is hereby **ORDERED** that the following deadlines and settings shall apply in the above referenced adversary:

   1.   All discovery in this case must be completed on or before _____.

   2.   The party with the burden of proof on an issue must serve its expert reports no later than _____. Rebuttal expert reports must be served no later than _____.

   3.   Dispositive motions may not be filed after _____. Any responses to dispositive motions must be filed within 20 days after a dispositive motion is filed. The Court additionally orders:

      A. _____ Courtesy copies of dispositive motions and responses must be mailed or delivered to the Court's chambers when they are filed with the Clerk.

      B. _____ Dispositive motions may not be filed until discovery is completed.

   4.   Witness and Exhibit Lists must be exchanged at least 2 working days prior to the face to face meeting required in the following paragraph. Copies of the exhibits shall be attached to the Exhibit List.

   5.   Counsel must meet face to face to attempt to resolve these issues amicably, to attempt to stipulate to as many facts and issues as possible, and to prepare the pretrial order. This face to face meeting must occur prior to _____. The court intends that this will be a substantive, good faith effort to resolve issues. Therefore trial counsel (lead counsel) are required to attend this meeting in person. Counsel who are not present at this meeting may not be permitted to participate in the trial.

   6.   The parties must jointly prepare and file a proposed form of pretrial statement not later than _____. The proposed form of statement must be signed by counsel for both parties and must be in the form set forth as Appendix C on the Court's website.

   7.   Copies of exhibits must be attached to the pretrial statement. Relevant portions of lengthy exhibits must be highlighted. Counsel must also attach succinct memoranda on disputed issues of law. A courtesy copy of the pretrial order must be delivered to chambers when the pretrial order is filed with the clerk.

   8.   A Pre-Trial Conference will:

      A. _____ Not be held.

B. _____ Be held on _____ at _____·____.m. Attendance by all parties is required, either in proper person (if not represented by counsel) or by an attorney who has authority to bind the party. Each party must have a representative present with full settlement authority.

9. Trial of this adversary proceeding will commence on _____ at _____ ____.m. It is estimated that trial can be completed in _____ hours of trial time.

IT IS FURTHER:

ORDERED that changes to this Scheduling Order may only be made by further order of this Court. A motion to extend any deadline and/or alter any hearing date will only be granted for good cause shown beyond the control of the lawyers and/or parties and only in very limited circumstances.

SIGNED:

_____

UNITED STATES BANKRUPTCY
JUDGE

ECF PROCEDURES
ADMINISTRATIVE PROCEDURES FOR THE FILING, SIGNING, AND VERIFYING OF DOCUMENTS BY ELECTRONIC MEANS IN TEXAS BANKRUPTCY COURTS

*[**Publisher's Note:** For electronic filing procedures, consult the "Administrative Procedures for the Filing, Signing, and Verifying of Documents by Electronic Means in Texas Bankruptcy Courts," published as part of the ECF Procedures for the United States Bankruptcy Court for the Northern District of Texas, ante.]*

SELECTED ORDERS AND PROCEDURES

GENERAL ORDER 2001–2. IN THE MATTER OF GUIDELINES FOR FEE APPLICATIONS FOR PROFESSIONALS—UNIFORM PRESUMPTIONS CONCERNING REIMBURSABLE EXPENSES

Guidelines for Attorneys Fee Applications–Reimbursement of Expenses

On November 28, 1998, the Court issued General Order 1998–5 providing for uniform presumptions among the divisions in this district concerning appropriate amounts for reimbursement of expenses. Since then, a bench/bar committee has reviewed those guidelines and suggested revisions.

After consideration of the proposed revisions, IT IS ORDERED THAT General Order 1998–5 is VACATED and the following order is substituted.

The following general guidelines are presented for the assistance of professionals in preparing fee applications to be presented to the Bankruptcy Court. These are merely presumptions, designed to assist in the efficient and inexpensive preparation and presentation of applications under all chapters of the Bankruptcy Code. In general, the Court will approve reimbursement of expenditures by professionals within the guidelines set forth below.

However, it should be understood that these are guidelines only. Any item appropriate for reimbursement that is not covered in the following guidelines must be alleged and proved in each case. In addition, if any professional believes that the guidelines are not applicable to that professional's application, the professional may assert and may present proof to the Court that a different allowance should be made. In addition, on its own motion or on request of a party in interest the Court may determine that a greater or lesser amount should be awarded in a particular case or that no reimbursement for one of the following items should be allowed in a particular case. The Court will ultimately be guided by the Bankruptcy Code, Federal Rules of Bankruptcy Procedure, and Bankruptcy Local Rules.

The following kinds of expenses are generally allowed or disallowed as indicated below. As to each type of expense, applicant shall state the amount or rate customarily charged to its non-bankruptcy clients as well as the rate or amount sought in the application:

A.   **Copy Costs—**

i.   Reimbursement is allowed at the same rate as is charged by the professional to its non-bankruptcy clients up to $.20 per page for copies made "in house."

ii. For large copy projects, an outside copy service should be used if the rate charged by the outside copy service is less than the rate the professional would charge to its non-bankruptcy clients or less than $.20 for basic copy services. Actual amounts charged by outside copy services will be allowed, including additional charges for collation, binding, mailing, delivery, etc.

B.   **Faxes—**The cost of both incoming and outgoing faxes will be allowed at the rationalized rate of $.25 per printed page. Long distance charges will be allowed in the same manner and amounts as long distance telephone charges, actual out-of-pocket charges.

C.   **Courier/Delivery Services—**will be allowed at actual cost when reasonable and appropriate.

D.   **Overnight Delivery—**will be allowed at actual cost when justified by delivery time necessity.

E.   **Clerical Services and Expenses—**

i. Professionals, other than trustees compensated under 11 U.S.C. § 326(a), may not be compensated for time associated with services that are essentially clerical or secretarial work, including, but not limited to, typing, filing, mailing and related activities, copying, faxing, etc.

ii Clerical overtime and related expenses will be allowed only upon justification in very exceptional circumstances, such as emergency preparation for major trials or other exigent circumstances. Multiple claims in the same case may be considered as indicative of inadequate work flow planning and inadequate staffing, and thus not allowed.

F.   **Overtime Utilities—** will be allowed according to the same principles as employee clerical overtime.

G.   **Telephone Expenses—**

i.   No allowance for local land line and carrier charges.

ii. Actual out-of-pocket expenses for long distance telephone, and conference call charges. The applicant must be able to produce documentation of charges on request.

iii. Cellular telephone charges will be allowed at the actual out-of-pocket rate up to $.25 a minute. The applicant must be able to produce documentation of charges on request.

iv. No allowance for air phone calls or charges except in very exceptional circumstances.

H. Electronic Research, Internet Research, Public Records Research, PACER/BANCAP Access—reimbursement allowed at actual out of pocket costs or, if compensated pursuant to a flat rate contract with the service provider, the per minute charge assessed to non-bankruptcy clients directly related to the client for which such research is more suitable, efficient or cost effective than traditional methods.

I. Postage & Supplies— postal charges, envelopes, paper, etc. for routine correspondence is considered an ordinary overhead expense, except for trustees compensated under 11 U.S.C. § 326. However postage and supplies for general and large mailings to multiple parties will be allowed at actual out-of-pocket cost.

J. Storage—

i. Trustees compensated under 11 U.S.C. § 326(a) who must store large volumes of documents or records (or other bulky items) may request reimbursement for actual storage charges offsite. The trustee should request the reimbursement in advance of making storage arrangements, should notice all creditors and parties in interest and should disclose the anticipated costs and duration of the storage arrangements. The stored items should be disposed of as quickly as reasonably possible under the circumstances.

ii All other professionals may not be reimbursed for storage fees except in very exceptional circumstances. If a professional believes that such circumstances apply, the professional should request authority in advance, as trustees are required to do.

K. Travel Time and Expenses—

i. Travel and meals within the metropolitan area in which the professional normally practices

(1) No allowance for normal commuting and daily parking expenses. Case related travel expenses, including mileage and parking, are allowable. Mileage is allowable at the rate permitted by the Internal Revenue Service at the time the travel is made and should be recorded at the time of travel for later verification. Parking is allowable at actual cost and receipts should be retained for verification.

(2) No allowance for meals in the town in which the professional normally practices.

ii. Travel charges outside the metropolitan area where the professional normally practices shall be allowed as follows—

(1) Travel by common carrier reimbursed only at the coach rate.

(2) Ground transportation and rental cars are allowable at actual cost and receipts should be retained for verification.

(3) Lodging and meals up to 300% of the approximate government per diem rate[1] except as otherwise specifically justified.

iii. Professionals may charge for time spent traveling out of town on a bankruptcy case at the same rate and on the same terms as they charge their non-bankruptcy clients provided however that the professional shall deduct from travel time any time spent working on another case or matter.

[Dated: May 3, 2001.]

[1] Refer to 41 CFR 301–11.303 and 301.305 or check the internet at http://www.dtlc.mil/perdiem or www.fpmi.com/pr/perdiemrates.

GENERAL ORDER 2008–2. IN RE: TERMINATING ADOPTION OF INTERIM BANKRUPTCY RULES AND ADOPTING BANKRUPTCY LOCAL RULE 5012

General Order 2005–6 was issued to adopt the interim rules promulgated by the Advisory Committee on Bankruptcy Rules following the passage of the Bankruptcy Abuse and Consumer

Protection Act of 2005. The interim rules are superseded by new national rules that will become effective on December 1, 2008. The new national rules do not address the matters covered by interim rule 5012. Accordingly, by majority vote of the Bankruptcy Judges, it is ordered that:

1. General Order 2005–6 is terminated.

2. The Court adopts new Bankruptcy Local Rule 5012, as follows:

> **Rule 5012. Communication and Cooperation With Foreign Courts and Foreign Representatives**
>
> Except for communications for scheduling and administrative purposes, the court in any case commenced by a foreign representative shall give at least 20 days' notice of its intent to communicate with a foreign court or a foreign representative. The notice shall identify the subject of the anticipated communication and shall be given in the manner provided by Rule 2002(q). Any entity that wishes to participate in the communication shall notify the court of its intention not later than 5 days before the scheduled communication.

3. This order is effective December 1, 2008.

[Dated: September 30, 2008.]

PROCEDURES FOR OBTAINING RELIEF FROM REQUIRED ATTENDANCE AT SECTION 341 MEETING OF CREDITORS (UNDATED)

The following procedures are mandated for efficient and expeditious treatment of requests for debtors to be excused from Bankruptcy Code § 341 meetings of creditors ("Creditors' Meetings"):

1. Debtors must attend Creditors' Meetings unless excused by the Court from attendance, Bankruptcy Code § 343. Failure to attend Creditors' Meetings, and to take appropriate measures to comply with this order, may be grounds for dismissal of a bankruptcy case, possibly with prejudice.

2. Prior to the date set for the Creditors' Meeting, the Court will **not** entertain motions to excuse the debtor's appearance at such meetings. The Court believes that such motions are premature prior to the scheduled time for the meeting. The Debtor must first attempt alternative methods of attending the meeting (as described below).

3. If attendance at the scheduled Creditors' Meeting is not possible, the Debtor must contact the trustee prior to the scheduled meeting and:

    a. Request that the meeting be rescheduled; or

    b. Request that the debtor be permitted to participate in the Creditors' Meeting by telephone in accordance with procedures established by the U.S. Trustee, including:

        i. Visiting a U.S. Trustee office, showing a picture ID, taking a testimonial oath, and participating in the Creditors' Meeting by telephone, or

        ii. Arranging with a notary public to appear in the notary's office, showing a picture ID, taking a testimonial oath, and participating in the Creditors' Meeting by telephone.

    c. A trustee is not required by this order to consent to Debtor's participation in the Creditors' Meeting by telephone. Even if the trustee initially consents to telephonic participation, the trustee may request attendance in person (or such other relief as the trustee may deem appropriate) if the participation by telephone is not satisfactory.

4. If the Debtor cannot attend the meeting in person and cannot arrange alternative methods of attending as provided in the proceeding paragraph, the Debtor may move for the Court to excuse the Debtor's attendance at a Creditors' Meeting. It is not anticipated that this motion would be granted except when it is impossible for the Debtor to attend, such as in case of the Debtor's death or complete physical or mental incapacity. Even when the Debtor is physically or mentally unable to participate in the Creditors' Meeting, a representative of the Debtor must appear and attempt to provide the trustee with all relevant information.

5. If the Debtor is unable to attend, and the Trustee agrees that the Debtor's attendance should be excused, and no creditor objects to excusing the Debtor's attendance:

    a. The Debtor must file a motion to excuse the Debtor's attendance, containing information in the detail suggested in the attached form; and

   b. The Chapter 7 trustee must sign the motion indicating:

     i. That a representative of the Debtor appeared and provided information satisfactory to the trustee,

     ii. That no creditor appeared at the Creditors' Meeting to question the Debtor, or else that the creditor(s) who did appear had no objection to excusing the Debtor's appearance, and

     iii. That the trustee has no opposition to the motion.

   6. If the Debtor is unable to attend, but the Trustee does not agree that the Debtor's attendance should be excused, or if any creditor objects at the Creditor's Meeting, the Debtor must file a motion to excuse the Debtor's appearance at the Creditors' Meeting. (Alternatively, the Debtor may move to dismiss the case.) The motion must contain the information in the detail suggested in the attached form, except that the motion must state why the Trustee does not agree to the relief requested in the motion. Any party in interest that objects to the motion shall file a response as required generally in contested matters.

   7. If the debtor does not attend the Creditors' Meeting in person or by telephone (to the satisfaction of the Trustee), and if the Trustee cannot join in the motion to excuse the Debtor's attendance at the Creditors' Meeting, the U.S. Trustee has instructed Trustees to file a motion to dismiss the case. The Clerk shall give notice of the motion to dismiss. If the Debtor objects to dismissal, the debtor shall file a response as required generally in contested matters.

   8. If a Debtor requests to be excused from attending a creditors' meeting, a judge may require substantiation of the Debtor's inability to attend, such as a doctor's certificate or other substantiation.

   9. If the Trustee files a motion to dismiss for failure of Debtor to appear at the Creditors' Meeting, the Clerk shall not issue a discharge for the non-appearing Debtor until the motion to dismiss is resolved.

UNITED STATES BANKRUPTCY COURT FOR THE SOUTHERN DISTRICT OF TEXAS

_____ DIVISION

IN RE _____   §
                        §   CASE #:_____
                        §
                        §

DEBTOR'S MOTION TO EXCUSE APPEARANCE AT § 341 MEETING

   1. The creditors' meeting under § 341 of the Bankruptcy Code in this case was conducted on _____, 200__.

   2. _____ (Debtor) did not appear at the creditors' meeting to be examined as required in the Bankruptcy Code. The Debtor did not appear because

_____

_____

_____

   3. It is not possible for Debtor to appear at the offices of the U.S. Trustee in any part of the United States to be sworn and to participate in the creditors' meeting by telephone, and it is not possible for the Debtor to appear at the offices of a notary public to be sworn and to participate in the creditors' meeting by telephone because:

_____

_____

_____

   4. The chapter 7 trustee in this case represents, by signing this motion, either (i) that no creditor appeared at the creditors' meeting to question the debtor, or (ii) that the creditor(s) that appeared at the 341 meeting stated that they do not object to excusing the debtor's appearance at the meeting. Further, by signing this motion, the trustee represents that the trustee is satisfied with the

information that was available at the creditors' meeting, and that the trustee has no objection to the Court excusing the requirement that the Debtor appear at the creditors' meeting.

_____
Debtor's Counsel

_____
Chapter 7 Trustee

UNITED STATES BANKRUPTCY COURT FOR THE SOUTHERN DISTRICT OF TEXAS

_____ DIVISION

IN RE _____   §   CASE #:_____
                            §
                            §
                            §

ORDER EXCUSING DEBTOR'S APPEARANCE AT § 341 MEETING

Considering (i) the Debtor's motion to excuse appearance at the § 341 meeting and the representations concerning why the Debtor cannot attend a 341 meeting, and (ii) the representations of the trustee in that motion,

IT IS ORDERED THAT THE DEBTOR'S APPEARANCE AT A MEETING OF CREDITORS UNDER § 341 OF THE BANKRUPTCY CODE IS HEREBY EXCUSED.

_____, 200__.

_____
UNITED STATES BANKRUPTCY
JUDGE

GENERAL ORDER 2012–6. IN RE: ORDER OF REFERENCE TO BANKRUPTCY JUDGES [DISTRICT COURT ORDER]

1. Bankruptcy cases and proceedings arising under Title 11 or arising in or related to a case under Title 11 of the United States Code are automatically referred to the bankruptcy judges of this district, except:

A. Civil actions pending before the United States District Court for the Southern District of Texas before a related bankruptcy petition is filed. With respect to these:

(1) The automatic stay applies until it is modified by an order; and

(2) The district judge may refer these to the Bankruptcy Court.

B. Civil actions, bankruptcy cases and proceedings specifically withdrawn from the general reference to the Bankruptcy Court.

C. Appeals from the Bankruptcy Court.

2. In civil actions, bankruptcy cases and proceedings referred to them, the bankruptcy judges may exercise the full authority allowed them by law.

3. Cases related to a bankruptcy may be *removed* only from state court to the United States District Court and not from other federal courts.

4. If a bankruptcy judge or district judge determines that entry of a final order or judgment by a bankruptcy judge would not be consistent with Article III of the United States Constitution in a particular proceeding referred under this order and determines that proceeding to be a core matter, the bankruptcy judge shall, unless otherwise ordered by the District Court, hear the proceeding and submit proposed findings of fact and conclusions of law to the District Court. The District Court

may treat any order of the Bankruptcy Court as proposed findings of fact and conclusions of law if the District Court concludes that the bankruptcy judge could not have entered a final order or judgment consistent with Article III of the United States Constitution.

5. This order supersedes General Order 2005–6.

[Dated: May 24, 2012.]

CHAPTER 13 PLAN. UNIFORM PLAN AND MOTION FOR VALUATION OF COLLATERAL

Uniform Modification of Confirmed Plan And Motion for Valuation of Collateral

CHAPTER 13 PLAN MODIFICATION
Date of Modified Plan: _____
[Date Must be Date that This Modified Plan is Signed by Debtor(s)]

1. Statement of Inclusion of Specific Provisions. The Debtor(s) propose this Modified Plan (the "Modified Plan") pursuant to 11 U.S.C. § 1329. The provisions of any previously approved plan remain binding unless inconsistent with this Modified Plan. Any valuations contained in any previously approved plan remain binding unless inconsistent with Paragraph 29 of this Modified Plan. The Debtor(s) disclose whether this Modified Plan includes certain provisions by checking the appropriate box:

Description of Provision	Included	Not Included
A. A "non-standard" provision contained in Paragraph 29.		
B. A provision limiting the amount of a secured claim based on a valuation of the collateral for the claim in Paragraph 14.		
C. A provision avoiding a security interest or a lien in Paragraph 8(C).		
D. A provision avoiding a security interest or lien in exempt property in Paragraph 15.		

2. Summary Attached. Attached as Exhibit "A" is a summary of the payments to the Chapter 13 Trustee ("Trustee") and the estimated disbursements to be made by the Trustee under this Modified Plan.

3. Description of Events Causing Need to Modify Plan. Modification is required to (check one or more):

☐ A. Provide for treatment of the following claims that were filed or amended after confirmation:
_____.

☐ B. Cure a post-petition payment default. The reason for the post-petition payment default is:
_____.

☐ C. Address a loss in income that requires a reduction in payments to the Trustee.

☐ D. Address an increase in income that requires an increase in payments to the Trustee.

☐ E. Other: _____.

4. Payments. The Debtor(s) must submit all or such portion of their future earnings and other future income to the supervision and control of the Trustee as is necessary for the execution of the Modified Plan.

A. *Pre–Modification Payments.* The Trustee's records reflect that, prior to the date of this modification, the Trustee has received $ _____ in payments from the Debtor(s). Of that total amount, $ _____ was placed into an emergency savings fund.

B. *Post–Modification Payments.* The amount, frequency, and duration of future payments to the Trustee are:

Beginning Month[1]	Ending Month	Total Amount of Monthly Payment[2]	Monthly Savings Fund Deposit	Total Forecast Emergency Savings Fund Deposits	Monthly Available for Creditors and Reserve Funds[3]	Total Available for Creditors and Reserve Funds
///////////////// /////////////////	///////////// /////////////	Grand Total:	///////////////// /////////////////		///////////////// /////////////////	

C. If the payments to be made by the Trustee pursuant to Paragraph 8(A)(ii) or 11(C) are adjusted in accordance with the Home Mortgage Payment Procedures defined and adopted pursuant to Bankruptcy Local Rule 3015–1(b) (whether on account of a change in any escrow requirement, a change in the applicable interest rate under an adjustable rate mortgage, or otherwise) or in accordance with the procedures set forth in Paragraphs 20(E) or 23(B), the payments to the Trustee under this Modified Plan will be changed as follows:

(i) The Debtor(s)' payments required by Paragraph 4 of this Modified Plan will be automatically increased or decreased by (i) the amount of the increase or decrease in the Paragraph 8(A)(ii), 11(C), 20(E) or 23(B) payments; and (ii) the amount of the increase or decrease in the Posted Chapter 13 Trustee Fee that is caused by the change.

(ii) The Posted Chapter 13 Trustee Fee is the percentage fee established by the Court and posted on the Court's web site from time to time.[4]

(iii) If a change to Paragraph 4(D), 8(a)(ii), 11(C), 20(E) or 23(B) is made and the monthly payment adjustment multiplied by the number of remaining months in the Modified Plan is less than $100, the payment adjustments required by Paragraph 4(C) will not be made.

C. If a Notice of Plan Payment Adjustment is required by Paragraph 8(a)(iii), the Debtor(s)' payments required by Paragraph 4 of this Modified Plan will be automatically increased by the amount of the adjustment.

D. Subject to an Order to the contrary, if the on-going monthly mortgage payment referenced in a timely filed proof of claim differs from the on-going monthly mortgage payment scheduled in this Modified Plan, the Trustee shall adjust the plan payment in order to reflect the on-going monthly mortgage payment amount provided for in the proof of claim.

E. If a secured or priority proof of claim is not timely filed, the amounts scheduled in this Plan will govern. If a secured or priority proof of claim is timely filed after confirmation of this Plan, the amounts shown on the timely filed proof of claim will govern. The procedures in Paragraph 4(D) govern monthly mortgage payment amounts.

F. In the event of a change in the monthly payment to the Trustee under this Modified Plan, the Trustee is directed to submit an amended wage withholding order or to amend any automated bank draft procedure to satisfy the automatic increase or decrease. The Debtor(s) must implement any appropriate amendments to any other form of payment.

G. Nothing in this Paragraph 4 precludes the Trustee from seeking to dismiss a case based on a timely filed proof of claim that renders this Modified Plan deficient.

5. Priority Claims for Domestic Support Obligations. From the payments made by the Debtor(s) to the Trustee, the Trustee shall pay in full all claims entitled to priority under 11 U.S.C. § 507(a)(1). The Remaining Claims[5] owed to the holders of a Domestic Support Obligation are the amounts reflected in this Modified Plan:

Name of Holder of Domestic Support Obligation	Remaining Claim	Post–Confirmation Claims not Included in Remaining Claim	Total Remaining Claims and Post Confirmation Claims	Interest Rate Under this Modified Plan	Amount of Periodic Payment	First Payment of this Amount in Mo. #	Last Payment of this Amount in Mo. #	Total

6. Priority Claims (Other than Domestic Support Obligations).

A.   From the payments made by the Debtor(s) to the Trustee, the Trustee shall pay in full all claims entitled to priority under 11 U.S.C. §§ 507(a)(2) through 507(a)(10).   The Remaining Claims owed to the holders of these priority claims are the amounts reflected in this Modified Plan:

Name of Holder of Priority Claim	Remaining Claim	Post–Confirmation Claims not Included in Remaining Claim	Total Remaining Claims and Post–Confirmation Claims	Interest Rate Under this Modified Plan	Amount of Periodic Payment	First Payment of this Amount in Mo. #	Last Payment of this Amount in Mo. #	Total

B.   Priority Claims arising under 11 U.S.C. § 503(b)(2) shall be paid only after entry of an order by the Bankruptcy Court approving payment of the claim.   If this case is dismissed, no Priority Claim arising under 11 U.S.C. § 503(b)(2) shall be allowed unless an application for allowance is filed on or before 21 days after entry of the order of dismissal, and such application is subsequently granted by the Court.

7. Secured Claims for which Collateral is Surrendered.   The Debtor(s) surrender the following collateral under this Modified Plan.   (If property was surrendered under a previously confirmed plan or modified plan, the property remains surrendered and should not be listed here.)

Name of Creditor	Description of Collateral

A.   Upon approval[6] of this Modified Plan, the Debtor(s) surrender the collateral and the automatic stay under 11 U.S.C. § 362(a) is terminated as to actions against any (i) collateral that is described in the preceding table; and (ii) escrow deposit held by the holder of a security interest to secure payment of taxes and insurance.   The automatic stay is not terminated under this Paragraph as to any other action.   The co-debtor stay under 11 U.S.C. § 1301(a) is terminated with respect to the collateral identified in the preceding table.

B.   Other than terminating the co-debtor stay, this Modified Plan does not affect any co-debtor's rights in the collateral or the obligation of any secured creditor to act with respect to such a co-debtor in compliance with applicable non-bankruptcy law.

C.   The Debtor(s) and the creditor asserting a security interest against the collateral must comply with Bankruptcy Local Rule 6007–1 with respect to the surrender of the collateral.

D.   The rights of a secured creditor to a deficiency claim will be determined (i) in accordance with the creditor's allowed unsecured claim in any timely filed proof of claim;   or (ii) by separate Court order.

8. Secured Claim for Claim Secured Only by a Security Interest in Real Property that is the Debtor(s)' Principal Residence (Property to be Retained).   For each such claim, utilize either A, B, or C, below:

☐ A.   This table sets forth the treatment of certain classes of secured creditors holding a claim secured only by a security interest in real property that is the Debtor(s)' principal residence located at (street address, city, state).

Name of	Remaining	Post–	Total	Modified	Security	Monthly Payment	Starting	Ending	Total

Holder of Secured Claim	Claim	Confirmation Claims not Included in Remaining Claim	Remaining Claims and Post Confirmation Claims	Plan Interest Rate	for Claim	Amount			Month #	Month #
						P&I	Escrow	Total		
	//////	//////	//////	//////		//////	//////	//////	//////	//////
Cure Claim7					//////					
Rule 3002.1(c) Amount			//////	//////	//////	//////				
Monthly Mtg. Payment8	//////	//////	//////	//////	//////					
Total Debt Claim				//////	//////					
	//////	//////	//////	//////		//////	//////	//////	//////	//////
Cure Claim					//////					
Rule 3002.1(c) Amount	//////	//////		//////	//////	//////				
Monthly Mtg. Payment	//////	//////	//////	//////	//////					
Total Debt Claim				//////	//////					

(i) Payment of these amounts will constitute a cure of all defaults (existing as of the date this Modified Plan is filed) of the Debtor(s)' obligations to the holder of the secured claim.

(ii) A claim secured only by a security interest in real property that is the Debtor(s)' principal residence (other than the Cure Claims or Total Debt Claim set forth in the above table) will be paid in accordance with the pre-petition contract. The claim includes all amounts that arose post-petition and that are authorized pursuant to Fed. R. Bankr. P. 3002.1. During the term of this Modified Plan, these payments will be made through the Trustee in accordance with the Home Mortgage Payment Procedures adopted pursuant to Bankruptcy Local Rule 3015–1(b). Each holder of a claim that is paid pursuant to this Paragraph must elect to either (i) apply the payments received by it to the next payment due without penalty under the terms of the holder's pre-petition note; or (ii) waive all late charges that accrue after the order for relief in this case. Any holder that fails to file an affirmative election within 30 days of entry of the order approving this Modified Plan has waived all late charges that accrue after the order for relief in this case. Notwithstanding the foregoing, the holder may impose a late charge that accrues following an event of default of a payment due under Paragraph 4 of this Plan.

(iii) Except as otherwise ordered by the Court, any amounts due as a result of the filing of a Rule 3002.1(c) Notice shall be paid after payment of all other secured and priority claims, but before payment of all general unsecured claims. If the payment of the amounts due under a Rule 3002.1(c) Notice would render this Modified Plan deficient because of a shortfall of available funds, the Trustee must file a Notice of Plan Payment Adjustment to provide sufficient funds to pay all secured and priority claims in full.

(iv) Each claim secured by a security interest is designated to be in a separate class.

(v) The Debtor(s) must timely provide the information required by the Trustee pursuant to the Home Mortgage Payment Procedures.

☐ B. The holder of the claim secured only by a security interest in real property that is the Debtor(s)' principal residence has agreed to refinance the security interest and claim on the terms set forth on the document attached as Exhibit "B". The refinancing brings the loan current in all respects. The terms of the loan that is being refinanced and the new loan are described below. (If the loan refinancing was approved under a previously confirmed plan or modified plan, the refinancing remains effective and should not be listed here. Amounts payable on a previously approved refinancing should be listed under Paragraphs 8A, 10 or 11, as appropriate.)

	Old Loan	New Loan
Current amount owed on old loan and total amount borrowed on new loan		
Interest rate is fixed or variable?		

Interest rate (in %)	
Closing costs paid by Debtor(s)	
Monthly principal and interest payment	
Monthly required escrow deposit	
Total monthly payment of principal, interest and escrow	

(i) Upon approval of this Modified Plan, the Debtor(s) are authorized to execute conforming documents with the holder of the security interest.

(ii) Payments made to the above referenced holder will be paid (check one, **only** if Debtor(s) have checked option **B**, above):

☐ **Through the Trustee.**

☐ **Directly to the holder of the claim, by the Debtor(s).** The holder of the claim may not impose any attorney's fees, inspection costs, appraisal costs or any other charges (other than principal, interest and ad valorem tax and property insurance escrows) if such charges arose (in whole or in part) during the period (i) when the case is open; (ii) after the closing of the refinanced loan; and (iii) prior to a further modification of this Plan (i.e., following a default by the Debtor(s) in payments to the holder of the claim) pursuant to which the Debtor(s) commence payments through the Trustee to the holder of the claim secured solely by a security interest in the Debtor(s)' principal residence. If the Debtor(s) default in direct payments following the refinancing, a proposed modification of this Plan must be filed.

☐ **C.** The following table sets forth the treatment of certain classes of secured creditors holding a claim secured only by a security interest in real property that is the Debtor(s)' principal residence. (If a lien has been avoided under a previously confirmed plan or modified plan, the lien remains avoided and should not be listed here.)

Name of Holder of Lien to which this provision applies		
Address of Principal Residence		
Debtor(s)' Stated Value of Principal Residence	$	
Description of all Liens Senior in Priority (List Holder and Priority)	Estimated Amount Owed on This Lien	///////////////////////
		///////////////////////
		///////////////////////
		///////////////////////
		///////////////////////
Total Owed—All Senior Liens		///////////////////////

(i) The Debtor(s) allege that the total amount of debt secured by liens that are senior in priority to the lien held by _____ exceeds the total value of the principal residence. Accordingly, the claim will receive (i) no distributions as a secured claim; and (ii) distributions as an unsecured claim only in accordance with applicable law.

(ii) Upon the Debtor(s)' completion of all payments set forth in this Modified Plan, the holder of the lien is required to execute and record a full and unequivocal release of its liens, encumbrances and security interests secured by the principal residence and to provide a copy of the release to the Debtor(s) and their counsel. Notwithstanding the foregoing, the holder of a lien that secures post-petition homeowners' association fees and assessments will be allowed to retain its lien, but only to secure (i) post-petition assessments; and (ii) other post-petition amounts, such as legal fees, if such other post-petition amounts are (a) incurred with respect to post-petition fees and assessments; and (b) approved by the Court, if incurred during the pendency of the bankruptcy case.

(iii) This Paragraph 8C will only be effective if the Debtor(s) perform each of the following:

(a) Mail a "Lien Stripping Notice," in the form set forth on the Court's website, to the holder of the lien that is governed by this Paragraph 8C. The Lien Stripping Notice must be mailed in a separate envelope from any other document. Service must be in a manner authorized by FED. R. BANKR. P. 7004.

(b) File a certificate of service at least 7 days prior to the modification hearing reflecting that the Lien Stripping Notice was mailed by both certified mail, return receipt requested and by regular US mail to the holder of the lien on **all** of the following, with the mailings occurring not later than 31 days prior to the hearing on this Plan:

The holder at the address for notices shown on any proof of claim filed by the holder and in accordance with FED. R. BANKR. P. 7004.

Any attorney representing the holder who has filed a request for notice in this bankruptcy case.

(iv) Third party costs incurred on behalf of the Debtor(s) such as the costs of performing a title or lien search or serving the motion and notices will be borne by the Debtor(s). If such third party costs are advanced by Debtor(s)' counsel, the Debtor(s) must promptly reimburse such costs, without the need for any further application or order.

9. Debt Incurred (a) within 910 Days Preceding Petition Date and Secured by a Lien on a Motor Vehicle or (b) within 1 Year Preceding Petition Date and Secured by Other Collateral for Which *Full Payment*, with Interest, is Required by 11 U.S.C. § 1325(a)(9) (hanging Paragraph). The following table sets forth each class of creditors holding a claim for a debt incurred within 910 days preceding the petition date and secured by a security interest on a motor vehicle or for a debt incurred within 1 year preceding the petition date and secured by a security interest on other collateral for which full payment is required by 11 U.S.C. § 1325(a)(9) (hanging Paragraph).

Name of Holder of Secured Claim	Remaining Claim	Post–Confirmation Claims not Included in Remaining Claim	Total Remaining Claims and Post Confirmation Claims	Modified Plan Interest Rate	Security for Claim	Monthly Payment Amount	Starting Month #	Ending Month #	Total
/////	/////	/////	/////			/////	/////	/////	/////
Cure Claim9					/////				
Monthly Contract Pmt.					/////				
Total Debt Claim					/////				
/////	/////	/////	/////			/////	/////	/////	/////
Cure Claim					/////				
Monthly Contract Pmt.					/////				
Total Debt Claim					/////				
/////	/////	/////	/////			/////	/////	/////	/////
Cure Claim					/////				
Monthly Contract Pmt.					/////				
Total Debt Claim					/////				

A. Payment of the amounts required in this section constitutes a cure of all defaults (existing as of the date this Modified Plan was filed) of the Debtor(s)' obligations to the holder of the claim. If the monthly payment in this proposed Modified Plan is less than the amount of the adequate protection payment ordered in this case, the actual payment will be the amount of the monthly adequate protection payment.

B. Each claim secured by a security interest is designated to be in a separate class.

10. Secured Debts on Which There is No Default and to be Paid Directly by the Debtor(s).

A. The claims held by the following secured creditors will be paid by the Debtor(s) (and not paid through the Trustee) in accordance with the pre-petition contracts between the Debtor(s) and the holder of the claim secured by a security interest:

Name of Holder	Collateral for Claim	Total Claim on Petition Date	Collateral Value on Petition Date	Contract Interest Rate	Monthly Payment	Date Last Payment is Due

B.   Each claim secured by a security interest is designated to be in a separate class.

11.   Other Secured Claims (Property to be Retained).   Payments on these claims will be made through the Trustee.   The secured claims treated by this Paragraph are in the following table:

Name of Holder of Secured Claim	Remaining Claim	Post–Confirmation Claims not Included in Remaining Claim	Total Remaining Claims and Post–Confirmation Claims	Modified Plan Interest Rate	Security for Claim	Monthly Payment Amount			Starting Month #	Ending Month #	Total
						P&I	Es-crow10	Total			
	/////////	/////////	/////////	/////////		/////////	/////////	/////////	/////////	/////////	/////////
Cure Claim11					/////////						
					/////////						
Monthly Contract Pmt.					/////////						
					/////////						
					/////////						
Total Debt Claim					/////////						
					/////////						
					/////////						

A.   The amount listed as "Escrow" will be adjusted to reflect $\frac{1}{12}$th of the annual ad valorem taxes and property insurance that is escrowed.   If there is an escrow shortage (for a RESPA Reserve or otherwise), the shortage is included in the Remaining Cure Claim listed above.

B.   Payment of the amounts required in this section constitutes a cure of all defaults (existing as of the date this proposed Modified Plan is filed) of the Debtor(s)' obligations to the holder of the secured claim.   If the monthly payment in this Modified Plan is less than the amount of the adequate protection payment ordered in this case, the actual payment will be the amount of the monthly adequate protection payment.

C.   If the pre-petition loan documents include a provision for an escrow account, the actual monthly payment is adjustable only in accordance with this Paragraph.   The Home Mortgage Payment Procedures must be followed, even though the claims treated in this Paragraph are not secured by the Debtor(s)' principal residence.

D.   Each claim secured by a security interest is designated to be in a separate class.

12.   Modification of Stay and Lien Retention.   The automatic stay is modified to allow holders of secured claims to send the Debtor(s): (i) monthly statements; (ii) escrow statements; (iii) payment change notices; and (iv) such other routine and customary notices as are sent to borrowers who are not in default.   The preceding sentence does not authorize the sending of any (i) demand letters; (ii) demands for payment; (iii) notices of actual or pending default.   The holder of an Allowed Secured Claim that is proposed to be paid under this Modified Plan shall retain its lien until the earlier of (i) the payment of the underlying debt as determined under nonbankruptcy law; or (ii) the entry of a discharge under 11 U.S.C. § 1328.   The holder of a claim secured by a valid lien may enforce its lien only if the stay is modified under 11 U.S.C. § 362 to allow the lender to enforce the lien.

13.   Maintenance of Taxes and Insurance.   The Debtor(s) must pay all ad valorem property taxes on property that is proposed to be retained under this Modified Plan, with payment made in accordance with applicable non-bankruptcy law not later than the last date on which such taxes may be paid without penalty.   The Debtor(s) must maintain insurance on all property that serves to secure a loan and that is proposed to be retained under this Modified Plan, as required by the underlying loan documents.   This Paragraph 13 does not apply to the extent that taxes and insurance are escrowed.   Any holder of a secured claim may request in writing, and the Debtor(s) must promptly provide proof of compliance with this Paragraph.   If the Debtor(s) fail to provide such proof within 30 days of receipt of a written request, the holder of the debt secured by a lien on the property may purchase such insurance or pay such taxes in accordance with its rights under applicable non-bankruptcy law.   Unless otherwise ordered by the Court, payment under this Paragraph may not be undertaken by a transfer of the tax lien on the property.

14. Secured Claims Satisfied by Transfer of Real Property in Satisfaction of Secured Claim. (If property was transferred under a previously confirmed plan or modified plan, the property remains transferred and should not be listed here.)

A. The secured claims set forth in this table will be satisfied by the transfer of title to the real property from the Debtor(s) to the transferee identified below.

Priority	Name and Address of Holder of Security Interest	Estimated Claim of Lien Holder
First lien		
Second lien		
Third lien		
Fourth lien		

B. The Transferee is _____.

C. The value to be credited to the Transferee's claim secured by the lien is:

Value of property	$
Total amounts owed to all holders of senior liens	$
Net value to be credited by Transferee	$

D. The address and legal description of the property to be transferred is _____.

E. This Paragraph applies only if 100% of the property to be transferred is included in the estate under 11 U.S.C. § 541(a), including without limitation community property included in the estate by 11 U.S.C. § 541(a)(2).

F. On or after the 30th day following entry of an order confirming this Modified Plan:

   (i) The Debtor(s) shall file as soon as practicable, a Notice of Transfer Pursuant to Bankruptcy Plan in the real property records of the County in which the property is located. A Notice of Transfer Pursuant to Bankruptcy Plan that attaches a certified copy of this Modified Plan and a certified copy of the Order approving this Modified Plan shall, when filed with a legal description of the property in the real property records of the County in which the property is located, constitute a transfer of ownership of the property to the holder of the Secured Claim. The transfer will be effective upon the later to occur of (i) the filing of the Notice of Transfer Pursuant to Bankruptcy Plan that attaches a certified copy of this Modified Plan and a certified copy of the Order approving this Modified Plan in the real property records of the applicable County; or (ii) if the Order is stayed pending appeal, the termination of the stay.

   (ii) The transferee of the transferred property must credit its claim with the Net Value to be credited by Transferee as shown in the preceding table (unless a different amount is ordered by the Court at the confirmation hearing on this Plan), not to exceed the balance owed on the claim on the date of the transfer. If the transfer is to the holder of a junior lien, the transfer is made subject to all senior liens. The holder of any senior lien may exercise its rights in accordance with applicable non-bankruptcy law. If the transfer is to the holder of a senior lien, the transfer is free and clear of the rights of the holder of any junior lien.[12]

   (iii) The senior liens must be satisfied, if at all, out of the property in accordance with applicable non-bankruptcy law. The transfer to the transferee and the relief granted by this Paragraph are in full satisfaction of the Debtor(s)' obligations to any holder of a security interest that is senior in priority to the security interest held by the transferee. No further payments by the Debtor(s) are required.

   (iv) The automatic stay is modified to allow any holder of a security interest or other lien on the property to exercise all of its rights against the property in accordance with applicable non-bankruptcy law.

G. Notwithstanding the foregoing Section F:

   (i) At its sole election prior to the 30th day following entry of an order approving this Modified Plan, the transferee may demand in writing, and the Debtor(s) must execute, a special warranty deed transferring the property to the transferee.

(ii) At its sole election prior to the 30th day following entry of an order approving this Modified Plan, the transferee may elect in writing to foreclose its security interest in the subject property. Any foreclosure must be completed within 90 days following entry of an order approving this Modified Plan. This Modified Plan, the order approving this Modified Plan and a proper election hereunder constitute a judicial authorization to proceed to foreclose to the extent required under applicable law. If an election is made under this subsection, the transferee shall be responsible for all loss associated with the property and all charges, liens, fees, etc. against the property from the 30th day following entry of an order confirming this Plan.

(iii) If a proper demand is made under this Section G, the provisions of Section F(i) are not applicable.

H. On and after the date on which the title to the real property (as reflected in the real property records) is not held by the Debtor(s), and except as otherwise agreed in writing between the Debtor(s) and the holder of the entity to which the property has been transferred, the Debtor(s) will immediately vacate the property.

I. The third party costs incurred on behalf of the Debtor(s) to obtain a lien search or title report and to file the Notice and certified copies will be borne by the Debtor(s). If such third party costs are advanced by Debtor(s)' counsel, the Debtor(s) must promptly reimburse such costs.

J. The Debtor(s) must file a certificate of service at least 7 days prior to the hearing on approval of this Modified Plan that a copy of this Modified Plan was mailed by both certified mail, return receipt requested and by regular US mail to all of the following, with the mailings to have occurred not later than 31 days prior to the hearing on approval of this Modified Plan to:

(i) Any attorney representing the holder of any security interest against the property who has filed a request for notice in this bankruptcy case.

(ii) The holder of any security interest against the property, in accordance with FED. R. BANKR. P. 7004 and the address for notice shown on any proof of claim filed by a holder. The identities of the holders must be identified from the deeds of trust filed in the real property records.

15. Secured Claims on Which Lien is Avoided Under 11 U.S.C. § 522(f). To the extent that the property described in this Paragraph is exempted under 11 U.S.C. § 522(b)(1), the following secured claims are avoided pursuant to 11 U.S.C. § 522(f) of the Bankruptcy Code. The only amount securing any such avoided lien is the lesser of (i) the amount shown as Remaining Value in this table; and (ii) the amount of the Allowed Claim secured by the lien. (If a lien was avoided under a previously confirmed plan or modified plan, the lien remains avoided and should not be listed here.)

Description of Property	Name and Address of Secured Creditor	Value of Property	Amount of Secured Claims Senior to Secured Claim to be Avoided	Amount Claimed as Exempt	Remaining Value

16. Specially Classified Unsecured Claims. The following unsecured claims will be treated as described below:

Name of Unsecured Creditor	Treatment and Reason for Special Classification

17. Unsecured Claims. Unsecured creditors not entitled to priority and not specially classified in Paragraph 16 shall comprise a single class of creditors. Allowed claims under this Paragraph 17 shall be paid a pro rata share of the amount remaining after payment of all secured, priority, and specially classified unsecured claims.

18. Executory Contracts. The following contracts were previously assumed. The amount and timing of any remaining cure payments will be made as shown (Contracts that were assumed and have been fully cured should not be listed):

Parties to Executory Contract	Amount of Remaining Cure	Remaining Cure to be Made Directly by the Debtor(s) in equal Monthly Installments of this Amount, with the First Installment Due on the 30th Day Following Entry of the Order Approving this Modified Plan

19. Asset Sales. The Debtor(s) are authorized—without the need for further Court order (except as provided by FED. R. BANKR. P. 2014 if applicable)—to sell their exempt property in accordance with this Paragraph. Any such sale shall provide for the full payment, at closing, of all liens on the property that is sold. If the Debtor(s) request and the Court so determines, an order confirming this authority may be granted by the Court, *ex parte*. Within 14 days following the closing of any sale of real property pursuant to this Paragraph, the Debtor(s) must provide to the Trustee a copy of the final closing statement. Any non-exempt proceeds received from the sale must be paid to the Trustee. Unless the sale was privately closed, the closing statement must be the statement issued by the title company or closing agent handling the sale. If the property that was sold was exempted as a homestead solely under Texas law, any proceeds of the sale that are not reinvested in a qualifying Texas homestead within 6 months of the closing of the sale must be paid to the Trustee within 14 days after the expiration of the 6-month period. If only a portion of the proceeds are reinvested in a qualifying Texas homestead prior to the expiration of the 6-month period, the balance of the proceeds must be paid to the Trustee within 14 days of the closing.

20. Surrender of Collateral during the Modified Plan Period. (If property was surrendered under a previously confirmed plan or modified plan, the property remains surrendered and should not be listed here.)

A. The Debtor(s) may surrender collateral to a secured creditor after approval of this Modified Plan by filing a Surrender Notice in the form set forth on the Court's website. The Surrender Notice will be effective upon the expiration of 21 days from the date that it is filed; provided, if an objection to the Surrender Notice is filed within the 21-day period, the Surrender Notice will become effective only upon entry of a Court order approving the Surrender Notice (the "Effective Date"). If a timely objection is filed, the Trustee will schedule the Surrender Notice for hearing on the next available Chapter 13 panel date. On the Effective Date, the automatic stay under 11 U.S.C. § 362(a) and the co-debtor stay under 11 U.S.C. § 1301(a) are terminated as to actions against surrendered property. The automatic stay is not terminated under this Paragraph as to any other action.

B. Bankruptcy Local Rule 6007–1 applies to the surrender of property under this Plan.

C. Other than terminating the co-debtor stay, this Modified Plan does not affect any co-debtor's rights in the collateral or the obligation of any secured creditor to act with respect to such a co-debtor in compliance with applicable non-bankruptcy law.

D. If payments on debt secured by the surrendered property were made through the Trustee, a Debtor(s)' Proposed Notice of Plan Payment Adjustment, in the form set forth on the Court's website, must be filed as an exhibit to the Surrender Notice. If the Trustee determines that the Debtor's Proposed Notice of Payment Adjustment is materially inconsistent with the following Paragraph, the Trustee must file a Trustee's Corrected Notice of Plan Payment Adjustment. Any such Corrected Notice must be filed within 30 days after the filing of the Debtor(s)' Proposed Notice of Plan Adjustment. The Trustee's Corrected Notice of Plan Payment Adjustment will be binding unless a party-in-interest files a motion and obtains an order to the contrary.

E. If the payment on the debt secured by the surrendered property was made through the Trustee, the payments to the Trustee under this Modified Plan will be adjusted. The adjusted payment will be effective with the next payment due to the Trustee after the Effective Date. The Plan Payment Adjustment will be a reduction equal to (i) the sum of (a) all remaining principal, interest and escrow payments that are due under this Modified Plan after the Effective Date and payable to the holder of the secured debt; plus (b) any Reserves required by Paragraph 23 for the payment of ad valorem taxes pertaining to the surrendered property; plus (c) the Posted Chapter 13 trustee fee applicable to the sum of such remaining payments of principal, interest, escrow and reserves; divided by (ii) the remaining number of monthly payments due under this Modified Plan after the Effective Date. No further ad valorem tax reserves will be established on surrendered property.

F.   On the Effective Date, no additional direct or Trustee payments will be made on the claim secured by the surrendered property. The rights of a secured creditor to a deficiency claim will be determined (i) in accordance with the creditor's allowed unsecured claim in any timely filed proof of claim; or (ii) by separate Court order.

G.   Within 14 days of the Effective Date, the Debtor(s) must file an amended Schedule I and J.

21.   Payments Under Plan. For the purposes of 11 U.S.C. § 1328(a) of the Bankruptcy Code, the Debtor(s) will have completed all payments under this Modified Plan by:

A.   Paying all amounts due under Paragraph 4 of this Modified Plan, as adjusted by this Modified Plan; and

B.   Paying all amounts due as direct payments under this Modified Plan, as adjusted by this Modified Plan.

22.   Emergency Savings Fund.

A.   Line 21 of Schedule J (the Debtor(s)' expense budget) includes a provision for an emergency savings fund by the Debtor(s). Deposits into the Emergency Savings Fund will be made to the Trustee. Withdrawals from the Emergency Savings Fund may be made by application to the Court, utilizing the form application from the Court's website. Withdrawals should be requested only in an emergency. The form application need only be served electronically, and only to persons subscribing to the Court's CM/ECF electronic noticing system. An application will be deemed granted on the 15th day after filing unless (i) an objection has been filed; or (ii) the Court has set a hearing on the application. The Debtor(s) may request emergency consideration of any application filed under this Paragraph. The balance, if any, in the Emergency Savings Fund will be paid to the Debtor(s) following (i) the completion of all payments under this Plan; (ii) the dismissal of this case; or (iii) the conversion of this case to a case under chapter 7, except under those circumstances set forth in 11 U.S.C. § 348(f)(2).

B.   The future deposits into the Emergency Savings Fund will be:

Month of First Deposit of this Amount following Plan Modification	Month of Last Deposit of this Amount	Amount	Total
/////////////////////////////////	/////////////////////////////////	TOTAL	

C.   Funds paid to the Trustee will not be credited to the Emergency Savings Fund unless, at the time of receipt by the Trustee, the Debtor(s) are current on payments provided for in this Modified Plan that are to be distributed to creditors or that are to be reserved under Paragraph 23. After funds have been credited to the Emergency Savings Fund, they may only be withdrawn in accordance with this Paragraph.

D.   All Emergency Savings Funds held by the Trustee as of the date this Modified Plan was filed will remain in place and be distributed in accordance with this Paragraph 22.

E.   The Debtor(s) may file a Notice reflecting any change into the Emergency Savings Fund deposits. Unless a party-in-interest objects within 14 days of the filing of the Notice, the Trustee must file a Notice of Plan Payment Adjustment to reflect the change.

23.   Reserves for Post–Petition Ad Valorem Taxes, Homeowners Association Fees or Other Periodic Post–Petition Obligations. (Check One or More):

☐ The Debtor(s) do not invoke this provision.

☐ The Debtor(s) will reserve for post-modification ad valorem taxes. The amount of each monthly reserve is shown on Schedule 23.[13]

☐ The Debtor(s) will reserve for post-modification homeowners' association fees. The amount of each monthly reserve is shown on Schedule 23.

☐ The Debtor(s) will reserve for post-modification federal income tax payments. The amount of each monthly reserve is shown on Schedule 23.

☐ The Debtor(s) will reserve for: _____.[14] The amount of each monthly reserve is shown on Schedule 23.

A. The Debtor(s)' expense budget shown on Schedule J includes a monthly provision for the payment of the post-petition Reserves identified above. The Debtor(s) must deposit the monthly amount shown on Schedule J for each of the designated Reserve items with the Trustee. Not less than 45 days before the date on which the payment is due to the taxing authority, homeowner's association or other person, the Debtor(s) must send a request to the Trustee, on a form promulgated by the Trustee, requesting a disbursement from the Reserves. Copies of the appropriate invoices or tax statements must be attached to the request. Not later than 45 days after receipt of an appropriate request, the Trustee must pay the lesser of (i) the amount shown on the invoices or tax statements; or (ii) the balance in the applicable Reserve. If the balance in the applicable Reserve is less than the amount due, then the Debtor(s) are responsible for payment of the balance due on the invoice or tax statements. The Chapter 13 Trustee's Fee will apply to any disbursements from these Reserves.

B. The Debtor(s) must file a Notice reflecting any change of the projected disbursement amount from the applicable Reserve. Unless a party-in-interest objects within 14 days thereafter, the Trustee must file a Notice of Plan Payment Adjustment to reflect the change.

C. Funds paid to the Trustee will not be credited to Reserves unless, at the time of receipt by the Trustee, the Debtor(s) are current on payments provided for in the Plan that are to be distributed to the holders of claims. If the monthly amount credited to Reserves is less than the total of all monthly reserves shown above, the Trustee will apply the credits to the Reserves pro rata. After funds have been credited to an applicable Reserve, they may only be withdrawn in accordance with this Paragraph.

D. If this Modified Plan provides for payment of a "Total Debt Claim" on real property and no lender-established escrow account is maintained, the Debtor(s) must establish Reserves under this Paragraph for the payment of ad valorem taxes. If the Debtor(s) subsequently surrender the real property, or if the automatic stay is terminated as to the real property, the amount of reserves for taxes on such property will be paid by the Trustee, without further Court Order, to the holder of the claim secured by the most senior security interest against the real property.

E. All Reserves held by the Trustee as of the date this Modified Plan was filed will be applied in accordance with this Paragraph 23.

F. Upon completion of all payments under this Modified Plan, the remaining balance on hand in the Reserves will be paid to the Debtor(s).

24. **Effect of a Motion to Convert to Chapter 7.** If, during the term of this Modified Plan, the Debtor(s) file a motion to convert this case to a case under Chapter 7 of the Bankruptcy Code, the motion may be included with a request to distribute to Debtor(s)' counsel the lesser of (i) the amount agreed between the Debtor(s) and Debtor(s)' counsel; and (ii) $750.00. If a motion to convert to chapter 7 has been filed and not yet granted by the Court, the Trustee must, within 35 days of the date on which the motion was filed, distribute any remaining funds (exclusive of Reserves and Emergency Savings Funds) (i) first to pay any unpaid adequate protection payments due to the holders of secured claims; and (ii) thereafter, the amount requested (not to exceed $750.00) to Debtor(s)' counsel for post-conversion services. Any amounts so distributed are subject to disgorgement if ordered by the Court. A motion to convert filed pursuant to this Paragraph 24 must be filed with a proposed order, in the form published on the Court's website. The Order, if submitted in accordance with this Paragraph, may be issued *ex parte* and without notice.

25. **Presence or Absence of a Proof of Claim.**

A. Secured and priority claims provided for in this Modified Plan will be paid without the necessity of the filing of a proof of claim. If this Modified Plan sets the amount of a monthly payment, monthly payments will be adjusted in accordance with the Court's Home Mortgage Payment Procedures as applied by Paragraphs 8 and 11 of this Plan.

B. Unless otherwise ordered by the Court (and subject to the claims objection process), the amounts shown on a timely filed proof of claim govern as to (i) the amount of that claim, (ii) the amount of any cure amount; and (iii) the amount of any monthly payment, which monthly payment is subject to adjustment in accordance with the Court's Home Mortgage Payment Procedures as applied by Paragraphs 8 and 11 of this Plan.

C.   Regardless of the filing of a proof of claim, any valuation in this Modified Plan of the collateral securing a claim controls over any contrary proof of claim.

D.   A determination made under this Modified Plan as to a claim does not constitute an order allowing or disallowing a claim against the estate for purposes of Rule 3008 or otherwise.

E.   Unless the Court orders otherwise, no general unsecured claim will be paid unless a proof of claim has been timely filed.

F.   The payment of Debtor(s)' attorney's fees are not governed by this Paragraph.

G.   No creditor, before or after completion of the Plan, shall be allowed to collect any payments, costs, fees, or expenses, from the Debtor(s), the estate, or their property, that are not provided for in this Plan.

26. Discharge and Vesting of Property. The Debtor(s) will be granted a discharge in accordance with 11 U.S.C. § 1328. Property of the estate shall vest in the Debtor(s) upon entry of the discharge order.

27. Effect of Dismissal. If this case is dismissed:

A.   Except for Paragraph 27(B), this Modified Plan is no longer effective.

B.   Any funds received by the Trustee after entry of the order of dismissal will be paid to the Debtor(s).

28. Modified Plan Not Altered from Official Form. By filing this Modified Plan, Debtor(s) and their counsel represent that the Modified Plan is in the official form authorized by the Court. There are no addenda or other changes made to the official form, except those contained in Paragraph 29.

29. Non–standard Provisions. _____

_____

_____

_____

_____

Except for provisions contained in Paragraph 29, any provision not contained in the official Southern District of Texas Uniform Modification of Confirmed Chapter 13 Plan and Motion for Valuation of Collateral is void. Any provision contained in this Paragraph 29 is void unless Paragraph 1 of this Modified Plan indicates that a non-standard provision has been included in this Modified Plan.

Submitted by

_____

Debtor Signature

_____

Joint Debtor Signature

_____

[Name, address, email and phone of Debtor(s) or of Debtor(s)' attorney]

Debtor(s)' Declaration Pursuant to 28 U.S.C. § 1746

I declare under penalty of perjury that the foregoing statements of value contained in this document are true and correct.

Dated: _____   _____

Signature of Debtor

Dated: _____   _____

Signature of Joint Debtor

CAPTION

NOTICE OF DEBTOR(S)' INTENTION TO STRIP YOUR LIEN

Notice to: [INSERT NAME OF HOLDER OF LIEN]

Regarding: Your lien that is alleged to be secured by the following real property:
                  [Street Address of Property]

Priority of the
Lien that Will
be Stripped: _____

[DEBTOR(S) NAMES] propose a modified chapter 13 plan that terminates your lien secured by the property located at [ADDRESS]. The proposed modified Plan alleges that the value of the property is less than the amount owed on all liens that are senior in priority to your lien.

You must file any objection to the termination of your lien within 28 days of the date of this notice. If you fail to do so, the Bankruptcy Court may approve the modified Plan without further notice. If you do object, you must appear at the hearing on approval of the proposed modified Plan. The hearing is scheduled for [INSERT DATE AND TIME] at the United States Courthouse, _____

You are urged to review the entire Plan. The provision of the Modified Plan that would terminate your lien is set forth below:

[INSERT ALL OF PARAGRAPH 8C VERBATIM]

CERTIFICATE OF SERVICE

On _____, a copy of this notice was sent by certified mail, return receipt requested, and by regular US mail to each of the following:

[List Name and Address of Each Recipient, as required by Paragraph 8C of the Modified Plan]

[SIGNATURE BLOCK]

Schedule 23

Month15	Ad Valorem Tax Reserve	HOA Reserve	Federal Income Tax Reserve	Other Reserves	Total Reserves This Month

Month15	Ad Valorem Tax Reserve	HOA Reserve	Federal Income Tax Reserve	Other Reserves	Total Reserves This Month

[Dated: December 1, 2017. Amended effective August 21, 2018.]

1 Throughout this Modified Plan, the first numbered month is the month in which the first payment is due under the proposed modification. For example, if the pre-modification plan period was 14 months, the beginning month number should ordinarily be 15.

2 The total amount of monthly payment includes savings and reserves.

3 Reserve funds are funds established under Paragraph 23 of this Modified Plan.

4 The Posted Chapter 13 Trustee Fee does not alter the amount of the actual trustee fee established under 28 U.S.C. § 586(e)(1).

5 Throughout this Modified Plan, the "Remaining Claim" must be the unpaid amount of the claim as reflected on the Trustee's website as of the date that this Modified Plan is filed.

6 This Modified Plan will be approved only upon entry of the order by the Bankruptcy Court that approves this Modified Plan pursuant to 11 U.S.C. § 1329.

7 In this Modified Plan, a "Cure Claim" is the amount required to cure any existing default. A "Total Debt Claim" is a claim that will be fully paid during the term of the proposed Plan. As to each claim secured by a security interest, the Debtor(s) must propose either (i) a Cure Claim and a monthly mortgage payment; (ii) a Total Debt Claim; or (iii) in cases in which there is no Cure Claim, a Monthly Mortgage Payment. The amount shown as "Cure Claim" should be equal to the total of all amounts required to cure the mortgage.

8 Including principal, interest, and escrow.

9 In this Modified Plan, a "Cure Claim" is the amount required to cure any existing default. A "Total Debt Claim" is a claim that will be fully paid during the term of the proposed Modified Plan. As to each claim secured by a security interest, the Debtor(s) must propose either (i) a Cure Claim and a Monthly Contract Payment; (ii) a Total Debt Claim; or (iii) in cases in which there is no Cure Claim, a Monthly Contractual Payment.

10 Only applicable if an escrow for ad valorem taxes or property insurance has been required by the holder of the security interest. If the collateral is a vehicle or other personal property, the "Escrow" amount should be $0.00.

11 In this Modified Plan, a "Cure Claim" is the amount required to cure any existing default. A "Total Debt Claim" is a claim that will be fully paid during the term of the Modified Plan. As to each claim secured by a security interest, the Debtor(s) must propose either (i) a Cure Claim and a Monthly Contract Payment; (ii) a Total Debt Claim; or (iii) in cases in which there is no Cure Claim, a Monthly Contractual Payment.

12 The property may not be transferred to the holder of an oversecured senior lien if there is a junior lien.

13 A Schedule 23 must be attached unless no Reserves are established.

14 Reserves may not be established under this Paragraph for the payment of insurance premiums.

15 See footnote 2 of the Modified Plan. The first listed number should be the month in which the first payment is due under the proposed modification. For example, if the pre-modification plan period was 14 months, the Beginning Month Number should ordinarily be 15.

EXHIBIT A. PLAN SUMMARY FOR PROPOSED PLAN

Disposable Income and Plan Payments

(A) Projected Schedule "I" Income (From most recently filed Schedule I)	(B) Projected Schedule "J" Expenses (From most recently filed Schedule J)	(C) Projected Disposable Income (Column A minus Column B)	(D) Payment Amount to Trustee	(E) Beginning Month #[1]	(F) Ending Month #	(G) Payments for the Benefit of Creditors and for Reserves[2]		(H) Savings Fund[3] Deposits Established Under Plan (Column D minus Column G)		(I) Total Monthly Trustee Payments (Column D multiplied by number of months paid)
						Per Month	Total	Per Month	Total	
				1						
				Grand Total						
			Less Posted Chapter 13 Trustee Fee[4]							
			Net Available to Creditors							

Projected Trustee Disbursements to Secured Creditors

Name of Holder	Description of Collateral	Claim	Plan Int. Rate	Monthly Payment Amount	Starting Month #	Ending Month #	Total
Holder's Name:							
Treated under Plan Section:							
Check One: ☐ Surrendered ☐ Transferred ☐ Retained (paid direct) ☐ Retained (paid through Trustee)[5]							
Cure Claim							
Monthly Payment							
Total Debt Claim							
Monthly Refinance Payment (¶ 8B)							

---

[1]   This is the month in which the first payment is due for this amount. The Debtor(s) must commence payments not later than 30 days after the petition date.

[2]   Reserves are established under Paragraph 23 of the Plan.

[3]   Savings funds are funds established under Paragraph 22 of the Plan.

[4]   The Posted Chapter 13 Trustee Fee is based on the percentage listed on the Court's website.

[5]   Amounts for Cure Claims, Monthly Payments, Total Debt Claims and Monthly Refinance Payments should be listed only if the box for "Retained (paid through Trustee)" is checked.

Name of Holder	Description of Collateral	Claim	Plan Int. Rate	Monthly Payment Amount	Starting Month #	Ending Month #	Total
Holder's Name: _____ Treated under Plan Section:							
Check One: ☐ Surrendered ☐ Transferred ☐ Retained (paid direct) ☐ Retained (paid through Trustee)							
Cure Claim							
Mortgage Payment							
Total Debt Claim							
Monthly Refinance Payment (¶ 8B)							
Total of Payments to Secured Creditors							

Projected Trustee Disbursements to Priority Creditors

Name of Holder	Nature of Priority (Taxes, Attorneys Fees, DSO, etc.)	Claim	Int. Rate	Monthly Payment Amount	Beg. Month #	End Month #	Total
Holder's Name: _____ Treated under Plan Section:							
Holder's Name: _____ Treated under Plan Section:							
Holder's Name: _____ Treated under Plan Section:							
Total of Payments to Priority Creditors							

Projected Trustee Reserve Funds

Reserve Fund Type (Ad Valorem Taxes, Insurance, HOA)	Total
Total of Reserve Funds	

SUMMARY

1	Total Payments to Trustee	
2	Less Total Savings Fund Deposits	
3	Net Trustee Payments (Line 1 minus line 2)	
4	Less Posted Chapter 13 Trustee Fee	
5	Less Total Payments by Trustee to Secured Creditors	
6	Less Total Payments by Trustee to Priority Creditors (§§507(a)(1) – (a)(10))	
7	Less Total Reserve Funds	
8	Net Available for General Unsecured Creditors (Line 3 minus lines 4-7)	

Unsecured Creditor Distribution Estimate

9	Estimated Total General Unsecured Claims	
10	Forecast % Dividend on General Unsecured Claims (Line 8 divided by line 9)	

Best Interest of Creditors Test

11	Total Non-Exempt Property	
12	Total Distributions to Administrative, Priority and General Unsecured Creditors (Line 4 plus lines 6 plus line 8 plus any direct payments by Debtor(s) under the Plan in satisfaction of prepetition priority claims)	

[Dated: December 1, 2017.]

GUIDELINES FOR COMMUNICATION AND COOPERATION BETWEEN COURTS IN CROSS–BORDER INSOLVENCY MATTERS

Introduction

A.   The overarching objective of these Guidelines is to improve in the interests of all stakeholders the efficiency and effectiveness of cross-border proceedings relating to insolvency or adjustment of debt opened in more than one jurisdiction ("Parallel Proceedings") by enhancing coordination and cooperation among courts under whose supervision such proceedings are being conducted. These Guidelines represent best practice for dealing with Parallel Proceedings.

B.   In all Parallel Proceedings, these Guidelines should be considered at the earliest practicable opportunity.

C.   In particular, these Guidelines aim to promote:

(i) the efficient and timely coordination and administration of Parallel Proceedings;

(ii) the administration of Parallel Proceedings with a view to ensuring relevant stakeholders' interests are respected;

(iii) the identification, preservation, and maximization of the value of the debtor's assets, including the debtor's business;

(iv) the management of the debtor's estate in ways that are proportionate to the amount of money involved, the nature of the case, the complexity of the issues, the number of creditors, and the number of jurisdictions involved in Parallel Proceedings;

(v) the sharing of information in order to reduce costs; and

(vi) the avoidance or minimization of litigation, costs, and inconvenience to the parties[1] in Parallel Proceedings.

D.   These Guidelines should be implemented in each jurisdiction in such manner as the jurisdiction deems fit.[2]

E.   These Guidelines are not intended to be exhaustive and in each case consideration ought to be given to the special requirements in that case.

F.   Courts should consider in all cases involving Parallel Proceedings whether and how to implement these Guidelines. Courts should encourage and where necessary direct, if they have the power to do so, the parties to make the necessary applications to the court to facilitate such implementation by a protocol or order derived from these Guidelines, and encourage them to act so as to promote the objectives and aims of these Guidelines wherever possible.

1. Adoption and Interpretation.

Guideline 1: In furtherance of paragraph F above, the courts should encourage administrators in Parallel Proceedings to cooperate in all aspects of the case, including the necessity of notifying the courts at the earliest practicable opportunity of issues present and potential that may (a) affect those proceedings and (b) benefit from communication and coordination between the courts. For the purpose of these Guidelines, "administrator" includes a liquidator, trustee, judicial manager, administrator in administration proceedings, debtor-in-possession in a reorganization or scheme of arrangement, or any fiduciary of the estate or person appointed by the court.

Guideline 2: Where a court intends to apply these Guidelines (whether in whole or in part and with or without modification) in particular Parallel Proceedings, it will need to do so by a protocol or an order,[3] following an application by the parties or pursuant to a direction of the court if the court has the power to do so.

Guideline 3: Such protocol or order should promote the efficient and timely administration of Parallel Proceedings. It should address the coordination of requests for court approvals of related decisions and actions when required and communication with creditors and other parties. To the extent possible, it should also provide for timesaving procedures to avoid unnecessary and costly court hearings and other proceedings.

Guideline 4: These Guidelines when implemented are not intended to:

(i) interfere with or derogate from the jurisdiction or the exercise of jurisdiction by a court in any proceedings, including its authority or supervision over an administrator in those proceedings;

(ii) interfere with or derogate from the rules or ethical principles by which an administrator is bound according to any applicable law and professional rules;

(iii) prevent a court from refusing to take an action that would be manifestly contrary to the public policy of the jurisdiction; or

(iv) confer or change jurisdiction, alter substantive rights, interfere with any function or duty arising out of any applicable law, or encroach upon any applicable law.

Guideline 5: For the avoidance of doubt, a protocol or order under these Guidelines is procedural in nature. It should not constitute a limitation on or waiver by the court of any powers, responsibilities, or authority or a substantive determination of any matter in controversy before the court or before the other court or a waiver by any of the parties of any of their substantive rights and claims.

Guideline 6: In the interpretation of these Guidelines or any protocol or order under these Guidelines, due regard shall be given to their international origin and to the need to promote good faith and uniformity in their application.

2. Communication Between Courts.

Guideline 7: A court may receive communications from a foreign court and may respond directly to them. Such communications may occur for the purpose of the orderly making of submissions and rendering of decisions by the courts, and to coordinate and resolve any procedural, administrative or preliminary matters relating to any joint hearing where Annex A is applicable. Such communications may take place through the following methods or such other method as may be agreed by the two courts in a specific case:

(i) Sending or transmitting copies of formal orders, judgments, opinions, reasons for decision, endorsements, transcripts of proceedings or other documents directly to the other court and providing advance notice to counsel for affected parties in such manner as the court considers appropriate.

(ii) Directing counsel to transmit or deliver copies of documents, pleadings, affidavits, briefs or other documents that are filed or to be filed with the instant court to the other court in such fashion as may be appropriate and providing advance notice to counsel for affected parties in such manner as the court considers appropriate.

(iii) Participating in two-way communications with the other court, in which case Guideline 8 should be considered.

<u>Guideline 8</u>: In the event of communications between courts, other than on procedural matters, unless otherwise directed by any court involved in the communications whether on an *ex parte* basis or otherwise, or permitted by a protocol, the following shall apply:

(i) In the normal case, parties may be present.

(ii) If the parties are entitled to be present, advance notice of the communications shall be given to all parties in accordance with the rules of procedure applicable in each of the courts to be involved in the communications and the communications between the courts shall be recorded and may be transcribed. A written transcript may be prepared from a recording of the communications that, with the approval of each court involved in the communications, may be treated as the official transcript of the communications.

(iii) Copies of any recording of the communications, of any transcript of the communications prepared pursuant to any direction of any court involved in the communications, and of any official transcript prepared from a recording may be filed as part of the record in the proceedings and made available to the parties and subject to such directions as to confidentiality as any court may consider appropriate.

(iv) The time and place for communications between the courts shall be as directed by the courts. Personnel other than judges in each court may communicate with each other to establish appropriate arrangements for the communications without the presence of the parties.

<u>Guideline 9</u>: A court may direct that notice of its proceedings be given to parties in proceedings in another jurisdiction. All notices, applications, motions, and other materials served for purposes of the proceedings before the court may be ordered to be provided to such other parties by making such materials available electronically in a publicly accessible system or by facsimile transmission, certified or registered mail or delivery by courier, or in such other manner as may be directed by the court in accordance with the procedures applicable in the court.

3. Appearance in Court.

<u>Guideline 10</u>: A court may authorize a party, or an appropriate person, to appear before and be heard by a foreign court, subject to approval of the foreign court to such appearance.

<u>Guideline 11</u>: If permitted by its law and otherwise appropriate, a court may authorize a party to a foreign proceeding, or an appropriate person, to appear and be heard on a specific matter by it without thereby becoming subject to its jurisdiction for any purpose other than the specific matter on which the party is appearing.

4. Consequential Provisions.

<u>Guideline 12</u>: A court shall, except on proper objection on valid grounds and then only to the extent of such objection, recognize and accept as authentic the provisions of statutes, statutory or administrative regulations, and rules of court of general application applicable to the proceedings in other jurisdictions without further proof. For the avoidance of doubt, such recognition and acceptance does not constitute recognition or acceptance of their legal effect or implications.

<u>Guideline 13</u>: A court shall, except upon proper objection on valid grounds and then only to the extent of such objection, accept that orders made in the proceedings in other jurisdictions were duly and properly made or entered on their respective dates and accept that such orders require no further proof for purposes of the proceedings before it, subject to its law and all such proper reservations as in the opinion of the court are appropriate regarding proceedings by way of appeal or review that are actually pending in respect of any such orders. Notice of any amendments, modifications, extensions, or appellate decisions with respect to such orders shall be made to the other court(s) involved in Parallel Proceedings, as soon as it is practicable to do so. For the avoidance of doubt, such recognition and acceptance does not constitute recognition or acceptance of their legal effect or implications.

<u>Guideline 14</u>: A protocol or order made by a court under these Guidelines is subject to such amendments, modifications, and extensions as may be considered appropriate by the court, and to reflect the changes and developments from time to time in any Parallel Proceedings. Notice of such amendments, modifications, or extensions shall be made to the other court(s) involved in Parallel Proceedings, as soon as it is practicable to do so.

5. Annex a (Joint Hearings).
Annex A to these Guidelines relates to guidelines on the conduct of joint hearings. Annex A shall be applicable to, and shall form a part of these Guidelines, with respect to courts that may signify their assent to Annex A from time to time. Parties are encouraged to address the matters set out in Annex A in a protocol or order.

Annex A: Joint Hearings

A court may conduct a joint hearing with another court. In connection with any such joint hearing, the following shall apply, or where relevant, be considered for inclusion in a protocol or order:

(i) The implementation of this Annex shall not divest nor diminish any court's respective independent jurisdiction over the subject matter of proceedings. By implementing this Annex, neither a court nor any party shall be deemed to have approved or engaged in any infringement on the sovereignty of the other jurisdiction.

(ii) Each court shall have sole and exclusive jurisdiction and power over the conduct of its own proceedings and the hearing and determination of matters arising in its proceedings.

(iii) Each court should be able simultaneously to hear the proceedings in the other court. Consideration should be given as to how to provide the best audio-visual access possible.

(iv) Consideration should be given to coordination of the process and format for submissions and evidence filed or to be filed in each court.

(v) A court may make an order permitting foreign counsel or any party in another jurisdiction to appear and be heard by it. If such an order is made, consideration needs to be given as to whether foreign counsel or any party would be submitting to the jurisdiction of the relevant court and/or its professional regulations.

(vi) A court should be entitled to communicate with the other court in advance of a joint hearing, with or without counsel being present, to establish the procedures for the orderly making of submissions and rendering of decisions by the courts, and to coordinate and resolve any procedural, administrative or preliminary matters relating to the joint hearing.

A court, subsequent to the joint hearing, should be entitled to communicate with the other court, with or without counsel present, for the purpose of determining outstanding issues. Consideration should be given as to whether the issues include procedural and/or substantive matters. Consideration should also be given as to whether some or all of such communications should be recorded and preserved

[Dated: January 31, 2019.]

1 The term "parties" when used in these Guidelines shall be interpreted broadly.

2 Possible modalities for the implementation of these Guidelines include practice directions and commercial guides.

3 In the normal case, the parties will agree on a protocol derived from these Guidelines and obtain the approval of each court in which the protocol is to apply.

UNITED STATES DISTRICT COURT FOR THE EASTERN DISTRICT OF TEXAS

Including Amendments Received Through
February 1, 2019

SECTION I.   CIVIL RULES

LOCAL RULE CV–1.   SCOPE AND PURPOSE OF RULES

(a) The rules of procedure in any proceeding in this court are those prescribed by the laws of the United States, the Federal Rules of Civil Procedure, these local rules, and any orders entered by the court. These local rules shall be construed as consistent with Acts of Congress and rules of practice and procedure prescribed by the Supreme Court of the United States and the United States Court of Appeals for the Fifth Circuit.

(b) Admiralty Rules. The Supplemental Rules for Certain Admiralty and Maritime Claims, as adopted by the Supreme Court of the United States, shall govern all admiralty and maritime actions in this court.

(c) Patent Rules. The "Rules of Practice for Patent Cases before the Eastern District of Texas" attached as Appendix B to these rules shall apply to all civil actions filed in or transferred to this court which allege infringement of a utility patent in a complaint, counterclaim, cross-claim, or third party claim, or which seek a declaratory judgment that a utility patent is not infringed, is invalid, or is unenforceable. Judges may opt out of this rule by entering an order

[Effective October 27, 1997. Amended effective December 1, 2000; May 6, 2015; December 1, 2015; December 1, 2018.]

LOCAL RULE CV–3.   COMMENCEMENT OF ACTION

(a) Habeas Corpus and 28 U.S.C. § 2255 Motions. The clerk may require that petitions for a writ of habeas corpus and motions filed pursuant to 28 U.S.C. § 2255 be filed on a set of standardized forms approved by this court and supplied, upon request, by the clerk without cost to the petitioner. Petitioners who do not proceed *in forma pauperis* must pay a $5.00 filing fee. *See* 28 U.S.C. § 1914(a). There is no filing fee for Section 2255 motions filed by prisoners in federal custody.

(b) Page Limitation for Petitions for a Writ of Habeas Corpus and 28 U.S.C. § 2255 Motions. Absent leave of court, 28 U.S.C. §§ 2241 and 2254 habeas corpus petitions and 28 U.S.C. § 2255 motions and the initial responsive pleadings thereto, shall not exceed thirty pages in non-death penalty cases, and one hundred pages in death penalty cases, excluding attachments. Replies and sur-replies, along with all other motions and responses thereto, shall not exceed fifteen pages in length in non-death penalty cases and thirty pages in length in death penalty cases, excluding attachments. Documents that exceed ten pages in length must include a table of contents and table of authorities, with page references. Tables and certificates of service and conference are not counted against the applicable page limit.

(c) Motions for Stay of Execution. A motion for stay of execution filed on behalf of a petitioner challenging a sentence of death must be filed at least seven days before the petitioner's scheduled execution date or recite good cause for any late filing.

(d) Page Limitations in Civil Rights Lawsuits. Absent leave of court, complaints and the initial responsive pleadings thereto filed in civil rights proceedings shall not exceed thirty pages, excluding attachments. Documents that exceed ten pages in length must include a table of contents and table of authorities, with page references. Tables and certificates of service and conference shall not be counted against the indicated page limit.

[Effective October 27, 1997. Amended effective December 1, 2000; October 24, 2001; January 14, 2008; March 19, 2008; March 19, 2014; December 1, 2018.]

LOCAL RULE CV–4.   COMPLAINT, SUMMONS, AND RETURN

(a) At the commencement of the action, counsel shall prepare and file the civil cover sheet, Form JS 44, along with the complaint. When filing a patent, trademark, or copyright case, counsel is also responsible for electronically filing an AO Form 120 or 121 using the event Notice of Filing of Patent/Trademark Form (AO 120) or Notice of Filing of Copyright Form (AO 121).

If service of summons is not waived, the plaintiff must prepare and submit a summons to the clerk for each defendant to be served with a copy of the complaint. The clerk is required to collect the filing fee authorized by federal statute before accepting a complaint for filing.

(b) Electronic Filing of Complaints. Attorneys must electronically file a civil complaint upon opening a civil case in CM/ECF.

(c) On the complaint, all litigants shall type or print all party names contained in the case caption with the accurate capitalization and spacing for each party (e.g., Martha van-Derkloot, James De Borne). This procedure seeks to ensure that accurate computer party name searches can later be performed.

(d) Service of civil process shall not be executed by the United States Marshal except for government initiated process, extraordinary writ, or when ordered to do so by a judge. The party requesting service is responsible for preparing all process forms to be supplied by the clerk. When process is to be served by the United States Marshal, the party seeking service shall complete the required U.S. Marshal Form 285.

[Effective October 27, 1997. Amended effective June 3, 1998; October 1, 2001; October 28, 2004; November 2, 2005; October 27, 2006; January 14, 2008; February 18, 2010; April 21, 2011; August 1, 2011; May 6, 2015; December 1, 2017; December 1, 2018.]

LOCAL RULE CV–5.   SERVICE AND FILING OF PLEADINGS AND OTHER DOCUMENTS

(a) Electronic Filing Required. Except as expressly provided or in exceptional circumstances preventing a Filing User from filing electronically, all documents filed with the court shall be electronically filed in compliance with the following procedures.

(1) *Exemptions From Electronic Filing Requirement.* The following are exempted from the requirement of electronic filing:

(A) In a criminal case, the charging documents, including the complaint, information, indictment, and any superseding indictment; affidavits in support of search and arrest warrants, pen registers, trap and trace requests, wiretaps, and other documentation; and *ex parte* documents filed in connection with ongoing criminal investigations;

(B) Documents filed by *pro se* litigants (prisoner and non-prisoner);

(C) Official administrative records or transcripts of prior court or administrative proceedings from other courts or agencies that are required to be filed by law, rule, or local rule; and

(D) Sealed civil complaints (these documents should be filed on a CD–ROM disk with the clerk along with a motion to seal the case). *See* LOCAL RULE CV–5(a)(7)(A).

(2) *Registration for Electronic Filing.*

(A) The clerk shall register all attorneys admitted to the bar of this court, including those admitted *pro hac vice*, as Filing Users of the court's Electronic Filing System. Registration as a Filing User constitutes consent to electronic service of all documents as provided in these rules in accordance with the Federal Rules of Civil and Criminal Procedure. The clerk shall provide Filing Users with a user log-in and password once registration is completed. Filing Users agree to protect the security of their passwords and immediately notify the clerk if they learn that their password has been compromised. After registration, attorneys are required to maintain their own account information, including changes in e-mail address. Documents sent from the court will be deemed delivered if sent to the last known e-mail address given to the court.

(B) With court permission, a *pro se* litigant may register as a Filing User in the Electronic Filing System solely for purposes of the action. If, during the course of the proceeding, the party retains an attorney who appears on the party's behalf, the attorney must advise the clerk to terminate the party's registration as a Filing User upon the attorney's appearance.

(C) A Filing User may apply to the court for permission to withdraw from participation in the Electronic Filing System for good cause shown.

(3) *Significance of Electronic Filing.*

(A) Electronic transmission of a document to the Electronic Filing System consistent with these rules, together with the transmission of a Notice of Electronic Filing from the court, constitutes filing of the document for all purposes and constitutes entry of the document on the docket kept by the clerk. Receipt by the filing party of a Notice of Electronic Filing from the court is proof of service of the document on all counsel who are deemed to have consented to electronic service.

(B) When a document has been filed electronically, the official record is the electronic recording of the document as stored by the court, and the filing party is bound by the document as filed. A document filed electronically is deemed filed at the "entered on" date and time stated on the Notice of Electronic Filing from the court.

(C) Service is deemed completed at the "entered on" date and time stated on the Notice of Electronic Filing from the court, except that documents filed electronically after 5:00 p.m. Central Time shall be deemed served on the following day.

(D) Filing a document electronically does not alter the filing deadline for that document. Filing must be completed before midnight Central Time in order to be considered timely filed that day.

(4) *File Size Limitations.* No single electronic file, whether containing a document or an attachment, may exceed fifteen megabytes in size. Documents or attachments in excess of fifteen megabytes must be divided into multiple files and accurately described to the court. *See* LOCAL RULE CV–7 (page requirements for motions and responses).

(5) *Signatures.* The user log-in and password required to submit documents to the Electronic Filing System serves as the Filing User's signature on all electronic documents filed with the court. The name of the Filing User under whose log-in and password the document is submitted must be preceded by either an image of the Filing User's signature or an "/s/" typed in the space where the signature would otherwise appear. *See* LOCAL RULE CV–11 (c), "Signing the Pleadings."

(6) *Attachments and Exhibits.* Filing Users must submit and describe each exhibit or attachment with specificity as a separate PDF document, unless the court permits conventional filing. *See* LOCAL RULES CV–5(a)(4) ("File Size Limitations"), CV–7(b) ("Documents Supporting Motions"), and CV–56(d) ("Proper Summary Judgment Evidence"). Non–documentary exhibits to motions (e.g., CD–ROM disks) should be filed with the clerk's office with a copy to the presiding judge.

(7) *Sealed Documents.*

(A) All sealed documents must state "Filed Under Seal" at the top of the document.

(B) Unless authorized by statute or rule, a document in a civil case shall not be filed under seal unless it contains a statement by counsel following the certificate of service that certifies that (1) a motion to seal the document has been filed, or (2) the court already has granted authorization to seal the document.

(C) A motion to file document(s) under seal must be filed separately and immediately before the document(s) sought to be sealed. If the motion to seal is granted, the document will be deemed to have been filed as of the original date of its filing. If the motion is denied, the document will be struck. A motion to seal that is filed as a sealed document does not need to include the certification specified in Section (B) above. *See* LOCAL RULE CR–49(b) (additional rules regarding the filing of sealed documents in criminal cases).

(D) Documents requested or authorized to be filed under seal or *ex parte* shall be filed in electronic form. Service in "electronic form" shall be of documents identical in all respects to the documents(s) filed with the court; service copies shall not include encryption, password security, or other extra steps to open or access unless the same are found in the document as filed. All sealed or *ex parte* documents filed with the court must comply with the file size and other form requirements of Local Rules CV–5(a) and CV–7. Counsel is responsible for serving documents under seal to opposing counsel and may do so in electronic form. Counsel is also responsible for complying with Local Rule CV–5(a)(9) regarding courtesy copies of filings. When a sealed order is entered by the court, the clerk will send by conventional mail a copy of the sealed order to the lead attorney only for each party who is responsible for distributing the order to all other counsel of record for that party. *See* Local Rule CV–11.

(E) Except as otherwise provided by Local Rule CR–49, a party filing a document under seal must publicly file a version of that document with the confidential information redacted within two days, unless the entire document is confidential information. For purposes of this rule, "confidential information" is information that the filing party contends is confidential or proprietary in a pending motion to file under seal; information that has been designated as confidential or proprietary under a protective order or nondisclosure agreement; or information otherwise entitled to protection from disclosure under a statute, rule, order, or other legal authority.

(8) *Entry of Court Orders.*

(A) All orders, decrees, judgments, and court proceedings will be filed electronically by the court or court personnel in accordance with these rules, which will constitute entry on the docket kept by the clerk. Any order filed electronically has the same force and effect as if the judge had signed a paper copy of the order and it had been entered on the docket in a conventional manner.

(B) A Filing User submitting a document electronically that requires a judge's signature must promptly deliver the document in such form as the court requires.

(9) *Paper Copies of Lengthy Documents.* Unless otherwise ordered by the presiding judge, if a document to be filed electronically exceeds ten pages in length, including attachments, a paper copy of the filed document must be sent contemporaneously to the presiding judge's chambers. A copy of the "Notice of Electronic Filing" must be attached to the front of the paper copy of the filed document. The paper copy should be sent directly to the judge's chambers and not to the clerk's office. *See* Local Rule CV–10(b) (regarding tabs and dividers for voluminous documents). Judges may opt out of this rule by entering an order. Such orders can be found on the court's website, located at *www.txed.uscourts.gov.*

(10) *Technical Failures.* A technical failure does not relieve a party from exercising due diligence to timely file and serve documents. A Filing User whose filing is made untimely as the result of a technical failure of the court will have a reasonable grace period to file from the time that the technical failure is cured. There will be a notice on the court's website indicating when the database was down and the duration of the grace period. A Filing User whose filing is made untimely as the result of a technical failure not attributable to the court may seek appropriate relief from the court.

(b) Filing by Paper. When filing by paper is permitted, the original pleadings, motions, and other papers shall be filed with the clerk.

(c) Certificates of Service. The certificate of service required by Fed. R. Civ. P. 5(d) shall indicate the date and method of service. Sealed documents in civil cases must indicate that the sealed document was promptly served by means other than the CM/ECF system, e.g., e-mail, conventional mail.

(d) Service by Facsimile or Electronic Means Authorized. Parties may serve copies of pleadings and other case related documents to other parties by facsimile or electronic means in lieu of service and notice by mail. Such service is deemed complete upon sending. Service after 5:00 p.m. Central Time shall be deemed served on the following day for purposes of calculating responsive deadlines.

(e) Service of Documents Filed by Pro Se Litigants. A document filed by a *pro se* litigant shall be deemed "served" for purposes of calculating deadlines under the Local Rules or Federal Rules of Civil Procedure on the date it is electronically docketed in the court's CM/ECF system.

[Effective October 27, 1997. Amended effective June 3, 1998; July 24, 1999; March, 2000; December 1, 2000; October 24, 2001; December 20, 2002; August 5, 2004; October 28, 2004; November 2, 2005; March 8, 2006; May 1, 2006; October 27, 2006; February 12, 2007; January 14, 2008; March 26, 2009; February 18, 2010; April 21, 2011; February 27, 2012; July 16, 2012; August 15, 2012; March 18, 2013; March 19, 2014; May 6, 2015; May 24, 2016; December 1, 2017; December 1, 2018.]

LOCAL RULE CV–5.2   PRIVACY PROTECTIONS FOR FILINGS MADE WITH THE COURT

(a) Electronic Filing of Transcripts by Court Reporters. The following procedures apply to all court transcripts filed on or after May 19, 2008. The court reporter or transcriber shall electronically file all court transcripts,[1] including a completed version of the attached "Notice of Filing of Official Transcript." Upon request, the clerk shall make an electronic version of any transcript available for public inspection without charge at the clerk's office public terminal. *See* 28 U.S.C. § 753(b).

(b) Availability of Transcripts of Court Proceedings. Electronically-filed transcripts of court proceedings are subject to the following rules:

(1) A transcript provided to a court by a court reporter or transcriber will be available at the clerk's office for inspection for a period of ninety days after it is electronically filed with the clerk. During the ninety-day inspection period, access to the transcript in CM/ECF is limited to the following users: (a) court staff; (b) public terminal users; (c) attorneys of record or parties who have purchased the transcript from the court reporter or transcriber; and (d) other persons as directed by the court. During the ninety-day period, court staff may not copy or print transcripts for a requester and the transcript may not be printed from the public computer terminals in the clerk's office.

(2) During the ninety-day period, a copy of the transcript may be obtained from the court reporter or transcriber at the

rate established by the Judicial Conference. The transcript will also be available within the court for internal use, and an attorney who obtains the transcript from the court reporter or transcriber may obtain remote electronic access to the transcript through the court's CM/ECF system for purposes of creating hyperlinks to the transcript in court filings and for other purposes.

(3) Within seven days of the filing of the transcript in CM/ECF, each party wishing to redact a transcript must inform the court, by filing the attached "Notice of Intent to Request Redaction," of the party's intent to redact personal data identifiers from the transcript as required by Fed. R. Civ. P. 5.2. If no such notice is filed within the allotted time, the court will assume redaction of personal data identifiers from the transcript is not necessary.

(4) If redaction is requested, a party is to submit to the court reporter or transcriber and file with the court, within twenty-one days of the transcript's delivery to the clerk, or longer if a court so orders, a statement indicating where the personal data identifiers to be redacted appear in the transcript. The court reporter or transcriber must redact the identifiers as directed by the party. These procedures are limited to the redaction of the specific personal identifiers listed in Fed. R. Civ. P. 5.2. If an attorney wishes to redact additional information, he or she must make a motion to the court. The transcript will not be electronically available until the court has ruled on any such motion.

(5) The court reporter or transcriber must, within thirty-one days of the filing of the transcript, or longer if the court so orders, perform the requested redactions and file a redacted version of the transcript with the clerk. Redacted transcripts are subject to the same access restrictions as outlined above during the initial ninety days after the first transcript has been filed. The original unredacted electronic transcript shall be retained by the clerk as a restricted document.

(6) If, after the ninety-day period has ended, there are no redacted documents or motions linked to the transcript, the clerk will remove the public access restrictions and make the unredacted transcript available for inspection and copying in the clerk's office and for download from the CM/ECF system.

(7) If, after the ninety-day period has ended, a redacted transcript has been filed with the court, the clerk will remove the access restrictions as appropriate and make the redacted transcript available for inspection and copying in the clerk's office and for download from the CM/ECF system or from the court reporter or transcriber.

[Effective May 9, 2008. Amended effective February 18, 2010; March 18, 2013; May 6, 2015; December 1, 2018.]

1 Contract court reporters may either file court transcripts electronically in the CM/ECF database or submit an electronic PDF version of the transcript to the clerk, who will thereupon file it.

LOCAL RULE CV-6.   COMPUTATION OF TIME

Deficient or Corrected Documents. When a document is corrected or re-filed by an attorney following a deficiency notice from the clerk's office (e.g., for a missing certificate of service or certificate of conference), the time for filing a response runs from the filing of the corrected or re-filed document, not the original document.

[Effective March 26, 2009. Amended effective February 18, 2010; December 1, 2015; May 24, 2016, effective December 1, 2016.]

LOCAL RULE CV-7.   PLEADINGS ALLOWED; FORM OF MOTIONS AND OTHER DOCUMENTS

(a) **Generally.** All pleadings, motions, and responses to motions, unless made during a hearing or trial, shall be in writing, conform to the requirements of LOCAL RULES CV-5 and CV-10, and shall be accompanied by a separate proposed order in searchable and editable PDF format for the judge's signature. Each pleading, motion, or response to a motion must be filed as a separate document, except for motions for alternative relief (e.g., a motion to dismiss or, alternatively, to transfer). The proposed order shall be endorsed with the style and number of the cause and shall not include a date or signature block. Motions, responses, replies, and proposed orders, if filed electronically, shall be submitted in "searchable PDF" format and shall not contain restrictions or security settings that prohibit copying, highlighting, or commenting. All other documents, including attachments and exhibits, should be in "searchable PDF" form whenever possible.

(1) *Case Dispositive Motions.* Case dispositive motions shall not exceed thirty pages, excluding attachments, unless leave of court is first obtained. Likewise, responses to such motions shall not exceed thirty pages, excluding attachments, unless leave of court is first obtained. *See* LOCAL RULE CV-56 (regarding attachments to motions for summary judgment and responses thereto). Any reply or sur-reply to an opposed case dispositive motion filed pursuant to Section (f) of this rule shall not exceed ten pages, excluding attachments.

Case dispositive motions shall contain a statement of the issues to be decided by the court. Responses to case dispositive motions must include a response to the movant's statement of issues.

(2) *Non-Dispositive Motions.* Non-dispositive motions shall not exceed fifteen pages, excluding attachments, unless leave of court is first obtained. Likewise, responses to such motions shall not exceed fifteen pages, excluding attachments, unless leave of court is first obtained. Any reply or sur-reply brief to an opposed non-dispositive motion filed pursuant to Section (f) of this rule shall not exceed five pages, excluding attachments. Non-dispositive motions include, among others, motions to transfer venue, motions for partial summary judgment, and motions for new trial pursuant to Fed. R. Civ. P. 59.

(3) *Total Page Limits for Summary Judgment Motions.* If a party files more than one summary judgment motion, the following additional limitations apply:

(A) a party's summary judgment motions shall not exceed sixty pages collectively, excluding attachments;

(B) a party's responses to summary judgment motions shall not exceed sixty pages collectively, excluding attachments;

(C) a party's reply briefing to summary judgment motions shall not exceed twenty pages collectively, excluding attachments; and

(D) a party's sur-reply briefing to summary judgment motions shall not exceed twenty pages collectively, excluding attachments.

(4) *Motions to Reconsider.* Motions to reconsider must specifically state the action and the docket sheet document number to be reconsidered in the title of the motion, e.g., "Motion to Reconsider Denial of Motion for Partial Summary Judgment (dkt #x)."

(b) Documents Supporting Motions. When allegations of fact not appearing in the record are relied upon in support of a motion, all affidavits and other pertinent documents shall be served and filed with the motion. The court strongly recommends that any attached materials have the cited portions highlighted or underlined in the copy provided to the court, unless the citation encompasses the entire page. The page preceding and following a highlighted or underlined page may be submitted if necessary to place the highlighted or underlined material in context. Only relevant, cited-to excerpts of attached materials should be attached to the motion or the response.

(c) Briefing Supporting Motions. The motion and any briefing shall be contained in one document. The briefing shall contain a concise statement of the reasons in support of the motion and citation of authorities upon which the movant relies. Briefing is an especially helpful aid to the judge in deciding motions to dismiss, motions for summary judgment, motions to remand, and post-trial motions.

(d) Response and Briefing. The response and any briefing shall be contained in one document. A party opposing a motion shall file the response, any briefing and supporting documents within the time period prescribed by Subsection (e) of this rule. A response shall be accompanied by a proposed order conforming to the requirements of Subsection (a) of this rule. Briefing shall contain a concise statement of the reasons in opposition to the motion and a citation of authorities upon which the party relies. A party's failure to oppose a motion in the manner prescribed herein creates a presumption that the party does not controvert the facts set out by movant and has no evidence to offer in opposition to the motion.

(e) Time to File Response. A party opposing a motion has fourteen days (twenty-one days for summary judgment motions) from the date the motion was served in which to file a response and any supporting documents, after which the court will consider the submitted motion for decision. Any party may separately move for an order of this court lengthening or shortening the period.

(f) Reply Briefs. Unless otherwise directed by the presiding judge, a party who has filed an opposed motion may serve and file a reply brief responding to the issues raised in the response within seven days from the date the response is served. A sur-reply responding to issues raised in the reply may be served and filed within seven days from the date the reply is served. The court need not wait for the reply or sur-reply before ruling on the motion. Absent leave of court, no further submissions on the motion are allowed.

(g) Oral Hearings. A party may in a motion or a response specifically request an oral hearing, but the allowance of an oral hearing shall be within the sole discretion of the judge to whom the motion is assigned.

(h) "Meet and Confer" Requirement. The "meet and confer" motions practice requirement imposed by this rule has two components, a substantive and a procedural component.

For opposed motions, the substantive component requires, at a minimum, a personal conference, by telephone or in person, between an attorney for the movant and an attorney for the non-movant. In any discovery-related motion, the substantive component requires, at a minimum, a personal conference, by telephone or in person, between the lead attorney and any local counsel for the movant and the lead attorney and any local counsel for the non-movant.

In the personal conference, the participants must give each other the opportunity to express his or her views concerning the disputes. The participants must also compare views and have a discussion in an attempt to resolve their differing views before coming to court. Such discussion requires a sincere effort in which the participants present the merits of their respective positions and meaningfully assess the relative strengths of each position.

In discovery-related matters, the discussion shall consider, among other things: (1) whether and to what extent the requested material would be admissible in a trial or is reasonably calculated to lead to the discovery of admissible evidence; (2) the burden and costs imposed on the responding party; (3) the possibility of cost-shifting or sharing; and (4) the expectations of the court in ensuring that parties fully cooperate in discovery of relevant information.

Except as otherwise provided by this rule, a request for court intervention is not appropriate until the participants have met and conferred, in good faith, and concluded, in good faith, that the discussions have conclusively ended in an impasse, leaving an open issue for the court to resolve. Good faith requires honesty in one's purpose to discuss meaningfully the dispute, freedom from intention to defraud or abuse the discovery process and faithfulness to one's obligation to secure information without court intervention. For opposed motions, correspondence, e-mails, and facsimile transmissions do not constitute compliance with the substantive component and are not evidence of good faith. Such materials, however, may be used to show bad faith of the author.

An unreasonable failure to meet and confer violates LOCAL RULE AT–3 and is grounds for disciplinary action. A party may file an opposed motion without the required conference only when the non-movant has acted in bad faith by failing to meet and confer.

The procedural requirement of the "meet and confer" rule is one of certification. It appears in Section (i) of this rule, entitled "Certificates of Conference."

(i) Certificates of Conference. Except as specified below, all motions must be accompanied by a "certificate of conference" at the end of the motion following the certificate of service. The certificate must state: (1) that counsel has complied with the meet and confer requirement in LOCAL RULE CV–7(h); and (2) whether the motion is opposed or unopposed.

Opposed motions shall include a statement in the certificate of conference, signed by the movant's attorney, that the personal conference or conferences required by this rule have been conducted or were attempted, the date and manner of such conference(s) or attempts, the names of the participants in the conference(s), an explanation of why no agreement could be reached, and a statement that discussions have conclusively ended in an impasse, leaving an open issue for the court to resolve. In discovery-related motions, the certificate of conference shall be signed by the lead attorney and any local counsel. In situations involving an unreasonable failure to meet and confer, the movant shall set forth in the certificate of conference the facts believed to constitute bad faith.

Neither the "meet and confer" nor the "certificate of conference" requirements are applicable to *pro se* litigants (prisoner or non–prisoner) or to the following motions:

(1) to dismiss;

(2) for judgment on the pleadings;

(3) for summary judgment, including motions for partial summary judgment;

(4) for judgment as a matter of law;

(5) for new trial;

(6) issuance of letters rogatory;

(7) objections to report and recommendations of magistrate judges or special masters;

(8) for reconsideration;

(9) for sanctions under Fed. R. Civ. P. 11, provided the requirements of Fed. R. Civ. P. 11(c)(2) have been met;

(10) for writs of garnishment, and

(11) any motion that is joined by, agreed to, or unopposed by, all the parties.

(j) Re–Urged Motions in Transferred/Removed Cases. Except in prisoner cases, any motions pending in another federal or state court made by any party will be considered moot at the time of transfer or removal unless they are re-urged in this court. *See* Local Rule CV–81(d).

(k) Motions for Leave to File. Motions for leave to file a document should be filed separately and immediately before the document for which leave is sought. If the motion for leave to file is granted, the document will be deemed to have been filed as of the original date of its filing. If the motion is denied, the document will be struck or, in the case of motions to file a document exceeding page limitations, the excess pages and attachments cited only therein will not be considered by the court. The time for filing any responsive documents will run from the date of the order on the motion for leave.

(*l*) Emergency Motions. Emergency motions are only those necessary to avoid imminent, irreparable harm such that a motion pursuant to LOCAL RULE CV–7(e) to shorten the period for a response is inadequate. Counsel filing an emergency motion should ensure that: (1) the caption of the motion begins with the word "emergency;" (2) the motion is electronically filed using the CM/ECF drop down menu option entitled "emergency;" (3) the motion clearly states the alleged imminent, irreparable harm and the circumstances making proceed-

ing under LOCAL RULE CV–7(e) inadequate; and (4) the chambers of the presiding judge is notified, either by telephone, e-mail, or fax, that an emergency motion has been filed.

(m) Motions in Limine. Motions *in limine* should be contained within a single document subject to the page limitations of LOCAL RULE CV–7(a)(2) for non-dispositive motions.

[Effective October 27, 1997. Amended effective June 3, 1998; January 14, 1999; July 24, 1999; October 6, 1999; December 1, 2000; March 26, 2001; October 24, 2001; December 20, 2002; August 13, 2004; October 28, 2004; November 2, 2005; October 27, 2006; February 12, 2007; January 14, 2008; March 19, 2008; March 26, 2009; April 6, 2010; February 18, 2010; April 21, 2011; February 27, 2012; March 18, 2013; March 19, 2014; May 6, 2015; December 1, 2015; May 24, 2016; December 1, 2017; December 1, 2018.]

LOCAL RULE CV–10. FORM OF PLEADINGS

(a) Generally. When offered for filing, all documents, excluding preexisting documentary exhibits and attachments, shall:

(1) be endorsed with the style and number of the action;

(2) have a caption containing the name and party designation of the party filing the document and a statement of the character of the document clearly identifying it (e.g., Defendant John Doe's Answer; Defendant John Doe's Motion to Dismiss under Rule 12(b)(6)) (*see* LOCAL RULE CV–38(a) (cases involving jury demands); *see also* LOCAL RULE CV–7(a) (each motion must be filed as a separate document, except when the motion concerns a request for alternative relief));

(3) be signed by the lead attorney or with his or her permission;

(4) when filed by paper, be plainly written, typed, or printed, double-spaced, on 8 1/2 inch by 11 inch white paper; and

(5) be double spaced and in a font no smaller than 12 point type.

(b) Tabs and Dividers. When filed by paper, original documents offered for filing shall not include tabs or dividers. The copy of the original that is required to be filed for the court's use, if voluminous, should have dividers or tabs, as should all copies sent to opposing counsel. *See* Fed. R. Civ. P. 5(a).

(c) Covers. "Blue backs" and other covers are not to be submitted with paper filings.

(d) Deficient Pleadings/Documents. The clerk shall monitor documents for compliance with the federal and local rules as to format and form. If the document sought to be filed is deficient as to form, the clerk shall immediately notify counsel, who should be given a reasonable opportunity, preferably within one day, to cure the perceived defect. If the perceived defect is not cured in a timely fashion, the clerk shall refer the matter to the appropriate district or magistrate judge for a ruling as to whether the documents should be made part of the record.

(e) Hyperlinks. Electronically filed documents may contain the following types of hyperlinks:

(1) Hyperlinks to other portions of the same document;

(2) Hyperlinks to CM/ECF that contains a source document for a citation;

(3) Hyperlinks to documents already filed in any CM/ECF database;

(4) Hyperlinks between documents that will be filed together at the same time;

(5) Hyperlinks that the clerk may approve in the future as technology advances.

Hyperlinks to cited authority may not replace standard citation format. Complete citations must be included in the text of the filed document. A hyperlink, or any site to which it refers, will not be considered part of the record. Hyperlinks are simply convenient mechanisms for accessing material cited in a filed document. The court accepts no responsibility for, and does not endorse, any product, organization, or content at any hyperlinked site, or at any site to which that site might be linked. The court accepts no responsibility for the availability or functionality of any hyperlink.

[Effective October 27, 1997. Amended effective December, 1997; June 3, 1998; July 24, 1999; March, 2000; December 1, 2000; October 24, 2001; December 20, 2002; April 15, 2004; October 28, 2004; November 2, 2005; October 27, 2006; January 14, 2008; May 9, 2008; March 26, 2009; April 21, 201; March 18, 2013; March 19, 2014; May 6, 2015; December 1, 2018.]

LOCAL RULE CV–11. SIGNING OF PLEADINGS, MOTIONS, AND OTHER DOCUMENTS

(a) Lead Attorney.

(1) *Designation.* On the first appearance through counsel, each party shall designate a lead attorney on the pleadings or otherwise.

(2) *Responsibility.* The lead attorney is responsible in that action for the party. That individual attorney shall attend all court proceedings or send a fully informed attorney with authority to bind the client.

(b) Signing the Pleadings. Every document filed must be signed by the lead attorney or by an attorney of record who has the permission of the lead attorney. Requests for postponement of the trial shall also be signed by the party making the request.

(1) *Required Information.* Under the signature, the following information shall appear:

    (A) attorney's individual name;

    (B) state bar number;

    (C) office address, including zip code;

    (D) telephone and facsimile numbers; and

    (E) e-mail address.

(c) Withdrawal of Counsel. Attorneys may withdraw from a case only by motion and order under conditions imposed by the court. Change of counsel will not be cause for delay.

(d) Change of Address. Notices will be sent only to an e-mail and/or mailing address on file. A *pro se* litigant must provide the court with a physical address (i.e., a post office box is not acceptable) and is responsible for keeping the clerk advised in writing of his or her current physical address. *Pro se* litigants must also advise the court of the case numbers of all pending cases in which they are participants in this district.

(e) Request for Termination of Electronic Notice. If an attorney no longer desires to receive electronic notification of filings in a particular case due to settlement or dismissal of his or her client, the attorney may file a request for termination of electronic notice.

(f) Sanctions Concerning Vexatious Pro Se Litigants. The court may make orders as are appropriate to control the conduct of a vexatious pro se litigant. *See* LOCAL RULE CV–65.1 (b).

[Effective October 27, 1997. Amended effective July 24, 1999; March, 2000; October 24, 2001; November 21, 2003; October 28, 2004; November 2, 2005; October 27, 2006; January 14, 2008; March 26, 2009; February 18, 2010; March 19, 2014; May 6, 2015; December 1, 2018.]

LOCAL RULE CV–12. FILING OF ANSWERS AND DEFENSES

An attorney may request that the deadline be extended for a defendant to answer the complaint or file a motion under Fed. R. Civ. P. 12(b). Unless otherwise ordered by the court, where the requested extension: (1) is not opposed; and (2) is not more than thirty days and does not result in an overall extension of the defendant's deadline exceeding forty-five days, the request shall be by application to the clerk, not motion. The application shall be acted upon with dispatch by the clerk on the court's behalf, and the deadline to answer or otherwise respond is stayed pending action by the clerk.

[Effective January 14, 2008. Amended effective March 19, 2014.]

LOCAL RULE CV–26. PROVISIONS GOVERNING DISCOVERY; DUTY OF DISCLOSURE

(a) No Excuses. Absent a court order to the contrary, a party is not excused from responding to discovery because there are pending motions to dismiss, to remand, or to change venue. Parties asserting the defense of qualified immunity may submit a motion to limit discovery to those materials necessary to decide the issue of qualified immunity.

(b) Disclosure of Expert Testimony.

(1) When listing the cases in which the witness has testified as an expert, the disclosure shall include the styles of the cases, the courts in which the cases were pending, the cause numbers, and whether the testimony was in trial or by deposition.

(2) By order in the case, the judge may alter the type or form of disclosures to be made with respect to particular experts or categories of experts, such as treating physicians.

(c) Notice of Disclosure. The parties shall promptly file a notice with the court that the disclosures required under Fed. R. Civ. P. 26(a)(1) and (a)(2) have taken place.

(d) Relevant to Any Party's Claim or Defense. The following observations are provided for counsel's guidance in evaluating whether a particular piece of information is "relevant to any party's claim or defense:"

(1) it includes information that would not support the disclosing parties' contentions;

(2) it includes those persons who, if their potential testimony were known, might reasonably be expected to be deposed or called as a witness by any of the parties;

(3) it is information that is likely to have an influence on or affect the outcome of a claim or defense;

(4) it is information that deserves to be considered in the preparation, evaluation or trial of a claim or defense; and

(5) it is information that reasonable and competent counsel would consider reasonably necessary to prepare, evaluate, or try a claim or defense.

(e) Discovery Hotline (903) 590–1198. The court shall provide a judge on call during business hours to rule on discovery disputes and to enforce provisions of these rules. Counsel may contact the duty judge for that month by dialing the hotline number listed above for any case in the district and get a hearing on the record and ruling on the discovery dispute, including whether a particular discovery request falls within the applicable scope of discovery, or request to enforce or modify provisions of the rules as they relate to a particular case.

[Effective October 27, 1997. Amended effective June 3, 1998; July 24, 1999; June 2, 2000; December 1, 2000; February 27, 2012; December 1, 2015; December 1, 2018.]

LOCAL RULE CV–30. DEPOSITIONS UPON ORAL EXAMINATION

In cases where there is a neutral non-party witness or a witness whom all parties must examine, the time limit shall be divided equally among plaintiffs and defendants. Depositions may be taken after 5:00 p.m., on weekends, or holidays with approval of a judge or by agreement of counsel. Unless permitted by Fed.R.Civ.P. 30(c)(2), a party may not instruct a deponent not to answer a question. Objections to questions during the oral deposition are limited to "Objection, leading" and "Objection, form." Objections to testimony during the oral deposition are limited to "Objection, nonresponsive." These objections are waived if not stated as phrased during the oral deposition. All other objections need not be made or recorded during the oral deposition to be later raised with the court. The objecting party must give a clear and concise explanation of an objection if requested by the party taking the oral deposition, or the objection is waived.

[Effective October 27, 1997. Amended effective July 24, 1999; December 1, 2000; March 26, 2009.]

LOCAL RULE CV–34. PRODUCTION OF DOCUMENTS AND THINGS

Authorizations. At any time after the parties have conferred as required by Fed. R. Civ. P. 26(f), a party may request medical records, wage and earning records, or Social Security Administration records of another party as follows:

(a) Where a party's physical or mental condition is at issue, that party shall provide to the opposing counsel either the party's medical records or a signed authorization so that records of health care providers which are relevant to injuries and damages claimed may be obtained. If additional records are desired, the requesting party must show the need for them.

(b) Where lost earnings, lost earning capacity, or back pay is at issue, the party making such claims shall furnish signed authorizations to the opposing party's counsel so that wage and earning records of past and present employers and the Social Security Administration records may be obtained.

(c) Copies of any records obtained with authorizations provided pursuant to Sections (1) or (2) above shall be promptly furnished to that party's counsel. Records obtained shall remain confidential. The attorney obtaining such records shall limit their disclosure to the attorney's client (or, in the case of an entity, those employees or officers of the entity necessary to prepare the defense), the attorney's own staff, and consulting and testifying experts who may review the records in connection with formulating their opinions in the case.

[Effective December 1, 2000. Amended effective May 6, 2015; December 1, 2018.]

LOCAL RULE CV–38. RIGHT TO A JURY TRIAL; DEMAND

(a) Jury Demand. A party demanding trial by jury pursuant to Fed. R. Civ. P. 38(b) is encouraged to do so by electronically filing a separate document styled as a "jury demand." If the jury demand is included in a pleading, that pleading must bear the word "jury" at the top, immediately below the case number. *See* Fed. R. Civ. P. 38(b)(1).

(b) Taxation of Jury Costs for Late Settlement. Except for good cause shown, whenever the settlement of an action tried by a jury causes a trial to be postponed, canceled, or terminated before a verdict, all juror costs, including attendance fees, mileage, and subsistence, may be imposed upon the parties unless counsel has notified the court and the clerk's office of the settlement at least one day prior to the day on which the trial is scheduled to begin. The costs shall be assessed equally against the parties and their counsel unless otherwise ordered by the court.

[Effective October 27, 1997. Amended effective December 1, 2000; March 18, 2013; August 2, 2013; March 19, 2014; May 6, 2015.]

LOCAL RULE CV–42. CONSOLIDATION; SEPARATE TRIALS

Consolidation of Actions.

(a) Duty to Notify Court of Collateral Proceedings and Re–Filed Cases. Whenever a civil matter commenced in or removed to the court involves subject matter that either comprises all or a material part of the subject matter or operative facts of another action, whether civil or criminal, then pending before this or another court or administrative agency, or previously dismissed or decided by this court, counsel for the filing party shall identify the collateral proceedings or re-filed case(s) on the civil cover sheet filed in this court. The duty to notify the court and opposing counsel of any collateral proceeding continues throughout the pendency of the action.

(b) Consolidation—Multiple Judges Involved. Upon the assignment of related actions to two or more different judges with the district, the affected judges may, in their discretion, agree to assign the related actions to one judge.

[Effective October 27, 1997; Amended effective December 4, 2006; May 6, 2015; December 1, 2018.]

LOCAL RULE CV-43. TAKING OF TESTIMONY

Interpreters in Civil Cases Not Instituted by the United States. The presiding judge shall approve the utilization of interpreters in all civil cases not instituted by the United States. Absent a judicial order to the contrary, the presiding judge shall encourage the use of certified interpreters, or when no certified interpreter is reasonably available, "otherwise qualified" interpreters. See 28 U.S.C. § 1827(b). The presiding judge may approve the use of an interpreter who is not certified or "otherwise qualified" if no certified or "otherwise qualified" interpreter is reasonably available. Upon request, the clerk shall make lists of certified and otherwise qualified interpreters available to parties.

[Effective October 24, 2001. Amended effective December 1, 2018.]

LOCAL RULE CV-47. SELECTING JURORS

Communication With Jurors

(a) No party or attorney for a party shall converse with a member of the jury during the trial of an action.

(b) After a verdict is rendered, an attorney must obtain leave of the court to converse with members of the jury.

[Effective October 27, 1997. Amended effective June 3, 1998; May 6, 2015; December 1, 2018.]

LOCAL RULE CV-50. JUDGMENT AS A MATTER OF LAW IN A JURY TRIAL

Total Page Limits for Motions for Judgment as a Matter of Law. The total page limits imposed by Local Rule CV-7(a)(3) on motions for summary judgment shall also apply to motions for judgment as a matter of law pursuant to Fed. R. Civ. P. 50.

[Effective February 18, 2010.]

LOCAL RULE CV-54. JUDGMENTS; COSTS

(a) A party awarded costs by final judgment or by judgment that a presiding judge directs be entered as final under Fed. R. Civ. P. 54(b) must apply to the clerk for taxation of such costs by filing a bill of costs. Unless otherwise provided by statute or by an order of the presiding judge, the bill of costs must be filed with the clerk and served on any party

entitled to such service no later than fourteen days after the clerk enters the judgment on the docket.

(b) Procedure for Contested Bill of Costs. Before filing a bill of costs, a party must:

(1) submit the proposed bill of costs to opposing counsel for review in light of the applicable law; and

(2) if there are any areas of disagreement, meet and confer with opposing counsel in an effort to submit an agreed bill of costs to the court. If the parties have a legitimate dispute on which they cannot agree, the parties have the option of filing either (A) a joint motion indicating areas of agreement and the areas of disagreement to be resolved by the court, or (B) a motion by the party requesting costs indicating the areas of agreement and the areas of disagreement to be resolved by the court, to which the opposing party may file a response. Either type of motion must contain a certificate confirming compliance with the conference requirements of this rule.

[Effective October 27, 2006. Amended effective January 14, 2008; February 27, 2012; December 1, 2018.]

LOCAL RULE CV-56. SUMMARY JUDGMENT

Procedure

(a) *Motion.* Any motion for summary judgment must include: (1) a statement of the issues to be decided by the court; and (2) a "Statement of Undisputed Material Facts." If the movant relies upon evidence to support its motion, the motion should include appropriate citations to proper summary judgment evidence as set forth below. Proper summary judgment evidence should be attached in accordance with Section (d) of this rule.

(b) *Response.* Any response to a motion for summary judgment must include: (1) a response to the statement of issues; and (2) a response to the "Statement of Undisputed Material Facts." The response brief should be supported by appropriate citations to proper summary judgment evidence as set forth below. Proper summary judgment evidence should be attached in accordance with Section (d) of this rule.

(c) *Ruling.* In resolving the motion for summary judgment, the court will assume that the facts as claimed and supported by admissible evidence by the moving party are admitted to exist without controversy, except to the extent that such facts are controverted in the response brief filed in opposition to the motion, as supported by proper summary judgment evidence. The court will not scour the record in an attempt to unearth an undesignated genuine issue of material fact.

(d) *Proper Summary Judgment Evidence.* As used within this rule, "proper summary judgment evidence" means excerpted copies of pleadings, depositions, documents, electronically stored information, answers to interrogatories, admissions, affidavits or declarations, stipulations (including those made for purposes of the motion only), and other admissible evidence cited in the motion for summary judgment or the response thereto. "Appropriate citations" means that any excerpted evidentiary materials that are attached to the motion or the response should be referred to by page and, if possible, by line. Counsel are strongly encouraged to highlight or underline the cited portion of any attached evidentiary materials, unless the citation encompasses the entire page. The page preceding and following a highlighted page may be submitted if necessary to place the highlighted material in context. Only relevant, cited-to excerpts of evidentiary materials should be attached to the motion or the response.

[Effective October 27, 1997; Amended effective February 12, 2007; January 14, 2008; April 21, 2011; May 6, 2015; December 1, 2018.]

LOCAL RULE CV-62. STAY OF PROCEEDINGS TO ENFORCE A JUDGMENT

(a) Bond or Other Security. Unless otherwise ordered by the presiding judge, a bond or other security staying execution of a money judgment shall be in the amount of the judgment, plus 20% of that amount to cover interest and any award of damages for delay, plus $250.00 to cover costs. The parties may waive the requirement of a bond or other security by stipulation.

The bond shall:

(1) confirm whether the security provider is on the Treasury Department's list of certified companies, unless the Court orders otherwise (a link to this list may be found on the court's website); and

(2) confirm the underwriting limitation, if applicable for the type of security.

(b) Electronic Filing Requirement for Bonds. When a bond or other security is posted for any reason, it must be electronically filed in the case by the posting party. The paper original of the security shall be retained by the posting party unless otherwise directed by the court.

[Effective January 23, 2008. Amended effective April 21, 2011; October 11, 2012; December 1, 2018.]

LOCAL RULE CV-63. INABILITY OF A JUDGE TO PROCEED REASSIGNMENT OF ACTIONS AFTER RECUSAL OR DISQUALIFICATION

(a) Single-Judge Divisions.

(1) Upon the disqualification or recusal of a judge from participation in an action or proceeding pending in a division wherein actions are assigned to only one judge, a reassignment of the action or matter shall be made in accordance with an order of the chief judge of the district.

(2) When the chief judge is the only judge who is assigned actions in a particular division and is disqualified or recuses himself in an action or proceeding pending in that division, the action or matter systematically shall be reassigned to the judge in active service, present in the district and able and qualified to act as chief judge, who is senior in precedence over the remaining judges in the district. Such action or matter may be reassigned by such acting chief judge as provided in Section (a)(1) above.

(b) Multi-Judge Divisions. Upon the disqualification of a judge from participation in an action or proceeding pending in a division wherein the caseload is divided between two judges, the action or matter systematically shall be randomly reassigned and transferred to the other judge sitting in that division. Where the caseload in the division is divided between more than two judges, the action or matter systematically shall be randomly reassigned and transferred to a judge in the division who is not disqualified. The clerk shall randomly assign another case to the recusing/disqualified judge in place of the case he or she recused in or was disqualified in. In instances where each judge in a two-judge or a multi-judge division recuses himself or herself or is disqualified, the action or matter systematically shall be reassigned and transferred in accordance with an order of the chief judge of the district to any judge in active service, in another division, who is not disqualified.

(c) All Judges Disqualified. If all judges in the district recuse themselves or are disqualified to preside over a particular civil or criminal action or matter, the clerk shall, without delay, so certify to the chief judge of the United States Court of Appeals for the Fifth Circuit, in order that he may re-assign such action or matter to a suitable judge.

(d) Recusal When Former Judge of This District Appears as Counsel. For a period of one year after the retirement or resignation of a former federal judge of this district, the judges of this court shall recuse themselves in any case in which the former colleague appears as counsel. See 28 U.S.C. § 455; Committee on Codes of Conduct Advisory Opinion No. 70.

[Effective October 27, 1997. Amended effective March 26, 2009; October 25, 2010; December 1, 2018.]

LOCAL RULE CV-65. INJUNCTIONS

An application for a temporary restraining order or for a preliminary injunction shall be made on an instrument separate from the complaint.

[Effective October 27, 1997.]

LOCAL RULE CV-65.1 SECURITY; PROCEEDINGS AGAINST SURETIES

(a) No Attorneys, Clerks, or Marshals as Sureties. No attorney, clerk, or marshal, or the deputies of any clerk or marshal shall be received as security on any cost, bail, attachment, forthcoming or replevy bond, without written permission of a judge of this court.

(b) Vexatious Litigants; Security for Costs. On its own motion or on motion of a party and after an opportunity to be heard, the court may at any time order a *pro se* litigant to give security in such amount as the court determines to be appropriate to secure the payment of any costs, sanctions, or other amounts which may be awarded against a vexatious *pro se* litigant.

[Effective October 27, 1997. Amended effective November 21, 2003; March 26, 2009; December 1, 2018.]

LOCAL RULE CV-72. MAGISTRATE JUDGES

(a) Powers and Duties of a United States Magistrate Judge in Civil Cases. Each United States magistrate judge of this court is authorized to perform the duties conferred by Congress or applicable rule.

(b) Objections to Non–Dispositive Matters—28 U.S.C. § 636(b)(1)(A). An objection to a magistrate judge's order made on a non-dispositive matter shall be specific. Any objection and response thereto shall not exceed five pages. A party may respond to another party's objections within fourteen days after being served with a copy; however, the court need not await the filing of a response before ruling on an objection. No further briefing is allowed absent leave of court.

(c) Review of Case Dispositive Motions and Prisoner Litigation—28 U.S.C. § 636(b)(1)(B). Objections to reports and recommendations and any response thereto shall not exceed eight pages. No further briefing is allowed absent leave of court.

(d) Assignment of Matters to Magistrate Judges. The method for assignment of duties to a magistrate judge and for the allocation of duties among the several magistrate judges of the court shall be made in accordance with orders of the court or by special designation of a district judge.

(e) Disposition of Civil Cases by Consent of the Parties—28 U.S.C. § 636(c).

(1) The clerk of court shall notify the parties in all civil cases that they may consent to have a magistrate judge conduct any or all proceedings in the case and order the entry of a final judgment. Additional notices may be furnished to the parties at later stages of the proceedings, and may be included with pretrial notices and instructions.

(2) The clerk shall not file consent forms unless they have been signed by all the parties or their respective counsel in a case. No consent form will be made available, nor will the contents be made known to any judge, unless all parties have consented to the reference to a magistrate judge. See Fed. R.Civ.P. 73(b); 28 U.S.C. § 636(c)(2).

[Effective October 27, 1997. Amended effective February 27, 2012; March 18, 2013; March 19, 2014; May 6, 2015; December 1, 2017.]

LOCAL RULE CV–77. DISTRICT COURTS AND CLERKS

Notice of Orders, Judgments, and Other Filings. The clerk may serve and give notice of orders, judgments, and other filings by e-mail in lieu of service and notice by conventional mail to any person who has signed a filed pleading or document and provided an e-mail address with his/her pleadings as specified in LOCAL RULE CV–11(b)(1)(E). Any other attorney who wishes to receive notice of judicial orders, judgments, and other filings must file a notice of appearance of counsel with the court.

By providing the court with an e-mail address, the party submitting the pleadings is deemed to have consented to receive service and notice of judicial orders and judgments from the clerk by e-mail. Lead attorneys who wish to be excluded from receiving judicial notices by e-mail may do so by filing a motion with the court; non-lead attorneys who wish to be excluded from e-mail noticing may do so by filing a notice with the court.

Notice of judicial orders, judgments, and other filings is complete when the clerk obtains electronic confirmation of the receipt of the transmission. Notice by e-mail by the clerk that occurs after 5:00 p.m. on any day is deemed effective as of the following day.

[Effective March, 2000. Amended effective April 10, 2003; October 28, 2004; October 27, 2006; January 14, 2008; March 18, 2013; May 6, 2015; December 1, 2017.]

LOCAL RULE CV–79. RECORDS KEPT BY THE CLERK

(a) Submission of Hearing/Trial Exhibits.

(1) The parties shall not submit exhibits to the clerk's office prior to a hearing/trial without a court order. The clerk shall return to the party any physical exhibits not complying with this rule.

(2) Exhibits shall be properly marked but not placed in binders. Multiple-paged documentary exhibits should be properly fastened. Additional copies of exhibits may be submitted in binders for the court's use.

(3) The parties shall provide letter-sized copies of any documentary, physical, or oversized exhibit to the court prior to the conclusion of a hearing/trial. At the conclusion of a hearing/trial, the parties shall provide the courtroom deputy with PDF copies of all exhibits that were admitted by the court, unless otherwise ordered. Oversized exhibits will be returned at the conclusion of the trial or hearing. If parties desire the oversized exhibits to be sent to the appellate court, it will be their responsibility to send them.

(b) Disposition of Exhibits by the Clerk. Thirty days after any direct appeal has been exhausted or the time for taking that appeal has lapsed and no further action is required by the trial court, the clerk is authorized to destroy any sealed or unsealed exhibits which have not been previously claimed by the attorney of record for the party offering the same in evidence at the hearing/trial.

(c) Hazardous Documents or Items Sent to the Court. Prisoners and other litigants shall not send to this court (including the district clerk, any judges, and any other court agency) documents or items that constitute a health hazard as defined below:

(1) The clerk is authorized to routinely and immediately dispose of, without seeking a judge's permission, any papers or items sent to the court by prisoners or other litigants that are smeared with or contain blood, hair, food, feces, urine, or other body fluids. Although "[t]he clerk must not refuse to file a paper solely because it is not in the form prescribed by these rules or by a local rule or practice," Fed. R. Civ.P. 5(d), papers or other items containing or smeared with excrement or body fluids are excepted from this rule on the ground that they constitute a health hazard and can be refused by the clerk for that reason, which is a reason other than improper form.

(2) In the event the clerk receives weapons or drugs that are intended to be filed as exhibits, the clerk shall notify the judge assigned to the case of that fact, or in the event that no case has been filed, the chief judge.

(3) The clerk shall maintain a log of the items that are disposed of pursuant to General Order 96–6. The log shall

contain the case number and style, if any, the name of the prisoner or litigant who sent the offending materials, and a brief description of the item disposed of. The clerk also shall notify the prisoner/litigant and, if applicable, the warden or other supervising official of the appropriate correctional facility that the item in question was destroyed and that sanctions may be imposed if the prisoner continues to forward papers, items, or physical exhibits in violation of General Order 96–6.

[Effective October 27, 1997. Amended effective July 24, 1999; December 1, 2000; October 1, 2001; November 2, 2005; October 27, 2006; January 14, 2008; June 18, 2014; May 6, 2015; May 24, 2016; December 1, 2018.]

LOCAL RULE CV–81. REMOVED ACTIONS

Parties removing cases from state court to federal court shall comply with the following:

(a) File with the clerk a notice of removal which reflects the style of the case exactly as it was styled in state court;

(b) If a jury was requested in state court, the removed action will be placed on the jury docket of this court provided the removing party or parties file a separate jury demand pursuant to LOCAL RULE CV–38(a);

(c) The removing party or parties shall furnish to the clerk the following information at the time of removal:

(1) a list of all parties in the case, their party type (e.g., plaintiff, defendant, intervenor, receiver, etc.) and current status of the removed case (e.g., pending, dismissed);

(2) a civil cover sheet and certified copy of the state court docket sheet; a copy of all pleadings that assert causes of action (e.g., complaints, amended complaints, supplemental complaints, petitions, counter-claims, cross-actions, third party actions, interventions, etc.); all answers to such pleadings and a copy of all process and orders served upon the party removing the case to this court as required by 28 U.S.C. § 1446(a);

(3) a complete list of attorneys involved in the action being removed, including each attorney's bar number, address, telephone number, and party or parties represented by that attorney;

(4) a record of which parties have requested jury trial (this information is in addition to filing a separate jury demand pursuant to LOCAL RULE CV–38(a)); and

(5) the name and address of the court from which the case was removed.

(d) Any motions pending in state court will be considered moot at the time of removal unless they are re-urged in this court.

[Effective October 27, 1997. Amended effective January 14, 1999; December 1, 2000; March 18, 2013; May 6, 2015; December 1, 2018.]

LOCAL RULE CV–83. RULES BY DISTRICT COURTS; JUDGE'S DIRECTIVES

(a) **Docket Calls.** Traditional docket calls are abolished. Each judge shall endeavor to set early and firm trial dates which will eliminate the need for multiple-case docket calls.

(b) **Transferred or Remanded Cases.** Absent an order to the contrary, no sooner than the twenty-first day following an order of the court transferring or remanding a case, the clerk shall transmit the case file to the directed court. Where a case has been remanded to state court, the clerk shall mail: (1) a certified copy of the court's order and docket sheet directing such action; and (2) all pleadings and other documents on file in the case. Where a case has been transferred to another federal district court, the electronic case file shall be transferred to the directed court. If a timely motion for reconsideration of the order of transfer or remand has been filed, the clerk shall delay mailing or transferring the file until the court has ruled on the motion for reconsideration.

(c) **Standing Orders.** Any standing order adopted by a judge pursuant to Fed. R. Civ. P. 83(b) must conform to any uniform numbering system prescribed by the Judicial Conference of the United States and be filed with the clerk. The court will periodically review all standing orders for compliance with Rule 83(b) and for possible inclusion in the local rules. This subsection does not apply to provisions in scheduling or other case-specific orders.

(d) **Courtroom Attire and Conduct.** All persons present in a courtroom where a trial, hearing, or other proceeding is in progress must dress and conduct themselves in a manner demonstrating respect for the court. The presiding judge has discretion to establish appropriate standards of dress and conduct.

(e) **Alternative Dispute Resolution.** Consistent with 28 U.S.C. § 651, the use of alternative dispute resolution processes in all civil actions, including adversary proceedings in bankruptcy, is authorized. Litigants in all civil actions shall consider the use of an alternative dispute resolution process at an appropriate stage in the litigation. This consideration shall include, but is not limited to, mediation as provided in the Court–Annexed Mediation Plan set forth on the court's website (per General Order 14–06) which is incorporated herein by reference.

[Effective October 27, 1997. Amended effective December 1, 2000; December 20, 2002; October 28, 2004; February 22, 2005; March 26, 2009; February 18, 2010; April 21, 2011; February 27, 2012; March 18, 2013; March 19, 2014; May 6, 2015; December 1, 2017; December 1, 2018.]

SECTION II. CRIMINAL RULES

LOCAL RULE CR–1. SCOPE

The rules of procedure in any criminal proceeding in this court are those prescribed by the laws of the United States, the Federal Rules of Criminal Procedure, these local rules, and any orders entered by the court. These rules shall be construed as consistent with acts of Congress and rules of practice and procedure prescribed by the Supreme Court of the United States and the United States Court of Appeals for the Fifth Circuit.

[Effective October 27, 1997. Amended effective December 1, 2000; March 19, 2014; May 6, 2015.]

LOCAL RULE CR–6. THE GRAND JURY

(a) Selection of Grand Jurors. Grand jurors shall be selected at random in accordance with a plan adopted by this court pursuant to applicable federal statute and rule.

(b) Grand Jury Subpoenas. Sealed grand jury subpoenas shall be kept by the clerk for three years from the date the witness is ordered to appear. After that time, the clerk may destroy the subpoenas.

(c) Signature of the Grand Jury Foreperson. The grand jury foreperson shall sign the indictment with initials rather than his or her whole name. The foreperson will continue to sign the concurrence of the grand jury using his or her whole name.

[Effective October 27, 1997. Amended effective December 1, 2000; December 4, 2006; March 19, 2014.]

LOCAL RULE CR–10. ARRAIGNMENTS

In the interest of reducing delays and costs, judges and magistrate judges may conduct the arraignment at the same time as the post-indictment initial appearance.

[Effective October 27, 1997. Amended effective December 1, 2000; May 6, 2015.]

LOCAL RULE CR–24. TRIAL JURORS

(a) Communication With Jurors.

(1) No party or attorney for a party shall converse with a member of the jury during the trial of an action.

(2) After a verdict is rendered, an attorney must obtain leave of court to converse with members of the jury.

(b) Signature of the Petit Jury Foreperson. The petit jury foreperson shall sign all documents or communications with the court using his or her initials.

[Effective October 27, 1997; Amended effective November 2, 2005; March 26, 2009; March 19, 2014; May 6, 2015; December 1, 2018.]

LOCAL RULE CR–47. MOTIONS

(a) Form and Content of a Motion. All motions and responses to motions, unless made during a hearing or trial, shall be in writing, conform to the requirements of LOCAL

RULES CV–5 and CV–10, and be accompanied by a separate proposed order for the judge's signature. The proposed order shall be endorsed with the style and cause number and shall not include a date or signature block. Dispositive motions— those which could, if granted, result in the dismissal of an indictment or counts therein or the exclusion of evidence— shall contain a statement of the issues to be decided by the court. Responses to dispositive motions must include a response to the movant's statement of issues. All motions, responses, replies, and proposed orders, if filed electronically, shall be submitted in "searchable PDF" format. All other documents, including attachments and exhibits, should be in "searchable PDF" form whenever possible.

(1) *Page Limits.*

(A) Dispositive Motions. Dispositive motions shall not exceed thirty pages, excluding attachments, unless leave of court is first obtained. Likewise, responses to such motions shall not exceed thirty pages, excluding attachments, unless leave of court is first obtained. Any reply brief shall not exceed ten pages, excluding attachments.

(B) Non–Dispositive Motions. Non-dispositive motions shall not exceed fifteen pages, excluding attachments, unless leave of court is first obtained. Likewise, a party opposing a non-dispositive motion shall limit the response to the motion to fifteen pages, excluding attachments, unless leave of court is first obtained. Any reply brief shall not exceed five pages, excluding attachments.

(2) *Briefing Supporting Motions and Responses.* The motion and any briefing shall be contained in one document. The briefing shall contain a concise statement of the reasons in support of the motion and citation of authorities upon which the movant relies. Likewise, the response and any briefing shall be contained in one document. Such briefing shall contain a concise statement of the reasons in opposition to the motion and a citation of authorities upon which the party relies.

(3) *Certificates of Conference.* Except as specified below, all motions must be accompanied by a "certificate of conference." It should be placed at the end of the motion following the certificate of service. The certificate must state: (1) that counsel has conferred with opposing counsel in a good faith attempt to resolve the matter without court intervention; and (2) whether the motion is opposed or unopposed. Certificates of conference are not required of *pro se* litigants (prisoner or non–prisoner) or for the following motions:

(A) motions to dismiss;

(B) motions for judgment of acquittal;

(C) motions to suppress;

(D) motions for new trial;

(E) any motion that is joined, by, agreed to, or unopposed by all the parties;

(F) any motion permitted to be filed *ex parte*;

(G) objections to report and recommendations of magistrate judges;

(H) motions for reconsideration; and

(I) dispositive motions.

(b) Timing of a Motion.

(1) *Responses.* A party opposing a motion has fourteen days from the date the motion was served in which to serve and file a response and any supporting documents, after which the court will consider the submitted motion for decision. Any party may separately move for a court order lengthening or shortening the period within which a response may be filed.

(2) *Reply Briefs and Sur–Replies.* Unless otherwise directed by the presiding judge, a party who has filed an opposed motion may serve and file a reply brief responding to issues raised in the response within seven days from the date the response is served. A sur-reply responding to issues raised in the reply may be served and filed within seven days from the date the reply is served. The court need not wait for the reply or sur-reply before ruling on the motion. Absent leave of court, no further submissions on the motion are allowed.

(c) Affidavit Supporting a Motion. When allegations of fact not appearing in the record are relied upon in support of a motion, all affidavits and other pertinent documents shall be served and filed with the motion. It is strongly recommended that any attached materials have the cited portions highlighted or underlined in the copy provided to the court, unless the citation encompasses the entire page. The page preceding and following a highlighted or underlined page may be submitted if necessary to place the highlighted or underlined material in context. Only relevant, cited-to excerpts of attached materials should be attached to the motion or the response.

[Effective October 27, 1997. Amended effective October 24, 2001; January 14, 2008; February 18, 2010; April 21, 2011; May 6, 2015; December 1, 2015; May 24, 2016; December 1, 2018.]

LOCAL RULE CR–49. SERVICE AND FILING

(a) Generally. All pleadings and documents submitted in criminal cases must conform to the filing, service, and format requirements contained in Local Rules CV–5, CV–10, and CV–11.

(1) *Defendant Number.* In multi-defendant cases, each defendant receives a "defendant number." The numbers are assigned in the order in which defendants are listed on the complaint or indictment. When filing documents with the court, parties shall identify by name and number each defendant to whom a document applies.

(2) *Sealed Indictments.* In multi-defendant cases involving one or more sealed indictments, the government should, at the time the sealed indictment is filed, provide the clerk with appropriately redacted copies of the indictment for each defendant. The goal of this procedure is to protect the confidential aspect of the sealed indictment with regard to any defendants not yet arrested.

(b) Public Access to Criminal Case Documents Generally. In order to serve the legal presumption of openness in criminal case proceedings, pleadings in this court are generally to be filed unsealed. Except for the documents listed in Section (c) of this rule, decisions as to whether to seal a particular pleading are made on a case-by-case basis by the court, with findings specific enough that a reviewing court can determine whether the sealing or closure was properly entered.

(1) Absent specific court findings to the contrary, all documents other than those specifically listed in paragraph (c) below and those submitted with a motion to seal in accordance with Local Rules CV–5(a)(7)(1) and CR–49(a) are to remain unsealed.

(c) Authorization to Routinely Seal Particular Types of Criminal Case Documents. Despite the general rule cited in Section (b) above, there is an overriding interest in routinely sealing certain types of criminal case documents, because public dissemination of the documents would substantially risk endangering the lives or safety of law enforcement officers, United States Marshals, agents, defendants, witnesses, cooperating informants, judges, court employees, defense counsel, prosecutors, or their respective family members, and could jeopardize continuing criminal investigations. The documents that trigger this overriding interest are:

(1) unexecuted summonses or warrants (e.g., search warrants, arrest warrants);

(2) pen register or a trap and trace device applications pursuant to either 18 U.S.C. § 3121 et seq. or 18 U.S.C. § 2516 et seq.;

(3) pretrial bail or presentence investigation reports and any addenda and objections thereto;

(4) the statements of reasons in the judgment of conviction;

(5) plea agreements,[2] which are governed by Section (d) below;

(6) addenda to plea agreements described in Section (e) below;

(7) motions for downward departure for substantial assistance, and responsive pleadings and orders granting or denying the same;

(8) motions pursuant to Section 5K1.1 of the United States Sentencing Guidelines, memoranda in support thereof, responsive pleadings and orders granting or denying the same;

(9) motions for reduction of sentence under Fed. R. Crim. P. 35(b), memoranda in support thereof, responsive pleadings and orders granting or denying the same;

(10) amended judgments pursuant to a grant of a Fed. R. Crim. P. 35(b) motion; and

(11) orders restoring federal benefits filed in conjunction with item 10 above.

The documents listed above shall be filed under seal without need of a motion to seal or a certification by counsel. Other than plea agreements, the documents shall remain sealed unless otherwise ordered by the court.

(d) Sealing and Unsealing of Plea Agreements (Item 5 Above).

(1) Until it is accepted by the court, a plea agreement is in the nature of an unaccepted offer of terms between parties. In addition to the findings of Section (c) above, making a plea agreement public before it has been accepted may lead to

publicity that would tend to prejudice a defendant who decides to exercise his right to trial by making it more difficult to select jurors who have not formed an opinion about the case. Such publicity may also provide details of the case pertinent to co-defendants who have not pled, thus prejudicing them. Therefore, plea agreements shall be filed under seal.

(2) The plea agreement shall be unsealed when the terms and conditions of the plea agreement are accepted absent a further court order finding that there is an overriding policy interest in keeping that particular plea agreement sealed and providing findings specific enough that a reviewing court can determine whether the sealing or closure was properly entered. The routine unsealing of sealed plea agreements is intended to serve the right of public access to criminal case documents.

(e) Sealed Addendums to Plea Agreements. Every plea agreement in this court shall have an addendum that is sealed (see section (c) 4 above). The addendum will either state "no provisions are included in this addendum," or it will contain specific provisions dealing with possible reductions in sentence in return for the defendant's substantial assistance to the government. This will allow each plea agreement to be unsealed upon sentencing without prejudicing or endangering a cooperating defendant or the defendant's family or other informants and defendants.

(f) In those instances where the court orders an entire criminal case sealed, case documents shall be e-mailed to the following addresses for filing by the relevant divisional clerk's office:

Beaumont	bmtcrimdocs@txed.uscourts.gov
Lufkin	lufcrimdocs@txed.uscourts.gov
Marshall	marcrimdocs@txed.uscourts.gov
Sherman	shrcrimdocs@txed.uscourts.gov
Texarkana	texcrimdocs@txed.uscourts.gov
Tyler	tylcrimdocs@txed.uscourts.gov

(g) Defendants proceeding pro se shall submit all sealed criminal case documents in paper format to the clerk's office for filing.

(h) Unless otherwise ordered by the presiding judge, counsel filing a document under seal must send a paper copy of that document to the presiding judge's chambers. The paper copy should be sent directly to the judge's chambers, not to the clerk's office.

[Effective October 27, 1997. Amended effective December, 1997; December 1, 2000; October 24, 2001; November 2, 2005; May 1, 2006; January 14, 2008; April 6, 2010; April 21, 2011; March 19, 2014; April 23, 2014; June 18, 2014; February 5, 2015; April 8, 2015; May 6, 2015; December 1, 2018.]

[2] The plea agreement does not include the factual basis of the offense and stipulation, and the elements of the offense, which are separate documents that are filed at the same time as the plea agreement.

LOCAL RULE CR–49.1 PRIVACY PROTECTION FOR FILINGS MADE WITH THE COURT

(a) Electronic Filing of Transcripts by Court Reporters. Any transcript of criminal proceedings in this court filed by a court reporter or transcriber shall be filed electronically, including a "Notice of Filing of Official Transcript." The clerk will post a "model notice" for the court reporter or transcribers use on the courts web site. Upon request, the clerk shall make an electronic version of any unsealed transcript available for public inspection without charge at the clerk's office. *See* 28 U.S.C. § 753(b).

(b) Availability of Transcripts of Court Proceedings. Electronically-filed transcripts of criminal court proceedings are subject to the following rules:

(1) A transcript provided to a court by a court reporter or transcriber will be available at the clerk's office for inspection for a period of ninety days after it is electronically filed with the clerk. During the ninety-day inspection period, access to the transcript in CM/ECF is limited to the following users: (a) court staff; (b) public terminal users; (c) attorneys of record or parties who have purchased the transcript from the court reporter or transcriber; and (d) other persons as directed by the court. Court staff may not copy or print transcripts for a requester during the ninety-day inspection period.

(2) During the ninety-day period, a copy of the transcript may be obtained from the court reporter or transcriber at the rate established by the Judicial Conference. The transcript will also be available within the court for internal use, and an attorney who obtains the transcript from the court reporter or transcriber may obtain remote electronic access to the transcript through the courts CM/ECF system for purposes of creating hyperlinks to the transcript in court filings and for other purposes.

(3) Within seven days of the filing of the transcript in CM/ECF, each party wishing to redact a transcript must inform the court, by filing the attached "Notice of Intent to Request Redaction," of the party's intent to redact personal data identifiers from the transcript as required by Fed. R. Crim. P. 49.1. If no such notice is filed within the allotted time, the court will assume redaction of personal data identifiers is not necessary.

(4) If redaction is requested, a party is to submit to the court reporter or transcriber and file with the court, within twenty-one days of the transcript's delivery to the clerk, or longer if a court so orders, a statement indicating where the personal data identifiers to be redacted appear in the transcript. The court reporter or transcriber must redact the identifiers as directed by the party. These procedures are limited to the redaction of the specific personal identifiers listed in Fed. R. Crim.P.49.1(a). If an attorney wishes to redact additional information, he or she may make a motion to the court. The transcript will not be electronically available until the court has ruled on any such motion.

(5) The court reporter or transcriber must, within thirty-one days of the filing of the transcript, or longer if the court so orders, perform the requested redactions and file a redacted version of the transcript with the clerk. Redacted transcripts are subject to the same access restrictions as outlined above during the initial ninety days after the first transcript has been filed. The original unredacted electronic transcript shall be retained by the clerk as a restricted document.

(6) If, after the ninety-day period has ended, there are no redaction documents or motions linked to the transcript, the clerk will remove the public access restrictions and make the

unredacted transcript available for inspection and copying in the clerk's office and for download from the CM/ECF system.

(7) If, after the ninety-day period has ended, a redacted transcript has been filed with the court, the clerk will remove the access restrictions as appropriate and make the redacted transcript available for inspection and copying in the clerk's office and for download from the CM/ECF system or from the court reporter or transcriber.

[Effective May 9, 2008. Amended effective March 18, 2013; May 6, 2015; December 1, 2017; December 1, 2018.]

LOCAL RULE CR–55. RECORDS

(a) **Submission of Hearing/Trial Exhibits.** The parties shall not submit exhibits to the clerk's office prior to a hearing/trial without a court order. The clerk shall return to the party any physical exhibits not complying with this rule. Exhibits shall be properly marked, but not placed in binders. Multiple-paged documentary exhibits should be properly fastened. Additional copies of trial exhibits may be submitted in binders for the court's use.

(b) **Post–Trial/Hearing Exhibit Procedures.** The parties shall provide letter-sized copies of any documentary, physical, or oversized exhibit to the court prior to the conclusion of a hearing/trial. At the conclusion of a hearing/trial, the parties shall provide the courtroom deputy with PDF copies of all exhibits that were admitted by the court, unless otherwise ordered. Oversized exhibits will be returned at the conclusion of the trial or hearing. If parties desire the oversized exhibits to be sent to the appellate court, it will be their responsibility to send them.

[Effective October 27, 1997. Amended effective December 1, 2000; October 24, 2001; November 2, 2005; October 27, 2006; January 14, 2008; March 19, 2014; June 18, 2014; May 6, 2015; May 24, 2016; December 1, 2017; December 1, 2018.]

LOCAL RULE CR–59. MATTERS BEFORE A MAGISTRATE JUDGE

(a) **Powers and Duties of a United States Magistrate Judge in Civil Cases.** Each United States magistrate judge of this court is authorized to perform the duties conferred by Congress or applicable rule.

(b) **Objections to Non–Dispositive Matters—28 U.S.C. § 636(b)(1)(A).** An objection to a magistrate judge's order made on a non-dispositive matter shall be specific. Any objection and response thereto shall not exceed five pages. A party may respond to another party's objections within fourteen days after being served with a copy; however, the court need not await the filing of a response before ruling on an objection. No further briefing is allowed absent leave of court.

(c) **Review of Case Dispositive Motions and Prisoner Litigation—28 U.S.C. § 636(b)(1)(B).** Objections to reports and recommendations and any response thereto shall not exceed eight pages. No further briefing is allowed absent leave of court.

(d) **Assignment of Criminal Matters to Magistrate Judges.** The method for assignment of duties to a magistrate judge and for the allocation of duties among the several magistrate judges of the court in criminal cases shall be made in accordance with orders of the court or by special designation of a district judge.

[Effective March 19, 2014. Amended effective May 6, 2015; December 1, 2017; December 1, 2018.]

SECTION III. ATTORNEYS

LOCAL RULE AT-1. ADMISSION TO PRACTICE

(a) An attorney who has been admitted to practice before the Supreme Court of the United States, a United States Court of Appeals, a United States District Court, or the highest court of a state, is eligible for admission to the bar of this court. He or she must be of good moral and professional character and must be a member in good standing of the state and federal bars in which he or she is licensed.

(b) Each applicant shall file an application on a form prescribed by the court. If the applicant has previously been subject to disciplinary proceedings, full information about the proceedings, the charges, and the result must be given.

(1) A motion for admission made by a member in good standing of the State Bar of Texas or the bar of any United States District Court shall accompany the completed admission form. The movant must state that the applicant is competent to practice before this court and is of good personal and professional character.

(2) The applicant must state in the application that he or she has read LOCAL RULE AT-3, the "Standards of Practice to be Observed by Attorneys," and the local rules of this court and that he or she will comply with the standards of practice adopted in LOCAL RULE AT-3 and with the local rules.

(3) The applicant must provide with the application form an oath of admission signed in the presence of a notary public on a form prescribed by the court. The completed application for admission, motion for admission, and oath of admission shall be submitted to the court, along with the admission fee required by law and any other fee required by the court. Upon investigation of the fitness, competency, and qualifications of the applicant, the completed application form may be granted or denied by the clerk subject to the oversight of the chief judge.

(c) The clerk shall maintain a complete list of all attorneys who have been admitted to practice before the court.

(d) An attorney who is not admitted to practice before this court may appear for or represent a party in any case in this court only upon an approved application to appear pro hac vice. When an attorney who is not a member of the bar of this court appears in any case before this court, he or she shall first submit electronically an application to appear *pro hac vice* with the clerk. The applicant must read and comply with LOCAL RULE AT-3, the "Standards of Practice to Be Observed by Attorneys," and the local rules of this court. The application shall be made using the form that is available on the court's website and must be signed by the applicant personally. Detailed instructions on how to e-file the application appear on the court's website, located at *www.txed.uscourts. gov.* Such application also shall be accompanied by a $100.00 local fee, which must be paid electronically. Any attachments to *pro hac vice* applications will be handled as electronic sealed documents by the clerk's office. The application shall be acted upon with dispatch by the clerk on the court's behalf. The clerk shall notify the applicant as soon as possible after the application is acted upon.

(e) **Federal Government Attorneys.** No bar admission fees shall be charged to attorneys who work for the United States government, including Assistant United States Attorneys, Assistant Federal Public Defenders, and CJA Panel attorneys. Bar admission fees cannot be waived for federal law clerks, however, as they do not appear in court on behalf of the United States but instead perform job duties that do not require admission to practice in the court. The clerk's office has no authority to waive bar admission fees for attorneys who work for state, county, or city governments.

[Effective October 27, 1997. Amended effective December 1, 2000; October 24, 2001; December 20, 2002; March 26, 2009; April 19, 2010; October 11, 2012; March 19, 2014; May 6, 2015; December 1, 2018.]

LOCAL RULE AT-2. ATTORNEY DISCIPLINE

(a) **Generally.** The standards of professional conduct adopted as part of the Rules Governing the State Bar of Texas shall serve as a guide governing the obligations and responsibilities of all attorneys appearing in this court. It is recognized, however, that no set of rules may be framed which will particularize all the duties of the attorney in the varying phases of litigation or in all the relations of professional life. Therefore, the attorney practicing in this court should be familiar with the duties and obligations imposed upon members of this bar by the Texas Disciplinary Rules of Professional Conduct, court decisions, statutes, and the usages customs and practices of this bar.

(b) **Disciplinary Action Initiated in Other Courts.**

(1) Except as otherwise provided in this subsection, a member of the bar of this court shall automatically lose his or her membership if he or she loses, either temporarily or permanently, the right to practice law before any state or federal court for any reason other than nonpayment of dues, failure to meet continuing legal education requirements, or voluntary resignation unrelated to a disciplinary proceeding or problem.

(2) When it is shown to the court that a member of its bar has lost his or her right to practice as described in subsection (1) above, the court shall issue an order directing the attorney to show cause within thirty days why the imposition of the identical discipline in this district should not be imposed, and imposing that identical discipline if no response is filed. If the attorney files a response, the court will consider the following defenses in determining whether the identical discipline is warranted in this court: that the procedure followed in the other jurisdiction deprived the attorney of due process; that the proof was so clearly lacking that the court determines it cannot accept the final conclusion of the other jurisdiction; that the imposition of the identical discipline would result in a grave injustice; that the misconduct established by the other jurisdiction warrants substantially different discipline in this court; that the misconduct for which the attorney was disciplined in the other jurisdiction does not constitute professional misconduct in this State or in this court. If the attorney fails to establish one or more of the defenses listed above, the court shall enter the identical discipline to the extent practicable. If the attorney establishes one or more of these defenses, the

court may impose whatever discipline it deems necessary and just.

(3) A member of this bar who has lost the right to practice law before any state or federal court, either permanently or temporarily, must advise the clerk of that fact within thirty days of the effective date of the disciplinary action. The clerk will thereafter proceed in accordance with this rule.

(c) Conviction of a Crime. A member of the bar of this court who is convicted of a felony offense in any state or federal court will be immediately and automatically suspended from practice and thereafter disbarred upon final conviction.

(d) Disciplinary Action Initiated in This Court.

(1) *Grounds for Disciplinary Action.* This court may, after an attorney has been given an opportunity to show cause to the contrary, take any appropriate disciplinary action against any attorney:

(A) for conduct unbecoming a member of the bar;

(B) for failure to comply with these local rules or any other rule or order of this court;

(C) for unethical behavior;

(D) for inability to conduct litigation properly; or

(E) because of conviction by any court of a misdemeanor offense involving dishonesty or false statement.

(2) *Disciplinary Procedures.*

(A) When it is shown to a judge of this court that an attorney has engaged in conduct which might warrant disciplinary action involving suspension or disbarment, the judge receiving the information shall bring the matter to the attention of the chief judge, who will poll the full court as to whether disciplinary proceedings should be held. If the court determines that further disciplinary proceedings are necessary, the disciplinary matter will be assigned to the chief judge, or a judge designated by the chief judge, who will notify the lawyer of the charges and give the lawyer opportunity to show good cause why he or she should not be suspended or disbarred. Upon the charged lawyer's response to the order to show cause, and after a hearing before the chief judge or a judge designated by the chief judge, if requested, or upon expiration of the time prescribed for a response if no response is made, the chief judge or a judge designate by the chief judge, shall enter an appropriate order.

(B) At any hearing before the chief judge or a judge designated by the chief judge, the charged lawyer shall have the right to counsel and at least fourteen days' notice of the time of the hearing and charges. Prosecution of the charges may be conducted by an attorney specially appointed by the court. Costs of the prosecutor and any fees allowed by the court shall be paid from the attorney admission fee fund.

(e) Notification of Disciplinary Action. Upon final disciplinary action by the court, the clerk shall send certified copies of the court's order to the State Bar of Texas, the United States Court of Appeals for the Fifth Circuit, and the National Discipline Data Bank operated by the American Bar Association.

(f) Reinstatement. Any lawyer who is suspended by this court is automatically reinstated to practice at the end of the period of suspension, provided that the bar membership fee required by Local Rule AT–1(b)(3) has been paid. Any lawyer who is disbarred by this court may not apply for reinstatement for at least three years from the effective date of his or her disbarment. Petitions for reinstatement shall be sent to the clerk and assigned to the chief judge for a ruling. Petitions for reinstatement must include a full disclosure concerning the attorney's loss of bar membership in this court and any subsequent felony convictions or disciplinary actions that may have occurred in other federal or state courts.

[Effective October 27, 1997. Amended effective June 8, 2004; October 27, 2006; January 14, 2008; March 18, 2013; May 6, 2015; December 1, 2017; December 1, 2018.]

LOCAL RULE AT–3. STANDARDS OF PRACTICE TO BE OBSERVED BY ATTORNEYS

Attorneys who appear in civil and criminal cases in this court shall comply with the following standards of practice in this district:[3]

(a) In fulfilling his or her primary duty to the client, a lawyer must be ever conscious of the broader duty to the judicial system that serves both attorney and client.

(b) A lawyer owes candor, diligence, and utmost respect to the judiciary.

(c) A lawyer owes, to opposing counsel, a duty of courtesy and cooperation, the observance of which is necessary for the efficient administration of our system of justice and the respect of the public it serves.

(d) A lawyer unquestionably owes, to the administration of justice, the fundamental duties of personal dignity and professional integrity.

(e) Lawyers should treat each other, the opposing party, the court, and court staff with courtesy and civility and conduct themselves in a professional manner at all times.

(f) A client has no right to demand that counsel abuse the opposite party or indulge in offensive conduct. A lawyer shall always treat adverse witnesses and suitors with fairness and due consideration.

(g) In adversary proceedings, clients are litigants and though ill feeling may exist between clients, such ill feeling should not influence a lawyer's conduct, attitude, or demeanor toward opposing lawyers.

(h) A lawyer should not use any form of discovery or the scheduling of discovery as a means of harassing opposing counsel or counsel's client.

(i) Lawyers will be punctual in communications with others and in honoring scheduled appearances and will recognize that neglect and tardiness are demeaning to the lawyer and to the judicial system.

(j) If a fellow member of the bar makes a just request for cooperation or seeks scheduling accommodation, a lawyer will not arbitrarily or unreasonably withhold consent. The court is not bound to accept agreements of counsel to extend deadlines imposed by rule or court order.

(k) Effective advocacy does not require antagonistic or obnoxious behavior, and members of the bar will adhere to the higher standard of conduct which judges, lawyers, clients, and the public may rightfully expect.

(*l*) The court also encourages attorneys to be familiar with the Codes of Pretrial and Trial Conduct promulgated by the American College of Trial Lawyers, which can be found on the court's website, located at *www.txed.uscourts.gov*, and to conduct themselves accordingly.

[Effective December 1, 2000; Amended effective November 2, 2005; March 19, 2014; May 6, 2015; December 1, 2018.]

3 The standards enumerated here are set forth in the en banc opinion in *Dondi Props. Corp. v. Commerce Sav. & Loan Ass'n.*, 121 F.R.D. 284 (N.D. Tex. 1988).

APPENDICES

APPENDIX A. UNITED STATES DISTRICT COURT FOR THE EASTERN DISTRICT OF TEXAS LOCAL ADMIRALTY RULES

Local Admiralty Rule (a). Authority and Scope.

LAR (a)(1) *Authority.* The local admiralty rules of the United States District Court for the Eastern District of Texas are promulgated by a majority of the judges as authorized by and subject to the limitation of Federal Rule of Civil Procedure 83 (Federal Rule or Rules).

LAR (a)(2) *Scope.* The local admiralty rules apply only to civil actions that are governed by Supplemental Rule A of the Supplemental Rules for Certain Admiralty and Maritime Claims (Supplemental Rule or Rules). All other local rules are applicable in these cases, but to the extent that another local rule is inconsistent with the applicable local admiralty rules, the local admiralty rules shall govern.

LAR (a)(3) *Citation.* The local admiralty rules may be cited by the letters "LAR" and the lower case letters and numbers in parentheses that appear at the beginning of each section. The lower case letter is intended to associate the local admiralty rule with the Supplemental Rule that bears the same capital letter.

LAR (a)(4) *Definitions.* As used in the Local Admiralty Rules, the word "Rule" followed by a numeral (*e.g.,* Rule 12) means a Federal Rule of Civil Procedure; the word "Rule" followed by a capital letter (*e.g.,* Rule C) means a Supplemental Rule for Certain Admiralty and Maritime Claims; the word "court" means the district court issuing these LARs; the term "judicial officer" means the United States district judge or a United States magistrate judge; the word "clerk" means the clerk of the district court and includes deputy clerks of court; the word "Marshal" means the United States Marshal and includes deputy Marshals; the word "keeper" means any person or entity appointed by the Marshal to take physical custody of and maintain the vessel or other property under arrest or attachment; and the term "substitute custodian" means the individual or entity who, upon motion and order of the court, assumes the duties of the Marshal or keeper with respect to the vessel or other property arrested or attached.

LAR (a)(5) *Bonds.* When a bond is posted under the Local Admiralty Rules for any reason, it should be electronically filed in the case by the posting party. The paper original of the bond shall be retained by the posting party unless otherwise directed by the court.

Local Admiralty Rule (b). Maritime Attachment and Garnishment.

LAR (b)(1) *Use of State Procedures.* When the plaintiff invokes a state procedure in order to attach or garnish as permitted by the Rules or the Supplemental Rules, the process of attachment or garnishment shall identify the state law upon which the attachment or garnishment is based.

Local Admiralty Rule (c). Actions In Rem: Special Provisions.

LAR (c)(1) *Intangible Property.* The summons to show cause why property should not be deposited in court issued pursuant to Supplemental Rule C(3)(c) shall direct the person having control of intangible property to show cause no later than seven days after service why the intangible property should not be delivered to the court to abide the judgment. A judicial officer for good cause shown may lengthen or shorten the time. Service of the warrant has the effect of arresting the intangible property and bringing it within the control of the court. Service of the summons to show cause requires a garnishee wishing to retain possession of the property to establish grounds for doing so, including specification of the measures taken to segregate and safeguard the intangible property arrested. The person who is served may, upon order of the court, deliver or pay over to the person on whose behalf the warrant was served or to the clerk of the court the intangible property proceeded against to the extent sufficient to satisfy the plaintiff's claim. If such delivery or payment is made, the person served is excused from the duty to show cause. The person asserting any ownership interest in the property or a right of possession may show cause as provided in Supplemental Rule C(6)(a) why the property should not be delivered to the court.

LAR (c)(2) *Publication of Notice of Action and Arrest.* The notice required by Rule C(4) shall be published at least once in a newspaper named in LAR (g)(2), and plaintiff's attorney shall file with the clerk a copy of the notice as it was published. The notice shall contain:

(A) The court, title, and number of the action;

(B) The date of the arrest;

(C) The identity of the property arrested;

(D) The name, address, and telephone number of the attorney for plaintiff;

(E) A statement that a person asserting any ownership interest in the property or a right of possession pursuant to Supplemental Rule C(6) must file a statement of such interest with the clerk and serve it on the attorney for plaintiff within fourteen days after publication;

(F) A statement that an answer to the complaint must be filed and served within twenty-one days after filing the statement of ownership interest in the property or right of possession, and that otherwise, default may be entered and condemnation ordered;

(G) A statement that applications for intervention under Federal Rule 24 by persons asserting maritime liens or other interests shall be filed within thirty days after publication; and

(H) The name, address, and telephone number of the Marshal, keeper, or substitute custodian.

LAR (c)(3) *Default In Action In Rem.*

(A) Notice Required. A party seeking a default judgment in an action in rem must satisfy the judge that due notice of the action and arrest of the property has been given:

(1) By publication as required in LAR (c)(2), and

(2) By service upon the Marshal and keeper, substitute custodian, master, or other person having custody of the property, and

(3) By mailing such notice to every other person who has not appeared in the action and is known to have an interest in the property.

(B) Persons with Recorded Interests.

(1) If the defendant property is a vessel documented under the laws of the United States, plaintiff must attempt to notify all persons named in the United States Coast Guard certificate of ownership.

(2) If the defendant property is a vessel numbered as provided in the Federal Boat Safety Act, plaintiff must attempt to notify the persons named in the records of the issuing authority.

(3) If the defendant property is of such character that there exists a governmental registry of recorded property interests and/or security interests in the property, the plaintiff must attempt to notify all persons named in the records of each such registry.

LAR (c)(4) *Entry of Default and Default Judgment.* After the time for filing an answer has expired, the plaintiff may move for entry of default under Federal Rule 55(a). Default will be entered upon showing that:

(A) Notice has been given as required by LAR (c)(3)(A); and

(B) Notice has been attempted as required by LAR (c)(3)(B), where appropriate; and

(C) The time to answer by claimants of ownership to or possession of the property has expired; and

(D) No answer has been filed or no one has appeared to defend on behalf of the property.

The plaintiff may move for judgment under Rule 55(b) at any time after default has been entered.

Local Admiralty Rule (d).   Possessory, Petitory, and Partition Actions.

LAR (d)(1) *Return Date.* In a possessory action under Rule D, a judicial officer may order that the statement of interest and answer be filed on a date earlier than twenty-one days after arrest. The order may also set a date for expedited hearing of the action.

Local Admiralty Rule (e).   Actions In Rem and Quasi In Rem. General Provisions.

LAR (e)(1) *Itemized Demand for Judgment.* The demand for judgment in every complaint filed under Rule B or C shall allege the dollar amount of the debt or damages for which the action was commenced. The demand for judgment shall also allege the nature of other items of damage. The amount of the special bond posted under Rule E(5)(a) may be based upon these allegations.

LAR (e)(2) *Salvage Action Complaints.* In an action for salvage award, the complaint shall allege the dollar value of the vessel, cargo freight, and other property salved or other basis for an award, and the dollar amount of the award sought.

LAR (e)(3) *Verification of Pleadings.* Every complaint in Rule B, C, and D actions shall be verified upon oath or solemn affirmation or in the form provided by 28 U.S.C. § 1746 by a party or by an authorized officer of a corporate party. If no party or authorized corporate officer is present within the district, verification of a complaint may be made by an agent, attorney in fact, or attorney of record, who shall state the sources of the knowledge, information, and belief contained in the complaint; declare that the document verified is true to the best of that knowledge, information, and belief; state why verification is not made by the party or an authorized representative thereof; and state that the affiant or declarant is authorized so to verify. A verification not made by a party or authorized corporate officer will be deemed to have been made by the party as if verified personally. If the verification was not made by a party or authorized representative, any interested party may move, with or without requesting a stay, for the personal oath of a party or an authorized representative, which shall be procured by commission or as otherwise ordered.

LAR (e)(4) *Review by Judicial Officer.* Unless otherwise required by the judicial officer, the review of complaints and papers called for by Rules B(1) and C(3) does not require the affiant party or attorney to be present. The applicant for review shall include a form of order to the clerk which, upon signature by the judicial officer, will direct the arrest, attachment, or garnishment sought by the applicant. In exigent circumstances, the certification of the plaintiff or his attorney under Rules B and C shall consist of an affidavit or a declaration pursuant to 28 U.S.C. § 1746 describing in detail the facts establishing the exigent circumstances.

LAR (e)(5) *Return of Service.* The party who requests a warrant of arrest or process of attachment or garnishment shall provide instructions to the Marshal. A person specially appointed by the court under Rules B or C who has served process of maritime attachment and garnishment or a warrant of arrest that seized property shall promptly file a verified return showing the name of the individual on whom the process or warrant was served, the identity of the person or entity on whom service was made, the documents served, the manner in which service was completed (*e.g.*, personal delivery), and the address, date, and time of service.

LAR (e)(6) *Property in Possession of United States Officer.* When the property to be attached or arrested is in the custody of an employee or officer of the United States, the Marshal will deliver a copy of the complaint and warrant of arrest or summons and process of attachment or garnishment to that officer or employee if present, and otherwise to the custodian of the property. The Marshal will instruct the officer or employee or custodian to retain custody of the property until ordered to do otherwise by a judicial officer.

LAR (e)(7) *Security for Costs.* In an action under the Rules, a party may move upon notice to all parties for an order to compel an adverse party to post security for costs with the clerk pursuant to Rule E(2)(b). Unless otherwise ordered, the amount of security shall be $500. The party so ordered shall post the security within seven days after the order is entered. A party who fails to post security when due may not participate further in the proceedings, except by order of the court. A party may move for an order increasing the amount of security for costs.

LAR (e)(8) *Adversary Hearing.* The adversary hearing following arrest or attachment or garnishment provided for in Supplemental Rule E(4)(f) shall be conducted by a judicial officer within three days, unless otherwise ordered. The person(s) requesting the hearing shall notify all persons known to have an interest in the property of the time and place of the hearing.

LAR (e)(9) *Appraisal.* An order for appraisal of property so that security may be given or altered will be entered upon motion. If the parties do not agree in writing upon an appraiser, a judicial officer will appoint the appraiser. The appraiser shall be sworn to the faithful and impartial discharge of the appraiser's duties before any federal or state officer authorized by law to administer oaths. The appraiser shall give one day's notice of the time and place of making the appraisal to counsel of record. The appraiser shall promptly file the appraisal with the clerk and serve it upon counsel of record. The appraiser's fee shall be paid in the first instance by the moving party, but it is taxable as an administrative cost of the action.

LAR (e)(10) *Security Deposit for Seizure of Vessels.* The first party who seeks arrest or attachment of a vessel or property aboard a vessel shall deposit a sum deemed sufficient by the Marshal to cover the expenses of the Marshal including, but not limited to, dockage, keepers, maintenance, and insurance. The security deposit for seizure of a vessel or property aboard a vessel is $5,000 if there is a substitute custodian, and $10,000 if the vessel or property is to remain in the custody of the Marshal. The Marshal is not required to execute process until the deposit is made. The party shall advance additional sums from time to time at the Marshal's request to cover estimated expenses. A party who fails to advance such additional costs as required by the Marshal may not participate further in the proceedings except by order of the court. The Marshal may, upon notice to all parties, petition the court for an order to be issued forthwith releasing the vessel if additional sums are not advanced within three days after the initial request.

LAR (e)(11) *Intervenor's Claims.*

(A) Presentation of Claim. When a vessel or other property has been arrested, attached, or garnished, and is in the hands of the Marshal or custodian substituted therefor, anyone having a claim against the vessel or property is required to present it by filing an intervening complaint and obtain a warrant of arrest, and not by filing an original complaint, unless otherwise ordered by a judicial officer. No formal motion is required. The intervening party shall serve a copy of the intervening complaint and warrant of arrest upon all parties to the action and shall forthwith deliver a conformed copy of the complaint and warrant of arrest to the Marshal, who shall deliver the copies to the vessel or custodian of the property. Intervenors shall thereafter be subject to the rights and obligations of parties, and the vessel or property shall stand arrested, attached, or garnished by the intervenor. An intervenor shall not be required to advance a security deposit to the Marshal for the intervenor's seizure of a vessel as required by LAR (e)(10), but will receive the funds back, less the intervenor's share of the Marshal's fees and expenses as stated in LAR (e)(11)(B).

(B) Sharing Marshal's Fees and Expenses. An intervenor shall owe a debt to the preceding plaintiffs and intervenors, enforceable on motion, consisting of the intervenor's share of the Marshal's fees and expenses in the proportion that the intervenor's claim bears to the sum of all the claims asserted against the property. If any party plaintiff permits vacation of an arrest, attachment, or garnishment, the remaining plaintiffs shall share the responsibility to the Marshal for fees and expenses in proportion to the remaining claims asserted against the property and for the duration of the Marshal's custody because of each such claim.

LAR (e)(12) *Custody of Property.*

(A) Safekeeping of Property. When a vessel or other property is brought to the Marshal's custody by arrest or attachment, the Marshal shall arrange for adequate safekeeping, which may include the placing of keepers on or near the vessel. A substitute custodian in place of the Marshal may be appointed by order of the court. Notice of the application to appoint a substitute custodian must be given to all parties and the Marshal. The application must show the name of the proposed substitute custodian, the fee, if any, to be charged by the proposed substitute custodian, the location of the vessel during the period of custody, and the proposed insurance coverage.

(B) Insurance. The Marshal may order insurance to protect the Marshal, his deputies, keepers, and substitute custodians, from liabilities assumed in arresting and holding the vessel, cargo, or other property, and in performing whatever services may be undertaken to protect the vessel, cargo, or other property, and in maintaining the court's custody. The arresting or attaching party shall reimburse the Marshal for premiums paid for the insurance and where possible shall be named as an additional insured on the policy. The party who applies for removal of the vessel, cargo, or other property to another location, for designation of a substitute custodian, or for other relief that will require an additional premium, shall reimburse the Marshal therefor. The premiums charged for the liability insurance shall be paid in the first instance by the initial party obtaining the arrest and holding of the property, but are taxable as administrative costs of the action while the vessel, cargo, or other property is in custody of the court.

(C)(i) Cargo Handling, Repairs, and Movement of the Vessel. Following arrest or attachment of a vessel, cargo handling will cease unless an order of the court is received by the Marshal. No movement of or repairs to the vessel shall take place without order of the court. The applicant for an order under this rule shall give notice to the Marshal and to all parties of record.

(ii) Insurance. If an applicant shows adequate insurance to indemnify the Marshal for liability, the court may order the Marshal to permit cargo handling, repairs, or movement of the vessel, cargo, or other property. The costs and expenses of such activities shall be borne as ordered by the court. Any party of record may move for an order to dispense with keepers or to remove or place the vessel, cargo, or other property at a specified facility, to designate a substitute custodian, or for similar relief. Notice of the motion shall be given to the Marshal and to all parties of record. The judicial officer will require that adequate insurances on the property will be maintained by the successor to the Marshal, before issuing the order to change arrangements.

(D) Claims by Suppliers for Payment of Charges. A person who furnishes supplies or services to a vessel, cargo, or other property in custody of the court who has not been paid and claims the right to payment or an expense of administration shall submit an invoice to the clerk in the form of a verified claim at any time before the vessel, cargo, or other property is released or sold. The supplier must serve copies of the claim on the Marshal, substitute custodian if one has been appointed, and all parties of record. The court may consider the claims individually or schedule a single hearing for all claims.

LAR (e)(13) *Sale of Property.*

(A) Notice. Unless otherwise ordered upon good cause shown or as provided by law, notice of sale of property in an action in rem shall be published on at least four days, between three and thirty-one days prior to the day of the sale.

(B) Payment of Bid. These provisions apply unless otherwise ordered in the order of sale:

(i) The person whose bid is accepted shall immediately pay the Marshal the full purchase price if the bid is $1000 or less.

(ii) If the bid exceeds $1,000, the bidder shall immediately pay a deposit of at least $1,000 or 10% of the bid, whichever is greater, and shall pay the balance within three days.

(iii) If an objection to the sale is filed within the period in LAR (e)(13)(F), the bidder is excused from paying the balance of the purchase price until three days after the sale is confirmed.

(iv) Payment shall be made by certified check or by cashier's check.

(C) Late Payment. If the successful bidder does not pay the balance of the purchase price within the time allowed, the bidder shall pay the Marshal the cost of keeping the property from the due date until the balance is paid, and the Marshal may refuse to release the property until this charge is paid.

(D) Default. If the successful bidder does not pay the balance of the purchase price within the time allowed, the bidder shall be in default, and the judicial officer may accept the second highest bid or arrange a new sale. The defaulting bidder's deposit shall be forfeited and applied to any additional costs incurred by the Marshal because of the default, the balance being retained in the registry of the court awaiting its order.

(E) Report of the Sale by Marshal. At the conclusion of the sale, the Marshal shall forthwith file a written report with the court setting forth the notice given of: the fact of sale; the date of the sale; the names, addresses, and bid amounts of the bidders; the price obtained; and any other pertinent information.

(F) Time and Procedure for Objection to Sale. An interested person may object to the sale by filing a written objection with the clerk within three days following the sale, serving the objection on all parties of record, the successful bidder, and the Marshal, and depositing a sum with the Marshal that is sufficient to pay the expense of keeping the property for at least seven days. Payment to the Marshal shall be by certified check or cashier's check. The court shall hold a hearing on the confirmation of the sale.

(G) Confirmation of Sale. If no objection to the sale has been filed, the sale shall be confirmed by order of the court no sooner than three days nor later than five days from the court's receipt of the Marshal's written report. The Marshal shall transfer title to the purchaser upon the order of the court.

(H) Disposition of Deposits.

(i) If the objection is sustained, sums deposited by the successful bidder will be returned to the bidder forthwith. The sum deposited by the objector will be applied to pay the fees and expenses incurred by the Marshal in keeping the property until it is resold, and any balance remaining shall be returned to the objector. The objector will be reimbursed for the expense of keeping the property from the proceeds of a subsequent sale.

(ii) If the objection is overruled, the sum deposited by the objector will be applied to pay the expense of keeping the property from the day the objection was filed until the day the sale is confirmed, and any balance remaining will be returned to the objector forthwith.

LAR (e)(14) *Presentation of Matters.* If the judge to whom a case has been assigned is not readily available, any matter under the Local Admiralty Rules may be presented to any other judge in the district without reassigning the case.

Local Admiralty Rule (f).   Limitation of Liability.

LAR (f)(1) *Security for Costs.* The amount of security for costs under Rule F(1) shall be $1,000, and security for costs may be combined with the security for value and interest unless otherwise ordered.

LAR (f)(2) *Order of Proof at Trial.* In an action where vessel interests seek to limit their liability, the damage claimants shall offer their proof first, whether the right to limit arises as a claim or as a defense.

Local Admiralty Rule (g).   Special Rules.

LAR (g)(1) *Newspapers for Publishing Notices.* Unless otherwise ordered by the court, every notice required to be published under the Local Admiralty Rules or any rules or statutes applying to admiralty and maritime proceedings shall be published in the following newspaper[s] of general circulation in the District:

Beaumont Enterprise

LAR (g)(2) *Use of State Procedures.* When the plaintiff invokes a state procedure in order to attach or garnish as permitted by the Federal Rules of Civil Procedure or the Supplemental Rules for Certain Admiralty and Maritime Claims, the process of attachment or garnishment shall identify the state law upon which the attachment or garnishment is based.

[Former Appendix J adopted effective August 18, 1998. Amended effective January 11, 2005; February 18, 2010; July 16, 2012. Redesignated Appendix A and amended effective March 19, 2014. Amended effective December 1, 2018.]

COMMENT

LAR (e)(13)(B)(iii) is amended to correct an incorrect cross-reference for its incorporated time requirement.

APPENDIX B. LOCAL PATENT RULES

1. SCOPE OF RULES

1–1. Title. These are the Rules of Practice for Patent Cases before the Eastern District of Texas. They should be cited as "P. R. ___."

1–2. Scope and Construction. These rules apply to all civil actions filed in or transferred to this Court which allege infringement of a utility patent in a complaint, counterclaim, cross-claim or third party claim, or which seek a declaratory judgment that a utility patent is not infringed, is invalid or is unenforceable. The Court may accelerate, extend, eliminate, or modify the obligations or deadlines set forth in these Patent Rules based on the circumstances of any particular case, including, without limitation, the complexity of the case or the number of patents, claims, products, or parties involved. If any motion filed prior to the Claim Construction Hearing provided for in P. R. 4–6 raises claim construction issues, the Court may, for good cause shown, defer the motion until after completion of the disclosures, filings, or ruling following the Claim Construction Hearing. The Civil Local Rules of this Court shall also apply to these actions, except to the extent that they are inconsistent with these Patent Rules. The deadlines set forth in these rules may be modified by Docket Control Order issued in specific cases.

1–3. Effective Date. These Patent Rules shall take effect on February 22, 2005 and shall apply to any case filed thereafter and to any pending case in which more than 9 days remain before the Initial Disclosure of Asserted Claims is made. The parties to any other pending civil action shall meet and confer promptly after February 22, 2005, for the purpose of determining whether any provision in these Patent Rules should be made applicable to that case. No later than 7 days after the parties meet and confer, the parties shall file a stipulation setting forth a proposed order that relates to the application of these Patent Rules. Unless and until an order is entered applying these Patent Local Rules to any pending case, the Rules previously applicable to pending patent cases shall govern.

2. GENERAL PROVISIONS

2–1. Governing Procedure.

(a) *Initial Case Management Conference.* Prior to the Initial Case Management Conference with the Court, when the parties confer with each other pursuant to Fed.R.Civ.P. 26(f), in addition to the matters covered by Fed.R.Civ.P. 26, the parties must discuss and address in the Case Management Statement filed pursuant to Fed.R.Civ.P. 26(f), the following topics:

(1) Proposed modification of the deadlines provided for in the Patent Rules, and the effect of any such modification on the date and time of the Claim Construction Hearing, if any;

(2) Whether the Court will hear live testimony at the Claim Construction Hearing;

(3) The need for and any specific limits on discovery relating to claim construction, including depositions of witnesses, including expert witnesses;

(4) The order of presentation at the Claim Construction Hearing; and

(5) The scheduling of a Claim Construction Prehearing Conference to be held after the Joint Claim Construction and Prehearing Statement provided for in P. R. 4–3 has been filed.

(6) Whether the court should authorize the filing under seal of any documents containing confidential information.

(b) *Further Case Management Conferences.* To the extent that some or all of the matters provided for in P. R. 2–1 (a)(1)-(5) are not resolved or decided at the Initial Case Management Conference, the parties shall propose dates for further Case Management Conferences at which such matters shall be decided.

(c) *Electronic Filings.* All patents attached as exhibits to any filing submitted electronically shall be in searchable PDF format. Any other documents attached as exhibits to any filing submitted electronically should be in searchable PDF format whenever possible.

2–2. Confidentiality. If any document or information produced under these Patent Local Rules is deemed confidential by the producing party and if the Court has not entered a protective order, until a protective order is issued by the Court, the document shall be marked "confidential" or with some other confidential designation (such as "Confidential—Outside Attorneys Eyes Only") by the disclosing party and disclosure of the confidential document or information shall be limited to each party's outside attorney(s) of record and the employees of such outside attorney(s).

If a party is not represented by an outside attorney, disclosure of the confidential document or information shall be limited to one designated "in house" attorney, whose identity and job functions shall be disclosed to the producing party 5 days prior to any such disclosure, in order to permit any motion for protective order or other relief regarding such disclosure. The person(s) to whom disclosure of a confidential document or information is made under this local rule shall keep it confidential and use it only for purposes of litigating the case.

2–3. Certification of Initial Disclosures. All statements, disclosures, or charts filed or served in accordance with these Patent Rules must be dated and signed by counsel of record. Counsel's signature shall constitute a certification that to the best of his or her knowledge, information, and belief, formed after an inquiry that is reasonable under the circumstances, the information contained in the statement, disclosure, or chart is complete and correct at the time it is made.

2–4. Admissibility of Disclosures. Statements, disclosures, or charts governed by these Patent Rules are admissible to the extent permitted by the Federal Rules of Evidence or Procedure. However, the statements or disclosures provided for in P. R. 4–1 and 4–2 are not admissible for any purpose other than in connection with motions seeking an extension or modification of the time periods within which actions contemplated by these Patent Rules must be taken.

2–5. Relationship to Federal Rules of Civil Procedure. Except as provided in this paragraph or as otherwise ordered, it shall not be a legitimate ground for objecting to an opposing party's discovery request (e.g., interrogatory, document request, request for admission, deposition question) or declining to provide information otherwise required to be disclosed pursuant to Fed.R.Civ.P. 26(a)(1) that the discovery request or disclosure requirement is premature in light of, or otherwise conflicts with, these Patent Rules. A party may object, however, to responding to the following categories of discovery requests (or decline to provide information in its initial disclosures under Fed.R.Civ.P. 26(a)(1)) on the ground that they are premature in light of the timetable provided in the Patent Rules:

(a) Requests seeking to elicit a party's claim construction position;

(b) Requests seeking to elicit from the patent claimant a comparison of the asserted claims and the accused apparatus, product, device, process, method, act, or other instrumentality;

(c) Requests seeking to elicit from an accused infringer a comparison of the asserted claims and the prior art; and

(d) Requests seeking to elicit from an accused infringer the identification of any opinions of counsel, and related documents, that it intends to rely upon as a defense to an allegation of willful infringement.

Where a party properly objects to a discovery request (or declines to provide information in its initial disclosures under Fed.R.Civ.P. 26(a)(1)) as set forth above, that party shall provide the requested information on the date on which it is required to provide the requested information to an opposing party under these Patent Rules, unless there exists another legitimate ground for objection.

2–6. Assignment of Related Cases. Separately filed cases related to the same patent shall be assigned to the same judge, i.e., the judge assigned to the first related case.

3. PATENT INITIAL DISCLOSURES

3–1. Disclosure of Asserted Claims and Infringement Contentions. Not later than 10 days before the Initial Case Management Conference with the Court, a party claiming patent infringement must serve on all parties a "Disclosure of Asserted Claims and Infringement Contentions." Separately for each opposing party, the "Disclosure of Asserted Claims and Infringement Contentions" shall contain the following information:

(a) Each claim of each patent in suit that is allegedly infringed by each opposing party;

(b) Separately for each asserted claim, each accused apparatus, product, device, process, method, act, or other instrumentality ("Accused Instrumentality") of each opposing party of which the party is aware. This identification shall be as specific as possible. Each product, device, and apparatus must be identified by name or model number, if known. Each method or process must be identified by name, if known, or by any product, device, or apparatus which, when used, allegedly results in the practice of the claimed method or process;

(c) A chart identifying specifically where each element of each asserted claim is found within each Accused Instrumentality, including for each element that such party contends is governed by 35 U.S.C. § 112(6), the identity of the structure(s), act(s), or material(s) in the Accused Instrumentality that performs the claimed function;

(d) Whether each element of each asserted claim is claimed to be literally present or present under the doctrine of equivalents in the Accused Instrumentality;

(e) For any patent that claims priority to an earlier application, the priority date to which each asserted claim allegedly is entitled; and

(f) If a party claiming patent infringement wishes to preserve the right to rely, for any purpose, on the assertion that its own apparatus, product, device, process, method, act, or other instrumentality practices the claimed invention, the party must identify, separately for each asserted claim, each such apparatus, product, device, process, method, act, or other instrumentality that incorporates or reflects that particular claim.

3–2. Document Production Accompanying Disclosure. With the "Disclosure of Asserted Claims and Infringement Contentions," the party claiming patent infringement must produce to each opposing party or make available for inspection and copying:

(a) Documents (e.g., contracts, purchase orders, invoices, advertisements, marketing materials, offer letters, beta site testing agreements, and third party or joint development agreements) sufficient to evidence each discussion with, disclosure to, or other manner of providing to a third party, or sale of or offer to sell, the claimed invention prior to the date of application for the patent in suit. A party's production of a document as required herein shall not constitute an admission that such document evidences or is prior art under 35 U.S.C. § 102;

(b) All documents evidencing the conception, reduction to practice, design, and development of each claimed invention, which were created on or before the date of application for the patent in suit or the priority date identified pursuant to P. R. 3–1(e), whichever is earlier; and

(c) A copy of the file history for each patent in suit. The producing party shall separately identify by production number which documents correspond to each category.

3–3. Invalidity Contentions. Not later than 45 days after service upon it of the "Disclosure of Asserted Claims and Infringement Contentions," each party opposing a claim of patent infringement, shall serve on all parties its "Invalidity Contentions" which must contain the following information:

(a) The identity of each item of prior art that allegedly anticipates each asserted claim or renders it obvious. Each prior art patent shall be identified by its number, country of origin, and date of issue. Each prior art publication must be identified by its title, date of publication, and where feasible, author and publisher. Prior art under 35 U.S.C. § 102(b) shall be identified by specifying the item offered for sale or publicly used or known, the date the offer or use took place or the information became known, and the identity of the person or entity which made the use or which made and received the offer, or the person or entity which made the information known or to whom it was made known. Prior art under 35 U.S.C. § 102(f) shall be identified by providing the name of the person(s) from whom and the circumstances under which the invention or any part of it was derived. Prior art under 35 U.S.C. § 102(g) shall be identified by providing the identities of the person(s) or entities involved in and the circumstances surrounding the making of the invention before the patent applicant(s);

(b) Whether each item of prior art anticipates each asserted claim or renders it obvious. If a combination of items of prior art makes a claim obvious, each such combination, and the motivation to combine such items, must be identified;

(c) A chart identifying where specifically in each alleged item of prior art each element of each asserted claim is found, including for each element that such party contends is governed by 35 U.S.C. § 112(6), the identity of the structure(s), act(s), or material(s) in each item of prior art that performs the claimed function; and

(d) Any grounds of invalidity based on indefiniteness under 35 U.S.C. § 112(2) or enablement or written description under 35 U.S.C. § 112(1) of any of the asserted claims.

3–4. Document Production Accompanying Invalidity Contentions. With the "Invalidity Contentions," the party opposing a claim of patent infringement must produce or make available for inspection and copying:

(a) Source code, specifications, schematics, flow charts, artwork, formulas, or other documentation sufficient to show the operation of any aspects or elements of an Accused Instrumentality identified by the patent claimant in its P. R. 3–1(c) chart; and

(b) A copy of each item of prior art identified pursuant to P. R. 3–3(a) which does not appear in the file history of the patent(s) at issue. To the extent any such item is not in English, an English translation of the portion(s) relied upon must be produced.

3–5. Disclosure Requirement in Patent Cases for Declaratory Judgment.

(a) *Invalidity Contentions If No Claim of Infringement.* In all cases in which a party files a complaint or other pleading seeking a declaratory judgment that a patent is not infringed, is invalid, or is unenforceable, P. R. 3–1 and 3–2 shall not apply unless and until a claim for patent infringement is made by a party. If the defendant does not assert a claim for patent infringement in its answer to the complaint, no later than 10 days after the defendant serves its answer, or 10 days after the Initial Case Management Conference, whichever is later, the party seeking a declaratory judgment must serve upon each opposing party its Invalidity Contentions that conform to P. R. 3–3 and produce or make available for inspection and copying the documents described in P. R. 3–4. The parties shall meet and confer within 10 days of the service of the Invalidity Contentions for the purpose of determining the date on which the plaintiff will file its Final Invalidity Contentions which shall be no later than 50 days after service by the Court of its Claim Construction Ruling.

(b) *Applications of Rules When No Specified Triggering Event.* If the filings or actions in a case do not trigger the application of these Patent Rules under the terms set forth herein, the parties shall, as soon as such circumstances become known, meet and confer for the purpose of agreeing on the application of these Patent Rules to the case.

(c) *Inapplicability of Rule.* This P. R. 3–5 shall not apply to cases in which a request for a declaratory judgment that a patent is not infringed, is invalid, or is unenforceable is filed in response to a complaint for infringement of the same patent.

3–6. Amending Contentions.

(a) *Leave Not Required.* Each party's "Infringement Contentions" and "Invalidity Contentions" shall be deemed to be that party's final contentions, except as set forth below.

(1) If a party claiming patent infringement believes in good faith that the Court's Claim Construction Ruling so requires, not later than 30 days after service by the Court of its Claim Construction Ruling, that party may serve "Amended Infringement Contentions" without leave of court that amend its "Infringement Contentions" with respect to the information required by Patent R. 3–1(c) and (d).

(2) Not later than 50 days after service by the Court of its Claim Construction Ruling, each party opposing a claim of patent infringement may serve "Amended Invalidity Contentions" without leave of court that amend its "Invalidity Contentions" with respect to the information required by P. R. 3–3 if:

(A) a party claiming patent infringement has served "Infringement Contentions" pursuant to P. R. 3–6(a), or

(B) the party opposing a claim of patent infringement believes in good faith that the Court's Claim Construction Ruling so requires.

(b) *Leave Required.* Amendment or supplementation of any Infringement Contentions or Invalidity Contentions, other than as expressly permitted in P. R. 3–6(a), may be made only by order of the Court, which shall be entered only upon a showing of good cause.

3–7. Opinion of Counsel Defenses. By the date set forth in the Docket Control Order, each party opposing a claim of patent infringement that will rely on an opinion of counsel as part of a defense shall:

(a) Produce or make available for inspection and copying the opinion(s) and any other documents relating to the opinion(s) as to which that party agrees the attorney-client or work product protection has been waived; and

(b) Serve a privilege log identifying any other documents, except those authored by counsel acting solely as trial counsel, relating to the subject matter of the opinion(s) which the party is withholding on the grounds of attorney-client privilege or work product protection.

A party opposing a claim of patent infringement who does not comply with the requirements of this P.R. 3–7 shall not be permitted to rely on an opinion of counsel as part of a defense absent a stipulation of all parties or by order of the Court, which shall be entered only upon a showing of good cause.

3–8. Disclosure Requirements for Patent Cases Arising Under 21 U.S.C. § 355 (Hatch–Waxman Act). The following provision applies to all patents subject to a Paragraph IV certification in cases arising under 21 U.S.C. § 355 (commonly referred to as "the Hatch–Waxman Act"). This provision takes precedence over any conflicting provisions in P.R. 3–1 to 3–5 for all cases arising under 21 U.S.C. § 355.

(a) Upon the filing of a responsive pleading to the complaint, the Defendant(s) shall produce to Plaintiff(s) the entire Abbreviated New Drug Application or New Drug Application that is the basis of the case in question.

(b) Not more than 7 days after the Initial Case Management Conference, Plaintiff(s) must identify the asserted claims.

(c) Not more than 14 days after the Initial Case Management Conference, the Defendant(s) shall provide to Plaintiff(s) the written basis for their "Invalidity Contentions" for any patents referred to in Defendant(s) Paragraph IV Certification. This written basis shall contain all disclosures required by P.R. 3–3 and shall be accompanied by the production of documents required by P.R. 3–4.

(d) Not more than 14 days after the Initial Case Management Conference, the Defendant(s) shall provide to Plaintiff(s) the written basis for any defense of non-infringement for any patent referred to in Defendant(s) Paragraph IV Certification. This written basis shall include a claim chart identifying each claim at issue in the case and each limitation of each claim at issue. The claim chart shall specifically identify for each claim those claim limitation(s) that are literally absent from the Defendant(s) allegedly infringing Abbreviated New Drug Application or New Drug Application. The written basis for any defense of non-infringement shall also be accompanied by the production of any document or thing that the Defendant(s) intend to rely upon in defense of any infringement allegations by Plaintiff(s).

(e) Not more than 45 days after the disclosure of the written basis for any defense of non-infringement as required by P.R. 3–8(c), Plaintiff(s) shall provide Defendant(s) with a "Disclosure of Asserted Claims and Infringement Contentions," for all patents referred to in Defendant(s) Paragraph IV Certification, which shall contain all disclosures required by P.R. 3–1 and shall be accompanied by the production of documents required by P.R. 3–2.

(f) Each party that has an ANDA application pending with the Food and Drug Administration ("FDA") that is the basis of the pending case shall: (1) notify the FDA of any and all motions for injunctive relief no later than three business days after the date on which such a motion is filed; and (2) provide a copy of all correspondence between itself and the FDA pertaining to the ANDA application to each party asserting infringement, or set forth the basis of any claim of privilege for such correspondence, no later than seven days after the date it sends or receives any such correspondence.

(g) Unless informed of special circumstances, the Court intends to set all Hatch–Waxman cases for final pretrial hearing at or near 24 months from the date of the filing of the complaint.

4. CLAIM CONSTRUCTION PROCEEDINGS

4–1. Exchange of Proposed Terms and Claim Elements for Construction.

(a) Not later than 10 days after service of the "Invalidity Contentions" pursuant to P. R. 3–3, each party shall simultaneously exchange a list of claim terms, phrases, or clauses which that party contends should be construed or found indefinite by the Court, and identify any claim element which that party contends should be governed by 35 U.S.C. § 112(f).

(b) The parties shall thereafter meet and confer for the purposes of finalizing this list, narrowing or resolving differences, and facilitating the ultimate preparation of a Joint Claim Construction and Prehearing Statement.

4-2. Exchange of Preliminary Claim Constructions and Extrinsic Evidence.

(a) Not later than 20 days after the exchange of "Proposed Terms and Claim Elements for Construction" pursuant to P. R. 4–1, the parties shall simultaneously exchange a preliminary proposed construction of each claim term, phrase, or clause which the parties collectively have identified for claim construction purposes. Each such "Preliminary Claim Construction" shall also, for each element which any party contends is governed by 35 U.S.C. § 112(f), identify the structure(s), act(s), or material(s) corresponding to that element.

(b) At the same time the parties exchange their respective "Preliminary Claim Constructions," they shall each also provide a preliminary identification of extrinsic evidence, including without limitation, dictionary definitions, citations to learned treatises and prior art, and testimony of percipient and expert witnesses they contend support their respective claim constructions or indefiniteness positions. The parties shall identify each such item of extrinsic evidence by production number or produce a copy of any such item not previously produced. With respect to any such witness, percipient or expert, the parties shall also provide the identity and a brief description of the substance of that witness' proposed testimony.

(c) The parties shall thereafter meet and confer for the purposes of narrowing the issues and finalizing preparation of a Joint Claim Construction and Prehearing Statement.

4-3. Joint Claim Construction and Prehearing Statement.

(a) Not later than 60 days after service of the "Invalidity Contentions," the parties shall complete and file a Joint Claim Construction and Prehearing Statement, which shall contain the following information:

(1) The construction of those claim terms, phrases, or clauses on which the parties agree;

(2) Each party's proposed claim construction or indefiniteness position for each disputed claim term, phrase, or clause, together with an identification of all references from the specification or prosecution history that support that position, and an identification of any extrinsic evidence known to the party on which it intends to rely either to support its position or to oppose any other party's position, including, but not limited to, as permitted by law, dictionary definitions, citations to learned treatises and prior art, and testimony of percipient and expert witnesses;

(3) The anticipated length of time necessary for the Claim Construction Hearing;

(4) Whether any party proposes to call one or more witnesses, including experts, at the Claim Construction Hearing and the identity of each such witness; and

(5) A list of any other issues which might appropriately be taken up at a prehearing conference prior to the Claim Construction Hearing, and proposed dates, if not previously set, for any such prehearing conference.

(b) Each party shall also simultaneously serve a disclosure of expert testimony consistent with Fed. R. Civ. P. 26(a)(2)(B)(i)–(ii) or 26(a)(2)(C) for any expert on which it intends to rely to support its proposed claim construction or indefiniteness position or to oppose any other party's proposed claim construction or indefiniteness position.

4-4. Completion of Claim Construction Discovery.
Not later than 30 days after service and filing of the Joint Claim Construction and Prehearing Statement, the parties shall complete all discovery relating to claim construction, including any depositions with respect to claim construction of any witnesses, including experts, identified in the Joint Claim Construction and Prehearing Statement.

4-5. Claim Construction Briefs.

(a) Not later than 45 days after serving and filing the Joint Claim Construction and Prehearing Statement, the party claiming patent infringement shall serve and file an opening brief and any evidence supporting its claim construction. All asserted patents shall be attached as exhibits to the opening claim construction brief in searchable PDF form.

(b) Not later than 14 days after service upon it of an opening brief, each opposing party shall serve and file its responsive brief and supporting evidence.

(c) Not later than 7 days after service upon it of a responsive brief, the party claiming patent infringement shall serve and file any reply brief and any evidence directly rebutting the supporting evidence contained in an opposing party's response.

(d) At least 10 days before the Claim Construction Hearing held pursuant to P.R. 4–6, the parties shall jointly file a claim construction chart.

(1) Said chart shall have a column listing complete language of disputed claims with disputed terms in bold type and separate columns for each party's proposed construction of each disputed term. The chart shall also include a fourth column entitled "Court's Construction" and otherwise left blank. Additionally, the chart shall also direct the Court's attention to the patent and claim number(s) where the disputed term(s) appear(s).

(2) The parties may also include constructions for claim terms to which they have agreed. If the parties choose to include agreed constructions, each party's proposed construction columns shall state "[AGREED]" and the agreed construction shall be inserted in the "Court's Construction" column.

(3) The purpose of this claim construction chart is to assist the Court and the parties in tracking and resolving disputed terms. Accordingly, aside from the requirements set forth in this rule, the parties are afforded substantial latitude in the chart's format so that they may fashion a chart that most clearly and efficiently outlines the disputed terms and proposed constructions. Appendices to the Court's prior published and unpublished claim construction opinions may provide helpful guidelines for parties fashioning claim construction charts.

(e) Unless otherwise ordered by the Court, the page limitations governing dispositive motions pursuant to Local Rule CV–7(a) shall apply to claim construction briefing.

4–6. Claim Construction Hearing. Subject to the convenience of the Court's calendar, two weeks following submission of the reply brief specified in P.R. 4–5(c), the Court shall conduct a Claim Construction Hearing, to the extent the parties or the Court believe a hearing is necessary for construction of the claims at issue.

[Former Appendix M effective February 22, 2005. Amended effective February 27, 2006; May 1, 2006; October 27, 2006; January 14, 2008; February 18, 2010; April 21, 2011; July 16, 2012; March 25, 2013. Redesignated Appendix B and amended effective March 19, 2014. Amended effective May 6, 2015; December 1, 2018.]

SELECTED FORMS

CIVIL COVER SHEET

JS 44 (Rev. 02/19)

CIVIL COVER SHEET

The JS 44 civil cover sheet and the information contained herein neither replace nor supplement the filing and service of pleadings or other papers as required by law, except as provided by local rules of court. This form, approved by the Judicial Conference of the United States in September 1974, is required for the use of the Clerk of Court for the purpose of initiating the civil docket sheet. *(SEE INSTRUCTIONS ON NEXT PAGE OF THIS FORM.)*

I. (a) PLAINTIFFS

DEFENDANTS

(b) County of Residence of First Listed Plaintiff _____
(EXCEPT IN U.S. PLAINTIFF CASES)

County of Residence of First Listed Defendant _____
(IN U.S. PLAINTIFF CASES ONLY)
NOTE: IN LAND CONDEMNATION CASES, USE THE LOCATION OF THE TRACT OF LAND INVOLVED.

(c) Attorneys *(Firm Name, Address, and Telephone Number)*

Attorneys *(If Known)*

II. BASIS OF JURISDICTION *(Place an "X" in One Box Only)*

- ☐ 1 U.S. Government Plaintiff
- ☐ 2 U.S. Government Defendant
- ☐ 3 Federal Question *(U.S. Government Not a Party)*
- ☐ 4 Diversity *(Indicate Citizenship of Parties in Item III)*

III. CITIZENSHIP OF PRINCIPAL PARTIES *(Place an "X" in One Box for Plaintiff and One Box for Defendant)*
(For Diversity Cases Only)

	PTF	DEF		PTF	DEF
Citizen of This State	☐ 1	☐ 1	Incorporated or Principal Place of Business In This State	☐ 4	☐ 4
Citizen of Another State	☐ 2	☐ 2	Incorporated and Principal Place of Business In Another State	☐ 5	☐ 5
Citizen or Subject of a Foreign Country	☐ 3	☐ 3	Foreign Nation	☐ 6	☐ 6

IV. NATURE OF SUIT *(Place an "X" in One Box Only)*   Click here for: Nature of Suit Code Descriptions.

CONTRACT	TORTS		FORFEITURE/PENALTY	BANKRUPTCY	OTHER STATUTES
☐ 110 Insurance	**PERSONAL INJURY**	**PERSONAL INJURY**	☐ 625 Drug Related Seizure of Property 21 USC 881	☐ 422 Appeal 28 USC 158	☐ 375 False Claims Act
☐ 120 Marine	☐ 310 Airplane	☐ 365 Personal Injury - Product Liability	☐ 690 Other	☐ 423 Withdrawal 28 USC 157	☐ 376 Qui Tam (31 USC 3729(a))
☐ 130 Miller Act	☐ 315 Airplane Product Liability	☐ 367 Health Care/ Pharmaceutical			☐ 400 State Reapportionment
☐ 140 Negotiable Instrument	☐ 320 Assault, Libel & Slander	Personal Injury		**PROPERTY RIGHTS**	☐ 410 Antitrust
☐ 150 Recovery of Overpayment & Enforcement of Judgment	☐ 330 Federal Employers' Liability	Product Liability		☐ 820 Copyrights	☐ 430 Banks and Banking
☐ 151 Medicare Act	☐ 340 Marine	☐ 368 Asbestos Personal Injury Product Liability		☐ 830 Patent	☐ 450 Commerce
☐ 152 Recovery of Defaulted Student Loans (Excludes Veterans)	☐ 345 Marine Product Liability	**PERSONAL PROPERTY**		☐ 835 Patent - Abbreviated New Drug Application	☐ 460 Deportation
☐ 153 Recovery of Overpayment of Veteran's Benefits	☐ 350 Motor Vehicle	☐ 370 Other Fraud	**LABOR**	☐ 840 Trademark	☐ 470 Racketeer Influenced and Corrupt Organizations
☐ 160 Stockholders' Suits	☐ 355 Motor Vehicle Product Liability	☐ 371 Truth in Lending	☐ 710 Fair Labor Standards Act	**SOCIAL SECURITY**	☐ 480 Consumer Credit
☐ 190 Other Contract	☐ 360 Other Personal Injury	☐ 380 Other Personal Property Damage	☐ 720 Labor/Management Relations	☐ 861 HIA (1395ff)	☐ 485 Telephone Consumer Protection Act
☐ 195 Contract Product Liability	☐ 362 Personal Injury - Medical Malpractice	☐ 385 Property Damage Product Liability	☐ 740 Railway Labor Act	☐ 862 Black Lung (923)	☐ 490 Cable/Sat TV
☐ 196 Franchise			☐ 751 Family and Medical Leave Act	☐ 863 DIWC/DIWW (405(g))	☐ 850 Securities/Commodities/ Exchange
			☐ 790 Other Labor Litigation	☐ 864 SSID Title XVI	☐ 890 Other Statutory Actions
REAL PROPERTY	**CIVIL RIGHTS**	**PRISONER PETITIONS**	☐ 791 Employee Retirement Income Security Act	☐ 865 RSI (405(g))	☐ 891 Agricultural Acts
☐ 210 Land Condemnation	☐ 440 Other Civil Rights	**Habeas Corpus:**		**FEDERAL TAX SUITS**	☐ 893 Environmental Matters
☐ 220 Foreclosure	☐ 441 Voting	☐ 463 Alien Detainee		☐ 870 Taxes (U.S. Plaintiff or Defendant)	☐ 895 Freedom of Information Act
☐ 230 Rent Lease & Ejectment	☐ 442 Employment	☐ 510 Motions to Vacate Sentence		☐ 871 IRS—Third Party 26 USC 7609	☐ 896 Arbitration
☐ 240 Torts to Land	☐ 443 Housing/ Accommodations	☐ 530 General			☐ 899 Administrative Procedure Act/Review or Appeal of Agency Decision
☐ 245 Tort Product Liability	☐ 445 Amer. w/Disabilities - Employment	☐ 535 Death Penalty	**IMMIGRATION**		☐ 950 Constitutionality of State Statutes
☐ 290 All Other Real Property	☐ 446 Amer. w/Disabilities - Other	**Other:**	☐ 462 Naturalization Application		
	☐ 448 Education	☐ 540 Mandamus & Other	☐ 465 Other Immigration Actions		
		☐ 550 Civil Rights			
		☐ 555 Prison Condition			
		☐ 560 Civil Detainee - Conditions of Confinement			

V. ORIGIN *(Place an "X" in One Box Only)*

- ☐ 1 Original Proceeding
- ☐ 2 Removed from State Court
- ☐ 3 Remanded from Appellate Court
- ☐ 4 Reinstated or Reopened
- ☐ 5 Transferred from Another District *(specify)*
- ☐ 6 Multidistrict Litigation - Transfer
- ☐ 8 Multidistrict Litigation - Direct File

VI. CAUSE OF ACTION
Cite the U.S. Civil Statute under which you are filing *(Do not cite jurisdictional statutes unless diversity)*:

Brief description of cause:

VII. REQUESTED IN COMPLAINT:
☐ CHECK IF THIS IS A CLASS ACTION UNDER RULE 23, F.R.Cv.P.
DEMAND $
CHECK YES only if demanded in complaint:
JURY DEMAND: ☐ Yes ☐ No

VIII. RELATED CASE(S) IF ANY
(See instructions)
JUDGE _____ DOCKET NUMBER _____

DATE _____ SIGNATURE OF ATTORNEY OF RECORD _____

FOR OFFICE USE ONLY

RECEIPT # _____ AMOUNT _____ APPLYING IFP _____ JUDGE _____ MAG. JUDGE _____

JS 44 Reverse (Rev. 02/19)

INSTRUCTIONS FOR ATTORNEYS COMPLETING CIVIL COVER SHEET FORM JS 44

Authority For Civil Cover Sheet

The JS 44 civil cover sheet and the information contained herein neither replaces nor supplements the filings and service of pleading or other papers as required by law, except as provided by local rules of court. This form, approved by the Judicial Conference of the United States in September 1974, is required for the use of the Clerk of Court for the purpose of initiating the civil docket sheet. Consequently, a civil cover sheet is submitted to the Clerk of Court for each civil complaint filed. The attorney filing a case should complete the form as follows:

I.(a) Plaintiffs-Defendants. Enter names (last, first, middle initial) of plaintiff and defendant. If the plaintiff or defendant is a government agency, use only the full name or standard abbreviations. If the plaintiff or defendant is an official within a government agency, identify first the agency and then the official, giving both name and title.

(b) County of Residence. For each civil case filed, except U.S. plaintiff cases, enter the name of the county where the first listed plaintiff resides at the time of filing. In U.S. plaintiff cases, enter the name of the county in which the first listed defendant resides at the time of filing. (NOTE: In land condemnation cases, the county of residence of the "defendant" is the location of the tract of land involved.)

(c) Attorneys. Enter the firm name, address, telephone number, and attorney of record. If there are several attorneys, list them on an attachment, noting in this section "(see attachment)".

II. Jurisdiction. The basis of jurisdiction is set forth under Rule 8(a), F.R.Cv.P., which requires that jurisdictions be shown in pleadings. Place an "X" in one of the boxes. If there is more than one basis of jurisdiction, precedence is given in the order shown below.
United States plaintiff. (1) Jurisdiction based on 28 U.S.C. 1345 and 1348. Suits by agencies and officers of the United States are included here.
United States defendant. (2) When the plaintiff is suing the United States, its officers or agencies, place an "X" in this box.
Federal question. (3) This refers to suits under 28 U.S.C. 1331, where jurisdiction arises under the Constitution of the United States, an amendment to the Constitution, an act of Congress or a treaty of the United States. In cases where the U.S. is a party, the U.S. plaintiff or defendant code takes precedence, and box 1 or 2 should be marked.
Diversity of citizenship. (4) This refers to suits under 28 U.S.C. 1332, where parties are citizens of different states. When Box 4 is checked, the citizenship of the different parties must be checked. (See Section III below; **NOTE: federal question actions take precedence over diversity cases.**)

III. Residence (citizenship) of Principal Parties. This section of the JS 44 is to be completed if diversity of citizenship was indicated above. Mark this section for each principal party.

IV. Nature of Suit. Place an "X" in the appropriate box. If there are multiple nature of suit codes associated with the case, pick the nature of suit code that is most applicable. Click here for: Nature of Suit Code Descriptions.

V. Origin. Place an "X" in one of the seven boxes.
Original Proceedings. (1) Cases which originate in the United States district courts.
Removed from State Court. (2) Proceedings initiated in state courts may be removed to the district courts under Title 28 U.S.C., Section 1441.
Remanded from Appellate Court. (3) Check this box for cases remanded to the district court for further action. Use the date of remand as the filing date.
Reinstated or Reopened. (4) Check this box for cases reinstated or reopened in the district court. Use the reopening date as the filing date.
Transferred from Another District. (5) For cases transferred under Title 28 U.S.C. Section 1404(a). Do not use this for within district transfers or multidistrict litigation transfers.
Multidistrict Litigation – Transfer. (6) Check this box when a multidistrict case is transferred into the district under authority of Title 28 U.S.C. Section 1407.
Multidistrict Litigation – Direct File. (8) Check this box when a multidistrict case is filed in the same district as the Master MDL docket. **PLEASE NOTE THAT THERE IS NOT AN ORIGIN CODE 7.** Origin Code 7 was used for historical records and is no longer relevant due to changes in statue.

VI. Cause of Action. Report the civil statute directly related to the cause of action and give a brief description of the cause. **Do not cite jurisdictional statutes unless diversity.** Example: U.S. Civil Statute: 47 USC 553 Brief Description: Unauthorized reception of cable service

VII. Requested in Complaint. Class Action. Place an "X" in this box if you are filing a class action under Rule 23, F.R.Cv.P.
Demand. In this space enter the actual dollar amount being demanded or indicate other demand, such as a preliminary injunction.
Jury Demand. Check the appropriate box to indicate whether or not a jury is being demanded.

VIII. Related Cases. This section of the JS 44 is used to reference related pending cases, if any. If there are related pending cases, insert the docket numbers and the corresponding judge names for such cases.

Date and Attorney Signature. Date and sign the civil cover sheet.

[Revised effective January 31, 2013; March 19, 2014; June 1, 2017; February 1, 2019.]

APPLICATION TO APPEAR PRO HAC VICE

Revised: 9/3/2015

UNITED STATES DISTRICT COURT
EASTERN DISTRICT OF TEXAS
Beaumont   **DIVISION**
APPLICATION TO APPEAR PRO HAC VICE

1.This application is being made for the following: Case #_____

Style/Parties:_____

2. Applicant is representing the following party/ics: _____

3.Applicant was admitted to practice in _____ (state) on _____ (date).

4. Applicant is in good standing and is otherwise eligible to practice law before this court.

5. Applicant is not currently suspended or disbarred in any other court.

6. Applicant ◯has ◯has not had an application for admission to practice before another court denied (please circle appropriate language). If so, give complete information on a separate page.

7. Applicant ◯has ◯has not ever had the privilege to practice before another court suspended (please circle). If so, give complete information on a separate page.

8. Applicant ◯has ◯has not been disciplined by a court or Bar Association or committee thereof that would reflect unfavorably upon applicant's conduct, competency or fitness as a member of the Bar (please circle). If so, give complete information on a separate page.

9. Describe in detail on a separate page any charges, arrests or convictions for criminal offense(s) filed against you. Omit minor traffic offenses and misdemeanor offenses committed prior to age 18. (See Page 3)

10. There are no pending grievances or criminal matters pending against the applicant.

11. Applicant has been admitted to practice in the following courts:

_____

12. Applicant has read and will comply with the Local Rules of the Eastern District of Texas, including Rule AT-3, the "Standards of Practice to be Observed by Attorneys."

13. Applicant understands that he/she is being admitted for the limited purpose of appearing in the case specified above only.

Application Oath:

     I, _____ do solemnly swear (or affirm) that the above information is true; that I will discharge the duties of attorney and counselor of this court faithfully; that I will demean myself uprightly under the law and the highest ethics of our profession; and that I will support and defend the Constitution of the United States.

Date _____   Signature _____ (s/Signature)

Name (please print) _____

Bar Number /State _____

Firm Name: _____

Address/P.O. Box: _____

City/State/Zip: _____

Telephone #: _____

Fax #: _____

E-mail Address: _____

Secondary E-Mail Address: _____

This application has been approved for the court on: _____

David A. O'Toole, Clerk

U.S. District Court, Eastern District of Texas

By _____

Deputy Clerk

Application Instructions
Complete page 1 and 2 of this application and email to pro@txed.uscourts.gov for approval. Once
approved, the clerk will email to you your new login and Password so that you will be able to
electronically file your application and pay the $100 fee on line. If you already have a login and
password, you will still need to wait for approval email from the clerk before filing your
electronic application. For Complete instructions please visit the website
http://www.txed.uscourts.gov/

| Email Application |

This may be used to answer question 9.

9. Describe in detail on a separate page any charges, arrests or convictions for criminal offense(s) filedagainst you. Omit minor traffic offenses and misdemeanor offenses committed prior to age 18.

[Effective October 24, 2001. Revised December 5, 2002; July 1, 2003; January 24, 2007; April 19, 2010; August 7, 2012; August 21, 2013; March 19, 2014; September 3, 2015.]

ORDER REGARDING E–DISCOVERY IN PATENT CASES

IN THE UNITED STATES DISTRICT COURT
EASTERN DISTRICT OF TEXAS
_____ DIVISION

Plaintiff,	§	
	§	
v.	§	Case No. _____
	§	
Defendant.	§	

[MODEL] ORDER REGARDING E–DISCOVERY IN PATENT CASES

The Court ORDERS as follows:

1. This order supplements all other discovery rules and orders. It streamlines Electronically Stored Information ("ESI") production to promote a "just, speedy, and inexpensive determination" of this action, as required by Federal Rule of Civil Procedure 1.

2. This order may be modified in the court's discretion or by agreement of the parties. The parties shall jointly submit any proposed modifications within 30 days after the Federal Rule of Civil Procedure 16 conference. If the parties cannot resolve their disagreements regarding these modifications, the parties shall submit their competing proposals and a summary of their dispute.

3. A party's meaningful compliance with this order and efforts to promote efficiency and reduce costs will be considered in cost-shifting determinations.

4. Absent a showing of good cause, general ESI production requests under Federal Rules of Civil Procedure 34 and 45, or compliance with a mandatory disclosure requirement of this Court, shall not include metadata. However, fields showing the date and time that the document was sent and received, as well as the complete distribution list, shall generally be included in the production if such fields exist.

5. Absent agreement of the parties or further order of this court, the following parameters shall apply to ESI production:

   A. **General Document Image Format**. Each electronic document shall be produced in single-page Tagged Image File Format ("TIFF") format. TIFF files shall be single page and shall be named with a unique production number followed by the appropriate file extension. Load files shall be provided to indicate the location and unitization of the TIFF files. If a document is more than one page, the unitization of the document and any attachments and/or affixed notes shall be maintained as they existed in the original document.

   B. **Text–Searchable Documents**. No party has an obligation to make its production text-searchable; however, if a party's documents already exist in text-searchable format independent of this litigation, or are converted to text-searchable format for use in this litigation, including for use by the producing party's counsel, then such documents shall be produced in the same text-searchable format at no cost to the receiving party.

   C. **Footer**. Each document image shall contain a footer with a sequentially ascending production number.

   D. **Native Files**. A party that receives a document produced in a format specified above may make a reasonable request to receive the document in its native format, and upon receipt of such a request, the producing party shall produce the document in its native format.

   E. **No Backup Restoration Required.** Absent a showing of good cause, no party need restore any form of media upon which backup data is maintained in a party's normal or allowed processes, including but not limited to backup tapes, disks, SAN, and other forms of media, to comply with its discovery obligations in the present case.

   F. **Voicemail and Mobile Devices.** Absent a showing of good cause, voicemails, PDAs and mobile phones are deemed not reasonably accessible and need not be collected and preserved.

6. General ESI production requests under Federal Rules of Civil Procedure 34 and 45, or compliance with a mandatory disclosure order of this court, shall not include e-mail or other forms of

electronic correspondence (collectively "e-mail"). To obtain e-mail parties must propound specific e-mail production requests.

7. E-mail production requests shall be phased to occur timely after the parties have exchanged initial disclosures, a specific listing of likely e-mail custodians, a specific identification of the fifteen most significant listed e-mail custodians in view of the pleaded claims and defenses,[1] infringement contentions and accompanying documents pursuant to P.R. 3–1 and 3–2, invalidity contentions and accompanying documents pursuant to P.R. 3–3 and 3–4, and preliminary information relevant to damages. The exchange of this information shall occur at the time required under the Federal Rules of Civil Procedure, Local Rules, or by order of the court. Each requesting party may also propound up to five written discovery requests and take one deposition per producing party to identify the proper custodians, proper search terms, and proper time frame for e-mail production requests. The court may allow additional discovery upon a showing of good cause.

8. E-mail production requests shall identify the custodian, search terms, and time frame. The parties shall cooperate to identify the proper custodians, proper search terms, and proper time frame. Each requesting party shall limit its e-mail production requests to a total of eight custodians per producing party for all such requests. The parties may jointly agree to modify this limit without the court's leave. The court shall consider contested requests for additional or fewer custodians per producing party, upon showing a distinct need based on the size, complexity, and issues of this specific case.

9. Each requesting party shall limit its e-mail production requests to a total of ten search terms per custodian per party. The parties may jointly agree to modify this limit without the court's leave. The court shall consider contested requests for additional or fewer search terms per custodian, upon showing a distinct need based on the size, complexity, and issues of this specific case. The search terms shall be narrowly tailored to particular issues. Indiscriminate terms, such as the producing company's name or its product name, are inappropriate unless combined with narrowing search criteria that sufficiently reduce the risk of overproduction. A conjunctive combination of multiple words or phrases (e.g., "computer" and "system") narrows the search and shall count as a single search term. A disjunctive combination of multiple words or phrases (e.g., "computer" or "system") broadens the search, and thus each word or phrase shall count as a separate search term unless they are variants of the same word. Use of narrowing search criteria (e.g., "and," "but not," "w/x") is encouraged to limit the production and shall be considered when determining whether to shift costs for disproportionate discovery.

10. Pursuant to Federal Rule of Evidence 502(d), the inadvertent production of a privileged or work product protected ESI is not a waiver in the pending case or in any other federal or state proceeding.

11. The mere production of ESI in a litigation as part of a mass production shall not itself constitute a waiver for any purpose.

12. Except as expressly stated, nothing in this order affects the parties' discovery obligations under the Federal or Local Rules.

[Effective February 27, 2012. Revised March 19, 2014.]

---

[1] A "specific identification" requires a short description of why the custodian is believed to be significant.

JOINT FINAL PRETRIAL ORDER

IN THE UNITED STATES DISTRICT COURT
FOR THE EASTERN DISTRICT OF TEXAS

_____ Division

_____,	*
Plaintiff(s)	*
	*
	*
v.	* Civil Action No. _____
	*
	*
_____,	*
Defendant(s)	*
	*

JOINT FINAL PRE–TRIAL ORDER

This cause came before the court at a pre-trial management conference held on ___, 20 ___, pursuant to Local Rule CV–16 and Rule 16 of the Federal Rules of Civil Procedure.

A. COUNSEL FOR THE PARTIES

Plaintiff(s):

Defendant(s):

B. STATEMENT OF JURISDICTION

(e.g., "Jurisdiction in this case is based on diversity of citizenship under Title 28 U.S.C. § 1332;" "Jurisdiction in this case is based on Title 28 U.S.C. § 1331 in that the plaintiff brings this action under Title 46 U.S.C. § 688, the Jones Act")

Jurisdiction is (not) disputed.

C. NATURE OF ACTION

(e.g., "This is a products liability case wherein the plaintiff seeks damages for personal injuries sustained when he fell from the driver's seat of a forklift. The plaintiff contends that the forklift was defectively designed and manufactured by the defendant and that the defects were a producing cause of his injuries and damages.")

D. CONTENTIONS OF THE PARTIES

(Note: The contentions of each party on those claims and issues approved for trial at the management conference shall be succinctly stated in a form suitable to be read to the jury.)

E. STIPULATIONS AND UNCONTESTED FACTS

F. CONTESTED ISSUES OF FACT AND LAW

G. LIST OF WITNESSES

(Note: Each party shall set forth a separate list of witnesses who (1) will be called to testify at trial; (2) may be called to testify at trial, and (3) may be presented by deposition testimony at trial. Those portions of the depositions that may be offered into evidence at trial shall be listed by page and line number.

H. LIST OF EXHIBITS

Counsel should fill out and submit to the Court an exhibit list containing the information in the form available on the court's website, located at _www.txed.uscourts.gov_, or at the clerk's office.

I. LIST OF ANY PENDING MOTIONS

J. PROBABLE LENGTH OF TRIAL

The probable length of trial is ___ days.

K. MANAGEMENT CONFERENCE LIMITATIONS

(Note: The parties shall set forth any limitations agreed upon or ordered by the court at or after the management conference set forth in Local Rule CV–16 such as a time limit on the length of trial, limitations on the number of experts a party may call, limitations on the length of video depositions, the use of deposition summaries, etc.)

L. CERTIFICATIONS

The undersigned counsel for each of the parties in this action do hereby certify and acknowledge the following:

(1) Full and complete disclosure has been made in accordance with the Federal Rules of Civil Procedure and the Court's orders;

(2) Discovery limitations set forth in the Federal Rules of Civil Procedure, the Local Rules, and the Court's orders have been complied with;

(3) Each exhibit in the List of Exhibits herein:

    (a) is in existence;

    (b) is numbered; and

    (c) has been disclosed and shown to opposing counsel.

Approved as to form and substance:

_____

Attorneys for Plaintiff(s)

_____

Attorneys for Defendant(s)

(Note: An attorney of record may sign and certify this order on behalf of opposing counsel "with permission.")

This Joint Pre–Trial Order is hereby approved this ____ day of [month],[year].

_____

United States District Judge

(Note: Where additional parties are joined or intervene pursuant to Rules 14, 19 and 24 of the Federal Rules of Civil Procedure, the style of the case and the various sections of the pre-trial order should be modified to reflect the additional parties and information pertaining to them.)

[Effective October 27, 1997. Revised December 1, 2000; December 20, 2002; February 22, 2005; November 2, 2005; May 1, 2006; March 19, 2014.]

JURY PLAN

PLAN FOR THE RANDOM SELECTION OF JURORS U.S. DISTRICT COURT FOR THE EASTERN DISTRICT OF TEXAS

Pursuant to the Jury Selection and Service Act of 1968, as amended, 28 U.S.C. § 1861 et seq.("the Act"), the following Plan for the Random Selection of Jurors is adopted by this Court superseding the plan now in effect, subject to approval of this Plan by a reviewing panel of members of the Fifth Judicial Circuit Council and to such rules and regulations as may be adopted from time to time by the Judicial Conference of the United States.

* * * * *

Section 1. Declaration of Policy. It is the policy of this Court that all litigants in this Court entitled to trial by jury shall have the right to grand and petit juries selected at random from a fair cross section of the community in the district or division wherein the court convenes. It is further the policy of this Court that all citizens shall have the opportunity to be considered for service on grand and petit juries and shall have an obligation to serve as jurors when summoned for that purpose.

No citizen shall be excluded from service as a grand or petit juror in this Court on account of race, color, religion, sex, national origin, or economic status.

Section 2. Application of Plan. The Eastern District of Texas is hereby divided for jury selection purposes into six jury divisions. Each county within the District is included in one of the following jury divisions:

Beaumont Division: Hardin, Jasper, Jefferson, Liberty, Newton and Orange Counties.

Marshall Division: Camp, Cass, Harrison, Marion, Morris and Upshur Counties.

Sherman Division: Delta, Fannin, Hopkins, Lamar, Collin, Cooke, Denton and Grayson Counties.

Texarkana Division: Red River, Bowie, Franklin and Titus Counties.

Tyler Division: Anderson, Cherokee, Gregg, Henderson, Panola, Rains, Rusk, Smith, Van Zandt and Wood Counties.

Lufkin Division: Angelina, Houston, Nacogdoches, Polk, Sabine, San Augustine, Shelby, Trinity and Tyler Counties.

Section 3. Management and Supervision of Jury Selection Process. The clerk of the court shall manage the jury selection process. The clerk shall act under the supervision and control of the judges of this district.

This district, by adoption of this plan, has elected to operate the jury selection process under a fully automated, electronic data processing system.

Section 4. Source of Names of Prospective Jurors. Texas law provides for a statutory registration of voters of the age of 18 years and upwards, which is uniform in all of the counties. Voter registration lists represent a fair cross section of the community in the Eastern District of Texas. Accordingly, the names of all grand and petit jurors serving on or after the time provided in this plan shall be selected at random from the Master Registration Lists maintained by the Secretary of the State of Texas of all persons registered to vote in the most recent federal general election held every two years.

The court finds that it is not necessary in this district to prescribe some other source or sources of names in addition to the official lists of registered voters in order to foster the policy and protect the rights secured by the provisions of the Act.

Section 5. Selecting of Names of Prospective Jurors from Source Lists. For each jury division, names of prospective jurors shall be determined by the following procedure. The voter registration lists shall be arranged numerically by voter certificate number within the county and the counties shall be arranged alphabetically to form one continuous list of names for each division. Each name shall then be numbered consecutively to form a Master Source List.

Random selections from the Master Source Lists may be made using a computer-generated random selection process to select the required number of names from the Master Source List in order to insure that (a), any group of names chosen will represent, in substantially correct proportions, the names on all voter registration lists of all counties comprising the master jury wheel; (b), that the mathematical odds of any single name being picked are substantially equal, and (c), that the possibility of human discretion or choice affecting the selection of any individual's name is eliminated.

Section 6. Master Jury Wheels. The clerk or any other person authorized by the court shall establish and maintain one Master Jury Wheel for each jury division. The physical form of records on which names for the Master Jury Wheel are kept may include such electronic data storage devices as magnetic tapes or magnetic disk files. The Master Jury Wheel shall contain the names, or numbers corresponding to names on file, of those persons selected at random for prospective jury duty.

The minimum number of names, or numbers corresponding to names, to be placed in each Master Jury Wheel shall be at least one thousand. The clerk shall insure that at all times a sufficient number of names are contained in each of the wheels so that grand and petit jury panels may be drawn at any time required by the court. Such additional names shall be selected at random from voter registration lists in compliance with the Act and this Plan.

Each master jury wheel shall be emptied and refilled every two years, immediately following federal general elections and as soon as complete and current voter registration lists are available from the Secretary of the State of Texas following such federal general elections. The emptying (removal) of unused names in the wheels shall be accomplished by July 1 unless the court should find it necessary to authorize the clerk to extend that time.

As required by the Judicial Conference of the United States, a report shall be prepared after each periodic refilling of each master jury wheel giving general data relating to the master jury wheel with an analysis of race and sex of prospective jurors based on juror qualification forms returned during the qualifying process. Such report shall not be made until six months after summoning the first panels from the jury wheels in order to provide sufficient data to complete the analysis. For the purposes of determining proportional representation in the master jury wheels, data from the most recent Bureau of Census information shall be used for comparisons. The clerk shall have the capacity to prepare an alphabetical list of the names drawn, which list shall not be disclosed to any person except pursuant to this Plan and the Act.

Upon completion of the random selection of names for the divisions' master jury wheels, the individual(s) who performed the task of randomly selecting the names pursuant to this Plan shall prepare and execute a certificate detailing their procedures and reporting on the performance and completion of the assignment and transmit the same promptly to the chief judge of the district.

Public notices shall be posted in each jury division of this district announcing the random selection of names for the master jury wheels as well as in the appropriate division(s) for the later random selection from the qualified wheels for jury panels as they are scheduled to occur.

Section 7. Qualification for Service. Any judge of this district shall determine whether a person is disqualified, exempt, excused, or excluded from inclusion on a jury panel or from service as a juror while presiding over his respective docket. The clerk and other authorized deputy clerks of this court in the management of the jury selection process and by compliance with the criteria set out below in this Plan shall determine at the time the qualified wheels are being established whether a person is unqualified, exempt, or excused from inclusion on the qualified wheels. Such determinations shall be made on the basis of information provided on the juror qualification form and other competent evidence. Only judges of this court may rule on exclusions from jury service.

Whenever a person is disqualified, excused, exempt, or excluded from jury service, the clerk shall note in the space provided on the juror qualification form the specific reason therefor. If a person did not appear in response to a summons, such fact shall be noted on the juror list.

a. *Disqualified for Service.* Any person shall be deemed qualified to serve on grand and petit juries in this district court unless he or she—

(1) is not a citizen of the United States eighteen years old who has resided for a period of one year within the judicial district;

(2) is unable to read, write, and understand the English language with a degree of proficiency sufficient to fill out satisfactorily the juror qualification form;

(3) is unable to speak the English language;

(4) is incapable, by reason of mental or physical infirmity, to render satisfactory jury service; or

(5) has a charge pending against him or her for the commission of, or has been convicted in a State or Federal court of record of a crime punishable by imprisonment for more than one year and his civil rights have not been restored.

b. *Exemptions from Jury Service (Barred from Service).* Pursuant to the provisions of Title 28 U.S.C. § 1863 (b)(6), the court hereby finds that exemptions of the following groups of persons or occupational classes is in the public interest and would not be inconsistent with sections 1861 and 1862 of the Act. Accordingly, members of the following groups are barred from jury service:

(1) members in active service in the Armed Forces of the United States;

(2) members of the fire or police departments of any State, district, territory, possession, or subdivision thereof;

(3) public officers in the executive, legislative, or judicial branches of the Government of the United States, or any State, district, territory, or possession or subdivision thereof, who are actively engaged in the performance of official duties. "Public officer" shall mean a person who is either elected to a public office or who is directly appointed by a person elected to public office.

c. *Excuses from Jury Service.* This district court, pursuant to section 1863 of the Act and by adoption of this Plan, finds that jury service by the following classes or groups would entail undue hardship or extreme inconvenience to the members thereof. Such excuse would not be inconsistent with sections 1861 and 1862 of the Act. Grounds for excuses upon individual request are:

(1) A person who is over 70 years of age;

(2) A person who has served in federal court as a grand or petit juror within the last two years;

(3) A person having active care and custody of a child or children under ten years of age whose health and/or safety would be jeopardized by his or her absence for jury service; or a person who is essential to the care of aged or infirm persons;

(4) A person whose services are so essential to the operation of a business, commercial, or agricultural enterprise that it must close or cease to function if he or she is required to perform jury duty; and

(5) A person actively practicing or engaged full-time in one of these occupations:

    (a) attorney

    (b) physician

    (c) dentist

    (d) registered nurse

    (e) member of the clergy or a religious order

(6) A person who serves as a volunteer (without compensation) in an official capacity as a firefighter or a member of a rescue squad or ambulance crew for a public agency. A "public agency" for this purpose means the United States, any State of the United States, the District of Columbia, Puerto Rico, the Virgin Islands, Guam, American Samoa, or other territory of the United States, or any unit of local government, department, or instrumentality of any of the foregoing.

(7) Full-time college students.

d. *Individual Excuse from Jury Service.* In addition to the members of classes or groups subject to excuse from jury service, any person summoned for jury service may be excused from service during the session for which the juror was summoned by the judge presiding over his respective docket or by the clerk based upon a showing of undue hardship or extreme inconvenience.

The names of those jurors who have been excused from a panel for hardship or extreme inconvenience reasons will be put back in the qualified jury wheel where they will be subject to subsequent random selection, unless the court should rule otherwise at the time of granting the excuse.

e. *Jurors Excluded by the Court.* Pursuant to the provisions of section 1866 of the Act, any juror who has been summoned for jury service may be excluded by the judge in open court upon the following grounds:

(1) that such person may be unable to render impartial jury service or that his or her service as a juror would be likely to disrupt the proceedings; or

(2) excluded upon peremptory challenge as provided by law; or

(3) excluded pursuant to the procedure specified by law upon a challenge by any party for good cause shown; or

(4) excluded upon determination by the court that his or her service as a juror would be likely to threaten the secrecy of the proceedings, or otherwise adversely affect the integrity of jury deliberations.

Any person excluded from a particular jury under clause (1), (2), or (3) of this section shall be eligible to sit on another jury if the basis for the person's initial exclusion would not be relevant to the person's ability to serve on such other jury.

Section 8. Qualified Jury Wheel. The clerk shall maintain or cause to be maintained a separate qualified jury wheel for each jury division in the district, and shall place in such wheels the names of all persons drawn from the Master Jury Wheel of the relevant jury division who are found not disqualified, exempt, or excused pursuant to this Plan. The clerk shall insure that at all times a sufficient number of names are contained in each of such wheels so that grand and petit jury panels may be drawn at any time required by the court.

Each time a jury division's master wheel is refilled, the qualified wheel then in use shall be emptied as soon as the process of qualifying jurors from the new Master Wheel has produced a sufficient number of qualified jurors to begin supplying the court's needs. The emptying (removal) of unused names in the qualified wheels shall be accomplished by July 1 unless the court should find it necessary to authorize the clerk to extend that time.

Section 9. Drawing of Names from Qualified Jury Wheels; The Issuance of Summonses; and Disclosure of Names.

a. *Drawing of Names.* As and when jurors are required by the court the clerk shall draw at random from the qualified jury wheel of the relevant jury division(s), the required number of names to serve on a petit or grand jury panel. Each name as it is drawn shall be counted in sequence, starting with number one, until the number of names required to fill the panel are drawn. These names shall then be arranged alphabetically on a list. The list may be printed or retained on a computer for future use. Each list shall also include the person's number, mailing address, and county. Such a list shall be prepared for each jury panel.

b. *Issuance of Summonses.* The clerk shall cause to be mailed to every person whose name is drawn from the master jury wheel a juror qualification form accompanied by instructions to fill out and return the form duly signed and sworn, to the clerk by mail within ten days. Procedures as set forth in the Act, section 1864, shall be followed in securing returns of the completed questionnaires.

Each person drawn for jury service will be served a summons by first-class mail addressed to such person at his usual residence or business address.

c. *Petit Jury Panels.* Names of all petit jurors drawn to fill a panel as provided in this Plan who are not disqualified, excluded, exempt or excused and who report for jury duty at a session of court, shall be randomly selected by the clerk for each jury case tried during the session as directed by the court.

When there is an unanticipated shortage of available petit jurors drawn from the qualified jury wheel, the court may require the marshal to summon a sufficient number of petit jurors selected at random from the voter registration lists in a manner ordered by the court consistent with sections 1861 and 1862 of the Act.

d. *Grand Jury Panels.* There will ordinarily be three grand juries sitting in the Eastern District of Texas; the Beaumont grand jury ordinarily hears cases arising from the counties of Hardin, Jasper, Jefferson, Liberty, Newton, Orange, Polk, Sabine, San Augustine, Trinity, and Tyler counties; the Sherman grand jury ordinarily hears cases arising from the counties of Collin, Cook, Delta, Denton, Fannin, Grayson, Hopkins, Lamar and Red River counties; and the Tyler grand jury ordinarily hears cases arising from the remaining counties of the district. When a particular grand jury is not in session but one of the other grand juries is, the court may direct that business which would normally come before the grand jury not in session will be handled by a grand jury currently in session. In the interest of achieving administrative economies, the court may at any time direct that one grand jury panel comprised of jurors drawn from the qualified jury wheel of only one jury division shall serve the entire judicial district.

The clerk, upon court order, will assemble a grand jury panel by randomly drawing or causing to be drawn, names from the appropriate qualified wheel(s) for a grand jury. The same selection process as outlined above for petit jury panels shall be used for grand jury panels. When a grand jury panel is drawn from the qualified wheels of more than one jury division, names shall be drawn in a proportionately appropriate number depending on the number of names of registered voters on the source list when the wheels were first filled. No list shall contain less than three names from each appropriate division.

When there is an unanticipated shortage of available grand jurors drawn from the qualified jury wheel(s), the court may require the marshal to summon a sufficient number of grand jurors selected at random from the voter registration lists in a manner ordered by the court consistent with sections 1861 and 1862 of the Act.

e. *Disclosure of Names.* The lists of all names drawn from any qualified wheel to fill a petit or grand jury panel shall not be disclosed and made available to parties and the public until jurors have been summoned, have responded, and have been found to be qualified and available to serve based on information secured from the qualification form sent with the summonses.

(1) Disclosure of Petit Jury Lists. The lists of names of prospective petit jurors shall be disclosed only by the Courtroom Deputy at the time of voir dire proceedings, and not prior to that time. All such lists shall be returned to the Courtroom Deputy at the conclusion of such voir dire proceedings. These restrictions shall not limit the authority of the Chief Judge of this District, or any judicial officer of this District while presiding over his or her respective docket, to release any such list of names at an earlier time where such earlier release is consistent with this Plan or other pertinent statute.

(2) Grand Jury Panels. The list of names of persons summoned to any court in this District for prospective grand juror service shall remain confidential. The names of persons chosen to serve as grand jurors in this District shall remain confidential in the interest of justice until otherwise ordered by the Court 28 U.S.C. § 1863(b)(7).

(3) Disclosure of Juror Information to the Media and the Public. A request for disclosure of juror names to the media or public may be made of the judge to whom the case is assigned in accordance with the above provisions relating to the timing of the release of juror information. The clerk shall not release juror names to the media or public unless specifically authorized by the assigned judge.

Section 10. Definitions and General Provisions. There is incorporated herein by reference as an integral portion of this Plan, the provisions of Sections 1861 to 1871, both inclusive, and Section 1878 of Title 28, United States Code, together with all amendments of said sections which may hereafter be made, and all laws hereafter enacted related to grand petit juries, and trial by jury in the United States.

[Effective March 21, 1997. Amended effective June 6, 2007; August 9, 2007; March 26, 2009; March 14, 2014.]

SPEEDY TRIAL PLAN
PLAN FOR ACHIEVING PROMPT DISPOSITION OF CRIMINAL CASES

THE SPEEDY TRIAL PLAN FOR THE EASTERN DISTRICT OF TEXAS

The Speedy Trial Plan for this district is based upon the Speedy Trial Act of 1974, the Speedy Trial Amendments Act of 1979, and the Federal Juvenile Delinquency Act as Amended in 1978, and is entitled "Plan for Achieving Prompt Disposition of Criminal Cases." The district's plan became effective June 1, 1980, adopting the time limits set forth on the following pages.

The Committee on the Administration of the Criminal Law of the Judicial Conference of the United States has provided numerous guidelines to the administration of the Speedy Trial Act, with revisions from 1974 through 1984. These guidelines are maintained in a separate binder under the label "Speedy Trial Act Guidelines" and should be referred to as needed.

PLAN FOR ACHIEVING PROMPT DISPOSITION OF CRIMINAL CASES
U.S. DISTRICT COURT, EASTERN DISTRICT OF TEXAS
(Speedy Trial Plan)

Pursuant to the requirements of Rule 50(b) of the Federal Rules of Criminal Procedure, the Speedy Trial Act of 1974 (18 U.S.C. Chapter 208), the Speedy Trial Act Amendments Act of 1979 (Pub. L. No. 96–43, 93 Stat. 327), and the Federal Juvenile Delinquency Act (18 U.S.C. Sections 5036, 5037), the Judges of the United States District court for the Eastern District of Texas have adopted the following time limits and procedures to minimize undue delay and to further the prompt disposition of criminal cases and certain juvenile proceedings:

Statement of Time Limits Adopted by the Court
And Procedures for Implementing Them

1. Applicability.

    (a) Offenses. The time limits set forth herein are applicable to all criminal offenses triable in this court,[1] including cases triable by United States Magistrates, except for petty offenses as defined in 18 U.S.C. Section 1(3). Except as specifically provided, they are not applicable to proceedings under the Federal Juvenile Delinquency Act. (Section 3172).

    (b) Persons. The time limits are applicable to persons accused who have not been indicted or informed against as well as those who have, and the word "defendant" includes such persons unless the context indicates otherwise.

2. Priorities in Scheduling Criminal Cases. Preferences shall be given to criminal proceedings as far as practicable as required by rule 50(a) of the Federal Rules of Criminal Procedure. The trial of defendants in custody solely because they are awaiting trial and of high-risk defendants as defined in section 5 should be given preference over other criminal cases. [S.3164(a)]

3. Time Within Which an Indictment or Information Must Be Filed.

    (a) Time Limits. If an individual is arrested or served with a summons and the complaint charges an offense to be prosecuted in this district, any indictment or information subsequently filed in connection with such charge shall be filed within 30 days of arrest or service. [S.3161(b)]

    (b) Grand Jury Not in Session. If the defendant is charged with a felony to be prosecuted in this district, and no grand jury in the district has been in session during the 30–day period prescribed in subsection (a), such period shall be extended an additional 30 days. [S.3161(b)]

    (c) Measurement of Time Periods. If a person has not been arrested or served with a summons on a Federal charge, an arrest will be deemed to have been made at such time as the person (i) is held in custody solely for the purpose of responding to a Federal charge; (ii) is delivered to the custody of a Federal official in connection with a Federal charge; or (iii) appears before a judicial officer in connection with a Federal charge.

(d) <u>Related Procedures</u>.

    (1) At the time of the earliest appearance before a judicial officer of a person who has been arrested for an offense not charged in an indictment or information, the judicial officer shall establish for the record the date on which the arrest took place.

    (2) In the absence of a showing to the contrary, a summons shall be considered to have been served on the date of service shown on the return thereof.

4. <u>Time within Which Trial Must Commence</u>.

(a) <u>Time Limits</u>. The trial of a defendant shall commence not later than 70 days after the last to occur of the following dates:

    (1) The date on which an indictment or information is filed in this district;

    (2) The date on which a sealed indictment or information is unsealed; or

    (3) The date of the defendant's first appearance before a judicial officer of this district. [S.3161(c)(1)].

(b) <u>Retrial: Trial After Reinstatement of an Indictment or Information</u>. The retrial of a defendant shall commence within 70 days from the date the order occasioning the retrial becomes final, as shall the trial of a defendant upon an indictment or information dismissed by a trial court and reinstated following an appeal. If the retrial or trial follows an appeal or collateral attack, the court may extend the period if unavailability of witnesses or other factors resulting from passage of time make trial within 70 days impractical. The extended period shall not exceed 180 days. [S.3161(d)(2),(e)]

(c) <u>Withdrawal of Plea</u>. If a defendant enters a plea of guilty or nolo contendre to any or all charges in an indictment or information and is subsequently permitted to withdraw it, the time limit shall be determined for all counts as if the indictment or information were filed on the day the order permitting withdrawal of the plea became final. [S.3161(i)]

(d) <u>Superseding Charges</u>. If, after an indictment or information has been filed, a complaint, indictment, or information is filed which charges the defendant with the same offense or with an offense required to be joined with that offense, the time limit applicable to the subsequent charge will be determined as follows:

    (1) If the original indictment or information was dismissed on motion of the defendant before the filing of the subsequent charge, the time limit shall be determined without regard to the existence of the original charge. [S.3161(d)(1)]

    (2) If the original indictment or information is pending at the time the subsequent charge is filed, the trial shall commence within the time limit for commencement of trial on the original indictment or information. [S.3161(h)(6)]

    (3) If the original indictment or information was dismissed on motion of the United States attorney before the filing of the subsequent charge, the trial shall commence within the time limit for commencement of trial on the original indictment or information, but the period during which the defendant was not under charges shall be excluded from the computations. Such period is the period between the dismissal of the original indictment or information and the date the time would have If commenced to run on the subsequent charge had there been no previous charge.[2] [S.3161(h)(6)]

If the subsequent charge is contained in a complaint, the formal time limit within which an indictment or information must be obtained on the charge shall be determined without regard to the existence of the original indictment or information, but earlier action may in fact be required if the time limit for commencement of trial is to be satisfied.

(e) <u>Measurement of Time Periods</u>. For the purpose of this section:

    (1) If a defendant signs a written consent to be tried before a magistrate and no indictment or information charging the offense has been filed, the time limit shall run from the date of such consent.

    (2) In the event of a transfer to this district under Rule 20 of the Federal Rules of Criminal Procedure, the indictment or information shall be deemed filed in this district when the papers in the proceeding or certified copies thereof are received by the clerk.

    (3) A trial in a jury case shall be deemed to commence at the beginning of voir dire.

    (4) A trial in a non-jury case shall be deemed to commence on the day the case is called, provided that some step in the trial procedure immediately follows.

(f) Related Procedures.

(1) At the time of the defendant's earliest appearance before a judicial officer of this district, the officer will take appropriate steps to assure that the defendant is represented by counsel and shall appoint counsel where appropriate under the Criminal Justice Act and Rule 44 of the Federal Rules of Criminal Procedure. Judicial officers may order defendants who are only partially indigent to pay some portion of the CJA defense costs.

(2) The court shall have sole responsibility for setting cases for trial after consultation with counsel. At the time of arraignment or as soon thereafter as is practicable, each case will be set for trial on a day certain or listed for trial on a weekly or other short-term calendar. [S.3161(a)]

(3) Individual calendars shall be managed so that it will be reasonably anticipated that every criminal case set for trial will be reached during the week of original setting. A conflict in schedules of Assistant United States Attorneys or defense counsel will be ground for a continuance or delayed setting only if approved by the court and called to the court's attention at the earliest practicable time.

(4) In the event that a complaint, indictment, or information is filed against a defendant charged in a pending indictment or information or in an indictment or information dismissed on motion of the United States Attorney, the trial on the new charge shall commence within the time limit for commencement of trial on the original indictment or information unless the court finds that the new charge is not for the same offense charged in the original indictment or information or an offense required to be joined therewith.

(5) At the time of the filing of a complaint, indictment, or information described in paragraph (4), the United States Attorney shall give written notice to the court of that circumstance and of his position with respect to the computation of the time limits.

(6) All pretrial hearings shall be conducted as soon after the arraignment as possible, consistent with the priorities of other matters on the court's criminal docket.

5. Defendants in Custody and High-Risk Defendants.[3]

(a) Time Limits. Notwithstanding any longer time periods that may be permitted under sections 3 and 4, the following time limits will also be applicable to defendants in custody and high-risk defendants as herein defined:

(1) The trial of a defendant held in custody solely for the purpose of trial on a Federal charge shall commence within 90 days following the beginning of continuous custody.

(2) The trial of a high-risk defendant shall commence within 90 days of the designation as high-risk. [S.3164(b)]

(b) Definition of "High-Risk Defendant." A high-risk defendant is one reasonably designated by the United States Attorney as posing a danger to himself or any other person or to the community.

(c) Measurement of Time Periods. For the purposes of this section:

(1) A defendant is deemed to be in detention awaiting trial when he is arrested on a Federal charge. Detention is deemed to be solely because the defendant is awaiting trial unless the person exercising custodial authority has an independent basis (not including a detainer) for continuing to hold the defendant.

(2) If a case is transferred pursuant to Rule 20 of the Federal Rules of Criminal Procedure and the defendant subsequently rejects disposition under Rule 20 or the court declines to accept the plea, a new period of continuous detention awaiting trial will begin at that time.

(3) A trial shall be deemed to commence as provided in sections 4(e)(3) and 4(e)(4).

(d) Related Procedures.

(1) If a defendant is being held in custody solely for the purpose of awaiting trial, the United States Attorney shall advise the court at the earliest practicable time of the date of the beginning of such custody.

(2) The United States Attorney shall advise the court at the earliest practicable time (usually at the hearing with respect to bail) if the defendant is considered by him to be high risk.

(3) If the court finds that the filing of a "high-risk" designation as a public record may result in prejudice to the defendant, it may order the designation sealed for such period as is necessary to protect the defendant's right to a fair trial, but not beyond the time that the court's judgment in the case becomes final. during the time the designation is under seal, it shall be made known to the defendant and his counsel but shall not be made known to other persons without the permission of the court.

6. <u>Exclusion of Time From Computations.</u>

(a) <u>Applicability.</u> In computing any time limit under section 3, 4, or 5, the periods of delay set forth in 18 USC S.3161(h) shall be excluded. Such periods of delay shall not be excluded in computing the minimum period for commencement of trial under section 7.

(b) <u>Records of Excludable Time.</u> The clerk of the court shall enter on the docket, in the form prescribed by the Administrative Office of the United States Courts, information with respect to excludable periods of time for each criminal defendant. With respect to proceedings prior to the filing of an indictment or information, excludable time shall be reported to the clerk by the United States Attorney.

(c) <u>Stipulations.</u>

(1) The attorney for the government and the attorney for the defendant may at any time enter into stipulations with respect to the accuracy of the docket entries recording excludable time.

(2) To the extent that the amount of time stipulated by the parties does not exceed the amount recorded on the docket for any excludable period of delay, the stipulation shall be conclusive as between the parties unless it has no basis in fact or law. It shall similarly be conclusive as to a codefendant for the limited purpose of determining, under 18 U.S.C. S.3161(h)(7), whether time has run against the defendant entering into the stipulation.

(3) To the extent that the amount of time stipulated exceeds the amount recorded on the docket, the stipulation shall have no effect unless approved by the court.

(d) <u>Pre–Indictment Procedures.</u>

(1) In the event that the United States Attorney anticipates that an indictment or information will not be filed within the time limit set forth in section 3, he may file a written motion with the court for a determination of excludable time. In the event that the United States Attorney seeks a continuance under 18 U.S.C. S.3161(h)(8), he shall file a written motion with the court requesting such a continuance.

(2) The motion of the United States Attorney shall state (i) the period of time proposed for exclusion, and (ii) the basis of the proposed exclusion. If the motion is for a continuance under 18 U.S.C.(h)(8),* it shall also state whether or not the defendant is being held in custody on the basis of the complaint. In appropriate circumstances, the motion may include a request that some or all of the supporting material be considered ex parte and in camera.

(3) The court may grant a continuance under 18 U.S.C. S.3161(h)(8) for either a specific period of time or a period to be determined by reference to an event (such as recovery from illness) not within the control of the government. If the continuance is to a date not certain, the court shall require one or both parties to inform the court promptly when and if the circumstances that justify the continuance no longer exist. In addition, the court shall require one or both parties to file periodic reports bearing on the continued existence of such circumstances. The court shall determine the frequency of such reports in the light of the facts of the particular case.

(e) <u>Post–Indictment Procedures.</u>

(1) At each appearance of counsel before the court, counsel shall examine the clerk's records of excludable time for completeness and accuracy and shall bring to the court's immediate attention any claim that the clerk's records is in any way incorrect.

(2) In the event that the court continues a trial beyond the time limit set forth in section 4 or 5, the court shall determine whether the limit may be recomputed by excluding time pursuant to 18 U.S.C. S.3161(h).

(3) If it is determined that a continuance is justified, the court shall set forth its findings in the record, either orally or in writing. If the continuance is granted under 18 U.S.C. S.3161(h)(8), the court shall also set forth its reasons for finding that the ends of justice served by granting the continuance outweigh the best interests of the public and the

defendant in a speedy trial. If the continuance is to a date not certain, the court shall require one or both parties to inform the court promptly when and if the circumstances that justify the continuance no longer exist. In addition, the court shall require one or both parties to file periodic reports bearing on the continued existence of such circumstances. The court shall determine the frequency of such reports in the light of the facts of the particular case.

7. Minimum Period for Defense Preparation.

Unless the defendant consents in writing to the contrary, the trial shall not commence earlier than 30 days from the date on which the indictment or information is filed or, if later, from the date on which counsel first enters an appearance or on which the defendant expressly waives counsel and elects to proceed pro se. In circumstances in which the 70–day time limit for commencing trial on a charge in an indictment or information is determined by reference to an earlier indictment or information pursuant to section 4(d), the 30–day minimum period shall also be determined by reference to the earlier indictment or information. When prosecution is resumed on an original indictment or information following a mistrial, appeal, or withdrawal of a guilty plea, a new 30–day minimum period will not begin to run. The court will in all cases schedule trials so as to permit defense counsel adequate preparation time in the light of all the circumstances. [S3161(c)(2)]

8. Time Within Which Defendant Should be Sentenced.

(a) [4]Time Limit. A defendant shall ordinarily be sentenced within twenty-one (21) days after submission of the presentence report to the sentencing judge.

(b) Related Procedures. If the defendant and his counsel consent thereto, a presentence investigation may be commenced prior to a plea of guilty or nolo contendre or a conviction.

9. Juvenile Proceedings.

(a) Time Within Which Trial Must Commence. An alleged delinquent who is in detention pending trial shall be brought to trial within 30 days of the date on which such detention was begun, as provided in 18 U.S.C. S.5036.

(b) Time of Dispositional Hearing. If a juvenile is adjudicated delinquent, a separate dispositional hearing shall be held no later than 20 days after trial, unless the court has ordered further study of the juvenile in accordance with 18 U.S.C. S.5037(c).

10. Sanctions.

(a) Dismissal or Release From Custody. Failure to comply with the requirements of Title I of the Speedy Trial Act may entitle the defendant to dismissal of the charges against him or to release from pretrial custody. Nothing in this plan shall be construed to require that a case be dismissed or a defendant released from custody in circumstances in which such action would not be required by 18 U.S.C. S.3162 and 3164.[5]

(b) High–Risk Defendants. A high-risk defendant whose trial has not commenced within the time limit set forth in 18 U.S.C. S.3164(b) shall, if the failure to commence trial was through no fault of the attorney for the government, have his release conditions automatically reviewed. A high-risk defendant who is found by the court to have intentionally delayed the trial of his case shall be subject to an order of the court modifying his nonfinancial conditions of release under chapter 207 of Title 18, U.S.C. to ensure that he shall appear at trial as required. [S. 3164(c)]

(c) Discipline of Attorneys. In a case in which counsel (1) knowingly allows the case to be set for trial without disclosing the fact that a necessary witness would be unavailable for trial, (2) files a motion solely for the purpose of delay which he knows is frivolous and without merit, (3) makes a statement for the purpose of obtaining a continuance which he knows to be false and which is material to the granting of the continuance, or (4) otherwise willfully fails to proceed to trial without justification consistent with 18 U.S.C. S.3161, the court may punish such counsel as provided in 18 U.S.C. S.3162(b) and (c).

(d) Alleged Juvenile Delinquents. An alleged delinquent in custody whose trial has not commenced within the time limit set forth in 18 U.S.C. S. 5036 shall be entitled to dismissal of his case pursuant to that section unless the Attorney General shows that the delay was consented to or caused by the juvenile or his counsel, or would be in the interest of justice in the particular case.

11. Persons Serving Terms of Imprisonment.

If the United States Attorney knows that a person charged with an offense is serving a term of imprisonment in any penal institution, he shall promptly seek to obtain the presence of the prisoner for trial, or cause a detainer to be filed, in accordance with the provisions of 18 U.S.C. S.3161(j).

12. Effective Dates.

(a) The amendments to the Speedy Trial Act made by Public Law 96–43 became effective August 2, 1979. To the extent that this revision of the district's plan does more than merely reflect the amendments, the revised plan shall take effect upon approval of the reviewing panel designated in accordance with 18 U.S.C. S.3165(c). However, the dismissal sanction and the sanctions against attorneys authorized by 18 U.S.C. S.3162 and reflected in sections 10(a) and (c) of this plan shall apply only to defendants whose cases are commenced by arrest or summons on or after June 1, 1980, and to indictments and informations filed on or after that date.

(b) If a defendant was arrested or served with a summons before July 1, 1979, the time within which an information or indictment must be filed shall be determined under the plan that was in effect at the time of such arrest or service.

(c) If a defendant was arraigned before August 2, 1979, the time within which the trial must commence shall be determined under the plan that was in effect at the time of such arraignment.

(d) If a defendant was in custody on August 2, 1979, solely because he was awaiting trial, the 90–day period under section 5 shall be computed from that date.

[Effective October 27, 1997. Amended effective March 18, 2013; March 19, 2014.]

CRIMINAL JUSTICE ACT PLAN

I. AUTHORITY

Pursuant to the Criminal Justice Act of 1964, as amended, (CJA), section 3006A of title 18, United States Code, and the Guidelines for the Administration of the *Criminal Justice Act*, Volume VII, *Guide to Judiciary Policies and Procedures* (CJA Guidelines), the judges of the United States District Court for the Eastern District of Texas adopt this Plan for furnishing representation in federal court for any person financially unable to obtain adequate representation in accordance with the CJA.

II. STATEMENT OF POLICY

A. Objectives.

1. The objective of this Plan is to attain the ideal of equality before the law for all persons. Therefore, this Plan shall be administered so that those accused of crime, or otherwise eligible for services pursuant to the CJA, will not be deprived, because they are financially unable to pay for adequate representation, of any element of representation necessary to an adequate defense.

2. The further objective of this Plan is to particularize the requirements of the CJA, the Anti-Drug Abuse Act of 1988 (codified in part at section 848(q) of title 21, United States Code), and the CJA Guidelines in a way that meets the needs of this district.

B. Compliance.

1. The court, its clerk, the federal public defender and private attorneys appointed under the CJA shall comply with the CJA Guidelines approved by the Judicial Conference of the United States and/or its Committee on Defender Services and with this Plan.

2. Each private attorney shall be provided by the clerk of court with a then-current copy of this Plan upon the attorney's first appointment under the CJA or designation as a member of the Panel of Private Attorneys under the Criminal Justice Act (CJA Panel). The clerk shall maintain a current copy of the CJA Guidelines for the use of members of the CJA Panel and shall make known to such attorneys its availability.

III. DEFINITIONS

A. "Representation" includes counsel and investigative, expert, and other services.

B. "Appointed attorney" includes private attorneys and the federal public defender.

IV. PROVISION OF REPRESENTATION

A. Circumstance.

1. *Mandatory.* Representation *shall* be provided for any financially eligible person who:

a. is charged with a felony or with a Class A misdemeanor;

b. is a juvenile alleged to have committed an act of juvenile delinquency as defined in section 5031 of title 18, United States Code;

c. is charged with a violation of probation, or faces a change of a term or condition of probation (unless the modification sought is favorable to the probationer and the government has not objected to the proposed change);

d. is under arrest, when such representation is required by law;

e. is entitled to appointment of counsel in parole proceedings;

f. is charged with a violation of supervised release or faces modification, reduction, or enlargement of a condition, or extension or revocation of a term of supervised release;

g. is subject to a mental condition hearing under chapter 313 of title 18, United States Code;

h. is in custody as a material witness;

i. is seeking to set aside or vacate a death sentence under sections 2254 or 2255 of title 28, United States Code;

j. is entitled to appointment of counsel in verification of consent proceedings pursuant to a transfer of an offender to or from the United States for the execution of a penal sentence under section 4109 of title 18, United States Code;

k. is entitled to appointment of council under the Sixth Amendment to the Constitution; or

l. faces loss of liberty in a case and federal law requires the appointment of counsel.

2. *Discretionary.* Whenever a judge or United States magistrate determines that the interests of justice so require, representation *may* be provided for any financially eligible person who:

a. is charged with a petty offense (Class B or C misdemeanor, or an infraction) for which a sentence to confinement is authorized;

b. is seeking relief, other than to set aside or vacate a death sentence under sections 2241, 2254, or 2255 of title 28, United States Code;

c. is charged with civil or criminal contempt who faces loss of liberty;

d. has been called as a witness before a grand jury, a court, the Congress, or a federal agency or commission which has the power to compel testimony, and there is reason to believe, either prior to or during testimony, that the witness could be subject to a criminal prosecution, a civil or criminal proceeding, or face loss of liberty;

e. is proposed by the United States attorney for processing under a pretrial diversion program;

f. is held for international extradition under chapter 209 of title 18, United States Code.

Representation may also be furnished for financially eligible persons in ancillary matters appropriate to the proceedings pursuant to subsection (c) of the CJA.

B. When Counsel Shall Be Provided. Counsel shall be provided to eligible persons as soon as feasible after they are taken into custody, when they appear before a magistrate or judge, when they are formally charged or notified of charges if formal charges are sealed, or when a magistrate or judge otherwise considers appointment of counsel appropriate under the CJA, whichever occurs earliest.

C. Number and Qualifications of Counsel.

1. *Number.* More than one attorney may be appointed in any case determined by the court to be extremely difficult. In a capital case, at least two attorneys should be appointed.

2. *Qualifications.* Except as provided by section 848(q)(7) of title 21, United States Code, at least one attorney appointed in a capital case shall meet the qualification requirements set forth in sections 848(q)(5) and (6) of title 21, United States Code. Pursuant to section 848(q)(7), the presiding judicial officer, for good cause, may appoint an attorney who may not qualify under sections 848(q)(5) and (6), but who has the background, knowledge, and experience necessary to represent the defendant properly in a capital case, giving due consideration to the seriousness of the possible penalty and to the unique and complex nature of the litigation.

D. Eligibility for Representation.

1. *Factfinding.* The determination of eligibility for representation under the CJA is a judicial function to be performed by a federal judge or magistrate after making appropriate inquiries concerning the person's financial condition.

2. *Disclosure of Change in Eligibility.* If, at any time after appointment, counsel obtains information that a client is financially able to make payment, in whole or in part, for legal or other services in connection with his or her representation, and the source of the attorney's information is not protected as a privileged communication, counsel shall advise the court.

V. FEDERAL PUBLIC DEFENDER ORGANIZATION

A. Establishment.

1. Pursuant to subsections (g)(1) and (g)(2)(A) of the CJA, the Federal Public Defender Organization for the Eastern District of Texas is hereby established. Upon organization of the

federal public defender's office, the federal public defender shall notify this court that he or she is available to accept appointments for representation.

2. The Federal Public Defender Organization shall be capable of providing legal services throughout the district and shall maintain offices in Tyler, Beaumont and Sherman, Texas.

B. Supervision of Defender Organization. The federal public defender shall be responsible for the supervision and management of the Federal Public Defender Organization. Accordingly, the federal public defender shall be appointed in all cases assigned to that organization for subsequent assignment to staff attorneys at the discretion of the federal public defender.

C. Management of CJA Plan. The United States District Clerk shall be responsible for the systematic distribution of cases to and for the management of the CJA Panel subject to the provisions of the Plan for the Composition, Administrators, and Management of the Panel of Private Attorneys under the Criminal Justice Act, found at Appendix I of this CJA Plan, until such time as the Chief Judge, in his discretion, shall determine that the federal public defender shall assume such responsibility.

VI. PRIVATE ATTORNEYS

A. Establishment of CJA Panel. The existing, previously established panel of attorneys (CJA panel) who are eligible and willing to be appointed to provide representation under the CJA is hereby recognized.

B. Organization. The Plan for the Composition, Administration, and Management of the Panel of Private Attorneys under the Criminal Justice Act is found at Appendix I of this CJA Plan.

C. Ratio of Appointments. Where practical and cost effective, private attorneys from the CJA Panel shall be appointed in a substantial proportion of the cases in which the accused is determined to be financially eligible for representation under the CJA. "Substantial" shall usually be defined as approximately 25% of the appointments under the CJA annually throughout the district.

D. Choice of Counsel by Defendant. Where counsel is appointed by the court from the CJA Panel, the Court is under no obligation to appoint a particular attorney solely because the defendant desires that attorney.

VII. REPRESENTATION IN STATE DEATH PENALTY HABEAS CORPUS PROCEEDINGS UNDER 28 U.S.C. S. 2254

A. Appointment of Counsel. The court shall appoint the federal public defender with his or her consent, or other attorney who qualifies for appointment pursuant to section 848(q) of title 21, United States Code to represent financially eligible persons seeking habeas corpus relief in state death penalty proceedings under section 2254 of title 28, United States Code.

VIII. DUTIES OF APPOINTED COUNSEL

A. Standards. The services to be rendered a person represented by appointed counsel shall be commensurate with those rendered if counsel were privately employed by the person.

B. Professional Conduct. Attorneys appointed pursuant to the CJA shall conform to the highest standards of professional conduct, including but not limited to the provisions of the American Bar Association's *Model Rules of Professional Conduct* and *Model Code of Professional Conduct.*

C. No Receipt of Other Payment. Appointed counsel may not require, request, or accept any payment or promise of payment or any other valuable consideration for representation under the appointment, unless such payment is approved by order of the court.

D. Continuing Representation. Once counsel is appointed under the CJA, counsel shall continue the representation until the matter, including appeals or review by certiorari, is closed; until substitute counsel has filed a notice of appearance; until an order has been entered allowing or requiring the person represented to proceed Pro se; or until the appointment is terminated by court order.

IX. DUTIES OF LAW ENFORCEMENT AND RELATED AGENCIES

A. Presentation of Accused for Appointment of Counsel. Federal law enforcement and prosecutorial agencies, probation officers, and pretrial services officers in this district, and those acting on their behalf, shall promptly ask any person who is in custody, or who otherwise may be entitled to counsel under the CJA whether he or she is financially able to secure representation, and shall, in such cases in which the person indicates that he or she is not able, arrange to have the person promptly presented before a magistrate or judge of this court for determination of financial eligibility and appointment of counsel.

B. Pretrial Services Interview. A person in custody shall have the right to appointed counsel at the pretrial services interview. The probation officer conducting the interview shall notify the person in custody of his right to have an attorney appointed if he is financially unable to afford counsel. If the person in custody states that he desires representation at that time but is unable to afford counsel, the pretrial services interview being conducted shall terminate at that time. The person in custody shall then be taken before the appropriate judicial officer, who may make a determination as to the financial status of the person in custody and may appoint the Federal Public Defender or counsel from the panel of private attorneys if appointment of counsel is warranted.

C. Notice of Indictment or Criminal Information. Upon the return or unsealing of an indictment, the filing of a criminal information, or the filing of a petition to modify or revoke probation, the United States attorney or the "probation officer", as appropriate, immediately shall mail or otherwise deliver a copy of the document to appointed counsel, or to the defendant if he is without counsel, at the address shown on defendant's bond papers or to the jail in which the defendant is incarcerated.

X. MISCELLANEOUS

A. Forms. Standard forms, pertaining to the CJA and approved by the Judicial Conference of the United States or its Committee on Defender Services and prescribed and distributed by the Director of the Administrative Office of the United States Courts, shall be used, where applicable, in all proceedings under this Plan.

B. Claims. Claims for compensation of private attorneys providing representation under the CJA shall be submitted on the appropriate CJA form, to the office of the clerk of the court. That office shall review the claim form for mathematical and technical accuracy and for conformity with the CJA Guidelines, and, if correct, shall forward the claim form for the consideration of the appropriate judge or magistrate. The court will exert its best effort to avoid delays in reviewing payment vouchers and in submitting them for further processing.

C. Supersession. This Plan supersedes all prior Criminal Justice Act Plans of this court.

XI. EFFECTIVE DATE

This Plan shall become effective when approved by the Judicial Council of the Fifth Circuit.

[Dated December 18, 1990. Approved by the Judicial Council of the Fifth Circuit February 21, 1991. Amended July 24, 1999; March 19, 2014.]

APPENDIX I. COMPOSITION ADMINISTRATION AND MANAGEMENT OF THE PANEL OF PRIVATE ATTORNEYS UNDER THE CRIMINAL JUSTICE ACT

I. COMPOSITION OF PANEL OF PRIVATE ATTORNEYS

A. CJA Panel.

1. *Approval.* The Court shall establish a panel of private attorneys (hereinafter referred to as the "CJA Panel") who are eligible and willing to be appointed to provide representation under the Criminal Justice Act. The Court shall approve attorneys for membership on the panel after receiving recommendations from the "Panel Selection Committee," established pursuant to paragraph B. of this Plan. Members of the CJA Panel shall serve at the pleasure of the Court.

2. *Size.* The Court shall fix, periodically, the size of the CJA Panel. The panel shall be large enough to provide a sufficient number of experienced attorneys to handle the CJA caseload, yet small enough so that panel members will receive an adequate number of appointments to maintain their proficiency in federal criminal defense work, and thereby provide a high quality of representation.

3. *Eligibility.* Attorneys who serve on the CJA Panel must be members in good standing of the federal bar of this district, and have demonstrated experience in, and knowledge of, the Federal Rules of Criminal Procedure, the Federal Rules of Evidence, and the Sentencing Guidelines.

Subsection (b) of the Act provides, in part, that:

> Counsel furnishing representation under the plan shall be selected from a panel of attorneys designated or approved by the court, or from a bar association, legal aid agency, or defender organization furnishing representation pursuant to the plan.

However, when the district judge presiding over the case, or the chief judge if a district judge has not yet been assigned to the case, determines that the appointment of an attorney, who is not a member of the CJA panel, is in the interest of justice, judicial economy or continuity of representation, or there is some other compelling circumstance warranting his or her appointment, the attorney may be admitted to the CJA panel pro hac vice and appointed to represent the CJA defendant. Consideration for preserving the integrity of the panel selection process suggests that such appointments should be made only in exceptional circumstances. Further, the attorney, who may or may not maintain an office in the district, should possess such qualities as would qualify him or her for admission to the district's CJA panel in the ordinary course of panel selection.

4. *Terms.* The CJA Panel established pursuant to this Plan will consist of those attorneys appointed by the Court. The term of service on the panel shall be determined by the Court for each attorney at the time of appointment. The Court may in its discretion appoint an attorney to an indeterminate term of service on the CJA panel.

5. *Reappointment.* A member of the CJA Panel appointed for a specific term of years shall not be eligible for reappointment to the panel for the one year period immediately following expiration of his or her term, unless waiver of this restriction is certified by the Court.

6. *Application.* Application forms for membership on the CJA Panel shall be made available, upon request, by the Clerk of the Court. Completed applications shall be submitted to the Clerk of the Court who will transmit the applications to the Chairperson of the Panel Selection Committee.

B. Panel Selection Committee.

1. *Membership.* A Panel Selection Committee shall be established by the Court. The Committee shall consist of a district judge, a magistrate judge, an attorney member of the CJA Panel, the Federal Public Defender, and other judicial and private lawyer members representative of the district's geographic regions. The Committee shall select its own Chairperson.

2. *Duties.*

a. The Panel Selection Committee shall meet at least once a year to consider applications for the vacancies created by the terms expiring each year. The Committee shall review the qualifications of applicants and recommend, for approval by the Court, those applicants best qualified to fill the vacancies.

At its annual meeting, the Committee shall also review the operation and administration of the panel over the preceding year, and recommend to the Court any changes deemed necessary or appropriate by the Committee regarding the appointment process and panel management. The Committee shall also inquire annually as to the continued availability and willingness of each panel member to accept appointments.

b. If, at any time during the course of a year, the number of vacancies due to resignation, removal, or death significantly decreases the size of the panel, the Committee shall solicit applications for the vacancies, convene a special meeting to review the qualifications of the applicants, and select prospective members for recommendation to the Court for approval. Members approved by the Court to fill mid-term vacancies shall serve until the expiration of the term that was vacated, and shall be immediately eligible for reappointment notwithstanding the one-year restriction imposed by paragraph A(5) above, if applicable.

Section B. amended by General Order 96–16 dated August 1, 1996.

C. CJA Training Panel. The Panel Selection Committee may establish a "CJA Training Panel," consisting of attorneys who do not have the experience required for membership on the CJA Panel.

Training Panel members may be assigned, by the Court, to assist members of the CJA Panel in a "second chair" capacity. Training Panel members are not eligible to receive appointments independently, and shall not be eligible to receive compensation for their services in assisting CJA Panel members. Prior service on the CJA Training Panel is not a requirement for membership on the CJA Panel, nor will service on the Training Panel guarantee admission of an attorney to the CJA Panel.

II. SELECTION FOR APPOINTMENT

A. Maintenance of List and Distribution of Appointments. The Clerk of the Court shall maintain a current list of all attorneys included on the CJA Panel, with current office addresses and telephone numbers, as well as a statement of qualifications and experience. The Clerk shall furnish a copy of this list to each judge and magistrate. The Clerk shall also maintain a public record of assignments to private counsel, and, when appropriate, statistical data reflecting the proration of appointments between attorneys from the Federal Public or Community Defender office and private attorneys, according to the formula described in the CJA Plan for the District. The Chief Judge may, in his discretion, assign the responsibilities listed in this paragraph to the Federal Public Defender.

B. Method of Selection. Appointments from the list of private attorneys should be made on a rotational basis, subject to the Court's discretion to make exceptions due to the nature and complexity of the case, an attorney's experience, and geographical considerations. This procedure should result in a balanced distribution of appointments and compensation among the members of the CJA Panel, and quality representation for each CJA defendant.

Upon the determination of a need for the appointment of counsel, the judge or magistrate shall notify the Clerk of Court or Federal Public Defender, where appropriate, of the need for counsel and the nature of the case.

The Clerk of Court or Federal Public Defender shall advise the judge or magistrate as to the status of distribution of cases, where appropriate, as between the Federal Public Defender and the panel of private attorneys. If the magistrate or district judge decides to appoint an attorney from the panel, the Clerk or Federal Public Defender shall determine the name of the next panel member on the list who has handled, or assisted in, a case of equal or greater complexity than the case for which appointment of counsel is required, and who is available for appointment, and shall provide the name to the appointing judge or magistrate.

In the event of an emergency, i.e., weekends, holidays, or other non-working hours of the Clerk of Court's office, the presiding judge or magistrate may appoint any attorney from the list. In all cases where members of the CJA Panel are appointed out of sequence, the appointing judge or magistrate shall notify the Clerk of Court or Federal Public Defender as to the name of the attorney appointed and the date of the appointment.

III. COMPENSATION—FILING OF VOUCHERS

Claims for compensation shall be submitted, on the appropriate CJA form, to the office of the Clerk of the Court. The Clerk of the Court shall review the claim form for mathematical and technical accuracy, and for conformity with the *Guidelines for the Administration of the Criminal Justice Act* (Volume VII, *Guide to Judiciary Policies and Procedures*) and, if correct, shall forward the claim form for the consideration and action of the presiding judge or magistrate.

[Amended effective March 19, 2014.]

COURT–ANNEXED MEDIATION PLAN

I. Purpose. It is the purpose of this Mediation Plan to provide an alternative resolution for civil disputes. This plan is not to be considered or construed to be any abridgement of a litigant's right to a trial by jury as guaranteed by the 7th Amendment. Rather, it is designed to encourage parties to:

(a) Confront the facts and issues in the case;

(b) Engage each other in a discussion of those issues;

(c) Analyze the risk of litigation;

(d) Consider all the costs, monetary and otherwise, involved in the dispute; and

(e) Discuss methods of resolving the dispute.

II. Mediation Defined. Mediation is a private process in which an impartial third party, the mediator, facilitates communication and negotiation and promotes voluntary decision-making by the parties to the dispute.

III. Qualifications. Any person may serve as a mediator who has been ordered by the court to serve as a mediator or is approved by the parties. Any person selected as a mediator may be disqualified by the court.

IV. Ethics. Any person serving as mediator pursuant to this plan is subject to the Model Standards of Conduct for Mediators that were adopted by the American Bar Association in August 2005 or similar ethical standards or guidelines. The mediator shall advise mediation participants what ethical standards he or she will follow.

V. Compensation. Mediators shall be compensated at a reasonable rate. Absent agreement of the parties to the contrary, the cost for the mediator's services shall be borne equally by the parties to the mediation. The court has the right to review the reasonableness and apportionment of the mediator's compensation.

VI. Mediation Referral. Any civil suit may be referred to mediation through the agreement of the parties and/or by order of the court. Where the court enters an order referring the parties to mediation, the court shall appoint the mediator and establish a deadline for convening the mediation.

VII. Scheduling Mediation and Attendance.

A. The parties shall cooperate with the mediator in scheduling the mediation.

B. Attendance. All parties or party representatives shall be present at the mediation. Where attendance of a party is required, a party other than a person satisfies the attendance requirement if it is represented by a person or persons, other than outside or local counsel, with authority to enter into stipulations, with reasonable settlement authority, and with sufficient stature in the organization to have direct access to those who make the ultimate decision about settlement. In addition, if an insurance company's approval is required by any party to settle a case, a representative of the insurance company with significant settlement authority shall attend in person.

If it appears to the mediator that a case is not being reasonably evaluated by the representative present, the mediator may meet privately with one or both sides to request the analysis that has gone into the evaluation of the case, including the names and authority of the individual involved in the analysis. The mediator may request identified individuals or designate a level of authority to be present if a subsequent mediation is scheduled.

The mediator may vary the mandates of this section, with respect to scheduling and attendance of parties or party representatives in accordance with law.

C. Rescheduling. The mediator may reschedule the mediation to any date before trial with or without the approval of the parties. Any rescheduling beyond the date of trial must be approved by the court.

VIII. Confidentiality. All proceedings of the mediation, including statements made by a party, attorney, or other participant, are privileged and confidential in all respects.

The mediation process is to remain confidential. Mediation proceedings may not be reported, recorded, placed in evidence, made known to the trial court or jury, or construed for any purpose as an admission against interest. A party is not bound by anything said or done at a mediation conference unless a settlement is reached.

A mediator shall protect confidential information obtained by virtue of the mediation process and shall not disclose such information to anyone else. Notwithstanding the foregoing, a mediator may disclose information (1) that is required to be disclosed by operation of law; (2) that he or she is permitted by the parties to disclose; or (3) that is related to an ongoing or intended crime or fraud. If confidential information is disclosed, the mediator shall advise the parties that disclosure is required and will be made.

IX.   Mediation Report. Within five (5) days following the conclusion of the mediation, the mediator shall electronically file the mediation report with the court using the CM/ECF filing system. The report shall indicate whether the case settled, was continued, or whether the mediator declared an impasse.

[Effective October 27, 1997. Amended effective June 3, 1998; February 3, 1999; November 5, 1999; February 12, 2007; November 19, 2007; March 19, 2014.]

OTHER SELECTED PLANS AND POLICIES
PLAN FOR REIMBURSEMENT OF ATTORNEY EXPENSES IN CIVIL CASES

I. Overview of the Plan. It is the policy of this court to encourage members of the bar to represent parties who cannot afford counsel. To further this policy, the court adopts this Plan for Reimbursement of Attorneys' Fees and Expenses in Non–CJA Cases ("Plan").

When an attorney has been appointed to represent an indigent party in a civil or criminal matter that is not governed by the CJA, that attorney will be allowed to petition the court for reimbursement of certain attorneys' fees and expenses. Attorneys' fees and expenses, as defined in this Plan, (1) must be incurred in the preparation and presentation of the case and (2) shall be reimbursed using forms, procedures and instructions developed by the clerk's office that conform to the forms, procedures and instructions governing fee and expense reimbursement under the CJA. The total amount that may be reimbursed for all fees and expenses per attorney per case under the Plan shall not exceed $2,500, unless a greater amount is approved by both the chief judge and the presiding judge. Funding for this Plan shall be obtained from this court's non-appropriated fund.

II. Restrictions.

1. Any attorneys' fees and costs that are either waived or recoverable under the provisions of Title 18, U.S.C. or Title 28, U.S.C. or which have been recovered under any other plan of reimbursement shall not be reimbursed from the non-appropriated fund.

2. In no case shall an appointed attorney for a party who has been awarded costs and/or fees pursuant to a judgment in a suit before this court be eligible for reimbursement of costs and/or fees from the non-appropriated fund.

3. Only those attorneys' fees and costs associated with the preparation or presentation of a civil or criminal action that is not governed by the CJA in the United States District Court for the Eastern District of Texas shall be approved for reimbursement. No attorneys' fees and costs associated with the preparation or presentation of an appeal to the United States Court of Appeals or the United States Supreme Court shall be reimbursed from the non-appropriated fund.

III. Procedure for Requesting Reimbursement. All requests for reimbursement of attorneys' fees and expenses pursuant to this Plan must be filed within forty-five (45) days of the entry of judgment or completion of the matter as determined by the appointing judge. No interim payments shall be made.

The appointed attorney shall file with the clerk a request for reimbursement of fees and expenses. This request shall be filed using worksheets and forms which will be made available from the clerk's office. The clerk will forward any request for reimbursement initially to the judge to whom the case was assigned. Upon approval of the judge, the clerk, as custodian of the non-appropriated fund, will arrange for payment of the appointed attorney.

If an appointed attorney has withdrawn or has been dismissed prior to the entry of judgment, that attorney shall file a request for reimbursement within thirty (30) days of withdrawal or dismissal. Any work product or services for which reimbursement is requested from the non-appropriated fund shall subsequently be provided to newly-appointed counsel or if no new counsel is appointed, to the party.

IV. Allowable and Non–Allowable Attorneys' Fees and Expenses.

1. Allowable and non-allowable attorneys' fees and expenses under this Plan are the same as the current allowable and non-allowable fees and expenses under the CJA, unless otherwise noted in this Plan. Likewise, the payment rates and procedures for reimbursement of expenses and fees in this Plan are the same as the current payment rates and procedures governing the CJA, unless otherwise noted in this Plan.

2. Any expense not properly documented with receipts or other proof may be disallowed by the district or magistrate judge assigned to the case or the non-appropriated fund custodian.

3. Expenses that may be statutorily recovered or costs or fees taxed against a party or appointed counsel shall not be reimbursed by this Plan.

[Adopted effective February 11, 1998. Amended effective February 14, 2002; April 5, 2010; March 19, 2014.]

PLAN FOR THE ADMINISTRATION OF NON–APPROPRIATED FUNDS

General Order # 18–07

The following plan shall guide the administration and operation of the court's Non–Appropriated Fund (the "Fund") pursuant to the *Guide to Judiciary Policies and Procedures, Vol. 4, Chapter 6: Fees, § 670, Court's Local Attorney Admission Funds.*

I. Source of the Fund: Fees paid by attorneys who apply to join or renew admission to the Bar of the Eastern District of Texas in excess of the basic fee set by the Judicial Conference and all income derived from the corpus shall be the source of the Fund. Neither the fees nor the increase of the corpus are monies appropriated by Congress.

A. Fees for the fund shall be collected from members of the Bar triennially, i.e., once every three years. The current fee is $10 per year ($30 for three years). The fee shall be pro-rated for attorneys who become new bar members after the date that triennial fees are collected, e.g., an attorney who becomes a new bar member during the second year of the triennial cycle will be charged $20, not $30. The amount of the fee may be changed by further order of the court. Attorneys who fail to pay the fee within a reasonable amount of time from a due date established by the Clerk will lose their bar membership, subject to reinstatement upon payment of the fee.

II. Expenditures from the Fund: The Fund has been created for the benefit of both the Eastern District bench and bar in the interest of justice. The Fund shall not be used to supplement appropriated funds or to supplement the salary of any court officer or court employee. Expenditures shall be approved by the Chief Judge (or designee) and the Custodian of the Fund in accordance with the general principles specified in the *Guide to Judiciary Policies and Procedures, Vol 4, Chapter 6: Fees, § 670.20 Policies for Fund Expenditures.*

III. Custodian of the Fund: Unless a different person is named in writing by the Court, the Clerk of Court shall be Custodian of the Fund. The Custodian shall follow this Plan.

IV. Reporting by the Custodian: The Custodian shall submit an annual report to the Court certifying compliance with the Plan including reports of income, expenditures, investments, and balances in the Fund.

V. Successor Custodian: When a successor custodian is appointed, the outgoing custodian will prepare and sign the following:

A. A report of the financial condition of the Fund as of the last day of service by the outgoing custodian;

B. A statement of operations for the period since the last annual report; and

C. A statement of the balance in the Fund as of the outgoing custodian's last day in office.

The Successor Custodian shall review the final reports and issue a receipt to the Outgoing Custodian when satisfied with the accuracy of the final reports.

VI. Fund Controls: The Custodian will:

A. Segregate responsibilities for approving, preparing and signing checks;

B. Assign responsibility for monthly bank reconciliation to an individual with no disbursing authority: and

C. Identify and report unusual reconciling items.

VII. Investment Controls: The Custodian will:

A. Invest funds in excess of planned disbursements in interest bearing accounts, government securities, or money market funds invested in government obligations;

B. Title investments: United States District Court Non–Appropriated Fund;

C. Compare the income received on investments with the income specified by the terms of the security; and

D. Report investment income and losses on the annual accounting statements.

VIII. Expenditures Controls: The Custodian will:

A. Record expenditures as they occur;

B. Insure that expenditures are authorized by the Plan;

C. Support expenditures with original invoices and other original documentation; and

D. Make certain that checks contain the signature of an authorized Chief Judge and the Custodian.

IX. Accounting Systems Controls: All transactions will be posted as they occur. Entries shall contain at minimum:

A. a transaction reference number (check number, deposit ticket number, journal voucher);

B. a brief description of the transaction; and

C. a dollar amount of the transaction.

X. Non–Appropriated Debit Card Usage: The court will use a debit card when purchases are not able to billed directly to the non-appropriated fund account. The debit card policy and procedure is attached to this plan as Exhibit A.

XI. Audit: The Fund is subject to audit by the Administrative Office of the United States Courts.

The Fund will be audited on an annual basis by a disinterested person or outside auditor appointed by the Court.

This General Order supersedes and revokes the following General Orders: 93–20, 04–4, 05–21, and 07–07.

EXHIBIT A

Non–Appropriated Funds Debit Card Policy

The non-appropriated fund (NAPF) has been established by *General Order 18–05* and is designated as the attorney admission fund for the Eastern District of Texas. This fund should only be used for purposes that benefit both the members of the bench and bar within this district in the administration of justice.

The Non–Appropriated Funds Debit Card Policy covers account establishment, account operations, card usage, card security, account reconciliation, separation of duties, and internal control requirements for NAPF account transactions made by debit cardholders. This policy will be used in conjunction with the Plan for the Administration of the Non–Appropriated Funds, *General Order 18–05* and the *Guide to Judiciary Policy.*

I. Purpose of NAPF Debit Card Account

A. *Account Establishment.*

1.) Objectives of this account are:

a. to simplify and streamline the purchase process for NAPF expenditures using a debit card;

b. to make purchases for items or services using a debit card to further the administration of justice as directed by the NAPF plan; and

c. to purchase items or services using a debit card directly from providers instead of employees or judges seeking reimbursement for purchases made on behalf of this account.

2.) Designated signers are:

a. Rodney Gilstrap, Chief Judge

b. David A. O'Toole, Clerk of Court

B. *Account Information.*

1.) Account information is as follows:

a. **Financial institution:**

Southside Bank
113 West Ferguson St.
Tyler, Texas 75702
Phone: (903) 533–7343

b. Maximum account balance to remain on deposit: $5,000.

    c. Account type: non–interest bearing simple checking.

2.) Account services included are:

    a. check withdrawals;

    b. deposits which will not exceed the $5,000 maximum balance requirement;

    c. MasterCard debit transactions; and

    d. mailed monthly statements.

3.) Account services not allowed are:

    a. ATM withdrawals;

    b. mobile banking; and

    c. overdraft protection.

II. Account Operations Related to Debit Card Transactions.

A. *Debit Cardholder Responsibilities:*

1.) Each cardholder is responsible for:

    a. verifying the debit card information upon receipt of a bank card and activating the account;

    b. maintaining current debit card information, i.e., name changes, address information, and phone numbers;

    c. for purchases over $1,000, obtaining prior approval in writing from one (1) of the designated signers on the account before using an assigned debit card;

    d. using the debit card for appropriate expenditures pertaining to the NAPF plan and in accordance with the *Guide to Judiciary Policy, Volume 4: Court and Case Administration § 670.20(a)(b)(c), Policies for Fund Expenditure;*

    e. verifying funds are available for approved purchases;

    f. providing a written purchase approval, a legible receipt, and a brief description for each debit card transaction;

    g. documenting the basis for the expenditure on the receipt or as an attachment;

    h. submitting receipts timely to the financial manager for accurate recording of expenditures;

    i. keeping the debit card and personal identification number (PIN) secure at all times when the card is not in the finance safe; and

    j. reporting any loss, theft, or unauthorized use of the card immediately to the financial institution, financial manager, or designated signer.

2.) Each debit card has a spending control based on:

    a. a transaction limit of $2,500 per expenditure per day; and

    b. a daily maximum of $2,500 in expenditures per cardholder.

B. *Financial Manager Responsibilities:*

1.) The Financial Manager is responsible for:

    a. creating debit card applications with the financial institution after receiving approval from the Chief Judge or Clerk of Court;

    b. maintaining up-to-date information related to debit cards, i.e., debit card numbers, names, addresses, and phone numbers;

    c. ensuring debit cardholders are familiar with appropriate NAPF policies and authorized uses of the account;

    d. monitoring account activity related to debit card purchases on a weekly basis;

    e. maintaining receipts and accurately recording expenditures in a timely manner;

    f. recording transactions with proper approvals and expenditure documentation;

    g. identifying any theft, misuse, or unauthorized activity related to expenditures;

    h. maintaining current financial institution contact information; and

i. communicating with the financial institution any changes to transactions limits, cardholder maintenance, or debit card cancellations with approval from designated signers;

j. monitoring that NAPF monies are not used to augment any court appropriated funding in accordance with the *Guide to Judiciary Policy, Volume 4: Court and Case Administration, § 670.30.*

2.) The Financial Manager will:

a. replenish the account when the balance falls below $2,000 up to the maximum balance of $5,000, after determining that the charges made were approved and in compliance with the purposes of the NAPF and no suspicious activity is noted;

b. reconcile monthly bank statements in a timely manner;

c. report any suspicious debit card activity to the Chief Judge and Clerk of Court; and

d. review the account, including transactions, for audit compliance and IRS reporting (if required).

III. Account Reconciliation Process.

A. *Account Balance Reconciliation.*

1.) Debit cardholders will:

a. maintain receipts and approval documents for submission to the financial manager for reconciliation purposes. Receipts should be provided within forty-eight (48) hours of an expenditure; and

b. notify the financial manager of any potential expenditure exceeding $1,000 prior to making a purchase. In these cases, coordination with the financial manager is necessary in order to maintain sufficient account balances.

2.) The financial manager will;

a. compare expenditure documentation to transactions listed on the monthly bank statement;

b. review documentation for required approvals, description of items or services purchased;

c. notate the reconciliation date on the monthly statement;

d. submit the monthly reconciliation to another financial deputy for review; and

e. retain all financial statements and documents in accordance with the *Guide to Judiciary Policy, Vol. 10, Chapter 6: Records Management.*

3.) Account balance will:

a. be reviewed, at a minimum, every thirty (30) days during the monthly reconciliation process;

b. replenished with PHV fees from the U.S. Treasury collections made directly to the Court; and

c. not exceed $5,000 at any time.

IV. Debit Cards, Separation of Duties, and Internal Controls.

A. *Debit Cards.*

1.) Debit card issuance and availability:

a. Debit cards can be issued to account signers or other designated personnel with written authorization from the Chief Judge or Clerk of Court.

b. Debit cards can be revoked or cancelled at any time by an account signer and with written notification to Southside Bank.

c. Cards should be limited to a minimum number of staff due to security and internal control concerns.

2.) Current Cardholders:

a. Debit cards have been approved and issued to:

(1) Maria Dozauer, Chief Deputy

(2) Loretta Rogers, Procurement Manager

    b. Debit card limits of $2,500 are applied to each cardholder. (See II. Account Operations Related to Debit Card Transactions.)

B. *Separation of Duties.*

1.) Separation of duties is a vital component of internal controls to safeguard assets. This policy is written to document procedures for audit compliance and will be used in conjunction with *Guide to Judiciary Policy, Vol. 11, Chapter 2: Financial Management.*

2.) In order to maintain separation of duties, accessibility concerns, and proper card usage, the Court has adopted the following:

    a. Debit cards will be maintained in the finance department when not in use. Debit cards are placed in an internal safe with a combination lock inside the finance safe with an additional combination behind a secured door.

    b. Two financial deputies, at a minimum, are required to open the finance staff, therefore, debit cards are under dual control when in the safe.

C. *Internal Controls.*

1.) This account is subject to internal control policies stated in the *Guide to Judiciary Policy, Vol. 11, Chapter 2: Financial Management* including other internal control procedures implemented by the Court.

2.) The Clerk of Court, as custodian, must ensure all funds are safeguarded and accounted for in accordance with this Court's approved NAPF plan contained in General Order 18–05.

3.) Funds considered non-appropriated funds may not be commingled with any other funds held by the Court. Examples of court held funds are: registry, deposit, and unclaimed monies.

4.) This account is subject to various types of audits. These audits are:

    a. an annual local self-assessment conducted by the Clerk of Court;

    b. an annual independent audit conducted by a local certified public accounting firm; and

    c. a cyclical audit performed by the Administrative Office of the U.S. Courts every 3–4 years.

5.) Each audit will be conducted by independent contractors or designated staff. Designated staff will be independent of all processes related to the management and oversight of NAPF funds.

6.) Results, findings, or recommendations will be documented in official reports submitted to the Chief Judge and Clerk of Court for review and further action if required.

7.) If the Court determines the Southside Bank account is no longer required, the Chief Judge or the Clerk of Court will make a request in writing to the financial manager to close the account. All remaining funds on deposit will be transferred to another NAPF account maintained by the Court.

[Effective December 5, 2005. Amended effective March 26, 2009; March 19, 2014; March 1, 2018.]

SELECTED ORDERS

GENERAL ORDER 07–08. GENERAL ORDER REGARDING TRANSCRIPT RATES

At its September 2007 session, the Judicial Conference of United States approved a ten percent increase to the maximum original and copy transcript fee rates to be effective in fiscal year 2008, therefore

It is hereby ORDERED that pursuant to Title 28 U.S.C. § 753, the following transcript rates per page for civil and criminal cases are prescribed by the Court and are effective as of the date of this order:

	Original	First Copy to Each Party	Additional Copy to Same Party
Ordinary Transcript (30 day)	$3.65	$0.90	$0.60
14–Day Transcript	4.25	0.90	0.60
Expedited Transcript (7 day)	4.85	0.90	0.60
Daily Transcript	6.05	1.20	0.90
Hourly Transcript	7.25	1.20	0.90
Real Time Transcript	3.05	1.20	

This order supercedes General Order 03–6.

[Dated: October 22, 2007.]

GENERAL ORDER 13–20. GENERAL ORDER ADOPTING MODEL ORDER FOCUSING PATENT CLAIMS AND PRIOR ART TO REDUCE COSTS

The attached Model Order Focusing Patent Claims and Prior Art to Reduce Costs is ADOPTED effective immediately. A redline/strikeout version of the Federal Circuit's model order and the Local Rules Committee's commentary regarding the Eastern District's model order have been included to provide background information.

Case No.: _____

Plaintiff,

v.

Defendant.

[MODEL] ORDER FOCUSING PATENT CLAIMS AND PRIOR ART TO REDUCE COSTS

The Court ORDERS[1] as follows:

1. This Order supplements all other discovery rules and orders. It streamlines the issues in this case to promote a "just, speedy, and inexpensive determination" of this action, as provided by Federal Rule of Civil Procedure 1.

Phased Limits on Asserted Claims and Prior Art References

2. By the date set for completion of claim construction discovery pursuant to P.R. 4–4, the patent claimant shall serve a Preliminary Election of Asserted Claims, which shall assert no more than ten claims from each patent and not more than a total of 32 claims. Not later than 14 days after service of the Preliminary Election of Asserted Claims, the patent defendant shall serve a Preliminary Election of Asserted Prior Art, which shall assert no more than twelve prior art references against each patent and not more than a total of 40 references.[2]

3. No later than 28 days before the service of expert reports by the party with the burden of proof on an issue, the patent claimant shall serve a Final Election of Asserted Claims, which shall identify no more than five asserted claims per patent from among the ten previously identified claims and no more than a total of 16 claims. By the date set for the service of expert reports by the party with the burden of proof on an issue, the patent defendant shall serve a Final Election of Asserted Prior Art, which shall identify no more than six asserted prior art references per patent from among the twelve prior art references previously identified for that particular patent and no more than a total of 20 references. For purposes of this Final Election of Asserted Prior Art, each obviousness combination counts as a separate prior art reference.

4. If the patent claimant asserts infringement of only one patent, all per-patent limits in this order are increased by 50%, rounding up.

Modification of this Order

5. Subject to Court approval, the parties may modify this Order by agreement, but should endeavor to limit the asserted claims and prior art references to the greatest extent possible. Absent agreement, post-entry motions to modify this Order's numerical limits on asserted claims and prior art references must demonstrate good cause warranting the modification. Motions to modify other portions of this Order are committed to the sound discretion of the Court.[3]

[1] The parties are encouraged to discuss limits lower than those set forth in this Model Order based on case-specific factors such as commonality among asserted patents, the number and diversity of accused products, the complexity of the technology, the complexity of the patent claims, and the complexity and number of other issues in the case that will be presented to the judge and/or jury. In general, the more patents that are in the case, the lower the per-patent limits should be. In cases involving several patent families, diverse technologies, disparate claims within a patent, or other unique circumstances, absent agreement of the parties, the court will consider flexibly whether circumstances warrant expanding the limits on asserted claims or prior art references. The parties shall jointly submit any proposed modifications by the deadline for submission of proposed docket control or discovery orders, but in no event later than the deadline for service of initial disclosures.

[2] For purposes of this Order, a prior art instrumentality (such as a device or process) and associated references that describe that instrumentality shall count as one reference, as shall the closely related work of a single prior artist.

[3] This Order contemplates that the parties and the Court may further narrow the issues during pretrial proceedings in order to present a manageable case at trial.

Case No.: _____

Plaintiff,

v.

Defendant.

[MODEL] ORDER ~~LIMITING EXCESS~~ FOCUSING
PATENT CLAIMS AND PRIOR ART
TO REDUCE COSTS

The Court ORDERS[1] as follows:

1. This Order supplements all other discovery rules and orders. It streamlines the issues in this case to promote a "just, speedy, and inexpensive determination" of this action, as provided by Federal Rule of Civil Procedure 1.

Phased Limits on Asserted Claims and Prior Art References

2.   ~~Not later than 40 days after the accused infringer is required to produce documents sufficient to show the operation of the accused instrumentalities~~ By the date set for completion of claim construction discovery pursuant to P.R. 4–4, the patent claimant shall serve a Preliminary Election of Asserted Claims, which shall assert no more than ten claims from each patent and not more than a total of 32 claims.   Not later than 14 days after service of the Preliminary Election of Asserted Claims, the patent defendant shall serve a Preliminary Election of Asserted Prior Art, which shall assert no more than twelve prior art references against each patent and not more than a total of 40 references.[2]

3.   ~~Not later than 28 days after the Court issues its Claim Construction Order~~ No later than 28 days before the service of expert reports by the party with the burden of proof on an issue, the patent claimant shall serve a Final Election of Asserted Claims, which shall identify no more than five asserted claims per patent from among the ten previously identified claims and no more than a total of 16 claims.   ~~Not later than 14 days after service of a Final Election of Asserted Claims~~ By the date set for the service of expert reports by the party with the burden of proof on an issue, the patent defendant shall serve a Final Election of Asserted Prior Art, which shall identify no more than six asserted prior art references per patent from among the twelve prior art references previously identified for that particular patent and no more than a total of 20 references. For purposes of this Final Election of Asserted Prior Art, each obviousness combination counts as a separate prior art reference.

4.   If the patent claimant asserts infringement of only one patent, all per-patent limits in this order are increased by 50%, rounding up.

Modification of this Order

5.   ~~Upon a showing of diligence, and with due consideration for prejudice, a party may seek to modify this order for good cause shown.   Any request to increase the limits contained in this order must specifically show why the inclusion of additional asserted claims or prior art references is warranted.   *See In re Katz Interactive Call Processing Patent Litig.*, 639 F.3d 1202, 1312–13 (Fed. Cir. 2011).   A failure to seek such a modification will constitute acquiescence to the limits contained in this Order~~ Subject to Court approval, the parties may modify this Order by agreement, but should endeavor to limit the asserted claims and prior art references to the greatest extent possible. Absent agreement, post-entry motions to modify this Order's numerical limits on asserted claims and prior art references must demonstrate good cause warranting the modification.   Motions to modify other portions of this Order are committed to the sound discretion of the Court.[3]

[1] The parties are encouraged to discuss limits lower than those set forth in this Model Order based on case-specific factors such as commonality among asserted patents, the number and diversity of accused products, the complexity of the technology, the complexity of the patent claims, and the complexity and number of other issues in the case that will be presented to the judge and/or jury.   In general, the more patents that are in the case, the lower the per-patent limits should be.   In cases involving several patent families ~~or~~, diverse technologies, ~~or~~ disparate claims within a patent, or other unique circumstances, absent agreement of the parties, the court ~~should~~ will consider flexibly whether circumstances warrant expanding the limits on asserted claims or prior art references.   The parties shall jointly submit any proposed modifications ~~in their Federal Rule of Civil Procedure 26(f) Discovery Plan~~ by the deadline for submission of proposed docket control or discovery orders, but in no event later than the deadline for service of initial disclosures.

[2] For purposes of this Order, a prior art instrumentality (such as a device or process) and associated references that describe that instrumentality shall count as one reference, as shall the closely related work of a single prior artist.   ~~In cases involving several patent families or diverse technologies, or disparate claims within a patent, the court should consider flexibly whether circumstances warrant expanding the limits on prior art.~~

[3] This ~~Model~~ Order contemplates that the parties and the Court may further narrow the issues during pretrial proceedings in order to present a manageable case at trial.

EASTERN DISTRICT OF TEXAS LOCAL RULES ADVISORY COMMITTEE COMMENTARY REGARDING MODEL ORDER FOCUSING PATENT CLAIMS AND PRIOR ART TO REDUCE COSTS

Based on a request from the court, a working group of the Local Rules Advisory Committee undertook a review of the Model Order Limiting Excess Patent Claims and Prior Art prepared by the Federal Circuit Advisory Council's Model Order Committee (the "Model Order").   The working group's goal was to determine whether the Model Order, or some portion or variation of it, should be recommended for inclusion in the Local Rules or practice of the Eastern District.   In this regard, the working group's task was similar to that of the working group formed to undertake a review of the Federal Circuit Advisory Council's Model Order Regarding E–Discovery in Patent Cases.

After consideration, the working group determined that a revised version of the Model Order could be helpful to practice in the Eastern District. However, rather than incorporating the revised version in the Local Rules, the working group recommended including it as an appendix to the Local Rules, much like the version of the Model Order Regarding E–Discovery which was adopted by the court. This approach allows flexibility for both litigants and the court to tailor limits on asserted claims and prior art references based on differing facts, case to case. This approach also allows the court to decide questions that may arise regarding the interpretation or application of the recommended limits in a particular case without having to generally construe or interpret a local rule.

Recognizing the substantial work that went into the Model Order, as well as the policy considerations that motivated it, the working group began its effort with the Model Order as the baseline. The working group then made the following changes to the Model Order based on its members' experience with practice in the Eastern District representing both plaintiffs and defendants in patent cases:

1. Revising the title to emphasize the goal of reducing the burden on the court and lowering the expense of the parties by focusing patent cases to the issues at the core of the dispute.

2. Revising footnote 1 to reflect that the initial consideration of the limitations for a given case should be flexible, taking account of all relevant and foreseeable case specific issues. This is achieved by: 1) relocating and amending language from footnote 2 to demonstrate that all pertinent issues presented by the parties should be considered before imposing case specific limitations, and 2) changes to paragraph 5 requiring that "post-entry" motions to modify the order's numerical limits require a showing of good cause, while committing all other modifications to the court's discretion. The last sentence of footnote 1 is revised to reflect the fact that many judges require the parties to submit joint proposed docket control and discovery orders rather than a Fed. R. Civ. P. 26(f) discovery plan.

3. Extending paragraph 2's deadline to serve a Preliminary Election of Asserted Claims to the date set for the completion of claim construction discovery pursuant to P.R. 4–4. In the experience of the members of the working group, the costs associated with invalidity contentions and claim construction are two of the most significant costs incurred in the pretrial phase of patent cases. However, reducing the cost of invalidity contentions through an early election has proved elusive considering the early stage at which invalidity contentions are served and the overriding need to give both plaintiffs and defendants sufficient information to make a meaningful election. Targeting the cost of claim construction therefore seems to be a more feasible object of the initial narrowing. The working group extended the Model Order's deadline for the preliminary election to the date for the completion of claim construction discovery. The working group made this extension for two reasons. First, the later preliminary election reflects the fact that the completeness of an accused infringer's initial production of documents sufficient to show the operation of the accused instrumentality is often subject to reasonable debate. The later preliminary election allows time to resolve such matters. Second, the later deadline allows initial claim construction disclosures to take place, giving the parties the benefit of each other's claim construction positions in making their preliminary elections. At the same time, the preliminary election is early enough to avoid undue expense from briefing and arguing excess claim construction issues. Significantly, the timing of the preliminary election will also lessen the court's burden in preparing for, hearing, and ruling on claim construction issues.

4. Relocating and amending the second sentence of footnote 2 to footnote 1 where it better fits with the discussion of the flexible considerations appropriate before imposing limits in a given case. The slight amendments to the relocated sentence avoid implication that the Model Order's identified circumstances warranting enlargement of the order's limitations are exhaustive or limited to expanding only the number of prior art references, not also the number of asserted claims.

5. Revising paragraph 3's deadline to serve a Final Election of Asserted Claims to not later than 28 days before the service of expert reports by the party with the burden of proof, rather than the Model Order's tethering of the deadline to the issuance of the claim construction order. The principal object of the final narrowing is lessening the costs associated with expert witnesses and final preparation of the case for trial. Requiring the plaintiff to make its final election 28 days before the deadline to serve opening expert reports permits the parties' experts to focus on those claims and references that will remain for trial. The timing of the final election also gives the parties maximum opportunity to consider discovery and claim construction in making their election, and may move the presentation of any discovery disputes to points earlier in the case. The anticipated cost savings is

necessarily dependent on the issuance of a claim construction order sufficiently far in advance of the narrowing date to permit the parties to make a meaningful election. In the experience of the members of the working group, this will be the usual situation. However, should the court's claim construction order be delayed, the parties may need to seek an extension of the deadline to make their final election until some period after the issuance of the order, a matter committed to the court's discretion as discussed in point 7, below. Revision of paragraph 3's deadline for the final election also reflects the reality that many judges set deadlines for expert reports which are not tied to the issuance of the claim construction order.

6. Supplementing paragraph 3 by stating that each obviousness combination counts as a separate prior art reference. A small number of prior art references can be combined to form an exponentially greater number of bases for invalidity. For the limit on prior art references to be meaningful, each obviousness combination should count as a separate prior art reference. Not imposing this requirement for purposes of the preliminary election gives defendants increased flexibility to develop the appropriate combinations as discovery proceeds. However, by the time of the final election, each basis for invalidity should be specifically identified.

7. Revising paragraph 5 to provide greater flexibility to modify the order's requirements depending on the circumstances of the case. Flexibility allows the order to account for such things as adjustments in the disclosure deadlines necessitated by the timing of the issuance of the claim construction order or other case specific events. However, post-entry motions to modify the numerical limits of the order remain subject to a showing of good cause.

[Dated: October 29, 2013.]

GENERAL ORDER 14–03. GENERAL ORDER REGARDING TRACK B INITIAL PATENT CASE MANAGEMENT ORDER

In service of the objectives of Fed. R. Civ. P. 1, this Court has developed and implemented specialized case management procedures for the efficient handling of patent litigation. In particular, the judges of this district have developed similar, though not identical, case management schemes that have provided predictability and structure to litigation that can otherwise be unwieldy. These now familiar case management schemes, which this Order will collectively refer to as "Track A," have proven effective in achieving their objective.

However, drawing on the experience gained implementing Track A, the Court expects that additional efficiencies and cost savings can be achieved through the use of alternative procedures in appropriate cases, while still ensuring a full and fair opportunity for the speedy determination of each case on its merits. This alternative, "Track B," is meant to complement the default procedures of Track A, by providing a choice. Accordingly, the Court hereby **ORDERS** the following:

To secure the just, speedy, and inexpensive determination of every action and proceeding pursuant to Fed. R. Civ. P. 1, the Court authorizes the use of the attached Track B Initial Patent Case Management order in all patent cases.

This Track B Initial Patent Case Management Order will be deemed effective and entered of record upon 1) all parties filing a joint notice electing its entry, or 2) an order of the Court. Notices of election shall be filed on or before the date by which all defendants have filed an answer or motion pursuant to Fed. R. Civ. P. 12(b), and shall be accompanied by an appropriately styled, though otherwise unaltered, version of the attached Order for the Court's signature. Upon a Track B election, the Court will also enter its Standard Protective Order to facilitate the required disclosures. Should additional parties be added or consolidated into a case after the filing of a Track B election, such new parties may file any objection to the election on or before the date by which the party files an answer or Rule 12(b) motion. The Court will then consider and dispose of any objection appropriately. Absent the Court's request, no response to the objection should be filed.

IN THE UNITED STATES DISTRICT COURT
EASTERN DISTRICT OF TEXAS
TYLER DIVISION

PLAINTIFF,   §
                              §
                              §
v.   §   Civil No.: _____
                              §
                              §
DEFENDANT.   §

TRACK B INITIAL PATENT CASE MANAGEMENT ORDER

Pursuant to Fed. R. Civ. P. 16(b), the Court ORDERS the following:

1. Infringement Contentions and Licensing Disclosures. Within 14 days of all defendants filing an answer or motion pursuant to Fed. R. Civ. P. 12(b), a party claiming patent infringement shall serve its infringement contentions and accompanying production in compliance with P.R. 3–1 and 3–2. A party claiming patent infringement shall also produce all licenses or settlement agreements concerning the patents-in-suit and any related patent.

2. Initial Disclosures and Summary Sales Information. Within 30 days of service of infringement contentions, all parties shall serve Initial Disclosures per Fed. R. Civ. P. 26(a)(1). Each party opposing a claim of patent infringement shall also produce summary sales information reflecting the quantity of accused products sold in the United States and the revenues from those sales. For purposes of this disclosure, accused products include all products identified in the infringement contentions and all reasonably similar products (i.e., other products that a party should reasonably expect to be accused of infringement of the asserted claims after a full opportunity for discovery).

3. Good Faith Damages Estimate. Within 14 days of the service of Initial Disclosures and summary sales information, each party claiming patent infringement shall file a good faith estimate of its expected damages, including a summary description of the method used to arrive at that estimate. This good faith estimate is non-binding in that it will not serve to limit the damages a party may recover.

4. Invalidity Contentions. Within 14 days of service of the good faith estimate of expected damages, each party opposing a claim of patent infringement shall serve its invalidity contentions and accompanying production in compliance with P.R. 3–3 and 3–4.

5. Notice of Readiness for Management Conference. Within 5 days of the service of invalidity contentions, Plaintiff shall file a notice that the case is ready for management conference, which will then be set by the Court. The parties shall proceed with claim construction related disclosures (P.R. 4–1 through 4–3) according to the timing set by the local patent rules. All local patent rule deadlines after the filing of the P.R. 4–3 joint claim construction statement will be set at the management conference.

6. Conference of the Parties and Discovery Plan. At least 14 days before the date set by the Court for the management conference, the parties shall confer pursuant to Fed. R. Civ. P. 26(f). At least 7 days before the date set by the Court for the management conference, the parties shall jointly file a discovery plan that addresses each of the following:

a. the existence of related cases and the appropriateness of consolidation;

b. appropriate discovery limitations considering the case facts and likely value, including written discovery limits, deposition limits, the number of expert witnesses, and whether expert depositions should be authorized;

c. whether document production should proceed by request for production or mandatory disclosure;

d. whether the court should enter the EDTX Model Order Focusing Patent Claims and Prior Art to Reduce Costs or modifications thereto;

e. whether the court should enter the EDTX Model Order Regarding E–Discovery or modifications thereto;

f. amendments to the Standard Protective Order or entry of an agreed protective order;

g. the scheduling of the case for claim construction, including an appropriate limit on the number of claim terms for construction, and trial scheduling;

h. the appointment of a mediator and an appropriate mediation schedule;

i. clearly dispositive issues that warrant special scheduling;

j. the appropriateness of an expedited trial, consolidated claim construction and trial procedure, trial on limited issues, or a stipulation for post-trial mediation before the entry of judgment on the verdict;

k. any existing or likely discovery disputes; and

l. whether the parties consent to trial before a magistrate judge.

For any areas of dispute, the report should clearly define the parties' respective positions so that all issues can be decided at the management conference.

7. Initial Discovery Limitations. Prior to the management conference, discovery is limited to 5 interrogatories, 5 requests for production, and 5 requests for admission per side, absent leave of court or stipulation of the parties.

8. Management Conference Requirements. At the management conference, the parties shall be prepared to discuss each of the items addressed in paragraph 6 and any other issues that may be set by the Court. In particular, the Court is interested in setting a schedule and discovery limitations that are fair and adequate, but that also bear an appropriate relationship to the likely value of the case.

9. Sanctions. Failure to comply with this order invites sanctions. Additionally, while the Court is cognizant that this order requires certain disclosures that depend on the exercise of judgment at an early stage of the case, should case development reveal that a party's disclosures under this order lacked a good faith basis, were unreasonably sparse, or were intentionally misleading, appropriate sanctions will be imposed.

[Dated: February 25, 2014.]

GENERAL ORDER 14–04. GENERAL ORDER REGARDING COURTHOUSE SECURITY POLICIES [SUPERSEDED EFFECTIVE APRIL 1, 2018]

GENERAL ORDER 14–07. GENERAL ORDER REGARDING PRESENTENCE INVESTIGATION REPORTS

The following rules and procedures shall be in effect for all cases sentenced pursuant to the Sentencing Act of 1987:

(a) Not less than 35 days prior to the date set for sentencing, the probation officer shall disclose the presentence investigation report to the defendant, counsel for the defendant, and counsel for the government. Within 14 days thereafter, either counsel shall file with the Clerk's Office any objection(s) they may have as to any material information, sentencing classifications, sentencing guideline ranges, and policy statements contained in or omitted from the report. Such communication shall be in affidavit form and shall state specific objection(s) and evidence relied upon to assert the stated objection(s). Copies of all objection(s) shall be served contemporaneously on the probation officer and opposing party by the filing party. The original objections shall be placed under seal by the clerk and made a part of the record. Any response to filed objections by either counsel shall likewise be filed with the Clerk's Office and placed under seal, and the filing party shall contemporaneously serve the probation officer and opposing counsel.

(b) The probation officer shall disclose the entire presentence investigation report including the recommendation and recommended conditions of supervision (if applicable). Excluded from this disclosure is the probation officer's justification for the recommendation and other information covered under Fed.R.Crim.P. 32(b) (5)(A), (B) and (C). In that the recommendation is not material to the calculation of the sentencing guidelines, it is not subject to objection by either counsel. However, either counsel may object to a proposed condition of supervision or lack thereof.

(c) After receiving counsel's objection(s), the probation officer shall conduct any further investigation and make any revisions to the presentence report that may be necessary. The officer may require counsel for both parties to meet with the probation officer to discuss unresolved factual and legal issues.

(d) Seven (7) days prior to the date of the sentencing hearing, the probation officer shall submit the presentence report to the sentencing judge. The report shall be accompanied by an addendum setting forth any objection(s) counsel may have made that have not been resolved, together with the officer's comments thereon. The probation officer shall certify that the contents of the report, including any revisions thereof, have been disclosed to the defendant, counsel for the defendant, and counsel for the government, and that the contents of the addendum have been communicated to counsel and that the addendum fairly states any remaining objection(s).

(e) Except with regard to any objection made under subdivision (a) that has not been resolved, the report of the presentence investigator may be accepted by the Court as accurate. The Court, however, for good cause shown, may allow a new objection to be raised at any time before the imposition of sentence. In resolving disputed issues of fact, the Court may consider any reliable information presented by the probation officer, the defendant, or the government.

(f) The times set forth in this rule may be modified by the Court for good cause shown.

(g) The presentence report shall be deemed to have been disclosed to the defendant, the defendant's counsel, and the government (1) when a copy of the report is physically delivered; (2) one (1) day after the report's availability for inspection is orally communicated; (3) three (3) days after a copy of the report or notice of its availability is mailed.

(h) The original presentence report presented to the Court shall be filed under seal with the Clerk of Court. The defendant, counsel for the defendant, and counsel for the government shall be allowed to retain copies of the presentence report unless otherwise directed by the Court.

This general order supersedes its predecessor, General Order 94–38.

[Dated: March 24, 2014.]

GENERAL ORDER 18–6. GENERAL ORDER REGARDING COURTHOUSE SECURITY POLICIES

The following courthouse security policies are hereby adopted:

Weapons

The United States Marshals Service is directed to:

(a) Adopt procedures excluding the carrying of weapons by any and all persons other than U.S. Marshals, Deputy U.S. Marshals and their designees, and Court Security Officers in all federal courthouses and off-site federal court facilities in the Eastern District of Texas, with the exception of off-site U.S. Probation facilities. *See* 18 U.S.C. § 930.

(b) Post an appropriate notice regarding the weapons and electronic communication device policies at the public entrances of the courthouses in the Eastern District of Texas.

Electronic Communication Devices

This policy pertains to the use of electronic devices by court staff, members of the bar, and the public in the courthouses of the United States District Court for the Eastern District of Texas. The presiding judge(s) of a particular courthouse or courtroom may deviate by general standing order or courtroom exemption order as they may find appropriate.

For purposes of this Order, electronic communication devices include, but are not limited to: cellular phones; smartphones (e.g., iPhones, Android devices, and other mobile phones that perform many of the functions of a computer); laptop computers; tablets (e.g., iPads); devices that wirelessly connect to computers and smartphones to transmit data (e.g., smartwatches, earpieces, headphones, and fitness trackers); and audio recorders, still cameras, and digital or other types of video cameras that connect wirelessly to other devices.

(a) Who May Regularly Possess: Law enforcement officers, court employees, and other tenants of the courthouse may bring electronic communication devices into the courthouses.

(b) Who May Possess Subject to Screening and Clearance: Possession of electronic communication devices in courthouses is prohibited, except by:

(1) attorneys who present photo identification and a current bar registration card from this or any other federal or state court;

(2) staff associated with such attorneys who are vouched for by such attorneys;

(3) only after selection for a jury panel, jurors who are selected to serve may be allowed to maintain possession of cellular or smartphones for the duration of the trial so long as the device(s) remain in the jury deliberation room and are not brought into the courtroom, and such is approved by the presiding judicial officer; and

(4) other individuals who are granted specific permission by the presiding judge(s).

(c) Unauthorized Use: No person shall use an electronic communication device to take photographs or make audio or video recordings or transmissions of court proceedings in any public area in the courthouse or any other location in which court business and proceedings are conducted, unless authorized by a judicial officer.

Electronic communication devices may not be used for phone calls in the courtroom and may not otherwise be used in any manner that disrupts or interferes with judicial proceedings. Ring tones and any other functional sound produced by devices must be disabled while in the courthouse.

Failure to adhere to this policy may result in confiscation of the device, removal from the courtroom or courthouse, or other sanctions by the court.

This Order supersedes General Order 14–4 and will be effective April 1, 2018.

[Dated: April 1, 2018.]

UNITED STATES BANKRUPTCY COURT FOR THE EASTERN DISTRICT OF TEXAS

Including Amendments Received Through
February 1, 2019

PART I. COMMENCEMENT OF CASE; PROCEEDINGS RELATING TO PETITION AND ORDER FOR RELIEF

LBR 1001–1. GENERAL SCOPE; APPLICABILITY OF DISTRICT COURT LOCAL RULES; ATTORNEY ADMISSIONS AND DUTIES; JUDGE'S REGULATIONS AND CLERK'S INTERNAL OPERATING PROCEDURES

(a) Title. These Local Rules of Bankruptcy Procedure and Forms govern procedure in the United States Bankruptcy Court for the Eastern District of Texas. These rules may be abbreviated in citations as "LBR," and the forms may be abbreviated as a "TXEB Local Form." These rules must be construed consistently with the Federal Rules of Bankruptcy Procedure ("Fed. R. Bankr. P.") to secure the just, speedy, and inexpensive determination of every case and proceeding.

(b) Scope and Effective Date.

1. These Local Rules of Bankruptcy Procedure, as amended, become effective December 1, 2017. They supersede all Local Rules of Bankruptcy Procedure issued prior to that date, and they govern a case, contested matter, or proceeding pending or commenced after such date.

2. Any appendix or local form to these Local Rules may be modified by the Court without the necessity of a formal amendment to the Local Rules.

3. On motion of a party in interest or acting *sua sponte*, the Court may — for the convenience of the parties or other good cause — suspend or modify any Local Rule of Bankruptcy Procedure in a particular case.

4. These Local Rules of Bankruptcy Procedure may be superseded or modified with respect to documents filed, signed or verified by electronic means in compliance with the *Administrative Procedures for the Filing, Signing, and Verifying of Documents by Electronic Means* as set forth in *TXEB Appendix 5005* and such Appendix controls in the event of a conflict between its procedures and these Local Rules. The procedures for electronic filing set forth in *TXEB Appendix 5005* may be modified by the Court from time to time without the necessity of a formal amendment to these Local Rules.

(c) Incorporated Local Court Rules of the United States District Court (the "District Court Rules").

1. The District Court Rules governing attorney admission, suspension, and disbarment apply in the Bankruptcy Court; provided, however, "Court" or "Clerk" in the District Court Rules means the Bankruptcy Court or Bankruptcy Clerk when an attorney appears in Bankruptcy Court. No decision by the Bankruptcy Court shall affect the ability of an attorney to appear before the District Court.

2. Other Local Court Rules of the United States District Court for the Eastern District of Texas do not apply in the Bankruptcy Court, except as specified in these Local Rules of Bankruptcy Procedure or in a separate order of the Court.

(d) Admission Pro Hac Vice. A request for temporary admittance when an attorney is not admitted to practice in the Eastern District of Texas is generally governed by the Eastern District Court Rule AT–1(d) except that:

(1) the Court will rule upon the application and the applicant must attach a separate proposed order to the request;

(2) the prescribed admission fee is waived if the attorney has not previously asked for temporary admittance within one year of the request;

(3) the applicant must list, by case style, case number and application filing date, all other *pro hac vice* applications

granted in the Bankruptcy Court within the year preceding the application.

Attorneys frequently appearing before the Bankruptcy Court must seek admission to practice in the Eastern District of Texas pursuant to Eastern District Court Rule AT–1. Unless otherwise authorized by the Court, an attorney may not be admitted to practice before the Bankruptcy Court on a *pro hac vice* basis on more than three (3) occasions in any given 12–month period.

(e) Attorney Obligation to Court. An attorney must promptly notify the Court of a formal grievance proceeding, disbarment, suspension, or other status change which impacts such person's eligibility to practice law.

(f) [Reserved for Future Use].

(g) Judges' Regulations. Each bankruptcy judge may adopt regulations in accordance with Fed. R. Bankr. P. 9029(b). *TXEB Appendix 1001–g* contains the current regulations and must be carefully reviewed as the regulations may make important additions or modifications to these Rules.

(h) Clerk's Internal Operating Procedures. *TXEB Appendix 1001–h* contains the Clerk's internal operating procedures.

(i) Standards of Litigation Conduct. The standards for attorney conduct set forth in the Local District Court Rule AT–3 and the Texas Lawyers Creed apply in the Bankruptcy Court.

[Effective February 1, 2000. Amended effective February 1, 2001; October 1, 2002; October 17, 2005; March 1, 2008; December 1, 2009; November 1, 2012; December 1, 2017.]

LBR 1002–1.   COMMENCEMENT OF CASE

(a) Filing Requirements. *TXEB Appendix 1002–a* outlines the requirements for commencing a new bankruptcy case.

(b) Filing a Bankruptcy Petition Without Counsel. An individual may file bankruptcy or appear in Bankruptcy Court without legal counsel. An attorney must sign the bankruptcy petition and appear for other types of debtors — including partnerships, corporations, and trusts. If a debtor who is not an individual files a bankruptcy petition without legal counsel, then the Court will dismiss the bankruptcy case *sua sponte* or on motion of a party in interest. Unless excused by order of the Court, all petitions filed by an individual debtor without legal counsel, shall include copies of a picture identification card.

[Effective February 1, 2000. Amended effective October 1, 2002; October 17, 2005; November 26, 2013; December 1, 2017.]

LBR 1005–1.   CAPTION OF PETITION

The petition caption must reflect the Title 11 bankruptcy chapter under which the debtor seeks relief.

[Effective February 1, 2000. Amended effective October 1, 2002; October 17, 2005.]

LBR 1006–1.   FILING FEES

(a) Basis for Fees and Method of Payment.

1. The Clerk collects fees as authorized by 28 U.S.C. § 1930, including those prescribed by the Judicial Conference of the United States under the *Bankruptcy Court Miscellaneous Fee Schedule* and the *Electronic Public Access Miscellaneous Fee Schedule*.

2. The Clerk accepts the following forms of payment:

- cash;
- cashier's check;
- money order;
- check drawn from account of attorney or attorney's law firm, accepted subject to collection;
- debit or credit card account of an attorney as authorized by the Court.

3. Items must be made payable to "Clerk, U.S. Bankruptcy Court."

4. The Clerk maintains a list of attorneys and law firms whose checks have been dishonored. The Clerk may refuse to accept a check from an attorney or law firm on the list.

5. Payment is due on the date the petition is filed.

(b) Chapter 11 Noticing and Claim Fees. The Clerk periodically invoices the fees imposed by the Bankruptcy Court Fee Schedule established by 28 U.S.C. § 1930. Fees are payable on invoice receipt.

(c) The United States Trustee Quarterly Fee. The United States Trustee invoices and collects the Chapter 11 quarterly fees imposed by 28 U.S.C. § 1930(a)(6).

(d) Application to Waive Filing Fee by Chapter 7 Individual Debtor. A request by an individual debtor to waive the filing fee for Chapter 7 relief must be indicated on the Voluntary Petition and accompanied by an application and proposed order that substantially conform to Official Form 103B. If granted, the waiver shall apply to all fees prescribed by the Judicial Conference of the United States to be paid by a debtor in a Chapter 7 case, excluding a Chapter 7 debtor's request to convert the case to another chapter, which must be accompanied by the full filing fee for relief under that chapter.

(e) Application to Pay Filing Fee in Installments. A request by an individual debtor to pay a filing fee in installments must be indicated on the Voluntary Petition and accompanied by an application and proposed order that substantially conform to Official Form 103A. Such an application should be accompanied by an initial payment of not less than $75.

[Effective February 1, 2000. Amended effective February 1, 2001; October 1, 2002; October 17, 2005; November 1, 2012; December 1, 2015.]

LBR 1007–1.   LISTS, SCHEDULES, STATEMENTS, AND OTHER DOCUMENTS; TIME LIMITS

(a) Master Mailing List (Matrix).

1. *General Requirements.*

(A) At the time of filing a voluntary petition [or within 14 days after the entry of an order for relief following the filing of an involuntary petition], the debtor [or petitioning creditor or partner, upon order of the Court] must file an alphabetized creditor list which includes the name and last known mailing address for every creditor.

(B) A master mailing list (matrix) must also include those agencies and officers of the United States required to receive notice in Fed. R. Bankr. P. 2002(j).

(C) The designated national address for service upon the Internal Revenue Service is contained in *TXEB Appendix 1007–b–1.*

2. *Partnership Filings.* If a debtor is a partnership, the master mailing list (matrix) must contain the names and current mailing addresses of each general and limited partner.

3. *Corporate Filings.* If a debtor is a corporation, the master mailing list (matrix) must contain:

(A) the names and current mailing addresses of the present officers and directors or, if none, the immediate past officers and directors;

(B) the name and last known address or place of business of each equity security holder.

4. *Form of Mailing List.* The master mailing list (matrix) must be in the format prescribed by *TXEB Appendix 1007–b–5.* The format may be changed from time to time without amendments to these Local Rules of Bankruptcy Procedure.

5. *Accuracy of Information.*

(A) The debtor and debtor's attorney [or petitioning creditor or partner, upon order of the Court] are responsible for the preparation of the master mailing list required by this Local Rule of Bankruptcy Procedure.

(B) The debtor must verify the list attesting to the accuracy and completeness of the information. The Verification of the Master Mailing List (Matrix) must conform to *TXEB Appendix 1007–b–6* and shall serve as the cover page to the master mailing list (matrix).

(C) A debtor should exercise care to insure that designated creditor addresses as described in § 342(c)(2) are utilized in the master mailing list (matrix).

6. *Amendment of Master Mailing List (Matrix).*

(A) When an amended schedule is filed which adds or deletes a new entity, an amended master mailing list (matrix) must be filed in the same format as the original list. The amendment must be limited to the names and addresses to be added or deleted.

(B) The Notice of Change in Schedule of Creditors must be in the format shown in *TXEB Appendix 1007–b–7,* and it must be the cover page to the amended mailing list (matrix) and amended schedule of creditors.

(b) Motion for Extension of Time to File Schedules and Statements.

1. An initial motion by a debtor to obtain an extension of the 14–day deadline to file schedules, statements and other documents under Fed. R. Bankr. P. 1007(c) shall not require

negative notice language and must be served only upon the case or standing trustee, any committee elected under § 705 or appointed under § 1102 of the Bankruptcy Code, and in a case under Chapter 7 or Chapter 11, the United States Trustee.

2. Though governed by the service requirements set forth in the preceding paragraph, any motion for an additional extension, including a motion filed pursuant to § 521(i)(3) or § 1116(3), shall be supported by the debtor's affidavit or unsworn declaration under penalty of perjury as provided in 28 U.S.C. § 1746 establishing the existence of extraordinary and compelling circumstances necessitating an extension beyond twenty-eight (28) days from the petition date.

3. Any untimely motion for extension of time shall be subject to immediate dismissal absent evidence of excusable neglect.

(c) Redaction of Personal Identifiers. Pursuant to Fed. R. Bankr. P. 9037 and the exemptions contained therein, a debtor must refrain from including, or shall redact where inclusion is necessary, the following personal identifiers from all lists, schedules and statements filed with the Court, unless ordered by the Court to do otherwise:

- **Social Security Numbers:** if disclosure of a social security number is required, only the last four digits of that number should be used;

- **Names of Minor Children:** if disclosure of the identity of any minor child is required, only the initials of that child should be used;

- **Dates of Birth:** if disclosure of an individual's date of birth is required by any statement or schedule, only the year should be used;

- **Financial Account Numbers:** if disclosure of any financial account number is required, only the last four digits of that number should be used.

The responsibility for redacting these personal identifiers rests solely with the debtor and debtor's counsel. The Court will not review documents for compliance with this rule. Parties are cautioned that failure to redact these personal identifiers may subject them to the full disciplinary power of the Court.

(d) Alphabetical Listing of Creditors. All creditors listed on Schedules D, E/F must be arranged in alphabetical order.

(e) Payment Advices Required by § 521(a)(1)(B)(iv). Copies of all payment advices or other evidence of payment from any employer received by an individual debtor in a Chapter 7 or Chapter 13 case within 60 days before the filing of the petition shall not be filed with the Court unless otherwise ordered. In lieu thereof, such payment advices shall be provided by the debtor:

(1) to the case or standing Trustee at least seven (7) days prior to the first date set for the § 341 meeting of creditors and, only upon request, to the United States Trustee; and

(2) to any creditor who serves upon the debtor a written request for such copies within seven (7) days following the conclusion of the § 341 meeting of creditors.

[Effective February 1, 2000. Amended effective October 1, 2002; October 17, 2005; March 1, 2008; December 1, 2009; November 1, 2012; December 1, 2015; December 1, 2017.]

LBR 1009–1. AMENDMENTS OF VOLUNTARY PETITIONS, LISTS, SCHEDULES, AND STATEMENTS

(a) **Titles and Effect of Amendment.** An amendment to the petition, lists, schedules or statements required under the Federal or Local Rules of Bankruptcy Procedure must be entitled "AMENDMENT TO (name of document)" and the amended document should clearly reveal the nature of the change being effectuated by the amendment [**i.e., designations of ADDED, DELETED, ALTERED, etc.**]. The Notice of Change in schedule of creditors must be in the format shown in *TXEB Appendix 1007–b–7*, and it must be the cover page to the new list and amended schedule of creditors. Additional copies are no longer required.

(b) **Required Service.**

1. A debtor must serve any amended schedule, statement, master mailing list (matrix), or list of the twenty (20) largest unsecured creditors upon the case or standing trustee, if any, the United States Trustee, and any party affected by such amendment.

2. If an amendment adds a creditor to the schedule of assets and liabilities, a debtor should exercise care to insure that the full tax identification number is provided in the copy of any amended schedule served upon any added creditor as described in § 342(c), while redacting such tax identification number in the amended schedule filed with the Court.

(c) **Notice to Newly Scheduled or Added Entities.** In addition to all parties entitled to notice of such amendments under the Federal Rules of Bankruptcy Procedure, a debtor must serve a notice of the filing of amended schedules and/or statements on each entity which has been newly added to the matrix or newly scheduled in the amended documents, and must also attach a copy of: (1) the *Notice of Chapter # Bankruptcy Case*; (2) any *Order Fixing Last Date for Filing Claims*; (3) any *Order Confirming Plan*; and/or (4) any *Discharge of Debtor* which have been entered in the case.

(d) **Notice of Amendment to Exemptions.** An amended Schedule of Property Claimed as Exempt (Schedule C) must be served on the master mailing list (matrix) as constituted by the Court on the date of service or it will be stricken.

(e) **Certificate of Service.** When notice of an amendment is required by this Local Rule of Bankruptcy Procedure, a certificate of service must be filed. LBR 9013(e) governs the format of a certificate of service.

[Effective February 1, 2000. Amended effective October 1, 2002; October 17, 2005; December 1, 2017.]

LBR 1015–1. CONSOLIDATION OR JOINT ADMINISTRATION OF CASES PENDING IN SAME COURT

(a) **Related Debtors.** When a joint administration or consolidation motion is filed, the bankruptcy judge with the lowest case filing number determines the motion.

(b) **Filing by Spouses.** When spouses file a joint petition, the Court deems the joint petition an order directing joint administration, unless the Court orders otherwise based on a party in interest's motion.

(c) **Related Entities.** A motion requesting joint administration of two or more pending bankruptcy cases must be filed in each such case and:

(1) contain the name and case number of cases sought to be jointly administered;

(2) address whether the practicalities of providing professional services to the jointly-administered estates preclude any professional person from effectively or accurately separating the services rendered solely for the benefit of one bankruptcy estate vis-a-vis another, thus justifying the submission of a consolidated application for compensation to be filed solely in the main case, accompanied by a proposal for proper apportionment of accumulated fees and expenses between/among the respective bankruptcy estates, subject to the right of any party-in-interest to object to the proposed apportionment;

(3) identify any existing administrative or scheduling order which might require modification; and

(4) attach a proposed consolidated master mailing list (matrix) in the affected cases for future noticing requirements.

[Effective February 1, 2000. Amended effective October 17, 2005; December 1, 2009.]

LBR 1017–1. DISMISSAL OR CONVERSION OF CASE; SUSPENSION

(a) **Definition of "Want of Prosecution".** For purposes of Fed. R. Bankr. P. 1017 and as used in these Local Rules of Bankruptcy Procedure, "want of prosecution" includes, but is not limited to, the following:

- failure to timely file schedules, statements and other required documents, including the Chapter 12 or 13 plan;

- failure to timely and diligently prosecute the filing of a plan or disclosure statement;

- failure to timely and diligently prosecute the confirmation of a plan or approval of a disclosure statement;

- failure to appear at any hearing as ordered by the Court, including the first meeting of creditors;

- failure to pay fees required under 28 U.S.C. § 1930; or

- failure to furnish to the case or standing trustee, if any, or to the United States Trustee information which is reasonably required to supervise the administration of the estate, including, but not limited to, monthly operating reports, proof of insurance on estate assets and evidence of payment of post-petition taxes.

(b) Dismissals.

1. A motion to dismiss a case filed by any party in interest must be served upon the master mailing list (matrix) as constituted by the Court on the date of service unless the dismissal is sought under § 707(a)(3), § 707(b), § 1307(b), § 1307(c), § 1307(e) or for failure to pay the required filing fee, in which service of the motion pursuant to the applicable section of LBR 9013(f)(1) shall suffice.

2. A trustee or the United States Trustee is given the discretion to schedule and provide notice of a hearing to consider a dismissal motion which he/she has filed. Such hearing may only be scheduled on the regularly-scheduled docket date for trustee dismissal motions under that chapter which is not less than: (1) 14 days from the date of filing for dismissal motions under § 707(a)(3) or § 707(b); or (2) 21 days from the date of filing for all other dismissal motions. Such trustee shall give notice of that scheduled hearing in boldface, large font on the initial page of the dismissal motion in lieu of the negative notice language otherwise required.

3. Any dismissal motion, other than one filed by the trustee with a designated hearing date, must contain the following 14–day negative notice language, which must appear as presented and be located in the motion text — preferably on the initial page:

14–DAY NEGATIVE NOTICE—LBR 1017(b):

Your rights may be affected by the relief sought in this pleading. You should read this pleading carefully and discuss it with your attorney, if you have one in this bankruptcy case. If you oppose the relief sought by this pleading, you must file a written objection, explaining the factual and/or legal basis for opposing the relief.

No hearing will be conducted on this Motion unless a written objection is filed with the Clerk of the United States Bankruptcy Court and served upon the party filing this pleading *WITHIN FOURTEEN (14) DAYS FROM THE DATE OF SERVICE* shown in the certificate of service unless the Court shortens or extends the time for filing such objection. If no objection is timely served and filed, this pleading shall be deemed to be unopposed, and the Court may enter an order granting the relief sought. If an objection is filed and served in a timely manner, the Court will thereafter set a hearing with appropriate notice. If you fail to appear at the hearing, your objection may be stricken. The Court reserves the right to set a hearing on any matter.

4. If a motion is requesting dismissal with prejudice to re-filing for any period of time, such request must be referenced in both the title of the motion and in the title of the proposed order.

5. A movant requesting dismissal of a case pursuant to Bankruptcy Code § 1112(b) may waive the 30–day hearing requirement under § 1112(b)(3), if desired, in the title of the motion.

Title Example: Motion to Convert or Dismiss Chapter 11 Case, Waiver of 30–Day Hearing Requirement, and Request for Hearing in Beaumont, Texas

If a waiver is not filed, the Court will convene a hearing within the required 30 days in the division most convenient to the Court.

(c) Trustee's Motion to Waive Automatic Dismissal of Case. A motion by a Chapter 7 trustee or the Chapter 13 trustee to waive the automatic dismissal provisions of § 521(i)(1), pursuant to the grounds set forth in § 521(i)(4), shall contain 14–day negative notice language, as utilized in LBR 1017(b)(3), and contain a certificate of service reflecting service on the master mailing list (matrix) as constituted by the Court on the date of service.

(d) Conversion.

1. A debtor's right to convert a case from Chapter 12 to Chapter 7 pursuant to Bankruptcy Code § 1208(a), or from Chapter 13 to Chapter 7 pursuant to Bankruptcy Code § 1307(a), is accomplished by the filing of a notice of conversion served upon the master mailing list (matrix) as constituted by the Court on the date of service. A debtor's motion to convert pursuant to § 1208(a) or § 1307(a) shall be deemed a notice of conversion.

2. Any other conversion motion, including one filed by the debtor pursuant to § 706(a) or § 1112(a), must be served upon the master mailing list (matrix) as constituted by the Court on the date of service and must contain the following 14–day negative notice language, must appear as presented, and it must be located in the motion text — preferably on the initial page:

14–DAY NEGATIVE NOTICE—LBR 1017(d):

Your rights may be affected by the relief sought in this pleading. You should read this pleading carefully and discuss it with your attorney, if you have one in this bankruptcy case. If you oppose the relief sought by this pleading, you must file a written objection, explaining the factual and/or legal basis for opposing the relief.

No hearing will be conducted on this Motion unless a written objection is filed with the Clerk of the United States Bankruptcy Court and served upon the party filing this pleading *WITHIN FOURTEEN (14) DAYS FROM THE DATE OF SERVICE* shown in the certificate of service unless the Court shortens or extends the time for filing such objection. If no objection is timely served and filed, this pleading shall be deemed to be unopposed, and the Court may enter an order granting the relief sought. If an objection is filed and served in a timely manner, the Court will thereafter set a hearing with appropriate notice. If you fail to appear at the hearing, your objection may be stricken. The Court reserves the right to set a hearing on any matter.

3. A movant requesting conversion of a case pursuant to Bankruptcy Code § 1112(b) may waive the 30–day hearing requirement under § 1112(b)(3), if desired, in the title of the motion.

Title Example: Motion to Convert or Dismiss Chapter 11 Case, Waiver of 30–Day Hearing Requirement, and Request for Hearing in Beaumont, Texas

If a waiver is not filed, the Court will convene a hearing within the required 30 days in the division most convenient to the Court.

[Effective February 1, 2000. Amended effective February 1, 2001; October 1, 2002; October 17, 2005; March 1, 2008; December 1, 2009; January 26, 2011; December 1, 2015; December 1, 2017.]

LBR 1019–1. FILING OF CHAPTER 13 TRUSTEE FINAL REPORTS UPON CONVERSION TO CHAPTER 7

If a fee application is pending at the time that a Chapter 13 case is converted to a case under Chapter 7, the period under Fed. R. Bankr. P. 1019(5)(B)(ii) for the filing of a final report by the Chapter 13 Trustee is extended to 60 days, with further extensions available upon proper motion.

[Effective November 1, 2012.]

LBR 1020–1. SMALL BUSINESS CHAPTER 11 REORGANIZATION CASE

(a) Determination of "Small Business Debtor" Status. A party seeking to object to a Chapter 11 debtor's statement in its petition regarding whether it meets the definition of a "small business debtor" under § 101(51D) of the Bankruptcy Code shall file a Motion to Determine Small Business Debtor Status. The motion must contain the 21–day negative notice language described in LBR 9007(a) and shall be served upon the parties designated by LBR 9013(f). A proposed order shall accompany the motion.

(b) Determination of Status of Unsecured Creditors' Committee. A party seeking to challenge the effectiveness of an official committee of unsecured creditors appointed under § 1102(a)(1) of the Bankruptcy Code for the purpose of imposing the designation of a "small business debtor" under § 101(51D) shall file a Motion for Determination of Status of Unsecured Creditors' Committee. The motion must contain the 21–day negative notice language described in LBR 9007(a) and shall be served upon the parties designated by LBR 9013(f). A proposed order shall accompany the motion.

[Effective October 17, 2005. Amended effective December 1, 2009.]

PART II. OFFICERS AND ADMINISTRATION; NOTICES; MEETINGS; EXAMINATIONS; ELECTIONS; ATTORNEYS AND ACCOUNTANTS

LBR 2002–1. NOTICES TO CREDITORS, EQUITY SECURITY HOLDERS, UNITED STATES, AND UNITED STATES TRUSTEE

(a) 21–Day Notice. Unless otherwise ordered by the Court, the Clerk notices the matters listed in Fed. R. Bankr. P. 2002(a).

(b) 28–Day Notice. Unless otherwise ordered by the Court, the Clerk notices all matters listed in Fed. R. Bankr. P. 2002(b).

(c) Notice Content. A hearing notice must identify the matter set for hearing, the court location, the hearing date, and the hearing commencement time.

(d) Returned Notices. Upon receipt of a returned undeliverable notice of the meeting of creditors, the debtor or debtor's counsel must attempt to find correct addresses for each returned notice and re-serve the affected parties. A debtor must confirm the fulfillment of this duty by filing a certificate of service within 14 days after the conclusion of the first meeting of creditors. At the time of certification, a debtor must also amend the master mailing list (matrix) pursuant to LBR 1007(b)(7). If corrected addresses cannot be found, the debtor or counsel must identify the creditors who cannot be found by written notification to the Clerk. The Clerk then may remove these creditors from the master mailing list.

(e) Service and Notice to the United States Trustee. The United States Trustee has a standing request not to receive service of pleadings nor notice of hearings in a Chapter 12 or Chapter 13 case.

[Effective February 1, 2000. Amended effective October 1, 2002; October 17, 2005; December 1, 2009.]

LBR 2004–1. EXAMINATION

(a) Motion and Notice. A motion for an examination under Fed. R. Bankr. P. 2004 must:

(1) contain the following 14–day negative notice language, which must appear as presented, and it must be located in the motion text — preferably on the initial page:

14–DAY NEGATIVE NOTICE—LBR 2004(a):

Your rights may be affected by the relief sought in this pleading. You should read this pleading carefully and discuss it with your attorney, if you have one in this bankruptcy case. If you oppose the relief sought by this pleading, you must file a written objection, explaining the factual and/or legal basis for opposing the relief.

No hearing will be conducted on this Motion unless a written objection is filed with the Clerk of the United States Bankruptcy Court and served upon the party filing this pleading *WITHIN FOURTEEN (14) DAYS FROM THE DATE OF SERVICE* shown in the certificate of service unless the Court shortens or extends the time for filing such objection. If no objection is timely served and filed, this pleading shall be deemed to be unopposed, and the Court may enter an order granting the relief sought. If an objection is filed and served in a timely manner, the Court will thereafter set a hearing with appropriate notice. If you fail to appear at the hearing, your objection may be stricken. The Court reserves the right to set a hearing on any matter.

(2) contain a certificate of conference tailored to one of the following three options:

(A) reflects that the parties agreed to a date, time, and place for examination;

(B) explains why the parties were unable to confer; or

(C) explains that the parties conferred but could not reach an agreement.

(3) describe the scope of examination;

(4) itemize requested document categories;

(5) provide a minimum of 28 days' written notice of the proposed examination date to the proposed examinee, the proposed examinee's counsel, the debtor's counsel, any trustee, any committee's counsel, and the United States Trustee; and

(6) attach a proposed order which contains the date, time, and location of the examination.

(b) Duration. Unless otherwise authorized by the Court or stipulated by the parties, an examination under Fed. R. Bankr. P. 2004 shall not exceed three (3) hours.

(c) Sanctions. The Court may impose sanctions if it finds that an examination request was unreasonably sought or resisted under Fed. R. Bankr. P. 2004 or LBR 2004.

(d) Exception. If a contested matter or an adversary proceeding is pending, then the adversary discovery rules govern, and Fed. R. Bankr. P. 2004 and LBR 2004 do not apply.

[Effective February 1, 2000. Amended effective October 1, 2002; October 17, 2005; December 1, 2009; December 1, 2017.]

LBR 2014–1. EMPLOYMENT OF PROFESSIONAL PERSONS

(a) Content of Application. In addition to the information required by Fed. R. Bankr. P. 2014, an application to employ a professional person shall:

(1) contain the following 14–day negative notice language, which must appear as presented, and it must be located in the application text — preferably on the initial page:

14–DAY NEGATIVE NOTICE—LBR 2014(a):

Your rights may be affected by the relief sought in this pleading. You should read this pleading carefully and discuss it with your attorney, if you have one in this bankruptcy case. If you oppose the relief sought by this pleading, you must file a written objection, explaining the factual and/or legal basis for opposing the relief. No hearing will be conducted on this Application unless a written objection is filed with the Clerk of the United States Bankruptcy Court and served upon the party filing this pleading *WITHIN FOURTEEN (14) DAYS FROM THE DATE OF SERVICE* shown in the certificate of service unless the Court shortens or extends the time for filing such objection. If no objection is timely served and filed, this pleading shall be deemed to be unopposed, and the Court may enter an order granting the relief sought. If an objection is filed and served in a timely manner, the Court will thereafter set a hearing with appropriate notice. If you fail to appear at the hearing, your objection may be stricken. The Court reserves the right to set a hearing on any matter.

(2) identify the petition filing date;

(3) identify the chapter under which the petition was filed;

(4) identify the mailing address, state bar number (if an attorney), telephone number, and e-mail address of the professional to be employed;

(5) identify the name(s) of any other professionals in the same profession employed pursuant to court order by the same applicant and, if there is any overlap in proposed services, provide an explanation of why additional professionals are needed;

(6) provide a description or disclosure of any compensation or promise of compensation already given to the professional, or of any security or pledge given; including a highlighted disclosure of any agreement to compensate the proposed professional under specified terms and conditions pursuant to § 328 of the Bankruptcy Code rather than § 330;

(7) attach the statements required by Fed. R. Bankr. P. 2014(a) and 2016(b);

(8) attach a certificate of service reflecting service as required by subsection (b) of this Local Rule;

(9) attach, if there has been a waiver of conflicts in a Chapter 11 case, an adequate description of the waiver and a copy of any written waiver;

(10) provide a description of any party in interest that has a connection with the applicant; and;

(11) attach a proposed order approving the employment which substantially conforms to *TXEB Local Form 2014.*

(b) Service of Applications. An application made under subsection (a) or (c) of this Local Rule shall be served on the parties designated by LBR 9013(f), as well as any entity described in Fed. R. Bankr. P. 2016 with whom the applicant has agreed to share compensation for services rendered in the case.

(c) Substitute Court Approved Professional. If a court-approved professional withdraws, then the substitute professional must file a motion for substitution of professional person which also contains the elements of an application to employ under Fed. R. Bankr. P. 2014 and LBR 2014.

(d) *Nunc Pro Tunc* Approval. If a professional applies for approval more than 30 days after employment and the professional seeks retroactive approval to the employment date, then the professional seeks approval *nunc pro tunc.* In addition to the general application content requirements, the *nunc pro tunc* application must contain:

(1) an explanation of why the application was not filed earlier;

(2) an explanation of why the order authorizing employment is required *nunc pro tunc*;

(3) an explanation — to the best of the applicant's knowledge — of how approval of the application will or will not prejudice any parties-in-interest;

(4) the 21–day negative notice language described in LBR 9007(a); and

(5) a certificate of service reflecting service on the master mailing list (matrix) as constituted by the Court on the date of service.

(e) Professionals Employable Without Application. Professionals on the payroll of an operating business at the time of the order for relief are exempt from the provisions of this Local Rule of Bankruptcy Procedure except that the professionals' annual salary and other compensation must be disclosed. This information must be contained in a separate pleading filed with the Court. The debtor is responsible for filing this pleading at the same time schedules are filed. Service of this pleading shall be on the same parties entitled to notice of an order approving employment of professionals. When cash collateral issues are not implicated, a debtor-in-possession or trustee of an operating business may also apply for an order waiving the provisions of this rule as to professionals of a type who are regularly employed in the ordinary course of a debtor's business and who are to provide services not directly related to the reorganization proceedings (e.g., collection agents or attorneys, accountants, geologists, appraisers, realtors, eviction attorneys, etc.).

[Effective February 1, 2000. Amended effective October 1, 2002; October 17, 2005; December 1, 2009; December 1, 2017.]

LBR 2015–1. DUTY TO KEEP RECORDS, MAKE REPORTS, AND GIVE NOTICE OF CASE

(a) Required Monthly Operating Reports When a Business Is Operated. When a business is operated by a trustee or debtor-in-possession in a Chapter 11 or 12 case, by a trustee in a Chapter 7 case, or by a debtor in a Chapter 13 case, a monthly operating report must be filed with the Court and served upon the United States Trustee [or, in lieu thereof, upon the standing trustee in a Chapter 12 or 13 case] not later than the 21st day of the month following the month for which the report is submitted. The first report is due the month following the month that the order for relief is granted or that a trustee qualifies. A report must be filed in the format approved by the United States Trustee [or, in lieu thereof, by the standing trustee in a Chapter 12 or 13 case].

(b) Disposition of Books and Records. Except in cases involving the disposal of patient records governed by § 351 of the Bankruptcy Code, a trustee who is in possession of books and records of the debtor may destroy, abandon, store, or return to the debtor all or a portion of those books and records on 21 days' notice to the Court, the debtor, the attorney for the debtor, the United States Trustee, the United States Attorney, and the appropriate Internal Revenue Service Special Procedures Staff office. A notice must include the 21–day negative notice language described in LBR 9007(a) and a detailed description of the books and records. If no objection to the proposed disposition is filed with the Court and served on the trustee, the disposition may be made without court order or further notice.

(c) Post Confirmation Requirements in Chapter 11 Cases.

1. In cases filed under Chapter 11 in which the debtor is a partnership or corporation, the proponent of a confirmed plan must:

(A) file a post confirmation report within 28 days after the date of the order confirming the plan and serve that report upon the master mailing list (matrix) as constituted by the Court on the date of service. The report must inform the Court of the post-confirmation actions taken by the confirmed debtor or the trustee and the progress made toward consummation of the plan; and

(B) within 180 days after the date of the confirmation order, file either an application for a final decree showing that the plan has been consummated with a proposed final decree or a subsequent post-confirmation report explaining why an application for final decree is not yet appropriate and requesting a continuance of any status conference previously scheduled.

2. In cases filed under Chapter 11 in which the debtor is an individual, the proponent of a confirmed plan must:

(A) file an annual status report on each anniversary date of the entry of the confirmation order which outlines the status of payments made by the individual debtor in the past year and any other post-confirmation action taken toward consummation of the plan; and

(B) file a "Notice of Plan Completion and § 522(q) Statement By Individual Debtor" in a Chapter 11 Case" (no service required) in a format substantially conforming to *TXEB Local Form 4004–b* under which each individual debtor declares that all payments under the confirmed Chapter 11 plan have been completed and that all prerequisites for the entry of an order of discharge pursuant to 11 U.S.C. § 1141(d)(5) have been fulfilled.

[Effective February 1, 2000. Amended effective February 1, 2001; October 17, 2005; December 1, 2009.]

LBR 2016–1. COMPENSATION FOR SERVICES RENDERED AND REIMBURSEMENT OF EXPENSES

(a) Form of Application. An application for compensation and reimbursement of expenses must:

(1) contain all information required by Fed. R. Bankr. P. 2016(a);

(2) disclose the name, hourly rate and work experience of each professional performing services for which compensation is sought;

(3) comply with the United States Trustee guidelines, when total requested fees and expenses exceed $10,000.00;

(4) bill travel time at half-rate unless work was done during travel, in which case the time may be billed at full rate;

(5) comply with the expense guidelines set forth in *TXEB Appendix 2016*;

(6) contain the 21–day negative notice language described in LBR 9007(a);

(7) contain a certificate of service reflecting service as required under subsection (c) of this rule; and

(8) attach a proposed order granting the application.

(b) Time Records Required. All professionals submitting an application under this rule, except auctioneers, real estate brokers, and appraisers, or professionals retained on a fixed-fee or contingent-fee basis, must keep accurate and contemporaneous time records.

(c) Service. A complete copy of the application, including all exhibits thereto, must be served on the debtor or the debtor's counsel, the trustee or the trustee's counsel, attorneys for any court-appointed committees, and the United States Trustee. The applicant must serve a summary of the fee application upon the master mailing list (matrix) as constituted by the Court on the date of service which:

(1) identifies the applicant and the capacity of such applicant;

(2) identifies the title of the application and the date it was filed,

(3) identifies the amounts sought by the application;

(4) identifies the time period covered by the application;

(5) contains the 21–day negative notice language described in LBR 9007(a); and

(6) contains a notice that a complete copy of the application will be sent to any requesting party at no charge.

If the fee exhibit to the application exceeds twenty-five (25) pages, the applicant must deliver a paper copy of the complete application, including all exhibits thereto, to the Clerk for use by the assigned judge per *TXEB Appendix 5005*.

(d) Multiple Cases. In cases involving multiple estates — absent substantive consolidation or special court order — a separate fee application must be filed for each case, and the detail of services and expenses must be apportioned to each estate or charged to the appropriate estate.

(e) Pre–Petition Retainers.

1. Any professional, regardless of whether employment of that professional must be approved under §§ 327 or 1103 of the Bankruptcy Code, must deposit any pre-petition payment for prospective services (i.e., a "security retainer") into a trust or IOLTA account. Except as otherwise authorized under these Local Rules, the security retainer must remain in the account until the Court enters an order allowing removal.

2. This requirement shall not apply to pre-petition payments constituting a classic or advance payment (flat fee) retainer, although such retainer must be disclosed pursuant to Fed. R. Bankr. P. 2016(b) and is subject to review under § 329 of the Bankruptcy Code.

(f) Post–Petition Retainers.

1. Unless otherwise authorized by the Court or these Rules, any post-petition payment received by a professional from the debtor or any other person for the benefit of the debtor must be disclosed to the Court and deposited into a trust or IOLTA account as a security retainer. This rule shall not apply to a post-petition payment tendered by a Chapter 7 debtor with funds which do not constitute property of the bankruptcy estate.

2. Unless the Court orders otherwise, any post-petition payment must remain in the trust or IOLTA account until the

Court enters an order allowing its removal. Any motion seeking such removal may be combined with an application for an award of post-petition fees and expenses. The motion must contain the 21–day negative notice language described in LBR 9007(a) and shall be served upon the parties designated by LBR 9013(f). A proposed order shall accompany the motion.

(g) Motion for Distribution of Retainer in Chapter 11 and 12 Cases. A motion for distribution of a retainer received by a professional in a Chapter 11 or 12 case may be filed on a monthly basis. Such motion must, at a minimum:

(1) contain all information required by Fed. R. Bankr. P. 2016(a);

(2) disclose the name, hourly rate and work experience of each professional performing services for which compensation is sought;

(3) meet the travel time and expense guidelines referenced in LBR 2016(a);

(4) utilize the 14–day negative notice language described in LBR 2014(a);

(5) contain a certificate of service reflecting service on the United States Trustee, the trustee (if one has been appointed), the ten (10) largest unsecured creditors or any committee appointed under the Bankruptcy Code or its authorized agent, and any party which has filed a notice of appearance or request for notice in the case; and

(6) attach a proposed order granting the motion.

The motion for distribution of retainer shall be treated as an application for interim compensation under § 331 of the Bankruptcy Code and, if no objection is filed within 14 days of the service thereof, the filing professional may withdraw from the retainer the amounts set forth as interim compensation without the necessity of a formal order.

(h) Attorney's Fees in Chapter 13 Cases.

1. The allowance of compensation and expense reimbursements for an attorney for a Chapter 13 debtor shall encompass pre-petition and post-petition services rendered and expenses incurred prior to the earlier of: (1) the first successful post-confirmation modification of a Chapter 13 plan which occurs subsequent to the filing of the Trustee's Reconciliation Concerning Claims; or (2) the filing of a certification by the Chapter 13 Trustee that all proofs of claim have been reconciled with the terms of the confirmed plan without the necessity of a plan modification (the "Benchmark Fee Period"). Such compensation shall be determined by the timely filing of a formal fee application in compliance with the requirements of this rule unless the attorney elects in the plan for the compensation to be determined by the benchmark fee amounts listed below according to the applicable circumstances:

(A) If the attorney has not rendered legal services pertaining to automatic stay litigation arising during the Benchmark Fee Period, a formal fee application is not required so long as the attorney requests $3,500 or less for the Benchmark Fee Period. The $3,500 benchmark fee shall include all pre-petition payments received by such attorney. This threshold amount may be increased by $500 in a case involving a debtor engaged in business when so certified by the Chapter 13 Trustee.

(B) If the attorney has rendered legal services pertaining to automatic stay litigation arising during the Benchmark Fee Period, a formal fee application is not required so long as the attorney requests $4,000 or less for the Benchmark Fee Period. The $4,000 benchmark fee shall include all pre-petition payments received by such attorney. This threshold amount may be increased by $500 in a case involving a debtor engaged in business when so certified by the Chapter 13 Trustee.

2. If an attorney for a Chapter 13 debtor elects to file a formal fee application for fees and expenses incurred during the Benchmark Fee Period, such application shall be filed no later than 30 days after the expiration of the Benchmark Fee Period as outlined in subsection (h)(1). If no formal fee application is filed by that deadline, the allowed compensation awarded to the debtor's attorney for services rendered in the Benchmark Fee Period shall revert to the applicable benchmark amounts authorized by subsection (h)(1) without the necessity of any further motion, notice or hearing.

3. The Chapter 13 trustee shall review a formal fee application and may file an objection or a comment.

4. Unless the Court orders otherwise, the entry of a Chapter 13 confirmation order shall authorize an attorney for a Chapter 13 debtor to withdraw a retainer in full or partial satisfaction of the attorney's outstanding fee without the necessity of a formal order.

5. Fees in excess of the retainer held by an attorney for a Chapter 13 debtor must be paid through the Chapter 13 plan as a Bankruptcy Code § 503(b)(2) administrative expense.

6. To obtain compensation for legal services rendered to a Chapter 13 debtor during any period subsequent to the Benchmark Fee Period outlined in subsection (h)(1), a formal fee application must be filed for allowance of such fees and expenses, unless such services pertain to a successful post-confirmation modification of a Chapter 13 plan achieved during such subsequent time period and such modification motion contains a detailed request for the award of such fees.

7. To obtain a fee award from the funds held by the Chapter 13 Trustee that are otherwise subject to return to the debtor under § 1326(a)(2) because the case has been dismissed prior to the entry of a plan confirmation order, the attorney must file an "Application for Administrative Expense by Chapter 13 Debtor's Attorney" which shall contain 21–day negative notice language and shall be served only upon the debtor(s) and any other party otherwise entitled to a share of those funds pursuant to an order of the Court. Unless otherwise ordered by the Court, such application must be filed prior to the dismissal of the case or it will be terminated without notice. If the application has not completed the required notice period prior to the dismissal of the case, the Court shall retain jurisdiction to consider the application when ripe for adjudication pursuant to the authority recognized in *Querner v. Querner (In re Querner)*, 7 F.3d 1199 (5th Cir. 1993) without the necessity of an order specifically retaining jurisdiction for that purpose.

8. A party in interest always has the right to object to the reasonableness of a fee request. This rule does not establish minimum, maximum, or average fees, nor does it establish the reasonableness of a fee in a particular case.

(i) Substitution of Attorney for Debtor. In addition to filing a statement under Fed. R. Bankr. P. 2016(b), an attorney who enters a case as substitute counsel for the debtor shall file a Notice of Appearance in that case, with notice to the master mailing list (matrix) as constituted by the Court on the date of service, which clearly sets forth the substitution of counsel.

(j) Application for Chapter 7 Trustee's Compensation and Expenses. Consideration of an application for compensation (commission) and reimbursement of expenses filed by a Chapter 7 Trustee shall be governed by the 30–day process outlined in the "Notice of Trustee's Final Report and Application for Compensation and Deadline to Object to TFR" issued in such Chapter 7 case.

[Effective February 1, 2000. Amended effective October 1, 2002; October 17, 2005; March 1, 2008; December 1, 2009; November 1, 2012; June 1, 2015; December 1, 2015; December 1, 2017.]

PART III.   CLAIMS AND DISTRIBUTION TO CREDITORS AND EQUITY INTEREST HOLDERS; PLANS

LBR 3002–1.   FILING PROOF OF CLAIM OR INTEREST

(a) Redaction of Personal Identifiers. The requirements of LBR 9013(d) regarding the redaction of personal identifiers applies to proofs of claim, and attachments thereto, filed with the Court.

(b) Service. A copy of a proof of claim or interest, with attachments, must be served on the debtor, evidenced by a certificate of service filed with the Court. Service upon the debtor's counsel and the case trustee shall be accomplished by electronic means through the transmission facilities of the Court.

[Effective February 1, 2000. Amended effective October 1, 2002; October 17, 2005; December 1, 2009.]

LBR 3003–1.   FILING OF PROOF OF CLAIM OR EQUITY SECURITY INTEREST IN CHAPTER 9 OR CHAPTER 11 REORGANIZATION CASES

(a) Time for Filing. A proof of claim is timely filed in a Chapter 9 or Chapter 11 case if it is filed not later than 120 days after the entry of the order for relief under that chapter, except as follows:

1. a proof of claim by a governmental unit is timely filed if it is filed not later than 180 days after the date of the order for relief; or

2. the Court may set a different bar date for a creditor or creditors. Notice of a different bar date for all creditors must comply with Fed. R. Bankr. P. 2002.

(b) Bar Date Notice.

1. The Clerk is authorized and directed to stamp the Court's signature and notify creditors of the Chapter 11 bar dates set forth in subsection (a) of this Rule.

2. If the Court orders a different bar date for filing proofs of claim or interest, then the order will conspicuously reflect that a new date has been set and that the new date differs from the deadline established in subsection (a) of this Rule.

[Effective February 1, 2000. Amended effective February 1, 2001; October 1, 2002; October 17, 2005; December 1, 2009; December 1, 2017.]

LBR 3007–1.　OBJECTIONS TO CLAIMS

(a) Contents. A claims objection must comply with the requirements of LBR 9013 and must contain the following:

(1) a copy of the proof of claim (without exhibits) to which the objection pertains;

(2) an affidavit and/or other documentary proof in support of the objection which is sufficient to overcome the presumption of validity imposed by Fed. R. Bankr. P. 3001(f) and, if pertaining to the valuation of collateral, a clear identification of the basis of any valuation opinion asserted;

(3) a certificate of service evidencing service of the claims objection upon the person most recently designated on the claimant's proof of claim as the person to receive notices, at the notice address indicated thereon, and upon all other parties entitled to notice under other applicable service rules; and

(4) a proposed order substantially conforming to TXEB Local Form 3007.

(b) Hearings. A party filing an objection to claim, other than an objection for which the filing of an adversary proceeding is required, may elect to utilize the following 30-day negative notice language which must be located in the objection text—preferably on the initial page:

30–DAY NEGATIVE NOTICE – LBR 3007(b):

ATTENTION: YOUR CLAIM MAY BE REDUCED, MODIFIED, OR ELIMINATED. Accordingly, you should read this pleading carefully and discuss it with your attorney, if you have one in this bankruptcy case. If you do not wish for the Court to eliminate or change your claim, you must file a written response opposing the claim objection, explaining the factual and/or legal basis for that response.

No hearing will be conducted on this claim objection unless a written response in opposition is filed with the Clerk of the United States Bankruptcy Court and served upon the party filing this pleading WITHIN THIRTY (30) DAYS FROM THE DATE OF SERVICE listed in the certificate of service unless the Court shortens or extends the time for filing such response. If no response in opposition is timely served and filed, this claim objection shall be deemed to be unopposed, and the Court may enter an order sustaining the objection to your claim. If a response in opposition is filed and served in a timely manner, the Court will thereafter set a hearing with appropriate notice. If you fail to appear at the hearing, your response in

opposition may be stricken. The Court reserves the right to set a hearing on any matter.

If the objection meets the requirements mandated by subsection (a) of this rule and no response in opposition to the claim objection is timely filed under the terms of the negative notice provided, the objection may be sustained by the Court without further notice or hearing. If a response to the claim objection is timely filed, the claim objection shall be set for hearing on not less than 30 days' notice. If a claim objection does not contain negative notice language, then the claim objection shall immediately be set for hearing on not less than 30 days' notice.

(c) Omnibus Claim Objections Prohibited. Except as authorized by Fed. R. Bankr. P. 3007 or unless otherwise authorized by the Court, omnibus claim objections to groups of claims are not allowed. Each claims objection must deal with one specific claim.

(d) Claim Procedures in Chapter 13 Cases. The procedure for adjudication of claims in Chapter 13 cases, including the establishment of a bar date for the filing of claim objections in Chapter 13 cases, is governed by LBR 3015(g).

[Effective February 1, 2000. Amended effective October 1, 2002; October 17, 2005; March 1, 2008; December 1, 2009.]

LBR 3012–1.　DETERMINING THE AMOUNT OF SECURED CLAIMS

(a) Contents. A motion to determine the amount of a secured claim under § 506(a), through the valuation of the collateral upon which such claim is based, must contain:

(1) a title which:

(A) identifies the holder of the lien or security interest upon the collateral sought to be valued; and

(B) adequately describes the collateral sought to be valued

Title Example: Motion for Valuation of Collateral of ABC Finance Corp. (2016 Ford Focus);

(2) a proposed valuation amount for the referenced collateral that the motion seeks to impose;

(3) an affidavit and/or other documentary proof in support of the motion that clearly identifies a credible, objective basis for the affiant's stated belief as to valuation of the referenced collateral;

(4) the 21–day negative notice language described in LBR 9007(a);

(5) a certificate of service reflecting service of the motion in accordance with LBR 9013(f), including upon the person most recently designated on the claimant's proof of claim as the person to receive notices, at the notice address indicated thereon; and

(6) be accompanied by a proposed order incorporating the title information from the pleading and otherwise substantially complying with *TXEB Local Form 9007–a.*

(b) Claim Procedures in Chapter 13 Cases. The procedure for the determination of claims in Chapter 13 cases, including the establishment of a deadline for the filing of any motion for valuation of collateral to determine the amount of a secured claim in a Chapter 13 case, is governed by LBR 3015(g).

[Effective December 1, 2017.]

LBR 3015–1. FILING, OBJECTION TO CONFIRMATION, EFFECT OF CONFIRMATION, AND MODIFICATION OF A PLAN IN A CHAPTER 12 OR A CHAPTER 13 CASE

(a) **Plan and Confirmation Order Format—Chapter 13.** Every Chapter 13 debtor shall file a proposed Chapter 13 plan in a format which substantially conforms to *TXEB Local Form 3015–a.* Any proposed confirmation order must substantially conform to *TXEB Local Form 3015–b.*

(b) **Service and Notice.** A debtor filing an original or modified Chapter 12 or 13 plan must serve such plan upon the master mailing list (matrix) as constituted by the Court on the date of service, including the standing trustee. A certificate of service evidencing the proper service of the plan on the matrix must be filed with the Court or such plan will be stricken. If a plan summary is not filed concurrently with a proposed plan, the plan summary must clearly identify by date of filing the proposed plan which it summarizes.

(c) **Plan Payments.**

1. Except to the extent that a proposed Chapter 13 plan provides for retention of collateral and direct payments by the debtor to the holder of a claim secured thereby or is otherwise authorized by the Court, no Chapter 13 debtor may provide adequate protection payments directly to a holder of a secured claim under the provisions of § 1326(a)(1)(C) but shall instead tender required adequate protection payments to the Chapter 13 Trustee in an amount equivalent to 1.50% of the value of the utilized collateral on the Petition Date and accruing for each 30–day period from the Petition Date until the month in which equal monthly payments to such holder are initiated under a confirmed plan, or as otherwise ordered by the Court.

2. Any adequate protection payment tendered to the Chapter 13 Trustee pursuant to this rule shall be held solely for the benefit of the affected secured creditor to the exclusion of the debtor and shall be tendered to that secured creditor by the Chapter 13 Trustee at the earliest practicable time, notwithstanding any failure of a debtor to confirm a Chapter 13 plan.

(d) **Chapter 12—Initial Confirmation Process.**

1. In a Chapter 12 case, the initial confirmation hearing date will be established by separate order.

2. An objection to confirmation by a creditor or party-in-interest must be filed no later than seven (7) days prior to confirmation, and untimely objections may not be considered by the Court.

3. The Chapter 12 Trustee must submit a confirmation recommendation and report, in which the Trustee must set forth all objections to the confirmation of the proposed Chapter 12 plan. This report must be filed with the Court and served on the debtor and the debtor's attorney at least seven (7) days prior to the scheduled confirmation hearing.

(e) **Chapter 13—Initial Confirmation Process.**

1. The notice of the initial § 341 meeting of creditors in a Chapter 13 case contains notice of the initial hearing to consider confirmation of a proposed Chapter 13 plan.

2. An objection to confirmation by a creditor or party-in-interest, other than the Chapter 13 Trustee, must be filed no later than fourteen (14) days prior to the scheduled hearing to consider confirmation of the plan, and untimely objections may not be considered by the Court.

3. No later than seven (7) days prior to the scheduled hearing to consider confirmation of the plan, a debtor shall:

(A) tender to the Chapter 13 Trustee a proposed confirmation order in a format which substantially conforms to *TXEB Local Form 3015–b;*

(B) file with the Court a declaration under penalty of perjury from the Debtors regarding the status of post-petition mortgage obligations which substantially conforms to *TXEB Local Form 3015–c;*

4. No later than seven (7) days prior to the scheduled hearing on confirmation of the plan, the Chapter 13 Trustee must determine whether to recommend confirmation of the proposed plan to the Court:

(A) if the Chapter 13 Trustee wishes to object to the confirmation of a proposed plan, a confirmation report must be filed in which the Trustee must set forth all objections to the confirmation of the proposed Chapter 13 plan. This report must be filed with the Court and served on the debtor and the debtor's attorney at least seven (7) days prior to the scheduled confirmation hearing;

(B) if the Chapter 13 Trustee wishes to recommend confirmation of the proposed plan and if all objections have been resolved, the Chapter 13 Trustee may upload an approved proposed confirmation order to the Court and such action will constitute a recommendation by the Trustee for confirmation of the proposed plan without the necessity of presenting additional documentation.

5. Upon the upload of an approved confirmation order by the Chapter 13 Trustee, the confirmation of the plan shall be considered unopposed, the attendance of the Debtor and the Debtor's counsel at the scheduled confirmation hearing shall be excused, and the Court may enter the submitted confirmation order without further hearing. Upon its review of the proposed plan and confirmation order, the Court reserves the right to reschedule the confirmation hearing with notice to all parties.

6. Upon the entry of an order denying confirmation of any original or amended Chapter 13 plan, any objection previously filed to that plan is resolved for all purposes and any objection by a creditor or party-in-interest to the confirmation of a subsequently-proposed Chapter 13 plan must be filed no later than seven (7) days prior to the scheduled hearing to consider that subsequently-proposed plan.

(f) **Pre–Confirmation Amendment Process.**

1. If a Chapter 12 or Chapter 13 plan is amended in the pre-confirmation period with less than 35 days' notice before

the confirmation hearing, the confirmation hearing will proceed only if the Court determines that:

(a) the modification does not adversely affect any creditors;

(b) any adversely affected creditor has consented; or

(c) the adverse impact of the modification on creditors is de minimis.

If a pre-confirmation plan amendment does not meet one of the three preceding requirements and additional notice of the amended plan is therefore required, a new confirmation hearing shall be scheduled, the deadline for filing an objection to the amended plan shall be extended to seven (7) days prior to the new confirmation hearing date, and the debtor shall provide notice of the new confirmation hearing date and the corresponding new 7–day objection deadline to the master mailing list (matrix) as constituted by the Court on the date of service. A certificate of service evidencing that proper notice has been given must be filed with the Court.

2. In the event that a new confirmation hearing is required to be scheduled due to a pre-confirmation amendment of the plan, and unless the Court orders otherwise, the continuation of the confirmation hearing in that context shall establish a final dismissal deadline for achieving confirmation of the proposed amended plan without the necessity of the entry of an independent order and, in the event that the debtor fails to confirm such an amended plan upon consideration by the Court at the rescheduled confirmation hearing, the underlying bankruptcy case shall be immediately dismissed, pursuant to § 349(a) of the Bankruptcy Code, without further notice or hearing and with prejudice to the rights of the debtor to file a subsequent petition under any chapter of Title 11, United States Code, for a period of 120 days from the entry of the order of dismissal.

(g) Claims Adjudication in Chapter 13 Cases.

1. A Trustee's Reconciliation Concerning Claims ("TRCC") shall be filed by the Chapter 13 Trustee within 45 days following the latter of: (a) the expiration of the time allowed for the filing of a proof of claim by a governmental unit; (b) the entry of an order confirming the Chapter 13 plan. The Chapter 13 Trustee is authorized to extend the TRCC deadline to a specified future date without leave of court on one occasion in any case by filing a notification with the Court which outlines the necessity for such an extension.

2. A TRCC shall serve primarily as a reconciliation device between the claims registry and the terms of the confirmed Chapter 13 plan.

3. As set forth below, the TRCC shall also provide prominent notice of the deadline by which challenges to claims filed in a Chapter 13 case must be filed by any party-in-interest, regardless of the means utilized to bring such challenge.

4. Absent a court order to the contrary, the deadline in a Chapter 13 case for any party-in-interest to:

(i) file an objection to the allowance of any proof of claim;

(ii) file a motion under Rule 3012 to determine the amount of a secured claim through the valuation of collateral; or

(iii) avoid or otherwise challenge the validity of any security interest claimed in any proof of claim,

shall be the twenty-first (21st) day following the date of service of the TRCC.

5. A TRCC shall therefore contain the following notice:

Notice of Filing Deadline for Challenging Claims.

YOU ARE NOTIFIED that, pursuant to LBR 3015(g), the deadline for: (1) filing an objection to the allowance of any proof of claim filed in this case; (2) filing a motion for valuation of collateral to determine the amount of a secured claim filed in this case pursuant to Rule 3012; or (3) filing an appropriate pleading to avoid or otherwise challenge the validity of any security interest claimed in any proof of claim filed in this case, is the **twenty-first (21st) day following the date of service of this document.**

6. Since a TRCC serves as a reconciliation document which requires no court approval, no negative notice language nor any proposed order is required.

7. A certificate of service is required, evidencing service of the TRCC upon the master mailing list (matrix) as constituted by the Court on the date of service.

8. Any claim objection filed by a party-in-interest in a Chapter 13 case must comply with the requirements of LBR 3007.

9. When any claim is challenged by a proper objection, the Chapter 13 Trustee shall reserve funds otherwise attributable to that claim until the dispute regarding such claim has been resolved. If the claim resolution results in an increase of money available for distribution to any class of creditors under the confirmed plan, the Chapter 13 Trustee may accordingly adjust payments to be made on allowed claims without the necessity of filing an additional TRCC.

(h) Post Confirmation Modification.

1. In a Chapter 13 case, a proponent requesting the post-confirmation modification of a Chapter 13 plan shall file a proposed *Motion to Modify Confirmed Chapter 13 Plan* in a format which substantially conforms to *TXEB Local Form 3015-d*. The motion must be accompanied by a proposed *Order Modifying Confirmed Chapter 13 Plan* in a format which substantially conforms to *TXEB Local Form 3015-e*.

2. In a Chapter 12 case, a proponent requesting the post-confirmation modification of a Chapter 12 plan must file a modified plan as an attachment to a motion seeking confirmation of the modified plan which specifies the precise changes sought by the modification including, but not limited to: (A) the purpose of or the necessity for the modification; (B) the changes being made as to the plan payment, the term of the plan; the proposed distribution to any class, or any other substantive provision; and (C) the amount of additional attorneys' fees requested for services pertaining to the modification, subject to the provisions and limitations of LBR 2016(h)(5).

3. In either a Chapter 12 or 13 case, the standing trustee is authorized during the pendency of a post-confirmation modification motion to maintain payments on allowed claims the treatment of which stands unaffected by the proposed modification.

4. In a Chapter 13 case, a debtor seeking a modification of a confirmed plan must contemporaneously file with the Court:

(a) a declaration under penalty of perjury regarding the status of post-petition mortgage obligations which substantially conforms to *TXEB Local Form 3015–c*;

(b) an amended Schedule I and an amended Schedule J in order to verify current income and expenditure information or, in the alternative, certify under penalty of perjury in the modification motion filed with the Court that the information contained in Schedule I and Schedule J as previously filed with the Court remains true and correct.

5. In either a Chapter 12 or 13 case, a proponent seeking a modification of a confirmed plan must serve the proposed modification, together with any attachments, to the master mailing list (matrix) as constituted by the Court on the date of service and file a certificate of service evidencing such service. The motion must also contain the following 28–day negative notice language, which must appear as presented and be located in the motion text — preferably on the initial page:

28–DAY NEGATIVE NOTICE—LBR 3015(h):

Your rights may be affected by the plan modifications sought in this pleading. You should read this pleading carefully and discuss it with your attorney, if you have one in this bankruptcy case. If you oppose the relief sought by this pleading, you must file a written objection, explaining the factual and/or legal basis for opposing the relief.

No hearing will be conducted on this Motion unless a written objection is filed with the Clerk of the United States Bankruptcy Court and served upon the party filing this pleading *WITHIN TWENTY–EIGHT (28) DAYS FROM THE DATE OF SERVICE* shown in the certificate of service unless the Court shortens or extends the time for filing such objection. If no objection is timely served and filed, this pleading shall be deemed to be unopposed, and the Court may enter an order confirming this plan modification. If an objection is filed and served in a timely manner, the Court will thereafter set a hearing with appropriate notice. If you fail to appear at the hearing, your objection may be stricken. The Court reserves the right to set a hearing on any matter.

5.* With the exception of the expanded response time, modifications shall be handled in accordance with the Court's usual motion procedures.

[Effective February 1, 2000. Amended effective October 1, 2002; October 17, 2005; March 1, 2008; December 1, 2009; November 1, 2012; June 1, 2015; December 1, 2015; December 1, 2017.]

* [Publisher's Note: So in original.]

LBR 3016–1. FILING OF PLAN AND DISCLOSURE STATEMENT IN CHAPTER 9 MUNICIPALITY AND CHAPTER 11 REORGANIZATION CASES

The plan proponent must deliver a paper copy of the proposed plan of reorganization and the accompanying disclosure statement, including all exhibits thereto, to the Clerk for use by the assigned judge pursuant to *TXEB Appendix 5005*.

[Effective October 17, 2005.]

LBR 3017–1. COURT CONSIDERATION OF DISCLOSURE STATEMENT IN CHAPTER 9 MUNICIPALITY AND CHAPTER 11 REORGANIZATION CASES

The solicitation package containing the documents and notice required by Fed. R. Bankr. P. 3017(d) must be served by the plan proponent upon the master mailing list (matrix) as constituted by the Court on the date of service. The notice must contain all instructions regarding the return of the ballot, including the name and address of the party to which the ballot must be returned as designated by LBR 3018(a) or by court order.

[Effective February 1, 2000. Amended effective October 1, 2002; October 17, 2005.]

LBR 3017.1–1. COURT CONSIDERATION OF DISCLOSURE STATEMENT IN A SMALL BUSINESS CASE

(a) Conditional Approval. A plan proponent in a small business case may seek conditional approval of a disclosure statement, subject to final approval after notice and hearing, by filing a request with the Court contemporaneously with the filing of the proposed plan of reorganization. Such request shall contain a certificate of service evidencing service upon the parties designated by LBR 9013(f) and shall be accompanied by a proposed order substantially conforming to *TXEB Local Form 3017.1*. The request will not require negative notice language and will be presented to the Court for immediate consideration

(b) Waiver. A plan proponent in a small business case may seek to waive the requirement of a disclosure statement because the proposed plan of reorganization itself provides adequate information. Such waiver may be sought by motion to be filed contemporaneously with the proposed plan of reorganization. Such motion shall be served upon the parties designated by LBR 9013(f) and must contain the following 14–day negative notice language, to be located in the motion text — preferably on the initial page:

14–DAY NEGATIVE NOTICE—LBR 3017.1(b):

Your rights may be affected by the relief sought in this pleading. You should read this pleading carefully and discuss it with your attorney, if you have one in this bankruptcy case. If you oppose the relief sought by this pleading, you must file a written objection, explaining the factual and/or legal basis for opposing the relief.

No hearing will be conducted on this Motion unless a written objection is filed with the Clerk of the United States Bankruptcy Court and served upon the party filing this pleading *WITHIN FOURTEEN (14) DAYS FROM THE DATE OF SERVICE* shown in the certificate of service unless the Court shortens or extends the time for filing such objection. If no objection is timely served and filed, this pleading shall be deemed to be unopposed, and the Court may enter an order granting the relief sought. If an objection is filed and served in a timely manner, the Court will thereafter set a hearing with appropriate notice. If you fail to appear at the hearing, your objection may be stricken. The Court reserves the right to set a hearing on any matter.

[Effective October 17, 2005. Amended effective March 1, 2008; December 1, 2009; December 1, 2017.]

LBR 3018–1. ACCEPTANCE OR REJECTION OF PLAN IN A CHAPTER 9 MUNICIPALITY OR A CHAPTER 11 REORGANIZATION CASE

(a) Voting. Unless otherwise ordered by the Court, a ballot accepting or rejecting a proposed plan must be returned to the attorney for the plan proponent.

(b) Ballot Summary.

1. At the confirmation hearing, a plan proponent must tender to the Court a ballot summary which certifies the amount and number of allowed claims of each class accepting or rejecting the plan and the amount of allowed interest of each class accepting or rejecting the plan. The actual ballots must be attached to the ballot summary.

2. The ballot summary will be marked as an exhibit for the plan proponent at the confirmation hearing. Thus, the plan proponent must provide appropriate copies of the ballot summary pursuant to LBR 7016(d), as incorporated into contested matters by LBR 9014(d).

[Effective February 1, 2000. Amended effective October 17, 2005.]

LBR 3019–1. MODIFICATION OF ACCEPTED PLAN AFTER CONFIRMATION IN A CHAPTER 11 REORGANIZATION CASE INVOLVING AN INDIVIDUAL DEBTOR

(a) Required Information. A proponent requesting the post-confirmation modification of a Chapter 11 plan of reorganization involving an individual debtor must file the modified plan, together with a motion seeking confirmation of the modified plan which specifies the precise changes sought by the modification including, but not limited to, the following:

(1) the purpose of, or the necessity for, the modification, together with sufficient information regarding such circumstances that would enable a hypothetical investor to make an informed judgment regarding the legitimacy of the need for the modification; and

(2) the changes being made as to the plan payment, the term of the plan; the proposed distribution to any class, or any other substantive provision.

(b) Service. A proponent requesting the post-confirmation modification of a Chapter 11 plan of reorganization involving an individual debtor must serve the proposed modification and the accompanying motion upon the master mailing list (matrix) as constituted by the Court on the date of service and file a certificate of service evidencing such service. The motion must also contain the following 28–day negative notice language, which must appear as presented and be located in the motion text — preferably on the initial page:

28–DAY NEGATIVE NOTICE—LBR 3019(b):

Your rights may be affected by the plan modifications sought in this pleading. You should read this pleading carefully and discuss it with your attorney, if you have one in this bankruptcy case. If you oppose the relief sought by this pleading, you must file a written objection, explaining the factual and/or legal basis for opposing the relief.

No hearing will be conducted on this Motion unless a written objection is filed with the Clerk of the United States Bankruptcy Court and served upon the party filing this pleading *WITHIN TWENTY–EIGHT (28) DAYS FROM THE DATE OF SERVICE* shown in the certificate of service unless the Court shortens or extends the time for filing such objection. If no objection is timely served and filed, this pleading shall be deemed to be unopposed, and the Court may enter an order confirming this plan modification. If an objection is filed and served in a timely manner, the Court will thereafter set a hearing with appropriate notice. If you fail to appear at the hearing, your objection may be stricken. The Court reserves the right to set a hearing on any matter.

Modifications shall be handled in accordance with the Court's usual motion procedures.

[Effective October 17, 2005. Amended effective December 1, 2009; December 1, 2017.]

PART IV. THE DEBTOR: DUTIES AND BENEFITS

LBR 4000–1. IMPOSITION, CONTINUATION OR STATUS OF THE AUTOMATIC STAY

(a) Imposition/Continuation Motions Scheduled for Hearing Upon Filing.

1. The following motions to impose or to continue the automatic stay shall not require negative notice language but instead shall be scheduled for an accelerated hearing upon filing:

(A) Motion to impose automatic stay pursuant to § 362(c)(4)(B) of the Code;

(B) Motion to impose automatic stay by small business debtor pursuant to § 362(n)(2) of the Code;

(C) Motion to continue automatic stay in consecutive individual case under chapter 7, 11 or 13 pursuant to § 362(c)(3)(B); and

(D) Motion to continue automatic stay on personal property of individual debtor by trustee pursuant to § 362(h)(2) and § 521(a)(6).

2. A stay imposition or continuation motion shall disclose in the body of the motion the following information regarding the dismissal of the debtor's prior bankruptcy case(s):

(A) the prior case number and the court in which it was filed;

(B) the circumstances upon which the dismissal was based;

(C) whether a request for relief from automatic stay had been granted or was pending in the prior case at the time of the dismissal;

(D) the identity and mailing address for any attorney (or pro se creditor) who had filed a request for relief from automatic stay for any party in the prior case; and

(E) the identity and mailing address for any attorney who had filed a notice of appearance in the prior case;

3. A stay imposition or continuation motion shall contain a certificate of service reflecting service of the motion upon the master mailing list (matrix) as constituted by the Court on the date of service if the stay is to be imposed or continued as to all parties in the case, or otherwise in accordance with LBR 9013(f), and in a manner consistent with Fed. R. Bankr. P. 7004(b); provided, however, that the motion shall also be served upon any attorney who had filed a request for relief from automatic stay or a notice of appearance in the debtor's prior bankruptcy case(s) and any party who filed a proof of claim in debtor's prior bankruptcy case shall be served at the address disclosed by such claimant in its prior proof of claim.

4. The motion must be accompanied by:

(A) a proposed deadline order which substantially conforms to *TXEB Local Form 4000–a*; and

(B) a proposed order granting the requested relief which substantially conforms to *TXEB Local Form 4000–b*.

5. Consideration of any stay imposition or continuation motion shall either be governed by an "Order Establishing Deadline for Objection to Motion for Continuation/Imposition of Automatic Stay and Setting Possible Hearing Date on Such Motion" through which the Court shall establish a deadline for filing an objection to the motion and a potential hearing date for the motion which shall be served upon the matrix or the Court shall proceed to schedule an accelerated hearing on the Motion upon filing.

6. If a hearing is so scheduled by the Court without the establishment of a deadline for objections, any such objection to the stay imposition or continuation motion must be filed and served no later than two (2) business days prior to the scheduled hearing; provided, however, that if the hearing is held on notice of seven (7) days or less, no formal objection shall be required.

(b) Petition–Date Certification of Compliance: Lease of Residential Real Property.

1. A petition-date certification of compliance necessary for a debtor to invoke the protection of the automatic stay regarding a lease of real property in which the debtor resides as a tenant pursuant to § 362(l)(1)—in addition to the requirements imposed by the Code—shall contain:

(A) the following 14–day negative notice language, which must be in boldface, large font and located in the text of the motion — preferably on the initial page:

This Petition Date Certification is self-executing and shall defer the applicability of 11 U.S.C. § 362(b)(22) to this lease of residential real property for a period of 30 DAYS FROM THE PETITION DATE absent an order of the Court to the contrary. No hearing will be conducted regarding this Certification unless a written objection is filed with the Clerk of the United States Bankruptcy Court and served upon the party filing this pleading WITHIN FOURTEEN (14) DAYS FROM THE DATE OF SERVICE unless the Court shortens or extends the time for filing such objection. If an objection is filed and served in a timely manner, the Court will thereafter set a hearing. If you fail to appear at the hearing, your objection may be stricken. The Court reserves the right to set a hearing on any matter.

and

(B) contain a certificate of service reflecting service of the petition date certification upon the affected lessor.

2. A lessor objecting to a debtor's petition-date certification of compliance may waive the 10–day hearing requirement, if desired, in the caption of the objection. If a waiver is not filed, the Court will convene a hearing within the required 10 days in the division most convenient to the Court.

Title Example: Objection to Debtor's Petition–Date Certification of Compliance Regarding Lease of Residential Real Property, Waiver of 10–Day Hearing Requirement, and Request for Hearing in Beaumont, Texas.

(c) Post–Petition Certification of Compliance: Lease of Residential Real Property.

1. A post-petition certification of compliance necessary for a debtor to continue the protections of the automatic stay regarding a lease of real property in which the debtor resides as a tenant for a period beyond 30 days from the petition date pursuant to § 362(l)(2) of the Code—in addition to the requirements imposed by the Code—shall contain:

(A) the following 14–day negative notice language, which must be in boldface, large font and located in the text of the motion — preferably on the initial page:

This post-petition certification is self-executing and shall defer the applicability of 11 U.S.C. § 362(b)(22) to this lease of residential real property for the duration of this bankruptcy case absent an order of the Court to the contrary. No hearing will be conducted regarding this Certification unless a written objection is filed with the Clerk of the United States Bankruptcy Court and served upon the party filing this pleading WITHIN FOURTEEN (14) DAYS FROM THE DATE OF SERVICE unless the Court shortens or extends the time

for filing such objection. If an objection is filed and served in a timely manner, the Court will thereafter set a hearing. If you fail to appear at the hearing, your objection may be stricken. The Court reserves the right to set a hearing on any matter.

and

(B) contain a certificate of service reflecting service of the post-petition certification upon the affected lessor.

2. A lessor objecting to a debtor's post-petition certification of compliance may waive the 10–day hearing requirement, if desired, in the title of the objection. If a waiver is not filed, the Court will convene a hearing within the required 10 days in the division most convenient to the Court.

Title Example: Objection to Debtor's Post–Petition Certification of Compliance Regarding Lease of Residential Real Property, Waiver of 10–Day Hearing Requirement, and Request for Hearing in Beaumont, Texas.

(d) Requests to Confirm Status of Automatic Stay. Any request for the Court to confirm the status of the automatic stay, including a request for an order pursuant to § 362(c)(4)(A)(ii) to confirm that the automatic stay is not in effect, or a request for an order pursuant to § 362(j) to confirm that the automatic stay has been previously terminated, shall be in writing and filed with the Clerk. Such requests shall not require negative notice language, nor a certificate of service, but shall require a proposed order substantially conforming to *TXEB Local Form 4000–d.*

(e) Notice of Termination of Automatic Stay. Any creditor which asserts that the automatic stay has been terminated by operation of law as against its interests shall file a Notice of Termination with the Court to evidence such termination of the automatic stay. Such Notice of Termination shall cite the statutory basis for the asserted termination.

[Effective October 17, 2005. Amended effective March 1, 2008; December 1, 2009; December 1, 2017.]

LBR 4001–1.   RELIEF FROM AUTOMATIC STAY; PROHIBITING OR CONDITIONING THE USE, SALE, OR LEASE OF PROPERTY; USE OF CASH COLLATERAL; OBTAINING CREDIT; AGREEMENTS

(a) Use of 14–Day Negative Notice Language. The following motions:

1. Motion to provide adequate protection;

2. Motion to prohibit or condition the use, sale, or lease of property pursuant to § 363(e) of the Code;

3. Motion for relief from automatic or co-debtor stay;

4. Motion for authority to use or to prohibit use of cash collateral;

5. Motion to obtain credit pursuant to § 364 of the Code; and

6. Motion to approve a stipulation regarding any of the above

must contain the following 14–day negative notice language, which must appear as presented and be located in the motion text — preferably on the initial page:

14–DAY NEGATIVE NOTICE—LBR 4001(a):

Your rights may be affected by the relief sought in this pleading. You should read this pleading carefully and discuss it with your attorney, if you have one in this bankruptcy case. If you oppose the relief sought by this pleading, you must file a written objection, explaining the factual and/or legal basis for opposing the relief.

No hearing will be conducted on this Motion unless a written objection is filed with the Clerk of the United States Bankruptcy Court and served upon the party filing this pleading *WITHIN FOURTEEN (14) DAYS FROM THE DATE OF SERVICE* shown in the certificate of service unless the Court shortens or extends the time for filing such objection. If no objection is timely served and filed, this pleading shall be deemed to be unopposed, and the Court may enter an order granting the relief sought. If an objection is filed and served in a timely manner, the Court will thereafter set a hearing with appropriate notice. If you fail to appear at the hearing, your objection may be stricken. The Court reserves the right to set a hearing on any matter.

The use of 14–day negative notice language does **not** apply to a motion for authority (or a notice of intention) to use, sell or lease property of the estate pursuant to § 363(b) of the Code or a motion to sell property of the estate free and clear of liens or other interests pursuant to § 363(f) of the Code. Such motions must contain **21–day** negative notice language described in LBR 9007(a), and contain a certificate of service reflecting service on the master mailing list (matrix) as constituted by the Court on the date of service. See LBR 6004.

(b) Content: Motion for Relief From Automatic Stay. A motion for relief from the automatic stay must:

(1) contain a title which:

(A) reflects that relief from the stay is sought against property, and

(B) waives the 30–day automatic stay hearing requirement, if desired. If a waiver is not filed, the Court will convene a hearing within the required 30 days in the division most convenient to the Court;

Title Example: Motion for Relief from Automatic Stay Against 2002 Ford Taurus, Waiver of 30–Day Hearing Requirement, and Request for Hearing in Beaumont, Texas.

(2) contain the 14–day negative notice language described in LBR 4001(a);

(3) contain a certificate of service reflecting service of the motion in accordance with LBR 9013(f) and in a manner consistent with Fed. R. Bankr. P. 7004(b);

(4) be accompanied by an affidavit which details the date and amount of each post-petition payment which:

(i) has become due since the filing of the petition; and

(ii) has been received by the Movant since the filing of the petition, if relief from the stay is sought "for cause" in a case under Chapter 11, 12, or 13 based upon an alleged failure of the debtor to tender a required post-petition payment; and

(5) be accompanied by a proposed order substantially complying with *TXEB Local Form 4001.*

(c) Motion to Use Cash Collateral.

1. *General Requirements.* A motion to use cash collateral must include:

(A) the amount of cash collateral sought to be used;

(B) name and address of each entity having an interest in the cash collateral;

(C) name and address of any entity in control or having possession of the cash collateral;

(D) facts demonstrating the need to use cash collateral;

(E) nature of the protection to be provided to those parties having an interest in the cash collateral; and

(F) a proposed budget exhibit which itemizes the proposed use of the cash collateral; accompanied by

(G) a proposed order.

2. *Emergency Affidavit Requirements.* A request for an emergency hearing regarding a motion for use of cash collateral must comply with the standards in LBR 9007(b) and, in compliance with such standards, the affidavit or unsworn declaration under penalty of perjury attesting to the emergency facts in a cash collateral context must reflect the following:

(A) names and addresses of all creditors holding or asserting an interest in the collateral and their attorneys, if known;

(B) efforts made to contact the affected creditor(s) or its/their attorneys with regard to the motion;

(C) the nature of the immediate and irreparable injury, loss, or damage;

(D) verification of a 30–day budget of emergency items; and

(E) the adequate protection to be provided to the affected creditors.

(d) Agreements. If a stipulation involves relief beyond the scope of that requested in any motion governed by this rule, a motion to approve the stipulation must be filed. The motion must contain 14–day negative notice language pursuant to LBR 4001(a), a certificate of service which evidences service upon the master mailing list (matrix) as constituted by the Court on the date of service, and attach the stipulation and a proposed order which grants the motion for approval.

(e) Lengthy Agreed Cash Collateral or Financing Orders. Agreed orders regarding a motion for authority to use cash collateral or to obtain credit pursuant to § 364 of the Code which are in excess of ten (10) pages in length must be accompanied by an executed attorney checklist of provisions in substantial conformity with Exhibit J of *TXEB Appendix 9007,* regardless of whether the underlying case has been designated as a complex Chapter 11 case by the Court.

[Effective February 1, 2000. Amended effective October 1, 2002; October 17, 2005; December 1, 2009; November 1, 2012; December 1, 2017.]

LBR 4002–1. DUTIES OF DEBTOR

(a) Individual Debtor's Duty to Provide Advance Documentation.* Upon written notification that the § 341 meeting of creditors shall be conducted by the trustee or United States Trustee via video conference, an individual debtor shall provide an enlarged (150%), legible (photo setting) copy of his/her picture identification and evidence of his/her social security number to the presiding trustee no later than seven (7) days prior to the first date set for the § 341 meeting of creditors. Such copy shall reference the date and time of the scheduled meeting at which time the debtor must present the original documents.

(b) Tax Return Required by § 521(e)(2)(A). Upon request, an individual debtor in a Chapter 7 case shall provide a copy of the federal tax return required under § 521(e)(2)(A) to the United States Trustee at the time that a copy is provided to the case trustee under that statute.

(c) Request for Debtor to File Tax Information With Court.

1. Any request by a party-in-interest to compel an individual debtor in a case under Chapter 7, 11, or 13 to file a copy of a federal tax return with the Court pursuant to § 521(f) shall be in writing and filed with the Clerk. Such request shall not require negative notice language, but shall require a certificate of service evidencing service upon the debtor(s) and his/her counsel of record, and shall be accompanied by a proposed order.

2. An individual debtor who is directed to file tax information with the Court shall redact from such tax information all personal identifiers pursuant to LBR 1007(c) prior to filing.

(d) Motion to Obtain Access to Debtor's Tax Information. A motion by party-in-interest to obtain access to a debtor's tax information tendered to the Court pursuant to § 521(f) must:

(1) contain the 14–day negative notice language described in LBR 4001(a);

(2) describe the movant's status in the case in order to allow the Court to ascertain whether the movant may properly be given access to the requested information;

(3) contain a description of the specific tax information sought;

(4) contain a statement indicating that the tax information sought cannot be obtained by the movant from any other source;

(5) contain a statement showing a demonstrated need for the tax information sought;

(6) contain a certificate of service reflecting service of the motion upon the debtor and any counsel for the debtor; and

(7) be accompanied by a proposed order.

Any party obtaining tax information from the Court through this process must safeguard the confidentiality of the information provided and sanctions may be imposed for any improper use, disclosure or dissemination of the tax information provided.

[Effective October 17, 2005. Amended effective March 1, 2008; December 1, 2009.]

* [Publisher's Note: *See also* General Order 08–2, *post.*]

LBR 4003–1. EXEMPTIONS

(a) **Claim of Exemptions.** The exemption list in Schedule C must itemize, describe and separately value each item claimed as exempt, except that household supplies, linens, cooking utensils, clothing and other items with an aggregate value of less than $500 may be placed in generic categories.

(b) **Notice of Amendment to Exemptions.** Any amendment to Schedule C must be accompanied by a certificate of service which evidences service of the amended schedule upon the master mailing list (matrix) as constituted by the Court on the date of service or it will be stricken.

(c) **Objection to Claim of Exemptions.** An objection to a debtor's claim of exemption is a "contested matter" governed by Fed. R. Bankr. P. 9014 and LBR 9014. It must contain the following 21–day negative notice language which must be located in the objection text — preferably on the initial page:

21–DAY NEGATIVE NOTICE—LBR 4003(c):

Your rights may be affected by the relief sought in this pleading. You should read this pleading carefully and discuss it with your attorney, if you have one in this bankruptcy case. If you oppose the relief sought by this objection, you must file a written response in opposition to the exemption objection, explaining the factual and/or legal basis for opposing the relief.

No hearing will be conducted on this Objection to Exemption unless a written response in opposition to it is filed with the Clerk of the United States Bankruptcy Court and served upon the party filing this pleading _WITHIN TWENTY–ONE (21) DAYS FROM THE DATE OF SERVICE_ listed in the certificate of service unless the Court shortens or extends the time for filing such response. If no response in opposition to the objection is timely served and filed, this objection to exemption shall be deemed to be unopposed, and the Court may enter an order sustaining the objection. If a response in opposition is filed and served in a timely manner, the Court will thereafter set a hearing with appropriate notice. If you fail to appear at the hearing, your response in opposition may be stricken. The Court reserves the right to set a hearing on any matter.

An objection must otherwise comply with the requirements of LBR 9013, including the submission of a certificate of service and be accompanied by a proposed order. The proposed order must specify the basis for disallowance and must not generically recite that the objection is sustained.

(d) **Responsive Pleading.** Any debtor who opposes the relief sought by an objection to a claim of exemption must file a *response* within the designated negative notice period. Any response must conform to the requirements of Fed. R. Civ. P. 8(b).

(e) **Lien Avoidance.** A motion to avoid a judicial lien or a non-possessory, non-purchase money security interest that impairs a claim of exemption must:

(1) delineate the extent to which the debtor seeks to avoid the referenced interest;

(2) identify in the title of the pleading whether the allegedly avoidable interest is a judicial lien or a non-possessory, non-purchase money security interest;

(3) either specifically describe the property subject to the lien/non–PMSI or attach the security documentation which describes the property;

(4) state whether the debtor claimed federal or state exemptions and state that the exemption objection period has expired;

(5) attach sufficient information regarding the formation of the allegedly avoidable lien to validate the sufficiency of service of the motion (e.g., copy of abstract of judgment, etc.); and

(6) cite to § 522(f).

As explained in Fed. R. Bankr. P. 4003 and the Advisory Committee notes, only a § 522(f) lien avoidance action may be sought by motion. Lien avoidance under the Texas Constitution or by statutory authority other than § 522(f) must be sought by an adversary complaint.

[Effective February 1, 2000. Amended effective October 1, 2002; October 17, 2005; March 1, 2008; December 1, 2009; December 1, 2017.]

LBR 4004–1. GRANT OR DENIAL OF DISCHARGE

(a) **Motion for Extension of Time.** In addition to stating the justification for the requested extension, a motion for an extension of time to file a complaint objecting to the debtor's discharge pursuant to § 727(a) of the Bankruptcy Code shall state the deadline for filing such a complaint in that case as established under Fed. R. Bankr. P. 4004(a) and the specific date to which an extension is requested.

(b) **Discharge Process for Chapter 11 Individual Debtors.**

1. Upon completion of all plan payments required of an individual debtor under a confirmed Chapter 11 plan, the individual debtor(s) shall file a "Notice of Plan Completion and § 522(q) Statement By Individual Debtor in a Chapter 11 Case" (no service required) in a format substantially conforming to *TXEB Local Form 4004–b.*

2. Upon the filing of the Notice of Plan Completion, an opportunity to object to the entry of the discharge order shall be given by the Clerk to all parties on the master mailing list (matrix) as constituted by the Court on that date.

3. Upon the entry of a discharge order on behalf of an individual debtor, and in the absence of any unresolved administrative issue, a final decree closing the case shall be entered by the Clerk.

(c) **Discharge Process in Chapter 12 or Chapter 13.**

1. Upon receipt of all plan payments from the debtor, the Trustee shall file a Notice of Plan Completion which verifies to the Court that the debtor has completed all payments under the confirmed plan for which the Trustee served as the disbursing agent and that the process to determine the entitlement of the debtor to an order of discharge should be initiated pursuant to 11 U.S.C. § 1228(a) or § 1328(a).

2. Upon the filing of the Notice of Plan Completion, a 60–day opportunity to object to the entry of the discharge order shall be given by the Clerk to all parties on the master mailing list (matrix) as constituted by the Court on that date.

3. Within 30 days after the filing of the Notice of Plan Completion by the Trustee, the Debtor must file:

(A) a "Statement of Debtor(s) Regarding Applicability of 11 U.S.C. § 522(q) in a Chapter 12 or 13 Case" in a format substantially conforming to *TXEB Local Form 4004–c;* and

(B) a "Certification of Debtor Regarding Status of Domestic Support Obligations in a Chapter 12 or 13 Case" in a format substantially conforming to *TXEB Local Form 4004–d.*

(d) Motion for Hardship Discharge. Any motion by an individual debtor for a discharge under § 1111(d)(5)(B), § 1228(b) or § 1328(b) of the Bankruptcy Code must be accompanied by a proposed order which substantially conforms to the bankruptcy form indicated:

Chapter 11: adapt Bankruptcy Director's Form B–3180FH (Chapter 12 form) until one is actually promulgated for Chapter 11 cases

Chapter 12: Bankruptcy Director's Form B–3180FH

PART V. COURTS AND CLERK

LBR 5001–1. COURTS AND CLERKS' OFFICES

"Clerk" means the Clerk of the Bankruptcy Court for the Eastern District of Texas or the Deputy Clerk in charge of the division in which such case or proceeding is pending or their designee.

[Effective February 1, 2000. Amended effective October 17, 2005.]

LBR 5003–1. RECORDS KEPT BY THE CLERK

(a) Electronic Files and Duty to Confirm. The Clerk shall keep and maintain all filed documents, bankruptcy dockets, and claim registers in an electronic format, unless otherwise ordered by the Court. Any document submitted to the Clerk in a paper format shall be converted into an electronic format prior to docketing. It is the duty of the filing party to confirm that such document has been accurately submitted into the Court's electronic file. If no challenge regarding the presentation of the document in the Court's electronic file is communicated to the Clerk within 14 days of the date of docketing, then the document as presented is conclusively confirmed as the document submitted, unless otherwise ordered by the Court.

(b) Retention of Paper Documents. Upon conversion of a paper document to an electronic format, such paper document shall be thereafter maintained by the Clerk by date of filing

Chapter 13: Bankruptcy Director's Form B–3180WH.

These forms are available at www.uscourts.gov/forms/bankruptcy-forms.

In Chapter 13 cases, the proposed order shall also contain the following paragraph:

"IT IS FURTHER ORDERED that a complaint to determine the dischargeability of any debt pursuant to § 523(a)(6) of the Bankruptcy Code shall be filed on or before [**DATE**], which is not later than 60 days from the date of the entry of this Order."

[Effective February 1, 2000. Amended effective October 1, 2002; October 17, 2005; March 1, 2008; December 1, 2009; November 1, 2012; December 1, 2015.]

LBR 4007–1. DETERMINATION OF DISCHARGEABILITY OF A DEBT

(a)* Motion for Extension of Time. In addition to stating the justification for the requested extension, a motion for an extension of time to file a complaint to determine the dischargeability of a debt pursuant to § 523(c) of the Bankruptcy Code shall state the deadline for filing such a dischargeability complaint in that case as established under Fed. R. Bankr. P. 4007(c) and the specific date to which an extension is requested.

[Effective February 1, 2000. Amended effective October 17, 2005.]

* **[Publisher's Note:** So in original. No subsection (b) promulgated.]

(as opposed to case number) for a retention period of not less than 30 days. Paper documents shall not be available for examination by the public during the retention period and shall thereafter be destroyed.

[Effective October 1, 2002. Amended effective October 17, 2005; December 1, 2009.]

LBR 5005–1. FILING AND TRANSMITTAL OF DOCUMENTS

Documents may be filed, signed or verified by electronic means that are consistent with technical standards established by the Judicial Conference of the United States and are in compliance with the *Administrative Procedures for the Filing, Signing, and Verifying of Documents by Electronic Means* as set forth in TXEB Appendix 5005.

[Effective October 1, 2002. Amended effective October 17, 2005.]

LBR 5009–1. DECLARATIONS REGARDING SATISFACTION OF SECURED CLAIM AND RELEASE OF LIEN

A motion seeking a declaration that a secured claim has been satisfied and the corresponding lien has been released under the terms of a confirmed plan must contain:

(1) a title which identifies the holder of the lien or security interest which is alleged to have been fully satisfied and which adequately describes the property upon which the lien had existed

Title Example: Motion for Order Declaring Release of Lien of ABC Finance Corp. Upon 1813 Falcon Blvd., Anytown, Texas Due to Full Satisfaction of Secured Claim [Claim #4–1];

(2) an affidavit and/or other documentary proof in support of the motion that demonstrates that: (1) the total satisfaction of the underlying indebtedness has occurred under non-bankruptcy law; (2) a discharge has been granted to the debtor-movant under § 1328; or (3) other circumstances exist that establish the complete satisfaction of the secured claim of the claimant;

(3) the 21–day negative notice language described in LBR 9007(a);

(4) a certificate of service reflecting service of the motion in accordance with LBR 9013(f), including upon the person most recently designated on the secured claimant's proof of claim as the person to receive notices, at the notice address indicated thereon; and

(5) be accompanied by a proposed order incorporating the title information from the pleading and otherwise substantially complying with *TXEB Local Form 9007–a.*

[Effective December 1, 2017.]

LBR 5010–1.   REOPENING CASES

(a) Filing Fee.   A motion to reopen must be accompanied by the filing fee. If a party contends the filing fee is not required, then the motion to reopen must state the facts supporting a finding that the reopening corrects an administrative error or relates to the debtor's discharge.

(b) Trustee Appointment.   In a Chapter 7, 12, or 13 case, the motion to reopen also must state whether or not a trustee is needed.

(c) Proposed Order.   A proposed order must be attached to a motion to reopen, and the proposed order must contain instructions to the Clerk about the filing fee and — in a Chapter 7, 12, or 13 case — to the United States trustee about appointment of a trustee.

[Effective February 1, 2000. Amended effective October 1, 2002; October 17, 2005.]

PART VI.   COLLECTION AND LIQUIDATION OF THE ESTATE

LBR 6004–1.   USE, SALE OR LEASE OF PROPERTY

(a) Contents.   A notice or motion required by Fed. R. Bankr. P. 6004(a), (c), or (d), in addition to the requirements of Fed. R. Bankr. P. 2002(c)(1), must contain:

(1) the 21–day negative notice language described in LBR 9007(a);

(2) a certificate of service reflecting service on the master mailing list (matrix) as constituted by the Court on the date of service;

and, to the extent applicable:

(3) the name and address of the proposed buyer;

(4) the proposed sale price, estimated costs of the sale or lease, including commissions, auctioneer's fees, costs of document preparation and recordation, etc.;

(5) the names and addresses of all parties including judgment creditors who claim an interest in the property, the nature of the claimed interest, and the balance due.

Any motion to sell pursuant to Fed. R. Bankr. P. 6004(c) must also state with particularity the provision of 11 U.S.C. § 363(f) upon which movant relies and be accompanied by a proposed order.

(b) Motion to Sell Personally Identifiable Information.

1. A motion to sell property which includes personally identifiable information under the conditions set forth in § 363(b)(1) of the Bankruptcy Code, shall not require negative notice language but instead shall be scheduled for hearing upon filing.

2. Such motion shall contain a certificate of service reflecting service of the motion upon the master mailing list (matrix) as constituted by the Court on the date of service and must be accompanied by two (2) proposed orders:

(A) one proposed order shall acknowledge the filing of the motion and shall order the United States Trustee to appoint a consumer privacy ombudsman pursuant to Fed. R. Bankr. P. 6004(g); and

(B) the other proposed order shall grant the relief requested by the motion.

3. Any objection to a motion which seeks to sell personally identifiable information must be filed and served no later than seven (7) days prior to the scheduled hearing.

(c) Authority to Pay Estate Expenses.   A Chapter 7 trustee who has not been authorized to operate the business of the debtor under § 721 of the Bankruptcy Code may advance from bankruptcy estate funds:

(1) payment of expenses incurred by the estate and owed to unrelated third parties in an aggregate amount not to exceed $1,000; provided that no single expense shall exceed $500 and that all such expenses are subsequently subjected to court approval for reasonableness after notice and a hearing;

(2) adversary filing fees; or

(3) payment of bond premiums as authorized by the United States Trustee.

[Effective February 1, 2000. Amended effective October 1, 2002; October 17, 2005; December 1, 2009.]

LBR 6007–1. ABANDONMENT OF PROPERTY

(a) Abandonment by Chapter 7 Trustee at First Meeting of Creditors.

1. A trustee in a case under Chapter 7 may, at the first meeting of creditors, announce an intention to abandon property of the estate having an aggregate value of not more than $1,500.00. All other abandonment actions are governed by subsection (b) below.

2. Any objection to such a proposed abandonment must be in writing and filed with the Clerk and served upon the trustee, debtor, debtor's attorney, and any known lienholders of the property no later than 14 days after the first meeting of creditors.

3. If an objection is timely filed and served, the Court shall schedule a hearing with notice to the trustee, debtor, debtor's attorney, any lienholder, and to the objecting party. If no objection is filed, the property will be deemed abandoned without further notice.

4. A statement or summary of this Local Rule shall be included in the notice of the first meeting of creditors.

(b) Abandonment Generally.

1. A notice of intent to abandon (filed by the trustee or debtor-in-possession) or motion to compel abandonment (filed by any other entity) must be filed with the Clerk and served in accordance with Fed. R. Bankr. P. 6007.

2. The notice/motion must describe the property, state its value, if known, and the justification for the proposed abandonment.

3. The notice/motion must contain the following 14–day negative notice language, which must appear as presented and be located in the motion text — preferably on the initial page:

14–DAY NEGATIVE NOTICE—LBR 6007(b):

Your rights may be affected by the relief sought in this pleading. You should read this pleading carefully and discuss it with your attorney, if you have one in this bankruptcy case. If you oppose the relief sought by this pleading, you must file a written objection, explaining the factual and/or legal basis for opposing the relief.

No hearing will be conducted on this Motion unless a written objection is filed with the Clerk of the United States Bankruptcy Court and served upon the party filing this pleading *WITHIN FOURTEEN (14) DAYS FROM THE DATE OF SERVICE* shown in the certificate of service unless the Court shortens or extends the time for filing such objection. If no objection is timely served and filed, this pleading shall be deemed to be unopposed, and the Court may enter an order granting the relief sought. If an objection is filed and served in a timely manner, the Court will thereafter set a hearing with appropriate notice. If you fail to appear at the hearing, your objection may be stricken. The Court reserves the right to set a hearing on any matter.

[Effective February 1, 2000. Amended effective October 1, 2002; October 17, 2005; December 1, 2009; December 1, 2017.]

LBR 6008–1. REDEMPTION OF PROPERTY FROM LIEN OR SALE

(a) Contents of Motion. A motion for redemption of property pursuant to § 722 of the Bankruptcy Code shall contain the 21–day negative notice language described in LBR 9007(a) and be accompanied by an affidavit of the debtor which discloses the following information:

(1) the date of the purchase and purchase price of the item(s) of property sought to be redeemed, as well as the account number by which the secured creditor can identify the particular loan transaction(s);

(2) a specific description of the condition of such item(s) of property;

(3) the Debtor's opinion of the fair market value of such item(s);

(4) the basis for the Debtor's opinion of the value of such item(s); and

(5) the creditor's valuation of such item(s) as indicated in its proof of claim, if any.

(b) Service. Service of a motion for redemption of property shall be made upon any affected creditor and the Chapter 7 Trustee.

[Effective February 1, 2000. Amended effective October 17, 2005; December 1, 2009.]

PART VII. ADVERSARY PROCEEDINGS

LBR 7003–1. COMMENCEMENT OF ADVERSARY PROCEEDING

(a) Filing Requirements. A party filing an adversary proceeding must file the following documents with the Clerk:

1. The complaint or notice of removal;

2. A completed adversary proceeding cover sheet, the form for which is available at the Court's website [www.txeb. uscourts.gov]; and

3. A summons for each defendant.

(b) Filing Fees.

1. A filing fee must be paid at the time the adversary proceeding is commenced unless no fee is required pursuant to 28 U.S.C. § 1930.

2. If funds are available in an estate, the trustee must pay the filing fee. If no funds are available, the trustee must file, at the time of filing the adversary complaint, a motion to defer payment of the filing fee. Such motion to defer shall be filed in the underlying bankruptcy case and be accompanied by a proposed order.

3. The provisions of Title 28 U.S.C. § 1915 apply to adversary proceedings filed in cases under the Bankruptcy Code.

(c) Caption and Form. The caption and form of pleading must comply with the provisions of LBR 7010.

[Effective February 1, 2000. Amended effective October 1, 2002; October 17, 2005.]

LBR 7005–1. SERVICE BY ELECTRONIC MEANS

Documents filed in any adversary proceeding subsequent to the original complaint may be served upon another party by electronic means that are consistent with technical standards established by the Judicial Conference of the United States and are in compliance with the *Administrative Procedures for the Filing, Signing, and Verifying of Documents by Electronic Means* as set forth in *TXEB Appendix 5005*. The transmission facilities of the Court may be utilized to accomplish such service.

[Effective October 1, 2002. Amended effective October 17, 2005.]

LBR 7007–1. PLEADINGS ALLOWED; FORM OF MOTIONS

Unless otherwise ordered by the Court or the provisions of this rule, all motions filed in adversary proceedings shall be governed by the requirements of LBR 9004, 9007 and 9013. Except for the following motions which are not required to contain negative notice language,

Motion for Summary Judgment	Motion to Quash
Application for Preliminary Injunction	Motion for Protective Order
Application for Temporary Restraining Order	Motion for Default Judgment

any motion filed in an adversary proceeding shall contain the following 14–day negative notice language, which must appear as presented and be located in the motion text — preferably on the initial page:

14–DAY NEGATIVE NOTICE—LBR 7007:

No hearing will be conducted on this Motion unless a written objection is filed with the Clerk of the United States Bankruptcy Court and served upon the party filing this pleading *WITHIN FOURTEEN (14) DAYS FROM THE DATE OF SERVICE* shown in the certificate of service unless the Court shortens or extends the time for filing such objection. If no objection is timely served and filed, this pleading shall be deemed to be unopposed, and the Court may enter an order granting the relief sought. If an objection is filed and served in a timely manner, the Court will thereafter set a hearing with appropriate notice. If you fail to appear at the hearing, your objection may be stricken. The Court reserves the right to set a hearing on any matter.

[Effective February 1, 2000. Amended effective October 1, 2002; October 17, 2005; December 1, 2009; December 1, 2017.]

LBR 7010–1. CAPTION AND FORM OF PLEADING IN ADVERSARY PROCEEDINGS

The caption of each pleading in an adversary proceeding must identify:

1. the district and division in which the proceeding was filed;

2. the style of the bankruptcy case including the name, address, and last four (4) digits of the taxpayer identification number of the debtor, the case number and the applicable chapter of the bankruptcy proceeding;

3. the name of the plaintiffs and the defendants in the adversary proceeding;

4. a space for the case number assigned to the adversary proceeding; and

5. a descriptive title indicating the nature of the relief being sought.

[Effective February 1, 2000. Amended effective October 17, 2005.]

LBR 7016–1. PRETRIAL PROCEDURES AND ORDERS

(a) Discovery. Discovery conducted in adversary proceedings must not be filed with the Clerk.

(b) Scheduling Order. A scheduling order controls the course of an adversary proceeding and may not be amended without Court approval. To the extent that a scheduling order is inconsistent with a provision in the Local Rules of Bankruptcy Procedure, the scheduling order controls. If a scheduling order is not issued, the provisions of this rule shall apply.

(c) Pretrial Conference. A pretrial conference may be scheduled, on written motion to the Court, or on the Court's own motion. A party's request for a pretrial hearing or conference must be made no later than 28 days prior to the date scheduled for the trial.

(d) Exhibits.

1. Exhibits which are to be introduced into evidence must be:

(A) individually marked for identification on the first page of the exhibit as set forth below prior to the hearing;

(B) tendered through digital (electronic) media, such as a USB flash drive or compact disc (CD), or otherwise bound in a booklet format, but a minimum of one copy of the exhibits must be tendered to the Court in a digital format;

(C) if tendered in booklet format, separated by tabs or other appropriate dividers;

(D) if tendered in digital format, indexed by bookmark or other appropriate dividing mechanism;

(E) presented in numerical or alphabetical sequence and preceded by an exhibit list in the format prescribed by *TXEB Local Form 7016*; and

(F) tendered in a minimum number of four (4) sets: two for the Court (one of which must be in a digital format); one for the witness box (which must be in a paper format); and one set for each opposing counsel who appears.

2. Exhibits for the Plaintiff shall be designated by number. In the event of multiple plaintiffs, then each exhibit shall be designated by a specific plaintiff's name, followed by a number [i.e. Smith, Inc. — 1].

3. Exhibits for the Defendant shall be designated by letter. In the event of multiple defendants, then each exhibit shall be designated by a specific defendant's name, followed by a letter [i.e. Smith, Inc. — A].

4. Copies of all exhibits must be provided to each party not less than 14 days prior to trial.

5. Failure to comply with the exhibit requirements in this Local Rule may result in the refusal of the Court to admit exhibits into evidence or other sanctions.

(e) Proposed Findings of Facts and Conclusions of Law. Unless excused by the Court, each party shall prepare proposed findings of fact and conclusions of law in a detailed format based upon the evidence anticipated to be offered at trial. The Court shall direct the time and the means for such submission through its scheduling order.

(f) Briefs. Any legal brief must be filed by the pretrial order deadline and must be served on opposing counsel.

(g) Pretrial Order. A pretrial or joint pretrial order caption must include the date set for trial, if known, and the estimated time required for trial of the issues. Unless otherwise established by the Court, a pretrial order is due 14 days prior to trial.

(h) Continuances in Adversary Proceedings. A motion for continuance in an adversary proceeding will require a proper certificate of service, but will not require any negative notice language.

[Effective February 1, 2000. Amended effective October 1, 2002; October 17, 2005; December 1, 2009; November 26, 2013; December 1, 2015; December 1, 2017.]

LBR 7021–1. MISJOINDER AND NON-JOINDER OF PARTIES

A plaintiff prosecuting an adversary complaint against multiple defendants shall set forth in its complaint the justifications for permissive joinder of such parties under the provisions of Fed. R. Bankr. P. 7020. Upon review of the complaint, and after maintaining the adversary proceeding against the first defendant named therein, the Court may, pursuant to Fed. R. Bankr. P. 7021 and without notice or hearing, either sever, or dismiss without prejudice, all claims against any misjoined parties in the adversary proceeding.

[Effective October 17, 2005.]

LBR 7041–1. SETTLEMENT AND DISMISSAL

(a) Settlement of Controversies Which Impact Bankruptcy Estate. A motion to compromise must comply with Federal and Local Rules of Bankruptcy Procedure 2002(a), 9014, and 9019. Such motion, and any proposed order approv-

ing such a motion, shall be filed in the underlying bankruptcy case.

(b) Disposition of Adversary Upon Settlement Approval. Upon the entry of an order approving a compromise and settlement in the underlying bankruptcy case, the parties shall submit to the Court either a final judgment based upon the approved settlement or an agreed order dismissing the adversary proceeding.

[Effective February 1, 2000. Amended effective October 17, 2005.]

LBR 7055–1. DEFAULT JUDGMENTS—AFFIDAVITS

Subject to the terms of Fed. R. Bankr. P. 7055, damages may be awarded without further hearing only if damages are liquidated and evidenced by an affidavit. Attorney's fees may be awarded if an affidavit satisfactory to the Court is submitted which details the fees incurred or other grounds for such award.

[Effective February 1, 2000. Amended effective October 1, 2002; October 17, 2005.]

LBR 7056–1. SUMMARY JUDGMENTS

(a) Length. A motion for summary judgment and brief in support thereof shall not exceed 30 pages in length, excluding attachments; however, a party may submit multiple motions, with each motion addressing a particular cause of action or defense.

(b) Response. Any response in opposition to a motion for summary judgment must be filed within 28 days of the filing of the motion. A response in opposition shall not exceed 30 pages in length, excluding attachments.

(c) Reply. Any reply brief to an opposed summary judgment motion must be filed within 14 days of the filing of the response in opposition. Any such reply brief shall not exceed 10 pages in length, excluding attachments. No sur-replies shall be filed without leave of court and such shall not be granted in the absence of exigent circumstances.

(d) Format. Each motion for summary judgment, or response and reply thereto, shall comply in format and content with the requirements of Local District Court Rule CV–56 and shall be decided under the procedures stated therein. A paper copy of the complete motion or response, including all exhibits thereto, must be delivered to the Clerk for use by the assigned judge per *TXEB Appendix 5005*.

(e) Hearing. The Court does not normally require nor permit oral argument in connection with a motion for summary judgment. In the absence of the granting of a motion to allow oral argument, no formal hearing on a motion for summary judgment will be conducted and the Court shall proceed to consider the merits of any such motion upon the expiration of the reply deadline set forth in subsection (c) above.

[Effective February 1, 2000. Amended effective October 17, 2005; December 1, 2009; November 1, 2012.]

LBR 7065–1. INJUNCTIONS

An application for a temporary restraining order or a preliminary injunction filed in an adversary proceeding does not require the negative notice language of LBR 9007, but must be accompanied by a request for emergency hearing under LBR 9007(b) in order to obtain the immediate attention of the Court.

[Effective February 1, 2000. Amended effective October 1, 2002; October 17, 2005.]

PART VIII. APPEALS TO DISTRICT COURT

LBR 8006–1. RECORD AND ISSUES ON APPEAL

A designation of record filed by any party must include the docket entry number and the filing or entry date for each item to be included in the appellate record. Payment must be made for all transcripts or copies prior to inclusion in the record.

[Effective February 1, 2000. Amended effective October 17, 2005; March 1, 2008.]

LBR 8007–1. COMPLETION AND TRANS-MISSION OF THE RECORD; DOCK-ETING OF THE APPEAL

If a party fails to designate the appellate record or to request transcript preparation, the Clerk must certify the omission when the appellate record is transmitted to the District Court. The omission does not stay transmittal of the record.

[Effective February 1, 2000. Amended effective October 17, 2005.]

LBR 8011–1. MOTIONS PENDING DOCKETING OF THE APPEAL

Except for motions which may be filed directly with the District Court pursuant to Fed. R. Bankr. P. 8005, until an appeal is docketed by the District Clerk, all pleadings must be filed with the Bankruptcy Clerk and acted upon by the bankruptcy judge.

[Effective February 1, 2000. Amended effective October 1, 2002; October 17, 2005.]

PART IX. GENERAL PROVISIONS

LBR 9001–1. GENERAL DEFINITIONS

The Bankruptcy Code and Federal Rules of Bankruptcy Procedure definitions of words and phrases and rules of construction govern their use in these rules. In addition, the following words and phrases used in these local rules have the meanings indicated:

(a) **Bankruptcy Court or Court** means the United States Bankruptcy Court for the Eastern District of Texas.

(b) **Clerk** means the United States Bankruptcy Clerk for the Eastern District of Texas. [See LBR 5001.]

(c) **District** means the Eastern District of Texas.

(d) **District Court** means the United States District Court for the Eastern District of Texas.

(e) **District Court Rules** means the Local Court Rules of the United States District Court for the Eastern District of Texas in effect on the effective date of these local rules and as subsequently amended.

(f) **Trustee** means the Chapter 7, 11, 12, or 13 trustee unless these Bankruptcy Rules specify the "United States Trustee."

[Effective February 1, 2000. Amended effective October 1, 2002; October 17, 2005.]

LBR 9004–1. GENERAL REQUIREMENTS OF FORM

(a) **Caption of Pleading.** The caption of each pleading must identify:

1. the district and division in which the proceeding was filed;

2. the name, address, and last four (4) digits of the taxpayer identification number of the debtor;

3. the bankruptcy case number; and

4. the applicable chapter of the bankruptcy proceeding.

(b) **Title of Pleading.** The title of a pleading must designate the relief sought in the motion and proposed order. Substantial variance between the title and the relief sought in the pleading may result in dismissal, denial, or sanctions.

(c) **Separate Motions Required.** A separate motion is required for each form of relief requested, and multiple forms of relief may not be contained in one motion, with the following exceptions:

(1) Motion for Relief from Automatic Stay, for Adequate Protection, and for Relief from Co–Debtor Stay;

(2) Motion to Use Cash Collateral and for Adequate Protection;

(3) Motion to Dismiss or to Convert Case;

(4) Trustee's Motion to Approve Compromise and Settlement Under Fed. R. Bankr. P. 9019 and Application for Compensation of Special Counsel Pertaining Thereto Based Upon Approved Contingent Fee Contract; and

(5) Motion for Contempt and/or for Sanctions.

(d) **Stay Relief Motions.** If filing a motion for relief from stay, refer to LBR 4001.

(e) Omission of Negative Notice Language. If a motion is amended after a hearing has been scheduled, such amended motion shall contain the date, time and location of the scheduled hearing in lieu of any negative notice language otherwise required by these Local Rules.

[Effective February 1, 2000. Amended effective October 1, 2002; October 17, 2005.]

LBR 9007-1. GENERAL AUTHORITY TO REGULATE NOTICES

(a) 21-Day Negative Notice Language. If relief may be granted "after notice and hearing" as defined in 11 U.S.C. § 102, *and unless otherwise specifically provided in these rules,* the pleading must contain the following 21-day negative notice language which must be located in the pleading text — preferably on the initial page:

21-DAY NEGATIVE NOTICE—LBR 9007(a):

Your rights may be affected by the relief sought in this pleading. You should read this pleading carefully and discuss it with your attorney, if you have one in this bankruptcy case. If you oppose the relief sought by this pleading, you <u>must</u> file a written objection, explaining the factual and/or legal basis for opposing the relief.

No hearing will be conducted on this Motion/Objection/Application unless a written objection is filed with the Clerk of the United States Bankruptcy Court and served upon the party filing this pleading *WITHIN TWENTY-ONE (21) DAYS FROM THE DATE OF SERVICE* shown in the certificate of service unless the Court shortens or extends the time for filing such objection. If no objection is timely served and filed, this pleading shall be deemed to be unopposed, and the Court may enter an order granting the relief sought. If an objection is filed and served in a timely manner, the Court will thereafter set a hearing with appropriate notice. If you fail to appear at the hearing, your objection may be stricken. The Court reserves the right to set a hearing on any matter.

Proposed orders for motions with 21-day language should substantially comply with *TXEB Local Form 9007-a.*

The following motions will require proper certificates of service, but will not require any suspense language, and will be presented to the Court for immediate consideration:

- Request for Emergency Hearing;
- Request for Expedited Hearing;
- Request for Conditional Approval of Disclosure Statement for Small Business Debtor;
- Motion for Continuance of Hearing;
- Motion/Application to Shorten or to Extend Notice Period;
- Motion for Extension of Time to File Schedules;
- Motion for Extension of Bar Date for Filing Claims;
- Motion by Debtor to Convert Chapter 12 Case to Chapter 7 (or Notice of Conversion);
- Motion by Debtor to Convert Chapter 13 Case to Chapter 7 (or Notice of Conversion);
- Motion by Debtor to Dismiss Chapter 12 Case;
- Motion by Debtor to Dismiss Chapter 13 Case;
- Motion for Approval of Reaffirmation Agreement;
- Motion to Quash;
- Motion for Protective Order;
- Motion to Reopen Estate;
- Motion to Defer Payment of Filing Fee;
- Application/Motion for Admission *Pro Hac Vice;*
- Motion to Deposit Funds in Court Registry (or for Disposition of Funds);
- Motion to Waive Debtor's Appearance at Section 341 Meeting (or similar).

(b) Request for Emergency Hearing.

1. If a motion requires an emergency hearing, it should still contain any applicable negative notice language and a separate request for emergency hearing must be filed.

2. An "emergency" is a matter which requires a hearing in less than seven (7) days, and which involves an irreparable injury which outweighs procedural due process concerns. A request for an emergency hearing is given the highest priority by the Court. Abuse of the emergency process may subject parties and/or attorneys to sanctions, contempt, or other disciplinary powers of the Court.

3. A request for emergency hearing must contain the following:

(A) sufficient factual information for the Court to find just cause for the scheduling of an emergency hearing;

(B) a certificate of conference reflecting inability to agree or inability to confer;

(C) a certificate of service reflecting service by e-mail or facsimile, if possible, and by first class mail;

(D) an affidavit or an unsworn declaration under penalty of perjury as provided in 28 U.S.C. § 1746 by the party or the attorney attesting to the emergency facts;

(E) a form order substantially conforming to *TXEB Local Form 9007-b.*

(c) Request for Expedited Hearing. If a motion requires a hearing on shortened notice but does not require an emergency hearing, the motion should still contain any applicable negative notice language and an application to shorten notice and/or to schedule an expedited hearing must be filed in accordance with Fed. R. Bankr. P. 9006(c). The request for expedited hearing must be accompanied by a proposed order substantially conforming to *TXEB Local Form 9007-c.*

(d) Complex Chapter 11 Cases. Procedures set forth in these Local Rules may be superseded in complex Chapter 11 cases by the procedures set forth in *TXEB Appendix 9007.*

[Effective February 1, 2000. Amended effective February 1, 2001; October 1, 2002; October 17, 2005; March 1, 2008; December 1, 2009; December 1, 2017.]

LBR 9011-1. SIGNING PLEADINGS

In addition to the requirements of Fed. R. Bankr. P. 9011, every pleading must contain the attorney's state bar number. Failure to comply with Fed. R. Bankr. P. 9011 or this local rule may result in dismissal of the pleading by the Court or other appropriate sanctions.

[Effective February 1, 2000. Amended effective October 1, 2002; October 17, 2005.]

LBR 9013–1. MOTION PRACTICE

(a) Form. A motion or application, an objection to a proof of claim, or an objection to a debtor's claim of exemption, must contain all information required under these Local Rules of Bankruptcy Procedure including any applicable negative notice language. A failure to include required information may result in the dismissal of that pleading.

(b) Proposed Orders.

1. Any motion, application, or objection shall be accompanied by a proposed order with a title that describes the relief and refers to the pleading which it accompanies.

2. A proposed order must clearly delineate that the motion is being granted or denied, or that an objection is being sustained or denied, and avoid non-descriptive titles such as "Order On" or "Order Regarding" in order to provide effective notification of the entry of such order to affected parties.

3. A failure to attach a proposed order may result in the dismissal of the referenced pleading.

(c) [Reserved for future use]

(d) Redaction of Personal Identifiers. Pursuant to Fed. R. Bankr. P. 9037 and the exemptions contained therein, as well as policies adopted by the Judicial Conference of the United States, all parties must refrain from including, or shall redact where inclusion is necessary, the following personal identifiers from all pleadings and exhibits filed with the Court, unless ordered by the Court to do otherwise:

- **Social Security Numbers:** if disclosure of a social security number is required, only the last four digits of that number should be used;
- **Names of Minor Children:** if disclosure of the identity of any minor child is required, only the initials of that child should be used;
- **Dates of Birth:** if disclosure of an individual's date of birth is required by any statement or schedule, only the year should be used;
- **Financial Account Numbers:** if disclosure of any financial account number is required, only the last four digits of that number should be used.
- **Driver's License Numbers:** parties should redact license numbers when attaching a copy of any driver's license to any pleading, including motions pertaining to unclaimed funds.

The responsibility for redacting these personal identifiers rests solely with counsel and the parties. The Court will not review each pleading for compliance with this rule. Parties are cautioned that failure to redact these personal identifiers may subject them to the full disciplinary power of the Court.

(e) Notices: Certificate of Service.

1. A motion, application, or other document filed with the Court when notice to interested parties is required under applicable law, or in which the relief requested may adversely affect an interested party, must contain a certificate of service.

2. The certificate of service must indicate specifically the parties served (including their addresses), the method of service, the date of service, and shall be signed by an attorney or an agent thereof.

3. Failure to include a certificate of service in compliance with this rule may result in the dismissal, denial or striking of the affected pleading.

(f) Notices: Parties–in–Interest Served.

1. When a motion or application is filed which can only be authorized or granted on notice or "after notice and hearing" as such phrase is defined in Bankruptcy Code § 102 (other than motions relating to appeals from orders or for new trial), including motions for relief from automatic stay, the movant shall serve a copy of the motion, or a summary of the motion, upon all parties entitled to service of such motion or any hearing on such a motion under any Federal Rule or Local Rule of Bankruptcy Procedure. Such service includes the following parties at a minimum:

(A) In a Chapter 7 case: the debtor, the trustee, the United States Trustee, all members of any official committee, and their respective attorneys; all parties who have filed a notice of appearance or request for notice in the case; and, if the motion involves relief from the stay with respect to property, any other parties claiming a security interest of record in the same property;

(B) In a Chapter 11 case: the debtor, the United States Trustee, the case trustee (if one has been appointed), all members of any official committee, and their respective attorneys; all secured creditors; all governmental units, the twenty (20) largest unsecured creditors (only in the event that no official committee of unsecured creditors has been formed); and all parties who have filed a notice of appearance or request for notice in the case;

(C) In a Chapter 12 or 13 case: the debtor, the debtor's attorney, the Chapter 12 or 13 Trustee, all parties who have filed a notice of appearance or request for notice in the case, and, if the motion involves relief from the stay or a motion for valuation with respect to property, any party claiming a security interest of record in the same property [no service upon United States Trustee is required].

For further information, parties should consult this Court's Guide to Practice and Procedures which is available at the Court's website [**www.txeb.uscourts.gov**].

2. Any summary of a motion or application issued to parties entitled to service shall contain:

(A) the relevant facts regarding the motion or application;

(B) appropriate negative notice language as designated in these Local Rules for that type of motion or application; and

(C) a notification that a complete copy of the motion or application will be sent to any requesting party at no charge.

(g) Briefs. Authorities and argument may be briefed in a motion, application or responsive pleading, and a separate brief or memorandum of authorities is not required. However, any party wishing to submit a separate brief must do so no later than three (3) business days prior to a hearing.

(h) Service by Electronic Means. Documents filed in any matter governed by this rule may be served upon another party by electronic means that are consistent with technical standards established by the Judicial Conference of the United States and are in compliance with the *Administrative Procedures for the Filing, Signing, and Verifying of Documents by Electronic Means* as set forth in *TXEB Appendix 5005*. The transmission facilities of the Court may be utilized to accomplish such service.

[Effective February 1, 2000. Amended effective February 1, 2001; October 1, 2002; October 17, 2005; March 1, 2008; November 1, 2012.]

LBR 9014–1.   CONTESTED MATTERS

(a) Summons. A summons is not required in a contested matter, but service otherwise must comply with Fed. R. Bankr. P. 7004.

(b) Responsive Pleadings.

1. Excluding the filing of a *response* to an objection to claim under LBR 3007 or to an objection to the debtor's claim of exemption under LBR 4003, any party who opposes the relief requested in any pleading containing negative notice language must file an *objection* within the designated negative notice period.

2. An objection — or a "response" under LBR 3007 or 4003 only — must conform to the requirements of Fed. R. Civ. P. 8(b) and is the only responsive pleading in a contested matter which constitutes a request for hearing. Any other type must be properly denominated as a *comment* and will not trigger the scheduling of a hearing before the Court.

3. If no objection — or no "response" under LBR 3007 or 4003 only— is filed within the designated negative notice period, the Court will deem the pleading unopposed and proceed to consider the merits of the pleading without a hearing in light of any comments which have been filed.

4. The title of a responsive pleading must state the respondent's name and incorporate the title of the original pleading. For example, "Big Bank's Objection [or Comment] to Deborah Debtor's Motion to Avoid Lien."

5. A responsive pleading must contain a certificate of service under LBR 9013(e) which documents that appropriate service has been accomplished under LBR 9013(f).

6. A responsive pleading does not require a proposed order.

(c) Scheduling of Hearings.

1. Hearings before the Court are generally scheduled and noticed by the Clerk through the auspices of the Bankruptcy Noticing Center.

2. The Courtroom Deputy must be contacted if the parties anticipate that a hearing scheduled to be conducted on a general docket date will exceed one (1) hour.

3. Once a hearing has been scheduled, any amendment of the pleading scheduled for hearing shall comply with LBR 9004(e) and become the operative pleading for the hearing.

The amendment of a pleading scheduled for hearing shall not result in the cancellation of the hearing unless otherwise ordered by the Court.

(d) Trial Preparation.

1. Subsections (a) and (f) of Fed. R. Bankr. P. 7026 and all other provisions of Fed. R. Bankr. P. 7026 pertaining to or based upon those subsections, shall not apply in a contested matter unless the Court orders otherwise.

2. Each party to a hearing on a contested matter shall provide to every other party:

(A) a witness list;

(B) an exhibit list presented in an electronic or booklet format as prescribed by TXEB Local Form 7016; and

(C) a copy of all exhibits, properly identified by number or letter as required by LBR 7016(d), which that party may seek to introduce at the hearing.

Such disclosures shall be made by 5:00 p.m, prevailing central time, at least three (3) business days prior to the hearing in compliance with the following schedule:

Hearing Day	Disclosure and Production Deadline
Monday	Prior Wednesday at 5:00 p.m.
Tuesday	Prior Thursday at 5:00 p.m.
Wednesday	Prior Friday at 5:00 p.m.
Thursday	Prior Monday at 5:00 p.m.
Friday	Prior Tuesday at 5:00 p.m.

3. In the face of a timely objection, and unless the Court orders otherwise, the testimony of any witness not timely identified under this rule or any exhibit not timely identified and produced to every other party under this rule at least three (3) business days prior to a hearing shall be inadmissible for any purpose at such hearing.

4. Excluding the time established for the exchange of exhibits among the parties as set forth in this subsection, the presentation of exhibits to the Court in contested matters shall be governed by LBR 7016(d).

5. Any brief must be filed at least three (3) business days prior to the hearing.

6. Witnesses may present testimony at any scheduled hearing on a contested matter except for preliminary hearings on motions for relief from the automatic stay and hearings to determine the adequacy of a Chapter 11 disclosure statement, although the Court may grant leave upon proper motion to allow witnesses to testify at any scheduled hearing.

[Effective February 1, 2000. Amended effective February 1, 2001; October 1, 2002; October 17, 2005; March 1, 2008.]

LBR 9017–1.   EVIDENCE

Exhibits introduced into evidence may be withdrawn from the custody of the Clerk only upon order of the Court. Any exhibit not withdrawn 30 days after final disposition of the proceedings may be destroyed without further order or notice.

[Effective February 1, 2000. Amended effective October 17, 2005.]

LBR 9018–1. FILING DOCUMENTS UNDER SEAL

No document shall be placed under seal unless authorized by the Court. A motion to place a document under seal shall not require service nor negative notice language, but shall be accompanied by a proposed order. Parties seeking to submit documents under seal should also consult Section III(A) of *TXEB Appendix 5005* regarding the submission of documents under seal by electronic means. Any party may seek to vacate or modify the order and the Court, after hearing on notice, shall determine such motion in a manner designed to preserve the confidential nature of the information sought to be protected.

[Effective October 17, 2005.]

LBR 9019–1. COMPROMISE AND ARBITRATION

A motion to approve compromise must:

(A) contain an analysis of the settlement factors invoked in this context by decisions of the United States Supreme Court and the Fifth Circuit Court of Appeals: *See, e.g., Protective Comm. For Indep. Stockholders of TMT Trailer Ferry, Inc. v. Anderson,* 390 U.S. 414, 425 (1968); *Official Comm. of Unsecured Creditors v. Cajun Electric Power Coop., Inc. (In re Cajun Elec. Power Coop., Inc.),* 119 F.3d 349, 355–56 (5th Cir. 1997); *Connecticut Gen. Life. Ins. Co. v. United Cos. Fin. Corp. (In re Foster Mortgage Corp.),* 68 F.3d 914, 917 (5th Cir. 1995);

(B) cite any adversary proceeding, by style and number, and provide trial setting information;

(C) attach a copy of the settlement agreement;

(D) contain an affidavit or an unsworn declaration under penalty of perjury as provided in 28 U.S.C. § 1746 by the debtor or trustee recommending settlement approval under the case law guidelines.

(E) contain the 21–day negative notice language described in LBR 9007(a); and

(F) attach a certificate of service reflecting service on the master mailing list (matrix) as constituted by the Court on the date of service.

[Effective February 1, 2000. Amended effective October 1, 2002; October 17, 2005; December 1, 2009.]

LBR 9022–1. AGREED ORDERS

(a) **Presentation.** When a disputed matter has been set for hearing and the parties have resolved the matter, in order to excuse the parties from appearance at the scheduled hearing, the agreed order: (1) must be reduced to writing, signed by the parties or their attorneys and submitted to the division where the case is pending prior to the hearing; (2) must be submitted to the Court at the hearing; or (3) if the agreement has not been reduced to writing, the terms of the agreement must be read into the record by at least one interested party or such party's attorney.

(b) **Service.** The Court may direct an agreed order or summary thereof be served by the movant on all parties upon whom service of the motion was required under these Local Rules, giving those parties an opportunity to object before the Court will enter the order.

[Effective February 1, 2000. Amended effective October 1, 2002; October 17, 2005.]

LBR 9027–1. REMOVALS

When a Notice of Removal is filed pursuant to Fed. R. Bankr. P. 9027(a), setting forth bankruptcy jurisdiction under 28 U.S.C. § 1334 as the ground for removal, the removing party is responsible for tendering the following items as **separate** attachments to the Notice of Removal:

1. the complete docket sheet from the prior court;

2. the operative petition or complaint;

3. all operative answers to the petition or complaint;

4. all operative counterclaims or cross-claims;

5. all operative answers to pending counterclaims or cross-claims;

6. any pending motion and any objections or replies thereto;

Documents other than those enumerated above may be tendered to the Court in a unified format. Unless the subject of a pending motion in need of resolution, or unless otherwise ordered by the Court, no discovery request or discovery response shall be filed in the removed action.

[Effective February 1, 2000. Amended effective October 1, 2002; October 17, 2005; December 1, 2017.]

APPENDICES

APPENDIX 1001–h. EXTERNAL OPERATING PROCEDURES—CLERK'S OFFICE

UNITED STATES BANKRUPTCY COURT
EASTERN DISTRICT OF TEXAS

External Operating Procedures—Clerk's Office

I. Clerk's Office Locations

A. *United States Bankruptcy Court—Tyler office*—(903) 590–3200

110 N. College Avenue, Ninth Floor

Tyler, Texas 75702–7226

(Tyler and Marshall Divisions)

{Counties of: Camp, Cass, Harrison, Marion, Morris, Upshur}

{Counties of: Anderson, Cherokee, Gregg, Henderson, Panola, Rains, Rusk, Smith, Van Zandt, Wood}

B. *United States Bankruptcy Court—Beaumont office*—(409) 654–7060

Jack Brooks Federal Building

300 Willow Street, First Floor

Beaumont, Texas 77701–2222

(Beaumont and Lufkin Divisions)

{Counties of: Hardin, Jasper, Jefferson, Liberty, Newton, Orange}

{Counties of: Angelina, Houston, Nacogdoches, Polk, San Augustine, Shelby, Trinity, Tyler, Sabine}

C. *United States Bankruptcy Court—Plano office*—(972) 509–1240

660 North Central Expressway, Third Floor

Plano, Texas 75074–6795

(Sherman and Texarkana Divisions)

{Counties of: Collin, Cooke, Delta, Denton, Fannin, Grayson, Hopkins, Lamar}

{Counties of: Bowie, Franklin, Red River, Titus}

II. Office Hours

A. The Clerk's Office is open for conducting official business from 8:00 AM to 4:00 PM daily, Monday through Friday, except official holidays and during such other times as the Chief Judge may designate. The doors close at 4:00 PM. We do not close for lunch.

B. With few exceptions, all documents submitted for filing at the front counter of any Clerk's Office must be scanned by the filer using a public scanner in order for that document to be filed. We strongly encourage the filing of new petitions early in the day.

C. With few exceptions, parties are required to submit documents by electronic means. Electronic filing is generally available 24 hours per day, 7 days per week. For more information, see LBR Appendix 5005 and the Court's website at www.txeb.uscourts.gov.

III. Filing Requirements

A. All papers and pleadings presented for filing are accepted, unless the document is not accompanied by the proper fee. Documents filed on paper by filers required to file such documents electronically are referred to the assigned judge. Voluntary petitions for individuals without payment in full must be accompanied by either an *Application to Pay Filing Fee in Installments*

(Official Form 3A) or *Application for Waiver of the Chapter 7 Filing Fee* (Official Form 3B). Also, fee-related documents filed by a case trustee without payment in full must be accompanied by an *Application to Defer the Filing Fee*.

B.   Every pleading must contain the attorney's state bar number (LBR 9011).

C.   Parties who are not required to file documents electronically and are requesting a file-stamped document copy must include an additional copy and a stamped, self-addressed envelope large enough and with sufficient postage attached to accommodate the return document.

D.   Documents filed on paper by an individual without an attorney must be accompanied by a valid picture ID.

E.   Documents may not be removed from the physical confines of the Court.

F.   The Court discards and does not file documents received using a facsimile machine.

G.   A *Notice of Change in Schedule of Creditors* prepared in accordance with LBR Appendix 1007–b–7 must be filed by the debtor to add or delete creditors, to notify the Court of creditor address changes, to amend schedules due to a chapter conversion, for other changes in the status of original scheduled debt, and with each amendment to Schedules I, J, and/or C.

IV.   Financial Transactions

A.   The Clerk's Office charges all fees according to the *Official Bankruptcy Fee Schedule*, including the *Bankruptcy Court Miscellaneous Fee Schedule* and the *Fee Schedule for Electronic Public Access*. 28 U.S.C. 1930.

B.   The Clerk's Office does not provide change.

C.   With the exception of pages printed from the public printer in the public area of each office, all services must be paid for in advance.

D.   For pages printed from the public printers in the public area of each office, payment must be tendered prior to any departure from the Clerk's Office.

E.   The Clerk's Office promptly deposits all cash, checks, and money orders, including those received with a *Motion to Reopen Case*.

F.   The Clerk's Office periodically invoices *Chapter 11 Noticing and Claim Fees*. Fees are payable upon invoice receipt.

G.   The Clerk's Office maintains a list of attorneys and law firms that may not pay fees with personal checks or checks from their law firm. These persons must pay for all services with cash, money order, cashier's check or credit/debit card.

H.   All fees due for documents filed electronically must be paid on-line within 72 hours of filing with a credit/debit card. Documentation is available for electronic filers to pay filing fees on-line in the On–Line Credit Card Payment Guide available on the Court's website.

I.   All Attorneys will pay filing fees and be able to review their payment histories and outstanding fees over the Internet any time of day. Filing fees must be paid with a credit/debit card transaction on-line; checks will no longer be mailed to the Court. We (the Court) will automatically docket the Internet credit card receipt number when fees are paid online, thus eliminating tasks such as maintaining and securing attorney credit card numbers and manually posting fee payments. During the unusual times when a document is scanned and filed at the front counter at a divisional office, the applicable filing fee must be paid with cash, check, money order, or credit card physically tendered at the time of filing.

V.   Copy Requests

A.   Various commercial service providers may perform research and make copies on your behalf. These companies usually charge a fee for their services. The Clerk's Office does not endorse any company nor will the Clerk's Office warrant their suitability to perform the work provided. The most current information is listed on our website at www.txeb.uscourts.gov.

B.   Generally speaking, paper documents are NOT available for examination. The Clerk's Office may charge the applicable search fee under the Bankruptcy Court Miscellaneous Fee Schedule for retrieval of a paper case file or any documents that are available in paper format. The Clerk's Office will charge the full applicable copy fees for all copies made from paper documents.

C. The Clerk's Office maintains public access computer terminals at each of its divisional offices. There is no charge to use one of these terminals; however, print fees may be charged for printed copies of documents stored in an electronic format.

VI. Informational Queries

A. Information about open and closed cases is available from a variety of mediums. The best medium for a user depends on the kind of information being sought and the type of access available.

B. **WebPACER**—The WebPACER system provides Public Access to Court Electronic Records via the Internet using any standard browser. Scanned document images and electronically filed documents are also available via our WebPACER service. Persons interested in using this service must first register with the PACER Service Center at 800—676–6856 or on the Internet at the PACER Service Center. There is a charge of $.10 per page for information retrieved from this site. If you need help using the WebPACER system, there is a user's guide available. To register for WebPACER, go to http://pacer.txeb.uscourts.gov.

C. **VCIS**—VCIS is the Voice Case Information System. VCIS uses an automated voice response system to read a limited amount of bankruptcy case information (debtor, debtor's attorney, case trustee and current case status) directly from the court's database in response to Touch–Tone telephone inquiries. Call toll-free 1–866–222–8029.

D. **National Case Party Index**—The U.S. Party/Case Index is a national index for U.S. district, bankruptcy, and appellate courts. This index allows searches to determine whether or not a party is involved in federal litigation almost anywhere in the nation. The U.S. Party/Case Index provides the capability to perform national or regional searches on party name and social security number in the bankruptcy index, party name and nature of suit in the civil index, and party name in the criminal and appellate indices. The search will provide a list of case numbers, filing locations and filing dates for those cases matching the search criteria. The U.S. Party/Case Index is available on the Internet at http://pacer.uspci.uscourts.gov. For more information on the U.S. Party/Case Index, please visit the USPCI Overview. In accordance with Judicial Conference policy, the PACER Service Center charges $.10 per page for Internet service. Persons desiring to use this service must also first register with the PACER Service Center at 1–800 676–6856 or on the Internet at pacer.psc.uscourts. gov/register.html.

E. **Federal Records Center**—The paper case files for all closed cases were sent to the Federal Records Center in Fort Worth, Texas, for long term storage. The physical location of closed paper case files should always be determined using the Court's electronic records. Please visit the Court's FRC Search Page on its website to determine the location of a file. You may request to have a file retrieved from FRC.

F. **Unclaimed Funds**—Unclaimed funds are monies deposited with the Clerk's Office by a case trustee pursuant to § 347, Title 11 of the United States Code. Generally, these monies are unclaimed because the trustee does not have a current address for the creditor. Funds may be claimed pursuant to § 2042, Title 28 of the United States Code. For further assistance, our Finance Office can be reached at (903) 590–3219. In almost all instances, the Court's Unclaimed Funds Database on the Court's website is the best source of information. Instructions and sample required forms are also posted on the Court's website.

VII. Electronic Document Filing

A. Registration forms to file documents electronically are available at any of the three divisional offices or from the Court's website at www.txeb.uscourts.gov.

B. All fees due for documents filed electronically must be paid for on-line with a credit/debit card.

VIII. Noticing

A. The Clerk's Office uses the Bankruptcy Noticing Center (BNC) under contract with the Administrative Office of the United States Courts (AOUSC) for noticing.

B.   Notice recipients generally receive notices that are printed and mailed first class using the United States Postal Service (USPS).   Notice requests are generated daily in the Clerk's Office and sent electronically to the BNC each evening.   Notices are printed and mailed on the following day at the BNC print facilities around the country.

C.   High volume users, those organizations receiving more than 200 notices on a monthly basis, are strongly encouraged to receive notices using Electronic Data Interchange (EDI).   Noticing data transmitted via EDI is automatically sent to a user-defined electronic destination.   This EDI information can then be processed by the user's computers, providing the capability for automated processing of at a fraction of the cost of manual methods.   This service is available at no cost to users and results in notices being received the same day or the next morning by the user.   A Trading Partner Agreement (TPA) must be signed by both the user and the Clerk's Office and be on file with the BNC.   The standard TPA is not authorized to be modified in any way.

D.   Users receiving between 20 and 200 notices on a monthly basis are strongly encouraged to receive notices either though their email system or through their facsimile machine.   These notices are usually received the same day the notice request is sent to the BNC or the next morning.

E.   There is a special Electronic Bankruptcy Noticing (EBN) website at www. ebnuscourts.com for detailed information about these free electronic noticing services.   Users may also contact the BNC directly at 800–837–3424.   These electronic notices will provide notices to users days faster than the usual USPS first class service.

F.   In all instances where the BNC does not receive an acknowledgment of receipt from a user's electronic system (EDI, email, or fax) by the time the notice is printed for all other notice recipients, the BNC will print and mail the notice.

G.   In certain limited situations, the Clerk's Office will fax or mail certain orders to small groups of notice recipients.

H.   National Creditor Registration Service—the National Creditor Registration Service (NCRS) is a free service provided by the U.S. Bankruptcy Courts to give creditors options to specify a preferred U.S. mail or email address, or a fax number to which bankruptcy notices should be sent.   The creditor specifies a preferred mailing address to be used by all bankruptcy courts or by particular bankruptcy courts for providing notices.   Creditors may also specify that notices be transmitted electronically, thereby reducing mailed paper notices.   A registration form for this service is available on our website.   The NCRS has a website EBN.uscourts.gov and a toll-free number 1–877–837–3424.

IX.   Criminal Referrals

Pursuant to 18 U.S.C. § 157(d), when judges refer cases that may contain a materially fraudulent statement in a bankruptcy schedule to the Clerk, the Clerk will notify the United States Attorney and the designated field office agent of the FBI.

The address for the United States Attorney is listed in TXEB Appendix 1007–b–1.

The designated field office of the FBI is at 3301 Golden Road in Tyler.

X.   Issuance of Summons

When a summons is received with an adversary complaint or upon the filing of a request for summons, the clerk's office will sign and seal the document electronically.   The summons will be emailed to the filing attorney.   The attorney should print the summons and serve it.   For pro se parties, the summons will be printed on paper, signed and sealed, then mailed to the pro se party. The pro se party must serve the summons.

XI.   Correcting a Social Security Number

The debtor must file on paper an amended verified statement (Official Form 21) with the correct full social security number.   The full SSN must be noticed to all creditors, the U.S. Trustee and the case trustee.   A redacted copy (showing only the last four digits of the SSN) of this notice with a certificate of service evidencing such service must also be filed.   This filing must be done even if the last four digits of the SSN did not change.

Only when a mistake occurs in the last four digits of the SSN should an amended petition and certificate of service evidencing service to all parties be filed. An amended petition filed electronically also requires another Declaration to be filed on paper, per exhibit B–3 to TXEB Appendix 5005.

The clerk's office will notify the three credit reporting agencies that the originally filed number was incorrect and ask that this number be corrected in their files.

[Effective February 1, 2000. Amended effective October 1, 2002; April 9, 2004; January 18, 2006; December 1, 2009; February 27, 2013; December 17, 2013.]

APPENDIX 1002–A. REQUIREMENTS FOR COMMENCING
A NEW BANKRUPTCY CASE

I. Before You File

Notice Required by 11 U.S.C. § 342(b) for Individuals Filing for Bankruptcy (Form 2010)

This notice is for you if:

☐ **You are an individual filing for bankruptcy,** and

☐ **Your debts are primarily consumer debts.** *Consumer debts* are defined in 11 U.S.C. § 101(8) as "incurred by an individual primarily for a personal, family, or household purpose."

The types of bankruptcy that are available to individuals

Individuals who meet the qualifications may file under one of four different chapters of the Bankruptcy Code:

● Chapter 7 — Liquidation

● Chapter 11 — Reorganization

● Chapter 12 — Voluntary repayment plan for family farmers or fishermen

● Chapter 13 — Voluntary repayment plan for individuals with regular income

You should have an attorney review your decision to file for bankruptcy and the choice of chapter.

Chapter 7:		Liquidation
	$245	filing fee
	$75	administrative fee
+	$15	trustee surcharge
	$335	total fee

Chapter 7 is for individuals who have financial difficulty preventing them from paying their debts and who are willing to allow their non-exempt property to be used to pay their creditors. The primary purpose of filing under chapter 7 is to have your debts discharged. The bankruptcy discharge relieves you after bankruptcy from having to pay many of your pre-bankruptcy debts. Exceptions exist for particular debts, and liens on property may still be enforced after discharge. For example, a creditor may have the right to foreclose a home mortgage or repossess an automobile.

However, if the court finds that you have committed certain kinds of improper conduct described in the Bankruptcy Code, the court may deny your discharge.

You should know that even if you file chapter 7 and you receive a discharge, some debts are not discharged under the law. Therefore, you may still be responsible to pay:

● most taxes;

● most student loans;

● domestic support and property settlement obligations;

● most fines, penalties, forfeitures, and criminal restitution obligations; and

● certain debts that are not listed in your bankruptcy papers.

You may also be required to pay debts arising from:

● fraud or theft;

● fraud or defalcation while acting in breach of fiduciary capacity;

● intentional injuries that you inflicted; and

● death or personal injury caused by operating a motor vehicle, vessel, or aircraft while intoxicated from alcohol or drugs.

If your debts are primarily consumer debts, the court can dismiss your chapter 7 case if it finds that you have enough income to repay creditors a certain amount. You must file *Chapter 7 Statement of Your Current Monthly Income* (Official Form 122A–1) if you are an individual filing for bankruptcy under chapter 7. This form will determine your current monthly income and compare whether your income is more than the median income that applies in your state.

If your income is not above the median for your state, you will not have to complete the other chapter 7 form, the *Chapter 7 Means Test Calculation* (Official Form 122A–2).

If your income is above the median for your state, you must file a second form —the *Chapter 7 Means Test Calculation* (Official Form 122A–2). The calculations on the form—sometimes called the *Means Test*—deduct from your income living expenses and payments on certain debts to determine any amount available to pay unsecured creditors. If your income is more than the median income for your state of residence and family size, depending on the results of the *Means Test*, the U.S. trustee, bankruptcy administrator, or creditors can file a motion to dismiss your case under § 707(b) of the Bankruptcy Code. If a motion is filed, the court will decide if your case should be dismissed. To avoid dismissal, you may choose to proceed under another chapter of the Bankruptcy Code.

If you are an individual filing for chapter 7 bankruptcy, the trustee may sell your property to pay your debts, subject to your right to exempt the property or a portion of the proceeds from the sale of the property. The property, and the proceeds from property that your bankruptcy trustee sells or liquidates that you are entitled to, is called *exempt property*. Exemptions may enable you to keep your home, a car, clothing, and household items or to receive some of the proceeds if the property is sold.

Exemptions are not automatic. To exempt property, you must list it on *Schedule C: The Property You Claim as Exempt* (Official Form 106C). If you do not list the property, the trustee may sell it and pay all of the proceeds to your creditors.

Chapter 11:		**Reorganization**
	$1,167	filing fee
+	$550	administrative fee
	$1,717	total fee

Chapter 11 is often used for reorganizing a business, but is also available to individuals. The provisions of chapter 11 are too complicated to summarize briefly.

Read These Important Warnings

Because bankruptcy can have serious long-term financial and legal consequences, including loss of your property, you should hire an attorney and carefully consider all of your options before you file. Only an attorney can give you legal advice about what can happen as a result of filing for bankruptcy and what your options are. If you do file for bankruptcy, an attorney can help you fill out the forms properly and protect you, your family, your home, and your possessions.

Although the law allows you to represent yourself in bankruptcy court, you should understand that many people find it difficult to represent themselves successfully. The rules are technical, and a mistake or inaction may harm you. If you file without an attorney, you are still responsible for knowing and following all of the legal requirements.

You should not file for bankruptcy if you are not eligible to file or if you do not intend to file the necessary documents.

Bankruptcy fraud is a serious crime; you could be fined and imprisoned if you commit fraud in your bankruptcy case. Making a false statement, concealing property, or obtaining money or property by fraud in connection with a bankruptcy case can result in fines up to $250,000, or imprisonment for up to 20 years, or both. 18 U.S.C. §§ 152, 1341, 1519, and 3571.

Chapter 12:		**Repayment plan for family farmers or fishermen**
	$200	filing fee
+	$75	administrative fee
	$275	total fee

Similar to chapter 13, chapter 12 permits family farmers and fishermen to repay their debts over a period of time using future earnings and to discharge some debts that are not paid.

Chapter 13:		**Repayment plan for individuals with regular income**
	$235	filing fee
+	$75	administrative fee
	$310	total fee

Chapter 13 is for individuals who have regular income and would like to pay all or part of their debts in installments over a period of time and to discharge some debts that are not paid. You are eligible for chapter 13 only if your debts are not more than certain dollar amounts set forth in 11 U.S.C. § 109.

Under chapter 13, you must file with the court a plan to repay your creditors all or part of the money that you owe them, usually using your future earnings. If the court approves your plan, the court will allow you to repay your debts, as adjusted by the plan, within 3 years or 5 years, depending on your income and other factors.

After you make all the payments under your plan, many of your debts are discharged. The debts that are not discharged and that you may still be responsible to pay include:

- domestic support obligations,

- most student loans,

- certain taxes,

- debts for fraud or theft,

- debts for fraud or defalcation while acting in a fiduciary capacity,

- most criminal fines and restitution obligations,

- certain debts that are not listed in your bankruptcy papers,

- certain debts for acts that caused death or personal injury, and

- certain long-term secured debts.

Warning: File Your Forms on Time

Section 521(a)(1) of the Bankruptcy Code requires that you promptly file detailed information about your creditors, assets, liabilities, income, expenses and general financial condition. The court may dismiss your bankruptcy case if you do not file this information within the deadlines set by the Bankruptcy Code, the Bankruptcy Rules, and the local rules of the court.

For more information about the documents and their deadlines, go to: http://www.uscourts.gov/bkforms/bankruptcy_forms.html#procedure.

Bankruptcy crimes have serious consequences

- If you knowingly and fraudulently conceal assets or make a false oath or statement under penalty of perjury—either orally or in writing—in connection with a bankruptcy case, you may be fined, imprisoned, or both.

- All information you supply in connection with a bankruptcy case is subject to examination by the Attorney General acting through the Office of the U.S. Trustee, the Office of the U.S. Attorney, and other offices and employees of the U.S. Department of Justice.

Make sure the court has your mailing address

The bankruptcy court sends notices to the mailing address you list on *Voluntary Petition for Individuals Filing for Bankruptcy* (Official Form 101). To ensure that you receive information about your case, Bankruptcy Rule 4002 requires that you notify the court of any changes in your address.

A married couple may file a bankruptcy case together—called a *joint case*. If you file a joint case and each spouse lists the same mailing address on the bankruptcy petition, the bankruptcy court generally will mail you and your spouse one copy of each notice, unless you file a statement with the court asking that each spouse receive separate copies.

Understand which services you could receive from credit counseling agencies

The law generally requires that you receive a credit counseling briefing from an approved credit counseling agency. 11 U.S.C. § 109(h). If you are filing a joint case, both spouses must receive the briefing. With limited exceptions, you must receive it within the 180 days **before** you file your bankruptcy petition. This briefing is usually conducted by telephone or on the Internet.

In addition, after filing a bankruptcy case, you generally must complete a financial management instructional course before you can receive a discharge. If you are filing a joint case, both spouses must complete the course.

You can obtain the list of agencies approved to provide both the briefing and the instructional course from: http://www.justice.gov/ust/list–approved–providers–personal–financial–management–instructional–cou

If you do not have access to a computer, the clerk of the bankruptcy court may be able to help you obtain the list.

II. Filing a Bankruptcy Case for Individuals (Chapters 7, 11, 12 and 13)

A. *Voluntary Petition for Individuals Filing for Bankruptcy (Official Form 101).*

Clerk's Note: A separate Exhibit D is no longer required. Exhibit D is included in Part 5 of Official Form 101 as of December 1, 2015.

B. *Filing Fee*

Chapter 7—$335.00

Chapter 11 (non–railroad) - $1,717.00

Chapter 11 (railroad) - $1,550.00

Chapter 12 - $275.00

Chapter 13 - $310.00

Or

Application for Individuals to Pay the Filing Fee in Installments (Official Form 103A) with proposed order. Debtor(s) must be individual and must submit a signed Application for Court approval. Rule 1006(b), Fed.R.Bankr.P.

Or

Application to Have the Chapter 7 Filing Fee Waived (Official Form 103B) with proposed order 11 USC § 1930(f)(1). Use this form only if you are filing under chapter 7 and you meet the criteria to have the chapter 7 filing fee waived.

C. *Declaration for Electronic Filing* (Exhibit B–1 or B–2 to LBR Appendix 5005)

If case is filed electronically, must be executed by the debtor(s) and original submitted to the Court within seven (7) days in paper format. LBR, Appendix 5005, Part II (Electronic Filing and Service of Documents) paragraph C. (Signatures) sub-section 3.

Or

Statement About Your Social Security Numbers (Official Form 121)

If case is filed by pro se debtor(s) and received via the U.S. mail, must be executed by the individual debtor(s) and original submitted to the Court within seven (7) days in paper format.

D. *Notice to Individual Consumer Debtor(s)* (Director's Form 2010)

Clerk's Note: For individual debtor(s) without attorney representation only. Individual debtor(s) without attorney representation must review form 2010 and certify that notice has been obtained and read by signing Part 7 of Official Form 101. See Part I above for Form 2010.

E. *Certificate of Budget and Credit Counseling Course with any Debtor Repayment Plan developed with credit agency*

Required at filing for all individual debtors; 11 USC § 521

Or

Motion for Exemption from Credit Counseling with Certificate of Exigent Circumstances.

See line 15 of the *Voluntary Petition for Individuals Filing for Bankruptcy* (Official Form 101).

F. *List of Creditors* (Master Mailing List "Matrix")

Names and addresses of all creditors of the debtor. Must be submitted with the petition. Rule 1007(a), Fed.R.Bankr.P. and LBR Appendix 1007–b–5.

For Individual Chapter 11 Cases Only: List of Creditors Who Have the 20 Largest Unsecured Claims Against You and Are Not Insiders (Official Form 104).

G. *Initial Statement About an Eviction Judgment Against You (101A) and Statement About Payment of an Eviction Judgment Against You (101B).*

Clerk's Note: Use Form 101A if your landlord has an eviction judgment against you. If you complete Form 101A and you want to stay in your residence for the first 30 days after you file, you must indicate that on the form. Use Form 101B if you have completed Form 101A and you want to stay in your rented residence for more than 30 days after you file for bankruptcy.

H. *Schedules* (Official Forms 106–Summary, 106–Declaration, A/ B, C, D, E/ F, G, H, I, J, J–2)

- Summary—Summary of Your Assets and Liabilities and Certain Statistical Information (Individuals)

- Declaration—Declaration About an Individual Debtor's Schedules (Official Form 106–Declaration)

- Schedule A/B—Property (Official Form 106A/B)

- Schedule C—The Property You Claim as Exempt (Official Form 106C)

- Schedule D—Creditors Who Have Claims Secured by Your Property (Official Form 106D)

- Schedule E/F—Creditors Who Have Unsecured Claims (Official Form 106E/F)

- Schedule G—Executory Contracts and Unexpired Leases (Official Form 106G)

- Schedule H—Your Co–Debtors (Official Form 106H)

- Schedule I—Your Income (Official Form 106I)

- Schedule J- Your Expenses (Official Form 106J); and Schedule J–2- Expenses for Separate Household of Debtor 2 (Official Form 106J–2)

Must be submitted within 14 days. Rule 1007(b) & (c), Fed.R.Bankr.P.

I. *Your Statement of Financial Affairs for Individuals Filing for Bankruptcy* (Official Form 107). Must be submitted within 14 days. Rule 1007(b) & (c), Fed.R.Bankr.P.

J. *Disclosure of Compensation of Attorney for Debtor.*

Must be submitted within 14 days. 11 USC § 329 and Rule 2016(b), Fed.R.Bankr.P.

Or

Declaration and Signature of Non–Attorney Bankruptcy Petition Preparer with Notice to Debtor by Non–Attorney Bankruptcy Petition Preparer (Official Forms 119). Declaration must be submitted with the petition. 11 USC § 110.

Clerk's Note: If filed electronically at the front counter, no additional copies are required. If filed by a pro se debtor using the U.S. Mail and a file stamped copy is to be returned to the debtor, an additional copy is required, plus a suitably sized, self-addressed envelope with sufficient postage affixed.

If you file under chapter 7, you must also file:

- ***Statement of Intention for Individuals Filing Under Chapter 7*** (Official Form 108). Required if the debtor is an individual and the schedule of assets and liabilities contains consumer debts secured by property of the estate. Must be submitted within 30 days of filing of the petition or by the date set for the Section 341 first meeting of creditors, whichever is earlier. 11 USC § 521(2).

- ***Chapter 7 Statement of Your Current Monthly Income (Official Form 122A–1) and Means Test Calculation (Official Form 122A–2)***

Or

- **Motion for Exemption from Means Test** 11 USC § 707

If you file under chapter 11, you must also file:

- ***Chapter 11 Statement of Your Current Monthly Income*** (Official Form 122–B)

If you file under chapter 11 and qualify as a small business debtor (see LR 1020 (a)), within 14 days after you file your bankruptcy forms to open your case, you must also file your most recent:

☐ Balance sheet

☐ Statement of operations

☐ Cash-flow statement

☐ Federal income tax return

Clerk's Note: If you do not have these documents, you must file a statement made under penalty of perjury that you have not prepared a balance sheet, statement of operations, or cash-flow statement or you have not filed a federal tax return. If you file under chapter 11, you must file additional documents beyond the scope of these instructions. You should consult your attorney.

If you file under chapter 12, you must also file:

- **Chapter 12 Plan** (within 90 days after you file your bankruptcy forms to open your case)

If you file under chapter 13, you must also file:

- *Chapter 13 Statement of Your Current Monthly Income and Calculation of Commitment Period* (Official Form 122C–1)
- *Chapter 13 Calculation of Your Disposable Income* (Official Form 122C–2)
- *Chapter 13 Plan*

III. **Filing a Bankruptcy Case for Non–Individuals (Chapters 7 and 11)**

A. *Voluntary Petition for Non–Individuals Filing for Bankruptcy (Official Form 201).*

With *Attachment to Voluntary Petition for Non–Individuals Filing for Bankruptcy Under Chapter 11* (Official Form 201A)

Clerk's Note: Must be attached to petition if debtor is required to file periodic reports (e.g. forms 10K and 10Q) with the Securities & Exchange Commission pursuant to Sections 13 or 15(d) of the Securities Act of 1934 and is requesting relief under chapter 11 of the Bankruptcy Code.

B. **Filing Fee**

Chapter 7—$335.00

Chapter 11 (non–railroad) - $1,717.00

Chapter 11 (railroad) - $1,550.00

Or

Application for Individuals to Pay the Filing Fee in Installments (Official Form 103A) with proposed order. Debtor(s) must be individual and must submit a signed Application for Court approval. Rule 1006(b), Fed.R.Bankr.P.

Or

Application to Have the Chapter 7 Filing Fee Waived (Official Form 103B) with proposed order 11 USC § 1930(f)(1). Use this form only if you are filing under chapter 7 and you meet the criteria to have the chapter 7 filing fee waived.

C. *Declaration for Electronic Filing* (Exhibit B–1 or B–2 to LBR Appendix 5005)

If case is filed electronically, must be executed by the debtor(s) and original submitted to the Court within seven (7) days in paper format. LBR, Appendix 5005, Part II (Electronic Filing and Service of Documents) paragraph C. (Signatures) sub-section 3.

Or

Statement About Your Social Security Numbers (Official Form 121)

If case is filed by pro se debtor(s) and received via the U.S. mail, must be executed by the individual debtor(s) and original submitted to the Court within seven (7) days in paper format.

D. *List of Creditors* (Master Mailing List "Matrix")

Names and addresses of all creditors of the debtor. Must be submitted with the petition. Rule 1007(a), Fed.R.Bankr.P. and LBR Appendix 1007–b–5.

E. *Schedules* (Official Forms 206–Summary, Declaration, A/ B, C, D, E/ F, G, H)

- Summary—Summary of Your Assets and Liabilities and Certain Statistical Information (Non–Individuals) (Official Form 206–Summary)
- Declaration—Declaration Under Penalty of Perjury for Non–Individual Debtors (Official Form 202)
- Schedule A/B—Property (Official Form 206A/B)
- Schedule D—Creditors Holding Secured Claims (Official Form 206D)
- Schedule E/F—Creditors Who Have Unsecured Claims (Official Form 206E/F)
- Schedule G—Executory Contracts and Unexpired Leases—Individuals (Official Form 206G)
- Schedule H—Your Co–Debtors (Official Form 206H)

Must be submitted within 14 days.   Rule 1007(b) & (c), Fed.R.Bankr.P.

F.   Statement of Financial Affairs (Official Form 207).

Must be submitted within 14 days.   Rule 1007(b) & (c), Fed.R.Bankr.P.

G.   Disclosure of Compensation of Attorney for Debtor.

Must be submitted within 14 days.   11 USC § 329 and Rule 2016(b), Fed.R.Bankr.P.

Or

Declaration and Signature of Non–Attorney Bankruptcy Petition Preparer with Notice to Debtor by Non–Attorney Bankruptcy Petition Preparer (Official Form 119).

Must be submitted with the petition.   11 USC § 110.

Clerk's Note: If filed electronically at the front counter, no additional copies are required. If filed by a pro se debtor using the U.S. Mail and a file stamped copy is to be returned to the debtor, an additional copy is required, plus a suitably sized, self-addressed envelope with sufficient postage affixed.

H.   Statement of current income and current expenditures *(use forms specific to the chapter being filed)*

If you file under chapter 11 and qualify as a small business debtor, you must also file:

If you file under chapter 11 and qualify as a small business debtor (see Local Rule 1020(a)), within 14 days after you file your bankruptcy forms to open your case, you must also file your most recent:

☐ Balance sheet

☐ Statement of operations

☐ Cash-flow statement

☐ Federal income tax return

Clerk's Note: If you do not have these documents, you must file a statement made under penalty of perjury that you have not prepared a balance sheet, statement of operations, or cash-flow statement or you have not filed a federal tax return. If you file under chapter 11, you must file additional documents beyond the scope of these instructions. You should consult your attorney.

IV.   Voluntary Chapter 15 Case

A.   Petition for Recognition of Foreign Proceeding (Official Form 401).

B.   Filing Fee of $1,717.00

C.   Chapter 15 Service List

V.   Involuntary Chapter 7 or 11 Case—Individual/Non–Individual

A.   Involuntary Petition Against an Individual (Official Form 105).11 USC § 303.

Or

Involuntary Petition Against a Non–Individual (Official Form 205).   11 USC § 303.

B.   Declaration for Electronic Filing (Exhibit B–1 or B–2 to LBR Appendix 5005)

If case is filed electronically, must be executed by the debtor and submitted to the Court within seven (7) days in paper format.   LBR, Appendix 5005, Part II (Electronic Filing and Service of Documents) paragraph C. (Signatures) sub-section 3.

C.   Filing Fee

For a Chapter 7 case, Filing Fee of $335.00

Or

For a Chapter 11 non-railroad case, Filing Fee of $1,717.00.   For a Chapter 11 railroad case, Filing Fee of $1,550.00

Fee may not be paid in installments Rule 1006(b), Fed.R.Bankr.P.

D.   Completed Summons to Debtor in Involuntary Case (Procedural Form 2500E)

Clerk's Note: If filed electronically at the front counter, no additional copies are required. If filed by a pro se debtor using the U.S. Mail and a file stamped copy is to be returned to the debtor, an additional copy is required, plus a suitably sized, self-addressed envelope with sufficient postage affixed.

VI. Adversary Case

A. *Filing fee* of $350.00 for complaint.

[Effective December 13, 2005. Amended effective October 3, 2007; December 1, 2009; December 1, 2012; December 1, 2015.]

APPENDIX 1007–B–1. REGISTRY OF MAILING ADDRESSES
OF FEDERAL AND STATE GOVERNMENTAL UNITS

1. **United States Trustee's Office**
    110 North College Avenue, Suite 300
    Tyler, Texas 75702–7231

2. **United States Attorney's Office** (for all chapters in Beaumont and Lufkin divisions)
    350 Magnolia Avenue, Suite 150
    Beaumont, Texas 77701–2248

3. **United States Attorney's Office** (for all chapters in Marshall, Sherman, Texarkana and Tyler)
    110 North College Avenue, Suite 700
    Tyler, Texas 75702–0204

4. **Internal Revenue Service**
    PO Box 7346
    Philadelphia, PA 19101–7346

5. **Michigan Department of Treasury, Tax Policy Division**
    Attn: Litigation Liaison
    2nd Floor, Austin Building
    430 West Allegan Street
    Lansing, Michigan 48922

6. **Oklahoma Tax Commission**
    Office of the General Counsel, Bankruptcy Section
    120 N. Robinson, Suite 2000W
    Oklahoma City, OK 73102

7. **Social Security Administration**
    Attn: Bankruptcy Coordinator
    Office of the General Counsel, Region VI
    1301 Young Street, Ste. A702
    Dallas, TX 75202–5433

8. **Chief Council, Franchise Tax Board**
    Attn: General Counsel Section
    P.O.   Box 1720, MS A–260
    Rancho Cordova, CA 95741–1720

9. **Franchise Tax Board**
    Attn: Bankruptcy Unit
    P.O.   Box 2952, MS A–340
    Sacramento, CA 959812–2952

[Effective February 1, 2000. Amended effective October 1, 2002; June 13, 2005; December 1, 2009; November 3, 2011; April 15, 2013; December 17, 2013; May 13, 2015; November 19, 2015.]

APPENDIX 1007–b–5. GUIDELINES FOR SUBMISSION
OF A MASTER MAILING LIST

UNITED STATES BANKRUPTCY COURT
EASTERN DISTRICT OF TEXAS

GUIDELINES FOR SUBMISSION OF A MASTER MAILING LIST

I. GENERAL

A. FORMAT FOR FILING

1. The Clerk of the Court strongly urges the original or amended Master Mailing Lists be submitted in electronic format via the Court's Electronic Case Filing system. (See Reports in CM/ECF)

2. Mailing lists submitted incorrectly may be required to be resubmitted.

3. The Clerk of Court may authorize other electronic media in the future.

B. NAME AND ADDRESS STANDARDS

The following standards apply to all Master Mailing lists submitted to this Court:

1. All names and addresses must be complete and accurate. Notices shall not be sent out by the Clerk to any entity with an incomplete or missing address.

2. If the case number is known it should appear on the first line, followed by two (2) blank lines. Begin the first creditor on the fourth line.

3. When listing creditors in care of an attorney, always put the creditor's name on line 1 and the attorney's name on line 2. For example:

	CORRECT	INCORRECT
	ABC Supply Company	Debra Jones
	c/o Debra Jones, Attorney	Attorney for ABC Supply Company

4. Do not include the debtor, joint debtor, attorney(s) for the debtor(s), the district court clerk, case trustee, or United States Trustee on the Master Mailing List. These parties will be entered by the Clerk's Office at the time of case opening.

5. Creditors shall be listed ONLY ONCE, even if they have more than one account with, or claim against, the debtor.

6. Each name and address must consist of at least two but not more than five lines, each forty characters or less in length. For example:

Line 1: XXXXXXXXXXXXXXXXXXXX

Line 2: XXXXXXXXXXXXXXXXXXXX

Line 3: XXXXXXXXXXXXXXXXXXXX

Line 4: XXXXXXXXXXXXXXXXXXXX

Line 5: City, State ZIP or ZIP + 4

7. "Care of" and "attention" designations may be included ONLY on the second line of the name and address, as long as the complete name and address block consists of no more than five lines.

8. No personal forms of address, titles, indefinite articles, or definite articles should precede the name. Personal forms of address and titles may be used *after* the name, but only as necessary to specifically identify someone.

9. Names of individuals must appear in the following order: first name, middle name or initial, last name.

10. Creditors must be listed alphabetically, according to the first letter of the company name or first name.

11. Only postal standard abbreviations, as directed by the United States Postal Service in the official USPS Publication *Postal Addressing Standards*, shall be used in addresses. The

name of the state must be abbreviated using the upper case, two-letter state identifier prescribed by the United States Postal Service (e.g. TX not Tex or Tx). City names less than 15 characters in length shall not be abbreviated.

12. The use of ZIP codes is MANDATORY. All domestic addresses must include the correct five-digit ZIP code. Domestic addresses that do not include a ZIP code will be treated as incomplete (See item 1, above). All ZIP code extensions must follow a hyphen and shall consist of four digits (for example, 75702–0012 NOT 75702–12). DO NOT use the ZIP code extension "0000" unless it is valid for the creditor.

13. For domestic mail, the last line of every address MUST contain EACH of the following items IN THIS ORDER: the city, the two character state abbreviation WITHOUT periods BUT in ALL CAPITAL LETTERS, and AT THE END, the ZIP code. *DO NOT* include any information for the creditor below the city, state, and ZIP.

14. All foreign addresses shall include the COMPLETE name of the country to which the mail will be sent. Country names *SHALL NOT* be abbreviated.

15. Except for hyphens in nine digit zip codes, no special character shall be included in names or addresses:

DO NOT use the letter "l" as a substitute for the number "1"

DO NOT use the % (percent sign) as a substitute for c/o ("in care of")

DO NOT use \ (backslash) as a substitute for / (slash or forward slash)

DO NOT use + (plus sign) for either "and" or & (ampersand)

DO NOT use ˜ (tilde) as a substitute for - (dash)

DO NOT use { } (braces) or [ ] (brackets) as a substitute for ( ) parentheses

16. Like correspondence, names and address shall be typed in both upper and lower case letters. Except to abbreviate the name of the state, do not use all uppercase letters.

17. There should be no punctuation included, except the hyphen in the ZIP code

18. Lists shall be typed in a single aligned column.

19. There must be two blank lines between one creditor's name and address and another's. Do not leave blank lines within an address.

II. GUIDELINES FOR SUBMITTING A HARD (PAPER) COPY

A. *ACCEPTABLE*

1. The hard-copy list shall be printed in black, on a white 8.5″ × 11″ bond or standard copy paper.

2. Font should be Times New Roman, Courier New, Universe, or Arial, 12 point.

3. The type must be of high quality. Poor quality type from a depleted printer cartridge, dot matrix printer, photocopy or carbon, exhausted typewriter ribbon, or fabric typewriter ribbons are electronically unreadable and must not be used.

4. If the case number is known it should appear on the first line, followed by two (2) blank lines. Begin the first creditor on the fourth line

5. The hard-copy list shall contain no handwriting, stray marks, correction fluid or tape.

6. Names and addresses must appear on one side of each page only. Do not use the back of the paper.

7. The first name and address on each page of the list may not be closer than two inches from the top of the page and should be no closer that one-half inch from the left side, right side, or bottom of the page.

8. The hard-copy Master Address List must be submitted as a clean, totally separate document. Any marks (including letterhead, dates, names, pager numbers, coffee stains, handwriting or multiple columns) must be avoided as they may cause the entry of incorrect data.

9. DO NOT STAPLE TOGETHER OR TWO–HOLE PUNCH PAGES OF THE <u>ORIGINAL</u> HARD–COPY MASTER ADDRESS LIST.

10. Although the court is using sophisticated equipment and software to insure accuracy in creditor list reading, certain problems can still occur. By following these guidelines, the court will avoid delays or additional effort in mailing notices.

B. UNACCEPTABLE

The following problems can prevent your matrix from being read by the optical scanner, requiring you to re-submit your creditor list in an acceptable form.

1. *Extra marks on the lists*—such as letterhead, dates, coffee stains, handwritten marks, page number.

2. *Non-standard paper* such as onionskin, half-sized paper, or colored paper. 8½ by 11″, 20 lb. paper is acceptable

3. *Poor quality printing* caused by low toner in the printer cartridge.

4. *Unreadable type fonts* or print types such as dot matrix or exotic fonts. Please use: Times New Roman .12, Courier .12, or Universe .12

5. *Misaligned lists* caused by inserting the paper in the printer crooked.

6. *Zip Code* not on the last line. Nine digit zip codes should be used with a hyphen separating the two groups of digits. Attention lines, in care of (c/o) should NOT be on the last line, they should be on the second line if needed. The zip code must be at the end of the last line.

7. *Punctuation*—There should be no commas or periods in any part of the address. There should be 2 spaces between the state and zip code. When typing a post office box (PO) do not use periods.

8. *Upper Case Only* (all capital letters) should be avoided. Type in upper and lower case as you would on a letter. Left justify all lines.

III. GUIDELINES FOR ELECTRONIC FILING OF THE MATRIX

A. *File matrix separately*

1. Save the file as generic *ASCII Text format*. The extension that your word processing application or bankruptcy software gives it is usually compatible with the Court's Electronic Filing System.

2. You must include the case number issued by the Court on the first line of the matrix followed by two (2) blank lines. You can then begin with the first creditor on the fourth line.

3. Name the file any name that is consistent with the naming standards of your company or that will be readily recognizable to you when searching for the file during the upload process.

B. *Case Upload*

1. If you are using a bankruptcy software program such as Bankruptcy Pro, the matrix will automatically be uploaded in proper format when the case is uploaded. It should not be filed separately per LBR 1007(a)1(A), because the case upload program satisfies that requirement.

[Effective February 1, 2000. Amended effective August 2001; October 1, 2002; December 1, 2009; May 16, 2011.]

APPENDIX 1007–b–6.   VERIFICATION OF CREDITOR MATRIX

UNITED STATES BANKRUPTCY COURT
EASTERN DISTRICT OF TEXAS

IN RE:

_____   _____
           Debtor(s)   Bankruptcy Case Number

VERIFICATION OF CREDITOR MATRIX

The above named Debtor(s) hereby verifies that the attached list of creditors is true and correct to the best of my/our knowledge.

Date: _____   _____

                                               Debtor Signature

Date: _____   _____

                                               Joint Debtor Signature

[Effective February 1, 2000. Amended effective February 1, 2001; July 2001; December 1, 2009.]

APPENDIX 1007–b–7. NOTICE OF CHANGE IN SCHEDULES OF CREDITORS

IN RE:

_____   _____
Debtor(s)   Bankruptcy Case Number

NOTICE OF CHANGE IN SCHEDULE OF CREDITORS

In accordance with LBR 1007(b)7, the attached amended schedule is filed for the following reason (check only one):

☐ Add Creditor(s) [requires $30.00 filing fee]

☐ Delete Creditor(s) [requires a $30.00 filing fee]

☐ Change the amount of a debt [requires a $30.00 filing fee]

☐ Change the classification of a debt [requires a $30.00 filing fee]

☐ Change the address of Creditor(s) or add Attorney for a Creditor [no fee required]

☐ Amendment to Schedule C—Property Claimed as Exempt [requires service on matrix]

☐ Amendment to Schedule I—Current Income of Individual Debtor(s)

☐ Amendment to Schedule J—Current Expenditures of Individual Debtor(s)

☐ Initial Amended Schedules due to Chapter Conversion

> Instructions: A separate Notice of Change is required when both adding and deleting creditors. An amended (partial) matrix is required to add or delete creditors. **ANNOTATE CLEARLY SO CHANGES ARE EASILY UNDERSTANDABLE.** Do not file a complete new matrix. Only those creditors affected by the amended schedule should be shown on the matrix. If the $30.00 filing fee is required, multiple filings of a Notice of Change filed in the same case at the same time require only a single $30.00 fee. Adding or deleting creditors at different times requires a fee each time.

I, or each of us, declare under penalty of perjury, that I/we have read the changes to the List of Creditors (Master Mailing List (matrix)) and to the schedules and statements as attached hereto, and that they are correct to the best of my/our knowledge, information and belief.

Date: _____
Debtor Signature

Date: _____
Joint Debtor Signature

[Effective February 1, 2000. Amended effective October 1, 2002; November 1, 2003; October 17, 2005; December 1, 2009; October 31, 2011.]

APPENDIX 2016. GUIDELINES FOR REIMBURSABLE EXPENSES

1. *Firm Practice.* The Court will consider the customary practice of the firm in charging or not charging non–bankruptcy/insolvency clients for particular expense items. Where any other clients, with the exception of pro–bono clients, are not billed for a particular expense, the estate should not be billed. Where expenses are billed to all other clients, reimbursement should be sought at the least expensive rate the firm or professional charges to any client for comparable services or expenses. It is recognized that there will be differences in billing practices among professionals.

2. *Actual Cost.* This is defined as the amount paid to a third party provider of goods or services without enhancement for handling or other administrative charge.

3. *Documentation.* This must be retained and made available upon request for all expenditures in excess of $50.00. Where possible, receipts should be obtained for all expenditures.

4. *Office Overhead.* This is not reimbursable. Overhead includes: secretarial time, secretarial overtime (where clear necessity for same has not been shown), word processing time, charges for after–hour and weekend air conditioning and other utilities, and cost of meals or transportation provided to professionals and staff who work late or on weekends.

5. *Word Processing.* This is not reimbursable.

6. *Computerized Research.* This is reimbursable at actual cost. For large amounts billed to computerized research, significant explanatory detail should be furnished.

7. *Paraprofessional Services.* These services may be compensated as a paraprofessional under § 330, but not charged or reimbursed as an expense.

8. *Professional Services.* A professional employed under § 327 may not employ, and charge as an expense, another professional (e.g., special litigation counsel employing an expert witness) unless the employment of the second professional is approved by the Court prior to the rendering of service.

9. *Photocopies (Internal).* Charges must be disclosed on an aggregate and per–page basis. If the per–page cost exceeds $.20, the professional must demonstrate to the satisfaction of the Court, with data, that the per–page cost represents a good faith estimate of the actual cost of the copies, based upon the purchase or lease cost of the copy machine and supplies therefor, including the space occupied by the machine, but not including time spent in operating the machine.

10. *Photocopies (Outside).* This item is reimbursable at actual cost.

11. *Postage.* This is reimbursable at actual cost.

12. *Overnight Delivery.* This is reimbursable at actual cost where it is shown to be necessary. The court acknowledges that in complex chapter 11 cases overnight delivery or messenger services may often be appropriate, particularly when shortened notice of a hearing has been requested.

13. *Messenger Service.* This is reimbursable at actual cost where it is shown to be necessary. An in–house messenger service is reimbursable, but the estate cannot be charged more than the cost of comparable services available outside the firm.

14. *Facsimile Transmission.* The actual cost of telephone charges for outgoing transmissions is reimbursable. Transmissions received are reimbursable on a per–page basis. If the per–page cost exceeds $0.20, the professional must demonstrate, with data, to the satisfaction of the Court, that the per–page cost represents a good faith estimate of the actual cost of the copies, based upon the purchase or lease cost of the facsimile machine and supplies therefor, including the space occupied by the machine, but not including time spent in operating the machine.

15. *Long Distance Telephone.* This is reimbursable at actual cost.

16. *Parking.* This is reimbursable at actual cost.

17. *Air Transportation.* Air travel is expected to be at regular coach fare for all flights.

18. *Hotels.* Due to wide variation in hotel costs in various cities, it is not possible to establish a single guideline for this type of expense. All persons will be required to exercise reasonable discretion and prudence in connection with hotel expenditures.

19. *Meals (Travel).* Reimbursement may be sought for the reasonable cost of breakfast, lunch and dinner while traveling.

20. *Meals (Working).* Working meals at restaurants or private clubs are not reimbursable. Reasonable reimbursement may be sought for working meals only where food is catered to the professional's office in the course of a meeting with clients, such as a Creditors' Committee, for the purpose of allowing the meeting to continue through a normal meal period.

21. *Amenities.* Charges for entertainment, alcoholic beverages, newspapers, dry cleaning, shoe shines, etc. are not reimbursable.

22. *Filing Fees.* These are reimbursable at actual cost.

23. *Court Reporter Fees.* These are reimbursable at actual cost.

24. *Witness Fees.* These are reimbursable at actual cost.

25. *Process Service.* This is reimbursable at actual cost.

26. *UCC Searches.* These are reimbursable at actual cost.

[Effective February 1, 2000. Amended effective October 17, 2005.]

APPENDIX 5005. ADMINISTRATIVE PROCEDURES FOR THE FILING, SIGNING, AND VERIFYING OF DOCUMENTS BY ELECTRONIC MEANS IN TEXAS BANKRUPTCY COURTS

*[**Publisher's Note:** For electronic filing procedures applicable in this Court, please consult the Administrative Procedures for the Filing, Signing, and Verifying of Documents by Electronic Means in Texas Bankruptcy Courts, published as part of the local rules for the United States Bankruptcy Court for the Northern District of Texas, ante.]*

APPENDIX 9007. PROCEDURES FOR COMPLEX CHAPTER 11 CASES IN TEXAS BANKRUPTCY COURT

These procedures for complex Chapter 11 cases shall apply to cases filed on or after October 17, 2005:

1. Complex Chapter 11 Case: is defined as a case filed in this district under Chapter 11 of the Bankruptcy Code that requires special scheduling and other procedures because of a combination of the following factors:

(a) the size of the case (usually total debt of more than $10 million);

(b) the large number of parties in interest in the case (usually more than 50 parties in interest in the case);

(c) the fact that claims against the debtor and/or equity interests in the debtor are publicly traded (with some creditors possibly being represented by indenture trustees); or

(d) any other circumstances justifying complex case treatment.

2. Expedited: is defined as a matter which, for cause shown, should be heard on less than 23 days' notice.

3. Emergency: is defined as a matter which, for cause shown, should be heard on less than 5 business days' notice.

4. Notice of Designation: If any party filing a Chapter 11 bankruptcy petition believes that the case should be classified as a complex Chapter 11 case, the party shall file with the bankruptcy petition a "Notice of Designation as Complex Chapter 11 Case" in the form* attached as Exhibit A.

5. First Day Matters: If a party has "First Day" matters requiring emergency consideration by the court, it should submit a "Request for Emergency Consideration of Certain 'First Day' Matters" in the form attached as Exhibit B.

6. First Day Emergency Hearings: Each judge shall arrange the judge's calendar so that "first day" emergency hearings, as requested in the court-approved form entitled "Request for Emergency Consideration of Certain 'First Day' Matters," can be conducted consistent with the Bankruptcy Code and Rules, including Rule 4001, as required by the circumstances, but not more than two business days after the request for emergency "first day" hearings.

7. Court Determination of Complex Case Designation: When a party has filed a Chapter 11 case and filed a Notice of Designation as Complex Chapter 11 Case, the Clerk of Court shall:

(a) generally assign the case to a judge in accordance with the usual procedures and general orders of the district or division;

(b) immediately confer with the court about designating the case as a complex

Chapter 11 case and setting hearings on emergency or first day motions:

(1) if the court determines that the case does not qualify as a complex Chapter 11 case, the court shall issue an "Order Denying Complex Case Treatment" in the form attached as **Exhibit C.**

(2) if the court determines that the case appears to be a complex Chapter 11 case, the court shall issue an "Order Granting Complex Chapter 11 Case Treatment" in the form attached as **Exhibit D;** and

(c) notify and serve counsel for the debtor with the order entered by the Court relating to the complex case treatment and notify counsel for the debtor regarding the hearing settings for emergency first day matters.

8. Duties of Debtor's Counsel: Counsel for the debtor, upon receipt of notice of entry of an order regarding complex Chapter 11 case treatment, shall:

(a) serve the order granting or denying complex chapter 11 case treatment on all parties in interest within seven (7) days; and

(b) provide notice of the first day emergency hearings in accordance with the procedures shown in the form attached as **Exhibit E.**

9. Guidelines: Counsel shall follow the agenda guidelines for hearings in complex Chapter 11 cases attached as **Exhibit E** and the guidelines for mailing matrices and shortened service lists attached as **Exhibit G.**

* All order exemplars attached as exhibits are furnished for the purpose of prescribing content. Actual formatting of orders should follow the formatting requirements for the district in which the case is filed.

EXHIBIT A: NOTICE OF DESIGNATION AS COMPLEX CHAPTER 11 BANKRUPTCY CASE

IN THE UNITED STATES BANKRUPTCY
COURT FOR THE
EASTERN DISTRICT OF TEXAS
_____ DIVISION

IN RE:)
)
_____)   Case No. _____
)
      Debtor   )   Chapter 11

NOTICE OF DESIGNATION AS COMPLEX
CHAPTER 11 BANKRUPTCY CASE

This bankruptcy case was filed on _____, 200__. The undersigned party in interest believes that this case qualifies as a complex Chapter 11 case because:

___ The debtor has total debt of more than $10 million;

___ There are more than 50 parties in interest in this case;

___ Claims against the debtor are publicly traded;

___ Other (Substantial explanation is required. (Attach additional sheets if necessary.)

_____

_____

DATED: ___, 200__   Address

_____   _____

Name

_____   Telephone, Fax Numbers, and Email

EXHIBIT B: REQUEST FOR EMERGENCY CONSIDERATION
OF CERTAIN "FIRST DAY" MATTERS

IN THE UNITED STATES BANKRUPTCY
COURT FOR THE
EASTERN DISTRICT OF TEXAS
_____ DIVISION

IN RE:)
)
_____   )   Case No. ____
)
                        Debtor)   Chapter 11

REQUEST FOR EMERGENCY CONSIDERATION
OF CERTAIN "FIRST DAY" MATTERS

On *[date]*, *[debtor]* filed a petition for relief under Chapter 11 of the Bankruptcy Code. Counsel for the debtor believes that the case qualifies as a "Complex Chapter 11 Case." The debtor needs emergency consideration of the following initial case matters (check those that apply):

___ JOINT MOTION FOR JOINT ADMINISTRATION

___ MOTION FOR ORDER EXTENDING TIME TO FILE SCHEDULES AND STATEMENT OF FINANCIAL AFFAIRS

___ MOTION RE MAINTENANCE OF BANK ACCOUNTS AND EXISTING CASH MANAGEMENT, ATTACHING NOTICE OF CONFERENCE WITH U.S. TRUSTEE

___ MOTION TO PAY PRE–PETITION WAGES, SALARIES, ET AL., ATTACHING NOTICE OF CONFERENCE WITH U.S. TRUSTEE AND DETAILED EXHIBIT SHOWING WHO DEBTOR PROPOSES TO PAY AND AMOUNTS

___ MOTION FOR ENTRY OF INTERIM ORDER AUTHORIZING USE OF CASH COLLATERAL

___ MOTION FOR INTERIM APPROVAL OF POST–PETITION SECURED AND SUPER PRIORITY FINANCING PURSUANT TO SECTION 364(c) OF THE BANKRUPTCY CODE

___ MOTION PURSUANT TO 11 U.S.C. § 366, FOR ENTRY OF INTERIM ORDER (1) DETERMINING ADEQUATE ASSURANCE OF PAYMENT FOR FUTURE UTILITY SERVICES AND (2) RESTRAINING UTILITY COMPANIES FROM DISCONTINUING, ALTERING, OR REFUSING SERVICE

___ MOTION TO ESTABLISH INTERIM NOTICE PROCEDURES

___ MOTION FOR ORDER APPROVING INTERIM RETENTION OF PROFESSIONALS MOTION FOR ORDER APPROVING PAYMENT OF PRE–PETITION CLAIMS OF CERTAIN CRITICAL VENDORS

___ OTHERS (LIST):

_____

_____

_____

_____

_____, 200___   Address
_____   _____
Name   Telephone, Fax Numbers and EMail
_____

NOTE: The court expects the parties to exercise judgment regarding which motions are applicable.

EXHIBIT C: ORDER DENYING COMPLEX CASE TREATMENT

IN THE UNITED STATES BANKRUPTCY
COURT FOR THE
EASTERN DISTRICT OF TEXAS
_____ DIVISION

IN RE:)
)
_____   )   Case No. _____
)
                        Debtor   )   Chapter 11

ORDER DENYING CHAPTER 11 COMPLEX CASE TREATMENT

This bankruptcy case was filed on _____, 200___. A Notice of Designation as Complex Chapter 11 Case was filed. After review of the initial pleadings filed in this case, the court concludes that the case does not appear to qualify as a complex Chapter 11 case. Therefore, the case will proceed under the local bankruptcy rules and procedures generally applicable to bankruptcy cases without special scheduling orders. The court may reconsider this determination on motion, after hearing.

[SPACE FOR JUDGE SIGNATURE BLOCK]

The Clerk shall notice:
Debtor
Debtor's Counsel
U.S. Trustee

EXHIBIT D: ORDER GRANTING COMPLEX CASE TREATMENT

IN THE UNITED STATES BANKRUPTCY
COURT FOR THE
EASTERN DISTRICT OF TEXAS
_____ DIVISION

IN RE:)
)
_____) Case No. _____
)
      Debtor) Chapter 11

ORDER GRANTING CHAPTER 11 COMPLEX CASE TREATMENT

This bankruptcy case was filed on _____, 200___. A Notice of Designation as Complex Chapter 11 Case was filed. After review of the initial pleadings filed in this case, the court concludes that this case appears to be a complex Chapter 11 case. Accordingly, unless the court orders otherwise,

IT IS ORDERED:

1. The debtor shall maintain a service list identifying the parties that must be served whenever a motion or other pleading requires notice. Unless otherwise required by the Bankruptcy Code or Rules, notices of motions and other matters will be limited to the parties on the service list.

a. The service list shall initially include the debtor, debtor's counsel, counsel for the unsecured creditors' committee, the U.S. Trustee, all secured creditors, the 20 largest unsecured creditors of each debtor, any indenture trustee, and any party that requests notice;

b. Any party in interest that wishes to receive notice, other than as listed on the service list, shall be added to the service list by filing and serving the debtor and debtor's counsel with a notice of appearance and request for service.

c. Parties on the service list, who have not otherwise consented to service by e-mail, through the act of becoming a registered e-filer in this district, are encouraged to provide an e-mail address for service of process and to authorize service by e-mail; consent to e-mail service may be included in the party's notice of appearance and request for service; in the event a party has not consented to e-mail service, a "hard copy" shall be served by fax or by regular mail.

d. The initial service list shall be filed within 3 days after entry of this order. A revised list shall be filed 7 days after the initial service list is filed. The debtor shall update the service list, and shall file a copy of the updated service list, (i) at least every 7 days during the first 30 days of the case; (ii) at least every 15 days during the next 60 days of the case; and (iii) at least every 30 days thereafter throughout the case.

2. [The court sets ___ of [each week] [every other week, commencing [Month and Day] [each month] at ___ am/pm as the pre-set hearing day and time for hearing all motions and other matters in these cases.] The court sets the following dates and times for the next two months as the pre-set hearing date and time for hearing all motions and other matters in these cases [insert dates and times]. Settings for the following months will be published by the court no later than 30 days prior to the first hearing date in the said following months. (There may be exceptions; those exceptions will be noted on the court's internet schedule, available at www.txeb.uscourts.gov.

a. All motions and other matters requiring hearing, but not requiring expedited or emergency hearing, shall be noticed for hearing, on the next hearing day that is at least 23 days after the notice is mailed. As a preface to each pleading, just below the case caption, [in lieu of the language required by any Local Bankruptcy Rule] the pleading shall state:

A HEARING WILL BE CONDUCTED ON THIS MATTER ON_____ AT ___ AM/PM IN THE UNITED STATES BANKRUPTCY COURTROOM, [COURTHOUSE NAME & ADDRESS], ___, TEXAS. IF YOU OBJECT TO THE RELIEF REQUESTED, YOU MUST RESPOND IN WRITING, SPECIFICALLY ANSWERING EACH PARAGRAPH OF THIS PLEADING. UNLESS OTHERWISE DIRECTED BY THE COURT, YOU MUST FILE YOUR RESPONSE WITH THE CLERK OF THE BANKRUPTCY COURT WITHIN TWENTY–THREE DAYS FROM THE DATE YOU WERE SERVED WITH THIS PLEAD-

ING. YOU MUST SERVE A COPY OF YOUR RESPONSE ON THE PERSON WHO SENT YOU THE NOTICE; OTHERWISE, THE COURT MAY TREAT THE PLEADING AS UNOPPOSED AND GRANT THE RELIEF REQUESTED.

b. All motions and other matters requiring expedited or emergency hearing shall comply with the usual court requirements for explanation and verification of the need for emergency or expedited hearing. Specifically, if a party in interest has a situation that it believes requires consideration on less than 23–days' notice, or an emergency that it believes requires consideration on less than 5 business days' notice, then the party should file and serve a separate, written motion for expedited hearing, with respect to the underlying motion. The court will make its best effort to rule on the motion for expedited or emergency hearing within 24 hours of the time it is presented. If the court grants the motion for expedited or emergency hearing, the underlying motion will be set by the courtroom deputy at the next available pre-set hearing day or at some other appropriate shortened date approved by the court. The party requesting the hearing shall be responsible for providing proper notice in accordance with this order and the Bankruptcy Code and Rules.

3. Emergency and expedited hearings (and other hearings in limited circumstances) in this case may be conducted by telephone or, where available, video. Parties must request permission to participate by telephone by calling the courtroom deputy, _____, at ____.

4. If a matter is properly noticed for hearing and the parties reach a settlement of the dispute prior to the final hearing, the parties may announce the settlement at the scheduled hearing. If the court determines that the notice of the dispute and the hearing is adequate notice of the effects of the settlement, (i.e., that the terms of the settlement are not materially different from what parties in interest could have expected if the dispute were fully litigated) the court may approve the settlement at the hearing without further notice of the terms of the settlement.

5. The debtor shall give notice of this order to all parties in interest within 7 days. If any party in interest, at any time, objects to the provisions of this order, that party shall file a motion articulating the objection and the relief requested. After hearing the objection and any responses the court may reconsider any part of this order and may grant relief, if appropriate.

[SPACE FOR JUDGE SIGNATURE BLOCK]

The Clerk shall notice:
Debtor
Debtor's Counsel
U.S. Trustee

EXHIBIT E: PROCEDURES FOR OBTAINING HEARINGS IN COMPLEX CHAPTER 11 CASES

1. **Hearing on First Day Matters—Official Form for Request for Expedited Consideration of Certain First Day Matters:** Upon the filing of a complex Chapter 11 case, if the debtor has matters that require immediate emergency consideration ("first day" or "near first day" relief), the debtor should file a "Request for Emergency Consideration of Certain 'First Day' Matters" using the form of Exhibit B to the Procedures for Complex Chapter 11 Cases ("First Day Hearing Request"). The first day hearing request will be immediately forwarded by the clerk of court to the judge who has been assigned the complex Chapter 11 case (or if there are multiple, related debtor cases, to the judge assigned to the first-filed case). The court will hold a hearing within 2 business days for the time requested by the debtor's counsel and the courtroom deputy will notify counsel for the debtor of the time of the setting. If the judge assigned to the complex Chapter 11 case is not available to hold the hearing within 2 business days of the time requested by the debtor's counsel, an available judge will hold a hearing within 2 business days of the time requested by the debtor's counsel and the courtroom deputy will notify counsel for the debtor of the time of the setting. If no judge is available to hold a hearing within 2 business days, then a hearing date will be scheduled at the earliest possible date that a judge is available. The debtor's counsel should (1) serve electronically, if the e-mail address is available (or by facsimile or immediate hand-delivery) a copy of the first day hearing request on all affected parties, including the U.S. Trustee, simultaneously with its filing; and (2) notify electronically, if the e-mail address is available, or by fax or telephonically (or by immediate hand-delivery) all affected parties of the hearing time on first day matters as soon as possible after debtor's counsel has received confirmation from the court. The court will allow parties in interest to participate telephonically at the hearing on first day matters whenever (and to the extent) practicable, and debtor's counsel will be responsible for the coordination of the telephonic participation.

2. **Pre–Set Hearing Dates.** The debtor may request (as one of its first day matters or otherwise) that the court establish in a complex Chapter 11 case a weekly/bi-monthly/monthly setting time ("Pre–Set Hearing Dates") for hearings in the complex Chapter 11 case (e.g., every Wednesday at 1:30 p.m.). The court will accommodate this request for pre-set hearing dates in a complex Chapter 11 case if it appears justified. After pre-set hearing dates are established, all matters in the complex Chapter 11 case (whether initiated by a motion of the debtor or by another party in interest) will be set on pre-set hearing dates that are at least 23 days after the filing/service of a particular motion (unless otherwise requested by a party or ordered by the court) and the movant shall indicate the hearing date and time on the face of the pleading. Movant shall advise the courtroom deputy of all such settings prior to filing, and the courtroom deputy will advise the movant whether there is enough time on the docket that day to accommodate the matter.

3. **Notice of Hearing.** Notice of hearing of matters scheduled for pre-set hearing dates shall be accomplished in the following manner in each district:

Northern District: Consult the Local Rules.

Western District: By the moving party, who shall file a certificate that the notice has been accomplished in accordance with these procedures.

Southern District: Consult the Local Rules.

Eastern District: By the moving party, who shall file a certificate that the notice has been accomplished in accordance with these procedures.

4. **Case Emergencies (Other than the First–Day Matters).** If a party in interest has an expedited or emergency situation that it believes requires consideration on less than 23–days' notice, the party must file and serve a separate, written motion for expedited or emergency hearing, with respect to the underlying motion, which must comply with the usual court requirements for explanation and verification of the need for expedited or emergency hearing. The court will make its best effort to rule on the motion for expedited or emergency hearing within 24 hours of the time it is presented. If the court grants the motion for expedited or emergency hearing, the underlying motion will be set by the courtroom deputy at the next available pre-set hearing date or at some other appropriate shortened date approved by the court. Motions for expedited and emergency hearings will only be granted for clear cause shown and presented with particularity in the body of the motion.

EXHIBIT F: AGENDA GUIDELINES FOR HEARINGS IN COMPLEX CHAPTER 11 CASES

In complex Chapter 11 cases where five or more matters are noticed for the same hearing date, counsel for the debtor-in-possession, the party requesting the hearings, or trustee shall file and serve an agenda describing the nature of the items set for hearing.

1. **Timing of Filing.** Counsel shall file an agenda at least 24 hours prior to the date and time of the hearing. At the same time, counsel shall also serve the agenda (or confirm electronic service has been effectuated) upon all attorneys who have filed papers with respect to the matters scheduled and upon the service list.

2. **Sequence of Items on Agenda.** Uncontested matters should be listed ahead of contested matters. Contested matters should be listed in the order in which they appear on the court's docket.

3. **Status Information.** For each motion filed in the complex Chapter 11 case, each motion filed in an adversary proceeding concerning the Chapter 11 case, each objection to claim, or application concerning the case, the agenda shall indicate the moving party, the nature of the motion, the docket number of the pleadings, if known, the response deadline, and the status of the matter. The status description should indicate whether the motion is settled, going forward, whether a continuance is requested (and any opposition to the continuance, if known) and any other pertinent information.

4. **Information for Motions in the Case.** For each motion that is going forward, or where a continuance request is not consensual, the agenda shall also list all pleadings in support of the motion, and any objections or responses. Each pleading listed shall identify the entity that filed the pleading, and the docket number of the pleading, if known. If any entity has not filed a responsive pleading, but has engaged in written or oral communications with the debtor, that fact should be indicated on the agenda, as well as the status or outcome of those communications. For an omnibus objection to claims, responses to the objection which have been continued by consent may be listed collectively (e.g., "the following responses have been continued by consent:").

5. **Changes in Agenda Information.** After the filing of the agenda, counsel shall notify judge's chambers by phone or letter of additional related pleadings that have been filed, and changes in the status of any agenda matter.

6. The requirements listed above should not be construed to prohibit other information of a procedural nature that counsel thinks would be helpful to the court.

ALL MOTIONS AND PLEADINGS SHALL CONTAIN THE HEARING DATE AND TIME BELOW THE CASE/ADVERSARY NUMBER.

EXHIBIT G: GUIDELINES FOR SERVICE LISTS AND SHORTENED SERVICE LISTS IN COMPLEX CHAPTER 11 CASES

I. Bankruptcy Rule 2002 Notice/Service List

A. Helpful Hints Regarding Whom to Include on the Service List in a Complex Chapter 11 Case. There are certain events and deadlines that occur in a Chapter 11 case which Federal Rules of Bankruptcy Procedure 2002 requires be broadly noticed to all creditors, indenture trustees, equity interest holders, and other parties in interest ("Rule 2002 notice list"). To facilitate this, debtor's counsel shall evaluate and consider whether the following persons and entities need to be included on the Rule 2002 notice list:

1. creditors (whether a creditor's claim is disputed, undisputed, contingent, non-contingent, liquidated, unliquidated, matured, unmatured, fixed, legal, equitable, secured or unsecured);

2. indenture trustees;

3. financial institutions at which the debtor has maintained accounts (regardless of whether such institutions are creditors);

4. vendors with whom the debtor has dealt, even if the debtor's records currently indicate no amount is owed;

5. parties to contracts, executory contracts or leases with the debtor;

6. federal, state, or local taxing authorities with which the debtor deals, including taxing authorities in every county in which the debtor owns real or personal property with regard to which ad valorem taxes might be owed;

7. governmental entities with which the debtor might interact (including, but not limited to, the U.S. Trustee and the SEC);

8. any party who might assert a lien against property of the debtor;

9. parties to litigation involving the debtor;

10. parties with which the debtor might be engaged in some sort of dispute, whether or not a claim has formally been made against the debtor;

11. tort claimants or accident victims;

12. insurance companies with whom the debtor deals or has policies;

13. active and retired employees of the debtor;

14. officers or directors of the debtor;

15. customers who are owed deposits, refunds, or store credit;

16. utilities;

17. shareholders (preferred and common), holders of options, warrants or other rights or equitable interests in the debtor;

18. miscellaneous others who, in debtor counsel's judgment, might be entitled to "party in interest" status or who have requested notice.

B. Flexible ("User Friendly") Format Rules for Mailing Matrix or Creditor List in a Complex Debtor 11 Case in Which Debtor's Counsel Serves Notices. In a complex Chapter 11 case, where the mailing matrix (or creditor list) is likely to be very lengthy, the following special format rules will apply, [in lieu of any applicable local bankruptcy rule, save and except the Administrative Procedures for the Filing, Signing and Verifying of Documents by Electronic Means in Texas Bankruptcy Courts, adopted by local rule or general order in all federal districts in Texas] whenever it is the debtor's responsibility to serve notices in the case. The debtor (since it will typically be the party serving all notices in the Chapter 11 case rather than the clerk of court) may create the mailing matrix or creditor list in whatever format it finds convenient so long as it is neatly typed in upper and lower case letter-quality characters (in no smaller than 10 point and no greater than 14 point type, in either Courier, Times Roman, Helvetica or Orator font) in a format equivalent to 8½ inch by 11 inch blank, unlined, standard white paper. The mailing matrix or creditor list, if lengthy, should ideally include separate subheadings throughout, to help identify categories of parties in interest. By way of example, the following subheadings (among others) might be used:

> Debtor and its Professionals
> Secured Creditors
> Indenture Trustees
> Unsecured Creditors
> Governmental Entities
> Current and Retired Employees
> Officers and Directors
> Tort Claimants
> Parties to Executory Contracts
> Equity Interest Holders
> Other

Parties in interest within each category/subheading should be listed alphabetically.

Also, the mailing matrix or creditor list may be filed in separate volumes, for the separate categories of parties in interest, if the mailing matrix or creditor list is voluminous. Finally, if there are multiple, related debtors and the debtors intend to promptly move for joint administration of their cases, the debtors may file a consolidated mailing matrix or creditor list, subject to later being required to file separate mailing matrices if joint administration is not permitted.

C. When Inclusion of Certain Parties in Interest on a Mailing Matrix is Burdensome. If inclusion of certain categories of parties in interest on the mailing matrix or creditor list would be extremely impracticable, burdensome and costly to the estate, the debtor may file a motion, pursuant to FRBP. 2002(*l*), and on notice to the affected categories of parties in interest, requesting authority to provide notices to certain categories of parties in interest and may forego including those categories of parties in interest on the mailing matrix if the court grants the motion.

II. Shortened Service List Procedure in a Complex Chapter 11 Case.

A. Procedures/Contents/Presumptions. If the court has entered an order granting complex Chapter 11 case treatment, the debtor shall provide service as required by ¶ 1 of that order. If the court has not entered such an order, the debtor may move to limit notice–that is, for approval of a shortened service list–that will be acceptable for noticing most events in the bankruptcy case, other than those events/deadlines that Federal Rules of Bankruptcy Procedure 2002 contemplates be served on all creditors and equity interest holders. At a minimum, the shortened list should include the debtor and its professionals, the secured creditors, the 20 largest unsecured creditors, any official committees and the professionals for same, the U.S. Trustee, the IRS and other relevant governmental entities, and all parties who have requested notice. Upon the court's approval of a shortened service list in a complex Chapter 11 case, notice in any particular situation during a case shall be presumed adequate if there has been service on (1) the most current service list on file in the case; plus (2) any other party directly affected by the relief requested and not otherwise included on the service list.

B. Obligation to Update, File and Serve Service List. The debtor must update the service list as parties request to be added to it or as circumstances otherwise require. To be added to the list, a party must file a notice of appearance and request for service and serve the notice on debtor's counsel. Parties should include e-mail transmission information if they wish to receive expedited service of process during the case. Additionally, the debtor must file an updated service list and must serve a clean and redlined copy of the updated service list on all parties on the service list weekly for the first month after filing, then bi-monthly for the next 60 days, then monthly thereafter during the pendency of the case. If, in a particular month, there are no changes to the service list, the debtor must file a notice with the court so stating.

EXHIBIT H: GUIDELINES FOR COMPENSATION AND EXPENSE REIMBURSEMENT OF PROFESSIONALS IN COMPLEX CHAPTER 11 CASES

The following guidelines govern the most significant issues relating to applications for compensation and expense reimbursement. The guidelines cover the narrative portion of an application, time records, and expenses. It applies to all professionals, but is not intended to cover every situation. All professionals are required to exercise reasonable billing judgment, notwithstanding total hours spent.

If, in a chapter 11 case, a professional to be employed pursuant to section 327 or 1103 of the Bankruptcy Code desires to have the terms of its compensation approved pursuant to section 328(a) of the Bankruptcy Code at the time of such professional's retention, then the application seeking such approval should so indicate and the Court will consider such request after an evidentiary hearing on notice to be held after the United States trustee has had an opportunity to form a statutory committee of creditors pursuant to section 1102 of the Bankruptcy Code and the debtor had such committee have had an opportunity to review and comment on such application. At a hearing to consider whether a professional's compensation arrangement should be approved pursuant to section 328(a), such professional should be prepared to produce evidence that the terms of compensation for which approval under section 328(a) is sought comply with the certification requirements of section I.G(3) of these guidelines.

I. NARRATIVE

A. Employment and Prior Compensation. The application should disclose the date of the order approving applicant's employment and contain a clear statement itemizing the date of each prior request for compensation, the amount requested, the amount approved, and the amount paid.

B. Case Status. With respect to interim requests, the application should briefly explain the history and the present posture of the case, including a description of the status of pending litigation and the amount of recovery sought for the estate.

In chapter 11 cases, the information furnished should describe the general operations of the debtor; whether the business of the debtor, if any, is being operated at a profit or loss; the debtor's cash flow; whether a plan has been filed, and if not, what the prospects are for reorganization and when it is anticipated that a plan will be filed and a hearing set on the disclosure statement.

In chapter 7 cases, the application should contain a report of the administration of the case including the disposition of property of the estate; what property remains to be disposed of; why the estate is not in a position to be closed; and whether it is feasible to pay an interim dividend to creditors.

In both chapter 7 and chapter 11 cases, the application should state the amount of money on hand in the estate and the estimated amount of other accrued expenses of administration. On applications for interim fees, the applicant should orally supplement the application at the hearing to inform the Court of any changes in the current financial status of the debtor's estate since the filing of the application. All retainers, previous draw downs, and fee applications and orders should be listed specifying the date of the event and the amounts involved and drawn down or allowed.

With respect to final requests, applications should meet the same criteria except where a chapter 7 trustee's final account if being heard at the same time, the financial information in the final account need not be repeated.

Fee applications submitted by special counsel seeking compensation from a fund generated directly by their efforts, auctioneers, real estate brokers, or appraisers do not have to comply with the above. For all other applications, when more than one application is noticed for the same hearing, they may, to the extent appropriate, incorporate by reference the narrative history furnished in a contemporaneous application.

C. Project Billing. This is required in all cases where the applicant's professional fee is expected to exceed $10,000.00. The narrative should be categorized by subject matter, and separately discuss each professional project or task. All work for which compensation is requested should be in a category. Miscellaneous items may be included in a category such as "Case Administration." The professional may use reasonable discretion in defining projects for this purpose, provided that the application provides meaningful guidance to the Court as to the complexity and difficulty of the task, the professional's efficiency, and the results achieved. With respect to each project or task, the number of hours spent and the amount of compensation and expenses requested should be set forth

at the conclusion of the discussion of that project or task. In larger cases with multiple professionals, efforts should be made by the professionals for standard categorization.

D. Billing Summary. Hours and total compensation requested in each application should be aggregate and itemized as to each professional and paraprofessional who provided compensable services. Dates of changes in rates should be itemized as well as reasons for said changes.

E. Paraprofessionals. Fees may be sought for paralegals, professional assistants and law clerks only if identified as such and if the application includes a resume or summary of the paraprofessional's qualifications.

F. Preparation of Application. Reasonable fees for preparation of a fee application and responding to objections thereto may be requested. The aggregate number of hours spent, the amount requested, and the percentage of the total request which the amount represents must be disclosed. If the actual time spent will be reflected and charged in a future fee application, this fact should be stated, but an estimate provided, nevertheless.

G. Certification. Each application for compensation and expense reimbursement must contain a certification by the professional designated by the applicant with the responsibility in the particular case for compliance with these guidelines ("Certifying Professional") that 1) the Certifying Professional has read the application; 2) to the best of the Certifying Professional's knowledge, information and belief, formed after reasonable inquiry, the compensation and expense reimbursement sought is in conformity with these guidelines, except as specifically noted in the application; and 3) the compensation and expenses reimbursement requested are billed at rates, in accordance with practices, no less favorable than those customarily employed by the applicant and generally accepted by the applicant's clients.

H. Interim Compensation Arrangements in Complex Cases. In a complex case, the Court may, upon request, consider at the outset of the case approval of an interim compensation mechanism for estate professionals that would enable professionals on a monthly basis to be paid up to 80% of their compensation for services rendered and reimbursed up to 100% of their actual and necessary out of pocket expenses. In connection with such a procedure, if approved in a particular complex case, professionals shall be required to circulate monthly billing statements to the US Trustee and other primary parties in interest, and the Debtor in Possession or Trustee will be authorized to pay the applicable percentage of such bill not disputed or contested by a party in interest.

II. TIME RECORDS

A. Time Records Required. All professionals, except auctioneers, real estate brokers, and appraisers must keep accurate contemporaneous time records.

B. Increments. Professionals are required to keep time records in minimum increments no greater than six minutes. Professionals who utilize a minimum billing increment greater than .1 hour are subject to a substantial reduction of their requests.

C. Descriptions. At a minimum, the time entries should identify the person performing the service, the date(s) performed, what was done, and the subject involved. Mere notations of telephone calls, conferences, research, drafting, etc., without identifying the matter involved, may result in disallowance of the time covered by the entries.

D. Grouping of Tasks. If a number of separate tasks are performed on a single day, the fee application should disclose the time spent for each such task, i.e., no "grouping" or "clumping." Minor administrative matters may be lumped together where the aggregate time attributed thereto is relatively minor. A rule of reason applies as to how specific and detailed the breakdown needs to be. For grouped entries, the applicant must accept the Court inferences therefrom.

E. Conferences. Professionals should be prepared to explain time spent in conferences with other professionals or paraprofessionals in the same firm. Relevant explanation would include complexity of issues involved and the necessity of more individuals' involvement. Failure to justify this time may result in disallowance of all, or a portion of, fees related to such conferences.

F. Multiple Professionals. Professionals should be prepared to explain the need for more than one professional or paraprofessional from the same firm at the same court hearing, deposition, or meeting. Failure to justify this time may result in compensation for only the person with the lowest billing rate. The Court acknowledges, however, that in complex chapter 11 cases the need for multiple professionals' involvement will be more common and that in hearings involving multiple or complex issues a law firm may justifiably be required to utilize multiple attorneys as the circumstances of the case require.

G. Travel Time. Travel time is compensable at one-half rates, but work actually done during travel is fully compensable.

H. Administrative Tasks. Time spent in addressing, stamping and stuffing envelopes, filing, photocopying or "supervising" any of the foregoing is generally not compensable, whether performed by a professional, paraprofessional, or secretary.

III. EXPENSES

A. Firm Practice. The Court will consider the customary practice of the firm in charging or not charging non-bankruptcy/insolvency clients for particular expense items. Where any other clients, with the exception of pro-bono clients, are not billed for a particular expense, the estate should not be billed. Where expenses are billed to all other clients, reimbursement should be sought at the least expensive rate the firm or professional charges to any client for comparable services or expenses. It is recognized that there will be differences in billing practices among professionals.

B. Actual Cost. This is defined as the amount paid to a third party provider of goods or services without enhancement for handling or other administrative charge.

C. Documentation. This must be retained and made available upon request for all expenditures in excess of $50.00. Where possible, receipts should be obtained for all expenditures.

D. Office Overhead. This is not reimbursable. Overhead includes: secretarial time, secretarial overtime (where clear necessity for same has not been shown), word processing time, charges for after-hour and weekend air conditioning and other utilities, and cost of meals or transportation provided to professionals and staff who work late or on weekends.

E. Word Processing. This is not reimbursable.

F. Computerized Research. This is reimbursable at actual cost. For large amounts billed to computerized research, significant explanatory detail should be furnished.

G. Paraprofessional Services. These services may be compensated as a paraprofessional under § 330, but not charged or reimbursed as an expense.

H. Professional Services. A professional employed under § 327 may not employ, and charge as an expense, another professional (e.g., special litigation counsel employing an expert witness) unless the employment of the second professional is approved by the Court prior to the rendering of service.

I. Photocopies (Internal). Charges must be disclosed on an aggregate and per-page basis. If the per-page cost exceeds $.20, the professional must demonstrate to the satisfaction of the Court, with data, that the per-page cost represents a good faith estimate of the actual cost of the copies, based upon the purchase or lease cost of the copy machine and supplies therefor, including the space occupied by the machine, but not including time spent in operating the machine.

J. Photocopies (Outside). This item is reimbursable at actual cost.

K. Postage. This is reimbursable at actual cost.

L. Overnight Delivery. This is reimbursable at actual cost where it is shown to be necessary. The court acknowledges that in complex chapter 11 cases overnight delivery or messenger services may often be appropriate, particularly when shortened notice of a hearing of a hearing has been requested.

M. Messenger Service. This is reimbursable at actual cost where it is shown to be necessary. An in-house messenger service is reimbursable, but the estate cannot be charged more than the cost of comparable services available outside the firm.

N. Facsimile Transmission. The actual cost of telephone charges for outgoing transmissions is reimbursable. Transmissions received are reimbursable on a per-page basis. If the per-page cost exceeds $.20, the professional must demonstrate, with data, to the satisfaction of the Court, that the per-page cost represents a good faith estimate of the actual cost of the copies, based upon the purchase or lease cost of the facsimile machine and supplies therefor, including the space occupied by the machine, but not including time spent in operating the machine.

O. Long Distance Telephone. This is reimbursable at actual cost.

P. Parking. This is reimbursable at actual cost.

Q. Air Transportation. Air travel is expected to be at regular coach fare for all flights.

R. Hotels. Due to wide variation in hotel costs in various cities, it is not possible to establish a single guideline for this type of expense. All persons will be required to exercise reasonable discretion and prudence in connection with hotel expenditures.

S. Meals (Travel). Reimbursement may be sought for the reasonable cost of breakfast, lunch and dinner while traveling.

T. Meals (Working). Working meals at restaurants or private clubs are not reimbursable. Reasonable reimbursement may be sought for working meals only where food is catered to the professional's office in the course of a meeting with clients, such as a Creditors' Committee, for the purpose of allowing the meeting to continue through a normal meal period.

U. Amenities. Charges for entertainment, alcoholic beverages, newspapers, dry cleaning, shoe shines, etc. are not reimbursable.

V. Filing Fees. These are reimbursable at actual cost.

W. Court Reporter Fees. These are reimbursable at actual cost.

X. Witness Fees. These are reimbursable at actual cost.

Y. Process Service. This is reimbursable at actual cost.

Z. UCC Searches. These are reimbursable at actual cost.

EXHIBIT I: GUIDELINES FOR EARLY DISPOSITION OF ASSETS IN CHAPTER
11 CASES; THE SALE OF SUBSTANTIALLY ALL ASSETS UNDER
SECTION 363; AND OVERBID AND TOPPING FEES.

The following guidelines are promulgated as a result of the increasing use of pre-negotiated or pre-packaged plans and 11 U.S.C. § 363 sales to dispose of substantially all assets of a Chapter 11 debtor shortly after the filing of the petition. The guidelines recognize that parties in interest perceive the need at times to act expeditiously on such matters. In addition, the guidelines are written to provide procedural protection to the parties in interest. The court will consider requests to modify the guidelines to fit the circumstances of a particular case.

A. OVERBIDS AND TOPPING FEES

1. Topping Fees and Break-up Fees. Any request for the approval of a topping fee or a break-up fee provision shall be supported by a statement of the precise conditions under which the topping fee or break-up fee would be payable and the factual basis on which the seller determined the provision was reasonable. The request shall also disclose the identities of other potential purchasers, the offers made by them (if any), and the nature of the offer, including, without limitation, any disclosure of their plans as it relates to retention of debtor's employees.

2. Topping fees, break-up fees, overbid amounts and other buyer protection provisions will be reviewed on a case by case basis and approved if supported by evidence and case law. Case law may not support buyer protection provisions for readily marketable assets.

3. In connection with a request to sell substantially all assets under § 363 within 60 days of the filing of the petition, buyer protections may be considered upon motion, on an expedited basis.

B. THE SALE OF SUBSTANTIALLY ALL ASSETS UNDER SECTION 363 WITHIN 60 DAYS OF THE FILING OF THE PETITION

1. **The Motion to Sell.** In connection with any hearing to approve the sale of substantially all assets at any time before 60 days after the filing of the petition, a motion for an order authorizing a sale procedure and hearing or the sale motion itself when regularly noticed, should include factual information on the following points:

a. *Creditors' Committee.* If a creditors' committee existed pre-petition, indicate the date and manner in which the committee was formed, as well as the identity of the members of the committee and the companies with which they are affiliated.

b. *Counsel for Committee.* If the pre-petition creditors' committee retained counsel, indicate the date counsel was engaged and the selection process, as well as the identity of committee counsel.

c. *Sale Contingencies.* Statement of all contingencies to the sale agreement, together with a copy of the agreement.

d. *Creditor Contact List.* If no committee has been formed, a list of contact persons, together with fax and phone numbers for each of the largest 20 unsecured creditors.

e. *Administrative Expenses.* Assuming the sale is approved, an itemization and an estimate of administrative expenses relating to the sale to be incurred prior to closing and the source of payment for those expenses.

f. *Proceeds of Sale.* An estimate of the gross proceeds anticipated from the sale, together with an estimate of the net proceeds coming to the estate with an explanation of the items making up the difference. Itemize all deductions that are to be made from gross sale proceeds and include a brief description of the basis for any such deductions.

g. *Debt Structure of Debtor.* A brief description of the debtor's debt structure, including the amount of the debtor's secured debt, priority claims and general unsecured claims.

h. *Need for Quick Sale.* An extensive description of why the assets of the estate must be sold on an expedited basis. Include a discussion of alternatives to the sale.

i. *Negotiating Background.* A description of the length of time spent in negotiating the sale, and which parties in interest were involved in the negotiation, along with a description of the details of any other offers to purchase, including, without limitation, the potential purchaser's plans in connection with retention of the debtor's employees.

j. *Marketing of Assets.* A description of the manner in which the assets were marketed for sale, including the period of time involved and the results achieved.

k. *Decision to Sell.* The date on which the debtor accepted the offer to purchase the assets.

l. *Relationship of Buyer.* A statement identifying the buyer and setting forth all of the buyer's (including its officers, directors and shareholders) connections with the debtor, creditors, any other party in interest, their respective attorneys, accountants, the United States Trustee or any person employed in the office of the United States Trustee.

m. *Post Sale Relationship with Debtor.* A statement setting forth any relationship or connection the debtor (including its officers, directors, shareholders and employees) will have with the buyer after the consummation of the sale, assuming it is approved.

*m. *Relationship with Secured Creditors.* If the sale involves the payment of all or a portion of secured debt(s), a statement of all connections between debtor's officers, directors, employees or other insiders and each secured creditor involved (for example, release of insider's guaranty).

o. *Insider Compensation.* Disclosure of current compensation received by officers, directors, key employees or other insiders pending approval of the sale.

p. *Notice Timing.* Notice of the hearing on the motion to approve the motion to sell will be provided as is necessary under the circumstances.

2. Proposed Order Approving Sale. A proposed order approving the sale must be included with the motion or the notice of hearing. A proposed final order and redlined version of the order approving the sale should be provided to chambers twenty-four hours prior to the hearing.

3. Good Faith Finding. There must be an evidentiary basis for a finding of good faith under 11 U.S.C. § 363(m).

4. Competing Bids. Unless the court orders otherwise, competing bids may be presented at the time of the hearing. The motion to sell and the notice of hearing should so provide.

5. Financial Ability to Close. Unless the court orders otherwise, any bidder must be prepared to demonstrate to the satisfaction of the court, through an evidentiary hearing, its ability to consummate the transaction if it is the successful bidder, along with evidence regarding any financial contingencies to closing the transaction.

6. Hearing and Notice Regarding Sale. Unless the court orders otherwise, all sales governed by these guidelines, including auctions or the presentation of competing bids, will occur at the hearing before the court. The court may, for cause, including the need to maximize and preserve asset value, expedite a hearing on a motion to sell substantially all assets under § 363.

*[**Publisher's Note:** So in original.]

EXHIBIT J: CHECKLIST FOR LENGTHY MOTIONS AND ORDERS PERTAINING
TO CASH COLLATERAL AND POST–PETITION FINANCING.

IN THE UNITED STATES BANKRUPTCY
COURT FOR THE
EASTERN DISTRICT OF TEXAS
_____ DIVISION

IN RE:)
)
_____)   CASE NO. ____
)
       DEBTOR   )   HEARING: ____

ATTORNEY CHECKLIST CONCERNING MOTIONS AND ORDERS PERTAINING
TO USE OF CASH COLLATERAL AND POST–PETITION FINANCING
(WHICH ARE IN EXCESS OF TEN (10) PAGES)

Motions and orders pertaining to cash collateral and post-petition financing matters tend to be lengthy and complicated. Although the Court intends to read such motions and orders carefully, it will assist the Court if counsel will complete and file this checklist. All references are to the Bankruptcy Code (§) or Rules (R). PLEASE NOTE:

* Means generally not favored by Bankruptcy Courts in this District.

** Means generally not favored by Bankruptcy Courts in this District without a reason and a time period for objections.

If your motion or order makes provision for any of the following, so indicate in the space provided:

CERTIFICATE BY COUNSEL

This is to certify that the following checklist fully responds to the Court's inquiry concerning material terms of the motion and/or proposed order:

Yes, at Page/Exhibit
Y means yes; N means no
N/A means not applicable
(Page Listing Optional)

1. Identification of Proceedings:
    (a) Preliminary or final motion/order (circle one) .... ____
    (b) Continuing use of cash collateral (§ 363) .... ____
    (c) New financing (§ 364) .... ____
    (d) Combination of §§ 363 and 364 financing .... ____
    (e) Emergency hearing (immediate and irreparable harm) .... ____
2. Stipulations:
    (a) Brief history of debtor's businesses and status of debtor's prior
        relationships with lender .... ____
    (b) Brief statement of purpose and necessity of financing .... ____
    (c) Brief statement of type of financing (i.e., accounts receivable,
        inventory)... ____
** (d) Are lender's pre-petition security interest(s) and liens deemed
        valid, fully perfected and non-avoidable .... ____
            (i) Are there provisions to allow for objections to above?......... ____
    (e) Is there a post-petition financing agreement between lender and
        debtor?.. ____
            (i) If so, is agreement attached? .... ____
** (f) If there is an agreement are lender's post-petition security
        interests and liens deemed valid, fully perfected and non-avoid-
        able? .... ____

Yes, at Page/Exhibit
Y means yes; N means no
N/A means not applicable
(Page Listing Optional)

(g) Is lender undersecured or oversecured? (circle one) . . . . _____

(h) Has lender's non-cash collateral been appraised? . . . . _____

    (i) Insert date of latest appraisal . . . . _____

(i) Is debtor's proposed budget attached? . . . . _____

(j) Are all pre-petition loan documents identified? . . . . _____

(k) Are pre-petition liens on single or multiple assets? (circle one) . . . . . . _____

(*l*) Are there pre-petition guaranties of debt? . . . . _____

    (i) Limited or unlimited? (circle one) . . . . _____

3.   Grant of Liens:

*   (a) Do post-petition liens secure pre-petition debts? . . . . _____

*   (b) Is there cross-collateralization? . . . . _____

**   (c) Is the priority of post-petition liens equal to or higher than existing liens? . . . . _____

**   (d) Do post-petition liens have retroactive effect? . . . . _____

    (e) Are there restrictions on granting further liens or liens of equal or higher priority? . . . . _____

*   (f) Is lender given liens on claims under §§ 506(c), 544–50 and §§ 522? . . . . _____

**   (i) Are lender's attorneys fees to be paid? . . . . _____

       (ii) Are debtor's attorneys fees excepted from § 506(c)? . . . . _____

*   (g) Is lender given liens upon proceeds of causes of action under §§ 544, 547 and 548? . . . . _____

4.   Administrative Priority Claims:

    (a) Is lender given an administrative priority? . . . . _____

    (b) Is administrative priority higher than § 507(a)? . . . . _____

    (c) Is there a conversion of pre-petition secured claim to post-petition administrative claim by virtue of use of existing collateral? . . . . _____

5.   Adequate Protection (§ 361):

    (a) Is there post-petition debt service? . . . . _____

    (b) Is there a replacement/addition 361(*l*) lien? (circle one or both) . . . . _____

**   (c) Is the lender's claim given super-priority? (§ 364(c) or (d)) [designate] . . . . _____

    (d) Are there guaranties? . . . . _____

    (e) Is there adequate Insurance coverage? . . . . _____

    (f) Other? . . . . _____

6.   Waiver/Release Claims v. Lender:

**   (a) Debtor waives or release claims against lender, including, but not limited to, claims under §§ 506(c), 544–550, 552, and 553 of the Code? . . . . _____

**   (b) Does the debtor waive defenses to claim or liens of lender? . . . . _____

7.   Source of Post–Petition Financing (§ 364 Financing):

    (a) Is the proposed lender also the pre-petition lender? . . . . _____

    (b) New post-petition lender? . . . . _____

    (c) Is the lender an insider? . . . . _____

8.   Modification of Stay:

**   (a) Is any modified lift of stay allowed? . . . . _____

**   (b) Will the automatic stay be lifted to permit lender to exercise self-help upon default without further order? . . . . _____

    (c) Are there any other remedies exercisable without further order of court? . . . . _____

    (d) Is there a provision that any future modification of order shall not affect status of debtor's post-petition obligations to lender? . . . . _____

9.   Creditors' Committee:

    (a) Has creditors' committee been appointed? . . . . _____

    (b) Does creditors' committee approve of proposed financing? . . . . _____

10.   Restrictions on Parties in Interest:

Yes, at Page/Exhibit
Y means yes; N means no
N/A means not applicable
(Page Listing Optional)

** (a) Is a plan proponent restricted in any manner, concerning modification of lender's rights, liens and/or causes? .... _____

** (b) Is the debtor prohibited from seeking to enjoin the lender in pursuant of rights? .... _____

** (c) Is any party in interest prohibited from seeking to modify this order? .... _____

(d) Is the entry of any order conditioned upon payment of debt to lender? .... _____

(e) Is the order binding on subsequent trustee on conversion? .... _____

11. Nunc Pro Tunc:

(a) Does any provision have retroactive effect? .... _____

12. Notice and Other Procedures:

(a) Is shortened notice requested? .... _____

(b) Is notice requested to shortened list? .... _____

(c) Is time to respond to be shortened? .... _____

(d) If final order sought, have 15 days elapsed since service of motion pursuant to Rule 4001(b)(2)? .... _____

(e) If preliminary order sought, is cash collateral necessary to avoid immediate and irreparable harm to the estate pending a final hearing? .... _____

(f) Is a Certificate of Conference included? .... _____

(g) Is a Certificate of Service included? .... _____

(h) Is there verification of transmittal to U.S. Trustee included pursuant to Rule 9034? .... _____

(i) Has an agreement been reached subsequent to filing motion? .... _____

(i) If so, has notice of the agreement been served pursuant to Rule 4001(d)(4)? .... _____

(ii) Is the agreement in settlement of motion pursuant to Rule 4001(d)(4)? .... _____

(iii) Does the motion afford reasonable notice of material provisions of agreement pursuant to Rule 4001(d)(4)? .... _____

(iv) Does the motion provide for opportunity for hearing pursuant to Rule 9014? .... _____

SIGNED this the _____ day of _____, 200__.

[ATTORNEY SIGNATURE BLOCK]

COMMENTS TO CASH COLLATERAL AND DIP FINANCING CHECKLIST

1. Interim vs. Final Orders

a. Stipulations in preliminary or interim orders should be minimized. Notice is generally not adequate to test the validity of stipulations, and they should be avoided to the extent not absolutely necessary to the interim approval process.

b. Simply state the nature of notice given; do not recite notice was "sufficient and adequate" since that is usually not the case particularly on the first day. The order should simply note that the financing is being approved pursuant to Bankruptcy Rule 4001(c)(2) authorizing such financing to avoid immediate and irreparable harm.

c. Adequate protection for the use of pre-petition cash collateral may be granted to the extent of a diminution of collateral. The court will not approve on an interim basis language that adequate protection is granted in the form of replacement liens on post-petition assets based on stipulations that "use of cash collateral shall be deemed a dollar for dollar decrease in the value of the pre-petition collateral." At the final hearing the court will consider evidence to determine the extent to which the lender's pre-petition collateral has or is likely to diminish in value. That evidence will inform the extent to which adequate protection will be granted.

d. The court expects that other parties in interest will be involved in the process of developing an interim cash collateral order to the extent practicable. If the court finds that the debtor and lender have not made reasonable efforts to afford the best notice possible, preliminary relief will not be granted until parties in interest have had a reasonable opportunity to review and comment on any proposed interim order.

e. Bankruptcy Rule 4001(b) and (c) limit the extent to which the court may grant relief on less than 15 days' notice. The debtor and the lender must negotiate interim orders within the confines of that authority. Interim orders shall be expressly without prejudice to the rights of parties in interest at a final hearing.

2. Stipulations

a. The lender may request a stipulation as to the amount, validity, priority and extent of the pre-petition documents. The stipulation will only be approved if the order provides the stipulation is binding on other parties in interest only after the passage of an appropriate period of time (customarily 90 days) during which the parties in interest will have the opportunity to test the validity of the lien and the allowance of the claim.

3. Grant of Liens

a. Liens granted in the cash collateral and DIP financing orders may not secure prepetition debts. Financing orders should not be used to elevate a pre-petition lender's collateral inadequacy to a fully secured status.

b. Avoidance actions are frequently one of the few sources of recovery for creditors other than secured lenders. Orders granting liens on these unencumbered assets for the benefit of the lender will require a showing of extraordinary circumstances. In most cases the adequate protection grant will protect the lender since the lender will have a superpriority under § 507(b) that will give the lender who suffers a failure of adequate protection a first right to payment out of the proceeds from such actions before payment of any other expenses of the Chapter 11 case. Avoidance actions in the event of a conversion to Chapter 7 may be the only assets available to fund the trustee's discharge of his or her statutory duties.

c. Similarly, limitations on the surcharge of the lender's collateral under § 506(c) are disfavored. The secured creditor may be the principal beneficiary of the proceedings in Chapter 11. Since the burden to surcharge requires a showing of direct benefit to the lender's collateral, lenders are not unreasonably exposed to surcharges of their collateral. And in light of the decision in Hartford Underwriter's Insurance Co. v. Union Planters Bank N.A. (In re Hen House Interstate Inc.), ___ U.S. ___, 120 S.Ct. 1942 (2000), only the DIP or the trustee may recover under § 506(c).

4. Modification of Stay

a. Authority for unilateral action by lender without necessity to return to court to establish post-petition default or breach or at least a notice to parties in interest will not be approved. If the cash collateral or financing order provides for a termination of the automatic stay in the event of a default, parties in interest must have an opportunity to be heard before the stay lifts.

5. Restrictions on Plan Process

a. The court will not approve cash collateral orders (or post-petition financing orders that are in substance cash collateral orders that have the effect of converting all the pre-petition liens and claims to post-petition liabilities under the guise of collecting pre-petition accounts and readvancing them post-petition) that have the effect of converting pre-petition secured debt into post-petition administrative claims that must be paid in full in order to confirm a plan. That type of provision unfairly limits the ability and flexibility of the debtor and other parties in interest to formulate a plan. That type of provision, granted at the outset of a case, effectively compels the debtor to pay off the secured lender in full on the effective date and has the consequence of eviscerating § 1129(b).

b. On the other hand, persons who are advancing new money to the debtor postpetition may include in financing orders provisions that the post-petition loans have a § 364(c)(1) super-super priority.

6. Loan Agreements

a. If there will be a loan agreement, the language of the financing order does not need to restate all of the terms of the loan agreement. The financing motion should, however, summarize the essential elements of the proposed borrowing or use of cash collateral, such as, amount of loan facility, sublimits on availability, borrowing base formula, conditions to new advances, interest rate, maturity, events of default, limitation on use of funds and description of collateral.

7. Professional Fees

a. To the extent consistent with the market for similar financings, the lender may request reimbursement of reasonable professional fees. The lender should provide reasonably detailed invoices to the debtor and the committees so a proper assessment of reasonableness can be made.

b. The parties may agree on carve-outs for estate professionals. Lenders may exclude from the carve-out payment of professional fees for litigation of the extent, validity or perfection of the lender's claim as well as prosecution of lender liability suits. The carve-out should not, however, exclude the due diligence work by the committee or its professionals to determine whether a challenge to the lender is justified.

8. Work Fees/Loan Fees

a. Underwriting a substantial DIP loan may involve both direct out-of-pocket expenses and, at times, a certain lost opportunity cost. The debtor may move for the reimbursement of its lender's direct out-of-pocket expenses. The debtor and lender must be prepared to establish actual out-of-pocket costs, the reasonableness of the costs, and that the type of costs are actually paid in the market. On a case-by-case basis, the court will consider on an expedited basis the debtor's request to pay a reasonable up-front fee to a prospective DIP lender to reimburse it for direct out-of-pocket costs. In addition, in connection with approving a DIP loan facility, on motion of the debtor, the court will consider evidence of market rates and pricing for comparable loans in determining whether commitment fees, facility or availability fees, and other up-front or periodic loan charges are appropriate. The lender must provide evidence that it actually has provided or will provide the services customarily associated with these fees.

[Effective October 17, 2005.]

SELECTED GENERAL ORDERS

GENERAL ORDER 04–1.　IMPLEMENTATION OF MANDATORY ELECTRONIC FILING OF DOCUMENTS BY ATTORNEYS AND OTHER FILERS

In fulfillment of the mandate for an orderly transition to electronic case filing and pursuant to the notice issued to attorneys and other frequent participants before the Court in October, 2002 regarding this Court's intent to require at some future date the filing of documents exclusively by electronic means:

IT IS HEREBY ORDERED THAT:

(1) **EFFECTIVE MARCH 1, 2004,** parties wishing to file documents with the United States Bankruptcy Court for the Eastern District of Texas shall file such documents exclusively by electronic means;

(2) the only parties generically exempted from the scope of this requirement shall be non-attorney parties with very limited involvement with the Court and for whom an Electronic Filer authorization would likely be denied; and

(3) except as excused by the Court, any document filed by non-electronic means by any party for whom filing by electronic means is mandatory under this general order may be stricken without further notice.

[Dated:　February 19, 2004.]

GENERAL ORDER 08–2.　COPIES OF DOCUMENTS BY INDIVIDUAL DEBTORS IN CHAPTER 7 CASES

In recognition that the disclosure of certain documents to the United States Trustee should be made by individual debtors in Chapter 7 cases in order to facilitate a review for abusive case filings and that the transmittal of such documents should begin immediately without regard to the effective date of any revisions to the Local Rules of Bankruptcy Procedure contemplated by the Court,

IT IS THEREFORE ORDERED that, for all Chapter 7 cases filed on or after January 1, 2008, an individual debtor shall provide to the United States Trustee:

(**A**) copies of all payment advices or other evidence of payment from any employer received by an individual debtor in a Chapter 7 or Chapter 13 case within 60 days before the filing of the petition; and

(**B**) a copy of the federal tax return required under § 521(c)(2)(A).

Such copies shall be provided to the United States Trustee at the same time as copies are provided by the debtor to the Chapter 7 trustee under the Bankruptcy Code and the Federal and Local Rules of Bankruptcy Procedure.

This General Order shall remain in effect pending the further order of the Court.

Executed and entered on behalf of all divisions of the Court.

[Dated:　January 1, 2008.]

GENERAL ORDER 08–3.　RESCISSION OF GENERAL ORDER 05–2 REGARDING ADOPTION OF INTERIM BANKRUPTCY RULES

In recognition of the fact that the revised Federal Rules of Bankruptcy Procedure, designated to become effective on December 1, 2008, have now incorporated rule amendments reflecting the substantive and procedural changes mandated by the passage of the Bankruptcy Abuse Prevention and Consumer Protection Act of 2005 (the "Act"); and the fact that the Interim Bankruptcy Rules previously promulgated by the Advisory Committee on Bankruptcy Rules of the Judicial Conference of the United States, and adopted by this Court through General Order 05–2 shall be superseded by such amendments to the Federal Rules of Bankruptcy Procedure,

IT IS THEREFORE ORDERED that General Order 05–2 of this Court, under which the Interim Bankruptcy Rules were adopted as a subset of the Local Rules of Bankruptcy Procedure, is hereby **RESCINDED** in its entirety.

[Dated:　December 1, 2008.]

GENERAL ORDER 12–1. ADOPTION OF AMENDMENTS
TO INTERIM BANKRUPTCY RULE 1007–I

By General Order dated December 8, 2008, this Court adopted Interim Bankruptcy Rule 1007–I, and by General Order dated December 1, 2010, this Court adopted amendments to Interim Bankruptcy Rule 1007–I to conform to an amendment to Bankruptcy Rule 1007. In recognition that Federal Rule of Bankruptcy Procedure 1007 will be amended again effective December 1, 2012, and in order to conform Interim Bankruptcy Rule 1007–I to such amendment, the Committee on Rules of Practice and Procedure of the Judicial Conference of the United States has prepared and recommended adoption of amendments to Interim Rule 1007–I (a copy of which is attached to this Order) pursuant to the authority granted to local bankruptcy courts to adopt local rules under Rule 9029 of the Federal Rules of Bankruptcy Procedure.

IT IS THEREFORE ORDERED that General Orders 08–4 and 10–2 are supplemented and amended as set forth in this Order;

IT IS FURTHER ORDERED that Interim Bankruptcy Rule 1007–I, including the amendments to Interim Bankruptcy Rule 1007–I, as approved by the Committee on Rules of Practice and Procedure of the Judicial Conference of the United States, is hereby **ADOPTED** in its entirety without change, as a subset of the Local Rules of Bankruptcy Procedure, to become effective on December 1, 2012.

Interim Rule 1007–I.[1] Lists, Schedules, Statements, and Other Documents; Time Limits; Expiration of Temporary Means Testing Exclusion[2]

* * * * *

(b) Schedules, Statements, and Other Documents Required.

* * * * *

(4) *Unless either*: (A) § 707(b)(2)(D)(I) applies, or (B) § 707(b)(2)(D)(ii) applies and the exclusion from means testing granted therein extends beyond the period specified by Rule 1017(e), an individual debtor in a chapter 7 case shall file a statement of current monthly income prepared as prescribed by the appropriate Official Form, and, if the current monthly income exceeds the median family income for the applicable state and household size, the information, including calculations, required by § 707(b), prepared as prescribed by the appropriate Official Form.

* * * * *

(c) Time Limits. In a voluntary case, the schedules, statements, and other documents required by subdivision (b)(1), (4), (5), and (6) shall be filed with the petition or within 14 days thereafter, except as otherwise provided in subdivisions (d), (e), (f), (h), and (n) of this rule. In an involuntary case, the list in subdivision (a)(2), and the schedules, statements, and other documents required by subdivision (b)(1) shall be filed by the debtor within 14 days of the entry of the order for relief. In a voluntary case, the documents required by paragraphs (A), (C), and (D) of subdivision (b)(3) shall be filed with the petition. Unless the court orders otherwise, a debtor who has filed a statement under subdivision (b)(3)(B), shall file the documents required by subdivision (b)(3)(A) within 14 days of the order for relief. In a chapter 7 case, the debtor shall file the statement required by subdivision (b)(7) within 60 days after the first date set for the meeting of creditors under § 341 of the Code, and in a chapter 11 or 13 case no later than the date when the last payment was made by the debtor as required by the plan or the filing of a motion for a discharge under § 1141(d)(5)(B) or § 1328(b) of the Code. The court may, at any time and in its discretion, enlarge the time to file the statement required by subdivision (b)(7). The debtor shall file the statement required by subdivision (b)(8) no earlier than the date of the last payment made under the plan or the date of the filing of a motion for a discharge under §§ 1141(d)(5)(B), 1228(b), or 1328(b) of the Code. Lists, schedules, statements, and other documents filed prior to the conversion of a case to another chapter shall be deemed filed in the converted case unless the court directs otherwise. Except as provided in § 1116(3), any extension of time to file schedules, statements, and other documents required under this rule may be granted only on motion for cause shown and on notice to the United States trustee, any committee elected under § 705 or appointed under § 1102 of the Code, trustee, examiner, or other party as the court may direct. Notice of an extension shall be given to the United States trustee and to any committee, trustee, or other party as the court may direct.

* * * * *

(n) Time Limits for, and Notice to, Debtors Temporarily Excluded from Means Testing.

(1) An individual debtor who is temporarily excluded from means testing pursuant to § 707(b)(2)(D)(ii) of the Code shall file any statement and calculations required by subdivision (b)(4) no later than 14 days after the expiration of the temporary exclusion if the expiration occurs within the time specified by Rule 1017(e) for filing a motion pursuant to § 707(b)(2).

(2) If the temporary exclusion from means testing under § 707(b)(2)(D)(ii) terminates due to the circumstances specified in subdivision (n)(1), and if the debtor has not previously filed a statement and calculations required by subdivision (b)(4), the clerk shall promptly notify the debtor that the required statement and calculations must be filed within the time specified in subdivision (n)(1).

[Dated: December 1, 2012.]

[1] Interim Rule 1007–I has been adopted by the bankruptcy courts to implement the National Guard and Reservists Debt Relief Act of 2008, Public Law No: 110–438, as amended by Public Law No. 112–64. The amended Act, which provides a temporary exclusion from the application of the means test for certain members of the National Guard and reserve components of the Armed Forces, applies to bankruptcy cases commenced in the seven-year period beginning December 19, 2008.

[2] Incorporates (1) time amendments to Rule 1007 which took effect on December 1, 2009, and (2) an amendment, effective December 1, 2010, which extended the time to file the statement of completion of a course in personal financial management in a chapter 7 case filed Try an individual debtor, and (3) a conforming amendment, effective December 1, 2012, which removed an inconsistency created by the 2010 amendment.

UNITED STATES DISTRICT COURT FOR THE WESTERN DISTRICT OF TEXAS

Including Amendments Received Through
February 1, 2019

Divisions of the Western District.

Order Adopting Amended Plan for the Payment of Attorney Fees and Reimbursement of Attorney Expenses in Civil Cases.

Re: Pro Hac Vice Fees.

DIVISIONS OF THE WESTERN DISTRICT

The **UNITED STATES DISTRICT COURT FOR THE WESTERN DISTRICT OF TEXAS** is comprised of seven divisions.

(1) The **AUSTIN DIVISION** comprises the following counties: Bastrop, Blanco, Burleson, Burnet, Caldwell, Gillespie, Hays, Kimble, Lampasas, Lee, Llano, Mason, McCulloch, San Saba, Travis, Washington and Williamson.

Court for the Austin Division shall be held at Austin. The addresses and telephone numbers for the residing U.S. District Judges and the U.S. District Clerk at Austin are as follows:

Hon. Lee Yeakel
U.S. District Judge
501 West 5th Street, Suite 7300
Austin, Texas 78701
(512) 916–5756

Hon. Robert L. Pitman
U.S. District Judge
501 West 5th Street, Suite 5300
Austin, Texas 78701
(512) 391–8824

Hon. Sam Sparks
Senior Judge
501 West 5th Street, Suite 4120
Austin, Texas 78701
(512) 916–5230

Hon. James R. Nowlin
Senior Judge
501 West 5th Street, Suite 6400
Austin, Texas 78701
(512) 916–5675

U.S. District Clerk
U.S. Courthouse
501 West 5th Street, Suite 1100
Austin, Texas 78701
(512) 916–5896

(2) The **DEL RIO DIVISION** comprises the following counties: Edwards, Kinney, Maverick, Terrell, Uvalde, Val Verde and Zavala.

Court for the Del Rio Division shall be held at Del Rio. The addresses and telephone numbers for the residing U.S. District Judge and the U.S. District Clerk at Del Rio are as follows:

Hon. Alia Moses
U.S. District Judge
111 East Broadway, Room A–202
Del Rio, Texas 78840
(830) 703–2038

U.S. District Clerk
U.S. Courthouse
111 East Broadway, Room 100
Del Rio, Texas 78840
(830) 703–2054

(3) The **EL PASO DIVISION** comprises the following counties: El Paso and Hudspeth.

Court for the El Paso Division shall be held at El Paso. The addresses and telephone numbers for the residing U.S. District Judges and the U.S. District Clerk at El Paso are as follows:

Hon. Philip R. Martinez
U.S. District Judge
Albert Armendariz, Sr. U.S. Courthouse
525 Magoffin Avenue, Suite 661
El Paso, Texas 79901
(915) 534–6736

Hon. Kathleen Cardone
U.S. District Judge
Albert Armendariz, Sr. U.S. Courthouse
525 Magoffin Avenue, Suite 561
El Paso, Texas 79901
(915) 534–6740

Hon. Frank Montalvo

Hon. David C. Guaderrama

U.S. District Judge
Albert Armendariz, Sr. U.S. Courthouse
525 Magoffin Avenue, Suite 461
El Paso, Texas 79901
(915) 534–6600

Hon. David Briones
Senior Judge
Albert Armendariz, Sr. U.S. Courthouse
525 Magoffin Avenue, Suite 761
El Paso, Texas 79901
(915) 534–6744

U.S. District Judge
Albert Armendariz, Sr. U.S. Courthouse
525 Magoffin Avenue, Suite 361
El Paso, Texas 79901
(915) 534–6005

U.S. District Clerk
Albert Armendariz, Sr. U.S. Courthouse
525 Magoffin Avenue, Suite 105
El Paso, Texas 79901
(915) 534–6725

(4) The **PECOS DIVISION** comprises the following counties: Brewster, Culberson, Jeff Davis, Loving, Pecos, Presidio, Reeves, Ward and Winkler.

Court for the Pecos Division shall be held at Pecos. The address and telephone number for the U.S. District Clerk at Pecos is:

U.S. District Clerk
Lucius D. Bunton, III U.S. Courthouse
410 South Cedar Street
Pecos, Texas 79772
(432) 445–4228

(5) The **SAN ANTONIO DIVISION** comprises the following counties: Atascosa, Bandera, Bexar, Comal, Dimmit, Frio, Gonzales, Guadalupe, Karnes, Kendall, Kerr, Medina, Real and Wilson.

Court for the San Antonio Division shall be held at San Antonio. The addresses and telephone numbers for the residing U.S. District Judges and the U.S. District Clerk at San Antonio are as follows:

Hon. Orlando L. Garcia
Chief U.S. District Judge
John H. Wood, Jr., U.S. Courthouse

655 E. Cesar E. Chavez Blvd.
San Antonio, Texas 78206

(210) 472–6565
Hon. Xavier Rodriguez
U.S. District Judge
John H. Wood, Jr., U.S. Courthouse

655 E. Cesar E. Chavez Blvd.
San Antonio, Texas 78206
(210) 472–6575

Hon. Fred Biery
U.S. District Judge
John H. Wood, Jr., U.S. Court-
house
655 E. Cesar E. Chavez Blvd.
San Antonio, Texas 78206

(210) 472–6505
Hon. David A. Ezra
Senior Judge
John H. Wood, Jr., U.S. Court-
house
655 E. Cesar E. Chavez Blvd.
San Antonio, Texas 78206
((210) 472–5870

U.S. District Clerk
John H. Wood, Jr., U.S. Courthouse
655 E. Cesar E. Chavez Blvd.,
Room G–65
San Antonio, Texas 78206
(210) 472–6550

(6) The **WACO DIVISION** comprises the following counties: Bell, Bosque, Coryell, Falls, Freestone, Hamilton, Hill, Leon, Limestone, McLennan, Milam, Robertson and Somervell.

Court for the Waco Division shall be held at Waco. The addresses and telephone number for the residing U.S. District Judge and the U.S. District Clerk at Waco are as follows:

Hon. Alan D Albright
U.S. District Judge
800 Franklin Avenue, Room 301
Austin, Texas 78701
(512) 391–8824

U.S. District Clerk
U.S. Courthouse, Room 380
800 Franklin Avenue
Waco, Texas 76701
(254) 750–1501

(7) The **MIDLAND/ODESSA DIVISION** comprises the following counties: Andrews, Crane, Ector, Martin, Midland and Upton.

Court for the Midland/Odessa Division shall be held at Midland. Court may be held, in the discretion of the Court, in Odessa, when courtroom facilities are made available at no expense to the government. The addresses and telephone numbers for the residing Sr. U.S. District Judge and the U.S. District Clerk at Midland are as follows:

Hon. David Counts
U.S. District Judge
U.S. Courthouse
200 E. Wall, Room 301
Midland, Texas 79701
(432) 686–4020

Hon. Robert A. Junell
Senior Judge
200 E. Wall, Room 317
Midland, Texas 79701
(432) 686–4020

U.S. District Clerk
U.S. Courthouse
200 E. Wall, Room 222
Midland, Texas 79701
(432) 686–4001

[Effective January 1, 1994. Amended February 17, 1995; January 28, 1997; June 1, 1998; January 2, 2001; December 1, 2002; December 1, 2009; December 2, 2011; April 16, 2012; January 17, 2019.]

SECTION I. CIVIL RULES

RULE CV–1. SCOPE OF RULES

(a) The rules of procedure in any proceeding in this court shall be prescribed by the laws of the United States, the rules of the Supreme Court of the United States, any applicable rules of the United States Court of Appeals for the Fifth Circuit, and these rules.

(b) Where in any proceeding or in any instance there is no applicable rule of procedure, a judge may prescribe same.

(c) These rules may be cited as Local Court Rules.

(d) Unless otherwise provided, any revision to these rules applies to all cases pending on or filed after the date of the revision.

(e) Any judge of this court may waive any requirement of these rules regarding the administration of that judge's docket.

[Effective January 1, 1994. Amended effective January 2, 2001; December 2, 2011; April 26, 2012.]

RULE CV–3. COMMENCEMENT OF ACTION

(a) **Civil Cover Sheet.** The clerk is authorized and instructed to require a complete and executed AO Form JS 44, Civil Cover Sheet, which shall accompany each civil case to be filed. If the filing of a civil case is not accompanied by a complete and executed Civil Cover Sheet, the clerk must accept the case for filing, but must promptly inform the filing party that the filing party must complete and execute the Civil Cover Sheet. If the filing party fails to do so not later than 7 days after being informed, the clerk must so advise the court. An unrepresented person who files a civil case or a person who, when filing a civil case, is in the custody of a civil, state or federal institution, need not complete and execute the Civil Cover Sheet. All parties are required to advise the court of any related cases, through means of the Civil Cover Sheet or otherwise.

(b) **Habeas Corpus and Motions Pursuant to 28 U.S.C. § 2255.**

(1) Petitions for writ of habeas corpus and motions filed pursuant to 28 U.S.C. § 2255 by persons in custody shall be in writing, signed, and verified.

(2) Such petitions and motions shall be made on forms supplied by the court or set forth in detail all the information requested in the court's forms.

(3) The petition or motion must be filed with the clerk's office in the proper division.

(4) If any issue is raised in a habeas corpus petition that was not raised or has not been fully exhausted in state court, the petition shall state the reasons why such action has not been taken.

(5) If the same petitioner or movant has previously filed in this court a petition for habeas corpus relief or a motion pursuant to 28 U.S.C. § 2255 challenging the same state court judgment or federal sentence, the case shall be assigned to the judge who considered the prior matter.

(6) A second or successive petition for habeas corpus relief or motion for relief pursuant to 28 U.S.C. § 2255 will be dismissed without prejudice unless accompanied by a certificate issued by a panel of the Fifth Circuit.

(7) This court's opinion in any such action shall separately state each issue raised by the habeas corpus petition or motion pursuant to 28 U.S.C. § 2255 and rule expressly on each issue, stating the reasons for each ruling made.

(8) If a certificate of appealability is issued by this court in a death penalty case with a pending execution date, the court shall, upon request, grant a stay of execution to continue until such time as the court of appeals expressly acts with reference to the case.

(c) Motions to Stay Execution of State Court Judgments.

(1) A petitioner or plaintiff who seeks a stay of enforcement or execution of a state court judgment or order shall attach to the motion requesting the stay a copy of each state court judgment that the petitioner or plaintiff seeks to have stayed.

(2) The motion for stay of execution or stay of enforcement must state whether the same petitioner or plaintiff has previously sought relief arising out of the same matter from this court or from any other federal court. The reasons for denying relief given by any court that has considered the matter, including any written opinion issued by said court, must also be attached to the motion for stay of execution or enforcement. If reasons for the ruling were not given in a written opinion, a copy of the relevant portions of the transcripts must be supplied to this court.

(3) A motion for stay of execution filed on behalf of a petitioner challenging a sentence of death must be filed at least 7 days before the petitioner's scheduled execution date or recite good cause for any late filing.

(4) If the same petitioner or plaintiff has previously filed in this court a motion for stay of execution or enforcement of the same state court judgment challenged in the petitioner's or plaintiff's motion for stay, the case shall be assigned to the judge who considered the prior matter.

[Effective January 1, 1994. Amended effective December 1, 2000; December 1, 2009; December 2, 2011; April 26, 2012.]

RULE CV–5. SERVICE AND FILING OF DOCUMENTS AND OTHER PAPERS

(a) Filing Requirements.

(1) *Electronic.* The court accepts documents by electronic means that comply with the *Administrative Policies and Procedures for Electronic Filing in Civil and Criminal Cases* ("Electronic Filing Procedures").

(2) *Traditional.* All documents submitted for traditional filing shall be furnished to the clerk in duplicate, the "original" of which shall be marked and filed, and the remaining copy shall be sent to the judge on whose docket the case is placed.

(b) Proof of Service.

(1) *Electronic.* Pursuant to Section 15(a) of the Electronic Filing Procedures, the Notice of Electronic Filing ("NEF") generated by the court's electronic filing system constitutes service of the document on those registered as Filing Users. Proof of service shall be provided as set out in Section 15(c) of the Electronic Filing Procedures.

(2) *Traditional.* All documents presented for traditional filing shall contain an acknowledgment of service by the person served, or proof of service in the form of a statement of the date and the manner of service and of the names of the persons served, certified by the person who made service.

Proof of service may appear on, or be affixed to the documents filed. The clerk may permit documents to be filed without acknowledgment of proof of service but shall require such to be filed promptly thereafter.

(c) Orders. All orders and decrees submitted for settlement or signature must be presented through the clerk's office, and not sent directly to the judge. In case of contest as to form or substance, the clerk will give notice of any hearing that may be required by the judge.

(d) Nonconforming Documents. If a document that fails to conform with these rules is submitted, the clerk shall file the document, and shall promptly inform the filing party that the document is not in compliance with these rules.

[Effective January 1, 1994. Amended effective December 1, 2000; February 6, 2006; December 1, 2009; December 2, 2011; April 26, 2012.]

RULE CV–5.2 DOCUMENTS FILED UNDER SEAL

(a) In appropriate circumstances a party may need to submit a sealed document for consideration by the court. For purposes of this rule, the term "sealed document" may include any pleading, motion, paper, physical item, or other submission that the Federal Rules of Civil Procedure or these rules permit or require to be filed. If the sealed document is associated with a pleading, motion or other submission requesting or opposing relief from the court, as in the case of an exhibit to such submission, the sealed document must not be filed with the submission. Instead, the sealed document must be separately filed as an exhibit to a motion requesting permission to keep the document under seal (a "sealing motion"). All documents intended to be kept under seal must be filed as an exhibit to a sealing motion.

(b) Motions to keep pleadings, motions, or other submissions requesting or opposing relief from the court under seal are disfavored. The court expects parties to draft such submissions in a manner that does not disclose confidential information.

(c) The sealing motion must identify the submission the sealed document is associated with, if applicable. The sealing motion and the accompanying sealed document must be filed under seal, state the factual basis for the requested sealing order, and otherwise comply with the requirements of Rules CV–7 and CV–10 and the procedures governing electronic or paper filings, as applicable to the submission. The court expects parties to draft sealing motions in a manner that does not disclose confidential information because the sealing motion, without the sealed document, may subsequently be unsealed by court order.

(d) If the court grants a sealing motion, the clerk will keep the sealed document under seal unless and until otherwise ordered by the court, and, if appropriate, the clerk shall link the sealed document to its associated pleading, motion, or other submission. The court may order that the sealing motion, without the sealed document, be unsealed. If the court denies a sealing motion, the clerk, on order of the court, shall delete the sealed document.

(e) Counsel for the party moving to keep any document under seal is responsible for serving a copy of the sealed document on all counsel of record, but may not use the court's electronic notice facilities to serve the sealed document.

[Effective December 2, 2011. Amended effective April 26, 2012.]

RULE CV–6. COMPUTING TIME

In computing any time period in any civil case, the provisions of Federal Rule of Civil Procedure 6, as amended, shall be applied.

[Effective December 1, 2009. Amended effective December 2, 2011; April 26, 2012.]

RULE CV–7. PLEADINGS ALLOWED; FORM OF MOTIONS

(a) Generally. Unless made during a hearing or trial, a pleading, motion, or other submission must meet the requirements of Rule CV–10.

(b) Leave to File. When a motion for leave to file a pleading, motion, or other submission is required, an executed copy of the proposed pleading, motion, or other submission shall be filed as an exhibit to the motion for leave. Unless otherwise ordered, if the motion for leave is granted, the clerk shall promptly file the pleading, motion, or other submission. After leave is granted, any applicable time limits triggered by the pleading, motion, or other submission shall run from the filing of the pleading, motion, or other submission by the clerk or otherwise.

(c) Dispositive Motion Defined. For purposes of this rule, a "dispositive motion" is a motion to dismiss, a motion for judgment on the pleadings, a motion for summary judgment or partial summary judgment, a motion for new trial, or a motion for judgment as a matter of law.

(d) Motions.

(1) *Generally.* Legal authorities supporting any motion must be cited in the motion. An appendix may be filed with the motion specifying any factual basis relied upon. If filed, the appendix must include all affidavits, deposition transcripts, or other documents supporting the relied upon facts. All motions must state the grounds therefor and cite any applicable rule, statute, or other authority, if any, justifying the relief sought.

(2) *Motions Not Requiring Citation of Legal Authorities.* Legal authorities are not required to be cited in any of the following motions:

(a) for extension of time for the performance of an act required or allowed to be done, provided request therefor is made before the expiration of the period originally prescribed, or as extended by previous orders;

(b) to continue a pretrial conference hearing or motion or the trial of an action;

(c) for a more definite statement;

(d) to join additional parties;

(e) to amend pleadings;

(f) to file supplemental pleadings;

(g) to appoint next friend or guardian ad litem;

(h) to intervene;

(i) for substitution of parties;

(j) relating to discovery including but not limited to motions for the production and inspection of documents, specific objections to interrogatories, motions to compel answers or further answers to interrogatories, and motions for physical or mental examination;

(k) to stay proceedings to enforce judgment;

(*l*) joint motions to dismiss;

(m) to withdraw as counsel;

(n) for mediation or other form of alternative dispute resolution; and

(o) for approval of an agreed protective order.

(3) *Page Limits.* Unless otherwise authorized by the court, a dispositive motion is limited to 20 pages and a nondispositive motion is limited to 10 pages. These page limits are exclusive of the caption, signature block, any certificate, and accompanying documents.

(e) Responses.

(1) *Generally.* Any party opposing a motion shall file a response and supporting documents as are then available. The response must contain a concise statement of the reasons for opposition to the motion and citations of the legal authorities on which the party relies.

(2) *Time Limits.* A response to a dispositive motion shall be filed not later than 14 days after the filing of the motion. A response to a nondispositive motion shall be filed not later than 7 days after the filing of the motion. If there is no response filed within the time period prescribed by this rule, the court may grant the motion as unopposed.

(3) *Page Limits.* Unless otherwise authorized by the court, a response to a dispositive motion is limited to 20 pages and a response to a nondispositive motion is limited to 10 pages. These page limits are exclusive of the caption, signature block, any certificate, and accompanying documents.

(f) Replies.

(1) *Generally.* A party may file a reply in support of a motion. Absent leave of court, no further submissions on the motion are allowed.

(2) *Time Limit.* A reply in support of a motion shall be filed not later than 7 days after the filing of the response to the motion. The court need not wait for a reply before ruling on a motion.

(3) *Page Limits.* Unless otherwise authorized by the court, a reply in support of a dispositive motion is limited to 10 pages and a reply in support of a nondispositive motion is limited to 5 pages. These page limits are exclusive of the caption, signature block, any certificate, and accompanying documents.

(g) Proposed Orders. A proposed order shall be filed with all nondispositive motions. When a motion is one that requires a proposed order, any response to the motion shall also be accompanied by a proposed order.

(h) Oral Hearings. A movant or respondent may request an oral hearing. The allowance of an oral hearing is within the sole discretion of the court.

(i) Conference Required. The court may refuse to hear or may deny a nondispositive motion unless the movant advises the court within the body of the motion that counsel for the parties have first conferred in a good-faith attempt to resolve the matter by agreement and, further, certifies the specific reason that no agreement could be made. Movants are encouraged to indicate in the title of the motion whether the motion is opposed. A motion is unopposed only if there has been an actual conference with opposing counsel and there is no opposition to any of the relief requested in the motion.

(j) Claims for Attorney's Fees.

(1) Unless the substantive law requires a claim for attorney's fees and related nontaxable expenses to be proved at trial as an element of damages to be determined by a jury, a claim for fees shall be made by motion not later than 14 days after entry of judgment pursuant to Federal Rule of Civil Procedure 54(d)(2) and pursuant to the following provisions. Counsel for the parties shall meet and confer for the purpose of resolving all disputed issues relating to attorney's fees prior to making application. The application shall certify that such a conference has occurred. If no agreement is reached, the applicant shall certify the specific reason why the matter could not be resolved by agreement. The motion shall include a supporting document organized chronologically by activity or project, listing attorney name, date, and hours expended on the particular activity or project, as well as an affidavit certifying (1) that the hours expended were actually expended on the topics stated, and (2) that the hours expended and rate claimed were reasonable. Such application shall also be accompanied by a brief memo setting forth the method by which the amount of fees was computed, with sufficient citation of authority to permit the reviewing court the opportunity to determine whether such computation is correct. The request shall include reference to the statutory authorization or other authority for the request.

(2) An objection to a motion for attorney's fees shall be filed on or before 14 days after the date of filing of the motion. If there is no timely objection, the court may grant the motion as unopposed.

(3) A motion for award of attorney's fees filed beyond the 14 day period may be deemed untimely and a waiver of entitlement to fees.

[Effective January 1, 1994. Amended effective May 16, 1994; December 1, 2000; January 2, 2001; December 1, 2009; December 2, 2011; April 26, 2012; October 21, 2013.]

RULE CV–10. FORM OF PLEADINGS

(a) A pleading, motion, or other submission shall be typed or printed in 12 point or larger font (including footnotes), double-spaced, on paper sized 8½″ × 11″ with one-inch margins on all sides and shall be endorsed with the style of the case and the descriptive name of the document. Headings, footnotes, and quotations more than two lines long may be single-spaced.

(b) A pleading, motion, or other submission filed by a represented party shall contain the mailing address, e-mail address, signature, state bar card number, and telephone and fax numbers, including area code, of the attorney.

(c) A pleading, motion, or other submission filed by an unrepresented party shall contain the party's mailing address, e-mail address, signature, and telephone and fax numbers, including area code.

(d) An unrepresented party and any attorney representing a party must timely inform the court of any change in the party's or attorney's mailing address, e-mail address, signature, or telephone or fax number. The court may sanction a party for the party's or the attorney's failure to do so, including dismissal of the party's claims or defenses.

[Effective January 1, 1994. Amended effective December 2, 2011; April 26, 2012; October 21, 2013.]

RULE CV–16. PRETRIAL CONFERENCES; SCHEDULING; MANAGEMENT

(a) A scheduling order must be entered in every case except those exempted in Section (b) of this rule. The form of the scheduling order should conform to the form prescribed by the judge and posted on the court's website. If the judge has not posted a form scheduling order on the website, the scheduling order may conform to the form set out in Appendix B of these rules.

(b) The same types of cases that are exempt from mandatory disclosure requirements under Federal Rule of Civil Procedure 26 are exempt from the scheduling order requirement of Rule 16. In addition, the following categories of cases are also exempt from the scheduling order requirement: (1) bankruptcy appeals; (2) civil forfeiture cases; (3) land condemnation cases; (4) naturalization proceedings filed as civil cases; (5) interpleader cases; and (6) any other case where the judge finds that the ends of justice would not be served by using the scheduling order procedure of Rule 16.

(c) Not later than 60 days after any appearance of any defendant, the parties shall submit a proposed scheduling order to the court in the form described in Section (a). The parties first shall confer as required by Rule 26(f). The content of the proposed scheduling order shall include proposals for all deadlines set out in the described form. The parties shall endeavor to agree concerning the contents of the proposed order, but in the event they are unable to do so, each party's position and the reasons for the disagreement shall be included in the proposed schedule submitted to the court. In the event the plaintiff has not yet obtained service on all defendants, the plaintiff shall include an explanation of why all parties have not been served. The scheduling proposals of the parties shall be considered by the court, but the setting of all dates is within the discretion of the court.

(d) Unopposed discovery may continue after the deadline for discovery contained in the scheduling order, provided that discovery does not delay other pretrial preparations or the trial setting. Absent exceptional circumstances, no motions relating to discovery, including motions under Rules 26(c), 29, and 37, shall be filed after the expiration of the discovery deadline, unless they are filed within 7 days after the discovery deadline and pertain to conduct occurring during the final 7 days of discovery. Written discovery is not timely unless the response to that discovery would be due before the discovery deadline. The responding party has no obligation to respond and object to written discovery if the response and objection would not be due until after the discovery deadline. Depositions must be completed before the discovery deadline. Notices served before the discovery deadline which purport to schedule depositions after the discovery deadline will not be enforced.

(e) Unless otherwise ordered by the court, each party shall serve and file the following information at least 14 days before the scheduled date for trial, jury selection, docket call, or the final pretrial conference, whichever is first:

(1) A list of questions the party desires the court to ask prospective jurors.

(2) In cases to be tried to a jury, a statement of the party's claims or defenses to be used by the court in conducting voir dire. The statement shall be no longer than ½ page with type double-spaced.

(3) A list of stipulated facts.

(4) An appropriate identification of each exhibit as specified in this rule (except those to be used for impeachment only), separately identifying those that the party expects to offer and those that the party may offer if the need arises.

(5) The name and, if not previously provided, the address and telephone number of each witness (except those to be used for impeachment only), separately identifying those whom the party expects to present and those whom the party may call if the need arises.

(6) The name of those witnesses whose testimony is expected to be presented by means of a deposition and designation by reference to page and line of the testimony to be offered (except those to be used for impeachment only) and, if not taken stenographically, a transcript of the pertinent portions of the deposition testimony.

(7) Proposed jury instructions and verdict forms.

(8) In nonjury trials, Proposed Findings of Fact and Conclusions of Law.

(9) Any motions in limine.

(10) An estimate of the probable length of trial.

(f) At least 7 days prior to the scheduled date for trial, jury selection, docket call, or the final pretrial conference, whichever is first, each party shall serve and file the following:

(1) A list disclosing any objections to the use under Rule 32(a) of deposition testimony designated by the other party.

(2) A list disclosing any objection, together with the grounds therefore, that may be made to the admissibility of any exhibits. Objections not so disclosed, other than objections under Federal Rules of Evidence 402 and 403 shall be deemed waived unless excused by the court for good cause shown.

(g) All trial exhibits must be marked with an identifying sequence, followed by a dash, followed by a number; for example, Exhibit P–1 and Exhibit D–1. The identifying sequence (e.g., "P" and "D") will identify the party who will offer the exhibit. Parties will assign numbers to their exhibits consecutively, beginning with the number 1. The letter "G" will be assigned to the government for identification purposes. In cases involving more complex pleading relationships (e.g., consolidated cases, intervenors, and third party actions), it is the responsibility of counsel for the plaintiff, in consultation with the judge's courtroom deputy clerk, to coordinate the assignment of the unique identification sequences.

[Effective January 1, 1994. Amended effective December 1, 2000; January 2, 2001; December 1, 2009; December 2, 2011; April 26, 2012.]

RULE CV–23.   CLASS ACTIONS

A motion to certify a class must include the information enumerated in Appendix A to these rules.

[Effective January 1, 1994. Amended effective December 2, 2011; April 26, 2012.]

RULE CV–26.   GENERAL PROVISIONS GOVERNING DISCOVERY

(a) Relief. If relief is sought under Federal Rules of Civil Procedure 26(c) or 37(a)(3), concerning any interrogatories, requests for production or inspection, requests for admissions, answers to interrogatories or responses to requests for admissions, copies of the portions of the interrogatories, requests, answers or responses in dispute shall be attached to the motion.

(b) Definitions and Rules of Construction. The full text of the definitions and rules of construction set forth in this paragraph is deemed incorporated by reference into all discovery requests, but shall not preclude (i) the definition of other terms specific to the particular litigation, (ii) the use of abbreviations or (iii) a more narrow definition of a term defined in this paragraph. This rule is not intended to broaden or narrow the scope of discovery permitted by the Federal Rules of Civil Procedure. The following definitions apply to all discovery requests:

(1) *Communication.* The term "communication" means the transmittal of information (in the form of facts, ideas, inquiries or otherwise).

(2) *Document.* The term "document" is defined to be synonymous in meaning and equal in scope to the usage of this term in Federal Rule of Civil Procedure 34(a). A draft of a nonidentical copy is a separate document within the meaning of this term.

(3) *Identify (With Respect to Persons).* When referring to a person, to "identify" means to give, to the extent known, the person's full name, present or last known address, e-mail address, and telephone number, and when referring to a natural person, additionally, the present or last known place of employment. Once a person has been identified in accordance with this subparagraph, only the name of that person need be listed in response to subsequent discovery requesting the identification of that person.

(4) *Identify (With Respect to Documents).* When referring to documents, "to identify" means to give, to the extent known, the (i) type of document; (ii) general subject matter; (iii) date

of the document; and (iv) author(s), addressee(s), and recipient(s).

(5) *Parties.* The terms "plaintiff" and "defendant" as well as a party's full or abbreviated name or pronoun referring to a party mean the party and, where applicable, its officers, directors, employees, partners, corporate parent, subsidiaries or affiliates. This definition is not intended to impose a discovery obligation on any person who is not a party to the litigation.

(6) *Person.* The term "person" is defined as any natural person or business, legal or governmental entity or association.

(7) *Concerning.* The term "concerning" means relating to, referring to, describing, evidencing or constituting.

(c) Protective Orders. Upon motion by any party demonstrating good cause, the court may enter a protective order in the form set out in Appendix H or any other appropriate form. In cases where the parties agree to a protective order, the form set out in Appendix H is approved.

(d) Authentication of Documents. A party's production of a document in response to written discovery authenticates the document for use against that party in any pretrial proceeding or at trial unless not later than 14 days or a period ordered by the court or specified by Rule CV-16(e), after the producing party has actual notice that the document will be used—the party objects to the authenticity of the document, or any part of it, stating the specific basis for objection. An objection must be either on the record or in writing and must have a good faith factual and legal basis. An objection made to the authenticity of only part of a document does not affect the authenticity of the remainder. If objection is made, the party attempting to use the document should be given a reasonable opportunity to establish its authenticity.

[Effective January 1, 1994. Amended effective December 1, 2000; December 1, 2009; December 2, 2011; April 26, 2012.]

RULE CV-30. DEPOSITIONS UPON ORAL EXAMINATION

(a) Notice. The notice for a deposition shall be in the form prescribed in Federal Rule of Civil Procedure 30, and in addition shall state the identity of persons who will attend other than the witness, parties, spouses of parties, counsel, employees of counsel, and the officer taking the deposition. If any party intends to have any other persons attend, that party must give reasonable notice to all parties of the identity of such other persons.

(b) Procedures, Examinations and Objections. The parties are permitted to stipulate on the record of the deposition any agreement regarding the rules for the deposition. Objections during depositions shall be stated concisely and in a nonargumentative and nonsuggestive manner. An attorney shall not, in the presence of the deponent, make objections or statements that might suggest an answer to the deponent. An attorney for a deponent shall not initiate a private conference with the deponent regarding a pending question, except for the purpose of determining whether a claim of privilege should be asserted. An attorney who instructs a deponent not to answer a question shall state, on the record, the legal basis for

the instruction consistent with Federal Rule of Civil Procedure 30(d)(1). If a claim of privilege has been asserted as a basis for an instruction not to answer, the attorney seeking discovery shall have reasonable latitude during the deposition to question the deponent and establish relevant information concerning the appropriateness of the assertion of the privilege, including (i) the applicability of the privilege being asserted, (ii) the circumstances that may result in the privilege having been waived, and (iii) circumstances that may overcome a claim of qualified privilege. A violation of the provisions of this Rule may be deemed to be a violation of a court order and may subject the violator to sanctions under Federal Rule of Civil Procedure 37(b)(2).

(c) Videotaped and Audiotaped Depositions. If the deposition is to be recorded by videotape or audiotape, the party noticing the deposition or subpoenaing the witness shall be responsible for ensuring that the equipment used is adequate to produce a clear record. If the deposition is to be recorded by videotape, the procedures set out in Appendix I shall govern the deposition proceedings, except upon stipulation of the parties or order of the court upon motion and showing of good cause.

[Effective January 1, 1994. Amended effective December 1, 2000; January 2, 2001; December 2, 2011; April 26, 2012.]

RULE CV-33. INTERROGATORIES TO PARTIES

(a) All answers to interrogatories must be signed under oath by the party to whom they are directed. If circumstances prevent a party from signing the answers, the party's attorney may serve the answers without the party's signature with a statement that properly executed answers will be served on the requesting party not later than 21 days after serving the unexecuted answers. This time may be extended by order of the court.

(b) A party that serves written interrogatories under Federal Rule of Civil Procedure 33 may use any of the following approved interrogatories. The court will not consider objections to these interrogatories, except upon a showing of exceptional circumstances. Each approved interrogatory counts as one question. Other interrogatories are counted in accordance with Federal Rule of Civil Procedure 33(a).

(1) Identify all persons who you believe have knowledge of relevant facts and identify the issues upon which you believe they have knowledge.

(2) Identify all persons or legal entities who have a subrogation interest in the cause of action set forth in your complaint [or counterclaim], and state the basis and extent of said interest.

(3) If [name of party to whom the interrogatory is directed] is a partner, a partnership, or a subsidiary or affiliate of a publicly owned corporation that has a financial interest in the outcome of this lawsuit, list the identity of the parent corporation, affiliate, partner, or partnership and the relationship between it and [the named party]. If there is a publicly owned corporation or a holding company not a party to the case that has a financial interest in the outcome, list the identity of such corporation and the nature of the financial interest.

(4) If the defendant is improperly identified, give its proper identification and state whether you will accept service of an amended summons and complaint reflecting the information furnished by you in answer hereto.

(5) If you contend that some other person or legal entity is, in whole or in part, liable to [the plaintiff or defendant] in this matter, identify that person or legal entity and describe in detail the basis of said liability.

[Effective January 1, 1994. Amended effective December 1, 2000; December 1, 2009; December 2, 2011; April 26, 2012.]

RULE CV-36. REQUESTS FOR ADMISSIONS

Requests for admissions made pursuant to Federal Rule of Civil Procedure 36 are limited to 30 requests. The court may permit further requests upon a showing of good cause.

[Effective January 1, 1994. Amended effective December 1, 2000; December 2, 2011; April 26, 2012.]

RULE CV-54. COSTS

(a) Unless otherwise determined by the court, costs will be assessed in the final judgment in a case. A party awarded costs shall prepare and file a proposed bill of costs no later than 14 days after the entry of judgment. The proposed bill of costs shall be served on all parties.

(b) Any party opposing a proposed bill of costs must file an objection no later than 14 days after a proposed bill of costs is filed.

(c) If no objection to the proposed bill of costs is filed, the clerk shall not tax costs until the expiration of 21 days after the filing of the proposed bill of costs. If the clerk fails to tax costs within 28 days after the proposed bill of costs is filed, and there being no objection filed, then costs will be deemed taxed as proposed.

(d) If objection to the proposed bill of costs is timely filed by a party, the clerk will forward the proposed bill of costs and the objection to the presiding judge in the case for final resolution.

(e) A party dissatisfied with the clerk's action may file a motion to review the clerk's action no later than 7 days after the clerk has taxed costs.

[Effective December 2, 2011. Amended effective April 26, 2012.]

RULE CV-55. FAILURE TO OBTAIN DEFAULT JUDGMENT

If a defendant is in default, the court may require the plaintiff to move for entry of a default and a default judgment. If the plaintiff fails to do so within the prescribed time, the court may dismiss the action, without prejudice, as to the defendant.

[Effective December 2, 2011. Amended effective April 26, 2012.]

RULE CV-65. INJUNCTIONS

An application for a temporary restraining order or preliminary injunction shall be made in an instrument separate from the complaint.

[Effective December 1, 2000. Amended effective December 2, 2011; April 26, 2012.]

RULE CV-65.1 SECURITY; PROCEEDINGS AGAINST SURETIES

(a) No clerk, marshal, attorney, or officer of this court will be accepted as surety, either directly or indirectly, on any bond or undertaking in any action or proceeding in this court, nor shall any such person advance or provide money or other thing of value for any cost, bail, attachment or replevy bond taken in this court.

(b) The clerk shall make available a list of corporations or other entities authorized by the Secretary of the Treasury to act as surety on official bonds on the district's website, or in such other manner as the clerk deems sufficient public notice.

(c) Unless the court otherwise directs, every bond furnished in connection with any matter must be done in one of the following manners, either:

(1) Cash or United States Government Bonds deposited in the registry of the court in lieu of sureties; or

(2) Surety bonds that have:

(A) A corporation authorized by the Secretary of the Treasury of the United States to act as surety on official bonds;

(B) An individual resident of the Western District of Texas who satisfied the court that he owns real or personal property not exempt by law within the district sufficient to justify the full amount of the suretyship.

(d) Each person who is to act as a principal or as a surety on an official bond shall undertake to:

(1) Prosecute the claim or action with effect;

(2) Abide by the decision of the court; and

(3) Pay the damages sustained, to the full extent of the face amount of the bond, if the court finds that the order secured by the bond was wrongfully applied for or wrongfully made.

[Effective January 1, 1994. Amended effective December 2, 2011; April 26, 2012.]

RULE CV-67. DEPOSIT AND DISBURSEMENT OF REGISTRY FUNDS

Deposits into and disbursements from the registry of the court must be made in compliance with Federal Rule of Civil Procedure 67 and Federal Rule of Bankruptcy Procedure 7067. The following procedures also govern any such deposits and disbursements:

(a) All funds tendered for deposit into the registry of the court, with the exception of cash bail, shall be placed in an interest bearing account.

(b) A motion requesting leave of court to deposit funds into the registry must be filed and served on all interested parties to the proceeding. The motion and proposed order shall set out with particularity the information found on the court's website, www.txwd.uscourts.gov, in the drop-down menu "For Attorneys" under "Registry Funds Information".

(c) The clerk is the designated beneficiary and custodian of the invested accounts.

(d) After the order is entered permitting deposit and investment or reinvestment of funds, the party presenting the order shall deliver a copy of said order on the clerk, either personally or by certified mail or in his absence, the divisional office manager. It shall also be incumbent on the presenting party to confirm that the appropriate action has been accomplished by the clerk in accordance with the provisions of the order.

(e) Upon entry of an order directing the clerk to disburse funds on deposit in the registry of the court, it will be the responsibility of the movant to serve a copy of said order on the clerk as set forth in subparagraph (d) above and in accordance with the information found on the court's website, www.txwd.uscourts.gov, in the drop-down menu "For Attorneys", under "Registry Funds Information".

[Effective January 1, 1994. Amended effective January 2, 2001; December 2, 2011; April 26, 2012; August 16, 2013.]

RULE CV-72. MAGISTRATE JUDGES, PRETRIAL MATTERS

The magistrate judges of this court are authorized to perform all the duties allowed to magistrate judges under the Federal Magistrates Act as amended in 28 United States Code § 636. The magistrate judges of this court are designated to exercise civil jurisdiction under section 636(c)(1) upon consent of the parties. Whenever applicable, the "Local Rules of the Assignment of Duties to United States Magistrate Judges" found at Appendix C shall apply to proceedings before the magistrate judges.

[Effective January 1, 1994. Amended effective December 2, 2011; April 26, 2012.]

RULE CV-79. REMOVAL AND DESTRUCTION OF RECORDS AND EXHIBITS

(a) Nothing in the files of the court shall be taken from the office or custody of the clerk, except on written order of the court. The party offering any exhibit or deposition shall be responsible for its removal from the clerk's office within 60 days after the final disposition of the case, including appeal thereof. A detailed receipt shall be given by the party to the clerk. Any exhibit or deposition remaining more than 60 days after final disposition of the case, including appeal, may be destroyed or otherwise disposed of by the clerk.

(b) Documents filed under seal in civil actions must remain sealed with the clerk, unless otherwise ordered by the court.

[Effective January 1, 1994. Amended effective December 2, 2011; April 26, 2012.]

RULE CV-88. ALTERNATIVE DISPUTE RESOLUTION

(a) ADR Methods Available. The court may approve any ADR method the parties suggest or the court believes is suited to the litigation.

(b) ADR Report. Upon order of the court, the parties shall submit a report addressing the status of settlement negotiations, disclosing the identity of the person responsible for settlement negotiations for each party, and evaluating whether alternative dispute resolution is appropriate in the case. In the event the parties conclude that ADR is appropriate and agree upon a method of ADR and an ADR provider, they should identify both the method of ADR and the provider they have selected, the method by which the provider was selected, and how the provider will be compensated.

(c) Referral to ADR. The court may refer a case to ADR on the motion of a party, on the agreement of the parties, or on its own motion; however, the court may refer a case to arbitration only with the consent of the parties (including but not limited to their consent by contract to arbitration). If the parties agree upon an ADR method or provider, the court will respect the parties' agreement unless the court determines that another ADR method or provider is better suited to the case and parties. If the parties are unable to agree on an ADR provider, the court will select a provider.

(d) Attendance; Authority to Settle. Counsel, party representatives with authority to negotiate a settlement, and all other persons necessary to negotiate a settlement, including insurance carriers, must attend the ADR session in person, unless the parties agree or the court orders otherwise.

(e) Fees. The provider and the litigants will determine the fees for the ADR. The court reserves the right to review the reasonableness of the fees. If the provider and litigants are unable to agree, the court will determine an appropriate fee.

(f) Disqualification. No person shall serve as a provider if any of the circumstances specified in 28 U.S.C. § 455 of the Judicial Code of Conduct exist, or if the provider believes in good faith that such circumstances exist.

(g) Relief From Referral. A party opposing either the ADR referral or the appointed provider must file written objections with the court not later than 14 days after receiving notice of the referral or provider. Any party may obtain relief from an order upon a showing of good cause. Good cause may include a showing that the expenses relating to alternative dispute resolution would cause undue hardship to the party seeking relief from the order. In that event, the court may in its discretion appoint a provider from the list of providers to serve at a reduced fee, or without fee and at no cost to the party or parties.

(h) Confidentiality. Except as otherwise provided herein, or as agreed by the participants, a communication relating to the subject matter of any civil or criminal dispute made by any participant during an alternative dispute resolution procedure, whether before or after the institution of formal judicial proceedings, is confidential, may not be disclosed, may not be used as evidence against the participant in any judicial or administrative proceeding, and does not constitute a waiver of any existing privileges or immunities.

(1) Any record made at an alternative dispute resolution procedure is confidential, and the participants or the third party facilitating the procedure may not be required to testify in any proceedings relating to or arising out of the matter in dispute or be subject to process requiring the disclosure of confidential information or data relating to or arising out of the matter in dispute.

(2) An oral communication or written material used in or made a part of an alternative dispute resolution procedure is admissible or discoverable if it is admissible or discoverable independent of the procedure.

(3) If this section conflicts with other legal requirements for disclosure of communications or materials, the issue of confidentiality may be presented to the court having jurisdiction of the proceedings to determine, in camera, whether the facts, circumstances, and context of the communications or materials sought to be disclosed warrant a protective order of the court or whether the communications or materials are subject to disclosure.

(i) Final ADR Report. At the conclusion of each ADR proceeding, the provider shall submit to the court a notice of outcome, including the style and number of the case, the type of case, the method of ADR, whether the case has settled, and the provider's fees.

(j) Sanctions. The sanctions available under Federal Rule of Civil Procedure 16(f) shall apply to any violation of this rule.

[Effective January 1, 1994. Amended effective December 1, 2000; January 2, 2001; December 1, 2009; December 2, 2011; April 26, 2012.]

SECTION II. CRIMINAL RULES

RULE CR-1. SCOPE AND APPLICABILITY OF RULES

(a) Scope. These rules apply in all criminal proceedings before the district and magistrate judges of the Western District of Texas.

(b) Applicability.

(1) *Conflicts with Other Laws or Rules.* To the extent any of these rules conflict with a law of the United States, or an applicable rule of the Supreme Court of the United States or the United States Court of Appeals for the Fifth Circuit, the rule must not apply.

(2) *Waiver of Rules.* Any judge of this court may waive a requirement of any of these rules when it is in the interest of justice.

(3) *Absence of Rule.* When no specific rule governs a procedural matter, the judge may prescribe the procedure for that case.

(c) Citation. These rules may be cited as the Western District of Texas Rules.

Committee Notes

1. The language of Rule CR-1 has been amended as part of the general restyling of the local criminal rules to make them more easily understood and to make style and terminology consistent throughout the rules. These changes are intended to be stylistic only, except as noted below.

2. The rules apply to cases then pending, unless applying a rule is not in the interest of justice.

3. Subsection (f) of the former rule, setting forth authority of magistrate judges is omitted from the proposed revision. The delegation of magistrate authority is not related to the general scope and applicability of the local rules and logically should be placed in its own rule. The style of subsection (f) has been revised as proposed Rule CR-58, consistent with proposed revisions to the Fed. R. Crim. P., which place matters pertaining to proceedings before a magistrate judge in Fed. R. Crim. P. 58.

[Effective January 1, 1994. Amended effective December 1, 2002.]

RULE CR-5A. PRETRIAL SERVICES INTERVIEW AND REPORT

(a) Interview.

(1) *Notice to Defendant.* Before conducting a pretrial services interview, the pretrial services officer must notify the defendant of:

(A) the circumstances under which the information the defendant provides must be disclosed; and

(B) the defendant's rights during the interview, including:

(i) the defendant's right not to be questioned regarding the charges in the case;

(ii) the defendant's right to decline to speak or provide any information to the officer; and

(iii) the defendant's right to counsel during the interview.

(2) *Notification Form.* A form notifying the defendant of the rights set out in subsection (a)(1) is appended to this rule.

(3) *Presence of Counsel.* If the defendant wishes to have the assistance of counsel during the interview, the pretrial services officer must afford a reasonable opportunity for counsel to be present.

(b) Use and Disclosure of Pretrial Service Report and Related Information.

(1) *In General.* The use and disclosure of the pretrial services report, and any information obtained by the pretrial services officer in the course of performing the pretrial services function, are governed by 18 U.S.C. § 3153(c). The pretrial services officer must limit disclosure to the minimum information and the minimum number of persons necessary to carry out the purpose of the disclosure.

(2) *Disclosure of the Pretrial Services Report.* The pretrial services report must be disclosed to the attorney for the defendant and the attorney for the government. The report should not be re-disclosed to other persons by the attorney for the defendant or the attorney for the government.

(3) *Disclosure of the Pretrial Services Recommendation.* Unless otherwise ordered by the court, the pretrial services officer's recommendation as to the propriety and conditions of release will be disclosed to the parties with the pretrial services report.

UNITED STATES DISTRICT COURT
WESTERN DISTRICT OF TEXAS
NOTICE TO DEFENDANTS

I, _____, am being asked questions about myself by a Pretrial Services Officer. I will not be questioned about the charges and I should avoid talking about them at this time. I understand I am under no obligation to give any information and I may decline to answer any particular question or all questions. However, I also understand the Pretrial Services Officer is required to provide a report to the court on my general background whether or not I choose to provide information at this time and that the absence of background information for consideration by the court could affect my chances for pretrial release. I further understand the report provided to the court will be made available to my attorney and the attorney for the government.

Any answers to these questions will be used by the court to decide whether I will be released or kept in jail pending my trial and whether I will have to take part in treatment programs such as for drug or alcohol abuse.

Statements I make to the Pretrial Services Officer in the course of the pretrial services function cannot be used against me on the issue of guilt in a criminal judicial proceeding. Any information could affect the decision regarding suitability for pretrial release.

If I am found guilty, either after trial or after pleading guilty, the information I provide to the Pretrial Services Officer will be made available to a U.S. Probation Officer for the purpose of investigating my background and preparing a presentence report and that information may affect my sentence.

I know I have the right to speak with a lawyer before answering any questions. If I cannot afford a lawyer, one will be appointed to represent me during questioning.

I have read this form, or had it read to me, and I understand my rights.

Date: _____

_____
Defendant's Signature

Time: _____ a.m.
p.m.   Pretrial Services Officer

TXW/11/95

TRIBUNAL DE JUSTICIA DE LOS ESTADOS UNIDOS DE AMERICA DISTRITO OESTE DE TEXAS

AVISO A LOS ACUSADOS

Yo, _____, sé que un Agente de Servicios Previos al Juicio me está haciendo preguntas acerca de mi mismo. No me interrogará acerca de los cargos en mi contra y por el momento deberé evitar hablar de ellos. Comprendo que no estoy obligado a dar información alguna y puedo declinar contestar alguna pregunta en partícular o todas las preguntas. Sin embargo, también comprendo que el Agente de Servicios Previos al Juicio está obligado a presentar un informe al tribunal. Este informe tratará de mis antecedentes personales ya sea que yo decida darle o no darle información en este momento. Además, comprendo que la falta de información acerca de mis antecedentes personales para la consideración del tribunal podría afectar la posibilidad de obtener libertad previa al juicio. Además, comprendo que el informe presentado al tribunal será puesto a la disposición de mi abogado y la del abogado del gobierno.

Cualquier respuesta a estas preguntas será usada por el tribunal para decidir si seré puesto en libertad o si permaneceré encarcelado mientras esté pendiente mi juicio y si tendré que participar en programas de tratamiento, por ejemplo, por abuso de drogas o alcohol.

Las declaraciones que yo le dé al Agente de Servicios Previos al Juicio durante el curso de las funciones de esos servicios no podrán ser usadas en mi contra con respecto a la decisión de culpabilidad en un procedimiento judicial penal. Cualquier información podría afectar la decisión respecto a la aptitud para recibir la libertad previa al juicio.

Si hay fallo de culpabilidad, ya sea después de un juicio o después de haberme declarado culpable, la información que yo le dé al Agente de Servicios Previos al Juicio se pondrá a la disposición del Agente de Libertad Condicional para los propósitos de investigar mis antecedentes personales y para preparar un informe precondenatorio y esa información podría afectar mi sentencia.

Sé que tengo el derecho de hablar con un abogado antes de contestar cualquier pregunta. Si no puedo costear los servicios de un abogado, se me asignará uno para que me represente durante el interrogatorio.

He leído este formulario o me lo han leído y entiendo mis derechos.

_____   _____
FECHA   FIRMA (DELA) ACUSADO(A)

_____   FIRMA DEL OFICIAL
HORA AM PM   AGENTE DE SERVICIOS
                    PREVIOS AL JUICIO

Committee Notes

1. Rule CR-5A is a new rule that prescribes procedures for pretrial services' interview and report, and the management of defendants on supervision who are confidential informants.

2. Subsection (a) ensures that a defendant knows of his rights, and has the opportunity to invoke them, before being interviewed by the pretrial services officer. Appended to the rule is a form pretrial services uses to notify the defendant of his rights, and to advise the defendant that no adverse inference will be drawn from his invocation of his rights.

3. Subsection (b) provides the parties with easier access to pretrial services information, subject to the confidentiality requirements of 18 U.S.C. § 3153(c). The Committee believes that it is consistent with the statute for the pretrial services officer to provide a copy of the pretrial services report and recommendation to both the government and defense attorneys, and that the statute does not require the return of the report at the conclusion of any bail or other pretrial hearing. Cf. 12 Administrative Office of the U.S. Courts, Guide to Judiciary Policies and Procedures, Ch. 3, Pt. A(4)(D)(1) (1999) (subject to district court's practice and procedure, report must be returned to pretrial services officer at conclusion of hearing).

[Effective December 1, 2002. Amended effective March 21, 2007.]

RULE CR–5B. INITIAL APPEARANCE OF UNDOCUMENTED ALIEN DETAINED AS MATERIAL WITNESS

(a) Appearance. Upon the filing of an affidavit under 18 U.S.C. § 3144 alleging that an undocumented alien is a material witness, the witness must be brought before the court without unnecessary delay.

(b) Procedure. Upon presentation of an undocumented alien witness, the court must:

(1) consider, with the assistance of pretrial services, whether the witness may be released under 18 U.S.C. § 3142, including release under an available community release program; and

(2) appoint counsel to represent the witness under the Criminal Justice Act, 18 U.S.C. § 3006A, if the court determines that:

(A) the witness is financially unable to retain counsel, and

(B) the witness does not waive counsel.

(c) Detention. If the witness is ordered detained, the detention must accord with the provisions of Rule CR–15B.

Committee Note

Rule CR–5B is a new rule that prescribes procedures for initial appearances of undocumented aliens detained as material witnesses. Because undocumented alien material witnesses are illegally in the United States, the feasibility of their conditional release under 18 U.S.C. § 3142 depends on the continued cooperation of U.S. Pretrial Services Office, the U.S. Attorney, and the Department of Homeland Security.

[Effective December 1, 2002.]

RULE CR–6A. THE GRAND JURY

Grand jurors' selection, qualification, summoning, and exemption or excuse from service are governed by Appendix D.

Committee Note

The language of Rule CR–6A has been amended as part of the general restyling of the local criminal rules to make them more easily understood and to make style and terminology consistent throughout the rules. These changes are intended to be stylistic only.

[Effective December 1, 2002.]

RULE CR–6B. DIVISION IN WHICH INDICTMENT MAY BE PRESENTED AND FILED

(a) In General. A case may be presented to a grand jury and may be filed in the following divisions:

(1) any division in which the offense was committed, in whole or in part; or

(2) with leave of the district judge supervising the grand jury before which the case is presented, any division whose borders are contiguous to any division in which the offense was committed, in whole or in part.

(b) Multiple Offenses. A case involving multiple offenses committed in separate divisions that are joined for indictment under Federal Rule of Criminal Procedure 8(a), may be presented to a grand jury in, and may be filed in, any division in which any one of the joined offenses could be presented and filed under subsection (a).

(c) Multiple Defendants. A case involving multiple defendants who are joined under Federal Rule of Criminal Procedure 8(b), may be presented to a grand jury in, and may be filed in, any division in which any one of the joined defendants could be charged under subsection (a).

Committee Notes

1. Rule CR–6B is a new rule that prescribes procedures for presentment and filing of indictments in divisions of the district. The rule allows, in certain circumstances, for an indictment to be presented and filed in a division contiguous to the one in which the offense was committed.

2. Leave of the district judge under subsection (a)(2) will normally be sought only when indictment in a division other than that in which the crime was committed is thought necessary to ensure a speedy trial, to avoid prejudice against the defendant, or when doing so would be in the interest of justice. The Committee contemplates that leave of the district judge will be documented in writing. Prosecution in

contiguous divisions is currently allowed in Appendix D, the Amended Plan for the Random Selection of Grand and Petit Jurors in the Western District of Texas. Subsection (a)(2) deviates from the procedures in Appendix D, which currently requires the approval of the chief judge.

[Effective December 1, 2002.]

RULE CR–12. PRETRIAL MOTIONS

(a) Motion by Defendant. Unless otherwise ordered by the court, the defendant must file any pretrial motion:

(1) within 14 days after arraignment; or

(2) if the defendant has waived arraignment, within 14 days after the latest scheduled arraignment date.

(b) Motion by the Government. Unless otherwise ordered by the Court, the government must file any pretrial motion by the latest of the following dates:

(1) within 14 days after receiving defendant's motions;

(2) within 21 days after the arraignment; or

(3) if the defendant has waived arraignment, within 21 days after the latest scheduled arraignment date.

Committee Notes

1. The language of Rule CR–12 has been amended as part of the general restyling of the local criminal rules to make them more easily understood and to make style and terminology consistent throughout the rules. These changes are intended to be stylistic only, except as noted below.

2. The form of motions and responses, and the time for filing a response, are governed by CR–47.

3. Notwithstanding the preference in the Federal Rules of Criminal Procedure for case-specific scheduling orders (see Committee Note, proposed amendment to Fed. R. Crim. P. 12(c)), the rule retains the practice of setting motions deadlines by local rule, recognizing that the practice is suitable for the vast majority of criminal cases filed in this district, and that the district court may set specific deadlines different from the rule in appropriate cases.

[Effective January 1, 1994. Amended effective May 16, 1994; December 1, 2002; December 1, 2009.]

RULE CR–15A. DEPOSITION OF WITNESS OTHER THAN MATERIAL WITNESSES

(a) Manner Taken. Except in the case of the deposition of a material witness, an oral deposition ordered by the court under Federal Rule of Criminal Procedure 15, may be recorded stenographically or on videotape if taken in accordance with the "Guidelines for Non–Stenographic Deposition," set forth in Appendix I.

(b) Stenographic Deposition. The original of a stenographic deposition must be delivered to the party who sought the deposition after one of the following has occurred:

(1) the deponent has signed the original deposition;

(2) the deponent and all interested parties have waived on the record the signing by the deponent; or

(3) the stenographic reporter has certified that the deponent has failed to sign the deposition after giving reasonable

notice of the availability of the transcript to the deponent and the deponent's attorney (if any).

(c) Videotape Deposition. The original of a videotape deposition must be delivered to the party who sought the deposition after one of the following has occurred:

(1) the deponent has reviewed the videotape and certified its accuracy; or

(2) the deponent and all interested parties have waived review and certification in writing; or

(3) the reporter has certified that the deponent has failed to sign an acknowledgment of review of the deposition after giving reasonable notice of the availability of the videotape to the deponent and the deponent's attorney (if any).

(d) Custody. The party who sought to take a deposition must maintain custody of the original transcript, or the original videotape deposition and certification, or any written waiver of certification. That party must make the deposition available for appropriate use by any party in a hearing or a trial of the case.

(e) Material Witnesses. The deposition of a material witness is governed by CR–15B.

Committee Note

The language of Rule CR–15A has been amended as part of the general restyling of the local criminal rules to make them more easily understood and to make style and terminology consistent throughout the rules. The rule has been revised to add procedures for the videotaping of depositions.

The rule does not govern the depositions of detained material witnesses, which is addressed by Rule CR–15B.

[Effective December 1, 2002.]

RULE CR–15B. DEPOSITION AND RELEASE OF MATERIAL WITNESS IN CUSTODY

(a) Scope.

(1) This rule provides for the deposition and release of a material witness who:

(A) is held pursuant to 18 U.S.C. § 3144;

(B) is found by the court to be an alien illegally in the United States; and

(C) has not been released on conditions under 18 U.S.C. § 3142.

(2) This rule does not affect the determination whether a material witness should be released under 18 U.S.C. § 3142.

(b) Deposition.

(1) *Entry and Service of Order.*

(A) Immediately after a material witness described in subsection (a) makes his or her first appearance before the court, the officer must enter an order setting the time and place for taking the deposition of the witness. No motion or notice is required by either the witness or any party. The order must comply with Federal Rule of Criminal Procedure 15. A form order is appended to this rule.

(B) An order entered under subsection (b)(1)(A) will serve as the notice of deposition required by Federal Rule of

Criminal Procedure 15(b). The clerk of the court must serve the order on counsel for all parties; on counsel for the material witness; on an interpreter; and on the U.S. Marshals Service.

(2) *When Taken; Cancellation or Continuance.*

(A) The court must order that the deposition be taken not later than 35 days after the witness first appeared before the officer.

(B) The deposition may be continued or canceled only on order of the court. If the government and the defendant or defendants reach an agreement disposing of related criminal charges before the deposition is taken, they must notify the court, which will then promptly determine whether to cancel or continue the deposition. The deposition cannot be continued beyond the 45–day deadline for release of the witness set out in subsection (c)(1).

(C) Subject to a finding of additional exceptional circumstances under Federal Rule of Criminal Procedure 15(a), the court must cancel the deposition if the material witness is released on conditions of release before the scheduled date of the deposition.

(3) *Discovery.* The parties must exchange all required discovery reasonably in advance of the date of the deposition.

(4) *Location.* Unless impracticable, the deposition should be taken in a court facility.

(5) *Attendance.*

(A) All parties and persons served under subsection (b)(1)(B) of this rule must attend the deposition, except that any defendant may waive attendance by filing a written waiver before the date of the deposition, in accordance with Federal Rule of Criminal Procedure 15(c)(1).

(B) The U.S. Marshals Service must make available the witness and defendant in its custody, at the time and place of the deposition ordered by the court.

(6) *How Taken.* The deposition must be recorded by videotape. The U.S. Attorney's Office must provide a videographer to record the deposition, and will bear the costs and expenses of taking the deposition. Other expenses will be borne by the parties, except as provided in Federal Rule of Criminal Procedure 15(d).

(7) *Review and Certification.*

(A) After the deposition is completed, the videotape recording must immediately be played back in the presence of the witness, the interpreter, and all parties attending the deposition, and their attorneys. Any corrections or modifications to the deposition must be recorded on the same videotape used to record the deposition, and should immediately follow the deposition on the recording.

(B) The deposition must be certified consistent with Federal Rule of Civil Procedure 30, except as otherwise provided by this rule or ordered by the court. It is not required for certification that the videotape recording be transcribed.

(C) The material witness and all interested parties may waive review and certification in writing, in accordance with Rule CR–15.

(8) *Custody of Deposition.* The government must maintain custody of the videotape deposition and certification, or any waiver of certification. Upon request, the government must provide a copy of the deposition to the witness or any defendant.

(9) *Use as Evidence.* The use and admissibility of the deposition are governed by Federal Rule of Criminal Procedure 15, the Federal Rules of Evidence, and applicable court precedent. The presiding judge should rule on any objections to the deposition at or before trial. Nothing in this rule relieves the proponent's burden of demonstrating the unavailability of the material witness under Federal Rule of Evidence 804(a).

(c) Release.

(1) *Mandatory Deadline for Release.* A material witness described in subsection (a) must be ordered released from the custody of the U.S. Marshals Service by the first to occur of the following deadlines:

(A) within 24 hours of the taking, and the certification or waiver of certification, of the witness' deposition; or

(B) within 45 days of the witness' first appearance before a court.

(2) *Earlier Release.* If the deposition is canceled under subsection (b)(2)(B), the court should determine promptly whether to order the release of the material witness from U.S. Marshals Service custody.

[Effective December 1, 2002.]

Committee Notes

1. Rule CR–15B is a new rule that prescribes procedures for deposing and releasing material witnesses in custody. The Committee notes that there is a conflict between Appendix I and CR–15B in that the appendix, which likely was drafted with civil depositions in mind, imposes the cost of copies on the party seeking the copy whereas CR–15B requires the government to furnish copies to the witness and defendant upon request. This conflict is addressed by language on the form order.

2. Notwithstanding subsection (b)(2)(B), the court may continue the deposition for "good cause." See Rule CR–1(e).

3. Subsection (b)(3) does not provide for discovery other than that ordered by the court. The Committee contemplates that the parties will exchange information as would be required as if the witness were testifying at trial, including discovery required by Fed. R. Crim. P. 15(e), Fed. R. Crim. P. 16, and Fed. R. Crim. P. 26.2; statements covered by the Jencks Act, 18 U.S.C. § 3500; and impeachment information under Brady v. Maryland, 373 U.S. 83, 83 S. Ct. 1194 (1963), and Giglio v. United States, 405 U.S. 150, 92 S. Ct. 763 (1972).

4. The use of an interpreter should accord with 28 U.S.C. § 1827 and applicable directives of the Administrative Office of the U.S. Courts. The government bears the burden of providing an interpreter for the deposition.

5. The rule does not require a written transcript of the deposition but leaves to the court and the parties to determine whether a written transcript is necessary in any given case. The Committee notes that, unlike the U.S. Attorney and the Federal Public Defender, private counsel appointed under the Criminal Justice Act, 18 U.S.C. § 3006A, cannot obtain a written transcript without a court order. See 28 U.S.C. § 1915(c). The proposed order appended to the rule provides that a Criminal Justice Act panel attorney may request a written transcript.

APPENDIX TO LOCAL COURT RULE CR–15B

UNITED STATES DISTRICT COURT
WESTERN DISTRICT OF TEXAS
SAN ANTONIO DIVISION

UNITED STATES OF AMERICA,) Plaintiff,) v.) Defendants.)	CRIMINAL NO. SA–CR–

ORDER SETTING MATERIAL WITNESS DEPOSITION

Before the Court is the matter of the taking of the deposition of material witnesses in the above-styled and numbered cause. The Court finds that _____ (names of material witnesses) are aliens not lawfully admitted to the United States, that they are material witnesses in the case styled United States v. (Name of Defendant, cause no.), being held pursuant to 18 U.S.C. § 3144, and that they have not been released on conditions pursuant to 18 U.S.C. § 3142. As such, the Court finds that this case presents "exceptional circumstances" and that the "interest of justice" requires the taking of the deposition of the material witnesses. Rule 15(a), Fed.R.Crim.P. The Court further finds that there will be no failure of justice if the material witnesses are released after their depositions have been taken and certified in accordance with 18 U.S.C. § 3144 and Local Court Rule CR–15B.

IT IS THEREFORE ORDERED that the depositions of _____(names of material witnesses) are set for ____(date and time) at _____(place).

IT IS FURTHER ORDERED that the depositions shall be recorded by videotape. The videotape must provide an electronic sound recording which is sufficient to comply with 28 U.S.C. § 1827(d)(2). They also may be recorded by stenographic means at the party's own expense. Notwithstanding the foregoing, subsequent to the completion of the deposition, a CJA panel attorney may request that a stenographic transcript of all or part of a deposition. Each deposition shall be certified consistent with Rule 30, Fed.R.Civ.P. and Local Rule CR–15B, and shall be accomplished by the immediate playback of the videotape recording in the presence of the material witness, the interpreter, all parties attending the deposition, and their attorneys. Any corrections or modifications to the deposition shall be recorded on the same videotape, following the recording of the deposition. Playback of the recording and certification may be waived in writing in accordance with Local Rule CR–15A. The government shall retain custody of the videotape depositions and written statements of certification or waiver of certification pending trial. Notwithstanding Appendix I to the Local Rules, the government shall, upon request, promptly provide to any defendant, material witness or counsel, copies of the videotape deposition and written statements of certification or waivers of certification.

IT IS FURTHER ORDERED that the Clerk of the Court shall serve a copy of this order on the following: All defendants, counsel for defendants, the material witnesses, counsel for the material witnesses, counsel for the government, an interpreter, and the United States Marshals Service.

IT IS FURTHER ORDERED that the United States Marshals Service shall make the named witnesses and defendants in their custody available on the date, time and place in conformity with this order. If any defendant desires to waive appearance, that defendant must file a written waiver with the Clerk of the Court prior to the date of the deposition.

IT IS FURTHER ORDERED that within 24 hours after the deposition and certification or waiver have been completed, the material witness shall be brought before the court for release from the custody of the U.S. Marshals Service.

[Effective December 1, 2002.]

RULE CR–16. DISCOVERY AND INSPECTION

(a) Discovery Conference and Agreement.

(1) The parties need not make standard discovery requests, motions, or responses if, not later than the deadline for filing pretrial motions (or as otherwise authorized by the court), they confer, attempt to agree on procedures for pretrial discovery, and sign and file a copy of the Disclosure Agreement Checklist appended to this rule.

(2) If the Disclosure Agreement Checklist indicates that a party intends to disclose, but does not currently possess, certain listed information, that party must disclose the information as soon as practicable.

(3) If the Disclosure Agreement Checklist indicates that a party refuses to disclose information, the other party may file motions regarding the undisclosed information within 14 days after filing of the checklist.

(4) Filing of the Disclosure Agreement Checklist does not preclude a party from filing motions relating to information not listed in the checklist.

(b) Timing of Discovery.

(1) *Discovery Deadlines.* Unless otherwise ordered by the court, or agreed to by the parties in writing:

(A) The parties must provide discovery in connection with pretrial release or detention not later than the commencement of a hearing on pretrial release or detention;

(B) The parties must provide discovery in connection with a pretrial hearing, other than a pretrial release or detention hearing, not later than 48 hours before the hearing; and

(C) The parties must provide discovery in connection with trial, whether agreed to by the parties or otherwise required, not later than:

(i) 14 days after arraignment; or

(ii) if the defendant has waived arraignment, within 14 days after the latest scheduled arraignment date.

(2) *Earlier Disclosure.* The court encourages prompt disclosure, including disclosure before the deadlines set out in this rule.

(3) *Disclosure After Motions Deadline.* The disclosure of information after the expiration of a motions deadline usually provides good cause for an extension of time to file motions based on that information.

(4) *Continuing Duty to Disclose.* The parties have a continuing duty to disclose promptly to opposing counsel all newly discovered information the party is required to disclose, or has agreed to disclose in the Disclosure Agreement Checklist.

(c) Late Disclosure.

(1) The late disclosure of material information under this rule is not usually a ground for exclusion of evidence, unless:

(A) the information was within the party's possession, custody or control, and its existence was known, or by the exercise of due diligence could have been known, to the party's attorney; and

(B) the party's attorney has not made good faith efforts to obtain and disclose the information on time.

(2) If not excluded under subsection (c)(1), material information that is not timely disclosed usually provides good cause for:

(A) extending the time to file a motion or notice, or to request a hearing, based on the late-disclosed information;

(B) extending a deadline for reaching a plea-bargain agreement; and

(C) continuing the trial setting.

[Effective March 26, 2003. Amended effective December 1, 2009.]

Committee Notes

1. Subsection (a) and the appended checklist provide a formal means by which the parties can, by agreement, regulate their discovery practice. This is not intended to preclude other agreed discovery methods (such as the open-file discovery regularly practiced in some divisions).

2. Subsection (c) deals with the problem of late—disclosed discovery. The rule recognizes that, when late disclosure of evidence is done in good faith, it should not usually provide grounds for excluding the evidence, but usually does provide cause for a continuance or other extension of time. Subsection (c) is not intended to limit the court's discretion under Federal Rule of Criminal Procedure 16(d).

3. The disclosure agreement checklist appended to the rule does not include specific reference to confidential informants. There are some cases in which an "informant" category on the checklist would not capture the unique circumstances regarding cooperating individuals; in those cases, any reference to informants on the checklist could be prejudicial to the Government, or misleading to the defense. Nevertheless, the identity and location of informants are important, recurring discovery issues. Subsection (a)(4) allows the defense to file discovery motions regarding informants; alternatively, the parties may address the issue in the "other matters" section of the checklist. If the checklist indicates that the Government refuses to disclose information regarding an informant, subsection (a)(3) would provide the defendant additional time to file a motion for disclosure.

UNITED STATES v. _____

CRIMINAL NO. ____

PARTIES' DISCLOSURE AGREEMENT CHECKLIST									
	Disclosed		Will Disclose Upon Receipt		Refuse to Disclose		Not Applicable		Comments
	Gov't	Def	Gov't	Def	Gov't	Def	Gov't	Def	
Police/Agent Reports									
Rule 12(d)(2) material									
Intercepted communications (18 U.S.C. § 2510, consensual)									
Rule 16 material:									
Defendant statement									
Defendant record									
Documents									
Tangible Objects									
Examination/ test reports									
Experts									
FRE 404(b) material									
Immigration file									
Eyewitness ID (lineup, showup, photo spread)									
Exculpatory material (*Brady*)									
Impeachment material (*Giglio, Napue,* FRE 608, 609)									
Witness list									
Witness statements (Rule 26.2, 18 U.S.C. § 3500)									
Guideline calculation material (U.S.S.G. § 6B1.2)									
Other matters:									

_____   _____   _____   _____
DEFENDANT'S ATTORNEY   DATE   ASSISTANT U.S. ATTORNEY   DATE

RULE CR–17.1 MARKING EXHIBITS

A party must mark any exhibit it offers at a trial or hearing in accordance with Rule CV–16(g).

Committee Notes

1. Rule CR–17.1 is a new rule, consisting of the substance of former Rule CR–55(b), renumbered as Rule CR–17.1, to conform more closely to the organizational structure of the Federal Rules of Criminal Procedure. The language of Rule CR–17.1 has been amended as part of the general restyling of the local criminal rules to make them more easily understood and to make style and terminology consistent throughout the rules. The changes are intended to be stylistic only, except as noted below.

2. The rule extends the requirement to premark exhibits to hearings as well as trials, to reflect current practice.

[Effective December 1, 2002.]

RULE CR–18. PLACE OF TRIAL WITHIN DISTRICT

(a) **Division in Which Prosecution and Trial May Occur.**

(1) Unless a statute, other rule, or court order requires otherwise, the government may prosecute a case in any division in the district in which the offense was committed, in whole or in part.

(2) The court may fix trial in:

(A) any division within the district consistent with Federal Rule of Criminal Procedure 18; or

(B) any other division within the district, if the court is satisfied that there exists in the division where the prosecution is pending so great a prejudice against the defendant that the defendant cannot obtain a fair and impartial trial.

(b) **Multiple Offenses.** In cases involving multiple offenses joined for trial under Federal Rule of Criminal Procedure 8(a), the court may fix the place of trial in any division in which any one of the joined offenses may be tried.

(c) **Multiple Defendants.** In cases involving multiple defendants joined for trial under Federal Rule of Criminal Procedure 8(b), the court may fix the place of trial in any division in which any one of the joined defendants may be tried.

Committee Notes

1. Rule CR–18 is a new rule that prescribes procedures for fixing the place of trial within the district.

2. Subsection (a)(2) does not limit the court's duty or discretion to transfer a proceeding to another district, as provided by Fed. R. Crim. P. 21(a). Subsection (a)(2)(B) is intended to clarify a specific circumstance in which transfer to another division may be required for the "prompt administration of justice" provided by Fed. R. Crim. P. 18.

3. Subsections (b) and (c) are not intended to affect or limit the court's discretion to sever as provided by Fed. R. Crim. P. 14.

4. The Committee contemplates that when a case is assigned for trial in another division, the clerk will cause the case to be assigned to a district judge in the transferee division in accordance with the plan for the random assignment of cases, unless the transferring judge orders that he or she will continue to handle the case after transfer.

[Effective December 1, 2002.]

RULE CR–24. TRIAL JURORS

(a) **Selecting Trial Jurors.**

(1) Trial jurors' selection, qualification, summoning, and exemption or excuse from service are governed by Appendix D.

(2) To assist the court in selecting a jury, each prospective juror must complete the juror information form set out in Appendix D–1.

(b) **Bailiff's Oath.** The bailiff, or other special officer appointed to attend upon a jury, must take the following oath:

"You solemnly swear that you will keep this jury during their retirement, in some convenient place removed from the presence of other persons; that you will not, without leave of the Court, suffer any person to speak to them; that you will not without such leave, hold or have any communication with them yourself, except to ascertain whether they have agreed upon their verdict and to attend to their needs; and that you will well and faithfully discharge your duties as bailiff. So help you God."

Committee Notes

1. The language of Rule CR–24 has been amended as part of the general restyling of the local criminal rules to make them more easily understood and to make style and terminology consistent throughout the rules. These changes are intended to be stylistic only.

2. Subsection (a) of the restyled rule deletes as unnecessary the reference to the statute and the title of the Plan of Implementation.

3. The revised rule removes the reference to the clerk administering the oath and changed the text of the oath only to reflect that the bailiff shall attend to the "needs" of the jurors, without further specification.

[Effective January 1, 1994. Amended effective December 1, 2002.]

RULE CR–32. SENTENCE AND JUDGMENT

(a) **Time of Sentencing.** Except for good cause, the court should sentence the defendant within 60 days after the date of the verdict or entry of guilty plea.

(b) **Time Limits Regarding the Presentence Report.** If the defendant and the government waive the time limits under Federal Rule of Criminal Procedure 32, the following time limits apply.

(1) *Disclosing the Report.* The probation officer must give the presentence report to the defendant, the defendant's attorney, and the attorney for the government at least 24 days before sentencing. Delivery of an extra copy of the presentence report to the defendant's attorney constitutes giving the report to the defendant.

(2) *Reviewing the Report.* Within 10 days after the presentence report is given, the attorney for the defendant must certify to the probation officer that the defendant has reviewed the presentence report and consulted with the attorney regarding the report.

(3) *Objecting to the Report.* Within 10 days after the presentence report is given, the parties must state in writing any objections to the report.

(4) *Acting on Objections.* Within 10 days after receiving objections, the probation officer may meet with the parties to discuss the objections, investigate further, and revise the presentence report as appropriate.

(5) *Submitting the Report.* At least 4 days before sentencing, the probation officer must submit the presentence report, any revision to the report, and any addendum to the court and the parties.

(c) Changing Time Limits. The court may, for good cause, change any time limit prescribed in subsection (b), except that the time limit for objecting to the presentence report may be shortened only with the consent of the defendant, the defendant's attorney, and the attorney for the government.

(d) Sentencing. At sentencing, the court may:

(1) allow a party, for good cause, to make a new objection before sentence is imposed;

(2) accept the presentence report as accurate, except with regard to any unresolved objection; and

(3) in resolving an objection, consider any reliable information presented by the probation officer, the defendant, or the government.

(e) Post–Sentencing Disclosures.

(1) *Presentence Report.* After sentencing, the presentence report and its contents must remain confidential, except that the probation officer may disclose the presentence report or its contents to:

(A) the U.S. Sentencing Commission;

(B) the U.S. Parole Commission;

(C) the U.S. Pretrial Services Office;

(D) another U.S. Court;

(E) the Federal Bureau of Prisons, if a term of imprisonment is imposed; or

(F) any person as ordered by the court.

(2) *Confidential Sentencing Recommendation.* Except as ordered by the sentencing judge, the probation officer's confidential sentencing recommendation must not be disclosed.

[Effective January 1, 1994. Amended effective February 17, 1995; September 1, 1995; June 11, 1998; December 1, 2002; December 1, 2009.]

Committee Notes

1. The language of Rule CR–32 has been amended as part of the general restyling of the local criminal rules to make them more easily understood and to make style and terminology consistent throughout the rules. These changes are intended to be stylistic only, except as noted below.

2. Subsection (a) extends the usual time for sentencing after a finding of guilt from 45 days to 60 days. The U.S. Probation Office indicates that a 60–day time frame would better reflect current practice across the district. The subsection also adds a "good cause" proviso, expressly allowing for variation from the 60–day practice.

3. Subsection (b)(3) deletes the former rule's reference to what must be included in the objections to the presentence report. This matter is covered by subsection (f)(1) of the restyled version of Fed. R. Crim. P. 32.

4. Subsection (b)(5) deletes the former rule's reference to what must be included in the addendum to the presentence report. This matter is covered by subsection (g) of the restyled version of Fed. R. Crim. P. 32.

5. Subsections (d)(1) and (d)(2) are taken from the former rule; they are substantially the same as subsections (h)(1)(D) and (h)(3)(A) of the restyled version of Fed. R. Crim. P. 32.

6. Subsection (e) deletes the former rule's prohibition on disclosing the presentence report to an inmate, instead providing generally that the presentence report remains confidential. Under subsection (e)(1)(F), any court of the district can order disclosure of a presentence report; under subsection (e)(2), by contrast, only the sentencing judge may order disclosure of the probation officer's confidential sentencing recommendation.

RULE CR–45. COMPUTING TIME

In computing any time period in any criminal case, the provisions of Rule 45, Federal Rules of Criminal Procedure (as amended effective December 1, 2009) shall be applied.

[Effective December 1, 2009.]

RULE CR–46. RELEASE FROM CUSTODY; REPORTS OF DETAINED MATERIAL WITNESSES

(a) Management by Pretrial Services Officers of Defendants Working as Informants. The following procedures apply to a defendant under supervision of pretrial services working as an informant for a law enforcement agency:

(1) The law enforcement agency using a defendant as an informant must promptly notify the defendant's pretrial services officer.

(2) The pretrial services officer must provide the law enforcement agency a copy of the defendant's conditions of release and the pretrial services officer's intended supervision activities.

(3) The law enforcement agency must advise the pretrial services officer of any requirements of the investigation that will affect supervision activities or require a change in the conditions of release.

(4) The law enforcement agency must inform the pretrial services officer of any violations by the defendant of any conditions of release.

(b) Reports of Detained Material Witnesses.

(1) *Government Report.* Unless otherwise ordered by the court, government reports regarding detained witnesses under Federal Rule of Criminal Procedure 46(h) must be sent to:

(A) the judge presiding over the case in which the detainee is a witness;

(B) the judge who ordered the witness detained; and

(C) the Pretrial Services Office.

(2) *Pretrial Services Office Recommendation.* Unless otherwise ordered by the court, the Pretrial Services Office, within 7 days of receiving a government report regarding detained witnesses, must provide a recommendation as to each witness's continued detention or release. The recommendation must be provided to:

(A) the judge presiding over the case in which the detainee is a witness;

(B) the judge who ordered the witness detained; and

(C) if the Pretrial Services Office recommends a change in status, the attorneys for the detainee and for the parties to the case in which the detainee is a witness.

[Effective December 1, 2002.]

Committee Note

1. Rule CR–46 is a new rule that prescribes procedures for release from custody of informants and for making reports on detained material witnesses.

2. Subsection (a) incorporates into the local rules the terms of the July 18, 1995 Standing Order Regarding Management by Pretrial Services Officers of Defendants who are Confidential Informants.

3. Disclosure of a recommendation for change of status under (b)(2)(C) does not require that the basis for the recommendation be disclosed.

RULE CR–47. MOTIONS AND RESPONSES

(a) **Requirements.** When filing a motion or response, a party must:

(1) cite the legal authority upon which the party relies; and

(2) submit a proposed order stating the relief the party seeks.

(b) **Time for Filing Response.** If a party opposes a motion, the party must file its response with the clerk and serve a copy on all parties within 11 days of service of the motion.

[Effective December 1, 2002. Amended effective December 1, 2009.]

Committee Notes

1. Rule 47 is a new rule consisting of portions of the substance of former CR–12, renumbered as CR–47 to conform more closely to the organizational structure of the Federal Rules of Criminal Procedure and to make it clear that the requirements apply to all motions and responses and not only pretrial motions and responses. These changes are intended to be stylistic only, except as noted below.

2. The rule requires the submission of a proposed order with motions and responses.

RULE CR–49. SERVING AND FILING DOCUMENTS

(a) **Filing and Service Requirements.** Rule CV–5 of the Local Court Rules of the United States District Court for the Western District of Texas is applicable to criminal cases.

(b) **Format of Documents.**

(1) Any document presented to the clerk for filing must:

(A) be typed or printed, double-spaced, without erasures or interlineation materially defacing it, and, if by traditional filing, on 8½ by 11 inch paper;

(B) be endorsed with the style of the case and the descriptive name of the pleading or document; and

(C) contain either:

(i) the mailing address, signature, state bar card number and telephone and fax numbers (including area code) of the attorney, if filed by an attorney; or

(ii) the mailing address, signature, and telephone number (including area code) of the pro se party, if filed pro se.

(2) Any proposed order submitted with a traditionally filed document must be completely separate from any other paper or document.

(c) **Nonconforming Documents.** The clerk must file any document not conforming to this rule and advise the court of the violation of the rule.

[Effective January 1, 1994. Amended effective December 1, 2002; January 30, 2006.]

RULE CR–55. REMOVAL OF RECORDS AND EXHIBITS

(a) **Records.**

(1) Except upon approval of the court, no record or paper in court files may be removed from the clerk.

(2) A party removing any record or paper must provide the clerk a receipt signed by the party or the party's attorney reflecting each record or paper removed from the clerk.

(b) **Exhibits.**

(1) *Removal After Final Disposition.* Within 60 days after final disposition of the case, including appeal, and denial of, or expiration of the time in which to file, a petition for writ of certiorari in the U.S. Supreme Court, the party who offered an exhibit must remove it from the clerk.

(2) *Failure to Remove.* Failure to remove any exhibit within 60 days of final disposition of the case may result in the clerk destroying or otherwise disposing of the exhibit.

[Effective January 1, 1994. Amended effective January 2, 2001; December 1, 2002.]

Committee Notes

1. The language of Rule CR–55 has been amended as part of the general restyling of the local criminal rules to make them more easily understood and to make style and terminology consistent throughout the rules. These changes are intended to be stylistic only, except as noted below.

2. "Final disposition" has been clarified in subsection (b)(2) to include exhaustion of the pursuit of, or expiration of the time for seeking relief in the Supreme Court. This definition of final disposition is consistent with the interpretation of the one-year limitation applicable to a judgment of conviction becoming final for purposes of seeking post-conviction relief pursuant to 28 U.S.C. § 2255. See United States v. Gamble, 208 F.3d 536 (5th Cir. 2000).

3. The requirement that the receipt evidencing return of exhibits be signed by the party or attorney reflects current practice.

4. Former Rule CR–55(b) has been restyled as Rule CR–17.1 to conform more closely to the organizational structure of the Federal Rules of Criminal Procedure.

5. As a matter of practice exhibits often are removed by the parties immediately after trial. The clerk's policy and practice are set out in the Clerk's Guidelines for Handling Exhibits, which may be

found at the Western District of Texas website at www.txwd.uscourts. gov.

RULE CR–58. PROCEEDINGS BEFORE MAGISTRATE JUDGES

(a) Authority of Magistrate Judges.

(1) The magistrate judges of this district are authorized to perform all duties assignable to magistrate judges as set forth in 28 U.S.C. § 636.

(2) The magistrate judges of this district are specially designated to exercise jurisdiction over misdemeanor offenses as provided by 18 U.S.C. § 3401.

(3) Proceedings before the magistrate judges are governed by the "Local Rules for the Assignment of Duties to United States Magistrate Judges," set forth in Appendix C.

(b) Paying a Fixed Sum in Lieu of Appearance.

(1) *Waiver of Appearance and Forfeiture of Collateral.* Unless otherwise ordered by a magistrate judge, a person charged with a petty offense as defined in 18 U.S.C. § 19, and listed in subsection (b)(2), may, in lieu of appearance:

(A) post collateral in the amount indicated for the offense;

(B) waive appearance before the magistrate judge; and

(C) consent to forfeiture of collateral.

(2) *Offenses Subject to Forfeiture in Lieu of Appearance.* The offenses for which collateral may be posted and forfeited in lieu of appearance by the person charged, together with the amounts of collateral to be posted, are identified in the exhibits referred to below,* copies of which are available in the office of the clerk in each division of this court:

(A) any petty offense listed in the schedule of offenses designated as Exhibit A, occurring on a U.S. Military Installation within the Western District of Texas;

(B) any violation listed in Exhibit B, and set forth in Title 36, Code of Federal Regulations, Chapters 2–5, occurring in a National Park or National Recreation area situated within the Western District of Texas;

(C) any violation of Fish and Wildlife laws listed in Exhibit C, and set forth in 16 U.S.C. § 703, 16 U.S.C. § 718a, 16 U.S.C. § § 851–856, 18 U.S.C. § § 41, 42, 44 and Parts 10 and 16 of Title 50, Code of Federal Regulations, occurring within the Western District of Texas;

(D) any petty offense listed in the schedule of offenses designated as Exhibit D, involving the public use of Veterans Administration properties, occurring within the Western District of Texas;

(E) any violation of Title 36, Code of Federal Regulations, Chapter III, Part 327, (Corps of Engineers), listed in Exhibit E, occurring within the Western District of Texas;

(F) any petty offense listed in Exhibit F, set forth in 40 U.S.C. § 318 and Title 41, Code of Federal Regulations, Chapter 101, occurring on General Services Administration property within the Western District of Texas;

(G) any petty offense listed in Exhibit G, set forth in 16 U.S.C. §§ 433, 460, 670, 18 U.S.C. §§ 1361, 1852, 1853, 1856, 1857, 1858, 43 U.S.C. § 1061 and Title 43, Code of Federal Regulations, occurring on Bureau of Land Management property within the Western District of Texas; and

(H) any petty offense listed in Exhibit H, set forth in 39 U.S.C. § 401 and Title 39, Code of Federal Regulations, as made available to the United States Postal Service by Title VI of Public Law 93–143, State. 525, occurring on Postal Service property within the Western District of Texas;

(I) any petty offense listed in Exhibit I, set forth in Title 32, Code of Federal Regulations, occurring on National Security Agency property within the Western District of Texas.

(3) *Punishment Other Than Forfeiture of Collateral.* If a person charged with an offense described in subsection (b)(2) fails to post and forfeit collateral, any punishment, including fine, imprisonment, or probation, may be imposed within the limits established by law upon conviction.

(4) *Other Offenses.* A person charged with a petty offense which is not listed in subsection (b)(2) must appear before a magistrate judge.

(5) *Arrest and Appearance Before Magistrate Judge.* Nothing contained in this rule prohibits a law enforcement officer from:

(A) arresting a person for the commission of any offense covered by this rule; or

(B) requiring the person arrested or charged for any offense covered by this rule to appear before a magistrate judge.

(6) *Special Assessment.* The collateral amounts set forth in Exhibits A through I include any special assessment required by 18 U.S.C. § 3013.

[Effective December 1, 2002. Amended effective January 20, 2010; April 28, 2016.]

* [**Publisher's Note:** For a copy of the most current version of exhibits referred to in this rule, please contact the Clerk's Office.]

Committee Notes

1. Rule CR–58 is a new rule, consisting of the substance of former Rules CR–1(f) and CR–61. The language of Rule CR–58 has been amended as part of the general restyling of the local criminal rules to make them more easily understood and to make style and terminology consistent throughout the rules. The changes are intended to be stylistic only.

2. Subsections (b)(2)(F) and (b)(2)(H) correspond to subsection (a)(6) of former Rule CR–61 and conform to the separate schedules of collateral currently on file as Exhibits F and H. Exhibits A through H are also available on the Western District of Texas website at www. txwd.uscourts.gov in the Local Rules area.

SECTION III. ATTORNEYS

RULE AT–1. ADMISSION OF ATTORNEYS

(a) Eligibility for Admission.

(1) *In General.* An attorney may be admitted to the bar of the U.S. District Court for the Western District of Texas if the attorney is licensed to practice by the highest court of a state, is in good standing in that bar; and has good personal and professional character. An applicant who is not licensed to practice by the highest court of any state may apply for admission, however, if admitted, such an attorney must obtain a license from the highest court of any state within one year after being admitted to the bar of this Court.

(2) *Bankruptcy Court.* An attorney seeking to practice before the Bankruptcy Court for the Western District of Texas must make application to the U.S. District Court for the Western District of Texas as this rule requires.

(b) Application for Admission.

(1) *Contents.* An application for admission must be made on the form prescribed by the court. It must be supported by a certificate of good standing (or equivalent documentation) from the highest state court and the United States district court, if licensed, where the applicant practices. All certificates of good standing must be dated no earlier than 60 days before the date the application is filed. The application must also be supported by two letters of recommendation in the form prescribed by the court. For an applicant residing in this district, the letters must be from attorneys admitted to practice and in good standing in the bar of this court. For an applicant practicing in another federal judicial district, the letters must be from attorneys admitted to practice and in good standing in the bar of that court. The letters must be written and dated no earlier than 6 months before the date the application is filed.

(2) *Seminar Requirement.* Within one year before the application is filed, the applicant must complete a live, video or on-line continuing legal education program on federal court practice approved by the court, and must certify that attendance on a form prescribed by the court. This requirement does not apply to a nonresident applicant who is admitted to practice and in good standing in the bar of another U.S. district court. In the event that the applicant was previously admitted to this Court and previously fulfilled the CLE requirement, this requirement is waived.

(3) *Filing.* An applicant residing in this district must file the application with the clerk in the division where he or she resides. An applicant residing outside this district may file the application in any division of the district.

(4) *Time for Completing Application.* An applicant must complete all requirements for admission (including any requested supplemental or explanatory information) within one year after filing an application. If the applicant fails to do so, the application expires. In that event, an applicant who seeks admission again must file a new application.

(c) Divisional Committee on Admissions. In each division of this court there is constituted a committee on admissions, which reviews applications for admission to the bar of this court and makes appropriate recommendations to the court.

(1) *Composition.* Each committee on admissions has five or more members, including a chair. To the extent possible, the committee should include civil, criminal, and bankruptcy practitioners. Those eligible for service on the committee are attorneys licensed to practice in this district and in good standing, and maintaining a law office in the division served. The members and chair are appointed by the judges resident in, or responsible for, the division.

(2) *Terms.* Membership terms should be staggered so that approximately one third of the members' terms expire each year. The term is 3 years, unless a shorter period is required to achieve staggered terms. The terms of members and the chair may be renewed one or more times.

(3) *Quorum.* A quorum of a committee consists of three members, participating either in person or by electronic means.

(d) Action on Applications.

(1) *Clerk's Duties.* The clerk will inspect applications for completeness, and may request the applicant to provide supplemental or explanatory information. The clerk will forward completed applications to the committee chair.

(2) *Examination by the Committee.* The committee will meet with reasonable frequency to examine applications referred to it. The committee may request the applicant to provide supplemental or explanatory information, and may request that the applicant appear before it. If the committee determines that an applicant meets all requirements for admission, it will report that recommendation to the judge or judges of the division. If the committee does not recommend an applicant for admission, the chair of the Divisional Committee will promptly inform the applicant.

(3) *Review by the Court.* An applicant who is not recommended for admission may request that the court review the application. A request for review must be made in writing within 30 days of receipt of the committee's notification, addressed to the judge or judges of the division, with a copy to the committee chair. Upon receipt of a request for court review, the chair will send the committee's file on the applicant to the court.

(e) Procedure for Admission.

(1) *In General.* After approval by the committee, and upon motion of a member of the bar of this court made in open court, an attorney may be admitted to practice. To complete admission, the attorney must pay the prescribed admission fee, and must take in open court the following oath or affirmation:

"I do solemnly [swear or affirm] that I will discharge the duties of attorney and counselor of this court faithfully, that I will demean myself uprightly under the law and the highest ethics of our profession, and that I will support and defend the Constitution of the United States."

(2) *Special Procedure for Non–Resident Attorney.* A non-resident attorney who has completed all other requirements for admission may, with the approval of a judge of the division where the application was filed, have the oath or affirmation of admission administered by a judge in another federal judicial district. When the attorney files the oath or affirmation with the clerk and pays the prescribed admission fee, the attorney will be admitted to practice in this district.

(f) Appearance Pro Hac Vice.

(1) *In General.* An attorney who is licensed by the highest court of a state or another federal district court, but who is not admitted to practice before this court, may represent a party in this court pro hac vice only by permission of the judge presiding. Unless excused by the judge presiding, an attorney is ordinarily required to apply for admission to the bar of this court.

(2) *Procedure.* An attorney seeking admission pro hac vice must make application on a form prescribed by the court, and must pay the prescribed fee to the clerk. An attorney admitted pro hac vice must read and comply with the Local Court Rules for the Western District of Texas. By appearing in any case, an attorney becomes subject to the rules of this Court.

(3) *Bankruptcy Court.* Admission to practice pro hac vice before the district's bankruptcy court rests in the sole discretion of the bankruptcy judge to whom the motion is addressed. Such admission is limited to the particular case or matter for which it is approved; it is not a general admission to practice before the bankruptcy court or the district court.

(g) Special Procedures for an Attorney Employed by a Governmental Entity. An application for admission by an attorney employed by the U.S. Department of Justice, the Attorney General of Texas, the Federal Public Defender for the district, or other governmental entity must be made on the form prescribed by the court, and supported with the required certificate of good standing. In lieu of submitting two letters of recommendation, an attorney covered by this subdivision need only submit a letter of recommendation from his or her supervising attorney. In addition, such an attorney is exempt while so employed from payment of any fee for admission, pro hac vice appearance, or membership renewal.

(h) Renewal of Membership. A member of the bar of this court must renew the membership every 3 years after admission by paying the prescribed renewal fee to the clerk. If the renewal fee is not timely paid, the attorney will be removed from the rolls of the court. An attorney so removed who wishes to practice in this court must reapply for admission.

[Effective January 1, 1994. Amended effective February 17, 1995; September 1, 1995; January 2, 2001; April 17, 2007.]

RULE AT–2. LOCAL COUNSEL

A judge presiding has discretion to require, upon notice, that an attorney who resides outside the district designate as local counsel an attorney who is licensed in this Court and maintains a law office in this district. Local counsel must have authority to act as attorney of record for all purposes, and

must be prepared to present and argue the party's position at any hearing or status conference called.

[Effective April 17, 2007.]

RULE AT–3. WITHDRAWAL OF ATTORNEY

An attorney seeking to withdraw from a case must file a motion specifying the reasons for withdrawal and providing the name and office address of the successor attorney. If the successor attorney is not known, the motion must set forth the client's name, address, and telephone number, and must bear either the client's signature or a detailed explanation why the client's signature could not be obtained after due diligence.

[Effective April 17, 2007.]

RULE AT–4. STANDARDS FOR PRETRIAL CONDUCT

(a) Obligation to Cooperate. Before noticing or scheduling a deposition, hearing, or other pretrial event, a lawyer should consult and work with opposing counsel to accommodate the needs and reasonable requests of all witnesses and participating lawyers. In scheduling a pretrial event, lawyers should strive to agree upon a mutually convenient time and place, seeking to minimize travel expense and to allow adequate time for preparation. If a lawyer needs to reschedule a deposition or other pretrial event, the lawyer should give prompt notice to all other counsel, explaining the conflict or other compelling reason for rescheduling.

(b) Requests for Extensions of Time. The court expects a lawyer to grant other lawyers' requests for reasonable extensions of time to respond to discovery, pretrial motions, and other pretrial matters. Opposing such requests wastes resources, unless the client's legitimate interests will be adversely affected.

(c) Written Submissions. Briefs and memoranda should not refer to or rely on facts that are not properly of record. A lawyer may, however, present historical, economic, or sociological data if the applicable rules of evidence support the data's admissibility. Neither written submissions nor oral presentations should disparage the integrity, intelligence, morals, ethics, or personal behavior of an adversary unless such matters are directly relevant under the controlling substantive law.

(d) Communication With Adversaries. A lawyer's role is to zealously advance the legitimate interests of the client, while maintaining appropriate standards of civility and decorum. In dealing with others, a lawyer should not reflect any ill feelings that the client may have toward the adversary. A lawyer should treat all other lawyers, all parties, and all witnesses courteously, not only in court, but also in other written and oral communication. A lawyer should refrain from acting upon or manifesting bias or prejudice toward any person involved in the litigation.

(e) Discovery. A lawyer should conduct discovery to elicit relevant facts and evidence, and not for an improper purpose, such as to harass, intimidate, or unduly burden another party or a witness. When a discovery dispute arises, opposing lawyers should attempt to resolve it by working cooperatively together. A lawyer should refrain from filing motions to compel or for sanctions unless all reasonable efforts to resolve the dispute with opposing counsel have been exhausted.

(f) Motion Practice. Before filing a non-dispositive motion, a lawyer should make a reasonable effort to resolve the issue without involving the court. A lawyer who has no valid objection to an opponent's proposed motion should promptly make this position known to opposing counsel. If, after opposing a motion, a lawyer determines that the opposition was mistaken, then the lawyer should promptly so advise opposing counsel and the court.

(g) Settlement and Alternative Dispute Resolution.

(1) A lawyer should educate the client early in the legal process about various methods of resolving disputes without trial, including mediation and neutral case evaluation. A lawyer should advise the client of the benefits of settlement, including savings to the client, greater control over the process and the result, and a more expeditious resolution of the dispute. At the earliest practicable time, a lawyer should provide the client with a realistic assessment of the potential outcome of the case so that the client may effectively assess various approaches to resolving the dispute. As new information is obtained during the pretrial phase, the lawyer should revise the assessment as necessary. When enough is known about the case to make settlement negotiations meaningful, a lawyer should explore settlement with the client and with opposing counsel.

(2) A lawyer must promptly inform the court of any settlement, whether partial or entire, with any party, or the discontinuance of any issue.

(h) Stipulations; Expediting Trial. In civil cases, a lawyer should stipulate in advance with opposing counsel to all non-controverted facts; give opposing counsel, on reasonable request, an opportunity to inspect, in advance, all non-impeaching evidence as the law permits; and, in general, take reasonable steps to avoid delays and to expedite the trial.

[Effective April 17, 2007.]

RULE AT–5. STANDARDS FOR CONDUCT BEFORE THE JUDGE AND JURY

The dignity, decorum and courtesy that traditionally characterize the courts of civilized nations are not empty formalities. They are essential to a courtroom atmosphere in which justice can be achieved. Accordingly, this court requires the following:

(a) A lawyer must be punctual in making all court appearances and fulfilling all professional commitments. In case of tardiness or absence from a court appearance, a lawyer should promptly notify the court and opposing counsel.

(b) An attorney must be attired in a proper and dignified manner, and should abstain from any apparel or ornament calculated to attract attention. A lawyer should refrain from assuming an undignified posture.

(c) A lawyer must display a courteous, dignified and respectful attitude toward the judge presiding, not for the sake of the judge's person, but to show respect for and confidence in the judicial office. A lawyer must rise when addressing, or being addressed by, the judge.

(d) A lawyer must never be unfair or abusive or inconsiderate to adverse witnesses or opposing litigants, or ask any question not intended to legitimately impeach but only to insult or degrade the witness.

(e) A lawyer must avoid disparaging personal remarks or acrimony toward opposing counsel.

(f) A lawyer must advise the client, witnesses, and spectators of the behavior and decorum required in the courtroom, and take all reasonable steps to prevent disorder or disruption of court proceedings.

(g) A lawyer must disclose to the judge and opposing counsel any information of which the lawyer is aware that a juror or a prospective juror has or may have any interest, direct or indirect, in the outcome of the case, or is acquainted or connected in any manner with any lawyer in the case or any partner or associate or employee of the lawyer, or with any litigant, or with any person who has appeared or is expected to appear as a witness, unless the judge and opposing counsel have previously been made aware of that fact by voir dire examination or otherwise.

(h) During the trial of a case a lawyer connected with the case must not communicate with or cause another to communicate with any member of the jury, and a lawyer who is not connected with the case must not communicate with or cause another to communicate with a juror concerning the case.

(i) A lawyer should avoid, as much as possible, approaching the bench. A lawyer should anticipate questions that may arise during the trial, and take them up with the court and opposing counsel in a pretrial hearing. If, however, it becomes necessary for an attorney to confer with the court at the bench, leave of court should be requested.

(j) A lawyer must question witnesses and deliver jury arguments from the lectern, which may be moved to face the jury. If it becomes necessary to question or argue from another location, leave of court should be requested.

(k) A lawyer must hand all papers intended for the court to see to the courtroom deputy clerk, who will pass them up to the judge. Hand to the clerk, rather than the court reporter, any exhibits to be marked which have not previously been identified; and give the clerk, as soon as convenient before the trial, a list of witnesses showing the probable order in which they will be called.

(*l*) Photographing, broadcasting or televising any judicial proceeding or any person directly or indirectly involved in a proceeding, whether court is in session or not, in or from any part of a United States Courthouse, is prohibited, except with the permission of the judge presiding.

(m) Audio recorders, audio- or video-recording cell phones, or other means of recording the proceedings must not be brought into a courtroom, except with the permission of the judge presiding. This rule does not apply to such recorders or other devices used by, and under the direction and control of, a judicial officer or the official court reporter.

(n) Cell phones, pagers, e-mail devices, and music players must be turned off while inside a courtroom.

(o) The following are prohibited in a courtroom:

(1) using tobacco in any form;

(2) consuming or possessing beverages or edibles (except as permitted by the judge presiding);

(3) chewing gum while court is in session;

(4) unnecessary talking or other unnecessary noises while court is in session.

Effective April 17, 2007.]

RULE AT–6. PUBLICITY AND TRIAL MANAGEMENT

(a) **In General.** A lawyer should try a case in court and not in the news media. A lawyer must not make an extrajudicial statement that a reasonable person would expect to be disseminated by means of public communication if the lawyer knows or reasonably should know that the statement has a substantial likelihood of materially prejudicing an adjudicative proceeding.

(b) **Criminal Investigation.** With respect to a grand jury or other pending investigation of a criminal matter, a lawyer participating in the investigation must refrain from making any extrajudicial statement, for dissemination by any means of public communication, that goes beyond the public record or that is not necessary to inform the public that the investigation is underway, to describe the general scope of the investigation, to warn the public of any dangers, to obtain assistance in the apprehension of a suspect, or to otherwise aid in the investigation.

(c) **Criminal Prosecution.** From time of arrest, issuance of an arrest warrant, or filing of a complaint, information, or indictment in any criminal matter until the commencement of trial or disposition without trial, a lawyer associated with the prosecution or defense must not release or authorize the release of any extrajudicial statement, for dissemination by any means of public communication, related to that matter and concerning:

(1) the prior criminal record (including arrests and criminal charges), or the character or reputation of the accused, except that the lawyer may make a factual statement of the accused's name, age, residence, occupation, and family status, and if the accused has not been apprehended, a lawyer associated with the prosecution may release any information necessary to aid in his apprehension or to warn the public of dangers he may present;

(2) the existence or contents of any confession, admission, or statement given by the accused, or the refusal or failure of the accused to make any statement;

(3) the performance of any examinations or tests or the accused's refusal or failure to submit to an examination or test;

(4) the identity, testimony, or credibility of prospective witnesses, except that the lawyer may announce the identity of the victim if the announcement is not otherwise prohibited by law;

(5) the possibility of a plea of guilty to the offense charged or a lesser offense; or

(6) any opinion as to the accused's guilt or innocence or as to the merits of the case or the evidence in the case.

(d) **Criminal Trial.** During the trial of any criminal matter, including jury selection, a lawyer associated with the prosecution or defense must not give or authorize any extrajudicial statement or interview, relating to the trial or the parties or issues in the trial, for dissemination by any means of public communication, except that the lawyer may quote from or refer without comment to public records filed in the case.

(e) **Sentencing Phase.** After guilt is found in a criminal case and before sentence is imposed, a lawyer associated with the prosecution or defense must not make or authorize any extrajudicial statement for dissemination by any means of public communication if there is a reasonable likelihood that the statement will affect the sentence.

(f) **Permitted Statements in Criminal Matters.** This rule does not preclude the lawyer, in the proper discharge of his or her official or professional duty, from:

(1) announcing the fact and circumstances of arrest (including time and place of arrest, resistance, pursuit, and use of weapons), the identity of the investigating and arresting officer or agency, and the length of the investigation;

(2) making an announcement, at the time of seizure of any physical evidence other than a confession, admission or statement, limited to a description of the evidence seized;

(3) disclosing the nature, substance, or text of the charge, including a brief description of the offense charged;

(4) quoting or referring without comment to public records of the court in the case;

(5) announcing the scheduling or result of any stage in the judicial process;

(6) requesting assistance in obtaining evidence; or

(7) announcing without elaboration that the accused denies the charges made against him.

(g) **Special Orders.** In a widely publicized or sensational case, the court on motion of either party or its own motion, may issue a special order governing extrajudicial statements by participants likely to interfere with the rights of the accused to a fair trial by an impartial jury, the courtroom seating and conduct of spectators and news media representatives, the management and sequestration of jurors and witnesses, and any other matters the court may deem appropriate. The order might address some or all of the following subjects, among others:

(1) a proscription of extrajudicial statements by participants in the trial, including lawyers, parties, witnesses, jurors, and court officials, which have a substantial likelihood of divulging prejudicial matter not of public record in the case;

(2) specific directives regarding the clearing of courthouse entrances and hallways and the management of the jury and witnesses during the course of the trial to avoid their mingling with or being in proximity of reporters, photographers, par-

ties, lawyers, and others, both in entering and leaving the courtroom and courthouse, and during recesses in the trial;

(3) a specific directive that the jurors refrain from reading, listening to, or watching news reports concerning the case, and that they similarly refrain from discussing the case with anyone during the trial and from communicating with others in any manner during their deliberations;

(4) sequestration of the jury on motion of either party or on the court's own, without disclosing any movant's identity;

(5) a directive that the names and addresses of jurors or prospective jurors not be publicly released except as required by statute, and that no photograph be taken or sketch made of any juror within the environs of the court;

(6) insulation of witnesses from news interviews during the trial period;

(7) specific directives regarding the seating of spectators and representatives of the news media.

[Effective April 17, 2007.]

RULE AT–7. DISCIPLINE OF ATTORNEYS

(a) **Standards of Professional Conduct.** Members of the bar of this court and any attorney permitted to practice before this court must comply with the standards of professional conduct set out in the Texas Disciplinary Rules of Professional Conduct, Texas Government Code, Title 2, Subtitle G, App. A, art. X, sec. 9 (Vernon) which are hereby adopted as the standards of professional conduct of this court. This specification is not exhaustive of the standards of professional conduct. For matters not covered by the Texas rules, the American Bar Association's Model Rules of Professional Conduct should be consulted.

(b) **District Disciplinary Committee.** There is constituted a District Disciplinary Committee, which assists the district court and the bankruptcy court in investigating complaints about the qualification, conduct, and performance of members of their bar.

(1) *Composition.* The committee has 15 members. Those eligible for service on the committee are attorneys licensed to practice in this district and in good standing, and residing within the district. The committee should include civil, criminal, and bankruptcy practitioners. Five members must be residents of the Austin and Waco Divisions, five members must be residents of the San Antonio and Del Rio Divisions, and five members must be residents of the El Paso, Midland–Odessa and Pecos Divisions. The members are appointed by the active judges resident in, or responsible for, those divisions. The chair and vice-chair are designated by the chief judge of the district.

(2) *Terms.* Membership terms should be staggered so that one third of the members' terms expire each year. The term is 3 years, unless a shorter period is required to achieve staggered terms. The terms of members and the chair may be renewed one or more times.

(c) **Grounds for Referral to the District Disciplinary Committee.** An attorney may be referred by any Magistrate Judge, Bankruptcy Judge or District Judge to the District Disciplinary Committee for appropriate review, investigation, and recommendation if there is reason to believe that the attorney:

(1) has been convicted of a felony offense or a crime involving dishonesty or false statement in any state or federal court;

(2) had his or her license to practice law in any jurisdiction suspended, revoked, or otherwise limited by any appropriate disciplinary authority;

(3) resigned his or her license to practice law in any state or any federal court;

(4) has engaged in conduct that violates the Texas Disciplinary Rules of Professional Conduct;

(5) fails to comply with any rule or order issued by a judge of this court;

(6) presents an impediment to the orderly administration of justice or the integrity of the court; or

(7) represents a client in such a manner as to raise a serious question concerning the quality of the attorney's professional performance.

(d) **Discipline Imposed by a Judge Presiding.** Notwithstanding any other provision of these rules, any judge, including a bankruptcy judge or a magistrate judge, has inherent authority to discipline an attorney who appears before him or her. However, any judge contemplating disbarring an attorney or preventing an attorney from practicing district-wide will refer the attorney to the District Disciplinary Committee. If a judge believes emergency circumstances exist that require the immediate suspension of an attorney, that judge may request that all active district judges immediately consider the matter. Upon a majority vote of the active district judges, an attorney may immediately be suspended from practicing in the district pending a report and recommendation from the District Disciplinary Committee. If a bankruptcy judge believes emergency circumstances exist that requires the immediate suspension of an attorney, that bankruptcy judge may request that all active district and bankruptcy judges immediately consider the matter. Upon a majority vote of the active district and bankruptcy judges, an attorney may immediately be suspended from practicing in the district pending a report and recommendation from the District Disciplinary Committee.

(e) **Self–Reporting by Attorneys.** A member of the bar of this court must promptly report in writing to the clerk, with full details and copies of pertinent documents, if any of the following occur:

(1) the attorney is convicted of a felony or a crime involving dishonesty or false statement;

(2) the attorney loses or relinquishes, temporarily or permanently, the right to practice in any court of record (other than voluntarily relinquishment, not under any disciplinary order or threat of discipline); or

(3) the attorney is disciplined, publicly or privately, by any bar, court, court agency, or court committee.

(f) Procedure Upon a Referral.

(1) *Notice.* Promptly upon receipt of a referral, the chair of the District Disciplinary Committee must inform the subject attorney in writing of the nature of the referral and the attorney's obligations under this rule.

(2) *Answer.* Within 14 days after receiving notice of a referral under this rule, the attorney must respond in writing to the committee chair. The respondent attorney must admit or deny each claim asserted, and state concisely any defense to a claim.

(3) *Screening.* The chair will assign the referral along with the respondent's response to a screening subcommittee. The subcommittee consists of one or more members of the full committee designated by the chair who reside in the same region as the referred attorney (e.g., Austin/Waco; San Antonio/Del Rio; West Texas). At least one member of the screening subcommittee must be an attorney who practices in the same area as the referred attorney (e.g., civil, criminal or bankruptcy). The subcommittee will conduct such preliminary inquiry it deems appropriate and may request the respondent to meet with it informally to provide an explanation. After this screening, if the subcommittee determines no further investigation is required and no discipline should be imposed, it will so inform the committee chair. The chair will then inform the chief judge and the respondent of the recommendation.

(4) *Assignment to a Panel.* If the screening subcommittee determines that the matter may warrant disciplinary action, it will inform the committee chair. The chair will then designate a panel and assign the matter to it. The panel must include three or more members of the full committee who reside in the same region as the respondent (e.g., Austin/Waco; San Antonio/Del Rio; West Texas). At least one member of the panel must be an attorney who practices in the same area as the referred attorney (e.g. civil, criminal or bankruptcy). Members of the initial screening subcommittee may serve as members of the panel. The chair will notify the respondent in writing of this assignment and what matters will be investigated.

(5) *Investigation.* No earlier than 10 days after notice to the respondent of the assignment, the panel will conduct such investigation it deems appropriate including questioning witnesses and holding a hearing with the respondent present. Full cooperation with any committee investigation is an obligation of any member of the bar of this court.

(6) *Panel Report and Recommendation.* After investigation the panel will render a report and recommendation as to whether the respondent committed any violation and what disciplinary action, if any, should be imposed. Absent good cause shown by the chair of the District Disciplinary Committee, the court expects that a report and recommendation will be completed within 6 months after the referral. The chair will send the complete report and recommendation to the chief judge and a summary of the report and recommendation to the respondent.

(7) *Objections to Report and Recommendation.* Within 14 days after receipt of the summary report and recommendation, the respondent may submit objections to it, seek revisions, and suggest alternatives to the recommendation. The panel, after considering the response, may modify, amend, revoke, or adhere to its original recommendation and will so inform the committee chair. The chair will then send a copy of the final report and recommendation to the chief judge and a summary final report and recommendation to the respondent.

(g) Determination by a District Judge. Within 7 days after receipt of the summary final report and recommendation, the respondent may contest any recommendation by written submission to the chief judge. Whether contested or not, the chief judge will assign the matter to a district judge for determination. The judge may conduct a hearing, and may appoint any member of the court's bar to assist in the hearing. The judge's decision as to whether disciplinary action is warranted, and what sanction to impose, is a final ruling of the court.

(h) Confidentiality. All papers pertaining to a matter referred to the committee must be kept confidential, except as otherwise provided above, unless the respondent requests in writing that the papers be opened to the public.

(i) Referral to Other Disciplinary Authority. The chief judge may forward a copy of the committee's records and any court action regarding an attorney to the appropriate disciplinary authority of any bar or court that authorizes the attorney to practice law.

[Effective April 17, 2007. Amended effective December 1, 2009.]

RULE AT–8. QUALIFIED LAW STUDENTS AND UNLICENSED LAW SCHOOL GRADUATES

(a) A qualified law student or a qualified unlicensed law school graduate who has been certified under Texas Government Code § 81.102 and the Texas Supreme Court's "Rules and Regulations Governing the Participation of Qualified Law Students and Qualified Unlicensed Law School Graduates in the Trial of Cases in Texas" may be allowed to participate in hearings in this Court, with the permission of the judge presiding, under the following terms:

(1) The student or unlicensed graduate must provide the Clerk's Office a copy (front and back) of his or her State Bar of Texas identification card. In so doing, the student or unlicensed graduate certifies that he or she has read and is familiar with the Western District of Texas Local Rules and will abide by them.

(2) The Clerk's Office must retain copies of the identification card on file.

(3) The supervising attorney named on the identification card and accompanying the student or unlicensed graduate in court must be a member in good standing of the bar of this court.

(b) If the student or unlicensed law graduate is appearing with an attorney employed by a governmental entity, the requirement for errors and omissions insurance is waived.

(c) The scope of participation of a student or unlicensed graduate in any hearing rests within the discretion of the judge presiding.

[Effective January 1, 1994. Amended effective April 17, 2007.]

RULE AT–9. CHANGE OF ADDRESS

An attorney who changes his or her office address, telephone number, facsimile number, or e-mail address must, within 30 days after the change, file with the clerk a notice of the change, along with any new information.

[Effective January 1, 1994. Amended effective April 17, 2007.]

SECTION IV. APPENDICES
APPENDIX A. INFORMATION REQUIRED—MOTION FOR CLASS ACTION CERTIFICATION

A motion to certify a class must include, but is not limited to, the following:

(1) A brief statement of the case.

(2) A statement defining the class plaintiff seeks to have certified including its geographical and temporal scope.

(3) A description of plaintiff's particular grievance and why that claim qualifies plaintiff as a member of the class as defined.

(4) Whether the plaintiff contends that the action may be maintained under Rule 23(b)(1), Rule 23(b)(2), or Rule 23(b)(3) and why.

(5) A statement respecting the four prerequisites of Federal Rule of Civil Procedure 23(a). The statement shall set forth: a. The anticipated number of class members and how this number was determined. b. The common questions of law and fact involved. c. The reasons why plaintiff's claim is typical of those of the other class members. d. The reason why representation by the named plaintiff is adequate to protect the interests of the class. This part of the statement shall specifically answer the following questions:

(i) Is the claim of the named plaintiff presently or potentially in conflict with that of any members of the class?

(ii) Will the claims of the class require subclasses presently or in the future?

(iii) What is the prior experience of counsel for the plaintiff that would indicate capability to handle the lawsuit?

(iv) Is counsel presently representing or has he at any time represented, a class in any other class action, and if so, when and how many instances?

(v) How many cases is plaintiff's counsel now handling in which class action allegations are made?

(6) A statement describing any other pending actions in any court against the defendants alleging the same or similar causes of action.

(7) A statement that the attorney for the named plaintiff has discussed and thoroughly explained to the plaintiff the nature of a class action and potential advantages and disadvantages to the named plaintiff by proceeding in a class action rather than individually.

(8) A statement of the proposed notices to the members of the class and how and when the notices will be given, including a statement regarding security deposit for the cost of notices.

(9) A description of the extent of any settlement negotiations that have taken place and the likelihood of settlement with the named plaintiff on an individual basis. If such settlement is likely, include a statement specifying: a. Whether or not counsel have any knowledge of any person who has relied on the fact that this suit was initially filed as a class action. b. The manner in which counsel will protect the class in the event of settlement with the named plaintiff on an individual basis.

(10) A statement of any other matters that the plaintiff deems necessary and proper to the expedition of a decision on the motion and the speedy resolution of the case on the merits.

[Effective January 1, 1994. Amended effective December 1, 2009; December 2, 2011; April 26, 2012.]

APPENDIX B. SCHEDULING ORDER

UNITED STATES DISTRICT COURT
WESTERN DISTRICT OF TEXAS
_____ DIVISION

_____	§
Plaintiff,	§
	§
	§
NO.	§
_____	§
Defendant.	§

SCHEDULING ORDER

Pursuant to Rule 16, Federal Rules of Civil Procedure, the Court issues the following Scheduling Order:

1. A report on alternative dispute resolution in compliance with Rule CV-88 shall be filed by __.

2. The parties asserting claims for relief shall submit a written offer of settlement to opposing parties by __, and each opposing party shall respond, in writing, by _____.

3. The parties shall file all motions to amend or supplement pleadings or to join additional parties by _____.

4. All parties asserting claims for relief shall file their designation of testifying experts and shall serve on all parties, but not file, the materials required by Federal Rule of Civil Procedure 26(a)(2)(B) by _____. Parties resisting claims for relief shall file their designation of testifying experts and shall serve on all parties, but not file, the materials required by Federal Rule of Civil Procedure 26(a)(2)(B) by _____. All designations of rebuttal experts shall be filed within 14 days of receipt of the report of the opposing expert.

5. An objection to the reliability of an expert's proposed testimony under Federal Rule of Evidence 702 shall be made by motion, specifically stating the basis for the objection and identifying the objectionable testimony, not later than ___ days of receipt of the written report of the expert's proposed testimony, or not later than days of the expert's deposition, if a deposition is taken, whichever is later.

6. The parties shall complete all discovery on or before _____. Counsel may by agreement continue discovery beyond the deadline, but there will be no intervention by the Court except in extraordinary circumstances, and no trial setting will be vacated because of information obtained in post-deadline discovery.

7. All dispositive motions as defined in Rule CV-7(c) shall be filed no later than _____.

8. This case is set for trial [docket call, or jury selection] on at ___.m. The parties should consult Rule CV-16 regarding matters to be filed in advance of trial.

SIGNED this day of _____.

UNITED STATES DISTRICT JUDGE

[Amended effective May 16, 1994; December 17, 2000; April 3, 2001; December 17, 2009; April 26, 2012.]

APPENDIX B–1. NOTICE OF RIGHT TO CONSENT TO TRIAL BY MAGISTRATE JUDGE

UNITED STATES DISTRICT COURT
WESTERN DISTRICT OF TEXAS
_____ DIVISION

_____,	)
Plaintiff,	)
	)
vs.	) NO. _____
	)
_____,	)
Defendant.	)

NOTICE OF RIGHT TO CONSENT TO TRIAL BY MAGISTRATE JUDGE

Pursuant to 28 U.S.C. § 636(c)(1), all full-time United States Magistrate Judges are authorized and empowered to try any civil case, jury or nonjury, with the consent of all parties to the lawsuit. Because of the crowded condition of the criminal docket in this District and the difficulty in reaching civil cases for trial, you may wish to consent to the trial of your case by a United States Magistrate Judge. Your decision should be communicated to the United States District Clerk's Office. Consent forms are available in the Clerk's office. Your consent to trial by a Magistrate Judge must be voluntary, and you are free to withhold consent without suffering any adverse consequences. If all parties do consent to trial of this case by a Magistrate Judge, the Court will enter an order referring the case to a Magistrate Judge for trial and for entry of judgment.

_____
UNITED STATES DISTRICT JUDGE

_____
Date

[Effective January 1, 1994. Amended effective April 3, 2001; April 26, 2012.]

APPENDIX C. LOCAL RULES FOR THE ASSIGNMENT OF DUTIES TO UNITED STATES MAGISTRATE JUDGES

RULE 1. AUTHORITY OF UNITED STATES MAGISTRATE JUDGES

(a) Duties Under 28 U.S.C. § 636(a). Each United States Magistrate Judge of this Court is authorized to perform the duties prescribed by 28 U.S.C. § 636(a), and may:

(1) Exercise all the powers and duties conferred or imposed upon United States Commissioners by law and the Federal Rules of Criminal Procedure.

(2) Administer oaths and affirmations, impose conditions of release under 18 U.S.C. § 3146, and take acknowledgments, affidavits and depositions; and

(3) Conduct extradition proceedings, in accordance with 18 U.S.C. § 3184.

(b) Disposition of Misdemeanor Cases—18 U.S.C. § 3401. A magistrate judge may:

(1) Try persons accused of, and sentence persons convicted of, misdemeanors committed within this district in accordance with 18 U.S.C. § 3401;

(2) Direct the probation service of the court to conduct a presentence investigation in any misdemeanor case; and

(3) Conduct a jury trial in any misdemeanor case where the defendant so requests and is entitled to trial by jury under the Constitution and laws of the United States.

(c) Determination of Non–Dispositive Pretrial Matters—28 U.S.C. § 636(b)(1)(A). A magistrate judge may hear and determine any procedural or discovery motion or other pretrial matter in a civil or criminal case, other than the motions which are specified in subsection 1(d), infra, of these rules.

(d) Recommendations Regarding Case—Dispositive Motions–28 U.S.C. § 636(b)(1)(B).

(1) A magistrate judge may submit to a judge of the court a report containing proposed findings of fact and recommendations for disposition by the judge of the following pretrial motions in civil and criminal cases:

A. Motions for injunctive relief, including temporary restraining orders and preliminary and permanent injunctions;

B. Motions for judgment on the pleadings;

C. Motions for summary judgment;

D. Motions to dismiss or permit the maintenance of a class action;

E. Motions to dismiss for failure to state a claim upon which relief may be granted;

F. Motions to involuntarily dismiss an action;

G. Motions for review of default judgments;

H. Motions to dismiss or quash an indictment or information made by a defendant; and

I. Motions to suppress evidence in a criminal case.

(2) A magistrate judge may determine any preliminary matters and conduct any necessary evidentiary hearing or other proceeding arising in the exercise of the authority conferred by this subsection.

(e) Prisoner Cases Under 28 U.S.C. §§ 2254 and 2255. A magistrate judge may perform any or all of the duties imposed upon a judge by the rules governing proceedings in the United States District Courts under § 2254 and § 2255 of Title 28, United States Code. In so doing, a magistrate judge may issue any preliminary orders and conduct any necessary evidentiary hearing or other appropriate proceeding and shall submit to a judge a report containing proposed findings of fact and recommendations for disposition of the petition by the judge. Any order disposing of the petition may be made only by a judge.

(f) Prisoner Cases Under 42 U.S.C. § 1983 and 28 U.S.C. § 2241. A magistrate judge may issue any preliminary orders and conduct any necessary evidentiary hearing or other appropriate proceeding and shall submit to a judge a report containing proposed findings of fact and recommendations for the disposition of petitions filed by prisoners pursuant to 42 U.S.C. § 1983 and 28 U.S.C. § 2241.

(g) Special Master References. A magistrate judge may be designated by a judge to serve as a special master in appropriate civil cases in accordance with 28 U.S.C. § 636(b)(2) and Rule 53 of the Federal Rules of Civil Procedure. Upon the consent of the parties, a magistrate judge may be designated by a judge to serve as a special master in any civil case, notwithstanding the limitations of Rule 53(b) of the Federal Rules of Civil Procedure.

(h) Review of Administrative Agency Proceedings. In a suit for judicial review of a final decision of an administrative agency, a magistrate judge may be designated by a judge to review the record of administrative proceedings and submit to the district judge a report and recommendation concerning (a) any defects in the agency proceedings which constitute a violation of statute or regulation or a violation of due process, (b) whether the matter should be remanded to the agency for additional factual determinations, and (c) whether the record contains substantial evidence in support of the agency decision.

(i) Conduct of Trials and Disposition of Civil Cases Upon Consent of the Parties—28 U.S.C. § 636(c). Upon the consent of the parties, a full-time magistrate judge may conduct any or all proceedings in any civil case which is filed in this court, including the conduct of a jury or non-jury trial, and may order the entry of a final judgment, in accordance with 28 U.S.C. § 636(c). In the course of conducting such proceedings upon consent of the parties, a magistrate judge may hear and determine any and all pretrial and post-trial motions which are filed by the parties, including case-dispositive motions.

(j) Other Duties. A magistrate judge is also authorized to:

(1) Exercise general supervision of civil and criminal calendars, conduct calendar and status calls, and determine motions to expedite or postpone the trial of cases for the judges;

(2) Conduct pretrial conferences, settlement conferences, omnibus hearings, and related pretrial proceedings in civil and criminal cases;

(3) Conduct arraignments in criminal cases not triable by the magistrate judge and take not guilty pleas in such cases;

(4) Receive grand jury returns in accordance with Rule 6(f) of the Federal Rules of Criminal Procedure;

(5) Accept waivers of indictment, pursuant to Rule 7(b) of the Federal Rules of Criminal Procedure;

(6) Accept petit jury verdicts in the absence of a judge;

(7) Conduct necessary proceedings leading to the potential revocation of misdemeanor probation and revocation of felony or misdemeanor supervised release;

(8) Issue subpoenas, writs of habeas corpus ad testificandum or habeas corpus ad prosequendum, or other orders necessary to obtain the presence of parties, witnesses or evidence needed for court proceedings;

(9) Order the exoneration or forfeiture of bonds;

(10) Perform the functions specified in 18 U.S.C. § 4107, 4108, 4109, regarding proceedings for verification of consent by offenders to transfer to or from the United States and the appointment of counsel therein;

(11) Preside over a naturalization ceremony and administer the oath required by 8 U.S.C. § 1448(a);

(12) Supervise proceedings on requests for letters rogatory in civil and criminal cases if designated by a district judge under 28 U.S.C. § 1782(a);

(13) Consider and rule upon applications for administrative inspection warrants and orders permitting entry upon a taxpayer's premises to effect levies in satisfaction of unpaid tax deficits;

(14) Issue orders authorizing the installation and use of pen registers, traps and traces, and issue orders directing a communications common carrier, including a telephone company, to provide assistance to a named federal investigative agency in accomplishing the installation of traps, traces and pen registers; and

(15) Perform any additional duty as is not inconsistent with the Constitution and laws of the United States.

RULE 2.   ASSIGNMENT OF MATTERS TO MAGISTRATE JUDGES

(a) General. The method of assignment of duties to a magistrate judge and for the allocation of duties among the several magistrate judges of the court shall be made in accordance with orders of the court or by special designation of a judge.

(b) Misdemeanor Cases. All misdemeanor cases shall be assigned, upon the filing of an information, complaint, or violation notice, or the return of an indictment, to a magistrate judge, who shall proceed in accordance with the provisions of 18 U.S.C. § 3401 and Rule 58, Federal Rules of Criminal Procedure.

RULE 3.   PROCEDURE BEFORE THE MAGISTRATE JUDGE

(a) In General. In performing duties for the court, a magistrate judge shall conform to all applicable provisions of federal statutes and rules, to the local rules of this court, and to the requirements specified in any order of reference from a judge.

(b) Special Provisions for the Disposition of Civil Cases by a Magistrate Judge on Consent of the Parties—28 U.S.C. § 636(c).

(1) *Notice.* The clerk of court shall notify the parties in all civil cases that they may consent to have a magistrate judge conduct any or all proceedings in the case and order the entry of a final judgment. Such notice shall be handed or mailed to the plaintiff or his/her representative at the time an action is filed and to other parties as attachments to copies of the complaint and summons, when served. Additional notices may be furnished to the parties at later stages of the proceedings, and may be included with pretrial notices and instructions.

(2) *Execution of Consent.* The parties may sign separate consent forms; however, consent forms signed by all the parties or their representatives will also be accepted. The consent forms should be sent to the clerk of court. Unless all parties have consented to the reference, the decision of each party as indicated on the consent forms shall not be made known to any judge or magistrate judge. No magistrate judge, judge, or other court official may attempt to persuade or induce any party to consent to the reference of any matter to a magistrate judge. This rule, however, shall not preclude a judge or magistrate judge from informing the parties that they have the option of referring a case to a magistrate judge.

(3) *Reference.* After the consent form has been executed and filed, the clerk shall transmit it to the judge to whom the case has been assigned for approval and referral of the case to a magistrate judge. Once the case has been assigned to a magistrate judge, the magistrate judge shall have the authority to conduct any and all proceedings to which the parties have consented and to direct the clerk of court to enter a final judgment in the same manner as if a judge had presided.

RULE 4.   REVIEW AND APPEAL

(a) Appeal of Non–Dispositive Matters—28 U.S.C. § 636(b)(1)(A). Any party may appeal from a magistrate judge's order determining a motion or matter under subsection 1(c) of these rules, supra, within 14 days after issuance of the magistrate judge's order, unless a different time is prescribed by the magistrate judge or a judge. Such party shall file with the clerk of court, and serve on the magistrate judge and all parties, a written statement of appeal which shall specifically designate the order, or part thereof, appealed from and the basis for any objection thereto. A judge of the court shall consider the appeal and shall set aside any portion of the magistrate judge's order found to be clearly erroneous or contrary to law. The judge may also reconsider sua sponte any matter determined by a magistrate judge under this rule.

(b) Review of Case–Dispositive Motions and Prisoner Litigation—28 U.S.C. § 636(b)(1)(B). Any party may object to a magistrate judge's proposed findings, recommendations or report under subsections 1(d), (e), (f) and (h) of these rules, supra, within 14 days after being served with a copy thereof. The clerk of court shall notify the parties of this right when serving copies of the report. Such party shall file with the clerk of court, and serve on the magistrate judge and all parties, written objections which shall specifically identify the portions of the proposed findings, recommendations or report to which objection is made and the basis for such objections. A judge shall make a de novo determination of those portions of the report or specified proposed findings or recommendations to which objection is made and may accept, reject, or modify, in whole or in part, the findings or recommendations made by the magistrate judge. The judge, however, need conduct a new hearing only in his/her discretion or where required by law, and may consider the record developed before the magistrate judge, making his/her own determination on the basis of that record. The judge may also receive further evidence, recall witnesses or recommit the matter to the magistrate judge with instructions.

(c) Special Master Reports—28 U.S.C. § 636(b)(2). Any party may seek review of, or action on, a special master report filed by a magistrate judge in accordance with the provisions of Rule 53(e) of the Federal Rules of Civil Procedure.

(d) Appeal From Judgments in Misdemeanor Cases—18 U.S.C. § 3402. A defendant may appeal a judgment of conviction by a magistrate judge in a misdemeanor case by filing a notice of appeal to the District Court within 14 days after entry of the judgment, and by serving a copy of the notice upon the United States Attorney. The scope of appeal shall be the same as on an appeal from a judgment of the district court of the court of appeals.

(e) Appeal From Judgments in Civil Cases Disposed of on Consent of the Parties—28 U.S.C. § 636(c).

(1)* *Appeal to the Court of Appeals.* Upon the entry of judgment in any civil case disposed of by a magistrate judge on consent of the parties under authority of 28 U.S.C. § 636(c) and subsection 1(i) of these rules, supra, an aggrieved party shall appeal directly to the United States Court of Appeals for this circuit in the same manner as an appeal from any other judgment of this court.

(f) Appeals From Other Orders of a Magistrate Judge. Appeals from any other decisions and orders of a magistrate judge not provided for in this rule should be taken as provided by a governing statute, rule, or decisional law.

ADDENDUM

General Order of July 17, 1981

ON THIS DATE came on to be considered those causes in which Plaintiff, pursuant to 42 U.S.C. § 405(g) and 5 U.S.C. §§ 701 et seq., seeks review of a decision by the Secretary of the Department of Health and Human Services upon an application for benefits under Title 42, Chapter 7, Subchapter II, United States Code, and

In accordance with the authority vested in the United States Magistrate Judge pursuant to the Amended Order for the Adoption of Rules for the exercise of Powers and Performance of Duties by United States Magistrate Judges, adopted in the Western District of Texas on April 17, 1980.

IT IS HEREBY ORDERED that all matters in which Plaintiff, pursuant to 42 U.S.C. § 405(g) and 5 U.S.C. §§ 701 et seq., seeks review of a decision by the Secretary of the Department of Health and Human Services upon an application for benefits under Title 42, Chapter 7, Subchapter II, United States Code, be referred by the Clerk to the United States Magistrate Judges sitting in the San Antonio Division in accordance with a random assignment procedure approved by the judges residing in the San Antonio Division.

IT IS FURTHER ORDERED that the United States Magistrate Judge is authorized to issue all orders necessary to his/her review, and that, upon completion of his/her review, he/she shall prepare a recommendation to the Court concerning the adjudication of these causes.

[Effective January 1, 1994. Amended effective December 1, 2009; April 25, 2012.]

* [**Publisher's Note:** So in original. No subsection (e)(2) promulgated.]

APPENDIX E–1. APPLICATION FOR ADMISSION

IN THE UNITED STATES DISTRICT COURT
FOR THE WESTERN DISTRICT OF TEXAS

APPLICATION FOR ADMISSION

Instructions: Type or print your answers. Answer all questions fully. If the question does not apply to you, answer "NA". An incomplete response will delay processing of your application. Where the space provided is insufficient, answer on additional sheets, with reference to the question.

Applicant Information

1.   (a) Full Name _____

                     (Last)   *(First)*   *(Middle)*

     (b)   If you have ever been known by any other name, state the name and the reason for using it:

         _____

     (c)   Your name as you wish it to appear on the register:

         _____

2.   (a)   Date of Birth: _____

     (b)   Place of Birth: _____

     (c)   If not native born, give date and place of naturalization:

         _____

3.   Business Name: _____

4.   Business Address: _____

     City, State, Zip: _____ County: _____

5.   (a)   Business Telephone: (   ) _____

     (b)   Business Fax: (   ) _____

     (b)   Business e-mail: _____

6.   State Bar I.D. Number: _____

7.   Residence Address: _____

     City, State, Zip: _____ County: _____

8.   Residence Telephone: (   ) _____

9.   Social Security Number[1]: _____

---

[1] Attorneys are requested to provide their Social Security Number in order to assist the court in maintaining the integrity of its records.

Bar Affiliation

10. List states, federal possessions and territories in which you have been admitted to practice law by the highest court. Indicate the year admitted, status, and areas of certified specialization.

State	Year Admitted	Current Standing	Specialization

11. List federal courts to which you have been admitted. Indicate the year admitted and current status.

Court	Year Admitted	Current Standing

Education

12. List your law school, the date of graduation, and the degree received. If you did not graduate from a law school, please describe your law study in detail.

_____

_____

_____

Good Standing

13. Indicate any grievances or involuntary removals filed against you as a lawyer. Describe the circumstances in detail.

_____

_____

_____

14. Describe in detail charges, arrests, or convictions for criminal offense(s). Omit minor traffic offenses.

_____

_____

_____

Rev: April 29, 2014

Page 2 of 4

ANSWER THE FOLLOWING QUESTIONS "YES" OR "NO" IN THE BLANK PROVIDED; IF "YES", EXPLAIN FULLY ON A SEPARATE SHEET.

15. (a) Have you ever been denied admission to the bar of any State (including the District of Columbia) or any federal court? _____

    (b) Have you ever been disbarred, suspended from practice, reprimanded, censured or otherwise disciplined or disqualified as an attorney? _____

    (c) Has any adverse action, formal or informal, been taken against you or your license to practice law by any grievance committee, court, or other disciplinary body or committee? _____

16. (a) Have you ever held a bonded position in connection with which anyone has sought to recover on your bond, or made a claim for any alleged default? _____

17. In connection with questions 17(a) through (c), the detailed explanation of any affirmative answers shall include dates, exact name and address of the court, if any, the case number, and disposition.

    (a) Have you ever been charged with any violation of any law, other than minor traffic violations? _____

    (b) Have you ever been charged with fraud, formally or otherwise, in any civil, criminal, bankruptcy, or administrative case or proceeding? _____

    (c) Have you ever been denied a discharge in bankruptcy, or had your discharge in bankruptcy revoked? _____

18. Are there any unsatisfied judgments against you, whether barred by limitation or not? _____

    (If so, give names and addresses of creditors, amounts, dates and nature of judgments, courts, and reasons for non-payment.)

Electronic Case Filing Registration

By submitting this form, I agree to abide by all Court rules, orders, policies and procedures governing the use of the electronic filing system. I also consent to service by electronic means in the circumstances permitted under those rules, orders, policies, and procedures. I further consent to allow the court to provide e-mail notifications on my behalf to all parties registered with the ECF System in lieu of providing certificate of service per Local Court Rule CV-5 and CR-49. I understand that the combination of user id and password will serve as the signature of the filing user filing the documents pursuant to Rule 11 of the Federal Rules of Civil Procedure, the Federal Rules of Criminal Procedure and the Local Rules of this court. Therefore as a filing user, I agree to protect the security of my password and immediately notify the Court if I suspect my password has been compromised.

I already have an ECF login that I use at another Court, which is _____. Please assign the same login, if possible. **(Important Note: This login cannot be your current PACER login.)**

_____   _____
Signature of Registrant   *Date Signed*

_____   _____   _____
Primary E-mail Address   *Courtesy E-Mail Address*   *Courtesy E-Mail #2 Address*

Rev: April 29, 2014 Page 3 of 4

Certification and Signature

I swear that the information provided in the foregoing application including attachments, if any, is true and correct. I acknowledge that by accepting admission to this Court I am subjecting myself to the discipline of this Court. I further certify that I have read and am familiar with the Federal Rules of Civil Procedure and Local Rules of this court and alternative dispute resolution procedures of the Western District of Texas and will advise clients in any actions pending in this court regarding alternative dispute resolution procedures. I further certify, if requested, I am willing to appear before this court or any Committee appointed to test the qualifications of applicants for admission to practice before this Court.

I declare under penalty of perjury that the foregoing is true.

_____   _____
Date   *Signature*

SUBSCRIBED AND SWORN TO BEFORE ME THIS _____ DAY OF _____ 20___, at

_____.

(SEAL)   _____
                                         Notary Public or Deputy Clerk of this Court

Rev: April 29, 2014   Page 4 of 4

[Effective February 15, 2018.]

APPENDIX E–2. APPLICATION FOR ADMISSION
TO PRACTICE IN THE DEL RIO DIVISION

IN THE UNITED STATES DISTRICT COURT
FOR THE WESTERN DISTRICT OF TEXAS

<u>APPLICATION FOR ADMISSION</u>
<u>TO PRACTICE IN THE DEL RIO DIVISION</u>

<u>Instructions:</u> Type or print your answers. Answer all questions fully. If the question does not apply to you, answer "NA." An incomplete response will delay processing of your application. Where the space provided is insufficient, answer on additional sheets, with reference to the question. Accompanying this application, you must provide the following:

(1)   Proof of completion of the seminar requirement of Local Rule AT-1(b)(2);
(2)   Certificate of good standing in a state bar; and
(3)   Two letters of recommendation from attorneys licensed and in good standing in the Del Rio Division.

1.   (a) Full Name _____
                        (Last)   (First)   (Middle)

        (b) If you have ever been known by any other name, state the name and the reason for using it:

        _____

        (c) Your name as you wish it to appear on the register:

        _____

2.   (a) Date of birth: _____

        (b) Place of birth: _____

        (c) If not native born, give date and place of naturalization:

        _____

3.   Business Name: _____

4.   Business Address: _____

      _____ Zip Code _____ County _____

5.   (a) Business Telephone : (____) _____

      (b) Business Fax: (____)_____

      (c) Business e-mail: _____

6.   State Bar I.D. Number: _____
                              (Specify state if other than Texas)

7.   Residence Address: _____

      _____Zip Code _____ County _____

8.   Residence Telephone: (____) _____

9.   Social Security Number: [1] _____

10.   List states, federal possessions and territories in which you have been admitted to practice
      law by the highest court.   Indicate the year admitted, status and areas of certified
      specialization.

      State   Year Admitted   Current Standing   Specialization

      _____

      _____

      _____

_____

      [1] Attorneys are requested to provide their Social Security Number in order to assist the
court in maintaining the integrity of its records.

11.   List federal courts to which you have been admitted. Indicate the year admitted and current status.

Court   Year Admitted   Current Standing

_____

_____

_____

12.   List your law school, the date of graduation, and the degree received. If you did not graduate from a law school, please describe your law study in detail.

_____

_____

_____

13.   List three felony jury trials wherein you served as first or second chair **OR** why you believe you are otherwise qualified.

_____

_____

_____

14.   Indicate any grievances or involuntary removals filed against you as a lawyer. Describe the circumstances in detail.

_____

_____

_____

15.   Describe in detail charges, arrests, or convictions for criminal offenses(s). Omit minor traffic offenses.

_____

_____

_____

ANSWER THE FOLLOWING QUESTIONS "YES" OR "NO" IN THE BLANK PROVIDED; IF "YES", <u>EXPLAIN FULLY</u> ON A SEPARATE SHEET.

16.   (a)   Have you ever been denied admission to the bar of any State (including the District of Columbia) or any other federal court?   _____

       (b)   Have you ever been disbarred, suspended from practice, reprimanded, censured or otherwise disciplined or disqualified as an attorney?   _____

       (c)   Has any adverse action, formal or informal, been taken against you or your license to practice law by any grievance committee, court, or other disciplinary body or committee?   _____

17.   Have you ever held a bonded position in connection with which anyone has sought to recover on your bond, or made a claim for any alleged default?   _____

18.   In connection with questions 18(a) through ©) , the detailed explanation of any affirmative answers shall include dates, exact name and address of the court, if any, the case number, and disposition.

       (a)   Have you ever been charged with any violation of any law, other than minor traffic violations?   _____

       (b)   Have you ever been charged with fraud, formally or otherwise, in any civil, criminal, bankruptcy, or administrative case or proceeding?   _____

       (c)   Have you ever been denied a discharge in bankruptcy, or had your discharge in bankruptcy revoked?   _____

19. Are there any unsatisfied judgments against you, whether barred by limitation or not? ⎯⎯⎯⎯

   (If so, give names and addresses of creditors, amounts, dates and nature of judgments, courts, and reasons for non-payment.)

20. Please provide the date of completion of the Federal Court Practice Seminar, as required by Local Rule AT-1(b)(2):

   Date Completed:_____ Course # _____

21. If approved, in which District/Division do you prefer to take the Oath?

   _____ District _____ Division

I swear that the information provided in the foregoing application including attachments, if any, is true and correct. I acknowledge that by accepting admission to this Court I am subjecting myself to the discipline of this Court. I further certify that I have read and am familiar with the Federal Rules of Civil Procedure and Local Rules of this court and alternative dispute resolution procedures of the Western District of Texas and will advise clients in any actions pending in this court regarding alternative dispute resolution procedures. I further certify, if requested, I am willing to appear before this court or any Committee appointed to test the qualifications of applicants for admission to practice before this Court.

I declare under penalty of perjury that the foregoing is true.

_____   _____
Date   Signature

SUBSCRIBED AND SWORN TO BEFORE ME this ____ day of _____, 20___,
at _____.

(SEAL)   _____
                                  Notary Public or Deputy Clerk of this Court

[Effective February 15, 2018.]

APPENDIX H.   CONFIDENTIALITY AND PROTECTIVE ORDER

IN THE UNITED STATES DISTRICT COURT
FOR THE WESTERN DISTRICT OF TEXAS
_____ **DIVISION**

_____ ,	§ § §	
Plaintiff,	§ §	CIVIL ACTION NO. _____
	§ §	
_____ ,	§ §	
Defendant.	§ §	

CONFIDENTIALITY AND PROTECTIVE ORDER

Before the court is the joint motion of the parties for the entry of a confidentiality and protective order ("Protective Order"). After careful consideration, it is hereby ORDERED as follows:

1. Classified Information. "Classified Information" means any information of any type, kind, or character that is designated as "Confidential", "For Counsel Only", or "Attorneys Eyes Only" by any of the supplying or receiving persons, whether it be a document, information contained in a document, information revealed during a deposition, information revealed in an interrogatory answer, or otherwise.

2. Qualified Persons. "Qualified Persons" means:

a. For Counsel or Attorneys Only information:

i. retained counsel for the parties in this litigation and their respective staff;

ii. actual or potential independent experts or consultants (and their administrative or clerical staff) engaged in connection with this litigation (which shall not include the current employees, officers, members, or agents of parties or affiliates of parties) who, prior to any disclosure of Classified Information to such person, have signed a document agreeing to be bound by the terms of this Protective Order (such signed document to be maintained by the attorney retaining such person) and have been designated in writing by notice to all counsel;

iii. this court and its staff and any other tribunal or dispute resolution officer duly appointed or assigned in connection with this litigation.

b. For Confidential information:

i. the persons identified in subparagraph 2(a);

ii. the party, if a natural person;

iii. if the party is an entity, such officers or employees of the party who are actively involved in the prosecution or defense of this case who, prior to any disclosure of Confidential information to such person, have been designated in writing by notice to all counsel and have signed a document agreeing to be bound by the terms of this Protective Order (such signed document to be maintained by the attorney designating such person);

iv. litigation vendors, court reporters, and other litigation support personnel;

v. any person who was an author, addressee, or intended or authorized recipient of the Confidential information and who agrees to keep the information confidential, provided that such persons may see and use the Confidential information but not retain a copy.

c. Such other person as this court may designate after notice and an opportunity to be heard.

3. Designation Criteria.

a. *Nonclassified Information.* Classified Information shall not include information that either:

i. is in the public domain at the time of disclosure, as evidenced by a written document;

ii. becomes part of the public domain through no fault of the recipient, as evidenced by a written document;

iii. the receiving party can show by written document was in its rightful and lawful possession at the time of disclosure; or

iv. lawfully comes into the recipient's possession subsequent to the time of disclosure from another source without restriction as to disclosure, provided such third party has the right to make the disclosure to the receiving party.

b. *Classified Information.* A party shall designate as Classified Information only such information that the party in good faith believes in fact is confidential. Information that is generally available to the public, such as public filings, catalogues, advertising materials, and the like, shall not be designated as Classified.

Information and documents that may be designated as Classified Information include, but are not limited to, trade secrets, confidential or proprietary financial information, operational data, business plans, and competitive analyses, personnel files, personal information that is protected by law, and other sensitive information that, if not restricted as set forth in this order, may subject the producing or disclosing person to competitive or financial injury or potential legal liability to third parties.

Correspondence and other communications between the parties or with nonparties may be designated as Classified Information if the communication was made with the understanding or reasonable expectation that the information would not become generally available to the public.

c. *For Counsel or Attorneys Only.* The designation "For Counsel Only" or "Attorneys Eyes Only" shall be reserved for information that is believed to be unknown to the opposing party or parties, or any of the employees of a corporate party. For purposes of this order, so-designated information includes, but is not limited to, product formula information, design information, non-public financial information, pricing information, customer identification data, and certain study methodologies.

d. *Ultrasensitive Information.* At this point, the parties do not anticipate the need for higher levels of confidentiality as to ultrasensitive documents or information. However, in the event that a court orders that ultrasensitive documents or information be produced, the parties will negotiate and ask the court to enter an ultrasensitive information protocol in advance of production to further protect such information.

4. Use of Classified Information. All Classified Information provided by any party or nonparty in the course of this litigation shall be used solely for the purpose of preparation, trial, and appeal of this litigation and for no other purpose, and shall not be disclosed except in accordance with the terms hereof.

5. Marking of Documents. Documents provided in this litigation may be designated by the producing person or by any party as Classified Information by marking each page of the documents so designated with a stamp indicating that the information is "Confidential", "For Counsel Only", or "Attorneys Eyes Only". In lieu of marking the original of a document, if the original is not provided, the designating party may mark the copies that are provided. Originals shall be preserved for inspection.

6. Disclosure at Depositions. Information disclosed at (a) the deposition of a party or one of its present or former officers, directors, employees, agents, consultants, representatives, or independent experts retained by counsel for the purpose of this litigation, or (b) the deposition of a nonparty may be designated by any party as Classified Information by indicating on the record at the deposition that the testimony is "Confidential" or "For Counsel Only" and is subject to the provisions of this Order.

Any party also may designate information disclosed at a deposition as Classified Information by notifying all parties in writing not later than 30 days of receipt of the transcript of the specific pages and lines of the transcript that should be treated as Classified Information thereafter. Each party shall attach a copy of each such written notice to the face of the transcript and each copy thereof in that party's possession, custody, or control. All deposition transcripts shall be treated as For Counsel Only for a period of 30 days after initial receipt of the transcript.

To the extent possible, the court reporter shall segregate into separate transcripts information designated as Classified Information with blank, consecutively numbered pages being provided in a nondesignated main transcript. The separate transcript containing Classified Information shall have page numbers that correspond to the blank pages in the main transcript.

Counsel for a party or a nonparty witness shall have the right to exclude from depositions any person who is not authorized to receive Classified Information pursuant to this Protective Order, but such right of exclusion shall be applicable only during periods of examination or testimony during which Classified Information is being used or discussed.

7. Disclosure to Qualified Persons.

a. *To Whom.* Classified Information shall not be disclosed or made available by the receiving party to persons other than Qualified Persons except as necessary to comply with applicable law or the valid order of a court of competent jurisdiction; ***provided, however,*** that in the event of a disclosure compelled by law or court order, the receiving party will so notify the producing party as promptly as practicable (if at all possible, prior to making such disclosure) and shall seek a protective order or confidential treatment of such information. Information designated as For Counsel Only shall be restricted in circulation to Qualified Persons described in subparagraph 2(a).

b. *Retention of Copies During this Litigation.* Copies of For Counsel Only information shall be maintained only in the offices of outside counsel for the receiving party and, to the extent supplied to experts described in subparagraph 2(a)(ii), in the offices of those experts. Any documents produced in this litigation, regardless of classification, that are provided to Qualified Persons shall be maintained only at the office of such Qualified Person and only necessary working copies of any such documents shall be made. Copies of documents and exhibits containing Classified Information may be prepared by independent copy services, printers, or illustrators for the purpose of this litigation.

c. Each party's outside counsel shall maintain a log of all copies of For Counsel Only documents that are delivered to Qualified Persons.

8. Unintentional Disclosures.
Documents unintentionally produced without designation as Classified Information later may be designated and shall be treated as Classified Information from the date written notice of the designation is provided to the receiving party.

If a receiving party learns of any unauthorized disclosure of Confidential information or For Counsel Only information, the party shall immediately upon learning of such disclosure inform the producing party of all pertinent facts relating to such disclosure and shall make all reasonable efforts to prevent disclosure by each unauthorized person who received such information.

9. Documents Produced for Inspection Prior to Designation.
In the event documents are produced for inspection prior to designation, the documents shall be treated as For Counsel Only during inspection. At the time of copying for the receiving parties, Classified Information shall be marked prominently "Confidential", "For Counsel Only", or "Attorneys Eyes Only" by the producing party.

10. Consent to Disclosure and Use in Examination.
Nothing in this order shall prevent disclosure beyond the terms of this order if each party designating the information as Classified Information consents to such disclosure or if the court, after notice to all affected parties and nonparties, orders such disclosure. Nor shall anything in this order prevent any counsel of record from utilizing Classified Information in the examination or cross-examination of any person who is indicated on the document as being an author, source, or recipient of the Classified Information, irrespective of which party produced such information.

11. Challenging the Designation.

a. *Classified Information.* A party shall not be obligated to challenge the propriety of a designation of Classified Information at the time such designation is made, and a failure to do so shall not preclude a subsequent challenge to the designation. In the event that any party to this litigation disagrees at any stage of these proceedings with the designation of any information as Classified Information, the parties shall first try to resolve the dispute in good faith on an informal basis, such as by production of redacted copies. If the dispute cannot be resolved, the objecting party may invoke this Protective Order by objecting in writing to the party who designated the document or information as Classified Information. The designating party shall then have 14 days to move the court for an order preserving the designated status of the disputed information. The disputed information shall remain Classified Information unless and until the court orders otherwise. Failure to move for an order shall constitute a termination of the status of such item as Classified Information.

b. *Qualified Persons.* In the event that any party in good faith disagrees with the designation of a person as a Qualified Person or the disclosure of particular Classified Information to such person, the parties shall first try to resolve the dispute in good faith on an informal basis. If the dispute cannot be resolved, the objecting party shall have 14 days from the date of the designation or, in the event particular Classified Information is requested subsequent to the designation of the Qualified Person, 14 days from service of the request to move the court for an order denying the disputed person (a) status as a Qualified Person, or (b) access to particular Classified Information. The objecting person shall have the burden of demonstrating that disclosure to the disputed person would expose the objecting party to the risk of serious harm. Upon the timely filing of such a motion, no disclosure of Classified Information shall be made to the disputed person unless and until the court enters an order preserving the designation.

12. Manner of Use in Proceedings. In the event a party wishes to use any Classified Information in affidavits, declarations, briefs, memoranda of law, or other papers filed in this litigation, the party shall do one of the following: (1) with the consent of the producing party, file only a redacted copy of the information; (2) where appropriate (e.g., in connection with discovery and evidentiary motions) provide the information solely for *in camera* review; or (3) file such information under seal with the court consistent with the sealing requirements of the court.

13. Filing Under Seal. The clerk of this court is directed to maintain under seal all documents, transcripts of deposition testimony, answers to interrogatories, admissions, and other papers filed under seal in this litigation that have been designated, in whole or in part, as Classified Information by any party to this litigation consistent with the sealing requirements of the court.

14. Return of Documents. Not later than 120 days after conclusion of this litigation and any appeal related to it, any Classified Information, all reproductions of such information, and any notes, summaries, or descriptions of such information in the possession of any of the persons specified in paragraph 2 (except subparagraph 2(a)(iii)) shall be returned to the producing party or destroyed, except as this court may otherwise order or to the extent such information has been used as evidence at any trial or hearing. Notwithstanding this obligation to return or destroy information, counsel may retain attorney work product, including document indices, so long as that work product does not duplicate verbatim substantial portions of the text of any Classified Information.

15. Ongoing Obligations. Insofar as the provisions of this Protective Order, or any other protective orders entered in this litigation, restrict the communication and use of the information protected by it, such provisions shall continue to be binding after the conclusion of this litigation, except that (a) there shall be no restriction on documents that are used as exhibits in open court unless such exhibits were filed under seal, and (b) a party may seek the written permission of the producing party or order of the court with respect to dissolution or modification of this, or any other, protective order.

16. Advice to Clients. This order shall not bar any attorney in the course of rendering advice to such attorney's client with respect to this litigation from conveying to any party client the attorney's evaluation in a general way of Classified Information produced or exchanged under the terms of this order; provided, however, that in rendering such advice and otherwise communicating with the client, the attorney shall not disclose the specific contents of any Classified Information produced by another party if such disclosure would be contrary to the terms of this Protective Order.

17. Duty to Ensure Compliance. Any party designating any person as a Qualified Person shall have the duty to reasonably ensure that such person observes the terms of this Protective Order and shall be responsible upon breach of such duty for the failure of such person to observe the terms of this Protective Order.

18. Waiver. Pursuant to Federal Rule of Evidence 502, neither the attorney-client privilege nor work product protection is waived by disclosure connected with this litigation.

19. Modification and Exceptions. The parties may, by stipulation, provide for exceptions to this order and any party may seek an order of this court modifying this Protective Order.

It is SO ORDERED this _____ day of _____, 20___.

_____
United States District Judge

[Amended effective May 16, 1994; March 13, 1998; December 1, 2000; March 15, 2002; December 2, 2011; April 26, 2012; January 14, 2019.]

APPENDIX I. GUIDELINES FOR NON–STENOGRAPHIC DEPOSITION

Depositions recorded by non-stenographic means, including videotape, are authorized without the prior necessity of a motion and court order if taken under the following guidelines:

1. The beginning of the videotape shall contain an announcement or other indication of the style of the case, the cause number, the name of the court where the case is pending, the physical location of the deposition, and an introduction of the witness, the attorneys, any parties or party representative who may be present, the court reporter, the video technician, and any other persons present at the deposition.

2. The witness will be sworn on camera.

3. The camera shall remain on the witness in standard fashion throughout the deposition. Close-ups and other similar techniques are forbidden unless agreed to by the parties or ordered by the court.

4. The arrangement of the interrogation should be such that, in responding to the interrogating attorney, the witness will look as directly into the camera as possible.

5. No smoking shall be allowed during the videotape, and there should be no unnecessary noise or movement.

6. The party issuing the notice of the videotape deposition shall be responsible for the original of the videotape, and other parties shall have the option to obtain copies at their cost.

7. A time-date generator or other suitable indexing method must be used throughout the course of recording the deposition.

8. An announcement of the time on the videotape shall be made each time the videotape is begun and is stopped.

9. The time of conclusion of the videotape must be announced on the videotape.

[Effective January 1, 1994. Amended effective December 2, 2011; April 26, 2012.]

APPENDIX J. NOTICE REGARDING COMPLAINTS
OF JUDICIAL MISCONDUCT OR DISABILITY

To improve the administration of justice in the federal courts, Congress passed the Judicial Conduct and Disability Act of 1980, codified at 28 U.S.C. § 372(c). The law authorizes complaints against United States circuit, district, bankruptcy, and magistrate judges who have "engaged in conduct prejudicial to the effective and expeditious administration of the business of the courts" or who are "unable to discharge all the duties of office by reason of mental or physical disability." The conduct to which the law is addressed does not include making wrong judicial decisions, for the law provides that a complaint may be dismissed if it is "directly related to the merits of a decision or procedural ruling." The Judicial Council of the Fifth Circuit has adopted Rules Governing Complaints of Judicial Misconduct or Disability. These rules apply to judges of the U.S. Court of Appeals for the Fifth Circuit and to the district, bankruptcy, and magistrate judges of federal courts within the Fifth Circuit. The circuit includes the states of Texas, Louisiana, and Mississippi.

These rules may be obtained from,* and written complaints filed at, the following office:

Clerk
U.S. Court of Appeals, Fifth Circuit
600 Camp Street, Room 102
New Orleans, Louisiana 70130

[Effective January 1, 1994. Amended effective April 26, 2012.]

* [**Publisher's Note:** The Rules for Judicial–Conduct and Judicial–Disability Proceedings are included in this publication preceding the Index to the Fifth Circuit Rules, ante.]

APPENDIX K. PLAN FOR PROMPT DISPOSITION OF CRIMINAL CASES PURSUANT TO THE SPEEDY TRIAL ACT OF 1974—18 U.S.C. § 3165(e)(3)

SECTION II. STATEMENT OF TIME LIMITS ADOPTED BY THE COURT AND PROCEDURES FOR IMPLEMENTING THEM

Pursuant to the requirements of Rule 50(b) of the Federal Rules of Criminal Procedure, the Speedy Trial Act of 1974 (18 U.S.C. Chapter 208), the Speedy Trial Act Amendments Act of 1979 (Pub.L. No. 96–43, 93 Stat. 327), and the Federal Juvenile Delinquency Act (18 U.S.C. §§ 5036, 5037), the Judges of the United States District Court for the Western District of Texas have adopted the following time limits and procedures to minimize undue delay and to further the prompt disposition of criminal cases and certain juvenile proceedings:

A. Applicability.

(1) *Offenses.* The time limits set forth herein are applicable to all criminal offenses triable in this Court,[1] including cases triable by United States Magistrates, except for petty offenses as defined in 18 U.S.C. § 1(3). Except as specifically provided, they are not applicable to proceedings under the Federal Juvenile Delinquency Act. [§ 3172]

(2) *Persons.* The time limits are applicable to persons accused who have not been indicted or informed against as well as those who have, and the word "defendant" includes such persons unless the context indicates otherwise.

B. Priorities in Scheduling Criminal Cases.
Preference shall be given to criminal proceedings as far as practicable as required by Rule 50(a) of the Federal Rules of Criminal Procedure. The trial of defendants in custody solely because they are awaiting trial and of high-risk defendants as defined in Section E should be given preference over other criminal cases. [§ 3164(a)]

C. Time Within Which an Indictment or Information Must Be Filed.

(1) *Time Limits.* If an individual is arrested or served with a summons and the complaint charges an offense to be prosecuted in this district, any indictment or information subsequently filed in connection with such charge shall be filed within 30 days of arrest or service. [§ 3161(b)]

(2) *Grand Jury Not in Session.* If the defendant is charged with a felony to be prosecuted in this district, and no grand jury in the district has been in session during the 30–day period prescribed in subsection (1), such period shall be extended an additional 30 days. [§ 3161(b)]

(3) *Measurement of Time Periods.* If a person has not been arrested or served with a summons on a Federal charge, an arrest will be deemed to have been made at such time as the person (i) is held in custody solely for the purpose of responding to a Federal charge; (ii) is delivered to the custody of a Federal official in connection with a Federal charge; or (iii) appears before a judicial officer in connection with a Federal charge.

(4) *Related Procedures.*

(a) At the time of the earliest appearance before a judicial officer of a person who has been arrested for an offense not charged in an indictment or information, the judicial officer shall establish for the record the date on which the arrest took place.

(b) In the absence of a showing to the contrary, a summons shall be considered to have been served on the date of service shown on the return thereof.

D. Time Within Which Trial Must Commence.

(1) *Time Limits.* The trial of a defendant shall commence not later than 70 days after the last to occur of the following dates:

(a) The date on which an indictment or information is filed in this district;

(b) The date on which a sealed indictment or information is unsealed; or

(c) The date of the defendant's first appearance before a judicial officer of this district. [§ 3161(c)(1)]

(2) *Retrial: Trial After Reinstatement of an Indictment or Information.* The retrial of a defendant shall commence within 70 days from the date the order occasioning the retrial becomes final, as shall the trial of a defendant upon an indictment or information dismissed by a trial court and reinstated

following an appeal. If the retrial or trial follows an appeal or collateral attack, the court may extend the period if unavailability of witnesses or other factors resulting from passage of time make trial within 70 days impractical. The extended period shall not exceed 180 days. [§§ 3161(d)(2), (e)]

(3) *Withdrawal of Plea.* If a defendant enters a plea of guilty or nolo contendere to any or all charges in an indictment or information and is subsequently permitted to withdraw it, the time limit shall be determined for all counts as if the indictment or information were filed on the day the order permitting withdrawal of the plea became final. [§ 3161(i)]

(4) *Superseding Charges.* If, after an indictment or information has been filed, a complaint, indictment, or information is filed which charges the defendant with the same offense or with an offense required to be joined with that offense, the time limit applicable to the subsequent charge will be determined as follows:

(a) If the original indictment or information was dismissed on motion of the defendant before the filing of the subsequent charge, the time limit shall be determined without regard to the existence of the original charge. [§ 3161(d)(1)]

(b) If the original indictment or information is pending at the time the subsequent charge is filed, the trial shall commence within the time limit for commencement of trial on the original indictment or information. [§ 3161(h)(6)]

(c) If the original indictment or information was dismissed on motion of the United States Attorney before the filing of the subsequent charge, the trial shall commence within the time limit for commencement of trial on the original indictment or information, but the period during which the defendant was not under charges shall be excluded from the computations. Such period is the period between the dismissal of the original indictment or information and the date the time would have commenced to run on the subsequent charge had there been no previous charge.[2] [§ 3161(h)(6)]

If the subsequent charge is contained in a complaint, the formal time limit within which an indictment or information must be obtained on the charge shall be determined without regard to the existence of the original indictment or information, but earlier action may in fact be required if the time limit for commencement of trial is to be satisfied.

(5) *Measurement of Time Periods.* For the purposes of this section:

(a) If a defendant signs a written consent to be tried before a magistrate and no indictment or information charging the offense has been filed, the time limit shall run from the date of such consent.

(b) In the event of a transfer to this district under Rule 20 of the Federal Rules of Criminal Procedure, the indictment or information shall be deemed filed in this district when the papers in the proceeding or certified copies thereof are received by the clerk.

(c) A trial in a jury case shall be deemed to commence at the beginning of voir dire.

(d) A trial in a nonjury case shall be deemed to commence on the day the case is called, provided that some step in the trial procedure immediately follows.

(6) *Related Procedures.*

(a) At the time of the defendant's earliest appearance before a judicial officer of this district, the officer will take appropriate steps to assure that the defendant is represented by counsel and shall appoint counsel where appropriate under the Criminal Justice Act and Rule 44 of the Federal Rules of Criminal Procedure.

(b) The court shall have sole responsibility for setting cases for trial after consultation with counsel. At the time of arraignment or as soon thereafter as is practicable, each case will be set for trial on a day certain or listed for trial on a weekly or other short-term calendar. [§ 3161(a)]

(c) Individual calendars shall be managed so that it will be reasonably anticipated that every criminal case set for trial will be reached during the week of original setting. A conflict in schedules of Assistant United States Attorneys or defense counsel will be ground for a continuance or delayed setting only if approved by the court and called to the court's attention at the earliest practicable time.

(d) In the event that a complaint, indictment, or information is filed against a defendant charged in a pending indictment or information or in an indictment or information dismissed on motion of the United States Attorney, the trial on the new charge shall commence within the time limit for commencement of trial on the original indictment or information unless the court finds that the new charge is not for the same offense charged in the original indictment or information or an offense required to be joined therewith.

(e) At the time of the filing of a complaint, indictment, or information described in paragraph (d), the United States Attorney shall give written notice to the court of that circumstance and of his position with respect to the computation of the time limits.

(f) All pretrial hearings shall be conducted as soon after the arraignment as possible, consistent with the priorities of other matters on the court's criminal docket.

E. Defendants in Custody and High–Risk Defendants.[3]

(1) *Time Limits.* Notwithstanding any longer time periods that may be permitted under sections C and D, the following time limits will also be applicable to defendants in custody and high-risk defendants as herein defined:

(a) The trial of a defendant held in custody solely for the purpose of trial on a Federal charge shall commence within 90 days following the beginning of continuous custody.

(b) The trial of a high-risk defendant shall commence within 90 days of the designation as high-risk. [§ 3164(b)]

(2) *Definition of "High–Risk Defendant."* A high-risk defendant is one reasonably designated by the United States Attorney as posing a danger to himself or any other person or to the community.

(3) *Measurement of Time Periods.* For the purposes of this section:

(a) A defendant is deemed to be in detention awaiting trial when he is arrested on a Federal charge or otherwise held for the purpose of responding to a Federal charge. Detention is deemed to be solely because the defendant is awaiting trial unless the person exercising custodial authority has an independent basis (not including a detainer) for continuing to hold the defendant.

(b) If a case is transferred pursuant to Rule 20 of the Federal Rules of Criminal Procedure and the defendant subsequently rejects disposition under Rule 20 or the court declines to accept the plea, a new period of continuous detention awaiting trial will begin at that time.

(c) A trial shall be deemed to commence as provided in section D(5)(c) and D(5)(d).

(4) *Related Procedures.*

(a) If a defendant is being held in custody solely for the purpose of awaiting trial, the United States Attorney shall advise the court at the earliest practicable time of the date of the beginning of such custody.

(b) The United States Attorney shall advise the court at the earliest practicable time (usually at the hearing with respect to bail) if the defendant is considered by him to be high risk.

(c) If the court finds that the filing of a "high-risk" designation as a public record may result in prejudice to the defendant, it may order the designation sealed for such period as is necessary to protect the defendant's right to a fair trial, but not beyond the time that the court's judgment in the case become final.

During the time the designation is under seal, it shall be made known to the defendant and his counsel but shall not be made known to other persons without the permission of the court.

F. Exclusion of Time From Computations.

(1) *Applicability.* In computing any time limit under section C (Interval I), D (Interval II), or E (Custody/High–Risk), the periods of delay set forth in 18 U.S.C. § 3161(h) shall be excluded. Such periods of delay shall not be excluded in computing the minimum period for commencement of trial under section G.

(2) *Records of Excludable Time.* The clerk of the court shall enter on the docket, in the form prescribed by the Administrative Office of the United States Courts, information with respect to excludable periods of time for each criminal defendant.

(3) *Stipulations.*

(a) The attorney for the government and the attorney for the defendant may at any time enter into stipulations with respect to the accuracy of the docket entries recording excludable time.

(b) To the extent that the amount of time stipulated by the parties does not exceed the amount recorded on the docket for any excludable period of delay, the stipulation shall be conclusive as between the parties unless it has no basis in fact or law. It shall similarly be conclusive as to a codefendant for the limited purpose of determining, under 18 U.S.C. § 3161(h)(7), whether time has run against the defendant entering into the stipulation.

(c) To the extent that the amount of time stipulated exceeds the amount recorded on the docket, the stipulation shall have no effect unless approved by the court.

(4) *Pre-indictment Procedures.*

(a) In the event that the United States Attorney anticipates that an indictment or information will not be filed within the time limit set forth in section C (Interval I), he may file a written motion with the court for a determination of excludable time. In the event that the United States Attorney seeks a continuance under 18 U.S.C. § 3161(h)(8), he shall file a written motion with the court requesting such a continuance.

(b) The motion of the United States Attorney shall state (i) the period of time proposed for exclusion, and (ii) the basis of the proposed exclusion. If the motion is for a continuance under 18 U.S.C. § 3161(h)(8), it shall also state whether or not the defendant is being held in custody on the basis of the complaint. In appropriate circumstances, the motion may include a request that some or all of the supporting material be considered ex parte and in camera.

(c) The court may grant a continuance under 18 U.S.C. § 3161(h)(8) for either a specific period of time or a period to be determined by reference to an event (such as recovery from illness) not within the control of the government. If the continuance is to a date not certain, the court shall require one or both parties to inform the court promptly when and if the circumstances that justify the continuance no longer exist. In addition, the court shall require one or both parties to file periodic reports bearing on the continued existence of such circumstances. The court shall determine the frequency of such reports in the light of the facts of the particular case.

(5) *Post-indictment Procedures.*

(a) At each appearance of counsel before the court, counsel shall examine the clerk's records of excludable time for completeness and accuracy and shall bring to the court's immediate attention any claim that the clerk's record is in any way incorrect.

(b) In the event that the court continues a trial beyond the time limit set forth in section D or E, the court shall determine whether the limit may be recomputed by excluding time pursuant to 18 U.S.C. § 3161(h).

(c) If it is determined that a continuance is justified, the court shall set forth its findings in the record, either orally or in writing. If the continuance is granted under 18 U.S.C. § 3161(h)(8), the court shall also set forth its reasons for finding that the ends of justice served by granting the continuance outweigh the best interest of the public and the defendant in a speedy trial. If the continuance is to a date not certain, the court shall require one or both parties to inform the court promptly when and if the circumstances that justify the continuance no longer exist. In addition, the court shall require one or both parties to file periodic reports bearing on the continued existence of such circumstances. The court shall determine the frequency of such reports in the light of the facts of the particular case.

G. Minimum Period for Defense Preparation. Unless the defendant consents in writing to the contrary, the trial shall not commence earlier than 30 days from (i) the date on which the indictment or information is filed or (ii), if later, from the date on which counsel first enters an appearance, or (iii) the date on which the defendant expressly waives counsel and elects to proceed pro se. In circumstances in which the 70-day time limit for commencing trial on a charge in an indictment or information is determined by reference to an earlier indictment or information pursuant to section D(4), the 30-day minimum period shall also be determined by reference to the earlier indictment or information. When prosecution is resumed on an original indictment or information following a mistrial, appeal, or withdrawal of a guilty plea, a new 30-day minimum period will not begin to run. The court will in all cases schedule trials so as to permit defense counsel adequate preparation time in the light of all the circumstances. [§ 3161(c)(2)]

H. Time Within Which Defendant Should Be Sentenced.

(1) *Time Limit.* A defendant shall ordinarily be sentenced within (45) days of the date of his conviction or plea of guilty or nolo contendere.

(2) *Related Procedures.* If the defendant and his counsel consent thereto, a presentence investigation may be commenced prior to a plea of guilty or nolo contendere or a conviction.

I. Juvenile Proceedings.

(1) *Time Within Which Trial Must Commence.* An alleged delinquent who is in detention pending trial shall be brought to trial within 30 days of the date on which such detention was begun, as provided in 18 U.S.C. § 5036.

(2) *Time of Dispositional Hearing.* If a juvenile is adjudicated delinquent, a separate dispositional hearing shall be held no later than 20 court days after trial, unless the court has ordered further study of the juvenile in accordance with 18 U.S.C. § 5037(c).

J. Sanctions.

(1) *Dismissal or Release From Custody.* Failure to comply with the requirements of Title I of the Speedy Trial Act may entitle the defendant to dismissal of the charges against him or to release from pretrial custody. Nothing in this plan shall be construed to require that a case be dismissed or a defendant released from custody in circumstances in which such action would not be required by 18 U.S.C. §§ 3162 and 3164.[4]

(2) *High–Risk Defendant.* A high-risk defendant whose trial has not commenced within the time limit set forth in 18 U.S.C. § 3164(b) shall, if the failure to commence trial was through no fault of the attorney for the government, have his release conditions automatically reviewed. A high-risk defendant who is found by the court to have intentionally delayed the trial of his case shall be subject to an order of the court modifying his nonfinancial conditions of release under Chapter 207 of Title 18, U.S.C., to ensure that he shall appear at trial as required. [§ 3164(c)]

(3) *Discipline of Attorneys.* In a case in which counsel (a) knowingly allows the case to be set for trial without disclosing the fact that a necessary witness would be unavailable for trial, (b) files a motion solely for the purpose of delay which he knows is frivolous and without merit, (c) makes a statement for the purpose of obtaining a continuance which he knows to be false and which is material to the granting of the continuance, or (d) otherwise willfully fails to proceed to trial without justification consistent with 18 U.S.C. § 3161, the court may punish such counsel as provided in 18 U.S.C. §§ 3162(b) and (c).

(4) *Alleged Juvenile Delinquents.* An alleged delinquent in custody whose trial has not commenced within the time limit set forth in 18 U.S.C. § 5036 shall be entitled to dismissal of his case pursuant to that section unless the Attorney General shows that the delay was consented to or caused by the juvenile or his counsel, or would be in the interest of justice in the particular case.

K. Persons Serving Terms of Imprisonment. If the United States Attorney knows that a person charged with an offense is serving a term of imprisonment in any penal institution, he shall promptly seek to obtain the presence of the prisoner for trial, or cause a detainer to be filed, in accordance with the provisions of 18 U.S.C. § 3161(j).

L. Effective Dates.

(1) The amendments to the Speedy Trial Act made by Public Law 96–43 became effective August 2, 1979. To the extent that this revision of the district's plan does more than merely reflect the amendments, the revised plan shall take effect upon approval of the reviewing panel designated in accordance with 18 U.S.C. § 3165(c). However, the dismissal sanction and the sanctions against attorneys authorized by 18 U.S.C. § 3162 and reflected in sanctions J(1) and (2) of this plan shall apply only to defendants whose cases are commenced by arrest or summons on or after July, 1980, and to indictments and information filed on or after that date.

(2) If a defendant was arrested or served with a summons before July 1, 1979, the time within which an information or indictment must be filed shall be determined under the plan that was in effect at the time of such arrest or service.

(3) If a defendant was arraigned before August 2, 1979, the time within which the trial must commence shall be determined under the plan that was in effect at the time of such arraignment.

(4) If a defendant was in custody on August 2, 1979, solely because he was awaiting trial, the 90–day period under section E shall be computed from that date.

[Effective January 1, 1994. Amended effective April 26, 2012.]

---

[1] 18 U.S.C. § 3172 defines offenses as "any Federal criminal offense which is in violation of any Act of Congress ..."

[2] Under the rule of this paragraph, if an indictment was dismissed on motion of the prosecutor on May 1, with 20 days remaining within which trial must be commenced, and the defendant was arrested on a new complaint on June 1, the time remaining for trial would be 20 days from June 1: the time limit would be based on the original indictment, but the period from the

dismissal to the new arrest would not count. Although the 30–day arrest-to-indictment time limit would apply to the new arrest as a formal matter, the short deadline for trial would necessitate earlier grand jury action.

3 If a defendant's presence has been obtained through the filing of a detainer with state authorities, the Interstate Agreement on Detainers, 18 U.S.C., Appendix, may require that trial commence before the deadline established by the Speedy Trial Act. See U.S. v. Mauro, 436 U.S. 340, 356–57 n. 24 (1978).

4 Dismissal may also be required in some cases under the Interstate Agreement on Detainers, 18 U.S.C., Appendix.

APPENDIX L.   LOCAL COURT RULES OF THE UNITED STATES BANKRUPTCY COURT FOR THE WESTERN DISTRICT OF TEXAS

*[**Publisher's Note:** The Local Rules of the U.S. Bankruptcy Court for the Western District of Texas follow the Selected Orders of the U.S. District Court for the Western District of Texas.]*

APPENDIX M.   ADOPTION OF THE TEXAS LAWYER'S CREED

On November 7, 1989, the Texas Supreme Court and the Texas Court of Criminal Appeals adopted the Texas Lawyer's Creed to encourage honorable conduct among Texas lawyers and to discourage abusive litigation tactics. A copy of the Creed is attached. The four Chief Judges of the federal districts in Texas signed the attached proclamation on November 9, 1994, commending the Creed to lawyers practicing in Texas federal courts. In light of the wide acceptance of the Texas Lawyer's Creed, United States District Judges of the Western District of Texas hereby adopt the Creed and commend it for observance to all lawyers practicing in this District. It should be understood that the Creed is aspirational and that any failure to follow it cannot be the basis for any sanction or other remedy.

PROCLAMATION
OF
THE UNITED STATES DISTRICT COURT
FOR THE EASTERN, NORTHERN, SOUTHERN AND WESTERN
DISTRICTS OF TEXAS

WHEREAS, on November 7, 1989, the Supreme Court of Texas and the Texas Court of Criminal Appeals adopted "The Texas Lawyer's Creed—A Mandate for Professionalism"; and

WHEREAS, the purpose of the Creed is to eliminate abusive litigation tactics which are a disservice to our citizens, harmful to clients, and demeaning to our profession; and

WHEREAS, the Texas Lawyer's Creed has aspirational standards and encourages attorneys to adhere to the highest principles of professionalism in their dealings with the legal system, clients, judges and other lawyers; and

WHEREAS, many lawyers and courts across the state have embraced the Texas Lawyer's Creed and adopted its tenets for conducting themselves with integrity, civility and courtesy; and

WHEREAS, most attorneys practicing in the Texas federal courts are Texas attorneys subject to the recommendations of the Texas Lawyer's Creed;

THEREFORE, Be It Resolved that United States District Courts for the Eastern, Northern, Southern, and Western Districts of Texas commend to attorneys practicing in these Districts a thorough study of The Texas Lawyer's Creed; and

Be It Further Resolved, as stated in the Creed, that all attorneys of the Eastern, Northern, Southern, and Western Districts rededicate themselves to practice law so that they can enhance public confidence in the legal profession, faithfully serve their clients, and fulfill their responsibility to the legal system.

ASPIRATIONAL GOALS: THE TEXAS LAWYER'S CREED —
A MANDATE FOR PROFESSIONALISM
ADOPTED BY THE SUPREME COURT OF TEXAS AND
THE COURT OF CRIMINAL APPEALS
NOVEMBER 7, 1989

I am a lawyer, I am entrusted by the People of Texas to preserve and improve our legal system. I am licensed by the Supreme Court of Texas. I must therefore abide by the Texas Disciplinary Rules of Professional Conduct, but I know that Professionalism requires more than merely avoiding the violation of laws and rules. I am committed to this Creed for no other reason than it is right.

I. OUR LEGAL SYSTEM

A lawyer owes to the administration of justice personal dignity, integrity, and independence. A lawyer should always adhere to the highest principles of professionalism.

1. I am passionately proud of my profession. Therefore, "My word is my bond."

2. I am responsible to assure that all persons have access to competent representation regardless of wealth or position in life.

3. I commit myself to an adequate and effective pro bono program.

4. I am obligated to educate my clients, the public, and other lawyers regarding the spirit and letter of this Creed.

5. I will always be conscious of my duty to the judicial system.

II. LAWYER TO CLIENT

A lawyer owes to a client allegiance, learning, skill, and industry. A lawyer shall employ all appropriate means to protect and advance the client's legitimate rights, claims, and objectives. A lawyer shall not be deterred by any real or imagined fear of judicial disfavor or public unpopularity, nor be influenced by mere self-interest.

1. I will advise my client of the contents of this Creed when undertaking representation.

2. I will endeavor to achieve my client's lawful objectives in legal transactions and in litigation as quickly and economically as possible.

3. I will be loyal and committed to my client's lawful objectives, but I will not permit that loyalty and commitment to interfere with my duty to provide objective and independent advice.

4. I will advise my client that civility and courtesy are expected and are not a sign of weakness.

5. I will advise my client of proper and expected behavior.

6. I will treat adverse parties and witnesses with fairness and due consideration. A client has no right to demand that I abuse anyone or indulge in any offensive conduct.

7. I will advise my client that we will not pursue conduct which is intended primarily to harass or drain the financial resources of the opposing party.

8. I will advise my client that we will not pursue tactics which are intended primarily for delay.

9. I will advise my client that we will not pursue any course of action which is without merit.

10. I will advise my client that I reserve the right to determine whether to grant accommodations to opposing counsel in all matters that do not adversely affect my client's lawful objectives. A client has no right to instruct me to refuse reasonable requests made by other counsel.

11. I will advise my client regarding the availability of mediation, arbitration, and other alternative methods of resolving and settling disputes.

III. LAWYER TO LAWYER

A lawyer owes to opposing counsel, in the conduct of legal transactions and the pursuit of litigation, courtesy, candor, cooperation, and scrupulous observance of all agreements and mutual understandings. Ill feelings between clients shall not influence a lawyer's conduct, attitude, or demeanor toward opposing counsel. A lawyer shall not engage in unprofessional conduct in retaliation against other unprofessional conduct.

1. I will be courteous, civil, and prompt in oral and written communications.

2. I will not quarrel over matters of form or style, but I will concentrate on matters of substance.

3. I will identify for other counsel or parties all changes I have made in documents submitted for review.

4. I will attempt to prepare documents which correctly reflect the agreement of the parties. I will not include provisions which have not been agreed upon or omit provisions which are necessary to reflect the agreement of the parties.

5. I will notify opposing counsel, and, if appropriate, the Court or other persons, as soon as practicable, when hearings, depositions, meetings, conferences or closings are cancelled.

6. I will agree to reasonable requests for extensions of time and for waiver of procedural formalities, provided legitimate objectives of my client will not be adversely affected.

7. I will not serve motions or pleadings in any manner that unfairly limits another party's opportunity to respond.

8. I will attempt to resolve by agreement my objections to matters contained in pleadings and discovery requests and responses.

9. I can disagree without being disagreeable. I recognize that effective representation does not require antagonistic or obnoxious behavior. I will neither encourage nor knowingly permit my client or anyone under my control to do anything which would be unethical or improper if done by me.

10. I will not, without good cause, attribute bad motives or unethical conduct to opposing counsel nor bring the profession into disrepute by unfounded accusations of impropriety. I will avoid disparaging personal remarks or acrimony towards opposing counsel, parties and witnesses. I will not be influenced by any ill feeling between clients. I will abstain from any allusion to personal peculiarities or idiosyncrasies of opposing counsel.

11. I will not take advantage, by causing any default or dismissal to be rendered, when I know the identity of an opposing counsel, without first inquiring about that counsel's intention to proceed.

12. I will promptly submit orders to the Court. I will deliver copies to opposing counsel before or contemporaneously with submission to the court. I will promptly approve the form of orders which accurately reflect the substance of the rulings of the Court.

13. I will not attempt to gain an unfair advantage by sending the Court or its staff correspondence or copies of correspondence.

14. I will not arbitrarily schedule a deposition, Court appearance, or hearing until a good faith effort has been made to schedule it by agreement.

15. I will readily stipulate to undisputed facts in order to avoid needless costs or inconvenience for any party.

16. I will refrain from excessive and abusive discovery.

17. I will comply with all reasonable discovery requests. I will not resist discovery requests which are not objectionable. I will not make objections nor give instructions to a witness for the purpose of delaying or obstructing the discovery process. I will encourage witnesses to respond to all deposition questions which are reasonably understandable. I will neither encourage nor permit my witness to quibble about words where their meaning is reasonably clear.

18. I will not seek Court intervention to obtain discovery which is clearly improper and not discoverable.

19. I will not seek sanctions or disqualification unless it is necessary for protection of my client's lawful objectives or is fully justified by the circumstances.

IV. LAWYER AND JUDGE

Lawyers and judges owe each other respect, diligence, candor, punctuality, and protection against unjust and improper criticism and attack. Lawyers and judges are equally responsible to protect the dignity and independence of the Court and the profession.

1. I will always recognize that the position of judge is the symbol of both the judicial system and administration of justice. I will refrain from conduct that degrades this symbol.

2. I will conduct myself in court in a professional manner and demonstrate my respect for the Court and the law.

3. I will treat counsel, opposing parties, the Court, and members of the Court staff with courtesy and civility.

4. I will be punctual.

5. I will not engage in any conduct which offends the dignity and decorum of proceedings.

6. I will not knowingly misrepresent, mischaracterize, misquote or miscite facts or authorities to gain an advantage.

7. I will respect the rulings of the Court.

8. I will give the issues in controversy deliberate, impartial and studied analysis and consideration.

9. I will be considerate of the time constraints and pressures imposed upon the Court, Court staff and counsel in efforts to administer justice and resolve disputes.

121 F.R.D. 284
57 USLW 2058, 2 Tex.Bankr.Ct.Rep. 518
(Cite as: 121 F.R.D. 284)

United States District Court,
N.D. Texas,
Dallas Division.

DONDI PROPERTIES CORPORATION and the
Federal Savings and Loan Insurance
Corporation as Receiver for Vernon Savings and
Loan Association, FSA,
Plaintiffs,
v.
COMMERCE SAVINGS AND LOAN
ASSOCIATION, et al., Defendants.
Jean Rinard KNIGHT, Plaintiff,
v.
PROTECTIVE LIFE INSURANCE COMPANY,
Defendant.

Civ. A. Nos. CA3-87-1725-H, CA3-87-2692-D.

July 14, 1988.

At request of one its members, the United States
District Court for the Northern District of Texas
convened en banc for purpose of establishing
standards of litigation conduct to be observed in civil
actions in district. The District Court held that
standards of litigation conduct would be adopted.

Ordered accordingly.

West Headnotes

[1] Federal Civil Procedure 25
170Ak25 Most Cited Cases

Standards of litigation conduct to be observed in civil
actions litigated in Northern District of Texas would
be adopted. 28 U.S.C.A. § 2072.

[2] Federal Civil Procedure 1636.1
170Ak1636.1 Most Cited Cases
(Formerly 170Ak1636)

Plaintiffs' failure to comply with magistrate's
previous discovery orders did not require dismissal of
civil action presenting complex legal and factual
theories involving hundreds of thousands of
documents, absent showing of intentional or willful
conduct on part of plaintiffs or their counsel.
Fed.Rules Civ.Proc.Rule 37(b), 28 U.S.C.A.

[3] Federal Civil Procedure 2795
170Ak2795 Most Cited Cases
(Formerly 45k24)

Attorney's failure to identify himself or his client to
prospective witness prior to making inquiries about
transaction pertinent to client's civil action did not
require sanctions. U.S.Dist.Ct.Rules N.D.Tex., Rule
5.1(a).

[4] Federal Civil Procedure 1105.1
170Ak1105.1 Most Cited Cases
(Formerly 170Ak1105)

Filing reply brief without district court's permission
did not require that brief be stricken, where court had
not yet considered underlying substantive motions.
U.S.Dist.Ct.Rules N.D.Tex., Rules 5.1, 5.1(a, c-f).

*284 Don T. O'Bannon of Arter, Hadden & Witts,
Dallas, Tex., and Jerome A. Hochberg and Douglas
M. Mangel of Arter & *285 Hadden, Washington,
D.C., for Dondi Properties Corp., et al.

Ernest E. Figari, Alan S. Loewinsohn, and James A.
Jones of Figari & Davenport, Dallas, Tex., for Gerald
Stool, et al.

Gordon M. Shapiro, Michael L. Knapek, and Patricia
J. Kendall of Jackson & Walker, Dallas, Tex., for
Commerce Sav. Assn.

Paul E. Coggins and Weston C. Loegering of Davis,
Meadows, Owens, Collier & Zachry, Dallas, Tex., for
W. Deryl Comer.

Randall L. Freedman, Dallas, Tex., for Jack Franks.

Christopher M. Weil and Amy Brook Ganci of Weil
& Renneker, P.C., Dallas, Tex., for R.H.
Westmoreland.

Mark T. Davenport of Figari & Davenport, Dallas,
Tex., for Jean Rinard Knight.

David M. Kendall of Thompson & Knight, Austin,
Tex., for Protective Life Ins. Co.

Before PORTER, Chief Judge, SANDERS, Acting

Chief Judge, and WOODWARD, MAHON, BELEW, ROBINSON, BUCHMEYER, FISH, MALONEY, FITZWATER, and CUMMINGS, District Judges.

PER CURIAM:

We sit en banc to adopt standards of litigation conduct for attorneys appearing in civil actions in the Northern District of Texas.

I.

Dondi Properties is a suit for recovery based upon civil RICO, common law and statutory fraud, the Texas Fraudulent Transfer Act, federal regulations prohibiting affiliate transactions, civil conspiracy, negligent misrepresentation, and usury, arising in connection with activities related to the failed Vernon Savings and Loan Association. *Knight* is an action for violations of the Texas Insurance Code and Texas Deceptive Trade Practices— Consumer Protection Act, and for breach of duty of good faith and breach of contract, arising from defendant's refusal to pay plaintiff the proceeds of a life insurance policy.

In *Dondi Properties*, the following motions have been referred to the magistrate pursuant to 28 U.S.C. § 636(b) and N.D.Tex.Misc.Order No. 6, Rule 2(c): the Stool defendants' [FN1] third motion for sanctions or, in the alternative, to compel (and supplement to the motion); the third motion for sanctions of defendant, Commerce Savings Association (and supplement to the motion); defendant, W. Deryl Comer's, first motion for sanctions or, in the alternative, motion to compel (and supplement to the motion); the Stool defendants' motion for sanctions against plaintiffs' attorney; defendant, Jack Franks', first motion for sanctions or, in the alternative, motion to compel; defendant, R.H. Westmoreland's, motion for sanctions and, in the alternative, to compel; and various submissions containing additional authorities in support of the motions and briefs already filed. Plaintiffs have responded to the motions, and the Stool defendants have filed a motion for leave to file reply to plaintiffs' response.

> FN1. The Stool defendants are Gerald Stool, Donald F. Goldman, AMF Partnership, Ltd., Park Cosmopolitan Associates, Duck Hook Associates, Turnpike Waldrop Joint Venture, Alamo Associates, and Seven Flags Partnership.

The sanction motions complain of plaintiffs' failure to answer interrogatories, failure to comply with prior orders of the court pertaining to discovery, misrepresenting facts to the court, and improperly withholding documents. The magistrate had previously entered orders on March 29, 1988 and April 28, 1988 and defendants contend plaintiffs' conduct with respect to prior orders of the magistrate warrants dismissing their action or awarding other relief to movants.

In *Knight,* there is pending before a judge of this court plaintiff's motion to strike a reply brief that defendant filed without leave of court. On April 8, 1988, defendant filed four motions, including motions for separate trials and to join another *286 party. [FN2] On April 27, 1988, plaintiff filed her response to the motions. Thereafter, without leave of court, defendant, on May 26, 1988, filed a reply to plaintiff's response. On June 3, 1988, plaintiff filed a motion to strike the reply, to which motion defendant has filed a response.

> FN2. The other motions are motions to compel and for protective order.

Plaintiff contends the reply brief should be stricken because defendant did not, as required by Local Rule 5.1(f), obtain leave to file a reply, because defendant failed to seek permission immediately upon receipt of plaintiff's response, and, alternatively, because defendant's reply was filed in excess of 20 days after plaintiff filed her response. In the event the court does not strike the reply, plaintiff requests leave to file an additional response.

At the request of a member of the court, we convened the en banc court [FN3] for the purpose of establishing standards of litigation conduct to be observed in civil actions litigated in the Northern District of Texas. In section II of the opinion we establish such standards. In section III the magistrate decides the *Dondi Properties* motions, and in section IV a judge of the court decides the *Knight* motion, in accordance with the standards we adopt. [FN4]

> FN3. We concede the unusual nature of this procedure. We note, however, that the U.S. District Court for the Central District of California recently sat en banc to decide the

constitutionality of the sentencing guidelines promulgated pursuant to the Sentencing Reform Act of 1984. See United States v. Ortega Lopez, 684 F.Supp. 1506 (C.D.Cal.1988) (en banc).

FN4. While we adopt en banc the standards for civil litigation conduct, the decisions regarding the particular motions are those of the magistrate and district judge, respectively, before whom the motions are pending.

II.

[1] The judicial branch of the United States government is charged with responsibility for deciding cases and controversies and for administering justice. We attempt to carry out our responsibilities in the most prompt and efficient manner, recognizing that justice delayed, and justice obtained at excessive cost, is often justice denied. [FN5]

FN5. We do so in the spirit of Fed.R.Civ.P. 1, which provides that the federal rules "shall be construed to secure the just, speedy, and inexpensive determination of every action."

We address today a problem that, though of relatively recent origin, is so pernicious that it threatens to delay the administration of justice and to place litigation beyond the financial reach of litigants.

With alarming frequency, we find that valuable judicial and attorney time is consumed in resolving unnecessary contention and sharp practices between lawyers. Judges and magistrates of this court are required to devote substantial attention to refereeing abusive litigation tactics that range from benign incivility to outright obstruction. Our system of justice can ill-afford to devote scarce resources to supervising matters that do not advance the resolution of the merits of a case; nor can justice long remain available to deserving litigants if the costs of litigation are fueled unnecessarily to the point of being prohibitive.

As judges and former practitioners from varied backgrounds and levels of experience, we judicially know that litigation is conducted today in a manner far different from years past. Whether the increased

size of the bar has decreased collegiality, or the legal profession has become only a business, or experienced lawyers have ceased to teach new lawyers the standards to be observed, or because of other factors not readily categorized, we observe patterns of behavior that forebode ill for our system of justice. [FN6] We now adopt standards designed to end such conduct.

FN6. Nor are we alone in our observations. In December 1984 the Texas Bar Foundation conducted a "Conference on Professionalism." The conference summary, issued in March 1985, recounts similar observations from leading judges, lawyers, and legal educators concerning the subject of lawyer professionalism.

A.

We begin by recognizing our power to adopt standards for attorney conduct in *287 civil actions and by determining, as a matter of prudence, that we, rather than the circuit court, should adopt such standards in the first instance.

By means of the Rules Enabling Act of 1934, now codified as 28 U.S.C. § 2072, Congress has authorized the Supreme Court to adopt rules of civil procedure. The Court has promulgated rules that empower district courts to manage all aspects of a civil action, including pretrial scheduling and planning (Rule 16) and discovery (Rule 26(f)). We are authorized to protect attorneys and litigants from practices that may increase their expenses and burdens (Rules 26(b)(1) and 26(c)) or may cause them annoyance, embarrassment, or oppression (Rule 26(c)), and to impose sanctions upon parties or attorneys who violate the rules and orders of the court (Rules 16(f) and 37). We likewise have the power by statute to tax costs, expenses, and attorney's fees to attorneys who unreasonably and vexatiously multiply the proceedings in any case. 28 U.S.C. § 1927. We are also granted the authority to punish, as contempt of court, the misbehavior of court officers. 18 U.S.C. § 401. In addition to the authority granted us by statute or by rule, we possess the inherent power to regulate the administration of justice. See Batson v. Neal Spelce Associates, Inc., 805 F.2d 546, 550 (5th Cir.1986) (federal courts possess inherent power to assess attorney's fees and litigation costs when losing party has acted in bad faith, vexatiously, wantonly, or for oppressive reasons); Thomas v. Capital Security Services, Inc., 836 F.2d 866, 875

(5th Cir.1988) (en banc) (district court has inherent power to award attorney's fees when losing party has acted in bad faith in actions that led to the lawsuit or to the conduct of the litigation).

We conclude also that, as a matter of prudence, this court should adopt standards of conduct without awaiting action of the circuit court. We find support for this approach in *Thomas,* where, in the Rule 11 context, the Fifth Circuit noted the singular perspective of the district court in deciding the fact intensive inquiry whether to impose or deny sanctions. The court noted that trial judges are "in the best position to review the factual circumstances and render an informed judgment as [they are] intimately involved with the case, the litigants, and the attorneys on a daily basis." 836 F.2d at 873. We think the circuit court's rationale for eschewing "second-hand review of the facts" in Rule 11 cases may be applied to our adopting standards of litigation conduct: " 'the district court will have a better grasp of what is acceptable trial-level practice among litigating members of the bar than will appellate judges.' ". Id. at 873 (quoting Eastway Construction Corp. v. City of New York, 637 F.Supp. 558, 566 (E.D.N.Y.1986)).

B.

We next set out the standards to which we expect litigation counsel to adhere.

The Dallas Bar Association recently adopted "Guidelines of Professional Courtesy" and a "Lawyer's Creed" [FN7] that are both sensible and pertinent to the problems we address here. From them we adopt the following as standards of practice [FN8] to be observed by attorneys appearing in civil actions in this district:

> FN7. We set out in an appendix pertinent portions of the guidelines and the creed in the form adopted by the Dallas Bar Association.

> FN8. We also commend to counsel the American College of Trial Lawyers' Code of Trial Conduct (rev. 1987). Those portions of the Code that are applicable to our decision today are set out in the appendix.

(A) In fulfilling his or her primary duty to the client, a lawyer must be ever conscious of the broader duty to the judicial system that serves both attorney and client.

(B) A lawyer owes, to the judiciary, candor, diligence and utmost respect.

(C) A lawyer owes, to opposing counsel, a duty of courtesy and cooperation, the observance of which is necessary for the efficient administration of our system of justice and the respect of the public it serves.

(D) A lawyer unquestionably owes, to the administration of justice, the fundamental *288 duties of personal dignity and professional integrity.

(E) Lawyers should treat each other, the opposing party, the court, and members of the court staff with courtesy and civility and conduct themselves in a professional manner at all times.

(F) A client has no right to demand that counsel abuse the opposite party or indulge in offensive conduct. A lawyer shall always treat adverse witnesses and suitors with fairness and due consideration.

(G) In adversary proceedings, clients are litigants and though ill feeling may exist between clients, such ill feeling should not influence a lawyer's conduct, attitude, or demeanor towards opposing lawyers.

(H) A lawyer should not use any form of discovery, or the scheduling of discovery, as a means of harassing opposing counsel or counsel's client.

(I) Lawyers will be punctual in communications with others and in honoring scheduled appearances, and will recognize that neglect and tardiness are demeaning to the lawyer and to the judicial system.

(J) If a fellow member of the Bar makes a just request for cooperation, or seeks scheduling accommodation, a lawyer will not arbitrarily or unreasonably withhold consent.

(K) Effective advocacy does not require antagonistic or obnoxious behavior and members of the Bar will adhere to the higher standard of conduct which judges, lawyers, clients, and the public may rightfully expect.

Attorneys who abide faithfully by the standards we adopt should have little difficulty conducting themselves as members of a learned profession whose unswerving duty is to the public they serve and to the system of justice in which they practice. [FN9] Those litigators who persist in viewing themselves solely as combatants, or who perceive that they are retained to win at all costs without regard to fundamental principles of justice, will find that their conduct does not square with the practices we expect of them. Malfeasant counsel can expect instead that their conduct will prompt an appropriate response from the court, including the range of sanctions the Fifth Circuit suggests in the Rule 11 context: "a warm friendly discussion on the record, a hard-nosed reprimand in open court, compulsory legal education, monetary sanctions, or other measures appropriate to the circumstances." Thomas, 836 F.2d at 878. [FN10]

FN9. We note that these standards are consistent with both the American Bar Association and State Bar of Texas Codes of Professional Responsibility. *See, e.g.,* ethical considerations EC 7-10, EC 7-36, EC 7- 37, and EC 7-38 set out in the appendix.

FN10. We draw the parallel to Fed.R.Civ.P. 11 with the *caveat* that we are not adopting Rule 11 jurisprudence in the context presented here.

We do not, by adopting these standards, invite satellite litigation of the kind we now see in the context of Fed.R.Civ.P. 11 motions. To do so would defeat the fundamental premise which motivates our action. We do intend, however, to take the steps necessary to ensure that justice is not removed from the reach of litigants either because improper litigation tactics interpose unnecessary delay or because such actions increase the cost of litigation beyond the litigant's financial grasp. [FN11]

FN11. We note, by way of example, the Dallas Bar Association guideline that eliminates the necessity for motions, briefs, hearings, orders, and other formalities when "opposing counsel makes a reasonable request which does not prejudice the rights of the client." This salutary standard recognizes that every contested motion, however simple, costs litigants and the court time and money. Yet our court has experienced an increasing number of instances in which attorneys refuse to agree to an extension of time in which to answer or to respond to a dispositive motion, or even to consent to the filing of an amended pleading, notwithstanding that the extension of time or the amended pleading would delay neither the disposition of a pending matter nor the trial of the case.

Similarly, we do not imply by prescribing these standards that counsel are excused from conducting themselves in any manner otherwise required by law or by court rule. We think the standards we now adopt are a *289 necessary corollary to existing law, and are appropriately established to signal our strong disapproval of practices that have no place in our system of justice and to emphasize that a lawyer's conduct, both with respect to the court and to other lawyers, should at all times be characterized by honesty and fair play.

III.

The *Dondi Properties* motions referred to the magistrate for determination raise issues concerning plaintiffs' compliance with prior discovery orders of the court and the conduct of one of plaintiffs' attorneys in contacting a possible witness.

A.
Discovery Issues

[2] Although in excess of 20 pleadings and letters from counsel have been presented to the court involving various defendants' motions for sanctions, the common denominator of all is whether or not plaintiffs have complied with the previous discovery orders of the magistrate.

The case at hand presents complex legal and factual theories involving hundreds of thousands of documents. The logistical problems presented in discovery are compounded by several factors, among them being that (a) none of the Receiver (FSLIC)'s employees were employed by either Vernon Savings and Loan Association, FSA, or its predecessor; (b) prior to the Receiver's receipt of documents they were not kept in a complete and orderly manner; (c) that plaintiffs have had three sets of attorneys of record in this case; and (d) plaintiffs and their counsel, past and present, have not taken adequate measures to assure compliance with the court's prior orders.

In seeking dismissal of plaintiffs' case, the moving defendants have categorized plaintiffs' conduct and that of their counsel as being in "bad faith" and "in defiance" of the court's prior orders. Such characterization of a party opponent's conduct should be sparingly employed by counsel and should be reserved for only those instances in which there is a sound basis in fact demonstrating a party's deliberate and intentional disregard of an order of the court or of obligations imposed under applicable Federal Rules of Civil Procedure. Such allegations, when inappropriately made, add much heat but little light to the court's task of deciding discovery disputes.

Although there are conceded instances of neglect on the part of plaintiffs and their counsel and instances of lack of communication or miscommunication among counsel for the parties in the present discovery disputes, there is no showing of intentional or willful conduct on the part of plaintiffs or their counsel which warrants dismissal under Rule 37(b), Federal Rules of Civil Procedure. However, the disputes which exist amply demonstrate an inadequate utilization of Local Rule 5.1(a). [FN12]

> FN12. In part Local Rule 5.1(a) reads as follows: "Before filing a motion, counsel for a moving party shall confer with the counsel of all parties affected by the requested relief to determine whether or not the contemplated motion will be opposed."

Local Rule 5.1(a) implicitly recognizes that in general the rules dealing with discovery in federal cases are to be self-executing. The purpose of the conference requirement is to promote a frank exchange between counsel to resolve issues by agreement or to at least narrow and focus the matters in controversy before judicial resolution is sought. Regrettably over the years, in many instances the conference requirement seems to have evolved into a *pro forma* matter. With increased frequency I observe instances in which discovery disputes are resolved by the affected parties after a hearing has been set-- sometimes within minutes before the hearing is to commence. If disputes can be resolved after motions have been filed, it follows that in all but the most extraordinary circumstances, they could have been resolved in the course of Rule 5.1(a) conferences.

A conference requires the participation of counsel for all affected parties. An attorney's refusal to return a call requesting a Rule 5.1(a) conference will not be *290 tolerated. Of course, the conference requirement may be satisfied by a written communication as well. The manner in which the conference is held and the length of the conference will be dictated by the complexity of the issues and the sound judgment of attorneys in their capacities as advocates as well as officers of the court, with the objective of maximizing the resolution of disputes without court intervention. Properly utilized Rule 5.1(a) promotes judicial economy while at the same time reducing litigants' expenses incurred for attorneys' time in briefing issues and in preparing and presenting pleadings. [FN13]

> FN13. When Rule 5.1(a) conferences result in agreements, counsel may wish to memorialize such agreements in writing.

Because the present controversies may well be resolved, or appreciably narrowed, following further communications among counsel and because the court is not presented with circumstances which warrant dismissal under Rule 37, the movant defendants' motions will be denied at this time.

B.
Motion for Sanctions

[3] In their motion filed on May 18, 1988, defendants, Goldman, Stool, AMF Partnership Ltd., et al. (the Stool defendants) seek an order sanctioning the conduct of David Hammond, an attorney practicing with the firm which is counsel of record for plaintiffs.

The undisputed facts are that on or about May 9, 1988, plaintiffs' attorney had a telephone conversation with Carl Edwards in which the attorney made inquiries about transactions pertinent to the present case, but the attorney did not identify himself as an attorney representing the plaintiffs.

As stated in the opinion issued in Ceramco, Inc. v. Lee Pharmaceuticals, 510 F.2d 268, 271 (2d Cir.1975): "the courts have not only the supervisory power but also the duty and responsibility to disqualify counsel for unethical conduct *prejudicial to his adversaries.*" (Emphasis added). However, in the present case movants do not seek to disqualify plaintiffs' counsel nor have they shown any prejudice resulting from the communication. Except in those instances in which an attorney's conduct prejudicially affects the interests of a party opponent or impairs the administration of justice, adjudication of alleged ethical violations is more appropriately left to grievance committees constituted for such purpose. Deferring to such bodies permits proper resolution of attorneys' conduct while at the same time relieving courts of deciding matters which are unrelated or at most peripheral to the cases before them. As reflected in the pleadings pertinent to this motion, there are both legal issues and factual conflicts which must be resolved in deciding whether ethical standards were violated. Indeed, following the filing of the motion movants have sought to depose the attorney whose conduct is at issue, which has in turn precipitated a motion for protective order filed by the plaintiffs.

Insuring that members of the legal profession comply with ethical standards should be a matter of concern to all attorneys, and alleged breaches should be brought to the attention of the grievance committee by an attorney without charge to a client, which is appropriate only when resolution by a court is warranted. *Ceramco, Inc., supra.* By the same token, absent a motion to disqualify, which if granted would adversely affect his client's interests, an attorney whose conduct is called into question must himself bear the cost of defending his actions before a grievance committee.

For the foregoing reasons movants' motion for sanctions will be denied, but without prejudice to their counsel's right to present the allegations of misconduct to the grievance committee. The refusal to grant sanctions should not be understood as condoning an attorney's failure to identify himself and his client to a prospective witness. Had the attorney done so in the present case, the present issue may not *291 have arisen. An attorney is held to a higher standard of conduct than non-lawyers, and unlike non-lawyers, if rebuffed by a prospective witness, the attorney may use available discovery procedures to obtain the information sought.

It is, therefore, ordered that the defendants' motions relating to discovery are denied, but without prejudice to their right to file subsequent motions, if disputes remain after their counsel and plaintiffs' counsel have engaged in a Rule 5.1(a) conference consistent with this order.

It is further ordered that the Stool defendants' motion for sanctions against plaintiffs' attorney is denied, but without prejudice to presentation of the issues raised to the appropriate grievance committee.

It is further ordered that neither the Stool defendants' counsel nor the plaintiffs' attorneys will charge their clients for any time or expenses incurred relating in any manner to the Stool defendants' motion for sanctions against plaintiffs' attorney.

IV.

[4] In *Knight,* plaintiff moves to strike a reply brief that defendant filed without the court's permission. In the alternative, plaintiff seeks leave to file a response to the reply brief.

A.

It is undisputed that defendant did not obtain court permission to reply to plaintiff's response to defendant's motions for separate trials and to join a party. Defendant explains in its response to the motion to strike that "because of the flurry of activity in this case, it failed to secure permission from the Presiding Judge to file the reply." Although defendant clearly violated a Local Rule of this court, the court concludes that the error did not warrant plaintiff's filing a motion to strike.

The en banc court has adopted standards of civil litigation conduct that apply to attorneys who practice before this court. One standard requires that attorneys cooperate with one another in order to promote "the efficient administration of our system of justice." This and the other standards adopted by the court attempt to satisfy the goals of reducing litigation costs and expediting the resolution of civil actions. The attorneys in *Knight* did not cooperate in connection with the filing of the reply brief, and there resulted a dispute that has presumably increased counsel's fees to their clients, has unquestionably required of the court an unnecessary expenditure of time, and has not materially advanced the resolution of the merits of this case.

In Local Rule 5.1 we have established the briefing and decisional regimens for contested motions. Rules 5.1(a), (c), and (d) prescribe the movant's obligations. Rule 5.1(e) dictates the deadline for filing a response and provides when contested motions shall be deemed ready for disposition. A movant may not, as of right, file a reply to a response; instead, Rule 5.1(f) requires the movant to obtain permission to do so immediately upon receipt of a response. In the present case, defendant's counsel failed to cooperate with plaintiff's counsel because he did not ask him to agree [FN14] to the filing of a reply. Plaintiff's counsel failed to cooperate when he filed the motion to strike the reply. [FN15]

FN14. The court is not to be understood as holding that the parties can, by agreement, bind the presiding judge to grant permission to file a reply. Where the parties have so agreed, however, the court will usually grant such permission.

FN15. Plaintiff's motion to strike contains a certificate of conference that states that defendant and plaintiff could not agree regarding the motion to strike. Defendant disputes in its response that plaintiff and defendant had such a conference, but states that had there been one, defendant would have opposed the motion to strike.

While our court has decided that the determination whether to permit a reply is discretionary with each judge, the principle is well-established that the party with the burden on a particular matter will normally be permitted to open and close the briefing. *See, e.g.,* Sup.Ct.R. 35(3); Fed.R.App.P. 28(c). It should thus be rare that a party *292 who opposes a motion will object to the movant's filing a reply.

In the present case, the parties have presumably incurred the expense of preparing, and the court has expended time considering, pleadings that go *not* to a question that will advance the merits of this case but instead to a collateral determination whether the court should consider a particular pleading. In isolation, such expenditures may appear inconsequential. Considered in the proper context of numerous civil actions and frequent disputes, it is apparent that cooperation between opposing counsel is essential to the efficient operation of our justice system.

B.

Turning to the merits of the motion to strike, the court concludes that the reply brief should not be stricken and that plaintiff should not be permitted to file a further response. Although defendant did not immediately seek permission to file a reply, the court has yet to consider the underlying substantive motions; it thus will not interfere with the court's decisional process to consider the reply. The court declines to permit plaintiff to file a further response because the burden on the motions is upon the defendant, who should thus be given the opportunity to open and close the argument.

SO ORDERED.

APPENDIX
Excerpts from the **Dallas Bar Association Guidelines of Professional Courtesy**

PREAMBLE
A lawyer's primary duty is to the client. But in striving to fulfill that duty, a lawyer must be ever conscious of the broader duty to the judicial system that serves both attorney and client.

A lawyer owes, to the judiciary, candor, diligence and utmost respect.

A lawyer owes, to opposing counsel, a duty of courtesy and cooperation, the observance of which is necessary for the efficient administration of our system of justice and the respect of the public it serves.

A lawyer unquestionably owes, to the administration of justice, the fundamental duties of personal dignity and professional integrity.

In furtherance of these fundamental concepts, the following Guidelines of Professional Courtesy are hereby adopted.

COURTESY, CIVILITY AND PROFESSIONALISM

1. General Statement
(a) Lawyers should treat each other, the opposing party, the court and members of the court staff with courtesy and civility and conduct themselves in a professional manner at all times.
(b) The client has no right to demand that counsel abuse the opposite party or indulge in offensive conduct. A lawyer shall always treat adverse witnesses and suitors with fairness and due consideration.
(c) In adversary proceedings, clients are litigants and though ill feeling may exist between clients, such ill feeling should not influence a lawyer's conduct, attitude, or demeanor towards opposing lawyers.

2. Discussion
(a) A lawyer should not engage in discourtesies or offensive conduct with opposing counsel, whether at hearings, depositions or at any other time when involved in the representation of clients. In all contacts with the court and court personnel, counsel should treat the court and its staff with courtesy and respect and without regard to whether counsel agrees or disagrees with rulings of the court in any specific case. Further, counsel should not denigrate the court or opposing counsel in private conversations with their own client. We should all remember that the disrespect we bring upon our fellow members of the Bar and the judiciary reflects *293 on us and our profession as well.
(b) Lawyers should be punctual in fulfilling all professional commitments and in communicating with the court and fellow lawyers.

DEPOSITIONS, HEARINGS, AND DISCOVERY MATTERS

1. General Statement
(a) Lawyers should make reasonable efforts to conduct all discovery by agreement.
(b) A lawyer should not use any form of discovery, or the scheduling of discovery, as a means of

harassing opposing counsel or his client.

(c) Requests for production should not be excessive or designed solely to place a burden on the opposing party, for such conduct in discovery only increases the cost, duration, and unpleasantness of any case.

2. Scheduling Lawyers should, when practical, consult with opposing counsel before scheduling hearings and depositions in a good faith attempt to avoid scheduling conflicts.

3. Discussion

(a) General Guidelines

(1) When scheduling hearings and depositions, lawyers should communicate with the opposing counsel in an attempt to schedule them at a mutually agreeable time. This practice will avoid unnecessary delays, expense to clients, and stress to lawyers and their secretaries in the management of the calendars and practice.

(2) If a request is made to clear time for a hearing or deposition, the lawyer to whom the request is made should confirm that the time is available or advise of a conflict within a reasonable time (preferably the same business day, but in any event before the end of the following business day).

(3) Conflicts should be indicated only when they actually exist and the requested time is not available. The courtesy requested by this guideline should not be used for the purpose of obtaining delay or any unfair advantage.

(b) Exceptions to General Guidelines

(1) A lawyer who has attempted to comply with this rule is justified in setting a hearing or deposition without agreement from opposing counsel if opposing counsel fails or refuses promptly to accept or reject a time offered for hearing or deposition.

(2) If opposing counsel raises an unreasonable number of calendar conflicts, a lawyer is justified in setting a hearing or deposition without agreement from opposing counsel.

(3) If opposing counsel has consistently failed to comply with this guideline, a lawyer is justified in setting a hearing or deposition without agreement from opposing counsel.

(4) When an action involves so many lawyers that compliance with this guideline appears to be impractical, a lawyer should still make a good faith attempt to comply with this guideline.

(5) In cases involving extraordinary remedies where time associated with scheduling agreements could cause damage or harm to a client's case, then a lawyer is justified in setting a hearing or deposition without agreement from opposing counsel.

*294 4. Minimum Notice for Depositions and Hearings

(a) Depositions and hearings should not be set with less than one week notice except by agreement of counsel or when a genuine need or emergency exists.

(b) If opposing counsel makes a reasonable request which does not prejudice the rights of the client, compliance herewith is appropriate without motions, briefs, hearings, orders and other formalities and without attempting to exact unrelated or unreasonable consideration.

5. Cancelling Depositions, Hearings and Other Discovery Matters

(a) General Statement Notice of cancellation of depositions and hearings should be given to the court and opposing counsel at the earliest possible time.

(b) Discussion

(1) Calling at or just prior to the time of a scheduled hearing or deposition to advise the court or opposing counsel of the cancellation lacks courtesy and consideration.

(2) Early notice of cancellation of a deposition or a hearing avoids unnecessary travel and expenditure of time by opposing counsel, witnesses, and parties. Also, early notice of cancellation of hearings to the Court allows the time previously reserved to be used for other matters.

* * *

TIME DEADLINES AND EXTENSIONS

1. General Statement Reasonable extensions of time should be granted to opposing counsel where such extension will not have a material, adverse effect on the rights of the client.

2. Discussion

(a) Because we all live in a world of deadlines, additional time is often required to complete a given task.

(b) Traditionally, members of this bar association have readily granted any reasonable request for an extension of time as an accommodation to opposing counsel who, because of a busy trial schedule, personal emergency or heavy work load, needs additional time to prepare a response or comply with a legal requirement.

(c) This tradition should continue; provided, however, that no lawyer should request an extension of time solely for the purpose of delay or to obtain any unfair advantage.

(d) Counsel should make every effort to honor previously scheduled vacations of opposing counsel which dates have been established in good faith.

* * *

Dallas Bar Association Lawyer's Creed:

1. I revere the Law, the System, and the Profession, and I pledge that in my private and professional life, and in my dealings with fellow members of the Bar, I will uphold the dignity and respect of each in my behavior toward others.

2. In all dealings with fellow members of the Bar, I will be guided by a fundamental sense of integrity and fair play; I know that effective advocacy does not mean hitting below the belt.

3. I will not abuse the System or the Profession by pursuing or opposing discovery through arbitrariness or for the purpose of harassment or undue delay.

4. I will not seek accommodation from a fellow member of the Bar for the rescheduling of any Court setting or discovery ***295** unless a legitimate need exists. I will not misrepresent conflicts, nor will I ask for accommodation for the purpose of tactical advantage or undue delay.

5. In my dealings with the Court and with fellow counsel, as well as others, my word is my bond.

6. I will readily stipulate to undisputed facts in order to avoid needless costs or inconvenience for any party.

7. I recognize that my conduct is not governed solely by the Code of Professional Responsibility, but also by standards of fundamental decency and courtesy.

8. I will strive to be punctual in communications with others and in honoring scheduled appearances, and I recognize that neglect and tardiness are demeaning to me and to the Profession.

9. If a fellow member of the Bar makes a just request for cooperation, or seeks scheduling accommodation, I will not arbitrarily or unreasonably withhold consent.

10. I recognize that effective advocacy does not require antagonistic or obnoxious behavior, and as a member of the Bar, I pledge to adhere to the higher standard of conduct which we, our clients, and the public may rightfully expect.

The **American College of Trial Lawyers' Code of Trial Conduct** (rev. 1987) provides, in pertinent part:

PREAMBLE

Lawyers who engage in trial work have a specific responsibility to strive for prompt, efficient, ethical, fair and just disposition of litigation....

* * *

To his client, a lawyer owes undivided allegiance, the utmost application of his learning, skill and industry, and the employment of all appropriate legal means within the law to protect and enforce legitimate interests. In the discharge of this duty, a lawyer should not be deterred by any real or fancied fear of judicial disfavor, or public unpopularity, nor should he be influenced directly or indirectly by any considerations of self-interest.

To opposing counsel, a lawyer owes the duty of courtesy, candor in the pursuit of the truth, cooperation in all respects not inconsistent with his client's interests and scrupulous observance of all mutual understandings.

To the office of judge, a lawyer owes respect, diligence, candor and punctuality, the maintenance of the dignity and independence of the judiciary, and protection against unjust and improper criticism and attack, and the judge, to render effective such conduct, has reciprocal responsibilities to uphold and protect the dignity and independence of the lawyer who is also an officer of the court.

To the administration of justice, a lawyer owes the maintenance of professional dignity and independence. He should abide by these tenets and conform to the highest principles of professional rectitude irrespective of the desires of his client or others.

This Code expresses only minimum standards and should be construed liberally in favor of its fundamental purpose, consonant with the fiduciary status ***296** of the trial lawyer, and so that it shall govern all situations whether or not specifically mentioned herein.

* * *

12. DISCRETION IN COOPERATING WITH OPPOSING COUNSEL

The lawyer, and not the client, has the sole discretion to determine the accommodations to be granted opposing counsel in all matters not directly affecting the merits of the cause or prejudicing the client's rights, such as extensions of time, continuances, adjournments and admission of facts. In such matters no client has a right to demand that his counsel shall be illiberal or that he do anything therein repugnant to his own sense of honor and propriety.

13. RELATIONS WITH OPPOSING COUNSEL

(a) A lawyer should adhere strictly to all express promises to and agreements with opposing counsel, whether oral or in writing, and should adhere in good faith to all agreements implied by the circumstances or by local custom.   When he knows the identity of a lawyer representing an opposing party, he should not take advantage of the lawyer by causing any default or dismissal to be entered without first inquiring about the opposing lawyer's intention to proceed.

(b) A lawyer should avoid disparaging personal remarks or acrimony toward opposing counsel, and should remain wholly uninfluenced by any ill feeling between the respective clients.   He should abstain from any allusion to personal peculiarities and idiosyncracies of opposing counsel.

* * *

American Bar Association and **State Bar of Texas Codes of Professional Responsibility** ethical considerations:

EC 7-10. The duty of a lawyer to represent his client with zeal does not militate against his concurrent obligation to treat with consideration all persons involved in the legal process and to avoid the infliction of needless harm.

EC 7-36. Judicial hearings ought to be conducted through dignified and orderly procedures designed to protect the rights of all parties.   Although a lawyer has the duty to represent his client zealously, he should not engage in any conduct that offends the dignity and decorum of proceedings. While maintaining his independence, a lawyer should be respectful, courteous, and above-board in his relations with a judge or hearing officer before whom he appears.   He should avoid undue solicitude for the comfort or convenience of judge or jury and should avoid any other conduct calculated to gain special consideration.

EC 7-37. In adversary proceedings, clients are litigants and though ill feeling may exist between clients, such ill feeling should not influence a lawyer in his conduct, attitude, and demeanor towards opposing lawyers. A lawyer should not make unfair or derogatory personal reference to opposing counsel.   Haranguing and offensive tactics by lawyers interfere with the orderly administration of justice and have no proper place in our legal system.

EC 7-38. A lawyer should be courteous to opposing counsel and should accede to reasonable requests regarding court proceedings, settings,

continuances, waiver of procedural formalities, and similar matters which do not prejudice the rights of his client.   He should follow local customs of courtesy or practice, unless he gives timely notice to opposing counsel of his intention not to do so. A lawyer should be punctual in fulfilling all professional commitments.

EC 7-39. In the final analysis, proper functioning of the adversary system depends upon cooperation between lawyers and tribunals in utilizing procedures which will preserve the impartiality of the tribunal and make their decisional processes prompt and just, without impinging upon the obligation of the lawyer to represent his client zealously within the framework of the law.

END OF DOCUMENT

[Effective February 15, 2018.]

JURY PLAN
AMENDED PLAN PROVIDING FOR THE RANDOM SELECTION OF GRAND AND PETIT JURORS IN THE WESTERN DISTRICT OF TEXAS

This amended plan for the random selection of grand and petit jurors in the United States District Court for the Western District of Texas is hereby adopted subject to the approval of the Reviewing Panel of the Fifth Circuit Judicial Council as required by the Jury Selection and Service Act of 1968 and the Jury System Improvements Act of 1978 (Title 28 U.S.C. §§ 1861, et seq.). There is incorporated herein by reference all provisions of Chapter 121, sections 1861, et seq., Title 28, United States Code, and all other laws which hereinafter may be enacted relating to juries and trial by jury.

I. POLICY

It is the policy of this Court that all litigants in any division of this District entitled to trial by jury shall have the right to grand and petit juries selected at random from a fair cross section of the community wherein this Court convenes; and that all citizens shall have the opportunity to be considered for service on grand and petit juries and shall have an obligation to serve as jurors when summoned for that purpose. The use of the word "Court" in this plan shall contemplate any district judge assigned to any division in this District. The phrase "Chief Judge of this District" wherever used in this Plan shall mean the Chief Judge of the Western District of Texas, or in the event of the Chief Judge's absence, disability, or inability to act, the active district judge who is present in the district and has been in service for the greatest length of time.

II. DISCRIMINATION PROHIBITED

No citizen shall be excluded from service as a grand or petit juror on account of race, color, religion, sex, national origin, or economic status.

III. APPLICABILITY OF THE PLAN

This plan shall be applicable to each of the divisions of this Court as established by section 124 (d), Title 28, United States Code. A master and qualified jury wheel shall be maintained for each division. The counties comprising each division of this District are as follows:

(1)	AUSTIN DIVISION:	Bastrop, Blanco, Burleson, Burnet, Caldwell, Gillespie, Hays, Kimble, Lampasas, Lee, Llano, Mason, McCulloch, San Saba, Travis, Washington and Williamson.
(2)	DEL RIO DIVISION:	Edwards, Kinney, Maverick, Terrell, Uvalde, Val Verde and Zavala.
(3)	EL PASO DIVISION:	El Paso and Hudspeth[1]
(4)	PECOS DIVISION:	Brewster, Culberson, Jeff Davis, Loving, Pecos, Presidio, Reeves, Ward and Winkler.
(5)	SAN ANTONIO DIVISION:	Atascosa, Bandera, Bexar, Comal, Dimmit, Frio, Gonzales, Guadalupe, Karnes, Kendall, Kerr, Medina, Real and Wilson.
(6)	WACO DIVISION:	Bell, Bosque, Coryell, Falls, Freestone, Hamilton, Hill, Leon, Limestone, McLennan, Milam, Robertson and Somervell.
(7)	MIDLAND–ODESSA DIVISION:	Andrews, Crane, Ector, Martin, Midland and Upton.

IV. RANDOM SELECTION FROM VOTER REGISTRATION LISTS

The random selection of names of prospective jurors to serve on grand and petit juries shall be drawn from the General Election Voter Registration Lists ("voter registration lists") of the counties comprising each division by the Clerk, any duly authorized deputy clerk, or any other person authorized by the Court to assist the Clerk, either manually or through the use of an electronic data processing system, or through a combination of manual and computer methods. The selection of names shall commence by a purely randomized process through routines approved by the National Institute of Standards and Technology ("NIST"). This Plan is based on the considered conclusion and judgment by the Court that the policy, purpose, and intent of the Jury Selection and Service Act of 1968 will be fully accomplished and implemented by the use of voter registration lists, as supplemented by the inclusion of subsequent registrants to the latest practicable date, as the exclusive source of names of prospective grand and petit jurors, drawn at random and being representative of a fair cross-section of the community.

The voter registration lists referred to shall be those compiled and maintained by the County Tax Assessor–Collector, Elections Administrator, or other such duly elected official for that county reflecting the names of those persons registered to vote in the last general election as supplemented by the inclusion of subsequent registrants to the latest practicable date. Such voter registration information is supplied by the Tax Assessor–Collector, Elections Administrator, or other such duly elected official from voter registration lists for each precinct within such county to the Office of the Secretary of State for the State of Texas in Austin, Texas. It is the judgment of this Court that the voter registration data used to construct each Master Jury Wheel may be acquired either directly from the County Tax Assessor–Collector, Elections Administrator, or other such duly elected official for each county within the District or from the Office of the Secretary of State for the State of Texas in Austin, Texas, provided the data acquired from either source is reflective of the most current information available and has been updated to the last practicable date.

V. MANAGEMENT AND SUPERVISION OF JURY SELECTION PROCESS

The Clerk of Court, one or more designated deputy clerks, or other authorized representative as directed by the Clerk, is empowered to perform every act required or permitted by law or this Plan to manage the jury selection process in the various divisions of this District under the general supervision and control of the Chief Judge, who will perform all duties imposed which cannot be lawfully delegated in accordance with the provisions of the Jury Selection and Service Act of 1968.

The Court finds it advantageous to use an electronic data processing system to maintain the Master Jury Wheels and Qualified Jury Wheels and to perform other clerical services related to the management and use of the jury system. Accordingly, the Clerk is authorized to make such arrangements and procure such assistance as necessary to establish an electronic data system, or combination of manual and electronic records system, to perform the duties of Clerk to achieve the same results as following a manual selection procedure.

VI. MASTER JURY WHEEL

For each division, the Clerk shall provide a Master Jury Wheel into which the names or the identifying numbers of those selected at random from the voter registration lists for that division shall be placed.

The Clerk shall select names from the complete source list databases by electronic media for each Master Jury Wheel by a purely randomized process. An electronic data processing system for pure randomized selection shall be used to select names from each Master Jury Wheel for the purpose of determining qualification for jury service, and from each Qualified Jury Wheel for the purpose of summoning persons to serve as grand or petit jurors. Such random selections of names from the source list for inclusion in each Master Jury Wheel must ensure that each county within the jury division is substantially proportionately represented in the Master Jury Wheel in accordance with the provisions of 28 U.S.C. § 1863 (b)(3). The selections of names from the source list, the Master Jury Wheels, and the Qualified Jury Wheels must also ensure that the mathematical odds of any single name being picked are substantially equal.

The total number of names placed in the Master Jury Wheel for each division shall be determined by the Clerk after consultation with the Chief Judge. To arrive at the total number of names to be placed in the Master Jury Wheel at each division, the Clerk, or a duly authorized deputy clerk, will determine the total number of registered voters for the particular division. The number taken as the total for each county will be based on the official count of voters registered by county. The Clerk will divide the total number of names on the voter registration lists by the number of persons needed to fill the Master Jury Wheel for each division. The selection of names shall commence by a purely randomized process through routines approved by the NIST.

The total number of names for each Master Jury Wheel shall not be less than one-half of one percent of the total number of persons on the voter registration lists in each division. In no event shall the number of names placed in the Master Jury Wheel for any division be less than one thousand (1,000). The Chief Judge may order additional names to be placed in the Master Jury Wheel as and when needed. From time to time, as directed by the Chief Judge, the Clerk shall draw at random from the Master Jury Wheel the names of as many persons as may be required for jury service. The Clerk shall post a general notice, both in the Clerk's office and on the Court's public website, with an explanation of the process by which names are randomly drawn. The Clerk shall mail to every person whose name is so drawn, a Juror Qualification Questionnaire Form ("juror qualification form"), with instructions to fill out and return the form, duly signed and sworn, to the Clerk by mail within ten (10) days. If the person is unable to fill out the form, another shall do it for that person and shall indicate the reason therefor. In drawing the names, allowance should be made for the possibility that some forms will not be returned, that some individuals may be exempt by law, and that others may not be able to comply with the statutory qualifications. Any person who fails to return a completed juror qualification form as instructed may be summoned by the Clerk to appear and fill out such a form; provided, that any person who returns an executed juror qualification form by mail, and who is subsequently summoned for jury service, may be required at the time of his appearance to fill out another juror qualification form in the presence of the Clerk. Any person who fails to appear as directed, or who willfully misrepresents a material fact on a juror qualification form for the purpose of avoiding or securing service as a juror, shall be subject to the provisions of Section 1864(b) of Title 28 U.S.C.

The Master Jury Wheel shall be emptied and refilled, pursuant to the procedure set forth in the Plan, not later than September 1, 2007; and thereafter every two years between January and October 1.

VII. JUROR QUALIFICATION QUESTIONNAIRE FORM

The juror qualification form shall elicit the information contemplated by the questions reflected on the form furnished by the Administrative Office of the United States Courts and as approved by the Judicial Conference of the United States, pursuant to Section 1869(h) of Title 28, United States Code. Upon recommendation of the Clerk, or on its own initiative, the Court shall determine solely on the basis of information provided on the juror qualification form, and other competent evidence, whether a person is unqualified for, or exempt, or to be excused or excluded from jury service; and such determination shall be entered by the Clerk in the space provided on the juror qualification form.

Upon determination of disqualification based on non-citizenship, the Clerk will provide such non-citizenship information to the Elections Division of the Secretary of State for the State of Texas in Austin, Texas in compliance with the provisions of section 1867(f), Title 28, United States Code.

If a juror has changed residence from one division in this District to another division within this District, that juror shall be disqualified from the division of original residence and the juror's name shall be placed into the Qualified Jury Wheel of the division in which that juror resides, provided that the responses on the juror qualification form or follow-up questionnaire otherwise render that person qualified to serve as a juror. If the responses render this person unqualified, then that juror shall be pulled from the Qualified Jury Wheel of the original division and designated disqualified.

VIII. QUALIFICATIONS TO SERVE

Any person shall be deemed qualified to serve on grand and petit juries in this Court unless that person: (1) is not a citizen of the United States; or (2) is not eighteen years of age; or (3) has not resided for a period of one year within the judicial district; or (4) is unable to read, write, and understand the English language with a degree of proficiency sufficient to fill out satisfactorily the juror qualification form; or (5) is unable to speak the English language; or (6) is incapable, by reason of mental or physical infirmity, to render satisfactory jury service; or (7) has a charge pending for the commission, or has been convicted in a State or Federal Court of record, of a crime punishable by imprisonment for more than one year and that person's civil rights have not been restored.

In any two-year period, no person shall be required to: (1) serve or attend court for prospective service as a petit juror for a total of more than thirty days, except when necessary to complete service in a particular case; or (2) serve on more than one grand jury; or (3) serve as both a grand and petit juror.

IX. EXCLUSIONS OR EXCUSES FROM JURY SERVICE

Except as provided herein, no person or class of persons shall be disqualified, excluded, excused or exempted from service as jurors; however, any person summoned for jury service may be: (1) excused by the Court or the clerk under supervision of the Court, upon a showing of undue hardship or extreme inconvenience, for such period as the Court deems necessary, at the conclusion of which such person shall be summoned again for jury service; or (2) excluded by the Court on the ground that such person may be unable to render impartial jury service or that his service as a juror would be likely to disrupt the proceedings; or (3) excluded upon peremptory challenge as provided by law; or (4) excluded pursuant to the procedure specified by law upon a challenge by any party for good cause shown; or (5) excluded upon determination by the Court that such service as a juror would be likely to threaten the secrecy of the proceedings, or otherwise adversely affect the integrity of jury deliberations. Any exclusion pursuant to clause (5) shall be in accordance with 28 U.S.C. Section 1866(c).

Jury service by members of the following occupational classes or groups of persons would entail undue hardship or extreme inconvenience to the members thereof, and the excuse of such members will not be inconsistent with the Act, and may be granted upon individual request:

(1) Person over seventy (70) years of age.

(2) Any student enrolled in a public or private secondary school and any full-time student enrolled at an institution of higher education.

(3) Persons who serve without compensation as a volunteer firefighter or member of a rescue squad or ambulance crew for a federal, state or local government agency.

In accordance with 28 U.S.C. Section 1866(c)(1), the Court, or the clerk under supervision of the Court, may temporarily excuse or defer any qualified juror from jury service upon a showing of undue hardship or extreme inconvenience. The names of deferred persons are to be reinserted into the qualified jury wheel. Whenever a person is excused for reason of undue hardship or extreme inconvenience, the clerk must note the reason for the excuse in the electronic juror record. At the conclusion of a juror's excuse period, he or she will either be summoned again for jury service or his or her name will be reinserted into the qualified jury wheel for possible re-summoning.

X. EXEMPTIONS FROM JURY SERVICE

The Court finds that the exemption of members of the following occupational classes or groups of persons is in the public interest, consistent with law, and not inconsistent with the Act; accordingly, members of such groups are barred from jury service.

(1) Members in active service in the Armed Forces of the United States;

(2) Members of the fire or police departments of the State or any subdivision thereof;

(3) Public officers in the executive, legislative or judicial branches of the government of the United States, or of any State, district, territory, or possession or subdivision thereof, who are actively engaged in the performance of official duties. ("Public Officer" shall mean a person who is either elected to public office or who is directly appointed by a person elected to public office.)

XI. QUALIFIED JURY WHEEL

The Clerk shall maintain separate Qualified Jury Wheels for each division in the District, and shall place in such wheels the names of all persons drawn from the respective Master Jury Wheels who are not disqualified, exempt or excused pursuant to this Plan. The names of both grand and petit jurors for each division shall be drawn at random, as defined in 28 U.S.C. 1869(k), from the Qualified Jury Wheels which shall contain the names of not less than 300 qualified persons in such division at the time of each drawing. The Clerk shall post a general notice, both in the Clerk's office and on the Court's public website, with an explanation of the process by which names are randomly drawn. Into such Qualified Jury Wheel shall be placed from time to time as needed the names of persons drawn from the Master Jury Wheel, who are deemed to be qualified as jurors and not exempted or excused. The Qualified Jury Wheel shall be emptied and refilled, pursuant to the procedure herein prescribed, after the Master Jury Wheel has been emptied and refilled but not later than October 1, 2007, and thereafter every two years between January 1 and October 1. Any unanticipated shortage of petit jurors can be supplied only by drawing the names of additional jurors from the Master Jury Wheel for that division.

In drawing names from the Qualified Jury Wheels for the purpose of summoning persons to serve as grand or petit jurors, the Clerk shall maintain a properly programmed electronic data processing system which provides for names to be selected in a purely randomized process through routines approved by the NIST. Such random selections of names from the Qualified Jury Wheel must ensure that the mathematical odds of any single name being picked are substantially equal in accordance with the purely randomized process.

Prospective jurors in each division may be summoned separately to serve exclusively as either grand or petit jurors; or prospective jurors may be summoned to appear at the same time for later assignment to either the grand jury or the petit jury panel. In the latter event, the Clerk shall draw at random the names of all persons summoned for service as either grand or petit jurors, a sufficient number to be then and there sworn as grand jurors, and the remainder shall be sworn as petit jurors. In either event, the Clerk shall prepare a separate list of names of persons assigned to grand and petit juries. A properly programmed electronic data processing system for pure randomized selection will be used to draw names from the qualified wheel.

When the Court orders a grand and/or petit jury to be drawn for any division or divisions, the Clerk shall issue summonses for the required number of jurors. Service of summonses may be made by personal service, first class mail, or by registered or certified mail. If service is to be made by first class mail or by registered or certified mail, the summonses may be served by the Clerk or a duly designated deputy clerk who shall make affidavit of service. If service is effected by registered or certified mail the addressee's receipt shall be filed with the affidavit of service.

However, upon approval of the district judge supervising the grand jury before which a case is presented, nothing herein shall preclude a grand jury exclusively drawn and empaneled in one division of this District from considering a matter chargeable in another division of this District provided that the borders of said division are contiguous to the division in which the offense was committed, in whole or in part.

XII. DISCLOSURE OF NAMES OF JURORS

In each division of this District, the names of prospective grand jurors and/or petit jurors drawn from the Qualified Jury Wheel shall not be disclosed prior to the date of appearance and qualification of such jurors, unless otherwise directed by the Court; however, the Court in any case may keep such names confidential for such period of time as the interests of justice may require or as otherwise required by the privacy provisions found in the E–Government Act of 2002.

XIII. UTILIZATION OF PETIT JURORS IN MULTI–JUDGE DIVISIONS

It is the policy of this Court to utilize the services of all qualified jurors summoned to appear for jury service as fully and efficiently as circumstances permit. To that end, it is contemplated that the judicial officers in multi-judge divisions of this District will coordinate their jury settings to permit the same pool of petit jurors to serve more than one judge. Jurors summoned for jury service shall appear at the time and place designated in the summons.

XIV. CHALLENGING COMPLIANCE WITH SELECTION PROCEDURES

In all civil and criminal cases, the exclusive method of challenging any jury on grounds that such jury was not selected in conformity with the provisions of Chapter 121 of Title 28, United States

Code, shall be that provided by any existing statute and rule of civil and criminal procedure, including but not limited to section 1867, Title 28, United States Code. Requests to inspect, reproduce, and copy records or papers used by the Clerk in the jury selection process must be submitted in writing to the Clerk or by properly filed motion, for determination by the Court.

XV. MAINTENANCE OF JURY RECORDS

The Clerk shall retain and, upon request, provide access to the following public documents:

(1) the Court's "Amended Plan for the Random Selection of Grand and Petit Jurors";

(2) a verbal description, flow chart, or algorithm of the procedure(s) employed in the automated selection process;

(3) a copy of the Court's order authorizing or instructing the effectuation of the automated, random selection of names from the Qualified Jury Wheel; and

(4) a copy of the public notice.

After any Master Jury Wheel is emptied and refilled as provided above, and after all persons selected to serve as jurors before such Master Jury Wheel was emptied have completed their service, all papers and records compiled and maintained by the Clerk before the Master Jury Wheel was emptied shall be preserved in the custody of the Clerk for four (4) years, or for such longer period as may be ordered by the Court, and shall be available for public inspection for the purpose of determining the valid selection of any jury. At the conclusion of such four year period, unless a longer period has been ordered by the Court, such records and papers shall be destroyed.

XVI. REPORTING STATEMENT

This Plan is based on the conclusion and judgment of the Court that the policy, purpose and intent of the Jury Selection and Service Act of 1968 will be fully accomplished and implemented by the use of voter registration lists, as supplemented by the inclusion of subsequent registrants to the latest practicable date, as the source of an at-random selection of prospective grand and petit jurors who represent a fair cross section of the community. This determination is supported by all the information this Court has been able to obtain after diligent effort on its part and after review of information received from the Office of the General Counsel of the Administrative Office of the United States Courts and the Judicial Council of the Fifth Circuit.

As required by the Judicial Conference of the United States, a report will be made within six months after each periodic refilling of the Master Jury Wheels in this District, in a format acceptable to the Judicial Conference, providing general data relating to each Master Jury Wheel, the time and manner of name selection, the source and number of names placed in the wheel and related information, and an analysis of the race and sex of prospective jurors based on returns of juror qualification forms mailed to a statistically reliable sample of persons chosen at random.

XVII. Effective Date

The provisions of any plan now in effect are superseded and this amended plan shall become effective upon the approval of the reviewing panel of the Judicial Council of the United States Court of Appeals for the Fifth Circuit, as required by 28 U.S.C. § 1863(a), at which time a copy shall be filed with the Clerk in each division of the District.

Adopted this 10th day of February, 2017, by unanimous consent of the Court.

[Dated: March 21, 2017.]

1 On August 22, 2003, the judges of the Western District of Texas entered an order based on a determination that it would be in the best interests of the judicial administration of justice in the El Paso and Pecos Divisions of this Court to have all criminal cases arising in Hudspeth County files in the El Paso Division as opposed to the Pecos Division, wherein Hudspeth County lies. On May 13, 2006, a second order was entered which supplemented the first order to further provide that all civil causes of action arising in Hudspeth County be filed in the El Paso Division as well. As a consequence of these orders, prospective jurors residing in Hudspeth County have been removed from the Pecos Division Qualified Jury Wheel and placed into the El Paso Division Qualified Jury Wheel. Copies of the above and foregoing orders are included as Attachment "I" and Attachment "II".

ECF PROCEDURES

AMENDED PRIVACY POLICY AND PUBLIC ACCESS TO ELECTRONIC FILES

Notice of Electronic Availability of Case File Information

In compliance with the directives of the E–Government Act of 2002, the United States District Court for the Western District of Texas will soon permit electronic public access to documents filed in matters before the court.[1] The Judicial Conference of the United States adopted a policy regarding privacy and public access to electronic files,which becomes effective November 1, 2004, and is applicable to all parties doing business with this court as set out below.

Privacy Policy

I. In order to protect personal privacy and other legitimate interests, parties should either **exclude** sensitive information in any documents filed with the court, or **partially redact** such sensitive information where inclusion is necessary and relevant to the case. Parties should realize that any personal information not otherwise protected will be made available electronically or at the courthouse. The following personal data identifiers should be excluded from all pleadings filed with the court including any exhibits thereto, whether filed electronically or in paper, unless otherwise ordered by the Court: [2]

a. Social Security numbers. If an individual's Social Security number must be included in a pleading, only the last four digits of that number should be used.

b. Names of minor children. If the name of a minor child must be mentioned in a pleading, only the initials of that child should be used.

c. Dates of birth. If an individual's date of birth must be included in a pleading, only the year should be used.

d. Financial account numbers. If financial account numbers are required in any pleading, only the last four digits of these numbers should be used.

e. Home Addresses (in criminal cases). If a home address must be included, only the city and state should be listed.

II. As provided by the E–Government Act of 2002, if a party wishes to file a document containing the full and complete personal data identifiers listed above, that party may,

a. file an unredacted version of the document under seal with the following heading "SEALED DOCUMENT PURSUANT TO E–GOVERNMENT ACT OF 2002"; or

b. file a reference list under seal with the same heading as above. The reference list shall contain the complete personal data identifier(s) and the redacted identifier(s) used in its(their) place in the filing. All references in the case to the redacted identifiers included in the reference list will be construed to refer to the corresponding complete personal data identifier. The reference list must be filed under seal, and may be amended as of right. The unredacted version of the document or the reference list shall be retained by the court as part of the record.

The reference list is intended to serve as a type of "key." For example, if an individual's full Social Security Number is 123–45–6789, the list would include the complete number with the corresponding partially redacted number of XXX–XX–6789, which would be used in future filings. This is beneficial to the court and the clerk's office because it eliminates the filing of two versions of a document—one unredacted (and automatically under seal) and one redacted. The listing can be filed in civil and criminal cases.

Note, however, that in either instance, the court may require the party to also file a redacted copy of the sealed document for the public file (which would be available electronically and at the courthouse).

III. In addition, parties should exercise caution when filing documents that contain the following:

1. any personal identifying number, such as driver's license number;

2. medical records, treatment and diagnosis;

3. employment history;

4. individual financial information;

5. proprietary or trade secret information;

6. information regarding an individual's cooperation with the government;

7. information regarding the victim of any criminal activity;

8. national security information; and

9. sensitive security information as described in 49 U.S.C. See, 114(s).

Counsel is strongly urged to share this notice and privacy policy with all clients so that an informed decision about the inclusion of certain materials may be made. If a redacted document is filed, it is the sole responsibility of counsel and the parties to ensure that all documents and pleadings comply with the rules of this court requiring redaction of personal data identifiers. The Office of the Clerk will not review filings for compliance with this rule.

[Dated: October 29, 2004.]

1 The Western District of Texas is scheduled to become an electronic filing court permitting attorneys to file pleadings and documents electronically in 2005. Documents that are electronically filed will be available to attorneys of record in a case and to registered users of the PACER service. Notice of the court's implementation of the electronic filing program will follow. Social Security cases shall be excluded from electronic public access except to judiciary employees, the United States Attorney or his/her representative, and all litigants in said cases.

2 In order to further comply with the Judicial Conference Policy, in addition to items listed in paragraphs a. through e., the clerk's office shall not, absent an order of the court, provide public access (electronically or at the courthouse) to records determined by the Judicial Conference to be "Non–Public" (e.g., unexecuted criminal summonses and warrants of any kind; documents containing identifying information about jurors or potential jurors; juvenile records; financial affidavits; etc.), as well as sealed documents.

ADMINISTRATIVE POLICIES AND PROCEDURES FOR ELECTRONIC FILING IN CIVIL AND CRIMINAL CASES

Section 1. Title

These Procedures may be known and cited as Administrative Policies and Procedures for Electronic Filing in Civil and Criminal Cases in the United States District Court for the Western District of Texas ("Electronic Filing Procedures").

Section 2. Definitions and Related Requirements

a. Court is defined as the "United States District Court for the Western District of Texas."

b. Court User is defined as an employee of the "United States District Court for the Western District of Texas" who is authorized use of the Court's automated system (CM/ECF).

c. Electronic Filing is defined as uploading a pleading or document, in PDF format, directly from the registered user's computer, using the Court's Internet-based system to file that pleading or document in the Court's case file. Sending a document or pleading to the Court via electronic mail (e-mail) as an attachment does not constitute "electronic filing."

d. Electronic Filing System refers to the Court's automated system that receives and stores documents filed in electronic form. The program is part of the CM/ECF (Case Management/Electronic Case Files) software developed for the Federal Judiciary by the Administrative Office of the United States Courts. When a document has been filed electronically, the official record is the electronic recording of the document as stored in the Court's electronic filing system.

e. Electronically Created Document is defined as a document generated from computer software programs. The document is available, and/or stored by means of a computer device, such as disks, CD's, or DVD's and can be transmitted in an electronic data interchange in various formats between computers utilizing computer software.

f. Filing User is defined as a person who has registered to file documents electronically with the Court. Filing Users must be one of the following: (1) admitted to practice before the United States District Court for the Western District of Texas and a member in good standing of the Court pursuant to Local Court Rule AT–1; (2) admitted pro hac vice; (3) authorized to represent the United States of America; or (4) proceeding as a nonprisoner pro se litigant approved as a Filing

User by the Court. A Filing User must receive a login and password from this district to use the Court's electronic filing system.

g. Hyperlink is a reference in a hypertext document to another document or other resource. It is similar to a citation in literature. However, combined with a data network and suitable access protocol, it can be used to retrieve the resource referenced. A Hyperlink document can be saved, viewed, or displayed as part of the referencing document.

h. Notice of Electronic Filing ("NEF") is an electronic notice automatically generated by the Electronic Filing System at the time a document is docketed. The NEF includes the time of filing and docketing, the name of the party and Filing User filing the document, the type of document, the text of the docket entry, the name of the party and Filing User receiving the notice. If a document is attached to the docket entry, the NEF will contain a Hyperlink to the filed document allowing recipients to retrieve the document.

i. Notice Only Party is someone who is not an attorney of record, but may be an interested third person. Examples of Notice Only Parties include but are not limited to: Administrative Law Judges, Social Security Liaisons, Trustees, and Victim's Coordinators.

j. PACER ("Public Access to Court Electronic Records") is an automated system that allows a person to view, print and download Court docket information over the Internet. Users must register with the PACER Service Center at http://pacer.psc.uscourts.gov/.

k. Portable Document Format ("PDF") is a document file created with a word processor, or a paper document that has been scanned and converted to PDF. Documents must be converted into PDF format to be filed electronically with the Court. Converted files contain the file name extension ".pdf".

l. Pro Se Litigant is defined as a person who represents himself or herself in a Court proceeding without the assistance of an attorney. A Pro Se Litigant who is incarcerated or on probation or supervised release may not participate in the Electronic Filing System and must file all documents by Traditional Filing.

m. Scanned Documents are defined as paper documents that are converted to PDF via a scanner or multifunction copier or scanner, as opposed to converting an electronic document from a word processor. When scanning paper documents that will subsequently be filed electronically, Filing Users should make certain their scanners are configured for 300 pixels per inch (ppi) and black and white rather than color scanning. PDF Files submitted for electronic filing shall not exceed a file size of 5 megabytes. Larger electronic documents shall be divided into smaller PDF files. For example, an eight (8) megabyte PDF File could be divided into one 5 megabyte file and one 3 megabyte file. Files exceeding 5 megabytes will be rejected by the CM/ECF system.

n. Technical Failure is defined as a malfunction of Court owned or leased hardware, software, or telecommunications equipment that results in the inability of a Filing User to submit a document electronically. Technical Failure does not include malfunctioning of a Filing User's hardware, software or telecommunications equipment.

o. Traditional Filing or Traditionally Filed, also referred to as "conventional filing," is defined as submitting paper copies of pleadings and documents in the traditional or conventional manner either in person, by courier, or via United States Postal Service. Traditional Filing includes submitting pleadings and documents via drop boxes.

Section 3. Scope of Electronic Filing

a. Effective date. Electronic Filing in accordance with these Electronic Filing Procedures began September 1, 2006. On November 1, 2006, all documents submitted for filing in all new or pending matters were required to be filed electronically using the Electronic Filing System, unless otherwise permitted by these Electronic Filing Procedures or authorized by the Court.

b. These Electronic Filing Procedures do not supersede the FEDERAL RULES OF CIVIL PROCEDURE, or the FEDERAL RULES OF CRIMINAL PROCEDURE, or the FEDERAL RULES OF APPELLATE PROCEDURE. However, in the event of a conflict with the Local Court Rules for the Western District of Texas ("Local Court Rules"), these Electronic Filing Procedures govern.

c. All civil, criminal, and miscellaneous cases will be assigned to the Electronic Filing System. Except as expressly provided in section 5.a. below, or elsewhere in these Electronic Filing

Procedures, or in other exceptional circumstances, a Filing User must file electronically all documents in PDF format.

(1) Word processing documents converted to PDF format must be converted with a fully licensed PDF conversion program. Documents converted by unlicensed (trial) versions will be rejected.

(2) All documents submitted for electronic filing shall maintain a minimum one inch margin at the top of each page to allow room for the electronic file stamp to be affixed to the document.

(3) Paper documents larger than 8.5″ × 11″ shall not be electronically reduced in size prior to or during the scanning process. Paper documents larger than 8.5″ × 11″ shall be filed traditionally.

(4) The text for all electronically created documents shall be created with a font size of 12.

(5) All documents submitted for filing shall be double spaced.

d. Social Security Cases. All documents in social security cases must be filed electronically, except as noted below:

(1) *Complaint.* The complaint and other documents typically submitted at the time a social security case is initiated in Federal Court may be filed either electronically or in the traditional manner.

(2) Social security transcripts of administrative hearings may be filed either electronically or in the traditional manner. Traditionally Filed transcripts will not be placed into the ECF system, but will be available in paper format with the Clerk.

(3) *Privacy.* To address the privacy issues inherent in a social security review, Internet access to documents other than judgments, opinions and orders, will be limited to counsel and Court staff. Docket sheets will be available over the Internet to nonparties. Nonparties will continue to have direct access to view documents on file in the Clerk's Office.

(4) *Good Cause.* Upon a showing of good cause approved by the Court, the parties may file documents by Traditional Filing.

e. The Filing User is responsible for the legibility of the scanned document. If a scanned document is not legible, the Filing User must file the paper document by Traditional Filing.

f. Pursuant to Judicial Conference Policy regarding the electronic availability of transcripts of court proceedings and the Court's General Order on Electronic Filing of Transcripts, entered May 8, 2008, all transcripts of court proceedings are to be filed electronically. This includes transcripts of sealed proceedings, which must also be filed electronically under seal.

g. With the exception of motions for leave to file detailed under section 4(c), each filing must consist of only one pleading. Multiple pleadings (e.g., an answer and a motion to dismiss, or a notice of appeal and a motion for certificate of appealability) must be filed as separate documents.

Section 4. Method of Electronic Filing

a. Docketing by Filing Users.

(1) The Electronic Filing System requires Filing Users to prepare the electronic docket entry for all electronically filed documents.

(2) Docket entries prepared by Filing Users are immediately posted to the official Court docket and made available to the Court, parties, and the public via PACER.

(3) If a document is submitted in error, the Filing User must file a motion to amend the pleading or a motion to strike the pleading in its entirety. If the Court grants such motion, the Filing User may resubmit the corrected document.

b. In order to preserve the integrity of the Court record, Filing Users who insert Hyperlinks shall also cite the authority by the traditional citation method. A Hyperlink reference is extraneous to any filed document and is not part of the record.

c. If the filing of a document requires leave of Court, the Filing User must include for the Court's review the document as a PDF attachment to the motion requesting leave to file. If the Court grants the motion, the Clerk will file the document, unless the Filing User is otherwise required to file traditionally as set forth in section 5.a. below or by order of the Court.

(1) For purposes of any deadline, a document is deemed filed on the date the Court grants the motion for leave to file, unless otherwise ordered by the Court.

(2) For purposes of service and computation of time for any response, a document is not deemed filed until filed by the Clerk or Filing User, unless otherwise ordered by the Court.

d. Filing Users must comply with the provisions of this Court's General Order dated October 29, 2004 regarding the E–Government Act of 2002.

Section 5. Traditionally Filed Documents: Filing, Scanning and Service

a. The following documents must be submitted traditionally unless otherwise noted:

(1) Civil complaints and notice of removal may be filed traditionally or electronically (all other civil initiating documents must be filed in the traditional manner);

(2) all criminal case initiating documents;

(3) answers, amended answers, amended complaints and other civil pleadings which add parties, (if no new parties are added, these documents shall be filed electronically);

(4) motions to intervene;

(5) motions to appear amicus curiae;

(6) documentary exhibits submitted at trial;

(7) waivers (except waiver of arraignment, waiver of preliminary examination, waiver of detention hearing and waiver of preliminary revocation hearing may be filed electronically);

(8) writs; and

(9) transcript orders (forms DKT–13 and AO 435).

b. Traditionally Filed documents will be scanned by the Clerk when possible and made part of the electronic record.

c. Unless otherwise ordered by the Court, the following Traditionally Filed documents will not be scanned by the Clerk and will not be available on the electronic docket:

(1) documents including attachment or exhibits exceeding 200 unbound pages or 10 megabytes;

(2) documents bound by a binding machine;

(3) documents greater than 8½ by 11 inches;

(4) two-sided documents; and

(5) illegible documents.

d. Paper clips or binder clips are preferred over the use of staples for all Traditionally Filed documents.

e. Traditionally Filed documents must be served in accordance with Rule 5, FEDERAL RULES OF CIVIL PROCEDURE, Rule 49, FEDERAL RULES OF CRIMINAL PROCEDURE, and Local Court Rules CV–5(b)(2) and CR–49(a). (Note: Although a NEF will be generated for Traditionally Filed documents that are scanned by the Clerk, the NEF does not constitute service of Traditionally Filed documents.)

Section 6. Eligibility, Registration, Passwords

a. Attorneys admitted or otherwise authorized to practice in this Court must register as Filing Users. Newly admitted attorneys must register within 10 days of their admission. Attorneys admitted pro hac vice must register within 10 days of the order granting the motion to proceed pro hac vice. An eligible Pro Se Litigant may file papers with the Clerk by Traditional Filing, but is not precluded from filing electronically as approved by the Court.

b. The registration form prescribed by the Clerk and located at www.txwd.uscourts.gov requires:

(1) the Filing User's name, address, and telephone number;

(2) the Filing User's Internet e-mail address; and

(3) a declaration that the attorney is admitted or authorized to practice in this Court or that the party has been approved to register as a Pro Se Litigant.

The Filing User will receive notification of the Filing User's login and password within 48 hours of receipt of the registration form by the Clerk.

c. Registration as a Filing User constitutes consent to electronic service on all documents as provided both in these procedures and by Rule 5(b)(2)(E), FEDERAL RULES OF CIVIL PROCEDURE, and Rule 49(b), FEDERAL RULES OF CRIMINAL PROCEDURE.

d. A Filing User agrees to protect the security of the Filing User's login and password, and shall immediately notify the Clerk if either the login or password has been compromised. The Court may sanction a Filing User for failure to comply with this provision.

e. A Filing User shall update the Filing User's Internet e-mail address and access password via the Electronic Filing System and must keep this information current to ensure timely electronic noticing of case activity. Filing Users may make firm address and phone number changes via the Electronic Filing System, thus superceding Local Rule AT–9.

f. Any attorney who is not a Filing User must submit to the Court in writing good cause why it is necessary that the attorney be authorized to file and serve documents by Traditional Filing.

g. If a Pro Se Litigant retains an attorney, the attorney must advise the Clerk to terminate the Pro Se Litigant's registration as a Filing User upon the attorney's appearance.

h. If it is determined by the Court that the Filing User is abusing the privilege to electronically file documents or is consistently error prone in electronic filing, the Filing User's registration may be rescinded.

i. An attorney no longer licensed in this Court shall withdraw from participating as a Filing User by providing the Clerk with a notice of withdrawal.

j. The registration of an attorney's admission to proceed pro hac vice will be rescinded 60 days after the termination of the case, unless that attorney has a pending application for admission to practice in the Western District of Texas.

Section 7. Consequences of Electronic Filing

a. Electronic transmission of a document through the Electronic Filing System constitutes the filing of the document pursuant to Rule 5(d)(3), FEDERAL RULES OF CIVIL PROCEDURE, and Rule 49, FEDERAL RULES OF CRIMINAL PROCEDURE.

b. The transmission of a NEF constitutes entry on the docket pursuant to Rules 58 and 79, FEDERAL RULES OF CIVIL PROCEDURE, and Rules 49 and 55, FEDERAL RULES OF CRIMINAL PROCEDURE.

c. Filing a document electronically does not alter the filing deadline for that document. Filing must be completed before midnight, Court's local time, to be considered timely filed that day.

Section 8. Entry of Case–Related Documents by the Court

All documents signed by the Court will be filed in accordance with these procedures and will constitute entry on the docket maintained by the Clerk pursuant to Rules 58 and 79, FEDERAL RULES OF CIVIL PROCEDURE, and Rules 49 and 55, FEDERAL RULES OF CRIMINAL PROCEDURE. Any document electronically signed by a Judge or Clerk has the same force and effect as if the Judge or Clerk had signed a paper copy of the document and the document had been entered by the Clerk on the docket in the traditional manner.

Section 9. Attachments and Exhibits

a. A Filing User must submit in electronic form all documents referenced as exhibits or attachments, unless the Court permits Traditional Filing. A Filing User must submit as exhibits or attachments only those excerpts of the referenced documents that are relevant to the matter under consideration by the Court.

b. The record of an administrative agency or judicial proceeding may be filed by Traditional Filing.

c. PDF Files submitted as attachments for electronic filing shall not exceed a file size of 5 megabytes. Larger electronic documents shall be divided into smaller PDF files. For example, an eight (8) megabyte PDF File could be divided into one 5 megabyte file and one 3 megabyte file. Files exceeding 5 megabytes will be rejected by the CM/ECF system.

d. Proposed orders for electronically filed motions must be filed in PDF as an electronic attachment to the motion or included with the motion, unless otherwise directed by the Court. Other documents must be submitted as separate PDF documents; e.g., an Appendix, an Exhibit, an Affidavit, a Supplement, or a Volume.

e. Unless authorized by the Court, trial exhibits will not be placed into the Electronic Filing System, but will be available in paper or electronic format with the Clerk.

Section 10. Sealed Documents

a. Sealed documents shall be electronically filed in cases that are not sealed. A sealed document in a civil case requires leave of the Court before being filed. Therefore, a Motion to Seal must be electronically filed and the Filing User must include for the Court's review the document as a PDF attachment to the motion. If the Court grants the Motion to Seal, the sealed document will be filed by the Clerk unless otherwise ordered by the Court. Unless otherwise directed by a specific divisional office standing order, a sealed document in a criminal case does not require leave of court. (Effective January 20, 2009)

b. Sealed documents cannot be electronically accessed by attorneys or the public. A NEF will be generated for the sealed document, but the document will not be viewable. When a sealed plea agreement is filed, a NEF will be generated to the Government and applicable defendant only. Accordingly, parties may not use the Court's electronic notice facilities to serve sealed documents. Service must be by other means. (Effective January 20, 2009)

Section 11. Consent to Proceed Before a U.S. Magistrate Judge

Abrogated by unanimous vote at Judges Meeting, July 11, 2008.

Section 12. Ex Parte Documents

Ex Parte documents shall be electronically filed in cases that are not sealed. When an ex parte motion or document is filed, a NEF is generated only to the Filing User. Sealed Ex parte document(s) cannot be electronically accessed by attorneys or the public, including the Filing User. (Effective January 20, 2009)

Section 13. Electronic Document Size Limitation

a. Filings including attachments or exhibits that exceed ten (10) megabytes in size, or 200 pages, shall be Traditionally Filed with the Court. (See Section 5.) This limit includes the main document and attachments in toto if applicable. It is the responsibility of the Filing User to ensure that PDF Files meet file size restrictions.

b. PDF Files submitted for electronic filing shall not exceed a file size of 5 megabytes, shall be created with a font size of 12, and shall be double spaced. Larger electronic documents shall be divided into smaller PDF files. For example, an eight (8) megabyte PDF File could be divided into one 5 megabyte file and one 3 megabyte file. Files exceeding 5 megabytes will be rejected by the CM/ECF system.

c. With leave of the Court, a Filing User encountering technical difficulties in electronically filing a voluminous document may file the document by Traditional Filing.

Section 14. Signatures and Retention Requirements

a. A Filing User's login and password will serve as the Filing User's signature for any purpose. An electronically filed document must include a signature block in compliance with Local Court Rule

CV–7(a). The name of the Filing User under whose login and password the document is submitted must include an electronic signature image or be preceded by a /s/, which is typed in the space where the signature would otherwise normally appear.

b. A Filing User must not permit the Filing User's password to be used by anyone other than an agent authorized by the Filing User.

c. Unless otherwise required by law, a Filing User who electronically files any document requiring the signature of other individuals must either (1) submit a scanned document containing the necessary signatures; or (2) indicate on the filed document by the designation /s/ that the original document has been signed. A designation on a document that one person has affixed another person's signature "by permission" may be used under circumstances when signing by permission would be acceptable on a document filed by Traditional Filing.

d. A document containing the signature of a defendant in a criminal case must be filed in a scanned format that contains an image of the defendant's actual signature. The original document must be retained for one year after final resolution of the action, including any appeal.

e. A Filing User filing a document electronically or traditionally must retain, in paper or electronic form, a copy of the filed document for one year after final resolution of the action, including any appeal.

Section 15. Service of Documents by Electronic Means

a. The NEF constitutes service of the unsealed electronically filed document on Filing Users. A Filing User may also notify another Filing User of electronically filed documents by other means, but the service date will be determined by the NEF. Parties who are not Filing Users must be served in accordance with the Federal Rules and the Local Court Rules.

b. A NEF will be generated when a sealed document is filed, but the document will not be viewable. Accordingly, parties may not use the court's electronic notice facilities to serve sealed documents. Service must be by other means.

c. A certificate of service must be included with all filed documents reflecting that service on known Filing Users will be accomplished through the NEF and indicating the manner of service on any party who is not a Filing User. For sample language to use in the certificate of service, see Exhibit 1.

d. For purposes of creating the certificate of service, Filing Users can determine who is registered with the Electronic Filing System using three methods:

(1) the Electronic Filing System includes a program called "Mailing Information for a Case" that the Filing User can execute to list registered users on a case-by-case basis;

(2) the docket includes the party's e-mail address if the party is a registered user of the Electronic Filing System; and

(3) the NEF details who will and who will not receive electronic service by the Court.

e. If a NEF has not been successfully transmitted to an intended recipient, the Clerk will notify the Filing User who originated the filing of the failure in transmission. Service by electronic means is not effective if the Filing User learns that attempted service did not reach an intended recipient.

f. For the purpose of computation of time, the three-day mailing provision found in Rule 6(d), FEDERAL RULES OF CIVIL PROCEDURE, does not apply to service by electronic means.

g. In multidefendant criminal cases, all Filing Users will receive all NEFs, except when a sealed plea agreement is filed. When a sealed plea agreement is filed, a NEF will be generated to the Government and applicable defendant only.

Section 16. Notice of Court Orders and Judgments

a. Immediately upon entry of an order or judgment, the Clerk will transmit a NEF to Filing Users. Transmission of the NEF constitutes the notice required by Rule 77(d), FEDERAL RULES OF CIVIL PROCEDURE, and Rule 49(c), FEDERAL RULES OF CRIMINAL PROCEDURE. The Clerk will send paper copies of orders and judgments to non-Filing Users.

b. The Statement of Reasons page of the Judgment in a Criminal Case will not be available electronically. The Clerk will send a paper copy of the Statement of Reasons to the parties.

Section 17.   Technical Failures/Difficulties

a.   Due to the possibility of Technical Failure or system outage, a Filing User is cautioned not to attempt to electronically file a document on a due date after the Clerk's office has closed for that day. Known Court system outages will be posted at www.txwd.uscourts.gov.

b.   A Filing User whose electronic filing is or would be made untimely as the result of a technical failure in the Court's electronic filing system may seek appropriate relief from the Presiding Judge in the case.

c.   Technical difficulties with the Filing User's system or Internet service provider do not excuse an untimely filing.   A Filing User who cannot file a document electronically because of difficulties with the Filing User's system or Internet service provider must file the document by Traditional Filing <u>and</u> submit a "declaration of technical difficulties" (see Exhibit 2) to the Clerk.

d.   Undeliverable NEF to a Primary E–Mail Address.

(1) If a NEF cannot be delivered to a recipient's primary e-mail address due to difficulties with the recipient's system or Internet service provider, the Clerk will attempt to resend the NEF, but there cannot be any guarantee of timely transmission.   If the second attempt fails, the Clerk will attempt to contact the recipient to resolve the problem.   If the problem cannot be resolved, the Court will be notified of the recipient's noncompliance with these procedures.

(2) If a NEF cannot be delivered due to difficulties with Court's System, the NEF will be resent as soon as possible (normally within one business day) with an explanation for the delay.

e.   Undeliverable NEF to a Secondary E–Mail Address or Notice Only Party.

(1) Because a secondary e-mail address is optional, the Clerk will not attempt to correct problems resulting from an undeliverable NEF, and the e-mail address will be deleted from the profile of the recipient without notification.

(2) For Notice Only Parties, an undeliverable NEF will result in one attempt by the Clerk to have the recipient correct the problem.

(3) Failing timely action by the Notice Only recipient, that address will be deleted from the profile of the recipient without further notification.

f.   Due to the possibility of unsuccessful transmissions of the NEF, parties are strongly encouraged to check the docket at regular intervals.   A PACER account is necessary to check the electronic docket.

Section 18.   Confidentiality and Public Access

a.   A Filing User must comply with the provisions of this Court's General Order dated October 29, 2004, regarding the E–Government Act of 2002, a copy of which is available for review at: http://www.txwd.uscourts.gov/rules/stdord/district/paef_order.pdf

b.   All public filings are available for review.   A person may access the Electronic Filing System at http://www.txwd.uscourts.gov/ by obtaining a PACER login and password.   A person who has PACER access may retrieve docket sheets and documents.

c.   A person may purchase copies of documents filed by Traditional Filing, or certified and exemplified copies of electronically filed documents, from the Clerk in person or by mailing a request designating the case number and document by title or docket number.   Requests submitted by mail must include the payment of the applicable fee as set forth in 28 U.S.C. § 1914.

Section 19.   Support Issues

The Clerk will provide assistance to Filing Users via online support documentation and email at http://www.txwd.uscourts.gov/ecf/.   Court personnel cannot and will not provide any advice, direction, or guidance on the Filing User's computer system, or any legal matter or the content of legal documents.   Support is limited to the administration and proper use of the Electronic Filing System.

EXHIBIT 1
Certificate of Service

(Sample Language)
CERTIFICATE OF SERVICE

I hereby certify that on the 27th day of October, 2004, I electronically filed the foregoing with the Clerk of Court using the CM/ECF system which will send notification of such filing to the following:

Jacob Smith
Attorney at Law
123 South St. Mary's Street
San Antonio, Texas 78212

and I hereby certify that I have mailed by United States Postal Service the document to the following non-CM/ECF participants:

JoAnn JoHansson
Attorney at Law
745 East Mulberry Avenue
San Antonio, Texas 78212
Attorney for James Jameson

_____

/s/Peter Peterson

EXHIBIT 2
DECLARATION THAT FILING USER WAS UNABLE TO FILE
IN A TIMELY MANNER DUE TO TECHNICAL DIFFICULTIES

IN THE UNITED STATES DISTRICT COURT
FOR THE WESTERN DISTRICT OF TEXAS
_____ DIVISION

DECLARATION THAT FILING USER WAS UNABLE TO FILE
IN A TIMELY MANNER DUE TO TECHNICAL DIFFICULTIES

Case Number: _____ Party: _____

Filing User: _____ State Bar Number: _____

E-mail Address: _____ Telephone Number: _____

Title of Document: _____

_____

Filing Deadline Date: (if any): _____

Please take notice that the above named Filing User was unable to file the attached document in a timely manner due to technical difficulties. The reason(s) that I was unable to file this document(s) in an electronic format and the good faith efforts I made prior to the filing deadline to both file in a timely manner and to inform the Court and the other parties that I could not do so are set forth below.

Please check all that apply:

_____ Malfunction of Filing User's computer hardware

_____ Malfunction of Filing User's scanner

_____ Malfunction of Filing User's software

_____ Malfunction of Filing User's telecommunications capability

_____

_____

_____

_____

I declare under penalty of perjury that the foregoing is true and correct.

_____

EXHIBIT 3
NOTICE OF ELECTRONIC FILING

U.S. District Court [LIVE]
Western District of Texas

Notice of Electronic Filing

The following transaction was entered on 10/14/2005 at 4:42 PM CDT and filed on 10/14/2005

Case Name:	Jones v. Doe
Case Number:	1:05–cv–150
Filer:	James Doe
Document Number:	10

Docket Text:
MOTION TO Dismiss by James Doe. (James, Doe)

The following document(s) are associated with this transaction:

Document description: Main Document
Original filename: n/a
Electronic document Stamp:

[STAMP dcecfStamp_ ID="1080075687" [Date=10/14/2005] [FileNumber=71428–0
[40a012c27475ba6fb0d1a468a60f5962228243fbc57e1ff2c42e51ed9dfdf5a17bfcc831fb5a747c4834dc
51e8a5b7957a40e44746c31f9a05cb9aa2b07d0cd5]]

1:05–cv–150 Notice will be electronically mailed to:

William B. Smith smith@lawfirm.net, peterson@lawfirm.net

1:05–cv–150 Notice will be delivered by other means to:

Mary Simmons
Attorney at Law
111 2nd Street
Austin, TX 78745

APPENDIX A.   DOCUMENT REVISION HISTORY

Date	Revision
May 22, 2006	Added language to 17.d. to include Notice Only Parties.
May 22, 2006	Changed 17.d.1 regarding undeliverable NEF"s.
May 22, 2006	Added definition 2.m. Notice Only Parties
August 1, 2006	Significant revisions regarding traditionally filed documents (see 5.a.)
August 1, 2006	Revised electronic filing specifications for size of documents (see 2.j., 9.c., and 13.)
August 1, 2006	Revised e-filing start date to September 1, 2006.
October 6, 2006	Revised section 3.c., added paragraphs 1–3.
October 6, 2006	Added nonconsents to 5.a.8.
July 11, 2008	Added new definition 2.b. "Court User"; added new definition 2.e. "Electronically Created Document"; added font size requirement of 12 to 3.c. (4); revised transcript policy in 3.f.; revised traditionally filed document section 5.a.; added 10 megabyte requirement, 5.c.(1); added 6.j. regarding pro hac vice attorney; added on year requirement; modified pdf file size requirement to 5 megabytes at 9.c. and 13.b.; deleted section 11, consents; modified document retention requirement to include traditionally filed document of 14.e.
December 11, 2008	Added documents submitted for filing shall be double spaced to 3.c.; deleted Section 5.e., retention of traditionally filed documents by Clerk; authorized e-filing of sealed documents section 10; authorized e-filing of ex parte documents section 12; added one year retention requirement for document containing signature of a defendant in a criminal case section 14(c); added parties may not use NEF for service in sealed documents section 14(b); added NEF will not be sent when a sealed plea agreement is filed to all defendants section 15(g); modified section 17 to include procedures for court technical failures with ecf system.
November 4, 2009	Per AO recommendation modified that scanner settings of 300 pixels per in ch (ppi) be used rather than 200 dpi, paragraph m of Section 2.
April 1, 2010	Section 2.d. A statement was added to the effect that electronic documents recorded in CM are the official record of the Court. Section 5. Paragraph a.(1) was revised to advise attorneys that civil complaints and notices of removal may be filed either traditionally or electronically. Paragraph a.(2) revised to remove reference to civil cases as they are addressed individually in the preceding subsection. Section 16 b. is removed in its entirety as its provisions are no longer applicable. Subsection 16 c. and now 16. B clarifies that the SOR will not be available electronically.
June 2, 2011	Section 3.d (1). A statement was added to allow for Social Security complaints to be filed either electronically or in the traditional manner. Section 3.d (2) A statement was added to allow for Social Security transcripts to be filed either electronically or in the traditional manner Section 5. Paragraph a.(7) was deleted to allow attorneys that notices of appeals be filed electronically. Paragraph a.(8) was modified to allow for some waivers to be filed electronically.

	Section 6c. Changed Rule 5(b)(2)(D) to Rule 5(b)(2)(E). Section 7a. Changed Rule 5(c) to Rule 5(d)(3).
November 17, 2013	Section 18(c) Removed requirement for "self-addressed, stamped return envelope' when requesting copies of documents per General Counsel.
December 1, 2016	Section 15(f) removed three-day mailing provision from electronic service pursuant to change in Civil Rule 6(d).

[Effective January 20, 2006. Amended effective October 6, 2006; January 19, 2009; November 4, 2009; April 1, 2010; June 2, 2011; November 17, 2013; December 1, 2016.]

CRIMINAL JUSTICE ACT PLAN

AMENDED CRIMINAL JUSTICE ACT PLAN

I. Authority

Under the Criminal Justice Act ("CJA") of 1964, as amended, 18 U.S.C. § 3006A, and Guide to Judiciary Policy ("Guide"), Volume 7, the judges of the United States District Court for the Western District of Texas, adopt this Plan ("District Plan"), as approved by the Judicial Council of the Fifth Circuit Court of Appeals, for furnishing representation in federal court for any person financially unable to obtain adequate representation in accordance with the CJA. This District Plan supersedes all prior district and divisional CJA plans, including the Modification of Plan for the Implementation of the Criminal Justice Act (W.D. Tex. Feb. 24, 1975).

II. Statement of Policy

A. Objectives. The objectives of the District Plan are:

1. to attain the goal of equal justice under the law for all persons;

2. to provide all eligible persons with timely appointed counsel services that are consistent with the best practices of the legal profession, are cost-effective, and protect the independence of the defense function so that the rights of individual defendants are safeguarded and enforced; and

3. to particularize the requirements of the CJA, the USA Patriot Improvement and Reauthorization Act of 2005 (recodified at 18 U.S.C. § 3599), and the Guide, Vol. 7, in a way that meets the needs of this district.

The District Plan must therefore be administered so that those accused of a crime, or otherwise eligible for services under the CJA, will not be deprived of the right to counsel, or any element of representation necessary to an effective defense, due to lack of financial resources.

B. Compliance.

1. The Court, its Clerk, employees of the Federal Public Defender, and private attorneys appointed under the CJA must comply with the Guide, Vol. 7, and with the District Plan, except as provided in paragraphs 3 and 4 of this subsection.

2. The Court will ensure that a current copy of the District Plan is made available on the Court's website, and provided to CJA counsel upon the attorney's designation as a member of the CJA panel of private attorneys.

3. *Divisional Plans.* The judges of any division of this District may adopt a divisional plan for implementation of the CJA. Any divisional plan will be incorporated into the District Plan as an appendix upon approval by the Fifth Circuit Judicial Council. If there is a conflict between a divisional plan and the District Plan, or an inconsistency between the plans in which the District Plan's requirement is stricter, the District Plan will control.

4. In any individual case, any judge of this Court may vary from the practice or procedure prescribed for by the District Plan, or any divisional plan, so long as the resulting proceedings comply with the U.S. Constitution, the CJA, the Guide and any applicable federal statute, regulation, or federal or local rule of procedure.

III. Definitions

A. Representation. "Representation" includes representation by counsel as well as investigative, expert, and other services.

B. Appointed Attorney. "Appointed attorney" is an attorney designated to represent a financially eligible person under the CJA and the District Plan. Such attorneys include private attorneys and the Federal Public Defender.

IV. Determination of Eligibility for CJA Representation

A. Subject Matter Eligibility.

1. *Mandatory.* Representation must be provided for any financially eligible person who:

a. is charged with a felony or with a Class A misdemeanor;

b. is a juvenile who is detained, or who is alleged to have committed an act of juvenile delinquency as defined in 18 U.S.C. § 5031;

c. is charged with a violation of probation, or faces a change of a term or condition of probation (unless the modification sought is favorable to the probationer and the government has not objected to the proposed change);

d. is under arrest, when such representation is required by law;

e. is entitled to appointment of counsel in parole proceedings;

f. is charged with a violation of supervised release or faces modification, reduction, or enlargement of a condition, or extension or revocation of a term of supervised release;

g. is subject to a mental condition hearing under 18 U.S.C. chapter 313;

h. is in custody as a material witness;

i. is seeking to set aside or vacate a death sentence under 28 U.S.C. § 2254 or § 2255;

j. is entitled to appointment of counsel under 18 U.S.C. § 4109;

k. is entitled to appointment of counsel under the Sixth Amendment to the Constitution; or

l. faces loss of liberty in a case and federal law requires the appointment of counsel.

2. *Discretionary.* Whenever a district judge or magistrate judge determines that the interests of justice so require, representation may be provided for any financially eligible person who:

a. is charged with a petty offense (Class B or C misdemeanor, or an infraction) for which a sentence to confinement is authorized;

b. is seeking relief under 28 U.S.C. §§ 2241, 2254, or 2255 other than to set aside or vacate a death sentence;

c. is charged with civil or criminal contempt and faces loss of liberty;

d. has been called as a witness before a grand jury, a court, the Congress, or a federal agency or commission which has the power to compel testimony, and there is reason to believe, either prior to or during testimony, that the witness could be subject to a criminal prosecution, a civil or criminal contempt proceeding, or face loss of liberty;

e. has been advised by the United States Attorney or a law enforcement officer that they are the target of a grand jury investigation;

f. is proposed by the United States Attorney for participation in a pretrial diversion program; or

g. is held for international extradition under 18 U.S.C. chapter 209.

3. *Ancillary Matters.* Representation may also be provided for financially eligible persons in ancillary matters appropriate to the proceedings under 18 U.S.C. § 3006A(c). In determining whether representation in an ancillary matter is appropriate to the proceedings, the Court should consider whether such representation is reasonably necessary:

a. to protect a constitutional right;

b. to contribute in some significant way to the defense of the principal criminal charge;

c. to aid in preparation for the trial or disposition of the principal criminal charge;

d. to enforce the terms of a plea agreement in the principal criminal charge;

e. to preserve the claim of the CJA client to an interest in real or personal property subject to civil forfeiture proceeding under 18 U.S.C. § 983,19 U.S.C. § 1602, 21 U.S.C. § 881, or similar statutes, which property, if recovered by the client, may be considered for reimbursement under 18. U.S.C. § 3006A(f); or

f. effectuate the return of real or personal property belonging to the CJA client, which may be subject to a motion for return of property under Fed. R. Crim. P. 41(g), which property, if recovered by the client, may be considered for reimbursement under 18 U.S.C. § 3006A(f).

B. Financial Eligibility.

1. *Presentation of Accused for Financial Eligibility Determination.*

    a. Duties of Law Enforcement.

    (i) Upon arrest of an individual in connection with a federal criminal charge, where the individual has not retained counsel, federal law enforcement officials must promptly notify the appropriate court personnel.

    (ii) Employees of law enforcement agencies should not participate in the completion of the financial affidavit or seek to obtain information concerning financial eligibility from a person requesting the appointment of counsel.

    b. Duties of United States Attorney's Office.

    (i) Upon the return or unsealing of an indictment or the filing or unsealing of a criminal information, where the defendant has not retained counsel, the United States Attorney, or his or her delegate, will promptly notify appropriate court personnel.

    (ii) Upon issuance of a target letter, and where the individual has not retained counsel, the United States Attorney, or his or her delegate, must promptly notify, the appropriate court personnel.

    (iii) Employees of the United States Attorney's Office should not participate in the completion of the financial affidavit or seek to obtain information concerning financial eligibility from a person requesting the appointment of counsel.

    c. Duties of Pretrial Services Office.

    (i) When practicable, the pretrial services officer will not conduct the pretrial service interview of a financially eligible defendant until counsel has been appointed, unless the right to counsel is waived or the defendant otherwise consents to a pretrial service interview without counsel.

    (ii) Once counsel has been appointed, the pretrial services officer will provide counsel notice and a reasonable opportunity to attend any interview of the defendant by the pretrial services officer prior to the initial pretrial release or detention hearing.

2. *Factual Determination of Financial Eligibility.*

    a. In every case where appointment of counsel is authorized under 18 U.S.C. § 3006A(a) and related statutes, the Court must advise the person that he or she has a right to be represented by counsel throughout the case and that, if so desired, counsel will be appointed to represent the person if he or she is financially unable to obtain counsel.

    b. The determination of eligibility for representation under the CJA is a judicial function to be performed by the Court after making appropriate inquiries concerning the person's financial eligibility. Other court personnel may be designated to obtain or verify the facts relevant to the financial eligibility determination.

    c. In determining whether a person is "financially unable to obtain counsel," consideration should be given to the cost of providing the person and his or her dependents with the necessities of life, the cost of securing pretrial release, asset encumbrance, and the likely cost of retained counsel.

    d. The initial determination of eligibility must be made without regard to the financial ability of the person's family to retain counsel unless their family indicates willingness and ability to do so promptly.

    e. Any doubts about a person's eligibility should be resolved in the person's favor; erroneous determinations of eligibility may be corrected at a later time.

    f. Relevant information bearing on the person's financial eligibility should be reflected on a financial affidavit (Form CJA 23).

    g. If, at any time after the appointment of counsel, a judge finds that a person provided representation is financially able to obtain counsel or make partial payment for the representation, the judge may terminate the appointment of counsel or direct that any funds available to the defendant be paid as provided in 18 U.S.C. § 3006A(f).

h. If, at any stage of the proceedings, a judge finds that a person is no longer financially able to pay retained counsel, counsel may be appointed in accordance with the general provisions set forth in the District Plan.

i. If, at any stage of the proceedings, a judge finds that a person who can afford retained counsel cannot afford investigatory, expert, or other needed services, such services may be approved in accordance with the general provisions set forth in the District Plan. *See also* Section XIII(A).

V. Timely Appointment of Counsel

A. Timing of Appointment. Counsel must be provided to eligible persons as soon as feasible in the following circumstances, whichever occurs earliest:

1. after they are taken into custody;

2. when they appear before a magistrate or district court judge;

3. when they are formally charged, or notified of charges if formal charges are sealed; or

4. when a magistrate or district court judge otherwise considers appointment of counsel appropriate under the CJA and related statutes.

B. Court's Responsibility. The Court, in cooperation with the Federal Public Defender, the CJA Panel Attorney District Representative,[1] and the United States Attorney, will make such arrangements with federal, state, and local investigative and police agencies as will ensure timely appointment of counsel.

C. Pretrial Service Interview. When practicable, unless the right to counsel is waived or the defendant otherwise consents to a pretrial service interview without counsel, financially eligible defendants will be provided appointed counsel prior to being interviewed by a pretrial services officer.

D. Retroactive Appointment of Counsel. Appointment of counsel may be made retroactive to include representation provided prior to appointment.

VI. Provision of Representational Services

A. Federal Public Defender and Private Counsel. The District Plan provides for representational services by the Federal Public Defender and for the appointment and compensation of private counsel from the CJA panel list(s) maintained by the Court in cases authorized under the CJA and related statutes.

B. Apportionment of Cases. Where practical and cost effective, private attorneys from the CJA panel list(s) will be appointed in a substantial proportion of the cases in which the accused is determined to be financially eligible for representation under the CJA. "Substantial" will usually be defined as a minimum of twenty-five percent (25%) of the annual CJA appointments.

C. Number of Counsel. In an extremely difficult case, the Court may appoint more than one attorney to represent an individual in the interest of justice.

D. Capital Cases. Procedures for appointment of counsel in cases where the defendant is charged with a crime that may be punishable by death, or is seeking to vacate or set aside a death sentence in proceedings under 28 U.S.C. §§ 2254 or 2255, are set forth in Section XIV.

VII. The Federal Public Defender

A. Establishment. The Federal Public Defender for the Western District of Texas, established in 1975, is responsible for rendering defense services by appointment throughout this district.

B. Standards. The Federal Public Defender must provide high quality representation consistent with the best practices of the legal profession and commensurate with those services rendered when counsel is privately retained. See *Polk Cnty. v. Dodson*, 454 U.S. 312, 318 (1981) ("'Once a lawyer has undertaken the representation of an accused, the duties and obligations are the same whether the lawyer is privately retained, appointed, or serving in a legal aid or defender program.'" (quoting ABA Standards for Criminal Justice § 4–3.9 (2d ed. 1980))).

C. Workload. The Federal Public Defender will continually monitor the workloads of its staff to ensure high quality representation for all clients.

D. Professional Conduct. The Federal Public Defender must conform to the highest standards of professional conduct, including but not limited to the *Code of Conduct for Federal Public Defender Employees* and the standards set out in Section XI(A)(2).

E. Private Practice of Law. Neither the Federal Public Defender nor any defender employee may engage in the private practice of law except as authorized by the Code of Conduct for Federal Public Defender Employees.

F. Supervision of the Defender Organization. The Federal Public Defender will be responsible for the supervision and management of the defender organization. Accordingly, the Federal Public Defender will be appointed in all cases assigned to that organization for subsequent assignment to staff attorneys at his or her discretion.

G. Training. The Federal Public Defender will assess the training needs of defender staff and provide training opportunities and other educational resources for the defender organization.

VIII. District and Divisional CJA Panel Committees

A. District CJA Panel Committee.

1. The District CJA Panel Committee is an advisory committee reporting directly to the Chief Judge. It is comprised of the following members:

   a. The Federal Public Defender;

   b. The Panel Attorney District Representative; and

   c. At least one private defense attorney member from each of the Divisional CJA Panel Committees described in Section VIII(B) below.

The Federal Public Defender and Panel Attorney District Representative constitute permanent members of the committee. The private defense attorney members will serve for three-year terms, which may be extended for an additional three years. Terms may be staggered if necessary to ensure continuity on the committee. The Court should make a diligent effort to ensure that the composition of the committee reflects the racial, ethnic, gender, and geographic diversity of the District.

2. The District CJA Panel Committee will meet at least once a year and at any time the Court asks the Committee to consider an issue.

3. The District CJA Panel Committee has the following duties:

   a. **Annual Report.** Reviewing the operation and administration of the District Plan over the preceding year, and recommending any necessary or appropriate changes to the Chief Judge concerning recurring issues or difficulties encountered by CJA panel members or their clients.

   b. **Training.** Assisting the Court in providing training for the CJA panel in each division on substantive and procedural legal matters affecting representation of CJA clients.

   c. **Voucher Review.** At the request of the Court or any Divisional CJA Panel Committee, reviewing and, if necessary, making recommendations to the Chief Judge regarding the processing and payment of CJA vouchers in those cases when the Court, for reasons other than mathematical or technical errors, authorizes payment for less than the amount of compensation claimed by CJA counsel.

   d. **Other Duties.** At the request of the Court or any Divisional CJA Panel Committee, assisting in the performance of the duties set out in Section VIII(B)(3).

B. Divisional CJA Panel Committees.

1. Each Division must establish a Divisional CJA Panel Committee. Membership of the committee is to be determined by the Court in each division, but must include at least one judicial officer, one attorney from the Federal Public Defender's office in the division (if applicable), and one criminal defense attorney who is a member of the panel in that division and who practices regularly there.[2] The committee may also include an employee of the Clerk's Office in the division. The Court should make a diligent effort to ensure that the composition of the committee reflects the racial, ethnic, gender, and geographic diversity of the division.

The judicial officer and defender representative constitute permanent members of the Divisional CJA Panel Committee. The criminal defense attorney member(s) will serve for three-year terms, which may be extended for an additional three years. Terms will be staggered if necessary to ensure continuity on the committee.

2. The Divisional CJA Panel Committee will meet at least twice a year and at any time the Court asks the Committee to consider an issue.

3. Duties of the Divisional CJA Panel Committee may include the following:

a. Membership. Examining the qualifications of applicants for membership on the CJA Panel in each respective division of the District, and recommending the approval of applications of those attorneys who are deemed qualified and the rejection of the applications of those attorneys deemed unqualified.

b. Recruitment. Engaging in recruitment efforts to establish a diverse panel and ensure that all qualified attorneys are encouraged to participate in the furnishing of representation in CJA cases.

c. Removal. Recommending to the presiding district judge in the division the removal of any CJA panel member who fails to satisfactorily fulfill the requirements of CJA panel membership during their term of service, including the failure to provide high quality representation to CJA clients, or who has engaged in other conduct such that his or her continued service on the CJA panel is inappropriate. *See also* Section IX.C.7.

d. Training. Assisting the Court, the Federal Public Defender, the Panel Attorney District Representative, and the District CJA Panel Committee in providing training for the CJA Panel on substantive and procedural legal matters affecting representation of CJA clients.

e. Voucher Review. Assisting the Court, upon request, when the Court contemplates reduction of a CJA voucher for reasons other than technical or mathematical errors. *See also* Section XII.B.6.

f. Mentoring. Appointing experienced CJA panel members to serve in a mentoring program designed to identify and help prepare viable candidates to qualify for consideration for appointment to the CJA panel. Experienced members of the criminal defense bar who have practiced extensively in the federal courts will be selected to serve as mentors. The Divisional CJA Panel Committee may review the mentee applications, make recommendations concerning their participation in the mentoring program, identify appropriate cases for the mentoring program, evaluate the success of the mentoring program, and provide guidance to the mentors.

IX. Establishment of CJA Panels

A. Approval of CJA Panels.

1. The existing, previously established panels of attorneys who are eligible and willing to be appointed to provide representation under the CJA in each division of the District are hereby recognized.

2. Either the presiding district judge in each division, or a majority of the district judges regularly handling criminal matters in that division, may approve attorneys for membership on the CJA panel(s) after receiving recommendations from the Divisional CJA Panel Committee.

B. Size of CJA Panels.

1. The size of the CJA panel(s) for each division will be determined by the Divisional CJA Panel Committee based on the caseload and activity of the panel members, subject to review by the Court.

2. The CJA panel(s) must be large enough to provide a sufficient number of experienced attorneys to handle the CJA caseload, yet small enough so that CJA panel members will receive an adequate number of appointments to maintain their proficiency in federal criminal defense work enabling them to provide high quality representation consistent with the best practices of the legal profession and commensurate with those services rendered when counsel is privately retained.

C. Qualifications and Membership on the CJA Panels.

1. *Application.* The Clerk of Court shall ensure that applications for membership on the CJA panel(s) in each division are available from the Court, including online.

2. *Equal Opportunity.* All qualified attorneys are encouraged to participate in the furnishing of representation in CJA cases.

3. *Eligibility.*

a. Applicants for CJA panel membership must be members in good standing with the federal bar of this District and, when applicable, the Fifth Circuit Court of Appeals.

b. Unless otherwise authorized by the Court, applicants must maintain an office in the division to which they seek to be admitted.

c. Applicants must possess strong litigation skills and demonstrate proficiency with the federal sentencing guidelines, federal sentencing procedures, the Bail Reform Act, the Federal Rules of Criminal Procedure, and the Federal Rules of Evidence.

d. Applicants must have significant experience representing persons charged with serious criminal offenses and demonstrate a commitment to the defense of people who lack the financial means to hire an attorney.

e. Attorneys who do not possess the experience set forth above but believe they have equivalent other experience are encouraged to apply and set forth in writing the details of that experience for the Divisional CJA Panel Committee's consideration.

4. *Appointment to CJA Panels.* Approval of attorneys for membership on CJA panel(s) for each division, in accordance with Section IX(A)(2), will be made after consideration of the recommendation of the Divisional CJA Panel Committee. Due to the highly complex and demanding nature of capital and habeas corpus cases, special procedures will be followed for the eligibility and appointment of counsel in such cases. *See* Section XIV.

5. *Terms of CJA Panel Members.* To establish staggered CJA membership terms, the current CJA panel in each Division will be divided into three groups, equal in number. Initially, members will be assigned to one of the three groups on a random basis. Members of the first group will continue to serve on the CJA panel for a term of one year, members of the second group will continue to serve on the CJA panel for a term of two years, and members of the third group will continue to serve on the CJA panel for a term of three years. Thereafter, attorneys admitted to membership on the CJA panel will each serve for a term of three years, subject to the reappointment procedures set forth in the District Plan.

6. *Reappointment of CJA Panel Members.*

a. The court will notify CJA panel members, prior to the expiration of their current term, of the need to apply for reappointment to the CJA panel.

b. A member of a CJA panel who wishes to be considered for reappointment must apply for appointment to an additional term prior to the expiration of his or her current term.

c. The Divisional CJA Panel Committee may solicit input concerning the quality of representation provided by attorneys seeking reappointment.

d. In making recommendations to the presiding judge regarding reappointment, the Divisional CJA Panel Committee also may consider how many cases the CJA panel member has accepted and declined during the review period, whether the member has participated in training opportunities, whether the member has been the subject of any complaints, and whether the member continues to meet the prerequisites and obligations of CJA panel members as set forth in the District Plan.

7. *Disciplinary Suspension or Removal from a CJA Panel.*

a. Mandatory suspension or removal. Any member of a CJA panel who is suspended or disbarred from the practice of law by any state or federal court will immediately be suspended or removed from the CJA panel.

b. Automatic review. The CJA Committee will conduct an automatic review of any CJA panel member against whom any licensing authority, grievance committee, or administrative body has taken action, or when a finding of contempt, sanction, or reprimand has been issued against the panel member by any state or federal court.

c. Complaints.

(i) Initiation. A complaint against a panel member may be initiated by any member of a District or Divisional CJA Panel Committee, a judge, another panel member, a defendant, or a member of the Federal Public Defender's office. A complaint need not follow any particular form, but it must be in writing and state the alleged deficiency with specificity. Any complaint should be directed to the Divisional CJA Panel Committee, which will determine whether further investigation is necessary.

(ii) Notice. When conducting an investigation, the Divisional CJA Panel Committee will notify the panel member of the specific allegations.

(iii) Response. A panel member subject to investigation may respond in writing and appear, if so directed, before the Divisional CJA Panel Committee or its subcommittee.

(iv) Protective Action. Prior to disposition of any complaint, the Divisional CJA Panel Committee may recommend temporary suspension or removal of the panel member from any pending case, or from the panel, and may take any other protective action that is in the best interest of the client or the administration of the District Plan.

(v) Review and recommendation. After investigation, the Divisional CJA Panel Committee may recommend dismissing the complaint, or recommend appropriate remedial action, including removing the attorney from the panel, limiting the attorney's participation to particular types or categories of cases, directing the attorney to complete specific CLE requirements before receiving further panel appointments, limiting the attorney's participation to handling cases that are directly supervised or overseen by another panel member or other experienced practitioner, or any other appropriate remedial action. The Divisional CJA Panel Committee may also refer any matter to the District CJA Panel Committee or the District Disciplinary Committee for further action.

(vi) Final disposition by the Court. The Divisional CJA Panel Committee will forward its recommendation either to the Chief Judge, or to the presiding judge of the appropriate division, for consideration and final disposition.

(vii) Confidentiality. Unless otherwise directed by the court, any information acquired concerning any possible disciplinary action, including any complaint and any related proceeding, will be confidential.

(viii) None of these procedures create a property interest in being on or remaining on a CJA panel.

8. *Non–Disciplinary Suspension or Removal.* In the event of physical or other incapacity, the Court may suspend or remove a panel member in the interests of justice. In the event that a panel member is suspended or removed under this provision, the Divisional CJA Panel Committee may be called upon to assist the Court in arranging for reassignment of the panel member's pending cases.

X. CJA Panel Attorney Appointment in Non–Capital Cases

A. Appointment List. The Court will maintain, for each division of the District, a current list of all attorneys included on the CJA panel(s), with current office addresses, email addresses, and telephone numbers. These lists will be provided to the District CJA Panel Committee, and to the Divisional CJA Panel Committee for the respective division.

B. Appointment Procedures.

1. The Court is responsible for overseeing the appointment of cases to panel attorneys. The Court will maintain a record of panel attorney appointments and, when appropriate, data reflecting the apportionment of appointments between attorneys from the Federal Public Defender's office and panel attorneys.

2. Appointment of cases to CJA panel members will ordinarily be made on a rotational basis.

3. Under special circumstances, the Court may appoint counsel outside of the normal rotation, and may appoint an attorney who is not a member of a CJA panel. Such special circumstances may include cases in which the Court determines that the appointment of a particular attorney is in the interests of justice, judicial economy, or continuity of representation, or for any other compelling reason. For example, a special appointment may be appropriate due to the particular needs of a defendant or a case, or the specialized knowledge, expertise, or language ability of a particular attorney. It is not anticipated that special circumstances will arise often, and the procedures set forth in the District Plan are presumed to be sufficient in the vast majority of cases in which counsel are to be appointed. Appointments made under this section must be reported to the Divisional CJA Panel Committee.

XI. Duties of CJA Panel Members

A. Standards and Professional Conduct.

1. CJA panel members must provide high quality representation consistent with the best practices of the legal profession and commensurate with those services rendered when counsel is privately retained. *See Polk Cnty. v. Dodson*, 454 U.S. at 318. ("'Once a lawyer has undertaken the representation of an accused, the duties and obligations are the same whether the lawyer is privately retained, appointed, or serving in a legal aid or defender program.'" (quoting ABA Standards for Criminal Justice § 4–3.9 (2d ed. 1980))).

2. Attorneys appointed under the CJA must conform to the highest standards of professional conduct as set out in the Texas Disciplinary Rules of Professional Conduct which have been adopted by the Western District of Texas as the standards of professional conduct. This specification is not exhaustive of the standards of professional conduct. For matters not covered by the Texas rules, the American Bar Association's Model Rules of Professional Conduct should be consulted.

3. A CJA panel member must notify the Divisional CJA Panel Committee within 30 days (i) when charged with or convicted of a felony, or any other serious crime as defined in Texas Rule of Disciplinary Procedure 1.06(AA), or (ii) when any licensing authority, grievance committee, or administrative body has taken action against them, or when a finding of contempt, sanction, or reprimand has been issued against the panel member by any state of federal court.

B. Training and Continuing Legal Education.

1. CJA panel members are expected to remain current with developments in federal criminal defense law, practice, and procedure, including the Recommendations for Electronically Stored Information Discovery Production in Federal Criminal Cases, available at https://www.fd.org.

2. Attorneys appointed to a CJA panel are expected to attend trainings on federal criminal practice sponsored by the court and the Federal Public Defender's office.

3. CJA panel members must attend at least 6 continuing legal education ("CLE") hours relevant to federal criminal practice annually.

4. While low-cost or no-cost CLE may be made available to panel members, the responsibility for timely compliance with the CLE requirements of this Plan rests with the panel member.

5. Failure to timely comply with the training and legal education requirements of this Plan may be grounds for removal from the CJA panel.

C. Facilities and Technology Requirements.

1. CJA panel attorneys must have facilities, resources, and technological capability to effectively and efficiently manage assigned cases.

2. CJA panel attorneys must comply with the requirements of electronic filing and eVoucher.

3. CJA panel attorneys must know and abide by procedures related to requests for investigative, expert, and other services.

D. Continuing Representation. Once counsel is appointed under the CJA, counsel will continue the representation until (1) the matter, including appeals or review by certiorari, is closed; (2) substitute counsel has been approved by the Court, and a notice of appearance has been entered; or (3) the appointment is terminated by Court order.

E. Miscellaneous.

1. *Case Budgeting.* In non-capital representations of unusual complexity that are likely to become extraordinary in terms of cost, the Court may require development of a case budget consistent with the Guide, Vol. 7A, Ch. 2, §§ 230.26.10–20.

2. *No Receipt of Other Payment.* Appointed counsel may not require, request, or accept any payment or promise of payment or any other valuable consideration for representation under the CJA, unless such payment is approved by Court order.

3. *Redetermination of Need.* If, at any time after appointment, counsel has reason to believe that a party is financially able to obtain counsel, or make partial payment for counsel, and the source of counsel's information is not protected as a privileged communication, counsel must advise the Court.

XII. Compensation of CJA Panel Attorneys

A. Policy of the Court Regarding Compensation. Providing fair compensation to appointed counsel is a critical component of the administration of justice. CJA panel attorneys must be compensated for time expended in court and time reasonably expended out of court, and reimbursed for expenses reasonably incurred.

B. Payment Procedures.

1. Claims for compensation must be submitted on the appropriate CJA form through the Court's eVoucher system.

2. Claims for compensation should be submitted no later than 45 days after final disposition of the case, unless good cause is shown.

3. The Clerk's Office will review the claim for mathematical and technical accuracy and for conformity with the Guide, Vol. 7A and, if correct, will forward the claim for consideration and action by the presiding judge.

4. Absent extraordinary circumstances, the Court should act on CJA compensation claims within 30 days of submission. Vouchers should not be delayed or reduced for the purpose of diminishing Defender Services program costs in response to adverse financial circumstances.

5. Except in cases involving mathematical or technical corrections, no claim for compensation submitted for services provided under the CJA may be reduced without affording counsel notice and the opportunity to be heard.

6. The Court, when contemplating reduction of a CJA voucher for other than technical or mathematical reasons, may refer the voucher to the Divisional CJA Committee for review and recommendation before final action on the claim is taken. If any claim for compensation is reduced, either the Court or the Divisional CJA Committee may refer the matter to the District CJA Committee for review and, if needed, recommendation to the Chief Judge.

7. Notwithstanding the procedure described above, the Court may, in the first instance, contact appointed counsel regarding questions or concerns with a claim for compensation.

C. Compensation Under a Mentoring Program. A mentoring programs established under Section VIII(f) may provide compensation for attorney mentees, either (1) at the prevailing hourly CJA rate when the mentee is appointed as second counsel in appropriate cases as determined by the Court; or (2) under the CJA at a reduced rate with prior authorization by the Court.

XIII. Investigative, Expert, and Other Services

A. Financial Eligibility. Counsel for a person who is financially unable to obtain investigative, expert, or other services necessary for an adequate defense may request such services as provided in 18 U.S.C. § 3006A(e)(1), regardless of whether counsel is appointed under the CJA. Upon finding that the services are necessary, and that the person is financially unable to obtain them, the Court must authorize counsel to obtain the services. In seeking investigative, expert, or other services, counsel must comply with Judicial Conference policies set forth in the Guide, Vol. 7A, Ch. 3.

B. Ex Parte Applications. In non-capital cases,[3] requests for authorization of funds for investigative, expert, and other services must be submitted in an *ex parte* application to the Court and must not be disclosed except with the consent of the person represented or as required by law or Judicial Conference policy.

C. Division of Labor. Appointed counsel are encouraged to seek authorization to use law clerks, paralegals, investigators, and other cost-effective service providers to reduce costs for those tasks that, in the attorney's view, need not be performed directly by the attorney.

D. Spanish Language Services. Services under this section include Spanish-language interpretation services in the appropriate case. An attorney who seeks to be appointed to represent Spanish-speaking persons without interpretation services may be required to establish the language proficiency of the attorney or the attorney's staff.

XIV. Federal Capital Prosecutions and Death Penalty Federal Habeas Corpus Proceedings

A. Applicable Legal Authority. The appointment and compensation of counsel in capital cases and the authorization and payment of persons providing investigative, expert, and other services are governed by 18 U.S.C. §§ 3005, 3006A, and 3599[4]; Guide, Vol. 7A, Ch. 6; and the Special Procedures for Reviewing Attorney Compensation Requests in Death Penalty Cases promulgated by the Judicial Council of the Fifth Circuit.

B. Number of Counsel.

1. *Federal Capital Prosecutions.* Pursuant to 18 U.S.C. § 3005, a person charged with a capital offense is entitled to the appointment of two attorneys, at least one of whom must be learned in the law applicable to capital cases. Pursuant to 18 U.S.C. § 3599, if necessary for adequate representation, more than two attorneys may be appointed to represent a defendant in such a case.

2. *Habeas Corpus Proceedings.* Pursuant to 18 U.S.C. § 3599(a)(2), a financially eligible person seeking to vacate or set aside a death sentence in proceedings under 28 U.S.C. §§ 2241, 2254, 2255, or related provisions, is entitled to appointment of one or more qualified attorneys.

C. Procedures for Appointment.

1. *Federal Capital Prosecutions.* Pursuant to 18 U.S.C. § 3005, counsel must promptly be appointed to represent whoever is indicted for a capital crime. In assigning counsel, the presiding judicial officer must consider the recommendation of the Federal Public Defender.

2. *Habeas Corpus Proceedings.*

   a. The Federal Public Defender's Capital Habeas Unit ("CHU") should ordinarily be appointed as either sole counsel or lead counsel in all federal death penalty habeas corpus proceedings in the District. The CHU may also be appointed to handle federal death penalty habeas corpus proceedings outside the District.

   b. If the CHU is not appointed in a federal death penalty habeas corpus proceeding in the District, the presiding judicial officer must consider the recommendation of the Federal Public Defender as to the appointment of counsel.

D. Qualifications for Appointed Counsel in Capital Cases.

1. *Appointment of Counsel Prior to Judgment.* Pursuant to 18 U.S.C. § 3599, at least one of the attorneys appointed must have been admitted to practice in the court in which the case will be prosecuted for not less than five years, and must have had not less than three years' experience in the actual trial of felony prosecutions in that court. Pursuant to 18 U.S.C. § 3005, at least one of the attorneys appointed must be knowledgeable in the law applicable to capital cases.

2. *Appointment of Counsel After Judgment.* Pursuant to 18 U.S.C. § 3599(c), at least one of the attorneys appointed must have been admitted to practice in the court of appeals for not less than five years, and must have had not less than three years' experience in the handling of appeals in felony cases in the court.

3. *Attorney Qualification Waiver.* Pursuant to 18 U.S.C. § 3599(d), the presiding judicial officer, for good cause, may appoint an attorney who may not qualify under 18 U.S.C. § 3599(b) or (c), but who has the background, knowledge, and experience necessary to represent the defendant properly in a particular capital case, giving due consideration to the seriousness of the possible penalty and the unique and complex nature of the litigation.

XV. Effective Date

The District Plan will become effective when approved by the Judicial Council of the Fifth Circuit.

[Approved by the Judicial Council of the Fifth Circuit and effective July 24, 2018.]

1 The Panel Attorney District Representative is a member of a CJA panel in the District who is selected by the Federal Public Defender, with acquiescence from the Chief Judge, to serve as the representative of the District's CJA panels for the national Defender Services CJA program.

2 In divisions that do not have a Federal Public Defender office, the Divisional CJA Panel Committee must include more than one criminal defense attorney.

3 For requests in capital cases, see Section XIV(A) & note 4, *infra*.

4 As to investigative, expert, and other services, Section 3599(f) provides:

Upon a finding that investigative, expert, or other services are reasonably necessary for the representation of the defendant, whether in connection with issues relating to guilt or the sentence, the court may authorize the defendant's attorneys to obtain such services on behalf of the defendant and, if so authorized, shall order the payment of fees and expenses therefor under subsection (g). No *ex parte* proceeding, communication, or request may be considered pursuant to this section unless a proper showing is made concerning the need for confidentiality. Any such proceeding, communication, or request shall be transcribed and made a part of the record available for appellate review.

SELECTED ORDERS
GENERAL ORDER RE: ELECTRONIC FILING OF TRANSCRIPTS
I. Public Access; Attorney Responsibility to Redact

The Judicial Conference of the United States adopted a policy regarding the electronic availability of transcripts of court proceedings at its September 2007 session (*see*: Attachment 1). Under this policy, transcripts will be available electronically to anyone holding a login and password to the judiciary's public access to electronic records system ("PACER") and to anyone using a public terminal in a district clerk's office. Therefore, attorneys must take specific steps to keep personal data identifiers out of transcripts.

To implement the Judicial Conference's policy, the U.S. District Court for the Western District of Texas has adopted the following procedures that apply to all transcripts filed with the court beginning May 15, 2008.

A. Once a transcript has been ordered by an attorney and produced by a court reporter, the court reporter will then electronically file the transcript with the clerk's office, and all attorneys in the case will be notified of such filing through the court's Case Management / Electronic Case Files (CM/ECF) system.

B. An electronically filed transcript will immediately be available for viewing at public terminals in the clerk's office. However, the transcript **may not be copied or reproduced** in the clerk's office for a period of **90 calendar days** from the date of filing with the clerk.

C. Each attorney in the case must review the electronically filed transcript and determine if any of the personal data identifiers listed in the Judicial Conference's policy are included in the transcript. An attorney is generally only responsible for reviewing and indicating redactions in the testimony of the witnesses called on behalf of the party represented by the attorney and in the opening statement and closing argument made on behalf of the party; however, both the attorney for the government and attorney for the defendant must review the entire transcript of a sentencing proceeding. An attorney serving as "standby counsel" to assist a pro se defendant has the same responsibility for redaction as if the attorney was representing the pro se defendant.

D. If an attorney determines that a transcript contains a Social Security number, financial account number, date of birth, name of a minor child, or a home address in a criminal case, the attorney must file a "Redaction Request" with the clerk's office on the approved form (*see*: Attachment 2). This form must be filed within **21 calendar days** of the date the transcript was filed. An attorney may petition the court, by way of a properly filed motion, if the attorney wants information other than the personal identifiers listed above to be redacted from a transcript.

E. A court reporter must redact each personal data identifier as requested by an attorney and electronically file a redacted transcript within **31 calendar days** after the filing of the transcript.

F. Restrictions on an electronically filed transcript, or a redacted version of the transcript if a redaction request was filed, will be removed 90 calendar days after the transcript was filed unless a redaction request is still pending or the presiding judge otherwise directs. The transcript will then be available remotely to view, download or print from PACER or CM/ECF or to obtain from the district clerk's office.

II. Administrative Procedures

The clerk of court is authorized to establish administrative procedures regarding access and use of the ECF system.

[Dated: May 8, 2008.]

ORDER RE: CELLULAR PHONE USE

It having come to the attention of the Court that this district's local rules do not regulate cellular telephones in courthouses and courtrooms, and that recent technology has developed cellular telephones that have the capacity to make photographs and record sound, it is therefore,

ORDERED:

(1) All cellular telephones must be turned off before being taken into any courtrooms.

(2) No cellular telephone that has the capacity to take photographs or record sound is allowed in any courthouse or courtroom.

(3) A violation of this order shall result in a fine of at least $100.00 or confiscation of the cellular telephone, at the discretion of the judge presiding at the time the offense occurs.

[Dated: August 1, 2003.]

ORDER ADOPTING AMENDED PLAN FOR THE PAYMENT OF ATTORNEY FEES AND REIMBURSEMENT OF ATTORNEY EXPENSES IN CIVIL CASES

On this day came on for consideration the proposed "Amended Plan for the Payment of Attorney fees and Reimbursement of Attorney Expenses in Civil Cases". Having previously forwarded copies of the proposed amended plan to the district judges of this Court for review and comment, and having further discussed the terms and provisions of this amended plan at the Judges Meeting held in San Antonio. Texas on May 5, 2011, a vote of the district judges was taken and all district judges in attendance voted in favor of adopting the amended plan. Upon such approval and there being no objection to the revisions proposed, the Court finds that the following orders should be entered:

IT IS ORDERED that the attached "Amended Plan for the Payment of Attorney Fees and Reimbursement of Attorney Expenses in Civil Cases" be, and is hereby **APPROVED** and **ADOPTED** by the Court.

IT IS FURTHER ORDERED that this amended plan is effective immediately and made applicable to all pending attorney appointments in civil cases, and requests for payment of attorney fees and reimbursement of expenses hereinafter submitted in accordance with the terms and provisions of this amended plan.

IT IS FURTHER ORDERED that the Clerk shall post a copy of this order and the amended plan to this Court's Internet site and further make a certified copy available in each divisional office of the United States District Clerk for the Western District of Texas, as well as any other place in this district where the Court does business.

[Dated: July 29, 2011.]

UNITED STATES DISTRICT COURT
WESTERN DISTRICT OF TEXAS

AMENDED PLAN FOR THE PAYMENT OF ATTORNEY'S FEES AND REIMBURSEMENT EXPENSES IN CIVIL CASES

I. Overview of the Program

It has long been the policy of this Court to encourage members of the bar to represent parties who cannot afford counsel. In furtherance of this policy, the Judges of this Court first adopted a "Plan for the Reimbursement of Attorney Expenses in Civil Cases" (hereinafter, "the Plan") on May 15, 1985.

At that time, it was determined that when an attorney is appointed to represent an indigent party in a civil matter, that attorney would be allowed to petition the Court for reimbursement of certain expenses. These were expenses, as initially defined in the policy section of the Plan, that would be incurred in the preparation and presentation of the case. Funding for this program would be obtained from the Court's Non–Appropriated Fund, and the total limit allowable under this program, as originally enacted, was $300 per case.

In August of 2002, it appearing to the Judges of this Court that the maximum allowable amount of $300 was grossly inadequate, and further noting that the newly initiated Attorney Renewal Fee requirement would significantly increase funding into the Non–Appropriated Fund, the Plan was amended to increase the maximum allowable amount of reimbursement for attorney "expenses" to $1,500.

It now appears to the Judges of this Court that the prompt and efficient administration of justice would be advanced by providing, in addition to certain allowable expenses, reimbursement of attorney's fees to those members of the bar called upon by the Court to (1) represent parties in civil cases who cannot afford counsel or (2) serve in an *ad litem* capacity for a minor child or mentally incompetent person. At this time, and until modification by this Court, the total amount of payment of allowable and approved attorney's fees and reimbursable expenses under these provisions **cannot exceed $3,500** for any one attorney in any one case, and said fees must be supported by an itemized listing of the time spent and reasonable description of services rendered on specified legal services. Attorney's fees will be claimed at a rate not to exceed the hourly rate allowed under the Criminal Justice Act, current at the time the services were provided.

Further, the maximum amount for payment of attorney expenses under the provisions of this Plan remains at **$1,500 per case** and is inclusive in the total amount of $3,500 awarded in any one case. **Only in rare and exceptional circumstances can this maximum amount be exceeded with the unanimous approval of the Non–Appropriated Fund Committee.**

II. Restrictions of the Program

A. Only reasonable and necessary attorney's fees and expenses or investigative fees actually incurred by the claimant are payable under the provisions of this Plan.

B. Any costs or fees that are either waived or recoverable under the provisions of Title 18 or Title 28, United States Code, or which have been recovered under any other plan of reimbursement shall not be reimbursed from the Non–Appropriated Fund. Specifically, in any proceeding in which fees and expenses are covered by the Criminal Justice Act, 18 U.S.C. § 3006A, such fees and expenses shall be paid from such funds in accordance with the CJA guidelines and not from this Court's Non–Appropriated Fund.

C. In no case shall an appointed attorney for a party who has been awarded costs or expert or investigative fees pursuant to a judgment in a suit before this Court be eligible for reimbursement of costs or expert or investigative fees from the Non–Appropriated Fund.

D. Only those fees and expenses associated with the preparation and presentation of a civil action in the United States District Court for the Western District of Texas shall be approved for payment. No fees, expenses, or costs associated with the preparation or presentation of an appeal to the United States Court of Appeals for the Fifth Circuit or the Supreme Court of the United States shall be reimbursed from the Non–Appropriated Fund.

III. Procedure for Requesting Reimbursement

A. All requests for payment of attorney's fees or reimbursement of expenses in civil cases must be filed not later than 30 days of the entry of the judgment. The appointed attorney shall file with the Clerk's office a request for payment of attorney's fees or reimbursement of expenses incurred in the preparation or presentation of the case. The appointed attorney shall first submit the request to the Judge to whom the case was assigned for review and approval. Upon approval from that Judge, the Clerk will then forward the request to the Non–Appropriated Fund Committee for final approval.

B. In cases in which an appointed attorney has withdrawn or has been dismissed prior to entry of judgment, that attorney shall file a request for payment of attorney's fees or reimbursement of expenses not later than 30 days of withdrawal or dismissal. A copy of any work product or written product of services obtained for which reimbursement or payment is requested from the Non–Appropriated Fund shall subsequently be provided to newly appointed counsel or, where no new counsel is appointed, to the party for whom counsel had been previously appointed.

C. No interim payments shall be made to counsel for attorney's fees or expenses, absent a showing to the Judge to whom the case is assigned of extreme hardship on the appointed counsel. Attorney's fees and expenses may only otherwise be reimbursed upon the conditions indicated in the next section of the Plan.

IV. Allowable Fees and Expenses

Attorneys appointed by the Court in civil cases may request payment for the following fees and reimbursement for the following expenses, subject to approval by the Judge who is assigned the case and the Non–Appropriated Fund Committee:

A. Attorney's Fees. The maximum total compensation for attorney's fees and expenses in a civil proceeding is $3,500. If multiple or successive attorneys were appointed by the Court to represent an indigent party in a civil proceeding (*e.g.*, if appointed counsel is allowed to withdraw for good cause as determined by the Court, and substitute counsel is appointed), each appointed attorney may be compensated for fees up to $3,500. All requests seeking compensation for attorney's fees shall be accompanied by sufficient documentation to permit the Court and the Non–Appropriated Fund Committee to determine that the time and services claimed for attorney's fees were expended and were appropriate and reasonable. To the extent that the services rendered include a legal assistant performing nonclerical support services, the legal assistant's time and services may be submitted at a rate not to exceed $50 per hour; however, such a claim for legal assistant services are included within the maximum compensation of $3,500.

B. Depositions and Transcripts. Appointed counsel may order written transcripts or depositions necessary in the preparation of the case. Cost of such transcripts shall not exceed the page rate for ordinary copy established in the Western District of Texas. Only the cost of the original of any transcript shall be allowed; the costs of additional copies shall not be reimbursed. In the interest of efficiency and cost effectiveness, appointed attorneys are encouraged to use audio tapes for depositions. If audio-tape depositions are used, transcription of the deposition may be reimbursed at the ordinary page rate established in the Western District of Texas. The cost of video depositions must be approved in advance by the Judge or the Non–Appropriated Fund Committee, if reimbursement is to be requested.

C. Investigative or Expert Services

1. Counsel may request investigative or expert services necessary for the reasonable preparation of a matter. Such services must have prior court approval by the Judge to whom the case is assigned to be considered for reimbursement under this Plan by the Non–Appropriated Fund Committee. If necessary, the request for approval may be made ex parte so that the applicant can avoid revealing trial or case strategy. The trial court shall approve such a request if it determines that the services are reasonably necessary to the prosecution of the applicant's claim. In making this determination, the Court may look by analogy to the standard set for approval of investigative or expert services in 21 U.S.C. §§ 848(q)(9).

2. Counsel should note that approval for this type of expenditure from the Non–Appropriated Fund is not automatic and should be prepared to explain and justify the reasons for its use.

3. Failure on the part of counsel to obtain prior approval of the request may result in a denial of reimbursement by the Judge or the Non–Appropriated Fund Committee.

D. Travel Expenses. Travel by privately owned vehicle for trips in excess of 50 miles each way may be claimed at the mileage rate authorized for federal employees current at the time of travel. In addition, out-of-pocket expenses for reasonable parking fees may also be reimbursed.

E. Fees for Service of Process. Fees for service of papers and the appearance of witnesses that are not otherwise voided, waived, or recovered may be reimbursed from the Non–Appropriated Fund in accordance with the applicable procedures.

F. Interpreter Services. Costs of interpreter services not otherwise voided, waived, or recoverable, may be reimbursed from the Non–Appropriated Fund in accordance with the applicable procedures.

G. Photocopying, Telephone Calls, Etc. Actual out-of-pocket expenses incurred for items such as photocopying, photographs used in the case, toll calls, and the like may be reimbursed from the Non–Appropriated Fund in accordance with the applicable procedures. Such expenses must be reasonably necessary to the preparation of the case.

H. Computer–Assisted Legal Research. Actual out-of-pocket expenses related to computer-assisted legal research must be accompanied by usage statements, along with an explanation of the amount claimed (*e.g.*, proration of a monthly charge or charges identifiable to the specific research), and the total time spent using the computerized system for research, and the applicable database and rate, relating to the civil proceeding the subject of the court appointment. Such expenditure may be considered to be reimbursed from the Non–Appropriated Fund in accordance with the applicable procedures.

V. Non–Allowable Expenses

The following expenses shall be considered to be nonallowable for reimbursement out of the Non–Appropriated Fund pursuant to this Plan:

A. General office expenses, including office overhead, secretarial overhead, payroll costs, equipment depreciation, basic telephone service, and the like shall not be reimbursable under this Plan.

B. Any expenses not properly documented with receipts or other proof may be disallowed by the Judge or the Non–Appropriated Fund Committee.

C. Expenses that may be statutorily recovered, or costs or fees taxed against a party or appointed counsel shall not be reimbursed by this Plan.

VI. Appendices: Fees and Expenses Claim Documents

The following documents, copies of which are attached hereto as Appendices "A" through "C", should be used when submitting a claim under the provisions of this plan.

Appendix A: Claim For Payment of Attorney's Fees and Expenses.

Appendix B: NAF Civil Case Expense Worksheet and Instructions.

Appendix C: NAF Civil Case Hourly Fees Worksheet.

APPENDIX: A

UNITED STATES DISTRICT COURT
WESTERN DISTRICT OF TEXAS

_____ Division

	§	
	§	
INSERT STYLE OF CASE	§	*INSERT CIVIL ACTION NO.*
	§	
	§	
	§	

CLAIM FOR REIMBURSEMENT OF ATTORNEY'S FEES AND EXPENSES

I was appointed by the Honorable (Insert Name or Judge), United States District Judge, to represent (Insert Name of Client) in the above captioned case. Final judgment was entered on (Insert date of Judgment) or I withdrew or was dismissed from the case on (Insert date of withdrawal or dismissal) prior to entry of a judgment. (Strike out inapplicable wording.)

In accordance with the provisions of the *Amended Plan for the Payment of Attorney's Fees and Reimbursement of Expenses in Civil Cases*, I am requesting reimbursement for fees and expenses as follows:

Attorney's Fees Claimed:	
Expenses Claimed:	
Total Amount Claimed:	$0.00

I have attached to this Claim a detailed Hourly Fees Worksheet (with a description of services rendered) or a Report of Expenses Claimed Worksheet, as appropriate, along with all required receipts.

I certify the above attorney's fees and expenses were incurred in the preparation and presentation of this case; that these attorney's fees and expenses do not include any costs either waived or recoverable under the provisions of Title 18 or Title 28, United States Code, or which have been recovered under any other plan; and no attorney's fees or expenses were awarded pursuant to a judgment before this Court.

INSERT SIGNATURE BLOCK OF
ATTORNEY AND SIGN

☐   Pending approval from the Non–Appropriated fund Committee, the above claim for payment of attorney's fees is APPROVED in the amount of $ _____.

☐   Pending approval from the Non–Appropriated Fund Committee, the above claim for reimbursement of expenses is APPROVED in the amount of $ _____.

☐   The above claim for reimbursement is DENIED.

_____
Date

_____
UNITED STATES DISTRICT JUDGE

APPENDIX: B

CIVIL CASE HOURLY FEES WORKSHEET

Support for Claim of Reimbursement of Attorney's Fees from the Non-Appropriated Fund

Case Number: _____

DATE	DESCRIPTION OF SERVICE	SERVICES PROVIDED							
		PREPARE AND REVIEW CASE DOCUMENTS	PREPARE AND REVIEW PLEADINGS	PREPARE AND ATTEND DEPOSITIONS	PREPARE FOR AND ATTEND MEDIATION	PREPARE AND/OR REVIEW PRETRIAL MATERIALS	INVESTIGATIVE WORK	TRAVEL TIME	OTHER
Page Total		0.0	0.0	0.0	0.0	0.0	0.0	0.0	0.0
Grand Total		0.0							

INSTRUCTIONS

Date Column

Insert actual date of service. Dates must be in chronological order.

Description Column

Attorney must provide brief, but appropriately detailed description of services noted in "Services Provided" columns per following examples:

Services Provided Column Headings	Description Column Example
Prepare and Review Case Documents	Interrogatory's Request for Production of Documents Request for Admissions Discovery
Prepare and Review Pleadings	Motion to Compel Motion for Summary Judgement Motion for Dismissal Motion to Transfer Judgment Motion for Continuance
Prepare For and Attend Depositions	
Prepare For and Attend Mediation	
Prepare and/or Review Pretrial Materials:	Motions in Limine Witness Lists Exhibit Lists
Travel Time	
Investigative Work:	Interviews Review Private Investigator Reports
Other:	Other services not classified above.

Columns

Indicate hours logged on each date, for each service provided, in appropriate column.

Note: Prepare separate worksheets for different CJA hourly rates. Multiply hours by CJA rate effective on date of service. Current and historical CJA rate information can be found at http://www.1swd.uscourts.gov/cja/default.asp

APPENDIX: C

CLAIM FOR REIMBURSEMENT OF ATTORNEY'S FEES AND/OR REIMBURSEMENT OF EXPENSES FROM THE NON–APPROPRIATED FUND

Civil Case Number:

Date Court Approved Expenses:

TYPE OF EXPENSE	AMOUNT
Depositions and Transcripts:	
Investigative or Expert Services:	
Investigative:	
Expert:	
Travel Expenses	
Mileage at $ _____ per mile:	
Parking:	
Lodging:	
Fees For Service of Process:	
Interpreter Services:	
Other	
Photocopying:	
Photographs:	
Telephone Toll Calls:	
TOTAL EXPENSES CLAIMED: $	0.00

X _____

Signature   **Date**

Supporting documentation, such as receipts, must be attached to this worksheet

RE: PRO HAC VICE FEES

Came on for consideration by the active and senior district judges of the United States District Court for the Western District of Texas a proposal to increase the current pro hac vice fee of $25.00 to $100.00.

For purposes of historical perspective, the payment of a pro hac vice fee by attorneys not admitted to practice in the Western District of Texas for one specific matter was first adopted by this Court on August 29, 2003. The amount of this fee was set at $25.00. There has been no change to that amount since the fee was first adopted in 2003.

With the exception of one dissenting vote submitted by a senior judge, the district judges in this district have otherwise unanimously agreed to increase the amount of the pro hac vice fee to **$100.00.**

ACCORDINGLY, IT IS HEREBY ORDERED that, **effective beginning Monday, January 13, 2014,** any attorney not admitted to the bar of this Court who is currently representing a party in any matter pending before this Court is required to submit the $100.00 pro hac vice fee if that attorney intends to actively continue representation. Further, if that attorney wishes to practice in this Court in subsequent matters, then the full and complete admissions requirements as set forth in Local Court Rule AT–1 must be met.

[Dated: January 6, 2014.]

UNITED STATES BANKRUPTCY COURT FOR THE
WESTERN DISTRICT OF TEXAS

Including Amendments Received Through
February 1, 2019

Amended Standing Order Regarding Privacy Related Rules.
Standing Order Regarding Mandatory Electronic Filing.
Standing Order Relating to Declarations for Electronic Filing.

SELECTED ORDERS

Standing Order Relating to Payment of Filing Fees in Installments.

Consolidated Standing Order for the Adoption of a District Form Chapter 13 Plan.
Chapter 13 Plan and Motions for Valuation and Lien Avoidance.
Standing Order Regarding Objections to Proofs of Claim.

L. RULE 1001. SCOPE OF RULES AND FORMS; SHORT TITLE

(a) Title. The Rules that follow are adopted as the Local Rules to govern procedure of the Bankruptcy Court until further order, and shall be cited as the "Bankruptcy Local Rules" or "L. Rule."

(b) Scope and Effective Date of Rules.

(1) These Rules supplement or, as permitted, modify the Federal Rules of Bankruptcy Procedure, and shall be construed consistently with those Rules and to promote the just, efficient and economical determination of every action and proceeding.

(2) On motion or on the Court's own initiative, a judge may waive the provisions of these Rules in any case for the convenience of the parties in interest or in the interest of justice. The Appendices may be supplemented or modified from time to time.

(3) These Rules shall govern all actions and proceedings pending or commenced after the effective date cited in the Standing Order adopting the changes to the Local Rules.

(c) Adoption of Certain Local Rules of the United States District Court. The Local Rules of the United States District Court for the Western District of Texas shall not apply to any proceedings in the United States Bankruptcy Court, except as hereinafter adopted. In the event of a conflict between the Local Rules of the United States District Court for the Western District of Texas and these Rules, these Rules shall control.

(d) Definitions.

(1) "District Court" shall mean the United States District Court.

(2) "Court" and "Judge" shall mean the United States Bankruptcy Court and bankruptcy judge, except when a matter is pending before a District Court Judge.

(3) "Trustee" shall mean the trustee appointed in a Chapter 7, 11, 12 or 13 case, except where specifically designated as "U.S. Trustee."

(4) The Local Rules of the United States District Court shall be referenced as "District Court Local Rules."

(5) The Federal Rules of Bankruptcy Procedure shall be referenced as "FRBP" and the Federal Rules of Civil Procedure shall be referenced as "FRCP."

(e) Reference. See the Standing Order of Reference on the Court's website at: http://www.txwb.uscourts.gov/district-court-standing-orders-affecting-bankruptcy-court.

(f) Standards of Conduct. The provisions of Rule AT 5 of the United States District Court Local Rules, which govern Standards of Professional Conduct, are adopted.

(g) Standing Orders.

(1) Standing orders of the Bankruptcy Court apply to practice before and procedures in the Bankruptcy Court for this District, including procedures relating to Chapter 13 practices in the various divisions thereof. These orders may be modified from time to time and are available at each divisional office and at the Court's website at: http://www.txwb.uscourts.gov/standing-orders-index.

(2) In the event of a conflict between a standing order of this Court and these Rules, the standing order shall prevail.

(h) Mediation and Alternative Dispute Resolution Provisions.

(1) The Court on its own motion or upon the motion of any party or party-in-interest may order parties to participate in mediation and may order the parties to bear expenses in such proportion as the Court finds appropriate.

(2) The ADR provisions found at Appendix L–1001–h are adopted.

(i) Court's Website. The most current Local Rules and their appendices, standing orders, and forms may be found on the Court's official website at: http://www.txwb.uscourts.gov.

[Effective November 7, 2005. Amended effective December 1, 2009; November 1, 2013.]

L. RULE 1002. COMMENCEMENT OF CASE

All debtors, other than individuals, must be represented by counsel as of the date a case is filed with regard to all pleadings and hearings (including the bankruptcy petition itself). Petitions filed without counsel by entities other than individuals may be dismissed by the Court on its own motion.

[Effective November 7, 2005. Amended effective November 1, 2013.]

L. RULE 1004. PARTNERSHIP PETITIONS

If a partnership case is commenced by the filing of an involuntary petition by its partner(s) and an order for relief is entered by default, the petitioning partner(s) shall be responsible for timely filing the schedules and statement of financial affairs for the debtor entity. If schedules are not timely filed, the petition may be dismissed by the Court on its own motion.

[Effective November 7, 2005. Amended effective November 1, 2013.]

L. RULE 1005. CAPTION OF PETITION

In addition to the requirements of Bankruptcy Rule 1005, the caption of the petition and all other pleadings and papers accompanying the petition shall include the division in which it is filed (Austin, El Paso, Midland/Odessa, San Antonio, or Waco).

[Effective November 7, 2005. Amended effective November 1, 2013.]

L. RULE 1007. LISTS, SCHEDULES AND STATEMENTS

(a) Creditor List.

(1) *General Requirements.* The master creditor list shall include those agencies and offices of the United States required to receive notice in FRBP 2002. Addresses for proper notice to major United States Government agencies are listed on the Court's website at: http://www.txwb.uscourts.gov/local-rules-attachments.

(2) *Form of Creditor List.* The creditor list shall be in such form as prescribed from time to time by the Clerk of the Court. The format may be found at the Court's website at: http://www.txwb.uscourts.gov/list-creditors-specifications.

(b) Counseling Certificate Required Under § 521(b)(1). If an individual debtor fails to file with the petition commencing the case the certificate, required under 11 U.S.C. § 521(b)(1), from an approved nonprofit budget and credit counseling agency, the Clerk of the Court shall refer the case to the presiding judge for action, which may include dismissal without further notice or hearing.

(c) Small Business Financial Report (Monthly Operating Report). Unless the Court orders otherwise, the filing of a completed Monthly Operating Report in the form required by the Office of the United States Trustee shall be deemed to satisfy the small business debtor's obligation under 11 U.S.C. § 308(b) to file periodic financial and other reports as described therein.

[Effective November 7, 2005. Amended effective December 1, 2009; November 1, 2013.]

L. RULE 1009. AMENDMENTS OF VOLUNTARY PETITIONS, LISTS, SCHEDULES AND STATEMENTS

(a) Required Service. Any amended petition, creditor list, list of 20 largest creditors, or amended or late-filed Schedules or Statements, shall be served by the party filing same on the parties listed in L. Rule 9013(d) and as provided below.

(b) Notice to Newly Scheduled or Added Entities. Copies of amended or late-filed Schedules or Statements shall be served within 3 days of filing, on each entity newly scheduled, newly added, or newly affected. The entity filing same shall also attach a copy of the "Order For and Notice of § 341(a) Meeting," "Discharge of Debtor," "Order Confirming Plan," and "Order Fixing Date for Filing Claims" if such orders have been entered in the case.

(c) Amendment of Creditor Lists. Whenever schedules or amendments add new entities or correct mailing addresses, the debtor shall file with the document an amended creditor list which shall include only the names and addresses of the entities added, deleted, or corrected.

(d) Notice of Amendment of Exemptions and Deadline for Objections. If a debtor's schedule of exemptions is amended, notice of such amendment shall be sent by the debtor to all creditors and to any trustee appointed in the case. Objections to the amended schedule must be filed within 30 days from the date of service of such notice.

[Effective November 7, 2005. Amended effective November 1, 2013.]

L. RULE 1010. SERVICE OF INVOLUNTARY PETITIONS AND SUMMONS

If service of the summons is not filed by the petitioning entity within the time allowed by FRBP 7004, the Court may dismiss the case on its own motion.

[Effective November 7, 2005. Amended effective November 1, 2013.]

L. RULE 1014. DISMISSAL AND CHANGE OF VENUE

Upon motion by any party-in-interest or upon the Court's own motion, the Court may, for cause, transfer venue to another division within the District.

[Effective November 7, 2005.]

L. RULE 1015. CONSOLIDATION OR JOINT ADMINISTRATION OF CASES PENDING IN SAME COURT

To request joint administration of two or more pending bankruptcy cases, a motion setting out the following shall be filed in each case:

(1) the name and case number of each case sought to be jointly administered;

(2) the proposed style and case number to be used on subsequent pleadings if joint administration is ordered;

(3) a summary of any administrative or scheduling orders previously entered in the affected cases which may require modification; and

(4) the need to propose amendments or consolidation of mailing lists in the affected cases for future noticing requirements.

A party seeking consolidation or joint administration must use the form of order prescribed by the Court on the Court's website at: http://www.txwb.uscourts.gov/official-forms-westerndistrict-texas.

[Effective November 7, 2005. Amended effective November 1, 2013.]

L. RULE 1017. DISMISSAL OR CONVERSION OF THE CASE

(a) Any motion to dismiss or convert shall state whether the case has been previously converted from another Chapter of Title 11.

(b) A motion to convert a case filed pursuant to 11 U.S.C. § 1112(a) shall state whether:

(1) the debtor is a debtor-in-possession;

(2) the case was commenced by an involuntary petition; and

(3) the case was previously converted to Chapter 11 other than on the debtor's request.

(c) **Section 521(i)(1) Dismissals.** The Court will enter an order dismissing a case voluntarily filed by an individual debtor under Chapter 7 or 13 under § 521(i)(1) only upon motion of a creditor or party in interest. If no motion is filed, the case will be deemed not to have been dismissed. A motion seeking an order of dismissal under § 521(i)(1) must be filed no later than the 65th day after the date of filing of the case in order for the case to be deemed to have been dismissed effective on the 46th day after the date of filing of the petition. A motion filed later than the 65th day, if granted, will result in a dismissal effective the date of entry of the order dismissing the case. A motion filed pursuant to this Local Rule shall be served on the debtor, the debtor's counsel, the trustee, the United States Trustee, and all creditors and parties in interest.

(d) **Section 521(e)(2)(A) Dismissals.** A party in interest seeking dismissal of a case for failure to comply with § 521(e)(2)(A) must do so by motion. Such motion must be served upon the trustee, the debtor, the debtor's counsel, and the United States Trustee.

[Effective November 7, 2005. Amended effective November 1, 2013.]

L. RULE 1019. CONVERSION OF CHAPTER 11 REORGANIZATION CASE, CHAPTER 12 FAMILY FARMER'S DEBT ADJUSTMENT CASE, OR CHAPTER 13 INDIVIDUAL'S DEBT ADJUSTMENT CASE TO CHAPTER 7 LIQUIDATION CASE

Within 14 days after the effective date of conversion, the debtor shall file an amended schedule indicating any changes to its creditor list, schedules, and statements of financial affairs, as may be applicable, or amend such items to reflect any changes, including but not limited to the inclusion of any property acquired or disposed of since the entry of the order for relief under the previous Chapter. If no amendments are necessary, debtor shall file a certificate to that effect during the 14–day period.

[Effective November 7, 2005. Amended effective December 1, 2009; November 1, 2013.]

L. RULE 1020.1 COMPLEX CHAPTER 11 CASES

Procedures for the administration of complex Chapter 11 cases are governed by the Texas Procedures for Complex Chapter 11 Cases. A copy of the Procedures is attached to these Local Rules as Appendix L–1020.1 and is also available on the Court's website at: http://www.txwb.uscourts.gov/appendix-1-10201-procedures-complex-chapter-11-cases.

[Effective November 7, 2005. Amended effective November 1, 2013.]

L. RULE 1021. HEALTH CARE BUSINESS CASE

In addition to the notice required by Rule 9013, the movant shall serve any motion to determine whether the debtor is a health care business on the designated representative of the Texas state agency responsible for regulating the health care business. A list of Texas state agencies is available on the Court's website at: http://www.txwb.uscourts.gov/1-rule-1021-health-care-business-case.

[Effective November 1, 2013. Amended effective June 3, 2015.]

L. RULE 2002. NOTICES TO CREDITORS, EQUITY SECURITY HOLDERS, UNITED STATES, AND UNITED STATES TRUSTEE

(a) **Returned Notices.** Notices of the Meeting of Creditors and Orders of Discharge which are undelivered shall be returned to the debtor or debtor's counsel. The debtor shall be responsible for re-serving such notices and is responsible for attempting to determine the correct address for each returned notice. The debtor shall file a certificate of service and file an amended creditor list with the Clerk, adding corrected addresses for the entities for whom notice was returned. If corrected addresses are unavailable, debtor or debtor's counsel shall file an amended creditor matrix with the Clerk, who is then authorized to remove from the mailing list on file any such address.

(b) **Section 342(b) Notice to Individual Consumer Debtors.** The notice required under 11 U.S.C. § 342(b) to be given by the Clerk is hereby delegated, and it shall be debtor's counsel's responsibility to give such notice in cases where the debtor is represented by counsel before filing the petition commencing the bankruptcy case.

[Effective November 7, 2005. Amended effective December 1, 2009; November 1, 2013.]

L. RULE 2004. EXAMINATION

(a) **Inapplicable to Adversary Proceedings.** The provisions for examination under FRBP 2004 shall be inapplicable to adversary proceedings.

(b) **Notice.** Not less than 14 days written notice of a proposed examination shall be given to the entity to be examined, and its counsel. The notice shall have a certificate of conference attached indicating what efforts were made to obtain an agreeable date, time and place for the 2004 examination. The entity to be examined shall object to the proposed examination within 7 days after service of the notice. The notice shall describe the scope of the examination and describe any documents requested.

(c) **No Order Required.** Unless a motion to quash or for a protective order is granted the noticed examination shall be, by this Local Rule, deemed ordered by the Court. The notice of intent to conduct Rule 2004 Examination need not be filed. Attendance and production of documentary evidence requested of an entity other than the debtor shall comply with FRBP 9016.

(d) **Motions to Quash.** If an entity objects to the examination for any reason, it must file a motion to quash, and request and obtain an expedited hearing on such motion before the scheduled date and time of the examination. Notwithstanding the filing of a motion to quash, the party to be examined must appear for the noticed examination unless otherwise excused by the Court, or if the notice provides less than 14 days notice.

[Effective November 7, 2005. Amended effective December 1, 2009; November 1, 2013.]

L. RULE 2007.1 APPOINTMENT OF A TRUSTEE OR EXAMINER IN A CHAPTER 11 REORGANIZATION CASE

(a) If a request has been made for the election of a trustee in a Chapter 11 case, pursuant to § 1104(b), the United States Trustee shall schedule a meeting for the purposes of the election.

(b) The party requesting the election shall be responsible for notice.

(c) An application for approval of the election results or, in the event of a dispute, a report summarizing the election and any disputes regarding the validity thereof shall be filed within 14 days after the conclusion of the election.

[Effective November 7, 2005. Amended effective December 1, 2009; November 1, 2013.]

L. RULE 2007.2 APPOINTMENT OF PATIENT CARE OMBUDSMAN IN A HEALTH CARE BUSINESS CASE

(a) In a chapter 7, chapter 9, or chapter 11 case in which the debtor is a health care business, the Court will enter an order no earlier than 22 days and no later than 30 days after commencement of the case directing the United States Trustee to appoint a patient care ombudsman, unless a party has filed a motion to find the appointment of a patient care ombudsman unnecessary under FRBP 2007.2. The Court will conduct a hearing within 30 days after commencement of the case on any motion to find the appointment of a patient care ombudsman unnecessary. A motion to expedite under L. Rule 9014 is required. If the motion to find the appointment of a patient care ombudsman unnecessary is denied, the Court will thereafter enter an order directing the United States Trustee to appoint a patient care ombudsman.

(b) For any motion filed under FRBP 2007.2, the movant shall serve the designated representative of the Texas agency(ies) which regulate the health care business at the address designated at the following website: http://www.txwb.uscourts. gov/1-rule-1021-health-care-business-case.

(c) Unless otherwise ordered by the Court, the patient care ombudsman's appointment will terminate on (i) entry of an order dismissing the case or (ii) the effective date of any chapter 11 plan. If a chapter 11 plan is confirmed, the plan proponent shall notify the patient care ombudsman of the occurrence of the effective date.

[Effective November 1, 2013. Amended effective June 3, 2015.]

L. RULE 2014. EMPLOYMENT OF PROFESSIONAL PERSONS

(a) By Whom Application Made. An application to approve the employment of a professional person shall be made and signed by the entity seeking to employ that person.

(b) Content of Application.

(1) In addition to the information required by FRBP 2014, the application must also contain the following:

(A) the date the petition was filed, the Chapter under which the petition was filed, and (if applicable), the date the case was converted and the Chapter under which the application is currently pending;

(B) the mailing address, telephone number, fax number, and email address (if available) of the professional person to be employed; and

(C) a disclosure of other persons in the same profession who are already or will be employed by the applicant, and an explanation of the reason an additional professional is required.

(2) An application to employ any professional under 11 U.S.C. § 327, 1103, or 1114 shall include a copy of the contract setting forth the terms of compensation and the FRBP 2016(b) disclosure of compensation. The Court recommends that any proposed form of order granting an application to employ include language stating that settlement funds shall not be disbursed without prior court approval.

(c) Nunc Pro Tunc Application. An application filed within 30 days after the professional's commencing services is deemed contemporaneous. Any later application is deemed nunc pro tunc and may be granted only for cause shown, and after notice and an opportunity for hearing.

(d) Procedure. An application to employ a professional person is a contested matter. The application or a summary of the application in the form of Appendix L–2014 must be served on entities pursuant to L. Rule 9013(d). The application may be granted by the Court without hearing. A party in interest who opposes an application for employment may file an objection within 21 days after the date of service of the application summary, and such objection shall be set for hearing notwithstanding the Court's order granting the application to employ.

(e) Withdrawal and Substitution of Counsel.

(1) Withdrawal from representation of, or substitution as, counsel for the debtor, an official creditors' committee, or the trustee must be done upon motion with notice pursuant to L. Rule 9013 and opportunity for hearing. Such motion may be filed with 21–day negative notice as provided in L. Rule 9014(a).

(2) Withdrawal from representation of, or substitution as, counsel for parties other than those described in subparagraph (1) above may be accomplished by notice filed with the Clerk and served pursuant to L. Rule 9013(d).

[Effective November 7, 2005. Amended effective December 1, 2009; November 1, 2013.]

L. RULE 2015. DUTY TO KEEP RECORDS, MAKE REPORTS, AND GIVE NOTICE OF CASE

(a) Maintenance and Disposition of Records. Unless otherwise ordered by the Court on notice and hearing, a debtor shall maintain all books and records until the entry of an order closing the case. A trustee who is in possession of books and records of the debtor may, on notice and hearing, destroy, abandon, store or return to the debtor all or a portion of those books and records. Such notice shall include a detailed description of the books and records and the objection period language as provided in L. Rule 9014(a). Notice shall be given to the United States Attorney, the United States Trustee, and the Special Procedures Office for the Internal Revenue Service, in addition to those persons otherwise entitled to notice under L. Rule 9013.

(b) Debtor's Duty to Report. In a Chapter 11 case, and in an operating Chapter 7 case, the debtor-in-possession or the trustee shall file a Monthly Operating Report, in the form prescribed by the United States Trustee. The Monthly Operating Report shall be filed on or before the 20th day of each month following the month the subject of the report until a plan is confirmed, or the case is converted or dismissed. A signed copy of the Monthly Operating Report shall be furnished to the United States Trustee.

[Effective November 7, 2005.]

L. RULE 2015.1   PATIENT CARE OMBUDSMAN

A patient care ombudsman may satisfy the notice requirements of FRBP 2015. 1(a) by stating that after the forthcoming report, the patient care ombudsman will file reports at least every 60 days during his or her appointment and no further notice of such reports will be given, except to new patients who have not received this notice.

[Effective November 1, 2013.]

L. RULE 2015.2   TRANSFER OF PATIENT IN HEALTH CARE BUSINESS CASE

Unless the Court orders otherwise, any notice served under FRBP 2015.2 shall at the same time be served on the (i) Texas Human Health and Human Services Commission, (ii) Texas Medicaid and Healthcare Partnership, and (iii) designated representative of the agency responsible for regulating the debtor at the address designated at the following website: http://www.txwb.uscourts.gov/1-rule-1021-health-care-business-case.

The health care business shall also provide for the orderly transfer to the new facility of all records relating to any affected patients, subject to applicable patient privacy or other law.

[Effective November 1, 2013. Amended effective June 3, 2015.]

L. RULE 2016.   COMPENSATION OF PROFESSIONALS

(a) Form of Application. Unless otherwise ordered by the Court, an application for compensation and reimbursement of expenses for a professional retained pursuant to Court order shall also include:

(1) A Fee Application Summary in the form of Appendix L–2016–a–2; the Summary must include a summary description of the services rendered by category, reflecting the total cost of each category of services and summarizing the nature and purpose of each category of services rendered, and the results obtained;

(2) A Compensation Support Exhibit reflecting contemporaneous time records itemizing services rendered by category, in a format which reflects a description of each service entry, the amount of time spent rendering that service, the date the service was performed, who performed that service, and the hourly rate of the person performing that service; and

(3) A Reimbursement Support Exhibit, reflecting invoices, records and/or receipts for expenses incurred. The date, time, and amount of each expense shall be shown. Any single expense in excess of $100.00 shall be supported by a receipt or invoice, except for in-house postage, telephone, and photocopying charges.

(b) Procedure for Applying for Compensation in Chapter 11 and Chapter 7 Cases.

(1) The Fee Application Summary must be served pursuant to L. Rule 9013 upon any secured creditor whose cash collateral is used by the estate (and such creditor's counsel), any committee appointed in the case (and such committee's counsel), the twenty largest unsecured creditors, any trustee appointed in the case (and such trustee's counsel), the debtor (and debtor's counsel), and the United States Trustee.

(2) Any party in interest may obtain a copy of the Compensation Support Exhibit and Reimbursement Support Exhibit at no charge by requesting a copy of same from the professional seeking compensation.

(3) A joint application can be filed for jointly administered cases. The Court reserves the right to order that fees be allocated at the time of the final fee application.

(c) Procedure for Compensation in Chapter 13 Cases.

(1) The Chapter 13 trustee shall review the attorney's fee charged in each case and shall make a recommendation concerning the reasonableness of the compensation requested. If the Court agrees with the trustee's recommendation, then confirmation of the Chapter 13 plan shall also constitute Court approval of the fees requested. The Court may, on its own motion, set a hearing to review the attorney's fee requested, which hearing may be conducted at the same time as the confirmation hearing scheduled in the case. The Court in each division may set a flat fee for routine non-business Chapter 13 cases, and a flat fee for routine business Chapter 13 cases. Notwithstanding said flat fee, an attorney may, for cause shown, request a higher fee.

(2) An attorney representing a debtor under Chapter 13 shall be the attorney of record from the filing of the petition for relief under Chapter 13, if signed by the attorney, or from the filing of a notice of appearance until the close or dismissal of the case (including disposition of motions to reinstate), unless relieved from representation by order of the Court.

(3) Standing Orders for each division govern compensation in Chapter 13 cases and are posted on the Court's website at: http://www.txwb.uscourts.gov/standingorders- index.

[Effective November 7, 2005. Amended effective November 1, 2013.]

L. RULE 2090. ADMISSION PRO HAC VICE

(1) **In General.** An attorney who is licensed by the highest court of a state, but who is not admitted to practice in the Western District of Texas, may represent a party in this Court pro hac vice by permission of the judge presiding. Admission to practice is limited to the particular case or adversary proceeding for which it is approved; it is not a general admission to practice before the Bankruptcy Court or the District Court. An attorney admitted pro hac vice must read and comply with the Local Court Rules for the Bankruptcy Court for the Western District of Texas. By appearing in any case, an attorney becomes subject to the rules of this Court.

(2) **Procedure.** An attorney seeking admission pro hac vice must use the form of motion and order prescribed by the Court, which may be found on the Court's website at: http://www.txwb.uscourts.gov/official-forms-western-district-texas.

(3) The motion may be filed ex parte.

[Effective November 1, 2013.]

L. RULE 3001. PROOF OF CLAIM

For the sole purpose of section 8 of the B 10 official proof of claim form, "creditor" and "debtor" shall include counsel for the creditor and for the debtor.

[Effective November 1, 2013.]

L. RULE 3002. FILING PROOF OF CLAIM OR INTEREST

(a) **Service of Claim.** A copy of each proof of claim or interest shall be served with any attachments on the debtor's attorney (or on the debtor, if the debtor is not represented by counsel) and any trustee appointed in the case.

(b) **Secured Proofs of Claim.** A secured creditor (or the debtor) in Chapter 12 and Chapter 13 must file a proof of claim for the claim to be allowed. Such proof of claim must be filed within the time frame set forth in FRBP 3002(c).

[Effective November 7, 2005. Amended effective November 1, 2013.]

L. RULE 3002.1 NOTICE RELATING TO CLAIMS SECURED BY SECURITY INTEREST IN THE DEBTOR'S PRINCIPAL RESIDENCE

(a) If the Court grants relief from the automatic stay with respect to property subject to this Rule, the Notices set forth in FRBP 3002.1(b), (c) and (f) are no longer required.

(b) If the holder of a claim, as defined in FRBP 3002.1, files a response which disagrees with the Notice of Final Cure Payment under 3002.1(f), or otherwise asserts that unpaid post-petition amounts are outstanding, and neither the debtor nor the trustee timely file a motion pursuant to FRBP 3002.1(h), the trustee is authorized to close the case.

(c) For provisions relating to payment of such fees and expenses, see divisional Standing Orders Relating to Bankruptcy Rule 3002.1.

[Effective November 1, 2013.]

L. RULE 3003. TIME FOR FILING PROOF OF CLAIM OR EQUITY SECURITY INTEREST IN CHAPTER 9 MUNICIPALITY OR CHAPTER 11 REORGANIZATION CASE; CLAIMS PROCEDURE FOR ADMINISTRATIVE CLAIMS

(a) **Bar Date for Proof of Claim or Interest in Notice of First Meeting.** Proofs of claim or interests in Chapter 11 cases shall be filed by the date established in the Notice of the Meeting of Creditors pursuant to 11 U.S.C. § 341, unless the Court, upon motion and after notice and an opportunity for hearing, orders otherwise.

(b) **Bar Date for Administrative Claims.** The Court, after notice and an opportunity for hearing, may establish a bar date for filing an application for allowance and payment of an administrative claim, either on its own motion or on motion of a party in interest, filed pursuant to L. Rules 9013 and 9014.

[Effective November 7, 2005.]

L. RULE 3004. FILING OF CLAIMS BY DEBTOR OR TRUSTEE

A proof of claim filed under FRBP 3004 need not comply with Bankruptcy Rule 3001(c).

[Effective November 1, 2013.]

L. RULE 3005. FILING OF CLAIM, ACCEPTANCE, OR REJECTION BY GUARANTOR, SURETY, ENDORSER, OR OTHER CREDITOR

A proof of claim filed under FRBP 3005 need not comply with Bankruptcy Rule 3001(c).

[Effective November 1, 2013.]

L. RULE 3007. OBJECTIONS TO CLAIM

(a) Objections to claims are contested matters and may be made on negative notice as set forth in L. Rule 9014. If negative notice is not used or if a timely response to the objection is filed, a hearing on the objection will be set in pursuant to FRBP 3007.

(b) All Objections to claims shall specifically set forth all bases for the objection. General denials regarding the accuracy of the claim without specific contentions regarding the disputed items may result in the Court denying the Objection.

[Effective November 7, 2005. Amended effective November 1, 2013.]

L. RULE 3011. UNCLAIMED FUNDS IN CHAPTER 7 LIQUIDATION, CHAPTER 12 FAMILY FARMER'S DEBT ADJUSTMENT, AND CHAPTER 13 INDIVIDUAL'S DEBT ADJUSTMENT CASES

An application seeking withdrawal of funds must comply with the procedures set forth by the clerk's office, which may be found on the Court's website at: http://www.txwb.uscourts.gov/unclaimed-funds.

[Effective November 7, 2005. Amended effective November 1, 2013.]

L. RULE 3012. VALUATION OF SECURITY

All motions for valuation shall include the name of the creditor and the claim number, if any, in the title of the motion.

[Effective November 7, 2005. Amended effective November 1, 2013.]

L. RULE 3015. CHAPTER 13 PLAN AND CONFIRMATION HEARINGS

(a) **Timely Filing of Plan.** If the plan is not timely filed, the Court may summarily dismiss the case without notice or hearing. A motion to extend the time for filing the plan must be filed before the expiration of the time provided in FRBP 3015(b).

(b) **Notice.** Unless provided otherwise by standing order, the debtor shall serve a copy of the plan and any amended plan on the Trustee, all creditors, and all parties requesting notice.

(c) **Pay Orders and Waivers of Pay Orders.** Pay orders are required in all Chapter 13 cases, except as provided herein or as otherwise ordered by the Court. The Chapter 13 trustee may waive the requirement of a pay order at the Meeting of Creditors on request of the debtor. If the Chapter 13 trustee declines to waive the requirement of a pay order, then the debtor may request a waiver of the pay order from the Court on motion and notice to the trustee and with opportunity for a hearing.

(d) **Modification of Plan After Confirmation.** Any modification to a plan after confirmation shall be upon motion and shall comply with the provisions of L. Rule 9014 and the requirements imposed by any applicable standing order affecting Chapter 13 practice in the division in which the case is pending. Contemporaneously with the motion to modify, amended schedules I and J must be filed with the Court as a separate entry on the docket. The filing of amended I and J only applies to the debtor, and not the Chapter 13 trustee.

(e) **Excused Attendance at Confirmation Hearings.** If all of the following conditions are met, the debtor and the debtor's attorney are excused from attending the scheduled Chapter 13 plan confirmation hearing:

(1) the plan has been filed and requirements imposed by any applicable standing order affecting Chapter 13 practice in the division in which the case is pending have been complied with;

(2) no party in interest has timely filed an objection or any such objection has been resolved before confirmation;

(3) the Chapter 13 trustee has recommended confirmation; and

(4) the Declaration Concerning Confirmation Requirements is filed no later than 7 days before the confirmation hearing to the extent that the Chapter 13 trustee requires a Declaration Concerning Confirmation Requirements.

[Effective November 7, 2005. Amended effective November 1, 2013.]

L. RULE 3017. APPROVAL OF DISCLOSURE STATEMENT IN CHAPTER 11 CASES

Unless otherwise ordered by the Court, any objection to a disclosure statement shall be filed and served not less than 3 days before the hearing on the disclosure statement.

[Effective November 7, 2005. Amended effective December 1, 2009; November 1, 2013.]

L. RULE 3018. ACCEPTANCE OR REJECTION OF A PLAN IN CHAPTER 11 REORGANIZATION CASES

(a) **Voting.** No ballots shall be filed with the Clerk of the Court, except as provided by this Rule or order of the Court. The notice which is required by FRBP 3017(d) shall direct that all ballots be submitted to the plan proponent at a specified mailing address.

(b) **Ballot Summary.** For all confirmation hearings the plan proponent must prepare a written ballot summary in substantially the same form as Appendix L–3018–b. In addition to indicating how each class and each claimant voted, the summary shall attach each ballot. The plan proponent shall file the ballot summary 3 days before the confirmation hearing, unless the Court orders otherwise.

[Effective November 7, 2005. Amended effective November 1, 2013.]

L. RULE 3022. FINAL DECREE IN CHAPTER 11 CASES

Motions requesting the entry of a final decree in Chapter 11 cases may be filed using the negative notice language set forth in L. Rule 9014(a). Such motions must be served as required under L. Rule 9013.

[Effective November 7, 2005.]

L. RULE 3023. DISPOSITION OF FEDERAL INCOME TAX REFUNDS IN CHAPTER 13 CASES

(a) Except as may be provided by standing order, any tax refund not necessary to pay tax obligations may be first applied to cure any delinquency in the Chapter 13 plan, and the balance of the refund shall be remitted to the debtor.

(b) With respect to all pending Chapter 13 bankruptcy cases:

(1) the Internal Revenue Service is authorized to apply any tax refunds of debtors to the payment of any tax obligations due and owing by the debtors, regardless of whether such tax obligations or tax refunds arose before or after the filing of the case, so long as such tax claims are entitled to priority status under § 507(a);

(2) the terms "taxes" and "refunds" include all penalties and interest associated with taxes and refunds; and

(3) the Internal Revenue Service shall be entitled to charge its normal rate of interest and penalties for tax obligations arising after the filing of the Chapter 13 petition.

For Austin, see the related standing order on the Court's website at: http://www.txwb.uscourts.gov/1-rule-3023-disposition-federal-income-tax-refundschapter-13-cases.

For Midland, see the related standing order on the Court's website at: http://www.txwb.uscourts.gov/1-rule-3023-disposition-federal-income-tax-refundschapter-13-cases.

[Former L. Rule 3025 adopted effective November 7, 2005. Redesignated as L. Rule 3023 and amended effective November 1, 2013.]

L. RULE 4001. RELIEF FROM AUTOMATIC STAY; PROHIBITING OR CONDITIONING USE, SALE OR LEASE OF PROPERTY; USE OF CASH COLLATERAL; OBTAINING CREDIT

(a) Motions for Relief From Stay under 11 U.S.C. § 362(d).

(1) *Motions.*

(A) Motions seeking relief from the automatic stay shall state the specific relief requested, shall state with specificity the facts that support the relief requested, shall state the provision of § 362(d) under which relief is sought, and shall state Movant's belief as to the value of any collateral and the basis for such belief.

(B) If the motion is filed in a Chapter 11 or Chapter 13 case with respect to residential real property and if non-payment of any post-petition payment is a ground for relief, at the time the motion is filed the movant shall serve the debtor, debtor's counsel, and trustee with an affidavit and a pay history showing, at a minimum, the months in which the default was alleged to have occurred and the amount and character of the default, in a form substantially in compliance with Appendix L–4001.

(C) By signing the certificate of service on the motion, the movant certifies that the affidavit and pay history were served on the debtor, debtor's counsel, and trustee in accordance with this Rule. Failure to serve the affidavit and pay history in accordance with this Rule may be grounds for the denial of the relief requested in the motion.

(D) A creditor moving for relief from stay under § 362(d)(1) in a case shall file with the motion, where applicable, an affidavit specifying the month(s) in which the debtor failed to make a payment, any failure to satisfy an escrow shortage (including the amount of the shortage and the period of time involved), and any failure to maintain insurance (including the amount of shortage and the period of time involved).

(E) Motions for relief from stay shall not be combined with other forms of relief except those allowed by §§ 362 and 1205. Movants wishing to waive the 30 day hearing requirement of § 362(e) must include such waiver in the caption of the motion.

(2) *Negative Notice.* A movant may file a motion seeking relief from stay using the following 14–day negative notice language:

This pleading requests relief that may be adverse to your interests.

If no timely response is filed within 14 days from the date of service, the relief requested herein may be granted without a hearing being held.

A timely filed response is necessary for a hearing to be held.

If this negative notice language is used, the movant will be deemed to have waived entitlement to an initial hearing within 30 days. If negative notice language is not used, then the motion will be set within 30 days of its filing, as provided in § 362(e), unless the movant waives the thirty day hearing requirement in the caption of the motion.

(3) *Responses.* If the motion includes negative notice language, a hearing will be held only if a timely response is filed, or if the Court decides that a hearing is appropriate. A response shall comply with Local Rule 9014(b). Furthermore, if the party filing a response disagrees with the value of collateral set forth in the motion, the party shall state its belief as to the value of any collateral and the basis for such belief.

(4) *Use of Affidavits.*

(A) Pursuant to FRCP 43(e), a movant may use affidavits as evidence at the hearing in support of the factual allegations in the motion. The affidavits should not be filed with the Clerk, but must be served pursuant to L. Rule 9013 when the motion is served.

(B) A respondent may also use affidavits as evidence at the hearing. The affidavits should not be filed with the Clerk, but must be served pursuant to L. Rule 9013 either (i) at the same time the response is filed, if one is required under this Rule or (ii) within 14 days of the date of service of the motion, if no response is required under this Rule.

(C) The use of affidavits does not preclude the use of witnesses at the hearing.

(5) *Value.* The statement of belief as to value of any collateral and the basis for such belief that is required to be included in the motion or response is for notice purposes only, shall not be construed as or deemed to be a judicial admission, shall not be used in any other proceeding, and may be amended by further evidence offered at the hearing on the motion (or any other hearing).

(6) *Hearings.* A § 362(e) hearing on a motion for relief from automatic stay shall be consolidated with the § 362(d) final hearing unless the Court, for cause, rules otherwise at the time of the hearing.

(b) Motions for Extensions of Stay Under § 362(c)(3)(B). A party in interest seeking relief under § 362(c)(3)(B) shall file a motion styled "Motion for Extension of Stay Pursuant to § 362(c)(3)(B)." If the motion is filed within 7 days after the petition was filed, the Court will set an expedited hearing and debtor's counsel shall give notice of the expedited hearing. If the motion is filed more than 7 days after the petition was filed, the motion must be accompanied by a separate motion for expedited hearing.

(c) Motions for Imposition of Stay Under § 362(c)(4)(B). A party in interest seeking relief under § 362(c)(4)(B) shall file a motion styled "Motion for Imposition of Stay Pursuant to § 362(c)(4)(B)." If the motion is filed within 7 days after the petition was filed, the Court will set an expedited hearing and debtor's counsel shall give notice of the expedited hearing. If the motion is filed more than 7 days after the petition was filed, the motion must be accompanied by a separate motion for expedited hearing.

(d) Motions for Orders Confirming Termination of Automatic Stay Under § 362(c). A party in interest requesting an order under § 362(j) shall file a verified motion styled "Motion for Order Confirming Termination of Automatic Stay Under § 362(c)." The verified motion shall specifically allege the grounds for contending that the stay has terminated under the provisions of § 362(c). The motion shall be served on the debtor, the trustee, the United States Trustee, and all creditors and parties in interest.

(e) Incurring Debt in a Chapter 13 Case.

(1) A motion by a debtor in a Chapter 13 case to incur debt shall include the following information:

(A) the amount of debt sought to be incurred, and the reasons why the debtor believes it necessary;

(B) the percentage to be paid to unsecured creditors under the plan before and after the proposed debt to be incurred; and

(C) a copy of the debtor's Schedules I and J, before and after the debt incurrence.

(2) The motion shall be served upon all creditors and parties in interest and may, upon a showing of need, be served on 14 days negative notice.

(3) A motion and order to incur debt shall not be required for any debtors wishing to proceed with a loan modification of their existing mortgage.

[Effective November 7, 2005. Amended effective December 1, 2009; November 1, 2013; June 3, 2015.]

L. RULE 4002. DUTIES OF DEBTOR

(a) Redaction.

(1) Debtors complying with the disclosure requirements of FRBP 4002, or of 11 U.S.C. §§ 521 and 1308, are required to redact personal information from the documents to be produced to the trustee, filed with the Court, or given to any creditor, consistent with the Guidelines for Safeguarding Confidentiality established by the Director of the Administrative Office of the United States Courts, as they may be amended from time to time. The Guidelines for Privacy are available at: http://www.pacer.gov/privacy/bk.html.

(2) A trustee or the United States Trustee may request authority to review the unredacted versions of any such documents, upon motion setting forth the grounds therefore, and notice to the debtor. The debtor may submit such documents to the Court for in camera inspection.

(b) Access to Debtor's Tax and Other Personal Information.

(1) A creditor or other party in interest desiring access to any tax information filed by the debtor pursuant to 11 U.S.C. § 521 must file a motion with the Court, served upon the trustee, the debtor, debtor's counsel, and the United States Trustee. The motion must state why such information is needed, why such information is not otherwise available to the creditor, and how the movant proposes to protect the privacy of the debtor and others consistent with the Guidelines for Safeguarding Confidentiality established by the Director of the Administrative Office of the United States Courts. Any motion filed pursuant to this subparagraph shall be set for hearing.

(2) A creditor or other party in interest may not directly request from a trustee copies of any materials submitted to the trustee pursuant to the debtor's duties under 11 U.S.C. § 521 or § 1308 or under Rule 4002(b), and all such materials are privileged from discovery in any Court proceeding. A trustee shall not produce such documents to any creditor or party in interest except on order of the Court. A trustee may produce such documents or materials to any law enforcement officer as part of any criminal investigation.

(3) A creditor or other party in interest may request from the Court permission to obtain access to materials submitted to a trustee pursuant to 11 U.S.C. § 521 or § 1308 or pursuant to the duties imposed by Rule 4002(b) or these Local Rules. Any such motion must set forth why such information is needed, why such information is not otherwise available to the creditor, and how the movant proposes to protect the privacy of the debtor and others, consistent with the Guidelines for Safeguarding Confidentiality established by the Director of the Administrative Office of the United States Courts.

(4) If the Court grants a creditor's request made pursuant to subparagraph (b)(3) of this Rule, then the debtor in responding to the order may redact such materials in accordance with subparagraph (a)(1) of this Rule, unless the Court orders otherwise.

[Effective November 7, 2005. Amended effective December 1, 2009; November 1, 2013.]

L. RULE 4004. GRANT OR DENIAL OF DISCHARGE

(a) Chapter 7. In a Chapter 7 case, a motion to delay or postpone discharge under § 727(a)(12) must be filed not later than 30 days before the deadline for filing a complaint objecting to discharge, and must be served on the debtor, any trustee serving in the case, and on the United States Trustee. An untimely motion will not be deemed to be pending, for purposes of Rule 4004(c)(1)(I), unless the Court orders otherwise before the entry of the discharge. To be timely considered, the motion must be accompanied by a separate motion to expedite the hearing in accordance with L. Rule 9014(e).

(b) Chapter 12 or 13. In a Chapter 12 or 13 case, a debtor who completes and timely submits to the trustee a pre-discharge questionnaire in the form specified by the trustee will be deemed to have complied with the filing requirements of Rule 1007(b)(8).

The trustee's motion to enter discharge shall be deemed to be notice under Rule 2002(f)(11) of the time to request delay in the entry of discharge under § 1228(f) or § 1328(h).

(c) Chapter 11. An individual debtor in a Chapter 11 case, in order to receive a discharge, must file a motion requesting entry of a discharge. The motion must contain a verified statement addressing the requirements of § 1141(d)(5)(A) or (B). The motion must also include the statements specified in Rule 4004(c)(1)(H) and (I). The motion (and all attachments) must be served on all creditors and parties in interest, and must include a conspicuous notice that any objections to the entry of discharge, or any request to delay entry of the discharge under § 1141(d)(5)(C) must be filed with the Clerk and served on the debtor within 21 days after the date of service of the statement. Service of the motion with the required notice in accordance with this Rule shall satisfy the requirements of Rule 2002(f)(11).

If an objection to the entry of discharge, or a request to delay entry of discharge is timely filed, then no discharge will be entered until a hearing has been held under § 1141(d)(5)(C). If no such objection or request is timely filed, then a discharge may be entered without further hearing, unless the Court orders otherwise.

[Effective November 7, 2005. Amended effective December 1, 2009; November 1, 2013.]

L. RULE 5005. ADMINISTRATIVE PROCEDURES FOR ELECTRONIC FILING

By standing order, the Court has adopted administrative procedures for electronic filing, which are posted on the Court's website at: http://www.txwb.uscourts.gov/1-rule-5005-administrative-procedures-electronic-filing.

[Effective November 7, 2005. Amended effective November 1, 2013.]

L. RULE 5011. WITHDRAWAL OF REFERENCE

(a) Filing. A motion to withdraw the reference and any responses thereto shall be filed under the style and number of the bankruptcy case or adversary proceeding in which reference is sought to be withdrawn and shall be filed with the Clerk of the Bankruptcy Court. The Clerk of the Bankruptcy Court will transmit the motion to withdraw the reference and timely filed responses to the District Court.

(b) Contents of Motion. The motion shall list all pleadings which may be relevant to the Court's disposition of the motion, including docket entry numbers. The motion shall be accompanied by a form of order for entry by the District Court.

(c) Responses. Any response or objection to a motion for withdrawal of the reference shall be filed within 14 days after the date of service.

(d) Standing Orders of Reference. The Standing Order of Reference is posted on the Court's website at: http://www.txwb.uscourts.gov/district-court-standing-orders-affecting-bankruptcy-court.

[Effective November 7, 2005. Amended effective December 1, 2009; November 1, 2013.]

L. RULE 6004. USE, SALE OR LEASE OF PROPERTY

(a) Trustee's Use of Estate Funds.

(1) A Chapter 7 trustee may, without prior approval of the Court, pay from funds of the estate routine expenses for preservation of the estate, such as insurance premiums on property, locksmith charges, storage space rental, filing fees for adversary proceedings, and other routine charges. Expenses included within this provision do not include reimbursement of internal operating expenses of the trustee. Payments made under this provision in each case shall not exceed an aggregate of $2,400.00 in any twelve month period.

(2) In addition to the expenses authorized in (a)(1) above, a Chapter 7 Trustee may, without prior approval of the Court, incur and pay funds of an estate, on an ongoing basis, any actual, necessary expense for bank fees and service charges imposed by third party depositories, related to the administration of the estate's accounts. The Court retains authority to review and approve bank fees and service charges during the administration of an estate.

(b) Notice of Proposed Use, Sale, or Lease of Property. Notice of a motion to use, sell, or lease property shall contain the negative notice language set forth in L. Rule 9014(a). In addition to the requirements of FRBP 2002(c)(1), the notice shall contain:

(1) The name and address of the proposed buyer or lessee;

(2) The proposed consideration to be received by the estate, including estimated costs of the sale or lease, including commissions, auctioneer's fees, costs of document preparation and recording and any other customary closing costs; and

(3) A description of the estimated or possible tax consequences to the estate, if known, and how any tax liability generated by the use, sale or lease of such property will be paid.

(c) Motions in Chapter 12 and 13 Cases. In Chapter 12 and Chapter 13 cases, a motion for proposed use, sale, or lease of property shall indicate consent or lack of consent of the trustee and of any affected secured creditor.

[Effective November 7, 2005. Amended effective November 1, 2013.]

L. RULE 6008. REDEMPTION OF PROPERTY FROM LIEN OR SALE

All motions seeking redemption of property under 11 U.S.C. § 722 must be verified or accompanied by an affidavit of the debtor which discloses:

(1) the purchase price of the item(s) sought to be valued;

(2) a description of the condition of the item(s);

(3) the movant's opinion of the value of the item(s);

(4) the basis for that opinion; and

(5) the last four digits of the account number by which the creditor can identify the loan transaction.

[Effective November 7, 2005. Amended effective November 1, 2013.]

L. RULE 6011. DISPOSAL OF PATIENT RECORDS IN HEALTH CARE BUSINESS CASE

Any notice served by mail under § 351(1)(B) shall also be served on the designated representative for the Texas state agency responsible for regulating the health care business at the address designated at the following website: http://www.txwb.uscourts.gov/1-rule-1021-health-care-business-case.

[Effective November 1, 2013. Amended effective June 3, 2015.]

L. RULE 7005. SERVICE AND FILING OF PLEADINGS AND OTHER PAPERS

Parties are permitted to make service through the Bankruptcy Court's electronic means, as permitted by FRCP 5(b)(2)(E). This rule is not applicable to the service of process of a summons and complaint, which must be served in accordance with Bankruptcy Rule 7004.

[Effective November 1, 2013.]

L. RULE 7007. PLEADINGS ALLOWED

Motions filed in adversary proceedings are governed by Local Rule 9013 and 9014, except as otherwise provided in these Rules. Service of the motion, responses, and replies is limited to all counsel and parties without counsel in the adversary proceeding. If a response is not timely filed, the relief requested may be granted without further notice and hearing.

(a) Motions.

(1) *Dispositive Motions.* For purposes of this rule, a "dispositive motion" is a motion filed pursuant to FRBP 7012 and 7056. Any other motions filed in an adversary proceeding are deemed non-dispositive for purposes of these Rules.

(2) *Page Limits.* A dispositive motion is limited to 20 pages and a non-dispositive motion is limited to 10 pages, unless otherwise authorized by the Court. These page limits are exclusive of the caption, signature block, any certificate, and accompanying documents.

(b) Responses.

(1) *Generally.* Any party opposing a motion shall file a response and supporting documents as are then available. The response must contain a concise statement of the reasons for opposition to the motion and citations of the legal authorities on which the party relies.

(2) *Time Limits.* A response to a dispositive motion shall be filed not later than 21 days after the filing of the motion. A response to a non-dispositive motion shall be filed not later than 14 days after the motion is filed, except to the extent the Court or these Rules provide otherwise. If there is no response filed within the time period prescribed by this rule, the Court may grant the motion as unopposed.

(3) *Page Limits.* A response to a dispositive motion is limited to 20 pages and a response to a non-dispositive motion is limited to 10 pages, unless otherwise authorized by the Court. These page limits are exclusive of the caption, signature block, any certificate, and accompanying documents.

(c) Replies.

(1) *Generally.* A party may file a reply in support of a motion. No further submissions on the motion are allowed, absent leave of the Court.

(2) *Time Limit.* A reply in support of a motion shall be filed not later than 7 days after the filing of the response to the motion. The Court need not wait for a reply before ruling on a motion.

(3) *Page Limits.* A reply in support of a dispositive motion is limited to 10 pages and a reply in support of a non-dispositive motion is limited to 5 pages, unless otherwise authorized by the Court. These page limits are exclusive of the caption, signature block, any certificate, and accompanying documents.

[Effective November 1, 2013.]

L. RULE 7012. DEFENSES AND OBJECTIONS—WHEN AND HOW PRESENTED—BY PLEADING OR MOTION—MOTION FOR JUDGMENT ON THE PLEADINGS

A response to a motion under FRBP 7012 must be filed within 21 days after service of the motion. The failure to timely file a response will be treated as consent to entry of an order granting the motion. The Court may set a motion under FRBP 7012 for hearing or may rule on such motion without a hearing.

[Effective November 7, 2005. Amended effective December 1, 2009; November 1, 2013.]

L. RULE 7015. AMENDED AND SUPPLEMENTAL PLEADINGS

(a) Attachments. Any motions to amend or to supplement pleadings must attach a complete copy of the amended or supplemental pleading the movant proposes to file. The failure to attach a copy may be grounds for denial of relief, without further hearing.

(b) Filing of Allowed Amendments. After an order is entered allowing the amendment, the amended or supplemental pleading which conforms with the Court's order must be filed and served by the movant within 7 days after the entry of the order.

[Effective November 7, 2005. Amended effective December 1, 2009; November 1, 2013.]

L. RULE 7016. PRETRIAL PROCEDURES; FORMULATING ISSUES

(a) Scheduling Order. After the filing of an answer or upon motion of a party, the Court shall issue its scheduling order, which will set forth deadlines, hearing dates, and limitations on discovery. Unopposed discovery may continue after the deadline for discovery contained in the scheduling order, provided that discovery does not delay other pretrial preparations or the trial setting.

(b) Pretrial Conferences. A pretrial conference will not be held, unless otherwise provided in the scheduling order. A pretrial conference may be scheduled upon written motion or upon the Court's own motion.

(c) Joint Pretrial Order. A joint pretrial order shall be filed at least 7 days before trial docket call, unless otherwise directed by the Court. Counsel shall exchange proposed Pretrial Orders 14 days before docket call, except to the extent counsel agree otherwise. If counsel cannot agree on a joint pretrial order, counsel shall file separate proposed Pretrial Orders on or before the deadline. The Pretrial Order shall contain the following:

(1) a concise description of the dispute;

(2) a statement as to jurisdiction, including whether the matter is core or non-core;

(3) a statement as to whether the parties consent to the entry of a final order or judgment by the Bankruptcy Court;

(4) a summary of the claims and defenses of each party;

(5) a statement of stipulated facts;

(6) a summary of the disputed factual issues;

(7) a summary of the agreed applicable law;

(8) a list of contested issues of law. This list shall include specific reference to applicable bankruptcy code provisions, state or federal statutes and/or regulations, applicable rules of procedure and conflict questions, if any. (Copies of regulations must be attached);

(9) A list of witnesses who may be called, accompanied by a concise statement of their proposed testimony. If a witness's testimony will be presented by a deposition, the Pretrial Order must designate by reference to page and line of the testimony to be offered (except those to be used for impeachment only), and if not taken stenographically, a transcript of the pertinent portions of the deposition testimony;

(10) an estimate of the length of trial. **If counsel's estimate of trial time is 5 hours or more, a pretrial conference must be requested. It will be the parties' burden to file a written request for the pretrial conference in such instance, within 30 days after the date of the initial scheduling order;**

(11) a list of any additional matters that might aid in the disposition of the case;

(12) a list and description of each exhibit upon which the parties intent to rely upon at trial of their case in chief; and

(13) a signature of an attorney for each party.

(d) Proposed Findings of Fact and Conclusions of Law. Proposed findings of fact and conclusions of law shall be filed by each party at least 7 days before trial docket call and emailed to the Courtroom Deputy in word processing format.

(e) Conflict Between Scheduling Order and Local Rule. In any conflict between a scheduling order and these Local Bankruptcy Rules, the scheduling order controls. If the Pretrial Order is not timely filed, a default judgment may be rendered or the proceeding may be dismissed for want of prosecution.

(f) Briefs. Any briefs to be considered by the Court at the trial on the merits of an adversary complaint shall be filed contemporaneously with the pretrial order, but as a separate document with service on all counsel and parties without counsel, unless otherwise provided in the scheduling order or other order of the Court.

(g) Exhibits and Number of Copies Required.

(1) All exhibits shall be appropriately marked and **either be provided in an electronic format agreed to by counsel or** be bound in booklet form which will lie flat when opened. Exhibits shall be separately tabbed and identified in numerical order, and shall be indexed at the front of each exhibit book or books.

(2) **Tabbed and marked copies** of exhibits shall be provided to each party not less than 5 days before trial.

(3) Exhibits shall not be filed with the Clerk before trial. **In addition to exhibits exchanged with opposing counsel, a complete set of exhibits shall be provided for the Court, the Law Clerk, the Courtroom Deputy and the witness stand.**

(4) Failure to comply with these rules may result in the refusal of the Court to admit exhibits into evidence, or in sanctions.

[Effective November 7, 2005. Amended effective December 1, 2009; November 1, 2013.]

L. RULE 7026. GENERAL PROVISIONS GOVERNING DISCOVERY

(a) Relief Under FRCP 26(c) or 37(a)(3). If relief is sought under FRCP 26(c) or 37(a)(3), concerning any interrogatories, requests for production or inspection, requests for admissions, answers to interrogatories or responses to requests for admissions, copies of the relevant portions of the interrogatories, requests, answers or responses in dispute shall be attached to the motion.

(b) Definitions and Rules of Construction. The full text of the definitions and rules of construction set forth in this paragraph is deemed incorporated by reference into all discovery requests, but shall not preclude (i) the definition of other terms specific to the particular litigation, (ii) the use of abbreviations or (iii) a more narrow definition of a term defined in this paragraph. This rule is not intended to broaden or narrow the scope of discovery permitted by the FRCP.

The following definitions apply to all discovery requests:

(1) *Communication.* The term "communication" means the transmittal of information (in the form of facts, ideas, inquiries, or otherwise).

(2) *Document.* The word "document" is synonymous—and equal in scope to the use of this term in FRCP 34(a). A draft of a non-identical copy is a separate document within the meaning of this term.

(3) *Identify (With Respect to Persons).* When referring to a person, to "identify" means to give, to the extent known, the person's full name, present or last known address, e-mail address, and telephone number, and when referring to a natural person, additionally, the present or last known place of employment. Once a person has been identified in accordance

with this subparagraph, only the name of that person need be listed in response to subsequent discovery requesting the identification of that person.

(4) *Identify (With Respect to Documents).* When referring to documents, "to identify" means to give, to the extent known, the (i) type of document; (ii) general subject matter; (iii) date of the document; and (iv) author(s), addressee(s), and recipient(s).

(5) *Parties.* The terms "plaintiff" and "defendant" as well as a party's full or abbreviated name or pronoun referring to a party mean the party and, where applicable, its officers, directors, employees, partners, corporate parent, subsidiaries, or affiliates. This definition is not intended to impose a discovery obligation on any person who is not a party to the litigation.

(6) *Person.* The term "person" is defined as any natural person or business, legal, or governmental entity or association.

(7) *Concerning.* The term "concerning" means relating to, referring to, describing, evidencing, or constituting.

(c) Protective Orders. Upon motion by any party demonstrating good cause, the Court may enter a protective order or any other appropriate order.

(d) Authentication of Documents. A party's production of a document in response to written discovery authenticates the document for use against that party in any pretrial proceeding or at trial unless within 14 days or a longer or shorter period ordered by the Court, after the producing party has actual notice that the document will be used—the party objects to the authenticity of the document, or any part of it, stating the specific basis for objection. An objection must be either on the record or in writing and must have a good faith factual and legal basis. An objection made to the authenticity of only part of a document does not affect the authenticity of the remainder. If objection is made, the party attempting to use the document should be given a reasonable opportunity to establish its authenticity.

(e) Discovery. Discovery shall not be filed with the Clerk. Absent exceptional circumstances, no motions relating to discovery, including motions under Rules FRCP 26(c), 29, and 37, shall be filed after the expiration of the discovery deadline, unless they are filed within 7 days after the discovery deadline and pertain to conduct occurring during the final 7 days of discovery. Written discovery is not timely unless the response to that discovery would be due before the discovery deadline. The responding party has no obligation to respond or object to written discovery if the response and objection would not be due until after the discovery deadline. Depositions must be completed before the discovery deadline. Any notices served before the discovery deadline scheduling depositions after the discovery deadline will not be enforced.

[Effective November 7, 2005. Amended effective December 1, 2009; November 1, 2013.]

L. RULE 7030. DEPOSITIONS UPON ORAL EXAMINATION

(a) Notice. The notice for a deposition shall be in the form prescribed in FRCP 30, and in addition shall state the identity of persons who will attend other than the witness, parties, spouses of parties, counsel, employees of counsel, and the officer taking the deposition. If any party intends to have any other persons attend, that party must give reasonable notice to all parties of the identity of such other persons.

(b) Procedures, Examinations and Objections. The parties are permitted to stipulate on the record of the deposition any agreement regarding the rules for the deposition. Objections during depositions shall be stated concisely and in a nonargumentative and non-suggestive manner. An attorney shall not, in the presence of the deponent, make objections or statements that might suggest an answer to the deponent. An attorney for a deponent shall not initiate a private conference with the deponent regarding a pending question, except for the purpose of determining whether a claim of privilege should be asserted. An attorney who instructs a deponent not to answer a question shall state, on the record, the legal basis for the instruction consistent with FRCP 30(d)(1). If a claim of privilege has been asserted as a basis for an instruction not to answer, the attorney seeking discovery shall have reasonable latitude during the deposition to question the deponent and establish relevant information concerning the appropriateness of the assertion of the privilege, including (i) the applicability of the privilege being asserted, (ii) the circumstances that may result in the privilege having been waived, and (iii) circumstances that may overcome a claim of qualified privilege. A violation of the provisions of this local Rule may be deemed to be a violation of a Court order and may subject the violator to sanctions under FRCP 37(b)(2).

[Effective November 1, 2013.]

L. RULE 7033. INTERROGATORIES TO PARTIES

(a) All answers to interrogatories must be signed under oath by the party except that, if circumstances prevent a party from signing responses to interrogatories, the attorney may serve the responses without the party's signature if an affidavit is served simultaneously stating that properly executed responses to interrogatories will be served within 21 days. Such time may be extended by order of the Court.

(b) Each party that chooses to submit written interrogatories pursuant to FRCP 33 may use the following questions. The Court will not entertain any objection to these approved interrogatories, except upon a showing of exceptional circumstances. Each of the following interrogatories counts as one question; as to all interrogatories other than those approved in this rule, subparts count as separate questions.

(1) Identify all persons who you believe have knowledge of relevant facts and identify the issues upon which you believe they have knowledge.

(2) Identify all persons or legal entities who have a subrogation interest in the cause of action set forth in your complaint [or counterclaim], and state the basis and extent of said interest.

(3) If [name of party to whom the interrogatory is directed] is a partner, a partnership, or a subsidiary or affiliate of a publicly owned corporation that has a financial interest in the

outcome of this lawsuit, list the identity of the parent corporation, affiliate, partner, or partnership and the relationship between it and [the named party]. If there is a publicly owned corporation or a holding company not a party to the case that has a financial interest in the outcome, list the identity of such corporation and the nature of the financial interest.

(4) If the defendant is improperly identified, give its proper identification and state whether you will accept service of an amended summons and complaint reflecting the information furnished by you in answer hereto.

(5) If you contend that some other person or legal entity is, in whole or in part, liable to [the plaintiff or defendant] in this matter, identify that person or legal entity and describe in detail the basis of said liability.

[Effective November 1, 2013.]

L. RULE 7036. REQUESTS FOR ADMISSION

Requests for admissions made pursuant to FRCP 36, are limited to 30 requests, which will include separate paragraphs and sub-parts contained within a numbered request. The Court may permit further requests upon a showing of good cause.

[Effective November 1, 2013.]

L. RULE 7054. CLAIMS FOR ATTORNEY'S FEES AND COSTS IN ADVERSARY PROCEEDINGS

(a) Claims for Attorney's Fees.

(1) All motions for an award of attorney's fees shall be filed and served no later than 14 days after entry of judgment pursuant to FRCP 54. Unless the substantive law requires a claim for attorney's fees and related nontaxable expenses to be proved at trial as an element of damages to be determined by a jury, a claim for fees shall be made by motion not later than 14 days after entry of judgment and pursuant to the following provisions. Counsel for the parties shall meet and confer for the purpose of resolving all disputed issues relating to attorney's fees before making application. The application shall certify that such a conference has occurred. If no agreement is reached, the applicant shall certify the specific reason(s) why the matter could not be resolved by agreement. The motion shall include a supporting document organized chronologically by activity or project, listing attorney name, date, and hours expended on the particular activity or project, as well as an affidavit certifying (1) that the hours expended were actually expended on the topics stated, and (2) that the hours expended and rate claimed were reasonable. Such application shall also be accompanied by a brief memo explaining how the fees were computed, with sufficient citation of authority to permit the reviewing court the opportunity to determine whether such computation is correct. The request shall include reference to the statutory authorization or other authority for the request. Detailed time sheets for each attorney for whom fees are claimed may be required to be submitted upon further order of the Court.

(2) An objection to any motion for attorney's fees shall be filed on or before 14 days after the date of filing of the motion. If there is no timely objection, the Court may grant the motion as unopposed.

(3) The motion shall be resolved without further hearing, unless an evidentiary hearing is requested, reasons therefore presented, and good cause shown, whereupon hearing on the motion may be granted.

(4) A motion for award of attorney's fees filed beyond the 14 day period may be deemed untimely and a waiver of entitlement to fees.

(b) Costs.

(1) Costs will be assessed in the final judgment in a proceeding, unless otherwise determined by the Court. A party awarded costs shall prepare and file a proposed bill of costs no later than 14 days after the entry of judgment. The proposed bill of costs shall be served on all parties. Suggested guidelines can be found at: http://www.txwb.uscourts.gov/local-rules attachments.

(2) Any party opposing a proposed bill of costs must file an objection no later than 14 days after a proposed bill of costs is filed.

(3) If no objection to the proposed bill of costs is filed, the clerk shall not tax costs until the expiration of 21 days after the filing of the proposed bill of costs. If the clerk fails to tax costs within 28 days after the proposed bill of costs is filed, and there being no objection filed, then costs will be deemed taxed as proposed.

(4) If objection to the proposed bill of costs is timely filed by a party, the clerk will forward the proposed bill of costs and the objection to the presiding judge in the case for final resolution.

(5) A party objecting to the clerk's action may file a motion to review the clerk's action no later than 7 days after the clerk has taxed costs.

[Effective November 7, 2005. Amended effective December 1, 2009; November 1, 2013.]

L. RULE 7056. SUMMARY JUDGMENT

Motions under FRCP 56 do not require negative notice. However, responses and responsive affidavits must be filed no later than 21 days after the date of service, unless the Court, for cause, extends or shortens the time. The Court may rule on the motion with or without a hearing.

[Effective November 7, 2005. Amended effective December 1, 2009; November 1, 2013.]

L. RULE 9004. GENERAL REQUIREMENTS OF FORM

(a) Number of Copies. Whenever any pleading is offered for filing, only the original shall be tendered to the Clerk, except as otherwise provided by applicable rules.

(b) Caption. Form 16 is modified to include the division where the case is pending (Austin, El Paso, Midland/Odessa,

San Antonio, or Waco) and the case number, including the initials of the judge assigned to the case.

(c) Titles of Pleadings and Proposed Forms of Orders. All pleadings and proposed forms of orders shall, within the title, designate the specific relief sought or granted. Orders shall contain within the title a reference to the motion or application to be granted.

(d) Non-Conforming Pleadings. Any pleading that fails to conform to the requirements of this or any other applicable rule may be dismissed by the Court on its own motion.

[Effective November 7, 2005. Amended effective November 1, 2013.]

L. RULE 9011. SIGNING OF PAPERS

All pleadings must be signed and shall include the signer's name, mailing address, email address, telephone and fax numbers including area code and, if the signer is an attorney, the attorney's State Bar Number (and the state from which the bar number is issued, if other than Texas). An electronic signature constitutes a signature for the purposes of FRBP 9011.

[Effective November 7, 2005. Amended effective November 1, 2013.]

L. RULE 9013. MOTIONS; FORM AND SERVICE

(a) Motions. The Court, in its discretion, may strike multifarious pleadings on its own motion.

(b) Forms of Orders. A form of proposed order must be submitted at the time of filing a request for relief, with the following exceptions:

(1) plans and objections to plans under Chapter 11 and Chapter 13;

(2) Chapter 11 disclosure statements; and

(3) motions requesting omnibus relief, such as an omnibus objection to claims.

A form of proposed order must be submitted both (1) attached as an exhibit to the motion and (2) separately uploaded for consideration by the Court.

(c) Certificates of Service. All motions, applications, objections to claims, and all responses to same must contain a certificate of service reflecting service on affected entities, as specified in paragraph (d) of this Local Rule.

(1) The certificate of service must be signed by an attorney or party (if appearing without counsel), certifying that service has been accomplished in the manner and on the date stated in the certificate and upon the parties required to be served.

(2) The certificate of service must list each of the entities served and their addresses.

(3) With Court approval, a party may serve a summary of a pleading where the pleading is voluminous, or the number of parties to be served is excessively large. In such cases, the summary shall be filed, and the certificate of service shall be appended to the summary.

(d) Entities to Be Served.

(1) When a pleading is filed, the following entities at a minimum shall be served unless otherwise specifically provided by these Rules, by the FRBP, by standing order, or by order of the Court.

(A) In a Chapter 7 case (except the Chapter 7 trustee's final reports before and after distribution and reports of sale): the debtor, the trustee, any court-approved committees, the counsel for each of these entities, and any other entities adversely affected by the relief requested.

(B) In a Chapter 11 case (except the plan and disclosure statement): the debtor, any court-approved committee, any Chapter 11 trustee, the counsel for each of these entities, the twenty largest unsecured creditors, parties who have filed a notice of appearance, the United States Trustee, and any other entities adversely affected by the relief requested.

(C) In a Chapter 12 or 13 case: the debtor, debtor's counsel, the trustee and any other entities adversely affected by the relief requested.

(2) In an adversary proceeding, service shall be made upon all counsel and parties without counsel, unless otherwise specifically provided by these rules, the FRBP, by standing order, or by order of the Court.

(3) Whenever a pleading governed by this Local Rule is to be served on the United States, or an officer or agency thereof, the service provisions of FRBP 7004(b)(4) apply.

(4) If a movant uses the negative notice language of L. Rule 9014(a), the following motions require service upon all creditors and parties in interest:

(A) motions to dismiss in Chapters 7, 9, and 11;

(B) motions to modify plans in Chapters 11, 12, and 13;

(C) motions to incur debt in Chapters 11, 12, and 13; and

(D) motions for hardship discharge.

(5) An attorney who is an electronic filer consents to service by electronic means within the meaning of FRCP 5.

[Effective November 7, 2005. Amended effective November 1, 2013.]

L. RULE 9014. CONTESTED MATTERS

(a) Negative Notice Language. Notice and an opportunity for hearing is accomplished by including the following form language presented conspicuously, in bold face type (at least 12 pt.) and placed immediately below the caption and before the body of the pleading.

This pleading requests relief that may be adverse to your interests.

If no timely response is filed within 21 days from the date of service, the relief requested herein may be granted without a hearing being held.

A timely filed response is necessary for a hearing to be held.

This language should not be used for:

(1) matters granted without a hearing as set forth in subsection (d);

(2) matters set forth in Appendix L-9014;

(3) matters upon which a hearing is specifically required by the Bankruptcy Code or by applicable rules; or

(4) matters that require the Court to act within a shortened time frame.

(b) Responses to Motions, Applications, and Objections to Claims and Any Reply Thereto.

(1) *Time of Filing a Response.* A party who opposes the relief requested must file a responsive pleading within the time set out in the negative notice (if applicable). If negative notice language is not used, a response is not required unless the Court or these rules direct. A responsive pleading shall specifically admit or deny each factual allegation or state that the party lacks knowledge or information sufficient to form a belief about the truth of an allegation.

(2) *Time of Filing a Reply.* Any reply to a response must be filed within 7 days after service of the response.

(c) Hearings. If a matter requires a hearing, the Clerk shall send notice of the hearing, unless otherwise directed by the Court. The Court may set any contested matter for hearing, even if negative notice language has been used and even if no party has requested a hearing.

(d) Matters Granted Without Hearing. The Court may rule, without further notice or hearing, on certain matters including the following:

(1) motions for admission pro hac vice, pursuant to L. Rule 2090;

(2) motions to shorten notice pursuant to FRBP 2002;

(3) motions to enlarge time pursuant to FRBP 9006;

(4) motions to expedite hearings;

(5) motions for new trial pursuant to FRBP 9023;

(6) motions for reconsideration pursuant to FRBP 9024; and

(7) motions for continuance.

(e) Expedited Hearing or Consideration. A motion for expedited hearing or expedited consideration of a matter, shall be filed as a separate pleading, except as otherwise provided by these Rules or by standing order. Such motions may be granted only for good cause stated in the pleading and shall contain a certificate of conference reflecting efforts to confer with adversely affected parties regarding the relief requested or the reasons why conferring was not possible or practical. Such motions shall also contain a detailed statement as to the need for an expedited hearing and the date by which relief is needed.

A proposed form of order shall accompany the motion for expedited hearing in substantially the following format:

ORDER GRANTING
MOTION OF [movant's name] TO EXPEDITE HEARING ON [name of underlying pleading][Docket No. ___]

On this date came on for consideration the Motion filed by [movant] ("Movant") requesting an expedited hearing on the [name of underlying pleading] filed on [date] [Docket No. ___].

The Court finds that the Motion should be granted as set forth below.

IT IS, THEREFORE, ORDERED that the [name of underlying pleading] is scheduled for expedited hearing on the date and time listed above.

The moving party is responsible for notice of hearing on expedited matters. Movant shall file a certificate of notice listing persons served. The certificate should be filed within 7 days of such service but in no event later than the date and time of the hearing.

(f) Continuances.

(1) *Time for Filing.* No continuance of any hearing will be granted except upon motion filed no later than 3 days before the scheduled hearing and upon good cause shown on the face of the pleading. The Court may consider such a motion filed less than 3 days prior, but only if the motion sets forth the emergency that explains why it was not timely filed. The motion shall contain a certificate of conference reflecting efforts to confer with affected parties regarding the relief requested or the reasons why conferring was not possible or practical.

(2) *Relief From Stay.* Parties to a motion for relief from stay are excused from filing a motion for continuance if it is their first request for continuance and the debtor, creditor, and any party that filed an objection or response to the motion for relief from stay are in agreement as to the continuance.

(3) *Agreement.* An agreement to continue is insufficient. The agreement of the parties to a continuance is not, in itself, good cause for granting a continuance.

(4) *Appearance Required.* Unless the Court grants the motion for continuance before the hearing, the parties are required to appear at the scheduled hearing. The filing of a motion for continuance of itself does not excuse appearance.

(5) *Certificate.* The moving party shall file a certificate signed by the party or the party's attorney reflecting the date of any hearing reset by the Court, and reflecting service of notice that reset hearing, within 7 days of such service.

(g) Exhibits for Hearings in Contested Matters.

(1) L. Rule 7016(g) applies in contested matters.

(2) Except as otherwise provided in these rules, witness and exhibit lists shall be exchanged 5 days in advance of the hearing.

(h) FRBP 7015, to the extent that it adopts FRCP 15(c), applies in contested matters.

(i) FRCP 26(b) and (c), as implemented by FRBP 7026, apply in contested matters and the remainder of FRCP 26 does not apply unless the Court orders otherwise.

[Effective November 7, 2005. Amended effective December 1, 2009; November 1, 2013.]

L. RULE 9015.   JURY TRIAL PROCEDURES

(a) Consent to Jury Trial Before Bankruptcy Court.

(1) *By the Party Demanding Jury Trial.* If a jury trial is requested in a matter pending before the Bankruptcy Court,

the requesting party shall file with the Court, in a separate pleading and contemporaneously with the jury demand, a separate pleading entitled "Statement Regarding Consent", setting forth the following:

(A) whether the requesting party consents to the conduct of the jury trial by the Bankruptcy Court;

(B) whether the matter is one to which the Seventh Amendment right to jury trial attaches, and the grounds therefore;

(C) whether the matter is a core or non-core proceeding, and the grounds therefore; and

(D) if the matter is a non-core proceeding, whether the party consents to the entry of a final order by the Bankruptcy Court.

(2) *By the Parties to the Litigation in Response to a Jury Demand.* Within 14 days after the filing of a jury demand and the Statement Regarding Consent required under paragraph (a)(1) of this Rule, each party to the litigation shall file with the Court in a separate contemporaneous pleading, a "Response Regarding Consent", addressing each of the four matters referenced above.

(b) Withdrawal of the Reference in the Event of Non–Consent. If the Court grants the jury demand and a party has refused to consent to the Bankruptcy Court's conduct of the jury trial, then any party may, within 14 days, file a motion to withdraw the reference, attaching a copy of the Court's order and a copy of the party's refusal to consent. If no party timely files such a motion, the Court shall strike the jury demand.

(c) Application of the District Court Local Rules Relating to Jury Trials. All rules relating to the conduct of a jury trial in the District Court shall apply to the conduct of such trials in Bankruptcy Court.

[Effective November 7, 2005. Amended effective December 1, 2009.]

L. RULE 9018. SECRET OR CONFIDENTIAL MATTERS

(a) Filing.

(1) Documents or proceedings may be sealed only by order of the Court, and on motion with notice to parties in interest.

(2) Documents to be sealed shall be presented to the Clerk after the order has been entered. The documents shall be contained in an envelope or other secure device, with the initials or signature of the submitting party or attorney written across the edge of the closure, and transparent tape placed on top of the mark for security. The envelope (or other secure device) shall have affixed to it a letter-size sheet of paper bearing the style and caption of the matter with reference to which the documents are being filed.

(3) The form of order submitted with the motion requesting a matter be sealed shall contain the following recitations:

(A) The matter shall remain under seal for no longer than one year from the date of entry of the order, unless the Court orders otherwise.

(B) The only entities permitted to review documents or transcripts of proceedings placed under seal are those entities specified in the order, except that the following entities shall also have access to matters placed under seal unless the Court specifically rules otherwise: (1) the judge presiding over the case, (2) the law clerk to whom the matter is assigned internally by the presiding judge, (3) the Courtroom Deputy responsible for the matter, (4) the Clerk of the Court, and (5) the presiding judge and staff of any appellate tribunal.

(b) Disposition of Sealed Documents.

(1) Documents or transcripts of proceedings under seal may be forwarded to an appellate court without the necessity of unsealing the matter. The matter so forwarded shall be accompanied by a true copy of the order placing the matter under seal. Further motions with regard to the sealing or unsealing of a matter shall be filed with the Court that entered the original order sealing the matter, notwithstanding the pendency of an appeal.

(2) Upon the entry of an order unsealing a matter (or upon the expiration of the time period specified in paragraph (a)(3)(A), supra), the Clerk (or other person responsible for the maintenance of the matter) shall place the document or transcript of proceedings in the file of the case or adversary proceeding.

[Effective November 7, 2005.]

L. RULE 9019. COMPROMISE

(a) Filing.

(1) An application to compromise an adversary proceeding shall be filed in the main bankruptcy case, not in the adversary proceeding. It shall bear the style of the main bankruptcy case, not the adversary proceeding.

(2) An application to compromise an adversary proceeding shall, within the body of the application, set out the style and number of the adversary proceeding.

(3) No application to compromise an adversary proceeding need be filed in order to settle a nondischargeability action filed pursuant to 11 U.S.C. § 523, unless the compromise creates an allowed claim to be paid in the bankruptcy case. The proposed order must set forth the name and address of the payee and the proposed treatment of the claim

(b) Notice.

(1) Applications to compromise adversary proceedings are governed by L. Rule 9014, and may include the negative notice language there specified.

(2) Applications to compromise and motions to dismiss an objection to discharge under 11 U.S.C. § 727 must identify the cause of action and any consideration paid or agreed to be paid.

(c) Order and Judgment. An application to compromise an adversary proceeding shall be submitted with both:

(1) an order to approve the application to compromise, bearing the style of the main bankruptcy case; and

(2) a proposed agreed judgment or order of dismissal, bearing the style of the adversary proceeding, for entry in the underlying adversary proceeding.

[Effective November 7, 2005. Amended effective November 1, 2013.]

L. RULE 9022. NON–ELECTRONIC SUBMISSION OF ORDERS OR JUDGMENTS

Order Submission Form. Agreed Orders submitted other than by electronic means must have a cover sheet in conformity with the standard form attached as Appendix L–9022.

[Effective November 7, 2005.]

L. RULE 9027. REMOVAL

(a) Abstention. A motion to abstain is filed with the Clerk of the Bankruptcy Court.

(b) Removal.

(1) *Filing.* A notice of removal pursuant to 28 U.S.C. § 1452(a) shall be filed with the Clerk of the Bankruptcy Court. A notice of removal grounded on any other federal provision (e.g., diversity of citizenship) shall be filed with the Clerk of the District Court.

(2) *Attachments.* A notice of removal pursuant to 28 U.S.C. § 1452(a) shall include a copy of the docket sheet and all pleadings, orders, and writs.

(3) *Motion for Remand.* Any motion for remand must be filed no later than 30 days after the date of filing of the notice of removal.

[Effective November 7, 2005.]

APPENDICES
APPENDIX L–1001–h.   ALTERNATIVE DISPUTE RESOLUTION

It is the intent of the Court to facilitate the use of alternative dispute resolution ("ADR") in all matters, including specifically contested matters and adversary proceedings, to the extent practicable, helpful and appropriate.

(a) ADR Report. Upon order of the Court entered in any contested matter or adversary proceeding, the Debtor and/or Trustee, and all parties (as well as all parties-in-interest affected thereby, including official Committees(s)) shall submit a report addressing the status of settlement negotiations, disclosing the identity of the person responsible for settlement negotiations for each party, and truthfully, candidly and realistically evaluating whether alternative dispute resolution is appropriate in the contested matter or adversary proceeding. Counsel shall certify in the report that their clients have been informed of the ADR procedures available in this district. In the event the parties conclude that ADR is appropriate and agree upon a method of ADR and a neutral, they should identify both the method of ADR and the neutral they have selected, the method by which the neutral was selected, and how the neutral will be compensated. If the parties agree upon an ADR method and neutral, the Court will defer to the parties' agreement, unless the Court finds that another ADR method or neutral is better suited to the contested matter, adversary proceeding or the parties.

(b) Referral to ADR. The Court on its own motion or upon the motion of any party or party-in-interest may order the participation in a non-binding alternative dispute resolution proceeding, including non-binding arbitration, early neutral evaluation, mediation, or mini-trial in accordance with Local Rule 1001(h). The order may further direct the parties to bear all expenses relating to alternative dispute resolution proceedings in such proportions as the Court finds appropriate, and may direct that portions thereof be allowed as an administrative expense entitled to priority in the case, but in no event should apportioning of costs constitute a penalty for failing to arrive at a settlement. The alternative dispute resolution proceeding shall begin at a date and time selected by the parties, subject to the schedule of the neutral or neutrals, but in no event later than forty-five (45) days after the entry of the order compelling participation in the proceeding.

(c) Attendance. Party representatives with authority to negotiate a settlement and all other persons necessary to negotiate a settlement must attend and participate in good faith in the alternative dispute proceeding, subject to the Court's power to assess appropriate sanctions.

(d) Selection of Neutral. Upon entry of an order compelling participation in alternative dispute resolution, or upon agreement of the parties where they have not selected a neutral or neutrals from the roster, the Clerk shall forthwith furnish to each party a list of neutrals. If the compelled procedure is nonbinding arbitration or moderated settlement conference, the list shall include five neutrals whose names have been selected from the roster of arbitrators maintained in the District Clerk's Office. If the compelled procedure is other than nonbinding arbitration or moderated settlement conference the list shall include three neutrals selected from general neutral roster. The parties shall then confer with each side entitled to strike one name from the three neutral list (two names from the five neutrals list). The person remaining shall be designated the neutral. The parties may by agreement reject the list furnished by the Clerk and instead unanimously select a neutral or neutrals from either roster. Failure of counsel to timely notify the Clerk of their strikes or selection shall result in the selection of the neutral or neutrals by the Clerk. The Clerk shall promptly notify the neutral or neutrals selected. If any person selected is unable or unwilling to serve the Clerk shall submit an additional list of names to the parties until a neutral or complete panel of neutrals is selected. When a neutral or full panel of neutrals have been selected and have agreed to serve, the Clerk shall promptly notify the neutral or neutrals and the parties of the selection. No person shall serve as a neutral if any of the circumstances specified in 28 U.S.C. § 455 of the Judicial Code of Conduct exist, or if the neutral believes in good faith that such circumstances exist. Any person whose name appears on the roster maintained in the Clerk's Office may ask at any time to have his or her name removed, or, if selected to serve in any case, decline to serve but remain on the roster.

Upon its own motion or upon motion and showing of good cause by any party, the Court may order appointment of a neutral or neutrals from outside the roster of qualified neutrals maintained by the Clerk's Office.

(e) Confidentiality. Except as otherwise provided herein, a communication relating to the subject matter of any case under Title 11, contested matter or adversary proceeding made by a participant in an alternative dispute resolution procedure, whether before or after the institution of formal judicial proceedings, is confidential, is not subject to disclosure, and may not be used as evidence against the participant in any judicial or administrative proceeding.

(1) Any record made at an alternative dispute resolution procedure is confidential, and the participants or the third party neutral(s) facilitating the procedure may not testify, or be required to testify, in any proceedings relating to or arising out of the matter in dispute or be subject to process requiring the disclosure of confidential information or data relating to or arising out of the matter in dispute.

(2) An oral communication or written material used in or made a part of an alternative dispute resolution procedure is only admissible or discoverable if it is admissible or discoverable independent of the procedure.

(3) If this section conflicts with other legal requirements for disclosure of communications or materials, the issue of confidentiality may be presented to any Court having jurisdiction of the proceedings to determine, in camera, whether the facts, circumstances, and context of the communications or materials sought to be disclosed warrant a protective order of the Court or whether the communications or materials are subject to disclosure.

(f) Summary Trial or Jury Trial. In cases where other alternative dispute resolution procedures have proved unsuccessful and a complex and lengthy trial is anticipated, the Court may conduct a summary trial or jury trial, provided that the Court finds that a summary trial or jury trial may produce settlement of all or a significant part of the issues and thereby effect a saving in time, effort and expense for all concerned. The Court should develop procedures, which may include referral to one or more neutrals on the roster of arbitrators (for report and recommendation), for such summary trial or jury trial with the advice of counsel.

(g) Report. At the conclusion of each ADR proceeding, the neutral or panel of neutrals shall submit to the Court a notice of outcome, including the style and number of the case, the date(s) of the ADR proceeding, the names of the participants and only whether the case has settled or not.

(h) Sanctions. All sanctions available under FRCP 16(f), FRBP 7016 and/or any Local Rule or previous Order of the Court shall apply to any violation of this rule.

(i) Court Authorization not Required. Nothing in this rule should be interpreted as limiting parties' ability to agree to a form of alternative dispute resolution or the selection of a neutral without a court order, through mutual consent. In fact, consent is preferred.

[Appendix L–1001–i effective December 1, 2000. Redesignated as Appendix L–1001–h and amended effective November 1, 2013; January 16, 2014.]

APPENDIX L–1020.1 PROCEDURES FOR COMPLEX CHAPTER 11 CASES

The following procedures shall apply in complex Chapter 11 cases:

1. A "complex Chapter 11 case" is defined as a case filed in this district under Chapter 11 of the Bankruptcy Code that requires special scheduling and other procedures because of a combination of the following factors:

a. the size of the case (usually total debt of more than $10 million);

b. the large number of parties in interest in the case (usually more than 50 parties in interest in the case);

c. the fact that claims against the debtor and/or equity interests in the debtor are publicly traded (with some creditors possibly being represented by indenture trustees); or

d. any other circumstances justifying complex case treatment.

2. "Expedited" means a matter which, for cause shown, should be heard on less than 21 days' notice. "Emergency" means a matter which, for cause shown, should be heard on less than 7 days' notice.

3. If any party filing a Chapter 11 bankruptcy petition believes that the case should be classified as a complex Chapter 11 case, the party shall file with the bankruptcy petition a Notice of Designation as Complex Chapter 11 Case in the form* attached as Exhibit A.

4. If a party has "First Day" matters requiring emergency consideration by the Court, it should submit a Request for Emergency Consideration of Certain "First Day" Matters in the form attached as Exhibit B.

5. Each judge shall arrange the judge's calendar so that "first day" emergency hearings, as requested in the Court-approved form entitled Request for Emergency Consideration of Certain First Day Matters, can be conducted consistent with the Bankruptcy Code and Rules, including Rule 4001, as required by the circumstances, but not more than two business days after the request for emergency "first day" hearings.

6. When a party has filed a Chapter 11 case and filed a Notice of Designation as Complex Chapter 11 Case, the Clerk of Court shall:

a. Generally assign the case to a judge in accordance with the usual procedures and general orders of the district or division;

b. Immediately confer with the Court about designating the case as a complex Chapter 11 case and about setting hearings on emergency or first day motions. If the Court determines that the case does not qualify as a complex Chapter 11 case, the Court shall issue an Order Denying Complex Case Treatment in the form attached as Exhibit C. If the Court determines that the case appears to be a complex Chapter 11 case, the Court shall issue an Order Granting Complex Chapter 11 Case Treatment in the form attached as Exhibit D; and

c. Notify and serve counsel for the debtor with the order entered by the Court relating to the complex case treatment and notify counsel for the debtor regarding the hearing settings for emergency first day matters.

7. Counsel for the debtor, upon receipt of notice of entry of an order regarding complex Chapter 11 case treatment, shall:

a. Serve the order granting or denying complex Chapter 11 case on all parties in interest within 7 days.

b. Provide notice of the first day emergency hearings in accordance with the procedures shown in the form attached as Exhibit E.

8. Counsel shall follow the agenda guidelines for hearings in complex Chapter 11 cases attached as Exhibit F and the guidelines for mailing matrices and shortened service lists attached as Exhibit G.

EXHIBIT A.
NOTICE OF DESIGNATION AS
COMPLEX CHAPTER 11 BANKRUPTCY CASE
IN THE UNITED STATES BANKRUPTCY COURT
FOR THE WESTERN DISTRICT OF TEXAS
_____ DIVISION

IN RE: §
                                §
                                §   CASE NO. _____
                                §
                                §
      DEBTOR.   §

NOTICE OF DESIGNATION AS COMPLEX
CHAPTER 11 BANKRUPTCY CASE

This bankruptcy case was filed on _____, 20 ___. The undersigned party in interest believes that this case qualifies as a complex Chapter 11 case because:

____ The debtor has total debt of more than $10 million;

____ There are more than 50 parties in interest in this case;

____ Claims against the debtor are publicly traded;

____ Other: (Substantial explanation is required. Attach additional sheets if necessary.)

_____

_____

_____

_____

_____, 20 __

_____
Name

_____
Address

_____
Telephone, Fax Numbers, and email

EXHIBIT B.
REQUEST FOR EMERGENCY CONSIDERATION
OF CERTAIN "FIRST DAY" MATTERS
IN THE UNITED STATES BANKRUPTCY COURT
FOR THE WESTERN DISTRICT OF TEXAS
_____ DIVISION

IN RE: §
                       §
                       §   CASE NO. _____
                       §
      DEBTOR.   §

REQUEST FOR EMERGENCY CONSIDERATION
OF CERTAIN "FIRST DAY" MATTERS

On _____, _____ filed a petition for relief under Chapter 11 of the Bankruptcy Code. Counsel for the debtor believes that the case qualifies as a "Complex Chapter 11 Case." The debtor needs emergency consideration of the following initial case matters (check those that apply*):

_____ JOINT MOTION FOR JOINT ADMINISTRATION

_____ MOTION FOR ORDER EXTENDING TIME TO FILE SCHEDULES AND STATEMENT OF FINANCIAL AFFAIRS

_____ MOTION RE MAINTENANCE OF BANK ACCOUNTS AND EXISTING CASH MANAGEMENT, ATTACHING NOTICE OF CONFERENCE WITH U.S. TRUSTEE

_____ MOTION TO PAY PRE–PETITION WAGES, SALARIES, ET AL., ATTACHING NOTICE OF CONFERENCE WITH U.S. TRUSTEE AND DETAILED EXHIBIT SHOWING WHO DEBTOR PROPOSES TO PAY AND AMOUNTS

_____ MOTION FOR ENTRY OF INTERIM ORDER AUTHORIZING USE OF CASH COLLATERAL

_____ MOTION FOR INTERIM APPROVAL OF POST–PETITION SECURED AND SUPER PRIORITY FINANCING PURSUANT TO SECTION 364(c) OF THE BANKRUPTCY CODE

_____ MOTION PURSUANT TO 11 U.S.C. § 366, FOR ENTRY OF INTERIM ORDER (1) DETERMINING ADEQUATE ASSURANCE OF PAYMENT FOR FUTURE UTILITY SERVICES AND (2) RESTRAINING UTILITY COMPANIES FROM DISCONTINUING, ALTERING, OR REFUSING SERVICE

_____ MOTION TO ESTABLISH INTERIM NOTICE PROCEDURES

_____ MOTION FOR ORDER APPROVING INTERIM RETENTION OF PROFESSIONALS

_____ MOTION FOR ORDER APPROVING PAYMENT OF PRE–PETITION CLAIMS OF CERTAIN CRITICAL VENDORS

_____ OTHERS (LIST):

_____
_____
_____
_____

—————————————————————, 20 —

—————————————————————
Name

—————————————————————
Address

—————————————————————
Telephone, Fax Numbers, and email

*NOTE: The Court expects the parties to exercise judgment regarding which motions are applicable.

EXHIBIT C.
ORDER DENYING COMPLEX
CASE TREATMENT
IN THE UNITED STATES BANKRUPTCY COURT
FOR THE WESTERN DISTRICT OF TEXAS
_____ DIVISION

IN RE: §
                §
                §   CASE NO. _____
                §
     DEBTOR.   §

ORDER DENYING COMPLEX
CASE TREATMENT

     This bankruptcy case was filed on _____, 20 ___. A Notice of Designation as Complex Chapter 11 Case was filed. After review of the initial pleadings filed in this case, the Court concludes that the case does not appear to qualify as a complex Chapter 11 case. Therefore, the case will proceed under the local bankruptcy rules and procedures generally applicable to bankruptcy cases without special scheduling orders. The Court may reconsider this determination on motion, after hearing.

     IT IS SO ORDERED.

# # #

The Clerk shall notice:
Debtor
Debtor's Counsel
U.S.   Trustee

EXHIBIT D.
ORDER GRANTING COMPLEX
CHAPTER 11 BANKRUPTCY CASE TREATMENT
IN THE UNITED STATES BANKRUPTCY COURT
FOR THE WESTERN DISTRICT OF TEXAS
_____ DIVISION

IN RE: §
         §
         §   CASE NO. _____
         §
         §
DEBTOR. §

ORDER GRANTING COMPLEX CHAPTER 11 BANKRUPTCY CASE TREATMENT

This bankruptcy case was filed on _____, 20 ___. A Notice of Designation as Complex Chapter 11 Case was filed. After review of the initial pleadings filed in this case, the Court concludes that this case appears to be a complex Chapter 11 case.

Accordingly, unless the Court orders otherwise,

IT IS ORDERED THAT:

1. The debtor shall maintain a service list identifying the parties that must be served whenever a motion or other pleading requires notice. Unless otherwise required by the Bankruptcy Code or Rules, notices of motions and other matters will be limited to the parties on the service list.

     a. The service list shall initially include the debtor, debtor's counsel, counsel for the unsecured creditors' committee, the U.S. Trustee, all secured creditors, the 20 largest unsecured creditors of each debtor, any indenture trustee, and any party that requests notice;

     b. Any party in interest that wishes to receive notice, other than as listed on the service list, shall be added to the service list by filing and serving the debtor and debtor's counsel with a notice of appearance and request for service.

     c. Parties on the service list, who have not otherwise consented to service by email, through the act of becoming a registered e-filer in this district, are encouraged to provide an e-mail address for service of process and to authorize service by email; consent to e-mail service may be included in the party's notice of appearance and request for service; in the event a party has not consented to email service, a "hard copy" shall be served by fax or by regular mail.

     d. The initial service list shall be filed within 3 days after entry of this order. A revised list shall be filed 7 days after the initial service list is filed. The debtor shall update the service list, and shall file a copy of the updated service list, (i) at least every 7 days during the first 30 days of the case; (ii) at least every 15 days during the next 60 days of the case; and (iii) at least every 30 days thereafter throughout the case.

2. [The Court sets _____ of [each week] [every other week, commencing [Month and Day] [each month] at _____ am/pm as the pre-set hearing day and time for hearing all motions and other matters in these cases.] The Court sets the following dates and times for the next two months as the pre-set hearing date and time for hearing all motions and other matters in these cases [insert dates and times]. Settings for the following months will be published by the Court no later than 30 days before the first hearing date in the said following months. (There may be exceptions; those exceptions will be noted on the Court's internet schedule, available at www.txwb.uscourts.gov.)

     a. All motions and other matters requiring hearing, but not requiring expedited or emergency hearing, shall be noticed for hearing, on the next hearing day that is at least 21 days after the notice is mailed. As a preface to each pleading, just below the case caption, in lieu of the language required by any Local Bankruptcy Rule, the pleading shall state:

A hearing will be conducted on this matter on _____ at __ am/pm in courtroom __, [courthouse name & address], _____, Texas.

If you object to the relief requested, you must respond in writing, specifically answering each paragraph of this pleading. Unless otherwise directed by the court, you must file your response with the clerk of the bankruptcy court within 21 days from the date you were served

with this pleading. **You must serve a copy of your response on the person who sent you the notice; otherwise, the court may treat the pleading as unopposed and grant the relief requested.**

    b.   All motions and other matters requiring expedited or emergency hearing shall comply with the usual Court requirements for explanation and verification of the need for emergency or expedited hearing. Specifically, if a party in interest has a situation that it believes requires consideration on less than 7 days' notice, then the party should file and serve a separate, written motion for expedited hearing, with respect to the underlying motion. The Court will make its best effort to rule on the motion for expedited or emergency hearing within 24 hours of the time it is presented. If the Court grants the motion for expedited or emergency hearing, the underlying motion will be set by the Courtroom Deputy at the next available preset hearing day or at some other appropriate shortened date approved by the Court. The party requesting the hearing shall be responsible for providing proper notice in accordance with this order and the Bankruptcy Code and Rules.

3.   Emergency and expedited hearings (and other hearings in limited circumstances) in this case may be conducted by telephone or, where available, video. Parties must request permission to participate by telephone by calling the Courtroom Deputy for the particular division at the number listed on the Court's website at www.txwb.uscourts.gov.

4.   If a matter is properly noticed for hearing and the parties reach a settlement of the dispute before the final hearing, the parties may announce the settlement at the scheduled hearing. If the Court determines that the notice of the dispute and the hearing is adequate notice of the effects of the settlement, (i.e., that the terms of the settlement are not materially different from what parties in interest could have expected if the dispute were fully litigated) the Court may approve the settlement at the hearing without further notice of the terms of the settlement.

5.   The debtor shall give notice of this order to all parties in interest within 7 days. If any party in interest, at any time, objects to the provisions of this order, that party shall file a motion articulating the objection and the relief requested. After hearing the objection and any responses the Court may reconsider any part of this order and may grant relief, if appropriate.

# # #

The Clerk shall notice:

Debtor

Debtor's Counsel

U.S. Trustee

EXHIBIT E. PROCEDURES FOR OBTAINING HEARINGS
IN COMPLEX CHAPTER 11 CASES

1. **Hearing on First Day Matters: Official Form for Request for Expedited Consideration of Certain First Day Matters.** Upon the filing of a complex Chapter 11 case, if the debtor has matters that require immediate emergency consideration ("first day" or "near first day" relief), the debtor should file a "Request for Emergency Consideration of Certain 'First Day' Matters" using the form of Exhibit B to the Procedures for Complex Chapter 11 Cases ("First Day Hearing Request"). The first day hearing request will be immediately forwarded by the Clerk of Court to the judge who has been assigned the complex Chapter 11 case (or if there are multiple, related debtor cases, to the judge assigned to the first-filed case). The Court will hold a hearing within 2 business days for the time requested by the debtor's counsel and the Courtroom Deputy will notify counsel for the debtor of the time of the setting. If the Judge assigned to the complex Chapter 11 case is not available to hold the hearing within 2 business days of the time requested by the debtor's counsel, an available judge will hold a hearing within 2 business days of the time requested by the debtor's counsel and the Courtroom Deputy will notify counsel for the debtor of the time of the setting. If no judge is available to hold a hearing within 2 business days, then a hearing date will be scheduled at the earliest possible date that a judge is available. The Debtor's Counsel should (1) serve electronically, if the e-mail address is available (or by facsimile or immediate hand–delivery) a copy of the first day hearing request on all affected parties, including the U.S. Trustee, simultaneously with its filing; and (2) notify electronically, if the e-mail address is available, or by fax or telephonically (or by immediate hand–delivery) all affected parties of the hearing time on first day matters as soon as possible after debtor's counsel has received confirmation from the Court. The Court will allow parties in interest to participate telephonically at the hearing on first day matters whenever (and to the extent) practicable, and Debtor's Counsel will be responsible for the coordination of the telephonic participation.

2. **Pre–Set Hearing Dates.** The debtor may request (as one of its first day matters or otherwise) that the Court establish in a complex Chapter 11 case a weekly/bimonthly/monthly setting time ("Pre–Set Hearing Dates") for hearings in the complex Chapter 11 case (e.g., every Wednesday at 1:30 p.m.). The Court will accommodate this request for pre-set hearing dates in a complex Chapter 11 case if it appears justified. After pre-set hearing dates are established, all matters in the complex Chapter 11 case (whether initiated by a motion of the debtor or by another party in interest) will be set on pre-set hearing dates that are at least 21 days after the filing/service of a particular motion (unless otherwise requested by a party or ordered by the Court) and the movant shall indicate the hearing date and time on the face of the pleading. Movant shall advise the Courtroom Deputy of all such settings before filing, and the Courtroom Deputy will advise the movant whether there is enough time on the docket that day to accommodate the matter.

3. **Notice of Hearing.** Notice of hearing of matters scheduled for pre-set hearing dates shall be accomplished by the moving party, who shall file a certificate that the notice has been accomplished in accordance with these procedures.

4. **Case Emergencies (Other Than the First–Day Matters).** If a party in interest has an expedited or emergency situation that it believes requires consideration on less than 21 days' notice, the party must file and serve a separate, written motion for expedited or emergency hearing, with respect to the underlying motion, which must comply with the usual Court requirements for explanation and verification of the need for expedited or emergency hearing. The Court will make its best effort to rule on the motion for expedited or emergency hearing within 24 hours of the time it is presented. If the Court grants the motion for expedited or emergency hearing, the underlying motion will be set by the Courtroom Deputy at the next available pre-set hearing date or at some other appropriate shortened date approved by the Court. Motions for expedited and emergency hearings will only be granted for clear cause shown and presented with particularity in the body of the motion.

EXHIBIT F.   AGENDA GUIDELINES FOR HEARINGS
IN COMPLEX CHAPTER 11 CASES

In complex Chapter 11 cases where five or more matters are noticed for the same hearing date, counsel for the debtor-in-possession, the party requesting the hearings, or trustee shall file and serve an agenda describing the nature of the items set for hearing.

1. **Timing of Filing.** Counsel shall file an agenda at least 24 hours before the date and time of the hearing. At the same time, counsel shall also serve the agenda (or confirm electronic service has been effectuated) upon all attorneys who have filed papers with respect to the matters scheduled and upon the service list.

2. **Sequence of Items on Agenda.** Uncontested matters should be listed ahead of contested matters. Contested matters should be listed in the order in which they appear on the Court's docket.

3. **Status Information.** For each motion filed in the complex Chapter 11 case, each motion filed in an adversary proceeding concerning the Chapter 11 case, each objection to claim, or application concerning the case, the agenda shall indicate the moving party, the nature of the motion, the docket number of the pleadings, if known, the response deadline, and the status of the matter. The status description should indicate whether the motion is settled, going forward, whether a continuance is requested (and any opposition to the continuance, if known) and any other pertinent information.

4. **Information for Motions in the Case.** For each motion that is going forward, or where a continuance request is not consensual, the agenda shall also list all pleadings in support of the motion, and any objections or responses. Each pleading listed shall identify the entity that filed the pleading, and the docket number of the pleading, if known. If any entity has not filed a responsive pleading, but has engaged in written or oral communications with the debtor, that fact should be indicated on the agenda, as well as the status or outcome of those communications. For an omnibus objection to claims, responses to the objection which have been continued by consent may be listed collectively (e.g., "the following responses have been continued by consent:")

5. **Changes in Agenda Information.** After the filing of the agenda, counsel shall notify judge's chambers by phone or letter of additional related pleadings that have been filed, and changes in the status of any agenda matter.

6. The requirements listed above should not be construed to prohibit other information of a procedural nature that counsel thinks would be helpful to the Court.

ALL MOTIONS AND PLEADINGS SHALL CONTAIN THE HEARING DATE AND TIME BELOW THE CASE/ADVERSARY NUMBER.

EXHIBIT G.   GUIDELINES FOR SERVICE LISTS
AND SHORTENED SERVICE LISTS IN
COMPLEX CHAPTER 11 CASES

I. Bankruptcy Rule 2002 Notice/Service List

A.   Helpful Hints Regarding Whom to Include on the Service List in a Complex Chapter 11 Case. There are certain events and deadlines that occur in a Chapter 11 case which FRBP 2002 requires be broadly noticed to all creditors, indenture trustees, equity interest holders, and other parties in interest ("Rule 2002 notice list"). To facilitate this, debtor's counsel shall evaluate and consider whether the following persons and entities need to be included on the Rule 2002 notice list:

1. creditors (whether a creditor's claim is disputed, undisputed, contingent, noncontingent, liquidated, unliquidated, matured, unmatured, fixed, legal, equitable, secured or unsecured);

2. indenture trustees;

3. financial institutions at which the debtor has maintained accounts (regardless of whether such institutions are creditors);

4. vendors with whom the debtor has dealt, even if the debtor's records currently indicate no amount is owed;

5. parties to contracts, executory contracts or leases with the debtor;

6. federal, state, or local taxing authorities with which the debtor deals, including taxing authorities in every county in which the debtor owns real or personal property with regard to which ad valorem taxes might be owed;

7. governmental entities with which the debtor might interact (including, but not limited to, the U.S. Trustee and the SEC);

8. any party who might assert a lien against property of the debtor;

9. parties to litigation involving the debtor;

10. parties with which the debtor might be engaged in some sort of dispute, whether or not a claim has formally been made against the debtor;

11. tort claimants or accident victims;

12. insurance companies with whom the debtor deals or has policies;

13. active and retired employees of the debtor;

14. officers or directors of the debtor;

15. customers who are owed deposits, refunds, or store credit;

16. utilities;

17. shareholders (preferred and common), holders of options, warrants or other rights or equitable interests in the debtor;

18. miscellaneous others who, in debtor counsel's judgment, might be entitled to "party in interest" status or who have requested notice.

B.   Flexible ("User Friendly") Format Rules for Mailing Matrix or Creditor List in a Complex Chapter 11 Case in Which Debtor's Counsel Serves Notices. In a complex Chapter 11 case, where the mailing matrix (or creditor list) is likely to be very lengthy, the following special format rules will apply, [in lieu of any applicable local bankruptcy rule, save and except the Administrative Procedures for the Filing, Signing and Verifying of Documents by Electronic Means in Texas Bankruptcy Courts, adopted by local rule or general order in all federal districts in Texas] whenever it is the debtor's responsibility to serve notices in the case. The debtor (since it will typically be the party serving all notices in the Chapter 11 case rather than the Clerk of Court) may create the mailing matrix or creditor list in whatever format it finds convenient so long as it is neatly typed in upper and lower case letter-quality characters (in no smaller than 10 point and no greater than 14 point type, in either Courier, Times Roman, Helvetica or Orator font) in a format equivalent to 8 1/2 inch by 11 inch blank, unlined, standard white paper. The mailing matrix or creditor list, if lengthy, should ideally include separate subheadings throughout, to help identify categories of parties in interest. By way of example, the following subheadings (among others) might be used:

Debtor and its Professionals

Secured Creditors
Indenture Trustees
Unsecured Creditors
Governmental Entities
Current and Retired Employees
Officers and Directors
Tort Claimants
Parties to Executory Contracts
Equity Interest Holders
Other

Parties in interest within each category/subheading should be listed alphabetically.

Also, the mailing matrix or creditor list may be filed in separate volumes, for the separate categories of parties in interest, if the mailing matrix or creditor list is voluminous. Finally, if there are multiple, related debtors and the debtors intend to promptly move for joint administration of their cases, the debtors may file a consolidated mailing matrix or creditor list, subject to later being required to file separate mailing matrices if joint administration is not permitted.

C. When Inclusion of Certain Parties in Interest on a Mailing Matrix is Burdensome. If inclusion of certain categories of parties in interest on the mailing matrix or creditor list would be extremely impracticable, burdensome and costly to the estate, the debtor may file a motion, pursuant to FRBP 2002(*l*), and on notice to the affected categories of parties in interest, requesting authority to provide notices to certain categories of parties in interest and may forego including those categories of parties in interest on the mailing matrix if the Court grants the motion.

II. Shortened Service List Procedure in a Complex Chapter 11 Case.

A. Procedures/Contents/Presumptions. If the Court has entered an order granting complex Chapter 11 case treatment, the debtor shall provide service as required by ¶ 1 of that order. If the Court has not entered such an order, the debtor may move to limit notice—that is, for approval of a shortened service list—that will be acceptable for noticing most events in the bankruptcy case, other than those events/deadlines that Federal Rules of Bankruptcy Procedure 2002 contemplates be served on all creditors and equity interest holders. At a minimum, the shortened list should include the debtor and its professionals, the secured creditors, the 20 largest unsecured creditors, any official committees and the professionals for same, the U.S. Trustee, the IRS and other relevant governmental entities, and all parties who have requested notice. Upon the Court's approval of a shortened service list in a complex Chapter 11 case, notice in any particular situation during a case shall be presumed adequate if there has been service on (1) the most current service list on file in the case; plus (2) any other party directly affected by the relief requested and not otherwise included on the service list.

B. Obligation to Update, File and Serve Service List. The debtor must update the service list as parties request to be added to it or as circumstances otherwise require. To be added to the list, a party must file a notice of appearance and request for service and serve the notice on debtor's counsel. Parties should include e-mail transmission information if they wish to receive expedited service of process during the case. Additionally, the debtor must file an updated service list and must serve a clean and redlined copy of the updated service list on all parties on the service list weekly for the first month after filing, then bi-monthly for the next 60 days, then monthly thereafter during the pendency of the case. If, in a particular month, there are no changes to the service list, the debtor must file a notice with the Court so stating.

EXHIBIT H.   GUIDELINES FOR COMPENSATION
AND EXPENSE REIMBURSEMENT OF
PROFESSIONALS IN COMPLEX CHAPTER 11 CASES

The following are guidelines govern the most significant issues relating to applications for compensation and expense reimbursement.   The guidelines cover the narrative portion of an application, time records, and expenses.   It applies to all professionals, but is not intended to cover every situation.   All professionals are required to exercise reasonable billing judgment, notwithstanding total hours spent.

If, in a chapter 11 case, a professional to be employed pursuant to section 327 or 1103 of the Bankruptcy Code desires to have the terms of its compensation approved pursuant to section 328(a) of the Bankruptcy Code at the time of such professional's retention, then the application seeking such approval should so indicate and the Court will consider such request after an evidentiary hearing on notice to be held after the United States trustee has had an opportunity to form a statutory committee of creditors pursuant to section 1102 of the Bankruptcy Code and the debtor had such committee have had an opportunity to review and comment on such application.   At a hearing to consider whether a professional's compensation arrangement should be approved pursuant to section 328(a), such professional should be prepared to produce evidence that the terms of compensation for which approval under section 328(a) is sought comply with the certification requirements of section I.G(3) of these guidelines.

I. NARRATIVE

A.   Employment and Prior Compensation. The application should disclose the date of the order approving applicant's employment and contain a clear statement itemizing the date of each prior request for compensation, the amount requested, the amount approved, and the amount paid.

B.   Case Status. With respect to interim requests, the application should briefly explain the history and the present posture of the case, including a description of the status of pending litigation and the amount of recovery sought for the estate.

In chapter 11 cases, the information furnished should describe the general operations of the debtor; whether the business of the debtor, if any, is being operated at a profit or loss; the debtor's cash flow; whether a plan has been filed, and if not, what the prospects are for reorganization and when it is anticipated that a plan will be filed and a hearing set on the disclosure statement.

In chapter 7 cases, the application should contain a report of the administration of the case including the disposition of property of the estate; what property remains to be disposed of; why the estate is not in a position to be closed; and whether it is feasible to pay an interim dividend to creditors.

In both chapter 7 and chapter 11 cases, the application should state the amount of money on hand in the estate and the estimated amount of other accrued expenses of administration.   On applications for interim fees, the applicant should orally supplement the application at the hearing to inform the Court of any changes in the current financial status of the debtor's estate since the filing of the application.   All retainers, previous draw downs, and fee applications and orders should be listed specifying the date of the event and the amounts involved and drawn down or allowed.

With respect to final requests, applications should meet the same criteria except where a chapter 7 trustee's final account if being heard at the same time, the financial information in the final account need not be repeated.

Fee applications submitted by special counsel seeking compensation from a fund generated directly by their efforts, auctioneers, real estate brokers, or appraisers do not have to comply with the above. For all other applications, when more than one application is noticed for the same hearing, they may, to the extent appropriate, incorporate by reference the narrative history furnished in a contemporaneous application.

C.   Project Billing. This is required in all cases where the applicant's professional fee is expected to exceed $10,000.00.   The narrative should be categorized by subject matter, and separately discuss each professional project or task.   All work for which compensation is requested should be in a category.   Miscellaneous items may be included in a category such as "Case Administration." The professional may use reasonable discretion in defining projects for this purpose, provided that the application provides meaningful guidance to the Court as to the complexity and difficulty of the task, the professional's efficiency, and the results achieved.   With respect to each project or task, the number of hours spent and the amount of compensation and expenses requested should be set forth at the conclusion of the discussion of that project or task. In larger cases with multiple professionals, efforts should be made by the professionals for standard categorization.

D. Billing Summary. Hours and total compensation requested in each application should be aggregate and itemized as to each professional and paraprofessional who provided compensable services. Dates of changes in rates should be itemized as well as reasons for said changes.

E. Paraprofessionals. Fees may be sought for paralegals, professional assistants and law clerks only if identified as such and if the application includes a resume or summary of the paraprofessional's qualifications.

F. Preparation of Application. Reasonable fees for preparation of a fee application and responding to objections thereto may be requested. The aggregate number of hours spent, the amount requested, and the percentage of the total request which the amount represents must be disclosed. If the actual time spent will be reflected and charged in a future fee application, this fact should be stated, but an estimate provided, nevertheless.

G. Certification. Each application for compensation and expense reimbursement must contain a certification by the professional designated by the applicant with the responsibility in the particular case for compliance with these guidelines ("Certifying Professional") that 1) the Certifying Professional has read the application; 2) to the best of the Certifying Professional's knowledge, information and belief, formed after reasonable inquiry, the compensation and expense reimbursement sought is in conformity with these guidelines, except as specifically noted in the application; and 3) the compensation and expenses reimbursement requested are billed at rates, in accordance with practices, no less favorable than those customarily employed by the applicant and generally accepted by the applicant's clients.

H. Interim Compensation Arrangements in Complex Cases. In a complex case, the Court may, upon request, consider at the outset of the case approval of an interim compensation mechanism for estate professionals that would enable professionals on a monthly basis to be paid up to 80% of their compensation for services rendered and reimbursed up to 100% of their actual and necessary out of pocket expenses. In connection with such a procedure, if approved in a particular complex case, professionals shall be required to circulate monthly billing statements to the US Trustee and other primary parties in interest, and the Debtor in Possession or Trustee will be authorized to pay the applicable percentage of such bill not disputed or contested by a party in interest.

II. TIME RECORDS

A. Time Records Required. All professionals, except auctioneers, real estate brokers, and appraisers must keep accurate contemporaneous time records.

B. Increments. Professionals are required to keep time records in minimum increments no greater than six minutes. Professionals who utilize a minimum billing increment greater than .1 hour are subject to a substantial reduction of their requests.

C. Descriptions. At a minimum, the time entries should identify the person performing the service, the date(s) performed, what was done, and the subject involved. Mere notations of telephone calls, conferences, research, drafting, etc., without identifying the matter involved, may result in disallowance of the time covered by the entries.

D. Grouping of Tasks. If a number of separate tasks are performed on a single day, the fee application should disclose the time spent for each such task, i.e., no "grouping" or "clumping." Minor administrative matters may be lumped together where the aggregate time attributed thereto is relatively minor. A rule of reason applies as to how specific and detailed the breakdown needs to be. For grouped entries, the applicant must accept the Court inferences therefrom.

E. Conferences. Professionals should be prepared to explain time spent in conferences with other professionals or paraprofessionals in the same firm. Relevant explanation would include complexity of issues involved and the necessity of more individuals' involvement. Failure to justify this time may result in disallowance of all, or a portion of, fees related to such conferences.

F. Multiple Professionals. Professionals should be prepared to explain the need for more than one professional or paraprofessional from the same firm at the same Court hearing, deposition, or meeting. Failure to justify this time may result in compensation for only the person with the lowest billing rate. The Court acknowledges, however, that in complex chapter 11 cases the need for multiple professionals' involvement will be more common and that in hearings involving multiple or complex issues a law firm may justifiably be required to utilize multiple attorneys as the circumstances of the case require.

G. Travel Time. Travel time is compensable at one-half rates, but work actually done during travel is fully compensable.

H. Administrative Tasks. Time spent in addressing, stamping and stuffing envelopes, filing, photocopying or "supervising" any of the foregoing is generally not compensable, whether performed by a professional, paraprofessional, or secretary.

III. EXPENSES

A. Firm Practice. The Court will consider the customary practice of the firm in charging or not charging non–bankruptcy/insolvency clients for particular expense items. Where any other clients, with the exception of pro-bono clients, are not billed for a particular expense, the estate should not be billed. Where expenses are billed to all other clients, reimbursement should be sought at the least expensive rate the firm or professional charges to any client for comparable services or expenses. It is recognized that there will be differences in billing practices among professionals.

B. Actual Cost. This is defined as the amount paid to a third party provider of goods or services without enhancement for handling or other administrative charge.

C. Documentation. This must be retained and made available upon request for all expenditures in excess of $50.00. Where possible, receipts should be obtained for all expenditures.

D. Office Overhead. This is not reimbursable. Overhead includes: secretarial time, secretarial overtime (where clear necessity for same has not been shown), word processing time, charges for after-hour and weekend air conditioning and other utilities, and cost of meals or transportation provided to professionals and staff who work late or on weekends.

E. Word Processing. This is not reimbursable.

F. Computerized Research. This is reimbursable at actual cost. For large amounts billed to computerized research, significant explanatory detail should be furnished.

G. Paraprofessional Services. These services may be compensated as a paraprofessional under § 330, but not charged or reimbursed as an expense.

H. Professional Services. A professional employed under § 327 may not employ, and charge as an expense, another professional (e.g., special litigation counsel employing an expert witness) unless the employment of the second professional is approved by the Court before the rendering of service.

I. Photocopies (Internal). Charges must be disclosed on an aggregate and per page basis. If the per-page cost exceeds $.20, the professional must demonstrate to the satisfaction of the Court, with data, that the per-page cost represents a good faith estimate of the actual cost of the copies, based upon the purchase or lease cost of the copy machine and supplies therefore, including the space occupied by the machine, but not including time spent in operating the machine.

J. Photocopies (Outside). This item is reimbursable at actual cost.

K. Postage. This is reimbursable at actual cost.

L. Overnight Delivery. This is reimbursable at actual cost where it is shown to be necessary. The Court acknowledges that in complex chapter 11 cases overnight delivery or messenger services may often be appropriate, particularly when shortened notice of a hearing of a hearing has been requested.

M. Messenger Service. This is reimbursable at actual cost where it is shown to be necessary. An in-house messenger service is reimbursable, but the estate cannot be charged more than the cost of comparable services available outside the firm.

N. Facsimile Transmission. The actual cost of telephone charges for outgoing transmissions is reimbursable. Transmissions received are reimbursable on a per-page basis. If the per-page cost exceeds $.20, the professional must demonstrate, with data, to the satisfaction of the Court, that the per-page cost represents a good faith estimate of the actual cost of the copies, based upon the purchase or lease cost of the facsimile machine and supplies therefore, including the space occupied by the machine, but not including time spent in operating the machine.

O. Long Distance Telephone. This is reimbursable at actual cost.

P. Parking. This is reimbursable at actual cost.

Q. Air Transportation. Air travel is expected to be at regular coach fare for all flights.

R. Hotels. Due to wide variation in hotel costs in various cities, it is not possible to establish a single guideline for this type of expense. All persons will be required to exercise reasonable discretion and prudence in connection with hotel expenditures.

S. Meals (Travel). Reimbursement may be sought for the reasonable cost of breakfast, lunch and dinner while traveling.

T. Meals (Working). Working meals at restaurants or private clubs are not reimbursable. Reasonable reimbursement may be sought for working meals only where food is catered to the professional's office in the course of a meeting with clients, such as a Creditors' Committee, for the purpose of allowing the meeting to continue through a normal meal period.

U. Amenities. Charges for entertainment, alcoholic beverages, newspapers, dry cleaning, shoe shines, etc. are not reimbursable.

V. Filing Fees. These are reimbursable at actual cost.

W. Court Reporter Fees. These are reimbursable at actual cost.

X. Witness Fees. These are reimbursable at actual cost.

Y. Process Service. This is reimbursable at actual cost.

Z. UCC Searches. These are reimbursable at actual cost.

EXHIBIT I.   GUIDELINES FOR EARLY DISPOSITION
OF ASSETS IN CHAPTER 11 CASES
THE SALE OF SUBSTANTIALLY ALL ASSETS UNDER SECTION 363
AND OVERBID AND TOPPING FEES

The following guidelines are promulgated as a result of the increasing use of prenegotiated or pre-packaged plans and 11 U.S.C. § 363 sales to dispose of substantially all assets of a Chapter 11 debtor shortly after the filing of the petition. The guidelines recognize that parties in interest perceive the need at times to act expeditiously on such matters. In addition, the guidelines are written to provide procedural protection to the parties in interest. The Court will consider requests to modify the guidelines to fit the circumstances of a particular case.

A. OVERBIDS AND TOPPING FEES

1.   Topping Fees and Break-up Fees. Any request for the approval of a topping fee or a break-up fee provision shall be supported by a statement of the precise conditions under which the topping fee or break-up fee would be payable and the factual basis on which the seller determined the provision was reasonable. The request shall also disclose the identities of other potential purchasers, the offers made by them (if any), and the nature of the offer, including, without limitation, any disclosure of their plans as it relates to retention of debtor's employees.

2.   Topping fees, break-up fees, overbid amounts and other buyer protection provisions will be reviewed on a case by case basis and approved if supported by evidence and case law. Case law may not support buyer protection provisions for readily marketable assets.

3.   In connection with a request to sell substantially all assets under § 363 within 60 days of the filing of the petition, buyer protections may be considered upon motion, on an expedited basis.

B. THE SALE OF SUBSTANTIALLY ALL ASSETS UNDER SECTION 363 WITHIN 60 DAYS OF THE FILING OF THE PETITION

1.   The Motion to Sell. In connection with any hearing to approve the sale of substantially all assets at any time before 60 days after the filing of the petition, a motion for an order authorizing a sale procedure and hearing or the sale motion itself when regularly noticed, should include factual information on the following points:

a.   Creditors' Committee. If a creditors' committee existed pre-petition, indicate the date and manner in which the committee was formed, as well as the identity of the members of the committee and the companies with which they are affiliated.

b.   Counsel for Committee. If the pre-petition creditors' committee retained counsel, indicate the date counsel was engaged and the selection process, as well as the identity of committee counsel.

c.   Sale Contingencies. Statement of all contingencies to the sale agreement, together with a copy of the agreement.

d.   Creditor Contact List. If no committee has been formed, a list of contact persons, together with fax and phone numbers for each of the largest 20 unsecured creditors.

e.   Administrative Expenses. Assuming the sale is approved, an itemization and an estimate of administrative expenses relating to the sale to be incurred before closing and the source of payment for those expenses.

f.   Proceeds of Sale. An estimate of the gross proceeds anticipated from the sale, together with an estimate of the net proceeds coming to the estate with an explanation of the items making up the difference. Itemize all deductions that are to be made from gross sale proceeds and include a brief description of the basis for any such deductions.

g.   Debt Structure of Debtor. A brief description of the debtor's debt structure, including the amount of the debtor's secured debt, priority claims and general unsecured claims.

h.   Need for Quick Sale. An extensive description of why the assets of the estate must be sold on an expedited basis. Include a discussion of alternatives to the sale.

i.   Negotiating Background. A description of the length of time spent in negotiating the sale, and which parties in interest were involved in the negotiation, along with a description of the details of any other offers to purchase, including, without limitation, the potential purchaser's plans in connection with retention of the debtor's employees.

j.   Marketing of Assets.   A description of the manner in which the assets were marketed for sale, including the period of time involved and the results achieved.

k.   Decision to Sell.   The date on which the debtor accepted the offer to purchase the assets.

l.   Relationship of Buyer.   A statement identifying the buyer and setting forth all of the buyer's (including its officers, directors and shareholders) connections with the debtor, creditors, any other party in interest, their respective attorneys, accountants, the United States Trustee or any person employed in the office of the United States Trustee.

m.   Post Sale Relationship with Debtor.   A statement setting forth any relationship or connection the debtor (including its officers, directors, shareholders and employees) will have with the buyer after the consummation of the sale, assuming it is approved.

n.   Relationship with Secured Creditors.   If the sale involves the payment of all or a portion of secured debt(s), a statement of all connections between debtor's officers, directors, employees or other insiders and each secured creditor involved (for example, release of insider's guaranty).

o.   Insider Compensation.   Disclosure of current compensation received by officers, directors, key employees or other insiders pending approval of the sale.

p.   Notice Timing.   Notice of the hearing on the motion to approve the motion to sell will be provided as is necessary under the circumstances.

2. Proposed Order Approving Sale.   A proposed order approving the sale must be included with the motion or the notice of hearing.   A proposed final order and redlined version of the order approving the sale should be provided to chambers twenty-four hours before the hearing.

3. Good Faith Finding.   There must be an evidentiary basis for a finding of good faith under 11 U.S.C. § 363(m).

4. Competing Bids.   Unless the Court orders otherwise, competing bids may be presented at the time of the hearing.   The motion to sell and the notice of hearing should so provide.

5. Financial Ability to Close.   Unless the Court orders otherwise, any bidder must be prepared to demonstrate to the satisfaction of the Court, through an evidentiary hearing, its ability to consummate the transaction if it is the successful bidder, along with evidence regarding any financial contingencies to closing the transaction.

6. Hearing and Notice Regarding Sale.   Unless the Court orders otherwise, all sales governed by these guidelines, including auctions or the presentation of competing bids, will occur at the hearing before the Court.   The Court may, for cause, including the need to maximize and preserve asset value, expedite a hearing on a motion to sell substantially all assets under § 363.

EXHIBIT J.
CHECKLIST FOR LENGTHY MOTIONS AND ORDERS PERTAINING TO
CASH COLLATERAL AND POST–PETITION FINANCING
IN THE UNITED STATES BANKRUPTCY COURT
FOR THE WESTERN DISTRICT OF TEXAS
_____ DIVISION

IN RE: §
                               §
                               §   CASE NO. _____
                               §
                               §
         DEBTOR.   §   HEARING: _____

ATTORNEY CHECKLIST CONCERNING MOTIONS AND ORDERS
PERTAINING TO USE OF CASH COLLATERAL AND POST–PETITION
FINANCING (WHICH ARE IN EXCESS OF TEN (10) PAGES)

Motions and orders pertaining to cash collateral and post- petition financing matters tend to be lengthy and complicated. Although the Court intends to read such motions and orders carefully, it will assist the Court if counsel will complete and file this checklist. All references are to the Bankruptcy Code (§) or Rules (R).
PLEASE NOTE:
"*"   Means generally not favored by Bankruptcy Courts in this District.
"**"   Means generally not favored by Bankruptcy Courts in this District without a reason and a time period for objections.

If your motion or order makes provision for any of the following, so indicate in the space provided:

CERTIFICATE BY COUNSEL

This is to certify that the following checklist fully responds to the Court's inquiry concerning material terms of the motion and/ or proposed order:
Yes, at Page/Exhibit
Y means yes; N means no
N/A means not applicable
(Page Listing Optional)

1. **Identification of Proceedings:**
    (a) Preliminary or final motion/order (circle one)   ____

    (b) Continuing use of cash collateral (§ 363)   ____

    (c) New financing (§ 364)   ____

    (d) Combination of §§ 363 and 364 financing   ____

    (e) Emergency hearing (immediate and irreparable harm)

2. **Stipulations:**
    (a) Brief history of debtor's businesses and status of debtor's
         prior relationships with lender   ____

    (b) Brief statement of purpose and necessity of financing   ____

    (c) Brief statement of type of financing (i.e., accounts receiv-
         able, inventory)   ____
** (d) Are lender's pre-petition security interest(s) and liens
         deemed valid, fully perfected and non–avoidable   ____

    (i) Are there provisions to allow for objections to above? ____

    (e) Is there a post-petition financing agreement between lender
         and debtor?   ____
         (i) If so, is agreement attached?   ____

** (f) If there is an agreement are lender's post-petition security interests and liens deemed valid, fully perfected and non–avoidable?   ____

(g) Is lender undersecured or oversecured? (circle one)   ____

(h) Has lender's non-cash collateral been appraised?
    (*i*) Insert date of latest appraisal   ____

(i) Is debtor's proposed budget attached?   ____

(j) Are all pre-petition loan documents identified?   ____

(k) Are pre-petition liens on single or multiple assets? (circle one)   ____

(*l*) Are there pre-petition guaranties of debt?
    (*i*) Limited or unlimited? (circle one)   ____

3. Grant of Liens:

* (a) Do post-petition liens secure pre-petition debts?   ____

* (b) Is there cross–collateralization?   ____

** (c) Is the priority of post-petition liens equal to or higher than existing liens?   ____

** (d) Do post-petition liens have retroactive effect?   ____

(e) Are there restrictions on granting further liens or liens of equal or higher priority?

* (f) Is lender given liens on claims under §§ 506(c), 544–50 and §§ 522?

**   (*i*) Are lender's attorney's fees to be paid?   ____
    (*ii*) Are debtor's attorney's fees excepted from § 506(c)?   ____

* (g) Is lender given liens upon proceeds of causes of action under §§ 544, 547 and 548?

4. Administrative Priority Claims:

(a) Is lender given an administrative priority?   ____

(b) Is administrative priority higher than § 507(a)?   ____

(c) Is there a conversion of pre-petition secured claim to post-petition administrative claim by virtue of use of existing collateral?   ____

5. Adequate Protection (§ 361):

(a) Is there post-petition debt service?   ____

(b) Is there a replacement/addition 361(*l*) lien? (circle one or both)   ____

** (c) Is the lender's claim given super–priority? (§ 364(c) or (d)) [designate]   ____

(d) Are there guaranties?   ____

    (e) Is there adequate insurance coverage?   _____

    (f) Other?   _____

6. Waiver/Release Claims v. Lender:

**   (a) Debtor waives or release claims against lender, including, but not limited to, claims under §§ 506(c), 544–550, 552, and 553 of the Code?   _____

**   (b) Does the debtor waive defenses to claim or liens of lender?   _____

7. Source of Post–Petition Financing (§ 364 Financing):

    (a) Is the proposed lender also the pre-petition lender?   _____

    (b) New post-petition lender?   _____

    (c) Is the lender an insider?   _____

8. Modification of Stay:

**   (a) Is any modified lift of stay allowed?   _____

**   (b) Will the automatic stay be lifted to permit lender to exercise self-help upon default without further order?   _____

    (c) Are there any other remedies exercisable without further order of the Court?   _____

    (d) Is there a provision that any future modification of order shall not affect status of debtor's post-petition obligations to lender?   _____

9. Creditors' Committee:

    (a) Has creditors' committee been appointed?   _____

    (b) Does creditors' committee approve of proposed financing?   _____

10. Restrictions on Parties in Interest:

**   (a) Is a plan proponent restricted in any manner, concerning modification of lender's rights, liens and/or causes?   _____

**   (b) Is the debtor prohibited from seeking to enjoin the lender in pursuant of rights?   _____

**   (c) Is any party in interest prohibited from seeking to modify this order?   _____

    (d) Is the entry of any order conditioned upon payment of debt to lender?   _____

    (e) Is the order binding on subsequent trustee on conversion?   _____

11. Nunc Pro Tunc:

    (a) Does any provision have retroactive effect?   _____

12. Notice and Other Procedures:

    (a) Is shortened notice requested?   _____

    (b) Is notice requested to shortened list?   _____

    (c) Is time to respond to be shortened?   _____

(d) If final order sought, have 14 days elapsed since service of motion pursuant to Rule 4001(b)(2)?   ____

(e) If preliminary order sought, is cash collateral necessary to avoid immediate and irreparable harm to the estate pending a final hearing?   ____

(f) Is a Certificate of Conference included?   ____

(g) Is a Certificate of Service included?   ____

(h) Is there verification of transmittal to U.S. Trustee included pursuant to Rule 9034?   ____

(i) Has an agreement been reached subsequent to filing motion?   ____
     (*i*) If so, has notice of the agreement been served pursuant to Rule 4001(d)(4)?   ____
     (*ii*) Is the agreement in settlement of motion pursuant to Rule 4001(d) (4)?   ____
     (iii) Does the motion afford reasonable notice of material provisions of agreement pursuant to Rule 4001(d)(4)?   ____
     (iv) Does the motion provide for opportunity for hearing pursuant to Rule 9014?   ____

SIGNED this ___ day of _____, 20 ___.
               [Enter Firm Name]

               By: _____
               [Enter Attorney's Name]
               [Enter Texas Bar No.]
               [Enter Address]
               [Enter Telephone Number]
               [Enter Email Address]
               [Enter Identification Role in Case]

COMMENTS TO CASH COLLATERAL AND DIP FINANCING CHECKLIST

1. Interim vs. Final Orders

a. Stipulations in preliminary or interim orders should be minimized. Notice is generally not adequate to test the validity of stipulations, and they should be avoided to the extent not absolutely necessary to the interim approval process.

b. Simply state the nature of notice given; do not recite notice was "sufficient and adequate" since that is usually not the case particularly on the first day. The order should simply note that the financing is being approved pursuant to Bankruptcy Rule 4001(c)(2) authorizing such financing to avoid immediate and irreparable harm.

c. Adequate protection for the use of pre-petition cash collateral may be granted to the extent of a diminution of collateral. The Court will not approve on an interim basis language that adequate protection is granted in the form of replacement liens on post-petition assets based on stipulations that "use of cash collateral shall be deemed a dollar for dollar decrease in the value of the pre-petition collateral." At the final hearing the Court will consider evidence to determine the extent to which the lender's pre-petition collateral has or is likely to diminish in value. That evidence will inform the extent to which adequate protection will be granted.

d. The Court expects that other parties in interest will be involved in the process of developing an interim cash collateral order to the extent practicable. If the Court finds that the debtor and lender have not made reasonable efforts to afford the best notice possible, preliminary relief will not be granted until parties in interest have had a reasonable opportunity to review and comment on any proposed interim order.

e. Bankruptcy Rule 4001(b) and (c) limit the extent to which the Court may grant relief on less than 14 days' notice. The debtor and the lender must negotiate interim orders within the confines of that authority. Interim orders shall be expressly without prejudice to the rights of parties in interest at a final hearing.

2. Stipulations

The lender may request a stipulation as to the amount, validity, priority and extent of the pre-petition documents. The stipulation will only be approved if the order provides the stipulation is binding on other parties in interest only after the passage of an appropriate period of time (customarily 90 days) during which the parties in interest will have the opportunity to test the validity of the lien and the allowance of the claim.

3. Grant of Liens

a. Liens granted in the cash collateral and DIP financing orders may not secure prepetition debts. Financing orders should not be used to elevate a pre-petition lender's collateral inadequacy to a fully secured status.

b. Avoidance actions are frequently one of the few sources of recovery for creditors other than secured lenders. Orders granting liens on these unencumbered assets for the benefit of the lender will require a showing of extraordinary circumstances. In most cases the adequate protection grant will protect the lender since the lender will have a superpriority under § 507(b) that will give the lender who suffers a failure of adequate protection a first right to payment out of the proceeds from such actions before payment of any other expenses of the Chapter 11 case. Avoidance actions in the event of a conversion to Chapter 7 may be the only assets available to fund the trustee's discharge of his or her statutory duties.

c. Similarly, limitations on the surcharge of the lender's collateral under § 506(c) are disfavored. The secured creditor may be the principal beneficiary of the proceedings in Chapter 11. Since the burden to surcharge requires a showing of direct benefit to the lender's collateral, lenders are not unreasonably exposed to surcharges of their collateral. And in light of the decision in *Hartford Underwriter's Insurance Co. v. Union Planters Bank N.A. (In re Hen House Interstate Inc.)*, 530 U.S. 1 (2000), only the DIP or the trustee may recover under § 506(c).

4. Modification of Stay

Authority for unilateral action by lender without necessity to return to Court to establish post-petition default or breach or at least a notice to parties in interest will not be approved. If the cash collateral or financing order provides for a termination of the automatic stay in the event of a default, parties in interest must have an opportunity to be heard before the stay lifts.

5. Restrictions on Plan Process

a. The Court will not approve cash collateral orders (or post-petition financing orders that are in substance cash collateral orders that have the effect of converting all the prepetition liens and claims to post-petition liabilities under the guise of collecting prepetition accounts and readvancing them post–petition) that have the effect of converting prepetition secured debt into post-petition adminis-trative claims that must be paid in full in order to confirm a plan. That type of provision unfairly limits the ability and flexibility of the debtor and other parties in interest to formulate a plan. That type of provision, granted at the outset of a case, effectively compels the debtor to pay off the secured lender in full on the effective date and has the consequence of eviscerating § 1129(b).

b. On the other hand, persons who are advancing new money to the debtor postpetition may include in financing orders provisions that the post-petition loans have a § 364(c)(1) super-super priority.

6. Loan Agreements

If there will be a loan agreement, the language of the financing order does not need to restate all of the terms of the loan agreement. The financing motion should, however, summarize the essential elements of the proposed borrowing or use of cash collateral, such as, amount of loan facility, sublimits on availability, borrowing base formula, conditions to new advances, interest rate, maturity, events of default, limitation on use of funds and description of collateral.

7. Professional Fees

a. To the extent consistent with the market for similar financings, the lender may request reimbursement of reasonable professional fees. The lender should provide reasonably detailed invoices to the debtor and the committees so a proper assessment of reasonableness can be made.

b. The parties may agree on carve-outs for estate professionals. Lenders may exclude from the carve-out payment of professional fees for litigation of the extent, validity or perfection of the lender's claim as well as prosecution of lender liability suits. The carve-out should not, however, exclude the due diligence work by the committee or its professionals to determine whether a challenge to the lender is justified.

8. Work Fees/Loan Fees

Underwriting a substantial DIP loan may involve both direct out-of-pocket expenses and, at times, a certain lost opportunity cost. The debtor may move for the reimbursement of its lender's direct out-of-pocket expenses. The debtor and lender must be prepared to establish actual out-of-pocket costs, the reasonableness of the costs, and that the type of costs are actually paid in the market. On a case-by-case basis, the Court will consider on an expedited basis the debtor's request to pay a reasonable up-front fee to a prospective DIP lender to reimburse it for direct out-of-pocket costs. In addition, in connection with approving a DIP loan facility, on motion of the debtor, the Court will consider evidence of market rates and pricing for comparable loans in determining whether commitment fees, facility or availability fees, and other up-front or periodic loan charges are appropriate. The lender must provide evidence that it actually has provided or will provide the services customarily associated with these fees.

[Amended effective December 1, 2009; January 16, 2014.]

* All order exemplars attached as exhibits are furnished for the purpose of prescribing content. Actual formatting of orders should follow the formatting requirements for the district in which the case is filed.

APPENDIX L–2014. NOTICE OF EMPLOYMENT OF PROFESSIONAL

(STYLE)

NOTICE OF EMPLOYMENT OF PROFESSIONAL

This pleading requests relief that may be adverse to your interests.

If no timely response is filed within 21 days from the date of service, the relief requested in the motion may be granted without a hearing being held.

A timely filed response is necessary for a hearing to be held.

Name of client:

Identity of professional: (Name, address, phone)

Nature of profession: (Attorney, accountant)

Conflicts: None or specify

Retainer:

Proposed compensation: (e.g. hourly rates (specified), flat fee, contingency fee)

List of other professionals in case:

   Signed: (professional)

[Effective December 1, 2000. Amended effective December 1, 2009; January 16, 2014.]

APPENDIX L–2016–a–2.   FEE APPLICATION SUMMARY

(Case No.)

(Case Name)

(Hearing Date, if known)

FEE APPLICATION SUMMARY

I.   CLIENT—(Name of party represented)

Example: DIP, Bankruptcy Estate

II.   REQUESTING APPLICANT/FIRM—(Give attorney/accountant name and nature of representation.)

Example: Collier & Norton, attorneys for the Debtor, on behalf of Penny & Dollar, Court-approved CPA.

III.   TOTAL AMOUNT OF FEES REQUESTED–

   a.   Fees: $

   b.   Expenses: $

   c.   Pre–petition retainer, if any: $ ___; (of this amount, $ ___ has previously been offset pursuant to prior fee applications)

   d.   Time period covered: ___ to ___.

IV.   BREAKOUT OF CURRENT APPLICATION

NAME/CAPACITY	TOTAL HOURS	RATE	TOTAL
(Collier, Atty.	20.00	$100.00	$2,000.00)
(Norton, Paralegal	10.00	35.00	350.00)
	30.00		$2,350.00

MINIMUM FEE INCREMENTS—(Give minimum fee increment. Explain fully fee increments other than. 1 or any other flat or unusual rates).

EXPENSES—(Give total amounts requested for expenses and specifically charge for photocopy and any in-house services such as delivery fees).

AMOUNT ALLOCATED FOR PREPARATION OF THIS FEE APPLICATION: _____

  V.   PRIOR APPLICATIONS:

Date of hearing (e.g., 1/5/87)	Amount requested $2,510.00	Amount authorized *$2,400.00

    * (Explain if any of the previous authorized amounts still remain to be paid.)

VI.   OTHER CO–EQUAL OR ADMINISTRATIVE CLAIMANTS IN THIS CASE:

    Name   Party Represented

Explain whether allowance of your Application will or will not result in this estate not being able to pay all co-equal or superior administrative claims in this ease.

VII.   RESULT OBTAINED–

For the time period covered by this Application, briefly identify the various matters for which services were rendered. For each identified matter, summarize the work performed and estimate the amount of fees allocated to such work during the time period in question. This estimate need not be exactly accurate, however the total of estimated fees must equal the amount of fees sought in this Application.

[Effective December 1, 2000. Amended effective January 16, 2014.]

APPENDIX L–3018–B. BALLOT SUMMARY

IN THE UNITED STATES BANKRUPTCY COURT
FOR THE WESTERN DISTRICT OF TEXAS
_____ DIVISION

IN RE	)	
	)	
	)	CASE NO.
	)	
DEBTOR(S)	)	
	)	

BALLOT SUMMARY FOR (PLAN PROPONENT'S NAME   )
PLAN OF REORGANIZATION

BALLOT SUMMARY (BY CLAIM)

NAME	CLASS		ALLOWED CLAIM			VOTE
(alphabetized)	(per plan)	p/c	sched	ct ord	Sec 502(c)	

BALLOT SUMMARY (BY CLASS)

CLASS	TOTAL #	TOTAL AMOUNT	TOTAL # (Y)/(N) (YES) (NO)	TOTAL AMNT (Y)/(N) (YES) (NO)	CLASS VOTE

[Effective December 1, 2000.]

APPENDIX L–4001. AFFIDAVIT

IN THE UNITED STATES BANKRUPTCY COURT FOR THE WESTERN DISTRICT OF TEXAS

_____ DIVISION

IN RE:
§
§
§
§
Debtor
§
§
§
§
§
Movant
§
§
v.
§
§
_____, §
§
Respondent
§

CASE NO.

Chapter

Hearing Date:
Time:

Judge:

Affidavit of [Affiant's name]
FOR [Movant] _____

STATE OF TEXAS   §
COUNTY OF   §
                              §
                              §

"Affiant, being duly sworn, deposes and says that:

1. My name is _____, I am of sound mind, capable of making this affidavit, and am personally acquainted with the facts herein stated.

2. I am a custodian of the records of _____ ("Movant").

3. Attached hereto as Exhibit "A" are ___ page(s) of the Payment History, prepared by me from records of Movant kept by it in the regular course of its business, and it was the regular course of business of Movant for an employee or a representative of said business, with knowledge of the acts, conditions, or opinions records, to make those records or to transmit the information to be included in such records; and such records were made at or near the time or reasonably soon after the acts, conditions or opinions records.

4. The records summarized in the Payment History, or copies thereof, have been or will be made available to any respondent on Movant's Motion for Relief from Stay upon request.

Further Affiant sayeth not."

_____
(Affiant)

Subscribed and sworn to me the undersigned authority of this ___ day of _____.
My Commission Expires:

_____
Notary Public in and for the State of
_____.

Certificate of Service

I hereby certify that a copy of the foregoing Affidavit was served on _____. Service was accomplished by the method(s) and on the persons indicated below.

/s/ _____
ATTORNEY FOR MOVANT

BY ELECTRONIC NOTICE OR REGULAR FIRST CLASS MAIL:

Debtor's Attorney: Persons filing notices of appearance:

Debtor: Other persons with an interest in the subject matter of the Motion for Relief from Stay:

Trustee:

Exhibit A— "Payment History"

Applied to	Date Rec'd	Amt due	Amt rec'd	Over/short	To Suspense	Suspense Balance	Comments

[Amended effective September 19, 2013.]

APPENDIX L–7016. FORM SCHEDULING ORDER

UNITED STATES BANKRUPTCY COURT
WESTERN DISTRICT OF TEXAS

	§	
	§	
	§	
	§	
V.	§	ADVERSARY NO.
	§	
	§	
	§	
	§	

SCHEDULING ORDER

Pursuant to Rule 16, Federal Rules of Civil Procedure, the Court issues the following scheduling order.

IT IS ORDERED THAT:

1. The parties shall file all amended or supplemental pleadings and shall join additional parties on or before [60 days after Scheduling Order]. *See* L. Rule 7015.

2. All parties asserting or resisting claims for relief shall file and serve on all other parties, but not file, the disclosures required by Federal Rule of Civil Procedure 26(a)(1) on or before [14 days after Scheduling Order].

3. The parties shall complete discovery on or before [90 days from the issuance of the Scheduling Order]. Counsel may, by agreement, continue discovery beyond the deadline, but there will be no intervention by the Court except in extraordinary circumstances.

4. All dispositive motions shall be filed and served on all other parties on or before [100 days from the issuance of the Scheduling Order] and shall be limited to 20 pages. *See* L. Rule 7007(a) for the definition of dispositive motions and page limits. Responses shall be filed and served on all other parties not later than 21 days of the service of the motion and shall be limited to 20 pages. *See* L. Rule 7007(b)(2). Any replies shall be filed and served on all other parties not later than 7 days of the service of the response and shall be limited to 10 pages, but the Court need not wait for the reply before ruling on the motion. *See* L. Rule 7007(c).

5. Motions other than Rule 12 or 56 are governed by L. Rule 7007, 9013, and 9014 where applicable.

6. Docket call for trial is set [125 days from issuance of the Scheduling Order]. Parties will be required to discuss at docket call any objections to the use of deposition testimony and stipulations regarding the use of experts for trial.

7. A Joint Pre-trial Order and proposed findings of fact and conclusions of law are due 7 days before docket call. *See* L. Rule 7016(c) and (d).

8. Exhibits and a witness list are to be exchanged five business days in advance of trial. *See* L. Rule 7016(g)(2). In addition, counsel are encouraged to present and provide electronic versions of exhibits where practicable. Use and presentation of electronic exhibits should be coordinated through the courtroom deputy.

9. Counsel are reminded that, with regard to any paper that is filed, compliance with Fed. R. Civ. P. 5.2 is mandatory. As such, counsel should ensure that appropriate redactions are made.

10. This Scheduling Order does not specifically address the discovery of electronically stored information (ESI). To the extent the parties believe that ESI is subject to discovery, the parties are directed to reach an agreement on production of ESI. The parties are encouraged to use the template developed by the Seventh Circuit Electronic Discovery Pilot Program. *See* www.discoverypilot.com. Any party may bring any dispute regarding the discovery of ESI, but it must be brought to the Court's attention by motion 30 days after Rule 26(a)(1) disclosures are made.

11. Counsel residing outside the State of Texas may designate local counsel in writing, giving the street address, telephone number and mailing address. The designation shall be filed with the Clerk of the Court in this proceeding, and a copy shall be sent to all other counsel of record in this proceeding. This provision may be waived by the Court upon motion of counsel and service upon other parties.

12. **All discovery must be commenced and completed by the discovery deadline provided in this Order.**

    a. Designation of experts shall be an issue at any pretrial conference.

    b. Counsel are encouraged to resolve discovery disputes by agreement. Motions to compel, motions for protective orders and similar motions, while not prohibited, may result in sanctions being imposed on the losing party or both parties as provided in Fed. R. Bankr. P. 7037 & 9011 or 28 U.S.C. § 1927, if a hearing is required thereon.

    c. If applicable, parties may file dispositive motions under Fed. R. Bankr. P. 7012 & 7056 and Fed. R. Civ. P. 12(b) & 56. Such motions, if filed, must be filed by the deadline for dispositive motions in this Order. Responses to motions under FRBP 12 and 56 must be filed within 21 days after the Motion is filed. **All other motions in this adversary proceeding, unless unopposed, require the filing of a written response within 14 days, or the motion may be granted without a hearing.**

    d. All discovery shall be commenced at a time which allows for the full response time provided by applicable rules on or before the discovery deadline.

    E.g., if the discovery deadline is July 15, interrogatories must be actually delivered on or before June 15 in order to allow thirty days for answers. If the interrogatories are mailed, then they must be mailed on or before June 12, pursuant to Fed. R. Bankr. P. 9006(f), to allow three additional days for service by mail.

    e. The Court may, upon motion and for cause shown, extend, reduce, or otherwise modify the deadlines set out in the Scheduling Order. Mere agreement of the parties to such extensions or modifications is not of itself sufficient cause.

13. Counsel and unrepresented parties must confer prior to the date the Pre–Trial Order is required to be filed, to fully explore the possibility of settlement, to stipulate to matters not in dispute and to simplify the issues. The Pre–Trial Order shall contain a certificate to the effect that the conference of counsel has been held. Counsel must also confer in an effort to determine whether the original time estimate for trial is correct or should be revised. If the parties wish to have a pre-trial conference with the Court, a pre-trial conference should be requested as early as possible, but at least 60 days prior to the trial.

14. Docket call is set on the docket call date provided in the scheduling order. **The only matters to be considered by the Court at docket call are as follows:**

    a. Date, time and place of trial following docket call.

    b. Properly and timely-filed motions for continuance or for default judgment.

    c. Motions not previously ruled on under Fed. R. Civ. P. 12 and Fed. R. Bankr. P. 7012.

    d. Settlement announcements.

Failure to attend docket call may result in dismissal or rendition of final judgment. You may, however, authorize any member of the Bar of this Court, including opposing counsel, to make an appearance on your behalf at docket call, if there are no contested motions for continuance, motions for default judgment or motions under Fed. R. Civ. P. 12 and Fed. R. Bankr. P. 7012.

Dated: _____   Yvette M. Taylor
                                            Clerk, US Bankruptcy Court

                                             by: _____
                                                   Courtroom Deputy

[Effective January 16, 2014.]

APPENDIX L-9014.   MATTERS DEEMED CONTESTED

Hearings must be held on the following matters:

1.   Reaffirmation Agreements (if the Court deems necessary to set).

2.   Disclosure statement and confirmation proceedings under Chapters 9, 11 and 12.

3.   Adversary proceedings generally, except as provided in Local District Rules or the Bankruptcy Rules.

4.   Motions for contempt or sanctions, including motions under Rule 9011.

5.   Objections to confirmation in Chapters 9, 11, 12, and 13.

6.   Motions to appoint a Trustee or examiner in Chapter 11 cases.

[Effective December 1, 2000. Amended effective January 16, 2014.]

APPENDIX L–9022. ORDER SUBMISSION FORM
UNITED STATES BANKRUPTCY COURT WESTERN DISTRICT OF TEXAS
_____ DIVISION
ORDER SUBMISSION FORM

(Order Submission Forms must have all required fields filled in. Order Submission
Forms that are not complete may be returned with the Order unsigned.)

RE: [Case Name and/or Adversary Style, as applicable]   Case Number: _____

Adversary Number: _____

_____

Related Document Number: _____

(The document number of the related matter for which the order is being submitted)

You *must* select one of the following order types:

___ **Ex Parte (no hearing required)** an order on a matter which is not going to be set for hearing
and which does not have negative notice language.

___ **Expedited** an order on a expedited or emergency matter.

___ **Hearing Held** an order on a matter for which a hearing has already been held.

Hearing Date

___ **Hearing Scheduled** an order on a matter for which a hearing has been set but not yet held.

Hearing Date

Suspense (obj language) an order on a matter that was filed with "negative response language"

Check one of the following: ___ **14 day** ___ **21 day** ___ **30 day** ___ **60 day**

Submitted By: _____

[Effective December 1, 2000. Amended effective December 1, 2009; January 16, 2014.]

ECF PROCEDURES
ORDER ADOPTING NEW ADMINISTRATIVE PROCEDURES FOR ELECTRONIC FILING

The United States Bankruptcy Court for the Western District of Texas hereby adopts the attached *Administrative Procedures for the Filing, Signing, and Verifying of Documents by Electronic Means in Texas Bankruptcy Courts.* These procedures shall become effective on December 1, 2004. The court has adopted these procedures to provide more uniformity in electronic filing with the Texas Eastern, Texas Northern, and Texas Southern Bankruptcy Courts. These procedures may be amended from time to time by order of the court.

IT IS ORDERED that the court adopts the attached *Administrative Procedures for Electronic Case Filing,* effective December 1, 2004.

[Dated: November 30, 2004.]

ADMINISTRATIVE PROCEDURES FOR THE FILING, SIGNING, AND VERIFYING OF DOCUMENTS BY ELECTRONIC MEANS IN TEXAS BANKRUPTCY COURTS

*[**Publisher's Note:** For electronic filing procedures, consult the "Administrative Procedures for the Filing, Signing and Verifying of Documents by Electronic Means in Texas Bankruptcy Courts," published as part of the local rules for the United States Bankruptcy Court for the Northern District of Texas, ante.]*

AMENDED STANDING ORDER REGARDING PRIVACY RELATED RULES

Effective November 15, 2004, the following procedures will apply to all documents filed in the Western District of Texas.

1. Official Form 21, Statement of Social Security Number(s):

A. Paper Submission: Voluntary petitions submitted in paper format must be accompanied by Form 21, Statement of Social Security Number. If the required statement is not submitted at the time of the filing of the voluntary petition, the case is subject to dismissal unless the same statement is submitted in the required format no later than one (1) business day after the filing of the petition.

B. Electronic Submission: When filing a new case electronically, the filing attorney shall provide the full nine digit social security number in the case opening screen, or if using case upload software, the "debtor.txt" file should continue to contain the full social security number. Form 21, Statement of Social Security Number, shall not be filed electronically. Electronic filers shall submit this document in paper format to the clerk within five (5) business days after the filing of the petition. Failure to submit the required statement within the time prescribed may result in the case being dismissed or other appropriate sanction.

2. Amended Form 21, Statement of Social Security Number: The debtor shall service all creditors copies of any amended Statement of Social Security Number. The debtor shall provide proof of service by filing a certificate of service indicating notice of the amended statement. The form of service shall comply with Local Rule 9013(f).

3. Wage Claims: Wage claimants shall provide the trustee with their full social security number by including it in the copy of the proof of claim that is served on the trustee pursuant to Local Rule 3002(a).

4. Personal Data Identifiers in All Documents and Pleadings: In compliance with the policy of the Judicial Conference of the United States, and the E–Government Act of 2002, and in order to promote electronic access to case files while also protecting personal privacy and other legitimate interests, parties shall refrain from including, or shall partially redact where inclusion is necessary, the following personal data identifiers from all documents and pleadings filed with the court, except with regard to Form 21, Statement of Social Security Number, as stated above. This includes exhibits, whether filed electronically or in paper, unless otherwise ordered by the Court or required by statute, the Federal Rules of Bankruptcy Procedure or the Official Bankruptcy Forms.

A.   Social Security Numbers: If an individual's social security number must be included in a pleading, including the voluntary petition, only the last four digits of that number should be used.

B.   Names of Minor Children: If the involvement of a minor child must be mentioned, only the initials of that child should be used. On Schedule I of Official Bankruptcy Form 6, list relationship and age of the debtor's dependents (i.e., son, age 6).

C.   Dates of Birth: If an individual's date of birth must be included in a pleading, only the year should be used. On Schedule I of Official Bankruptcy Form 6, list the age of each of the debtor's dependents.

D.   Financial Account Numbers: If financial account numbers are relevant, only the last four digits of these numbers should be used. On Schedules D, E, and F of Official Bankruptcy Forms 6, debtors, if they so choose, may include their full account numbers to assist the trustee and creditors.

In compliance with amendments to the E–Government Act of 2002, a party wishing to file a document containing the personal data identifiers listed above may:

(a) file an unredacted document under seal. The sealed document must be filed in a manner that is in compliance with Local Rule 9018(a). This document shall be retained by the court as part of the record. or

(b) file a reference list under seal. The reference list shall contain the complete personal data identifier(s) and the redacted identifier(s) used in its(their) place in the filing. All references in the case to the redacted identifiers included in the reference list will be construed to refer to the corresponding complete identifier. The reference list must be filed under seal, and may be amended as of right. The sealed reference list must be filed in a manner that is in compliance with Local Rule 9018(a). It shall be retained by the court as part of the record. The court may, however, still require the party to file a redacted copy for the public file. The responsibility for redacting these personal identifiers rests solely with counsel and the parties. The Clerk will not review each document for compliance with this rule.

[Dated: November 15, 2004.]

STANDING ORDER REGARDING MANDATORY ELECTRONIC FILING

IT IS HEREBY ORDERED that effective **July 1, 2011**, all petitions, motions, pleadings, briefs, proofs of claim and other documents must be filed electronically pursuant to electronic filing procedures established by this court's Administrative Procedures for Filing, Signing and Verifying Documents by Electronic Means—except as expressly provided below:

1.   Pro Se Debtor Filing.   Debtors without legal representation may not file pleadings and other papers in a case electronically.

2.   Pro Se Creditor Filing.   Creditors that are not represented by counsel are not required to file documents electronically, unless the number of documents filed by an individual creditor exceeds six (6) per month.   These documents include but are not limited to reaffirmation agreements, proofs of claims, transfers of claims, notice requests, notice of change of payment address and notice of payment changes.

3.   Documents Filed Under Seal.   A motion to file a document(s) under seal shall be filed electronically; however the actual document(s) to be sealed shall be filed conventionally, on paper after the order granting the motion has been entered as in accordance with L.R. 9018.   IT IS FURTHER ORDERED that the Clerk of Court is directed to decline to accept for filing any pleading and other documents submitted in paper format after the mandatory date except by those filers specifically set forth above.   In an emergency, an attorney not admitted to practice before the Western District of Texas and not having an office in this district, may file a document(s) in paper form if it is impracticable to become a ECF registrant or engage local counsel prior to filing the document(s).   However, the paper filing must be accompanied by a separate motion seeking leave to file in paper form and showing cause for not becoming a ECF registrant and for not engaging local counsel in time to file the document(s) electronically.   If the motion for leave is not granted, the document(s) may be stricken by the court without prior notice.

IT IS FURTHER ORDERED that if the Court's ECF site is unable to accept filings for an extended period of time, a party whose filing is made untimely as the result of a technical failure may seek appropriate relief from the Court through the filing of a motion. The Court shall determine whether a technical failure has occurred on a case-by-case basis.

IT SO ORDERED that the Clerk of Court shall give notice of this Order by service through the Clerk's electronic mailing list manager and posting a copy on the Court's official website. A notice regarding the effective date of mandatory electronic filing will be posted in the public intake area of each divisional office.

[Dated: April 27, 2011.]

STANDING ORDER RELATING TO DECLARATIONS FOR ELECTRONIC FILING

This Standing Order relates to the filing of "Declarations for Electronic Filing" (commonly known as Declaration(s), eDec or DEF) electronically into the Court's CM/ECF system. It also sets forth the document retention requirements for electronically filed Declarations.

IT IS HEREBY ORDERED:

I. Filing of Declaration by Electronic Filers.

A. Contemporaneous with the filing by electronic means of a bankruptcy petition, list, schedule, or statement that requires verification or an unsworn declaration under Fed. R. Bankr. P. 1008, the Electronic Filer shall file with the Court in electronic format the appropriate Declaration which has been executed by any individual debtor or by the authorized representative of any corporate or partnership debtor.

B. Such Declaration shall substantially conform to either Exhibit B–1, B–2, or B–3 to Appendix 5005, as set forth in Bankruptcy Local Rule 5005 and the Administrative Procedures for Electronic Filing.

C. Such Declaration shall be an exact image of the original containing the ink signature of any individual debtor or the ink signature of the authorized representative of any corporate or partnership debtor.

D. Since a Declaration contains personally identifiable information it must not be attached to the petition, list, schedule, or statement. Rather, the Declaration must be electronically filed as a separate document using the specific CM/ECF docketing event "Declaration for Electronic Filing (Restricted Document)" and linked to the petition, list, schedule, or statement to which the Declaration pertains. Filing the Declaration in this precise manner ensures that the document is restricted from public view upon filing.

II. Document Retention.

An executed Declaration containing the original ink signature of the debtor(s) or authorized representative of any corporate or partnership debtor shall be retained by the Electronic Filer for a period of not less than five (5) years after the case or adversary proceeding is closed. Upon request, the original Declaration must be provided to the Court or other parties for review.

III. Effective Date and Scope.

This Standing Order is effective as of **March 1, 2018** and is applicable to all cases in all Divisions of the United States Bankruptcy Court for the Western District of Texas. This Standing Order shall control to the extent that it conflicts with Bankruptcy Local Rule 5005 and the Administrative Procedures for Electronic Filing as related to "Declarations for Electronic Filing."

#

[Effective March 1, 2018.]

SELECTED ORDERS
STANDING ORDER RELATING TO PAYMENT
OF FILING FEES IN INSTALLMENTS

This Standing Order supersedes the Standing Order Relating to Payment of Filing Fees in Installments dated November 8, 2013 and is effective as to all cases filed on and after December 1, 2017.

Section 1930(a)(7) of Title 28 of the United States Code allows an individual to pay the filing fee in installments. Bankruptcy Rule 1006(b) permits an individual to file a signed application, along with the petition, stating that the Debtor is unable to pay the filing fee except in installments. Accordingly, it is ORDERED that:

At least fifty percent of the filing fee must be paid within seven days of the filing of the petition for debtors applying to pay the filing fee in installments. Noncompliance may result in dismissal of the bankruptcy case without further notice or hearing.

[Dated: December 1, 2017.]

CONSOLIDATED STANDING ORDER FOR THE ADOPTION
OF A DISTRICT FORM CHAPTER 13 PLAN

The Bankruptcy Judges for the Western District of Texas have determined that, in addition to any Division Standing Orders Relating to Chapter 13 Practices, a Standing Order adopting a District Form Chapter 13 Plan in accordance with proposed Fed. R. Bankr. P. 3015.1 and 3015(c)(2) is necessary for the efficient and orderly administration of Chapter 13 cases. This Consolidated Standing Order supersedes all prior standing orders in every Division regarding District form chapter 13 plans for all cases filed on or after the Effective Date of this Order. Attached as Exhibit #1 to this Consolidated Standing Order is the Form Chapter 13 Plan (hereinafter the "Form Plan") which shall be used by all chapter 13 debtors in cases filed in this District on and after the Effective Date of this Order. *The Form Plan may be revised periodically.* The clerk shall make available to the public the Form Plan and any revised Form Plans.

Creditors are hereby notified that the Plan may be amended at any time before confirmation. Any amendment may affect your status as a creditor. Debtor's estimate of how much the Plan will pay, projected payments, and estimates as to the payment or distribution to a particular class may change.

I. Plan Payments

A. Debtor shall propose to pay to the Trustee the indicated base amount by paying the indicated monthly payment ("Plan Payment"). Debtor shall submit such portion of future earnings or other future income of the Debtor to the supervision and control of the Trustee as is necessary for the execution of the Plan. [§ 1306(a)(2)].

B. Debtor shall commence making Plan Payments to the Trustee not later than thirty (30) days after the date the Petition is filed. [§ 1326(a)(1)]

II. Other Plan Provisions

A. Lien Avoidance Powers. The confirmation of the Plan shall not limit the ability of the Trustee or Debtor from exercising any lien avoidance powers pursuant to the Bankruptcy Code.

B. Debtor Request for Moratoriums of Plan Payments. Debtor may request a one-time moratorium on Plan payments not to exceed sixty (60) days. Debtor shall file a Motion with the Court with fourteen (14) days negative notice to all creditors. The Motion must state with specificity the basis for the request and the impact on a class or classes of creditors. The Motion must state when the debtor will resume payments and how the missed payment(s) will be cured. The purpose of such Motion is to assist Debtor in the performance under the Plan and to meet emergency situations that arise during the term of the Plan. The duration of the Plan may be extended, but not beyond sixty (60) months from confirmation. This provision may also be governed by the Standing Order for Chapter 13 Administration for the division in which this case is pending.

C. Incurring Post–Petition Debt. Debtor shall not, without Court or Trustee approval, incur debt, except in the ordinary course of business if Debtor is engaged in business pursuant to § 1304.

D. Transfer of Assets Post–Petition. Debtor shall not, without Court approval, transfer or dispose of assets, unless it is an exempt asset with a value of less than $2,500.00. Debtor shall not transfer or sell any property claimed as exempt homestead unless approved by order of the Court.

E. Late Filed Claims, Amended Claims, or Deficiency Claims. If a late claim, an amended claim, or a deficiency claim is filed and allowed; and the Trustee has disbursed to other claims within that class or junior classes, such creditor's allowed claim shall be paid at the same percentage as was paid to other creditors with allowed claims in the same class before recommencing payments to other creditors, but only to the extent possible without recovery of payment from other creditors in the same class. The Trustee shall not be required to recover any payments made to other creditors as a result of the filing of an allowed late claim, amended claim, or a deficiency claim.

F. Termination of the Automatic Stay. If the automatic stay applicable to a creditor is terminated either by confirmation of the Plan or order of the Court (or a notice filed pursuant to the terms of a Court order), the Trustee shall cease payments to all secured creditors having a lien on such collateral. Those creditors having a lien on the collateral shall have ninety (90) days from the date the automatic stay is terminated to file an unsecured deficiency claim.

G. Debtor Engaged in Business. If Debtor is self-employed, Debtor shall comply with the duties required under § 1304(b) and (c) regarding the operation of the business. The duties imposed on Debtor are incorporated herein by reference, including the submission of periodic reports to the Trustee, if required.

H. Additional Attorney Fees. If the Court approves additional attorney fees, such fees are to be paid as an administrative claim. Further, to the extent the Trustee has disbursed to other classes of creditors, including general unsecured creditors, the Trustee shall not be required to recover such funds previously disbursed in order to assure full payment of the additionally allowed attorney fees.

I. Order of Payment. Unless the Plan states otherwise, the Trustee shall disburse the funds received as follows:

(i) Trustee Fees on receipt

(ii) Ongoing Mortgage Payments

(iii) Adequate Protection Payments

(iv) § 503 Administrative Claims (Attorney Fees and other Administrative Claims)—subject to the Standing Order for Chapter 13 Administration for the Division

(v) Secured Claims

(vi) § 507 Priority Claims

(vii) General Unsecured Claims

J. Date of Plan. Every original, amended or modified plan shall be dated.

The Effective Date of this Standing Order is _____. The Form Plan shall be used in every case filed in this District on and after the Effective Date of this Standing Order.
[Dated: November 1, 2017.]

CHAPTER 13 PLAN AND MOTIONS FOR VALUATION AND LIEN AVOIDANCE

UNITED STATES BANKRUPTCY COURT
FOR THE WESTERN DISTRICT OF TEXAS
_____ DIVISION

IN RE:	§	CASE NO.
	§	
	§	Chapter 13
Debtor(s)	§	

CHAPTER 13 PLAN AND MOTIONS FOR VALUATION AND LIEN AVOIDANCE

☐ **AMENDED**

If you oppose the Plan's treatment of your claim or any provisions of this Plan, YOU MUST FILE AN OBJECTION to confirmation no later than fourteen (14) days before the confirmation hearing date.

Use of the singular word "Debtor" in this Plan includes the plural where appropriate. All section references ("§") are to the Bankruptcy Code unless otherwise noted.

The following matters may be of particular importance. *Debtors must check one box on each line to state whether or not the Plan includes each of the following items.* If an item is checked as "Not Included" or if both boxes are checked, the provision will be ineffective if set out later in the Plan.

1. Plan Overview

1.1	A limit on the amount of secured claim based on valuation of collateral for the claim, set out in Sections 7.8 and 7.9, which may result in a partial payment or no payment at all to the secured creditor	☐ Included	☐ Not Included
1.2	Avoidance of a wholly unsecured lien or judicial lien or nonpossessory, nonpurchase-money security interest, set out in Sections 7.9 and 7.10	☐ Included	☐ Not Included
1.3	Nonstandard provisions, set out in Section 8	☐ Included	☐ Not Included

2. Plan Summary

2.1 Debtor's Plan payment will be $ _____ per month, paid by ☐ 3rd Party Epay (if accepted by Trustee), ☐ Payroll Order, or ☐ Direct (Money Order or Cashier's Check). Variable payments, if applicable, are proposed as follows:

EXAMPLE:

Months	Amount of Monthly Payment
1–24	$500
25–60	$750

The term of the Plan is _____ months. The gross amount to be paid to the Trustee (sometimes, the "base amount") is $ _____.

2.2 Under this Plan, the Trustee will pay all allowed priority claims in full; all allowed secured claims to the extent of the value of the collateral or the amount of the claim, whichever amount is provided for in Sections 7.7 and 7.8; and approximately _____ % to allowed general unsecured claims. The specific treatment for each class of creditors is set forth below in the Plan.

This Plan does not allow claims. A creditor must file a proof of claim by the applicable deadline to receive distributions under the plan as confirmed. Creditors are referred to the Federal Rules of Bankruptcy Procedure, the Local Bankruptcy Rules for the Western District of Texas, and the Standing Order for Chapter 13 Administration for this Division for information on procedures and deadlines.

2.3 The aggregate value of Debtor's non-exempt assets is: $ _____.

3. Vesting of Estate Property

☐ Upon confirmation of the Plan, all property of the estate **shall** vest in the Debtor, shall not remain property of the estate, and shall not be subject to the automatic stay of § 362; provided however, in the event of conversion of this case to chapter 7 the property of the Debtor as of the petition date should revest in the estate.

☐ Upon confirmation of the Plan, all property of the estate **shall not** vest in the Debtor, shall remain property of the estate, and shall remain subject to the automatic stay of § 362.

4. Tax Refunds and Annual Tax Returns

4.1 Tax Refunds. All tax refunds received by Debtor (or either Debtor if a joint case) while the chapter 13 case is pending shall be allocated as set forth below:

1) The total amount of the aggregate tax refund(s) received for any tax period that exceeds $2,000.00 shall, upon receipt, be paid and turned over to the Trustee as additional disposable income and such amount shall increase the base amount of the Plan. The Plan shall be deemed modified accordingly, and the Trustee will file a notice of plan modification within 21 days of receipt of the tax refund;

2) This $2,000.00 annual limit shall apply to both joint-debtor and single-debtor cases;

3) The $2,000.00 otherwise retained by Debtor must first be applied to any Plan arrearages;

4) Notwithstanding subparagraph (1) above, Debtor may file a notice to retain the portion of the tax refund otherwise payable to the Plan under subparagraph (1) with twenty-one (21) day negative notice as set forth in Local Rule 9014(a) if, at the time of receipt of a refund, Debtor's Plan provides for the payment of 100% of allowed general unsecured claims within the term of this Plan. If the Trustee does not object within the twenty-one (21) day negative notice period, Debtor may retain that portion of the tax refund.

The Trustee is hereby authorized to endorse a tax refund check if the check is made payable to Debtor.

4.2 Annual Tax Returns. Debtor shall provide a copy of the annual post-petition income tax return to the Trustee if requested to do so or if required to do so pursuant to the Standing Order for Chapter 13 Administration for the division in which this case is pending. If this is a joint case, each Debtor shall comply with this provision if separate returns are filed.

5. Pre–Confirmation Adequate Protection Payments

Pre-confirmation adequate protection payments under § 1326(a)(1) and § 502(b) shall be made as provided below, and pursuant to the Standing Order for Chapter 13 Administration for the division in which this case is pending:

A. All pre-confirmation payments if required by § 1326(c) and proposed below will be made by the Chapter 13 Trustee without further order of the Court. Such payments shall be considered payments pursuant to § 1326(a) and 28 U.S.C. § 586(e).

B. If the Debtor fails to make the required plan payments and funds on hand are not sufficient to pay all pre-confirmation adequate protection payments due, then such payments shall be paid on a pro rata basis, with the exception of ongoing monthly mortgage payments made by the Trustee.

C. Monthly pre-confirmation adequate protection payments will be calculated from the date the first plan payment is due. To receive adequate protection payments, a secured creditor must have on file with the Clerk of the Court a timely filed and allowed proof of claim. The proof of claim must include proof of the creditor's security interest and shall be served on the Chapter 13 Trustee, the Debtor and Debtor's attorney. The Trustee will thereafter commence disbursement of pre-confirmation adequate protection payments in the next regularly scheduled monthly disbursement following the filing of the claim, subject to normal operating procedures.

D. The Debtor proposes the following pre-confirmation adequate protection ("AP") payments. The Trustee shall apply pre-confirmation adequate protection payments to accrued interest, if applicable, and then to principal. AP payments shall cease upon confirmation of the Plan.

Creditor & Collateral	Monthly Payment	AP	Interest Rate, If Claim is Over Secured	Other Treatment Remarks

6. Executory Contracts / Unexpired Leases / Contracts for Deed

6.1 Pursuant to § 1322(b)(7) and § 365, Debtor hereby elects to assume the following executory contracts, unexpired leases, and/or contracts for deed as follows:

Creditor	Property or Contract Description	Current Monthly Payment to be Paid Directly by the Debtor

6.2 Pursuant to § 1322(b)(7) and § 365, Debtor hereby elects to reject the following executory contracts, unexpired leases, and/or contracts for deed:

Creditor	Property

7. Treatment of Claims

7.1 Administrative Claims & Request for Attorney Fees. The Trustee shall collect the allowed statutory Trustee fee upon receipt of all monies paid by or on behalf of Debtor. All other administrative claims, including Debtor's attorney fees, shall be paid according to the terms of this Plan.

Upon confirmation of the Plan, the Court approves and awards $ _____ to Debtor's attorney as an administrative claim for legal services performed in this case in accordance with the applicable benchmark. Debtor's attorney may file applications for an additional award of attorney fees pursuant to the Bankruptcy Code, Local Bankruptcy Rules for the Western District of Texas, and the Standing Order for Chapter 13 Administration for the division in which this case is pending. If additional monies are available, the Trustee may, within his or her discretion, disburse such funds to this class on a pro rata basis. The Trustee shall disburse payments to the attorney as follows:

Debtor's Attorney	Amount of Fee Paid Through the Plan	Payment Method:	Additional Provisions
		☐ Standing Order ☐ Other	

7.2 Priority Claims. All allowed claims entitled to priority under § 507(a), except § 507(a)(2), shall be paid in full in deferred distributions by the Trustee, unless: (1) the holder of a particular claim agrees to a different treatment of such claim; or (2) such claim is provided for under § 1322(a)(4). Unless the Plan provides otherwise, the distributions shall be made by the Trustee. If the Plan identifies a creditor's claim as a priority claim and the creditor files the claim as a general unsecured claim, the claim shall be treated as a general unsecured claim unless otherwise ordered by the Court. If any priority claim is filed for a debt that was either not scheduled or scheduled as a general unsecured claim, the claim shall be allowed as a priority claim unless otherwise ordered by the Court. Allowed priority claim(s) shall be paid without interest, unless otherwise ordered by the Court or unless specifically allowed under § 1322(b)(10) and provided for below.

The amount set forth in the Plan is an estimate and if the actual allowed claim is in a different amount, the amount to be paid pursuant to the Plan shall be the amount due on the allowed claim.

<u>Domestic Support Obligations ("DSO").</u> The Trustee shall pay all pre-petition DSO claims through the Plan unless the Court orders otherwise. Debtor shall pay all DSO payments that accrue post-petition directly to the holder, or the holder's agent, pursuant to the terms of the DSO.

The Trustee shall disburse payments to the following creditors holding priority claims:

EXAMPLE:

Creditor	Description	Est. Claim Amount	Est. Monthly Payment
Attorney General	Child Support	$5,000	Pro Rata
IRS	Income Tax (2013)	$5,000	Pro Rata

If additional monies are available, the Trustee may, within his or her discretion, disburse such funds to this class on a pro rata basis.

7.3 Arrears on Assumed Executory Contracts/Leases/Contracts for Deed. The Trustee shall disburse payments for arrears to creditors holding assumed executory contracts, leases, and/or contracts for deeds. The amounts listed below by Debtor are estimates. If a creditor files a proof of claim and the claim for arrears or the ongoing monthly payment is in a different amount than stated below, the payments under the Plan shall be based on the creditor's claim unless a different amount is established by court order.

Those creditors holding claims within this class are as follows:

Creditor & Collateral	Arrears & Treatment of Arrears Through the Plan	Amount of Ongoing Monthly Payment Through the Plan

7.4 Collateral to be Surrendered. Upon the entry of an order confirming the Plan or an order modifying the Plan, the stay shall automatically terminate with regard to the collateral surrendered. Upon the entry of such order, the creditor shall have ninety (90) days from the date of the order to file a claim or amended claim as to any deficiency balance that may remain, and such deficiency balance will be paid as a general unsecured claim. Any such claim is subject to objection.

Debtor surrenders the following collateral:

Creditor	Collateral	Location of Collateral

7.5 Creditors to be Paid Directly by Debtor (Other Than Mortgage Creditors), by a Third Party, or by a Co–Debtor. [USE ONLY IF THERE IS NO DEFAULT]

Creditors within this class shall retain their liens on the collateral that is security for the claim until the claim has been paid in full as determined by the note and/or applicable non-bankruptcy law.

If certain claims are paid directly by Debtor to creditor, Debtor shall be deemed acting as a disbursing agent under the Plan for payment of such claim. Such payments shall be made in addition to the payments by Debtor to the Trustee and are deemed to be payments made pursuant to the Plan.

The following creditors shall be paid directly by Debtor, a Third Party, or a Co–Debtor:

Creditor	Collateral	Debt Owed	Monthly Payment	Remarks	Identify Payer

7.6 Mortgage Creditors: Ongoing Mortgage Payments & Direct Mortgage Payments on Debtor's Principal Residence.

Unless the Debtor is current on the mortgage on the petition date, or otherwise provided for under PLAN PROVISIONS 8. **Nonstandard Plan Provisions**, the Trustee shall pay all post-petition monthly mortgage payments to the mortgagee. Ongoing mortgage payments will be in the amount stated in the allowed proof of claim or pursuant to a Court Order. If Debtor makes a Plan payment that is insufficient for the Trustee to disburse all ongoing mortgage payments required below, the Trustee shall hold plan payments until a sufficient amount is received to make a full ongoing mortgage payment. Debtor shall provide to the Trustee all notices received from Mortgage Creditors including, statements, escrow notices, default notifications, and notices concerning changes of the interest rate if a variable rate mortgage. The automatic stay is modified to permit Mortgage Creditors to issue such notices.

The Trustee shall be authorized to make changes to the ongoing monthly mortgage payments based on Notice filed pursuant to Bankruptcy Rule 3002.1(b) and to pay fees, expenses, and charges based on Notice filed pursuant to Bankruptcy Rule 3002.1(c). The Trustee may request that the Debtor file amended Schedules I and J, and the Debtor shall do so on or within thirty (30) days after receiving such a request from the Trustee. If Debtor lacks the disposable income to pay the ongoing mortgage payment, the Trustee may seek dismissal. The Debtor or the Trustee may seek to modify the Plan based on Debtor's current income, Debtor's ongoing mortgage payment obligations, or as otherwise provided in § 1329.

Alternatively, upon the filing by a Mortgage Creditor of a Notice pursuant to Bankruptcy Rule 3002.1(b) or 3002.1(c), the Trustee may file a Notice of Increase of Plan Payment with the Court if the Trustee reasonably believes that, under the circumstances, the increased payment should be Debtor's responsibility. The Trustee shall serve the Notice of Increase of Plan Payment on Debtor and Debtor's counsel. Such circumstances include but are not limited to: (1) increase in the mortgage payment or claim for expense is caused by Debtor's failure to pay tax, insurance or other obligations to the mortgagee that the Debtor was required to pay directly; (2) cases in which the Debtor is paying less than the Debtor's full disposable income because the Debtor has agreed to pay a 100% dividend to general unsecured creditors; and (3) cases where, because of the increase due the Mortgage Creditor, the current Plan would fail to pay fully the amount provided under the Plan to allowed secured, priority, and administrative claims and any required amount to be paid to general unsecured claims under the terms of the confirmed Plan by reason of § 1325(a)(4) or otherwise.

The amount set forth in a Notice of Increase of Plan Payment shall become the modified Plan payment, and the Plan base shall be correspondingly increased. The Debtor must file a motion to modify Plan, supported by amended Schedules I and J as well as income verification, if the Debtor believes there is not, at that time, sufficient disposable income to pay the increased Plan payment or there is otherwise basis to amend the Plan rather than pay the increased Plan payment. The Debtor's motion to modify Plan shall be filed no later than thirty (30) days after Trustee's Notice of Increase in Plan Payment is filed.

It is possible that a change in the ongoing mortgage payment will affect the distribution to the unsecured creditors, and this provision of the Plan shall serve as adequate notice of the possibility.

If Debtor is current as of the petition date and elects to pay the ongoing mortgage directly but subsequently defaults, Debtor should file a motion to modify the Plan within thirty (30) days of receiving notice of the default to provide for the payment of the post-petition mortgage arrears. The future ongoing mortgage payments shall be paid by the Trustee. The motion to modify the

Plan must state the name, address, and account number of the Mortgage Creditor to whom payments are to be made; the date the Trustee is to commence the ongoing mortgage payments; and the treatment of the post-petition delinquency including the gap between the date when Debtor modified the Plan and the date on which the Trustee is to commence the ongoing mortgage payments. The Trustee may also file a motion to modify the Plan in the event of a post-petition default.

The Standing Order for Chapter 13 Administration for the division in which this case is pending as to ongoing mortgage payments shall also apply.

For cause shown, Debtor may deviate from the procedures set forth in this provision of the Plan provided that Debtor sets forth cause, with specificity, in <u>PLAN PROVISIONS 8</u>. **Nonstandard Plan Provisions.** The Trustee and any party in interest may object. Debtor shall have the burden of proving at any hearing on confirmation of the Plan cause for such deviation. Avoidance of administrative fees alone shall not be considered cause.

The amounts set forth below are Debtor's estimate and the allowed claim shall control as to the amounts. Those creditors holding a secured claim with ongoing mortgage payments are as follows:

Creditor	Property Address	Monthly Mortgage Payment	Interest Rate (for informational purposes only)	Payment Due Date (per contract)	Paid By:
					☐ Trustee (Conduit)
					☐ Debtor (Direct)

7.7 Secured Claims: Cure Arrears on Long Term Debt and Mortgage Arrears on Debtor's Principal Residence.

Arrears on long term debt and pre-petition mortgage arrearage claims shall be paid pursuant to the payment schedule set forth below. Upon discharge, if the pre-petition arrears and the post-petition ongoing payments are current on Debtor's Principal Residence, the default will be deemed cured and the note reinstated according to its original terms, including the retention of any security interest. The pre-petition arrears set forth below is an estimate only and the Trustee shall pay the pre-petition arrears based on the proof of claim as filed by the creditor, unless a different amount is allowed pursuant to a court order.

If there are insufficient funds to pay the monthly payment to claims within this class, creditors in this class shall be paid on a pro rata basis. If additional monies are available, the Trustee may, within his or her discretion, disburse such funds to this class on a pro rata basis.

The following secured creditors hold claims for arrears in this class:

Creditor	Collateral Description	Estimated Arrearage	Monthly Payment or Method of Distribution	Interest Rate (If applicable)	Remarks

7.8 Secured Claims: Treatment of Claim and Motion to Value Collateral Pursuant to § 506; and 910 Day Claims/1 Year Claims.

Creditors within this class shall retain their liens on the collateral that is security for their claims until the earlier of: (1) the date the underlying debt, as determined by non-bankruptcy law, has been paid in full; or (2) the date discharge is entered under § 1328. If the case is dismissed or converted without completion of all Plan payments, the liens shall be retained by the creditors pursuant to applicable non-bankruptcy law.

Debtor moves to value the collateral described below in the amounts indicated. The values as stated below represent the fair market value of the collateral pursuant to § 506(a)(2). Objections to the valuation of collateral proposed by this Motion and the Plan must be filed no later than fourteen (14) days before the confirmation hearing date. If no timely objection is filed, the relief requested may be granted in conjunction with the confirmation of the Plan.

The Trustee shall pay the allowed secured claims, which require the filing of a proof of claim, to the extent of the value of the collateral or the full payment of the claim as specified below, plus interest thereon at the rate specified in this Plan. **Failure of the secured creditor to object will be deemed acceptance of the plan under § 1325(a)(5)(A)** Except for secured claims for which provision is made to pay the full amount of the claim notwithstanding the value of the collateral, the portion of any allowed claim that exceeds the value of the collateral shall be treated as an unsecured claim under Section 7.11 below.

Creditor	Collateral Description	Amount of Debt (Est)	Fair Market Value	Interest Rate	Equal Monthly Payment	Unsecured Claim	910 Claim? ***
							☐

*** Debtor indicates, by notation ([/]) that the collateral which secures the claim was purchased within 910 days if a vehicle or within 1 year if personal property pursuant to § 1325(a) (hanging paragraph).

If additional monies are available, the Trustee may, within his or her discretion, disburse such funds to this class on a pro rata basis.

If any secured proof of claim is timely filed for a debt that was either not scheduled or scheduled as unsecured, the claim shall be allowed as secured unless otherwise ordered by the Court. Said claim shall be paid under the Plan with interest at _____ % per annum and shall be paid on a pro rata basis as funds become available after payment of any fixed equal monthly payments payable to other secured creditors listed above.

7.9 Wholly Unsecured Claims.

NOTICE OF DEBTOR'S INTENTION TO STRIP A WHOLLY UNSECURED LIEN

Debtor proposes a Chapter 13 plan that strips your lien secured by real property to a wholly unsecured claim. The Plan alleges that the value of the real property is less than the amount owed on all liens that are senior in priority to your lien. Your claim will receive no distributions as a secured claim but will receive distributions as a general unsecured claim.

If you disagree with the treatment proposed by the Plan that will terminate your lien and that will pay your claim as a general unsecured claim, you must file an objection to the Plan no later than fourteen (14) days before the confirmation hearing date. If you fail to object, the Bankruptcy Court may approve the Plan without further notice.

Upon entry of a Discharge Order, the holder of the lien is required to execute and record a full and unequivocal release of its liens, encumbrances and security interests secured by the real property and to provide a copy of the release to the Trustee, Debtor, and Debtor's counsel. Notwithstanding the foregoing, the holder of a lien that secures post-petition homeowners' association fees and assessments will be allowed to retain its lien, but only to secure (i) post-petition assessments; and (ii) other post-petition amounts, such as legal fees, if such post-petition amounts are incurred with respect to post-petition fees and assessments, and are approved by the Court, if incurred during the pendency of the bankruptcy case.

This provision does not apply if a secured creditor does not file a proof of claim.

Notice of this Plan provision must be provided by the Debtor to the secured creditor in accordance with Fed. R. Bankr. P. 7004.

The following claims shall be paid as a general unsecured claim as there is no equity in the collateral to secure the claim.

If the case is dismissed or converted without completion of all Plan payments, the liens shall be retained by the creditors pursuant to applicable non-bankruptcy law.

Those creditors holding secured claims that are wholly unsecured and are within this class are as follows:

Creditor	Collateral	Fair Market Value	Amount of Senior Lien(s)

7.10   **Motions to Avoid Lien Pursuant to § 522(f).** The Bankruptcy Code allows certain liens to be avoided. If a lien is avoided, the creditor's claim, to the extent allowed, will be treated as a general unsecured claim under Section 7.11. The amount of the debt set forth in the Plan is Debtor's estimate and if the actual allowed claim is in a different amount, the unsecured amount to be treated pursuant to the Plan shall be the amount due on the allowed claim.

If the case is dismissed or converted without completion of all Plan payments, the liens shall be retained by the creditors pursuant to applicable non-bankruptcy law.

Debtor moves under § 522(f) to avoid the following liens that impair exemptions. Objections to this treatment must be filed no later than fourteen (14) days before the confirmation hearing date. If no timely objection is filed, the relief requested may be granted in conjunction with the confirmation of the Plan. (Debtor must list the specific exempt property that the lien impairs and the basis of the lien—e.g. judicial lien, non–PMSI, etc.).

Creditor	Property Subject to Lien	Lien Amount to be Avoided	Secured Amount Remaining	Type of Lien

7.11   **General Unsecured Claims.** Creditors within this class hold general unsecured claims that are not otherwise provided for in the Plan, including but not limited to creditors' unsecured claims arising by reason of lien avoidance or lien strip, rejection of executory contracts or leases, or bifurcation of a claim. Payments to holders of allowed claims within this class shall be disbursed on a pro rata basis and shall be disbursed after payment of other creditors. The amounts set forth as unsecured claims in Debtor's schedules are estimates only, and payments to holders of allowed general unsecured claims shall be based upon allowed claim amounts.

8. Nonstandard Plan Provisions

Nonstandard Plan Provisions.

The following Plan provisions will be effective only if there is a check in the box in Section 1.3 of the Plan.

<u>**Failure to place any nonstandard provision in this section results in the nonstandard provision being void.**</u>

I certify that all nonstandard plan provisions are contained in this section of the Plan.

_____   Date: _____
Debtor's Attorney or Pro Se Debtor
State Bar No. _____

_____
Debtor

_____
Joint Debtor

Certificate of Service

Debtor shall be responsible for service of the Plan on the Trustee and all parties in interest.
[Dated: November 1, 2017.]

STANDING ORDER REGARDING OBJECTIONS TO PROOFS OF CLAIM

To implement Rule 3007(a) of the Federal Rules of Bankruptcy Procedure, as amended effective December 1, 2017, this Standing Order is hereby adopted by the United States Bankruptcy Court for the Western District of Texas.

IT IS HEREBY ORDERED:

1. Objections to Claim.

A. An objection to a proof of claim shall be titled "OBJECTION TO CLAIM # (CLAIMS DOCKET NUMBER) OF (NAME OF CLAIMANT), WITH NOTICE THEREOF."

B. An objection to a proof of claim must state, in bold print immediately below the title:

This is an objection to your claim in this bankruptcy case. This objection asks the Court to disallow (eliminate), reduce, or modify your claim as set forth in this objection. If you do not file a written response to this objection within 30 days from the date of mailing of this objection, the Court may disallow (eliminate), reduce, or modify your claim as set forth in this objection, without a hearing being held.

Any response to this objection must explain your position and be timely filed with the United States Bankruptcy Clerk, Western District of Texas, mailing address of applicable Clerk's office. If a timely response is filed, the Court will then set a hearing on the objection and you will be provided with notice of the date, time, and place of the hearing. If you do not attend the hearing, the Court may decide that you do not oppose the objection to your claim.

C. Unless otherwise ordered by the Court in a particular case: (1) if a timely response is filed to an objection to a proof of claim, then the objecting party and the claimant will be provided with at least 30 days notice of the hearing on the objection; and (2) a hearing will not be automatically set on an objection to claim unless a timely response is filed to the objection.

2. Effective Date and Applicability. This Standing Order is effective immediately upon the date of its entry. This Standing Order is applicable to all cases in all Divisions of the United States Bankruptcy Court for the Western District of Texas. This Standing Order supersedes and replaces Bankruptcy Local Rule 3007(a).

[Dated: December 19, 2017.]

RULES OF PROCEDURE OF THE JUDICIAL PANEL ON MULTIDISTRICT LITIGATION

Renumbered and Amended Effective November 2, 1998

Including Amendments Effective
October 4, 2016

I. RULES FOR MULTIDISTRICT LITIGATION
UNDER 28 U.S.C. § 1407

RULE 1.1 DEFINITIONS

(a) "Panel" means the members of the United States Judicial Panel on Multidistrict Litigation appointed by the Chief Justice of the United States pursuant to 28 U.S.C. § 1407.

(b) "Chair" means the Chair of the Panel appointed by the Chief Justice of the United States pursuant to Section 1407, or the member of the Panel properly designated to act as Chair.

(c) "Clerk of the Panel" means the official that the Panel appoints to that position. The Clerk of the Panel shall perform such duties that the Panel or the Panel Executive delegates.

(d) "Electronic Case Filing (ECF)" refers to the Panel's automated system that receives and stores documents filed in electronic form. All attorneys filing pleadings with the Panel must do so using ECF. All pro se individuals are non-ECF users, unless the Panel orders otherwise.

(e) "MDL" means a multidistrict litigation docket which the Panel is either considering or has created by transferring cases to a transferee district for coordinated or consolidated pretrial proceedings pursuant to Section 1407.

(f) "Panel Executive" means the official appointed to act as the Panel's Chief Executive and Legal Officer. The Panel Executive may appoint, with the approval of the Panel, necessary deputies, clerical assistants and other employees to perform or assist in the performance of the duties of the Panel Executive. The Panel Executive, with the approval of the Panel, may make such delegations of authority as are necessary for the Panel's efficient operation.

(g) "Pleadings" means all papers, motions, responses, or replies of any kind filed with the Panel, including exhibits attached thereto, as well as all orders and notices that the Panel issues.

(h) "Tag-along action" refers to a civil action pending in a district court which involves common questions of fact with either (1) actions on a pending motion to transfer to create an MDL or (2) actions previously transferred to an existing MDL, and which the Panel would consider transferring under Section 1407.

(i) "Transferee district" is the federal district court to which the Panel transfers an action pursuant to Section 1407, for inclusion in an MDL.

(j) "Transferor district" is the federal district court where an action was pending prior to its transfer pursuant to Section 1407, for inclusion in an MDL, and where the Panel may remand that action at or before the conclusion of pretrial proceedings.

[Former Rule 1 adopted May 3, 1993, effective July 1, 1993. Renumbered Rule 1.1 September 1, 1998, effective November 2, 1998. Amended September 8, 2010, effective October 4, 2010.]

RULE 2.1   RULES AND PRACTICE

(a) Customary Practice. The Panel's customary practice shall govern, unless otherwise fixed by statute or these Rules.

(b) Failure to Comply With Rules. When a pleading does not comply with these Rules, the Clerk of the Panel may advise counsel of the deficiencies and set a date for full compliance. If counsel does not fully comply within the established time, the Clerk of the Panel shall file the non-complying pleading, but the Chair may thereafter order it stricken.

(c) Admission to Practice Before the Panel. Every member in good standing of the Bar of any district court of the United States is entitled to practice before the Panel, provided, however, that he or she has established and maintains a CM/ECF account with any United States federal court. Any attorney of record in any action transferred under Section 1407 may continue to represent his or her client in any district court of the United States to which such action is transferred. Parties are not required to obtain local counsel.

(d) Pendency of Motion or Conditional Order. The pendency of a motion, order to show cause, conditional transfer order or conditional remand order before the Panel pursuant to 28 U.S.C. § 1407 does not affect or suspend orders and pretrial proceedings in any pending federal district court action and does not limit the pretrial jurisdiction of that court. An order to transfer or remand pursuant to 28 U.S.C. § 1407 shall be effective only upon its filing with the clerk of the transferee district court.

(e) Reassignment. If for any reason the transferee judge is unable to continue those responsibilities, the Panel shall make the reassignment of a new transferee judge.

[Former Rule 5 adopted May 3, 1993, effective July 1, 1993. Renumbered Rule 1.2 September 1, 1998, effective November 2, 1998. Former Rule 4 adopted May 3, 1993, effective July 1, 1993. Renumbered Rule 1.3 and amended September 1, 1998, effective November 2, 1998. Former Rule 6 adopted May 3, 1993, effective July 1, 1993. Renumbered Rule 1.4 September 1, 1998, effective November 2, 1998. Former Rule 18 adopted May 3, 1993, effective July 1, 1993. Renumbered Rule 1.5 September 1, 1998, effective November 2, 1998. Former Rules 1.2, 1.3, 1.4, and 1.5 redesignated and amended September 8, 2010, effective October 4, 2010.]

RULE 3.1   ELECTRONIC RECORDS AND FILES; COPY FEES

(a) Electronic Record. Effective October 4, 2010, the official Panel record shall be the electronic file maintained on the Panel's servers. This record includes, but is not limited to, Panel pleadings, documents filed in paper and then scanned and made part of the electronic record, and Panel orders and notices filed. The official record also includes any documents or exhibits that may be impractical to scan. These documents and exhibits shall be kept in the Panel offices.

(b) Maintaining Records. Records and files generated prior to October 4, 2010, may be (i) maintained at the Panel offices, (ii) temporarily or permanently removed to such places at such times as the Clerk of the Panel or the Chair shall direct, or (iii) transferred whenever appropriate to the Federal Records Center.

(c) Fees. The Clerk of the Panel may charge fees for duplicating records and files, as prescribed by the Judicial Conference of the United States.

[Former Rule 2 adopted May 3, 1993, effective July 1, 1993. Renumbered Rule 5.1 and amended September 1, 1998, effective November 2, 1998. Former Rule 5.1 redesignated and amended September 8, 2010, effective October 4, 2010.]

RULE 3.2   ECF USERS: FILING REQUIREMENTS

(a) Form of Pleadings. This Rule applies to pleadings that ECF users file with the Panel.

(i) Each pleading shall bear the heading "Before the United States Judicial Panel on Multidistrict Litigation," the identification "MDL No.___" and the descriptive title designated by the Panel. If the Panel has not yet designated a title, counsel shall use an appropriate description.

(ii) The final page of each pleading shall contain the name, address, telephone number, fax number and email address of the attorney or party designated to receive service of pleadings in the case, and the name of each party represented.

(iii) Each brief submitted with a motion and any response to it shall not exceed 20 pages, exclusive of exhibits. Each reply shall not exceed 10 pages and shall address arguments raised in the response(s). Absent exceptional circumstances and those set forth in Rule 6.1(d), the Panel will not grant motions to exceed page limits.

(iv) Each pleading shall be typed in size 12 point font (for both text and footnotes), double spaced (text only), in a letter size document (8½ × 11 inch) with sequentially numbered pages.

(v) Each exhibit shall be separately numbered and clearly identified.

(vi) Proposed Panel orders shall not be submitted.

(b) Place of Filing. Counsel shall sign and verify all pleadings electronically in accordance with these Rules and the Panel's Administrative Policies and Procedures for Electronic Case Filing found at www.jpml.uscourts.gov. A pleading filed electronically constitutes a written document for the purpose of these Rules and the Federal Rules of Civil Procedure and is deemed the electronically signed original thereof. All pleadings, except by pro se litigants, shall conform with this Rule beginning on October 4, 2010.

(i)* Pleadings shall not be transmitted directly to any Panel member.

(c) Attorney Registration. Only attorneys identified, or to be identified, pursuant to Rule 4.1, shall file pleadings. Each of these attorneys must register as a Panel CM/ECF user through www.jpml.uscourts.gov. Registration/possession of a CM/ECF account with any United States federal court shall be deemed consent to receive electronic service of all Panel orders and notices as well as electronic service of pleadings from other parties before the Panel.

(d) Courtesy Copy of Specified Pleadings. Counsel shall serve the Clerk of the Panel, for delivery within 1 business day of filing, with a courtesy paper copy of any of the following pleadings: (i) a motion to transfer and its supporting brief; (ii) a response to a show cause order; (iii) a motion to vacate a conditional transfer order or a conditional remand order; and (iv) any response, reply, supplemental information or interested party response related to the pleadings listed in (i), (ii) and (iii). No courtesy copies of any other pleadings are required. Courtesy copies of pleadings totaling 10 pages or less (including any attachments) may be faxed to the Panel. The courtesy copy shall include all exhibits, shall be clearly marked "Courtesy Copy–Do Not File," shall contain the CM/ECF pleading number (if known), and shall be mailed or delivered to:

Clerk of the Panel
United States Judicial Panel on Multidistrict Litigation
Thurgood Marshall Federal Judiciary Building
One Columbus Circle, NE, Room G–255, North Lobby
Washington, DC 20002–8041

(e) Privacy Protections. The privacy protections contained in Rule 5.2 of the Federal Rules of Civil Procedure shall apply to all Panel filings.

[Former Rule 3 adopted May 3, 1993, effective July 1, 1993. Renumbered Rule 5.11 and amended September 1, 1998, effective November 2, 1998; renumbered Rule 5.1.1 and amended March 25, 2010, effective April 1, 2010. Former Rule 7 adopted May 3, 1993, effective July 1, 1993. Renumbered Rule 5.12 and amended September 1, 1998, effective November 2, 1998. Amended April 2, 2001, effective April 2, 2001; paragraph (a) suspended in part by Order filed April 19, 2005; renumbered Rule 5.1.2 and amended March 25, 2010, effective April 1, 2010. Former Rule 9 adopted May 3, 1993, effective July 1, 1993. Renumbered Rule 7.1 and amended September 1, 1998, effective November 2, 1998. Amended April 2, 2001, effective April 2, 2001. Former Rules 5.1.1, 5.1.2, and 7.1 redesignated in part and amended September 8, 2010, effective October 4, 2010. Amended effective July 6, 2011; October 4, 2016.]

* [**Publisher's Note:** So in original. No subdivision (ii) promulgated.]

RULE 3.3 NON–ECF USERS: FILING REQUIREMENTS

(a) Definition of Non–ECF Users. Non–ECF users are all pro se individuals, unless the Panel orders otherwise. This Rule shall apply to all motions, responses and replies that non-ECF users file with the Panel.

(b) Form of Pleadings. Unless otherwise set forth in this Rule, the provisions of Rule 3.2 shall apply to non-ECF users.

(i) Each pleading shall be flat and unfolded; plainly written or typed in size 12 point font (for both text and footnotes), double spaced (text only), and printed single-sided on letter size (8 ½ × 11 inch) white paper with sequentially numbered pages; and fastened at the top-left corner without side binding or front or back covers.

(ii) Each exhibit shall be separately numbered and clearly identified. Any exhibits exceeding a cumulative total of 50 pages shall be bound separately.

(c) Place of Filing. File an original and one copy of all pleadings with the Clerk of the Panel by mailing or delivering to:

Clerk of the Panel
United States Judicial Panel on Multidistrict Litigation
Thurgood Marshall Federal Judiciary Building
One Columbus Circle, NE,
Room G–255, North Lobby
Washington, DC 20002–8041

(i) Pleadings not exceeding a total of 10 pages, including exhibits, may be faxed to the Panel office.

(ii) The Clerk of the Panel shall endorse the date for filing on all pleadings submitted for filing.

[Former Rule 3 adopted May 3, 1993, effective July 1, 1993. Renumbered Rule 5.11 and amended September 1, 1998, effective November 2, 1998; renumbered Rule 5.1.1 and amended March 25, 2010, effective April 1, 2010. Former Rule 7 adopted May 3, 1993, effective July 1, 1993. Renumbered Rule 5.12 and amended September 1, 1998, effective November 2, 1998. Amended April 2, 2001, effective April 2, 2001; paragraph (a) suspended in part by Order filed April 19, 2005; renumbered Rule 5.1.2 and amended March 25, 2010, effective April 1, 2010. Former Rule 9 adopted May 3, 1993, effective July 1, 1993. Renumbered Rule 7.1 and amended September 1, 1998, effective November 2, 1998. Amended April 2, 2001, effective April 2, 2001. Former Rules 5.1.1, 5.1.2, and 7.1 redesignated in part and amended September 8, 2010, effective October 4, 2010.]

RULE 4.1 SERVICE OF PLEADINGS

(a) Proof of Service. The Panel's notice of electronic filing shall constitute service of pleadings. Registration/possession by counsel of a CM/ECF account with any United States federal court shall be deemed consent to receive electronic service of all pleadings. All pleadings shall contain a proof of service on all other parties in all involved actions. The proof of service shall indicate the name and manner of service. If a party is not represented by counsel, the proof of service shall indicate the name of the party and the party's last known address. The proof of service shall indicate why any person named as a party in a constituent complaint was not served with the Section 1407 pleading.

(b) Service Upon Transferor Court. The proof of service pertaining to motions for a transfer or remand pursuant to 28 U.S.C. § 1407 shall certify that counsel has transmitted a copy of the motion for filing to the clerk of each district court where an affected action is pending.

(c) Notice of Appearance. Within 14 days after the issuance of a (i) notice of filing of a motion to initiate transfer under Rule 6.2, (ii) notice of filed opposition to a CTO under Rule 7.1, (iii) a show cause order under Rules* 8.1, (iv) notice of filed opposition to a CRO under Rule 10.2, or (v) notice of filing of a motion to remand under Rule 10.3, each party or designated attorney as required hereinafter shall file a Notice of Appearance notifying the Clerk of the Panel of the name, address and email address of the attorney designated to file and receive service of all pleadings. Each party shall designate only one attorney. Any party not represented by counsel shall be served by mailing such pleadings to the party's last known address. Except in extraordinary circumstances, the Panel will not grant requests for an extension of time to file the Notice of Appearance.

(d) Liaison Counsel. If the transferee district court appoints liaison counsel, this Rule shall be satisfied by serving each party in each affected action and all liaison counsel. Liaison counsel shall receive copies of all Panel orders concerning their particular litigation and shall be responsible for distribution to the parties for whom he or she serves as liaison counsel.

[Former Rule 8 adopted May 3, 1993, effective July 1, 1993. Renumbered Rule 5.2 and amended September 1, 1998, effective November 2, 1998; March 26, 2009, effective December 1, 2009. Former Rule 5.2 redesignated and amended September 8, 2010, effective October 4, 2010. Technical revisions effective July 6, 2011.]

* [**Publisher's Note:** So in original.]

RULE 5.1 CORPORATE DISCLOSURE STATEMENT

(a) Requirements. A nongovernmental corporate party must file a disclosure statement that: (1) identifies any parent corporation and any publicly held corporation owning 10% or more of its stock; or (2) states that there is no such corporation.

(b) Deadline. A party shall file the corporate disclosure statement within 14 days after issuance of a notice of the filing of a motion to transfer or remand, an order to show cause, or a motion to vacate a conditional transfer order or a conditional remand order.

(c) Updating. Each party must update its corporate disclosure statement to reflect any change in the information therein (i) until the matter before the Panel is decided, and (ii) within 14 days after issuance of a notice of the filing of any subsequent motion to transfer or remand, order to show cause, or motion to vacate a conditional transfer order or a conditional remand order in that docket.

[Former Rule 2 adopted May 3, 1993, effective July 1, 1993. Renumbered Rule 5.1 and amended September 1, 1998, effective November 2, 1998. Former Rule 5.3 redesignated and amended September 8, 2010, effective October 4, 2010. Amended effective July 6, 2011.]

RULE 5.1.3 FILING OF PAPERS: COMPUTER GENERATED DISK REQUIRED [DELETED SEPT. 8, 2010, EFF. OCT. 4, 2010]

[Added May 22, 2000, effective June 1, 2000. And amended July 30, 2007, effective July 30, 2007; renumbered Rule 5.1.3 and amended March 25, 2010, effective April 1, 2010. Deleted September 8, 2010, effective October 4, 2010.]

RULE 6.1 MOTION PRACTICE

(a) Application. This Rule governs all motions requesting Panel action generally. More specific provisions may apply to motions to transfer (Rule 6.2), miscellaneous motions (Rule 6.3), conditional transfer orders (Rule 7.1), show cause orders (Rule 8.1), conditional remand orders (Rule 10.2) and motions to remand (Rule 10.3).

(b) Form of Motions. All motions shall briefly describe the action or relief sought and shall include:

(i) a brief which concisely states the background of the litigation and movant's factual and legal contentions;

(ii) a numbered schedule providing

(A) the complete name of each action involved, listing the full name of each party included as such on the district court's docket sheet, not shortened by the use of references such as "et al." or "etc.";

(B) the district court and division where each action is pending;

(C) the civil action number of each action; and

(D) the name of the judge assigned each action, if known;

(iii) a proof of service providing

(A) a service list listing the full name of each party included on the district court's docket sheet and the complaint, including opt-in plaintiffs not listed on the docket sheet; and

(B) in actions where there are 25 or more plaintiffs listed on the docket sheet, list the first named plaintiff with the reference "et al." if all the plaintiffs are represented by the same attorney(s);

(iv) a copy of all complaints and docket sheets for all actions listed on the Schedule; and

(v) exhibits, if any, identified by number or letter and a descriptive title.

(c) Responses and Joinders. Any other party may file a response within 21 days after filing of a motion. Failure to respond to a motion shall be treated as that party's acquiescence to it. A joinder in a motion shall not add any action to that motion.

(d) Replies. The movant may file a reply within 7 days after the lapse of the time period for filing a response. Where a movant is replying to more than one response in opposition, the movant may file a consolidated reply with a limit of 20 pages.

(e) Alteration of Time Periods. The Clerk of the Panel has the discretion to shorten or enlarge the time periods set forth in this Rule as necessary.

(f) Notification of Developments. Counsel shall promptly notify the Clerk of the Panel of any development that would partially or completely moot any Panel matter.

[Former Rule 10 adopted May 3, 1993, effective July 1, 1993. Renumbered Rule 7.2 and amended September 1, 1998, effective November 2, 1998. Amended April 2, 2001, effective April 2, 2001; March 26, 2009, December 1, 2009. Former Rule 7.2 redesignated in part and amended September 8, 2010, effective October 4, 2010.]

RULE 6.2 MOTIONS TO TRANSFER FOR COORDINATED OR CONSOLIDATED PRETRIAL PROCEEDINGS

(a) Initiation of Transfer. A party to an action may initiate proceedings to transfer under Section 1407 by filing a motion in accordance with these Rules. A copy of the motion shall be filed in each district court where the motion affects a pending action.

(b) Notice of Filing of Motion to Transfer. Upon receipt of a motion, the Clerk of the Panel shall issue a "Notice of Filing of Motion to Transfer" to the service list recipients. The Notice shall contain the following: the filing date of the motion, caption, MDL docket number, briefing schedule and pertinent Panel policies. After a motion is filed, the Clerk of the Panel shall consider any other pleading to be a response unless the pleading adds an action. The Clerk of the Panel may designate such a pleading as a motion, and distribute a briefing schedule applicable to all or some of the parties, as appropriate.

(c) Notice of Appearance. Within 14 days of issuance of a "Notice of the Filing of a Motion to Transfer," each party or designated attorney shall file a Notice of Appearance in accordance with Rule 4.1(c).

(d) Notice of Potential Tag-along Actions. Any party or counsel in a new group of actions under consideration for transfer under Section 1407 shall promptly notify the Clerk of the Panel of any potential tag-along actions in which that party is also named or in which that counsel appears.

(e) Interested Party Responses. Any party or counsel in one or more potential tag-along actions as well as amicus curiae may file a response to a pending motion to transfer. Such a pleading shall be deemed an Interested Party Response.

(f) Amendment to a Motion. Before amending a motion to transfer, a party shall first contact the Clerk of the Panel to ascertain whether such amendment is feasible and permissible considering the Panel's hearing schedule. Any such amendment shall be entitled "Amendment to Motion for Transfer," and shall clearly and specifically identify and describe the nature of the amendment.

   (i) Where the amended motion includes new civil actions, the amending party shall file a "Schedule of Additional Actions" and a revised Proof of Service.

   (ii) The Proof of Service shall state (A) that all new counsel have been served with a copy of the amendment and all previously-filed motion papers, and (B) that all counsel previously served with the original motion have been served with a copy of the amendment.

   (iii) The Clerk of the Panel may designate the amendment with a different denomination (*e.g.*, a notice of potential tag-along action(s)) and treatment.

(h) Oral Argument*. The Panel shall schedule oral arguments as needed and as set forth in Rule 11.1.

[Former Rule 10 adopted May 3, 1993, effective July 1, 1993. Renumbered Rule 7.2 and amended September 1, 1998, effective November 2, 1998. Amended April 2, 2001, effective April 2, 2001; March 26, 2009, December 1, 2009. Former Rule 15 adopted May 3, 1993, effective July 1, 1993. Renumbered Rule 6.2 and amended September 1, 1998, effective November 2, 1998. Former Rule 7.2 redesignated in part and amended September 8, 2010, effective October 4, 2010. Technical revisions effective July 6, 2011.]

* [Publisher's Note: So in original.]

RULE 6.3 MOTIONS FOR MISCELLANEOUS RELIEF

(a) Definition. Motions for miscellaneous relief include, but are not limited to, requests for extensions of time, exemption from ECF requirements, page limit extensions, or expedited consideration of any motion.

(b) Panel Action. The Panel, through the Clerk, may act upon any motion for miscellaneous relief, at any time, without waiting for a response. A motion for extension of time to file a pleading or perform an act under these Rules must state specifically the revised date sought and must be filed before the deadline for filing the pleading or performing the act. Any party aggrieved by the Clerk of the Panel's action may file objections for consideration. Absent exceptional circumstances, the Panel will not grant any extensions of time to file a notice of opposition to either a conditional transfer order or a conditional remand order.

[Former Rule 15 adopted May 3, 1993, effective July 1, 1993. Renumbered Rule 6.2 and amended September 1, 1998, effective November 2, 1998. Former Rule 6.2 redesignated and amended September 8, 2010, effective October 4, 2010.]

RULE 7.1 CONDITIONAL TRANSFER ORDERS (CTO) FOR TAG–ALONG ACTIONS

(a) Notice of Potential Tag-along Actions. Any party or counsel in actions previously transferred under Section 1407 shall promptly notify the Clerk of the Panel of any potential tag-along actions in which that party is also named or in which that counsel appears. The Panel has several options: (i) filing a CTO under Rule 7.1, (ii) filing a show cause order under Rule 8.1, or (iii) declining to act (Rule 7.1(b)(i)).

(b) Initiation of CTO. Upon learning of the pendency of a potential tag-along action, the Clerk of the Panel may enter a conditional order transferring that action to the previously designated transferee district court for the reasons expressed in the Panel's previous opinions and orders. The Clerk of the Panel shall serve this order on each party to the litigation but shall not send the order to the clerk of the transferee district court until 7 days after its entry.

   (i)* If the Clerk of the Panel determines that a potential tag-along action is not appropriate for inclusion in an MDL proceeding and does not enter a CTO, an involved party may move for its transfer pursuant to Rule 6.1.

(c) Notice of Opposition to CTO. Any party opposing the transfer shall file a notice of opposition with the Clerk of the Panel within the 7–day period. In such event, the Clerk of the Panel shall not transmit the transfer order to the clerk of the transferee district court, but shall notify the parties of the briefing schedule.

(d) Failure to Respond. Failure to respond to a CTO shall be treated as that party's acquiescence to it.

(e) Notice of Appearance. Within 14 days after the issuance of a "Notice of Filed Opposition" to a CTO, each opposing party or designated attorney shall file a Notice of Appearance in accordance with Rule 4.1(c).

(f) Motion to Vacate CTO. Within 14 days of the filing of its notice of opposition, the party opposing transfer shall file a motion to vacate the CTO and brief in support thereof. The Clerk of the Panel shall set the motion for the next appropriate hearing session. Failure to file and serve a motion and brief shall be treated as withdrawal of the opposition and the Clerk of the Panel shall forthwith transmit the order to the clerk of the transferee district court.

(g) Notification of Developments. Parties to an action subject to a CTO shall notify the Clerk of the Panel if that action is no longer pending in its transferor district court.

(h) Effective Date of CTO. CTOs are effective when filed with the clerk of the transferee district court.

[Former Rule 12 adopted May 3, 1993, effective July 1, 1993. Renumbered Rule 7.4 and amended September 1, 1998, effective November 2, 1998. Amended April 2, 2001, effective April 2, 2001; March 26, 2009, December 1, 2009. Former Rule 7.4 redesignated and amended September 8, 2010, effective October 4, 2010. Technical revisions effective July 6, 2011.]

* [**Publisher's Note:** So in original. No subdivision (ii) promulgated.]

RULE 7.2 MISCELLANEOUS PROVISIONS CONCERNING TAG–ALONG ACTIONS

(a) Potential Tag-alongs in Transferee Court. Potential tag-along actions filed in the transferee district do not require Panel action. A party should request assignment of such actions to the Section 1407 transferee judge in accordance with applicable local rules.

(b) Failure to Serve. Failure to serve one or more of the defendants in a potential tag-along action with the complaint and summons as required by Rule 4 of the Federal Rules of Civil Procedure does not preclude transfer of such action under Section 1407. Such failure, however, may constitute grounds for denying the proposed transfer where prejudice can be shown. The failure of the Clerk of the Panel to serve a CTO on all plaintiffs or defendants or their counsel may constitute grounds for the Clerk to reinstate the CTO or for the aggrieved party to seek § 1407(c) remand.

[Former Rule 13 adopted May 3, 1993, effective July 1, 1993. Renumbered Rule 7.5 and amended September 1, 1998, effective November 2, 1998. Amended April 2, 2001, effective April 2, 2001. Former Rule 7.5 redesignated and amended September 8, 2010, effective October 4, 2010. Amended effective July 6, 2011.]

RULE 8.1 SHOW CAUSE ORDERS

(a) Entry of Show Cause Order. When transfer of multidistrict litigation is being considered on the initiative of the Panel pursuant to 28 U.S.C. § 1407(c)(i), the Clerk of the Panel may enter an order directing the parties to show cause why a certain civil action or actions should not be transferred for coordinated or consolidated pretrial proceedings. Any party shall also promptly notify the Clerk of the Panel whenever they learn of any other federal district court actions which are similar to those which the show cause order encompasses.

(b) Notice of Appearance. Within 14 days of the issuance of an order to show cause, each party or designated attorney shall file a Notice of Appearance in accordance with Rule 4.1(c).

(c) Responses. Unless otherwise provided by order, any party may file a response within 21 days of the filing of the show cause order. Failure to respond to a show cause order shall be treated as that party's acquiescence to the Panel action.

(d) Replies. Within 7 days after the lapse of the time period for filing a response, any party may file a reply.

(e) Notification of Developments. Counsel shall promptly notify the Clerk of the Panel of any development that would partially or completely moot any matter subject to a show cause order.

[Former Rule 7.3 adopted May 3, 1993, effective July 1, 1993. Renumbered Rule 7.3 and amended September 1, 1998, effective November 2, 1998; March 26, 2009, effective December 1, 2009. Former Rule 7.3 redesignated and amended September 8, 2010, effective October 4, 2010.]

RULE 9.1 TRANSFER OF FILES; NOTIFICATION REQUIREMENTS

(a) Notice to Transferee Court Clerk. The Clerk of the Panel, via a notice of electronic filing, will notify the clerk of the transferee district whenever a Panel transfer order should be filed in the transferee district court. Upon receipt of an electronically certified copy of a Panel transfer order from the clerk of the transferee district, the clerk of the transferor district shall transmit the record of each transferred action to the transferee district and then, unless Rule 9.1(b) applies, close the transferred action in the transferor district.

(b) Retention of Claims. If the transfer order provides for the separation and simultaneous remand of any claim, cross-claim, counterclaim, or third-party claim, the clerk of the transferor district shall retain jurisdiction over any such claim and shall not close the action.

(c) Notice to Clerk of Panel. The clerk of the transferee district shall promptly provide the Clerk of the Panel with the civil action numbers assigned to all transferred actions and the identity of liaison counsel, if or when designated. The clerk of the transferee district shall also promptly notify the Clerk of the Panel of any dispositive ruling that terminates a transferred action.

[Former Rule 19 adopted May 3, 1993, effective July 1, 1993. Renumbered Rule 1.6 and amended September 1, 1998, effective November 2, 1998. Former Rule 1.6 redesignated in part and amended September 8, 2010, effective October 4, 2010.]

RULE 10.1 TERMINATION AND REMAND

(a) Termination. Where the transferee district court terminates an action by valid order, including but not limited to summary judgment, judgment of dismissal and judgment upon stipulation, the transferee district court clerk shall transmit a copy of that order to the Clerk of the Panel. The terminated action shall not be remanded to the transferor court and the transferee court shall retain the original files and records unless the transferee judge or the Panel directs otherwise.

(b) Initiation of Remand. Typically, the transferee judge recommends remand of an action, or a part of it, to the transferor court at any time by filing a suggestion of remand with the Panel. However, the Panel may remand an action or any separable claim, cross-claim, counterclaim or third-party claim within it, upon

(i) the transferee court's suggestion of remand,

(ii) the Panel's own initiative by entry of an order to show cause, a conditional remand order or other appropriate order, or

(iii) motion of any party.

[Former Rule 14 adopted May 3, 1993, effective July 1, 1993. Renumbered Rule 7.6 and amended September 1, 1998, effective November 2, 1998. Amended April 2, 2001, effective April 2, 2001; March 26, 2009, effective December 1, 2009. Former Rule 7.6 redesignated in part and amended September 8, 2010, effective October 4, 2010.]

RULE 10.2 CONDITIONAL REMAND ORDERS (CRO)

(a) Entering a CRO. Upon the suggestion of the transferee judge or the Panel's own initiative, the Clerk of the Panel shall enter a conditional order remanding the action or actions to the transferor district court. The Clerk of the Panel shall serve this order on each party to the litigation but shall not send the order to the clerk of the transferee district court for 7 days from the entry thereof.

(i)* The Panel may, on its own initiative, also enter an order that the parties show cause why a matter should not be remanded. Rule 8.1 applies to responses and replies with respect to such a show cause order.

(b) Notice of Opposition. Any party opposing the CRO shall file a notice of opposition with the Clerk of the Panel within the 7–day period. In such event, the Clerk of the Panel shall not transmit the remand order to the clerk of the transferee district court and shall notify the parties of the briefing schedule.

(c) Failure to Respond. Failure to respond to a CRO shall be treated as that party's acquiescence to it.

(d) Notice of Appearance. Within 14 days after the issuance of a "Notice of Filed Opposition" to a CRO, each opposing party or designated attorney shall file a Notice of Appearance in accordance with Rule 4.1(c).

(e) Motion to Vacate CRO. Within 14 days of the filing of its notice of opposition, the party opposing remand shall file a motion to vacate the CRO and brief in support thereof. The Clerk of the Panel shall set the motion for the next appropriate Panel hearing session. Failure to file and serve a motion and brief shall be treated as a withdrawal of the opposition and the Clerk of the Panel shall forthwith transmit the order to the clerk of the transferee district court.

(f) Effective Date of CRO. CROs are not effective until filed with the clerk of the transferee district court.

[Former Rule 14 adopted May 3, 1993, effective July 1, 1993. Renumbered Rule 7.6 and amended September 1, 1998, effective November 2, 1998. Amended April 2, 2001, effective April 2, 2001; March 26, 2009, effective December 1, 2009. Former Rule 7.6 redesignated in part and amended September 8, 2010, effective October 4, 2010. Technical revisions effective July 6, 2011.]

* [Publisher's Note: So in original. No subdivision (ii) promulgated.]

RULE 10.3 MOTION TO REMAND

(a) Requirements of the Motion. If the Clerk of the Panel does not enter a CRO, a party may file a motion to remand to the transferor court pursuant to these Rules. Because the Panel is reluctant to order a remand absent the suggestion of the transferee judge, the motion must include:

(i) An affidavit reciting whether the movant has requested a suggestion of remand and the judge's response, whether the parties have completed common discovery and other pretrial proceedings, and whether the parties have complied with all transferee court orders.

(ii) A copy of the transferee district court's final pretrial order, if entered.

(b) Filing Copy of Motion. Counsel shall file a copy of the motion to remand in the affected transferee district court.

(c) Notice of Appearance. Within 14 days of the issuance of a "Notice of Filing" of a motion to remand, each party or designated attorney shall file a Notice of Appearance in accordance with Rule 4.1(c).

[Former Rule 14 adopted May 3, 1993, effective July 1, 1993. Renumbered Rule 7.6 and amended September 1, 1998, effective November 2, 1998. Amended April 2, 2001, effective April 2, 2001; March 26, 2009, effective December 1, 2009. Former Rule 7.6 redesignated in part and amended September 8, 2010, effective October 4, 2010. Technical revisions effective July 6, 2011.]

RULE 10.4 TRANSFER OF FILES ON REMAND

(a) Designating the Record. Upon receipt of an order to remand from the Clerk of the Panel, the parties shall furnish forthwith to the transferee district clerk a stipulation or designation of the contents of the record or part thereof to be remanded.

(b) Transfer of Files. Upon receipt of an order to remand from the Clerk of the Panel, the transferee district shall transmit to the clerk of the transferor district the following concerning each remanded action:

(i) a copy of the individual docket sheet for each action remanded;

(ii) a copy of the master docket sheet, if applicable;

(iii) the entire file for each action remanded, as originally received from the transferor district and augmented as set out in this Rule;

(iv) a copy of the final pretrial order, if applicable; and

(v) a "record on remand" as designated by the parties in accordance with 10.4(a).

[Former Rule 19 adopted May 3, 1993, effective July 1, 1993. Renumbered Rule 1.6 and amended September 1, 1998, effective November 2, 1998. Former Rule 1.6 redesignated in part and amended September 8, 2010, effective October 4, 2010.]

RULE 11.1 HEARING SESSIONS AND ORAL ARGUMENT

(a) Schedule. The Panel shall schedule sessions for oral argument and consideration of other matters as desirable or necessary. The Chair shall determine the time, place and agenda for each hearing session. The Clerk of the Panel shall give appropriate notice to counsel for all parties. The Panel may continue its consideration of any scheduled matters.

(b) Oral Argument Statement. Any party affected by a motion may file a separate statement setting forth reasons why oral argument should, or need not, be heard. Such statements shall be captioned "Reasons Why Oral Argument Should [Need Not] Be Heard" and shall be limited to 2 pages.

(i)* The parties affected by a motion to transfer may agree to waive oral argument. The Panel will take this into consideration in determining the need for oral argument.

(c) Hearing Session. The Panel shall not consider transfer or remand of any action pending in a federal district court when any party timely opposes such transfer or remand without first holding a hearing session for the presentation of oral argument. The Panel may dispense with oral argument if it determines that:

(i) the dispositive issue(s) have been authoritatively decided; or

(ii) the facts and legal arguments are adequately presented and oral argument would not significantly aid the decisional process.

Unless otherwise ordered, the Panel shall consider all other matters, such as a motion for reconsideration, upon the basis of the pleadings.

(d) Notification of Oral Argument. The Panel shall promptly notify counsel of those matters in which oral argument is scheduled, as well as those matters that the Panel will consider on the pleadings. The Clerk of the Panel shall require counsel to file and serve notice of their intent to either make or waive oral argument. Failure to do so shall be deemed a waiver of oral argument. If counsel does not attend oral argument, the matter shall not be rescheduled and that party's position shall be treated as submitted for decision on the basis of the pleadings filed.

(i) Absent Panel approval and for good cause shown, only those parties to actions who have filed a motion or written response to a motion or order shall be permitted to present oral argument.

(ii) The Panel will not receive oral testimony except upon notice, motion and an order expressly providing for it.

(e) Duty to Confer. Counsel in an action set for oral argument shall confer separately prior to that argument for the purpose of organizing their arguments and selecting representatives to present all views without duplication. Oral argument is a means for counsel to emphasize the key points of their arguments, and to update the Panel on any events since the conclusion of briefing.

(f) Time Limit for Oral Argument. Barring exceptional circumstances, the Panel shall allot a maximum of 20 minutes for oral argument in each matter. The time shall be divided among those with varying viewpoints. Counsel for the moving party or parties shall generally be heard first.

[Former Rule 16 adopted May 3, 1998, effective July 1, 1993. Renumbered Rule 16.1 and amended September 1, 1998, effective November 2, 1998. Amended April 2, 2001, effective April 2, 2001. Former Rule 16.1 redesignated and amended September 8, 2010, effective October 4, 2010.]

* [**Publisher's Note:** So in original. No subdivision (ii) promulgated.]

RULES 12 TO 15. [RESERVED]

II. RULES FOR MULTICIRCUIT PETITIONS FOR REVIEW UNDER 28 U.S.C. § 2112(a)(3)

RULE 25.1 DEFINITIONS

The Panel promulgates these Rules pursuant to its authority under 28 U.S.C. § 2112(a)(3) to provide a means for the random selection of one circuit court of appeals to hear consolidated petitions for review of agency decisions.

An "Agency" means an agency, board, commission or officer of the United States government, that has received two or more petitions for review in a circuit court of appeals to enjoin, set aside, suspend, modify or otherwise review or enforce an action.

[Former Rule 20 adopted May 3, 1993, effective July 1, 1993. Renumbered Rule 25.1 and amended September 1, 1998, effective November 2, 1998. Amended September 8, 2010, effective October 4, 2010.]

RULE 25.2 FILING OF NOTICES

(a) Submitting Notice. An affected agency shall submit a notice of multicircuit petitions for review pursuant to 28 U.S.C. § 2112(a)(3) to the Clerk of the Panel by electronic means in the manner these Rules require and in accordance with the Panel's Administrative Policies and Procedures for Electronic Case Filing, except that the portion of Rule 3.2(d) requiring a courtesy copy is suspended in its entirety.

(b) Accompaniments to Notices. All notices of multicircuit petitions for review shall include:

(i) a copy of each involved petition for review as the petition for review is defined in 28 U.S.C. § 2112(a)(2);

(ii) a schedule giving

(A) the date of the relevant agency order;

(B) the case name of each petition for review involved;

(C) the circuit court of appeals in which each petition for review is pending;

(D) the appellate docket number of each petition for review;

(E) the date of filing by the court of appeals of each petition for review; and

(F) the date of receipt by the agency of each petition for review; and

(iii) proof of service (see Rule 25.3).

(c) Scope of Notice. All notices of multicircuit petitions for review shall embrace exclusively petitions for review filed in the courts of appeals within 10 days after issuance of an agency order and received by the affected agency from the petitioners within that 10–day period.

(d) Filing at the Panel. The Clerk of the Panel shall file the notice of multicircuit petitions for review and endorse thereon the date of filing.

(e) Filing With Each Circuit Clerk. The affected agency shall file copies of notices of multicircuit petitions for review with the clerk of each circuit court of appeals in which a petition for review is pending.

[Former Rule 21 adopted May 3, 1993, effective July 1, 1993. Renumbered Rule 25.2 and amended September 1, 1998, effective November 2, 1998. Amended September 8, 2010, effective October 4, 2010. Technical revisions effective July 6, 2011.]

RULE 25.3 SERVICE OF NOTICES

(a) Proof of Service. Notices of multicircuit petitions for review shall include proof of service on all other parties in the petitions for review included in the notice. Rule 25 of the Federal Rules of Appellate Procedure governs service and proof of service. The proof of service shall state the name, address and email address of each person served and shall indicate the party represented by each and the manner in which service was accomplished on each party. If a party is not represented by counsel, the proof of service shall indicate the name of the party and his or her last known address. The affected party shall submit proof of service for filing with the Clerk of the Panel and shall send copies thereof to each person included within the proof of service.

(b) Service on Clerk of Circuit. The proof of service pertaining to notices of multicircuit petitions for review shall certify the affected party has mailed or delivered copies of the notices to the clerk of each circuit court of appeals in which a petition for review is pending that is included in the notice. The Clerk shall file the notice with the circuit court.

[Former Rule 22 adopted May 3, 1993, effective July 1, 1993. Renumbered Rule 25.3 September 1, 1998, effective November 2, 1998. Amended September 8, 2010, effective October 4, 2010.]

RULE 25.4 FORM OF NOTICES; PLACE OF FILING

(a) Unless otherwise provided here, Rule 3.2 governs the form of a notice of multicircuit petitions for review. Each notice shall bear the heading "Notice to the United States Judicial Panel on Multidistrict Litigation of Multicircuit Petitions for Review," followed by a brief caption identifying the involved agency, the relevant agency order, and the date of the order.

(b) Rule 3.2(b) and (c) govern the manner of filing a notice of multicircuit petitions for review.

[Former Rule 23 adopted May 3, 1993, effective July 1, 1993. Renumbered Rule 25.4 and amended September 1, 1998, effective November 2, 1998. Amended September 8, 2010, effective October 4, 2010.]

RULE 25.5 RANDOM SELECTION

(a) Selection Process. Upon filing a notice of multicircuit petitions for review, the Clerk of the Panel shall randomly select a circuit court of appeals from a drum containing an entry for each circuit wherein a constituent petition for review is pending. Multiple petitions for review pending in a single circuit shall be allotted only a single entry in the drum. A designated deputy other than the random selector shall witness the random selection. Thereafter, an order on behalf of the Panel shall be issued, signed by the random selector and the witness,

(i) consolidating the petitions for review in the court of appeals for the circuit that was randomly selected; and

(ii) designating that circuit as the one in which the record is to be filed pursuant to Rules 16 and 17 of the Federal Rules of Appellate Procedure.

(b) Effective Date. A consolidation of petitions for review shall be effective when the Clerk of the Panel enters the consolidation order.

[Former Rule 24 adopted May 3, 1993, effective July 1, 1993. Renumbered Rule 17.1 September 1, 1998, effective November 2, 1998. Former Rule 17.1 redesignated and amended September 8, 2010, effective October 4, 2010.]

RULE 25.6 SERVICE OF PANEL CONSOLIDATION ORDER

(a) The Clerk of the Panel shall serve the Panel's consolidation order on the affected agency through the individual or individuals, as identified in Rule 25.2(a), who submitted the notice of multicircuit petitions for review on behalf of the agency.

(b) That individual or individuals, or anyone else designated by the agency, shall promptly serve the Panel's consolidation order on all other parties in all petitions for review included in the Panel's consolidation order, and shall promptly submit a proof of that service to the Clerk of the Panel. Rule 25.3 governs service.

(c) The Clerk of the Panel shall serve the Panel's consolidation order on the clerks of all circuit courts of appeals that were among the candidates for the Panel's random selection.

[Former Rule 25 adopted May 3, 1993, effective July 1, 1993. Renumbered Rule 25.5 and amended September 1, 1998, effective November 2, 1998. Former Rule 25.5 redesignated and amended September 8, 2010, effective October 4, 2010.]

III. CONVERSION TABLE

New to Old:

New Rule / Previous Rule

New Rule	Previous Rule
1.1	1.1
2.1	1.2, 1.3, 1.4, 1.5
3.1	5.1
3.2	5.1.1, 5.1.2, 7.1
3.3	5.1.1, 5.1.2, 7.1
4.1	5.2
5.1	5.3
6.1	7.2
6.2	7.2
6.3	6.2
7.1	7.4
7.2	7.5
8.1	7.3

New Rule / Previous Rule

New Rule	Previous Rule
9.1	1.6
10.1	7.6
10.2	7.6
10.3	7.6
10.4	1.6
11.1	16.1
25.1	25.1
25.2	25.1, 25.2
25.3	25.3
25.4	25.1, 25.4
25.5	17.1
25.6	25.5

Old to New:

Previous Rule / New Rule

Previous Rule	New Rule
1.1	1.1
1.2	2.1
1.3	2.1
1.4	2.1
1.5	2.1
1.6	10.4
5.1	3.1
5.1.1	3.2, 3.3
5.1.2	3.2, 3.3
5.1.3	-
5.2	4.1
5.3	5.1
6.2	6.3

Previous Rule / New Rule

Previous Rule	New Rule
7.1	3.2, 3.3
7.2	6.1
7.3	8.1
7.4	7.1
7.5	7.2
7.6	10.1
16.1	11.1
17.1	25.5
25.1	25.1, 25.2, 25.4
25.2	25.2
25.3	25.3
25.4	25.4
25.5	25.6

[October 2010.]

ELECTRONIC CASE FILING ADMINISTRATIVE
POLICIES AND PROCEDURES

1. DEFINITIONS.

1.1 "ELECTRONIC FILING SYSTEM" (ECF) refers to the United States Judicial Panel on Multidistrict Litigation's (the Panel's) automated system that receives and stores documents filed in electronic form. The program is part of the CM/ECF (Case Management/Electronic Case Files) software which was developed for the Federal Judiciary by the Administrative Office of the United States Courts.

1.2 "CLERK OF THE PANEL" means the official appointed by the Panel to act as Clerk of the Panel and shall include those deputized by the Clerk of the Panel to perform or assist in the performance of the duties of the Clerk of the Panel.

1.3 "FILING USER" is an individual who has a Panel-issued login and password to file documents electronically. In accordance with Rule 1.4 of the Rules of Procedure of the United States Judicial Panel on Multidistrict Litigation (the Panel Rules), every member in good standing of the Bar of any district court of the United States is entitled to practice before the Judicial Panel on Multidistrict Litigation.

1.4 "NOTICE OF ELECTRONIC FILING" (NEF) is a notice automatically generated by the Electronic Filing System at the time a document is filed with the system, setting forth the time of filing, the date the document is entered on the docket, the name of the party and attorney filing the document, the type of document, the text of the docket entry, the name of the party and/or attorney receiving the notice, and an electronic link (hyperlink) to the filed document, which allows recipients to retrieve the document automatically. A document shall not be considered filed for the purposes of the Panel's Rules until the filing party receives a system generated Notice of Electronic Filing with a hyperlink to the electronically filed document.

1.5 "PACER" (Public Access to Court Electronic Records) is an automated system that allows an individual to view, print and download Panel docket information over the Internet.

1.6 "PDF" (Portable Document Format). A document file created with a word processor, or a paper document which has been scanned, must be converted to portable document format to be filed electronically with the Panel. Converted files contain the extension ".pdf".

1.7 "TECHNICAL FAILURE" is defined as a failure of Panel owned/leased hardware, software, and/or telecommunications facility which results in the inability of a Filing User to submit a filing electronically. Technical failure does not include malfunctioning of a Filing User's equipment.

2. SCOPE OF ELECTRONIC FILING.

(a) All multidistrict litigation matters (MDLs) brought before the Panel under 28 U.S.C. § 1407 shall be assigned to the Electronic Filing System. Effective October 1, 2010, all MDLs, proceedings, motions, memoranda of law and other pleadings or documents filed with the Panel in new and existing dockets must be filed using CM/ECF unless otherwise specified herein.

(b) The filing of all MDL papers shall be accomplished electronically under procedures outlined in the Panel's CM/ECF User Manual.

(c) A party proceeding pro se shall not file electronically, unless otherwise permitted by the Panel. Pro se filers shall file paper originals of all documents. The clerk's office will scan these original documents into the JPML's electronic system, unless otherwise sealed.

3. ELIGIBILITY, REGISTRATION, PASSWORDS.

(a) Any attorney admitted to the Bar of any United States district court is eligible to practice before the Panel. Unless otherwise exempt as set forth herein, to become a Filing User, an attorney must register as a Filing User by completing the prescribed registration form and submitting it to the Clerk of the Panel.

(b) Registration as a Filing User constitutes consent to electronic service of all documents filed with or issued by the Panel in accordance with the Panel Rules.

(c) By submitting the online registration form, the Filing Users certify that they have read and are familiar with the Panel Rules and these administrative policies and procedures governing electronic filing and the method of training in the System used prior to becoming a Filing User. Filing users must also have a PACER account. An individual may register more than one Internet email address. The clerk's office will email the login and password to the attorney.

(d) Once the registration is processed by the clerk, the Filing User shall protect the security of the User password and immediately notify the clerk if the Filing User learns that the password has been compromised. Filing Users may be subject to sanctions for failure to comply with this provision. After registering, attorneys may change their passwords. If an attorney comes to believe that the security of an existing password has been compromised and that a threat to the System exists, the attorney must change his or her password immediately.

(e) Exemptions from mandatory electronic filing may be granted upon submission of a written request to the clerk. The written request shall include a supporting affidavit showing a substantial undue hardship. Final authority to grant such request is vested in the Clerk of the Panel or his/her designee.

(f)(1) Each attorney is responsible for keeping his/her contact information up to date. If an attorney is leaving a law firm and is the attorney of record on an existing case and representation in the case will remain with the law firm, withdrawal and substitution of counsel must be made prior to the attorney's termination in the law firm, for the following reason:

The attorney leaving the firm has an email address with the law firm he or she is leaving on record with the Panel. This email address may be disabled by the law firm as soon as the attorney terminates his/her employment. The electronic notices in CM/ECF will continue to go to the terminated attorney's email address at the former firm. If the email address is disabled at the law firm, the attorney will not receive the electronic notice. If a withdrawal/substitution of counsel has not been filed prior to the attorney leaving the firm, the law firm should not disable the email account of the attorney leaving the firm until another attorney in the firm enters his/her appearance. The law firm should designate someone in the firm to check this email account for CM/ECF notices until substitution of counsel has been filed with the Panel.

(2) If the attorney leaving the firm is taking active cases from the firm, the attorney needs to change his/her email address as soon as possible, otherwise the attorney will not receive electronic notices from CM/ECF. The email will continue to be sent to the former law firm's email address still on record. Procedures for changing an email address may be found in the Panel's CM/ECF User Manual.

4. ELECTRONIC FILING AND SERVICE OF DOCUMENTS.

(a) Electronic transmission of a document to the Electronic Filing System in accordance with these procedures, together with the transmission of a (System) Notice of Electronic Filing from the Panel with a hyperlink to the electronically filed document, constitutes filing of the document for all purposes of the Panel Rules of Procedure.

(b) Emailing a document to the clerk's office does not constitute filing the document. A document shall not be considered filed until the System generates a Notice of Electronic Filing (NEF) with a hyperlink to the electronically filed document.

(c) Before filing a scanned document with the court, a Filing User must verify its legibility.

(d) When a document has been filed electronically, the official record of that document is the electronic recording as stored by the Panel and the filing party is bound by the document as filed. A document filed electronically is deemed filed on the date and time stated on the Notice of Electronic Filing (NEF) from the Panel.

(e) Filing a document electronically does not alter the filing deadline for that document. Filing must be completed before midnight, **EASTERN TIME**, in order to be considered timely filed that day. However, if time of day is of the essence, the Clerk of the Panel may order a document filed by a certain time.

(f) Upon the filing of a document, a docket entry will be created using the information provided by the Filing User. The clerk will, where necessary and appropriate, modify the docket entry description to comply with quality control standards. In the event a Filing User electronically files a document in the wrong MDL or associated civil action, or the incorrect PDF document is attached, the Clerk of the Panel, or his/her designee, shall be authorized to strike the document from the record. A notice of the action striking a document from the record shall be served on all parties in the case.

(g) By participating in the electronic filing process, the parties consent to the electronic service of all documents, and shall make available electronic mail addresses for service. Upon the filing of a document by a Filing User, a Notice of Electronic Filing (NEF), with a hyperlink to the electronic document and an email message will be automatically generated by the electronic filing system, and sent via electronic mail to the email addresses of all parties who have registered in the MDL. In addition to receiving email notifications of filing activity, the Filing User is strongly encouraged to sign on to the electronic filing system at regular intervals to check the docket in his/her MDL and/or civil action.

(h) If the filing of an electronically submitted document requires leave of the Panel, such as a request to file out-of-time, the attorney shall attach the proposed document as an attachment to the motion requesting leave to file. If the Clerk of the Panel grants the motion, the document will be electronically filed without further action by the Filing User.

(i) A certificate of service must be included with all documents filed electronically. Such certificate shall indicate that service was accomplished pursuant to the Panel's electronic filing procedures. Service by electronic mail shall constitute service pursuant to Panel Rule 5.2.

A party who is not a registered CM/ECF participant with any United States federal court is entitled to a paper copy of any electronically filed pleading, document, or order pursuant to Panel Rule 5.1.1.(b). The filing party must therefore provide the non-registered attorney or party, including a terminated party or attorney, if appropriate, with the pleading, document, or order pursuant to Panel Rule 5.2. Under the Rule, they can be served with a paper copy of the electronically filed document, or they can consent in writing to service by any other method, including other forms of electronic service such as fax or direct email.

The following is a suggested certificate of service for electronic filing:

CERTIFICATE OF SERVICE

On [Date], I electronically filed this document through the CM/ECF system, which will send a notice of electronic filing to: [Attorney Name (attach list if necessary)]; and I [mailed] [hand delivered] [faxed] this document and the notice of electronic filing to: [Attorney/Party Name], [Address], [Parties Represented], [Civil Action(s)] (attach list if necessary).

/s/ [typed name of attorney]
Attorney's name
Law Firm Name (if applicable)
Address
Phone Number
Fax Number
Attorney's Email address
Attorney for:

5. ENTRY OF PANEL DOCUMENTS.

(a) A document entered or issued by the Panel will be filed in accordance with these procedures and such filing shall constitute entry on the docket kept by the Clerk.

(b) All signed orders will be electronically filed or entered. An order containing the electronic signature of a Panel Judge or the Clerk of the Panel shall have the same force and effect as if the Panel Judge or Clerk of the Panel had affixed a signature to a paper copy of the order and the order had been entered on the docket in a conventional manner.

(c) Orders may also be issued as "text-only" entries on the docket, without an attached document. Such orders are official and binding.

6. NOTICE OF PANEL ORDERS AND NOTICES.

Immediately upon the entry of an order or notice by the Panel, the clerk will transmit to Filing Users in affected cases in the MDL, in electronic form, a Notice of Electronic Filing (NEF), with a hyperlink to the electronic document. Electronic transmission of the NEF, along with a hyperlink to the electronic document, constitutes the notice required by Panel Rule 5.2. The clerk must give notice in paper form to a pro se party or an attorney who is not a Filing User to the extent notice is required.

7. ATTACHMENTS AND EXHIBITS.

Documents referenced as exhibits or attachments shall be filed in accordance with these administrative policies and procedures and the Panel's CM/ECF User Manual, unless otherwise ordered by the Panel. A Filing User shall submit as exhibits or attachments only those excerpts of the referenced documents that are directly germane to the matter under consideration by the Panel. Excerpted material must be clearly and prominently identified as such. Filing Users who file excerpts of documents as exhibits or attachments under these procedures do so without prejudice to their right to file timely additional excerpts or the complete document. Responding parties may timely file additional excerpts or the complete document that they believe are directly germane. The Panel may require parties to file additional excerpts or the complete document.

8. SEALED DOCUMENTS.

To ensure proper storage of a document, a document subject to a sealing order must be filed with the Panel on paper in a sealed envelope marked "sealed", citing thereon the MDL docket number and title and the associated case caption and case number; or by attaching thereto a paper copy of the Panel's order sealing the document or a copy of the NEF citing the entry of the court's order sealing the document. The clerk may require the document to be accompanied by a disk or CD–ROM containing the document in .pdf format. Only a motion to file a document under seal may be filed electronically, unless prohibited by law. The order of the Panel authorizing the filing of documents under seal may be filed electronically, unless prohibited by law or otherwise directed by the Panel. If a document is filed under seal pursuant to the E–Government Act of 2002, the filing party is nevertheless required to file a redacted copy for the public record along with the unredacted sealed document.

9. SPECIAL FILING REQUIREMENTS AND EXCEPTIONS.

9.1 Special Filing Requirements

The documents listed below shall be presented for filing on paper. The clerk may require the document be accompanied by a disk or CD–ROM containing the document in .pdf format:

Sealed

MDL dockets involving Qui Tam Cases (under seal)

9.2 Exceptions

All documents shall be filed electronically unless otherwise ordered by the Panel or specifically exempt herein.

10. RETENTION REQUIREMENTS.

(a) A document that is electronically filed and requires an original signature other than that of the Filing User must be maintained in paper form by counsel and/or the firm representing the party on whose behalf the document was filed until one year after all periods for appeals expire. On request of the Panel, said counsel must provide the original document for review.

(b) The clerk's office may choose to discard certain documents brought to the clerk's office for filing in paper form after those documents are scanned and uploaded to the System (to include pro se filings). Therefore, counsel and pro se filers shall provide the Panel with a copy of the original documents with intrinsic value for scanning and maintain the original signature in accordance with 10(a).

11. SIGNATURES.

(a) The user login and password required to submit documents to the Electronic Filing System serve as the Filing User signature on all electronic documents filed with the court. They serve as a signature for purposes of the Panel Rules and any other purpose for which a signature is required in connection with proceedings before the Panel.

(b) Each document filed electronically must indicate in the caption that it has been electronically filed. An electronically filed document must include a signature block in compliance with Panel Rule 7.1(e), and must set forth the name, address, telephone number, fax number, and email address. In addition, the name of the Filing User under whose login and password the document is submitted must be preceded by an "/s/" and typed in the space where the signature would otherwise appear. No Filing User or other person may knowingly permit or cause to permit a Filing User password to be used by anyone other than an authorized agent of the Filing User.

(c) A document requiring signatures of more than one party must be filed either by:

(1) electronically filing a scanned document containing all necessary signatures; or

(2) representing the consent of the other parties on the document; or

(3) identifying on the document the party whose signature is required and by the submission of a notice of endorsement by the other parties no later than three (3) business days after filing; or

(4) any other manner approved by the Panel.

(d) A non-filing signatory or party who disputes the authenticity of an electronically filed document with a non-attorney signature, or the authenticity of the signature on that document; or the authenticity of an electronically filed document containing multiple signatures or the authenticity of the signature themselves, must file an objection to the document within fourteen (14) days of service of the document.

(e) Any party challenging the authenticity of an electronically filed document or the attorney's signature on that document must file an objection to the document within fourteen (14) days of service of the document.

(f) If a party wishes to challenge the authenticity of an electronically filed document or signature after the fourteen (14) day period, the party shall file a motion to seek a ruling from the Panel.

12. SERVICE OF DOCUMENTS BY ELECTRONIC MEANS.

12.1   Service

12.1.1   Filing User

Upon the electronic filing of a pleading or other document, the Panel's Electronic Case Filing System will automatically generate and send a Notice of Electronic Filing (NEF) to all Filing Users associated with that MDL and/or associated cases, along with a hyperlink to the electronic document. Transmission of the Notice of Electronic Filing with a hyperlink to the electronic document constitutes service of the filed document.

The NEF must include the time of filing, the date the document was entered on the docket, the name of the party and attorney filing the document, the type of document, the text of the docket entry, and an electronic link (hyperlink) to the filed document, allowing anyone receiving the notice by email to retrieve the document automatically. If the Filing User becomes aware that the NEF was not transmitted successfully to a party, or that the notice is deficient, *i.e.*, the electronic link to the document is defective, the filer shall serve the electronically filed document by email, hand, facsimile, or by first-class mail postage prepaid immediately upon notification of the NEF deficiency.

12.1.2   Individual who is not a Filing User

A non-registered participant is entitled to receive a paper copy of any electronically filed document from the party making such filing. Service of such paper copy must be made according to the Panel Rules.

13. TECHNICAL FAILURES.

(a) If the site is unable to accept filings continuously or intermittently for more than one (1) hour occurring after 12:00 noon Eastern Time that day, the Clerk of the Panel shall deem the Panel's Electronic Case Filing web site to be subject to a technical failure.

(b) If a Filing User experiences a technical failure as defined herein, the Filing User may submit the document to the Clerk of the Panel, provided that the document is accompanied by a certification, signed by the Filing User, that the Filing User has attempted to file the document electronically at least twice, with those unsuccessful attempts occurring at least one (1) hour apart after 12:00 noon Eastern Time that day. The Clerk may require the document to be accompanied by a disk or CD–ROM which contains the document in .pdf format.

(c) The initial point of contact for a Filing User experiencing technical difficulty filing a document electronically will be the Panel's CM/ECF Help Desk at the numbers listed on the Panel's web site and in the CM/ECF User Manual.

(d) A Filing User who suffers prejudice as a result of a technical failure as defined herein or a Filing User who cannot file a time-sensitive document electronically due to unforeseen technical difficulties, such as the malfunctioning of a Filing User's equipment, may seek relief from the Clerk of the Panel.

14. PUBLIC ACCESS.

14.1   (a) A person may receive information from the Electronic Filing System at the Panel's Internet site by obtaining a PACER login and password. A person who has PACER access may retrieve docket sheets and documents (unless otherwise sealed or restricted) in MDL dockets and associated civil cases. Any case or document under seal shall not be available electronically or through any other means.

(b) If a case or document has been restricted, a PACER user may retrieve the docket sheet over the Internet, but only a Filing User who is counsel of record may retrieve restricted documents electronically. However, a restricted case or document will be available for viewing by the public at the clerk's office.

(c) Electronic access to electronic docket sheets and all documents filed in the System, unless sealed, is available to the public for viewing at no charge during regular business hours at the clerk's office. A copy fee for an electronic reproduction is required in accordance with 28 U.S.C. § 1932.

(d) Conventional copies and certified copies of electronically filed documents may be purchased at the clerk's office. The fee for copying and certifying will be in accordance with 28 U.S.C. § 1932.

14.2   <u>Sensitive Information</u>

Since the public may access certain case information over the Internet through the Panel's Electronic Filing System, sensitive information should not be included in any document filed with the court unless such inclusion is necessary and relevant. In accordance with these Administrative Policies and Procedures, if sensitive information must be included, certain personal and identifying information such as Social Security numbers, financial account numbers, dates of birth and names of minor children shall be redacted from the pleading, whether it is filed electronically or on paper.

The Panel recognizes that parties may need to include in the record a document containing information such as driver's license number; medical records, treatment and diagnosis; employment history; individual financial information; and proprietary or trade secret information.

To avoid unnecessary disclosure of private, personal or financial information, a party may:

(a) **RESTRICTED MDL DOCKETS OR DOCUMENTS.**

File a "Motion to Seal" or "Motion to Seal Document". The motion must state the reason and show good cause for restricting remote access to the case. If the motion is granted, remote access to documents will be limited to Filing Users who are counsel of record. However, the MDL docket sheet and/or documents will be available for viewing by the public at the clerk's office.

(b) **EXHIBITS.**

File an exhibit containing private, personal or financial information as an attachment to a pleading entitled "Notice of Filing Restricted Exhibit". The notice and the attached exhibit shall be filed as a separate docket entry, rather than as an attachment to the pleading supported by the exhibit. Remote public access to the notice and exhibit will be limited to Filing Users who are counsel of record. The notice and exhibit will, however, be available for viewing by the public at the clerk's office.

(c) **DOCUMENTS UNDER SEAL.**

(1) File a redacted copy of a pleading or exhibit containing private, personal or financial information, whether electronically or on paper, while concurrently filing an unredacted copy under seal. This document shall be retained by the Panel as part of the record.

OR

(2) File a reference list under seal. The reference list shall contain the complete personal data identifier(s) and the redacted identifier(s) used in its (their) place in the filing. All references in the case to the redacted identifier(s) included in the reference list will be construed to refer to the corresponding complete identifier. The reference list must be filed under seal, and may be amended as of right. It shall be retained by the Panel as part of the record.

(d) **MOTION TO SEAL.**

File a motion to seal the document or MDL associated case. The motion must state the reason and show good cause for sealing the document or MDL associated case. If the motion to seal is granted, the document or case under seal will not be available electronically or through any other means.

It is the sole responsibility of counsel and the parties to ensure that all documents filed with the Panel comply with these Administrative Policies and Procedures, regarding public access to electronic case files. The Clerk will not review any document for redaction.

Counsel are strongly urged to share this information with all clients so that an informed decision about the inclusion, redaction, and/or exclusion of certain materials may be made.

[Effective May 2010.]

FEDERAL COURTS MISCELLANEOUS FEE SCHEDULES
COURT OF APPEALS FEE SCHEDULE
(Effective September 1, 2018)

The fees included in the Court of Appeals Miscellaneous Fee Schedule[1] are to be charged for services provided by the courts of appeals, including relevant services[2] provided by the bankruptcy appellate panels established under 28 U.S.C. § 158(b)(1).

- The United States should not be charged fees under this schedule, except as prescribed in Items 2, 4, and 5 when the information requested is available through remote electronic access.

- Federal agencies or programs that are funded from judiciary appropriations (agencies, organizations, and individuals providing services authorized by the Criminal Justice Act, 18 U.S.C. § 3006A, and bankruptcy administrators) should not be charged any fees under this schedule.

(1) For docketing a case on appeal or review, or docketing any other proceeding, $500.

- Each party filing a notice of appeal pays a separate fee to the district court, but parties filing a joint notice of appeal pay only one fee.

- There is no docketing fee for an application for an interlocutory appeal under 28 U.S.C. § 1292(b) or other petition for permission to appeal under Fed. R. App. P. 5, unless the appeal is allowed.

- There is no docketing fee for a direct bankruptcy appeal or a direct bankruptcy cross appeal, when the fee has been collected by the bankruptcy court in accordance with item 14 of the Bankruptcy Court Miscellaneous Fee Schedule.

- This fee is collected in addition to the statutory fee of $5 that is collected under 28 U.S.C. § 1917.

(2) For conducting a search of the court of appeals or bankruptcy appellate panel records, $31 per name or item searched. This fee applies to services rendered on behalf of the United States if the information requested is available through remote electronic access.

(3) For certification of any document, $11.

(4)

a. For reproducing any document and providing a copy in paper form, $.50 per page. This fee applies to services rendered on behalf of the United States if the document requested is available through remote electronic access.

b. For reproducing and transmitting in any manner a copy of an electronic record stored outside of the court's electronic case management system, including but not limited to, document files, audio and video recordings (other than a recording of a court proceeding), $31 per record provided.

(5) For reproducing recordings of proceedings, regardless of the medium, $31, including the cost of materials. This fee applies to services rendered on behalf of the United States if the recording is available through remote electronic access.

(6) For reproducing the record in any appeal in which the court of appeals does not require an appendix pursuant to Fed. R. App. P.30(f), (or, in appeals before a bankruptcy appellate panel, pursuant to Fed. R. Bankr. P. 8018(e)), $86.

(7) For retrieval of one box of records from a Federal Records Center, National Archives, or other storage location removed from the place of business of the court, $64. For retrievals involving multiple boxes, $39 for each additional box. For electronic retrievals, $10 plus any charges assessed by the Federal Records Center, National Archives, or other storage location removed from the place of business of the courts.

(8) For any payment returned or denied for insufficient funds, $53.

(9) For copies of opinions, a fee commensurate with the cost of printing, as fixed by each court of appeals.

(10) For copies of the local rules of court, a fee commensurate with the cost of distributing the copies. The court may also distribute copies of the local rules without charge.

(11) For filing:

- Any separate or joint notice of appeal or application for appeal from the bankruptcy appellate panel, $5;

- A notice of the allowance of an appeal from the bankruptcy appellate panel, $5.

(12) For counsel's requested use of the court's videoconferencing equipment in connection with each oral argument, the court may charge and collect a fee of $200 per remote location.

(13) For original admission of attorney to practice, including a certificate of admission, $181. For a duplicate certificate of admission or certificate of good standing, $19.

[1] Issued in accordance with 28 U.S.C. § 1913.

[2] Item 13 does not apply to bankruptcy appellate panels.

DISTRICT COURT FEE SCHEDULE

(Effective September 1, 2018)

The fees included in the District Court Miscellaneous Fee Schedule[1] are to be charged for services provided by the district courts.

- The United States should not be charged fees under this schedule, with the exception of those specifically prescribed in Items 2, 4 and 5, when the information requested is available through remote electronic access.

- Federal agencies or programs that are funded from judiciary appropriations (agencies, organizations, and individuals providing services authorized by the Criminal Justice Act, 18 U.S.C. § 3006 and bankruptcy administrators) should not be charged any fees under this schedule.

1. For filing any document that is not related to a pending case or proceeding, $47.

2. For conducting a search of the district court records, $31 per name or item searched. This fee applies to services rendered on behalf of the United States if the information requested is available through electronic access.

3. For certification of any document, $11. For exemplification of any document, $22.

4. a. For reproducing any record and providing a copy in paper form, $.50 per page. This fee shall apply to paper copies made from either: (1) original documents; or (2) microfiche or microfilm reproductions of the original records. This fee shall apply to services rendered on behalf of the United States if the record requested is available through electronic access.

   b. For reproducing and transmitting in any manner a copy of an electronic record stored outside of the court's electronic case management system, including but not limited to, document files, audio recordings, and video recordings, $31 per record provided. Audio recordings of court proceedings continue to be governed by a separate fee in item 5 of this schedule.

5. For reproduction of an audio recording of a court proceeding, $31. This fee applies to services rendered on behalf of the United States, if the recording is available electronically.

6. For each microfiche sheet of film or microfilm jacket copy of any court record, where available, $6.

7. For retrieval of one box of records from a Federal Records Center, National Archives, or other storage location removed from the place of business of the court, $64. For retrievals involving multiple boxes, $39 for each additional box. For electronic retrievals, $10 plus any charges assessed by the Federal Records Center, National Archives, or other storage location removed from the place of business of the courts.

8. For any payment returned or denied for insufficient funds, $53.

9. For an appeal to a district judge from a judgment of conviction by a magistrate judge in a misdemeanor case, $38.

10. For original admission of attorneys to practice, $181 each, including a certificate of admission. For a duplicate certificate of admission or certificate of good standing, $19.

11. The court may charge and collect fees commensurate with the cost of providing copies of the local rules of court. The court may also distribute copies of the local rules without charge.

12.

- For handling registry funds deposited with and held by the court, the clerk shall assess a charge from interest earnings, in accordance with the detailed fee schedule issued by the Director of the Administrative Office of the United States Courts.

- For management of registry funds invested through the Court Registry Investment System, a fee at an annual rate of 10 basis points of assets on deposit shall be assessed from interest earnings, excluding registry funds from disputed ownership interpleader cases deposited under 28 U.S.C. § 1335 and held in a Court Registry Investment System Disputed Ownership Fund.

- For management of funds deposited under 28 U.S.C. § 1335 and invested in a Disputed Ownership Fund through the Court Registry Investment System, a fee at an annual rate of 20 basis points of assets on deposit shall be assessed from interest earnings.

• The Director of the Administrative Office has the authority to waive these fees for cause.

13.   For filing an action brought under Title III of the Cuban Liberty and Democratic Solidarity (LIBERTAD) Act of 1996, P.L. 104–114, 110 Stat. § 785 (1996), $6,548. (This fee is in addition to the filing fee prescribed in 28 U.S.C. § 1914(a) for instituting any civil action other than a writ of habeas corpus.)

14.   Administrative fee for filing a civil action, suit, or proceeding in a district court, $50. This fee does not apply to applications for a writ of habeas corpus or to persons granted in forma pauperis status under 28 U.S.C. § 1915.

15.   Processing fee for a petty offense charged on a federal violation notice, $30.

¹ Issued in accordance with 28 U.S.C. § 1914.

BANKRUPTCY COURT MISCELLANEOUS FEE SCHEDULE

(Effective September 1, 2018)

The fees included in the Bankruptcy Court Miscellaneous Fee Schedule[1] are to be charged for services provided by the bankruptcy courts.

- The United States should not be charged fees under this schedule, with the exception of those specifically prescribed in Items 1, 3 and 5 when the information requested is available through remote electronic access.

- Federal agencies or programs that are funded from judiciary appropriations (agencies, organizations, and individuals providing services authorized by the Criminal Justice Act, 18 U.S.C. § 3006A, and bankruptcy administrators) should not be charged any fees under this schedule.

1.   a.   For reproducing any document and providing a copy in paper form, $.50 per page. This fee applies to services rendered on behalf of the United States if the document requested is available through electronic access.

    b.   For reproducing and transmitting in any manner a copy of an electronic record stored outside of the court's electronic case management system, including but not limited to, document files, audio recordings, and video recordings, $31 per record provided. Audio recordings of court proceedings continue to be governed by a separate fee under item 3 of this schedule.

2.   For certification of any document, $11. For exemplification of any document, $22.

3.   For reproduction of an audio recording of a court proceeding, $31. This fee applies to services rendered on behalf of the United States if the recording is available electronically.

4.   For filing an amendment to the debtor's schedules of creditors, lists of creditors, or mailing list, $31, except:

- The bankruptcy judge may, for good cause, waive the charge in any case.

- This fee must not be charged if -

  - the amendment is to change the address of a creditor or an attorney for a creditor listed on the schedules; or

  - the amendment is to add the name and address of an attorney for a creditor listed on the schedules.

5.   For conducting a search of the bankruptcy court records, $31 per name or item searched. This fee applies to services rendered on behalf of the United States if the information requested is available through electronic access.

6.   For filing a complaint, $350, except:

- If the trustee or debtor-in-possession files the complaint, the fee must be paid only by the estate, to the extent there is an estate.

- This fee must not be charged if -

  - the debtor is the plaintiff; or

  - a child support creditor or representative files the complaint and submits the form required by § 304(g) of the Bankruptcy Reform Act of 1994.

7.   For filing any document that is not related to a pending case or proceeding, $47.

8.   Administrative fee:

- For filing a petition under Chapter 7, 12, or 13, $75.

- For filing a petition under Chapter 9, 11, or 15, $550.

- When a motion to divide a joint case under Chapter 7, 12, or 13 is filed, $75.

- When a motion to divide a joint case under Chapter 11 is filed, $550.

9.   For payment to trustees pursuant to 11 U.S.C. § 330(b)(2), a $15 fee applies in the following circumstances:

- For filing a petition under Chapter 7.

- For filing a notice of conversion to a Chapter 7 case.
- For filing a motion to convert a case to a Chapter 7 case.
- For filing a motion to divide a joint Chapter 7 case.
- For filing a motion to reopen a Chapter 7 case.

10.   In addition to any fees imposed under Item 9, above, the following fees must be collected:

- For filing a motion to convert a Chapter 12 case to a Chapter 7 case or a notice of conversion pursuant to 11 U.S.C. § 1208(a), $45.
- For filing a motion to convert a Chapter 13 case to a Chapter 7 case or a notice of conversion pursuant to 11 U.S.C. § 1307(a), $10.

The fee amounts in this item are derived from the fees prescribed in 28 U.S.C. § 1930(a).

If the trustee files the motion to convert, the fee is payable only from the estate that exists prior to conversion.

If the filing fee for the chapter to which the case is requested to be converted is less than the fee paid at the commencement of the case, no refund may be provided.

11.   For filing a motion to reopen, the following fees apply:

- For filing a motion to reopen a Chapter 7 case, $245.
- For filing a motion to reopen a Chapter 9 case, $1167.
- For filing a motion to reopen a Chapter 11 case, $1167.
- For filing a motion to reopen a Chapter 12 case, $200.
- For filing a motion to reopen a Chapter 13 case, $235.
- For filing a motion to reopen a Chapter 15 case, $1167.

The fee amounts in this item are derived from the fees prescribed in 28 U.S.C. § 1930(a).

The reopening fee must be charged when a case has been closed without a discharge being entered.

The court may waive this fee under appropriate circumstances or may defer payment of the fee from trustees pending discovery of additional assets. If payment is deferred, the fee should be waived if no additional assets are discovered.

The reopening fee must not be charged in the following situations:

- to permit a party to file a complaint to obtain a determination under Rule 4007(b); or
- when a debtor files a motion to reopen a case based upon an alleged violation of the terms of the discharge under 11 U.S.C. § 524; or
- when the reopening is to correct an administrative error.
- to redact a record already filed in a case, pursuant to Fed. R. Bankr. P. 9037, if redaction is the only reason for reopening.

12.   For retrieval of one box of records from a Federal Records Center, National Archives, or other storage location removed from the place of business of the court, $64. For retrievals involving multiple boxes, $39 for each additional box. For electronic retrievals, $10 plus any charges assessed by the Federal Records Center, National Archives, or other storage location removed from the place of business of the courts.

13.   For any payment returned or denied for insufficient funds, $53.

14.   For filing an appeal or cross appeal from a judgment, order, or decree, $293.

This fee is collected in addition to the statutory fee of $5 that is collected under 28 U.S.C. § 1930(c) when a notice of appeal is filed.

Parties filing a joint notice of appeal should pay only one fee.

If a trustee or debtor-in-possession is the appellant, the fee must be paid only by the estate, to the extent there is an estate.

Upon notice from the court of appeals that a direct appeal or direct cross-appeal has been authorized, an additional fee of $207 must be collected.

15.   For filing a case under Chapter 15 of the Bankruptcy Code, $1167.

This fee is derived from and equal to the fee prescribed in 28 U.S.C. § 1930(a)(3) for filing a case commenced under Chapter 11 of Title 11.

16.   The court may charge and collect fees commensurate with the cost of providing copies of the local rules of court. The court may also distribute copies of the local rules without charge.

17.

- For handling registry funds deposited with and held by the court, the clerk shall assess a charge from interest earnings, in accordance with the detailed fee schedule issued by the Director of the Administrative Office of the United States Courts.

- For management of registry funds invested through the Court Registry Investment System, a fee at an annual rate of 10 basis points of assets on deposit shall be assessed from interest earnings, excluding registry funds from disputed ownership interpleader cases deposited under 28 U.S.C. § 1335 and held in a Court Registry Investment System Disputed Ownership Fund.

- For management of funds deposited under 28 U.S.C. § 1335 and invested in a Disputed Ownership Fund through the Court Registry Investment System, a fee at an annual rate of 20 basis points of assets on deposit shall be assessed from interest earnings.

- The Director of the Administrative Office has the authority to waive these fees for cause.

18.   For a motion filed by the debtor to divide a joint case filed under 11 U.S.C. § 302, the following fees apply:

- For filing a motion to divide a joint Chapter 7 case, $245.

- For filing a motion to divide a joint Chapter 11 case, $1167.

- For filing a motion to divide a joint Chapter 12 case, $200.

- For filing a motion to divide a joint Chapter 13 case, $235.

These fees are derived from and equal to the filing fees prescribed in 28 U.S.C. § 1930(a).

19.   For filing the following motions, $181:

- To terminate, annul, modify or condition the automatic stay;

- To compel abandonment of property of the estate pursuant to Rule 6007(b) of the Federal Rules of Bankruptcy Procedure;

- To withdraw the reference of a case or proceeding under 28 U.S.C. § 157(d); or

- To sell property of the estate free and clear of liens under 11 U.S.C. § 363(f).

This fee must not be collected in the following situations:

- For a motion for relief from the co-debtor stay;

- For a stipulation for court approval of an agreement for relief from a stay; or

- For a motion filed by a child support creditor or its representative, if the form required by § 304(g) of the Bankruptcy Reform Act of 1994 is filed.

20.   For filing a transfer of claim, $25 per claim transferred.

21.   For filing a motion to redact a record, $25 per affected case. The court may waive this fee under appropriate circumstances.

1 Issued in accordance with 28 U.S.C. § 1930.

JUDICIAL PANEL ON MULTIDISTRICT LITIGATION FEE SCHEDULE

(Effective September 1, 2018)

Following are fees to be charged for services to be performed by the clerk of the Judicial Panel on Multidistrict Litigation[1].

No fees are to be charged for services rendered on behalf of the United States, with the exception of those specifically prescribed in items 1 and 3. No fees under this schedule shall be charged to federal agencies or programs which are funded from judiciary appropriations, including, but not limited to, agencies, organizations, and individuals providing services authorized by the Criminal Justice Act, 18 U.S.C. § 3006A.

(1) For every search of the records of the court conducted by the clerk of the court or a deputy clerk, $31 per name or item searched. This fee shall apply to services rendered on behalf of the United States if the information requested is available through electronic access.

(2) For certification of any document or paper, whether the certification is made directly on the document or by separate instrument, $11.

(3)

a.   For reproducing any record and providing a copy in paper form, $.50 per page. This fee shall apply to paper copies made from either: (1) original documents; or (2) microfiche or microfilm reproductions of the original records. This fee shall apply to services rendered on behalf of the United States if the record requested is available through electronic access.

b.   For reproducing and transmitting in any manner a copy of an electronic record stored outside of the court's electronic case management system, including but not limited to, document files, audio recordings, and video recordings, $31 per record provided.

(4) For retrieval of one box of records from a Federal Records Center, National Archives, or other storage location removed from the place of business of the court, $64. For retrievals involving multiple boxes, $39 for each additional box. For electronic retrievals, $10 plus any charges assessed by the Federal Records Center, National Archives, or other storage location removed from the place of business of the courts.

(5) For any payment returned or denied for insufficient funds, $53.

[1] Issued in accordance with 28 U.S.C. § 1932.

ELECTRONIC PUBLIC ACCESS FEE SCHEDULE

(Issued in accordance with 28 U.S.C. §§ 1913, 1914, 1926, 1930, 1932)

(Effective April 1, 2017)

The fees included in the Electronic Public Access Fee Schedule are to be charged for providing electronic public access to court records.

Fees for Public Access to Court Electronic Records (PACER)

1. Except as provided below, for electronic access to any case document, docket sheet, or case-specific report via PACER: $0.10 per page, not to exceed the fee for thirty pages.

2. For electronic access to transcripts and non-case specific reports via PACER (such as reports obtained from the PACER Case Locator or docket activity reports): $0.10 per page.

3. For electronic access to an audio file of a court hearing via PACER: $2.40 per audio file.

Fees for Courthouse Electronic Access

4. For printing copies of any record or document accessed electronically at a public terminal in a courthouse: $0.10 per page.

PACER Service Center Fees

5. For every search of court records conducted by the PACER Service Center, $30 per name or item searched.

6. For the PACER Service Center to reproduce on paper any record pertaining to a PACER account, if this information is remotely available through electronic access: $0.50 per page.

7. For any payment returned or denied for insufficient funds, $53.

Free Access and Exemptions

8. Automatic Fee Exemptions:

- No fee is owed for electronic access to court data or audio files via PACER until an account holder accrues charges of more than $15.00 in a quarterly billing cycle.

- Parties in a case (including *pro se* litigants) and attorneys of record receive one free electronic copy, via the notice of electronic filing or notice of docket activity, of all documents filed electronically, if receipt is required by law or directed by the filer.

- No fee is charged for access to judicial opinions.

- No fee is charged for viewing case information or documents at courthouse public access terminals.

- No fee is charged for Chapter 13 bankruptcy trustees to download quarterly (i.e., once every 90 days) a list of the trustee's cases from the PACER Case Locator.

9. Discretionary Fee Exemptions:

- Courts may exempt certain persons or classes of persons from payment of the user access fee. Examples of individuals and groups that a court may consider exempting include: indigents, bankruptcy case trustees, pro bono attorneys, pro bono alternative dispute resolution neutrals, Section 501(c)(3) not-for-profit organizations, and individual researchers associated with educational institutions. Courts should not, however, exempt individuals or groups that have the ability to pay the statutorily established access fee. Examples of individuals and groups that a court should not exempt include: local, state or federal government agencies, members of the media, privately paid attorneys or others who have the ability to pay the fee.

- In considering granting an exemption, courts must find:
  - that those seeking an exemption have demonstrated that an exemption is necessary in order to avoid unreasonable burdens and to promote public access to information;
  - that individual researchers requesting an exemption have shown that the defined research project is intended for scholarly research, that it is limited in scope, and that it is not intended for redistribution on the internet or for commercial purposes.

- If the court grants an exemption:
  - the user receiving the exemption must agree not to sell the data obtained as a result, and must not transfer any data obtained as the result of a fee exemption, unless expressly authorized by the court; and
  - the exemption should be granted for a definite period of time, should be limited in scope, and may be revoked at the discretion of the court granting the exemption.
- Courts may provide local court information at no cost (e.g., local rules, court forms, news items, court calendars, and other information) to benefit the public.

Applicability to the United States and State and Local Governments

10. Unless otherwise authorized by the Judicial Conference, these fees must be charged to the United States, except to federal agencies or programs that are funded from judiciary appropriations (including, but not limited to, agencies, organizations, and individuals providing services authorized by the Criminal Justice Act [18 U.S.C. § 3006A], and bankruptcy administrators).

11. The fee for printing copies of any record or document accessed electronically at a public terminal ($0.10 per page) described in (4) above does not apply to services rendered on behalf of the United States if the record requested is not remotely available through electronic access.

12. The fee for local, state, and federal government entities, shall be $0.08 per page until April 1, 2015, after which time, the fee shall be $0.10 per page.

JUDICIAL CONFERENCE POLICY NOTES

The Electronic Public Access (EPA) fee and its exemptions are directly related to the requirement that the judiciary charge user-based fees for the development and maintenance of electronic public access services. The fee schedule provides examples of users that may not be able to afford reasonable user fees (such as indigents, bankruptcy case trustees, individual researchers associated with educational institutions, 501(c)(3) not-for-profit organizations, and court-appointed pro bono attorneys), but requires those seeking an exemption to demonstrate that an exemption is limited in scope and is necessary in order to avoid an unreasonable burden. In addition, the fee schedule includes examples of other entities that courts should not exempt from the fee (such as local, state or federal government agencies, members of the media, and attorneys). The goal is to provide courts with guidance in evaluating a requestor's ability to pay the fee.

Judicial Conference policy also limits exemptions in other ways. First, it requires exempted users to agree not to sell the data they receive through an exemption (unless expressly authorized by the court). This prohibition is not intended to bar a quote or reference to information received as a result of a fee exemption in a scholarly or other similar work. Second, it permits courts to grant exemptions for a definite period of time, to limit the scope of the exemptions, and to revoke exemptions. Third, it cautions that exemptions should be granted as the exception, not the rule, and prohibits courts from exempting all users from EPA fees.